THE CAMBRIDGE HANDBOOK OF CONSUMER PRIVACY

Businesses are rushing to collect personal data to fuel surging demand. Data enthusiasts claim that personal information obtained from the commercial Internet, including mobile platforms, social networks, cloud computing, and connected devices, will unlock pathbreaking innovation, including advanced data security. By contrast, regulators and activists contend that corporate data practices too often disempower consumers by creating privacy harms and related problems.

As the Internet of Things matures and facial recognition, predictive analytics, big data, and wearable tracking grow in power, scale, and scope, a controversial ecosystem exacerbates the acrimony over commercial data capture and analysis. The only productive way forward is to get a grip on key problems right now and change the conversation, which is exactly what Jules Polonetsky, Omer Tene, and Evan Selinger do. They bring together diverse views from leading academics, business leaders, and policymakers to discuss the opportunities and challenges of the new data economy.

EVAN SELINGER is Professor of Philosophy and Head of Research Communications, Community, and Ethics at the Center for Media, Arts, Games, Interaction, and Creativity at the Rochester Institute of Technology. Selinger is also Senior Fellow at the Future of Privacy Forum. His most recent book, co-written with Brett Frischmann, is *Re-Engineering Humanity* (Cambridge University Press, 2018). Selinger's primary research is on the ethical and privacy dimensions of emerging technology. A strong advocate of public philosophy, he writes regularly for magazines, newspapers, and blogs, including *The Guardian*, *The Atlantic*, *Slate*, and *Wired*.

JULES POLONETSKY is the CEO of the Future of Privacy Forum (FPF), a non-profit organization that serves as a catalyst for privacy leadership and scholarship, advancing principled data practices in support of emerging technologies. FPF is supported by the chief privacy officers of more than 130 leading companies and several foundations, as well as by an advisory board comprised of the country's leading academics and advocates. Polonetsky's previous roles have included serving as Chief Privacy Officer at AOL and before that at DoubleClick, as Consumer Affairs Commissioner for New York City, as an elected New York State legislator, and as an attorney.

OMER TENE is Vice President of Research and Education at the International Association of Privacy Professionals. He is a consultant to governments, regulatory agencies, and businesses on privacy, cybersecurity, and data management. He is an affiliate scholar at the Stanford Center for Internet and Society and Senior Fellow at the Future of Privacy Forum. He comes from Israel, where he was a professor at the College of Management School of Law.

The Cambridge Handbook of Consumer Privacy

Edited by

EVAN SELINGER
Rochester Institute of Technology

JULES POLONETSKY
Future of Privacy Forum

OMER TENE
International Association of Privacy Professionals

CAMBRIDGE
UNIVERSITY PRESS

CAMBRIDGE
UNIVERSITY PRESS

University Printing House, Cambridge CB2 8BS, United Kingdom

One Liberty Plaza, 20th Floor, New York, NY 10006, USA

477 Williamstown Road, Port Melbourne, VIC 3207, Australia

314-321, 3rd Floor, Plot 3, Splendor Forum, Jasola District Centre, New Delhi - 110025, India

79 Anson Road, #06-04/06, Singapore 079906

Cambridge University Press is part of the University of Cambridge.

It furthers the University's mission by disseminating knowledge in the pursuit of
education, learning and research at the highest international levels of excellence.

www.cambridge.org
Information on this title: www.cambridge.org/9781108971461
DOI:10.1017/9781316831960

© Cambridge University Press 2018

First published 2018
First paperback edition 2020

A catalogue record for this publication is available from the British Library

Library of Congress Cataloging in Publication data
NAMES: Selinger, Evan, 1974- editor. | Polonetsky, Jules, 1965- editor. | Tene, Omer, editor.
TITLE: The Cambridge handbook of consumer privacy / edited by Evan Selinger, Jules Polonetsky, Omer Tene.
DESCRIPTION: Cambridge, United Kingdom ; New York, NY : Cambridge University Press, 2018. | Includes
    bibliographical references and index.
IDENTIFIERS: LCCN 2017054702 | ISBN 9781107181106 (hardback : alk. paper)
SUBJECTS: LCSH: Consumer protection. | Consumer protection–Law and legislation. | Consumer profiling. |
    Privacy, Right of.
CLASSIFICATION: LCC HC79.C63 C36 2018 | DDC 381.3/4–dc23
    LC record available at https://lccn.loc.gov/2017054702

ISBN 978-1-107-18110-6 Hardback
ISBN 978-1-108-97146-1 Paperback

Contents

Contributors

Martin E. Abrams is Executive Director of the Information Accountability Foundation.

Alessandro Acquisti is Professor of Information Technology and Public Policy at Heinz College, Carnegie Mellon University.

Rebecca Balebako is an information scientist at Rand Corporation.

Stephen Balkam is Founder and CEO of the Family Online Safety Institute.

Jane R. Bambauer is Professor of Law at the University of Arizona James E. Rogers College of Law.

Alvaro Bedoya is Executive Director of the Center on Privacy and Technology at Georgetown University Law Center.

Franziska Boehm is Law professor at FIZ Karlsruhe, the Leibniz Institute of Information Infrastructure and the Karlsruhe Institute of Technology.

Frederik Zuiderveen Borgesius is a researcher at the Law, Science, Technology & Society group at the Vrije Universiteit Brussels, and a fellow of the Institute for Information Law at the University of Amsterdam.

Courtney Bowman is a civil liberties engineer at Palantir Technologies.

Laura Brandimarte is assistant professor of Management Information Systems at the University of Arizona.

Julie Brill is Corporate Vice President and Deputy General Counsel for Privacy and Regulatory Affairs at Microsoft.

Paula J. Bruening is Founder and Principal of Casentino Strategies LLC. She is the former Director of Global Privacy Policy at Intel Corporation.

Ryan Calo is Lane Powell and D. Wayne Gittinger Associate Professor at the University of Washington School of Law.

James C. Cooper is associate professor of Law and Director of the Program on Economics and Privacy at the Antonin Scalia Law School at George Mason University.

Lorrie Faith Cranor is FORE Systems Professor of Computer Science and of Engineering & Public Policy at Carnegie Mellon University.

Mary J. Culnan is Professor Emeritus of Information and Process Management at Bentley University.

Adam L. Durity is a privacy engineer at Google.

Kelsey Finch is Policy Counsel at the Future of Privacy Forum.

Jennifer Barrett Glasgow is Chief Privacy Officer Emeritus at Acxiom Corporation.

Lynn A. Goldstein is a senior strategist at the Information Accountability Foundation.

John Grant is a civil liberties engineer at Palantir Technologies.

Seda Gürses is a Flanders Research Foundation (FWO) Postdoctoral Fellow at the Computer Security and Industrial Cryptography Group (COSIC) at the University of Leuven and an affiliate at the Center for Information Technology and Policy (CITP) at Princeton University.

Paul De Hert is a professor at the Vrije Universiteit Brussel, Associated Professor at Tilburg Institute for Law, Technology, and Society at Tilburg University & Co-Director of Research Group on Law, Science, Technology, and Society (LSTS) at Vrije Universiteit Brussel.

Mike Hintze is a partner with Hintze Law and a part-time lecturer at the University of Washington School of Law. He is the former Chief Privacy Counsel at Microsoft, where he worked on privacy compliance, policy, and strategy from 1998 to 2016.

Joris van Hoboken is Chair of Fundamental Rights and the Digital Transformation at the Vrije Universiteit Brussels (VUB) and a Senior Researcher at the Institute for Information Law (IViR) at the University of Amsterdam.

David A. Hoffman is Associate General Counsel and Global Privacy Officer at Intel Corporation.

Chris Jay Hoofnagle is Adjunct Professor of Information and Law at the University of California, Berkeley.

J. Trevor Hughes is President and CEO of the International Association of Privacy Professionals.

Irene Kamara is attorney-at-law and doctoral Researcher at the Tilburg Institute for Law, Technology, and Society at Tilburg University and the Research Group on Law, Science, Technology and Society at the Vrije Universiteit Brussel.

Cobun Keegan is a Westin fellow at the International Association of Privacy Professionals.

Stefan Kulk is a doctoral researcher at Utrecht University School of Law.

George Lowenstein is Herbert A. Simon University Professor of Economics and Psychology at Carnegie Mellon University.

Mark MacCarthy is Senior Vice President for Public Policy at the Software and Information Industry Association and Adjunct Professor in the Communication, Culture, and Technology Program at Georgetown University.

Kirsten Martin is associate professor of Strategic Management and Public Policy at the George Washington University School of Business.

Aleecia M. McDonald is a privacy researcher and nonresident fellow at the Center for Internet and Society at Stanford University.

Michelle N. Meyer is assistant professor and Associate Director of Research Ethics at the Center for Translational Bioethics and Health Care Policy at Geisinger Health System.

Brian P. O'Connor is Senior Privacy Manager at Dell.

Aeryn Palmer is Senior Legal Counsel at the Wikimedia Foundation.

Bilyana Petkova is a postdoctoral researcher at the Information Law Institute at New York University.

Jules Polonetsky is CEO of the Future of Privacy Forum.

Patricia A. Rimo is Vice President of Public Affairs at RH Strategic Communications.

Ira Rubinstein is Adjunct Professor of Law and Senior Fellow at the Information Law Institute at the New York University School of Law.

Florian Schaub is assistant professor of Information and Electrical Engineering and Computer Science at the University of Michigan.

Evan Selinger is Professor of Philosophy at the Rochester Institute of Technology, where he also is Head of Research Communications, Community, and Ethics at the Media, Arts, Games, Interaction, Creativity Center (MAGIC). Selinger is also a Senior Fellow at the Future of Privacy Forum.

Katie Shilton is associate professor at the College of Information Studies at the University of Maryland.

Dale Skivington is Vice President for Global Compliance and Chief Privacy Officer at Dell.

Omer Tene is Senior Fellow at the Future of Privacy Forum. Tene is also Vice President of Research and Education at the International Association of Privacy Professionals and associate professor at the College of Management School of Law, Rishon Lezion, Israel.

Adam Thierer is a senior research fellow in the Technology Policy Program at the Mercatus Center at George Mason University.

Joseph Turow is Robert Lewis Shayon Professor of Communication at the Annenberg School for Communication at the University of Pennsylvania.

Yana Welinder is a nonresidential fellow at the Stanford Center for Internet and Society and affiliate at the Berkman Klein Center for Internet and Society at Harvard University.

Joshua D. Wright is University Professor and Executive Director of the Global Antitrust Institute at the Antonin Scalia Law School at George Mason University.

Elana Zeide is a visiting assistant professor at Seton Hall University School of Law.

Lisa Zolidis is Privacy Counsel for the Americas at Dell.

PART I

Introduction

Consumer Privacy and the Future of Society

Jules Polonetsky, Omer Tene, and Evan Selinger

In the course of a single day, hundreds of companies collect massive amounts of information from individuals. Sometimes they obtain meaningful consent. Often, they use less than transparent means. By surfing the web, using a cell phone and apps, entering a store that provides Wi-Fi, driving a car, passing cameras on public streets, wearing a fitness device, watching a show on a smart TV or ordering a product from a connected home device, people share a steady stream of information with layers upon layers of hardware devices, software applications, and service providers. Almost every human activity, whether it is attending school or a workplace, seeking healthcare or shopping in a mall, driving on a highway or watching TV in the living room, leaves behind data trails that build up incrementally to create a virtual record of our daily lives. How companies, governments, and experts should use this data is among the most pressing global public policy concerns.

Privacy issues, which are at the heart of many of the debates over data collection, analysis, and distribution, range extensively in both theory and practice. In some cases, conversations about privacy policy focus on marketing issues and the minutiae of a website's privacy notices or an app's settings. In other cases, the battle cry for privacy extends to diverse endeavors, such as the following: calls to impose accountability on the NSA's counterterrorism mission;[1] proposals for designing safe smart toys;[2] plans for enabling individuals to scrub or modify digital records of their pasts;[3] pleas to require database holders to inject noise into researchers' queries to protect against leaks that disclose an individuals' identity;[4] plans to use crypto currencies[5] or to prevent criminals and terrorists from abusing encryption tools;[6] proposals for advancing medical research

[1] Richard Clarke, Michael Morell, Geoffrey Stone, Cass Sunstein & Peter Swire, The NSA Report: Liberty and Security in a Changing World (The President's Review Group on Intelligence and Communications Technologies, Princeton University Press, 2014).
[2] *Kids and the Connected Home: Privacy in the Age of Connected Dolls, Talking Dinosaurs, and Battling Robots* (Future of Privacy Forum and Family Online Safety Institute, Dec. 2016), https://fpf.org/wp-content/uploads/2016/11/Kids-The-Connected-Home-Privacy-in-the-Age-of-Connected-Dolls-Talking-Dinosaurs-and-Battling-Robots.pdf.
[3] Case C-131/12 Google Spain v. Agencia Española de Protección de Datos (AEPD) and Mario Costeja González, ECLI: EU:C:2014:317.
[4] Cynthia Dwork, Frank McSherry, Kobbi Nissim & Adam Smith, *Calibrating Noise to Sensitivity in Private Data Analysis*, in Proceedings of the 3rd Theory of Cryptography Conference, 265–284 (2006).
[5] Arvind Narayanan, Joseph Bonneau, Edward Felten, Andrew Miller & Steven Goldfeder, Bitcoin and Cryptocurrency Technologies (Princeton University Press, 2016).
[6] In re Order Requiring Apple, Inc. to Assist in the Execution of a Search Warrant Issued by This Court, No. 15-mc-1902 (JO) (E.D.N.Y. Feb. 29, 2016).

and improving public health without sacrificing patients' control over their data;[7] and ideas for how scientists can make their data more publicly available to facilitate replication of studies without, at the same time, inadvertently subjecting entire populations to prejudicial treatment, including discrimination.[8]

At a time when fake news influences political elections, new and contentious forms of machine-to-machine communications are emerging, algorithmic decision-making is calling more of the shots in civic, corporate, and private affairs, and ruinous data breaches and ransomware attacks endanger everything from financial stability to patient care in hospitals, "privacy" has become a potent shorthand. Privacy is a boundary, a limiting principle, and a litmus test for identifying and adjudicating the delicate balance between the tremendous benefits and dizzying assortment of risks that insight-filled data offers.

DIVERSE PRIVACY PERSPECTIVES

The wide scope of perspectives found in this collection reflects the very diversity of privacy discourse.

Since privacy is front-page news, politicians regularly weigh in on it. Some politicians make privacy their signature issue by submitting legislative proposals, convening committee hearings, and sending letters to technology companies as they launch and test new tools. Interestingly, in the United States, privacy can be a bipartisan issue that brings together coalitions from opposite sides of the aisle. For example, on questions of national security surveillance, right wing libertarians side with left wing civil rights activists in opposing government powers and advocating for robust oversight mechanisms. However, in the consumer privacy space, traditional roles are often on display as supporters of regulation spar with free market activists on issues ranging from telecom regulation to the legitimacy of the data broker industry. In Europe, left wing parties, such as the German Greens or the Scandinavian Pirate Party, have played important roles in privacy advocacy by embracing an expansive reading of data protection principles. Conservatives, by contrast, have sought to balance data protection against economic interests and free trade. This political tension manifests itself in the twin, often conflicting objectives of the European data protection regime, which instructs Member States to "protect the fundamental rights and freedoms of natural persons, and in particular their right to privacy with respect to the processing of personal data," while, at the same time, "neither restrict[ing] nor prohibit[ing] the free flow of personal data between Member States."

Industry interest in privacy often aligns with businesses uniformly vying for more data use and less regulation. Even so, opinions still splinter across a broad spectrum. Some publishers believe that stronger limits on ad-tracking will advantage them to collect ad revenue that is earned today by advertising technology companies or large platforms. Other companies believe that new data portability rules will enable them to leverage data now held by platforms to better compete or to launch new services. Nevertheless, incumbents in many sectors worry that new regulations and more extensive liability will impede their digital strategies.

---

[7] Salil Vadhan, David Abrams, Micah Altman, Cynthia Dwork, Paul Kominers, Scott Duke Kominers, Harry Lewis, Tal Moran & Guy Rothblum, Comments on Advance Notice of Proposed Rulemaking: Human Subjects Research Protections: Enhancing Protections for Research Subjects and Reducing Burden, Delay, and Ambiguity for Investigators, Docket ID No. HHS-OPHS-2011–0005 (2011), https://privacytools.seas.harvard.edu/publications/comments-advance-notice-proposed-rulemaking-human-subjects-research.

[8] Daniel Goroff, Jules Polonetsky & Omer Tene, *Privacy Protective Research: Facilitating Ethically Responsible Access to Administrative Data*, 65 ANN. AM. ACAD. POL. & SOC. SCI. 46–66 (2018).

Regulators chase the flurry of market developments with carrots and sticks. Approaches vary, with some regulators, such as the UK Information Commissioner's Office, offering advice, best practices, and compliance tools. Others, such as the Canadian Federal Privacy Commissioner, enhance limited enforcement powers by actively engaging with the media to "name and shame" alleged violations of privacy laws. Some European data protection regulators are known to levy stiff fines and penalties even for technical violations of local statutes. The compliance risks for businesses will escalate sharply with the imposition of formidable sanctions under the General Data Protection Regulation. The Federal Trade Commission (FTC), the main federal privacy regulator in the United States, has developed a complex privacy and security regulatory approach that is built on two pillars. On the one hand, it includes a string of settlements referred to by Daniel Solove and Woodrow Hartzog as a "common law" of privacy.[9] On the other hand, the FTC issues a line of policy guidelines through workshops and reports on cutting-edge issues ranging from connected vehicles and consumer genetics to the sharing economy.

Privacy academics are a heterogeneous group who occupy a central place in policy debates. Some are data optimists. They see a bright future in data-intensive technologies and seek to facilitate their adoption while respecting individuals' rights. Others are data pessimists. They warn against the disruptive risk of data technologies and in extreme cases even see an inevitable decline toward a "database of ruin."[10] More traditionally, academics can be loosely categorized according to their disciplines. Law and policy scholars explore issues such as the Fourth Amendment, privacy legislation such as the Health Insurance Portability Act, the Family Educational Rights and Privacy Act, the Fair Credit Reporting Act, the Children's Online Privacy Protection Act, and the FTC's body of privacy law. Computer scientists deal with issues such as security and privacy in online, mobile operating systems and software, network security, anonymity, human–machine interaction, and differential privacy. Engineers work on network security, values in design, privacy by design, blockchain, and privacy-enhancing technologies. Economists assess the value and markets for data, as well as such issues as the value of privacy, privacy incentives and nudges, data-based price discrimination, privacy in credit and health markets, the behavioral economics of privacy, and more. Design schools innovate privacy messaging, information schools explore the role of privacy in media and culture, psychologists experiment on individuals' responses to incentives in cyber and real-world spaces, and ethicists weigh in on all of this.

CONSUMER PRIVACY

This book brings together academics, policy makers, and industry leaders to critically address the subset of issues that are raised in the context of *consumer privacy*. It purposefully sets aside the fateful dilemmas raised by government surveillance. This includes the continuing fallout from Edward Snowden's revelations about the prevalence of government access to private communications data. And it extends to newly emerging challenges, such as deploying military drones to assassinate suspected terrorists, using data-driven software for criminal sentencing, and monitoring people awaiting trial and serving court-mandated sentences in the seclusion of their homes. Yet, even narrowed to consumer privacy, this book still addresses a rich spectrum of issues triggered by an exceedingly broad swath of activities. While consumer privacy once was limited

---

[9] Daniel Solove & Woodrow Hartzog, *The FTC and the New Common Law of Privacy*, 114 COLUM. L. REV. 583 (2014).
[10] Paul Ohm, *Don't Build a Database of Ruin*, HARV. BUS. REV, Aug. 23, 2012, https://hbr.org/2012/08/dont-build-a-database-of-ruin.

to the realm of online tracking for targeted advertising,[11] the topic now extends to wearable technologies and implantable medical devices, smart homes and autonomous vehicles, facial recognition and behavioral biometrics, and algorithmic decision-making and the Internet of Things.[12] As companies collect massive amounts of data through the Internet, mobile communications, and a vast infrastructure of devices and sensors embedded in healthcare facilities, retail outlets, public transportation, social networks, workplaces, and homes, they use the information to test new products and services, improve existing offerings, and conduct research.

Given the wide scale and scope of consumer privacy, the topic can't be easily distinguished from government surveillance. With companies amassing huge warehouses of personal information, governments can swoop in when necessary to access the data through procurement, legal process, or technological capabilities. As Chris Hoofnagle observed more than a decade ago, "Accumulations of information about individuals tend to enhance authority by making it easier for authority to reach individuals directly. Thus, growth in society's record-keeping capability poses the risk that existing power balances will be upset."[13]

Since each new space and field of activity raises weighty policy, legal, ethical, economic, and technological questions and challenges, input on privacy is needed from experts across the disciplines. Philosophers, social scientists, legal theorists, geneticists, mathematicians, computer scientists, and engineers all have important roles to play. The pressing debates require a careful balancing of diverse values, interests, rights, and considerations. In many cases, individual benefits are pitted against the public good, and this tension tests the contours of autonomy and fundamental human rights in a constantly shifting techno-social environment.

The impact of technology on the economy and global markets cannot be overstated. Several of the most highly valued companies are data-driven innovators. That is why companies such as Apple, Google, Microsoft, Amazon, and Facebook, alongside traditional technology powerhouses, such as Intel, IBM and AT&T, and new upstarts, including Uber and Snap, are the focus of heated consumer discussion and regulatory debate.[14] This trend goes beyond the United States and, more broadly, the Western world. Chinese tech giants, such as Baidu, Alibaba, JD.com, and surging new entrants – notably, Didi Chuxing, and Lu.com – are shaking up the Asian economy and gaining a global footprint.[15] These companies have profound impacts our lives. Every day, they confront a host of complex value-laden choices when designing products that collect, analyze, process, and store information about every aspect of our behavior. Realizing the magnitude of these decisions, companies have begun to create ethical review processes, employ data ethicists and philosophers, and seek guidance from academics, think tanks, policymakers, and regulators.[16] The role of the chief privacy officer, once the domain of only a handful of

[11] Omer Tene & Jules Polonetsky, *To Track or "Do Not Track": Advancing Transparency and Individual Control in Online Behavioral Advertising*, 13 MINN. J. L. SCI. & TECH. 281 (2012).

[12] Woodrow Hartzog & Evan Selinger, *The Internet of Heirlooms and Disposable Things*, 17 N. C. J. L. & TECH. 581 (2016).

[13] Chris Jay Hoofnagle, *Big Brother's Little Helpers: How ChoicePoint and Other Commercial Data Brokers Collect, Process, and Package Your Data for Law Enforcement*, 29 N. C. J. INT'L L. & COM. REG. 595 (2004).

[14] Farhad Manjoo, *Tech's "Frightful 5" Will Dominate Digital Life for Foreseeable Future*, N.Y. TIMES, Jan. 20, 2016, https://www.nytimes.com/2016/01/21/technology/techs-frightful-5-will-dominate-digital-life-for-foreseeable-future.html.

[15] Brendon Kochkodin, *Chinese Big Five Tech Companies Gain on U.S. Counterparts*, BLOOMBERG BUSINESSWEEK, June 22, 2017, https://www.bloomberg.com/news/articles/2017-06-23/chinese-big-five-tech-companies-gain-on-u-s-counterparts.

[16] Jules Polonetsky, Omer Tene & Joseph Jerome, *Beyond the Common Rule: Ethical Structures for Data Research in Non-Academic Settings*, 13 COLO. TECH. L. J. 333 (2015); also see Ryan Calo, *Consumer Subject Review Boards: A Thought Experiment*, 66 STAN. L. REV. ONLINE 97, 102 (2013); Evan Selinger & Woodrow Hartzog, *Facebook's*

technology leaders, has emerged as a strategic C-suite position.[17] Within a decade, privacy has matured into a full-fledged profession with a body of knowledge, professional certifications, and formal legal status.[18]

Increasingly, not only companies but also government entities are transforming into data service providers for consumers. Consider smart cities, where local governments have become hubs of data that is collected through growing networks of sensors and connected technologies to generate actionable, often real-time information.[19] By relying on ubiquitous telecommunications technologies to provide connectivity to sensor networks and set actuation devices into operation, smart cities are increasingly collecting information on cities' air quality, temperature, noise, street and pedestrian traffic, parking capacity, distribution of government services, emergency situations, and crowd sentiments, among other data points. This information can now be cheaply aggregated, stored, and analyzed to draw conclusions about the intimate affairs of city dwellers. The more connected a city becomes, the more it will generate steady streams of data from and about its citizens and the environment they live in.[20]

The urban data revolution enables cities to better manage traffic congestion, improve energy efficiency, expand connectivity, reduce crime, and regulate utility flow. By analyzing data trends and auditing the performance of schools, public transportation, waste management, social services, and law enforcement, smart cities can better identify and respond to discriminatory practices and biased decision-making, empowering weakened populations and holding institutions to account. At the same time, the specter of constant monitoring threatens to upset the balance of power between city governments and city residents. At the extreme, it might destroy the sense of anonymity that has defined urban life over the past century. As Kelsey Finch and Omer Tene observe, "There is a real risk that, rather than standing as 'paragons of democracy,' [smart cities] could turn into electronic panopticons in which everybody is constantly watched."[21]

Smart community policy also highlights the tension between the push for open data mandates and public records acts and the desire citizens have for privacy. On the one hand, the transparency goals of the open data movement serve important social, economic, and democratic functions. Open and accessible public data can benefit individuals, companies, communities, and government by fueling new social, economic, and civic innovations, and improving government accountability and transparency. On the other hand, because the city collects and shares information about its citizens, public backlash over intrusive surveillance remains an ever-present possibility.[22] Due to these competing concerns, the consumer privacy discussion requires aligning potentially conflicting interests: maximizing transparency and accountability without forsaking individual rights.

Emotional Contagion Study and the Ethical Problem of Co-Opted Identity in Mediated Environments Where Users Lack Control, 12 RESEARCH ETHICS 35 (2016).

[17] Andrew Clearwater & J. Trevor Hughes, *In the Beginning . . . An Early History of the Privacy Profession*, 74 OHIO ST. L. J. 897 (2013).

[18] J. Trevor Hughes & Cobun Keegan, *Enter the Professionals: Organizational Privacy in a Digital Age* (see Chapter 22).

[19] Kelsey Finch & Omer Tene, *Welcome to Metropticon: Protecting Privacy in a Hyperconnected Town*, 41 FORDHAM URBAN L. J. 1581 (2015).

[20] Kelsey Finch & Omer Tene, *The City as a Platform: Enhancing Privacy and Transparency in Smart Communities* (see Chapter 7).

[21] Finch & Tene, *supra* note 16, at 1583.

[22] Ben Green, Gabe Cunningham, Ariel Ekblaw, Paul Kominers, Andrew Linzer & Susan Crawford, *Open Data Privacy: A Risk-Benefit, Process-Oriented Approach to Sharing and Protecting Municipal Data* (Berkman Klein Center for Internet & Society Research Publication, 2017), https://dash.harvard.edu/bitstream/handle/1/30340010/OpenData Privacy.pdf.

BEYOND PRIVACY

As we have been suggesting, arguments about privacy have become proxy debates for broader societal choices about fairness, equity, and power. Since data is central to economic activity across every sector – government, non-profit, and corporate – the privacy debate has spilled over to adjacent areas. Educational technology is a prime example.

Long confined to using textbooks, blackboards, and pencil-and-paper testing, schools now use new applications, hardware, and services. This includes online curricula and tools, social media and cloud applications for file sharing and storage, note taking, and collaboration platforms, and a variety of connected tablets and workstations. Student performance data is driving next-generation models of learning and measurements for teacher effectiveness. And connected learning is fast becoming a path for access to knowledge and academic achievement.

New educational technology offers many advantages for educators, teachers, parents, and students. Education has become more interactive, adaptive, responsive, and even fun. Parents can stay apprised of their child's performance, accomplishments, and difficulties without weighing down teachers' limited time resource. Teachers can connect to sophisticated learning management systems, while school administrations can obtain rich, measurable inputs to better calibrate resources to needs.[23]

However, from a privacy perspective, the confluence of enhanced data collection that contains highly sensitive information about children and teens also makes for a combustive mix. New data flows raise questions about who should have access to students' data and what are the legitimate uses of the information. Should a developer of a math app be authorized to offer high-performing students a version that covers more advanced material, or would that be considered undesirable marketing to children? Should an educational social network be permitted to feature a third-party app store for kids? Or, if an education service detects a security vulnerability on a website that is available for schools to use, should it be able to leverage its knowledge to protect schools as well as clients outside of the educational sector? And what about education technology developers who want to use the data they extract from students to develop software for the general market?

It is clear that when it comes to education, privacy means different things to different people and traditional privacy problems are only the tip of the policy iceberg. Activists have challenged data collection and use to debate school reform, common core curricula, standardized testing, personalized learning, teacher assessments, and more. Some critics even consider efforts to ramp up education technology misguided altogether, labeling them as the work of "corporate educa-tion reformers" who seek profit at the expense of public education. Ultimately, then, the challenge for educational technology entails differentiating problems that can be remedied with privacy solutions from problems that require other resolutions because they are, at bottom, proxies for conflicts about education policy.

Complex conversations also surround smart cars and autonomous vehicles. On the one hand, collecting data in cars is old hat. Vehicles have had computerized data systems since the 1960s. On the other hand, things are profoundly changing now that vehicles are becoming data hubs that collect, process, and broadcast information about drivers' performance, geolocation, tele-matics, biometrics, and even media consumption. Furthermore, vehicle-to-vehicle (V2V)

---

[23] Jules Polonetsky & Omer Tene, *Who is Reading Whom Now: Privacy in Education from Books to MOOCs*, 17 Vand. J. Ent. & Tech. L. 927 (2015); *also see* Jules Polonetsky & Omer Tene, *The Ethics of Student Privacy: Building Trust for Ed Tech*, 21 Int'l Rev. Info. Ethics 25 (2014).

technology introduces a new way for smart cars to seamlessly receive and analyze information about other vehicles. This capability is essentially transforming public thoroughfares into a seamless network of information about each vehicle's position, direction of travel, speed, braking, and other variables that telematics studies.[24]

Smart car data collection raises all kinds of issues. Consumers and advocates are concerned about cars extracting personal data that can be shared with government and law enforcement. Security experts are anxious about self-driving cars being vulnerable to hacking. At the same time, under the banner of privacy concerns, critics also discuss ethics, labor markets, insurance premiums, and tradeoffs between safety and autonomy. For example, while smart cars and autonomous vehicles can reduce traffic accidents, they will also need to make decisions with moral implications, such as choosing to prioritize the safety of passengers or pedestrians. Coding algorithms to make momentous moral choices is a formidable challenge that transcends the guidance traditional privacy frameworks offer.

Insurance companies are vigorously embracing the growth in vehicle-generated data by developing usage-based applications to harness information emanating from onboard diagnostic systems. These applications provide insurers with information on how a vehicle is driven, and they factor in this information when making decisions about safe driver programs and personalized insurance rates. While the Fair Credit Reporting Act applies to the process of using data to make insurance decisions, its standards cannot address all of the questions that are starting to arise. Concern is being expressed over allocations of risk and the process of creating categories of drivers who are uninsurable due to traits and tendencies that potentially can be correlated with health, genetics, race, and ethnicity. Also, within a generation, autonomous vehicles will fundamentally upend labor markets. Ostensibly consumers will benefit from increased fleet efficiency and huge savings in labor costs. At the same time, the economic changes seem poised to dramatically affect employment prospects, especially for the millions of taxi and truck drivers in the United States and beyond.[25] These policy issues clearly extend digital and cyber privacy debates into new realms and possibly transform them as well.

THE FUTURE OF SOCIETY

The upshot of the dynamics and processes highlighted here is that the chapters in this book are about much more than consumer privacy – which is to say, they go far beyond consumer privacy construed as a niche topic. Contributors fundamentally advance conversations about what paths should be paved in order to create flourishing societies in the future. With every aspect of human behavior being observed, logged, analyzed, categorized, and stored, technology is forcing legislatures, regulators, and courts to deal with an incessant flow of weighty policy choices. These debates have long spilled over from the contours of privacy, narrowly defined as a right to anonymity, seclusion and intimacy – a right to be let alone[26] – to a discussion about power and democracy, social organization, and the role humans should occupy in technologically mediated spaces. These tough discussions are about matters such as exposure, profiling and discrimination, self-expression, individual autonomy, and the relative roles of humans and machines.

---

[24] Lauren Smith & John Verdi, *Comments from the Future of Privacy Forum to the Federal Trade Commission and U.S. Department of Transportation* (National Highway Traffic Safety Administration, May 1, 2017), https://fpf.org/wp-content/uploads/2017/05/Future-of-Privacy-Forum-Comments-FTC-NHTSA-Workshop.pdf.

[25] *See, e.g., The Future of Jobs: Employment, Skills and Workforce Strategy for the Fourth Industrial Revolution* (World Economic Forum, Jan. 2016), http://www3.weforum.org/docs/WEF_Future_of_Jobs.pdf.

[26] Samuel Warren and & Louis Brandeis, *The Right to Privacy*, 4 HARV. L. REV. 193 (1890).

Consider what happened when a teacher was fired after a picture was posted on Facebook of her dressed as a drunk pirate. It was hard to know if the ensuing public debate was about privacy settings on the social network or the limits of assessing behavior in a world where every action is documented, tagged, and presented to the public to judge.[27] Similarly, it is hard to pinpoint what parents and teachers are concerned about when they recoil against ephemeral cyberbullying messages on apps such as Snapchat. Is it dismay about the software's privacy settings? Or might it be sadness over the cruel experiences of childhood being exposed and augmented through a new medium?[28] And what about autonomous vehicles engineers who design a real-life response to the longstanding trolley problem? Are they dealing with fair information practice principles or ethical challenges that have occupied philosophers from Aristotle to Immanuel Kant and John Stuart Mill?[29]

Advances in artificial intelligence and machine learning keep raising the stakes. Developers deploy artificial intelligence to improve organizations' performance and derive predictions in almost every area of the economy. This happens in domains ranging from social networks, autonomous vehicles, drones, precision medicine, and the criminal justice system. And it includes such processes as speech and image recognition, universal translators, and ad targeting, to name a few. Organizations leverage algorithms to make data-based determinations that impact individuals' rights as citizens, employees, seekers of credit or insurance, and so much more. For example, employers use algorithms to assess prospective employees by offering neuroscience-based games that are said to measure inherent traits. Even judges turn to algorithms for sentencing and parole decisions. They use data to predict a person's risk of recidivism, violence, or failure to appear in court based on a complicated mix of behavioral and demographic characteristics.[30]

Daniele Citron has written about the importance of creating appropriate standards of algorithmic due process that include transparency, a right to correct inaccurate information, and a right to appeal adverse decisions.[31] Unfortunately, this goal might be incredibly difficult to meet. Thanks to machine learning, sophisticated algorithmic decision-making processes arguably have become inscrutable, even to their programmers. The emergent gap between what humans and machines know has led some critics, such as Frank Pasquale, to warn against the risks of a *Black Box Society*[32] driven by what Cathy O'Neil dubs *Weapons of Math Destruction*.[33]

At the same time, breakthroughs in artificial intelligence have enabled disenfranchised groups to speak the truth to power by identifying biases and inequities that were previously hidden in

---

[27] Jeffrey Rosen, *The Web Means the End of Forgetting*, N.Y. TIMES, July 21, 2010, http://www.nytimes.com/2010/07/25/magazine/25privacy-t2.html.

[28] J. Mitchell Vaterlaus, Kathryn Barnett, Cesia Roche and & Jimmy Young, *"Snapchat is more personal": An Exploratory Study on Snapchat Behaviors and Young Adult Interpersonal Relationships*, 62 COMPUTERS HUM. BEHAV. 594 (2016); *also see* Evan Selinger, Brenda Leong & Bill Fitzgerald, *Schools Fail to Recognize Privacy Consequences of Social Media*, CHRISTIAN SCI. MONITOR, Jan. 20, 2016, https://www.csmonitor.com/World/Passcode/Passcode-Voices/2016/0120/Opinion-Schools-fail-to-recognize-privacy-consequences-of-social-media.

[29] *Why Self-Driving Cars Must Be Programmed to Kill*, MIT TECH. REV., Oct. 22, 2015, https://www.technologyreview.com/s/542626/why-self-driving-cars-must-be-programmed-to-kill/.

[30] Omer Tene & Jules Polonetsky, *Taming the Golem: Challenges of Ethical Algorithmic Decision Making*, 19 N. C. J. L. & TECH. (forthcoming 2019).

[31] Danielle Keats Citron, *Technological Due Process*, 85 WASH. U. L. REV. 1249 (2008).

[32] FRANK PASQUALE, THE BLACK BOX SOCIETY (Harvard University Press, 2015).

[33] CATHY O'NEIL, WEAPONS OF MATH DESTRUCTION: HOW BIG DATA INCREASES INEQUALITY AND THREATENS DEMOCRACY (Crown, 2016).

opaque databases or behind faceless human bureaucracies.[34] New uses of data can also save lives. For example, the United Nations Global Pulse project uses data from cell phones in developing countries to detect pandemics, relieve famine, and fight human trafficking.[35] New policy initiatives have been started that recognize the mixed blessings of artificial intelligence and the inevitable trade-offs created by using it. The Partnership on Artificial Intelligence, for example, is set "to address such areas as fairness and inclusivity, explanation and transparency, security and privacy, values and ethics, collaboration between people and artificial intelligence systems, interoperability of systems, and the trustworthiness, reliability, containment, safety, and robustness of the technology."[36]

In an ideal world, due process would be secured and every company would follow all of the technical privacy rules all of the time. But even in such a utopia, consumers and commentators probably still would be unsettled by "creepy" technologically mediated behavior. Attributions of "creepy" revolve around activities where people believe that harm is occurring even though privacy settings are not circumvented and data use technically remains within the scope of its intended purposes. These are instances where new technology further erodes cherished values, such as obscurity, or new uses of existing technologies produce novel outcomes, such as unexpected data use or customization.[37] People are rattled by such threats to traditional social norms and the prospect that unsettling new practices will be normalized. In these moments, they wonder why engineers and marketers fail to anticipate problems. Sometimes, they hold these groups accountable.

All of this suggests that, far from what a first glance at the title of this volume might lead readers to expect, the *Cambridge Handbook of Consumer Privacy* critically explores core issues that will determine how the future is shaped. To do justice to the magnitude and complexity of these topics, we have asked contributors to address as many parts and perspectives of the consumer privacy debate as possible. How we, all of us, collectively grapple with these issues will determine the fate of technology and course of humanity.[38]

CHAPTER SUMMARIES[39]

The Pervasiveness and Value of Tracking Technologies

In Chapter 2, "Data Brokers – Should They Be Reviled or Revered," Jennifer Barrett Glasgow defines the various types of data brokers as they exist today in the United States. She discusses where they get their data and how much of it is aggregated from multiple sources. Glasgow also describes how data brokers deliver data to the marketplace and who buys data from a data broker. She covers how data brokers are regulated by law or self-regulation and how they interact with consumers. Finally, Glasgow outlines the risks that data brokers pose, and briefly poses some thoughts about their future.

---

[34] *Big Data: A Tool for Fighting Discrimination and Empowering Groups* (Future of Privacy Forum and Anti-Defamation League Report, 2014), https://fpf.org/wp-content/uploads/Big-Data-A-Tool-for-Fighting-Discrimination-and-Empowering-Groups-FINAL.pdf.

[35] *The State of Mobile Data for Social Good Report* (United Nations Global Pulse, June 2017), http://unglobalpulse.org/sites/default/files/MobileDataforSocialGoodReport_29June.pdf.

[36] Goals statement, PARTNERSHIP ON AI, https://www.partnershiponai.org/.

[37] Woodrow Hartzog & Evan Selinger, *Surveillance as Loss of Obscurity*, 72 WASH. & LEE L. REV. 1343 (2015).

[38] *See, e.g.,* Evan Selinger & Brett Frischmann, *Utopia?: A Technologically Determined World of Frictionless Transactions, Optimized Production, and Maximal Happiness*, 64 UCLA L. REV. DISC. 372 (2016).

[39] To ensure all of the chapters are fairly summarized, we asked contributors to provide their own. What follows are versions of their summaries, in some cases verbatim.

In Chapter 3, "In Defense of Big Data Analytics," Mark MacCarthy argues that big data analytics, including machine learning and artificial intelligence, are natural outgrowths of recent developments in computer technology such as the availability of massive data sets, vast increases in computing power, and breakthroughs in analytical techniques. These techniques promise unprecedented benefits for consumers, workers, and society at large, but they also pose challenges for privacy and fairness. MacCarthy's chapter contains a short summary of the range of potential benefits made possible by these new analytic techniques and then discusses privacy and fairness challenges. Principles of privacy policy requiring data minimization and restricting secondary data use need to be reformulated to allow for both the successful delivery of big data benefits and effective privacy protection. Ubiquitous re-identification risks and information externalities reduce the ability of individuals to control the disclosure of information and suggest less reliance on notice and choice mechanisms. Big data analytics can pose fairness challenges, but these techniques are not exempt from existing antidiscrimination and consumer protection laws. Regulatory agencies and courts need to enforce these laws against any abuses accomplished through big data analysis. Disclosure of source code is not an effective way to respond to the challenges of designing and using unbiased algorithms. Instead, enterprises should develop and implement a framework for responsible use of data analytics that will provide for fairness by design and after-the-fact audits of algorithms in use. Such a framework will need to adopt standards of fairness and appropriate remedies for findings of disparate impact. This will require moving beyond technical matters to address sensitive normative issues where the interests of different groups collide and moral intuitions diverge. A collaborative effort of businesses, governments, academics, and civil rights and public interest groups might sharpen the issues and allow sharing of information and best practices in a way that would benefit all.

In Chapter 4, "Education Technology and Student Privacy," Elana Zeide argues that new education technology (ed tech) creates new ways to manage, deliver, and measure education that generate a previously unimaginable array and detail of information about students' actions both within and outside classrooms. She claims that data-driven education tools have the potential to revolutionize the education system – and, in doing so, provide more access to better quality, lower-cost education and broader socioeconomic opportunity. The information generated by such tools also provides fodder for more informed teacher, school, and policy decision-making. At the same time, Zeide maintains, these data practices go against traditional expectations about student privacy. The education context requires a tailored approach to data protection. Few students can opt out of school information practices, making consent-based protections potentially problematic. Maturing data subjects, Zeide cautions, raises concerns about creating modern day "permanent records" with outdated information that unfairly foreclose opportunities. Many fear for-profit providers will prioritize generating revenue over students' educational interests. Traditional student privacy regulations aren't designed for an era of the tremendous volume, variety, and velocity of big data, because they rely on privacy self-management and institutional oversight. Many newer state laws restrict commercial educational technology services to using student data only for "school purposes," but don't cover the potential unintended consequences and nuanced ethical considerations surrounding educational use of data. As a result, Zeide concludes, the responsibility rests on entities generating, collecting, and using student data to adopt best practices to meet the specific expectations and considerations of education environments.

In Chapter 5, "Mobile Privacy Expectations: How Privacy Is Respected in Mobile Devices," Kirsten Martin and Katie Shilton describe privacy challenges raised by mobile devices, explore user privacy expectations for mobile devices, and discuss developer responses to privacy concerns. Martin and Shilton argue that mobile technologies change social practices and introduce new surveillance concerns into consumers' everyday lives. Yet, consumers, regulators, and even the developers who build mobile applications struggle to define their expectations for the privacy of this data, and consumers and developers express different privacy expectations. The authors argue firms and regulators can help mitigate the gap between developers and consumers by making privacy by design part of corporate governance and establishing privacy as a first-order concern for protecting consumer trust.

In Chapter 6, "Face Recognition, Real-Time Identification, and Beyond," Yana Welinder and Aeryn Palmer provide an overview of face recognition technology and recent efforts to regulate its use. They first explain the process by which face recognition technology operates, including recent advancements in its capabilities through the use of neural networks. They then discuss various consumer applications of the technology, such as mobile apps and social network features that can identify people in photos. Next, they survey regulatory responses to face recognition technology across the globe, highlighting new developments and previewing possible trends to come in the United States, the European Union, Canada, China, and other jurisdictions. The discussion demonstrates the lack of regulation in some areas and reveals global uncertainty about how best to control face recognition technology under the law. The chapter concludes with recommendations to two types of stakeholders. First, it addresses policy-makers, encouraging them to balance support for innovation with protection of individual privacy rights. It stresses the importance of obtaining consent from all relevant parties, and of giving special consideration to government access to privately held face recognition data. Finally, Welinder and Palmer suggest that developers leverage User Experience Design as a notice tool, collect and retain a minimal amount of data, and keep the principles of security by design at the forefront of their minds.

In Chapter 7, "Smart Cities: Privacy, Transparency, Community," Kelsey Finch and Omer Tene argue that today's cities are pervaded by growing networks of connected technologies to generate actionable, often real-time data about the city and its citizens. The more connected a city becomes, the more it will generate a steady stream of data from and about its citizens. As smart city technologies are being rapidly adopted around the globe, we must determine how communities can leverage the benefits of a data-rich society while minimizing threats to individuals' privacy and civil liberties. Just as there are many methods and metrics to assess a smart city's livability, or sustainability, or efficiency, so too there are different lenses through which cities can evaluate their privacy preparedness. This chapter lays out three such perspectives, considering a smart city's privacy responsibilities in the context of its roles as a data steward, data platform, and government authority. By considering the deployment of smart city technologies in these three lights, communities will be better prepared to reassure residents of smart cities that their rights will be respected and their data protected.

Ethical and Legal Reservations about Tracking Technologies

In Chapter 8, "Americans and Marketplace Privacy: Seven Annenberg National Surveys in Perspective," Joseph Turow sketches the growing surveillance and personalized targeting of Americans carried out by marketers as well as the public arguments used to defend these activities. At the core of their justifications is the notion that despite professed concerns over privacy, people are rationally willing to trade information for the relevant benefit that marketers provide. Drawing on seven nationally representative telephone surveys from 1999 through 2015, Turow presents findings that tend to refute marketers' justifications for increased personalized surveillance and targeting of individuals. Contrary to the claim that a majority of Americans consent to data collection because the commercial benefits are worth the costs, he also shows that the 2015 survey supports a different explanation: a large pool of Americans feel resigned to the inevitability of surveillance and the power of marketers to harvest data. When they give up information as they shop it merely *appears* they are interested in tradeoffs. The overall message of the surveys is that legislators, regulators, and courts ought to rethink the traditional regulatory understanding of harm in the face of a developing American marketplace that ignores the majority of Americans' views and is making overarching tracking and surreptitious profiling an aspect of society taken for granted.

In Chapter 9, "The Federal Trade Commission's Inner Privacy Struggle," Chris Jay Hoofnagle's discusses the cultural and ideological conflicts on privacy internal to the FTC, and explains why the lawyers at the Commission are leading the privacy charge. This is because the Bureau of Economics is constitutionally skeptical of information privacy. Privacy skepticism reflects the economists' academic methods and ideological commitments. While information privacy is a deeply multidisciplinary field, the Bureau of Economics adheres to a disciplinarity that bounds its inquiry and causes it to follow a laissez faire literature. Commitments to "consumer welfare," concerns about innovation policy, lingering effects of Reagan-era leadership, the lack of a clearly-defined market for privacy, and the return of rule of reason analysis in antitrust also contribute to the Bureau of Economics' skepticism toward rights-based privacy regimes. Hoofnagle concludes with a roadmap for expanding the BE's disciplinary borders, for enriching its understanding of the market for privacy, and for a reinvigoration of the FTC's civil penalty factors as a lodestar for privacy remedies.

In Chapter 10, "Privacy and Human Behavior in the Information Age," Alessandro Acquisti, Laura Brandimarte, and George Lowenstein provide a review that summarizes and draws connections between diverse streams of empirical research on privacy behavior. They use three themes to connect insights from social and behavioral sciences: people's uncertainty about the consequences of privacy-related behaviors and their own preferences over those consequences; the context-dependence of people's concern, or lack thereof, about privacy; and the degree to which privacy concerns are malleable – manipulable by commercial and governmental interests. Organizing our discussion by these themes, the authors offer observations concerning the role of public policy in the protection of privacy in the information age.

In Chapter 11, "Privacy, Vulnerability, and Affordance," Ryan Calo argues that the relationship between privacy and vulnerability is complex. Privacy can be both a shield against vulnerability and a sword in its service. What is needed to capture this nuanced interaction is a theoretical lens rooted in the physical and social environments as they exist, but also sensitive to the differing ways people perceive and experience that environment. Calo further contends that James Gibson's theory of affordance is an interesting candidate to capture this complexity, including in the context of consumer privacy. Affordance theory, Calo demonstrates, helps generate and unify some of consumer privacy's most important questions and will perhaps one day lead to better answers.

In Chapter 12, "Ethical Considerations When Companies Study – and Fail to Study – Their Customers," Michelle N. Meyer provides an overview of the different ways in which businesses increasingly study their customers, users, employees, and other stakeholders, and the different reasons why they do so. Meyer argues, however, that a complete ethical analysis of business research requires consideration not only of the purpose, nature, and effects of such research but also of a business's choice *not* to study the effects of its products, services, and practices on stakeholders. Depending on a variety of criteria she discusses, a particular business study – even one conducted without study-specific informed consent – can fall on a spectrum from unethical to ethically permissible to ethically laudable or even obligatory. Although business research is now ubiquitous – in many ways, happily so – the fact that individual, study-specific informed consent is usually infeasible in this context means that a careful consideration of a study's risks and expected benefits is called for. For reasons that Meyer explains, the *content* of federal regulations that govern risk-benefit analyses of most academic and some industry research – the so-called Common Rule – is not easily translated to the business setting. But she argues that companies should consider adopting something like the *process* used by institutional reviews boards (IRBs) to prospectively review and oversee research, and provides recommendations about how such company "research review boards" might operate.

In Chapter 13, "Algorithmic Discrimination vs. Privacy Law," Alvaro Bedoya addresses the intersection of two pressing debates: the desire to eliminate bias in automated decision-making systems, and the recent industry-led push to enforce privacy protections at the point of data *use*, rather than the point of data *collection*. Bedoya highlights that most proposed solutions to the problem of algorithmic bias have tended to focus on *post*-collection remedies. Honing in on a specific technology, face recognition, Bedoya argues that correcting for algorithmic bias in this way will prove to be difficult, if not impossible. Instead, he says, the most effective means to counter algorithmic discrimination may come at the beginning of the data life cycle – at the point of collection. In making this argument, he emphasizes the importance of collection controls in any comprehensive privacy protection regime.

In Chapter 14, "Children, Privacy, and the New Online Realities," Stephen Balkam discusses the extraordinary challenges we all face in staying private in our hyperconnected lives. He emphasizes the difficulties parents, platforms, and policy makers face in keeping children's data private in an age of connected toys, devices, and always-on connectivity. Balkam looks at the history and evolution of the Children's Online Privacy Protection Act (COPPA) and addresses its benefits and shortcomings. He looks at how major social media platforms, such as Facebook, have responded to COPPA as well as some of the companies that have fallen foul of the law. In addition to considering the likes of Hello Barbie and Amazon's Echo, Balkam also considers the range of potential privacy issues brought by innovations in virtual, augmented, and mixed reality devices, apps and games. He concludes with a look at the future of children's privacy in an AI-infused, constantly monitored world. Balkam suggests that solutions will have to be found across the public, private, and non-profit sectors and then communicated clearly and consistently to parents and their digitally savvy children.

In Chapter 15, "Stakeholders and High Stakes: Divergent Standards for Do Not Track," Aleecia M. McDonald provides an in-depth look at the history of Do Not Track, informed by McDonald's personal experience as an original cochair of the World Wide Web Committee standards group. In the United States, the Do Not Call list is considered one of the big successes in consumer privacy. In contrast, Do Not Track was dubbed "worse than a miserable failure" before it even got out of the standards committee trying to define it. At this time, Do Not Track is a soon-to-be published standard from the World Wide Web Committee (W3C), where standards emerge for web technologies such as HTML, which is the language of web pages. Meanwhile, the Electronic Frontier Foundation (EFF), an online rights group, has devised its own privacy-enhanced version of Do Not Track, with multiple companies pledging to use it. Several ad blockers will permit ads from companies that honor EFF's Do Not Track, providing a carrot and stick approach to user privacy and control. In yet a third approach, Do Not Track was suggested as a way to signal compliance with European Union privacy laws, both in a recent international Privacy Bridges project, as well as in publications by this author and leading European privacy scholars. The best thing about standards, as the saying goes, is that there are so many to choose from. Yet from a user's perspective, how can the multiplicity of Do Not Track approaches be anything but confusion?

In Chapter 16, "Applying Ethics When Using Data Beyond Individuals' Understanding," Martin E. Abrams and Lynn A. Goldstein contend that with the expanding use of observational data for advanced analytics, organizations are increasingly looking to move beyond technical compliance with the law to the ethical use of data. Organizations need to understand the fair processing risks and benefits they create for individuals, whether they are ethically appropriate, and how they might be demonstrated to others. Their chapter explores the evolution of data-driven research and analytics, discusses how ethics might be applied in an assessment process, and sets forth one process for assessing whether big data projects are appropriate.

International Perspectives

In Chapter 17, "Profiling and the Essence of the Right to Data Protection," Bilyana Petkova and Franziska Boehm begin by reviewing the legislative history of the provision on automated decision-making in the 1995 EU Data Protection Directive (the 1995 Directive), as it was amended in the process of adopting a new EU General Data Protection Regulation that would enter into force in 2018. Next, they discuss profiling in the context of the case law of the Court of Justice of the European Union (CJEU) in the *Google Spain*, *Digital Rights Ireland*, and *Schrems* cases. Petkova and Boehm argue that the CJEU might be making a subtle move in its interpretation of the EU Charter of Fundamental Rights toward protecting against undesirable profiling measures instead of merely protecting against the identification of an individual. Finally, from the employment context, they discuss a few hypotheticals of algorithmic decision-making that illustrate how the relevant legislative framework might be applied.

In Chapter 18, "Privacy, Freedom of Expression, and the Right to be Forgotten in Europe," Stefan Kulk and Frederik Zuiderveen Borgesius discuss the relation between privacy and freedom of expression in Europe. In principle, the two rights have equal weight in Europe – which right prevails depends on the circumstances of a case. To illustrate the difficulties when balancing privacy and freedom of expression, Kulk and Borgesius discuss the *Google Spain* judgment of the Court of Justice of the European Union, sometimes called the "right to be forgotten" judgment. The court decided in *Google Spain* that, under certain conditions, people have the right to have search results for their name delisted. The authors discuss how Google and Data Protection Authorities deal with such delisting requests in practice. Delisting requests illustrate that balancing the interests of privacy and freedom of expression will always remain difficult.

In Chapter 19, "Understanding the Balancing Act Behind the Legitimate Interest of the Controller Ground: A Pragmatic Approach," Irene Kamara and Paul De Hert analyse the provision of the legitimate interest ground in the new EU data protection framework, the General Data Protection Regulation. The authors explain that the rationale of the legitimate interest ground is that under certain conditions, controllers' or third parties' interests might be justified to prevail over the interests, rights, and freedoms of the data subject. When and how the prevailing may take place under the GDPR provisions is not a one-dimensional assessment. De Hert and Kamara suggest a formalisation of the legitimate interest ground steps toward the decision of the controller on whether to base his or her processing on the legitimate interest ground. They argue that the legitimate interest ground should not be seen in isolation, but through the lens of the data protection principles of Article 5 GDPR and Article 8 Charter

Fundamental Rights EU. The authors further analyse the relevant case law of the Court of Justice EU, as well as the cases of Network and Information Security and Big Data and Profiling. Kamara and De Hert conclude that the legitimate interest of the controller is not a loophole in the data protection legislation, as has often been alleged, but an equivalent basis for lawful processing, which can distinguish controllers in bad faith from controllers processing data in good faith.

New Approaches to Improve the Status Quo

In Chapter 20, "The Intersection of Privacy and Consumer Protection," Julie Brill explores the intersection between privacy and consumer protection in the United States. She surveys the consumer protection laws that simultaneously address privacy harms, and also examines how the Federal Trade Commission's consumer protection mission has allowed the Commission to become a lead privacy regulator. Along the way, Brill delves into the challenges posed by data brokers, lead generators, and alternative credit scoring – as well as potential avenues for the United States to strengthen privacy protections.

In Chapter 21, "A Design Space for Effective Privacy Notices," Florian Schaub, Rebecca Balebako, Adam L. Durity, and Lorrie Faith Cranor argue that notifying users about a system's data practices is supposed to enable users to make informed privacy decisions. Yet, current notice and choice mechanisms, such as privacy policies, are often ineffective because they are neither usable nor useful, and are therefore ignored by users. Constrained interfaces on mobile devices, wearables, and smart home devices connected in an Internet of Things exacerbate the issue. Much research has studied the usability issues of privacy notices and many proposals for more usable privacy notices exist. Yet, there is little guidance for designers and developers on the design aspects that can impact the effectiveness of privacy notices. In this chapter, Schaub, Balebako, Durity, and Cranor make multiple contributions to remedy this issue. They survey the existing literature on privacy notices and identify challenges, requirements, and best practices for privacy notice design. Further, they map out the design space for privacy notices by identifying relevant dimensions. This provides a taxonomy and consistent terminology of notice approaches to foster understanding and reasoning about notice options available in the context of specific systems. Our systemization of knowledge and the developed design space can help designers, developers, and researchers identify notice and choice requirements and develop a comprehensive notice concept for their system that addresses the needs of different audiences and considers the system's limitations and opportunities for providing notice.

In Chapter 22, "Enter the Professionals: Organizational Privacy in a Digital Age," J. Trevor Hughes and Cobun Keegan observe that contemporary privacy professionals apply legal, technological, and management knowledge to balance the important concerns of citizens and consumers with the interests of companies and governments worldwide. They further note that the field of information privacy has rapidly matured into an organized, interdisciplinary profession with international reach. Their chapter compares the burgeoning privacy profession with other modern professions, describing its history and similar growth curve while highlighting the unique characteristics of a profession that combines law, policy, technology, business, and ethics against a rapidly shifting technological landscape. As it has grown into a profession, Hughes and Keegan argue that privacy has developed a broad body of knowledge with multiple specialties, gained recognition as a vital component of organizational management, and become formally organized through professional associations and credentialing programs. Government recognition and enforcement actions have legitimized the role of privacy professionals even as these professionals work collectively to synthesize comprehensive and lasting ethical norms. In an era increasingly fueled and defined by data, significant changes in the shape of our economy and professional workforce are inevitable. By guiding the governance and dissemination of personal information, Hughes and Keegan argue that the privacy profession is well situated to grow and mature in these rapidly changing times.

In Chapter 23, "Privacy Statements: Purposes, Requirements, and Best Practices," Mike Hintze addresses common criticisms of privacy statements and argues that many criticisms misunderstand the most important purposes of privacy statements, while others can be addressed through careful and informed drafting. Hintze suggests that while drafting a privacy statement may be considered by some to be one of the most basic tasks of a privacy professional, doing it well is no simple matter. One must understand and reconcile a host of statutory and self-regulatory obligations. One must consider different audiences who may read the statement from different perspectives. One must balance pressures to make the statement simple and readable against pressures to make it comprehensive and detailed. A mistake can form the basis for an FTC deception claim. And individual pieces can be taken out of context and spun into public relations debacles. Hintze's chapter explores the art of crafting a privacy statement. It explains the multiple purposes of a privacy statement. It lists and discusses the many elements included in a privacy statement – some required by law and others based on an organization's objectives. Finally, it describes different approaches to drafting privacy statements and suggests best practices based on a more complete understanding of a privacy statement's purposes and audiences.

In Chapter 24, "Privacy Versus Research in Big Data," Jane R. Bambauer analyzes how traditional notions of privacy threaten the unprecedented opportunity to study humans in the Big Data era. After briefly describing the set of laws currently constraining research, the chapter identifies puzzles and potential flaws in three popular forms of privacy protection. First, data protection laws typically forbid companies from repurposing data that was collected for a different, unrelated use. Second, there is a growing appreciation that anonymized data can be reidentified, so regulators are increasingly skeptical about using anonymization to facilitate the sharing of research data. And third, research law generally prohibits researchers from performing secret interventions on human subjects. Together, these restrictions will interfere with a great amount of Big Data research potential, and society may not get much in return for the opportunity costs.

In Chapter 25, "A Marketplace for Privacy: Incentives for Privacy Engineering and Innovation," Courtney Bowman and John Grant inquire into what drives businesses to offer technologies and policies designed to protect consumer privacy. The authors argue that in capitalist systems, the primary levers would be market demand supplemented by government regulation where the market fails. But when it comes to privacy, consumers' demand can appear inconsistent with their expressed preferences, as they ignore high-profile data breaches and gleefully download trivial smartphone apps in exchange for mountains of their own personal data. Yet, even in places where government regulation is light (such as the United States), many companies increasingly appear to be pursuing high profile – and sometimes costly – positions, practices, and offerings in the name of protecting privacy. Ultimately, Bowman and Grant suggest that in order to understand the true market for privacy, beyond consumer-driven demand, it is necessary also to consider the ethos of the highly skilled engineers who build these technologies and their level of influence over the high-tech companies that have created the data economy.

In Chapter 26, "The Missing Role of Economics in FTC Privacy Policy," James Cooper and Joshua Wright note that the FTC has been in the privacy game for almost twenty years. In that time span, the digital economy has exploded. As a consequence, the importance to the economy of privacy regulation has grown as well. Unfortunately, Cooper and Wright insist, its sophistication has yet to keep pace with its stature. As they see it, privacy stands today where antitrust stood in the 1970s. Antitrust's embrace then of economics helped transform it into a coherent body of law that – despite some quibbles at the margin – almost all agree has been a boon for consumers. Cooper and Wright thus argue that privacy at the FTC is ripe for a similar revolution. The chapter examines the history of FTC privacy enforcement and policy making, with special attention paid to the lack of economic analysis. It shows the unique ability of economic analysis to ferret out conduct that is likely to threaten consumer welfare, and provide a framework for FTC privacy analysis going forward. Specifically, Cooper and Wright argue that the FTC needs to be more precise in identifying privacy harms and to develop an empirical footing for both its enforcement posture and such concepts as "privacy by design" and "data minimization." The sooner that the FTC begins to incorporate serious economic analysis and rigorous empirical evidence into its privacy policy, the authors maintain, the sooner consumers will begin to reap the rewards.

In Chapter 27, "Big Data by Design: Establishing Privacy Governance by Analytics," Dale Skivington, Lisa Zolidis, and Brian P. O'Connor argue that a significant challenge for corporate big data analytics programs is deciding how to build an effective structure for addressing privacy risks. They further contend that privacy protections, including thoughtful Privacy Impact Assessments, add essential value to the design of such programs in the modern marketplace where customers demand adequate protection of personal data. The chapter thus provides a practical approach to help corporations weigh risks and benefits for data analytics projects as they are developed to make the best choices for the products and services they offer.

In Chapter 28, "The Future of Self-Regulation is Co-Regulation," Ira Rubinstein contends that privacy self-regulation – and especially voluntary codes of conduct – suffers from an overall lack of transparency, weak or incomplete realization of the Fair Information Practice Principles, inadequate incentives to ensure wide-scale industry participation, and ineffective compliance and enforcement mechanisms. He argues that the US experiment with voluntary codes has gone on long enough and that it is time to try a new, more co-regulatory approach. In co-regulation, firms still enjoy considerable flexibility in shaping self-regulatory guidelines, but consumer advocacy groups have a seat at the table, and the government retains general oversight authority to approve and enforce statutory requirements. Rubenstein examines three recent co-regulatory efforts: (1) privacy management programs designed by multinational firms to demonstrate accountability under both European and US privacy laws; (2) the NTIA multistakeholder process, under which industry and privacy advocates have sought to develop voluntary but enforceable privacy codes without any explicit legal mandate; and (3) Dutch codes of conduct under national data protection law, which allows industry sectors to draw up privacy codes specifying how statutory requirements apply to their specific sector. He concludes by identifying lessons learned and offering specific policy recommendations that might help shape any future consumer privacy legislation in the United States or abroad.

In Chapter 29, "Privacy Notices: Limitations, Challenges, and Opportunities," Mary J. Culnan and Paula J. Bruening contend that openness is the first principle of fair information practices. While in practice "notice" has been used to create openness, notices have been widely criticized as being too complex, legalistic, lengthy, and opaque. Culnan and Bruening argue that to achieve openness, data protection should move from a "notice" model to a model that requires organizations to create an environment of "transparency." They assert that while often used interchangeably, the terms "notice" and "transparency" are not synonymous. In their chapter, Culnan and Bruening review the history of notice in the United States, its traditional roles in data protection, the challenges and limitations of notice, the efforts to address them, and the lessons learned from these efforts. They examine the challenges emerging technologies pose for traditional notice and propose a move away from a reliance on notice to the creation of an environment of transparency that includes improved notices, attention to contextual norms, integrating notice design into system development, ongoing public education, and new technological solutions. Finally, Culnan and Bruening present arguments for business buy-in and regulatory guidance.

In Chapter 30, "It Takes Data to Protect Data," David A. Hoffman and Patricia A. Rimo note that we live in a world of constant data flow, and safeguarding data has never been more important. Be it medical records, financial information or simple online passwords, the amount of private data that needs to be protected continues to grow. Along with this growth in the need to secure data, Hoffman and Rimo insist, however, are the privacy concerns people have with their data. While some would pit security and privacy against each other, arguing that individuals must choose one over the other, the two actually can and should reinforce each other. It's this model that forms the basis of the chapter: Privacy and security should be pursued hand-in-hand as we move toward an increasingly connected, digital world. To fully realize the benefits of information technology, big data, and Internet of Things, Hoffman and Rimo argue individuals must be confident that their devices are designed in a way that protects their data and that any data being collected and processed from those devices is used responsibly. Using internationally recognized mechanisms such as the Fair Information Privacy Principles, public and private organizations can enable both the innovative and ethical use of data. The key is not avoiding data but using it mindfully. It takes data to protect data.

In Chapter 31, "Are Benefit-Cost Analysis and Privacy Protection Efforts Incompatible?" Adam Thierer argues that benefit-cost analysis (BCA) helps inform the regulatory process by estimating the benefits and costs associated with proposed rules. At least in the United States, BCA has become a more widely accepted part of regulatory policy-making process and is formally required before many rules can take effect. The BCA process becomes far more contentious, however, when the variables or values being considered are highly subjective in character. This is clearly the case as it pertains to debates over online data collection and digital privacy. The nature and extent of privacy rights and privacy harms remain open to widely different conceptions and interpretations. This makes BCA more challenging, some would say impossible. In reality, however, this same problem exists in many different fields and does not prevent BCA from remaining an important part of the rule-making process. Even when some variables are highly subjective, others are more easily quantifiable. Thierer thus contends that policymakers should conduct BCA for any proposed rules related to data collection and privacy protection to better understand the trade-offs associated with those regulatory proposals.

In Chapter 32, "Privacy After the Agile Turn," Seda Gürses and Joris van Hoboken explore how recent paradigmatic transformations in the production of everyday digital systems are changing the conditions for privacy governance. Both in popular media and in scholarly work, great attention is paid to the privacy concerns that surface once digital technologies reach consumers. As a result, the strategies proposed to mitigate these concerns, be it through technical, social, regulatory or economic interventions, are concentrated at the interface of technology consumption. The authors propose to look beyond technology consumption, inviting readers to explore the ways in which consumer software is produced today. By better understanding recent shifts in software production, they argue, it is possible to get a better grasp of how and why software has come to be so data intensive and algorithmically driven, raising a plethora of privacy concerns. Specifically, the authors highlight three shifts: from waterfall to agile development methodologies; from shrink-wrap software to services; and, from software running on personal computers to functionality being carried out in the cloud. Their shorthand for the culmination of these shifts is the "agile turn." With the agile turn, the complexity, distribution, and infrastructure of software have changed. What are originally intended to be techniques to improve the production of software development, e.g., modularity and agility, also come to reconfigure the ways businesses in the sector are organized. In fact, the agile turn is so tectonic, it unravels the authors' original distinction: The production and consumption of software are collapsed. Services bind users into a long-term transaction with software companies, a relationship constantly monitored and improved through user analytics. Data flows, algorithms, and user profiling have become the bread and butter of software production, not only because of business models based on advertisements, but because of the centrality of these features to a successful disruptive software product. Understanding these shifts has great implications for any intervention that aims to address, and mitigate, consumer privacy concerns.

PART II

The Pervasiveness and Value of Tracking Technologies

Data Brokers: Should They Be Reviled or Revered?

Jennifer Barrett Glasgow

Data brokers are largely unknown by the average individual and often accused by the press and privacy advocates for doing all kinds of unsavory things because they make money collecting and sharing personal data with others, often without the knowledge of the consumer.

In 2012, the Federal Trade Commission investigated the industry and published a report, "Data Brokers: A Call for Transparency and Accountability."[1] The report said, "In today's economy, Big Data is big business. Data brokers – companies that collect consumers' personal information and resell or share that information with others – are important participants in this Big Data economy." However, the report went on to say,

> Many of these findings point to a fundamental lack of transparency about data broker industry practices. Data brokers acquire a vast array of detailed and specific information about consumers; analyze it to make inferences about consumers, some of which may be considered sensitive; and share the information with their clients in a range of industries. All of this activity takes place behind the scenes, without consumers' knowledge.

The FTC also recommended that Congress consider legislation requiring data brokers to provide consumers access to their data, including sensitive data, and the ability to opt out from marketing uses.

The marketing community is an aggressive user of data about people. A study published in 2013 by John Deighton of the Harvard Business School and Peter Johnson of mLightenment Economic Impact Research, a recent Columbia University professor, "The Value of Data 2013: Consequences for Insight, Innovation, and Efficiency in the U.S. Economy," found that the data-driven marketing economy added $156 billion in revenue to the US economy and fueled more than 675,000 jobs in 2012. These issues were revisited in 2015 in the follow-up study, "The Value of Data 2015: Consequences for Insight, Innovation and Efficiency in the U.S. Economy," which found that in two years, revenue had grown to $202 billion, a 35 percent increase, and jobs had grown to 966,000, a 49 percent increase.

So, are data brokers doing great things for our economy or are they operating a personal data exchange behind the backs of consumers?

---

[1] FTC report, *Data Brokers: A Call for Transparency and Accountability*, https://www.ftc.gov/system/files/documents/reports/data-brokers-call-transparency-accountability-report-federal-trade-commission-may-2014/140527databrokerreport.pdf. (*Data Brokers*)

AN INTRODUCTION TO DATA BROKERS

Data brokers have been around since the 1960s. They are not homogeneous entities nor are they easily defined. Some are regulated entities, and some are not. Some companies that broker data are consumer facing; others are not. The key differences relate to where the data comes from, the types of data the brokers bring to the marketplace, and the various uses of the data by the buyer.

The definition of "data broker" has been debated for some time, and many companies work hard to avoid the label because it is easy to make data brokers sound scary or evil. For purposes of this handbook, we will use an expansive definition. Data brokers are companies that collect personal and non-personal information about individuals and license, sell, share or allow use of that information by another entity for the other entity's benefit or for their mutual benefit. One area of debate is over whether a company that allows other entities to "use" consumer data they posses to advertise on the company's websites should be considered a data broker. Such entities argue they are not a data broker since they don't actually "give" the data to the advertiser. However, for purposes of discussion, we will include them in the definition.

Historically, data brokers in the offline space in the 1960s dealt primarily with personally identifiable information (PII),[2] such as names, addresses, and telephone numbers. In the early 2000s, we began to see data brokers in the digital space dealing mainly with data collected anonymously through cookies and other digital markers, which is considered non-personally identifiable information (Non-PII).[3] Today, data brokers often combine offline and online data for their clients to use to market and advertise across all digital channels.

Some data brokers collect data directly through some type of relationship with the individual. These data brokers are considered "first-party" data brokers. Some data brokers are second parties and collaboratively share their customer data with each other for some mutual benefit. Third-party data brokers have no relationship with the individual, but instead buy or license data from public sources and from both first-party and third-party data brokers. It's worth noting that these definitions are not always mutually exclusive – the same data broker can act as a first-, second- and third-party source in different cases. Clearly, data can pass through a number of hands in the chain of custody for the data broker ecosystem. Also, it is common for data brokers to offer their clients multiple data products and ancillary data-related services, such as data hygiene.

Commercial data brokers generally fall into four categories.

- Providers of public information, including government agencies, professional organizations, and research, look-up and locate services (e.g., people-search services).
- Consumer reporting agencies (CRAs), including background screening services.
- Risk mitigation services (e.g., identity verification and anti-fraud services).
- Marketing data brokers, including general marketing data brokers, lead generation services, and large advertising-supported websites (e.g., social media and search engine sites).

---

[2] Personally Identifiable Information (PII) as used in US privacy law and information security, is "information that can be used on its own or with other information to identify, contact, or locate a single person, or to identify an individual in context," https://en.wikipedia.org/wiki/Personally_identifiable_information.

[3] "Non-Personal Information (Non-PII) is data that is linked or reasonably linkable to a particular computer or device. Non-PII includes, but is not limited to, unique identifiers associated with users' computers or devices and IP addresses, where such identifiers or IP addresses are not linked to PII. Non-PII does not include De-Identified Data." https://www.networkadvertising.org/understanding-online-advertising/glossary.

There are a variety of data sources for data brokers, ranging from public records and other publicly available information to digital behavior data. Different data brokers are interested in different combinations of data. However, one common thread for most data brokers, especially third-party brokers, is that they aggregate data from multiple sources to make it easier for the buyer – a kind of one-stop shopping.

The media have been known to focus on one of these categories of data brokers, often marketing data brokers, but will use the generic 'data broker' moniker as if there was one homogeneous industry. However, due to various regulations on some data and on certain uses of data, these categories differentiate quite significantly based on the data they broker and the use of the brokered data by the client. A discussion of each of these broad categories of data brokers follows.

PROVIDERS OF PUBLIC INFORMATION, INCLUDING GOVERNMENT AGENCIES, PROFESSIONAL ORGANIZATIONS, AND THIRD-PARTY RESEARCH, LOOK-UP, AND LOCATE SERVICES (E.G., PEOPLE-SEARCH SERVICES)

Many federal and state government agencies and most professional organizations are first-party data brokers. Government agencies provide access to and broker data that is considered public record. They may license this data to other agencies, companies, non-profit organizations and third-party data brokers for commercial and non-commercial purposes. A few examples of first-party government agencies that broker their data include state motor vehicle and driver's license divisions, state voter registration divisions, property deed agencies, tax agencies, courts, the Federal Aviation Administration, and even the Social Security Administration.

In addition, many professional organizations and licensing agencies broker their membership and licensing data. Examples include physician, nursing, dental, and realtor professional associations. A number of websites also provide directory information to look up and/or locate individuals. These are often referred to as people-search sites. They include many free sites, usually supported by advertising, such as yellowpages.com, as well as sites such as spokeo.com and peoplefinders.com where some basic data is free, but the user must pay for additional information related to the search. Ancestry sites offering genealogical information would also fall into this category.

Since this is a very broad category of data brokers, the type of data they bring to the market can vary drastically. Property ownership records contain identifying information about the owner along with characteristics of the property (number of bedrooms, baths, etc.), as well as information about any mortgages on the property. Voter records would contain name, address, date of birth, and party affiliation. Court proceedings would include such identifying information on the defendant as name, address, and possibly Social Security number (SSN), along with information about the charges and sentence.

Many consumers do not fully understand all the types of government records that are public. Some are dismayed at the level of personal detail that is available in these records. However, they also lack an understanding of the value public records and open access bring.

These agencies and organizations provide critical information that has been the bedrock of our democracy for decades. According to the Coalition for Sensible Public Record Access (CSPRA),[4] "The debate over access to public records focuses primarily on concerns about privacy and identity theft and fraud. Technology advances and the growing trend of providing electronic access to public records have helped advance this debate."

CSPRA further reports,

---

[4] Coalition for Sensible Public Record Access (CSPRA), http://cspra.org/.

Information and data compiled by private companies from public records, including Social Security numbers, addresses, dates of birth and phone numbers, are used every day to help combat identity theft. Social Security numbers have proven to be the most reliable tool in verifying an individual's identity. Certain public and court records contain this vital information, and provide a reliable source for data matching, which helps prevent the rapid increase in identity fraud victims. Further, commercial databases compiled using public records for identity verification are routinely used online and offline to detect credit card application fraud, and insurance application and claims fraud.

CSPRA points to additional benefits: "The use of public records improves the speed and accuracy of check acceptances, combats identity theft, and reduces check fraud, which has the combined effect of lowering costs for all consumers."

Public information providers give access to information that is also very valuable for research purposes. The National Public Records Research Association (NPRRA)[5] is a trade association of businesses engaged in an industry for which public records serve as the backbone. Its membership includes document filers, researchers, retrievers, corporate service providers, entity formation agents, and registered agents.

LexisNexis and Experian are two of the largest aggregators of public records; however, numerous smaller brokers focus on aggregating specific types of public records, such as property records and marriage and divorce records.

CONSUMER REPORTING AGENCIES (CRAs), INCLUDING BACKGROUND SCREENING SERVICES

The Fair Credit Reporting Act (FCRA)[6] was enacted in 1970 due to a lack of transparency in the credit industry in the 1960s, and has been amended numerous times since.[7] The law places a number of obligations on the category of data broker known in the law as a consumer reporting agency (CRA). CRAs provide data in the form of consumer reports for certain permissible purposes, decisions of eligibility for credit, employment, insurance, and housing, and similar determinations.

Credit bureaus are a type of CRA and provide consumer reports in the form of credit reports. Background screening brokers are another type of CRA that provides consumer reports in the form of background checks, when the screening is done for employment purposes.

CRAs have a number of obligations under the law. These include requirements to maintain reasonable procedures for maximum accuracy of consumer reports, provide access to the information they hold, handle disputes by a consumer, and remove negative information, such as bankruptcies, after ten years and other negative information after seven years.

Credit bureaus maintain information about the status of a consumer's credit accounts and some bill payment information. They maintain information about how often payments are made, how much credit is available, how much credit is currently in use, and any debts that are past due. They also maintain rental information and public records such as liens, judgments, and bankruptcies that are helpful in assessing a consumer's financial status. CRAs also use all this information to create a credit score, an easy way to summarize a consumer's credit history in one rating.

---

[5] National Public Records Research Association (NPRRA), http://www.nprra.org/.

[6] Fair Credit Reporting Act (FCRA), https://www.consumer.ftc.gov/articles/pdf-0111-fair-credit-reporting-act.pdf.

[7] Fair and Accurate Credit Transaction Act of 2003 (FACTA) PUBLIC LAW 108–159 — Dec. 4, 2003.

Background screening brokers verify the information provided by a job applicant for the prospective employer. The verification can range from past employment to education and criminal history. The applicant must authorize the screening and has the right to challenge any errors in the report prior to the employer taking any adverse action.

The passage of the FCRA led to significant consolidation in the credit bureau industry from thousands of small local CRAs to a much smaller number of large credit bureaus and specialty CRAs.

In addition to the three major credit bureaus, Experian, Equifax, and TransUnion, there are dozens of other specialty CRAs. These include companies that maintain medical records and payments, residential or tenant histories, and other publicly available information for permissible purposes. Some of the companies considered specialty CRAs include: First Data Telecheck, Innovis, MIB Group, and Milliman.

Although the major CRAs are required by law to provide a central source website for consumers to request a copy of the consumer report about them, the nationwide specialty consumer reporting agencies are not required to provide a centralized online source. Instead they must establish a streamlined process for consumers to request a report about them, which must include, at a minimum, a toll-free telephone number.

Because the decisions being made by users of consumer reports are very impactful on the consumer, the accuracy of the data is of paramount importance. The FCRA requires, "Whenever a consumer reporting agency prepares a consumer report it shall follow reasonable procedures to assure maximum possible accuracy of the information concerning the individual about whom the report relates."[8]

It should be mentioned that smaller companies who offer look-up and locate or background screening services must be careful to understand when they are subject to the FCRA. This occurs when they provide services for credit, employment, insurance, housing, and similar eligibility determinations. One such instance occurred in 2012 when Spokeo paid $800,000 to settle charges by the FTC that they marketed their consumer profiles to companies in the human resources, background screening, and recruiting industries without complying with the FCRA.[9]

RISK MITIGATION SERVICES (E.G., IDENTITY VERIFICATION AND ANTI-FRAUD)

There are third-party data brokers who provide identity verification services and, in some instances, identity information for use in detecting and preventing fraud. In order to guard against fraudulent transactions, a number of laws have been passed that require a company to "know your customer." In other instances it is just a smart business practice to screen customers and monitor suspicious transactions. Such legal obligations are common in the financial services sector. The Gramm-Leach-Bliley Act (GLBA)[10] regulating financial institutions is one such law.

According to the FTC report on Data Brokers, "Risk mitigation products provide significant benefit to consumers, by, for example, helping prevent fraudsters from impersonating unsuspecting consumers."[11]

---

[8] Fair Credit Reporting Act (FCRA) 15 U.S.C 1681, p. 34, Accuracy of Report, https://www.consumer.ftc.gov/articles/pdf-0111-fair-credit-reporting-act.pdf.

[9] Spokeo to Pay $800,000 to Settle FTC Charges, https://www.ftc.gov/news-events/press-releases/2012/06/spokeo-pay-800000-settle-ftc-charges-company-allegedly-marketed.

[10] Gramm-Leach-Bliley Act (GLBA), https://www.law.cornell.edu/uscode/text/15/chapter-94.

[11] FTC report, *Data Brokers*, p. v, https://www.ftc.gov/system/files/documents/reports/data-brokers-call-transparency-accountability-report-federal-trade-commission-may-2014/140527databrokerreport.pdf.

Most often, these services provide verification of data the user already has. They can verify that a name, address, SSN, and phone all belong to the same person. They may also identify whether the individual is on a money-laundering list or a terrorists watch list. In some cases, they assist the fraud department of a financial institution investigate suspected fraudulent transactions by providing a variety of identifying information about the individual, such as multiple SSNs associated with the person, or past addresses or phone numbers.

While these risk-mitigation services are able to identify and respond to most requests, they may not satisfy 100 percent of inquiries. Thus, the user of the service has to have alternative verification processes, usually manual ones, to handle inquires that cannot be serviced.

The consumer may or may not be aware that third-party verification is taking place, unless the verification is denied. Then they are usually referred to the data broker providing the service to determine if there are errors in their files.

The credit bureaus, along with LexisNexis, Acxiom, and Thompson Reuters, are a few of the largest third-party providers of these types of services.

MARKETING DATA BROKERS INCLUDING GENERAL MARKETING DATA BROKERS, LEAD GENERATION SERVICES, AND LARGE ADVERTISING-SUPPORTED WEBSITES (INCLUDING SOCIAL MEDIA AND SEARCH ENGINES)

There are tens of thousands of first-, second-, and third-party entities that provide data for marketing purposes. The number of players and the scope of the data they collect and bring to market make this the largest, most aggressive and sophisticated category of data brokers.

Many in the retail, catalog, and publishing industries rent some of their first-party customer data for marketing and advertising purposes. Financial institutions do a lot of second-party joint marketing with airlines, retailers, and other brands. Acxiom, Experian, and IMS Health are some of the largest third-party marketing data brokers, but there are thousands of smaller, more specialized ones, such as the real estate multi-listing service.

As the world becomes more digitally connected, a growing number of digital data brokers focus on providing data for online, mobile, and addressable TV advertising, and as the Internet of Things expands, advertising will support many other devices, including wearables,[12] smart devices,[13] and even smart cars.[14] This segment of the community is the fastest-growing segment.

---

[12] Wearables are the general category of "wearable devices, tech togs, or fashion electronics," i.e., clothing and accessories incorporating computer and advanced electronic technologies. The designs often incorporate practical functions and features. "Wearable devices such as activity trackers are a good example of the Internet of Things," since they are part of the network of physical objects or "things" embedded with "electronics, software, sensors, and connectivity" to "enable objects to exchange data … with a manufacturer, operator and/or other connected devices, without requiring human intervention," https://en.wikipedia.org/wiki/Wearable_technology.

[13] Smart devices are electronic devices, "generally connected to other devices or networks via different wireless protocols such as Bluetooth, NFC, Wi-Fi, #G, etc., that can operate to some extent interactively and autonomously. Several notable types of smart devices are smartphones, phablets, tablets, smart watches, smart bands, and smart key chains … Smart devices can be designed to support a variety of form factors, a range of properties pertaining to ubiquitous computing, and use in three main system environments: the physical world, human-centered environments, and distributed computing environments," https://en.wikipedia.org/wiki/Smart_device.

[14] Smart cars are automobiles with advanced electronics. Microprocessors have been used in car engines since the late 1960s and have steadily increased in usage throughout the engine and drivetrain to improve stability, braking, and general comfort. The 1990s brought enhancements such as GPS navigation, reverse sensing systems, and night vision (able to visualize animals and people beyond the normal human range). The 2000s added assisted parking, Web and e-mail access, voice control, smart card activation instead of keys, and systems that keep the vehicle a safe distance from cars and objects in its path. Of course, the ultimate smart car is the one that drives itself (see autonomous vehicle and connected cars), http://www.pcmag.com/encyclopedia/term/51503/smart-car.

General marketing data brokers provide PII and Non-PII data for both offline and digital marketing[15] purposes. They license a list of individuals who meet certain criteria to a marketer, a process known as "list rental," or they append specified data elements to a marketer's customer list, a process known as "enhancement."

These data brokers aggregate and provide data on individuals and households – identifying information (e.g., name, address, phone, and email), demographic information (e.g., age or date of birth, education, and ethnicity), household characteristics (e.g., identifying and demographic information on the spouse, how many children there are and their approximate ages, and how many people live in the house), general financial information (e.g., modeled ranges of estimated household income and modeled estimated net worth), interests (e.g., like to cook, read, water ski, travel abroad, or redecorate the house), lifestyle (e.g., types of cars, and information about property owned, such as price, value, size, age, features, and mortgage company), and major life events (e.g., recently got married, divorced, had a child, or bought a new house).

There are many first-party websites, known as lead generation services, that sell varying levels of qualified leads, meaning individuals inquiring about or shopping for certain products or services. These include individuals shopping for automobiles, insurance policies, hotel rooms, and much more. These websites typically provide competitive quotes from various providers and then sell the inquiry back to the provider and sometimes to others for marketing purposes. These data brokers provide identifying and contact information and some information related to the products of interest. For example, if the lead is for a used car, the type of car the individual is interested in would be included, or if the lead is for life insurance, the age of the individual may be provided.

Some websites, typically those with large user bases, monetize their site by allowing advertisers to market to their users based on data about their customers. As discussed, some of these first-party companies argue that they are not true data brokers, because the data does not actually end up in the hands of the advertiser. However, because they allow the use of consumer data for the advertiser's marketing purpose, we are including them in our definition of a data broker. This type of data broker includes many social media sites, including Facebook, search engines, such as Google, news and magazine sites, and many others.

Because data from data brokers has become a part of almost every marketing campaign, it is difficult to measure the precise value brought by exchanging marketing data. As cited previously, the DDMI's 2015 study, "The Value of Data," quantifies the value of the Data-Driven Marketing Economy (DDME), both in terms of revenues generated for the US economy and jobs fueled across the nation. The DDME contributed 966,000 jobs and $202 billion to the US economy in 2014. The report went on to point out that 70 percent of the value is in the exchange of data across the DDME, and if markets had to operate without the ability to broker data, our economy would be significantly less efficient. Because the study used a very conservative methodology, the actual impact could be even larger.

According to the FTC "Data Brokers" report, "Marketing products benefit consumers by allowing them to more easily find and enjoy goods and services they need and prefer. In addition, consumers benefit from increased and innovative product offerings fueled by increased

---

[15] Digital marketing is an umbrella term for "the marketing of products or services using digital technologies, mainly on the Internet, but also including mobile phones, display advertising, and any other digital medium," https://en .wikipedia.org/wiki/Digital_marketing.

competition from small businesses that are able to connect with consumers they may not have otherwise been able to reach."[16]

While acknowledging the benefits, the FTC and others have criticized the marketing data broker category for not being more transparent. The category has also been criticized because the data that brokers aggregate is not accurate.

All data has errors. Unavoidable errors can be introduced during the data aggregation process. However, marketing data from brokers is accurate enough to provide significant benefit, even with a reasonable percentage of errors. Furthermore, the negative impact from inaccurate marketing data is that someone may not see the ad they would consider relevant, or they may see an ad they would not consider relevant, a situation that is exacerbated when data is less available. Consumers often assume marketing data from brokers is completely accurate, but this is neither a reasonable expectation nor a marketplace need.

The 2014 FTC report on data brokers was critical of the extent to which marketing data brokers offered choices to consumers. While some data brokers offered consumers choices about how data was used, because the brokers are third parties, and not consumer facing, consumers did not always know about the choice. They went onto say that the opt-outs were sometimes unclear about the scope of the choice.

The report also acknowledged that, "marketing products benefit consumers by allowing them to more easily find and enjoy goods and services they need and prefer. In addition, consumers benefit from increased and innovative product offerings fueled by increased competition from small businesses that are able to connect with consumers they may not have otherwise been able to reach."

WHERE DO DATA BROKERS GET THEIR DATA?

Data brokers are often reported to have detailed dossiers on individuals. Certain types of data brokers, such as CRAs, do have extensive profiles. But because of laws, industry codes of conduct, and the basic economics of collecting or purchasing data, aggregating it from multiple sources, storing it, and making it available in the market, different types of data brokers collect or acquire different data.

The kind of data available in the offline space is quite different from the data available in the digital space. Offline data is almost entirely PII. However, in the digital space, much of the data is Non-PII, relating to a device rather than to an individual.

Finally, data brokers provide data that is legal, of interest, and relevant to their clients' ultimate uses. Furthermore, there must be a sufficient quantity of a data element for it to be of value to a data broker. An identity verification service that can only verify forty percent of the requests they get is not financially viable. Marketers don't market to a few individuals, instead they market to tens of thousands or millions of individuals. With the exception of lead generation services which don't need such high volumes to be viable, this means data has to be available on a substantial portion of the total audience before it is commercially feasible to collect, store, package, and sell it for marketing purposes.

The offline data sources of interest and available to a data broker vary with the type of data broker, often based on laws and industry codes of conduct as well as the type of data most valuable for the ultimate use.

---

[16] FTC report, *Data Brokers*, p. v, https://www.ftc.gov/system/files/documents/reports/data-brokers-call-transparency-accountability-report-federal-trade-commission-may-2014/140527databrokerreport.pdf.

In general, offline data comes from the following sources:

- Public Records and Publicly Available Information: Public records are a common source of offline data for all types of third-party data brokers. In the United States, we believe that certain government actions, licenses, and registrations should be available for all to view, both individuals and organizations. These include court proceedings, property ownership, census data, and much more, as described previously. Some believe such access should be curtailed, but today, this data supports our democracy and provides significant benefits ranging from locating missing individuals to assisting with business, legal, and personal affairs. According to CSPRA, public records are actually one of the best protections against criminal activity.

  The benefits of public records[17] are summarized in a CSPRA whitepaper. They include a reliable system of recording property owners and assessing the credit worthiness of buyers and sellers, the ability to recover a debt, enforce a law, collect child support, find witnesses and bail jumpers, identify sex offenders, find safe drivers, and hire responsible trustworthy employees. As indicated in the chart that follows this section, public records are used by every category of data broker.

  A variety of telephone directories, professional directories and listings, motor vehicle records, driver's license records, real property records, assessor information, court proceedings, voter registration records, birth records, and death records are a few of the common sources of public records. Many state-level public records are governed by state laws that restrict some uses of such data. Some of the best examples are motor vehicle records that are restricted by both federal and state Driver's Privacy Protection acts. For example, these records can be used for identity verification and anti-fraud purposes, but not for marketing. Another example would be voter registration records. In some states voter records generally can be used for election-related purposes by candidates and parties, but again, not for general marketing purposes. A third example is real property records that are very helpful to the real estate industry, but in some states are prohibited from use for other types of marketing.

  Data that is not a government public record, but is generally publicly accessible or viewable, can sometimes be used for many other purposes unless restrictions are put on it by the source. This includes directories on websites for professional organizations and publicly viewable data on social media sites. However, many such sites, especially social media sites, have terms of use that restrict commercialization without specific authorization. Anyone collecting this data should carefully review the site's terms of access and use before collecting and brokering this type of data. Just because you can view it doesn't mean you can legally use it.

- Surveys: Consumer surveys are conducted by survey companies and by consumer-facing entities such as manufacturers who provide a short survey when the buyer registers the product, often for warranty purposes.

  Responsible companies conducting surveys inform the individual at the time the survey is conducted about whether the answers will be used only by them or brokered to others and for what purposes. They also offer an opt-out from such brokering.

  Surveys are less accurate than other sources of data, so they are of value for marketing purposes, but not for such other purposes as risk mitigation.

[17] *The Benefits of Commercial and Personal Access to Public Records,* http://www.cspra.us/yahoo_site_admin/assets/docs/The_Benefits_of_Commercial_and_Personal_Access_to_Public_Records_2013.121143932.pdf.

- First and Second Parties: Consumer-facing brands in many industries including finance, media, publishing, catalog, retail, travel, entertainment, automotive, and, of course, lead generation entities, license some or all of their customer information for various purposes including consumer reports, risk mitigation, and marketing.

  For marketing purposes this information can be general, such as that a consumer subscribed to a certain magazine, or it can be fairly detailed, such as information about auto sales, service, and repairs. While the data would not contain a credit card number, it may contain a type of credit card, such as VISA Gold Card, and may include the amount of the purchase or flag the transaction in a range of amounts, along with some indication about the product(s) bought.

  For risk mitigation purposes the data may be limited to identifying information, such as name and address, phone number, email address, and SSN.

  Companies that offer credit furnish information to credit bureaus as governed by the GLBA and FCRA. Examples of these companies include credit card companies, auto finance companies, and mortgage banking institutions. Other examples include collection agencies, state and municipal courts, and employers. Under the FCRA, entities that furnish information to a credit bureau must provide complete and accurate information, inform consumers about negative information, and investigate consumer disputes.

- Other Third Party Data Brokers: It is typical for third-party data brokers to aggregate information from many sources that often include information from other data brokers, providing one-stop shopping for the data buyer. The FTC data brokers report said, "seven of the nine data brokers buy from or sell information to each other. Accordingly, it may be virtually impossible for a consumer to determine the originator of a particular data element."[18]

- Modeled (or Derived) Data: Data is also created by the data broker from statistical modeling activities using some or all of these data sources. Data is modeled when the desired data elements are not otherwise available. These analytical processes range from fairly simple derivations to highly sophisticated predictive analytics. There are primarily two forms of modeled data – directly modeled and look-alike models. Both types of modeled data are rapidly growing in variety and popularity.

  Directly modeled data is created by statistically analyzing a large number of data elements and determining which of them can predict the desired outcome, such as predicting a transaction is likely to be fraudulent or estimating the financial capacity of a household for marketing purposes. In general, the most common elements that are statistically modeled for marketing are estimated income and estimated net worth, since precise information is not available. Such elements may be modeled from data such as zip code, education/profession, price of the home, cars owned, and age. For risk mitigation purposes, fraud scores are an example of modeled data.

  Look-alike models are used to create data when a small target audience is known – say, people who traveled abroad more than two times a year for pleasure – but information on the total audience is unavailable. The known audience is enhanced with other available data, such as demographic, household, interest, and financial, and then statistically studied to determine which of the enhancement elements most predict the individuals in the target audience. Once the study is complete, the original audience data is discarded and the

---

[18] FTC report, *Data Brokers*, p. 14, https://www.ftc.gov/system/files/documents/reports/data-brokers-call-transparency-accountability-report-federal-trade-commission-may-2014/140527databrokerreport.pdf.

model is applied to a file with only the enhancement data to identify the target audience. While less precise than directly modeled data, look-alike data can be an excellent way to derive data that is unavailable otherwise or in sufficient quantities to be useful.

Scores are growing in popularity as more data is used to make predictions. A report by the World Privacy Forum, "The Scoring of America: How Secret Consumer Scores Threaten Your Privacy and Your Future,"[19] points out unexpected problems that arise from new types of predictive consumer scoring. These activities usually fall outside FCRA and other legal regulated practices, but use thousands of pieces of information to predict how consumers will behave. The report raises issues of fairness, discrimination, accuracy, and transparency.

The following chart depicts where different data brokers commonly get their offline data.

| | | | | | Other | |
Type of Data Broker	Individual	Public Records & Publicly Available	Surveys	First Parties	Data Brokers	Modeled Data
Where do offline data brokers get their information?						
Government/ Professional/People Search	X	X				
Consumer Reporting Agencies		X		X		X
Risk Mitigation		X		X	X	X
Marketing	X	X	X	X	X	X

The digital segment of the data broker community typically operates with data that is non-personally identifiable information (Non-PII). In addition to anonymizing all the offline data and using it in the digital ecosystem, digital data brokers also collect usage data (known as behavioral data) that relates to a device – a browser, an App, a mobile ID, IDs that identify TV set-top boxes, etc. – rather than to a person.

As we further embrace the Internet of Things (IoT), we will see an even wider variety of device-related data being brokered.

- Behavioral Data: Generally digital behavioral data is information collected about the sites/apps/TV shows with which a user of a device interacts over time. Companies who collect this type of data across multiple devices for advertising purposes are called network advertisers[20]. This type of data is referred to as "interest based advertising" (IBA) data[21] and is usually Non-PII. Because the individual is often unaware that their actions are being observed and recorded, robust self-regulation has been in place since the early 2000s to

[19] Pam Dixon & Robert Gellman, *The Scoring of America: How Secret Consumer Scores Threaten Your Privacy and Your Future*, http://www.worldprivacyforum.org/wp-content/uploads/2014/04/WPF_Scoring_of_America_April2014_fs.pdf.

[20] Network advertisers are third-party online advertising technology companies, including networks, exchanges, DMPs, SSPs, RTB platforms, analytics companies, and service providers. The advertising technologies deployed by 100 member companies in NAI provide considerable economic benefits across the online and mobile ecosystems, including for publishers, advertisers, and consumers, https://www.networkadvertising.org/about-nai/about-nai#7.

[21] Interest Based Advertising (IBA) means the collection of data across web domains owned or operated by different entities for the purpose of delivering advertising based on preferences or interests known or inferred from the data collected, p. 5, https://www.networkadvertising.org/sites/default/files/NAI_Code15encr.pdf.

provide individuals some level of awareness and control over these practices. Self-regulation for IBA is discussed in greater detail later in this chapter.

Behavioral data may also be collected for anti-fraud purposes. Monitoring behavioral activity on a website helps detect and prevent fraud by recognizing unusual and risky user patterns of activity. All activity is monitored and both typical or normal and atypical behavior is identified, so future activity correlating to high-risk behavioral patterns, or those inconsistent with normal patterns, can be identified.

HOW DO DATA BROKERS AGGREGATE DATA FROM MULTIPLE SOURCES?

Since one of the key aspects of third-party data brokers is the aggregation of data from many, sometimes thousands of sources, the processes used to aggregate data accurately are very important. What the data broker needs is a common data element – a name and address, a phone number, an email, a device ID, etc. – across all their data sources. When the data element is finite, such as a phone number or email address, the matching is straightforward. But when the elements are more free-form, such as a name and address, with various anomalies, such as initials or nicknames, the matching becomes much more complicated and introduces more chance for errors.

In the digital space, one method of aggregation is ID syncing. Any type of digital ID can be synced. For example, when party A gives party B permission to read their cookie on a browser where party B also has a cookie, the IDs in each cookie can be synced, creating the opportunity to aggregate information associated with both cookies. In the online world, this is called cookie syncing[22]. Across the digital ecosystem, syncing IDs across different media, such as browsers, Apps, and other addressable devices, is referred to as a cross-device graph.[23]

While all the offline data is considered PII, this data may be stripped of its personal identifying characteristics and tied to a Non-PII device through a process known as "onboarding." Once onboarded, offline data can be linked to digital data associated with the same device.

In the digital space, third-party IBA data relates to a device instead of to an individual. The IBA data is analyzed to create audience segments. A segment usually has multiple characteristics, such as women over fifty who like to play golf, or people making more than $100,000/year who have a college degree and like to travel abroad. The characteristics of a segment are based on what kind of IBA activity is available and what the marketplace wants to buy.

It is important to note that some types of data are typically not available or useful to marketers. Marketing data brokers do not typically sell specific details about a purchase. Instead they summarize purchase data into demographic, interest, and lifestyle data or ranges of financial data. They also shy away from more sensitive information such as credit information, medical information or Social Security numbers, most of which are regulated by law. They also typically focus on personal data about adults, individuals over the age of seventeen. While they may be interested in the family make-up, say how many kids there are in the household and of what ages, adults usually control the purse strings and marketing messages are directed to them, not the children.

With laws, such as the Children's Online Privacy Protection Act (COPPA), there has been interest in having the ability to know if a registered user is a child or not. However, since such data is unavailable on children, such verification services are not currently possible.

---

[22] Cookie syncing and how it works, http://clearcode.cc/2015/12/cookie-syncing/.
[23] DMA's Cross-Device Identity Solutions RFI Template, https://thedma.org/structured-innovation/cross-device-id/.

HOW DO DATA BROKERS DELIVER THEIR DATA TO THE MARKETPLACE?

There are various ways a data broker delivers their data or services supported by their data into the marketplace.

- User Search and View: Some data brokers allow clients to do real-time searches and view the response online or through a subscription service or app. A search can provide response data on one individual or a few individuals may meet the search criteria. Batch searches are also usually available for high-volume inquiries that are not time sensitive.
- Lists: Requests for lists can be placed with the data broker that give a count of how many individuals/households meet the criteria. The request can be refined so the result is within the usage parameters of the buyer. Once the specifications are set, the data broker pulls a list of relevant records and sends it to the buyer. Such lists are typically delivered for one-time use or for use over a specific period of time. Once the usage limits have been met, the list should be destroyed.
- Enhancement: The process known as enhancement takes place when the buyer sends the data broker the contact information for the consumers on whom they want information, such as name and address, email or phone number. The buyer also identifies the data elements they want to license from the data broker. The data broker matches the buyer's data to its master database. Where there is a match, the data broker appends the desired data elements from their database to the buyers file, or in other words, enhances the buyer's data with the specified data elements requested, and returns the information to the marketer. Enhancement data is usually provided under a rental contract with an expiration date, typically a six- or twelve-month period, after which the buyer needs to come back to the data broker and append fresh data.

In the digital space, data is delivered through digital connections. Such companies as Acxiom/LiveRamp and Datalogix facilitate connectivity between the advertiser and the site, app, or other digital device where the ad is displayed.

- Use on Site Only: Large search engines and social media sites often offer the ability for brands to advertise on their sites to users based on the information they have about the user. This information may be only the usage history of the site by the user, or it may be enhanced with other offline marketing data. While the advertiser does not actually take possession of the data, they do get the benefit of using it to target their messages on that site.
- Onboarding: This is the process of taking PII from offline sources and going through a process to strip away the identifying information, rendering it Non-PII before matching it to a cookie or other digital ID. It can then be used in the digital space and synced with other data for advertising purposes.
- Cookie and/or Device Syncing: Syncing digital IDs is done in several different ways, but results in one digital ID (e.g., cookie ID from company A) being connected to another digital ID (e.g., cookie ID from company B), thus allowing an exchange of data.

WHO BUYS DATA FROM DATA BROKERS?

The vast majority of data brokers sell only to qualified businesses, political organizations or government agencies. Virtually every consumer-facing company in the financial services, health care, retail, publishing, cataloging, travel and entertainment, telecommunications, and technology industries, regardless of size, are users of lists and enhancement data as well as onboarded data from data brokers. Many of these organizations use people search and risk mitigation services, as well.

However, few data brokers, such as research, look-up, and locate brokers, sell directly both to individuals and organizations. The individual may be searching for an old friend or family member, or the organization may be looking to track down a bad debt.

Ultimately, size does not matter. Almost every marketer, from mom-and-pop operations to the largest, most sophisticated financial institutions, buys lists and enhancement data from data brokers. For startups, data reduces barriers to market entry. The 2015 DDMI study, "The Value of Data," found that small businesses benefit significantly from third-party marketing data because it enables them to compete effectively with big players and enter markets with lower start-up costs. Prospect lists are a cost-effective way to build a customer base over time. Well-known brands, such as Montgomery Ward, built their businesses by buying prospect lists and sending them catalogs in the mail. For decades, the non-profit sector has also been a big user of lists and enhancement data to acquire new donors and raise funds for charitable causes.

For years, political candidates have used lists for fundraising purposes, but recently, they have become very sophisticated in their use of digital data from data brokers. Many states allow voter registration lists to be used by candidates for fundraising and to get out the vote. The Obama campaign was one of the most sophisticated users of data to motivate people to vote and raise support. Since then, almost all candidates and political parties have used these techniques.

Federal, state, and local government agencies use identity verification and risk mitigation services on a regular basis.

HOW DO CONSUMERS LEARN ABOUT AND INTERACT WITH DATA BROKERS?

How to make data brokers more transparent to consumers is a question and concern that has been hotly debated for many years. Each category of data broker has different levels of visibility and challenges for greater transparency.

Consumers learn over time about public records and publicly available information, as they encounter them in their daily lives. However, few consumers understand the full scope of this information or the benefits and risks associated with publicly available information. Furthermore, it is a difficult process for consumers either to correct or remove inaccurate information from public sources. They must know where the data came from and deal directly with the source. If the data a broker has is accurate with respect to the source, there is no obligation for the data broker to correct or delete it. Public records and publicly available information represent foundational data used by all categories of data brokers, therefore, the impact of inaccurate information can be quite widespread. Fortunately, public records are known for a pretty high degree of accuracy.

Most research, look-up, and locate services are on the Internet, so it is pretty easy for consumers to search and learn about these kinds of services. This is one of the few categories of data brokers that serve consumers as customers. However, consumers are unlikely to fully understand the scope of commercial use by this category of data broker. Some, but not all, of these data brokers offer consumers access, correction, and opt-out choices.

Consumer reporting agencies offer access and correction rights as prescribed by the FCRA. This is an important provision of the law because inaccurate information can have big negative effects on an individual. Since the United States has determined that there is societal good in having all of one's financial history part of a consumer report, individuals generally cannot opt out or have their data deleted, if it is accurate and up to date. Consumers can only correct or remove information in their consumer report if it is inaccurate or obsolete, or if the CRA is unable to verify the disputed information.

The consumer usually does not know there is a risk mitigation data broker involved in a transaction, unless their identity is not verified. In such instances, the company using the verification service will employ an alternate means to verify an individual's identity. The lack of information may never be reported back to the data broker providing the service. Fortunately, contentious users of risk mitigation services will refer the consumer to the data broker for access and correction, if the data is wrong or out of date.

Responsible marketing data brokers offer a choice to consumers to opt out of having information about them shared with others for marketing purposes. This is required by marketing self-regulatory codes of conduct. However, not all marketing data brokers are members of the trade associations endorsing these codes and some do not follow the guidance as carefully as they should.

In 2013, Acxiom launched the website www.aboutthedata.com, where individuals can provide identifying information, and once authenticated, view, correct or delete all the data Acxiom has about them that it sells for marketing purposes, both offline and in the digital space. Even after extensive news coverage of the site when it was first launched in 2013, and sporadic media reference ever since, fewer than a million consumers have actually visited the site, with about one-third actually logging in. Of those, just over 60 percent make some changes and about 5 percent opt out. Fewer than 20 percent return to the site to see what data may have changed or been added over time.

No other marketing data broker has followed Acxiom's lead with full disclosure about the data they have on consumers. While large companies offer the individual the ability to opt out from data about them being licensed for future marketing purposes, as called for by the codes of conduct put out by the Direct Marketing Association,[24] the Digital Advertising Alliance,[25] and the Network Advertisers Initiative,[26] they don't offer the ability to view the actual data.

In addition to offering an individual the ability to opt out from one broker, reputable marketing data brokers also use the Direct Marketing Association's industry-wide Mail Preference and E-mail Preference suppression files,[27] the Direct Marketing Association's Commitment to Consumer Choice opt-out service,[28] as well as state and federal do not call lists in the development of their marketing and advertising products. These are all industry-wide registries where the individual signs up requesting the opt-out.

Marketers are under one additional obligation when they use data from a data broker. If a consumer asks where they got the data, they are required under the Direct Marketing Association's code of conduct to tell the individual what data broker provided the data.

HOW ARE DATA BROKERS REGULATED?

Some say the data broker community is virtually unregulated, but this claim does not recognize the different categories of data brokers that are highly regulated, such as CRAs. While no one overarching federal law regulates all categories of data brokers, there are a host of sector- or data-specific

---

[24] *Direct Marketing Association (DMA) Guidelines for Ethical Business Practice*, https://thedma.org/wp-content/uploads/DMA_Guidelines_January_2014.pdf.

[25] *Digital Advertising Alliance (DAA) Self-Regulatory Program*, http://www.aboutads.info/.

[26] Network Advertiser's Initiative (NAI) Code of Conduct, http://www.networkadvertising.org/code-enforcement/code.

[27] DMA Mail Preference and Email Preference Suppression, https://dmachoice.thedma.org/index.php.

[28] DMA Commitment to Consumer Choice, https://dmachoice.thedma.org/static/pdf/CCC_other_DMA_requirements.pdf.

federal and state laws as well as a number of codes of conduct with which various data brokers must comply.

Generally, laws and self-regulations focus on either the data itself or its intended use. Many of these laws and codes apply to both data brokers and their clients. Some of the more important laws and codes of conduct that impact data brokers are briefly described below.

A number of federal and state laws focus on limiting the use of certain types of data.

- Gramm-Leach-Bliley Act (GLBA)[29] and Similar State Laws: Among other things, the Gramm-Leach-Bliley Act requires financial institutions – companies that offer consumers financial products or services such as loans, financial or investment advice, or insurance – to explain their information-sharing practices to their customers and to safeguard sensitive data. Customers are given a notice of the institution's practices and their rights at the time the relationship is established and whenever the policy changes. The GLBA Safeguards Rule requires financial institutions provide reasonable security for personal financial information.

  Personal financial information cannot be shared with third parties for marketing purposes (e.g., marketing data brokers) without notice and the offer of an opt-out choice to customers. The law allows personal financial information to be shared with credit bureaus and identity verification and anti-fraud services.

  GLBA allows states to pass more restrictive laws, and since the passage of the California Financial Information Privacy Act[30] that calls for opt-in for sharing financial information with third parties for marketing purposes, this has become the de facto choice for the whole country.

- Health Insurance Portability and Accountability Act (HIPAA):[31] The HIPAA Privacy Rule establishes national standards to protect individuals' medical records and other protected health information. The law applies to health plans, health care clearinghouses, and those health care providers that conduct certain health care transactions electronically. The law does not apply to the growing number of health device manufacturers unless the device is prescribed by a physician. The rule requires appropriate safeguards be in place and sets limits and conditions on the uses and disclosures that may be made of such information without patient authorization (e.g., to third-party marketing data brokers). The rule also gives patients rights over their health information, including rights to examine and obtain a copy of their health records, and to request corrections.

- Children's Online Privacy Protection Act (COPPA):[32] COPPA imposes requirements to obtain verifiable parental consent, with limited exceptions, when collecting personal information from a child under thirteen years of age. The requirements apply to websites, online services, and apps directed to children under thirteen and when they have actual knowledge that they are dealing with a child under thirteen. Parents must consent to the collection of personal information and must separately consent to that data being shared with a third party. Parents can also have access and deletion of their child's information. These websites, online services, and apps must also maintain the security of the information.

[29] FTC advice on GLBA, https://www.ftc.gov/tips-advice/business-center/privacy-and-security/gramm-leach-bliley-act.
[30] California Financial Information Privacy Act, Financial Code Section 4050–4060, http://www.leginfo.ca.gov/cgi-bin/displaycode?section=fin&group=04001-05000&file=4050-4060.
[31] Health Insurance Portability and Privacy Act (HIPPA), http://www.hhs.gov/hipaa/for-professionals/privacy/.
[32] Children's Online Privacy Protection Rule (COPPA), https://www.ftc.gov/enforcement/rules/rulemaking-regulatory-reform-proceedings/childrens-online-privacy-protection-rule.

- Social Security Death Master File (DMF):[33] As a result of a court case under the Freedom of Information Act, the Social Security Administration (SSA) is required to release its death information to the public. SSA's Death Master File contains all information in the official SSA database, as well as updates to the file of other persons reported to SSA as being deceased. SSA authorizes the use of this database in identity verification solutions. A recent law limits access to Death Master File records that are less than three years old.

- Driver's Privacy Protection Acts (DPPAs):[34] The federal DPPA and numerous state DPPAs protect the confidentiality and privacy of records from state departments of motor vehicles. These laws prohibit disclosure of personal information obtained by the department in connection with a motor vehicle record, except as expressly permitted in the law. The law allows disclosures to verify the accuracy of information provided by the consumer, thus allowing such records to be used by CRAs and other risk mitigation services.

- Voter Registration Files (Voter Files):[35] The use of state voter registration files is governed by laws that vary widely in each state. Some states restrict the use to political purposes or by political candidates and parties and prohibit their use for marketing purposes, while voter records in other states are not restricted, at all.

- Real Property Files (Property Files):[36] The use of property files is governed by laws that vary widely in each state. For example, in Arkansas anyone may look up a property record online and find current property value, previous sale price, and characteristics of the property, such as number of bedrooms and bathrooms, square feet, year built, land value, and nearby schools. Property files are widely used by marketing data brokers, especially in the real estate sector, and are also valuable for identity verification and anti-fraud services. In other states, property records cannot be used for general marketing purposes.

A number of federal and state laws focus on limiting data for specific uses.

- Fair Credit Reporting Act (FCRA):[37] This federal law requires third-party entities that provide information related primarily to consumer credit, employment, insurance, and other eligibility decisions, known as consumer reporting agencies (CRAs), to adopt reasonable procedures with regard to the confidentiality, accuracy, relevancy, and use of such information.

  This includes specific obligations related to the companies that can access the data, a consumer report, and for what purposes. Any access for purposes of credit, employment, insurance, and other eligibility decisions is covered by the law, regardless of the data. The law also includes specific obligations to respond to consumer inquiries about the data in a consumer report about them and rights to correct inaccurate data.

- FTC Do-Not-Call Registry (DNC):[38] The National Do Not Call Registry gives consumers a choice about whether to receive telemarketing calls on a land line or mobile phone. An individual can register their land line or mobile phone number for free.

[33] Social Security Administration Death Master File, http://www.ntis.gov/products/ssa-dmf/.

[34] Federal Driver's Privacy Protection Act (DPPA), https://www.law.cornell.edu/uscode/text/18/2721.

[35] Florida Voter Registration website, http://dos.myflorida.com/elections/for-voters/check-your-voter-status-and-polling-place/.

[36] Arkansas Real Property website, http://www.propertyrecord.com/property.php?utm_source=bing&utm_medium=cpc&utm_campaign=PropertyRecord.com%20-%20Tax&utm_term=property%20tax%20much&utm_content=how%20much%20is%20property%20tax.

[37] Fair Credit Reporting Act (FCRA), https://www.consumer.ftc.gov/sites/default/files/articles/pdf/pdf-0111-fair-credit-reporting-act.pdf.

[38] FTC Do-Not-Call Registry, https://www.donotcall.gov/.

Telemarketers should not call a number on the registry, unless there is a preexisting business relationship with the consumer. If they do, an individual can file a complaint at the FTC website. This law applies to information provided by data brokers for telemarketing.

- Federal Trade Commission Act Section 5 (FTC Unfair or Deceptive Powers):[39] Section 5 of the Federal Trade Commission Act (FTC Act) prohibits "unfair or deceptive acts or practices in or affecting commerce." The FTC can deem certain practices of a data broker to be unfair and/or deceptive. This is a broad authority and has been used to obtain consent agreements with a number of data brokers, such as ChoicePoint and Spokeo.

- State Unfair and Deceptive Practices Acts (UDAP Laws):[40] Every state has one or more consumer protection laws that are generally referred to as UDAP laws. For example, in Texas the attorney general files civil lawsuits under the Deceptive Trade Practices Act and other consumer protection statutes. The decision to investigate or file a lawsuit is based on a number of factors. Consumer complaints filed with the attorney general may form the basis for an investigation into a company's business practices. In some cases, significant numbers of complaints about a business may give rise to legal action, not on behalf of the individual complainants, but to enforce state law.

- California Online Privacy Protection Act (CalOPPA): This law requires operators of commercial website and mobile apps to conspicuously post a privacy policy if they collect personally identifiable information from Californians. The policy must describe the information collection, use and sharing practices of the company, how the site responds to Do Not Track signals, and whether third parties may collect personal information about consumers who use the site. The website should also describe the choices offered to the consumer regarding sharing of this information.

Note: This short list only represents a sample of the best-known and oft-cited federal and state laws applicable to certain data broker practices.

Where no laws govern either the data or certain uses of data, especially in the marketing space, but where regulators and the public have expressed concerns about certain commercial practices, industry has put forth self-regulatory codes of conduct that have been widely adopted. Some of the important codes of conduct that affect marketing data brokers are discussed here.

- Direct Marketing Association (DMA):[41] The DMA's Guidelines for Ethical Business Practice are intended to provide individuals and organizations involved in direct marketing across all media with generally accepted principles of conduct. The guidelines are used by DMA's Ethics Operating Committee, a peer review committee, as the standard by which DMA investigates consumer complaints against members and nonmembers. The guidelines include requirements provide information on its policies about the transfer of personally identifiable information for marketing purposes, respond to inquiries and complaints in a constructive, timely way, maintain appropriate security policies and practices to safeguard information, honor requests not to have personally identifiable information transferred for marketing purposes, and honor requests not to receive future solicitations from the organization.

---

[39] Federal Trade Commission Act Section 5, http://www.federalreserve.gov/boarddocs/supmanual/cch/ftca.pdf.

[40] State of Texas Deceptive Trace Practices Act, https://texasattorneygeneral.gov/cpd/consumer-protection.

[41] *Direct Marketing Association (DMA) Guidelines for Ethical Business Practice,* https://thedma.org/wp-content/uploads/DMA_Guidelines_January_2014.pdf.

- Digital Advertising Alliance (DAA):[42] The Digital Advertising Alliance establishes and enforces responsible privacy practices for certain types of digital advertising, providing consumers with enhanced transparency and control. DAA principles apply to data gathered from a particular device in either the desktop or mobile environments that involves multi-site data collection and use. The DAA is an independent non-profit organization led by the leading advertising and marketing trade associations.
- Network Advertiser's Initiative (NAI):[43] NAI is a non-profit organization that is the leading self-regulatory association dedicated to responsible data collection and its use for digital advertising. Since 2000, it has worked with the leaders in online advertising to craft policies that help ensure responsible data collection and use practices. The result is the development of high standards that are practical and scalable to benefit everyone. The NAI Code of Conduct is a set of self-regulatory principles that require NAI member companies to provide notice and choice with respect to interest-based advertising and ad delivery and reporting activities.

In recent years, there have been calls for data brokers to be more regulated. These initiatives usually focus on one type of data broker, often marketing data brokers due to the sheer quantity of information they collect. Regulators focused on shortcomings in the FCRA would like the FCRA to include practices that are on the fringe of the law. They also have concerns about medical devices that fall outside HIPPA. However, as of this writing, none of these initiatives have progressed.

The marketing self-regulatory bodies listed here continue to expand their codes as new mediums and new types of data enter the marketplace. Self-regulatory initiatives, in sectors such as smart cars, are starting to emerge more and more, and we expect these types of codes to continue to evolve as consumers embrace the IoT.

ARE THERE DATA BROKERS OUTSIDE THE UNITED STATES?

For a number of reasons, there are far more data brokers within than outside the United States. Other countries have fewer public records and publicly available information. Also, many countries, such as those in Europe, have broad data protections laws, which limit data sharing. Both attitudes and laws governing credit are quite different outside the United States. Laws requiring identity verification and background checks typically do not exist in other countries. Consequently, other countries have fewer first- and third-party data brokers.

In the credit bureau space, a research group known as PERC[44] reports, "approximately 3.5 billion of the world's adults do not use formal financial services. Even when access to a formal lending institution is possible – and many lack access, especially in rural areas – most of these persons are 'Credit Invisibles.' Credit Invisibles have no credit data, and mainstream lenders use automated underwriting systems requiring this data – such as a credit report. When none is available, lenders automatically reject an applicant."

The DDMI "Value of Data" study reports, "The DDME is a uniquely American creation. Just as the U.S. created digital market - making media by commercializing the Internet browser in the 1990s, so it created postal market - making media when Montgomery Ward developed the

---

[42] *Digital Advertising Alliance (DAA) Self-Regulatory Program*, http://www.aboutads.info/.

[43] *Network Advertiser's Initiative (NAI) Code of Conduct*, http://www.networkadvertising.org/code-enforcement/code.

[44] PERC drives financial inclusion by using innovative information solutions using original research that serve unmet needs in the market, http://www.perc.net.

mail order catalog in 1872. Today, data-driven marketing is a major export industry. The study's employment analysis confirms that the DDME is a Net (export) contributor to US economic well-being. DDME firms derive a considerable portion of their revenue abroad (sometimes upwards of 15%) while employing nearly all their workers in the U.S. The study confirms that the U.S. leads the world in data science applied to the marketplace. Ideas developed in the U.S. by American statisticians and econometricians, running on U.S.-designed hardware, and coded in algorithms developed and tested in the research offices of U.S. firms, are used to generate revenues throughout the world."

While this study was focused on marketing, and no comparable studies exist for other types of data brokers, the relative financial fraud rates are dropping, so there is likely value created in this sector. Thus we can extrapolate that at least some value can be applied to most types of data brokers.

There are a few self-regulatory efforts by direct marketing associations in Europe and other developed countries in Asia, and the DAA has expanded into Europe and Canada.

The US economy has enjoyed the innovation and positive economic benefits that come from the robust use of data provided by data brokers. As technology rapidly moves forward, continued advancements in self-regulation are needed to keep pace. Such guidance can respond to changes in the marketplace faster than can legislation and should be aggressively supported by industry.

WHAT RISKS DO DATA BROKERS POSE?

While the benefits that robust uses of information are significant, there are a number of very real risks involved with data brokering. While some risks are common across the data broker community, some are unique to certain categories of data brokers.

Risks Common to All Data Brokers:

- Security: Probably the biggest risk for data brokers is poor security, where fraudsters can compile enough of a profile on an individual to steal their identity or successfully pose as a trusted party. Reasonable and appropriate security is a requirement for every data broker.
- Potential Discrimination: As analytics gets more sophisticated, the second common risk is that we can no longer simply rely on not using certain defined data points, such as age, race or marital status, to avoid discriminatory consequences. Analytics can predict these characteristics with a fairly high degree of accuracy. This is actually a problem with big data in general, and not limited to data brokers, but data brokers contribute to the issue by bringing more data into the analytics process. As mentioned earlier, the World Privacy Report on the growth of consumer scores raises issues of discrimination. All companies taking advantage of big data, including data brokers, must look for ways to discover when their practices have adverse effects on certain at-risk classes. The 2016 FTC study, "Big Data – A Tool for Inclusion or Exclusion,"[45] provides an in-depth analysis of this issue.
- Non-Compliance: Large players in the community usually do a better job of following the rules than smaller players do. They have more at stake and usually better understand what is

---

[45] FTC report, *Big Data – A Tool for Inclusion or Exclusion?*, https://www.ftc.gov/system/files/documents/reports/big-data-tool-inclusion-or-exclusion-understanding-issues/160106big-data-rpt.pdf.

expected of them. As a greater number of smaller players enter the marketplace, the risk of more data brokers acting out of compliance with laws and self-regulation may grow.

A summary of risks to specific categories of data brokers follows.

Providers of Public Information, Including Government Agencies, Professional Organizations, and Research, Look-Up, and Locate Services:

These organizations rely primarily on public records and publically available information. The overall benefits of this information being available to the public outweigh any risks of identity theft and fraud by helping locate the perpetrators of these crimes.

- Opt-Out for High-Risk Individuals: While some avenues exist, there must be more ways for individuals who are at high risk (e.g., pubic officials, battered wives, and individuals in witness protection) to block public access to their personal information.

Consumer Reporting Agencies (CRAs):

Most of the risks associated with CRAs are addressed in the federal and state laws governing these practices.

- Accuracy: The biggest risk is the potentially devastating effects inaccurate information can have on individuals, financially and otherwise. The community has been under criticism for the accuracy of their records. The 2014 FTC study, "Report to Congress Under Section 319 of the Fair and Accurate Credit Transactions Act of 2003,"[46] in 2015, which was a follow-up to their 2012 study, highlights the findings.

Risk Mitigation Services:

- Accuracy: Obviously, the need for a high degree of information accuracy is also critical in this category of data broker. However, risks are low. Due to the inherent latency of information used for these purposes, the services that such data brokers provide is understood not to be 100 percent effective, so alternate methods of verification are always provided by the user of the service.

Marketing Data Brokers:

While accurate information is good, the consequences of inaccuracies are not nearly as important for this, the largest category of data broker.

- Transparency: As reported in the FTC report on data brokers, concerns relative to marketing data brokers relate primarily to transparency. Consumers do not generally read privacy policies, so they do not know or understand that first-party data brokers, survey companies, and ad-supported websites and apps are selling their information to marketers and advertisers, and third-party data brokers are aggregating it with public records. While

---

[46] FTC, *Report to Congress Under Section 319 of the Fair and Accurate Credit Transactions Act of 2003* (2015), https://www.ftc.gov/system/files/documents/reports/section-319-fair-accurate-credit-transactions-act-2003-sixth-interim-final-report-federal-trade/150121factareport.pdf.

self-regulation promotes more robust transparency, marketing data brokers need to consider even more creative ways to engage with consumers about both the benefits and risks of data sharing for advertising and marketing purposes, so consumers can make informed decisions about what they are comfortable allowing and where the line is for acceptable use.

- Education: While many self-regulatory codes call for the community to better educate consumers about marketing data brokers, privacy policies are not a good way to explain the ecosystem and how data actually is shared and impacts consumers. The Better Business Bureau Institute for Marketplace Trust recently launched Digital IQ[47] to help consumers easily access the information they want on the Internet, express their preferences, exercise informed choices, and shop smart. It provides a digital quiz and short, easily digestible education modules to help consumers be more savvy shoppers.

WHAT DOES THE FUTURE HOLD FOR DATA BROKERS?

So, are data brokers doing great things for our economy or are they operating a personal data exchange behind the backs of consumers? The answer to both questions, to some degree, is yes. Responsible use of data does provide great benefits to our economy, to innovation, and to consumer convenience. However, most individuals do not understand the data broker community, the risk it poses, and the benefits they derive from it.

With big data and the Internet of Things accelerating data collection at an increasingly rapid pace, more and more companies are going to become first-, second-, and third-party data brokers. This means it is getting harder and harder for individuals even to know about, much less control, how data about them is collected, created, used, and shared.

This begs the question: What, if anything, should be done to make the practices of the data broker community more transparent and less risky while preserving the benefits?

Data brokers must take an ethical, not just a compliance-oriented, approach to their practices and look for innovative ways to create a more transparent environment for regulators and provide more informed engagements that explain when and how consumers can participate in the use of data about them.

Fortunately, experience tells us that, if the practices of data brokers actually result in real harms, either tangible or reputational, or other risks to individuals, over time this will damage consumer confidence and is likely to lead to restrictive legislation and ultimately limit access to data. This will have a negative impact on the data broker community itself, and in turn, will have negative economic implications on society.

While new US federal legislation regulating data brokers is unlikely in the next few years, these moments in time represent a great opportunity for the data broker community to expand their self-regulatory practices. As appropriately protecting consumers against harm and other risks becomes more and more contextual, the data broker community, in all its various forms, working with regulators and advocates, has the best chance of writing workable guidelines that benefit everyone. Time will tell whether it seizes this window of opportunity or not.

---

[47] BBB Digital IQ, http://www.bbb.org/council/digitaliq/.

3

In Defense of Big Data Analytics

*Mark MacCarthy**

* The views expressed in this chapter are those of the author and not necessarily those of the Software & Information Industry Association (SIIA) or any of its member companies.

THE RISE OF BIG DATA ANALYTICS

Changes in Computer Technology

Today analytics firms, data scientists and technology companies have valuable new tools at their disposal, derived from three interlocking developments in computer technology. Data sets have dramatically increased in volume, variety and velocity. Processing capacity and storage capacity have increased, accommodating and reinforcing these changes. And new analytic techniques that were ineffective at lower scale and slower processing speeds have had spectacular successes.

Big data consists of data sets with increased volume, variety of formats and velocity.[1] Data sets, especially those derived from Internet activity containing video and images, are massive. The Internet of Things adds data from sensors embedded in everyday objects connected online. In addition, big data sets come in a variety of unstructured and semi-structured formats such as text, images, audio, video streams, and logs of web activity. Finally, big data sets change with astonishing rapidity in real time. A major driver of the increased availability of data is the computer communications networks that have been growing at astonishing rates since the Internet went commercial in the early 1990s.

According to IBM, increases in the amount of available data are staggering: "Every day, we create 2.5 quintillion bytes of data – so much that 90% of the data in the world today has been created in the last two years alone."[2] According to Cisco, the Internet of Things will generate more than 400 zetabytes of data per year by 2018.[3]

For more than fifty years, processing speeds and computer memory have doubled every eighteen to twenty-four months. The 1985 Nintendo Entertainment System had half the processing power of the computer that brought Apollo to the moon in 1969. The Apple iPhone

---

[1] The standard definition of big data includes volume (i.e., the size of the dataset); variety (i.e., data from multiple repositories, domains, or types); velocity (i.e., rate of flow); and variability (i.e., the change in other characteristics). National Institute of Standards and Technology (NIST) Big Data Public Working Group Definitions and Taxonomies Subgroup, *NIST Big Data Interoperability Framework, Volume 1: Definitions*, NIST Special Publication (SP) 1500–1, September 2015, p. 4, available at http://nvlpubs.nist.gov/nistpubs/SpecialPublications/NIST.SP.1500–1.pdf.

[2] "2.5 Quintillion Bytes of Data Created Every Day," *IBM*, April 24, 2013, available at https://www.ibm.com/blogs/insights-on-business/consumer-products/2-5-quintillion-bytes-of-data-created-every-day-how-does-cpg-retail-manage-it/

[3] "The Zetabyte Era: Trends and Analysis," *Cisco*, available at http://www.cisco.com/c/en/us/solutions/collateral/service-provider/visual-networking-index-vni/vni-hyperconnectivity-wp.html.

5 has 2.7 times the processing power of the 1985 Cray-2 supercomputer. Today's Samsung Galaxy S6 phone has five times the power of Sony's 2000 PS2. It would take 18,400 of today's PS4s to match the processing power of one of today's supercomputers, the Tianhe-2.[4] This rate of change has driven spectacular improvements in value for consumers, but most importantly it has allowed analysis to move in directions that had previously been thought to be unproductive.

New analytic techniques can discover in data connections and patterns that were often invisible with smaller data sets and with older techniques. Earlier researchers would approach a defined data set with a well-formulated hypothesis and proceed to test it using standard statistical techniques such as multi-variate regression analysis. Researchers brought background knowledge, theoretical understanding and intuitions into the process of hypothesis creation and hoped to find a pattern in the data that would verify this hypothesis. But the data themselves were silent and would tell him nothing. In contrast, new analytic techniques based on machine learning discover connections in the data that the researcher had not even dreamed of. The data speak for themselves, leading to completely novel and unexpected connections between factors that had previously been thought of as unrelated.

Machine Learning and Artificial Intelligence

Artificial intelligence and machine learning are examples of big data analytics. Machine learning is a programming technique that teaches machines to learn by examples and precedents. Artificial intelligence is a generic name for a variety of computational techniques that allow machines to exhibit cognitive capacities.[5] Its current success in pattern-recognition tasks such as speech or object recognition is a natural outgrowth of the developments in computer technology that we have just described.

The increase in the availability of data and computing power has enabled a previous version of AI research to move forward dramatically. The initial approaches to AI fit the model of structured programming prevalent in the 1950s. Computers could only do what they have been programmed to do. So the field focused on finding simplifying rules that were obtained from subject-matter experts, like doctors, lawyers or chess masters. However, the resulting "expert systems" were not very effective.

A different approach to programming was initially known as neural networks and came to be called machine learning. It sought to "create a program that extracts signals from noise in large bodies of data so those signals can serve as abstractions for understanding the domain or for classifying additional data."[6] This alternative approach required programmers simply to present

---

[4] "Processing Power Compared," *Experts Exchange*, available at http://pages.experts-exchange.com/processing-power-compared/.

[5] Related definitions focus on the ability of machines to function intelligently in their environment, where "intelligently" refers to elements of appropriate behavior and foresight. See Report of the 2015 Study Panel, *Artificial Intelligence and Life in 2030: One Hundred Year Study on Artificial Intelligence*, Stanford University, September 2016, p. 7, available at https://ai100.stanford.edu/sites/default/files/ai_100_report_0831fnl.pdf (Study Group Report). Artificial intelligence is not necessarily aimed at mimicking or reproducing human intelligence. One of the founders of AI, John McCarthy, said that the idea behind AI was to "get away from studying human behavior and to consider the computer as a tool for solving certain classes of problems." AI researchers weren't "considering human behavior except as a clue to possible effective ways of doing a task ... AI was created as a branch of computer science and as a branch of psychology." John McCarthy, "Book Review of B. P. Bloomfield, The Question of Artificial Intelligence: Philosophical and Sociological Perspectives," *Annals of the History of Computing*, vol. 10, no. 3 (1998), available at http://www-formal.stanford.edu/jmc/reviews/bloomfield.pdf.

[6] Jerry Kaplan, *Humans Need Not Apply: A Guide to Wealth and Work in the Age of Artificial Intelligence*, Yale University Press, 2015, p. 212 (Kaplan).

sufficient examples of the task they wanted the computer to solve. However, this alternative approach faced its own theoretical and practical limitations, and was largely abandoned in the 1980s. In the 1990s and 2000s, however, it reappeared and rapidly made progress in pattern recognition, displacing its rival approach as the dominant approach in the field.[7]

The structured approach to programming was suited for the size and scale of the computer capacity of its time – limited processing speeds, memory and data. The machine learning approach could not demonstrate results with this computer architecture. Computer memory and processing speeds were so limited, machine learning programs could recognize only very simple patterns. Data sets did not contain a sufficient number of examples to generate accurate pattern recognition.

The new computer infrastructure, however, allowed more flexible programming techniques. Faster computers with larger memory could begin to recognize complex patterns – if they had sufficient data to be trained on. The Internet provided just such a treasure trove of training data. In this new environment, machine learning rapidly developed.

Machine-learning programs get better as they are exposed to more data, which the spectacular growth of the Internet has been able to provide in ever increasing amounts. The programs adjust themselves as they are exposed to new data, evolving not only from the original design of the program but also from the weights developed from their exposure to earlier training data.

Because these new machine-learning techniques are not pre-programmed with humanly created rules, their operation can sometimes resist human comprehension. Often, it is "impossible for the creators of machine learning programs to peer into their intricate, evolving structure to understand or explain what they know or how they solve a problem."[8] In addition, they rely on correlations found in data, rather than on empirically or theoretically comprehensible causal connections: "In a big-data world ... we won't have to be fixated on causality; instead we can discover patterns and correlations in the data that offer us novel and invaluable insights."[9]

Despite the difficulty in discerning the logical or causal structure uncovered by these machine-learning algorithms, they are increasingly moving out of computer science departments and providing substantial benefits in real world applications.

Applications of Big Data Analytics

A common view is that big data analytics has a natural home in science and research institutes, information technology companies, analytics firms and Internet companies that use it for online behavioral advertising or recommendation engines for news, music and books. According to this view, big data analytics lives in computers or smart phones or communications networks such as the Internet, and we should look for its benefits and challenges there.

But this is to misunderstand the reality and potential of this disruptive technology. Big data analytics is not confined to separate devices called computers or smart phones, or used only in the information and communications technology industries. We are just at the beginning of the application of these techniques in all domains of economic, political and social life. It will transform everyday life for everyone, creating enormous opportunities and challenges for all of us.

---

[7] Kaplan, p. 25.
[8] Kaplan, p. 30.
[9] Viktor Mayer-Schonberger and Kenneth Cukier, *Big Data: A Revolution That Will Transform How We Live, Work, and Think*, Houghton Mifflin Harcourt, 2013, p. 14 (Mayer-Schonberger and Cukier).

Recent studies document the domains in which it is being used and where its impact is likely to be greatest in the coming years, including a 2014 big data report from the Obama administration[10] and a 2016 report by the AI Study Group, a panel of industry and academic experts.[11]

Transportation

The AI Study Group report predicts that in North American cities by 2030 autonomous transportation would be commonplace including cars, trucks, flying vehicles and personal robots. Cars will be better drivers than people, who will own fewer cars and live farther from work.[12] McKinsey reports that all major car manufacturers as well as technology companies such as Google are gearing up to provide autonomous vehicles, and that sometime between 2030 and 2050 autonomous vehicles will become the primary means of transportation, reducing accidents by 90 percent, thereby saving billions of dollars and billions of square meters in parking space.[13]

This development is especially striking because it illustrates the surprising capacity of AI systems to overcome problems of context and perception that were thought just a few years ago to be well beyond the capacity of computer programs. Computers could not handle driving, it was thought, because they could not process such a large amount of unstructured visual data and because the rules to mimic how humans assessed and reacted to traffic would be impossibly complex. A computer could never understand the context of driving well enough to know that "a ball rolling into the street is often followed by a young child chasing the ball so you step on the brakes."[14] But this is exactly what autonomous vehicles are able to do successfully – by following a model of computer programing that is not limited to pre-defined rules.

Speech Recognition

Several years ago, people noticed that an early version of Siri could not answer the question, "Can a dog jump over a house?" They explained this failure by saying that "engineers don't yet know how to put enough common sense into software."[15] But that is not how advanced versions of speech recognition work.

Older attempts to computerize speech recognition assumed that computers would have to understand the context of an utterance and absorb large amounts of cultural material in order to recognize speech. Newer versions look instead for how often words appear in certain combinations, taking advantage of the vast increase in available examples of language use. The distinctions between "to," "two" and "too" can be identified statistically, rather than through mimicking a human process of understanding contexts. Even rare combinations can be detected if the amount of training data is large enough.[16]

---

[10] United States, Executive Office of the President, *Big Data: Seizing Opportunities, Preserving Values*, The White House, May 2014, available at https://www.whitehouse.gov/sites/default/files/docs/big_data_privacy_report_may_1_2014.pdf (White House Big Data Report).

[11] Study Group Report.

[12] Study Group Report, p. 4.

[13] Michele Bertoncello and Dominik Wee, "Ten Ways Autonomous Driving Could Redefine the Automotive World," *McKinsey*, June 2016, available at http://www.mckinsey.com/industries/automotive-and-assembly/our-insights/ten-ways-autonomous-driving-could-redefine-the-automotive-world.

[14] Frank Levy and Richard J. Murnane, "Dancing with Robots: Humans Skills for Computerized Work," *Third Way*, 2013, p. 9, available at http://content.thirdway.org/publications/714/Dancing-With-Robots.pdf (Levy and Murnane).

[15] Levy and Murnane, p. 10.

[16] "A good speech recognition system that 'hears' the sentence 'my last visit to the office took two hours too long' can correctly spell the 'to,' 'two,' and 'too.' It can do this not because it understands the context of the usage of these words

Complete language fluency might still elude computerization.[17] But speech recognition is increasingly accurate with Baidu's Deep Speech 2 at 96 percent accuracy and Apple's Siri at 95 percent and is on the way to being used in search applications.[18] Speech recognition is ubiquitous today in our smart phones and increasingly in consumer devices such as Amazon's Echo that allow people to talk to their houses.[19]

Health Care

The AI Study Report finds that the last several years have seen an immense leap forward in collecting useful data from personal monitoring devices and mobile apps and from electronic health records in clinical settings. As a result, AI-based applications could improve health outcomes and the quality of life for millions of people in the coming years.[20]

Research hospitals are already using IBM's Watson as an oncology diagnosis and treatment advisor and to select patients for clinical trials. The system synthesizes vast amounts of data from textbooks, guidelines, journal articles, and clinical trials to help physicians make diagnoses and identify treatment options for cancer patients. Medical decision-making will become "ever more scientific" while remaining a creative activity for the doctors and health care professionals involved.[21] The promise of intelligent systems that can aid diagnosis and treatment of disease is better quality care and lower cost for all patients, but especially for those who currently face health care barriers.[22]

One particularly striking example involves the use of data analytics to save premature babies at risk. Medical researchers used pattern recognition to analyze data generated from premature babies such as heart rate, respiration rate, temperature, blood pressure and blood oxygen level – with startling results. The simultaneous stabilization of vital signs as much as twenty-four hours in advance was a warning of an infection to come, thereby allowing medical intervention well before a crisis had developed. AI had discovered a useful fact about the onset of fevers and infections in premature babies that can become standard practice for early intervention.[23]

Consumer Credit

Credit scoring models have been used for decades to increase the accuracy and efficiency of credit granting. They help as many people as possible to receive offers of credit on affordable

---

as human beings do, but because it can determine, statistically, that 'to' is much more likely immediately to precede 'the office' than 'two' or 'too'. And this probability is established, effectively, by very fast searching and sorting across a huge database of documents." Richard Susskind and Daniel Susskind, *The Future of the Professions: How Technology Will Transform the Work of Human Experts*, Oxford University Press, 2015, pp. 186–187 (Susskind and Susskind). Similarly, good speech recognition programs use frequency not context to distinguish between "abominable" and "a bomb in a bull" (p. 275).

[17] Will Knight, "AI's Language Problem," *MIT Technology Review*, August 9, 2016, available at https://www.technologyreview.com/s/602094/ais-language-problem/.

[18] Kevin J. Ryan, "Who's Smartest: Alexa, Siri, and or Google Now?" *Inc.*, June 3, 2016, available at http://www.inc.com/kevin-j-ryan/internet-trends-7-most-accurate-word-recognition-platforms.html.

[19] Ry Crist and David Carnoy, "Amazon Echo Review: The Smart Speaker That Can Control Your Whole House," *C|Net*, February 15, 2016, available at http://www.cnet.com/products/amazon-echo-review/.

[20] Study Panel Report, p. 4.

[21] John Kelly III and Steve Hamm, *Smart Machines: IBM's Watson and the Era of Cognitive Computing*, Columbia Business School Publishing, Columbia University Press, 2013, p. 138.

[22] Laura Lorenzetti, "Here's How IBM Watson Health Is Transforming the Health Care Industry," *Fortune*, April 5, 2016 available at http://fortune.com/ibm-watson-health-business-strategy/.

[23] Mayer-Schonberger and Cukier, p. 60.

terms; and they allow lenders to efficiently manage credit risk. The models improve upon the older judgmental systems that relied excessively on subjective assessments by loan officers.

Traditional credit scores are built from information in credit bureau reports and typically use variables relating to credit history. But these traditional credit scores are not able to score approximately 70 million individuals who lack credit reports or have "thin" credit reports without enough data to generate a credit score.

This inability to score no-file or thin-file individuals differentially affects historically disadvantaged minorities. A recent Lexis-Nexis study found that 41 percent of historically underserved minority populations of Hispanics and African-Americans could not be scored using traditional methods, while the unscorable rate for the general population was only 24 percent. Minorities face an unscorable rate that is 1.7 times – almost twice – the rate for the general population.[24]

To remedy this limitation, companies are looking beyond the information contained in credit reports to alternative data sources and building credit scores based on this additional data. For instance, RiskView, an alternative credit score built by Lexis-Nexis relies on public and institutional data such as educational history and professional licensing, property asset and ownership data such as home ownership, and court-sourced items such as foreclosures, evictions, bankruptcies and tax liens.

The Lexis-Nexis report demonstrated the extent to which credit risk scores built from alternative data can help to extend credit to unscorable consumers, finding that fully 81 percent of unscorable minorities received a RiskView score. A major benefit of alternative credit scores is the improvement in the availability of credit for historically underserved minority groups.

Not every new model based on alternative data will be as predictive as the standard credit scoring models.[25] But a number of checks are in place to prevent abuse. New scoring models based on alternative data are subject to the same regulatory scrutiny as traditional scores. Moreover, the market will not support inaccurate models. For instance, some rethinking is already taking place on the appropriate role of social media information in determining creditworthiness.[26]

Education

Big data analytics is improving education through personalizing learning and identifying students at risk of failing. New computer-based educational resources record student activity during learning and create user models and groupings that improve student learning.[27] Advanced online learning systems recommend the next learning activity and also predict how the student will perform on examinations.[28]

---

[24] Jeffrey Feinstein, "Alternative Data and Fair Lending," *Lexis-Nexis*, August 2013, available at http://www.lexisnexis.com/risk/downloads/whitepaper/fair_lending.pdf.

[25] A 2014 study by Robinson + Yu discusses these alternative data scores and their limitations. See Robinson + Yu, *Knowing the Score: New Data, Underwriting, and Marketing in the Consumer Credit Marketplace: A Guide for Financial Inclusion Stakeholders*, October 2014, available at https://www.teamupturn.com/static/files/Knowing_the_Score_Oct_2014_v1_1.pdf.

[26] See Telis Demos and Deepa Seetharaman, "Facebook Isn't So Good at Judging Your Credit After All," *Wall Street Journal*, February 24, 2016, available at http://www.wsj.com/articles/lenders-drop-plans-to-judge-you-by-your-facebook-friends-1456309801.

[27] Marie Bienkowski, Mingyu Feng and Barbara Means, *Enhancing Teaching and Learning Through Educational Data Mining and Learning Analytics: An Issue Brief*, US Department of Education Office of Educational Technology, October 2012, available at http://www.ed.gov/edblogs/technology/files/2012/03/edm-la-brief.pdf.

[28] Paul Fain, "Intel on Adaptive Learning," *Inside Higher Ed*, April 4, 2013, available at http://www.insidehighered.com/news/2013/04/04/gates-foundation-helps-colleges-keep-tabs-adaptive-learning-technology#disqus_thread.

These developments allow for various forms of individualized learning that can replace one-size-fits-all models of learning.[29] In addition, biometric information can be used for assessing various psychological characteristics, such as grit, tenacity and perseverance, linked to effective learning.[30]

The US Department of Education concluded that these new data-driven learning methods are effective, saying, "students taught by carefully designed systems used in combination with classroom teaching can learn faster and translate their learning into improved performance relative to students receiving conventional classroom instruction."[31]

Predictive analytics can also be used to find students at risk of failing a class or dropping out. Simple early warning indicator systems can identify most students who eventually drop out of high school as early as the sixth grade by their attendance, behavior and course performance. Even more can be identified by the middle of ninth grade.[32] Many schools throughout the country use these systems to identify students to improve their chances of graduation.[33]

Other systems use a broader range of factors and more advanced analytics to identify at-risk students to enable schools to intervene early to provide them with the right support and intervention. Using one of these systems developed by IBM, for instance, the Hamilton County, Tennessee Board of Education increased graduation rates by more than eight percentage points and increased standardized test scores in math and reading by more than 10 percent.[34]

Detecting and Remedying Discrimination

Human biases are notorious and often unconscious. Classical music orchestras were almost entirely male for generations, despite the denials of bias by conductors who apparently exhibited no gender bias in any other aspect of their lives. But arranging auditions to be held behind a screen that hid the gender of the aspiring musician produced a dramatic change toward gender neutrality. Eliminating information that biased human judgment led to fairer outcomes.[35]

More elaborate data analysis can also detect totally unconscious biases. Judges are trained to conscientiously make good faith efforts to be impartial. Still one study in Israel found that at the beginning of the workday, judges granted around two-thirds of parole requests, but that approvals fell steadily until food breaks, after which the judges again granted most parole requests.[36]

Moreover, statistical techniques can be used to assess whether employment hiring and promotion practices are fair and provide the bases for taking remedial steps. Google publishes

---

[29] US Department of Education, *Expanding Evidence: Approaches for Measuring Learning in a Digital World*, chapter 2, 2013, available at http://www.ed.gov/edblogs/technology/files/2013/02/Expanding-Evidence-Approaches.pdf.

[30] US Department of Education, *Promoting Grit, Tenacity and Perseverance: Critical Factors for Success in the 21st Century*, February 2013, p. 41, at http://pgbovine.net/OET-Draft-Grit-Report-2-17-13.pdf.

[31] US Department of Education, *Expanding Evidence: Approaches for Measuring Learning in a Digital World*, chapter 2, 2013, p. 28, available at https://tech.ed.gov/wp-content/uploads/2014/11/Expanding-Evidence.pdf.

[32] Robert Balfanz, "Stop Holding Us Back," *New York Times*, June 4, 2014, available at http://mobile.nytimes.com/blogs/opinionator/2014/06/07/stop-holding-us-back/?_php=true&_type=blogs&emc=edit_tnt_20140608&nlid=50637717&tntemailo=y&_r=0.

[33] Mary Bruce and John M. Bridgeland, "The Use of Early Warning Indicator and Intervention Systems to Build a Grad Nation," Johns Hopkins University, November 2011, available at http://www.civicenterprises.net/MediaLibrary/Docs/on_track_for_success.pdf.

[34] "IBM Predictive Analytics Solution for Schools and Educational Systems," *IBM*, available at http://www-01.ibm.com/common/ssi/cgi-bin/ssialias?htmlfid=YTS03068USEN&appname=wwwsearch.

[35] Malcolm Gladwell, *Blink: The Power of Thinking without Thinking*, Little, Brown and Company, 2005, pp. 245 ff.

[36] "'I think it's time we broke for lunch ...': Court Rulings Depend Partly on When the Judge Last Had a Snack," *The Economist*, Apr. 14, 2011, available at http://www.economist.com/node/18557594.

its diversity report regularly[37] and has pioneered efforts to diversify its workplace through workshops for employees on detecting and dealing with unconscious bias. Software recruiting tools can also be used to help employers correct the underrepresentation of certain groups in their workforces.[38]

Data analysis can detect whether a statistical model has disproportionate adverse effects on protected classes. For instance, non-mortgage financial institutions do not have information about the race and ethnicity of their applicants and customers. To assess whether their statistical models comply with fair lending rules they can use publicly available information on surnames and geo-location as reliable predictors of these characteristics, and advanced statistical techniques can improve the predictive accuracy of these factors.[39]

Future of Work

Computer-based systems today can outperform people in more and more tasks once considered within the exclusive competence of humans. Automation has historically produced long-term growth and full employment, despite initial job losses. But the next generation of really smart AI-based machines could create the sustained technological unemployment that John Maynard Keynes warned against in the 1930s.[40] This time it could be different – people could go the way of horses, and lose their economic role entirely.[41] One study summed up the issue this way, "if new technologies do not create many additional tasks, or if the tasks that they do create are of a type in which machines, rather than people, have the advantage, then technological (un)employment, to a greater or lesser extent, will follow."[42]

Carl Frey and Michael Osborne estimated that 47 percent of occupations are susceptible to automation, including the more advanced cognitive work of lawyers and writers.[43] A study from the Organization for Economicy Cooperation and Development (OECD) found that "9% of jobs are automatable."[44] McKinsey estimates that currently demonstrated technologies could automate 45 percent of work activities, and that in about 60 percent of all occupations currently

---

[37] Google's January 2016 report showed that its workforce was 59% white and 69% male. See Google Diversity Index, available at https://www.google.com/diversity/index.html.

[38] Jules Polonetsky and Chris Wolf, "Fighting Discrimination – With Big Data," *The Hill*, September 15, 2015, available at http://thehill.com/blogs/pundits-blog/technology/217680-fighting-discrimination-with-big-data. See also Future of Privacy Forum, "Big Data: A Tool for Fighting Discrimination and Empowering Groups," September 2015.

[39] CFPB recently revealed the methodology it uses to assess disparate impact for fair lending compliance. Consumer Financial Protection Board, *Using Publicly Available Information to Proxy for Unidentified Race and Ethnicity: A Methodology and Assessment*, Summer 2014, available at http://files.consumerfinance.gov/f/201409_cfpb_report_proxy-methodology.pdf (CFPB Methodology). It does not mandate that anyone use this methodology but companies seeking to assess fair lending compliance risk are now in a position to make these assessments more reliably.

[40] John Maynard Keynes, "Economic Possibilities for Our Grandchildren," in *Essays in Persuasion*, New York: W. W. Norton & Co., 1963, pp. 358–373, available at http://www.aspeninstitute.org/sites/default/files/content/upload/Intro_Session1.pdf.

[41] See Erik Brynjolfsson and Andrew McAfee, "Will Humans Go the Way of Horses? Labor in the Second Machine Age," *Foreign Affairs*, July/August 2015, available at https://www.foreignaffairs.com/articles/2015-06-16/will-humans-go-way-horses. See also by the same authors, *The Second Machine Age: Work, Progress, and Prosperity in a Time of Brilliant Technologies*, W. W. Norton & Company, 2014.

[42] Susskind and Susskind, p. 289.

[43] Carl Frey and Michael Osborne, "The Future of Employment: How Susceptible Are Jobs to Computerization?" *Oxford University*, September 2013, available at http://www.oxfordmartin.ox.ac.uk/downloads/academic/The_Future_of_Employment.pdf.

[44] Melanie Arntz, Terry Gregory and Ulrich Zierahn, "The Risk of Automation for Jobs in OECD Countries: A Comparative Analysis," OECD Social, Employment and Migration Working Papers No. 189, 2016, available at http://www.oecd-ilibrary.org/social-issues-migration-health/the-risk-of-automation-for-jobs-in-oecd-countries_5jlz9h56dvq7-en.

available technologies could automate 30 percent or more of their constituent activities.[45] The Council of Economic Advisors estimates that that 83 percent of jobs making less than $20 per hour would come under pressure from automation, as compared to only 4 percent of jobs making above $40 per hour.[46]

The fear that the economy will motor on without human labor in a completely post-work society is far-fetched, but the chances of a less labor-intensive economy are significant enough to warrant serious attention from policymakers. In the short term, increased efforts for education and training are important. Policymakers should also consider income support measures such as a universal basic income that break the link between work and income and could provide a fair distribution of the cornucopia of plenty made possible by the advances of machine learning and artificial intelligence.[47]

Companies will need to examine how job redesign and process reengineering can make full use of skilled human resources while taking advantage of the efficiencies of machine learning. One strand of thought emphasizes technology that complements human skills, systems that augment human ability rather than substitute for it.[48] The National Science Foundation's National Robotics Initiative provides an incentive for systems that work alongside or cooperatively with workers.[49]

PRIVACY

The history of privacy policy shows that policymakers need to adapt privacy principles in the face of significant technological changes. In the 1890s, Warren and Brandeis developed the right to privacy as the right to be left alone in reaction to the development of the snap camera and mass print media. Sixty years of case law produced Prosser's four privacy torts as a systematization of the harms from different privacy invasions.[50]

These legal structures proved inadequate to deal with the arrival of the mainframe computer, which allowed the collection, storage, and processing of large volumes of personal information to improve operations in business, government and education. A regulatory paradigm of fair information practices arose to fill this gap.[51]

---

[45] Michael Chui, James Manyika and Mehdi Miremadi, "Four Fundamentals of Workplace Automation," *McKinsey Quarterly*, November 2015, available at http://www.mckinsey.com/business-functions/business-technology/our-insights/four-fundamentals-of-workplace-automation; and Michael Chui, James Manyika and Mehdi Miremadi, "Where Machines Could Replace Humans – And Where They Can't (Yet)," *McKinsey Quarterly*, July 2016, available at http://www.mckinsey.com/business-functions/business-technology/our-insights/where-machines-could-replace-humans-and-where-they-cant-yet#.

[46] Jason Furman, "Is This Time Different? The Opportunities and Challenges of Artificial Intelligence," Remarks at AI Now: The Social and Economic Implications of Artificial Intelligence Technologies in the Near Term, July 7, 2016, available at https://www.whitehouse.gov/sites/default/files/page/files/20160707_cea_ai_furman.pdf.

[47] See Study Report, p. 9: "It is not too soon for social debate on how the economic fruits of AI technologies should be shared."

[48] One goal could be human–machine cooperation by design, where the developers would aim "to engineer a human/machine team from the very beginning, rather than to design a highly automated machine to which a user must adapt." David A. Mindell, *Our Robots, Ourselves: Robotics and the Myths of Autonomy*, Penguin Publishing Group, 2015, p. 210.

[49] "National Robotics Initiative (NRI): Program Solicitation 16–517," *National Science Foundation*, December 15, 2015, available at http://www.nsf.gov/pubs/2016/nsf16517/nsf16517.htm.

[50] See the short history of the evolution of privacy law in Paul Ohm, "Broken Promises of Privacy: Responding to the Surprising Failure of Anonymization," *UCLA Law Review*, vol. 57, p. 1701, 2010; University of Colorado Law Legal Studies Research Paper No. 9–12, pp. 1731–1739, available at http://ssrn.com/abstract=1450006 (Ohm, Broken Promises).

[51] Robert Gellman, "Fair Information Practices: A Basic History," available at http://bobgellman.com/rg-docs/rg-FIPShistory.pdf.

Today, artificial intelligence, machine learning, cloud computing, big data analytics and the Internet of Things rest firmly on the ubiquity of data collection, the collapse of data storage costs, and the astonishing power of new analytic techniques to derive novel insights that can improve decision-making in all areas of economic, social and political life. A reevaluation of regulatory principles is needed in light of these developments.

Data Minimization

A traditional privacy principle calls for enterprises and others to limit their collection of information to the minimum amount needed to accomplish a clearly specified specific purpose and then to discard or anonymize this information as soon as that purpose is accomplished.[52]

In an era of small data sets, expensive memory and limited computing power, privacy policymakers could enforce this data minimization principle to reduce privacy risks without sacrificing any significant social gains. With the increasing capacity of big data analytics to derive new insights from old data, this principle of collecting the minimum amount of information and throwing it away as soon as possible is no longer appropriate. The routine practice of data minimization would sacrifice considerable social benefit.

Full data minimization is not an ultimate moral principle that should endure through changes in technology. It is a practical guideline that grew up in a time when the dangers of computer surveillance and information misuse were not matched with the potential gains from data retention and analysis. Previously, we could not use data to perform the astonishing range of activities made possible by new machine learning and artificial intelligence techniques, including high-level cognitive functions that rival or surpass human efforts. Now we can do these things, provided we retain and analyze truly staggering amounts of information. It is now sensible to retain this information rather than routinely discarding it.

This does not mean that all constraints on data collection and retention should be abandoned. Good privacy-by-design practice suggests that a prior risk-based assessment of the extent of data collection and retention could prevent substantial public harm.

An example illustrates the point. Before the introduction of credit cards using a chip, a common way to make a counterfeit card was to hack into a merchant database in the hopes of finding enough information to make counterfeit cards. If the database contained the access codes that had been read from the cards' magnetic stripes, then the thieves could make the counterfeit cards, but without these security codes the fake cards would not work at the point of sale. This led to a very simple security rule: don't store the access code. There was no business reason for it to be retained and substantial risk in doing so.

This example suggests that a prior review of data collection and retention practices is warranted to avoid retaining information that could create an unnecessary risk of harm. In these cases, data controllers should assess the likely harm in retaining data compared to the likely gains and should throw away information or de-identify it when the risks of harm are too great.

---

[52] See, for instance, the European General Data Protection Regulation, where article 5(1)(c) provides that personal data shall be "adequate, relevant and limited to what is necessary in relation to the purposes for which they are processed" and is labeled "data minimization." A Regulation of the European Parliament and of the Council of the European Union on the Protection of Natural Persons with Regard to the Processing of Personal Data and on the Free Movement of Such Data, and Repealing Directive 95/46/EC (General Data Protection Regulation) April 27, 2016, Article 5(1)(c), available at http://eur-lex.europa.eu/legal-content/EN/TXT/PDF/?uri=CELEX:32016R0679&from=EN.

Secondary Use

Traditional privacy principles call for enterprises to request approval from data subjects when seeking to use information collected for one purpose for a purpose that is inconsistent with, unrelated to or even just different from the original purpose.[53]

One way to try to avoid a need to seek approval for secondary use would be to describe completely the purposes for which an enterprise might want to collect data. But this is exactly what cannot be done in an era of big data analytics. Often information gathered for one purpose is found to be useful for additional purposes. For example, health information gathered for the purpose of treatment has enormous value for medical research. Also, information used to assess student learning can be used to examine the effectiveness of new educational tools and programs.

As one commentator put it: "Since analytics are designed to extract hidden or unpredictable inferences and correlations from datasets, it becomes difficult to define *ex ante* the purposes of data processing ... a notice that explains all the possible uses of data is hard to be given to data subjects at the time of the initial data collection."[54]

A privacy principle restricting all secondary uses without further notice and consent would create unnecessary procedural barriers to beneficial uses made possible by new data analysis techniques.

This does not mean that any further use of information is legitimate. Secondary uses of personal information are legitimate when they do not pose a significant risk of harm to the data subject or when they are consistent with the context of information collection and use. Good privacy-by-design practice suggests a risk analysis of secondary uses to assess likely harms and benefits. When there is a significant risk of injury to data subjects, an appropriate level of control might be needed – prohibition, or opt-in or opt-out choice, depending on the severity of the risk. This risk-based secondary use principle is more appropriate to meet the challenges of privacy protection in an age of big data.

Anonymization: Privacy and Utility

Traditional privacy policy emphasizes the role of anonymization or de-identification as a way to protect privacy. De-identification is sound information management practice when there is little need for keeping data in identified form. But there are substantial limitations to the effectiveness of the technique of privacy protection in an age of big data analysis.

De-identification involves removing identifying information from a dataset so that the remaining data cannot be linked with specific individuals. If an individual-level record is stripped of such obvious identifiers as name, social security number, date of birth and zip code, then privacy interests are no longer at stake because the record cannot be recognized as being about a specific individual. For this reason, several privacy rules exempt de-identified information.[55] Various

---

[53] The consideration of secondary use usually arises in the context of applying the principle of purpose limitation. See Article 29 Data Protection Working Party, Opinion 03/2013 on purpose limitation, April 2, 2013, available at http://ec.europa.eu/justice/data-protection/article-29/documentation/opinion-recommendation/files/2013/wp203_en.pdf.

[54] Alessandro Mantelero and Giuseppe Vaciago, "Data Protection in a Big Data Society: Ideas for a Future Regulation," *Digital Investigation*, vol. 15, December 2015, pp. 104–109, Post-print version, available at http://dx.doi.org/10.1016/jdiin.2015.09.006.

[55] The restrictions on public release of student data imposed by the Family and Educational Records Privacy Act (FERPA) do not apply to de-identified student records. See "Dear Colleague Letter about Family Educational Rights and Privacy Act (FERPA) Final Regulations," US Department of Education, December 17, 2008, available at http://www2.ed.gov/policy/gen/guid/fpco/hottopics/ht12–17-08.html. The privacy requirements of the Health Insurance Portability and Accountability Act (HIPAA) Privacy Rule do not apply to de-identified health information. 42 CFR 164.514, available at https://www.law.cornell.edu/cfr/text/45/164.514.

studies have shown, however, that it is often possible to use available techniques, including information contained in other databases, to reidentify records in de-identified databases.[56]

The Federal Trade Commission (FTC) has addressed this issue through a policy that relieves enterprises using de-identified databases of various privacy requirements such as notice and consent, provided that their methods of anonymization are reasonable in light of current technical developments in the field, that they commit to not attempting to reidentify records and that they bind third parties to whom they make the data available to abide by the same commitment.[57]

A legislative proposal by Robert Gellman is similar to the FTC policy. It would have data providers include clauses in their data use agreements noting that the data had been de-identified and requiring the data user to keep it in de-identified form. Recipients would then face civil and criminal penalties if they attempted to reidentify the data.[58]

This contractual policy might work in certain circumstances when the data is released only to qualified individuals who can be clearly identified by the data provider. It does not provide sufficient protection when data is simply released to the public, which is legally required in certain circumstances and is often in the public interest to enable socially important scientific, social or medical research.

Moreover, reidentification techniques can be effective, even when the underlying data set is completely private and the only public information is the statistical model derived from the private data set. Often sensitive information is part of a model that can accurately predict nonsensitive information that has been voluntarily provided. The model can be run in reverse, using the value of the dependent variable and other independent variables in the model to predict the value of the sensitive variable. In this way, a person's health status, for instance, could be inferred from non-health information voluntarily provided to a third party.

Absolute privacy cannot be guaranteed if the data set and the models derived from it are to be publicly available and useful. A kind of relative privacy, differential privacy, can be obtained using various techniques, which reduces the risk of reidentifying a person's sensitive attribute to a level judged to be acceptably low.[59] Such privacy-preserving techniques, however, can prevent the effective use of the information in the database. A trade-off must be made between the utility of the data and the privacy of the data subjects. When the utility of the database is paramount, as in medical settings where the priority is setting a safe and effective dose of a lifesaving medicine, the notion of balancing the risk of revealing sensitive information versus the extra risk of mortality seems problematic. In these circumstances, release of the data or the statistical models based on them might need to be avoided.[60]

---

[56] See Ohm, Broken Promises for examples. See also Simpson Garfinkel, *De-Identification of Personal Information*, National Institute of Standards and Technology, NIST IR 8053, October 2015, available at http://nvlpubs.nist.gov/nistpubs/ir/2015/NIST.IR.8053.pdf.

[57] Federal Trade Commission report, *Protecting Consumer Privacy in an Age of Rapid Change: Recommendations for Businesses and Policymakers*, March 2012, p. 21, available at https://www.ftc.gov/sites/default/files/documents/reports/federal-trade-commission-report-protecting-consumer-privacy-era-rapid-change-recommendations/120326privacyreport.pdf.

[58] Robert Gellman, "The Deidentification Dilemma: A Legislative and Contractual Proposal," *Fordham Intellectual Property, Media & Entertainment Law Journal*, vol. 21, no. 33, 2010, available at http://iplj.net/blog/wp-content/uploads/2013/09/Deidentificatin-Dilemma.pdf.

[59] Cynthia Dwork, "Differential Privacy," 33rd International Colloquium on Automata, Languages and Programming, part II (ICALP 2006), pp. 1–12, available at https://www.microsoft.com/en-us/research/publication/differential-privacy/ (Dwork, Differential Privacy).

[60] See, for instance, Matthew Fredrikson et al., "Privacy in Pharmacogenetics: An End-to-End Case Study of Personalized Warfarin Dosing," Proceedings of the 23rd USENIX Security Symposium, August 20–22, 2014, available at https://www.usenix.org/system/files/conference/usenixsecurity14/sec14-paper-fredrikson-privacy.pdf. They conclude that differential privacy mechanisms cannot always be used to release data sets and statistical models based on them. "Differential privacy is suited to settings in which *privacy and utility requirements are not fundamentally at odds*, and

Information Externalities

The problem raised by the reidentification of public data sets is really part of a general problem of information externalities, where information disclosed by some people reveals information about others.[61] In principle, this has been a commonplace for years. If the police know that a perpetrator of a certain crime is left-handed and one of three people, and find out from the first two that they are right-handed, then they know that the third person is the guilty one, even though the third person has disclosed nothing at all. If I know the average height of Lithuanian women and that Terry Gross is two inches shorter than the average Lithuanian woman, I know Terry Gross's height.[62]

But information externalities are much more common than these curiosities suggest. Any statistical regularity about people creates a potential for an information externality. Social scientists know that people having a certain array of characteristics often have another characteristic that is of interest. The dependent variable of interest can be inferred from independent variables, even when that fact about a person is highly sensitive, that person never disclosed it and it cannot be found in public records.[63]

The new technology of big data analytics makes information externality the norm rather than a curiosity. The standard examples are well-known: pregnancy status can be inferred from shopping choices;[64] sexual orientation can be inferred from the characteristics of friends on social networks;[65] race can be inferred from name, and even more strongly from zip code and name.[66] As machine-learning algorithms improve they will be able to more accurately ferret out more and more personal traits that are of interest. In the age of big data analytics, it will be increasingly difficult to keep secret any personal characteristic that is important for classifying and making decisions about people.

One recommendation to fix to this problem, suggested earlier as a remedy for the de-anonymization problem, is to keep secret the statistical regularities, algorithms, and models that allow information externalities. This can in some circumstances mitigate the extent of the issue. After all, if the regularity is publicly available, then any researcher, enterprise or government agency can use it to create this kind of information externality. Keeping it secret limits the group of entities that can use it.

But secrecy is not the answer. If an organization develops a proprietary model or algorithm, but doesn't make it generally available, it can still generate information externalities. In many cases the algorithms that allow inference to previously hidden traits will be

can be balanced with an appropriate privacy budget . . . In settings where privacy and utility *are* fundamentally at odds, release mechanisms of any kind will fail, and restrictive access control policies may be the best answer," p. 19.

[61] See Mark MacCarthy, "New Directions in Privacy: Disclosure, Unfairness and Externalities," *I/S: A Journal of Law and Policy for the Information Society*, vol. 6, no. 3 (2011), pp. 425–512, available at http://www18.georgetown.edu/data/people/maccartm/publication-66520.pdf.

[62] Dwork, Differential Privacy.

[63] This well-known property is sometimes called inferential disclosure. See OECD Glossary of Statistical terms, available at https://stats.oecd.org/glossary/detail.asp?ID=6932: "Inferential disclosure occurs when information can be inferred with high confidence from statistical properties of the released data. For example, the data may show a high correlation between income and purchase price of a home. As the purchase price of a home is typically public information, a third party might use this information to infer the income of a data subject."

[64] Charles Duhigg, "How Companies Learn Your Secrets," *New York Times*, February 16, 2012, available at http://www.nytimes.com/2012/02/19/magazine/shopping-habits.html.

[65] Carter Jernigan and Behram F. T. Mistree, "Gaydar: Facebook Friends Expose Sexual Orientation," *First Monday*, vol. 14, no. 10, October 5, 2009, available at http://firstmonday.org/article/view/2611/2302.

[66] CFPB Methodology.

proprietary. The use will be restricted to a single company or its institutional customers and will be available only to those who have the most interest and need to make the inferences that expose previously hidden traits.

Information externalities challenge the traditional core privacy principle that individual control over the flow of information is the front line of defense against privacy violations. In the traditional view, privacy is just control over information.[67] Privacy policymakers aim to empower people to protect themselves and their privacy through a "notice and choice" mechanism. In practice, privacy policymakers focus on the best way to have companies tell people about the use of information and provide them a choice of whether or not to release information for that purpose.

But this tool of privacy policy will become increasingly ineffective in an age of ubiquitous information externalities. Fully informed, rational individuals could make the choice not to reveal some feature of their character or conduct, but as long as others are willing to reveal that information about themselves and contribute it to the huge data sets that form the input for increasingly sophisticated algorithms, data scientists will be able to make increasingly accurate predictions about that hidden feature of an individual's life.

This does not imply that notice and choice are always a mistake. They can sometimes provide an effective privacy protective mechanism. But policymakers are beginning to move away from heavy reliance on notice and choice. The Obama Administration's 2014 big data report urged privacy policymakers to "to look closely at the notice and consent framework that has been a central pillar of how privacy practices have been organized for more than four decades."[68] The accompanying report from the President's Council of Advisors on Science and Technology says plainly that the notice and choice framework is "increasingly unworkable and ineffective."[69]

As privacy moves away from reliance on notice and choice mechanisms, it moves toward other policy areas. Law and policy on minimum wage, non-discrimination, information security, occupational safety and health, and environmental protection, to name just a few, do not rely on consent mechanisms. In these areas, individual choice undermines the policy goal of a high level of equal protection for all. In the past, privacy policymakers have thought that privacy choices were individual and idiosyncratic and that regulation should allow space for differences in the value people placed on keeping information confidential. But the growing use of big data algorithms makes it increasingly likely that privacy cannot be provided on an individualized basis. In the age of big data analysis, privacy is a public good.[70]

Privacy policy makers can begin to rely more on two other approaches to supplement traditional privacy principles. A consequentialist framework focuses on the likely outcome of a proposed privacy requirement and uses an assessment of benefits and costs to decide when and how to regulate.[71] A social approach treats privacy as a collection of informational norms tied to

---

[67] Alan Westin famously defined privacy as "the claim of individuals, groups, or institutions to determine for themselves when, how, and to what extent information about them is communicated to others." Alan Westin, *Privacy and Freedom*, Atheneum, 1967, p. 7.

[68] White House Big Data Report, p. 54.

[69] Executive Office of the President, President's Council of Advisors on Science and Technology, *Report to the President: Big Data and Privacy: A Technological Perspective*, May 2014, p. 40, available at https://www.whitehouse.gov/sites/default/files/microsites/ostp/PCAST/pcast_big_data_and_privacy_-_may_2014.pdf.

[70] Joshua A. T. Fairfield and Christoph Engel, "Privacy as a Public Good," *Duke Law Journal*, vol. 65, p. 385, 2015, available at http://scholarship.law.duke.edu/dlj/vol65/iss3/1/.

[71] J. Howard Beales, III and Timothy J. Muris, "Choice or Consequences: Protecting Privacy in Commercial Information," *University of Chicago Law Review*, vol. 75, p. 109, 2008, especially pp. 109–120, available at https://lawreview.uchicago.edu/sites/lawreviewuchicago.edu/files/uploads/75.1/75_1_Muris_Beales.pdf.

specific contexts such as medicine, education, or finance and regulates to maintain or enforce these privacy norms.[72] The Software & Information Industry Association (SIIA) has issued guidelines for privacy policy makers that attempt to meld these two frameworks as a way to provide for effective privacy protection in an age of big data.[73]

FAIRNESS

Introduction

The increased use of big data analytics also raises concerns about fairness. Are the algorithms accurate? Do they utilize characteristics like race and gender that raise issues of discrimination? How do we know? Can people have redress if an algorithm gets it wrong or has a disparate impact on protected classes?[74]

Policymakers have issued reports and held workshops on these questions over the last two years. The Obama Administration's 2016 report on big data and civil rights highlighted concerns about possible discriminatory use of big data in credit, employment, education, and criminal justice.[75] The Federal Trade Commission held a workshop and issued a report on the possible use of big data as a tool for exclusion.[76]

Even when companies do not intend to discriminate and deliberately avoid the use of suspect classifications such as race and gender, the output of an analytical process can have a disparate impact on a protected class when a variable or combination of variables is correlated both with the suspect classification and the output variable. These correlations might be the result of historical discrimination that puts vulnerable people at a disadvantage. The end result is that analytics relying on existing data could reinforce and worsen past discriminatory practices.[77]

Concerned that the new techniques of data analysis will create additional challenges for minority groups, civil rights groups have developed principles aimed at protecting civil liberties in an age of big data[78] and have focused on the possibility that new techniques of analysis will be used to target minorities for discriminatory surveillance.[79]

---

[72] Helen Nissenbaum, *Privacy in Context*, Stanford University Press, 2009.

[73] SIIA, *Guidelines for Privacy Policymakers*, 2016, available at https://www.siia.net/Portals/0/pdf/Policy/SIIA%20Guidelines%20for%20Privacy%20Policymakers.pdf.

[74] See Cathy O'Neil, *Weapons of Math Destruction: How Big Data Increases Inequality and Threatens Democracy*, Crown/Archetype, 2016 and Frank Pasquale, *The Black Box Society: The Secret Algorithms That Control Money and Information*, Harvard University Press, 2015.

[75] Executive Office of the President, *Big Data: A Report on Algorithmic Systems, Opportunity, and Civil Rights*, May 2016, available at https://www.whitehouse.gov/sites/default/files/microsites/ostp/2016_0504_data_discrimination.pdf (Big Data and Civil Rights).

[76] Federal Trade Commission, *Big Data: A Tool for Inclusion or Exclusion? Understanding the Issues*, January 2016, available at https://www.ftc.gov/system/files/documents/reports/big-data-tool-inclusion-or-exclusion-understanding-issues/160106big-data-rpt.pdf.

[77] Solon Barocas and Andrew D. Selbst, "Big Data's Disparate Impact," *California Law Review*, vol. 104, p. 671, 2016, available at http://ssrn.com/abstract=2477899.

[78] Leadership Conference on Civil Rights, "Civil Rights Principles for the Era of Big Data," 2014, available at http://www.civilrights.org/press/2014/civil-rights-principles-big-data.html.

[79] On April 8, 2016, Georgetown Law and the Center on Privacy & Technology held a conference this issue of minority surveillance, entitled The Color of Surveillance: Government Monitoring of the African American Community. See https://www.law.georgetown.edu/academics/centers-institutes/privacy-technology/events/index.cfm.

Current Legal Framework

Any technology, new or old, can further illegal or harmful activities, and big data analysis is no exception. But neither are the latest computational tools an exception from existing laws that protect consumers and citizens from harm and discrimination.

The Fair Credit Reporting Act (FCRA) sets out requirements for credit reporting agencies, including access, correction and notification of adverse action.[80] FCRA was put in place to deal with computerized credit reporting agencies in the 1970s, but it applies to decisions made using big data and the latest machine-learning algorithms, including third-party companies that combine social media data with other information to create profiles of people applying for jobs.[81]

A second element of the current legal framework is the prohibition on discrimination against protected groups for particular activities. As statutory constraints on discrimination:

- Title VII of the Civil Rights Act of 1964 makes it unlawful for employers and employment agencies to discriminate against an applicant or employee because of such individual's "race, color, religion, sex, or national origin."[82]

- The Equal Credit Opportunity Act makes it unlawful for any creditor to discriminate against any applicant for credit on the basis of "race, color, religion, national origin, sex or marital status, or age."[83]

- Title VIII of the Civil Rights Act of 1968, the Fair Housing Act, prohibits discrimination in the sale, rental or financing of housing "because of race, color, religion, sex, familial status, or national origin."[84] The act also protects people with disabilities and families with children.

- The Age Discrimination in Employment Act of 1967 (ADEA) makes it unlawful for an employer to refuse to hire or to discharge or to otherwise discriminate against any individual because of the individual's age.[85]

- The Genetic Information Nondiscrimination Act of 2008 prohibits US health insurance companies and employers from discriminating on the basis of information derived from genetic tests.[86]

- Section 1557 of the Affordable Care Act of 2010 prohibits discrimination in health care and health insurance based on race, color, national origin, age, disability, or sex.[87]

These laws apply to the use of any statistical techniques, including big data analytics, as the Obama Administration recognized when they recommended that regulatory agencies "should expand their technical expertise to be able to identify practices and outcomes facilitated by big data analytics that have a discriminatory impact on protected classes, and develop a plan for investigating and resolving violations of law in such cases."[88]

---

[80] 15 U.S.C. § 1681 et seq.

[81] See Federal Trade Commission, "Spokeo to Pay $800,000 to Settle FTC Charges Company Allegedly Marketed Information to Employers and Recruiters in Violation of FCRA," press release, June 12, 2012, available at http://www.ftc.gov/opa/2012/06/spokeo.shtm. For more on the FCRA enforcement, see SIIA, *How the FCRA Protects the Public*, 2013 available at http://archive.siia.net/index.php?option=com_docman&task=doc_download&gid=4767&Itemid=318.

[82] 42 U.S.C. § 2000e-2, available at http://www.law.cornell.edu/uscode/text/42/2000e-2.

[83] 15 U.S.C. § 1691, available at http://www.law.cornell.edu/uscode/text/15/1691.

[84] 42 U.S.C. 3604, available at http://www.law.cornell.edu/uscode/text/42/3604.

[85] 29 U.S.C. § 623, available at https://www.law.cornell.edu/uscode/text/29/623.

[86] Pub. L. No. 110–233, 122 Stat. 881, available at http://www.gpo.gov/fdsys/pkg/PLAW-110publ233/pdf/PLAW-110publ233.pdf.

[87] 42 U.S.C. § 18116, available at https://www.law.cornell.edu/uscode/text/42/18116.

[88] White House Big Data Report, p. 60.

It is true that big data analytics might have discriminatory effects, even when companies do not intend to discriminate and do not use sensitive classifiers such as race and gender. But social scientists and policymakers have long known that statistical techniques and inferences can have discriminatory effects.[89] When discrimination arises indirectly through the use of statistical techniques, regulatory agencies and courts use disparate impact assessment to determine whether the practice is prohibited discrimination.[90]

Current rules provide for reasonable, contextually appropriate amounts of due diligence to ensure fairness in the use of statistical models. Credit scoring models, for instance, are routinely tested for compliance with fair lending laws and methodologies have been developed to assess the risk of failing a disparate impact test.[91] Reviews of some of these assessments have been made public.[92] Studies of disparate impact in the financial world include a Federal Trade Commission study on insurance credit scores,[93] a Payment Card Center study of credit cards,[94] and a Federal Reserve Board study of credit scores and the availability of credit.[95]

Existing rules for due diligence apply when newer techniques of big data analysis such as machine learning algorithms are used. When these techniques are used in the regulated contexts of housing, credit granting, employment and insurance, they are subject to the same regulatory controls and validation requirements that apply to any statistical methodology used in these contexts.

---

[89] NIST points out that information externalities can produce this kind of harm: "Inferential disclosure may result in **group harms** to an entire class of individuals, including individuals whose data do not appear in the dataset. For example, if a specific demographic group is well represented in a data set, and if that group has a high rate of a stigmatizing diagnosis in the data set, then all individuals in that demographic may be stigmatized, even though it may not be statistically appropriate to do so." NIST, p. 12.

[90] Disparate impact analysis is controversial because it focuses on the effects of a policy, practice or procedure rather than on its motivation or intent. Yet regulators and courts use disparate impact to assess discrimination in a wide variety of circumstances. For instance, Title VII of the Civil Rights Act of 1964 forbids any employment practice that causes a disparate impact on a prohibited basis if the practice is not "job related for the position in question and consistent with business necessity" or if there exists an "alternative employment practice" that could meet the employer or employment agency's needs without causing the disparate impact (42 U.S.C. § 2000e-2(k)(1)), available at https://www.eeoc.gov/laws/statutes/titlevii.cfm. On June 25, 2015, the Supreme Court, by a five-to-four margin, upheld the application of disparate impact under the Fair Housing Act in Texas Department of Housing & Community Affairs v. The Inclusive Communities Project, Inc., available at https://www.supremecourt.gov/opinions/14pdf/13-1371_m640.pdf.

[91] See, for instance, Charles River Associates, *Evaluating the Fair Lending Risk of Credit Scoring Models*, February 2014, available at http://www.crai.com/sites/default/files/publications/FE-Insights-Fair-lending-risk-credit-scoring-models-0214.pdf. The concern that big data analysis might discriminate inadvertently is explicitly recognized: "Ostensibly neutral variables that predict credit risk may nevertheless present disparate impact risk on a prohibited basis if they are so highly correlated with a legally protected demographic characteristic that they effectively act as a substitute for that characteristic" (p. 3).

[92] See, for instance, Center for Financial Services Innovation, *The Predictive Value of Alternative Credit Scores*, November 26, 2007, available at http://www.cfsinnovation.com/node/330262?article_id=330262.

[93] Federal Trade Commission, *Credit-Based Insurance Scores: Impacts on Consumers of Automobile Insurance*, July 2007, p. 3, available at http://www.ftc.gov/sites/default/files/documents/reports/credit-based-insurance-scores-impacts-consumers-automobile-insurance-report-congress-federal-trade/p044804facta_report_credit-based_insurance_scores.pdf.

[94] David Skanderson and Dubravka Ritter, *Fair Lending Analysis of Credit Cards*, Payment Card Center Federal Reserve Bank of Philadelphia, August 2014, available at http://www.philadelphiafed.org/consumer-credit-and-payments/payment-cards-center/publications/discussion-papers/2014/D-2014-Fair-Lending.pdf.

[95] Board of Governors of the Federal Reserve System, *Report to Congress on Credit Scoring and Its Effects on the Availability and Affordability of Credit*, August 2007, available at http://www.federalreserve.gov/boarddocs/rptcongress/creditscore/creditscore.pdf. See also Robert Avery, et al., "Does Credit Scoring Produce a Disparate Impact?" Staff Working Paper, Finance and Economics Discussion Series, Divisions of Research & Statistics and Monetary Affairs, Federal Reserve Board, October 2010, available at https://www.federalreserve.gov/pubs/feds/2010/201058/201058pap.pdf.

Algorithmic Transparency

To address these questions of fairness, some commentators have suggested moving beyond current rules, calling for a policy of algorithmic transparency that would require the disclosure of the source code embodied in a decision-making or classificatory algorithm. In this view, one of the major changes of rendering decision-making more computational under big data analysis is that the standards and criteria for making decisions have become more opaque to public scrutiny and understanding. Disclosure would allow outsiders an effective way to evaluate the bases for the decisions made by the programs. Along with a right to appeal a decision before an independent body, it would provide due process protection for people when algorithms are used to make decisions about them.[96]

Transparency in this sense of public disclosure of source code would be a mistake. Commercial algorithms are often proprietary and are deliberately kept as trade secrets in order to provide companies with a competitive advantage. In addition, revealing enough about the algorithm so that outside parties can predict its outcomes can defeat the goal of using the formula. For instance, the process and criteria for deciding whom to audit for tax purposes or whom to select for terrorist screening must be opaque to prevent people from gaming the system.[97]

In addition, transparency of code will not really address the problem of bias in decision-making. Source code is only understandable by experts. And even for them it is hard to understand what a program will do based solely on the source code. In machine learning algorithms, the decision rule is not imposed from outside, but emerges from the data under analysis. Even experts have little understanding of why the decisional output is what it is. In addition, the weights associated with each of the factors in a machine learning system change as new data is fed into the system and the program updates itself to improve accuracy. Knowing what the code is at any one time will not provide an understanding of how the system evolves in use.[98]

Still some understanding of the "narrative" behind algorithms might accomplish the goals of algorithmic transparency. Traditional credit scoring companies such as FICO routinely release the general factors that power their models and the rough importance of these factors. For instance, payment history contributes 35 percent to the overall score and amounts owed contributes 30 percent.[99] Designers and users of newer statistical techniques might consider the extent to which they could provide the public with a story to accompany the output of their statistical models. For instance, researchers at Carnegie Mellon University have developed a method for

[96] See, for example, Danielle Keats Citron and Frank Pasquale, "The Scored Society: Due Process for Automated Predictions," University of Maryland Francis King Carey School of Law, Legal Studies Research Paper, No. 2014–8. (2014) 89 Wash. L. Rev 1, http://papers.ssrn.com/sol3/papers.cfm?abstract_id=2376209; Danielle Keats Citron, "Technological Due Process," University of Maryland Legal Studies Research Paper No. 2007–26; *Washington University Law Review*, vol. 85, pp. 1249–1313, 2007, available at SSRN: http://ssrn.com/abstract=1012360; Kate Crawford and Jason Schultz, "Big Data and Due Process: Toward a Framework to Redress Predictive Privacy Harms," *Boston College Law Review*, vol. 55, p. 93, 2014, available at http://lawdigitalcommons.bc.edu/bclr/vol55/iss1/4.

[97] Christian Sandvig, Kevin Hamilton, Karrie Karahalios and Cedric Langbort, "Auditing Algorithms: Research Methods for Detecting Discrimination on Internet Platforms," Data and Discrimination: Converting Critical Concerns into Productive Inquiry, 2014, available at http://www-personal.umich.edu/~csandvig/research/Auditing%20Algorithms%20–%20Sandvig%20–%20ICA%202014%20Data%20and%20Discrimination%20Preconference.pdf (Auditing Algorithms).

[98] See the discussion in Joshua A. Kroll, Joanna Huey, Solon Barocas, Edward W. Felten, Joel R. Reidenberg, David G. Robinson and Harlan Yu, "Accountable Algorithms," 165 U. PA. L. REV. 633 (2017), available at http://scholarship.law.upenn.edu/penn_law_review/vol165/iss3/3.

[99] See, "What's in My Credit Score," *FICO*, available at http://www.myfico.com/crediteducation/whatsinyourscore.aspx.

determining why an AI system makes particular decisions without having to divulge the underlying workings of the system or code.[100]

Framework of Responsible Use

To help ensure algorithmic fairness, FTC Commissioner Terrell McSweeny has called for a framework of "responsibility by design" that would test algorithms – at the development stage – for potential bias. Fairness by design should be supplemented by audits after the fact to ensure that properly designed algorithms continue to operate properly.[101] The Obama Administration called for a similar practice of "equal opportunity by design."[102]

Individual enterprises could address the issues involved in the construction of a framework of responsible use, and in the end it might be a matter of balancing the business needs, legal risk and social responsibility in ways that best fit the context of the individual company. For instance, care in the use of statistical models that rely on commute time can be a matter of a company's own individual determination of how to manage legal risk and public perceptions, and some companies choose not to use that information in their hiring decisions.[103]

Nevertheless, a collaborative effort involving a range of stakeholders might sharpen the issues and allow sharing of information and best practices in a way that would benefit all. In such a collaborative effort, businesses, government, academics and civil rights and public interest groups would come together to establish a clear operational framework for responsible use of big data analytics. The tech industry has begun to organize itself for this task with the formation of a Partnership on AI "to advance public understanding of artificial intelligence technologies (AI) and formulate best practices on the challenges and opportunities within the field."[104]

It might be that there is no single framework for responsible use of big data analytics. It is certainly true that the risks and considerations involved in the use of a technique such as machine learning depends on the domain of use.[105] The legal standards differ as well.[106] Still a stakeholder group might assess whether there are actionable general principles that could be applied successfully in many fields.

It is important to begin to develop this framework now, and to get it right. The public needs to be confident in the fairness of algorithms, or a backlash will threaten the very real and substantial

---

[100] Byron Spice, "Carnegie Mellon Transparency Reports Make AI Decision-Making Accountable," Carnegie Mellon University, May 26, 2016, https://www.cs.cmu.edu/news/carnegie-mellon-transparency-reports-make-ai-decision-making-accountable.

[101] Terrell McSweeny, Keynote Remarks, "Tech for Good: Data for Social Empowerment," September 10, 2015, available at https://www.ftc.gov/system/files/documents/public_statements/800981/150909googletechroundtable.pdf.

[102] Big Data and Civil Rights, p. 5.

[103] Evolv, a waste management company, "is cautious about exploiting some of the relationships it turns up for fear of violating equal opportunity laws. While it has found employees who live farther from call-center jobs are more likely to quit, it doesn't use that information in its scoring in the U.S. because it could be linked to race." Joseph Walker, "Meet the New Boss: Big Data. Companies Trade In Hunch-Based Hiring for Computer Modeling," *Wall Street Journal*, September 2012, available at
    http://www.wsj.com/articles/SB10000872396390443890304578006252019616768.

[104] Partnership for AI, "Industry Leaders Establish Partnership on AI Best Practices," Press Release, September 28, 2016, available at http://www.partnershiponai.org/2016/09/industry-leaders-establish-partnership-on-ai-best-practices/.

[105] This dovetails with the idea that regulation of AI as such would be mistaken. See Study Group, p. 48: "attempts to regulate 'AI' in general would be misguided, since there is no clear definition of AI (it isn't any one thing), and the risks and considerations are very different in different domains."

[106] For instance, disparate impact analysis in employment is subject to a business necessity test, but disparate impact for age discrimination is subject to a less stringent "reasonableness" standard. See Smith v. City of Jackson, 544 U.S. 228 (2005), available at https://www.law.cornell.edu/supct/pdf/03-1160P.ZO.

benefits. Stakeholders need to do more to ensure the uses of the new technology are, and are perceived to be, fair to all.

Whether implemented by a single enterprise or developed as a collaborative effort, a framework would need to set out stakeholder roles, determine what metrics to use to assess fairness, the range of economic life to which these assessments should apply, the standards of fairness and what to do with a finding of disparate impact.

Stakeholder Roles

The framework would need to address the proper roles of the public, developers and users of algorithms, regulators, independent researchers, and subject matter experts, including ethics experts. How much does the public need to know about the inner workings of algorithms? What are the different responsibilities of the developers of analytics, the furnishers of data and the users? Should regulators be involved in the assessment of fairness? In areas where there are no legal responsibilities is there a role for government to act as a convener? What is the role of independent researchers? Should they have access to websites to test them for fairness?

Metrics

Fairness involves protecting certain classes of people against disproportionate adverse impacts in certain areas. But how do we measure this? Statisticians, economists, and computer scientists, among others, are working in the growing field of metrics designed to measure disparate impact.[107] Deviation from statistical parity is one measure. But there are others.[108] Sometimes analysis of training data can reveal the possibility of disparate impact in the use of algorithms.[109] Rules of thumb have been developed from some legal contexts, such as the 80 percent rule in employment contexts. It might be important to develop similar thresholds of disproportionate burden that suggest possible illegal discrimination in other fields. It is also important to measure how much loss of accuracy would result from using alternative statistical models. To assess the central normative questions we need good measurement of the size of the disparate impact and the loss of accuracy, if any, that might be involved in remedial action.

Individual enterprises or stakeholders will need to survey these methods, develop a process for keeping up with developments in the fast-moving field, and integrate the most effective methodologies into the process of auditing and testing.

Extent of Application

Current law does not protect people in suspect classifications in every area of economic and social life. Nevertheless, those who design, implement and use data analytics systems should be

---

[107] Kroll et al. have a good discussion of the field in Accountable Algorithms; Sandvig et al. discuss different auditing techniques in Auditing Algorithms. A good general framework from a computer science perspective is set out in Cynthia Dwork, et al., "Fairness through awareness," Proceedings of the 3rd Innovations in Theoretical Computer Science Conference, ACM, 2012, available at http://dl.acm.org/citation.cfm?id=2090255.

[108] For a comprehensive summary of these alternatives, see A. Romei and S. Ruggieri, "A Multidisciplinary Survey on Discrimination Analysis," *The Knowledge Engineering Review*, pp. 1–57, April 3, 2013, available at http://pages.di .unipi.it/ruggieri/Papers/ker.pdf; see also Salvatore Ruggieri, "Data Anonymity Meets Non-Discrimination," 2013 IEEE 13th International Conference on Data Mining Workshops, p. 876, available at http://pages.di.unipi.it/ ruggieri/Papers/icdmw2013.pdf.

[109] Michael Feldman, Sorelle Friedler, John Moeller, Carlos Scheidegger and Suresh Venkatasubramanian, "Certifying and Removing Disparate Impact," arXiv:1412.3756v3 [stat.ML], 2015, available at https://arxiv.org/abs/1412.3756.

thoughtful about the potential for discriminatory effects in any field. In many cases, businesses would want to know whether their use of these tools has disproportionate adverse impacts on protected classes. But a universal audit norm for all statistical models is too broad, since it would extend to areas where there is no consensus that making distinctions is an issue. In the stakeholder approach to developing a common framework of responsible use, interested parties would need to discuss which areas of social and economic life to include in a responsible use model.

Standards of Fairness

The FTC found that credit insurance scores have a disparate impact, and are also predictive of automobile insurance risk, not simply proxies for race and ethnicity.[110] The Federal Reserve Board had a similar finding that traditional credit scores had a disparate impact and were also accurate predictors of creditworthiness. These findings were viewed as confirmation that the scores were not discriminatory.[111] Still many think these uses are unfair and most states limit the use of credit insurance scores.[112]

Assessments of algorithms appear to be about data, statistics, and analytics. But in reality they are often disputes about contested standards of fairness. Is fairness a matter of reducing the subordination of disadvantaged groups or avoiding the arbitrary misclassification of individuals?[113] Should analytics aim only at accurate predictions or should it also aim at the statistical parity of protected groups?[114] Is fairness simply accuracy in classification? Or does fairness call for some sacrifice of accuracy in order to protect vulnerable groups?[115] Are there some factors other than suspect classifications that should not be taken into account even if they are predictive because to do so would be unfair? Should we be judged solely by what we do and never by who

---

[110] Federal Trade Commission, *Credit-Based Insurance Scores: Impacts on Consumers of Automobile Insurance*, July 2007, p. 3, available at http://www.ftc.gov/sites/default/files/documents/reports/credit-based-insurance-scores-impacts-con sumers-automobile-insurance-report-congress-federal-trade/p044804facta_report_credit-based_insurance_scores.pdf.

[111] Commissioner Julie Brill said that the FTC and a companion Federal Reserve study, "found that the scores they examined largely did *not* serve as proxies for race or ethnicity," Remarks of FTC Commissioner Julie Brill at the FTC Workshop, "Big Data: A Tool for Inclusion or Exclusion?" September 15, 2014, available at http://www.ftc.gov/system/files/documents/public_statements/582331/140915bigdataworkshop1.pdf.

[112] "As of June 2006, forty-eight states have taken some form of legislative or regulatory action addressing the use of consumer credit information in insurance underwriting and rating." FTC Study, p. 17.

[113] Jack M. Balkin and Reva B. Siegel, "The American Civil Rights Tradition: Anticlassification or Antisubordination?" *University of Miami Law Review*, vol. 58, p. 9, 2003, available at http://www.yale.edu/lawweb/jbalkin/articles/theamer icancivilrightstradition1.pdf. A study by Robinson + Yu frames the issue clearly: "Industry-standard credit scores accurately reflect underlying differences in credit risk between racial groups, which are themselves a reflection of social disparities and years of economic, political and other biases against racial minorities." Robinson + Yu, "Knowing the Score: New Data, Underwriting, and Marketing in the Consumer Credit Marketplace: A Guide for Financial Inclusion Stakeholders," October 2014, available at https://www.teamupturn.com/static/files/Knowing_the_ Score_Oct_2014_v1_1.pdf.

[114] See Jill Gaulding, "Race Sex and Genetic Discrimination in Insurance: What's Fair," *Cornell Law Review*, vol. 80, p. 1646, 1995, available at: http://scholarship.law.cornell.edu/clr/vol80/iss6/4: "From the efficient discrimination perspective, we have a right not to be classified for insurance purposes unless the classification corresponds to an accurate prediction of risk. From the anti-discrimination perspective, we have a right not to be classified for insurance purposes on the basis of unacceptable classifiers such as race, sex, or genetic factors."

[115] Dwork joins the accuracy group with her definition of individual fairness as closeness to an accurate assessment of ground truth about individuals and her rejection of statistical parity as an adequate notion of fairness. But her framework allows for a form of "affirmative action" by seeking ways to preserve statistical parity with the minimum sacrifice of accuracy.

we are?[116] Should we allow new evidence from statistical models to change our pre-existing notions of what is relevant to a certain decision?

Some strong moral intuitions regarding fairness are widely shared and can form a basis for responsible action even when they are not legal requirements. But this is an area where the interests of different groups collide and moral intuitions diverge. One advantage of a collaborative approach to a responsible use framework would be to facilitate discussions to air these differences and seek commonality, most productively under the guidance of philosophers and legal scholars who have a wide understanding of different approaches to ethical questions. Coming to some consensus or even isolating key differences in standards of fairness are not technical questions. They are normative and need to be approached as such in developing a framework of responsible use.

Remedies for Disparate Impact

Enterprises also need to determine a course of action following a finding of disproportionate adverse impact, discovered either in the design stage or as a result of an after-the-fact audit. While companies need to make their own decisions, a stakeholder approach might help to develop and share alternatives.

Current non-discrimination law applies only to certain industries and contexts, and even in those contexts, does not require designing away features of algorithms that pass a legal test for disparate impact. Still some designers and users of data analytics feel a need to do more than reflect the realities of what was, and in many respects still is, a discriminatory society. They are examining the extent to which they should take steps to free their algorithms as much as possible of what they view as harmful biases.

A conversation among stakeholders would help to clarify what steps are appropriate and in what situations they make sense.

These discussions must face squarely the question of what to do when steps to provide fair treatment for protected classes through adjustments in algorithms might disadvantage other citizens who feel that this treatment is itself a form of discrimination. These are contentious issues concerning the extent to which institutional practice should be race-conscious[117] and the extent to which efforts to avoid disparate impact run afoul of the duty to avoid discriminatory treatment.[118]

---

[116] Cathy O'Neil reflects widespread moral intuitions in saying that it is unjust to base sentencing on factors that could not be admitted in evidence, such as the criminal record of a defendant's friends and family. "These details should not be relevant to a criminal case or a sentencing," she says, because "(w)e are judged by what we do not by who we are." See *Weapons of Math Destruction*, at Kindle location 423. Eric Holder holds this view as well saying that criminal sentences "should *not* be based on unchangeable factors that a person cannot control." See Attorney General Eric Holder Speaks at the National Association of Criminal Defense Lawyers 57th Annual Meeting, August 1, 2014, available at https://www.justice.gov/opa/speech/attorney-general-eric-holder-speaks-national-association-criminal-defense-lawyers-57th.

[117] In Fisher v. University of Texas at Austin, 579 U.S. ___ (2016), available at https://www.supremecourt.gov/opinions/15pdf/14-981_4g15.pdf, the Supreme Court allowed the University of Texas to continue using a race-conscious admissions program, ruling that the program was permitted under the equal protection clause.

[118] Under the Supreme Court decision in Ricci v. DeStefano, 557 U.S. 557 (2009), available at https://www.supremecourt.gov/opinions/08pdf/07-1428.pdf, an employer might not be permitted to respond to a finding that an employment test has a disparate impact by taking steps that would consciously disadvantage other groups without a "strong basis in evidence to believe that it will be subject to disparate impact liability" if it continues to use that employment test. See Kroll, Accountable Algorithms, for further discussion of the idea that this "strong-basis-evidence" test counsels for building fairness into algorithms in the design stage rather than revising them after discovering a disparate impact in use.

Detecting disparate impact and designing alternatives that are less impactful are technical questions. But the decision to modify an algorithm to be fair is not. It involves legal, ethical, business and social matters that go beyond technical expertise in system design. For this reason, people from many disciplines and with a broad array of knowledge, expertise and experience need to be involved in assessing what to do with analytical structures that have or could have a disparate impact. Since the risks, laws and other considerations vary from domain to domain, it is unlikely that there will be one response to the question of what to do with an algorithm that has a disparate impact.

CONCLUSION

The powerful new tools of data analysis making their way through our social and economic life are designed and used by people, acting in their institutional capacities.[119] They can be designed and used in ways that preserve privacy and are fair to all, but this will not happen automatically. If we want these outcomes, we have to design these features into our algorithmic systems and use the systems in ways that preserve these values.

We cannot ignore or resist the inherent normative nature of this conversation, or reduce it to adventures in technical novelty. Ryan Calo got it right in his discussion of the use of a robot to intentionally kill Micah Johnson, the person who had shot five Dallas police officers in July 2016 and was cornered in a parking garage, saying, "rather than focus on the technology, we should focus on whether it was legitimate to kill Micah Johnson instead of incapacitating him. Because robots could do either."[120]

We are not driven willy-nilly by technology. The choices are up to us, acting through our current institutions, imperfect as they are, to put in place policies to protect privacy and preserve fairness in an age of big data analysis.

[119] Rob Atkinson emphasizes this key point of human agency: "AI systems are not independent from their developers and, more importantly, from the organizations using them." See Rob Atkinson, "Will Smart Machines Be Less Biased than Humans?" *Brink*, August 15, 2016, available at http://www.brinknews.com/will-smart-machines-will-be-less-biased-than-humans/?mc_cid=feaec2cdf1&mc_eid=aa397779d1.

[120] Ryan Calo, "Focus on Human Decisions, Not Technological Ethics of Police Robots," *New York Times*, July 14, 2016, available at http://www.nytimes.com/roomfordebate/2016/07/14/what-ethics-should-guide-the-use-of-robots-in-policing/focus-on-human-decisions-not-technological-ethics-of-police-robots.

4

Education Technology and Student Privacy

Elana Zeide

Education is increasingly driven by big data. New education technology (ed tech) creates virtual learning environments accessible online or via mobile devices. These interactive platforms generate a previously unimaginable array and detail of information about students' actions both within and outside of classrooms. This information not only can drive instruction, guidance, and school administration, but also better inform education-related decision-making for students, educators, schools, ed tech providers, and policymakers. This chapter describes the benefits of these innovations, the privacy concerns they raise and the relevant laws in place. It concludes with recommendations for best practices that go beyond mere compliance.

Data-driven education tools have the potential to revolutionize the education system – and, in doing so, provide more access to better quality, lower-cost education and broader socioeconomic opportunity. Learners can access world-class instruction online on demand without having to be physically present or enroll in expensive courses. "Personalized learning" platforms, for example, use detailed, real-time learner information to adjust instruction, assessment, and guidance automatically to meet specific student needs. Information collected during the learning process gives researchers fodder to improve teaching practices.

Despite their potential benefits, data-driven education technologies raise new privacy concerns. The scope and quantity of student information has exploded in the past few years with the rise of the ed tech industry.[1] Schools rely on educational software created by private companies that collect information about students both inside and outside of classroom spaces.

Three characteristics of the education context call for more stringent privacy measures than the caveat-emptor consumer regime. First, student privacy protects particularly vulnerable individuals – maturing children and developing learners. Traditional rules seek to prevent students' early mistakes or mishaps from foreclosing future opportunities – the proverbial "permanent record."

Second, students rarely have a choice regarding educational privacy practices. In America, education is compulsory in every state into secondary school. Most schools deploy technology on a classroom- and school-wide basis due to practical constraints and a desire to ensure pedagogical equality.

Third, the integration of for-profit entities into the school information flow is still novel in the education system. American education institutions and supporting organizations such as test

---

[1] TJ McCue, *Online Learning Industry Poised for $107 Billion in 2015*, FORBES, 2014.

providers and accreditors have traditionally been public or non-profit entities with a primary mission to promote learning and academic advancement. Today, educators want to take advantage of the latest technologies and give students the opportunity to develop digital literacy, but don't have the programming sophistication or resources to create data systems and apps internally. They instead turn to ed tech companies that often spring out of for-profit startup culture or from Silicon Valley stalwarts such as Google and Microsoft.

Traditional student privacy regulations aren't designed for an era of big data. They focus on the circumstances under which schools can share student information and giving parents and older students the right to review and request corrections to their education record. Student privacy regulations, most notably FERPA, which requires that parents, older students, teachers, or school administrators approve disclosure of personally identifiable student information can share personally identifiable information. In today's age of big data, however, the volume, variety, and velocity of data schools generate and share makes it difficult for parents and schools to keep track of information flow and data recipients' privacy policies. Stakeholders fear that companies share, or even sell, student data indiscriminately or create advertisements based on student profiles. Many fear that, following in the steps of several for-profit colleges, companies will prioritize generating revenue over students' educational interests.

Newer state laws supplement traditional student data protection. The most recent reforms prohibit school technology service providers from using student data for anything other than educational purposes. They don't, however, cover more nuanced questions. These include whether student data can be used by schools or for school purposes in ways that might still undermine students' education interests through unintentional bias or disparate impact. Data-driven ed tech allows schools and companies to test new approaches on student data subjects. Finally, student privacy rules do not apply to platforms and applications that learners use outside of school, which instead fall under the permissive consumer privacy regime. This chapter suggests best practices to cultivate the trust necessary for broad acceptance of new ed tech and effective learning spaces. These include accounting for traditional expectations that student information stays in schools, in contrast to the caveat emptor underpinning of the commercial context, as well as providing stakeholders with sufficient transparency and accountability to engender trust.

TODAY'S EDUCATION TECHNOLOGY

Schools, districts, and higher education institutions increasingly embrace digital and online services. New tools take advantage of the widespread adoption of networked systems, cloud storage, and mobile devices. Most outsource operation management to data-driven vendors. Identification cards, for example, use data to provide students with access to physical facilities and the ability to buy food at "cashless" cafeterias. They use outside software and platforms. Some, like G Suite for Education and Bing for Education, offer core functionalities like email, document creation, search engines, and social media specifically designed for school environments. Administrators rely on student information systems (SISs) to manage increasingly complex education records. These tools allow schools to draw upon outside expertise and maintain their focus on their primary task of providing students with high quality educational experiences.[2]

---

[2] Samantha Adams Becker et al., *NMC/CoSN Horizon Report: 2016 K-12 Edition* (The New Media Consortium), 2016 [hereinafter Adams Becker et al., *NMC/CoSN Horizon Report: 2016 K-12 Edition*]; Samantha Adams Becker et al., *NMC/CoSN Horizon Report: 2016 Higher Education Edition* (2016) [hereinafter Adams Becker et al., *NMC/CoSN*

Instructors adopt apps to track individual progress, monitor behavior, and develop lessons and learning materials. These are often free or freemium software that allow teachers to draw upon collective knowledge or communal resources to inform their own teaching. They create new pathways for educators to share information about pedagogical and classroom management practices that until recently remained siloed in individual classrooms or educational institutions.

Data-Based Education Platforms

Ed tech is moving from hardware like whiteboards and class computers to data-driven instructional software. Early learning management systems, like Blackboard, created tools to deliver digitized documents like syllabi and course readings. These evolved into interactive digital environments that provide multi-media instructional content, assessment tools, and discussion boards. Today's "intelligent" technologies go a step further and use data to assess students automatically and adapt instruction accordingly.[3]

Massive Open Online Courses (MOOCs)

In 2012, online education platforms gained public prominence through so-called Massive Open Online Courses (MOOCs). Huge enrollment in Stanford professors' internet-accessed computer science course prompted educators to adopt similar models.[4] They created companies or consortia that offered thousands of students (massive) internet access (online) to learning materials structured like traditional classes (courses) for free or nominal fees (open). Many schools, particularly in higher education, used MOOC platforms to provide courses to enrolled students.

The revolutionary aspect of MOOCs, however, lay in the fact that independent companies such as Coursera and Udacity, or non-profits such as edX, offered education directly and at no cost to learners outside the traditional education system. Many saw MOOCs as a way to give students in underserved communities or remote locations access to high quality educational resources at minimal, if any, cost. They hoped that this availability would provide new pathways that allowed learners to pursue their own educational goals regardless of their status and without requiring enrollment or acceptance at a school or university.[5]

Virtual Learning Environments

MOOCs have since shifted from strictly massive, open, online, complete courses to a variety of Virtual Learning Environments (VLEs) better tailored to specific institutions and student populations. Today's learning platforms may reach a smaller scope of students. They may limit enrollment or charge fees. They often supplement online work with physical instruction or

---

Horizon Report: 2016 Higher Education Edition]; Elana Zeide, *19 Times Data Analysis Empowered Students and Schools: Which Students Succeed and Why?* (Future of Privacy Forum), Mar. 22, 2016, available at https://fpf.org/wp-content/uploads/2016/03/Final_19Times-Data_Mar2016-1.pdf; Jules Polonetsky & Omer Tene, *Who Is Reading Whom Now: Privacy in Education from Books to MOOCs*, 17 Vand. J. Ent. & Tech. L. 927 (2014).

[3] Vincent Aleven et al., *Embedding Intelligent Tutoring Systems in MOOCs and E-Learning Platforms*, Int'l Conf. on Intelligent Tutoring Sys. 409 (Springer 2016).

[4] Jane Karr, *A History of MOOCs, Open Online Courses*, N.Y. Times, Oct. 30, 2014.

[5] Laura Pappano, *The Year of the MOOC*, N.Y. Times (Nov. 2, 2012).

assessment. Most offer education on specific topics in ways that are more modular than traditional courses, letting users create their own learning playlists. The entities creating these new technologies are predominantly for-profit companies, with Khan Academy's tutoring platform and edX's MOOCs as notable exceptions.

These VLEs are more integral to the education system than their predecessors. They increasingly supplement and, in some cases, replace physical classes in lower and higher education. Students can access thousands of explicitly education-oriented offerings directly online or through app stores. In the classroom, instructors increasingly employ digitally mediated learning tools on school computers or students' individual devices. They direct students to independent online education resources to supplement in-class activity.[6]

VLEs deliver coursework, references, and guidance, at scale and on demand. The flexibility of these anywhere, anytime, self-paced, playlist-style offerings offers more convenience to the nontraditional students who now make up the majority of the students in America. These individuals may be adult learners or younger students who balance education with family or work commitments. It also provides ways for workers to continue their education as employers' needs shift due to technological advances and increasingly automated functions.[7]

Data-Driven Education

With new technology, these interactive education platforms can conduct real-time assessment of student progress to adjust learning paths to suit students' specific needs instead of providing one-size-fits-all instruction. VLEs are increasingly interactive.[8] Students can choose to review specific content, solve problems, and answer questions. The learning platforms continuously collect information about students' actions, including not only explicit responses to questions and practice problems, but metadata about what pages they read, whether their mouse paused over a wrong answer, and the length of each learning session.[9] Education technologies capture detailed information about students' actions and performance during the learning process that has never before been possible in physical classrooms.[10]

To track student progress more precisely, these platforms use real-time monitoring and learning analytics. Most systems use algorithmic "learning analytics" to transform the flow of clickstream-level data into models that reflect student progress in defined areas.[11] They can, for example, examine Susan's answers to math problems over time to see how often she answers questions related to a certain algebraic concept correctly. By tracking student performance

---

[6] Adams Becker et al., *NMC/CoSN Horizon Report: 2016 K-12 Edition*, *supra* note 2; Adams Becker et al., *NMC/CoSN Horizon Report: 2016 Higher Education Edition*, *supra* note 2.

[7] *Competency-Based Learning or Personalized Learning* (Office of Educational Technology, U.S. Department of Education); *Competency-Based Education Reference Guide* (U.S. Department of Education, 2016).

[8] Dan Kohen-Vacs et al., *Evaluation of Enhanced Educational Experiences Using Interactive Videos and Web Technologies: Pedagogical and Architectural Considerations*, 3 SMART LEARN. ENV'T. 6 (2016).

[9] Daphne Koller: What we're learning from online education (TED Talks, Aug. 1, 2012), https://www.youtube.com/watch?v=U6FvJ6jMGHU.

[10] Barbara Means & Kea Anderson, *Expanding Evidence Approaches for Learning in a Digital World* (Office of Educational Technology, U.S. Department of Education, 2013).

[11] Ryan Baker, *Using Learning Analytics in Personalized Learning*, in HANDBOOK ON PERSONALIZED LEARNING FOR STATES, DISTRICTS, AND SCHOOLS (Center on Innovations in Learning, 2016); George Siemens, *Learning Analytics: The Emergence of a Discipline*, 57 AM. BEHAV. SCI. 1380–1400 (2013).

related to specific skills and concepts, these platforms can create virtual "knowledge maps" that that provide detailed diagnostics of student competencies and gaps over time.[12]

In doing so, they "embed" assessment within instruction. Instead of tests at the end of a chapter or semester, teachers can use performance information to gauge student mastery. This reduces reliance on periodic, high-stakes exams that may not accurately reflect learners' actual competencies. Digital platforms can display results for teachers to use or created automated systems that adapt instruction according to students' performance.[13]

"Personalized" learning platforms use these assessments in real-time to automatically adapt the pace and content of instruction and assessment based on how students perform.[14] This allows differentiation between learners at scale. Many educators see smart instruction and tutoring systems as the way to move past the factory model of education that often neglects individual learner differences.[15] The US Department of Education foresees that these technologies could eventually lead to an entirely new way of measuring and accounting for education based on competencies instead of degrees.[16] It is a stark contrast to the days when education records consisted of a few pieces of paper in school filing cabinets, report cards, and transcripts.

Data-Driven Education Decision-Making

Data collected and generated about students though ed tech also helps inform broader education-related decision-making.[17] "Academic analytics" allow parents and students, institutions, companies, and policymakers to examine trends over time and according to different types of student populations. This can help them make more evidence-based decisions to help students better maneuver the education system, schools make more informed institutional decisions, and companies optimize technologies and innovate according to marketplace needs.[18]

Student and parents can see what schools and degrees correspond with higher rates of employment and income long after graduation. They can get a sense of the likelihood of acceptance at a specific school. They can navigate the complicated options regarding enrollment and federal aid to find the school that best meets their needs and their budgets.[19]

---

[12] Bela Andreas Bargel et al., *Using Learning Maps for Visualization of Adaptive Learning Path Components*, 4 Int'l J. Computer Info. Sys. & Indus. Mgmt. Appl. 228 (2012); Debbie Denise Reese, *Digital Knowledge Maps: The Foundation for Learning Analytics through Instructional Games*, in Digital Knowledge Maps in Education 299 (Dirk Ifenthaler & Ria Hanewald eds., 2014); Kevin Wilson & Nicols Sack, Jose Ferreira, *The Knewton Platform: A General-Purpose Adaptive Learning Infrastructure* (Knewton, Jan. 2015).

[13] Aleven et al., *supra* note 3.

[14] Baker, *supra* note 12; Christina Yu, *What Personalized Learning Pathways Look Like at ASU*, Knewton Blog (Apr. 2, 2013), http://www.knewton.com/blog/education-videos/what-personalized-learning-pathways-look-like-at-asu/.

[15] Andrew Calkins & Kelly Young, *From Industrial Models and "Factory Schools" to … What, Exactly?*, EdSurge (Mar. 3, 2016), https://www.edsurge.com/news/2016-03-03-from-industrial-models-and-factory-schools-to-what-exactly; Monica Bulger, *Personalized Learning: The Conversations We're Not Having* (Data & Society Research Institute), Jul. 22, 2106.

[16] *Competency-Based Learning or Personalized Learning*, *supra* note 8.

[17] Zeide, *supra* note 2.

[18] Ellen B. Mandinach & Sharnell S. Jackson, Transforming Teaching and Learning through Data-Driven Decision Making (2012); Data Quality Campaign, *Executive Summary: All States Could Empower Stakeholders to Make Education Decisions with Data – But They Aren't Yet* (2012); Suhirman et al., *Data Mining for Education Decision Support: A Review*, 9 Int'l J. Emerging Tech. Learning 4 (2014).

[19] Zeide, *supra* note 2.

Schools can see which courses in the curricula students struggle with the most and adjust course requirements or tutoring resources accordingly.[20] Data mining can supplement this information by incorporating into analytics information outside of classrooms. Many schools, for example, monitor information on students' social media accounts. Others, particularly in higher education, incorporate administrative and operation data showing when students regularly attend school events or skip lunch to detect struggling learners and intervene before they drop out.[21]

Tracking students in detail and over time gives educators and education providers more insight into the learning process. Companies and other platform providers can determine what variations promote faster student progress and pinpoint where students struggle. Researchers use education data to analyze student and school success across the country to highlight lessons to learn and issues that require more attention.[22]

Policymakers can observe patterns in college readiness, enrollment, and attainment and make more informed reforms. They can use state longitudinal data systems to trace individual academic and workplace trajectories. Advocates can gather evidence supporting specific reforms. Recent reports, for example, revealed that many high school seniors say they intend to go to college, yet one in ten of those students never apply. As a result, some schools have simplified the federal student aid application process with positive outcomes.[23]

TODAY'S STUDENT PRIVACY CONCERNS

Some of the demand for stricter privacy protection is the shock of the new. New student information practices are often at odds with expectations about information practices in learning environments. Today's technology captures student information continuously and at a level of detail previously unheard of in learning environments. Schools share student data daily with a broad array of private service providers.[24]

Most students, parents, and educators have no specific sense of the data or privacy practices of school software providers.[25] They don't know what data companies collect about them, how that information might inform pedagogical or institutional decisions, and if anyone is truly looking out for their interests given the fast pace of technological change. Many companies make matters worse by being secretive about their practices or failing to consider the perspectives of different stakeholders in the education community. This lends itself to speculation, sensationalism, and confusion.

Poor preparation and communication brought down a $100 million, Gates Foundation–funded nonprofit which offered a secure data repository to districts and states to use at their own

[20] Ben Kei Daniel, *Overview of Big Data and Analytics in Higher Education, in* Big Data and Learning Analytics in Higher Education 1–4 (2017); Zeide, *supra* note 2; Maria Eliophotou Menon et al., Using Data to Improve Higher Education: Research, Policy and Practice (2014).

[21] Zeide, *supra* note 2.

[22] *Id.*

[23] *Id.*; see also *Nudging for Success: Using Behavioral Science to Improve the Postsecondary Student Journey* (ideas42), Jun. 2016.

[24] Joel R. Reidenberg et al., *Privacy and Cloud Computing in Public Schools* (Center on Law and Information Policy), Dec. 2013.

[25] *New FPF Survey Shows Parents Overwhelmingly Support Using Student Data to Improve Education,* Future of Privacy (Sept. 21, 2015), http://www.futureofprivacy.org/2015/09/21/new-fpf-survey-shows-parents-overwhelmingly-support-using-student-data-to-improve-education/.

discretion. The organization, inBloom, launched with considerable fanfare, trying to dazzle the technology industry and education reformers with the platform's capabilities.[26] However, its leaders did not consider how new practices might run counter to parental expectations and, accordingly, arouse suspicion and fear. The public debate that followed suffered from rampant speculation, media sensationalism, and outright confusion that conflated inBloom with the controversial adoption of the Common Core State Standards.[27] Most states and districts withdrew their association with the organization, which closed soon afterwards.[28]

Pervasive Surveillance

Many parents and advocates consider continuous student monitoring as intrusive, regardless of the possible benefits of pervasive data collection. Schools increasingly incorporate audiovisual information from security cameras or social media monitoring for pedagogical and research purposes.[29] As described earlier, they may also collect data from nonacademic sources. The wealth of information available will expand as the Internet of Things generates more data from wearables and connected devices.[30]

Concerns about student data collection surface even when information is publicly available. In 2015, for example, reports indicated that Pearson, the textbook and test publisher, monitored Twitter feeds to detect and prevent cheating on the Partnership for Assessment of Readiness for College and Careers tests which were administered at different times to students across the country.[31] While doing so was certainly legal, and arguably part of Pearson's duty to ensure a fair testing environment, some members of the public reacted with alarm.[32] While parents were aware that their children's posts were publicly accessible, they did not necessarily connect that understanding to the possibility that a company might systematically collect and analyze specific students' posts. The intentional, systematic nature of the surveillance changed how parents perceived the companies' reported privacy practices.

Permanent Records

New education technology also creates uncertainty about the accuracy, representativeness, and retention of student data. Data used to drive instruction and track student progress might be

---

[26] Benjamin Herold, *inBloom to Shut Down Amid Growing Data-Privacy Concerns*, EDUC. WEEK, 2014; Ki Mae Heussner, *Gates Foundation-Backed InBloom Frees up Data to Personalize K-12 Education*, GIGAOM (Feb. 5, 2013), http://gigaom.com/2013/02/05/gates-foundation-backed-inbloom-frees-up-data-to-personalize-k-12-education/.

[27] Elana Zeide, *Parsing Student Privacy*, TECHNOLOGY | ACADEMICS | POLICY (Sept. 18, 2015), http://www.techpolicy .com/Blog/Featured-Blog-Post/Parsing-Student-Privacy.aspx.

[28] Herold, *supra* note 27.

[29] Emmeline Taylor, *Surveillance Schools: A New Era in Education*, in SURVEILLANCE SCHOOLS: SECURITY, DISCIPLINE AND CONTROL IN CONTEMPORARY EDUCATION 15 (2013); Amelia Vance & J. William Tucker, *School Surveillance: The Consequences for Equity and Privacy* (National Association of State Boards of Education), Oct. 2016.

[30] Max Myers, *Can the Internet of Things Make Education More Student-Focused?*, GOVERNMENT 2020 (Dec. 3, 2014), http://government-2020.dupress.com/can-internet-things-make-education-student-focused/.

[31] Audrey Watters, *Pearson, PARCC, Privacy, Surveillance, & Trust*, HACKEDUCATION (Mar. 17, 2015), http://hackeduca tion.com/2015/03/17/pearson-spy; e-mail, Pearson is spying on students (Mar. 17, 2015).

[32] *Pearson Under Fire for Monitoring Students' Twitter Posts*, BITS BLOG, http://bits.blogs.nytimes.com/2015/03/17/ pearson-under-fire-for-monitoring-students-twitter-posts/; e-mail, Pearson is spying on students, *supra* note 33; Cynthia Liu, *Pearson Is Not Spying on Student Tweets; Instead Enlisting Public School Officials to Protect Its Tests*, K-12 NEWS NETWORK (Mar. 14, 2015), http://thewire.k12newsnetwork.com/2015/03/14/pearson-is-not-spying-on-student-tweets-its-enlisting-public-school-officials-to-defend-its-intellectual-property/.

inaccurate, nonrepresentative, or outdated. Because student information can be stored indefinitely and capture mistakes in much greater detail, it raises the possibility of outdated information unfairly limiting students' academic and employment opportunities – a contemporary version of the proverbial permanent record.[33]

Big Data Bias

Big data processing also creates new privacy concerns. Data-mining risks incorporating irrelevant or improper information into education decision-making. Subtle bias may also be unintentionally embedded into algorithmic data processing.[34] Seemingly neutral big data decision-making may have a disparate impact on different communities in ways that promote, rather than ameliorate, existing inequalities.[35] Most of the individuals who successfully completed early MOOCs, for example, were already educated, not part of the underserved community the learning platforms sought to serve.[36]

Experimentation Ethics

Digitally data-driven education is new and, like most innovative technologies, involves ongoing experimentation and improvement. Stakeholders want to know that ed tech actually achieves the promised result – that someone has tested a given system, hopefully over time and independent from the people who seek to profit from it. They want to know that developers and educators have considered potential unintended.[37] In the 1970s, similar concerns prompted academic researchers to create an ethical framework and review system governing human subject research.[38] No such rules apply, however, to companies' "optimization" and "experimentation."[39] Facebook, for example, was harshly criticized for conducting research that altered different readers' news feeds to promote positive or negative emotions.[40]

---

[33] Anthony Cody, *Will the Data Warehouse Become Every Student and Teacher's "Permanent Record"?*, Educ. Week (May 20, 2013), http://blogs.edweek.org/teachers/living-in-dialogue/2013/05/will_the_data_warehouse_become.html?cmp=SOC-SHR-FB; David Sirota, *Big Data Means Kids' "Permanent Records" Might Never Be Erased*, Motherboard (Oct. 24, 2013); Elana Zeide, *The Proverbial Permanent Record* (2014).

[34] danah boyd & Kate Crawford, *Six Provocations for Big Data* (2011).

[35] Solon Barocas & Andrew D. Selbst, *Big Data's Disparate Impact*, 104 Cal. L. Rev. 671 (2016).

[36] John D. Hansen & Justin Reich, *Democratizing Education? Examining Access and Usage Patterns in Massive Open Online Courses*, 350 Science 1245 (2015).

[37] Michael Zimmer, *Research Ethics in the Big Data Era: Addressing Conceptual Gaps for Researchers and IRBs*, in Beyond IRBs: Ethical Review Processes for Big Data Research (Future of Privacy Forum Washington, DC, Dec. 2, 2015); Katie Shilton, *Emerging Ethics Norms in Social Media Research*, in Beyond IRBs: Ethical Review Processes for Big Data Research (Future of Privacy Forum, Washington, DC, Dec. 2, 2015); Jacob Metcalf, *Big Data Analytics and Revision of the Common Rule*, 59 Comm. ACM 31 (2016).

[38] Department of Health, Education and Welfare Washington, DC, Ethical Principles and Guidelines for the Protection of Human Subjects of Research (1979).

[39] *See* Omer Tene & Jules Polonetsky, *Beyond IRBs: Ethical Guidelines for Data Research*, in Beyond IRBs: Ethical Review Processes for Big Data Research (Future of Privacy Forum, Washington, DC, Dec. 2015).

[40] Jeff T. Hancock, *The Facebook Study: A Personal Account of Data Science, Ethics and Change*, in Proceedings of the 18th ACM Conference on Computer Supported Cooperative Work & Social Computing 1 (CSCW '15, Mar. 14–18, 2015); Chris Chambers, *Facebook Fiasco: Was Cornell's Study of "Emotional Contagion" an Ethics Breach?*, The Guardian, Jul. 1, 2014, http://www.theguardian.com/science/head-quarters/2014/jul/01/facebook-cornell-study-emotional-contagion-ethics-breach; danah boyd [sic], *Untangling Research and Practice: What Facebook's "Emotional Contagion" Study Teaches Us*, 12 Res. Ethics 4–13 (2016); James Grimmelmann, *The Law and Ethics of Experiments on Social Media Users*, 13 J. Telecomm. & High Tech. L. 219 (2015).

Education-Specific Considerations

As society grapples with issues surrounding surveillance, discrimination, and the ethics of big data across sectors, several factors drive heightened concerns in the education context.[41]

The Difficulty of Opting Out of Mainstream School Data Policies

Using student or parental consent to ensure adequate privacy is particularly difficult in the context of formal education. School attendance is compulsory in every state into secondary school. Parents could theoretically switch schools or homeschool their children if they object to schools' technology and privacy policies, but few have the resources or incentive to do in practice. Schools, districts, and an education model based on classroom-wide instruction incentivize students and parents to participate in mainstream technological use, regardless of their individual privacy preferences.[42] Students who opt out of using the default class technology often end up at a social and academic disadvantage, so most parents eventually capitulate.

Vulnerable Children and Developing Learners

K-12 schools are sites of particular concern. Many students are children, an inherently vulnerable population. In other contexts, the law recognizes that students may make mistakes as they mature. The criminal justice system, for example, accords juveniles greater leniency and permits their records to be sealed or expunged so that offenders can move past early mistakes. Traditional student privacy rules against school disclosure function similarly by limiting the information available to outsiders. Today parents fear that students' second-grade performance or behavior might limit future opportunities through a modern day version of the proverbial permanent record. As noted in a recent report from the Executive Office of the President, "As learning itself is a process of trial and error, it is particularly important to use data in a manner that allows the benefits of those innovations, but still allows a safe space for students to explore, make mistakes, and learn without concern that there will be long term consequences for errors that are part of the learning process."[43]

Parents also have specific concerns about companies marketing to their children. The Children's Online Privacy Protection Rule (COPPA), for example, requires commercial websites to obtain parental consent prior to collecting, using, or disclosing personal information about children under 13 years old.[44] Another federal privacy statute, the Protection of Pupil Rights Amendment (PPRA), requires federally funded schools to obtain written consent before administering surveys that include such sensitive information as political beliefs or religious practices as well as collection, disclosure, or use of personal information for marketing or sales.[45]

---

[41] Elana Zeide, *Student Privacy Principles for the Age of Big Data: Moving beyond FERPA and FIPPs*, 8 Drexel L. Rev. 339 (2016); Polonetsky & Tene, *supra* note 2; Elana Zeide, *The Structural Consequences of Big Data-Driven Education*, 5 Big Data, 164–172 (2017).
[42] Zeide, *supra* note 43.
[43] John Podesta, *Big Data: Seizing Opportunities, Preserving Values* (Executive Office of the President), May 1, 2014.
[44] 15 U.S. C § 650.
[45] 20 U.S. § 1232h.

For-Profit Fears

After decades of scandals, Americans place little trust in for-profit education providers.[46] The norm is still public and non-profit schools that explicitly serve educational missions. The same is true of the organizations that traditionally offer data-dependent services, such as The College Board and National Clearinghouse. Most ed tech providers handling student data are for-profit companies, with Khan Academy and edX as notable exceptions.[47] Public schools and nonprofits are explicitly oriented and legally bound to education-oriented missions. For-profit education companies, in contrast, face the primary pressure of generating revenue, which they may do at the cost of educational quality. For-profit colleges, for example, have been repeatedly reprimanded for investing in marketing rather than in academics.[48]

STUDENT PRIVACY PROTECTION

Regulation of School Information

Parents and schools traditionally consider student privacy in terms of confidentiality. This informs the primary regulatory protection governing education data for the past forty years, the Family Educational Rights and Privacy Act (FERPA) and similar state statutes.[49] FERPA created rules restricting how federally funded schools, districts, and state educational agencies control access to personally identifiable student information.[50] It provides parents and students with nominal control over school disclosure of personally identifiable student information. In practice, however, most schools share information under the statute's School Official Exception, which requires the data recipient to be performing services on the schools' behalf and have what educators determine to be a legitimate educational interest in doing so.[51] FERPA's regulations also indicate that recipients should not re-disclose FERPA-covered personally identifiable student information, although they can do so with de-identified data.[52]

Today's Student Data Privacy

FERPA and similar state laws, however, do not address many issues raised by today's data-driven ed tech. They were designed for a world of paper records, not networked, cloud-based platforms

---

[46] *Why Do Americans Mistrust For-Profit Universities?*, THE ECONOMIST, July 50, 2013.

[47] Michelle Molnar, *K-12 For-Profits Increasingly "Cashing in on Kids,"* EDUCATION DIVE (Apr. 8, 2014), http://www.educationdive.com/news/k-12-for-profits-increasingly-cashing-in-on-kids/247645/.

[48] *See, e.g.,* Committee on Health, Labor, and Pensions, U.S. Senate, *For Profit Higher Education: The Failure to Safeguard the Federal Investment and Ensure Student Success,* Vol. 1. No. 1–3. U.S. Government Printing Office, 2012.

[49] 20 U.S. § 1232g.

[50] Personally identifiable information includes direct and indirect identifiers like names, parents or other family members' names, address and address of student or family, as well as "other personal identifiers information that alone or in combination, is linked to a specific student that would allow a reasonable person in the school community, who does not have personal knowledge of the relevant circumstances, to identify the student with reasonable certainty" (34 CFR §99.3).

[51] § 99.31(a)(1) (School Officials Exception); *FERPA Frequently Asked Questions: FERPA for School Officials* (Family Policy Compliance Office, U.S. Department of Education); *id.*; Brenda Leong, *Who Exactly IS a "School Official" Anyway?*, FUTURE OF PRIVACY FORUM Jan. 19, 2016; *The Family Educational Rights and Privacy Act: Guidance for Reasonable Method and Written Agreements* (Family Policy Compliance Office, U.S. Department of Education).

[52] FERPA's definition for de-identication is more stringent than simply stripping data of unique identifiers. The data also can't include information about such small groups of students that they would be easily recognizable by community members. § 99.3.

that collect information automatically.[53] This is a sharp contrast to long-standing expectations, supported by the federal student privacy regulatory regime, that personally identifiable information primarily remains within the confines of public or nonprofit educational institutions.

As discussed above, schools today outsource a broad variety of services that use student data – everything from administrative data systems to cafeteria billing. Individual educators adopt innovative apps, often without a concrete sense of what happens to the data they share.[54] Private, for-profit companies design and provide vast majority these technologies.

Networked and cloud-based platforms continuously and automatically collect a wide array of administrative and academic data about students. Even diligent educators find it difficult to understand exactly what information they share with the companies that provide these tools, let alone monitor and evaluate providers' own privacy practices.[55]

Different rules govern the disclosure and subsequent sharing and use of learner information obtained through schools or directly from learners. Schools can only share

Ed tech providers must meet different privacy requirements if they collect data about students using technologies in schools or learners independent of formal education institutions. User information shared under the auspices public and publicly-funded schools is subject to the student privacy regime. , most notably FERPA.[56] The less restrictive consumer privacy rules apply if a company obtains the exact same data points directly from users.[57] As a result, the Department of Education has no recourse against companies regarding their collection, use, disclosure, and protection of information from schools.

State legislators have responded with a wave of regulation that imposes more requirements on schools sharing student information. Some apply directly to commercial ed tech providers, limiting how can use the data they receive.[58]

Several state have passed rules limiting company use of student data for "educational" purposes. Most prominently, California law confined operators who knowingly provide services used primarily for K-12 "school purposes" to only use information, including creating profiles, to serve such purposes.[59] It defines "K-12 school purposes" as those "that customarily take place at

---

[53] Zeide, *supra* note 43; Elise Young, *Educational Privacy in the Online Classroom: FERPA, MOOCs, and the Big Data Conundrum*, 28 HARV. J. LAW & TEC. 549 (2015); Reidenberg et al., *supra* note 25; Daniel J. Solove, *FERPA and the Cloud: Why FERPA Desperately Needs Reform*, LINKEDIN (Dec. 11, 2012), https://www.linkedin.com/pulse/20121211124311-2259773-ferpa-and-the-cloud-why-ferpa-desperately-needs-reform.

[54] Zeide, *supra* note 43; Young, *supra* note 55; Reidenberg et al., *supra* note 25; Solove, *supra* note 55; Natasha Singer, *Privacy Pitfalls as Education Apps Spread Haphazardly*, N.Y. TIMES, Mar. 11, 2015, http://www.nytimes.com/2015/03/12/technology/learning-apps-outstrip-school-oversight-and-student-privacy-is-among-the-risks.html; Khaliah Barnes, *Why a "Student Privacy Bill of Rights" Is Desperately Needmed*, WASHINGTON POST, Mar. 6, 2014, http://www.washingtonpost.com/blogs/answer-sheet/wp/2014/03/06/why-a-student-privacy-bill-of-rights-is-desperately-needed/.

[55] Zeide, *supra* note 43; Young, *supra* note 55; Reidenberg et al., *supra* note 25; Solove, *supra* note 55; Singer, *supra* note 56; Barnes, *supra* note 56.

[56] While often discussed in terms of "prohibitions," FERPA technically does not bar certain practices but instead imposes conditions that schools, districts, and education agencies must meet in order to receive federal funding. 20 U.S.C. § 1232g(a)(1)(A); 20 U.S.C. § 1232g(a)(1)(B).

[57] Steve Kolowich, *Are MOOC-Takers "Students"? Not When It Comes to the Feds Protecting Their Data*, CHRON. HIGHER EDUC. BLOGS (Dec. 3, 2014), http://chronicle.com/article/Are-MOOC-Takers-Students-/150325/?cid=at&utm_source=at&utm_medium=en; Zeide, *supra* note 43; Young, *supra* note 55.

[58] *Student Data Privacy Legislation: A Summary of 2016 State Legislation* (Data Quality Campaign), Sept. 2016; *State Student Privacy Law Compendium* (Center for Democracy and Technology), Oct. 2016.

[59] The law specifically governs any "operator of an Internet Web site, online service, online application, or mobile application with actual knowledge that the site, service, or application is used primarily for K–12 school purposes and was designed and marketed for K–12 school purposes." CAL. BUS. & PROF. CODE § 22584(a).

the direction of the K-12 school, teacher, or school district or aid in the administration of school activities, including, but not limited to, instruction in the classroom or at home, administrative activities, and collaboration between students, school personnel, or parents or are for the use and benefit of the school."[60] The statute specifically carves out an exception for personalized learning platforms, stating that its provisions do "not limit the ability of an operator to use student data for adaptive learning or customized student learning purposes."[61] By regulating vendors directly, these types of laws address some concerns about commercial use of student data without increasing the burden on schools to keep track of data recipients' privacy practices. However, it remains to be seen how these will play out in practice.

Consumer Privacy Protection for "Learner" Data

Most student privacy protection, however, does not cover a wide variety of data collected directly from "learners" by independent education providers. These frequently present themselves as promoting educational missions, but are firmly within the commercial sphere – subject to financial pressures to turn a profit and more lenient consumer privacy regulations. Under these rules, companies can share and use data with anyone for any purpose in accordance with the terms of service accepted by their users.[62]

Many scholars and advocates, as well as the President's Council of Advisors on Science and Technology, question whether user acceptance of the vague fine print in privacy policies constitutes meaningful knowledge or consent.[63] Reading privacy policies is not only time consuming, but often provides little meaningful information about specific corporate information practices.[64] Further, users may have no realistic alternative to using a specific data-driven tool.[65] Finally, even providing such notice and consent may not be possible given the size and continuous collection capacity of sensor-based devices connected to the emerging Internet of Things.[66]

TOMORROW'S BEST PRACTICES

As discussed above, data-driven education technologies can provide tremendous benefit to students and the broader education system and labor markets. However, the volume, velocity, and

---

[60] CAL. BUS. & PROF. CODE § 22584(j); Amelia Vance, *Data Privacy Laws Follow Lead of Oklahoma and California*, 16 THE STATE EDUCATION STANDARD25, May 2016.

[61] CAL. BUS. & PROF. CODE § 22584(l); see also Jean-Louis Maritza, *California Breaks New Ground in Education Privacy Law with K-12 Student Data Privacy Bill*, NAT. L. REV, (Sept. 14, 2014).

[62] The Federal Trade Commission (FTC) and state attorney generals may impose fines or bring suits if they determine that companies have not upheld their promises and engage in deceptive business practices. The Federal Trade Commission Act, 15 U.S.C. § 45(a)(2) (section 5).

[63] President's Council of Advisors on Science & Technology, *Big Data and Privacy: A Technological Perspective*, THE WHITE HOUSE (May 1, 2014), whitehouse.gov/bigdata.

[64] Joel R. Reidenberg et al., *Disagreeable Privacy Policies: Mismatches between Meaning and Users' Understanding*, 30 BERKELEY TECH. L. J. 39 (2015); Norman Sadeh et al., *The Usable Privacy Policy Project* (Technical Report, CMU-ISR-13-119, Carnegie Mellon University, 2013).

[65] Joel R. Reidenberg et al., *Privacy Harms and the Effectiveness of the Notice and Choice Framework*, 11 ISJLP 485 (2015); Robert H. Sloan & Richard Warner, *Beyond Notice and Choice: Privacy, Norms, and Consent*, 14 J. HIGH TECH. L. 370 (2014).

[66] Carlo Maria Medaglia & Alexandru Serbanati, *An Overview of Privacy and Security Issues in the Internet of Things*, in THE INTERNET OF THINGS 389 (2010).

variety of big data limit the capacity of individuals and institutions to control, consent to, and oversee data collection, sharing, and quality that have traditionally protected "student privacy."[67]

As a result, companies and educators often struggle to determine which practices are not only legal but also acceptable to students, learners, and the education community. In the absence of specific rules or social consensus, it rests on traditional educators and independent education providers to determine what constitutes student privacy through their technological structures, day-to-day protocols, and formally articulated standards. The following best practices – considering education stakeholders' expectations, transparency, and accountability – are excellent places to start.

Consider Student Expectations and Education Values

It is important for commercial and private education technology providers and the educators and policymakers who rely on their services to consider the perspectives of multiple stakeholders across the educational context. This includes not only the school and administrator who are their clients, but also students, parents, educators, and the broader community. When creating technologies and communicating with stakeholders and the broader community, ed tech providers and data processors need to consider the considerations noted earlier, which make expectations different in education. Data policies and practices should accord with the high stakes of the education context and the trust required in learning environments. This may entail minimizing collection and retention to only essential information, or prohibiting data practices that do not explicitly serve school or student interests.

Transparency

A best practice to prevent panicked responses to new information practices is to provide as much transparency as possible regarding specific information practices in ways that the general public can understand, as well as providing more detailed information for those who seek more specifics.[68] In creating systems and implementing governance and ethical review protocols, companies should consider ways they can make their practices more transparent in terms of (1) data practices; (2) specific technologies; (3) decision-making; (4) security; and (5) oversight. This can be difficult given the velocity, variety, and volume of big data and the complexity of algorithmic and automated analysis. It is also complicated by the fact that many companies consider their data processing proprietary information they do not want to release for public scrutiny. However, the black box of big data decision-making creates considerable uncertainty that feeds public and parental fears.

Accountability

Since the Facebook's "emotional contagion" scandal in 2015, companies are under increasing pressure to put similar protocols or review mechanisms in place to ensure that they do not

---

[67] Zeide, *supra* note 43.
[68] Privacy Technical Assistance Center, *Protecting Student Privacy While Using Online Educational Services: Requirements and Best Practice* (Privacy Technical Assistance Center, U.S. Department of Education 2014), Feb. 25, 2014; Department of Education, Transparency Best Practices (PTAC 2014).

manipulate their users in exploitative or potentially harmful ways.[69] Facebook, for example, has implemented a formal review process before beginning certain user-based experiments and publishing the results.[70] Advocates and policymakers debate whether companies should be required to create such internal review systems or be accountable to external ethical review boards.[71] Regardless, it behooves companies – especially those dealing with children – to create review systems to consider ways that information practices might disadvantage student data subjects.

Companies should be prepared to account for their decision-making in terms of specific individuals and broader patterns. While the small decisions that drive personalized learning platforms or games might seem inconsequential, they have growing impact on students' academic progress, attainment, and, future opportunities. This is where self-regulation such as pledges and certifications – backed up by auditing and accountability – can be useful.

In a regulatory system that is fractured and difficult for companies, let alone stakeholders, to comprehend, many companies turn to self-regulation to reassure students and stakeholders that they take user privacy seriously. The Student Privacy Pledge organized by the Future of Privacy Forum and Software and Information Industry Association (SIIA), for example, has over 300 companies and organizations who have promised to abide by ten principles which include not selling personal information and "not build[ing] a personal profile of a student other than for supporting authorized educational/school purposes or as authorized by the parent/student."[72] Signatories who fail to abide by these principles may be subject to FTC enforcement.

Other companies take advantage of nonprofits and advocacy groups who offer "seals" signaling compliance with certain regulatory and security standards. These generally involve companies passing an internal audit of their practices before obtaining a certificate of compliance that they can then display on their websites and promotional material. Prominent privacy toolkit and audit providers include iKeepSafe and the Consortium of School Networks (CoSN) CoSN.[73] These self-regulatory mechanisms are, however, successful only to the degree that stakeholders trust that participants are actually audited and held accountable for noncompliance.[74]

CONCLUSION

Ed tech offers tremendous potential to provide a better education for students worldwide and of all ages. The data collected allows learning platforms to adjust course content, pacing, and testing automatically to suit individual student needs and better inform students, parents,

[69] Tene & Polonetsky, *supra* note 41; Ryan Calo, *Consumer Subject Review Boards: A Thought Experiment*, 66 Stan. L. Rev. Online 97 (2013).

[70] Molly Jackman & Lauri Kanerva, *Evolving the IRB: Building Robust Review for Industry Research*, 72 Wash. & Lee L. Rev. Online 442 (2016).

[71] Tene & Polonetsky, *supra* note 41; Camille Nebeker et al., *New Challenges for Research Ethics in the Digital Age*, in Beyond IRBs: Ethical Review Processes for Big Data Research (Future of Privacy Forum Washington, D.C.), Dec. 10, 2015.

[72] *Pledge to Parents & Students* (Future of Privacy Forum & Software & Information Industry Association), 2016.

[73] *FERPA – Ikeepsafe.org* (iKeepSafe); Consortium for School Networking, *Protecting Student Privacy* (Consortium of School Networks).

[74] Michele Molnar, *Student-Privacy Pledge for Ed-Tech Providers Draws Praise, Criticism*, Educ. Week (Oct. 12, 2014), http://blogs.edweek.org/edweek/marketplacek12/2014/10/student_privacy_pledge_for_ed-tech_providers_draws_praise_criticism.html?cmp=SOC-SHR-FB; Sophia Cope & Gennie Gebhart, *Loopholes and Flaws in the Student Privacy Pledge*, Electronic Frontier Found. (Oct. 20–2016), https://www.eff.org/deeplinks/2016/10/loopholes-and-flaws-student-privacy-pledge; Jules Polonetsky, *Student Privacy Pledge Loopholes? Nope. We Did Our Homework.*, Future of Privacy Forum (Oct. 21, 2016), https://fpf.org/2016/10/21/student-privacy-pledge-loopholes-nope-homework/.

schools, companies, and policymakers making education-related decisions. At the same time, schools' routine sharing of student information with outsiders and independent education providers' collection of learner data raise questions about unintended inequity, unforeseen consequences, and whose interests will be prioritized. Private companies can legally use student data in ways that worry parents and advocates, even under newer state laws that restrict processing information for noneducational purposes. Entities handling student data can take a proactive stance by considering different stakeholder perspectives, providing meaningful transparency, and ensuring accountability. Doing so helps reassure students, educators, and the broader community not only of their good intentions, but thoughtful implementation of data-driven systems. The transformative potential of data-driven ed tech requires sufficient stakeholder trust – and support. Tailoring privacy practices to the specific considerations of learning environments paves the way for truly revolutionary innovation.

5

Mobile Privacy Expectations

How Privacy Is Respected with Mobile Devices

Kirsten Martin and Katie Shilton

INTRODUCTION

Privacy expectations about the information collected by our mobile devices has been a specter in the popular press since the advent of smartphones in 2007 and in the academic literature for years before that (Curry, 2002). In this time, little has been solved and concerns have only grown. Consider recent news that antichoice groups have targeted women visiting Planned Parenthood locations with antiabortion advertisements using a technique based on phone location data (Coutts, 2016). Or news that a popular pregnancy app was exposing consumers to privacy threats due to a software bug (Beilinson, 2016). Mobile application company Uber was hit with criticism after journalists revealed it had access to all of its users' locations through a so-called "God view" (Bellware, 2016). A big data company gathered the mobile device IDs of Iowa caucus-goers and de-anonymized them by matching those IDs with real-world online profiles (Hill, 2016).

These incidents cause alarm because individuals use mobile devices to socialize, communicate, play, shop, bank, and monitor their own behavior, health, and moods. Mobile devices enable novel possibilities for human interaction while changing the privacy landscape in important ways. New types of information are available through smartphones, tablets, and e-readers, and mobile applications enable new data collection actors. Data may be collected by application developers (e.g., Rovio Games), mobile providers (e.g., AT&T), operating system providers (e.g., Google), and device manufacturers (e.g., Blackberry and Apple). These data may also be shared with third-party tracking or advertising companies.

Consumers and regulators both struggle to define their own expectations for the privacy of this data. When is it acceptable for companies to track, store, and sell data? Regulatory bodies such as the US Federal Trade Commission have suggested privacy approaches for developers (Federal Trade Commission, 2012), and industry groups have begun to make recommendations (Future of Privacy Forum & Center for Democracy & Technology, 2012). Meanwhile, watchdog groups defending consumer privacy rights have brought cases on behalf of consumers against companies such as a flashlight app that was recording users' locations (Kang, 2013). The European Union has taken a much more proactive regulatory stance. Beginning in 2018, the EU's General Data Protection Regulation will apply to any company processing the data of EU citizens, and will require measures such as strong forms of notice, strong privacy defaults, privacy impact assessments, and hiring of a data protection officer (Jones, 2016).

In this chapter, we focus on the ever-changing ecosystem of applications, hardware, operating systems, and telecommunication companies that collect increasing amounts of personal data

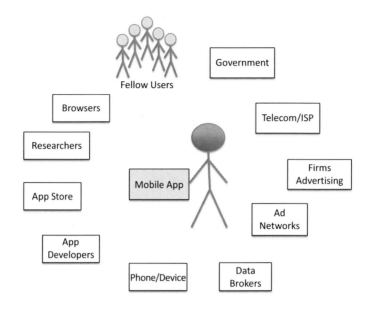

FIGURE 5.1 The mobile device ecosystem

(see Figure 5.1). Mobile developers are key agents impacting consumer privacy, deciding what data to collect and how to store and share it. Yet, application developers struggle to find a common understanding of users' privacy expectations (Greene & Shilton, 2017). In this chapter, we explore what we know about the privacy challenges raised by mobile devices; user privacy expectations in regards to mobile devices; and developer responses to those challenges. Through so doing, we illustrate the role of each actor in the mobile ecosystem in respecting privacy expectations.

WHAT WE KNOW ABOUT PRIVACY AND MOBILE DEVICES

1 *Mobile Technologies Have Technological Properties that Change Social Practices*

What's so new about mobile devices? They are host to increasingly prevalent digital activity. Consumers use their phones for a wide range of application-enabled activities, from accessing social media to banking and performing searches on health conditions. In 2015, 64% of Americans owned a smartphone(Smith, 2015). Between 2013 and 2015, mobile application usage grew 90% and contributed to 77% of the total increase in digital media time spent by US consumers. Two out of every three minutes Americans spend with digital media is on a mobile device, and mobile applications constitute just over half of those minutes (Lella & Lipsman, 2015). In many ways, mobile devices are simply pocket-sized laptops. But in other ways, their unique technological *affordances* – what actions they enable easily or disallow entirely (Friedman & Nissenbaum, 1996; Shilton, Koepfler, & Fleischmann, 2013) – matter because they shift social practices.

First, new types of information are available through smartphones, tablets, and e-readers. Data such as location, motion, communications content, in-application activities, and sound are easily gathered through mobile devices. Much of the literature on privacy and mobile devices, in particular, has focused on the fact that mobile devices uniquely enable the collection of *location* information. Using cell-tower triangulation, WiFi mapping, and GPS, mobile phones can record a user's location frequently and accurately (Barkhuus & Dey, 2003; Decker, 2008; He, Wu, & Khosla, 2004; Shilton, 2009).

Second, mobile applications enable new data collection *actors*. Data may be collected by a variety of companies: application developers, mobile providers, operating system providers, and device manufacturers. These data may also be shared with third-party tracking or advertising companies. Mobile data may be compelled from companies during law enforcement investigations (Soghoian, 2011), or "skimmed" from geographic locations using special devices that imitate cell towers ("Stingray Tracking Devices," 2016).

Finally, the smartphone or tablet is more personal and connected to the individual than are desktops or other computing devices. Many consumers carry their mobile devices with them at all times and the device is intimate to them in a way that differs from the shared personal computer at home or work. Tracking of user information gathered from phones may feel more personal, invasive, and ubiquitous than surveillance of work or home computers.

This personalization is important because how users relate to their mobile devices is different from how they relate to their desktop. Users have a more intimate relationship with devices they carry on their person, accessible everywhere (but also following them everywhere). This allows users to share a constant flow of information – where they are, who they are with, what they are doing, and what they are worried about – with the mobile device and, possibly, the entire ecosystem in Figure 5.1. This change in social practices leads us to point #2: surveillance and mobile devices.

2 *Surveillance Is Highly Salient for Mobile Device Users*

The personal and omnipresent nature of mobile devices, and their data collection capabilities, lend themselves to ubiquitous tracking. Mobile phones not only track online behaviors such as browsing and shopping habits, but they can also track previously offline activities such as commuting routes and habits, frequented locations, and interpersonal contacts. Practically, consumers' online life is as deeply integrated into their social life and as radically heterogeneous as their offline life (Nissenbaum, 2011). The ability to track both online and offline activities with mobile devices lends itself to concerns about *surveillance*.

Jeffery Rosen (2000) frames surveillance as the unwanted gaze from direct observations as well as from searches on stored records. Famously, Foucault used the architectures of hospitals and prisons as classic illustrations of surveillance, where persistent observation is used to maintain control (Foucault, 1977). Foucault's panopticon includes a centralized, hidden actor in a tall guard tower to watch prisoners in surrounding prison cells (see also Bentham, 1791). The individuals under observation begin to self-monitor and to curtail prohibited or even perfectly legal but socially stigmatized behaviors. Importantly, "spaces exposed by surveillance function differently than spaces that are not so exposed" (Cohen, 2008, p. 194) by changing how individuals behave and think due to the fear of being watched and judged by others.

As noted by Kirsten Martin (2016), surveillance is a concern because it frustrates the need of individuals to be unobserved (Benn, 1984), discourages expressions of uniqueness, and complicates individuals' development of a sense of self (Bloustein, 1964; Fried, 1970; Rachels, 1975). Unobserved personal space permits "unconstrained, unobserved physical and intellectual movement," enabling critical, playful individual development and relationship cultivation (Cohen, 2008, p. 195).

Mobile surveillance is particularly effective in changing behavior and thoughts when individuals (1) cannot avoid the gaze of the watcher and (2) cannot identify the watchers (Cohen, 2008).

In other words, both the breadth of information gathered and the tactic of invisibility contribute to the problem of surveillance with mobile devices (Martin, 2016). Further complicating the problem of surveillance is that mobile devices support aggregating data across disparate contexts and contribute to the perception that surveillance is impossible to avoid. Many of the actors in the ecosystem pictured in Figure 5.1 – data brokers, ISPs, and device manufacturers – have the capability to create a data record that tells a richer, more personalized story than any individual data points. The mosaic theory of privacy explains why privacy scholars are concerned with all elements of tracking, including transaction surveillance and purchasing behavior (Strandburg, 2011). The mosaic theory of privacy suggests that the whole of one's movements reveals far more than the individual movements comprising it (DC Circuit, p. 647; Kerr, 2012; United States v. Jones, 2012), where the aggregation of small movements across contexts is a difference in kind and not in degree (Strandburg, 2011).

Mobile devices allow for broad user surveillance across many areas of life and support tracking not only online activity but also the user's associated offline activity, such as where they are and who they are with. As Brunton and Nissenbaum (2011) note, "Innocuous traces of everyday life submitted to sophisticated analytics tools developed for commerce and governance can become the keys for stitching disparate databases together into unprecedented new wholes."

3 *Context Matters for Privacy Expectations for Mobile Devices*

A popular, yet outdated (Martin & Nissenbaum, 2016), approach to privacy attempts to group consumers by privacy preferences. Alan F. Westin famously claimed consumers ranged from "privacy fundamentalists" with greater concern for privacy, to "privacy pragmatists," willing to supposedly trade privacy for certain benefits, to "privacy unconcerned" (Westin, 1970). However, recent empirical research has shown Westin's privacy categories to be relatively unimportant in relation to contextual elements in privacy judgments (King, 2014; Martin & Nissenbaum, 2016). In one study, even "privacy unconcerned" respondents rated data collection vignettes as not meeting privacy expectations on average, and respondents across categories had a common vision of what constituted a privacy violation. In fact, how the information was used – within the stated context versus for commercial use – drove meeting privacy expectations rather than difference in privacy 'concerns' (Martin & Nissenbaum, 2016).

These theories – and empirical data to support them – apply to mobile application users, as well. Much of the research on user privacy expectations for mobile devices resides in the human–computer interaction and usability research areas (Anthony, Kotz, & Henderson, 2007; Palen & Dourish, 2003). Though early work in this space attempted to sort consumers into groups based on privacy or data-sharing preferences or policies (Sadeh et al., 2009), recently, much of this work has reflected the important movement in privacy scholarship that approaches privacy expectations less as personal preferences, and more as social, contextually dependent phenomena (Ahern et al., 2007; Khalil & Connelly, 2006; Mancini et al., 2009). This work posits that privacy expectations are based on social norms within particular information contexts (Nissenbaum, 2009). Those contextual privacy norms dictate what data it is acceptable to collect, who can have access to it, whether it should be kept confidential, and how it can be shared and reused.

When privacy expectations are context-specific, norms around what information should be disclosed and gathered and for what purpose are developed within a particular community or context. Shopping online, talking in the break room, and divulging information to a doctor are each governed by different information norms. As Nissenbaum states, "the crucial issue is not whether the information is private or public, gathered from private or public settings, but whether the action breaches contextual integrity" (Nissenbaum, 2004, p. 134).

This contextual approach is consistent with a social contract approach to privacy expectations (Culnan & Bies, 2003; Li, Sarathy, & Xu, 2010; Martin, 2012; Xu, Zhang, Shi, & Song, 2009) in which rules for information flow take into account the purpose of the information exchange as well as risks and harms associated with sharing information. This approach allows for the development of contextually dependent privacy norms between consumers and businesses. These norms have been shown to take into account (Martin, 2015b; Nissenbaum, 2010):

- Who/Recipients – the people, organizations, and technologies who are the senders, recipients, and subjects of information.
- What/Information – the information types or data fields being transmitted.
- How/Transmission principles – the constraints on the flow of information.
- Why – the purpose of the use of information.

Key to all contextual definitions of privacy is how the main components work together – who receives the information, what type of information, how it is used, and for what purpose – within a particular context.

Ongoing research that connects mobile devices to contextual privacy attempts to understand what contexts, actors, values, transmission principles, and information uses matter to users' mobile privacy expectations. For example, location data may be required for contexts such as navigation but inappropriate for a flashlight application (Kang, 2013); anonymity may be appropriate for a context such as Internet searching, but inappropriate in a context such as social networking. Contextual privacy also stipulates that data types cannot be deemed 'private' or 'public' across contexts. Tactics such as behavioral advertising, data collection and retention, and tracking may be appropriate and within the contextually defined privacy norms in one context while inappropriate in another. Importantly, mobile phones cross contexts as users carry them throughout their days, and use apps which may touch upon contexts such as banking, education, socializing, and leisure time.

Researchers such as Lin et al. (2012) have begun this effort by measuring sensitive data types and user reactions to the purpose of data collection in the mobile ecosystem. They found that the purpose of information use was a powerful factor in meeting individuals' expectations for an app, and that explanations of information use could allay users' concerns about data collection. We have also conducted empirical research in this space, including a factorial vignette survey that measured the impact of diverse real-world contexts (e.g., medicine, navigation, and music), data types, and data uses on user privacy expectations (Martin & Shilton, 2015; Martin & Shilton, 2016). Results demonstrate that individuals' general privacy preferences are of limited significance for predicting their privacy judgments in specific scenarios. Instead, the results present a nuanced portrait of the relative importance of particular contextual factors and information uses, and demonstrate how those contextual factors can be found and measured. The results also suggest that current common activities of mobile application companies, such as harvesting and reusing location data, images, and contact lists, do not meet users' privacy expectations.

In our study, each survey respondent was shown a series of vignettes that varied based on:

- Who: The data collection actor – the primary organization collecting information, such as application developer, third party placing an ad, app store, or mobile phone provider;
- What: The type of information received or tracked by the primary organization such as location, accelerometer, demographic data, contacts, keywords, user name, and images;

- Why: The application context – e.g., playing games, checking weather, participating in social networking, navigating using maps, listening to music, banking, shopping, and organizing personal productivity;
- How (used): How the data is reused or stored: the length of storage, whether the data was tied to a unique identifier for personalization, and the secondary use such as retargeting ads, social advertising, or selling to a data exchange.

This generated vignettes such as the following; underlining highlights the factors (independent variables) that would systematically change.

Targeting Vignette Sample:

While using your phone, you check updates on a social networking application that you have used occasionally for less than a month.
The social networking app shows you an advertisement for another application they sell based on your phone contact list.

We found that tracking scenarios met privacy expectations to a lesser extent than targeting scenarios (mean = –42.70 and –18.01, respectively) on the 'meeting privacy expectations' scale of –100 to +100. In addition, some data types were particularly sensitive regardless of context—or at least particularly surprising to respondents. Harvest of both images and contact information universally failed to meet user privacy expectations. This may be because it is not widely known that these data *can* be harvested by mobile applications, or it may be that these data types are particularly sensitive. Application developers engaged in privacy by design may wish to avoid collecting, using, or selling images or contact information from phones.

Among the contextual factors, generally, the type of information mattered most to respondents' privacy judgments. The use of contact information (β = –70.10) and image information (–78.84) were the most (negatively) influential types of information, followed by the individual's name (–19.51), friend information (–20.35), accelerometer (–15.17), and location (–13.33). All of these data types negatively impacted meeting privacy expectations for targeted advertising compared to using demographic information. However, using keywords (11.49) positively impacted meeting privacy expectations for targeted advertising compared to using demographic information. For tracking scenarios, the secondary use of information was the most important factor impacting privacy expectations. Selling to a data exchange (β = –47.17) and using tracked information for social advertising to contacts and friends (–21.61) both negatively impacted meeting privacy expectations.

The results indicate that very common activities of mobile application companies (harvesting and using data such as location, accelerometer readings, demographic data, contacts, keywords, name, images, and friends) do not meet users' privacy expectations. But users are not monolithic in their privacy expectations. For example, users expect navigation and weather applications to use location and accelerometer data, and users expect a link between harvesting keywords and targeted advertising. The results show that nuanced, contextual privacy concerns can be measured within an industry. For example, navigation applications should feel confident collecting users' location data, but should not collect image data. Navigation applications can make design changes to avoid data besides location, supporting privacy by design. These findings are important because regulators and companies should not rely on consumers as idiosyncratic as to their privacy preferences or privacy expectations. Consumers, when asked, can be fairly consistent as to the minimum protections they expect in regards to their information being accessed, stored, shared, and used.

The need to define appropriate contextual boundaries for mobile data privacy highlights the importance of "apps" as a contextual concept. Apps – single-purpose pieces of software – are a place where we can design for context in a device that otherwise spans multiple contexts.

CHALLENGES TO MEETING PRIVACY EXPECTATIONS WITH MOBILE DEVICES

4 *Government Regulations on Mobile Surveillance Have Been Slow to Catch Up*

Perhaps surprising given the sensitivity of mobile data and the fact that mobile data collection has been growing for almost ten years, mobile data collection and use are largely unregulated in the United States. Some health applications may be regulated under the Health Information Portability and Privacy Act (HIPPA) (Martínez-Pérez, Torre-Díez, & López-Coronado, 2014), and all applications must ensure that they do not collect data from children under 13. Beyond these restrictions, regulation of mobile data collection is left to the Federal Trade Commission (FTC) under its jurisdiction to punish unfair and deceptive trade practices (Solove & Hartzog, 2014). For example, the FTC fined a flashlight application that was tracking the location of its users (Kang, 2013) and has published recommended security best practice for mobile application developers (Bureau of Consumer Protection, 2013).

The FTC, however, only regulates private companies. US *government* rules and regulations about how the federal government may use mobile data for law enforcement are also in flux (Pell & Soghoian, 2012). Law enforcement regularly uses either cell tower data requested from phone providers, or increasingly, specialized devices called "stingrays" which mimic cell towers to track the location of individuals (Michael & Clarke, 2013).

Court decisions are increasingly recognizing the privacy rights of users of mobile devices. A 2014 Supreme Court case declared that law enforcement officers require a warrant to search mobile devices (Liptak, 2014). But in 2016, an appellate court declared that a warrant was not necessary to obtain a suspect's historical cell phone data from a phone company (Volz, 2016). The multi-actor ecosystem in which mobile data resides was used as the justification for the majority's decision; judges argued that once user location was stored by a third party, it was no longer protected under the Constitution's Fourth Amendment. The third-party doctrine dominates the current legal understanding of privacy expectations: information given to a third party is not considered to have legal privacy expectations (Kerr, 2009). However, recent scholarship has called into question the utility of relinquishing privacy protections of all information shared with a third party (Richards & King, 2016).

5 *Corporate Best Practices Also Slow to Adapt*

Governments are not the only actors in the mobile ecosystem struggling with questions of fairness and privacy while dealing with mobile data. How firms should best meet consumer privacy expectations in the mobile space is an unanswered question. This growing market lacks standards of practice for addressing privacy, as most uses of data collected by mobile applications are unregulated (Federal Trade Commission, 2012; Shilton, 2009).

Fair Information Principles (FIP), and in particular notice and choice, serve as one source of guidance for self-regulation within the industry (Bowie & Jamal, 2006; Culnan & Williams, 2009;

Milne & Culnan, 2002), and could be adapted to the mobile sector (Federal Trade Commission, 2012). However, relying on notice and choice raises both practical and philosophical problems. First, "choice" is a problematic concept when individuals perceive that opting out of application usage has more costs than benefits. In addition, surveys and experiments have shown that individuals make judgments about privacy expectations and violations regardless of the content of privacy notices (Beales & Muris, 2008; Martin, 2013; McDonald & Cranor, 2008; Milne, Culnan, & Greene, 2006; Nissenbaum, 2011). As noted in a study on the role of privacy notices in consumer trust (Martin, 2017), privacy notices are also frequently difficult to read (Ur, Leon, Cranor, Shay, & Wang, 2012), misleading (Leon, Cranor, McDonald, & McGuire, 2010), and difficult to find (Leon et al., 2012). Notices are also time consuming (McDonald & Cranor, 2008) and not always targeted towards consumers. Mobile devices, with their small screens and limited user interface features, exacerbate these issues (Schaub, Balebako, Durity, & Cranor, 2015).

Companies also struggle to identify who, in a complex data sharing ecosystem, should be responsible for user privacy. Platform providers such as Apple require independent app developers to provide privacy policies, and screens for these policies during its app stores approval process. While adhering to a notice-and-choice model, the app store approval process provides a clear signal that Apple views consumer privacy as a shared responsibility between users (who must read notices), developers (who must set policies), and the platform itself (which enforces compliance) (Shilton & Greene, 2016). In contrast, Google's popular Android marketplace does not screen apps submitted to its store (Google Play, 2016). While its developer policies emphasize that developers should include privacy notices, the open nature of its store signals much more reliance on developers and users to monitor their own application choices.

Individual developers also struggle to define and implement best-practice privacy. Low barriers to entry enable a vibrant but deprofessionalized development ecosystem (Cravens, 2012), and surveys of application developers have revealed that many lack knowledge of current privacy best practices (Balebako, Marsh, Lin, Hong, & Cranor, 2014). A recent study contrasting iOS and Android applications found that 73% of Android apps tested, and 47% of iOS apps tested, reported user location. Forty-nine percent of Android apps and 25% of iOS apps shared personally identifying information (Zang, Dummit, Graves, Lisker, & Sweeney, 2015).

In a study of privacy conversations in mobile development forums, Shilton and Greene (2016) found that many developers, particularly in the Android ecosystem in which hobbyists are very involved in development conversations, get feedback from users and take it quite seriously. However, developers don't have ready access to comprehensive or representative data on user privacy expectations. As a result, developers argue about how much privacy matters to users, as well as about privacy as an ethical principle more broadly.

Within these arguments, privacy tends to be defined rather narrowly. Developers focus on data collection or notice and consent, rather than on the contextual variables (particularly the actor collecting the data, the purpose of data collection, and the social context of the app) that have been shown to matter to users (Shilton & Greene, 2016). In our analysis of the discussion forums, it became evident that the platforms themselves – iOS and Android – were impacting how developers in each ecosystem defined privacy. iOS developers must pass a review by Apple that includes privacy requirements. As a result, iOS developers tend to define privacy according to Apple's regulations, which focus on notice and consent. The most frequently cited privacy definition in iOS discussions focused on transparency with users, particularly in the form of notice and consent. Developers frequently defined most kinds of data collection as allowable as long as users were informed. Developers also frequently credited Apple with authorizing this particular definition of privacy.

Android developers are much less regulated by the platform. Android lacks the stringent app store review process that was so critical to prompting privacy discussions in iOS. While Android developers must agree to the Developer Distribution Agreement (Google Play, 2016), and are asked to include privacy features such as a privacy policy and encryption for data in transmission, the agreement explicitly states that Google does not "undertake an obligation to monitor the Products or their content." Instead, Google reserves the right to remove (called "takedowns") violating apps from the store at their discretion. Interestingly, discussion of app takedowns was not prominent in the XDA forums. Instead, privacy was discussed as a *feature* that could provide consumer choice and could distinguish an application in the competitive marketplace. Defining privacy as a feature, particularly one enabling user choice, led to a wealth of privacy-enhancing options within the Android ecosystem. But privacy-enhancing or privacy-enhanced applications were often developed by hobbyists and open-source developers working on their own and then beta-testing with like-minded experts. This led to a marketplace in which consumer choice ran amok, but there was little indication of the level of professionalization, trustworthiness, product support, or long-term prospects of most applications.

TABLE 5.1 *Mobile devices and privacy: What we know, why it's hard, what is next*

WHAT WE KNOW ABOUT PRIVACY AND MOBILE DEVICES	CHALLENGES TO MEETING PRIVACY EXPECTATIONS WITH MOBILE DEVICES	THE FUTURE OF PRIVACY AND MOBILE DEVICES
Mobile Technologies Have Technological Properties that Change Social Practices: *Users have a more intimate relationship with mobile devices as the device is literally on their person, following them everywhere.*	Government regulations on mobile surveillance have been slow to catch up Notice-and-Choice as particularly limited with mobile Developers struggle to define privacy in a new sociotechnical setting:	**Focus of Users**: growing mistrust
Surveillance Is Highly Salient with Mobile Device Users: *Mobile devices allow for broad user surveillance across many areas of life and supports tracking not only the user online but also their associated offline activity such as where they are and who they are with.*		**Focus of Firms**: techniques to meet privacy expectations
Context Matters for Privacy Expectations for Mobile Devices: *Tactics such as behavioral advertising, data collection and retention, and tracking may be appropriate and within the contextually defined privacy norms in one context while inappropriate in another. Importantly, mobile phones cross contexts as users carry them throughout their days, and use apps which may touch upon contexts such as banking, education, socializing, and leisure time.*		**Focus of Regulators**: regulating themselves and others

THE FUTURE OF PRIVACY AND MOBILE DEVICES

Given the state of privacy and mobile devices and the challenges facing both industry and regulators, we see trends in the future focus of users, firms, and regulators. Users are growing more mistrustful of corporations and their use of mobile data. Firms should use increased focus on privacy as one way of regaining consumer trust.

Users: Growing Mistrust

Users are becomingly increasingly concerned with, frustrated at, and mistrustful of technology companies. Users have long rejected tracking of their information for targeted advertising (Turow, King, Hoofnagle, Bleakley, & Hennessy, 2009) and have become only more pessimistic over time (Turow, Hennessy, & Draper, 2015). Consumers care about privacy but do not believe their concerns will be addressed by commercial entities (Turow et al., 2015). These findings are reinforced by surveys measuring changing expectations over time (Urban, Hoofnagle, & Li, 2012).

We believe two additional issues will only become more prevalent with growing user awareness of mobile surveillance. First is the challenging issue of when the massive stores of information collected with mobile devices can be used beyond commercial purposes, for example, for research (Metcalf & Crawford, 2017; Vitak, Shilton, & Ashktorab, 2016; Zimmer, 2010). The assumption that information collected by one party is available for any use or by any other entity has been debunked (Martin & Nissenbaum, 2016). But this challenges researchers who hope to use these datasets to understand human behavior, health, and practices. Should corporations be the sole actors with access to these "small data" streams that can be useful for individual health and wellness (Estrin, 2014) as well as population-level research (boyd & Crawford, 2012)? If this data is to be made available for research, how can users ensure that their rights and dignity as research subjects are respected?

Second, it is increasingly difficult for individuals to resist government surveillance (Calo, 2016) or remain obscure from public or private interests (Hartzog & Selinger, 2015). As consumers seek to protect their information, their focus may turn to tools to obfuscate their activities. For example, Nissenbaum and Brunton created a user's guide to obfuscation with practical tips to thwart pervasive tracking (Nissenbaum & Brunton, 2015). Introducing widespread obfuscation into data streams may frustrate governments, corporations, and researchers reliant on this data. But it is a legitimate tool of protest for users who feel that their interests are overlooked by powerful data collectors.

Firms: Techniques to Meet Privacy Expectations

For the reasons outlined above, user trust is a primary issue that should concern firms in the mobile data ecosystem. Figure 5.2 illustrates the varying levels of trust within the mobile device ecosystem. Not all actors in the ecosystem are equally close to consumers, and therefore different actors might require different levels of trust. Gatekeepers, such as mobile applications, are the mechanism by which consumers enter the ecosystem, and such firms carry an additional obligation to respect consumer privacy expectations (Martin, 2016). Mobile devices and mobile platform providers similarly carry an obligation to uphold the trust of consumers, as these firms have the technological ability and unique regulatory position to enforce what sorts of data collection and sharing are permitted on the device.

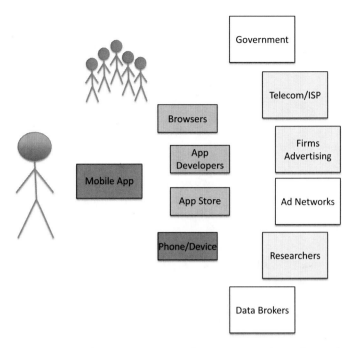

FIGURE 5.2 Mobile device ecosystem by consumer relationship and trust

For firms interested in increasing consumer trust, we predict several areas of focus. First, given the issues with adequate notice explained above, new types of notices around choice architecture, framing, and layered privacy choices will become the focus of firms (Adjerid, Acquisti, & Loewenstein, 2016). Increasingly, behavioral approaches and nudges are utilized for notice on mobile devices (Balebako et al., 2011). In addition, when the notice is given matters: recent research has illustrated the importance of timing when the notice is shown to the user. Showing the notice during app use significantly increased users' recall rates as opposed to showing the notice in the app store. Importantly, the results suggest that a notice is unlikely to be recalled by users if only shown in the app store (Balebako, Schaub, Adjerid, Acquisti, & Cranor, 2015)

Second, mobile platforms may become more interested in using their regulatory power to maintain consumer trust. Apple has recently announced a new internal emphasis on differential privacy, an innovative privacy protection technique that enables aggregate data use without identifying individuals (Simonite, 2016). Apple has long showed a willingness to regulate privacy policies for mobile applications, and their interest in incorporating advanced methods for privacy protection into the mobile ecosystem could help enhance consumer trust.

Consumer-facing organizations are uniquely positioned to manage consumer privacy, and firms face the risk of consumer backlash if privacy is not respected. In the past, efforts to place security concerns on the agendas of boards of directors have been fruitful to realigning consumer trust and corporate practice.[1] Privacy practices could soon be included in corporate governance. As privacy concerns and the associated perceptions of vulnerability begin to look similar to security concerns, corporate governance could begin to focus on the privacy practices of corporations as a form of risk management.

---

[1] https://www.sec.gov/News/Speech/Detail/Speech/1370542057946.

Regulators: Regulating Themselves and Others

US regulatory bodies are also starting to realize the importance of regulating privacy to maintain user trust. Documents such as the White House's Consumer Privacy Bill of Rights (Strickling, 2012) and the recent National Privacy Research Strategy (National Science and Technology Council, 2016) signal the interest of the executive branch in engaging privacy as a regulatory topic. Regulators have at least two areas of focus in the mobile data ecosystem: regulating corporate use of mobile data and regulating government use of that same data.

Regulators such as the FTC have long enforced the use of adequate notice and consumer choice (Solove & Hartzog, 2014). In addition, researchers' attention to privacy by design has also attracted the attention of regulators. Regulators could move beyond the limitations of notice to promote more creative approaches to privacy by design. For example, regulators might require corporate privacy programs to include identifying privacy risks as a step in all product design decisions. Regulators might also regulate the substance and adequacy of privacy notices, instead of only their compliance with corporate policy (Mulligan & Bamberger, 2013; Mulligan & King, 2011). Asking firms to detail their design decisions and ongoing data maintenance in official privacy programs will highlight the importance of thoughtful privacy design. Focusing less on the degree to which firms are truthful in their privacy notices (which is necessary, but not sufficient) will encourage firms to focus more on the substance of the notices and their adherence to the expectations of consumers.

Finally, US courts, and perhaps the US Congress, will also need to decide the limits to which governments can compel user data from private companies. As we have outlined, the specter of government surveillance of mobile data is real and realized. Governments must limit their access to this data for the good of *national* trust.

CONCLUSION

In this chapter, we examined privacy and the ecosystem of applications, hardware, operating systems, and telecommunication companies that collect increasing amounts of personal data. We explored what we know about the privacy challenges raised by mobile devices; user privacy expectations in regards to mobile devices; and developer responses to those challenges. Mobile device users have predictable privacy expectations, but these vary based on data type and application context. Mobile developers are positioned as key decision-makers about consumer privacy, but they struggle to find a common understanding of users' context-sensitive privacy expectations.

While mobile device technology is relatively new, recent research has revealed quite a bit about privacy expectations and mobile devices. Firms and regulators can help to mitigate the gap between developers and consumers by increasing attention to privacy by design at the level of corporate governance, making privacy a first-order concern in protecting consumer trust.

ACKNOWLEDGMENTS

Thanks to Karen Boyd for assistance with background research for this article. This work was supported in part by the US National Science Foundation awards, CNS-1452854, SES-1449351, and a Google Faculty Research Award.

REFERENCES

Adjerid, I., Acquisti, A., & Loewenstein, G. (2016). Choice architecture, framing, and layered privacy choices. *Framing, and Layered Privacy Choices*. Available at SSRN: https://ssrn.com/abstract=2765111.

Ahern, S., Eckles, D., Good, N. S., King, S., Naaman, M., & Nair, R. (2007). Over-exposed?: Privacy patterns and considerations in online and mobile photo sharing. In *Proceedings of the SIGCHI Conference on Human Factors in Computing Systems* (pp. 357–366). ACM. Retrieved from http://dl.acm.org/citation.cfm?id=1240683.

Anthony, D., Kotz, D., & Henderson, T. (2007). Privacy in location-aware computing environments. *Pervasive Computing*, 6(4), 64–72.

Balebako, R., Leon, P. G., Almuhimedi, H., Kelley, P. G., Mugan, J., Acquisti, A., … Sadeh, N. (2011). Nudging users towards privacy on mobile devices. In *Proceedings of the CHI 2011 Workshop on Persuasion, Nudge, Influence and Coercion*.

Balebako, R., Marsh, A., Lin, J., Hong, J., & Cranor, L. F. (2014). The privacy and security behaviors of smartphone app developers. In *USEC '14*. San Diego, CA: Internet Society. Retrieved from http://lorrie.cranor.org/pubs/usec14-app-developers.pdf.

Balebako, R., Schaub, F., Adjerid, I., Acquisti, A., & Cranor, L. F. (2015). The impact of timing on the salience of smartphone app privacy notices. In *Proceedings of the 5th Annual ACM CCS Workshop on Security and Privacy in Smartphones and Mobile Devices* (pp. 63–74). ACM.

Barkhuus, L., & Dey, A. (2003). Location-based services for mobile telephony: A study of users' privacy concerns. In *Proceedings of the INTERACT 2003: 9TH IFIP TC13 International Conference on Human-Computer Interaction* (Vol. 2003, pp. 709–712).

Beales, J. H., & Muris, T. J. (2008). Choice or consequences: Protecting privacy in commercial information. *The University of Chicago Law Review*, 75(1), 109–135.

Beilinson, J. (2016, July 28). Glow pregnancy app exposed women to privacy threats, *Consumer Reports* finds. *Consumer Reports*. Retrieved from http://www.consumerreports.org/mobile-security-software/glow-pregnancy-app-exposed-women-to-privacy-threats/.

Bellware, K. (2016, January 6). Uber settles investigation into creepy "God View" tracking program. *The Huffington Post*. Retrieved from http://www.huffingtonpost.com/entry/uber-settlement-god-view_us_568da2a6e4b0c8beacf5a46a.

Benn, S. I. (1984). Privacy, freedom, and respect for persons. In F. Schoeman (Ed.), *Philosophical dimensions of privacy*. (pp. 223–244). Cambridge, MA: Cambridge University Press.

Bentham, J. (1791). *Panopticon or the inspection house* (Vol. 2). Retrieved from http://sites.scran.ac.uk/ada/documents/castle_style/bridewell/bridewell_jeremy_bentham_panoption_vol1.htm.

Bloustein, E. J. (1964). Privacy as an aspect of human dignity: An answer to Dean Prosser. *NYU Law Review*, 39, 962.

Bowie, N. E., & Jamal, K. (2006). Privacy rights on the internet: Self-regulation or government regulation? *Business Ethics Quarterly*, 16(3), 323–342.

Boyd, D., & Crawford, K. (2012). Critical questions for big data. *Information, Communication & Society*, 15(5), 662–679.

Brunton, F., & Nissenbaum, H. (2011). Vernacular resistance to data collection and analysis: A political theory of obfuscation. *First Monday*, 16(5). Available at: http://www.ojphi.org/ojs/index.php/fm/article/view/3493/2955.

Bureau of Consumer Protection. (2013, February). Mobile App Developers: Start with security. Retrieved June 21, 2013, from http://business.ftc.gov/documents/bus83-mobile-app-developers-start-security.

Calo, R. (2016). Can Americans resist surveillance? *The University of Chicago Law Review*, 83(1), 23–43.

Cohen, J. E. (2008). Privacy, visibility, transparency, and exposure. *The University of Chicago Law Review*, 75(1), 181–201.

Coutts, S. (2016, May 25). Anti-choice groups use smartphone surveillance to target "abortion-minded women" during clinic visits. *Rewire*. Retrieved from https://rewire.news/article/2016/05/25/anti-choice-groups-deploy-smartphone-surveillance-target-abortion-minded-women-clinic-visits/.

Cravens, A. (2012, September 26). A demographic and business model analysis of today's app developer. Retrieved March 19, 2013, from http://pro.gigaom.com/2012/09/a-demographic-and-business-model-analysis-of-todays-app-developer/.

Culnan, M. J., & Bies, R. J. (2003). Consumer privacy: Balancing economic and justice considerations. *Journal of Social Issues*, 59(2), 323–342.

Culnan, M. J., & Williams, C. C. (2009). How ethics can enhance organizational privacy: Lessons from the ChoicePoint and TJX data breaches. *Management Information Systems Quarterly*, 33(4), 6.

Curry, M. R. (2002). Discursive displacement and the seminal ambiguity of space and place. In L. Lievrouw & S. Livingstone (Eds.), *Handbook of new media.* (pp. 502–517). London: Sage Publications.

Decker, M. (2008). Location privacy: An overview. In *Proceedings of the 2008 7th International Conference on Mobile Business* (pp. 221–230). Barcelona: IEEE Computer Society Press. Retrieved from http://csdl2.computer.org/persagen/DLAbsToc.jsp?resourcePath=/dl/proceedings/&toc=comp/proceedings/icmb/2008/3260/00/3260toc.xml&DOI=10.1109/ICMB.2008.14.

Estrin, D. (2014). Small data, where n = me. *Communications of the ACM*, 57(4), 32–34. http://doi.org/10.1145/2580944.

Federal Trade Commission (2012). *Protecting consumer privacy in an era of rapid change: Recommendations for businesses and policymakers.* Washington, DC: Federal Trade Commission.

Foucault, M. (1977). *Discipline and punish: The birth of the prison.* New York: Random House LLC.

Fried, C. (1970). *An anatomy of values: Problems of personal and social choice.* Cambridge, MA: Harvard University Press.

Friedman, B., & Nissenbaum, H. (1996). Bias in computer systems. *ACM Transactions on Information Systems (TOIS)*, 14(3), 330–347.

Future of Privacy Forum, & Center for Democracy & Technology. (2012). *Best practices for mobile application developers.* Washington, DC: Future of Privacy Forum. Retrieved from http://www.futureofprivacy.org/wp-content/uploads/Best-Practices-for-Mobile-App-Developers_Final.pdf.

Google Play (2016, July 2). Google Play developer distribution agreement. Retrieved August 9, 2016, from https://play.google.com/intl/ALL_us/about/developer-distribution-agreement.html.

Hartzog, W., & Selinger, E. (2015). Surveillance as loss of obscurity. *Washington and Lee Law Review*, 72(3), 1343.

He, Q., Wu, D., & Khosla, P. (2004). The quest for personal control over mobile location privacy. *IEEE Communications Magazine*, 42(5), 130–136.

Hill, K. (2016, February 12). How this company tracked 16,000 Iowa caucus-goers via their phones. Retrieved from https://www.huffingtonpost.com/entry/dstillery-iowa-caucus_us_56c12cafe4b08ffac125b591.

Jones, M. L. (2016). *Ctrl + z: The right to be forgotten.* New York and London: New York University Press.

Kang, C. (2013, December 6). Flashlight app kept users in the dark about sharing location data: FTC. *The Washington Post.* Retrieved from http://www.washingtonpost.com/business/technology/flashlight-app-kept-users-in-the-dark-about-sharing-location-data-ftc/2013/12/05/1be26fa6-5dc7-11e3-be07-006c776266ed_story.html.

Kerr, O. S. (2009). The case for the third-party doctrine. *Michigan Law Review*, 107, 561–601.

Kerr, O. S. (2012). The Mosaic Theory of the Fourth Amendment. *Michigan Law Review*, 110, 311–354.

Khalil, A., & Connelly, K. (2006). Context-aware telephony: Privacy preferences and sharing patterns. In *Proceedings of the 2006 20th anniversary conference on computer supported cooperative work* (pp. 469–478). New York: ACM. Retrieved from http://dl.acm.org/citation.cfm?id=1180947

King, J. (2014). Taken out of context: An empirical analysis of Westin's privacy scale. In *Symposium on Usable Privacy and Security (SOUPS) 2014.* Menlo Park, CA: ACM.

Lella, A., & Lipsman, A. (2015). *The 2015 U.S. Mobile App Report.* Retrieved from http://www.comscore.com/Insights/Presentations-and-Whitepapers/2015/The-2015-US-Mobile-App-Report.

Leon, P. G., Cranor, L. F., McDonald, A. M., & McGuire, R. (2010). Token attempt: The misrepresentation of website privacy policies through the misuse of p3p compact policy tokens. In *Proceedings of the 9th annual ACM workshop on privacy in the electronic society* (pp. 93–104). New York: ACM.

Leon, P. G., Cranshaw, J., Cranor, L. F., Graves, J., Hastak, M., Ur, B., & Xu, G. (2012). What do online behavioral advertising privacy disclosures communicate to users? In *Proceedings of the 2012 ACM workshop on privacy in the electronic society* (pp. 19–30). New York: ACM.

Li, H., Sarathy, R., & Xu, H. (2010). Understanding situational online information disclosure as a privacy calculus. *Journal of Computer Information Systems*, 51(1), 62.

Lin, J., Amini, S., Hong, J. I., Sadeh, N., Lindqvist, J., & Zhang, J. (2012). Expectation and purpose: Understanding users' mental models of mobile app privacy through crowdsourcing. In *Proceedings of the 2012 ACM Conference on Ubiquitous Computing* (pp. 501–510). New York: ACM. http://doi.org/10.1145/2370216.2370290.

Liptak, A. (2014, June 25). Supreme Court says phones can't be searched without a warrant. *The New York Times*. Retrieved from http://www.nytimes.com/2014/06/26/us/supreme-court-cellphones-search-privacy.html.

Mancini, C., Thomas, K., Rogers, Y., Price, B. A., Jedrzejczyk, L., Bandara, A. K., . . . Nuseibeh, B. (2009). *From spaces to places: Emerging contexts in mobile privacy*. New York: ACM Press. http://doi.org/10.1145/1620545.1620547.

Martin, K. (2017). Do privacy notices matter? Comparing the impact of violating formal privacy notices and informal privacy norms on consumer trust online. *Journal of Legal Studies*, 45(S2), 191–215.

Martin, K. (2013). Transaction costs, privacy, and trust: The laudable goals and ultimate failure of notice and choice to respect privacy online. *First Monday*, 18(12).

Martin, K. (2015). Ethical issues in the big data industry. *MIS Quarterly Executive*, 14(2): 67–85.

Martin, K. (2016a). Understanding privacy online: Development of a social contract approach to privacy. *Journal of Business Ethics*, 137(3), 551–569.

Martin, K. (2016b). Data aggregators, consumer data, and responsibility online: Who is tracking consumers online and should they stop? *The Information Society*, 32(1), 51–63.

Martin, K. (2012). Diminished or just different? A factorial vignette study of privacy as a social contract. *Journal of Business Ethics*, 111(4), 519–539. http://doi.org/10.1007/s10551-012-1215-8.

Martin, K. E., & Shilton, K. (2015). Why experience matters to privacy: How context-based experience moderates consumer privacy expectations for mobile applications. *Journal of the Association for Information Science and Technology*, 67(8), 1871–1882.

Martin, K. E., & Shilton, K. (2016). Putting mobile application privacy in context: An empirical study of user privacy expectations for mobile devices. *The Information Society*, 32(3), 200–216. http://doi.org/10.1080/01972243.2016.1153012.

Martin, K., & Nissenbaum, H. (2016). Measuring privacy: Using context to expose confounding variables. *Columbia Science and Technology Law Review*. Retrieved from http://papers.ssrn.com/sol3/papers.cfm?abstract_id=2709584.

Martínez-Pérez, B., Torre-Díez, I. de la, & López-Coronado, M. (2014). Privacy and security in mobile health apps: A review and recommendations. *Journal of Medical Systems*, 39(1), 181. http://doi.org/10.1007/s10916-014-0181-3.

McDonald, A. M., & Cranor, L. F. (2008). The cost of reading privacy policies. *I/S: A Journal of Law and Policy for the Information Society*, 4(3), 543.

Metcalf, J., & Crawford, K. (2016). Where are human subjects in Big Data research? The emerging ethics divide. *Big Data & Society*, 3(1). https://doi.org/10.1177/2053951716650211.

Michael, K., & Clarke, R. (2013). Location and tracking of mobile devices: Überveillance stalks the streets. *Computer Law & Security Review*, 29(3), 216–228.

Milne, G. R., & Culnan, M. J. (2002). Using the content of online privacy notices to inform public policy: A longitudinal analysis of the 1998–2001 US web surveys. *The Information Society*, 18(5), 345–359.

Milne, G. R., Culnan, M. J., & Greene, H. (2006). A longitudinal assessment of online privacy notice readability. *Journal of Public Policy & Marketing*, 25(2), 238–249.

Mulligan, D. K., & Bamberger, K. A. (2013). What regulators can do to advance privacy through design. *Communications of the ACM*, 56(11), 20–22.

Mulligan, D. K., & King, J. (2011). Bridging the gap between privacy and design. *University of Pennsylvania Journal of Constitutional Law*, 14 (4), 989.

National Science and Technology Council. (2016). *National privacy research strategy*. Washington, DC: National Science and Technology Council.

Nissenbaum, H. (2004). Privacy as contextual integrity. *Washington Law Review*, 79(1), 119–158.

Nissenbaum, H. (2010). *Privacy in context: Technology, policy, and the integrity of social life*. Stanford, CA: Stanford University Press.

Nissenbaum, H. (2011). A contextual approach to privacy online. *Daedalus*, 140(4), 32–48.

Nissenbaum, H., & Brunton, F. (2015). *Obfuscation: A user's guide for privacy and protest*. Cambridge, MA: MIT Press.

Palen, L., & Dourish, P. (2003). Unpacking "privacy" for a networked world. In *CHI 2003* (Vol. 5, pp. 129–136). Ft. Lauderdale, FL: ACM.

Pell, S. K., & Soghoian, C. (2012). Can you see me now?: Toward reasonable standards for law enforcement access to location data that Congress could enact. *Berkeley Technology Law Journal*, 27(1), 117–195.

Rachels, J. (1975). Why privacy is important. *Philosophy & Public Affairs*, 4(4), 323–333.

Richards, N. M., & King, J. H. (2016). Big data and the future for privacy. In F. X. Olleros & M. Zhegu (Eds.), *Research handbook on digital transformations*. (p. 272). Northhampton, MA: Edward Elgar Publishing.

Rosen, J. (2011). *The unwanted gaze: The destruction of privacy in America*. New York: Vintage Books.

Sadeh, N., Hong, J., Cranor, L., Fette, I., Kelley, P., Prabaker, M., & Rao, J. (2009). Understanding and capturing people's privacy policies in a mobile social networking application. *Personal and Ubiquitous Computing*, 13(6), 401–412.

Schaub, F., Balebako, R., Durity, A. L., & Cranor, L. F. (2015). A design space for effective privacy notices. In *Proceedings of the Eleventh Symposium On Usable Privacy and Security (SOUPS 2015)* (pp. 1–17).

Shilton, K. (2009). Four billion little brothers?: Privacy, mobile phones, and ubiquitous data collection. *Communications of the ACM*, 52(11), 48–53. http://doi.org/10.1145/1592761.1592778.

Shilton, K., & Greene, D. (2017). Linking platforms, practices, and developer ethics: levers for privacy discourse in mobile application development. *Journal of Business Ethics* (online first). https://doi.org/10.1007/s10551-017-3504-8.

Shilton, K., Koepfler, J. A., & Fleischmann, K. R. (2013). Charting sociotechnical dimensions of values for design research. *The Information Society*, 29(5), 259–271.

Simonite, T. (2016, August 3). Breakthrough privacy technology invented by Microsoft gets its first big test thanks to Apple. *MIT Technology Review*. Retrieved August 10, 2016, from https://www.technologyreview.com/s/602046/apples-new-privacy-technology-may-pressure-competitors-to-better-protect-our-data/?imm_mid=0e6973&cmp=em-data-na-na-newsltr_20160810.

Smith, A. (2015, April 1). U.S. smartphone use in 2015. Retrieved from www.pewinternet.org/2015/04/01/us-smartphone-use-in-2015/.

Soghoian, C. (2011, April 22). How can US law enforcement agencies access location data stored by Google and Apple? Retrieved April 23, 2011, from http://paranoia.dubfire.net/2011/04/how-can-us-law-enforcement-agencies.html.

Solove, D. J., & Hartzog, W. (2014). The FTC and the new common law of privacy. *Columbia Law Review*, 114: 583–676.

Stingray tracking devices: Who's got them? (2016). Retrieved August 19, 2016, from https://www.aclu.org/map/stingray-tracking-devices-whos-got-them

Strandburg, K. J. (2011). Home, home on the web: The Fourth Amendment and technosocial change. *Maryland Law Review*, 3, 614–680.

Strickling, L. (2012, June 15). Putting the Consumer Privacy Bill of Rights into practice. Retrieved from http://www.ntia.doc.gov/blog/2012/putting-consumer-privacy-bill-rights-practice.

Turow, J., Hennessy, M., & Draper, N. (2015). *The tradeoff fallacy: How marketers are misrepresenting American consumers and opening them up to exploitation* (pp. 1–24). Annenburg School of Communication. Retrieved from https://www.asc.upenn.edu/sites/default/files/TradeoffFallacy_1.pdf.

Turow, J., King, J., Hoofnagle, C. J., Bleakley, A., & Hennessy, M. (2009). Americans reject tailored advertising and three activities that enable it. *Available at SSRN* at https://ssrn.com/abstract=1478214 or http://dx.doi.org/10.2139/ssrn.1478214.

Ur, B., Leon, P. G., Cranor, L. F., Shay, R., & Wang, Y. (2012). Smart, useful, scary, creepy: Perceptions of online behavioral advertising. In *Proceedings of the 8th symposium on usable privacy and security* (p. 4). ACM.

Urban, J. M., Hoofnagle, C. J., & Li, S. (2012). *Mobile phones and privacy* (BCLT Research Paper Series). Berkeley, CA: University of California at Berkeley - Center for the Study of Law and Society. Retrieved from http://papers.ssrn.com/sol3/papers.cfm?abstract_id=2103405.

Vitak, J., Shilton, K., & Ashktorab, Z. (2016). Beyond the Belmont principles: Ethical challenges, practices, and beliefs in the online data research community. In *Proceedings of the 19th ACM Conference on Computer Supported Cooperative Work and Social Computing (CSCW 2016)*. San Francisco, CA: ACM.

Volz, D. (2016, May 31). U.S. court says no warrant needed for cellphone location data. *Reuters*. Retrieved from http://www.reuters.com/article/us-usa-court-mobilephones-idUSKCN0YM2CZ

Westin, A. F. (1970). *Privacy and freedom*. New York: Atheneum.

Xu, H., Zhang, C., Shi, P., & Song, P. (2009). Exploring the role of overt vs. covert personalization strategy in privacy calculus. *Academy of Management Proceedings*, 2009(1), 1–6. http://doi.org/10.5465/AMBPP.2009.44249857.

Zang, J., Dummit, K., Graves, J., Lisker, P., & Sweeney, L. (2015). Who knows what about me? A survey of behind the scenes personal data sharing to third parties by mobile apps. *Journal of Technology Science*, 30. Retrieved from http://jots.pub/a/2015103001/.

Zimmer, M. (2010). "But the data is already public": On the ethics of research in Facebook. *Ethics and Information Technology*, 12(4), 313–325.

6

Face Recognition, Real-Time Identification, and Beyond

*Yana Welinder and Aeryn Palmer**

INTRODUCTION

In China, you can access your bank account with your face.[1] A Russian app allows users to take a photo of a crowd and match people with their social media accounts.[2] And countries all over the world are adding face recognition software to the complement of tools used to identify travelers at the borders.[3]

Technology companies are racing to outpace each other and discover new, innovative ways of using face recognition technology. In the quest to discover what *can* be done, questions about what *should* be done may be left behind. Privacy and security concerns related to the massive scope of data collection and sharing are pushed aside, or addressed haphazardly with little consideration. Consumers may not understand the implications of using this technology, while regulators struggle to keep up.

Regulators and developers can both take steps to ensure that consumers understand the technology and make informed choices about its use. Companies can design intuitive data practices, minimize data collection and retention, and carefully protect biometric data from being misused. They are in the best position to ensure good privacy practices given that they know what data they collect and how they use it. They also have a business incentive to create solutions that build user trust and preempt impulsive overbroad government regulations that tend to be issued in response to abusive practices. Regulators, on their end, can mandate meaningful consent and focus on

* We would like to thank Anisha Mangalick, Gaëtan Goldberg, James Buatti, Jane Pardini, Jennifer Grace, and Tiffany Li for their excellent research assistance.

[1] Zhang Yuzhe, *Banks Face Obstacles to Using Biometric Data for ID Purposes*, CaixinOnline (May 25, 2015), http://english.caixin.com/2015–05–25/100812437.html; *see also Chinese regulators put brakes on facial-recognition for payment*, PYMNTS.com (May 26, 2015), http://www.pymnts.com/news/2015/chinese-regulators-put-brakes-on-face-recognition-for-payment/.

[2] Shawn Walker, *Face Recognition App Taking Russia by Storm May Bring End to Public Anonymity*, The Guardian (May 17, 2016), https://www.theguardian.com/technology/2016/may/17/findface-face-recognition-app-end-public-anonymity-vkontakte.

[3] *See, e.g.*, Jim Bronskill, *Candid Facial-Recognition Cameras to Watch for Terrorists at Border*, Toronto Metro (Jan. 8, 2016), http://www.metronews.ca/news/canada/2016/01/08/candid-facial-recognition-cameras-to-watch-for-terrorists-at-border.html (citing The Canadian Press); Peter B. Counter, *FaceFirst Expands Border Control Deployment in Panama*, FindBiometrics (Sept. 18, 2014), http://findbiometrics.com/facefirst-expands-border-control-deployment-in-panama/; Melinda Ham, *Face Recognition Technology*, University of Technology Sydney Faculty of Law (Nov. 17, 2015), https://www.uts.edu.au/about/faculty-law/news/face-recognition-technology; Stephen Mayhew, *Istanbul Atatürk Airport Deploys Biometric Border Control Gates*, BiometricUpdate.com (Jan. 26, 2015), http://www.biometricupdate.com/201501/istanbul-ataturk-airport-deploys-biometric-border-control-gates.

technology-neutral regulations that prevent harmful practices regardless of what technology they employ, and don't slow down innovation in specific classes of technology, such as computer vision.

This chapter will describe technological advances in the world of face recognition and biometric data collection, before laying out some recent regulatory efforts to control the technology's use. Finally, we will make a series of policy recommendations to regulators and technology companies, which could create a safer environment for consumers.

HOW FACE RECOGNITION TECHNOLOGY WORKS

Computer scientists have spent countless brain cycles to get computers to recognize faces. The main appeal of face recognition technology is convenience. You don't have to interact with a person to identify her by asking for her name or fingerprint.[4] More importantly, face recognition is how we humans tend to recognize each other.[5] So this research problem is a piece of the puzzle to get computers to simulate or preferably excel at human vision on the path towards artificial intelligence.

The Process of Face Recognition Technology

Most automatic face recognition methods involve a general step-by-step process, analyzing photos of already identified individuals to measure their facial features.[6] The measurements are "biometric data" that is compiled into a biometric database.[7] Face recognition technology refers to this database to be able to recognize the listed individuals in new photos.[8] It allows a user of the technology to recognize the listed individuals without actually knowing them. The user only needs to capture a photo of an individual and apply the technology.[9] The technology detects a face in the new photo and matches it against the database.[10] Traditionally, the technology would transform the size, position, illumination, and color-scale of the detected face to compare its measurements to biometric data gathered under other conditions.[11]

Over the last few years, the process of automatic face recognition has changed significantly with the use of neural networks. A neural network is a machine learning method that can be used to find an optimal function to solve a task from a large amount of inputs.[12] It is particularly helpful for complex tasks that require such extensive data analysis that a human would struggle to find the optimal function for the task.

As applied to face recognition, neural network models "learn" to recognize individuals based on large data sets of images. One such face recognition process trains the neural network on three images at a time, where two of the images are known to show the same person and the third shows a different person.[13] The network is instructed to extract vectors of biometric data

---

[4] *See* Tanzeem Choudhury, *History of Face Recognition*, MIT MEDIA LAB (Jan. 21, 2000), http://vismod.media.mit.edu/tech-reports/TR-516/node7.html.

[5] *Id.*

[6] *See* HANDBOOK OF FACE RECOGNITION 2–3 (Stan Z. Li & Anil K. Jain eds., 1st ed. 2005).

[7] *Id.*

[8] *Id.*

[9] Article 29 Data Protection Working Party, *Working Party 29 Opinion on Face Recognition in Online and Mobile Service*, 2012 00727/12 (WP 192) (EN), 2012 O.J. (L 727) 2 (EN) [hereinafter WP29 Opinion], http://ec.europa.eu/justice/data-protection/article-29/documentation/opinion-recommendation/files/2012/wp192_en.pdf.

[10] *See* HANDBOOK OF FACE RECOGNITION, *supra* note 7, at 2–3.

[11] *See id.*

[12] *Artificial Neural Network*, WIKIPEDIA, https://en.wikipedia.org/wiki/Artificial_neural_network.

[13] Florian Schroff et al., *FaceNet: A Unified Embedding for Face Recognition and Clustering*, COMPUTER VISION FOUNDATION, http://www.cv-foundation.org/openaccess/content_cvpr_2015/papers/Schroff_FaceNet_A_Unified_2015_CVPR_paper.pdf (2015).

from each image in a way that would allow it to distinguish the two images of the same person from the third image. It does this by extracting data such that the combined score of vectors for two images will be closer if they show the same person than if they show different people. This process is then repeated for millions or billions of images until the network establishes an optimized process for analyzing faces for similarity and can be applied to images of previously unidentified individuals. While certain parameters and the general architecture of the neural network are predetermined by the developer of the network, the network decides how to analyze each image to create the optimal score for determining similarity. Researchers have been able to peek under the hood of neural networks to see that a neural network usually starts with determining the edges of a face in an image in different orientations.[14] But most of the analysis that a network does to an image to recognize faces is still a black box and there is some research effort into trying to understand this complex analysis.[15]

The application of neural networks to the face recognition process has significantly improved the accuracy of automatic face recognition. It is now fair to say that networks that rely on huge datasets of images approach human capability in recognizing faces.[16] When trained on a massive data set of 4 million photos of 4,000 individuals, this process can identify faces with 97.35 percent accuracy on a popular face recognition dataset.[17]

Consumer Applications of Face Recognition Technology

As face recognition technology has improved over the years, it has started being used in various consumer applications.[18] At the most basic level, many digital cameras rely on parts of the face recognition process to focus the lens on a face.[19] Photo management apps have used face recognition to help users organize their photos.[20] Social networks such as Facebook and Google+ have integrated face recognition technology features to allow users to automatically identify their friends in photos that they upload and link to their friends' online profiles.[21]

---

[14] *See* Matthew Zeiler & Rob Fergus, *Visualizing and Understanding Convolutional Networks, in* Lecture Notes in Computer Science 8689, 818 (Springer International Publishing, 2014), https://scholar.google.com/citations?view_op=view_citation&hl=en&user=a2KklUoAAAAJ&citation_for_view=a2KklUoAAAAJ:YsMSGLbcyi4C; Hakka Labs, *Visualizing and Understanding Deep Neural Networks by Matt Zeiler,* YouTube (Feb. 2, 2015), https://www.youtube.com/watch?v=ghEmQSxT6tw.

[15] *See id.*

[16] Yanav Taigman et al., *DeepFace: Closing the Gap to Human-Level Performance in Face Verification,* Research at Facebook (June 24, 2014), https://research.facebook.com/publications/deepface-closing-the-gap-to-human-level-performance-in-face-verification/.

[17] *Id.*

[18] *See, e.g.,* Alessandro Acquisti et al., *Faces of Facebook: Privacy in the Age of Augmented Reality,* Black Hat Webcast 1 (Jan. 9, 2012), http://www.blackhat.com/docs/webcast/acquisti-face-BH-Webinar-2012-out.pdf; Larry Magid, *Google+ Adds Find My Face Feature,* Forbes (Dec. 8, 2011, 1:59 PM), http://www.forbes.com/sites/larrymagid/2011/12/08/google-adds-find-my-face-feature/. *See also* Douglas Gantenbein, *Helping Kinect Recognize Faces,* Microsoft Research (Oct. 31, 2011), http://research.microsoft.com/en-us/news/features/kinectfacereco-103111.aspx.

[19] *See, e.g., Face Detection,* Sony Cyber-shot User Guide, http://docs.esupport.sony.com/dvimag/DSCH70_guide/eng/contents/05/02/15/15.html; *DCRP Review: Canon PowerShot S5 IS,* Digital Camera Resource Page, http://www.dcresource.com/reviews/canon/powershot_s5-review/.

[20] *See, e.g.,* Russell Brandom, *Apple's New Facial Recognition Feature Could Spur Legal Issues,* The Verge (June 16, 2016, 8:11 AM), http://www.theverge.com/2016/6/16/11934456/apple-google-facial-recognition-photos-privacy-faceprint (addressing Apple's announcement of a new facial recognition system cataloging pictures according to faces and Google Photos' ability to auto-tag photos); Tom Simonite, *Apple Rolls Out Privacy-Sensitive Artificial Intelligence,* MIT Technology Review (June 13, 2016), https://www.technologyreview.com/s/601688/apple-rolls-out-privacy-sensitive-artificial-intelligence/.

[21] *See* Larry Magid, *supra* note 18.

Some apps and devices have used face recognition instead of passwords to allow users to quickly unlock and access their services.[22] Gaming devices use face recognition to keep track of different players so that friends can challenge each other in sports in their living rooms rather than just exercising their thumbs with the more traditional forms of video games.[23] So the applications of the technology are many and diverse and there is continuous innovation in this field.

The availability of ubiquitous camera phones with fast Internet connection have enabled mobile applications also to take advantage of face recognition technology. This means a phone user could take a photo of someone they see and instantly read information about that individual on the phone. A number of mobile apps have tapped into Facebook's massive photo database to allow users to do just that. One example is KLIK, an iPhone app offered by a company called Face.com in 2012.[24] KLIK was short-lived. It was acquired by Facebook, which promptly pulled the plug on the app after it turned out to have security vulnerabilities.[25] There was a similar app called Viewdle SocialCamera for Android users.[26] These and other apps allowed users to upload photos to social networks and link them to the user profiles of the individuals identified in the photos. Photos taken with a mobile phone often include metadata about where and when the photo was taken.[27] So uploading the images to social networks allowed social networks to track the location of the user, who presumably was there to take the photo, as well as the individuals identified in the photo. The location may also have been available to other social network users, depending on whether the social network in question made metadata publicly available. And even without metadata, the location can sometimes be obvious from landmarks in the background, potentially exposing more information than the uploader or people identified in the photo would anticipate.[28]

EMERGING REGULATORY RESPONSES TO FACE RECOGNITION TECHNOLOGY

Governments around the world are reacting to the new prevalence of face recognition technology. Some have created fairly specific rules for handling face recognition data. Others are

---

[22] *See e.g.*, John P. Pullen, *How Windows 10 Could Kill Passwords Forever*, Time (Nov. 30, 2015), http://time.com/4128834/windows-10-hello-facial-recognition/ (describing a Microsoft Windows 10 feature called "Hello," which allows device login using facial recognition).

[23] Douglas Gantenbein, *Helping Kinect Recognize Faces*, Microsoft Research (Oct. 31, 2011, 9:30 AM), http://web.archive.org/web/20160428231310/http://research.microsoft.com/en-us/news/features/kinectfacereco-103111.aspx.

[24] *See* David Goldman, *Real-Time Face Recognition Comes to Your iPhone Camera*, CNN Money (Mar. 12, 2012), http://money.cnn.com/2012/03/12/technology/iPhone-face-recognition/index.htm.

[25] *See* Ashkan Soltani, *Facepalm*, AshkanSoltani (June 18, 2012), http://ashkansoltani.org/2012/06/18/facepalm/ ("Face.com essentially allowed *anyone* to hijack a KLIK user's Facebook and Twitter accounts to get access to photos and social graph (which enables 'face prints'), even if that information isn't public." (Emphasis in the original.)); Steven Musil, *Facebook Shuts Down Face.com APIs, Klik App*, CNET News (July 8, 2012, 11:00 AM), http://news.cnet.com/8301-1023_3-57468247-93/facebook-shuts-down-face.com-apis-klik-app/.

[26] *See, e.g.*, Emily Steel, *A Face Launches 1,000 Apps*, Wall St. J. (Aug. 5, 2011), http://online.wsj.com/article/SB10001424053111903885604576488273434534638.html?mod=WSJ_Tech_LEFTTopNews; *Viewdle*, CrunchBase, http://www.crunchbase.com/company/viewdle.

[27] *See, e.g.*, *Facebook Data Use Policy: Information We Receive and How It Is Used*, Facebook, https://www.facebook.com/about/privacy/your-info#inforeceived (Facebook may get this information as a geotag uploaded with the photo, containing its exact latitude and longitude). *See also* Kate Murphy, *Web Photos That Reveal Secrets, Like Where You Live*, N.Y. Times, Aug. 12, 2010, at B6.

[28] *See Vice.com Publishes Exclusive with John McAfee Reveals Location in iPhone Metadata (EXIF)*, Mobile Privacy (Dec. 3, 2012), http://www.mobileprivacy.org/2012/12/vice-com-publishes-exclusive-with-john-mcafee-reveals-location-in-iphone-metadata-exif/; *see also* Hanni Fakhoury, *A Picture Is Worth a Thousand Words, Including Your Location*, Electronic Frontier Foundation (Apr. 20, 2012), https://www.eff.org/deeplinks/2012/04/picture-worth-thousand-words-including-your-location.

already using the technology to their own ends, but have yet to create laws controlling its use. In this section, we will detail some recent developments in legal responses to face recognition. Divided by region, the survey is a sample of current laws and practices, and does not cover the entire globe.

United States

In the United States, both state and federal laws regulate face recognition technology.[29] Chief among them are Section 5 of the Federal Trade Commission Act (FTC Act) and the Children's Online Privacy Protection Act (COPPA). Section 5 of the FTC Act protects consumers from "unfair or deceptive acts or practices in or affecting commerce."[30] In practice, this requirement means that technology companies must provide consumers with adequate notice and choice about practices that may affect their privacy. COPPA requires that websites targeting or knowingly collecting information from children must ensure that they have parental consent.[31] Neither law addresses face recognition specifically, although the FTC has released best practices regarding face recognition data that emphasize the importance of choice, transparency, and building in privacy at every stage of product development, a practice known as "Privacy by Design."[32]

Without comprehensive federal laws addressing the unique nature of biometric information, some states have passed their own laws, which consumers or state attorney generals may enforce.[33] Here, we will mostly focus on recent consumer litigation. Many of the recent cases were brought under the Illinois Biometric Information Privacy Act (BIPA), which provides rules for the collection, storage, and handling of biometric data. Consumers may sue for violations of the law, such as if their information is stored or used improperly, or disclosed without author-ization.[34] For example, in *Licata v. Facebook, Inc.*, the plaintiffs claimed that Facebook's face recognition feature, which helps users "tag" people in photos, violates the BIPA.[35] Facebook's motion to dismiss failed; they argued that digital photographs were not "face geometry" under the BIPA, but the court disagreed.[36]

This outcome mirrors the ruling on Shutterfly's motion to dismiss a similar case, *Norberg v. Shutterfly, Inc.*, the first to address such a claim.[37] There, the court held that online photos contain face geometry information, and found that the plaintiff's arguments could have merit:

---

[29] For a summary of these laws through 2013, see Yana Welinder, *A Face Tells More than a Thousand Posts: Developing Face Recognition Privacy in Social Networks*, 26 Harvard J. L. & T. 165 (2012); Yana Welinder, *Facing Real-Time Identification in Mobile Apps & Wearable Computers*, 30 Santa Clara High Tech. L.J. 89 (2014).

[30] 15 U.S.C. § 45(a)(1) (2006).

[31] 15 U.S.C. § 6502.

[32] *Facing Facts: Best Practices for Common Uses of Facial Recognition Technologies*, Fed. Trade Comm'n, https://www.ftc.gov/sites/default/files/documents/reports/facing-facts-best-practices-common-uses-facial-recognition-technologies/121022facialtechrpt.pdf.

[33] *See, e.g.*, TEX. BUS. & COM. CODE ANN. § 503.001(a) (2009); 740 Ill. Comp. Stat. 14 (2008).

[34] 740 Ill. Comp. Stat. 14.

[35] Venkat Balasubramani, *Facebook Gets Bad Ruling in Face-Scanning Privacy Case – In Re Facebook Biometric Information Privacy Litigation*, Tech. & Mktg. Law Blog (May 6, 2016), http://blog.ericgoldman.org/archives/2016/05/facebook-gets-bad-ruling-in-face-scanning-privacy-case-in-re-facebook-biometric-information-privacy-litigation.htm.

[36] *Id.*; *In re Facebook Biometric Information Privacy Litigation*, 2016 WL 2593853 (N.D. Cal. May 5, 2016).

[37] Venkat Balasubramani, *Shutterfly Can't Shake Face-Scanning Privacy Lawsuit*, Tech. & Mktg. Law Blog (Jan. 11, 2016), http://blog.ericgoldman.org/archives/2016/01/shutterfly-cant-shake-face-scanning-privacy-lawsuit.htm.

Plaintiff alleges that Defendants are using his personal face pattern to recognize and identify Plaintiff in photographs posted to Websites. Plaintiff avers that he is not now nor has he ever been a user of Websites, and that he was not presented with a written biometrics policy nor has he consented to have his biometric identifiers used by Defendants. As a result, the Court finds that Plaintiff has plausibly stated a claim for relief under the BIPA.[38]

Tech companies have unsuccessfully lobbied to amend BIPA;[39] without changes, the lawsuits continue. Facebook is now trying a new argument to defeat the claims in *Licata*. It is using the Supreme Court's *Spokeo v. Robins*[40] ruling to argue that any injury from scanning photographs is too speculative to warrant damages.[41] Another class action suit was filed in July 2016, this time against Snapchat. The plaintiff alleges that Snapchat's "Lenses" feature – which adds humorous animations to a person's image – is based upon scanning their face and retaining their biometric identifiers, in violation of BIPA.[42] Uses of face recognition technology will almost certainly continue to multiply, and it is likely that consumer lawsuits will do the same.

In June 2016, the US Department of Commerce National Telecommunications and Information Administration (NTIA) released best practices for commercial use of face recognition technology.[43] Among other considerations, the guide suggests that companies collecting, processing, or storing face recognition data prioritize good data management and security practices, and be transparent with consumers about the data's handling and use.[44] Perhaps if consumers were provided with better notice, some BIPA litigation could be prevented.

The NTIA guidelines do not apply to government entities. A recent report from the US Government Accountability Office begins to fill that gap, in addressing FBI use of automatic face recognition.[45] The FBI has a database of roughly 30 million photos, mostly from state, local, and other law enforcement agencies, to which face recognition analysis is applied in the course of criminal investigations.[46] The report found several ways in which oversight and transparency could be improved. It noted, for example, that required Privacy Impact Assessments were not carried out in a timely manner,[47] oversight audits of some systems had not been completed,[48] and the accuracy of some external analysis systems had not been assessed.[49]

---

[38] *Norberg v. Shutterfly, Inc.*, No. 15-CV-5351 (N.D. Ill. 2015). *See also* Venkat Balasubramani, *Shutterfly Can't Shake Face-Scanning Privacy Lawsuit*, TECH. & MKTG. LAW BLOG (Jan. 11, 2016), http://blog.ericgoldman.org/archives/2016/01/shutterfly-cant-shake-face-scanning-privacy-lawsuit.htm.

[39] *Id.*

[40] *Spokeo, Inc. v. Robins*, 578 U.S. ___ (2016)., https://www.supremecourt.gov/opinions/15pdf/13-1339_f2q3.pdf

[41] John J. Roberts, *Facebook and Google Really Want to Kill This Face-Scanning Law*, FORTUNE (10:17 AM EDT), http://fortune.com/2016/06/30/facebook-google-face-recognition-lawsuits/.

[42] Cyrus Farivar, *Does Snapchat's Lenses Feature Violate Illinois' Biometrics Law?*, ARS TECHNICA (July 17, 2016), http://arstechnica.com/tech-policy/2016/07/does-snapchats-lenses-feature-violate-illinois-biometrics-law/; *Martinez v. Snapchat, Inc.*, No. 2:16-CV-05182 (Cal. Super. Ct. 2016), https://www.documentcloud.org/documents/2993790-03112389o956.html.

[43] Hunton & Williams, *NTIA Releases Facial Recognition Technology Best Practices*, PRIVACY & INFORMATION SECURITY LAW BLOG (June 22, 2016), https://www.huntonprivacyblog.com/2016/06/22/ntia-releases-face-recognition-technology-best-practices/.

[44] National Telecommunications and Information Administration, *Privacy Best Practice Recommendations For Commercial Facial Recognition Use*, PRIVACY & INFORMATION SECURITY LAW BLOG (June 15, 2016), https://www.huntonprivacyblog.com/wp-content/uploads/sites/18/2016/06/privacy_best_practices_recommendations_for_commercial_use_of_facial_recogntion.pdf.

[45] U.S. Gov't Accountability Office, GAO-16–267, *Face Recognition Technology: FBI Should Better Ensure Privacy and Accuracy* (May 2016), UNITED STATES GOVERNMENT ACCOUNTABILITY OFFICE *available at* http://www.gao.gov/assets/680/677098.pdf.

[46] *Id.* at 10.

[47] *Id.* at 18.

[48] *Id.* at 23.

[49] *Id.* at 30.

Whether these recent publications will affect general practice in either corporate or government use of face recognition technology remains to be seen. For the moment, it is clear that efforts to respond to the technology in the United States are coming both from government agencies and also from consumers themselves. Those who use and develop the technology face a somewhat uncertain regulatory future.

Europe

In Europe, data collection and processing are governed by a framework of national laws that implement the European Union (EU) Data Protection Directive.[50] Article 29 of the directive establishes a working party to opine on how the directive should be applied to specific data practices.[51] In a 2012 opinion, the Article 29 working party provided guidance on the development of technologies that process biometric data.[52] The opinion provided specific requirements for companies to bear in mind.[53] These included a proportionality requirement and an accuracy requirement, which stressed the importance of preventing identity fraud.[54] Additionally, companies were encouraged to retain biometric data no longer than necessary.[55]

The opinion specifically singled out tagging software on social networks as a source of concern:

> Photographs on the internet, in social media, in online photo management or sharing applications may not be further processed in order to extract biometric templates or enrol them into a biometric system to recognise the persons on the pictures automatically (face recognition) without a specific legal basis (e.g. consent) for this new purpose. ... [If a data subject consents to being tagged] biometric data not needed anymore after the tagging of the images with the name, nickname or any other text specified by the data subject must be deleted. The creation of a permanent biometric database is a priori not necessary for this purpose.[56]

EU regulators have been cautious about the use of face recognition software for social media purposes – Facebook's "Moments" app was stripped of its automatic face scanning capabilities in its EU release. Users may identify friends one by one, and the app looks for other images with similarities, but does not compile a database of biometric information.[57]

The future of regulating biometric data in the EU depends upon the incoming General Data Protection Regulation (GDPR), which will supersede the Data Protection Directive. The GDPR has established baseline considerations for the processing of biometric information, defining it broadly to include face recognition data: "'biometric data' means personal data resulting from specific technical processing relating to the physical, physiological or behavioural

---

[50] Directive 95/46/EC of the European Parliament and of the Council of 24 October 1995 on the Protection of Individuals with Regard to the Processing of Personal Data and on the Free Movement of Such Data, Recital 3, 1995 O.J. (L 281) 31 (EC), http://eur-lex.europa.eu/LexUriServ/LexUriServ.do?uri=OJ:L:1995:281:0031:0050:EN:PDF. It should be noted that this directive is now superseded by Regulation (EU) 2016/679 of the European Parliament and of the Council of 27 April 2016 on the protection of natural persons with regard to the processing of personal data and on the free movement of such data.

[51] *Id.* at art. 29.

[52] Article 29 Data Protection Working Party, *Opinion on "Developments in Biometric Technologies,"* 2012 00720/12 (WP 193) (EN) 2012 O.J. (L 720) 17 (EN), http://ec.europa.eu/justice/data-protection/article-29/documentation/opin ion-recommendation/files/2012/wp193_en.pdf.

[53] *Id.*

[54] *Id.*

[55] *Id.*

[56] *Id.* at 7.

[57] Russell Brandom, *Facebook Strips Out Facial Recognition for the European Version of Moments,* THE VERGE (May 10, 2016, 5:38 PM), http://www.theverge.com/2016/5/10/11652940/facebook-moments-face-recognition-europe-canada-eu.

characteristics of a natural person, which allow or confirm the unique identification of that natural person, such as face images or dactyloscopic data."[58]

Biometric information processed "in order to uniquely identify a person" is considered sensitive data that requires particular protection.[59] Processing of sensitive information is only allowed under certain exceptions, for example if the data subject has given explicit consent,[60] or if the processing is necessary to uphold a "substantial public interest."[61] The GDPR makes it clear that these caveats are only a floor; each country may create further limitations.[62]

The current Data Protection Directive does not include biometric information among the categories of sensitive data. However, data protection authorities have already treated biometric data as a special case. For example, the Irish Data Protection Commissioner has strongly suggested that systems collecting biometric data in the workplace should undergo a privacy impact assessment.[63] The GDPR recommends similar assessments in its recitals.[64]

Outside of the EU, regulators in other European countries also think about how to address face recognition technology. In Turkey, a draft law that would regulate the protection of personal data has not yet been implemented.[65] Turkish law generally defines personal information as "any information relating to an identified or identifiable individual," using the definition in Article 2(a) of the Strasbourg Convention for the Protection of Individuals with Regard to Automatic Processing of Personal Data 1981.[66] Until the draft law comes into force, a patchwork of constitutional provisions, civil, and criminal laws may impact the collection and use of biometric and face recognition data in Turkey – which is already in use there. In 2015, biometric gate controls were added to Istanbul's Atatürk airport, with plans to expand the system from fingerprints to face recognition data.[67] The same year, Vodafone Turkey aimed to allow users to login to a payment app via eyeprint.[68]

In contrast to Turkey, some European countries seek to regulate biometric data with more specificity. For example, Azerbaijan has a specific law relating to biometric information, which includes "fingerprints of hands and palms, the image of the person, the retina, fragments of the voice and its acoustic parameters, analysis results of deoxyribonucleic acid (DNA), the sizes of the body, the description of special signs and shortcomings of the body, handwriting, the signature etc."[69] Similarly, Serbia's draft law on personal data protection defines biometric data

---

[58] Regulation (EU) 2016/679 of the European Parliament and of the Council on the Protection of Natural Persons with Regard to the Processing of Personal Data and on the Free Movement of Such Data, and Repealing Directive 95/46/EC, art. 4(14), (Apr. 27, 2016), http://eur-lex.europa.eu/legal-content/EN/TXT/HTML/?uri=CELEX:32016R0679& from=en [hereinafter "General Data Protection Regulation" or "GDPR"].

[59] *Id.* at art. 9(1).

[60] *Id.* at art. 9(2)(a).

[61] *Id.* at art. 9(2)(g).

[62] *Id.* at art. 9(4).

[63] The Office of the Data Protection Commissioner in Ireland, *Biometrics in the Workplace*, DATA PROTECTION COMMISSIONER IN IRELAND https://www.dataprotectionie/docs/Biometrics-in-the-workplace-/244.htm.

[64] GDPR Recital 91.

[65] Hakki Can Yildiz & Can Sözer, *Data Protection in Turkey: Overview*, PRACTICAL LAW (Nov. 1, 2015), http://uk .practicallaw.com/7-520-1896#a490337.

[66] *Id.* at § 3; *See also* Council of Europe, *Convention for the Protection of Individuals with Regard to Automatic Processing of Personal Data* ("Strasbourg convention"), European Treaty Series – No. 108 (Jan. 28, 1981), https:// www.coe.int/en/web/conventions/full-list/-/conventions/rms/0900001680078b37.

[67] Stephen Mayhew, *Istanbul Atatürk Airport Deploys Biometric Border Control Gates*, BIOMETRICUPDATE.COM (Jan. 26, 2015), http://www.biometricupdate.com/201501/istanbul-ataturk-airport-deploys-biometric-border-control-gates.

[68] Justin Lee, *Olcsan to Resell and Distribute EyeVerify Eye Recognition Products in Turkey and Europe*, BIOMETRICUPDATE.COM (June 8, 2015), http://www.biometricupdate.com/201506/olcsan-to-resell-and-distribute-eyever ify-eye-recognition-products-in-turkey-and-europe.

[69] The Law of the Azerbaijan Republic about Biometric Information, 2008, No. 651-IIIG, Article 1.1.2), http://cis-legislation.com/document.fwx?rgn=24349.

as "particularly [including] data relating to appearance, voice, fingerprint, signature, hand geometry, eye pupil and cornea, as well as DNA."[70]

Russia's Personal Data Law, which regulates both government and private businesses, provides a more general definition of biometric data, and does not single out face imagery. It encompasses "information characterizing physiological peculiarities of a human being and on which basis it is possible to establish his identity."[71] This data can only be processed without the data subject's consent under certain conditions, such as upon crossing the border.[72] Additionally, biometric data may only be stored using methods "that ensure protection of these data from unlawful or accidental access to them, destruction, modification, blocking, copying, distribution."[73]

Use of face recognition technology in Russia is expanding. FindFace is a wildly popular Russian app that allows users to discover social media profiles of individuals they photograph in public.[74] Its inventors are in talks with Moscow city officials to install the program on CCTV systems.[75] The software could be used by police to identify suspects by matching surveillance images with court records or even social media photos. The company also plans retail applications, which could allow shops to track individuals and market products to them based upon items in which they show interest online.[76] It remains to be seen how Russian law will handle such developments.

Canada

In Canada, the major federal privacy laws are the Privacy Act[77] and the Personal Information Protection and Electronic Documents Act (PIPEDA);[78] the former applies to the public sector, the latter to the private sector. Neither law specifically mentions face recognition. In 2013, the Research Group of the Office of the Privacy Commissioner of Canada (OPC)[79] issued a report stating that the Privacy Act prohibits face recognition data from being used for purposes beyond or inconsistent with those for which it was initially collected.[80] Further, the report confirms that PIPEDA would likely control any commercial use of face recognition technology.[81]

The report recommends that any party considering the use of face recognition technology should examine factors such as the purposes of the use, consent from data subjects, and reasonable security measures. It proposes a series of useful questions. For example, the OPC

---

[70] Draft Law on Data Protection, art. 3(12), http://www.mpravde.gov.rs/sekcija/53/radne-verzije-propisa.php (providing English and Serbian versions).

[71] Federal Law on Personal Data, 2006, No.152-FZ, art. 11(1), https://iapp.org/media/pdf/knowledge_center/Russian_Federal_Law_on_Personal_Data.pdf.

[72] *Id.* at art. 11(2).

[73] *Id.* at art. 19(4).

[74] Shaun Walker, *Face Recognition App Taking Russia by Storm May Bring End to Public Anonymity*, THE GUARDIAN (May 17, 2016, 4:39 EDT), https://www.theguardian.com/technology/2016/may/17/findface-face-recognition-app-end-public-anonymity-vkontakte.

[75] *Id.*

[76] *Id.*

[77] Canada Privacy Act, R.S.C. 1985, c. P-21, http://laws-lois.justice.gc.ca/eng/acts/P-21/.

[78] Canada Personal Information Protection and Electronic Documents Act, S.C. 2000, c. 5, http://laws-lois.justice.gc.ca/eng/acts/p-8.6/.

[79] *See generally* Office of the Privacy Commissioner of Canada Website, https://www.priv.gc.ca/index_e.asp.

[80] Research Group of the Office of the Privacy Commissioner of Canada, *Automated Facial Recognition in the Public and Private Sectors* (Mar. 2013), § 5(3), https://www.priv.gc.ca/information/research-recherche/2013/fr_201303_e.asp#heading-005-3 (addressing consistent use under facial recognition and the Privacy Act).

[81] *Id.* at § 7, https://www.priv.gc.ca/information/research-recherche/2013/fr_201303_e.asp#heading-007 (discussing face recognition and PIPEDA).

suggests that government agencies determine whether or not the use of the technology justifies the potential intrusion on subjects' privacy:

Is the measure demonstrably necessary to meet a specific need?

Is it likely to be effective in meeting that need?

Would the loss of privacy be proportionate to the benefit gained?

Is there a less privacy-invasive way of achieving the same end?[82]

The report notes that face recognition systems could be added to existing video surveillance, such as at the Canadian border.[83] This prediction seems to be coming true. In 2016, the Canadian Border Services Agency announced that it is testing the use of face recognition technology on travelers at the border.[84]

In addition to federal privacy laws, there are provincial privacy statutes. Some expressly mention face recognition or biometric data, and allow government use in association with an application for an identification card.[85] However, this use may not be unfettered; in Quebec, the collection of biometric information for identification purposes is allowed only with the express consent of the data subject.[86] Further, "only the minimum number of characteristics or measurements needed to link the person to an act and only such characteristics or measurements as may not be recorded without the person's knowledge may be recorded for identification purposes."[87]

In the absence of provincial laws that specifically mention face recognition technology, regulators must still evaluate its use. In 2001, the Ontario Alcohol and Gaming Commission allowed casinos to employ face recognition software to identify known cheats, as long as patrons had notice of the technology's use.[88] More recently, in a 2012 report, the Office of the Information and Privacy Commissioner for British Columbia examined police use of face recognition technology to identify suspects following a hockey riot.[89] The data in question had been collected by the Insurance Corporation of British Columbia (ICBC).[90] The report made several recommendations, including that ICBC cease using its database to identify individuals in images sent to them by police in the absence of a warrant or other order.[91] The report also encouraged ICBC to conduct a Privacy Impact Assessment and make structural changes that would establish better accountability and consideration of data subjects' privacy.[92]

---

[82] *Id.* at § 5(c), https://www.priv.gc.ca/information/research-recherche/2013/fr_201303_e.asp#heading-005-2.

[83] *Id.* at § 5, https://www.priv.gc.ca/information/research-recherche/2013/fr_201303_e.asp#heading-005.

[84] Jim Bronskill, *Candid Facial-Recognition Cameras to Watch for Terrorists at Border*, TORONTO METRO (Jan. 8, 2016), http://www.metronews.ca/news/canada/2016/01/08/candid-facial-recognition-cameras-to-watch-for-terrorists-at-border.html (citing The Canadian Press).

[85] *See, e.g.*, Identification Card Regulation, Alberta Reg. 221/2003 (Can.), § 7.3, https://www.canlii.org/en/ab/laws/regu/alta-reg-221-2003/latest/alta-reg-221-2003.html; Manitoba, The Drivers and Vehicles Act, CCSM c D104 §§ 149.1 *et seq.*

[86] An Act to Establish a Legal Framework for Information Technology, CQLR c. C-1.1 s. 44, https://www.canlii.org/en/qc/laws/stat/cqlr-c-c-1.1/latest/cqlr-c-c-1.1.html.

[87] *Id.*

[88] Ontario Alcohol and Gaming Commission, Investigation Report, PC-010005–1/2001 (Can.), http://www.canlii.org/en/on/onipc/doc/2001/2001canlii26269/2001canlii26269.html.

[89] *See* Elizabeth Denham, *Investigation Report F12–01: Investigation into the Use of Facial Recognition Technology by the Insurance Corporation of British Columbia*, INFORMATION AND PRIVACY COMMISSIONER (Feb. 16, 2012), https://www.oipc.bc.ca/investigation-reports/1245.

[90] *Id.* at 2.

[91] *Id.* at 35.

[92] *Id.* at 35–6.

Latin America

Face recognition technology has previously been used in Latin America for governmental and law enforcement purposes. For example, in 2000, the Mexican government used face recognition information to prevent voter fraud.[93] More recent activity in the country has involved the creation of systems to make analysis of biometric information easier and more efficient.[94]

With use has come an interest in laws to regulate such technology. Peru's personal data protection law, passed in 2010, includes in its definition of sensitive data biometric information that can be used to identify an individual.[95] Colombia's data protection law also classes biometric data as sensitive information.[96] Use of face recognition technology may be outpacing the passage of laws to regulate it. Colombian buses are fitted with a system designed by FaceFirst that can identify bus passengers whom the police may be seeking.[97] FaceFirst has also established a system at at Panama's Tocumen International Airport, which picks out passengers who are wanted in the country, or by Interpol.[98] In 2015, it was announced that Brazilian airports would see a similar project to improve security and create a more efficient immigration experience for travelers.[99] Brazil also provided officers with face recognition goggles at the 2014 World Cup.[100] Rio de Janeiro, host of the 2016 Summer Olympics, refused to be outdone; they contracted with a Chinese company that had supplied the 2014 World Cup with face recognition technology for security purposes.[101]

Law enforcement agencies are not the only parties using face recognition data in Latin America. Consumers are gaining access to it in their daily life. For example, in Costa Rica, Ecuador, and Peru, bank customers can authenticate their identity using their image.[102] FacePhi Biometría, a Spanish firm that has sold such technology to several banks in the region, describes

---

[93] *Mexican Government Adopts FaceIt Face Recognition Technology to Eliminate Duplicate Voter Registrations in Upcoming Presidential Election*, THE FREE LIBRARY (May 11, 2000), http://www.thefreelibrary.com/Mexican+Government+Adopts+FaceIt+Face+Recognition+Technology+to...-a062019954 (citing Business Wire).

[94] *See, e.g.*, Ryan Kline, *New Facial Recognition System in Mexico to Help Law Enforcement*, SECUREIDNEWS (July 23, 2007), http://www.secureidnews.com/news-item/new-face-recognition-system-in-mexico-to-help-law-enforcement/; Katitza Rodriguez, *Biometrics in Argentina: Mass Surveillance as a State Policy*, ELECTRONIC FRONTIER FOUNDATION (Jan. 10, 2012), https://www.eff.org/deeplinks/2012/01/biometrics-argentina-mass-surveillance-state-policy.

[95] *See* DLA Piper, *Data Protection Laws of the World: Peru*, in GLOBAL DATA PROTECTION HANDBOOK, https://www.dlapiperdataprotection.com/index.html#handbook/definitions-section/c1_PE, (accessed Sept. 5, 2015); *see also Peru Adopts New Data Protection Law*, IT LAW GROUP, http://www.dataguidance.com/uploads/Peru_Data_Protection_Law.pdf (last accessed Sept. 12, 2016).

[96] L. 1377/2013, art. 3, June 27, 2013, MINISTRY OF TRADE, INDUSTRY AND TOURISM (Colom.), https://iapp.org/media/pdf/knowledge_center/DECRETO_1377_DEL_27_DE_JUNIO_DE_2013_ENG.pdf (last accessed Sept. 12, 2016).

[97] Peter B. Counter, *FaceFirst Biometrics Deployed in Colombia*, FINDBIOMETRICS (Mar. 19, 2015), http://findbiometrics.com/facefirst-biometrics-deployed-in-colombia-23196/.

[98] Peter B. Counter, *FaceFirst Expands Border Control Deployment in Panama*, FINDBIOMETRICS (Sept. 18, 2014), http://findbiometrics.com/facefirst-expands-border-control-deployment-in-panama/.

[99] Justin Lee, *NEC to Provide Facial Recognition Technology for 14 Brazilian Airports*, BIOMETRICUPDATE (July 16, 2015), http://www.biometricupdate.com/201507/nec-to-provide-face-recognition-technology-for-14-brazilian-airports.

[100] Ariel Bogel, *Drones Are Keeping Their Eyes on the Ball, Too*, SLATE (June 13, 2014), http://www.slate.com/articles/technology/future_tense/2014/06/world_cup_security_brazil_has_spent_insane_amounts_on_surveillance_technology.html; *see also* Robin Yapp, *Brazilian Police to Use "Robocop-Style" Glasses at World Cup*, THE TELEGRAPH (Apr. 12, 2011), http://www.telegraph.co.uk/news/worldnews/southamerica/brazil/8446088/Brazilian-police-to-use-Robocop-style-glasses-at-World-Cup.html.

[101] Wuang Sujuan & Sun Muyao, *Made-in-China Security Equipment Safeguards Rio Olympics*, CHINA DAILY (May 10, 2016), http://www.chinadaily.com.cn/beijing/2016-05/10/content_25212912.htm.

[102] Tanya Andreasyan, *Banco Nacional of Costa Rica Implements FacePhi's Facial Recognition Technology*, IBS INTELLIGENCE (Jan. 13, 2016), https://ibsintelligence.com/ibs-journal/ibs-news/banco-nacional-of-costa-rica-implements-facephis-face-recognition-technology/.

the use as account access via selfie.[103] As consumer applications continue to crop up, we can expect more consumer biometric regulation in the region.

Asia and Oceania

In China, too, consumers may now use face recognition to access their bank accounts.[104] With such innovations serving as a backdrop, Asian countries have made strides towards covering face recognition data in their personal data protection laws in the past few years. Japan, China, and Hong Kong have amended existing laws, passed new ones, and issued agency guidance that may address the use of face recognition data.

China's draft cybersecurity law includes a reference to "personal biometric information," which it fails to define.[105] Generally, the term has been understood to refer to genetic information and fingerprints.[106] Whether or not the draft law is intended to cover face recognition data, its regulation is already taking place. Face recognition is becoming a more popular method of identification in China – as mentioned earlier, banks are using it to verify customers' identities. However, regulators have expressed concern over the lack of a technological standard and prevented banks from using face recognition to identify new customers. Existing customers, however, can still use the technology to be identified by their bank for online transactions – or, in the phrasing of Alibaba affiliate Ant Financial Services Group, "smile to pay."[107]

In contrast to China's rather vague draft cybersecurity law, guidance issued by the Hong Kong Office of the Privacy Commissioner for Personal Data has made it clear that face recognition data is under the umbrella of personal information.[108] The guidance urges caution in the gathering of biometric data, and notes that individuals must have a "free and informed choice" in its collection.[109]

In Japan, amendments to the Personal Information Protection Act were suggested in 2014 that would expand the definition of "personal data."[110] Passed in October of the following year, the amendments added biometric data to the definition of Personally Identifiable Information.[111]

---

[103] *Id.*

[104] Zhang Yuzhe, *Banks Face Obstacles to Using Biometric Data for ID Purposes*, CAIXIN ONLINE (May 25, 2015), http://english.caixin.com/2015-05-25/100812437.html; *see also Chinese Regulators Put Brakes on Facial-Recognition for Payment*, PYMNTS (May 26, 2015), http://www.pymnts.com/news/2015/chinese-regulators-put-brakes-on-face-recognition-for-payment/.

[105] *See* Article 72(5); Eric Carlson, Sheng Huang & Ashwin Kaja, *China Releases Draft of New Network Security Law: Implications for Data Privacy & Security*, INSIDE PRIVACY (July 12, 2015), https://www.insideprivacy.com/uncategorized/chinas-releases-draft-of-new-network-security-law-implications-for-data-privacy-security/. The law received a second reading in June 2016, but the updated text does not provide more details. *See* Cybersecurity Law (draft) (second reading draft), CHINA LAW TRANSLATE, http://chinalawtranslate.com/cybersecurity2/?lang=en; *see also Second Reading of China's Draft of Cybersecurity Law*, HUNTON PRIVACY BLOG (June 30, 2016), https://www.huntonprivacyblog.com/2016/06/30/second-reading-of-chinas-draft-of-cybersecurity-law/.

[106] Carlson, Huang & Kaja, *supra* note 98.

[107] Yuzhe, *supra* note 97; *see also* PYMTS, *supra* note 97.

[108] *See* Office of the Privacy Commissioner for Personal Data, Hong Kong, *Guidance on Collection and Use of Biometric Data* (July 2015), https://www.pcpd.org.hk/english/resources_centre/publications/files/GN_biometric_e.pdf (last visited Aug. 29, 2016).

[109] *Id.*

[110] Mark Parsons & Peter Colegate, *2015: The Turning Point for Data Privacy Regulation in Asia?* (Feb. 18, 2015), CHRONICLE OF DATA PROTECTION (Feb. 18, 2015), http://www.hldataprotection.com/2015/02/articles/international-eu-privacy/2015-the-turning-point-for-data-privacy-regulation-in-asia/.

[111] Matthew Durham, *Japan Updates Privacy Law*, WINSTON (Oct. 20, 2015), http://www.winston.com/en/privacy-law-corner/japan-updates-privacy-law.html.

This aspect of the regulation will soon be tested; Japan has made plans to implement face recognition systems at its airports, in advance of hosting the 2020 Summer Olympics.[112]

To the south, Australia and New Zealand have begun using biometric data for national security and immigration purposes. Both countries' customs services use face recognition software at the border.[113] Australian law was amended in 2015 to explicitly allow this use. An explanatory memorandum for the Migration Amendment (Strengthening Biometrics Integrity) Bill defined personal identifiers as unique physical characteristics, such as fingerprints, iris scans, or face images.[114] The bill empowered the government to collect such information at the border, from both citizens and noncitizens.[115] Later in the year, Australia announced that it was creating a National Facial Biometric Matching Capability, which will allow some police and other government agencies to "share and match" photos in existing databases. Minister for Justice Michael Keenan hailed the tool as Australia's "newest national security weapon."[116]

The Middle East and North Africa

In some Middle Eastern countries, where biometric data and its appropriate uses have not yet been clearly defined in the law, face recognition is nevertheless part of the technological landscape.

In Egypt, no specific law explicitly regulates the use of face recognition technology. It may instead be covered by a patchwork of other laws.[117] A 2014 Privacy International report notes that "[t]he absence of definitions as to what consists personal data and sensitive personal data, [and] the lack of an independent national authority responsible for data protection in Egypt … raise significant concerns in view of the extensive access given to authorities of users' personal data."[118]

Egyptian authorities are already using biometric data to serve important governmental functions, such as verifying the identity of voters.[119] This is somewhat similar to the situation in Lebanon, which also lacks a broad privacy regime.[120] There has been little oversight by Lebanese courts regarding biometric data.[121] Yet, passports using face recognition information have been introduced.[122]

---

[112] Kamran Shah, *Japan Launches "Facial Recognition" Technology to Thwart Terrorism: Report*, INQUISITR (Mar. 23, 2016), http://www.inquisitr.com/2920433/japan-launches-face-recognition-technology-to-thwart-terrorism-report/.

[113] Melinda Ham, *Face Recognition Technology*, UNIVERSITY OF TECHNOLOGY SYDNEY FACULTY OF LAW (Nov. 17, 2015), https://www.uts.edu.au/about/faculty-law/news/face-recognition-technology.

[114] *See* Explanatory Memorandum, Migration Amendment (Strengthening Biometrics Integrity) Bill 2015, http://parlinfo.aph.gov.au/parlInfo/search/display/display.w3p;query=Id%3A%22legislation%2Fems%2Fr5421_ems_2e28605d-fbe5-401d-9039-ccead805c177%22 at 1.

[115] *Id.* at, e.g., 34.

[116] Ariel Bogle, *Facial Recognition Technology Is Australia's Latest "National Security Weapon,"* MASHABLE (Sep. 11, 2015), http://mashable.com/2015/09/10/australia-facial-recognition-problem/#jie23E65.aqW.

[117] Dyson et al., *Data Protection Laws of the World*, DLA PIPER, http://www.dlapiperdataprotection.com/#handbook/law-section/c1_EG (last visited Aug. 25, 2016).

[118] *See* Privacy International et al., *The Right to Privacy in Egypt*, PRIVACY INTERNATIONAL, https://www.privacyinternational.org/sites/default/files/UPR_Egypt.pdf at 11.

[119] Stephen Mayhew, *Mobile Biometric Solution MorphoTablet Secures the Voting Process in Egyptian Parliamentary Elections*, BIOMETRIC UPDATE (Dec. 17, 2015), http://www.biometricupdate.com/201512/mobile-biometric-solution-morphotablet-secures-the-voting-process-in-egyptian-parliamentary-elections.

[120] *See* Privacy International et al., *The Right to Privacy in Lebanon*, PRIVACY INTERNATIONAL, https://www.privacyinternational.org/sites/default/files/Lebanon_UPR_23rd_session_Joint_Stakeholder_submission_0.pdf (Mar. 2015).

[121] Alexandrine Pirlot de Corbion, *Lebanon: It's Time to Turn Your International Position on Privacy into Action at the National Level*, PRIVACY INTERNATIONAL (May 26, 2015), https://www.privacyinternational.org/node/586.

[122] Adam Vrankulj, *Lebanon to Introduce Biometric Passports in 2014*, BIOMETRIC UPDATE (Nov. 27, 2012), http://www.biometricupdate.com/201211/lebanon-to-introduce-biometric-passports-in-2014.

Other countries in the region have more established data protection laws. One example is Morocco.[123] While the Moroccan personal data law does not specifically refer to biometric or face recognition information, it is likely that such data would be covered by the definition of "personal information" in Article 1, which includes information relating to "several factors specific to the physical, physiological, genetic, mental, economic, cultural or social identity [of that natural person]."[124]

A 2014 report on data protection in various countries, commissioned by the United Kingdom Centre for the Protection of National Infrastructure, found Moroccan law largely to be in line with the EU Data Protection Directive.[125] Time will tell whether Morocco will update its laws to match the new GDPR's considerations regarding biometric data. Moroccan government officials have taken courses from the US FBI on topics including face recognition technology, so they may be looking for ways to use these capabilities.[126]

A detailed data protection law can also be found in the Dubai International Financial Centre (DIFC) in the United Arab Emirates. The DIFC Data Protection Law No. 1 of 2007,[127] amended by the DIFC Data Protection Law Amendment Law No. 5 of 2012,[128] prescribes rules for the handling of personal data. It also establishes a Commissioner of Data Protection, who issues relevant regulations.[129] Under the Data Protection Law, an "Identifiable Natural Person" is "a natural living person who can be identified, directly or indirectly, in particular by reference to an identification number or to one or more factors specific to his biological, physical, biometric, physiological, mental, economic, cultural or social identity."[130]

Despite the fact that more specific data protection laws are otherwise lacking in the United Arab Emirates,[131] one of the most famous recent uses of face recognition technology has occurred in Abu Dhabi, where police have been using such software since 2008. Information posted on the police department's website in 2013 explains that:

> with only a brief look from the individual in the direction of the camera, face characteristics such as the position, size and shape of the eyes, nose, cheekbones and jaw are recorded and the image is instantly secured. Biometric software allows for analysis and evaluation of the image by anyone: technicians do not need extensive training, unlike with other biometric technology.

---

[123] *See* Law no. 09–08 of 18 February 2009 relating to the protection of individuals with respect to the processing of personal data, http://www.cndp-maroc.org/images/lois/Loi-09-08-Fr.pdf; *see also* its implementation Decree n° 2–09–165 of 21 May 2009, http://www.cndp-maroc.org/images/lois/Decret-2-09-165-Fr.pdf.

[124] Law no. 09–08 of Feb. 2009 Article 1(1) ("plusieurs éléments spécifiques de son identité physique, physiologique, génétique, psychique, économique, culturelle ou sociale").

[125] *See* Centre for the Protection of National Infrastructure, *Personnel Security in Offshore Centres* (Apr. 2014) at 132–33, CENTRE FOR THE PROTECTION OF NATIONAL INFRASTRUCTURE https://www.cpni.gov.uk/system/files/documents/f4/75/personnel-security-in-offshore-centres-guidance.pdf.

[126] *See* Moroccan American Center for Policy, *State Department Terrorism Reports Lauds Moroccan Counterterrorism Strategy*, MARKET WIRED (June 23, 2015), http://www.marketwired.com/press-release/state-department-terrorism-report-lauds-moroccan-counterterrorism-strategy-us-morocco-2032292.htm.

[127] *See Dubai International Financial Centre Authority (DIFC) Data Protection Law*, DIFC Law No. 1 of 2007, https://www.difc.ae/files/5814/5448/9177/Data_Protection_Law_DIFC_Law_No._1_of_2007.pdf.

[128] *See DIFC Data Protection Law Amendment Law No. 5 of 2012*, DIFC, https://www.difc.ae/files/9514/5449/6834/Data_Protection_Law_Amendment_Law_DIFC_Law_No.5_of_2012.pdf (last visited Aug. 29, 2016).

[129] *See DIFC Data Protection Regulations*, DIFC, https://www.difc.ae/files/6514/5449/8311/Data_Protection_Regulations_0_0_0.pdf (last visited Aug. 29, 2016).

[130] *See DIFC Data Protection Law Amendment Law*, DIFC Law No. 5, 2012, Schedule 1.3, https://www.difc.ae/files/9514/5449/6834/Data_Protection_Law_Amendment_Law_DIFC_Law_No.5_of_2012.pdf.

[131] Dyson et al., *Data Protection Laws of the World Handbook*, DLA PIPER, http://dlapiperdataprotection.com/#handbook/law-section/c1_AE2/c2_AE.

This makes the Community Protection Face Recognition System in addition to being highly accurate exceptionally simple to use.[132]

Additional plans were made in 2015 to use face recognition technology at United Arab Emirates airports as well, in order to implement more efficient interactions between travelers and immigration officers.[133]

RECOMMENDATIONS FOR POLICY-MAKERS

As the previous section illustrates, there are currently no consistent and comprehensive rules governing applications that rely on face recognition technology. This section provides some general recommendations for how these applications should be addressed, recognizing that the best regulation will carefully balance innovation and privacy rights.

As a model for good balance between innovation and privacy, we can look at how the law around instantaneous photography has evolved over the past century. In a seminal 1890s piece articulating principles that became the foundation of current privacy law in the United States, Samuel Warren and Louis Brandeis observed that "since the latest advances in photographic art have rendered it possible to take pictures surreptitiously, the doctrines of contract and of trust are inadequate to support the required protection, and the law of tort must be resorted to."[134] Back then, instantaneous photography challenged the law just as face recognition does today.[135] It was up to lawmakers and the public to determine the norms to govern photography. In the United States, they did not in any way prohibit instantaneous photography or stop innovation in portable cameras. But they did regulate specific situations, such as photographing and videotaping private body parts without a person's consent.[136] We also witnessed the development of a body of case law that regulates specific situations when photographing or publishing a photo may invade a person's privacy.[137] Other jurisdictions have struck the balance differently based on the value their culture places on privacy. In France, for example, a photographer needs to get a person's consent before taking a photo focusing on that person, even if the photo is taken in public.[138]

With information flowing freely between state boundaries in our information age, finding a balance based on cultural norms will be more difficult and result in a battle of values. But ultimately, some balance will need to be reached.

Technology-Neutral Regulation

Our earlier publications on face recognition technology advise against a blanket prohibition on the technology because it also presents useful applications, many of which we are still to

---

[132] *See* Abu Dhabi Police GHQ, *Face Recognition* (Apr. 8, 2013), ABU DHABI POLICE https://www.adpolice.gov.ae/en/aboutadpolice/ourachievments/face.fingerprints.aspx.

[133] Caline Malek, *New Biometrics System to Speed Up Travel Through UAE*, THE NATIONAL (Mar. 12, 2015), http://www.thenational.ae/uae/new-biometrics-system-to-speed-up-travel-through-uae.

[134] Samuel D. Warren & Louis D. Brandeis, *The Right to Privacy*, 4 HARV. L. REV. 193, 211 (1890).

[135] *See id.*

[136] Video Voyeurism Prevention Act, 18 U.S.C. § 1801 (2004).

[137] *See, e.g.*, RESTATEMENT (SECOND) OF TORTS § 652B cmt. b (1977) ("The intrusion itself makes the defendant subject to liability, even though there is no publication or other use of any kind of the photograph or information outlined.").

[138] Logeais & Schroeder, at 526.

discover.[139] Face recognition technology can help photographers organize their photos, and enable more interactive video games, and certain aspects of the technology even provide basic functionality in digital cameras.[140]

Particular uses of face recognition technology, however, may raise privacy concerns. One invasive use would be if a person with criminal intent could automatically recognize strangers in public and access their personal information from a social network or a dating app, for example. Applications that enable this behavior may need to be regulated to prevent harmful uses. Any regulation that could overly burden or eliminate applications of technology needs to be preceded by very careful analysis. But more importantly, any such regulation should narrowly target specific *uses*, rather than *classes* of technology such as face recognition technology.

Technology neutrality is a well-established regulatory principle that is particularly beneficial for rapidly developing technologies.[141] One example of tech neutral regulation that has applied to specific uses of face recognition technology is the EU Data Protection Directive.[142] The directive regulates automatic processing of personal data, which can be done with a lot of different technologies. An advisory opinion of the EU Article 29 working party explains how this tech neutral directive applies to particular uses of face recognition technology.[143] A German Data Protection Agency has similarly enforced the directive as it has been implemented into German law against Facebook's use of face recognition technology.[144] But the directive could similarly have been applied if Facebook started enabling its users to identify other Facebook users in the street based on their scent or patterns in their fashion choices. At the same time, the directive does not apply to a camera function that identifies a person's face to focus the lens on the face, even though this function is one step of the face recognition process, because its application does not result in an identification.

In contrast to the EU directive, recommendations issued by the US FTC in 2012 broadly focus on face recognition technology to provide guidance for developing various applications that use the technology.[145] The guidance is based on a workshop that examined face recognition technology, rather than focusing on specific uses or particular privacy concerns.[146]

---

[139] *See* Yana Welinder, *A Face Tells More Than a Thousand Posts: Developing Face Recognition Privacy in Social Networks*, 26 HARV. J. L. & TECH. 165 (2012); *see also* Yana Welinder, *Facing Real-Time Identification in Mobile Apps & Wearable Computers*, 30 Santa Clara High Tech. L.J. 89 (2014).

[140] supra, at 104–105.

[141] *See* Bert-Jaap Koops, *Should ICT Regulation Be Technology-Neutral?*, *in* 9 IT & LAW SERIES, STARTING POINTS FOR ICT REGULATION, DECONSTRUCTING PREVALENT POLICY ONE-LINERS 77 (Bert-Jaap Koops et al., eds., 2006) (arguing that "legislation should abstract away from concrete technologies to the extent that it is sufficiently sustainable and at the same provides sufficient legal certainty"), http://ssrn.com/abstract=918746.

[142] Directive 95/46/EC of the European Parliament and of the Council of 24 October 1995 on the Protection of Individuals with Regard to the Processing of Personal Data and on the Free Movement of Such Data, Recital 3, 1995 O.J. (L 281) 31 (EC), http://eur-lex.europa.eu/LexUriServ/LexUriServ.do?uri=OJ:L:1995:281:0031:0050:EN:PDF. It should be noted that this Directive is now superseded by the Regulation (EU) 2016/679 of the European Parliament and of the Council of 27 April 2016 on the protection of natural persons with regard to the processing of personal data and on the free movement of such data.

[143] *See Opinion of the Article 29 Data Protection Working Party*, 2012 O.J. (C 727), http://ec.europa.eu/justice/data-protection/article-29/documentation/opinion-recommendation/files/2012/wp192_en.pdf.

[144] *See* Jon Brodkin, *Germany: Facebook Must Destroy Facial Recognition Database*, ARS TECHNICA (Aug. 15, 2012), http://arstechnica.com/tech-policy/2012/08/germany-facebook-must-destroy-facial-recognition-database/.

[145] *Facing Facts: Best Practices for Common Uses of Facial Recognition Technologies*, FED. TRADE COMM'N, https://www.ftc.gov/sites/default/files/documents/reports/facing-facts-best-practices-common-uses-facial-recognition-technologies/121022facialtechrpt.pdf.

[146] *Face Facts: A Forum on Facial Recognition Technology*, FED. TRADE COMM'N, http://www.ftc.gov/bcp/workshops/facefacts/.

Technology neutral regulation does not always mean that regulation has to be particularly broad. It could, for example, specifically address the instantaneous processing of biometric data, which would apply to real-time identification as well as to other similar processes. It may seem that broad regulation of face recognition technology will be more effective because it will cover new face recognition technology implementations as they evolve. But while broad regulation of automatic face recognition could provide regulation of new implementations as they crop up, that regulation may not be suitable for them because those uses would not have been anticipated when the regulation was developed. The regulation will likely unduly burden a new product development or may not address any of its real problems (if there are any such problems to be addressed).

In fact, technology neutral regulation may instead outlast seemingly timeless regulation of face recognition technology.[147] Consider, for example, a law that would regulate collection of data indicating a person's real-time location. If well drafted, such a law today would also apply to sensitive location data in geolocation apps, which raise similar concerns to apps that can identify a person in real time using face recognition technology. It would also apply to future applications that would expose individuals in the same manner, such as technologies that would identify individuals from a distance based on their smell or the rhythm of their heartbeat.[148] It would be more targeted at the relevant harm and address all new technologies that have similar uses. The law would not need to be *translated* into the language of the future.[149] Conversely, the regulation of face recognition technology would be useless with respect to future technologies even if they were to raise very similar concerns. Indeed, one day, regulation of face recognition technology could sound just as outdated as the regulation of gramophones or videocassette tapes sounds today.[150]

Mandating Meaningful Consent from the Right Person

Consent from the relevant person will be central to regulation of face recognition applications, which often identify individuals other than the user of the application. This is a tricky concept given that notice to and consent from the user of an application is such a fundamental principle in much privacy law. But a few regulatory recommendations with respect to face recognition applications have already emphasized the need to obtain consent from the person

---

[147] *See* Koops, *supra* note 13; *but see* Christian Laux, *Must RFID-Legislation Be Technology Neutral?*, THE CENTER FOR INTERNET AND SOCIETY AT STANFORD LAW SCHOOL (Apr. 12, 2007, 1:02 PM), http://cyberlaw.stanford.edu/blog/2007/04/must-rfid-legislation-be-technology-neutral.

[148] *See* Jacob Aron, *Your Heartbeat Could Keep Your Data Safe*, NEWSCIENTIST (Feb. 11, 2012), http://www.newscientist.com/article/mg21328516.500-your-heartbeat-could-keep-your-data-safe.html; JOHN R. VACCA, BIOMETRIC TECHNOLOGIES AND VERIFICATION SYSTEMS 215 (2007) (implying that odor recognition technology may one day recognize individuals, provided that they have unique bodily odors); *see also* Paul Marks, *Google Glass App Identifies You by Your Fashion Sense*, NEWSCIENTIST (Mar. 7, 2013), http://www.newscientist.com/article/mg21729075.600-google-glass-app-identifies-you-by-your-fashion-sense.html; *See* Koops, *supra* note 13 (noting that "particular attention must be given to the sustainability of laws that target technology, because there is a greater risk than usual that changes in the subject matter may soon make the law obsolete").

[149] *See* LAWRENCE LESSIG, CODE 157–169 (2d ed. 2006).

[150] For example, the regulation of "video cassette tapes" in the Video Privacy Protection Act (VPPA) has caused the legislation to quickly seem antiquated. However, the VPPA also regulates "similar audio-visual technology," which essentially means that this is regulation of a *use* rather than a *technology*. Therefore, it has been applied to various subsequent technologies such as DVDs and online video. Yana Welinder, *Dodging the Thought Police: Privacy of Online Video and Other Content Under the "Bork Bill,"* HARV. J. L. & TECH. DIG. (Aug. 14, 2012, 6:11 PM), http://jolt.law.harvard.edu/digest/legislation/dodging-the-thought-police-privacy-of-online-video-and-other-content-under-the-bork-bill.

who is identified using the application rather than from the app user. For example, a 2012 report by the FTC states that "only consumers who have affirmatively chosen to participate in [a system that allows others to recognize them in public] should be identified."[151] Similarly, an advisory opinion of the EU Article 29 working party explains the difference between getting consent from a user of a face recognition application and the "data subject" whose data is actually processed.[152]

To meaningfully consent, a person must know to what she is consenting. It is not reasonable to use small print hidden in a privacy policy to try put a person on notice that her social network profile can be used to identify her in the street with automatic face recognition. Users rarely read online terms.[153] So it is better to design consent around their general expectations of the services they use.[154] If the main purpose of an application is to organize photos by the individuals it spots in those photos, users who provide photos of themselves will expect their photos to be used in this manner. But if an application primarily serves a different purpose and its use of face recognition is not obvious, separate notice and consent may be needed.[155]

To be meaningful, consent should also be obtained before a person's data is processed for automatic face recognition. But sometimes, prior consent may not be possible or reasonable. For example, an app may need to match a face to a database to be able to determine whether that person has consented to being recognized by face recognition technology.[156] Similarly, face recognition technology can be used to find missing persons or to identify an injured individual who is unable to consent.[157] In those cases, it's important to limit the data processing to the minimum necessary and to delete all biometric data once it's no longer needed for the particular and limited purpose. There may also be ways to allow individuals to preemptively opt out of even these uses at the time that they originally provide images of themselves. One could also imagine face recognition free zones similar to prohibitions on photographing found in restrooms and gym locker rooms.[158]

Context-Centric Regulation

A helpful framework for determining when an application of face recognition technology may raise privacy concerns is Helen Nissenbaum's theory of contextual integrity.[159] Departing from the traditional distinction between "private" and "public" information, she focuses on the

---

[151] FACING FACTS, at iii.

[152] WP29 Opinion, at 5.

[153] *See* Alessandro Acquisti & Ralph Gross, *Imagined Communities: Awareness, Information Sharing, and Privacy on the Facebook*, 2006 PRIVACY ENHANCING TECH. WORKSHOP 16, *available at* http://citeseerx.ist.psu.edu/viewdoc/download?doi=10.1.1.93.8177&rep=rep1&type=pdf. ("Among current members, 30% claim not to know whether [Facebook] grants any way to manage who can search for and find their profile, or think that they are given no such control.").

[154] *See* WP29 Opinion, at 7.

[155] *See id.* The FTC has articulated a similar idea in its consumer privacy guidelines, which provide that separate consent may not be required when a data "practice is consistent with the context of [a] transaction or the consumer's existing relationship with the business." FTC CONSUMER PRIVACY REPORT, at 39.

[156] *See* WP29 Opinion, at 5.

[157] *See* EU Directive, art. 8(c) (providing an exception to the consent requirement when "processing is necessary to protect the vital interests of the data subject or of another person where the data subject is physically or legally incapable of giving his consent").

[158] Madelyn Chung, *Playboy Model Dani Mathers Slammed for Publicly Body Shaming Nude Woman at Gym*, HUFFINGTON POST CANADA (Jul. 15, 2016), http://www.huffingtonpost.ca/2016/07/15/dani-mathers-body-shaming_n_11015320.html.

[159] NISSENBAUM, PRIVACY IN CONTEXT, at 2.

context in which the information is shared and the norms governing that particular context.[160] Her analysis considers:

1. The context in which the information is being shared,
2. The sender, recipient, and the subject of the information,
3. The nature of the shared information, and
4. The transmission principles underlying the information sharing.[161]

Based on the answers to these questions, Nissenbaum considers whether there are societal norms for the information flow that have developed in analogous situations and applies those norms to the situation at hand.[162] If the flow doesn't follow the relevant norms, it violates contextual integrity.[163] This often happens when a flow alters the nature of the information, shares the information with additional individuals, or changes the transmission principles that were understood at the time when the information was shared.[164]

Nissenbaum explains that breaking social norms can sometimes be desirable, but only if it results in new norms that are morally or politically superior.[165] The new norms must benefit the society with respect to freedom, justice, fairness, equality, democracy, and similar important concerns.[166] Nissenbaum weighs the benefit to the society from the change against the interests protected by the previous norms.[167]

To illustrate how the theory of contextual integrity would apply to face recognition applications, we apply it to the use of face recognition technology in social networks. Social network applications may violate contextual integrity by transforming the nature of information from photos that users share with their friends to biometric data that could be used by anyone to identify them.[168] If a mobile app further taps into the biometric database of the social network to allow people to recognize the social network users on the street, it further violates contextual integrity by changing the transmission principles from a strictly online context to offline tracking of individuals.

This contextual analysis can be taken into account when designing regulation of face recognition applications. For example, the FTC applied a similar analysis in its recommendations on face recognition technology.[169] Noting that face recognition technology is not consistent with the context in which users share photos on a social network, the FTC stated that users must get separate notice and the ability to opt out before their photos are used for automatic face recognition.[170] Although the FTC does suggest that the ability to opt out can be can be used for this, it is far from ideal. Social media users rarely use opt-out settings.[171] A notice with the ability to opt in is therefore more preferable when data will be used in a new way outside the context in which it was originally shared.

---

[160] *Id.* at 125–126.
[161] *Id.* at 149–150.
[162] *Id.* at 138, 149–150.
[163] *Id.* at 10.
[164] *Id.* at 150.
[165] *Id.* at 165.
[166] *Id.* at 182.
[167] *Id.* at 182.
[168] Welinder, *A Face Tells More than a Thousand Posts*, at 186–88.
[169] Facing Facts, at 18.
[170] *Id.* at 18–19.
[171] *See* Michelle Madejski et al., *The Failure of Online Social Network Privacy Settings*, Future of Privacy Forum (July 2011), http://bit.ly/MlkhFT.

Consider Government Access to Privately Collected Biometric Data

When regulating collection and use of biometric data for consumer applications, we also need to make sure that it doesn't enable government agencies to unreasonably search private data.[172] The US Fourth Amendment jurisprudence that protects against unreasonable searches mostly developed before companies were collecting the vast amount of data that they collect today.[173] While a government agency would need a warrant to look for photos in a person's home, it only needs a subpoena or a court order issued pursuant to a lower standard than a warrant to obtain that person's photos when they are stored by a company.[174] The law in this area is clearly outdated, given that the photos stored by the company are likely to include more personal information than photos found in a person's home: digital photos often include time and location metadata and have labels identifying the people in the photos.

Photos stored for consumer applications enjoy even less protection from government search when an agency purports to be investigating something related to foreign intelligence.[175] As long as a foreign intelligence issue is a "significant purpose" of an investigation, even if not the primary purpose, ordinary electronic surveillance protections can be suspended.[176]

Regulation should plan for a future where government agencies continue tapping into privately collected biometric data because governments' own biometric databases may not be as effective at identifying individuals. There have been multiple reports that government agencies are developing their own biometric databases to identify suspects.[177] But unlike many consumer apps, the government's face recognition system will not be able to contextualize the matching of faces based on which people are more likely to appear in photos with particular friends.[178] Consumer apps can also rely on their users to confirm or deny automatic identification of their friends, training the identification algorithm every time. As a result, government agencies will continue seeking access to photos and biometric data stored in consumer apps.

Privately collected biometric data is simply inseparable from issues of government surveillance. To avoid having consumer apps become conduits for surveillance of their users, regulation should encourage the companies to design services to avoid collecting or retaining

---

[172] *See, e.g.*, Laura K. Donohue, *NSA Surveillance May Be Legal – But It's Unconstitutional*, WASH. POST (June 21, 2013), http://www.washingtonpost.com/opinions/nsa-surveillance-may-be-legal–but-its-unconstitutional/2013/06/21/b9ddec20-d44d-11e2-a73e-826d299ff459_story.html.

[173] *Digital Duplications and the Fourth Amendment*, 129 HARV. L. REV. 1046 (2016), http://harvardlawreview.org/2016/02/digital-duplications-and-the-fourth-amendment/.

[174] Stored Communications Act, 18 U.S.C. § 2703(b). To obtain a court warrant under this provision, a law enforcement agency only needs to provide "specific and articulable facts showing that there are reasonable grounds to believe that the contents of a wire or electronic communication, or the records or other information sought, are relevant and material to an ongoing criminal investigation" (18 U.S.C. § 2703(d)). Significantly, the agency does not need to show reasonable belief that evidence of a crime exists in the location to be searched, as it would need to do for a search warrant.

[175] *See* Foreign Intelligence Surveillance Act, 50 U.S.C. §§ 1804(a)(7)(B), 1823 (a)(7)(B), and 1881a(a).

[176] *Id.*; *In re* Sealed Case, 310 F.3d 717 (FISA Ct. Rev. 2002) ("FISA, as amended, does not oblige the government to demonstrate to the FISA court that its primary purpose in conducting electronic surveillance is not criminal prosecution.").

[177] *Next Generation Identification*, FED. BUREAU OF INVESTIGATION, http://www.fbi.gov/about-us/cjis/fingerprints_biometrics/ngi; *FBI Criminal Justice Information Services Division Staff Paper: Update on Next Generation Identification*, ELECTRONIC FRONTIER FOUND (June 2012), https://www.eff.org/document/fbi-cjis-staff-paper-next-generation-identification; *FBI Performs Massive Virtual Line-up by Searching DMV Photos*, ELECTRONIC PRIVACY INFO. CENTER (June 17, 2013), http://epic.org/2013/06/fbi-performs-massive-virtual-l.html.

[178] This may become less valuable given the recent advancement in face recognition technology that relies on neural networks.

unnecessary data.[179] They can also be encouraged to implement local storage and end-to-end encryption, when that is compatible with their services. This will ensure that government agencies have to obtain the data directly from the user, which is more analogous to when law enforcement collects fingerprints from a criminal suspect or searches for photos in the suspect's home pursuant to a specific warrant.

RECOMMENDATIONS FOR DEVELOPERS

The best privacy practices come from carefully designed apps rather than from regulation. Regulation of quickly evolving technology will always lag behind. This lag is actually desirable, because it gives regulators time to observe how technology evolves to adopt more meaningful regulations only when it is necessary and avoid blocking innovation. But that does not mean that companies should abuse personal data until their applications are regulated. Bad privacy practices result in poor service for the users and erode user trust. That is ultimately bad for business, particularly for a new application that is trying to build up its reputation. It can also provoke knee-jerk regulations, blocking further innovation in the field.

Developers should aim to create applications that protect personal data given that they are in the best position to know what data they collect and how they use it. In this section, we discuss three design principles that can help with developing more privacy protective applications when using face recognition technology. Additional design principles may later become relevant as we start seeing new applications of face recognition technology.

Leverage User Experience Design as a Notice Tool

When designing applications with face recognition technology, developers need to consider how their data collection and processing are experienced by users and those around the users. The best scenario is when the use of face recognition technology is consistent with the general context of the application as experienced by the user and the people they photograph. When the use is less obvious, developers should consider how they can actively notify users and other affected individuals through the interface. User experience design could help to instinctively make a user aware of data collection without the need to read or understand a privacy policy. It can also provide notice to individuals beyond the primary user of a product, which as discussed in Section IV(B) is particularly relevant for face recognition technology.

People tend to know that they are being photographed when a camera directed at them emits a shutter sound or a flash.[180] Another example of intuitive design is security cameras that have a video screen next to them directly showing people when they are being recorded.[181] Similar intuitive design could be created for devices equipped with face recognition technology. They could for example loudly state a person's name as they recognize her, as well as the source of the biometric data. Such an announcement would put the person on notice that she is being recognized, and allow her to take action if she doesn't want to be part of the biometric database. The device could also send an electronic message to the identified person stating the time and place of the identification as well as the identity of the user of the face recognition device to

---

[179] *See ECPA Reform: Why Now?* Digital Due Process, http://digitaldueprocess.org/index.cfm?objectid= 37940370-2551-11DF-8E02000C296BA163.

[180] *See* Calo, at 1036–37 ("Analog cameras make a click and, often, emit a flash when taking a picture.").

[181] *See Photo of Self-Checkout at Home Depot*, Flickr (Apr. 19, 2011), http://www.flickr.com/photos/ginger-jengibre/ 5635513442/in/photostream/.

provide mutual transparency. While the exact implementation of these types of features might vary, the general idea of notifying people when they are automatically recognized is a palpable example of privacy protective user experience design.

Another solution is to design an application to simulate people's preexisting expectations about who is able to recognize their face. For example, an application could allow a user to run face recognition only for the individuals whom this user had previously identified. This design would play on people's expectations that a person they interact with may remember them next time, no matter how brief the initial interaction. It would also allow the biometric data to be stored locally on one device, making it less susceptible to abuse.[182]

Collect Less; Delete More

Excessive data collection and retention create the risk that the data can be misused down the road. This is particularly problematic when dealing with sensitive data, such as biometrics. Applications with face recognition technology should therefore actively limit data collection to what is absolutely necessary to provide a service and regularly delete data when it is no longer needed. If a user were to delete her account with an application or turn off the face recognition function in an application with broader functionality, the biometric data is obviously no longer needed and should be deleted. Importantly, the data should be deleted from the biometric database and not only from the user interface of the application.[183]

When designing applications with face recognition technology, it is best to adopt data retention policies early in the development process. That way, the policy can be optimized before the application becomes overwhelmed with data. Having an effective data retention policy will allow a company to prevent data from being misused within the company, help safeguard the data from third parties, and make it easier to respond to law enforcement demands. If an application collects limited data and promptly deletes it when it is not necessary to serve the users, the company in charge of the application can easily reject government demands for data that it does not store.[184]

Security by Design

The data used by face recognition applications must be safeguarded carefully given that, unlike a compromised password or a stolen credit card, a person's facial features cannot just be replaced.[185] Ideally, it is good to store the biometric data locally in an encrypted format as much as possible.[186] But many applications require the data to be transferred between multiple servers. In that case, it is important to make sure that the data is encrypted and travels via encrypted

---

[182] Russel Brandom, *Apple's New Facial Recognition Feature Could Spur Legal Issues*, THE VERGE (June 16, 2016), http://www.theverge.com/2016/6/16/11934456/apple-google-facial-recognition-photos-privacy-faceprint.

[183] *See, e.g., Facebook Data Use Policy* (stating that "some information may remain in backup copies and logs for up to 90 days" after an account is deleted); *but see* FACING FACTS, at 18 n.70 (referring to Facebook's testimony that "Facebook deleted any previously collected biometric data" "if a user opted out of Facebook's 'Tag Suggest' feature").

[184] *See, e.g., Request for User Information Procedures & Guidelines*, THE WIKIMEDIA FOUNDATION (May 14, 2015), https://wikimediafoundation.org/wiki/Requests_for_user_information_procedures_%26_guidelines (explaining that user data requests to the Wikimedia Foundation may be futile because it "collects very little nonpublic information (if any) that could be used to identify its users offline and it retains that information for a limited amount of time").

[185] *See Face Facts: A Forum on Face Recognition Technology*, FED. TRADE COMM'N 1 (Dec. 8, 2011), http://www.ftc.gov/video-library/transcripts/120811_FTC_sess3.pdf (Alessandro Acquisti testifying, "It's much easier to change your name and declare 'reputational bankruptcy' than to change your face.").

[186] WP29 Opinion, at 8.

channels.[187] The multiple servers can be leveraged to store different pieces of a person's biometric data to make it more difficult for a third party to access the biometric data when only one of the servers is compromised.[188]

There has been significant research into designing biometric systems to protect personal data.[189] One approach is to distort an image during the face recognition process to avoid storing original images of individuals.[190] Another approach is to hash the biometric data in the course of the recognition process.[191] But both these methods have had a negative impact on the effectiveness of the face recognition process.[192] A more effective method is to transform biometric data into two components where the component that pertains to a person's identity is encrypted and can be entirely revoked if the system is compromised.[193]

CONCLUSION

Biometric technology is rapidly evolving, both in its capabilities and in its use. Consumers are presented with a dizzying array of advancements, from clever mobile apps to pervasive government surveillance. As difficult as it may be to track changes to the technology itself, it is almost as difficult to stay abreast of changes to the laws regulating the technology.

While consumer privacy is not always considered in this development, there are signs that consumers themselves, as well as governments, are working to address privacy concerns. For better or for worse, lawsuits under the Illinois Biometric Identification Privacy Act will likely continue to be filed in the United States, and courts seem willing to hear them. Data protection authorities have urged caution in gathering biometric data and said that consumers need the ability to make informed choices. Regulators should continue to emphasize the importance of transparency, notice, and consent. They should also focus on specific uses of face recognition technology, rather than on the technology in general, to avoid stifling innovation. Further, they need to ensure that law enforcement and other government agencies consider personal privacy interests in their efforts to access privately held databases of face recognition information.

Independent of regulation, application developers can take steps to inform and protect consumers. Good interface design can make it clear what data is being collected and when. Implementing security by design can help keep the information safe. Generally, developers should strive to collect less and delete more.

Face recognition technology is here to stay – and so are efforts to regulate it and litigate about it. We can only guess what steps the technology and the laws will take next; the last few years suggest that it will be a rocky, but interesting, path.

---

[187] Margarita Osadchy et al., *SCiFI: A System for Secure Face Identification*, BENNY PINKAS, 1 (May 2010), http://pinkas .net/PAPERS/scifi.pdf; *see also* WP29 Opinion, at 8.

[188] Osadchy et al., at 1.

[189] *See* T. Boult, *Robust Distance Measures for Face-Recognition Supporting Revocable Biometric Tokens*, UNIVERSITY OF COLORADO AT COLORADO SPRINGS AND SECURICS, INC, Preprint (2006), *available at* http://innovation.uccs.edu/ ~tboult/PAPERS/removed-Boult-IEEEFG06-preprint.pdf.

[190] Ratha et al., Enhancing Security and Privacy in Biometrics-Based Authentication Systems, 2001, http://ieeexplore .ieee.org/xpl/login.jsp?tp=&arnumber=5386935&url=http%3A%2F%2Fieeexplore.ieee.org%2Fiel5%2F5288519% 2F5386925%2F05386935.pdf%3Farnumber%3D5386935.

[191] Tulyakov et al., *Symmetric Hash Functions for Secure Fingerprint Biometric Systems*, 2004, PATTERN RECOGNITION LETTERS, 28(16):2427–2436, https://www.researchgatenet/publication/222570842_Symmetric_Hash_Functions_for_ Secure_Fingerprint_Biometric_Systems

[192] *See* Boult, *supra* note 182.

[193] *Id.* http://innovation.uccs.edu/~tboult/PAPERS/removed-Boult-IEEEFG06-preprint.pdf.

7

Smart Cities: Privacy, Transparency, and Community

*Kelsey Finch and Omer Tene**

INTRODUCTION

At the beginning of the 20th century, a group of Italian artists and poets called the Futurists sought to reshape the world around them to reflect a futuristic, technological aesthetic – transforming everything from cities, to train stations, to chess sets.[1] In the city of the future, they believed, technology would inspire and elevate the physical and mental world: "Trains would rocket across overhead rails, airplanes would dive from the sky to land on the roof, and skyscrapers would stretch their sinewed limbs into the heavens to feel the hot pulse of radio waves beating across the planet."[2]

But today's cities – and our train stations, self-driving cars, and chess sets – have moved far beyond artistic imagination. Today's cities are already pervaded by growing networks of connected technologies to generate actionable, often real-time data about themselves and their citizens. Relying on ubiquitous telecommunications technologies to provide connectivity to sensor networks and set actuation devices into operation, smart cities routinely collect information on cities' air quality, temperature, noise, street and pedestrian traffic, parking capacity, distribution of government services, emergency situations, and crowd sentiments, among other data points.[3]

While some of the data sought by smart cities and smart communities is focused on environmental or non-human factors (e.g., monitoring air pollution, or snowfall, or electrical outages), much of the data will also record and reflect the daily activities of the people living, working, and visiting the city (e.g., monitoring tourist foot traffic, or home energy usage, or homelessness). The more connected a city becomes, the more it will generate a steady stream of data from and about its citizens.

Sensor networks and always-on data flows are already supporting new service models and generating analytics that make modern cities and local communities faster and safer, as well as

---

* Kelsey Finch is Policy Counsel and Omer Tene is Senior Fellow at the Future of Privacy Forum. Tene is Vice President of Research and Education at the International Association of Privacy Professionals and Associate Professor at the College of Management School of Law, Rishon Lezion, Israel.

[1] *See* Adam Rothstein, *The Cities Science Fiction Built*, MOTHERBOARD (Apr. 20, 2015), https://motherboard.vice.com/read/the-cities-science-fiction-built; ITALIAN FUTURISM, 1909–1944: RECONSTRUCTING THE UNIVERSE (Vivian Greene, ed., 2014).

[2] Adam Rothstein, *The Cities Science Fiction Built*, MOTHERBOARD (Apr. 20, 2015), https://motherboard.vice.com/read/the-cities-science-fiction-built ("This artistic, but unbridled enthusiasm was the last century's first expression of wholesale tech optimism.").

[3] *See Shedding Light on Smart City Privacy*, THE FUTURE OF PRIVACY FORUM (Mar. 30, 2017), https://fpf.org/2017/03/30/smart-cities/.

more sustainable, more livable, and more equitable.[4] At the same time, connected smart city devices raise concerns about individuals' privacy, autonomy, freedom of choice, and potential discrimination by institutions. As we have previously described, "There is a real risk that, rather than standing as 'paragons of democracy, [smart cities] could turn into electronic panopticons in which everybody is constantly watched."[5] Moreover, municipal governments seeking to protect privacy while still implementing smart technologies must navigate highly variable regulatory regimes,[6] complex business relationships with technology vendors, and shifting societal – and community – norms around technology, surveillance, public safety, public resources, openness, efficiency, and equity.

Given these significant and yet competing benefits and risks, and the already rapid adoption of smart city technologies around the globe,[7] the question becomes: How can communities leverage the benefits of a data-rich society while minimizing threats to individuals' privacy and civil liberties?

Just as there are many methods and metrics to assess a smart city's livability, sustainability, or effectiveness,[8] so too there are different lenses through which cities can evaluate their privacy preparedness. In this article, we lay out three such perspectives, considering a smart city's privacy responsibilities in the context of its role as a data steward, as a data platform, and as a government authority. While there are likely many other lenses that could be used to capture a community's holistic privacy impacts, exploring these three widely tested perspectives can help municipalities better leverage existing privacy tools and safeguards and identify gaps in their existing frameworks. By considering the deployment of smart city technologies in these three lights, communities will be better prepared to reassure residents of smart cities that their rights will be respected and their data protected.

CITY AS DATA STEWARD

In many ways, smart communities are no different than other data-rich entities: they act as a data stewards, ensuring that data is always available, reliable, and useful to their organization. Data stewardship is well established in the information management field, denoting an individual or institution with control over the collection, handling, sharing, and analysis of data.[9] Increasingly, data governance in data-rich organizations concerns not only carrying out the day-to-day management of data assets, but also taking on fiduciary-like responsibilities to consider the

---

[4] *See, e.g., Smart Cities: International Case Studies*, INTER-AM. DEV. BANK, (2016), http://www.iadb.org/en/topics/emerging-and-sustainable-cities/international-case-studies-of-smart-cities,20271.html (last visited Mar. 31, 2017).

[5] Kelsey Finch & Omer Tene, *Welcome to the Metropticon: Protecting Privacy in a Hyperconnected Town*, 41 FORDHAM URB. L.J. 1581, 1583 (2015), http://ir.lawnet.fordham.edu/cgi/viewcontent.cgi?article=2549&context=ulj.

[6] Including regulatory regimes and principles that create sometimes competing obligations to keep personal data private while also making the data held by government more transparent and accessible to the public. *See, e.g., Report of the Special Rapporteur on the Right to Privacy, Annex II*, Human Rights Council, U.N. Doc. A/HRC/31/64 (May 8, 2016) (by Joseph A. Cannataci).

[7] *See* RESEARCH & MARKETS, GLOBAL SMART CITIES MARKET INSIGHTS, OPPORTUNITY ANALYSIS, MARKET SHARES AND FORECAST 2017–2023 (Jan. 2017).

[8] *See* ISO 37120:2014 SUSTAINABLE DEVELOPMENT IN COMMUNITIES: CITY INDICATORS FOR SERVICE DELIVERY AND QUALITY OF LIFE (2014), https://www.iso.org/files/live/sites/isoorg/files/archive/pdf/en/37120_briefing_note.pdf.

[9] *See* Mark Moseley, *DAMA_DBOK Functional Framework*, THE DATA MGMT. ASS'N. (Version 3.02, Sept. 10, 2008), https://www.dama.org/sites/default/files/download/DAMA-DMBOK_Functional_Framework_v3_02_20080910.pdf.

ethical and privacy impacts of particular data activities and to act with the best interests of individuals and society in mind.[10]

All organizations dealing with data must ensure that their data assets are appropriately secured, handled, and used. While privacy laws and commitments give organizations in both the private and public sectors clear motivations to protect personally identifying information (PII), non-personal data is oftentimes just as robustly safeguarded because of concerns for intellectual property and trade secrets. While this paper focuses on methods designed to protect PII, data governance and accountability mechanisms instituted throughout the data lifecycle often mitigate risks to both PII and non-PII.[11]

Companies, NGOs, and government agencies of all stripes are familiar to some extent with the variety of roles and responsibilities that accompany the day-to-day use and maintenance of data assets and that keep systems running smoothly: IT departments ensure that data is secure and uncorrupted, lawyers oversee compliance with privacy and other legal regimes, engineers architect new and better ways of developing data, researchers explore datasets for new insights, and business units and policy teams determine what data to collect and how to use it. In the municipal context, oftentimes it is a chief innovation officer (CIO), a chief technology officer (CTO), a chief data officer (CDO), or increasingly a chief privacy officer (CPO) who oversees this process and inculcates institutional norms around privacy and security.

Thus, the data steward model – and many of the data (and privacy) governance tools and terminology that accompany it – is already familiar to a wide set of IT, compliance, and privacy professionals in the private sector.[12] It is also familiar to career civil servants in public sector entities – especially data-intensive environments such as national security, healthcare and education.[13] As municipalities expand their technology and data capabilities, many of the professionals they hire will bring with them experience with data and privacy governance. Nevertheless, municipalities need to be forward-thinking and purposeful in planning, supervising, and controlling data management and use within – and between – their numerous departments, agencies, and public-private partnerships.

What tools and considerations, then, should smart cities take into account in their role as data stewards?

Privacy management. As data stewards, cities must devise privacy management programs to ensure that responsibility is established, accountability is maintained, and resources are allocated to successfully oversee, govern, and use individuals' data. Documenting and routinizing these principles and practices throughout the entire data lifecycle are critical to ensuring accountability.

---

[10] *See* Jan Whittington et al., *Push, Pull, and Spill: A Transdisciplinary Case Study in Municipal Open Government*, 30 (3) BERKELEY TECH. L.J. 1989 (2015), http://btlj.org/data/articles2015/vol30/30_3/1899–1966%20Whittington.pdf; Jack Balkin & Jonathan Zittrin, *A Grand Bargain to Make Tech Companies Trustworthy*, THE ATLANTIC (Oct. 3, 2016), https://www.theatlantic.com/technology/archive/2016/10/information-fiduciary/502346/.

[11] We note, as well, that the line between PII and non-PII is often indistinct, and that data traditionally considered non-identifying may become PII in the future as look-up databases or technical systems emerge to link that data to individuals. *See* Jules Polonetsky, Omer Tene & Kelsey Finch, *Shades of Gray: Seeing the Full Spectrum of Practical Data De-identification*, 56 SANTA CLARA L. REV. 593 (2016), http://digitalcommons.law.scu.edu/lawreview/vol56/iss3/3. Given these risks, instituting a variety of forward-thinking safeguards throughout the full data lifecycle is critical.

[12] *See, e.g.,* Moseley, *supra* note 9.

[13] *See, e.g.,* Susan Baird Kanaan & Justine M. Carr, *Health Data Stewardship: What, Why, Who, How*, NAT'L COMM. ON VITAL & HEALTH STATISTICS, U.S. DEP'T OF HEALTH & HUMAN SVCS. (Sept. 2009), http://www.ncvhs.hhs.gov/wp-content/uploads/2014/05/090930lt.pdf; *Data Governance and Stewardship*, PRIVACY TECHNICAL ASSISTANCE CTR., U.S. DEP'T OF EDUC. (Dec. 2011), http://ptac.ed.gov/sites/default/files/issue-brief-data-governance-and-stewardship.pdf.

The core of any privacy management program is establishing principles and practices that apply to collecting, viewing, storing, sharing, aggregating, analyzing, and using personal data. In order to strengthen public trust, some city leaders have used the process of developing core privacy principles as an opportunity to engage their communities. For example, as the City of Seattle developed its six citywide "Privacy Principles,"[14] the Seattle IT department created a Community Technology Advisory Board (CTAB), made up of local experts, business representatives, and academics from the University of Washington,[15] and invited their input, as well as that of local privacy advocacy groups.[16] The principles were ultimately adopted by City Council Resolution 31570,[17] and laid the foundation for a more in-depth, public-facing privacy policy detailing the city's privacy and security practices.[18]

Once their guiding principles are established, there are many models that city officials might turn to in building workable, auditable municipal privacy programs. In 2016, the Federal Office of Management and Budget (OMB) updated Circular A-130, the document governing the management of federal information resources.[19] Recognizing the impact of big data trends on government data management, the updated OMB Circular requires federal agencies to:

- Establish comprehensive, strategic, agency-wide privacy programs;
- Designate Senior Agency Officials for Privacy;
- Manage and train an effective privacy workforce;
- Conduct Privacy Impact Assessments (PIA);
- Apply NIST's Risk Management Framework to manage privacy risk throughout the information system development life cycle;
- Use Fair Information Practice Principles (FIPPs) when evaluating programs that affect privacy;
- Maintain inventories of personally identifiable information (PII); and
- Minimize the collection and usage of PII within agencies.[20]

Another leading example in the United States has emerged from the Federal Trade Commission's (FTC) body of privacy and security settlements. The FTC's model is likely to influence many of the technology vendors a city might partner with, who are expected to stay in line with their primary regulator's best practices or may be already under a settlement order themselves.[21] In broad strokes, the FTC has increasingly required settling companies to maintain a privacy program that:

---

[14] See *City of Seattle Privacy Principles*, City of Seattle (Mar. 2015), http://ctab.seattle.gov/wp-content/uploads/2015/03/Privacy-Principles-FINAL-RESOLUTION.pdf.

[15] See *CTAB Blog*, City of Seattle, http://ctab.seattle.gov/ (last visited Apr. 24, 2017).

[16] See *City of Seattle's Tech Board Restarts Privacy Committee*, Seattle Privacy Coal. (Sept. 27, 2016), https://www.seattleprivacy.org/city-of-seattles-tech-board-restarts-privacy-committee/.

[17] See Res. 31570, *A resolution adopting the City of Seattle Privacy Principles governing the City's operations, which will provide an ethical framework for dealing with current and future technologies that impact privacy, and setting timelines for future reporting on the development of a Privacy Statement and Privacy Toolkit for their implementation*, Seattle City Council (Mar. 3, 2015), http://clerk.seattle.gov/~legislativeItems/Resolutions/Resn_31570.pdf.

[18] See *Privacy*, City of Seattle, http://www.seattle.gov/tech/initiatives/privacy#x58255 (last visited Apr. 24, 2017).

[19] See Revision of OMB Circular A-130, "Managing Information as a Strategic Resource," FR Doc. 2016–17872 (July 28, 2016), https://obamawhitehouse.archives.gov/blog/2016/07/26/managing-federal-information-strategic-resource.

[20] See Circular No. A-130, *Managing Information as a Strategic Resource*, Appendix II, Office of Mgmt. & Budget, Exec. Office of the President (July 28, 2016), https://obamawhitehouse.archives.gov/sites/default/files/omb/assets/OMB/circulars/a130/a130revised.pdf.

[21] See Daniel Solove & Woodrow Hartzog, *The FTC and the New Common Law of Privacy*, 114 Colum. L. Rev. 583 (2014), https://papers.ssrn.com/sol3/papers.cfm?abstract_id=2312913.

- Is reasonably designed to: (1) address privacy risks related to the development and management of new and existing products and services for consumers, and (2) to protect the privacy and confidentiality of personal information;
- Is fully documented in writing;
- Contains privacy controls and procedures appropriate to the organization's size and complexity, the nature and scope of its activities, and the sensitivity of the personal information;
- Designates an employee or employees to coordinate and be accountable for the privacy program;
- Conducts a privacy risk assessment identifying reasonably foreseeable, material risks, both internal and external, that could result in the organization's unauthorized collection, use, or disclosure of personal information – specifically including risks related to employee training and management and product design, development, and research;
- Implements reasonable privacy controls and procedures to address the risks identified through the privacy risk assessment, and regularly tests or monitors their effectiveness;
- Takes reasonable steps to select and retain service providers capable of maintaining appropriate security practices, and requires service providers to contractually implement appropriate safeguards; and
- Reevaluates and adjusts the privacy program in light of any new material risks, material changes in the organization's operations or business arrangements, or any other circumstances that might materially impact the effectiveness of the privacy program.[22]

International standards and regulations add clarity on the importance of robust privacy programs. The OECD's 1980 privacy guidelines, amended in 2013, dictate that data controllers should "Have in place a privacy management programme that:

- Gives effect to these Guidelines for all personal data under its control;
- Is tailored to the structure, scale, volume and sensitivity of its operations;
- Provides for appropriate safeguards based on privacy risk assessment;
- Is integrated into its governance structure and establishes internal oversight mechanisms;
- Includes plans for responding to inquiries and incidents; [and]
- Is updated in light of ongoing monitoring and periodic assessment."[23]

The new European General Data Protection Regulation (GDPR), which goes into force in May 2018, will also require the appointment of Data Protection Officers within organizations of all shapes and sizes, and the establishment of structured accountability programs.[24] Indeed, the Article 29 Working Party believes that "the DPO is a cornerstone of accountability."[25] DPOs are at a minimum tasked with monitoring their organizations' compliance with the GDPR; advising their organizations in the course of conducting data protection impact assessments (DPIAs); taking risk-based approaches to their data protection activities; and maintaining records of all of their organizations' data processing operations.[26] While uncertainty remains as to the precise

---

[22] *See id.* at 617.
[23] *See OECD Guidelines Governing the Protection of Privacy and Transborder Flows of Personal Data*, THE OECD PRIVACY FRAMEWORK, 16 (July 11, 2013), https://www.oecd.org/sti/ieconomy/2013-oecd-privacy-guidelines.pdf.
[24] *See* Regulation 2016/679, General Data Protection Regulation, art. 37, 2016 O.J. (L. 119) 1, http://ec.europa.eu/justice/data-protection/reform/files/regulation_oj_en.pdf; ART. 29 DATA PROTECTION WORKING PARTY, GUIDELINES ON DATA PROTECTION OFFICERS (Dec. 13, 2016), http://ec.europa.eu/information_society/newsroom/image/document/2016–51/wp243_en_40855.pdf.
[25] ART. 29 WORKING PARTY, *supra* note 24, at 4.
[26] *Id.* at 16–18.

contours of the DPO role within EU data protection practice, the International Association of Privacy Professionals (IAPP) estimates that at least 28,000 new DPO positions will be created in the coming years in Europe alone in response to the GDPR.[27]

Privacy oversight. Designating a governance lead (such as a Chief Privacy Officer, a DPO or a Senior Agency Official for Privacy[28]) who oversees privacy responsibilities can create an authoritative hub where dedicated experts navigate relevant laws and regulations, advise other officials and departments, create documentation and policies, look for and remediate violations, and educate the public workforce on privacy policies and practices. As data stewards, smart cities should clearly establish governance structures and oversight mechanisms for granting access to data, analytics, and tracking technologies.

In addition to designating a privacy lead, smart cities should consider the value of establishing a privacy committee made up of a range of stakeholders, including members of the public. Such working groups are common within the privacy profession, and often stress interdisciplinary representation within the working groups to improve outcomes, make programs more inclusive, and generate buy-in throughout an organization.[29] Seattle's Community Technical Advisory Board is formalized in the Seattle Municipal Code,[30] and in January 2016 the Oakland City Council created and defined the duties of a formal Privacy Advisory Commission, tasked with (among other things): providing advice and technical assistance on privacy best practices for surveillance equipment and citizen data, providing annual reports and recommendations on the city's use of surveillance equipment, conducting public hearings, drafting reports, and making findings and recommendations to the city council.[31]

While only Seattle and Oakland have established formal citywide privacy advisory boards at this date, specific agencies within local government have also turned to their communities for input – local libraries, for instance, have long been on the forefront of progressive citizen-engaged privacy policymaking.[32] And the original Array of Things installation in Chicago, a partnership between the City of Chicago, the University of Chicago, and the Argonne National Laboratory, has convened independent governance boards responsible for overseeing the privacy and security practices of its distributed sensor arrays and data processing activities.[33]

Privacy Risk Management. Robust data governance requires identifying, assessing, and ultimately mitigating privacy risks. While many organizations have their own internal risk management structures, privacy-specific frameworks are less systematic and, given the largely subjective nature of privacy harms, more difficult to quantify.[34] One instructive risk management framework for municipal officials to consider is a recent effort by the US National Institute

---

[27] *See* Warwick Ashford, *GDPR Will Require 28,000 DPOs in Europe and US, Study Shows*, COMPUTER WEEKLY (Apr. 20, 2016), http://www.computerweekly.com/news/450283253/GDPR-will-require-28000-DPOs-in-Europe-study-shows.

[28] *See* OFFICE OF MGMT. & BUDGET, *supra* note 20.

[29] *See* IAPP-EY ANNUAL PRIVACY GOVERNANCE REPORT 7 (2015), https://webforms.ey.com/Publication/vwLUAssets/EY_-_IAPP_ey_privacy_governance_report_2015/$FILE/EY-IAPP-ey-privacy-governance-report-2015.pdf.

[30] SEATTLE COMMUNITY TECHNOLOGY ADVISORY BOARD (CTAB) – MEMBERSHIP AND DUTIES, SEATTLE MUNICIPAL CODE 3.23.060, https://www.municode.com/library/wa/seattle/codes/municipal_code?nodeId=TIT3AD_SUBTITLE_IIDEOF_CH3.23SEINTEDE_3.23.060SECOTEADBOCTEMDU (last visited Apr. 24, 2017).

[31] *Privacy Advisory Commission*, CITY OF OAKLAND, http://www2.oaklandnet.com/government/o/CityAdministration/d/PrivacyAdvisoryCommission/index.htm (last visited Apr. 24, 2017).

[32] *See, e.g.*, SAN FRANCISCO PUB. LIBRARY TECH. & PRIVACY ADVISORY COMM., SUMMARY REPORT: RADIO FREQUENCY IDENTIFICATION AND THE SAN FRANCISCO PUBLIC LIBRARY (Oct. 2005), http://sfpl.org/pdf/about/commission/RFID-and-SFPL-summary-report-oct2005.pdf.

[33] *See* ARRAY OF THINGS OPERATING POLICIES (Aug. 15, 2016), https://arrayofthings.github.io/final-policies.html.

[34] *See* NIST INTERNAL REPORT (NISTIR) 8062, PRIVACY RISK MANAGEMENT FOR FEDERAL INFORMATION SYSTEMS 1 (Jan. 4, 2017), http://csrc.nist.gov/publications/drafts/nistir-8062/nistir_8062_draft.pdf ("Although existing tools such as the Fair Information Practice Principles (FIPPs) and privacy impact assessments (PIAs) provide a foundation for taking

of Standards and Technology (NIST) to develop a comprehensive system for "Privacy Risk Management for Federal Information Systems."[35] NIST explicitly modeled this effort on its successful cybersecurity risk management framework (RMF) and accompanied the development of a privacy risk model with a foundation for "the establishment of a common vocabulary to facilitate better understanding of – and communication about – privacy risks and the effective implementation of privacy principles in federal information systems."[36]

A recurring challenge for smart communities in deploying risk mitigation strategies is that reducing privacy risk often entails impairing data utility, thus inhibiting potentially beneficial uses of data. For smart communities and other organizations, considering the *risks* of a project is merely one part of a balanced value equation; decision-makers must also take into count the project's *benefits* in order to make a final determination about whether to proceed.[37] In another article, we suggested that in addition to conducting a Privacy Impact Analysis (PIA), therefore, decision-makers need to conduct a Data Benefit Analysis (DBA), putting a project's benefits and risks on an equal footing.[38] This is especially true as cities, researchers, companies, and even citizens engage in the sort of big data analyses that promise tremendous – and often unexpected – benefits, but which also introduce new privacy and civil liberties concerns associated with large-scale data collection and analysis. On the one hand, if a city can provide free internet access for thousands of un- or underserved individuals, for example, it may be legitimate to deploy such a service even though not all of its privacy risks can be completely eliminated.[39] On the other hand, where smart city benefits are small or remote, larger privacy risks would not be justified.[40]

These assessments should take into account variables such as the nature of the prospective risk or benefit, the identity of the impacted subject(s), and the likelihood of success. These assessments should consider and document specific impacts to individuals, communities, organizations, and society at large, in part to help determine whether risks and benefits are accruing fairly and equitably across these populations.[41] Cities must also negotiate the difficult reality that social and cultural priorities and sensitivities may vary widely among their constituent communities, and ensure that all interested members of the public can legitimately have their voices heard on the potential impacts of civic projects.[42]

Vendor management. Public-private partnerships have also emerged as a leading driver for smart city developments. Rather than simply outsourcing technical work to service providers, cities are increasingly co-organizing, co-operating, co-funding, and co-branding data intensive projects with private enterprises.[43] In such high profile relationships, cities (and vendors) must

---

privacy into consideration, they have not yet provided a method for federal agencies to measure privacy impacts on a consistent and repeatable basis.").

[35] *Id.*

[36] *Id.* at 3.

[37] Jules Polonetsky, Omer Tene & Joseph Jerome, Benefit-Risk Analysis for Big Data Projects 1 (Sept. 2014), https://fpf.org/wp-content/uploads/FPF_DataBenefitAnalysis_FINAL.pdf [hereinafter "DBA"].

[38] *Id.*

[39] *See, e.g.,* Eillie Anzilotti, *To Court a Skeptical Public, New York Sends Wi-Fi Ambassadors,* CityLab (Aug. 12, 2016), http://www.citylab.com/navigator/2016/08/to-court-a-skeptical-public-new-york-sends-wi-fi-ambassadors/495623/.

[40] *See* DBA, *supra* note 37, at 4.

[41] *Id.* at 9.

[42] *Id.* at 7 ("For example, the relative value of a health or national security benefit may differ from society to society. Some societies may place a high value on individual benefits, while others give greater weight to community values.").

[43] *See* Inter-Sessional Panel on "Smart Cities and Infrastructure" and "Foresight for Digital Development," U.N. Conference on Trade & Dev. (Jan. 11–13, 2016), http://unctad.org/meetings/en/Presentation/CSTD_2015_ppt07_Bufi_en.pdf; *PPP for Cities Case Studies Quick Facts and PPP Learned Lessons,* Specialist Centre on PPP in Smart and Sustainable Cities (Nov. 17, 2016), http://www.pppcities.org/wp-content/uploads/2016/11/7.-PPP-for-Cities.pdf.

do their due diligence and clearly delineate each party's responsibilities (and capacities) for managing, using, sharing, securing, or destroying data; for communicating with the public about privacy; and for supervising other contractors or subcontractors.

Even when initiating projects on their own, smart cities rely extensively on vendors, particularly in deploying, maintaining, and analyzing emerging data tools and technologies (including procuring Internet of Things devices, maintaining sensor networks, and publishing open data to platforms). As scholars have noted, "Vendors have different capabilities and incentives than a municipal government; they may be more or less capable of keeping data secure, and are not likely to be as responsive to residents as their city government ... [and] stakeholders will ultimately hold cities responsible as stewards and expect them to uphold constituent values."[44]

An instructive example of how the dynamics between public sector agencies and technology vendors can lead to gaps in individual privacy protection was presented in a study by the Center for Law and Information Policy at Fordham Law School. In the study, researchers analyzed contracts between US public schools and cloud computing service providers and found that "only 25% of districts inform parents of their use of cloud services, 20% of districts fail to have policies governing the use of online services, and a sizeable plurality of districts have rampant gaps in their contract documentation, including missing privacy policies."[45] Their findings showed that vendors often produced commercial boilerplate contracts that did not adequately address the student data context[46]; that school districts lacked knowledgeable privacy officers and staff; and that each party to a transaction expected that the other would raise any relevant privacy and security concerns.[47] These findings – and the fierce public backlash that ensued – should serve as a warning sign for other smart community services, which leverage private sector vendor technologies and business models but could create or exacerbate privacy risks.

Standard contract terms, such as data use limitations, data ownership, data security policies, confidentiality statements, and commitments not to reidentify data are crucial tools for ensuring individuals' privacy in multilayered smart city ecosystems. Given that the technologies and data analysis and management tools required for smart city operations typically are sold or managed by third-party service providers, it is essential that city leaders carefully select, engage, and supervise their vendors. It is also essential that privacy and security obligations flow with the data, binding subcontractors to equivalent protections throughout the data lifecycle. City leaders must continue to regularly monitor, assess, and audit whether service providers and other partners continue to adhere to contracts and agreed-upon practices.

Another reason that city leaders must be forward thinking in selecting and contracting with their service providers is that – unlike dispersed public schools – cities are "market makers, not market takers."[48] Cities wield significant purchasing power, and by requiring commitments around privacy and security in their deals with vendors they can effectively set nationwide industry standards. Best practices and standard contractual clauses at the largest companies can then have a trickle-down effect. This is particularly true as cities turn to start-ups and smaller

---

[44] *See* Whittington et al., *supra* note 10, at 1947.

[45] *See* Joel Reidenberg et al., *Privacy and Cloud Computing in Public Schools*, FORDHAM CTR. ON L. AND INFO. POLICY (Dec. 12, 2013), http://www.immagic.com/eLibrary/ARCHIVES/GENERAL/FRDHM_US/F131213R.pdf.

[46] For example, including terms that would violate the Federal Educational Rights and Privacy Act, the Protection of Pupil Rights Amendment, and the Children's Online Privacy Protection Act. *See id.* at 35.

[47] *Id.*

[48] *See* Whittington et al., *supra* note 10, at 1954.

organizations for their technology services, which may not have the same institutional expertise with privacy and security as large enterprise vendors.[49]

Data research and ethical reviews. Smart cities are becoming storehouses of hugely valuable information for public and private researchers. But appropriating civic data that was originally collected for another purpose without citizens' knowledge or consent raises significant privacy concerns – and weighty ethical and technical questions.

Traditionally, privacy laws have envisioned researchers utilizing de-identification to unleash the value of data while protecting privacy.[50] In recent years, however, advances in reidentification science and the increasing availability of external datasets with potentially revealing elements have led scientists and policymakers to doubt the reliability of de-identification measures to appropriately reduce the risk of an individual being reidentified from a dataset.[51] A robust scholarly debate continues unabated to this day between data scientists, researchers, lawyers, and regulators over whether and to what extent data can be scientifically or legally considered de-identified.[52]

Nevertheless, even as the debate continues to rage, communities leveraging citizens' data for additional, secondary purposes, including conducting scientific research or business analytics, must do so while respecting individuals' privacy. If consent to use data in a particular manner is not feasible to obtain, or de-identification unduly degrades the data or offers inadequate guarantees, urban data stewards must evaluate and document risk benefit assessments as part of a structured ethical review process.

In the United States, federal and federally supported institutions conducting human subject research have been governed by the Common Rule since 1991, which is itself grounded in the principles articulated by the *Belmont Report* of the 1970s. Under the Common Rule guidelines, researchers who are studying human subjects seek the informed consent of their subjects or, where that is not feasible, obtain the approval of an institutional review board composed of trained experts from diverse backgrounds who are charged with balancing the risks to individuals against the benefits of a research project. To the extent that cities accept federal funding, they are also directly subject to the Common Rule.

At the same time, the sort of big data research and analysis that municipalities and even corporate institutions increasingly are interested in have challenged existing legal and ethical frameworks, including the Common Rule. For example, the Common Rule defines a human subject as "a living individual about whom an investigator . . . conducting research obtains (1) data through intervention or interaction with the individual, or (2) identifiable private information."[53] In the age of data-focused research, however, it is unclear whether research of large datasets collected from public or semi-public sources even constitutes human subject research, as it often requires no interaction with individuals or involves data that has been de-identified or

---

[49] *See, e.g., 80+ Startups Making Cities Smarter Across Traffic, Waste, Energy, Water Usage, and More*, CB INSIGHTS (Jan. 24, 2017), https://www.cbinsights.com/blog/iot-smart-cities-market-map-company-list/; Jason Shueh, *How Startups Are Transforming the Smart City Movement*, GOVTECH (Sept. 1, 2015), http://www.govtech.com/How-Startups-Are-Transforming-the-Smart-City-Movement.html; Ben Miller, *3 Reasons Some Local Governments Are Eschewing Big Tech Vendors for Startups*, GOVTECH (Oct. 27, 2016), http://www.govtech.com/civic/3-Reasons-Some-Local-Governments-are-Eschewing-Big-Tech-Vendors-for-Startups.html.

[50] *See, e.g.,* Paul Schwartz & Dan Solove, *The PII Problem: Privacy and a New Concept of Personally Identifiable Information*, 86 NYU L. REV. 1814 (2011).

[51] *See* Ira Rubinstein & Woodrow Hartzog, *Anonymization and Risk*, 91 WASH. L. REV. 703 (2015), https://papers.ssrn.com/sol3/papers.cfm?abstract_id=2646185.

[52] *See id.*

[53] 45 C.F.R. 46.102(f).

that was in the public domain.[54] The size and scope of the data that researchers can now access – often involving the mining of massive datasets that can be years old and gathered from around the world – also tends to render traditional "informed consent" mechanisms ineffective.[55] Furthermore, as research projects are initiated beyond traditional academic institutions, new ethical review processes and principles will continue to develop.[56] City officials who wish to enable data research should be aware of the robust and ongoing discussions within the research community about how to responsibly and ethically use data in the pursuit of knowledge.

Irrespective of the precise scope of the Common Rule, municipalities conducting data research must consider ethical review processes and benefit-risk analyses as critical parts of privacy and civil liberties protections, particularly when sensitive data or vulnerable populations are concerned. Part of the difficult calculus of data-based research is determining when the risks of using personal information in a particular way so strongly outweigh the benefits that a project becomes unethical and should not be allowed to proceed – or, conversely, when individuals must assume some risk for the greater good. Without robust ethical review processes to help researchers, data stewards, and publishers answer these questions, valuable data research results could become locked away or research projects never even started for fear of public backlash or regulatory action."[57] Cities that seek to conduct research or to enable research by others must address these difficult challenges, and should engage with researchers and ethicists to develop new approaches to ethical review and big data research.[58]

As communities begin to actively push their data out into the hands of researchers, citizens, businesses, and other civic constituencies, however, they move beyond the routine tools of enterprise data management. When they act as platforms for data inputs and outputs, smart cities must rely on additional tools to strike the right balance between protecting privacy and enabling data use for the public good.

CITY AS PLATFORM

Historically, communities have been governed by "nineteenth and twentieth-century ideas of civic organization and social norms … revolv[ing] around representative governance and centrally directed bureaucracies overseen by experts using strict, formal rules of procedure."[59] Municipal data management has followed similar trends: data was often lost in siloed, incompatible systems, inaccessible to other agencies, let alone the public. Even where data was made public, it was often buried in labyrinthine city websites, in non-searchable or cross-linkable formats.[60]

---

[54] OMER TENE & JULES POLONETSKY, BEYOND IRBs: ETHICAL GUIDELINES FOR BIG DATA RESEARCH 1 (Dec. 2015), https://bigdata.fpf.org/wp-content/uploads/2015/12/Tene-Polonetsky-Beyond-IRBs-Ethical-Guidelines-for-Data-Research1.pdf.

[55] *See id.*

[56] *See generally* CONFERENCE PROCEEDINGS: BEYOND IRBs: ETHICAL GUIDELINES FOR BIG DATA RESEARCH, FUTURE OF PRIVACY FORUM (Dec. 10, 2015), https://fpf.org/wp-content/uploads/2017/01/Beyond-IRBs-Conference-Proceedings_12-20-16.pdf.

[57] *See* Jules Polonetsky, Omer Tene & Joseph Jerome, *Beyond the Common Rule: Ethical Structures for Data Research in Non-Academic Settings*, 13 COLO. TECH. L.J. 333, 336 (2015), http://ctlj.colorado.edu/wp-content/uploads/2015/08/Polonetsky-Tene-final.pdf.

[58] *See* Matthew Zook et al., *Ten Simple Rules for Responsible Big Data Research*, PLoS COMPUT. BIO. 13 (2017), http://journals.plos.org/ploscompbiol/article?id=10.1371/journal.pcbi.1005399.

[59] David Bollier, *The City as Platform: How Digital Networks Are Changing Urban Life and Governance*, THE ASPEN INSTITUTE COMMC'NS & SOC'Y PROGRAM (2016), http://csreports.aspeninstitute.org/documents/CityAsPlatform.pdf.

[60] *See id.* at 8.

Today, however, technological progress is helping municipalities make a revolutionary shift. By mediating interactions between communities and their citizens, smart city technologies, apps, and datasets are helping cities position themselves not as fixed, distant decision-makers, but as vital, central platforms that support the efforts of citizens, businesses, and other organizations to play a direct role in community operations.[61] Rather than relying on "separate islands of software that don't communicate," cities are centralizing and interconnecting "all the digital functionality the city needs to serve internal operating requirements and to engage with citizens."[62] In the process, they are becoming massive data and computing platforms, controlling what can and cannot be done with data, whether data will flow in and out of the city, and how privacy and security protections will be embedded throughout its physical and digital infrastructure.

In an era in which "code is law,"[63] municipalities should embrace their roles as digital platforms and the opportunity to set norms and standards around privacy for emerging technologies. Smart cities sit at the convergence of every major technology trend: the Internet of Things, cloud computing, mobile connectivity, big data, crowdsourcing, artificial intelligence, algorithmic decision-making, and more. Just as the Apple iTunes and the Google Play platforms mediate interactions between consumers and apps,[64] municipalities are creating platforms to mediate interactions between citizens and the civic environment. Similarly to commercial platforms, too, cities have an opportunity to write their own terms of service and to embed privacy and security protections throughout their physical and digital infrastructures.

Given the political gridlock and the pace of technological advancement today, privacy policy is seldom written by lawmakers in Washington, DC, or faraway state capitols, but rather is being embedded into the deals that cities are striking with technology and analytics providers. Cities already deploy sensor networks to monitor air pollution and reduce asthma rates; they support smartphone apps to optimize bus routes (or 911 services, or snow removal, remedying potholes, or any number of things); they develop facial recognition and algorithms to make policing more efficient; they provide free (but often ad-supported) public Wi-Fi; they send drones to monitor road congestion; and they rely on citywide electric grids to self-report usage and maintenance needs.[65]

Many cities are already absorbing data from the urban environment – including existing infrastructure and systems, sensor networks, social media feeds, user-generated app data, and more – and then centralizing and repackaging it in accessible, usable interfaces for developers, civic hackers, researchers, businesses, other cities, and citizens to take advantage of.[66] Providing a city's many constituents with access to data from and about their lives promotes a more engaged polity. Importantly, it also helps prepares citizens to consider their own data footprint and how "the technologies that seamlessly connect individuals to their environments change how they interact with the city and how the city interacts with the world at large."[67]

---

[61] *See id.*

[62] *See* Barbara Thornton, *City-As-A-Platform: Applying Platform Thinking to Cities*, PLATFORM STRATEGY (http://platformed.info/city-as-a-platform-applying-platform-thinking-to-cities/ (last visited Apr. 24, 2017).

[63] Lawrence Lessig, *Code Is Law: On Liberty in Cyberspace*, HARVARD MAGAZINE (Jan. 1, 2000), http://harvardmagazine.com/2000/01/code-is-law-html.

[64] *See* Adrian Fong, *The Role of App Intermediaries in Protecting Data Privacy*, 25 INT'L J. L. & INFO TECH. 85 (2017), doi: 10.1093/ijlit/eax002.

[65] *See Shedding Light on Smart City Privacy*, THE FUTURE OF PRIVACY FORUM (Mar. 30, 2017), https://fpf.org/2017/03/30/smart-cities/.

[66] *See, e.g.*, Rob van der Meulen, *Developing Open-Data Governance in Smart Cities*, GARTNER (June 21, 2016), https://www.gartner.com/smarterwithgartner/developing-open-data-governance-in-smart-cities/ ("CitySDK, a project by the European Commission, and the Smart Nation API coLab from Singapore are two examples already in progress.").

[67] Matt Jones, *The City Is a Battlesuit for Surviving the Future*, I09 (Sept. 20, 2009), https://i09.gizmodo.com/5362912/the-city-is-a-battlesuit-for-surviving-the-future.

Another significant, technology-driven aspect of this policy shift is that many of these efforts rely on novel combinations of municipal data, consumer data, and corporate data. For example, the City of Los Angeles entered into a data-sharing partnership with Waze, the smartphone app that tracks traffic in real time, in which "Data flows upward from motorists to Waze about traffic accidents, police traps, potholes, etc., and the City shares with Waze its data about construction projects, big events and other things that may affect traffic."[68] Where partnerships with private companies are not established, local regulatory authorities may instead require data sharing by law. In New York, San Francisco, and Sao Paolo, for example, local governments have revised rules or brought bills requiring Uber to share granular data about individual trips for such purposes as guiding urban planning, regulating driver fatigue, or reducing traffic congestion.[69]

Thus, smart cities will increasingly find themselves situated as intermediaries in an ecosystem of complex data and analytics flows. Given cities' unique regulatory, market, and social positioning, they will become important gatekeepers, dictating when, how, and for what purposes civic data may flow from one entity to another. What tools and considerations, then, should smart cities take into account in their role as platform?

Data mapping. Before cities can begin mediating the complex flows of municipal data to and from individuals and other entities, city officials need to understand what data they are collecting and how it is used throughout the entire smart city ecosystem. While this task can be daunting for an entity with the size and complexity of a municipality, a central component of a successful privacy and security program is knowing what data is collected, how sensitive it is, how identifiable it is, where it is stored, who has access to it, when and how it might be disposed of, and what it is or will be used for. When the city is acting as a platform for sharing data, the complexity of mapping data increases – as do the consequences should a city fail to understand the legal, economic, and social impacts of citizens' data spilling out without clear oversight.[70]

In particular, although these categories remain hotly debated, it is important to classify data as personally identifiable, pseudonymous, or de-identified.[71] Whether data can be used to identify or single out an individual within the city will have major legal implications and will determine under what conditions and for what purposes data may be used. This sort of identifiability classification is increasingly popular as part of open data schemas,[72] even as cities should be aware that there is significant debate within privacy and data science communities over when and how to regard data as "de-identified" or "anonymous."[73]

Urban datascapes raise difficult questions about data ownership. Who owns civic data – the individual who generates the data? The technology system provider? The municipality that contracted for the technology system? The public? Cities and those in privity with them need to navigate these complex waters, while keeping abreast of related issues such as what capacity parties have to secure data systems (e.g., a small public school may lack the expertise of a global

---

[68] David Bollier, *The City as Platform*, BOLLIER.ORG (Feb. 19, 2016), http://bollier.org/blog/city-platform.

[69] *See* Assembly Bill A6661, 2017–2018 (NY), https://www.nysenate.gov/legislation/bills/2017/A6661; *Regulating Individual Transportation in Sao Paolo: What Is at Stake?*, INTERNETLAB (Jan. 12, 2016), http://www.internetlab.org.br/en/opinion/regulating-individual-transportation-in-sao-paulo-what-is-at-stake/; Joe Fitzgerald Rodriguez, *SF Wants Access to Uber and Lyft to Tackle Traffic Congestion*, SF EXAMINER (Mar. 31, 2017), http://www.sfexaminer.com/sf-wants-access-uber-lyft-data-tackle-traffic-congestion/; Lauren Smith, *NYC Taxi & Limousine Commission Proposal Requiring Drop-Off Location Data Raises Privacy Concerns*, FUTURE OF PRIVACY FORUM (Dec. 30, 2016), https://fpf.org/2016/12/30/privacy-implications-collecting-hire-vehicle-drop-off-location-data/.

[70] *See* Whittington et al., *supra* note 10.

[71] *See* Jules Polonetsky, Omer Tene & Kelsey Finch, *supra* note 11.

[72] *See, e.g., Data Classification Policy*, OFFICE OF THE CHIEF TECH. OFFICER (Mar. 30, 2011), https://octo.dc.gov/sites/default/files/dc/sites/octo/publication/attachments/DataClassificationPolicy.pdf.

[73] *See* Part III below ("Open Data").

technology firm); who should be liable in the event of a data breach; what extra-legal privacy or security commitments entities have made; what data can or may cross territorial borders; and under what circumstances a particular party might be compelled to turn data over to a third party (e.g., a company holding citizen data may provide data to law enforcement subject to a subpoena or warrant, and a municipality may provide it to an individual subject to a freedom of information request).

Privacy notices. Every city, no matter how sizable its smart technology stores, should also establish – and make publicly available – a comprehensive privacy policy. These policies help all community stakeholders understand how and why data will be collected and used throughout the city, encouraging accountability and building public trust. While the science of effective disclosures continues to develop,[74] privacy policies remain a foundational tool for businesses and government organizations.

These public-facing policies should describe urban data practices, including, but not limited to, the following key provisions:

- How data is collected, stored, used, secured, shared, and disclosed
- For what purposes data is collected and used
- Which data sets are owned by which stakeholders, and what data rights and protections accompany them
- Which data sets are private or require individuals' consent before being used
- Which data sets can be shared with the city or with authorized third parties
- How de-identified data can be shared
- What options, if any, individuals have to access, correct, or request the deletion of their personal data
- If personal data will be used for automated decision-making, meaningful information about the logic involved and the significance and envisaged consequences of such processing for the individual
- How data holders will respond to law enforcement requests for data
- The identity and the contact details of the data controller
- Whether data will be used for research
- The period for which personal data will be stored

Cities can and should experiment with additional features such as layered notices, just-in-time notifications, and explanatory illustrations and data visualizations, as well as ensure that privacy policies are consistent, easy to understand, and accessible to all members of the public, including individuals with disabilities. Determining *where* and *how* to place notices in public spaces can be challenging. For example, in many places around the world, CCTV cameras are accompanied by a printed card with the legal authority, a statement that the camera is in operation, and contact details for obtaining additional details about the data processing.[75] Once cities begin expanding to distributed devices and sensors, however, notice will become even more difficult – should citizens look for a license plate on a drone overhead? Should there be a sign at the entrance to every subway station with mobile location analytics systems? Should cities

---

[74] *See, e.g.*, Lorrie Cranor, *Reflections on the FTC's Disclosure Evaluation Workshop*, FED. TRADE COMM'N (Nov. 30, 2016), https://www.ftc.gov/news-events/blogs/techftc/2016/11/reflections-ftcs-disclosure-evaluation-workshop.

[75] *See Data Protection and CCTV*, DATA PROTECTION COMM'R (IRELAND), https://www.dataprotection.ie/docs/Data-Protection-CCTV/m/242.htm (last visited Apr. 24, 2017).

provide an app that will pop up notices about active data collection?[76] With a vast array of devices and sensors hovering around the cityscape, the public sphere can quickly become cluttered with an incomprehensible cacophony of privacy notices.

In addition to the challenge of balancing comprehensive disclosures against *readable* disclosures, smart city officials have sometimes struggled to draft disclosures that are temporally appropriate. That is, sometimes privacy policies describe not just the city's current technological and data collection capabilities, but also those that it hopes to roll out in the future (sometimes seeking to look years forward).[77] While cities should be commended for thinking about and making public the potential privacy impact of their new technologies and services suitably far in advance, making such disclosures in a privacy policy – without additional discussion – can muddy the water.

Much like their corporate counterparts, city attorneys that are not sure precisely how a new feature will work in practice often find themselves drafting privacy policies with the broadest possible terms, providing flexibility for when the city does finally roll out an ambitious project. Until the feature *is* available, however, such broad, permissive policies may give citizens, communities, and consumer and privacy advocates (and anyone else who reads the privacy policy)[78] cause for concern. Confusion and mistrust are only likely to compound when city officials (understandably) cannot describe any concrete privacy controls for as yet inactive features.

This is not to say that cities should withhold information about prospective privacy-impacting technologies or services; after all, constant updates to a privacy policy every time a new feature comes online may also fail to satisfy (or adequately notify) citizens and advocates. Rather, cities should aspire to publish privacy policies that are current and timely, but also to supplement them with additional transparency mechanisms.

Transparency. In a smart city, privacy policies are necessary but not sufficient for informing citizens about how data is collected and used. Municipalities must strive to be truly *transparent* to the public they serve. This requires engaging with communities and stakeholders early and often, seeking creative ways to alert citizens to data-driven activities, and increasing data literacy throughout the city's population.

When cities literally act as data platforms, they gain additional leverage to promote transparency throughout the smart city data ecosystem. Through their terms of service or contractual dealings, cities may condition other parties' access to civic data on maintaining appropriate transparency mechanisms. Consider, for example, the critical role played by the Apple iTunes and Google Play platforms, which require apps to provide privacy policies and link to them from

---

[76] *See, e.g.*, Art. 29 Data Protection Working Party, Opinion 8/2014 on the Recent Developments on the Internet of Things (Sept. 16, 2014), http://www.dataprotection.ro/servlet/ViewDocument?id=1088; Art. 29 Data Protection Working Party, Opinion 01/2015 on Privacy and Data Protection Issues relating to the Utilisation of Drones (June 16, 2015), http://ec.europa.eu/justice/data-protection/article-29/documentation/opin ion-recommendation/files/2015/wp231_en.pdf; *Opening remarks of FTC Chairwoman Edith Ramirez, Privacy and the IoT: Navigating Policy Issues*, Int'l. Consumer Electronics Show (Jan. 6, 2015), https://www.ftc.gov/system/files/ documents/public_statements/617191/150106cesspeech.pdf.

[77] For example, early versions of the privacy policy for LinkNYC, which offered free public Wi-Fi through sidewalk kiosks, contained language about camera and facial recognition for months before the cameras were turned on. *See* Brady Dale, *Meet the Brave Souls Who Read LinkNYC's Two Different Privacy Policies*, Observer (July 28, 2016), http://observer.com/2016/07/linknyc-intersection-sidewalk-labls-alphabet-google-privacy/.

[78] *Cf.* Aleecia McDonald & Lorrie Cranor, *The Cost of Reading Privacy Policies*, 4 I/S: A J. of L. and Policy for the Info. Soc'y 543 (2008), http://hdl.handle.net/1811/72839.

within the platforms themselves.[79] App platforms also tackle more sensitive data collection by requiring and prompting users with just-in-time notifications about particular data uses, such as location tracking or access to address book contacts.

Cities can also leverage their unique control over both physical and digital spaces to deploy multifarious messages about how civic data is collected and used. City officials should pro-actively and preemptively assess in what manner to provide information about data collection and use for every initiative that involves citizens' PII. Some uses may be appropriately disclosed via municipal publications or announcements, while other, more sensitive uses may require specific, on-site public disclosures or signage. The physical environment for cities' connected devices also provides creative opportunities, such as lights or noises, to indicate when data is being collected. Some devices will be more obvious than others; for example, a streetlight triggered by a motion detector likely does not need a more specific notification. A streetlight passively sensing a nearby smartphone's MAC signal, on the other hand, would raise a more significant concern.[80]

Cities can also invest in digital literacy and education campaigns, to help citizens understand and take advantage of technological offerings more generally while bridging the digital divide.

Purpose specification and data minimization. Finally, when designing systems to collect or use personal data, smart cities should specify the purpose of data collection and ensure data minimization to avoid collecting beyond what is necessary for those purposes. In situations where notice and choice may not be practical, or where data may leave the city's specific control and enter an unregulated ecosystem, narrowing collection and use of personal data in accordance with these principles will safeguard individuals' privacy and bar indiscriminate surveillance. At the same time, these principles should not be rigidly applied to hinder the ability of smart cities to improve and develop innovative new services. Smart cities should consider looking to the Federal Privacy Act of 1974 as a model for addressing the privacy impact of government databases.

City officials must also keep in mind their influence as custodians of a data and technology intermediary, where data practices, permissions, and assumptions written into a city's code can become *de facto* laws.[81] By controlling the pipeline of civic data and restricting the types and classes of data going into and out of their data platforms (whether internal or public-facing), cities will have tremendous power to set privacy-protective standards, norms, and technologies in place to enforce – or, conversely, to undercut – the principles of purpose specification and data minimization. This requires cities not only to implement these principles, but to enforce them and monitor data recipients and systems for compliance. At the same time, however, cities should be cognizant of their own limitations: data that enters city hands may be *more* susceptible to being made public via freedom of information requests or open data mandates.

---

[79] *See, e.g., Google API Terms of Service*, GOOGLE DEVELOPERS (Dec. 5, 2014), https://developers.google.com/terms/; *Terms and Conditions*, APPLE DEVELOPER, https://developer.apple.com/terms/ (last visited Apr. 24, 2017); *FPF Mobile Apps Study*, FUTURE OF PRIVACY FORUM (Aug. 2016), https://fpf.org/wp-content/uploads/2016/08/2016-FPF-Mobile-Apps-Study_final.pdf (showing upward trend of privacy policies in app stores).

[80] *See, e.g., Mobile Location Analytics Opt-Out*, SMART-PLACES, https://smart-places.org/ (last visited Apr. 24, 2017); *Wi-Fi Location Analytics*, INFO. COMM'R'S OFFICE (U.K.) (Feb. 16, 2016), https://ico.org.uk/media/1560691/wi-fi-location-analytics-guidance.pdf; U.S. v. InMobi Pte Ltd., Case No.: 3:16-cv-3474 (N.D. Cal. 2016), https://www.ftc.gov/system/files/documents/cases/160622inmobicmpt.pdf; *WiFi Tracking Technology in Shops and on Public Roads by Bluetrace: Investigation by the Dutch Data Protection Authority*, AUTORITEIT PERSOONSGEGEVENS (Oct. 2015), https://autoriteit persoonsgegevens.nl/sites/default/files/atoms/files/conclusions_bluetrace_investigation.pdf.

[81] *See* Martjin de Waal, *The City as an Interactive Platform*, THE MOBILE CITY (Oct. 9, 2009), http://themobilecity.nl/2009/10/09/593/.

Collecting data without an intent to use it in specific ways, or storing it after it has served its purpose, is risky behavior for any organization, but cities especially hold the keys to highly sensitive data, often from vulnerable populations.[82] The New York City municipal ID program, for example, was designed to help undocumented immigrants integrate into the city's residential fabric. Upon the election of President Trump and a policy shift by the federal government towards actively tracking and deporting undocumented immigrants, New York City officials have struggled over what to do to protect their database: challenge in court any attempt by the federal data to access it? Destroy it?[83] When cities choose to collect personal and sensitive data, they must consider how that information could be reused by others. It is common privacy gospel that if sensitive data cannot be adequately safeguarded, it should not be collected in the first place.

CITY AS GOVERNMENT

Even the most technologically advanced city in the world[84] is still ultimately a political entity, accountable to the needs and desires of its constituents. Unlike private sector data stewards or platforms, cities cannot pick and choose which populations to serve, and every misstep can have huge and lasting impacts on the urban life of citizens. The technologists' desire to "move fast and break things" is dangerous when real lives and the public interest are at stake.

In their more traditional role as a local governmental entity, cities must navigate their obligations to ensure the safe, efficient, and equitable administration of city services; to govern transparently; and to protect the civil liberties of city residents. Often, these goals need to be balanced against each other, as for example, transparency mandated by freedom of information laws may run up against individuals' privacy rights. Complicating this, cities must account for the competing public values and preferences of their highly diverse constituents: some citizens broadly support the use of body-worn cameras by police for improving accountability and public safety, for example, while others distrust and reject this measure for increasing government surveillance of vulnerable populations.[85]

Furthermore, municipalities' reliance on data-driven decision-making raises concerns that "technocratic governance" could supplant citizen-centered political processes.[86] Municipalities that are overeager to deploy technologically oriented solutions may inadvertently find themselves prioritizing some citizens over others.[87] The City of Boston, for example, developed a smartphone app that would use the phone's accelerometer and GPS data to automatically report

---

[82] *See, e.g.,* Deepti Hajela & Jennifer Peltz, *New York City Could Destroy Immigrant ID Card Data After Donald Trump Win,* THE DENVER POST (Nov. 15, 2016), http://www.denverpost.com/2016/11/15/new-york-city-destroy-immigrant-id-card-data/.

[83] *See* Liz Robbins, *New York City Should Keep ID Data for Now, Judge Rules,* N.Y. TIMES (Dec. 21, 2016), https://www.nytimes.com/2016/12/21/nyregion/new-york-city-should-keep-id-data-for-now-judge-rules.html.

[84] According to one recent study, Tokyo. IESE CITIES IN MOTION INDEX 25 (2016), http://www.iese.edu/research/pdfs/ST-0396-E.pdf/.

[85] *See* Harvard Law Review, *Considering Police Body Cameras,* 128 HARV. L. REV. 1794 (Apr. 10, 2015), http://harvardlawreview.org/2015/04/considering-police-body-cameras/.

[86] *See* Rob Kitchin, *The Real-Time City? Big Data and Smart Urbanism,* 79 GEOJOURNAL 1–14 (2014), https://pdfs.semanticscholar.org/6e73/7a0e5ef2930376oa565ba5e9d98510ab0976.pdf.

[87] *See* Jathan Sadowski & Frank Pasquale, *The Spectrum of Control: A Social Theory of the Smart City,* 20 FIRST MONDAY (2015), http://firstmonday.org/article/view/5903/4660 ("To take some obvious examples: should new forms of surveillance focus first on drug busts, or evidence of white-collar crime, or unfair labor practices by employers? . . . Do the cameras and sensors in restaurants focus on preventing employee theft of food, stopping food poisoning, and/or catching safety violations?").

potholes to the city's Public Works Department as users drove around town.[88] Before launching the app, however, the city and the app developers realized that variances in smartphone ownership could foster inequities in road improvement. The populations that were most likely to own a smart phone – the young and the wealthy – were at risk of diverting city services away from poor and elderly neighborhoods.[89] Instead, the city modified their rollout plans, "first handing the app out to city-road inspectors, who service all parts of the city equally, relying on the public for only additional supporting data."[90]

Municipalities must ever be conscious of how the deployment of data-collecting technologies will shift the balance of power maintained between citizens and the city. What tools and considerations, then, should smart cities take into account to protect individual privacy in their role as local government?

Open data. Many federal, state, and municipal governments have committed to making their data available to city partners, businesses, and citizens alike through Open Data projects and portals.[91] Open data efforts characterize themselves as providing the social, economic, and democratic values that cities often seek to embody[92]: they are about "living up to the potential of our information, about looking at comprehensive information management and making determinations that fall in the public interest," "unlock[ing] troves of valuable data – that taxpayers have already paid for," and establishing "a system of transparency, public participation, and collaboration."[93] As a practical matter, too, governments are uniquely situated to give back to their communities due to the quantity and centrality of the government's data collection, as well as the fact that most government data is public data by law.[94]

In the spirit of civic innovation and reform, many cities are not only making their databases public, they are increasingly doing so by default. The City of Louisville has a standing executive order for all data to be open,[95] for example, and the mayor and city council of the City of Palo Alto have also recently decreed data to be open by default.[96] The City of Seattle, which finds itself attempting to balance a stringent public records law against a robust civic tech ethos, has decreed that data will be made "open by preference."[97] Indeed, all levels of government are encouraging open data: in 2013, "President Obama signed an executive order that made open and machine-readable data the new default for government information,"[98] and the federal data.

---

[88] *See* Exec. Office of the President, Big Risks, Big Opportunities: the Intersections of Big Data and Civil Rights (May 2016), https://obamawhitehouse.archives.gov/sites/default/files/microsites/ostp/2016_0504_data_discrimination.pdf; John D. Sutter, *Street Bump App Detects Potholes, Tells City Officials*, CNN (Feb. 16, 2012), http://edition.cnn.com/2012/02/16/tech/street-bump-app-detects-potholes-tells-city-officials/index.html.

[89] *See* Kelsey Finch & Omer Tene, *supra* note 5, at 1604.

[90] *Id.*

[91] *See* Roberto Montano & Prianka Srinivasan, *The GovLab Index: Open Data*, GovLab (Oct. 6, 2016), http://thegovlab .org/govlab-index-on-open-data-2016-edition/.

[92] *See, e.g.*, Jane Jacobs, The Death and Life of Great American Cities (1961) ("Cities have the capability of providing something for everybody, only because, and only when, they are created by everybody.").

[93] *See Open Government* Initiative, The White House, https://obamawhitehouse.archives.gov/open (last visited Apr. 24, 2017), *Why Open Data?*, Open Data Handbook, http://opendatahandbook.org/guide/en/why-open-data/ (last visited Apr. 24, 2017).

[94] *See id.*

[95] Mayor of Louisville, Executive Order No. 1, Series 2013, *An Executive Order Creating an Open Data Plan* (Oct. 11, 2013), https://louisvilleky.gov/government/mayor-greg-fischer/read-open-data-executive-order.

[96] City of Palo Alto, *Proclamation of the Council Proclaiming the City of Palo Alto as Open [Data] by Default* (Feb. 10, 2014), http://www.cityofpaloalto.org/civicax/filebank/documents/38803.

[97] Office of the Mayor, City of Seattle, Executive Order 2016–01 (Feb. 27, 2016), http://murray.seattle.gov/wp-content/ uploads/2016/02/2.26-EO.pdf.

[98] *See Open Government Initiative*, The White House, https://obamawhitehouse.archives.gov/open (last visited Apr. 24, 2017).

gov catalog contains 5,610 datasets from nineteen contributing city governments, 1,392 datasets from seven county governments, and 9,619 datasets from twenty-one state governments.[99]

City leaders must also carefully evaluate local public records laws[100] to ensure that individuals' personal data is not inadvertently made public by open programs. The breadth of any relevant Freedom of Information Act or similar laws should also be considered in determining what personal information a city can or should collect. While freedom of information laws uniformly include exceptions to protect individuals from the "unwarranted invasion of personal privacy,"[101] they predate the advent of big data and smart city technologies. Consequently, cities – and governments more broadly – have struggled to adapt to the realities of modern de-identification and reidentification science in determining what constitutes protected personal information. In 2013, for example, the New York Taxi and Limousine Commission collected "pickup and drop off times, locations, fare and tip amounts, as well as anonymized (hashed) versions of the taxi's license and medallion numbers" for every taxi ride in the city.[102] The data was obtained via a freedom of information request and subsequently made public, at which point industrious data scientists began reidentifying trips made by particular celebrities (including exact fare and tipping data), as well as, more salaciously, detailing the travels of everyone who took a taxi to or from Larry Flynt's Hustler Club, "pinpointing certain individuals with a high probability."[103]

Open and accessible public data benefits citizens by helping cities uphold their promises towards efficient and transparent governance, but also poses a significant risk to individual privacy. One of the greatest risks of opening government datasets to the public is the possibility that individuals may be reidentified or singled out from those datasets, revealing data about them that would otherwise not be public knowledge and could be embarrassing, damaging or even life threatening.[104] Recent advances in smart city technologies, reidentification science, data market-places, and big data analytics raise those reidentification risks.[105]

These concerns loom all the larger as open data efforts continue to mature, no longer simply publishing historic data and statistics but increasingly making granular, searchable, *real-time* data about the city's – and its citizens' – activities available to anyone in the world. Databases of calls to emergency services – for 911, or fire departments, or civil complaints about building codes, restaurants, and even civil rights violations – are all obvious risks for the leakage of sensitive data. Data sets that are more bureaucratic may fail to raise the same privacy red flags, while still leaving individuals just as exposed. In 2017, for example, a parent who was examining expenditure files on the Chicago Public Schools website discovered that deep within the tens of thousands of rows of vendor payment data were some 4,500 files that identified students with Individualized Educational Programs – revealing in plain text the students' names, identification

---

[99] *Data Catalog*, DATA.GOV, https://catalog.data.gov/ (last visited Jan. 3, 2017).

[100] *See, e.g.*, *State Freedom of Information Laws*, NAT'L FREEDOM OF INFO. COAL., http://www.nfoic.org/state-freedom-of-information-laws (last visited Apr. 24, 2017).

[101] *See, e.g.*, *Exemption 6*, DEP'T OF JUSTICE GUIDE TO THE FREEDOM OF INFO. ACT, https://www.justice.gov/sites/default/files/oip/legacy/2014/07/23/exemption6_o.pdf (last visited Apr. 24, 2017).

[102] Anthony Tockar, *Riding with the Stars: Passenger Privacy in the NYC Taxicab Database*, NEUSTAR RESEARCH (Sept. 15, 2014), https://research.neustar.biz/2014/09/15/riding-with-the-stars-passenger-privacy-in-the-nyc-taxicab-dataset/.

[103] *Id.*

[104] *Report of the Special Rapporteur on the Right to Privacy*, Annex II, Human Rights Council, U.N. Doc. A/HRC/31/64 (May 8, 2016) (by Joseph A. Cannataci); BEN GREEN ET AL., OPEN DATA PRIVACY PLAYBOOK (Feb. 2017), https://cyber.harvard.edu/publications/2017/02/opendataprivacyplaybook.

[105] *See, e.g.*, ARVIND NARAYANAN & EDWARD FELTEN, NO SILVER BULLET: DE-IDENTIFICATION STILL DOESN'T WORK (July 9, 2014), http://randomwalker.info/publications/no-silver-bullet-de-identification.pdf.

numbers, the type of special education services that were being provided for them, how much those services cost, the names of therapists, and how often students met with the specialists.[106]

Governments and scholars have only recently begun to tackle the difficult question of publishing and de-identifying record-level government data.[107] In 2016, the National Institute of Standards and Technologies released a guide to de-identifying government datasets,[108] and de-identification expert Dr. Khaled El Emam published an "Open Data De-Identification Protocol."[109] The City of San Francisco also published the first iteration of an "Open Data Release Toolkit," which walks city officials through the process of classifying data's appropriateness for public output, identifying direct and indirect identifiers, applying de-identification techniques, and balancing the residual risks to individual privacy against the potential benefit and utility of the data.[110] The City of Seattle is currently producing an "Open Data Risk Assessment," which in collaboration with a community advisory board and local academics, examines the city's open data program, organizational structure, and data handling practices and identifies privacy risks and mitigation strategies.[111]

De-identification may be the single most difficult tool for cities to implement, and yet also one of the most important if data continues to be made open.[112] In addition to risk assessments, cities should consider alternatives to the "release and forget" model that most open data portals use.[113] Where possible, cities may condition access to data on the signing of a data use agreement (for example, prohibit attempted reidentification, linking to other data, or redistribution of the data), or set up a data enclave where researchers can run queries on de-identified information without ever acquiring it directly.[114]

Communications and engagement strategies. As smart city residents begin to interact with new technologies and data-driven services in their environment, misunderstandings around what data is collected and fears about how it may be used could risk the viability of valuable urban projects.

Smart city leaders should develop proactive strategies that anticipate potential privacy concerns and seek to address them in public. Materials that are easy for the public to access and understand should be available from the outset of a program to explain the purposes and societal benefits of using data in a particular way, as well as the range of safeguards available to mitigate residual privacy risks. Citizens should be given opportunities to comment publicly on the

---

[106] *See* Lauren FitzPatrick, *CPS Privacy Breach Bared Confidential Student Information*, CHICAGO SUN TIMES (Feb. 25, 2017), http://chicago.suntimes.com/news/cps-privacy-breach-bared-confidential-student-information/ (further database details on file with authors); Cassie Creswell, *How a Parent Discovered a Huge Breach by Chicago Public Schools – of Private School Students with Special Needs*, PARENT COAL. FOR STUDENT PRIVACY (Mar. 5, 2017), https://www.studentprivacymatters.org/how-a-parent-discovered-a-huge-breach-by-chicago-public-schools-of-private-school-students-with-special-needs/.

[107] *Cf.* The U.S. Census Bureau, which has been producing aggregated statistics and engaging with cutting-edge statistical disclosure control science for decades. *Statistical Disclosure Control*, U.S. CENSUS BUREAU, https://www.census.gov/srd/sdc/ (last visited Apr. 24, 2017).

[108] SIMSON GARFINKEL, NIST SPECIAL PUBLICATION 800–188, 57 (2ND DRAFT): DE-IDENTIFYING GOVERNMENT DATASETS (Dec. 2016), http://csrc.nist.gov/publications/drafts/800–188/sp800_188_draft2.pdf.

[109] Khaled El Emam, *A De-Identification Protocol for Open Data*, PRIVACY TECH (May 16, 2016), https://iapp.org/news/a/a-de-identification-protocol-for-open-data/.

[110] ERICA FINKLE, DataSF: OPEN DATA RELEASE TOOLKIT, https://drive.google.com/file/d/oBojc1tmJAlTcRoRMVo1PM2NyNDA/view (last visited Apr. 24, 2016).

[111] *See* GREEN ET AL., *supra* note 105, at 57.

[112] *See* GARFINKEL, *supra* note 108.

[113] *See* SIMSON GARFINKEL, NISTIR 8053: DE-IDENTIFICATION OF PERSONAL INFORMATION 14 (Oct. 2015), http://nvlpubs.nist.gov/nistpubs/ir/2015/NIST.IR.8053.pdf.

[114] *Id.*

development and deployment of smart city technologies, particularly where data will be collected in new or different ways. Where possible, cities should also consider including citizens in the development process through user research, hackathons, and other participatory design events, which will give them an opportunity for deeper and more collaborative engagement than a public comment period alone. These responses, together with a proactive and responsive communications strategy, can help explain urban data strategy to alleviate public concerns.

One instructive example is the City of Chicago's "Array of Things" project. In partnership with the University of Chicago and the Argonne National Laboratory, the city wanted to deploy "a network of interactive, modular sensor boxes around Chicago to collect real-time data on the city's environment, infrastructure, and activity for research and public use."[115] Given the breadth and novelty of this urban sensing network, concerns about privacy loomed large.[116]

In addition to taking technical measures to minimize any personally identifying data being captured by the sensors, and instituting a variety of governance tools, the Array of Things also developed a sophisticated civic engagement plan. Its goals were fourfold: to "educate Chicagoans about the Array of Things project, process, the potential of the research, and the sensors' capacities; inform future generations of the Array of Things sensors; understand what the people want out of the Internet of Things & these neighborhood data; and collect resident feedback on privacy and governance policies for Array of Things."[117] The project team partnered with local community organizations to engage and educate Chicagoans, provided several easily accessible in-person and digital mechanisms for individuals to comment on its draft privacy policy, and developed a curriculum for a local high school to educate students on the Array of Things, developing their technology skills and engaging them with their city's real-time data flows.[118] The result was a more sophisticated privacy policy, an engaged and informed populace, and a positive model for cities around the world.

In contrast, the implications of failure to communicate effectively and timely can be stark, as demonstrated by the quick rise and even quicker demise of education technology vendor inBloom. Only a year after its public launch, the high-profile educational nonprofit inBloom folded in the face of sustained parent, press, and regulatory pressure about student privacy.[119] inBloom, in fact had more sophisticated privacy and security processes than many of the public schools whose data it sought to warehouse "so that school officials and teachers could use it to learn about their students and how to more effectively teach them and improve their performance in school."[120] Yet the organization largely failed to communicate proactively and respond to concerns about privacy, assuming that the value proposition of its data tools was self-evident. In doing so, it lost sight of the need to involve parents in the creation and implementation of the project and failed to prepare its partners – school districts and states – to talk about privacy and new technologies at a time when student data analytics were new to many stakeholders (including students, parents, and teachers). The results of failing to engage and communicate

---

[115] *What Is the Array of Things*, ARRAY OF THINGS, https://arrayofthings.github.io (last visited Apr. 24, 2017).

[116] *See* Amina Elahi, *City Needs More Detail in Array of Things Privacy Policy, Experts Say*, CHICAGO TRIBUNE (June 20, 2016), http://www.chicagotribune.com/goo/bluesky/originals/ct-expert-array-of-things-privacy-policy-bsi-20160621-story .html.

[117] *Array of Things Civic Engagement*, SMART CHICAGO, http://www.smartchicagocollaborative.org/work/ecosystem/array-of-things-civic-engagement/ (Apr. 24, 2017).

[118] *Id.*

[119] *See* Natasha Singer, *InBloom Student Data Repository to Close*, N.Y. TIMES (Apr. 21, 2014), http://bits.blogs.nytimes .com/2014/04/21/inbloom-student-data-repository-to-close/.

[120] *See* Dan Solove, *Why Did inBloom Die? A Hard Lesson About Education Privacy*, LINKEDIN (Apr. 29, 2014), https:// www.linkedin.com/pulse/20140429042326-2259773-why-did-inbloom-die-a-hard-lesson-about-education-privacy.

with citizens were a $100 million failed project, a skeptical and distrusting populace, and a wave of legislation permanently restricting the sharing of student data.[121]

Surveillance and individual control. While ubiquitous and persistent monitoring technologies are increasingly available to cities – including CCTV and body-worn cameras, stingrays, facial recognition, and automated license plate readers – the important goals of security and efficiency should not open the door to unlimited surveillance of urban residents.[122] A recent study by the Georgetown Law Center on Privacy and Technology suggests that half of all US residents are in a police facial recognition database, but that the systems are typically unregulated and hidden from the public.[123] Troublingly, the report notes that "of 52 agencies, only four (less than 10%) have a publicly available use policy. And only one agency, the San Diego Association of Governments, received legislative approval for its policy," and that "only nine of 52 agencies (17%)" had an intent to log and audit officers' face recognition searches for improper use."[124] Further, the report underscores racial disparities built into the facial recognition technologies, which both "include a disproportionate number of African Americans" and "may be less accurate on black people."[125] The lack of transparency, lack of strict oversight, sensitivity of the data, and power imbalance inherent in surveillance programs significantly threatens civil liberties and undercuts public trust in all other civic technology programs. The report, along with further testimony before the House Committee on Oversight and Government Reform, also implicates the enhanced risk to privacy and transparency when local government joins forces with federal agencies – in this case, allowing the FBI access to state DMV photo databases through contractual memoranda with state governments.[126]

Wherever possible, cities should strive to give citizens detailed information and legitimate choices about how their data is collected and used. In some situations, however, cities may be faced with technologies and data services that make it impractical or infeasible to offer citizens traditional notices or choices. If citizens could opt out of automated tolling enforcement, or security cameras, or court records, important public safety and accountability goals could not be met.[127] If cities needed to inform citizens of every instance in which their smartphones' mobile identifiers were collected by a city-run Wi-Fi connection,[128] individuals would constantly be bombarded by information and grow unreceptive even to important notices. Nevertheless, cities should sometimes be prepared to trade off perfect data for individual privacy, in order to build trust. While citywide smart grids will not be as efficient without 100 percent participation, and many citizens may be perfectly happy to share their utility information for lower costs overall,

---

[121] *See* Brenda Leong & Amelia Vance, *inBloom: Analyzing the Past to Navigate the Future*, DATA & SOC'Y (Feb. 2, 2017), https://points.datasociety.net/inbloom-analyzing-the-past-to-navigate-the-future-77e24634bc34.

[122] *See* U.S. v. Jones, 132 S.Ct. 945 (2012) (J. Sotomayor, concurring).

[123] CLARE GARVIE, ALVARO BEDOYA & JONATHAN FRANKLE, THE PERPETUAL LINE-UP (Oct. 216), https://www.perpetual lineup.org/.

[124] *Id.*

[125] *Id.*

[126] *See Law Enforcement's Policies on Facial Recognition Technology: Hearing Before the H. Comm. on Oversight and Gov't Reform*, 115TH CONG. (2016), https://oversight.house.gov/hearing/law-enforcements-use-facial-recognition-tech nology/.

[127] Paradoxically, in order to maintain such opt-outs the government would need to maintain a database of individuals who did not want to be tracked in order to effectuate those choices.

[128] *See, e.g.*, Steven Irvine, *Wifi Data Trial – Understanding London Underground Customer Journeys*, TRANSPORT FOR LONDON DIGITAL BLOG (Nov. 23, 2016), https://blog.tfl.gov.uk/2016/11/23/wifi-data-trial-understanding-london-under ground-customer-journeys/.

cities have nevertheless found ways to offer free and easy opt-outs for those citizens who do not wish to participate.[129]

If cities cannot notify citizens about a specific data collection in advance or at the time of collection, they should consider alternatives to safeguard individual privacy and bar indeterminate surveillance. If notice or choice is not provided in a particular instance, cities should:

- Conduct a privacy impact assessment and document in writing why notice or choice was not provided[130] (and revisit the decision on a regular basis),
- Implement processes to aggregate or de-identify data as soon as possible,[131]
- Seek the input and approval of an independent ethical review board,
- Provide individuals with information about how their data was used within a reasonable period of time after it had been collected,[132] and/or
- Minimize data to only what is necessary for a particular purpose.

Indeed, given that citizens may have no reasonable alternatives to opt out of municipal information systems, smart cities should seek to minimize data collection, or otherwise restrict the use and retention of personal data. As we have discussed previously, "one of the fundamental principles of informational privacy is to prevent the creation of secret databases."[133]

In addition to broader, public access to open government datasets that provide aggregate data on city and citizen activities, *individual* access rights are critical drivers for establishing trust and support in smart city technologies. They can ensure that smart city surveillance is not adversarial and secretive by empowering users to see for themselves what information has been collected about them. Where cities rely on algorithms to make substantive decisions with individual impacts, they should make efforts to reveal which databases they maintain and what criteria are used in their decision-making processes. If individuals cannot understand how and why civic institutions use their data, individual access rights may ring hollow.

Equity, fairness, and antidiscrimination. City leaders increasingly rely on big data analytics and algorithms to make cities, e-government, and public services faster, safer, and more efficient.

---

[129] *See, e.g.,* U.S. ENERGY INFO. ADMIN., SMART GRID LEGISLATIVE AND REGULATORY POLICIES AND CASE STUDIES (Dec. 2011), https://www.eia.gov/analysis/studies/electricity/pdf/smartgrid.pdf; Cassarah Brown, *States Get Smart: Encouraging and Regulating Smart Grid Technologies,* NAT'L CONFERENCE OF STATE LEGISLATURES (July 2013), http://www.ncsl.org/research/energy/regulating-and-encouraging-smart-grid-technologies.aspx (listing states with legislative action creating smart grid opt-outs); Nancy King & Pernille Jessen, *For Privacy's Sake: Consumer Opt-Outs for Smart Meters,* 30 COMPUTER L. & SECURITY REV. 530 (2014), http://ir.library.oregonstate.edu/xmlui/bitstream/handle/1957/55599/KingNancyBusinessForPrivacy'sSake.pdf; jsessionid=9D15BA5022E662CA12B15F1FAC292B49?sequence=1.

[130] For example, the FBI's Privacy Impact Assessments often include this question: "Clear and conspicuous notice and the opportunity to consent to the collection and use of individuals' information provides transparency and allows individuals to understand how their information will be handled. Describe how notice for the system was crafted with these principles in mind, or if notice is not provided, explain why not." *See, e.g.,* PRIVACY IMPACT ASSESSMENT FOR THE FIRST (Firearms Information, Registration & Shooter Tracking) APPLICATION, FED. BUREAU OF INVESTIGATION, DEP'T OF JUSTICE (July 2013), https://www.fbi.gov/services/records-management/foipa/privacy-impact-assessments/first.

[131] *See, e.g.,* INFO. COMM'R'S OFFICE (U.K.), *supra* note 79 (recommending data from Wi-Fi analytics be aggregated or have identifiable elements removed as soon as possible); AUTORITEIT PERSOONSGEGEVENS, *supra* note 79 (suggesting that Wi-Fi tracking within shops would be "less intrusive if the personal data processed will be made anonymous as soon as possible, or at least within 24 hours.").

[132] *See, e.g.,* Lukasz Olejnik, *Switzerland's New Surveillance Law,* SECURITY, PRIVACY, & TECH INQUIRIES (Sept. 26, 2016), https://blog.lukaszolejnik.com/switzerlands-new-surveillance-law/.

[133] *See* Kelsey Finch & Omer Tene, *supra* note 5, at 1613 ("From its inception, information privacy law has been modeled to alleviate this concern, which arose in the Watergate period in the United States and the Communist era in Eastern Europe when secret databases were used to curtail individual freedoms.").

It is important that smart cities also use these tools to make their environments fairer, and not unfairly distribute resources or inadvertently discriminate against certain groups, including not only historic minorities, but also any group of individuals with a smaller digital footprint, who may otherwise be left out of data-driven analytics.[134] City leaders will need to be particularly forward-thinking as they consider the societal impact of revolutionary new technologies that may have conflicting impacts on different populations: automated vehicles, for example, promise to bring new freedom and mobility to the elderly and people with disabilities, and to rededicate urban spaces to people, rather than parking, but at the same time may eat up thousands of driving jobs.[135]

As municipal governments begin to gain real-time awareness of the people and activities within the city, that information feeds into policies with "profound social, political and ethical effects: introducing new forms of social regulation, control and governance; extending surveillance and eroding privacy; and enabling predictive profiling, social sorting and behavioural nudging."[136] With increasingly robust data and analytics, cities will be more equipped than ever to subtly "nudge" their citizens to modify their behavior in subtle, low-cost interventions – hopefully, for the common good.[137] For example, when the Center for Economic Opportunity in New York City implemented its $aveNYC initiative, it relied on behavioral economics to nudge low-income households to opening savings accounts, tying the accounts to financial incentives in the form of a 50 percent savings match, with results showing that "half of the program's participants reported no history of savings, 80% saved for at least one year to receive the match and 75% continued to save thereafter."[138] City leaders must be careful to nudge individual behavior in ethical ways, rather than in ways that will constrain individual behavior, or profile and discriminate against a certain class of people.

As cities increasingly rely on data to automate their decision-making, they must be careful to think holistically about why and how data is being used: bad data can lead to bad policies, even (or especially) in "smart" systems. Predictive policing and predictive sentencing, for example, have repeatedly been undercut by studies revealing racial bias in both their inputs (historic arrest and recidivism data, respectively) and their outputs, leading to institutional racial profiling.[139]

As we have discussed previously, big data and increased data flows may both exacerbate and alleviate governmental discrimination, whether intentional or inadvertent. Given this, it is more important than ever that cities engage citizens early and often in designing such systems, and

---

[134] *See* Exec. Office of the President, Big Risks, Big Opportunities: the Intersections of Big Data and Civil Rights (May 2016), https://obamawhitehouse.archives.gov/sites/default/files/microsites/ostp/2016_0504_data_discrimination.pdf; John D. Sutter, *Street Bump App Detects Potholes, Tells City Officials*, CNN (Feb. 16, 2012), http://edition.cnn.com/2012/02/16/tech/street-bump-app-detects-potholes-tells-city-officials/index.html.

[135] *See* Jackie Ashley, *The Driverless Car Revolution Isn't Just about Technology: It's about Society Too*, The Guardian (Jan. 1, 2017), https://www.theguardian.com/commentisfree/2017/jan/01/driverless-cars-boon-bane-coming-down-fast-lane.

[136] *See* Rob Kitchin, *Getting Smarter About Smart Cities: Improving Data Privacy and Data Security*, Data Protection Unit, Department of the Taoiseach (Jan. 2016), http://www.taoiseach.gov.ie/eng/Publications/Publications_2016/Smart_Cities_Report_January_2016.pdf.

[137] Monika Glowacki, *Nudging Cities: Innovating with Behavioral Science*, Data-Smart City Solutions (May 17, 2016), http://datasmart.ash.harvard.edu/news/article/nudging-cities-innovating-with-behavioral-science-833 ("At the 15th Convening of the Project on Municipal Innovation, mayoral chiefs of staff and leaders in the field discussed how behavioral science can be used as a tool to improve public policy.").

[138] *Id.*

[139] *See* Julia Angwin et al., *Machine Bias*, ProPublica (May 23, 2016), https://www.propublica.org/article/machine-bias-risk-assessments-in-criminal-sentencing; Kelsey Finch & Omer Tene, *supra* note 5, at 1602–1603.

provide individuals who may be adversely impacted be informed of the criteria used in the decision-making processes, if not necessarily the raw data or code behind the determination.

Municipalities must be constantly vigilant to ensure they are serving *all* of their citizens, however difficult it may be to strike a balance between smart city beneficiaries and smart city casualties.

CONCLUSION

As Jane Jacobs said half a century ago, "Cities have the capability of providing something for everybody, only because, and only when, they are created by everybody."[140] The goal of local governments, technology developers, and community organizations should be to empower and engage citizens – to ensure that the cities of the future *are* created by everybody. And while many technological innovations are emerging first in urban spaces, they hold the potential to transform communities of all shapes and sizes.

Smart and data-driven technologies launch new conversations – and new ways to converse – between community leaders and community residents, creating room for the cultural growth and democratic impulses that have caused modern cities to flourish. Through open data programs, hackathons, participatory governance, and innovative community engagement processes, local governments are giving individuals new ways to interact with themselves, each other, and the world around them. When individuals have more control of their own data for their own purposes, a culture of data-driven decision-making, civic participation, and empowerment takes hold.

At the same time, if citizens do not trust that their data will be protected or do not see the benefits of new technologies, they could begin to fear the smart city's sensors and services as tools of discipline and surveillance, rather than cherish them as vehicles for transparency and innovation. City officials will need to learn how to make thoughtful decisions about providing appropriate notices, choices, and security measures to protect citizens' data, and to compete on accountability and transparency as much as on technological advancement. They will need to act as data stewards, diligently and faithfully protecting the personal data that the city and its partners collect. They should embrace their roles as platforms for data and technology, setting the bar high for privacy and security practices. And they must always strive to govern both their citizens and their citizens' data legally, fairly, and ethically.

If city leaders, technology providers, community organizations, and other stakeholders work together to address core privacy issues and principles, they will be able to leverage the benefits of a data-rich society while minimizing threats to individual privacy and civil liberties.

---

[140] JANE JACOBS, THE DEATH AND LIFE OF GREAT AMERICAN CITIES 238 (1961).

PART III

Ethical and Legal Reservations about Tracking Technologies

8

Americans and Marketplace Privacy

Seven Annenberg National Surveys in Perspective

Joseph Turow

The arrival of the commercial internet on a broad scale in the mid-1990s marked the beginning of new opportunities for advertisers and retailers to interact with and follow shoppers. Beforehand, advertisements were typically one-way phenomena. A person could read, hear or view a media-delivered commercial message, but the sending organization couldn't immediately note the audience members and their responses; nor could it reply to those individuals. To be sure, the actual act of selling products was not devoid of immediate knowledge about purchasers or of a marketer's ability to present feedback to them. Store clerks have a tradition of working with visitors and even in individual cases remembering their preferences. Moreover, catalog firms have long been collecting data on the purchase patterns of customers and sending them catalogs based on previous purchases. Too, chain retailers such as supermarkets, department stores, and discount chains have since the 1980s been keeping tabs on the purchase patterns of repeat customers by linking their loyalty cards to the goods' barcode scans at checkout. Nevertheless, most retailers didn't explore their customers' shopping habits in detail, and none followed them individually through the aisles.

The commercial internet changed all that. Virtually from its start, it allowed an unprecedented level of interactivity and surveillance for both the advertising and retailing industries. Retailers' needs got early attention. It was for tracking the same person's multiple purchases on the same retailing website using a desktop browser that Netscape software experts created the cookie in 1993.[1] Advertising firms then quickly realized they could introduce cookies to sites on which they bought commercial messages and use the cookies to recognize individuals (or at least their devices) across different sites. Over the next twenty years, advertisers and retailers pushed the boundaries of tracking technology beyond the desktop to the laptop, smartphone, tablet, gaming console, television set, smart watch, and an accelerating number of devices worn by individuals or in their homes. The aim was to gain immediate feedback about what audiences and shoppers were doing on web browsers and in apps so they could learn about and target messages to small segments of the population and even individuals in ways previously impossible via earlier media. By the early 2010s, retailers and their technology partners had begun to introduce ways to bring to physical stores the kinds of interactions and tracking that had become common on the web and in apps.[2]

---

[1] See Joseph Turow, *The Daily You* (New Haven: Yale University Press, 2011), p. 47.

[2] See Joseph Turow, *The Aisles Have Aisles* (New Haven: Yale University Press, 2017), pp. 66–106.

Public advocates worried about this commercial surveillance from their start. They have complained to the government and the press that the activities are ethically problematic, are clearly raising concerns among the citizenry, and would raise greater alarm if the companies involved would tell the public openly what they are doing. Industry spokespeople have responded that their key motivation for tracking is relevance. They reason that if people find advertising and retailing messages relevant, they will be happy to receive them. Moreover, marketers have claimed that people understand the trade-off of their data for the benefits of relevant messages and discounts. They argue that young people, especially, don't mind because the upcoming generation takes such tracking for granted.

In the context of growing surveillance by advertisers and retailers, the aim of this chapter is to interrogate their justifications based on the results of seven nationally representative telephone surveys I have conducted with colleagues from 1999 through 2015.[3] The purpose of the surveys was to assess Americans' understanding of their commercial internet environment as well as to evaluate the claims by marketers that relevance and trade-offs compensated in people's minds for the tracking that takes place. In the following pages, I present findings that tend to refute marketers' justifications for increased personalized surveillance and targeting for commercial purposes. I also argue that Americans resist data collection and personalization based on data collection because they don't think those activities are right, even if not confronted with immediate quantifiable harm resulting from them. I also argue that, contrary to the claim that a majority of Americans consent to data collection because the commercial benefits are worth the costs, our data support a quite different explanation: a large pool of Americans feel resigned to the inevitability of surveillance and the power of marketers to harvest their data. When they shop it merely appears they are interested in trade-offs. The overall message of the surveys is that legislators, regulators, and courts ought to rethink the traditional regulatory understanding of harm in the face of a developing American marketplace that ignores the majority of Americans' views and is making overarching tracking and surreptitious profiling a taken-for-granted aspect of society.

THE COMMERCIAL SURVEILLANCE ENVIRONMENT

In the late 2010s, the advertising and retailing industries in the US are developing their abilities to monitor, profile, and differentially interact with individuals in ways that extend far beyond their capabilities during the early years of the cookie. Technology firms that didn't exist a decade ago are deeply involved in helping to create what many in the business call a new marketing ecosystem that gives advertisers and merchants increased ability to discriminate among niche population segments and individuals. The opportunity to target messages increasingly takes

---

[3] Joseph Turow and Lilach Nir, *The Internet and the Family 2000* (Philadelphia: Annenberg Public Policy Center, 2000); Joseph Turow, *Americans and Online Privacy: The System Is Broken* (Philadelphia: Annenberg Public Policy Center, 2003); Joseph Turow, Lauren Feldman, and Kimberly Meltzer, *Open to Exploitation: American Shoppers Online and Offline* (Philadelphia: Annenberg Public Policy Center, 2005); Joseph Turow, Jennifer King, Chris Jay Hoofnagle, and Michael Hennessy, *Americans Reject Tailored Advertising* (Philadelphia: Annenberg School for Communication, 2009); Joseph Turow, Michael X. Delli Carpini, Nora Draper, and Rowan Howard-Williams, *Americans Roundly Reject Tailored Political Advertising* (Philadelphia: Annenberg School of Communication, 2012); Joseph Turow, Michael Hennessy, and Nora Draper, *The Tradeoff Fallacy* (Philadelphia: Annenberg School of Communication, 2015). The first six reports are collected in Joseph Turow, Americans, Marketers, and the Internet, 1999–2012, http://papers.ssrn.com/sol3/papers.cfm?abstract_id=2423753. *The Tradeoff Fallacy* is available at http://papers.ssrn.com/sol3/papers.cfm?abstract_id=2820060. Methodological and statistical specific accompany every report.

place in so-called programmatic marketplaces where advertisers bid to reach individuals with specific characteristics, often in real time, as they are entering websites or apps. In tandem with the growth of new ways and places to reach people, the past few decades have seen the rise of a data cornucopia that marketers can combine for all sorts of personalized offers and other messages. Most programmatic domains claim to be able to match shopper names, e-mail addresses, cookies, or other unique customer documentation with the individuals whom the websites and apps are offering for targeting. They also tout the ability to find large numbers of "lookalikes" who have the characteristics of those known individuals.

Marketers who want even more information about their customers, including information that can potentially identify them on their sites and apps on different devices, can buy it from data brokers such as Acxiom and Experian who at mid-decade had put together their own ways of tracking individuals across digital devices. Acxiom, for example, introduced an offline/online cross-device tracking system in 2013 that, it said, continually gathers information about approximately 700 million identifiable individuals from three sources: Fortune 100 companies' records of people who "purchased something or signed up for a mailing list or some kind of offer"; "every data attribute you could gather publicly about consumers from public records"; and its own cross-device cookie-like system that can match the same individuals across a huge number of digital properties and gives Acxiom "access to the last 30 days of behavior on more than one billion consumers." The Acxiom executive in charge reported, "For every consumer we have more than 5,000 attributes of customer data." Mediapost editor-in-chief Joe Mandese asked him and the company's chief executive about the possibly "creepy" nature of Acxiom's aggressive quantification of individuals. As Mandese paraphrased their answers, he saw the work as "just a fact of modern consumer life, and all Acxiom is trying to do is make it more scientific so that the data works the way it should, friction is taken out of the process for marketers and agencies, and consumers – at least – get the most relevant offers and messages targeted at them." The Acxiom executive contended his firm can predict individuals' future behaviors because it knows demographic information about them, has actual offline and online purchase data about them, and can follow what they do on different digital devices. "We know what your propensity is to buy a handbag," he said. "We know what your propensity is to go on vacation or use a loyalty card."[4]

In addition to third-party database firms such as Acxiom that traffic in identifiable individuals, marketers can turn to digital advertising networks that claim to bring together data about individuals for marketers from a wide variety of places, find those people – or people like them – and send persuasive messages to them on a wide gamut of devices. Google and Facebook do this kind of work all the time. They follow individuals who "login" to them on multiple devices. (Facebook requires personal identification to enter, while Google requires it for Gmail, Google +, and a few others of its services.) Individuals typically need to login once, after which the identification and tracking are automatic. Based on these actions, the networks claim "deterministic" knowledge that they are locating the same person on their smartphone, tablet, laptop, and desktop, for example.

But Google, Facebook and a relatively few other firms are distinctive in their ability to insist that visitors identify themselves personally. Many networks, apps, and sites recognize people's unwillingness to take the time to register on every site or app that requires it. One solution is to piggyback their logins on Google+, Facebook or Twitter identifications. Janrain is one firm that facilitates the process by helping sites and apps exploit social network logins, in which people

---

[4] Joe Mandese, "Supplier of the Year: Acxiom," *Media*, January 8, 2014, http://www.mediapost.com/publications/article/216930/supplier-of-the-year-acxiom-whos-on-first-wha.html, accessed September 16, 2016.

register and sign in to the location with their passwords from one of the social networks to which they belong. Janrain claims that "more than half of people" worldwide do it, with 81 percent of them going through Facebook or Google+. One cost to people using the technique is that the social network logging them in learns where they are on the internet. Another is that "social login identity providers" such as Facebook and Google offer the site or app owners the ability to learn each person's name as well as "select specific pieces of customer data that go beyond the basic name and verified email address to include elements like a customer's birthday, Likes, relationship status, photos, and friends' lists, to name a few." Moreover, the social network updates the data every time the person return through the login. "Your customers simply select their preferred social identity from Facebook, Twitter, or other networks," Janrain notes, "and choose whether to share some of their information with you." Logging into the retailer on every device with the same social login gives the person a persistent identity that can be helpful in noting the person's interactions with the retailer across different devices.[5]

A drawback to the site or app using this approach is that in recent years privacy advocates have convinced Facebook, Google, and other social platforms to tell their users what kinds of data they transfer when they login with their social accounts. Calls for greater control over what gets sent led Facebook in 2015 to allow individuals to check off the specific types of data they don't feel comfortable sharing when logging into a site or app. A Janrain report noted, "Some consumers are discouraged from using social login when the personal data requested seems excessive for or irrelevant to the intended transaction." The best way to allay customer concerns, it said, is by asking the social media site to transfer only the data that will allow the retailer to recognize the individual. Once that basic material has crossed the threshold and allowed persistent identity the data floodgates would be open. At that point, Janrain advised, "build a supplemental strategy to collect everything else."[6]

Janrain listed nine ways to collect "everything else" when cross-device identities are persistent. E-mail service providers can provide the site with each individual's forwarding behavior, e-mail frequency preferences, newsletter opt-in, stated preferences, and inferred preferences. Content management systems can provide the person's content viewed, shared, and saved. Contest platforms can inform the marketer of sharing behavior. Games can point out referrals through sharing. E-commerce platforms can list products purchased, frequency of purchase, recentness of purchase, average order amount, discount code used, and the reviews the individual posted. Chat and comment possibilities on a website can provide a light on an individual's sentiment and frequency of participation. Firms that provide "social listening" services can report on an individual's follows and un-follows on Twitter, the person's sentiments on Facebook, the person's views and comments on YouTube. Ratings and review platforms can enlighten a marketer about an individual's sentiments regarding particular products, services, and companies. And on-site behavioral analytics can yield a person's frequency of visits, time spent, content viewed, abandonment rate, and the site from which the person arrived to that site.[7]

---

[5] "Identity-Driven Marketing: Best Practices for Marketing Continuity," *Janrain*, 2014, p. 6, http://www.janrain.com/ resources/white-papers/identity-driven-marketing-best-practices-for-marketing-continuity/, accessed September 26, 2016, http://marketingland.com/coalition-for-better-ads-google-facebook-iab-191619, accessed September 26, 2016,

[6] "Marketing Continuity," *Janrain*, May 1, 2014, p. 15, http://janrain.com/blog/marketing-continuity/, accessed September 26, 2016.

[7] "Identity-Driven Marketing: Best Practices for Marketing Continuity," *Janrain*, 2014, p. 6, http://www.janrain.com/ resources/white-papers/identity-driven-marketing-best-practices-for-marketing-continuity/, accessed September 26, 2016.

Not all targeting that takes places involves known individuals. The continual matching of people and their characteristics for the purpose of commercial messaging takes place in an odd world where those traded across sites, apps, and devices might be personally identified or anonymous. Some marketers, sensitive to being accused of trading their customers but wanting to make money from the information, will get around the issue by insisting that the companies buying them scrub the personally identifiable information from them. Although the database companies that buy those data do not have the deterministic knowledge of an individual that a Google or Facebook have, they claim that by using advanced statistics they can indeed identify and follow the same person across sites, apps, and devices.

Conversant, a subsidiary of the big database-marketing firm Experian, is one firm that revels in such statistical inferences. Its website states "We accurately recognize consumers like no one else," because of its use of " an unprecedented amount of data, including anonymized transactional [store] data (both online and off) from more than 4,000 brands." Because it has so many data points on every individual (including data about their devices), Conversant claims a 96 percent accuracy rate in statistically determining that a person it is following in one domain is the same as the person in another. "We track over 1 million online actions per second to build each profile across more than 7,000 dimensions – including web browsing, app usage, video plays, email activity, crosscreen engagement, life events, hobbies, ad interactions and product interests." In Conversant's constantly updating world, marketers can find individuals who do or could use their products and target them with ads personalized to their profiles and delivered "across 3.3 million websites … and on 173,000+ mobile apps." The company adds that "our reach is on par with Google. And our competitors can't come close to our scale or persistence of recognition." [8]

When anonymity is touted, left unstated is that in many cases the lack of personally identifiable information such as name and address may not matter for marketers' targeting purposes. Because people lead so much of their lives on Internet spaces, for many advertisers it is enough that Facebook, Conversant, and many other audience suppliers can deliver the targets they need as they interact with websites or apps on a variety of digital devices, and lead them to respond to the advertisements sent their way. It is common, moreover, for marketers to match anonymous ID tags (such as cookies) with providers such as Blue Kai that match them with other tags, add more information about the individuals to the original cookies, and return them to the providers. The marketer thereby learns a growing amount about the individual and has a broad ability to reach that person despite not knowing the name and address. Marketing executives realize, too, that commercial anonymity online need not at all be permanent. It is quite possible to cajole people who are anonymous to reveal their identities. One way is to send an ad encouraging the person to sign up for a sweepstakes or free report using name and e-mail address. Another is to match a cookie or other ID of the anonymous person with the cookie for that person at a website or app that knows the person's identity.

The armamentarium of techniques to track and identify people with the aim of sending them digital messages that convince them to buy continues to grow. Over the past half-decade many retailers have been increasingly involved in bringing the process into their physical stores. Although most also sell online, the merchants are aware that the great majority (in the US, about 90 percent) of retail sales still take place in the brick-and-mortar domain. They are consequently accelerating their ability to exploit tracking and data as people move with their

[8] Matt Martella, "Making True 1:1 Marketing Happen, at Scale," *Conversant*, December 1, 2015, pp. 5–6, http://www.conversantmedia.com/insights/making-true-11-marketing-happen-scale, accessed September 7, 2016.

smartphones from their homes through out-of-home places and into the retailers' aisles. The technologies to do that include cellular, GPS, WiFi, Bluetooth Low Energy, sound impulses that interact with the phone's microphone, light systems that work with the phone's camera, and indoor mapping systems that work with the phone's accelerometer. These tools are typically used to determine a device's indoor and outdoor locations with the aim of sending a shopper messages about the retailer's goods, or personalized discount coupons. One way retailers can reach potential customers is to bid on reaching them when they are near their stores; programmatic marketplaces auction the outdoor locations of devices along with certain characteristics of their owners in a process called geofencing. When known customers who use certain apps walk through the stores, merchants can detect them in front of certain products and persuade them with personalized messages and discriminatory pricing – price discounts based on the store's profile of them and evaluation of their importance.

It should be clear that none of these activities is straightforward; the process of tracking, profiling, and targeting is fraught with challenges for the entire digital ecosystem. Many in-store recognition systems, for example, depend on the shoppers' downloading of an app (not necessarily the retailer's app) that can interact with the location technologies in the store. (Facial recognition and other biometric identification systems exist but have so far not been distributed widely.) Apart from the need for shoppers' participation in some in-store tracking activities are the difficulties the technology firms helping advertisers reach people with messages on websites and apps have with click fraud and ad blocking. Click fraud takes place in pay-per-click advertising when the owners of digital locales that post ads are paid an amount of money based on the number of visitors to those domains who click on the ads. An unscrupulous site or app owner will pay people or create automated scripts to click on ads simply to accumulate money deceptively.[9] Ad blocking is the act of using a type of software (less commonly, computer hardware) to remove advertising content from a webpage or app.[10] While industry players debate the specific reasons for these activities, they agree they cause substantial economic losses.[11] A report from Distil Networks estimated that in 2015, for every $3 spent on advertising, $1 went to ad fraud, costing the industry about $18.5 billion dollars annually. [12] As for ad blocking, one report estimated that around a quarter of Americans and Europeans block ads. A study from Adobe and PageFair concluded that the number of people engaged in the activity worldwide rocketed from roughly 21 million in 2009 to 198 million in 2015, with $21.8 billion in global ad revenues stymied in the first six months of 2015.[13]

THE RHETORIC OF TRADE-OFFS AND RELEVANCE

These developments greatly worry US marketing organizations such as the Interactive Advertising Bureau, and they have mobilized to address them.[14] At the same time, the business' leaders

---

[9] https://en.wikipedia.org/wiki/Click_fraud, accessed September 13, 2016.

[10] https://en.wikipedia.org/wiki/Ad_blocking, accessed September 13, 2016.

[11] George Slefo, "Report: For Every $3 Spent on Digital Ads, Fraud Takes $1," *Advertising Age*, October 22, 2015, http://adage.com/article/digital/ad-fraud-eating-digital-advertising-revenue/301017/, accessed September 13, 2016, accessed September 13, 2016.

[12] Greg Sterling, "Ad-Blocking Report," *Marketing Land*, August 10, 2015, http://marketingland.com/ad-blocking-report-nearly-200-million-users-22-billion-in-lost-ad-revenue-138051, accessed September 13, 2016.

[13] Greg Sterling, "Ad-Blocking Report," *Marketing Land*, August 10, 2015, http://marketingland.com/ad-blocking-report-nearly-200-million-users-22-billion-in-lost-ad-revenue-138051, accessed September 13, 2016.

[14] Ginny Marvin, "Google, Facebook, IAB & Major Brands Form Coalition for Better Ads," *MarketingLand*, September 16, 2016, https://marketingland.com/coalition-for-better-ads-google-facebook-iab-191619, accessed September 16, 2016,

are confronting public advocates and policymakers who decry the very elements of digital targeting the executives see as succeeding: the tracking of actual individuals, the digital dossiers marketers create about them based on various forms of tracking, and the personalized messages that circulate daily to hundreds of millions of people based on ideas about them that those individuals don't know and might not even approve. Marketing, retailing, database, and technology executives – and organizations such as the Interactive Advertising Bureau that represent some of their firms – insist the public accepts their activities even as they acknowledge some Americans feel discomfort regarding the data firms gather about them.[15]

Central to their arguments is the privacy paradox. It's the idea that, as *New York Times* reporter Brad Stone put it, "normally sane people have inconsistent and contradictory impulses and opinions when it comes to their safeguarding their own private information."[16] The Accenture consulting firm highlighted this phenomenon in a March 2015 web survey of 1,000 US adults. The firm found that while "nearly 60% of consumers want real time promotions and offers," only 20 percent want retailers to "know their current location" so the retailers could tailor those offers.[17] The McCann Worldwide advertising network's Truth Central project underscored the same contradiction from "a global research study surveying over 10,000 people in eleven countries," including the United States. Not breaking down the results by country or detailing the survey method, McCann stated that while "71% worry about the amount online stores know about them, 65% are willing to share their data as long as they understand the benefits for them."[18] Such seeming contradictions have led firms, including McCann and Accenture, to argue that what people do should trump what they say when it comes to marketers' uses of their data. The editor for mCommerceDaily interpreted the findings to mean "the tracking of consumers all comes down to the trade-off in value."[19] Along the same lines, the president and chief strategy officer of Mobiquity, a mobile-strategy consultancy, wrote in 2012 that "the average person is more than willing to share their information with companies if these organizations see the overall gain for end-users as a goal, not just for themselves."[20] A May 2014 report by Yahoo Advertising followed this logic in interpreting its survey of "6,000 respondents ages 13–64, a representative sample of the U.S. online population." It highlighted the finding, "Roughly two-thirds of consumers find it acceptable or are neutral to marketers using online behavior or information to craft better ads." Digitally connected Americans, the study concluded, "demonstrate a willingness to share information, as more consumers begin to recognize the value and self-benefit of allowing advertisers to use their data in the right way."[21] Industry executives further argue that young adults – some specifically say Millennials, the huge population of Americans

---

[15] Pam Baker, "Shoppers OK with Online Tracking, Not So Much With In-Store Tracking," *FierceRetailIT*, July 15, 2013, http://www.fiercebigdata.com/story/shoppers-ok-online-tracking-not-so-much-store-tracking/2013-07-15, accessed September 26, 2016.

[16] Brad Stone, "Our Paradoxical Attitudes toward Privacy," *New York Times*, July 2, 2008, https://bits.blogs.nytimes.com/2008/07/02/our-paradoxical-attitudes-towards-privacy/, accessed April 6, 2015.

[17] "US Consumers Want More Personalized Retail Experience and Control Over Personal Information, Accenture Survey Shows," Accenture, March 9, 2015, https://newsroom.accenture.com/industries/retail/us-consumers-want-more-personalized-retail-experience-and-control-over-personal-information-accenture-survey-shows.htm, accessed December 17, 2017,

[18] "The Truth About Shopping," *McCann Truth Central*, August 20, 2014, http://truthcentral.mccann.com/wp-content/uploads/2014/09/McCann_Truth_About_Shopping_Guide.pdf, accessed May 8, 2015.

[19] Chuck Martin, "What the Shopper Gets Out of Being Tracked," mCommerceDaily, May 28, 2014, http://www.mediapost.com/publications/article/226734/what-the-shopper-gets-out-of-being-traked.html, accessed May 8, 2015.

[20] Scott Snyder, "Mobile Devices: Facing the 'Privacy Vs. Benefit' Trade-Off," *Forbes*, August 3, 2012, http://www.forbes.com/sites/ciocentral/2012/08/03/mobile-devices-facing-the-privacy-vs-benefit-trade-off/, accessed May 8, 2015.

[21] "The Balancing Act: Getting Personalization Right," *Yahoo! Advertising*, May 2014, p. 11, https://advertising.yahoo.com/Insights/BALANCING-ACT.html, accessed May 8, 2015.

born from 1980 through 1996 – are much more likely to be comfortable with data capture and the notion of trade-offs.

Marketers also insist relevance is an argument for carrying out tracking and targeting despite the audience's professed discomfort. Virtually all search engines, social media, and retailers use the term to justify to the public their digital tracking and targeting activities. Google's "privacy policy" states right up front, for example, that "When you share information with us, for example by creating a Google Account, we can make those services even better – to show you more relevant search results and ads, to help you connect with people or to make sharing with others quicker and easier."[22] Similarly, Facebook's "data policy" states that "We use the information we have [about you] to improve our advertising and measurement systems so we can show you relevant ads on and off our Services and measure the effectiveness and reach of ads and services."[23]

Relevance is also part of the rhetoric that firms within the tracking-and-targeting ecosystem use to increase the data-exchange business. A contention going back to the dawn of the commercial web is that the best way to engage possible customers with a brand is to follow them with messages that are tailored to be as close as possible to their behaviors, interests, backgrounds, and relationships.[24] An Acxiom brochure tells potential clients to "Imagine being able to match your customers at various life stages and across touch points to be an accurate, comprehensive view." It adds, "Now that you are marketing to them in personal and relevant ways they are more willing to offer their trust and loyalty to your brand."[25] Carrying this idea forward, a report from the Forrester Research consultancy urges marketers to link relevance to trade-offs. "Provide services that customers find useful," a report exhorted, "and get back data on product use and customer affinities." Carrying this idea forward, the managing director of Mobile at the Mindshare agency suggested that his clients persuade their audiences to give up their data through use of wearable technologies (e.g., digital watches and exercise bands) by asserting that they will find the data as relevant as the marketers. "The Truth will be present in everything," was the trade-off rhetoric he said they should use to their targets. "You'll know everything about yourself and your loved ones if you opt in."[26]

WHAT THE PUBLIC KNOWS AND THINKS OF TRACKING, RELEVANCE AND TRADE-OFFS

This image of a powerful consumer making rational decisions in the face of considered concerns has become a way for marketers and the publishers who serve them to claim to policymakers and the media that Americans accept widespread tracking of their backgrounds, behaviors, and lifestyles across devices. Industry actors, moreover, cite studies they say indicate that Americans, while wary, are nevertheless are quite willing in actual circumstances to countenance robust amounts of tracking, data storage, and profiling, in trade for messages and benefits personally

[22] "Privacy Policy," *Google*, August 29, 2016, https://www.google.com/policies/privacy/, accessed September 16, 2016.
[23] "Data Policy," *Facebook*, undated, https://www.facebook.com/policy.php, accessed September 16, 2016.
[24] See Joseph Turow, *The Daily You* (New Haven: Yale University Press, 2011), Chapter 2.
[25] "Welcome to a World of Marketing to One," *Acxiom*, 2016, https://marketing.acxiom.com/rs/982-LRE-196/images/BRO-AbiliTec_web.pdf, accessed September 16, 2016. See also Adobe, "New Day for TV Advertising," paid (TBrand-Studio) post in New York Times, 2016, http://paidpost.nytimes.com/adobe/new-day-for-tv-advertising.html?tbs_nyt=2016-august-nytnative_morein-adobe-0824-0831?module=MoreInSection&version=PaidPostDriver&region=Footer&pgType=article&action=click. accessed December 17, 2017.
[26] "The Wearable Future," *PricewaterhouseCoopers US*, http://www.pwc.com/us/en/technology/publications/wearable-technology.html, p. 42, accessed September 26, 2017.

relevant to them. Unfortunately the specific questions and methods of these studies often don't get reported with the findings, so it's hard to evaluate the results carefully. Sometimes the respondents are volunteers responding to web ads, and their comments have no statistical relationship to the population as a whole. Connected to this difficulty with the reported research is that the people they get to answer the questions are recruited online. It is quite possible that volunteers to fill out online surveys are more comfortable with giving up data than is the population at large. To cap it off, some of the survey results are inconsistent, and even marketing executives are sometimes loath to fully champion the trade-off view. An Accenture executive interpreted his company's survey to mean: "If retailers approach and market personalization as a value exchange, and are transparent in how the data will be used, consumers will likely be more willing to engage and trade their personal data."[27] The Bain consultancy was even more cautious about results it had, saying "customers' trust cannot be bought by companies offering compensation in exchange for selling or sharing personal data."

So what do Americans know and what are their attitudes when it comes to commercial tracking, trade-offs, and personalization? Over the years, valuable noncommercial research has touched on parts of this question. The focus here will be on the Annenberg National Internet Surveys, conducted seven times from 1999 through 2015, because they have uniquely drilled down into key issues relating to Internet commercialism. Together, they yield a wide as well as deep view of Americans' understanding of and attitudes toward the digital marketing world. I created the surveys with the help of a team at the school and at times academic colleagues at other academic venues, notably Berkeley Law School. Major polling firms – Roper, ICR, and Princeton Research Associates International – asked the questions in twenty-minute interviews with random, nationally representative samples of (typically) 1,500 Americans, eighteen years and older. The survey firms reached the people by phone – landlines in the early studies and in recent years a combination of cell phones and landlines to account for the rise of mobile-phone only households. We asked a number of questions across more than one survey to assess the questions' reliability and, sometimes, the extent of changing knowledge and attitudes. In our reports we present the specific questions with the results.[28]

The answers are consistent, possibly surprising, and may contradict marketers' key contentions. Below I present an overview of key interconnected findings from various surveys, leading up to data that challenge the pro-marketing implications of personalized relevance and trade-offs.

1. *People are nervous / concerned / disagreeable about the data marketers hold about them and their family members.*

As Table 8.1 indicates, in the early surveys we asked about general nervousness and concerns. Later surveys probed the extent of respondents' agreement or anger regarding specific activities by "companies" and "stores" as well as by Internet firms such as Facebook and Google. The findings are quite clear and consistent across the decade and a half. In high percentages, people acknowledge being nervous about firms having information about them, especially when the firms retrieve it online. People believe that what companies know about them can hurt them and find it unacceptable if a store charges a price based on what it knows about them, if an

---

[27] "US Consumers Want More Personalized Retail Experience and Control over Personal Information, Accenture Survey Shows," *Accenture*, March 9, 2015, http://newsroom.accenture.com/news/us-consumers-want-more-personalized-retail-experience-and-contol-over-personal-information-accenture-survey-shows.htm, accessed April 26, 2015.

[28] See Joseph Turow et al., "Americans, Marketers, and the Internet, 1999–2012," Annenberg School for Communication report, 2014, http://papers.ssrn.com/sol3/papers.cfm?abstract_id=2423753, accessed November 29, 2015.

TABLE 8.1 *Percentage of Americans agreeing or agreeing strongly to statements about the data marketers hold about them and their family members*

1999: The internet is a safe place for my children to spend time: 26%	2005: What companies know about me won't hurt me: 17%
2000: I am nervous about websites having information about me: 73%	2005: It's OK if a store charges me a price based on what it knows about me: 8%
2000: I worry more about what information a teenager would give away to a website than a younger child under 13 would: 61%	2009: It is ok for internet mapping websites, such as MapQuest or Google Maps, to include a photo of my home on an online map: 40%
2003: I am nervous about websites having information about me: 70%	2012: If I found out that Facebook was sending me ads for political candidates based on my profile information that I had set to private, I would be angry: 75%
2003: I would worry more about what information a teenager would give away to a web site than a younger child under 13 would. 58%	2012: If I knew a website I visit was sharing information about me with political advertisers, I would not return to the site: 77%
2005: I am nervous about websites having information about me: 79%	2015: It is OK if Facebook links what people do when they access the internet on a laptop computer with what they do on their cell phone's or tablet's apps: 28%
2005: I am more concerned about giving away sensitive information online than about giving away sensitive information any other way: 65%	2015: It's OK if a store charges me a price based on what it knows about me: 14%
2005: It would bother me if websites I shop at keep detailed records of my buying behavior: 57%	2015: What companies know about me from my behavior online cannot hurt me: 25%

internet mapping firm shows a photo of their home, and if Facebook sends them political ads based on their private profile information. (All of these take place regularly for many if not most Americans.) We found that people fret about the safety of their children online. They worry more about teens than children under age thirteen giving up data online. The responses also show Americans specifically pushing back against a retail environment in which companies collect personal information. In 2005 and 2015, low percentages of Americans (17 percent and 14 percent, respectively) agreed with the idea of a store charging prices based on what it knows about them.

  2. *Most people know they are being tracked but Americans don't grasp the complexity of what happens to data behind the screen.*

They don't understand data mining, the way companies plumb and merge data about individuals to come to broader conclusions about them. Our 2005 study found that 80 percent of Americans know that "companies today have the ability to follow my activity across sites on the web," and 62 percent know that "a company can tell I have opened its e-mail even if I don't respond." Similarly, in our 2003 study, 59 percent of adults who used the internet at home knew that websites collect information about them even if they don't register. They did not, however, understand more granular aspects of the tracking activities. For example, 49 percent could not detect illegal "phishing" – the activity where crooks posing as banks or other firms send e-mails to consumers that ask them to reveal crucial information about their account. Yet when presented with an everyday scenario of the way sites track, extract, and share information to make money from advertising, 85 percent of the respondents did not agree to accept it even on a site they valued. When offered a choice to obtain content from a valued site with such a policy or pay for the site and not have it collect information, 54 percent of adults who go online at home said that they would rather leave the web for that content than do either. Among the 85 percent who did not accept the policy, one in two (52 percent) had earlier said they gave or would likely give the valued site their real name and e-mail address – the very information a site needs to begin creating a personally identifiable dataset about them.

We did not repeat the scenario in subsequent years to see if this general awareness of tracking along with a low level of understanding about its particulars still holds. But answers to true–false questions about the nature of internet activities indicate it does. In 2015, we found (almost exactly as in 2003) that 61 percent of Americans know "that a company can tell I have opened its e-mail even if I don't respond." Further, 74 percent of Americans know that "it is possible for Facebook to link what people do when they access the internet on a laptop computer with what they do on their cell phones' or tablets' apps." Yet in 2015 fully 66 percent got the phishing question wrong – much higher than in 2005. Moreover 64 percent did not know the answer (false) to the statement, "If I want to be sure not to be tracked on my cell phone, I should clear the phone's cookies." By far the strongest indication that most Americans still don't understand the particulars of tracking and its relation to data mining comes from the following consistent finding:

3. *Most Americans do not understand the meaning of the label "privacy policy."*

In five separate national surveys from 2005 through 2015, we presented to our representative sample of US adults a true–false question regarding a statement about the meaning of the label *privacy policy*. In 2014, the Pew Internet and Society program did the same.[29] As Table 8.2 indicates, our surveys in 2009, 2012, and 2015 presented virtually the same false statement. In 2009 and 2012 we said, "If a website has a privacy policy, the site cannot share information about you with other companies, unless you give the website your permission." In 2015 the phrasing was, "When a website has a privacy policy, it means the site will not share my information with other websites or companies without my permission." The Annenberg studies of 2003 and 2005, as well as the Pew study, phrased the concept differently. They omitted the point about permission, and the 2003 question asked whether the respondent agreed or disagreed with the statement, as opposed to presenting the true–false formulation of the later years.

Table 8.2 shows that over 50 percent of Americans in every year affirmatively chose the wrong answer – that is, answered *true* (or *agree* in 2003) rather than *false, disagree,* or *don't know*. In two cases, the percentage of people choosing the wrong answer reached above 70 percent, and in two years it passed 60 percent. The years with relatively lower percentages involved the most unusual approaches to the question: the 2003 request for an agree/disagree answer, and the 2014 Pew statement, which used an exceptionally strict formulation of the privacy policy's meaning via the phrase "ensures that the company keeps confidential all the information it collects." The overall impression is clear, though: despite different characterizations of the label's meaning, well over half of American adults in six surveys across thirteen years get it wrong.

The most obvious implication of accepting the truth of these statements is that the label's mere presence on a site or app leads people to believe they are safe from unwanted sharing of

[29] See Aaron Smith, "Half of Online Americans Don't Know What a Privacy Policy Is," *Pew Research Center*, December 4, 2014, http://www.pewresearch.org/fact-tank/2014/12/04/half-of-americans-dont-know-what-a-privacy-policy-is/, accessed September 21, 2016.

TABLE 8.2 *Percent of incorrect answers to privacy policy questions, 2003–2015*

	Survey Creator & Sample Size*	Phrasing	% Incorrect Answer
2003	Annenberg (N=1,155)	When a web site has a privacy policy, I know that the site will not share my information with other websites or companies.	59% agree or agree strongly
2005	Annenberg (N=1,257)	When a website has a privacy policy, it means the site will not share my information with other websites or companies.	71% true
2009	Annenberg (N=842)	If a website has a privacy policy, it means that the site cannot share information about you with other companies, unless you give the website your permission.	73% true
2012	Annenberg (N=1,228)	If a website has a privacy policy, it means that the site cannot share information about you with other companies, unless you give the website your permission.	65% true
2014	Pew (N=1,034)	When a company posts a privacy policy, it ensures that the company keeps confidential all the information it collects on users.	54% true
2015	Annenberg (N=1,399)	When a web site has a privacy policy, it means the site will not share my information with other websites or companies without my permission.	63% true

* Does not include Don't Know/Not Sure or No Response.

data with third parties. As noted earlier, that's simply not the case. Search engines, social media sites, and retailers routinely trade data about their visitors in one way or another. Another possible consequence of many Americans' belief in the label's reassuring message is that they don't go on to try to read the actual documents and get a sense of the litany of surveillance activities taking place behind the screen. The operative words are "try to read." Lawyers see privacy policies as contractual documents, designed (a number have told me) to broadly protect the right of a site or app to carry out its business. The policies are filled with industry jargon such as *affiliates*, *third parties*, *tags*, *beacons*, and *cookies*, and their very length makes them difficult to digest, as Cranor and others have found.[30] Nevertheless, the label may well diminish even the chance of gaining knowledge about the tracking, profiling, selective targeting, and data sharing that many firms carry out. Lack of knowledge is certainly the case among contemporary American adults:

4. *Large percentages of Americans don't know the rules of the new digital marketplace, and they overestimate the extent to which the government protects them from discriminatory pricing.*

Our 2005 and 2015 surveys focused on these topics through true–false questions. Slightly higher percentages of American adults knew the correct answers in the latter year than in the former, so perhaps a bit more of the population is getting conversant with the new digital-commercial

[30] See, for example, Jonathan A. Obar and Anne Oeldorf-Hirsch, "The Biggest Lie on the Internet: Ignoring the Privacy Policies and Terms of Service Policies of Social Networking Services," July 2016, http://papers.ssrn.com/sol3/papers.cfm?abstract_id=2757465; Solon Barocas and Helen Nissenbaum, "On Notice: The Trouble With Notice And Consent." In *Proceedings of the Engaging Data Forum: The First International Forum on the Application and Management of Personal Electronic Information* (2009), https://www.nyu.edu/projects/nissenbaum/papers/ED_SII_On_Notice.pdf; and Aleecia McDonald and Lorrie Faith Cranor, "The Cost of Reading Privacy Policies," *I/S: A Journal of Law and Policy for the Information Society*, 4:3 (2008).

world. The lack of knowledge about basic topics is, however, still widespread. Our 2015 study noted that

- 49 percent of American adults who use the internet believe (incorrectly) that by law a supermarket must obtain a person's permission before selling information about that person's food purchases to other companies
- 69 percent do not know that a pharmacy does not legally need a person's permission to sell information about the over-the-counter drugs that person buys;
- 55 percent do not know it is legal for an online store to charge different people different prices at the same time of day;
- 62 percent do not know it is legal for an offline or physical store to charge different people different prices at the same time of day; and
- 62 percent do not know that price-comparison sites like Expedia or Orbitz are not legally required to include the lowest travel prices;

Despite this pervasive misunderstanding of the rules of their digital-commercial environment, Americans have consistent and strong opinions when these issues are brought to their attention. Especially noteworthy, and not at all predictable, are their attitudes about various forms of personalization that are increasingly hallmarks of that new world:

5. *Most people don't think personalization by marketers in general or retailers in particular is a good thing, especially when they are told how the data for personalization are obtained.*

We found definitively in the 2010 survey that, contrary to what many marketers claim, most adult Americans do not want advertisements, news, and discounts "tailored to their interests." The percentages were 66 percent, 57 percent, and 51 percent, respectively. Even the people who accepted the idea pushed back when they found out how the personalization is carried out. We presented these people with three common ways marketers gather data in order to tailor ads – "tracking the website you have just visited," "tracking you on other websites," and "tracking you offline (for example, in stores)." We found that when people understand how their data are mined for personalization, the overall percentage objecting to the activity skyrockets. For example, when the people who earlier approved of tailored advertising learned the data would come from tracking them on the website they had just visited, the percentage of all respondents saying they don't want personalized ads jumped to 73 percent. When told the data would come from watching what they had done offline, the total number saying no jumped even higher, to 86 percent. With discounts, the corresponding percentages were 62 percent and 78 percent, and with news, resistance rose from 71 percent to 85 percent.

Our 2012 survey replicated these results with respect to consumer ads, discounts, and news. Our aim in that election year was to add political advertising to the list. The findings in that sphere showed even more definitive public distaste for personalization: fully 80 percent of Americans said they do not want political campaigns to tailor advertising to their interests. When the relatively few who agreed to political tailoring were then told the data would come from following them on the website they had just visited, the total number saying no to personalization jumped to 89 percent. When told the data would come from watching three of their activities offline – purchases in stores, political party affiliation, and whether they voted in the past two elections – the total disapproving hit 93 percent, 90 percent, and 91 percent respectively.

Americans' distaste for tracking and the personalization that often goes along with it was also reflected in answers to the 2010 survey that presented them with targeting activities and asked whether or not (given the choice) they would allow them. Only 12 percent said that they would allow marketers to follow them "online in an anonymous way in exchange for content," only 10 percent said they would allow marketers to "share information about [their] internet use in exchange for free content," and only 9 percent said they would allow marketers to "use information about [their] internet activities to deliver advertisements on [their] cell phone or video game system in exchange for free content." Of course, internet marketers carry out these activities continually (and did back in 2010). The respondents' answers suggest that if they had their way these activities would not take place. Americans similarly indicated their dislike for common political tracking and personalization scenarios. In response to questions during our 2012 survey, 64 percent of Americans said their likelihood of voting for a candidate they support would decrease (37 percent said decrease a lot, 27 percent said decrease somewhat) if they learned a candidate's campaign organization buys information about their online activities and their neighbor's online activities – and then sends them different political messages it thinks will appeal to them. In a similar vein, 77 percent of Americans agreed (including 35 percent who agreed strongly) that "if I knew a website I visit was sharing information about me with political advertisers, I would not return to the site."

A broad set of findings, then, call into question marketers' claim that people value the personalization that, marketers argue, leads to relevant commercial messages. Additional findings from the surveys push back against another major pillar of marketers' justification of their tracking activities: that Americans agree that they are getting value in trading their data for free content and other internet benefits. To the contrary, we found that

6. *Most people philosophically do not agree with the idea of trade-offs*

In 2015 we presented a random cross-section of Americans everyday circumstances where marketers collect people's data. We phrased the situations as trade-offs and learned that very many feel those trade-offs are unfair.

- 91 percent disagreed (77 percent of the total sample strongly) that "if companies give me a discount, it is a fair exchange for them to collect information about me without my knowing";
- 71 percent disagreed (53 percent strongly) that "it's fair for an online or physical store to monitor what I'm doing online when I'm there, in exchange for letting me use the store's wireless internet, or Wi-Fi, without charge"; and
- 55 percent disagreed (38 percent strongly) that "it's okay if a store where I shop uses information it has about me to create a picture of me that improves the services they provide for me."

Further analysis of these responses indicates that a very small percentage of Americans agrees with the overall concept of trade-offs. In fact, only about 4 percent agreed or agreed strongly with all three propositions. If we use a broader definition of a belief in trade-offs – the average value of all three statements – even then only 21 percent of the respondents accept the idea. Despite this principled disagreement with trade-offs, we found in our survey that many would act as if they agreed with them. We presented the people interviewed with a real-life trade-off case, asking whether they would take discounts in exchange for allowing their supermarket to collect information about their grocery purchases. We found that 43 percent said yes to trade-offs there – more than twice as many who believe in the concept of trade-offs according to the broader definition. Underscoring the inconsistency, we found that 40 percent of the people who said they would accept the grocery-discount deal did not agree with the third trade-off statement listed earlier, even though the type of exchange it suggests is similar.

So what is going on? Why the inconsistency? Based on examining the findings carefully, our answer is:

6. *Contrary to the claim that a majority of Americans consent to discounts because the commercial benefits are worth the costs, we find a new explanation: a large pool of Americans feel resigned to the inevitability of surveillance and the power of marketers to harvest their data. When they shop it merely appears they are interested in trade-offs.*

The meaning of resignation we intend is, to quote a Google dictionary entry, "the acceptance of something undesirable but inevitable."[31] And, in fact, our 2015 study reveals that 58 percent of Americans agreed with the statement "I want to have control over what marketers can learn about me online," while at the same time they agreed "I've come to accept that I have little control over what marketers can learn about me online." Rather than feeling able to make choices, Americans believe it is futile to manage what companies can learn about them.

People who are resigned do not predictably decide to give up their data. Watching what shoppers do doesn't reveal their attitude. We found that while people who believe in trade-offs are quite likely to accept supermarket discounts, we couldn't predict whether a person who is resigned to marketers' data-gathering activities would accept or reject the discounts. Marketers want us to see all those who accept discounts as rational believers in trade-offs. But when we looked at those surveyed who agreed to give up their data for supermarket discounts, we found that well over half owere resigned rather than being believers in trade-offs. Ironically, and contrary to many academic claims about the reasons people give up their information, those who knew the most about these marketing practices were more likely to be resigned. Moreover, resigned people's decisions to accept supermarket discounts even when the supermarket collects increasingly personal information were also positively related to knowledge. When it comes to protecting their personal data, then, our survey found those with the wherewithal to accurately calculate the costs and benefits of privacy are likely to consider their efforts futile.

7. *Sex, education, income, race, and age tend not to separate Americans substantially when it comes to privacy issues.*

Age and gender showed no differences with regard to resignation. When it came to education and race, statistically significant differences did appear: higher resignation percentages for Whites compared to non-Whites and for more educated people compared with respondents with a high school education or less. Yet those comparisons still showed that one-half or more of the individuals in most categories of respondents were resigned. The same tendency showed up with regard to our questions relating to knowing the meaning of *privacy policy* as well as those about tracking and serving tailored political ads: despite some differences, most Americans of all these categories revealed misplaced assurance about giving up their data when they see the privacy policy label. Similarly, concern with aspects of tailored or targeted political advertising never fell below 50 percent for any of the social groupings and was frequently far above that proportion. In fact, the proportions of demographic segments saying no were typically in the 80–90 percent range with respect to the central question about the desire for tailored political advertising.

It is important to stress that being a young adult (aged twenty-two to twenty-four) makes little difference compared to other age groups when it comes to views on resignation, understanding of privacy policy, and attitudes toward tracking and tailoring with regard to political advertising.

[31] "Resignation," *Google*, https://www.google.com/?gws_rd=ssl#q=resignation, accessed May 18, 2015.

Marketing executives are wont to claim that young people "are less concerned with maintaining privacy than older people are."[32] One reason is that media reports teem with stories of young people posting salacious photos online, writing about alcohol-fueled misdeeds on social networking sites, and publicizing other ill-considered escapades that may haunt them in the future. Some commentators interpret these anecdotes as representing a shift among Millennials (those born between 1980 and 1996) and Generation Z (those born after 1996) in attitude away from information privacy compared to older Americans.

The findings noted earlier contradict this assertion, at least with regard to the young cohort of Millennials. A deeper analysis of our 2009 data with colleagues from Berkeley Law School found that expressed attitudes towards privacy by American young adults (aged eighteen to twenty-four) are not nearly as different from those of older adults as many suggest. With important exceptions, large percentages of young adults are in harmony with older Americans when it comes to sensitivity about online privacy and policy suggestions. For example, a large majority of young adults

- said they refused to give information to a business where they felt it was too personal or not necessary;
- said anyone who uploads a photo of them to the internet should get their permission first, even if the photo was taken in public;
- agreed there should be a law that gives people the right to know all the information websites know about them; and
- agreed there should be a law that requires websites to delete all stored information about an individual.

In view of these findings, why would so many young adults act in social networks and elsewhere online in ways that would seem to offer quite private information to all comers? Some research suggests that people twenty-four years and younger approach cost–benefit analyses related to risk differently than do individuals older than twenty-four.[33] An important part of the picture, though, must surely be our finding that higher proportions of eighteen-to-twenty-four-year-olds believe incorrectly that the law protects their privacy online and offline more than it actually does. This lack of knowledge in a tempting environment, rather than a cavalier lack of concern regarding privacy, may be an important reason large numbers of them engage with the digital world in a seemingly unconcerned manner.

CONCLUDING REMARKS

Over the past two decades, large sectors of the advertising and retailing industries have built opaque surveillance infrastructures to fuel ever-escalating competitions aimed at the efficient targeting of messages to likely customers. When critics and policymakers have confronted them about these activities, industry representatives have often played down the concerns. They present a portrait of a nation of rational shoppers uneasy about marketers' data capture in the abstract but at the same time quite aware of the data transfer taking place and willing to give up

---

[32] Ariel Maislos, chief executive of Pudding Media, quoted in Louise Story, "Company Will Monitor Phone Calls to Tailor Ads," *New York Times*, September 24, 2007, available at: http://www.nytimes.com/2007/09/24/business/media/24adcol.html.

[33] See Margo Gardner and Laurence Steinberg, "Peer Influence on Risk Taking, Risk Preference, and Risky Decision Making in Adolescence and Adulthood: An Experimental Study," *Developmental Psychology* 41:4 (2005), 625–635. No one 23 or 24 years of age was in the sample; and Jennifer Barrigar, Jacquelyn Burkell, and Ian Kerr, "Let's Not Get Psyched Out of Privacy," *Canadian Business Law Journal*, 44:54, pp. 2006–2007.

information about themselves in exchange for relevant information and discounts. The Annenberg surveys over the past decade and a half indicate consistently that this view of the American public is highly flawed. Most people are certainly nervous about data marketers capture about them, but they do not display the reasoned, knowing perspective the marketing establishment claims. They don't understand the particularities of tracking – alarmingly, most cannot detect a description of phishing – or basic aspects of data mining. They consistently mistake the label privacy policy for an assurance that marketers will not use information gleaned about them without their permission. And, surely in part because they misunderstand *privacy policy*, they believe it is illegal for marketers to gather data and personalize prices in ways that are actually quite common.

Even if Americans are approaching the new commercial digital world through rational lenses, then, our surveys show that the knowledge they have to apply their reasoning is slim and in important cases wrong. The Annenberg Internet Surveys also reveal the fallacy in marketers' insistence that individuals accept the idea of trade-offs. Quite the contrary: Americans reject the idea of trade-offs as unfair even as they sometimes act in their shopping as if they are making the trade-off between the qualms they have about giving up information and the desires they have to get good deals. We found, instead, that for most the explanation for giving up the data is resignation. They see no opportunity to get what they really want from digital marketers – the ability to control what the marketers know about them. In that context, their unpredictable responses to the blandishment of discounts reflects futility rather than rational trade-off strategies.

The resignation finding was not unanticipated. Members of our team have long heard discussions by people around us that reflect a dislike of marketers' surveillance, a powerlessness to do anything about it but a need to adapt to the new environment. (Often the discussion relates to Facebook.) Scholarly descriptions have also suggested resignation is at work in the new surveillance world.[34] In the face of markers' quite different claims, systematic national surveys show that most Americans do not feel in control of the information commercial entities have about them and would like to be. The logical next question is how to change that. One solution is that regulators should force greater corporate transparency and more personalized controls on data use. Unfortunately, the Annenberg surveys suggest that most people's knowledge about digital commerce is so low that it is highly unrealistic to expect them to get and keep up to speed with the ever-changing data-collecting dynamics of the advertising and retailing environments. Another solution is for regulators to step in to do that with the public interest in mind. Here we confront a key dilemma that has bedeviled the Federal Trade Commission and other government bodies: the nature of public harm involved in the retrieval of individuals' data for commercial purposes. In spite of a growing literature on the social as well as the individual functions of privacy, US regulatory bodies still define harm in terms that require evident and often quantifiably determined injury. Fifteen years of Annenberg national surveys strongly suggest that Americans dispute this view of harm. Americans plainly resist data collection and personalization based on data collection because they don't think it is the right thing to do even if they are not confronted with immediate and/or quantifiable harm. It will be useful to learn more about this set of expectations. Clearly, however, a desire for dignity, control, and respect pervades many of the responses we received about data use over the years. Implementing this desire should be a crucial next step for marketers, regulators, and others interested in a twenty-first century where citizens themselves have respect for the emerging new commercial sphere and the government officials who regulate it.

---

[34] See, for example, Julie E. Cohen, *aa* (New Haven: Yale University Press, 2011), p. 108; and Helen Nissenbaum, *Privacy in Context* (Stanford: Stanford University Press, 2007), pp. 1, 3, 20, and 65.

9

The Federal Trade Commission's Inner Privacy Struggle

Chris Jay Hoofnagle

INTRODUCTION

At the Federal Trade Commission (FTC), all privacy and security matters are assigned to a consumer protection economist from the agency's Bureau of Economics (BE). The BE is an important yet often ignored element of the FTC. Advocates and others operating before the commission have been inattentive to the BE, choosing to focus instead on persuading commissioners on policy matters, and staff attorneys, on case selection. This chapter shows how the BE's *evaluative* role is just as important as attorneys' case *selection* role.

This chapter describes the BE, discusses the contours of its consumer protection theories, and discusses how these theories apply to privacy matters. I explain why the FTC, despite having powerful monetary remedy tools, almost never uses them: this is because the BE sees privacy and security injuries as too speculative, because the FTC's lawyers prefer settlement for a variety of logistical and strategic reasons, and because the FTC's remedies come too late to deter platform-age services. The BE is also skeptical of information privacy rights because of their potential impact on innovation policy and because privacy may starve the market of information. In this, the BE hews to certain interpretations of information economics, ignoring research in traditional and behavioral economics that sometimes finds benefits from the regulation of information. Not surprisingly, calls for the BE to expand its role from case *evaluation* to case *selection* typically come from those wishing to curb the FTC's privacy-expanding enforcement agenda. Those calls may be strategic, but are not without merit.

We should expect President Donald Trump's administration to expand the role of the BE and to make its role more public. With newfound powers, the BE will argue that more cases should be pled under the unfairness theory. This will have the effect of blunting the lawyers' attempts to expand privacy rights through case enforcement.

But the answer is not to avoid the BE's preferred pleading theory. Instead, we need to foster a BE that can contemplate invasions of privacy and security problems as causing injuries worthy of intervention and monetary remedy. This chapter concludes with a roadmap to do so. Among other things, the roadmap includes the consideration of existing markets for privacy as a proxy for the value of personal information. For example, tens of millions of Americans pay money to keep nonsensitive information, such as their home address, secret. Additionally, the FTC's civil penalty factors, which consider issues such as how to deny a defendant the benefits from illegal activity, could justify interventions to protect privacy and security. Finally, the BE could explore how existing information practices have inhibited the kinds of control that could lead to a functioning market for privacy.

THE BUREAU OF ECONOMICS

The Bureau of Economics is tasked with helping the FTC evaluate the impact of its actions by providing analysis for competition and consumer protection investigations and rulemakings, and by analyzing the economic impact of government regulations on businesses and consumers. With commission approval, the BE can exercise spectacular powers. The BE can issue compulsory processes to engage in general and special economic surveys, investigations, and reports. Congress required the BE to perform some of its most interesting recent privacy activities, such as a study of accuracy in consumer reports. The study found that 13 percent of consumers had material errors in their files, meaning that tens of millions of Americans could be affected by inaccuracy in their credit reports.[1]

The BE is divided into three areas focusing on antitrust law, research, and consumer protection. About eighty economists educated at the PhD level work for the BE. Twenty-two economists and eight research analysts are tasked to the over 300 attorneys focused on the consumer protection mission. The economists help design compulsory process, evaluate evidence collected from process, provide opinions on penalties to be levied in cases, conduct analyses of cases independent of the lawyers, serve as expert witnesses, support litigation, and provide perspective on larger policy issues presented by enforcement. In this last category, the BE has been an important force in eliminating state laws that restrict certain types of price advertising.[2]

By deeply integrating principles of cost-benefit analysis in the FTC's decision-making, the BE has a disciplining effect on the agency's instinct to intervene to protect consumers.[3] As former Chairman William E. Kovacic and David Hyman explained, the BE "is a voice for the value of competition, for the inclusion of market-oriented strategies in the mix of regulatory tools, and for awareness of the costs of specific regulatory choices . . . BE has helped instill within the FTC a culture that encourages ex post evaluation to measure the policy results of specific initiatives."[4] According to Kovacic and Hyman, this disciplining effect is good. The duo explains that the BE's tempering role stops the agency from adopting an interventionist posture, warning that sister agencies (such as the Consumer Financial Protection Bureau) may become overzealous without economists acting in an evaluative role.

The most comprehensive history of the BE was written in 2015 by Dr. Paul Pautler, longtime FTC employee and deputy director of the BE.[5]

---

[1] FTC, Section 319 of the Fair and Accurate Credit Transactions Act of 2003: Third Interim Federal Trade Commission Report to Congress Concerning the Accuracy of Information in Credit Reports (Dec. 2008).

[2] For a general discussion of these contributions, *see* Janis K. Pappalardo, *Contributions by Federal Trade Commission Economists to Consumer Protection: Research, Policy, and Law Enforcement*, 33(2) J. Pub. Pol'y & Mktg 244 (2014).

[3] Jonathan Baker, *Continuous Regulatory Reform at the Federal Trade Commission*, 49(4) Admin. L. Rev. 859 (1997).

[4] David A. Hyman & William E. Kovacic, *Why Who Does What Matters: Governmental Design, Agency Performance, the CFPB and PPACA*, 82 Geo. Wash. L. Rev. 1446 (2014).

[5] *See* Paul A. Pautler, *A History of the FTC's Bureau of Economics*, AAI Working Paper No. 15–03, ICAS Working Paper 2015–3 (Sept. 2015).

The BE's Conceptions of Consumer Injury

If the BE is skeptical of privacy harms, why is it that the FTC brings so many privacy cases without evidence of pure fraud or out-of-pocket monetary loss? The answer is that staff-level FTC lawyers have broad discretion in target *selection*, and the lawyers have focused on expanding pro-privacy norms through enforcement. Privacy enforcement has often focused on large, mainstream, reputable companies such as Google, Facebook, and Microsoft rather than more marginal companies.

While the lawyers select the cases, the economists *evaluate* them and recommend remedies to the Commission. The BE has developed substantial policy thinking surrounding remedies. The BE wishes to achieve deterrence – both specific and general – with an emphasis on avoiding over-deterrence. This is tricky because risk of detection affects deterrence, and the FTC's small staff means that the vast majority of illegal practices will go undetected and unremedied. One thus might conclude that penalties should be massive, but large penalties might cause others to overinvest in compliance, making the entire economy less efficient.[6]

A number of factors are considered in the difficult calculus of balanced remedies. The BE weighs options that could make the consumer whole, by putting the consumer in the position she occupied before the illegal transaction. BE also considers how a deception shapes demand for a product, thereby inducing individuals to buy who would not make a purchase absent an illegal practice, or whether customers paid more for a product because of a deception.

In its evaluative activities, the BE's lodestar is "consumer welfare" and its economists claim that they have no other social agenda in their activities. The BE's approach "has traditionally focused on fostering 'informed consumer choice' in well-functioning markets."[7]

The special dynamics of personal information transactions make it difficult for the BE to justify monetary remedies in privacy cases. Consider a fraud where consumers are promised an 18-karat gold trinket but are delivered a 10-karat one. The FTC can easily calculate the injury to the consumer based on the price differential between the two products. A market exists that clearly differentiates between these products and assigns a higher price to the 18-karat object. The transaction is a simple, bounded one.

Turning to privacy cases, the calculation is not as simple. Many services provided to a consumer lack a price tag because they are "free."[8] The alleged deception might be unrelated to price, but rather to a subtle feature, such as the degree of publicity given to some fact about the user. Complicating matters is that the boundaries of the transaction are unclear because services change over time, and in the process, shift consumer expectations and desires.

Furthermore, individual privacy preferences vary. Some consumers may never have considered privacy attributes in their service selection or may not care a great deal about privacy. Unlike something as salient as the purity of a gold object, specific information uses may not enter into the consumer's awareness when selecting a service. These uses of information may never come into the consumer's mind until something goes wrong. When that happens, users often cannot point to an economic injury from unwanted disclosures. All of these problems are compounded by the fact that many services do not offer an alternative, "privacy friendly" feature set or comparative price point.

---

[6] Mallory Duncan, FTC Civil Penalties: Policy Review Session (1980).

[7] Paul A. Pautler, *A Brief History of the FTC's Bureau of Economics: Reports, Mergers, and Information Regulation*, 46 Rev. Ind. Org. 59 (2015).

[8] John M. Newman, The Myth of Free, 86 Geo. Wash. L. Rev. ___ (2017).

The above discussion shows that assigning a dollar value to a privacy violation is not a simple exercise. But other dynamics cause the BE to be skeptical of information privacy cases more generally.[9] This skepticism is expressed both in methods and in larger ideological issues. For instance, lawyers may point to surveys as evidence of privacy harm, but the BE systematically dismisses survey research in this field, because decisions about privacy can implicate complex short and long term trade-offs that are not well presented in surveys. Sometimes economists will argue that consumer behavior belies stated preferences for privacy. One oft-stated rationale is that if consumers really cared about privacy, they would read privacy notices.

Ideologically the BE has had a reputation of hewing to conservative economic norms.[10] This may be in part a problem of disciplinarity. Pautler's 2015 history of the BE notes that when it became active in consumer protection in the 1970s, economists had just started considering the topic. Similarly, Ippolito's 1986 survey only cites to three pre-1970 works on consumer protection economics.[11] This narrow view is strange, because the consumer protection literature spanned the 20th century, often describing economic problems in the language of psychology or marketing. Popular, pro-advertising works, such as David Ogilvy's *Confessions of an Advertising Man* (1963), provide credible insights about consumer psychology, decision-making, and the effect of FTC regulation. Similarly, Samuel Hopkins Adams's 1905 work explains the economic conflicts that prevented market forces from policing patent medicines.[12] Yet these kinds of works are not defined as being in the discipline.

Aside from a narrow view of disciplinary relevance, the literature has a conservative lens. Scanning BE literature reviews, the notable omissions are liberal and even centrist works on consumer protection – Albert Hirschman, Arthur Leff, Arthur Kallet and F.J. Schlink, Ralph Nader, David A. and George S. Day's multi-edition compilations on "consumerism," and the "ghetto marketplace" research (some of which was generated by the BE itself) of the 1960s.

President Reagan's appointment of economist James Miller to the chairmanship of the FTC in 1981 also added to the BE's reputation as conservative. The Miller-era leadership strengthened the FTC in some ways, making it more enforcement-oriented. But Miller also scaled back many consumer protection efforts and pursued aggressive policies reflecting great faith in contractual freedom.[13] Miller installed economists in consumer protection leadership positions to influence how the agency weighed case policy. Also, relevant to today's debates about case selection, Miller turned away from normative causes that the FTC might have pursued in favor of policing pure fraud cases.

Wendy Gramm was a director of the BE during Miller's tenure. To get a taste of the flavor of Miller-era consumer protection policy, consider Gramm's defense of debt collection tools such as the "blanket security interest." These were agreements that empowered creditors to show up at debtors' homes and seize household goods unrelated to the debt. The record showed that some

[9] Peter P. Swire, *Efficient Confidentiality for Privacy, Security, and Confidential Business Information*, BROOKINGS-WHARTON PAPERS ON FINANCIAL SERVICES 306 (2003)("… based on my experience in government service, graduate training in economics is an important predictor that someone will not 'get' the issue of privacy protection.").

[10] Patrick E. Murphy, *Reflections on the Federal Trade Commission*, 33(2) J. OF PUB. POL'Y & MKTG 225 (2014)(The economists had a "more conservative mindset [than the lawyers]; in general, they were more reluctant to support cases unless some economic harm could be proved. There seemed to be an ongoing battle between these two groups.").

[11] Pauline M. Ippolito, *Consumer Protection Economics: A Selective Survey, in* EMPIRICAL APPROACHES TO CONSUMER PROTECTION ECONOMICS pp. 1–33 (Pauline M. Ippolito and David T. Scheffman, eds)(1986).

[12] Among other reasons, advertisers banned publishers from running anti-patent-medicine content. *See* Samuel Hopkins Adams, *The Patent Medicine Conspiracy against the Freedom of the Press*, COLLIER'S, *in* THE GREAT AMERICAN FRAUD pp. 147 (American Medical Association) (n.d).

[13] THOMAS O. MCGARITY, FREEDOM TO HARM: THE LASTING LEGACY OF THE LAISSEZ FAIRE REVIVAL (2013).

creditors lorded the agreements over debtors, causing debtors psychological terror through the risk of arbitrary seizure of their possessions, most of which were valueless and would not satisfy the debt obligation. But Gramm reasoned that consumers accepted blanket security agreements in order to send important signals about the commitment to repay. If consumers really wanted to avoid the risk of their things being seized, perhaps they would shop elsewhere for credit. If denied the choice to agree to security agreements, perhaps consumers could not get credit at all.

There are three important points about the Miller-era BE ideology. First, institutions are shaped by people. The BE is typically directed by an academic economist with impeccable credentials.[14] But a thesis of my book, Federal Trade Commission Privacy Law and Policy is that FTC staff, who often remain at the agency for decades, have a profound role, one perhaps more powerful than even the appointed political leaders of the FTC.[15] The current staff leadership of the BE's consumer protection division all joined the FTC in the 1980s. Miller, and his similarly oriented successor, Daniel Oliver, hired all three of the economists currently responsible for privacy and security cases.

Second, one should not confuse Miller-era policy instincts with mainstream economics. I expand on this point in the next part of this chapter. For now, it is sufficient to observe that support for privacy and security rights and rules can be found outside the sometimes-maligned field of behavioral economics.[16] The BE marches to a different drum and has not incorporated scholarship from traditional economic fields that finds benefits to social welfare from privacy.

Third, the Miller-era emphasis on contractual freedom and consumer savvy frames consumer harm as a foreseeable risk assumed by calculating, even wily consumers. Returning to the example of the blanket security interest, through the Gramm/Miller lens, consumers in such relationships agreed to be subject to the indignity of having their things taken. The mother who had her baby furniture taken[17] may be harmed, but on the other hand there is some risk of moral hazard if consumers think the government might intervene in private ordering. When public attention turned to the unfairness of blanket security agreements, Gramm commented, "Consumers are not as ignorant as you might suspect."[18] Translated into consumer privacy, this attitude holds that consumers are happy to enjoy the benefits of free services that trade in personal information and have calculated the risks flowing from these services.

Finally, the Miller era had a partial revival with the election of President George W. Bush, who appointed Timothy Muris, a protégé of James Miller, as chairman in 2001. An eminently qualified Chairman, Muris focused the FTC on a "harms-based" approach. This approach was shaped by concerns about innovation policy, and in part by a kind of naïve belief in the power of information to lead markets to correct decisions.[19] A trade in personal information is necessary and indeed beneficial for enabling modern economic infrastructures, such as consumer reporting. Thus, the harms-based approach allowed information flows presumptively, and

---

[14] FTC Office of the Inspector General, Evaluation of the Federal Trade Commission's Bureau of Economics, OIG Evaluation Report 15–03 (June 30, 2015).

[15] Chris Jay Hoofnagle, Federal Trade Commission Privacy Law and Policy p. 82 (Cambridge Univ. Press 2016).

[16] Alessandro Acquisti, Curtis R. Taylor, & Liad Wagman, *The Economics of Privacy*, 54(2) J. Eco. Lit. 442 (Jun. 2016).

[17] Federal Trade Commission, Credit practices: final report to the Federal Trade Commission and proposed trade regulation rule (16 CFR part 444) (1980).

[18] Michael deCourcy Hinds, *The Rift over Protecting Consumers in Debt*, p. F8, N.Y. Times, May 8, 1983.

[19] Muris was part of a chorus of thinkers who downplayed the risks of the housing bubble, arguing that richer information in credit reporting enabled safe lending to "underserved" (i.e. subprime) prospects. *See e.g.* Fred H. Cate, Robert E. Litan, Michael Staten, & Peter Wallison, *Financial Privacy, Consumer Prosperity, and the Public Good* (AEI-Brookings Joint Center for Regulatory Studies 2003).

intervention was limited to situations where "harm" was present. "Harm," a thorny concept that seemingly has expanded over time, was never defined in a satisfying way. The Bush FTC found telemarketing to be "harmful" and adopted a dramatic policy intervention for sales calling: the National Do-Not-Call Registry. Yet, when it came to privacy, the Bush FTC's idea of harm did not justify adoption of a rights-based framework. Pautler marks 2008 as the end of the harms-based era.

Using the Freedom of Information Act, I obtained training materials for the BE and a literature review of privacy papers apparently used by the BE during the harms-based approach era. Some of the microeconomic work showing the costs to consumers from a lack of privacy protection, as well as work in behavioral economics or law regarding consumer challenges in shopping for privacy, make no appearance in the paper list – including articles by some of the best-known scholars in the field and articles published in journals familiar to economists who work on consumer protection.[20] Instead, the BE's literature had a distinctly laissez faire bent, with the first paper listing the product of an industry think tank supported by five- and six-figure donations from telecommunications companies and Silicon Valley firms.

The Bureau of Economics versus the Bureau of Consumer Protection

There is tension between the lawyers of the Bureau of Consumer Protection (BCP) and the economists of the BE over consumer injury, and thus case selection.[21] It is not obvious why lawyers and economists would be at loggerheads over damages in consumer cases. Lawyers are comfortable allowing judges and juries to determine damages for inherently subjective injuries, such as pain and suffering, and the loss of marital consortium. The law also provides remedy for mere fear of harm (such as assault).[22]

Yet, economists may have an even broader view of harm than do lawyers. As Sasha Romanosky and Alessandro Acquisti explain, "economic considerations of privacy costs are more promiscuous [than those of tort law]. From an economic perspective, the costs of privacy invasions can be numerous and diverse. The costs and benefits associated with information protection (and disclosure) are both tangible and intangible, as well as direct and indirect."[23]

Romanosky and Acquisti's observation positions economists as potentially more open to recognizing consumer injury than are lawyers. Their point is growing in persuasiveness as legal impediments to consumer lawsuits expand, particularly those requiring more proof of "injury" to gain standing, and thus jurisdiction in court. In a case decided by the Supreme Court in 2016, several information-intensive companies argued that they should not be subject to suit unless the consumer suffers financial injury – even if the company violates a privacy law intentionally.[24] Many consumer lawsuits for security breaches and other privacy problems have been tossed out

---

[20] Surprising omissions from the list include, James P. Nehf, *Shopping for Privacy on the Internet*, 41 J. CONSUMER AFF. 351 (2007); Alessandro Acquisti & Hal R. Varian, *Conditioning Prices on Purchase History*, 24(3) MKTG. SCI. 367 (2005).

[21] Joshua L. Wiener, *Federal Trade Commission: Time of Transition*, 33(2) J. PUB. POL'Y & MKTG 217 (2014)("Prior to working at the FTC, I naively thought in terms of FTC versus business. I quickly learned that a more adversarial contest was lawyers versus economists.").

[22] Ryan Calo, *Privacy Harm Exceptionalism*, 12(2) COLO. TECH. L. J. 361 (2014); Ryan Calo, *The Boundaries of Privacy Harm*, 86 IND. L. J. 1131 (2011).

[23] Sasha Romanosky and Alessandro Acquisti, *Privacy Costs and Personal Data Protection: Economic and Legal Perspectives*, 24(3) Berk. Tech. L. J. 1060 (2009).

[24] *See* amicus curie brief of eBay, Inc., Facebook, Inc., Google, Inc., and Yahoo! Inc. *in Spokeo v Robins*, No. 13–1339 (SCT 2015).

of court on jurisdictional grounds for lacking "injury"[25] – but economists may view these same cases as meritorious.

The BE sees each case selected as an important policy decision. From the BE's lens, those policy decisions should focus not on rule violations, but on the harm suffered. The BE's approach is thus more evaluative of and more critical of legal rules. The BE wants to see some detriment to consumer welfare as a result of rule breaking. This reflects a revolution in thinking about business regulation also present in the FTC's antitrust approaches. With per se antitrust rule violations out of favor, the FTC focuses now on rule-of-reason style approaches with more evaluation of consumer harm. In addition to reflecting policy commitments, adopting a harm approach empowers the economists structurally, because a focus on harm causes economists to be more deeply involved in consumer protection cases.[26]

Lawyers on the other hand are more moralistic, and likely to view a misrepresentation as an inherent wrong. Lawyers are trained and indeed ethically bound to uphold legal processes. In fact, many lawyers see the prosecution of cases as merely being "law enforcement," and are unwilling to acknowledge the policy issues inherent in case selection, as the BE correctly does.

The problem with the lawyers' approach is that the law can be applied inefficiently and produce perverse outcomes. The lawyers' approach can be rigid and out of touch with the market. The problem with the economists' approach is that it can supplant democratic processes. The word "harm" appears nowhere in Title 15 of the US Code, which governs the FTC, yet the economists have read the term into the fabric of the agency. Sometimes democratic processes create ungainly regulatory approaches, but setting these aside and reading harm into the statute is governance by philosopher king rather than rule of law.

The BE has a more academic culture than the BCP as well. Since at least the 1990s, the economists have been able to obtain leave for academic positions and for academic writing.[27] The economists are free to express their opinions, and even press them in situations where they are in disagreement with the FTC's actions. This internal questioning can cause attorneys to think that the economists are not fully participating in the consumer protection mission, and instead frustrating it by trying to engage in academic discourse about situations attorneys see as law enforcement matters.

Attorneys know that the agency's hand is weakened in litigation when it is apparent that a matter is controversial within the FTC. Attorneys also see economists as serving in an expert witness role, a service function that should be deferential to the strategic decisions of the litigators. Kenneth Clarkson and former Chairman Timothy Muris explain: "The economists' role is controversial. Many attorneys, sometimes even those the top of the bureau, are dissatisfied with the economists' substantive positions, with their right to comment, and what they perceive as the undue delay that the economists cause."[28] But if they truly are to be independent advisors, the kind accepted by courts as legitimate experts, the economists need to have the very comforts that attorneys find discomforting.

---

[25] Lexi Rubow, *Standing in the Way of Privacy Protections: The Argument for a Relaxed Article III Standing Requirement for Constitutional and Statutory Causes of Action*, 29 Berkeley Tech. L.J. 1007, 1008 (2014).

[26] Paul A. Pautler, *A History of the FTC's Bureau of Economics*, AAI Working Paper No. 15–03, ICAS Working Paper 2015-3 (Sept. 2015).

[27] Paul A. Pautler, *A History of the FTC's Bureau of Economics*, AAI Working Paper No. 15–03, ICAS Working Paper 2015-3 (Sept. 2015).

[28] Kenneth W. Clarkson & Timothy J. Muris, *Commission Performance, Incentives, and Behavior* 280–306, in The Federal Trade Commission Since 1970: Economic Regulation and Bureaucratic Behavior (Kenneth W. Clarkson & Timothy J. Muris, eds., 1981).

The lawyers' instinct to intervene also causes tension between the BCP and the BE. Economists are more likely to take a long view of a challenge, allowing the marketplace to work out the problem even where the law prohibits certain practices or gives the agency tools to redress the problem. The BE may also trust that consumers are more sophisticated in advertising interpretation than the lawyers do.

Beliefs about consumer sophistication and the ability to leave advertising representations to the market can go to extremes, however. Consider John Calfee, a long time expert with the American Enterprise Institute and former Miller-era BE advisor. Calfee thought that most regulation of advertising was perverse and thus consumer advocates harmed the public interest by attempting to police it. To press the point, he used cigarette advertising – the bête noir of consumer advocates – as a model. He argued that the cigarette industry's own health claims actually undermined tobacco companies. For instance, an advertising claim that there was, "Not a single case of throat irritation due to smoking Camels,"[29] is interpreted differently by consumers and lawyers. Lawyers assume that consumers are more ovine than vulpine. A lawyer views the claim as a simple form of deception that should not appear in advertising. But according to Calfee, consumers may read the same sentence and think that cigarettes are generally dangerous – after all, at least some of them cause throat irritation.

In Calfee's view cigarette advertising that mentioned any health issue taught consumers that all smoking was unhealthful. In fact, no amount of regulation could tell consumers about smoking's danger more effectively than the very ads produced by tobacco companies. According to Calfee, FTC regulation caused tobacco companies to stop mentioning health completely, and the industry's advertising became less information rich. In short, Calfee argued that regulation caused smoking to be portrayed in a kinder light.[30] But to the more legalistic culture of the BCP, Calfee's reasoning rejects the FTC's statutory mandate of preventing deceptive practices and false advertising.

Perhaps the different views of consumer sophistication also explain why the FTC has not updated guidelines on various forms of trickery for decades. The guidelines surrounding the use of the word "free" were introduced in 1971 and never updated. The "bait and switch" and "price comparison" ("sales" that misrepresent the regular price of an item) guidance have never been updated since their introduction in 1967. Within the commission, there is fear that updating these different informational remedies would cause them to be watered down by the BE. Yet, any user of the internet can see that free offers, bait and switch marketing, and fake price comparisons are rampant online.

Finally, the lawyers too can steer the FTC away from monetary awards and other dramatic remedies. Pursuing such remedies may force the agency into litigation. The FTC is a risk averse litigant because it has more to lose from bad precedent than do other actors, such as class action attorneys. The burdens of litigation can consume precious staff attorney time, slowing down or even stopping the investigation of other cases. In addition, a 1981 study by Sam Peltzman found that FTC actions, even those without civil penalties, have a dramatic, negative effect on

---

[29] R. J. REYNOLDS CORP., NOT ONE SINGLE CASE (1947) in Stanford School of Medicine, Stanford Research into the Impact of Tobacco Advertising, available at http://tobacco.stanford.edu/tobacco_main/images.php?token2=fm_st069 .php&token1=fm_img1636.php&theme_file=fm_mt004.php&theme_name=Scientific%20Authority&subtheme_ name=Not%20One%20Single%20Case.

[30] JOHN H. CALFEE, FEAR OF PERSUASION (1997); Posner too expressed qualified support for this reasoning, and argued that low-tar, improved filters, and new technology, such as lettuce-based cigarettes, might reduce the harms of smoking. *See* ABA, REPORT OF THE ABA COMMISSION TO STUDY THE FEDERAL TRADE COMMISSION (Sept. 15, 1969)(Separate Statement of Richard Posner).

respondents.[31] FTC attorneys may thus feel satisfied that respondent companies are punished enough by the bad press and legal bills that invariably come from a settled case.

THE BUREAU OF ECONOMICS' ECONOMICS OF PRIVACY AND SECURITY

The FTC has resolved over 150 matters involving privacy and security, using its authority to bring cases against deceptive and unfair trade practices. The BE is involved in every case to a varying degree. Under the Federal Trade Commission Act, "unfair practices" clearly call for cost-benefit analysis. The FTC has to show that a practice causes "substantial injury" and that it is not outweighed by benefits to consumers or competitors. This balancing between injury and benefits is nicely suited to economists' strengths.

The FTC's power to police deception is less burdened than the unfairness test. There is essentially no balancing involved, because across ideological lines, deception is believed to harm consumers and the marketplace. Because deception cases are easier to bring—indeed, only consumer "detriment" need be proven instead of injury—it is no surprise that the FTC relies on its deception power when wading into new areas, such as privacy. Doing so has another strategic, internal benefit for the lawyers: framing a wrong as deceptive essentially circumvents the BE. Deception cases receive much less economic attention.

There is growing tension at the FTC surrounding cases where the lawyers clothe unfairness cases in deception garb. Typically, this happens where a company engages in normatively objectionable behavior and some minor deception is present. The FTC enforces against the deception in order to quash the normatively objectionable practice. For instance, consider the 2015 Jerk.com matter, where the FTC brought an administrative action against a company that created a website that allowed users to rate people as "jerks." The FTC's basis for the matter was the false representation that the site was based on organic, user-generated content, when in reality, the profile data were scraped from Facebook. In another case, a company tracked consumers by monitoring unique identifiers emitted from phones. The company, Nomi, violated the law not because it tracked people, but because it failed to live up to promises of providing notices of its activities.

Why would anyone care about whether Jerk.com's data were organically generated user content? Why would anyone care about whether Nomi faithfully posted privacy notices? The real issue underlying these cases is our normative commitment to privacy: Do we really want websites that label people jerks or companies that collect unique identifiers from phones? The unfairness theory better fits the privacy problems presented by Jerk and Nomi. But the BCP lawyers realized that if they styled these practices as unfair, the BE would have to be convinced that overall consumer welfare was harmed by their activities. The easily satisfied deception power gave the FTC a simple path to policing these objectionable practices.

Returning to unfairness, the FTC has alleged such substantial injury in dozens of privacy and security cases. For instance, many FTC security cases involve the exposure of millions of credit card, debit card, and checking account identifiers. Yet, only a handful of security cases have involved monetary remedies of any type.

FTC observers might conclude that the lack of fines can be attributed to the agency's limits on civil penalties (for the most part, the FTC cannot levy civil penalties in privacy and security matters). But the FTC has a broad range of monetary and other remedies in addition to civil

---

[31] Sam Peltzman, *The Effects of FTC Advertising Regulation*, 24(3) J. L. ECON. 403 (Dec. 1981).

penalties. It can seek restitution, redress, disgorgement, asset freezes, the appointment of receivers, and the recession of contracts.

There are several reasons why various remedies go unused. First, the BE does not believe there is a market for privacy. This leads the BE to undervalue privacy wrongs. Without some kind of penalty, companies may find it economically efficient to violate privacy, in particular because privacy violations are so difficult to detect. Second, the BE's focus on providing information to the consumer at service enrollment finds its roots in standard, physical product marketing. Today, the approach is antiquated and deficient because so many transactions are based on personal information, with the ultimate goal of establishing a platform rather than selling a specific product or service. The next sections explain these problems in greater detail.

No Monetary Damages in a World with No Privacy Market

The BE's methods of evaluating relief drive monetary penalties to zero in most privacy matters. And even where civil penalties are applied, they tend to be too low to serve retributive or deterrent goals. One illustration comes from the agency's case against Google. In it, Google was found to have deceived users of the Apple Safari browser by tracking these users despite promising not to. Google was fined $22.5 million, one of the largest privacy-related recoveries by the commission.[32] Google's behavior was intentional, and the company was already under a consent decree for other privacy violations (thus making it possible for the FTC to apply civil penalties, as explained above).

Google derived clear benefits from tracking Apple users. Apple is a luxury brand in technology, thus Apple users are attractive to advertisers. In addition, eroding Apple's efforts to shield its users from Google tracking may have been strategically and psychologically valuable. Detection of Google's tracking required forensic analysis on a specific kind of software, and thus there was little risk that regulators would discover the practice. Google clearly had the ability to pay a much larger fine. In a way, the fine created incentives for bad behavior by setting such a low penalty for intentional misbehavior.

To a BE analyst the fine could be seen as disproportionately high. Consumers do not pay with money when they use search engines, and there is no option to pay extra to avoid the kind of tracking that Google used. Thus, the market did not set a price to avoid Google's deception. While millions of consumers who use both Safari and Google would have been affected by the practice, perhaps few of them had ever read Google's privacy policy, known of Google's statements on the matter, or even chosen Safari because of its privacy features. Only a small number were actually deceived by the representation and subsequent tracking. In sum, the practice justified a relatively small fine because any price on the tracking would be speculative, and because many who were tracked probably did not care about it. The absence of any kind of monetary damages in this and other privacy cases points to a general inability of the BE to consider privacy invasion a harm in itself.

Economic Reasoning for Physical-World Products in the Platform Age

The BE's privacy work appears still to operate in a pre-platform-economy era, with a fixation on price and on the information available to the user at enrollment in a service rather than on the complex interdependencies that develop between users and services as time goes on (this is not

---

[32] *In the Matter of Google*, FTC File No. 102 3136 (2011).

true of the BE's antitrust work).[33] For instance, a 2014 BE working paper modeled a market in which privacy policies were transparent and well understood by consumers – two key assumptions refuted by a wealth of research in consumer privacy.[34] The BE authors concluded that that under the two assumptions, a competitive marketplace could provide consumers privacy options.[35]

But the 2014 study is important for an entirely separate reason. The study reveals the shading of the BE's privacy lens. Recall from section 2 that the BE's economics is not necessarily "traditional," but rather grounded in relatively conservative economic work. This is reflected in the 2014 study's references. Reading over those references, one sees little overlap with the literature discussed in Acquisti et al., *The Economics of Privacy*.[36] Instead, the authors refer to the above-mentioned training materials and the *advertising* literature rather than the privacy literature.

Two problems emerge from the BE's view of the literature. First, it ignores the diverse array of traditional and empirical economic work that explores the potential welfare gains from privacy protection. Second, the focus on the economics of advertising is misplaced because privacy policies are not like price or product attribute advertising. Privacy features are much more complex, hidden, and most importantly, changeable. Today's technology market is not so much about an individual, discrete product. Instead, consumers are bargaining with platforms that are attempting to mediate many different aspects of consumer experience. These platforms are trying to influence how consumers understand and expect rights from technology.

If firms are strategic, they will compete to both capture benefits and deny them to competitors. Through this lens, Google's tracking of Safari users could be motivated by a desire to capture benefits from tracking, but also to deny Apple the ability to compete on privacy. Denying Apple the competitive benefit could also affect the psychology of consumers, leading them to think no company can protect privacy. This is what Joe Farrell has called a dysfunctional equilibrium,[37] a situation in which no firm is trusted to deliver on privacy, and therefore no one can compete on it.

Companies that are competing to be the dominant platform are constantly changing the bargain with the consumer through continuous transactions over time. Platforms build huge user bases with promises of privacy, often ones that distinguish the company from competitors on privacy. Once a large user base is obtained and competitors trumped, the company switches directions, sometimes adopting the very invasive practices protested against.[38]

---

[33] Although according to a critique by Maurice Stucke and Allen Grunes, antitrust authorities have systematically avoided examining the consumer-side of multi-sided transactions in data-driven mergers and acquisitions, leading to a focus on competitive effects on advertisers but not on privacy and quality issues that affect consumers. Maurice E. Stucke & Allen P. Grunes, Big Data and Competition Policy 103–4, 114, 153–154, 224 (Oxford Univ. Press 2016).

[34] Daniel J. Solove, *Privacy Self-Management and the Consent Dilemma*, 126 Harv. L. Rev. 1880 (2013); Aleecia M. McDonald & Lorrie Faith Cranor, *The Cost of Reading Privacy Policies*, 4 I/S J. L. Pol'y Info. Soc'y 543, 564 (2008); James P. Nehf, *Shopping for Privacy on the Internet*, 41 J. Consumer Aff. 351 (2007); George R. Milne, Mary J. Culnan, & Henry Greene, *A Longitudinal Assessment of Online Privacy Notice Readability*, 25 J. Pub. Pol'y Marketing 238, 243 (2006) (based on the growing length and complexity of privacy policies, a user would have to read eight pages of text per competitor to evaluate their privacy choices); Paul M. Schwartz, *Internet Privacy and the State*, 32 Conn. L. Rev. 815 (2000).

[35] Daniel P. O'Brien & Doug Smith, *Privacy in Online Markets: A Welfare Analysis of Demand Rotations*, FTC Bureau of Economics Working Paper No. 323 (Jul. 2014).

[36] Alessandro Acquisti, Curtis R. Taylor, & Liad Wagman, *The Economics of Privacy*, 54(2) J. Econ. Lit. 442 (Jun. 2016).

[37] Joseph Farrell, *Can Privacy Be Just Another Good*, 10 J. Telecomm. High Tech. L. 251 (2012).

[38] Paul Ohm, *Branding Privacy*, 97 Minn. L. Rev. 907 (2013)(describing the "privacy lurch").

Network effects, lock-in, and the power of platforms to shift user expectations enable dramatic policy lurches. But the BE's tools, forged in the era of valuing jewelry, the sizes of television screens, and so on, need adaptation to be applied to the problems posed by internet services.

In fact, the BE approach militates against remedy, because of the bureau's method for analysis of marketplace effects of remedies. Simply put, remedies are unlikely to be effective by the time the FTC gets involved, investigates a case, and litigates it. The delay involved in FTC processes gives respondents time to establish their platform and shut out competitors. By the time these steps are achieved, the BE is correct to conclude that remedies are likely to improve privacy options in the marketplace because no competitors are left standing.

HOW ACADEMICS COULD HELP SHAPE THE BE'S PRIVACY EFFORTS

The BE is proud of its engagement with the academic community. Unlike BCP attorneys, BE economists have biographies online that feature academic publications. BE economists also have academic traditions, such as taking leave from the FTC to visit at a college. The BE holds an annual conference on microeconomics open to outside academics. The President Trump administration is likely to elevate the role of the BE, making it more central to case selection, but also more public. The BE's posture gives academics opportunities to shape and expand the FTC's privacy outlook.

Documenting the Market for Pro-Privacy Practices

There are tremendous opportunities for research that would assist the BE and the American consumer. Inherently, the BE's monetary relief calculations are impaired because it perceives there to be no market for pro-privacy practices. Academics could document the contours of the privacy market where it currently exists, most notably, in the privacy differential between free, consumer-oriented services and for-pay, business-oriented services.

One example comes from Google, which offers a free level of service for consumers and another for businesses that is $5 a month. Google explains, "Google for Work does not scan your data or email ... for advertising purposes ... The situation is different for our free offerings and the consumer space."[39] Of course privacy is just one feature that flows from the $5 charge, yet it serves as evidence that the market puts some value on the avoidance of communications surveillance (Google's representation concerns the actual scanning of data and not just absence of advertising). Such surveillance must involve human review of e-mail at times in order to train advertising targeting systems. The inferences from automated scanning could contribute to Google's competitive intelligence.[40] Those who owe confidentiality duties to customers or clients need communications privacy, and so some portion of that $5 could be interpreted as a valuation of privacy.

Elucidating areas where some valuation of privacy exists – particularly in business-to-business scenarios where actors actually read policies and have the resources and time to protect rights – could help establish a value for privacy.

Another source for harm signals comes from the plaintiff bar, which has developed methods for measuring how consumers conceive of the value of personal information. For instance, in one case involving the illegal sale of driver record information, an economist polled citizens to

[39] Google, *Google for Work Help: Privacy* (2016), https://support.google.com/work/answer/6056650?hl=en.
[40] MAURICE E. STUCKE & ALLEN P. GRUNES, BIG DATA AND COMPETITION POLICY (Oxford Univ. Press 2016).

explore what kind of discounts they would accept in renewing their driver's license in exchange for this information being sold to marketers. In the state in question, drivers had to pay a $50 fee to renew their license. However, 60 percent of respondents said they would reject an offer of a $50 discount on their license in exchange for allowing the sale of their name and address to marketers.[41] Meanwhile, the state was selling this same information at $0.01 per record.

This survey method represented a plausible, real-life, bounded expense concerning information that is not even considered sensitive. Now, one may object to the survey as artificial – consumers, when presented in the moment with a $50 discount, may behave differently and allow the sale of personal information. But on the other hand, given the prevalence of domestic violence and stalking among other problems, it seems obvious that many drivers would be willing to pay $0.01 to prevent the sale of this information to others. There is thus some value to this information. There is also increased risk of harm to those whose home address is spread to others indiscriminately. The data could be copied endlessly and resold to entities not in privity with the state, making it impossible for people to trace stalkers or swindlers back to the sale of personal information by the state.

Some economists have studied the value of privacy options to individuals. Perhaps the most popular privacy option of all time was the FTC's establishment of the Telemarketing Do-Not-Call Registry. In the 1990s, technological advances in telemarketing made it easier for sales callers to ring many numbers at the same time, changing the fundamental dynamics of telemarketing. As Peter Swire explained, these calls externalized costs to consumers who were displeased with the calling, but also may have reduced the value of having a phone in general, because defensive techniques to avoid unwanted callers, such as call screening and not answering the phone, could get in the way of desirable calls.[42] One could also account for the positive value to consumers from avoiding these calls. Professor Ivan Png estimated this value to households as being between $13 and $98. Png's low estimate for the welfare created by telemarketing avoidance was $1.42 billion.[43]

Apart from telemarketing, there are many examples where individuals pay money in order to have enhanced information privacy options. For instance, while many people consider address information public, some homeowners take considerable expense to protect this information. "Land trusts" are used extensively by the affluent to shield home addresses from real estate websites and public records. Similarly, the private mailbox is a significant expense, often used to shield home addresses from marketers and others. One's listing in the phone book has been public for decades, yet about 30 percent of Americans pay $1.25 to $5.50 a month to unlist this information. The expenses from these interventions add up. Consider that paying the minimum unlisting fee for 10 years would be $150. Private mailboxes can cost more than that in a single year. These expenditures demonstrate that for tens of millions of Americans, privacy is worth real money, even for the protection of "public" data.

Finally, sophisticated actors use legal agreements in order to prevent secondary use of personal information. *The New York Times* reported in 2015 that Silicon Valley technology executives – who scoop up information with the most alacrity – use nondisclosure agreements in many contexts where domestic workers are employed.[44]

[41] *Richard Fresco v. Automotive Directions Inc, et al.* 2004 WL 3671355 (S.D.Fla.)(expert affidavit of Henry Fishkind).
[42] Peter P. Swire, *Efficient Confidentiality for Privacy, Security, and Confidential Business Information*, BROOKINGS-WHARTON PAPERS ON FINANCIAL SERVICES (2003).
[43] I.P.L. Png, *On the Value of Privacy from Telemarketing: Evidence from the "Do Not Call" Registry* (white paper) (Sept. 2007).
[44] Matt Richtel, *For Tech Titans, Sharing Has Its Limits* BU4, N.Y. TIMES, Mar. 14, 2015.

More Emphasis on the FTC's Civil Penalty Factors

A second area ripe for documenting injury in privacy cases comes from the economic dynamics in the FTC's civil penalty factors, which must be considered when the FTC seeks fines.[45] The factors inherently call for economic perspective and could be used more prominently in case evaluation. This article largely is a critique of the BE's emphasis on the second civil penalty factor: the injury to the public from the illegal practice. Courts consider four other factors, three of which could also benefit from academic analysis.

One factor concerns the "desire to eliminate the benefits derived by a violation." Recall the discussion earlier concerning the differences between physical-world products and platform-era services. In an era of platforms, denying the benefits of an illegal practice is a much more complex effort than addressing physical-world swindles. A physical-world swindle often can be cured by the reputational effects of a FTC action combined with disgorgement and restitution to victims. However, platform economy actors use a form of bait and switch that allows them to benefit from the momentum gained from a large base of subscribers who took the bait.

Both Facebook and Google are platforms that benefitted from a bait and switch. Facebook attracted a huge user base with promises of exclusivity and control but then relaxed these very features. The company changed its disclosure settings, making user profiles dramatically more public over time, while masking its own economic motives with claims that users wanted to be "more open." By the time Facebook made its major privacy changes in 2009, it had such a command of the market and such powerful network effects that users could not defect.

Google announced its search engine wearing opposition to advertising and its influence on search on its sleeve. The company's founders promised revolutions in both search and advertising. Google even presented its search service as more privacy-protective than those of competitors because it did not take users' browsing history into account when delivering search results.[46]

Consider how different the Google approach is today. It quietly started using behavioral data in search without telling the public.[47] It runs paid search ads prominently at the top of organic search results – mimicking the very thing it considered evil in the 1990s. Google even uses television-style commercials on YouTube – but these new commercials are worse because they can automatically pause if not kept in focus and because they track you individually.

Academics could provide research on just how much intervention is needed to address these platform-era bait and switches. Some of the tools used to police natural monopoly may be appropriate.

The interventions may need to be severe to undo the momentum gained from platform status. Consider the findings of a study written in part by two BE authors on the Suntasia Marketing case. That company enticed consumers with "free" trial offers to reveal their checking account numbers, but then Suntasia made many small, fraudulent charges on the checking accounts. The court allowed Suntasia to continue business but, in the process, the court segmented

---

[45] Several courts have approved a five-factor test for evaluating the reasonableness of FTC penalties: "(1) the good or bad faith of the defendants; (2) the injury to the public; (3) the defendant's ability to pay; (4) the desire to eliminate the benefits derived by a violation; and (5) the necessity of vindicating the authority of the FTC." *United States v. Reader's Digest Ass'n, Inc.* [1981] 662 F.2d 955, 967 (3d Cir.).

[46] Chris Jay Hoofnagle, *Beyond Google and Evil: How Policy Makers, Journalists and Consumers Should Talk Differently about Google and Privacy*, 14(4) First Monday (2009), http://firstmonday.org/article/view/2326/2156.

[47] Recall that Google presented its search services, which did not track users over time, as a privacy-friendly alternative to competitors. When Google changed strategies and used historical search data for targeting results, it did so secretly and the shift was discovered by an outside analyst. Saul Hansell, *Google Tries Tighter Aim for Web Ads*, C1, N. Y. Times, Jun. 27, 2008.

Suntasia's consumers into two groups, thereby setting up a natural experiment. Some Suntasia customers had to opt in to stay subscribed, while others were retained unless the customer opted out. Almost all of the customers who were required to opt in let their subscriptions cancel. But only about 40 percent of those given opt-out notices canceled, and thus the remainder kept on being charged for "essentially worthless" products. Minorities from low-socioeconomic-status (SES) areas were 8 percent less likely to opt out than whites in high-SES areas.[48] These findings speak to the idea that companies in continuous transactions with the consumer (such as platforms or companies that possess personal information) may require dramatic intervention to deny the benefits from deceptive practices.

Another civil penalty factor concerns whether the respondent company acted in good or bad faith. This raises the need for research into what kinds of fines are enough to deter bad faith – or whether fines can deter at all. Deterrence may vary based on industry, and on the size and maturity of the respondent company.

The final civil penalty factor concerns "the necessity of vindicating the authority of the FTC." Inherently, this factor considers respect for the law and for the consumer. The law presumes that natural and fictitious people are rational actors and that they respond sensibly to incentives and disincentives. Yet, we impose fines with almost no due process or economic analysis against natural persons for many violations of the law. The criminal law imposes drastic penalties on individuals even though many criminals lack the capacity to act rationally. Administrative penalties, such as the $50 parking ticket for forgetting to pay a $1 meter fee, are keyed to municipal revenue goals rather than economic loss to society or actual proof of harm. Oddly, such a disproportionate penalty would never survive constitutional review if applied against a company.

Turning to wrongdoing by companies, an economic analysis of harm and other factors is appropriate. But there is something substantively unfair and strange in how these analyses result in recommendations for no monetary penalties. The FTC need only make a "reasonable approximation" when specifying monetary relief,[49] and thus need not surmount a particularly high threshold to find that damages are in order. In addition, companies receive *ex ante* legal advice and engage in serious planning when deciding what to do with data. Many privacy lapses, such as Facebook's settings changes, are deliberate in a way that criminal acts and parking mater lapses are not. It would seem that economic actors would make the best case for monetary penalties in order to engender respect for the law.

Fostering A Market for Privacy

Finally, the BE could explore ways to foster a market for privacy. Part of that effort should concern the FTC's traditional approach of ensuring effective disclosures to consumers. But the more difficult challenge comes in addressing industry players who do not have incentives to fairly use data. For instance, data brokers engage in practices, such as reverse data appends, that render consumers' attempts at selective revelation ineffective. That is, reverse appends make it impossible to avoid having a retailer learn personal information about a consumer. The BE could use its empirical might to study how these information flows in the data broker market

---

[48] Robert Letzler, Ryan Sandler, Ania Jaroszewicz, Issac T. Knowles, and Luke M. Olson, *Knowing when to Quit: Default Choices, Demographics and Fraud*, 127 ECON. J. 2617–2640 (2017). doi:10.1111/ecoj.12377.

[49] *FTC v. Inc12.com Corp*, 475 F. App'x 106, 110 (9th Cir. 2012).

undermine alternatives that could result in better incentives and business practices more in line with consumer preferences.

Another area for rethinking BE approaches comes from behavioral economics. As early as 1969, Dorothy Cohen called for the creation of a "Bureau of Behavioral Studies," with the mission of gathering and analyzing data on "consumer buying behavior relevant to the regulation of advertising in the consumer interest."[50] The BE embraced this recommendation in several areas,[51] most visibly in false advertising. In the 1970s, the FTC began a program where marketing professors were embedded in the BCP. This led to greater sophistication in the interpretation of advertising, and, perhaps, the first agency use of copy testing (the evaluation of consumer interpretation of advertising by survey and lab experiments) in a matter.[52]

Today, when analyzing what a person might understand from a marketing representation, the FTC is quite humanistic in its outlook. It does not limit itself to disciplinary borders. It eschews rational choice theories and the idea that the consumer reads the small print. The FTC focuses on the overall impression of an advertisement. It acknowledges that consumers are not perfectly informed, and that they have limited resources to investigate advertising claims. However, this expansive view of consumer behavior and the subtleties of information products does not appear to have informed the BE's own privacy work.

CONCLUSION

This chapter has provided an overview of the Bureau of Economics, explained its case evaluation role in relationship to the lawyers' case selection role, and summarized reasons why BE economists might conclude that there is no harm from many privacy disputes.

The BE is key to effective enforcement of consumer privacy. Academics and advocates should pay more attention to this important institution because it shapes how privacy and security is protected. In the President Trump administration, it is likely to have a more public role, and it will perform cost-benefit analysis in more privacy cases. Helping the BE see economic injury in privacy and security violations could strengthen the agency's agenda and introduce disgorgement and restitution in matters currently settled with no monetary damages. The BE could also map an enforcement strategy that stimulates a market for privacy, one that helps consumers assign a different value to the attention and data they pour into "free" online services.

---

[50] Dorothy Cohen, *The Federal Trade Commission and the Regulation of Advertising in the Consumer Interest*, 33(1) J. MKTG 40 (1969).

[51] Consider the multidisciplinary approach taken in the FTC's tome on information remedies. FTC, CONSUMER INFORMATION REMEDIES: POLICY REVIEW SESSION (1979).

[52] William L. Wilkie, *My Memorable Experiences as a Marketing Academic at the Federal Trade Commission*, 33(2) J. Pub. Pol'y & Mktg 194 (2014).

10

Privacy and Human Behavior in the Information Age*

Alessandro Acquisti, Laura Brandimarte, and George Loewenstein

If this is the age of information, then privacy is the issue of our times. Activities that were once private or shared with the few now leave trails of data that expose our interests, traits, beliefs, and intentions. We communicate using e-mails, texts, and social media; find partners on dating sites; learn via online courses; seek responses to mundane and sensitive questions using search engines; read news and books on the cloud; navigate streets with geotracking systems; and celebrate our newborns, and mourn our dead, on social media profiles. Through these and other activities, we reveal information – both knowingly and unwittingly – to one another, to commercial entities, and to our governments. The monitoring of personal information is ubiquitous; its storage is so durable as to render one's past undeletable (1) – a modern digital skeleton in the closet. Accompanying the acceleration in data collection are steady advancements in the ability to aggregate, analyze, and draw sensitive inferences from individuals' data (2).

Both firms and individuals can benefit from the sharing of data once hidden and from the application of increasingly sophisticated analytics to larger and more interconnected databases (3). So too can society as a whole, for instance, when electronic medical records are combined to observe novel drug interactions (4). On the other hand, the potential for personal data to be abused – for economic and social discrimination, hidden influence and manipulation, coercion, or censorship – is alarming. The erosion of privacy can threaten our autonomy, not merely as consumers but as citizens (5). Sharing more personal data does not necessarily always translate into more progress, efficiency, or equality (6).

Because of the seismic nature of these developments, there has been considerable debate about individuals' ability to navigate a rapidly evolving privacy landscape, and about what, if anything, should be done about privacy at a policy level. Some trust people's ability to make self-interested decisions about information disclosing and withholding. Those holding this view tend to see regulatory protection of privacy as interfering with the fundamentally benign trajectory of information technologies and the benefits such technologies may unlock (7). Others are concerned about the ability of individuals to manage privacy amid increasingly complex trade-offs. Traditional tools for privacy decision-making such as choice and consent, according to this perspective, no longer provide adequate protection (8). Instead of individual responsibility, regulatory intervention may be needed to balance the interests of the subjects of data against the power of commercial entities and governments holding that data.

---

* This chapter previously appeared as Acquisti A, Brandimarte L, Loewenstein G, Privacy and human behavior in the age of information, *Science* vol. 347, no. 6221 (2015), 509–514.

Are individuals up to the challenge of navigating privacy in the information age? To address this question, we review diverse streams of empirical privacy research from the social and behavioral sciences. We highlight factors that influence decisions to protect or surrender privacy and how, in turn, privacy protections or violations affect people's behavior. Information technologies have progressively encroached on every aspect of our personal and professional lives. Thus, the problem of control over personal data has become inextricably linked to problems of personal choice, autonomy, and socioeconomic power. Accordingly, this chapter focuses on the concept of, and literature around, informational privacy (that is, privacy of personal data) but also touches on other conceptions of privacy, such as anonymity or seclusion. Such notions all ultimately relate to the permeable yet pivotal boundaries between public and private (9).

We use three themes to organize and draw connections between streams of privacy research that, in many cases, have unfolded independently. The first theme is people's uncertainty about the nature of privacy trade-offs, and their own preferences over them. The second is the powerful context-dependence of privacy preferences: The same person can in some situations be oblivious to, but in other situations be acutely concerned about, issues of privacy. The third theme is the malleability of privacy preferences, by which we mean that privacy preferences are subject to influence by those possessing greater insight into their determinants. Although most individuals are probably unaware of the diverse influences on their concern about privacy, entities whose interests depend on information revelation by others are not. The manipulation of subtle factors that activate or suppress privacy concern can be seen in myriad realms – such as the choice of sharing defaults on social networks, or the provision of greater control on social media – which creates an illusion of safety and encourages greater sharing.

Uncertainty, context-dependence, and malleability are closely connected. Context-dependence is amplified by uncertainty. Because people are often "at sea" when it comes to the consequences of, and their feelings about, privacy, they cast around for cues to guide their behavior. Privacy preferences and behaviors are, in turn, malleable and subject to influence in large part because they are context-dependent and because those with an interest in information divulgence are able to manipulate context to their advantage.

UNCERTAINTY

Individuals manage the boundaries between their private and public spheres in numerous ways: via separateness, reserve, or anonymity (10); by protecting personal information; but also through deception and dissimulation (11). People establish such boundaries for many reasons, including the need for intimacy and psychological respite and the desire for protection from social influence and control (12). Sometimes, these motivations are so visceral and primal that privacy-seeking behavior emerges swiftly and naturally. This is often the case when physical privacy is intruded – such as when a stranger encroaches on one's personal space (13–15) or demonstratively eavesdrops on a conversation. However, at other times (often including when informational privacy is at stake), people experience considerable uncertainty about whether, and to what degree, they should be concerned about privacy.

A first and most obvious source of privacy uncertainty arises from incomplete and asymmetric information. Advancements in information technology have made the collection and usage of personal data often invisible. As a result, individuals rarely have clear knowledge of what information other people, firms, and governments have about them or how that information is used and with what consequences. To the extent that people lack such information, or are aware of their ignorance, they are likely to be uncertain about how much information to share.

Two factors exacerbate the difficulty of ascertaining the potential consequences of privacy behavior. First, whereas some privacy harms are tangible, such as the financial costs associated with identity theft, many others, such as having strangers become aware of one's life history, are intangible. Second, privacy is rarely an unalloyed good; it typically involves trade-offs (16). For example, ensuring the privacy of a consumer's purchases may protect her from price discrimination but also deny her the potential benefits of targeted "offers and advertisements."

Elements that mitigate one or both of these exacerbating factors, by either increasing the tangibility of privacy harms or making trade-offs explicit and simple to understand, will generally affect privacy-related decisions. This is illustrated by one laboratory experiment in which participants were asked to use a specially designed search engine to find online merchants and purchase from them, with their own credit cards, either a set of batteries or a sex toy (17). When the search engine only provided links to the merchants' sites and a comparison of the products' prices from the different sellers, a majority of participants did not pay any attention to the merchants' privacy policies; they purchased from those offering the lowest price. However, when the search engine also provided participants with salient, easily accessible information about the differences in privacy protection afforded by the various merchants, a majority of participants paid a roughly 5 percent premium to buy products from (and share their credit card information with) more privacy-protecting merchants.

A second source of privacy uncertainty relates to preferences. Even when aware of the consequences of privacy decisions, people are still likely to be uncertain about their own privacy preferences. Research on preference uncertainty (18) shows that individuals often have little sense of how much they like goods, services, or other people. Privacy does not seem to be an exception. This can be illustrated by research in which people were asked sensitive and potentially incriminating questions either point-blank, or followed by credible assurances of confidentiality (19). Although logically such assurances should lead to greater divulgence, they often had the opposite effect because they elevated respondents' privacy concerns, which without assurances would have remained dormant.

The remarkable uncertainty of privacy preferences comes into play in efforts to measure individual and group differences in preference for privacy (20). For example, Alan Westin (21) famously used broad (that is, not contextually specific) privacy questions in surveys to cluster individuals into privacy segments: privacy fundamentalists, pragmatists, and unconcerned. When asked directly, many people fall into the first segment: They profess to care a lot about privacy and express particular concern over losing control of their personal information or others gaining unauthorized access to it (22, 23). However, doubts about the power of attitudinal scales to predict actual privacy behavior arose early in the literature (24). This discrepancy between attitudes and behaviors has become known as the "privacy paradox."

In one early study illustrating the paradox, participants were first classified into categories of privacy concern inspired by Westin's categorization based on their responses to a survey dealing with attitudes toward sharing data (25). Next, they were presented with products to purchase at a discount with the assistance of an anthropomorphic shopping agent. Few, regardless of the group they were categorized in, exhibited much reluctance to answering the increasingly sensitive questions the agent plied them with.

Why do people who claim to care about privacy often show little concern about it in their daily behavior? One possibility is that the paradox is illusory – that privacy attitudes, which are defined broadly, and intentions and behaviors, which are defined narrowly, should not be expected to be closely related (26, 27). Thus, one might care deeply about privacy in general but, depending on the costs and benefits prevailing in a specific situation, seek or not seek privacy protection (28).

This explanation for the privacy paradox, however, is not entirely satisfactory for two reasons. The first is that it fails to account for situations in which attitude–behavior dichotomies arise under high correspondence between expressed concerns and behavioral actions. For example, one study compared attitudinal survey answers to actual social media behavior (29). Even within the subset of participants who expressed the highest degree of concern over strangers being able to easily find out their sexual orientation, political views, and partners' names, 48 percent did in fact publicly reveal their sexual orientation online, 47 percent revealed their political orientation, and 21 percent revealed their current partner's name. The second reason is that privacy decision-making is only in part the result of a rational "calculus" of costs and benefits (16, 28); it is also affected by misperceptions of those costs and benefits, as well as social norms, emotions, and heuristics. Any of these factors may affect behavior differently from how they affect attitudes. For instance, present-bias can cause even the privacy-conscious to engage in risky revelations of information, if the immediate gratification from disclosure trumps the delayed, and hence discounted, future consequences (30).

Preference uncertainty is evident not only in studies that compare stated attitudes with behaviors, but also in those that estimate monetary valuations of privacy. "Explicit" investigations ask people to make direct trade-offs, typically between privacy of data and money. For instance, in a study conducted both in Singapore and the United States, students made a series of hypothetical choices about sharing information with websites that differed in protection of personal information and prices for accessing services (31). Using conjoint analysis, the authors concluded that subjects valued protection against errors, improper access, and secondary use of personal information between $30.49 and $44.62. Similarly to direct questions about attitudes and intentions, such explicit investigations of privacy valuation spotlight privacy as an issue that respondents should take account of and, as a result, give increased weight in their responses.

Implicit investigations, in contrast, infer valuations of privacy from day-to-day decisions in which privacy is only one of many considerations and is typically not highlighted. Individuals engage in privacy-related transactions all the time, even when the privacy trade-offs may be intangible or when the exchange of personal data may not be a visible or primary component of a transaction. For instance, completing a query on a search engine is akin to selling personal data (one's preferences and contextual interests) to the engine in exchange for a service (search results). "Revealed preference" economic arguments would then conclude that because technologies for information sharing have been enormously successful, whereas technologies for information protection have not, individuals hold overall low valuations of privacy. However, that is not always the case: Although individuals at times give up personal data for small benefits or discounts, at other times they voluntarily incur substantial costs to protect their privacy. Context matters, as further discussed in the next section.

In fact, attempts to pinpoint exact valuations that people assign to privacy may be misguided, as suggested by research calling into question the stability, and hence validity, of privacy estimates. In one field experiment inspired by the literature on endowment effects (32), shoppers at a mall were offered gift cards for participating in a nonsensitive survey. The cards could be used online or in stores, just like debit cards. Participants were either given a $10 "anonymous" gift card (transactions done with that card would not be traceable to the subject) or a $12 trackable card (transactions done with that card would be linked to the name of the subject). Initially, half of the participants were given one type of card, and half the other. Then, they were all offered the opportunity to switch. Some shoppers, for example, were given the anonymous $10 card and were asked whether they would accept $2 to "allow my name to be linked to transactions done with the card"; other subjects were asked whether they would accept a card with $2 less value to "prevent my name from being linked to transactions done with the card." Of the subjects who originally held the less valuable but anonymous card, five times as many (52.1 percent) chose it and kept it over the other card than did those who originally held the more valuable card (9.7 percent). This suggests that people value privacy more when they have it than when they do not.

The consistency of preferences for privacy is also complicated by the existence of a powerful countervailing motivation: the desire to be public, share, and disclose. Humans are social animals, and information sharing is a central feature of human connection. Social penetration theory (33) suggests that progressively increasing levels of self-disclosure are an essential feature of the natural and desirable evolution of interpersonal relationships from superficial to intimate. Such a progression is only possible when people begin social interactions with a baseline level of privacy. Paradoxically, therefore, privacy provides an essential foundation for intimate disclosure. Similar to privacy, self-disclosure confers numerous objective and subjective benefits, including psychological and physical health (34, 35). The desire for interaction, socialization, disclosure, and recognition or fame (and, conversely, the fear of anonymous unimportance) are human motives no less fundamental than the need for privacy. The electronic media of the current age provide unprecedented opportunities for acting on them. Through social media, disclosures can build social capital, increase self-esteem (36), and fulfill ego needs (37). In a series of functional magnetic resonance imaging experiments, self-disclosure was even found to engage neural mechanisms associated with reward; people highly value the ability to share thoughts and feelings with others. Indeed, subjects in one of the experiments were willing to forgo money in order to disclose about themselves (38).

CONTEXT-DEPENDENCE

Much evidence suggests that privacy is a universal human need (Box 1) (39). However, when people are uncertain about their preferences they often search for cues in their environment to provide guidance. And because cues are a function of context, behavior is as well. Applied to privacy, context-dependence means that individuals can, depending on the situation, exhibit anything ranging from extreme concern to apathy about privacy. Adopting the terminology of Westin, we are all privacy pragmatists, privacy fundamentalists, or privacy unconcerned, depending on time and place (40).

Box 1. Privacy: A Modern Invention?

Is privacy a modern, bourgeois, and distinctly Western invention? Or are privacy needs a universal feature of human societies? Although access to privacy is certainly affected by socioeconomic factors (87) (some have referred to privacy as a "luxury good" (15)), and privacy norms greatly differ across cultures (65, 85), the need for privacy seems to be a universal human trait. Scholars have uncovered evidence of privacy-seeking behaviors across peoples and cultures separated by time and space: from ancient Rome and Greece (39, 88) to preindustrialized Javanese, Balinese, and Tuareg societies (89, 90). Privacy, as Irwin Altman (91) noted, appears to be simultaneously culturally specific and culturally universal. Cues of a common human quest for privacy are also found in the texts of ancient religions: The Quran (49:12) instructs against spying on one another (92); the Talmud (Bava Batra 60a) advises home-builders to position windows so that they do not directly face those of one's neighbors (93); and the Bible (Genesis 3:7) relates how Adam and Eve discovered their nakedness after eating the fruit of knowledge and covered themselves in shame from the prying eyes of God (94) (a discussion of privacy in Confucian and Taoist cultures is available in [95]). Implicit in this heterogeneous selection of historical examples is the observation that there exist multiple notions of privacy. Although contemporary attention focuses on informational privacy, privacy has been also construed as territorial and physical, and linked to concepts as diverse as surveillance, exposure, intrusion, insecurity, and appropriation, as well as secrecy, protection, anonymity, dignity, or even freedom (a taxonomy is provided in [9]).

The way we construe and negotiate public and private spheres is context-dependent because the boundaries between the two are murky (*41*): The rules people follow for managing privacy vary by situation, are learned over time, and are based on cultural, motivational, and purely situational criteria. For instance, we may usually be more comfortable sharing secrets with friends, but at times we may reveal surprisingly personal information to a stranger on a plane (*42*). The theory of contextual "integrity" posits that social expectations affect our beliefs regarding what is private and what is public, and that such expectations vary with specific contexts (*43*). Thus, seeking privacy in public is not a contradiction; individuals can manage privacy even while sharing information, and even on social media (*44*). For instance, a longitudinal study of actual disclosure behavior of online social network users highlighted that over time, many users increased the amount of personal information revealed to their friends (those connected to them on the network) while simultaneously decreasing the amounts revealed to strangers (those unconnected to them) (Figure 10.1) (*45*).

Endogenous privacy behavior and exogenous shocks.

Percentage of profiles on the Carnegie Mellon University Facebook network who revealed birthday and high school over time, 2005–2011.

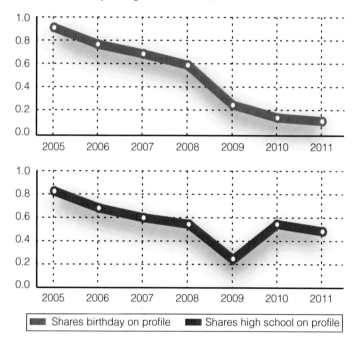

Shares birthday on profile ▮ Shares high school on profile

FIGURE 10.1 Endogenous privacy behavior and exogenous shocks. Privacy behavior is affected both by endogenous motivations (for instance, subjective preferences) and exogenous factors (for instance, changes in user interfaces). Over time, the percentage of members in the Carnegie Mellon University Facebook network who chose to publicly reveal personal information decreased dramatically. For instance, more than 80% of profiles publicly revealed their birthday in 2005, but less than 20% in 2011. The decreasing trend is not uniform, however. After decreasing for several years, the percentage of profiles that publicly revealed their high school roughly doubled between 2009 and 2010 – after Facebook changed the default visibility settings for various fields on its profiles, including high school (bottom), but not birthday (top) (*45*).

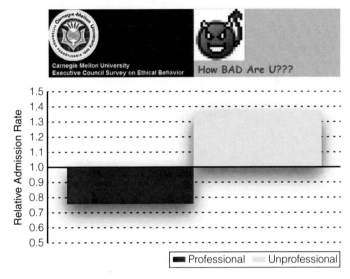

The impact of cues on disclosure behavior.

Relative admission rates, by experimental condition, in an experiment testing the impact of different survey interfaces on willingness to answer questions about the subject's engagement in various sensitive behaviors.

FIGURE 10.2 The impact of cues on disclosure behavior. A measure of privacy behavior often used in empirical studies is a subject's willingness to answer personal, sometimes sensitive questions – for instance, by admitting or denying having engaged in questionable behaviors. In an online experiment (47), individuals were asked a series of intrusive questions about their behaviors, such as "Have you ever tried to peek at someone else's e-mail without them knowing?" Across conditions, the interface of the questionnaire was manipulated to look more or less professional. The y-axis captures the mean affirmative admission rates (AARs) to questions that were rated as intrusive (the proportion of questions answered affirmatively) normed, question by question, on the overall average AAR for the question. Subjects revealed more personal and even incriminating information on the website with a more casual design, even though the site with the formal interface was judged by other respondents to be much safer. The study illustrates how cues can influence privacy behavior in a fashion that is unrelated, or even negatively related, to normative bases of decision-making.

The cues that people use to judge the importance of privacy sometimes result in sensible behavior. For instance, the presence of government regulation has been shown to reduce consumer concern and increase trust; it is a cue that people use to infer the existence of some degree of privacy protection (46). In other situations, however, cues can be unrelated, or even negatively related, to normative bases of decision-making. For example, in one online experiment (47) individuals were more likely to reveal personal and even incriminating information on a website with an unprofessional and casual design with the banner "How Bad R U" than on a site with a formal interface – even though the site with the formal interface was judged by other respondents to be much safer (Figure 10.2). Yet in other situations, it is the physical environment that influences privacy concern and associated behavior (48), sometimes even unconsciously. For instance, all else being equal, intimacy of self-disclosure is higher in warm, comfortable rooms, with soft lighting, than in cold rooms with bare cement and overhead fluorescent lighting (49).

Some of the cues that influence perceptions of privacy are one's culture and the behavior of other people, either through the mechanism of descriptive norms (imitation) or via reciprocity

(50). Observing as other people reveal information increases the likelihood that one will reveal it oneself (51). In one study, survey-takers were asked a series of sensitive personal questions regarding their engagement in illegal or ethically questionable behaviors. After answering each question, participants were provided with information, manipulated unknown to them, about the percentage of other participants who in the same survey had admitted to having engaged in a given behavior. Being provided with information that suggested that a majority of survey takers had admitted a certain questionable behavior increased participants' willingness to disclose their engagement in other, also sensitive, behaviors. Other studies have found that the tendency to reciprocate information disclosure is so ingrained that people will reveal more information even to a computer agent that provides information about itself (52). Findings such as this may help to explain the escalating amounts of self-disclosure we witness online: If others are doing it, people seem to reason unconsciously, doing so oneself must be desirable or safe.

Other people's behavior affects privacy concerns in other ways, too. Sharing personal information with others makes them "co-owners" of that information (53) and, as such, responsible for its protection. Mismanagement of shared information by one or more co-owners causes "turbulence" of the privacy boundaries and, consequently, negative reactions, including anger or mistrust. In a study of undergraduate Facebook users (54), for instance, turbulence of privacy boundaries, as a result of having one's profile exposed to unintended audiences, dramatically increased the odds that a user would restrict profile visibility to friends-only.

Likewise, privacy concerns are often a function of past experiences. When something in an environment changes, such as the introduction of a camera or other monitoring devices, privacy concern is likely to be activated. For instance, surveillance can produce discomfort (55) and negatively affect worker productivity (56). However, privacy concern, like other motivations, is adaptive; people get used to levels of intrusion that do not change over time. In an experiment conducted in Helsinki (57), the installation of sensing and monitoring technology in households led family members initially to change their behavior, particularly in relation to conversations, nudity, and sex. And yet, if they accidentally performed an activity, such as walking naked into the kitchen in front of the sensors, it seemed to have the effect of "breaking the ice"; participants then showed less concern about repeating the behavior. More generally, participants became inured to the presence of the technology over time.

The context-dependence of privacy concern has major implications for the risks associated with modern information and communication technology (58). With online interactions, we no longer have a clear sense of the spatial boundaries of our listeners. Who is reading our blog post? Who is looking at our photos online? Adding complexity to privacy decision-making, boundaries between public and private become even less defined in the online world (59), where we become social media friends with our coworkers and post pictures to an indistinct flock of followers. With different social groups mixing on the Internet, separating online and offline identities and meeting our and others' expectations regarding privacy becomes more difficult and consequential (60).

MALLEABILITY AND INFLUENCE

Whereas individuals are often unaware of the diverse factors that determine their concern about privacy in a particular situation, entities whose prosperity depends on the revelation of information by others are much more sophisticated. With the emergence of the information age, growing institutional and economic interests have developed around the disclosure of personal information, from online social networks to behavioral advertising. It is not surprising, therefore,

Changes in Facebook default profile settings over time, 2005–2014.

Degree of visibility of different fields of Facebook profiles based on default settings.

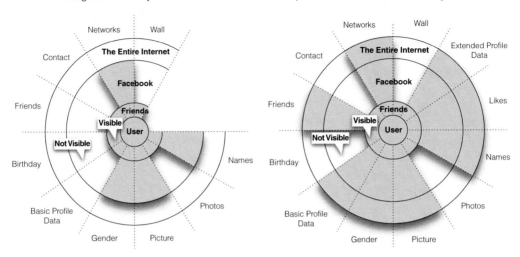

FIGURE 10.3 Changes in Facebook default profile visibility settings over time (2005–2014). Over time, Facebook profiles included an increasing amount of fields and, therefore, types of data. In addition, default visibility settings became more revelatory between 2005 (top) and 2014 (bottom), disclosing more personal information to larger audiences, unless the user manually overrode the defaults (fields such as "Likes" and "Extended Profile Data" did not exist in 2005). "Basic profile data" includes hometown, current city, high school, school (status, concentration, secondary concentration), interested in, relationship, workplace, about you, and quotes. Examples of "Extended profile data" include life events such as new job, new school, engagement, expecting a baby, moved, bought a home, and so forth. "Picture" refers to the main profile image. "Photos" refers to the additional images that users might have shared in their account. "Names" refers to the real name, the username, and the user ID. This figure is based on the authors' data and the original visualization created by M. McKeon, available at http://mattmckeon.com/facebook-privacy.

that some entities have an interest in, and have developed expertise in, exploiting behavioral and psychological processes to promote disclosure (61). Such efforts play on the malleability of privacy preferences, a term we use to refer to the observation that various, sometimes subtle, factors can be used to activate or suppress privacy concerns, which in turn affect behavior.

Default settings are an important tool used by different entities to affect information disclosure. A large body of research has shown that default settings matter for decisions as important as organ donation and retirement savings (62). Sticking to default settings is convenient, and people often interpret default settings as implicit recommendations (63). Thus, it is not surprising that default settings for one's profile's visibility on social networks (64), or the existence of opt-in or opt-out privacy policies on websites (65), affect individuals' privacy behavior (Figure 10.3).

In addition to default settings, websites can also use design features that frustrate or even confuse users into disclosing personal information (66), a practice that has been referred to as "malicious interface design" (67). Another obvious strategy that commercial entities can use to avoid raising privacy concerns is not to "ring alarm bells" when it comes to data collection. When companies do ring them – for example, by using overly fine-tuned personalized advertisements – consumers are alerted (68) and can respond with negative "reactance" (69).

Various so-called "antecedents" (70) affect privacy concerns and can be used to influence privacy behavior. For instance, trust in the entity receiving one's personal data soothes concerns.

Moreover, because some interventions that are intended to protect privacy can establish trust, concerns can be muted by the very interventions intended to protect privacy. Perversely, 62 percent of respondents to a survey believed (incorrectly) that the existence of a privacy policy implied that a site could not share their personal information without permission (40), which suggests that simply posting a policy that consumers do not read may lead to misplaced feelings of being protected.

Control is another feature that can inculcate trust and produce paradoxical effects. Perhaps because it is not a controversial concept, control has been one of the capstones of the focus of both industry and policy-makers in attempts to balance privacy needs against the value of sharing. Control over personal information is often perceived as a critical feature of privacy protection (39). In principle, it does provide users with the means to manage access to their personal information. Research, however, shows that control can reduce privacy concern (46), which in turn can have unintended effects. For instance, one study found that participants who were provided with greater explicit control over whether and how much of their personal information researchers could publish ended up sharing more sensitive information with a broader audience – the opposite of the ostensible purpose of providing such control (71).

Similar to the normative perspective on control, increasing the transparency of firms' data practices would seem to be desirable. However, transparency mechanisms can be easily rendered ineffective. Research has highlighted not only that an overwhelming majority of Internet users do not read privacy policies (72), but also that few users would benefit from doing so; nearly half of a sample of online privacy policies were found to be written in language beyond the grasp of most Internet users (73). Indeed, and somewhat amusingly, it has been estimated that the aggregate opportunity cost if US consumers actually read the privacy policies of the sites they visit would be $781 billion per year (74).

Although uncertainty and context-dependence lead naturally to malleability and manipulation, not all malleability is necessarily sinister. Consider monitoring. Although monitoring can cause discomfort and reduce productivity, the feeling of being observed and accountable can induce people to engage in prosocial behavior or (for better or for worse) adhere to social norms (75). Prosocial behavior can be heightened by monitoring cues as simple as three dots in a stylized face configuration (76). By the same token, the depersonalization induced by computer-mediated interaction (77), either in the form of lack of identifiability or of visual anonymity (78), can have beneficial effects, such as increasing truthful responses to sensitive surveys (79, 80). Whether elevating or suppressing privacy concerns is socially beneficial critically depends, yet again, on context (a meta-analysis of the impact of de-identification on behavior is provided in (81)). For example, perceptions of anonymity can alternatively lead to dishonest or prosocial behavior. Illusory anonymity induced by darkness caused participants in an experiment (82) to cheat in order to gain more money. This can be interpreted as a form of disinhibition effect (83), by which perceived anonymity licenses people to act in ways that they would otherwise not even consider. In other circumstances, though, anonymity leads to prosocial behaviour – for instance, higher willingness to share money in a dictator game, when coupled with the priming of religiosity (84).

CONCLUSIONS

Norms and behaviors regarding private and public realms greatly differ across cultures (85). Americans, for example, are reputed to be more open about sexual matters than are the Chinese, whereas the latter are more open about financial matters (such as income, cost of home, and possessions). And even within cultures, people differ substantially in how much they care about privacy and what information they treat as private. And as we have sought to highlight in this chapter, privacy concerns can vary dramatically for the same individual, and for societies, over time.

If privacy behaviors are culture- and context-dependent, however, the dilemma of what to share and what to keep private is universal across societies and over human history. The task of navigating those boundaries, and the consequences of mismanaging them, have grown increasingly complex and fateful in the information age, to the point that our natural instincts seem not nearly adequate.

In this chapter, we used three themes to organize and draw connections between the social and behavioral science literatures on privacy and behavior. We end with a brief discussion of the reviewed literature's relevance to privacy policy. Uncertainty and context-dependence imply that people cannot always be counted on to navigate the complex trade-offs involving privacy in a self-interested fashion. People are often unaware of the information they are sharing, unaware of how it can be used, and even in the rare situations when they have full knowledge of the consequences of sharing, uncertain about their own preferences. Malleability, in turn, implies that people are easily influenced in what and how much they disclose. Moreover, what they share can be used to influence their emotions, thoughts, and behaviors in many aspects of their lives, as individuals, consumers, and citizens. Although such influence is not always or necessarily malevolent or dangerous, relinquishing control over one's personal data and over one's privacy alters the balance of power between those holding the data and those who are the subjects of that data.

Insights from the social and behavioral empirical research on privacy reviewed here suggest that policy approaches that rely exclusively on informing or "empowering" the individual are unlikely to provide adequate protection against the risks posed by recent information technologies. Consider transparency and control, two principles conceived as necessary conditions for privacy protection. The research we highlighted shows that they may provide insufficient protections and even backfire when used apart from other principles of privacy protection.

The research reviewed here suggests that if the goal of policy is to adequately protect privacy (as we believe it should be), then we need policies that protect individuals with a minimal requirement of informed and rational decision-making – policies that include a baseline framework of protection, such as the principles embedded in the so-called fair information practices (86). People need assistance and even protection to aid in navigating what is otherwise a very uneven playing field. As highlighted by our discussion, a goal of public policy should be to achieve an equity of power between individuals, consumers, and citizens on the one hand and, on the other, the data holders such as governments and corporations that currently have the upper hand. To be effective, privacy policy should protect real people – who are naïve, uncertain, and vulnerable – and should be sufficiently flexible to evolve with the emerging unpredictable complexities of the information age.

ACKNOWLEDGMENTS

We are deeply grateful to the following individuals: R. Gross and F. Stutzman for data analysis; V. Marotta, V. Radhakrishnan, and S. Samat for research; W. Harsch for graphic design; and A. Adams, I. Adjerid, R. Anderson, E. Barr, C. Bennett, R. Boehme, R. Calo, J. Camp, F. Cate, J. Cohen, D. Cole, M. Culnan, R. De Wolf, J. Donath, S. Egelman, N. Ellison, A. Forget, U. Gasser B. Gellman, J. Graves, J. Grimmelmann, J. Grossklags, S. Guerses, J. Hancock,

E. Hargittai, W. Hartzog, J. Hong, C. Hoofnagle, J. P. Hubaux, A. Joinson, J. King, B. Knijnenburg, A. Kobsa, P. Leon, M. Madden, I. Meeker, D. Mulligan, C. Olivola, E. Peer, S. Petronio, S. Preibusch, J. Reidenberg, S. Romanosky, M. Rotenberg, I. Rubinstein, N. Sadeh, A. Sasse, F. Schaub, P. Shah, R. E. Smith, S. Spiekermann, J. Staddon, L. Strahilevitz, P. Swire, O. Tene, E. VanEpps, J. Vitak, R. Wash, A. Woodruff, H. Xu, and E. Zeide for enormously valuable comments and suggestions.

REFERENCES

1. V. Mayer-Schönberger, *Delete: The Virtue of Forgetting in the Digital Age* (Princeton Univ. Press, Princeton, 2011).
2. L. Sweeney, *Int. J. Uncert. Fuzziness Knowl. Based Syst.* 10, 557–570 (2002).
3. A. McAfee, E. Brynjolfsson, *Harv. Bus. Rev.* 90, 60–66, 68, 128 (2012).
4. N. P. Tatonetti, P. P. Ye, R. Daneshjou, R. B. Altman, *Sci. Transl. Med.* 4, 125ra31 (2012).
5. J. E. Cohen, *Stanford Law Rev.* 52, 1373–1438 (2000).
6. K. Crawford, K. Miltner, M. L. Gray, *Int. J. Commun.* 8, 1663–1672 (2014).
7. R. A. Posner, *Am. Econ. Rev.* 71, 405–409 (1981).
8. D. J. Solove, *Harv. Law Rev.* 126, 1880–1903 (2013).
9. D. J. Solove, *Univ. Penn. L. Rev.* 154, 477–564 (2006).
10. F. Schoeman, Ed., *Philosophical Dimensions of Privacy: An Anthology* (Cambridge Univ. Press, New York, 1984).
11. B. M. DePaulo, C. Wetzel, R. Weylin Sternglanz, M. J. W. Wilson, *J. Soc. Issues* 59, 391–410 (2003).
12. S. T. Margulis, *J. Soc. Issues* 59, 243–261 (2003).
13. E. Goffman, *Relations in Public: Microstudies of the Public Order* (Harper & Row, New York, 1971).
14. E. Sundstrom, I. Altman, *Hum. Ecol.* 4, 47–67 (1976).
15. B. Schwartz, *Am. J. Sociol.* 73, 741–752 (1968).
16. R. S. Laufer, M. Wolfe, *J. Soc. Issues* 33, 22–42 (1977).
17. J. Y. Tsai, S. Egelman, L. Cranor, A. Acquisti, *Inf. Syst. Res.* 22, 254–268 (2011).
18. P. Slovic, *Am. Psychol.* 50, 364–371 (1995).
19. E. Singer, H. Hippler, N. Schwarz, *Int. J. Public Opin. Res.* 4, 256–268 (1992).
20. V. P. Skotko, D. Langmeyer, *Sociometry* 40, 178–182 (1977).
21. A. Westin, Harris Louis & Associates, Harris-Equifax Consumer Privacy Survey (Tech. rep. 1991).
22. M. J. Culnan, P. K. Armstrong, *Organ. Sci.* 10, 104–115 (1999).
23. H. J. Smith, S. J. Milberg, S. J. Burke, *Manage. Inf. Syst. Q.* 20, 167–196 (1996).
24. B. Lubin, R. L. Harrison, *Psychol. Rep.* 15, 77–78 (1964).
25. S. Spiekermann, J. Grosslags, B. Berendt, *E-Privacy in 2nd Generation E-Commerce: Privacy Preferences versus Actual Behavior* (Third ACM Conference on Electronic Commerce, Tampa, 2001), pp. 38–47.
26. P. A. Norberg, D. R. Horne, D. A. Horne, *J. Consum. Aff.* 41, 100–126 (2007).
27. I. Ajzen, M. Fishbein, *Psychol. Bull.* 84, 888–918 (1977).
28. P. H. Klopfer, D. I. Rubenstein, *J. Soc. Issues* 33, 52–65 (1977).
29. A. Acquisti, R. Gross, in *Privacy Enhancing Technologies*, G. Danezis, P. Golle Eds. (Springer, New York, 2006), pp. 36–58.
30. A. Acquisti, *Privacy in Electronic Commerce and the Economics of Immediate Gratification* (Fifth ACM Conference on Electronic Commerce, New York, 2004), pp. 21–29.
31. I. Hann, K. Hui, S. T. Lee, I. P. L. Png, *J. Manage. Inf. Syst.* 24, 13–42 (2007).
32. A. Acquisti, L. K. John, G. Loewenstein, *J. Legal Stud.* 42, 249–274 (2013).
33. I. Altman, D. Taylor, *Social Penetration: The Development of Interpersonal Relationships* (Holt, Rinehart & Winston, New York, 1973).
34. J. Frattaroli, *Psychol. Bull.* 132, 823–865 (2006).
35. J. W. Pennebaker, *Behav. Res. Ther.* 31, 539–548 (1993).
36. C. Steinfield, N. B. Ellison, C. Lampe, *J. Appl. Dev. Psychol.* 29, 434–445 (2008).
37. C. L. Toma, J. T. Hancock, *Pers. Soc. Psychol. Bull.* 39, 321–331 (2013).

38. D. I. Tamir, J. P. Mitchell, *Proc. Natl. Acad. Sci. U.S.A.* 109, 8038–8043 (2012).
39. A. Westin, *Privacy and Freedom* (Athenäum, New York, 1967).
40. C. J. Hoofnagle, J. M. Urban, *Wake Forest Law Rev.* 49, 261–321 (2014).
41. G. Marx, *Ethics Inf. Technol.* 3, 157–169 (2001).
42. J. W. Thibaut, H. H. Kelley, *The Social Psychology of Groups* (Wiley, Oxford, 1959).
43. H. Nissenbaum, *Privacy in Context: Technology, Policy, and the Integrity of Social Life* (Stanford Univ. Press, Redwood City, 2009).
44. d. Boyd, *It's Complicated: The Social Lives of Networked Teens* (Yale Univ. Press, New Haven, 2014).
45. F. Stutzman, R. Gross, A. Acquisti, *J. Priv. Confidential.* 4, 7–41 (2013).
46. H. Xu, H. H. Teo, B. C. Tan, R. Agarwal, *J. Manage. Inf. Syst.* 26, 135–174 (2009).
47. L. K. John, A. Acquisti, G. Loewenstein, *J. Consum. Res.* 37, 858–873 (2011).
48. I. Altman, *The Environment and Social Behavior: Privacy, Personal Space, Territory, and Crowding* (Cole, Monterey, 1975).
49. A. L. Chaikin, V. J. Derlega, S. J. Miller, *J. Couns. Psychol.* 23, 479–481 (1976).
50. V. J. Derlega, A. L. Chaikin, *J. Soc. Issues* 33, 102–115 (1977).
51. A. Acquisti, L. K. John, G. Loewenstein, *J. Mark. Res.* 49, 160–174 (2012).
52. Y. Moon, *J. Consum. Res.* 26, 323–339 (2000).
53. S. Petronio, *Boundaries of Privacy: Dialectics of Disclosure* (SUNY Press, Albany, 2002).
54. F. Stutzman, J. Kramer-Duffield, *Friends Only: Examining a Privacy-Enhancing Behavior in Facebook* (SIGCHI Conference on Human Factors in Computing Systems, ACM, Atlanta, 2010), pp. 1553–1562.
55. T. Honess, E. Charman, *Closed Circuit Television in Public Places: Its Acceptability and Perceived Effectiveness* (Police Research Group, London, 1992).
56. M. Gagné, E. L. Deci, *J. Organ. Behav.* 26, 331–362 (2005).
57. A. Oulasvirta *et al.*, *Long-Term Effects of Ubiquitous Surveillance in the Home* (ACM Conference on Ubiquitous Computing, Pittsburgh, 2012), pp. 41–50.
58. L. Palen, P. Dourish, *Unpacking "Privacy" For a Networked World* (SIGCHI Conference on Human Factors in Computing Systems, ACM, Fort Lauderdale, 2003), pp. 129–136.
59. Z. Tufekci, *Bull. Sci. Technol. Soc.* 28, 20–36 (2008).
60. J. A. Bargh, K. Y. A. McKenna, G. M. Fitzsimons, *J. Soc. Issues* 58, 33–48 (2002).
61. R. Calo, *Geo. Wash. L. Rev.* 82, 995–1304 (2014).
62. E. J. Johnson, D. Goldstein, *Science* 302, 1338–1339 (2003).
63. C. R. McKenzie, M. J. Liersch, S. R. Finkelstein, *Psychol. Sci.* 17, 414–420 (2006).
64. R. Gross, A. Acquisti, *Information Revelation and Privacy in Online Social Networks* (ACM Workshop–Privacy in the Electronic Society, New York, 2005), pp. 71–80.
65. E. J. Johnson, S. Bellman, G. L. Lohse, *Mark. Lett.* 13, 5–15 (2002).
66. W. Hartzog, *Am. Univ. L. Rev.* 60, 1635–1671 (2010).
67. G. Conti, E. Sobiesk, *Malicious Interface Design: Exploiting the User* (19th International Conference on World Wide Web, ACM, Raleigh, 2010), pp. 271–280.
68. A. Goldfarb, C. Tucker, *Mark. Sci.* 30, 389–404 (2011).
69. T. B. White, D. L. Zahay, H. Thorbjørnsen, S. Shavitt, *Mark. Lett.* 19, 39–50 (2008).
70. H. J. Smith, T. Dinev, H. Xu, *Manage. Inf. Syst. Q.* 35, 989–1016 (2011).
71. L. Brandimarte, A. Acquisti, G. Loewenstein, *Soc. Psychol. Personal. Sci.* 4, 340–347 (2013).
72. C. Jensen, C. Potts, C. Jensen, *Int. J. Hum. Comput. Stud.* 63, 203–227 (2005).
73. C. Jensen, C. Potts, *Privacy Policies as Decision-Making Tools: An Evaluation of Online Privacy Notices* (SIGCHI Conference on Human factors in computing systems, ACM, Vienna, 2004), pp. 471–478.
74. A. M. McDonald, L. F. Cranor, *I/S: J. L. Policy Inf. Society.* 4, 540–565 (2008).
75. C. Wedekind, M. Milinski, *Science* 288, 850–852 (2000).
76. M. Rigdon, K. Ishii, M. Watabe, S. Kitayama, *J. Econ. Psychol.* 30, 358–367 (2009).
77. S. Kiesler, J. Siegel, T. W. McGuire, *Am. Psychol.* 39, 1123–1134 (1984).
78. A. N. Joinson, *Eur. J. Soc. Psychol.* 31, 177–192 (2001).
79. S. Weisband, S. Kiesler, *Self-Disclosure on Computer Forms: Meta-Analysis and Implications* (SIGCHI Conference Conference on Human Factors in Computing Systems, ACM, Vancouver, 1996), pp. 3–10.
80. R. Tourangeau, T. Yan, *Psychol. Bull.* 133, 859–883 (2007).
81. T. Postmes, R. Spears, *Psychol. Bull.* 123, 238–259 (1998).

82. C. B. Zhong, V. K. Bohns, F. Gino, *Psychol. Sci.* 21, 311–314 (2010).

83. J. Suler, *Cyberpsychol. Behav.* 7, 321–326 (2004).

84. A. F. Shariff, A. Norenzayan, *Psychol. Sci.* 18, 803–809 (2007).

85. B. Moore, *Privacy: Studies in Social and Cultural History* (Armonk, New York, 1984).

86. *Records, Computers and the Rights of Citizens* (Secretary's Advisory Committee, US Dept. of Health, Education and Welfare, Washington, DC, 1973).

87. E. Hargittai, in *Social Stratification*, D. Grusky Ed. (Westview, Boulder, 2008), pp. 936–113.

88. P. Ariès, G. Duby (Eds.), *A History of Private Life: From Pagan Rome to Byzantium* (Harvard Univ. Press, Cambridge, 1992).

89. R. F. Murphy, *Am. Anthropol.* 66, 1257–1274 (1964).

90. A. Westin, in *Philosophical Dimensions of Privacy: An Anthology*, F.D. Schoeman Ed. (Cambridge Univ. Press, Cambridge, 1984), pp. 56–74.

91. I. Altman, *J. Soc. Issues* 33, 66–84 (1977).

92. M. A. Hayat, *Inf. Comm. Tech. L.* 16, 137–148 (2007).

93. A. Enkin, "Privacy," www.torahmusings.com/2012/07/privacy (2014).

94. J. Rykwert, *Soc. Res. (New York)* 68, 29–40 (2001).

95. C. B. Whitman, in *Individualism and Holism: Studies in Confucian and Taoist Values*, D. J. Munro, Ed. (Center for Chinese Studies, Univ. Michigan, Ann Arbor, 1985), pp. 85–100.

11

Privacy, Vulnerability, and Affordance

Ryan Calo

A person without privacy is vulnerable. But what is it to be vulnerable? And what role does privacy or privacy law play in vulnerability?

This chapter, adapted from the Clifford Symposium at DePaul University, begins to unpack the complex, sometimes contradictory relationship between privacy and vulnerability. I begin by exploring how the law conceives of vulnerability – essentially, as a binary status meriting special consideration where present. Recent literature recognizes vulnerability not as a status but as a state – a dynamic and manipulable condition that everyone experiences to different degrees and at different times.

I then discuss various ways in which vulnerability and privacy intersect. I introduce an analytic distinction between vulnerability *rendering*, i.e., making a person more vulnerable, and the *exploitation* of vulnerability whether manufactured or native. I also describe the relationship between privacy and vulnerability as a vicious or virtuous circle. The more vulnerable a person is, the less privacy they tend to enjoy; meanwhile, a lack of privacy opens the door to greater vulnerability and exploitation.

Privacy can protect against vulnerability but can also be invoked to engender it. I next describe how privacy supports the creation and exploitation of vulnerability in ways literal, rhetorical, and conceptual. An abuser may literally use privacy to hide his abuse from law enforcement. A legislature or group may invoke privacy rhetorically to justify discrimination, for instance, against the transgender individuals who wish to use the bathroom consistent with their gender identity.[1] And courts obscure vulnerability conceptually when they decide a case on the basis of privacy instead of the value that is more centrally at stake.

Finally, building on previous work, I offer James Gibson's theory of affordances as a theoretical lens by which to analyze the complex relationships that privacy mediates. Privacy understood as an affordance permits a more nuanced understanding of privacy and vulnerability and could perhaps lead to wiser privacy law and policy.

VULNERABILITY

Vulnerability refers to exposure to emotional, physical, or other negative forces. We can imagine being vulnerable to a positive force: a person could be vulnerable to a plea for help. But this

---

[1] These laws simultaneously compromise the privacy of transgender individuals. For an analysis, see Scott Skinner-Thompson, *Outing Privacy*, 110 Nw. U. L. Rev. 159 (2015).

seems to stretch the meaning of vulnerable. Usually when we refer to a person as vulnerable we mean vulnerable to harm.[2] A person or group who is invulnerable, of course, cannot be harmed or moved.[3]

In privacy and elsewhere, the law often conceives of vulnerability as the product of a status or special relationship. A person with particular characteristics – for instance, a very young or old person – may be vulnerable to various harms and hence require greater protection. Privacy law reflects this view where, for instance, it protects children's consumer privacy online but withdraws that protection at the age of thirteen.[4] In criminal law, the same action directed at a vulnerable victim may result in higher penalties under sentencing guidelines.[5] And of course most "undue influence" involves victims who are elderly or otherwise lack capacity.[6]

The law also sees vulnerabilities in certain relationships between people. In privacy, Jack Balkin has explored the idea that custodians of sensitive consumer information be considered "information fiduciaries," complete with obligations of loyalty and care.[7] But generally a more narrow relationship is necessary to trigger these obligations. Thus, we understand subjects in an experiment to be vulnerable to the researcher and hence require special protections throughout and beyond the study. We also think of patients as vulnerable to doctors and lay clients as vulnerable to financial advisors.

This binary conception of vulnerability as either present or absent is hardly inevitable. We can imagine a more nuanced understanding that takes into account circumstance.[8] The legal literature is indeed replete with more nuanced discussions of vulnerability. For example, work by Florencia Luna conceives of vulnerability not as a label that applies or does not apply but as a layer of personhood. Thus, for Luna, the proper way to understand vulnerability "is not by thinking that someone *is* vulnerable, but by considering a particular situation that *makes or renders* someone vulnerable."[9]

The insight that vulnerability is not binary is critical. Several insights follow. The first is that no one is entirely invulnerable at all times and in all contexts. We are all vulnerable in degrees and according to circumstance. This is especially clear in the consumer context, as I describe in the chapter.

Some theorists – notably Martha Fineman – would leverage our shared human condition of vulnerability to supplant discrimination as a way to organize equality discourse and redress.[10]

---

[2] See Martha Albertson Fineman, *The Vulnerable Subject and the Responsive State*, 60 EMORY L.J. 251 (2010).

[3] Perhaps they are not even a person. As philosopher Martha Nussbaum argues, a capacity to be vulnerable is in some sense critical to the human condition. On her account, a person who is entirely hardened against society and incapable of trust essentially ceases to be human. See MARTHA C. NUSSBAUM, THE FRAGILITY OF GOODNESS: LUCK AND ETHICS IN GREEK TRAGEDY AND PHILOSOPHY (1986).

[4] Child Online Privacy Protection Act of 1998, 15 U.S.C. § 6501–6506.

[5] E.g., Sentence of Imprisonment for Offenses Against Children, Elder Persons, or Handicapped Persons, Haw. Rev. Stat. § 706–660.2.

[6] For a full if skeptical discussion of undue influence in the probate context, see Ray D. Madoff, *Unmasking Undue Influence*, 81 MINN. L. REV. 571 (1997).

[7] Jack M. Balkin, *Information Fiduciaries and the First Amendment*, 49 U.C. DAVIS L. REV. 1183 (2016). Woodrow Hartzog and Neil Richards have explored related concepts such as a greater role for confidentiality in digital privacy and, more recently, the importance of promoting trust between firms and consumers. Neil M. Richards & Woodrow Hartzog, *Taking Trust Seriously in Privacy Law*, 19 STAN. TECH. L. REV. (2016).

[8] For example, the Supreme Court for a time recognized the need for special protections from attorney solicitation while a person was recovering from injuries. See Ohralik v. Ohio State Bar Ass'n, 436 U.S. 447, 464–65 (1978).

[9] See Florencia Luna, *Elucidating the Concept of Vulnerability: Layers Not Labels*, INT'L J. FEMINIST APPROACHES TO BIOETHICS, Spring 2009, at 121, 129 (my emphasis).

[10] See Martha Albertson Fineman, *Beyond Identities: The Limits of an Antidiscrimination*, 92 B.U. L. REV. 1713 (2012); Martha Albertson Fineman, *The Vulnerable Subject and the Responsive State*, 60 EMORY L.J. 251 (2010).

The responsibility of the state becomes the recognition and redress of vulnerability as it arises in society according to social, physical, environmental, or other forces. At the same time, although everyone is vulnerable to a degree, some individuals and groups within society are more vulnerable than others. A person of color may lack privileges as basic as the benefit of doubt, which in turn renders him or her systematically vulnerable to abuses of government power.[11] Scholars have critiqued vulnerability theory on this basis.[12]

The second insight is that vulnerability is not entirely a product of happenstance. The circumstances that correlate to vulnerability can be controlled or engineered and, thus, so can vulnerability itself. Vulnerability is not, or at least not exclusively, a naturally occurring phenomenon. A person, group, or society could *exploit* the vulnerability it happens to come across in the world – as when an unscrupulous caretaker exploits the vulnerability of an elderly charge in an effort to divert her will. But, separate and apart, a person, group, or society could *render* a person more vulnerable by exposing that person to particular circumstances, actions, or information. Tal Zarsky furnishes the example of a consumer who receives a complementary pack of cigarettes with his groceries when the store figures out he is contemplating quitting.[13] And again, this choice to exploit or render vulnerable may in turn fall disproportionately across society on the basis of demographic or other factors.

The remainder of the chapter explores these two insights in greater depth.

PRIVACY AS A SHIELD

Lex Luthor, the great enemy of Superman, was originally depicted as a mad scientist with access to futuristic weaponry. By the time of Gene Hackman's famous portrayal in the 1978 film *Superman*, Luther is just a very clever businessperson.[14] He is nevertheless able to capture and almost kill Superman, who escapes only when Luthor's girlfriend frees him in order to save her family. How does an ordinary person such as Luthor nearly defeat the Man of Steel?

Knowledge about a person confers power over that person. It makes the person vulnerable. A straightforward enough example is physical vulnerability. If you know that a person is allergic to peanuts (or kryptonite) you could use that information to make them very sick. Absent this knowledge you have no such power.

Whether knowledge creates vulnerability can depend on context. Generally there is no threat to person A if person B knows her location. Unless, of course, person B is the perpetrator of intimate partner violence against person A. That is why mapping services such as Google Maps that make the world more discoverable work with anti-domestic violence groups to help ensure no information about them appears in the database.[15]

A second, related vulnerability is the prospect of blackmail. The FBI famously sought to blackmail Dr. Martin Luther King, Jr. by threatening to reveal alleged extramarital affairs evidenced through (illegal) wiretaps.[16] But one need not rely on this extreme, historic example regarding a highly visible individual. Paul Ohm speculates that nearly everyone has a fact about

---

[11] Cf. Cheryl I. Harris, *Whiteness as Property*, 106 HARV. L. REV. 1707 (1993).

[12] E.g., Frank Rudy Cooper, *Always Already Suspect: Revising Vulnerability Theory*, 93 N.C. L. REV. 1339, 1342 n.9 (2015) (critiquing vulnerability theory for its refusal to acknowledge the role of identity); Nancy E. Dowd, *Unfinished Equality: The Case of Black Boys*, 2 IND. J.L. & SOC. EQUALITY (2013).

[13] Tal Z. Zarsky, *Mine Your Own Business! Making the Case for the Implications of Data Mining of Personal Information in the Forum of Public Opinion*, 4 YALE J.L. & TECH. 5 (2002).

[14] SUPERMAN: THE MOVIE (Warner Bros. 1978).

[15] Ryan Singel, *Google Map Makers Reaches Out To Anti-Domestic Violence Community*, WIRED (May 19, 2007).

[16] For a discussion, see Neil M. Richards, *The Dangers of Surveillance*, 126 HARV. L. REV. 1934, 1953–55 (2013).

them that could be ruinous were it widely shared – what Ohm calls a database of ruin.[17] If so, this opens each of us open to the prospect of being made vulnerable through its discovery.

A third example involves persuasion. In his chilling book *Lexicon*, Max Barry dreams up a world in which Poets learn to overcome a subject's will through a particular string of words that break down the mind's resistance.[18] Each person's string is different in accordance to their segment, i.e., their particular psychological category. A skilled Poet need only determine a person's segment and is able to take them over completely. (Poets themselves take great care not to reveal anything about themselves – for instance, by selecting office décor at random.)

Lexicon is science fiction.[19] But the notion that understanding a person can lead to control over them is not. In previous work around consumer privacy, I have explored a different sense in which information about a person renders them vulnerable. We know from the study of behavioral economics that consumers do not always act rationally in their self-interest. Indeed, people often behave *irrationally* in largely predictable ways due to so-called cognitive biases. Presumably, not everyone has the same cognitive biases, or to the same degrees. Thus, a firm (company) with access to how a particular consumer deviates from rational decision making has both the incentive and the means to extract rent from that consumer by manipulating the circumstances of their interaction – what I call digital market manipulation, after the work of Jon Hanson and Douglas Kysar.[20]

Privacy acts as a shield in these and other contexts by placing barriers in the way of discovering or rendering vulnerability. Precisely how Lex Luther discovered Superman's susceptibility to kryptonite is unclear. But presumably Superman could have used better information security. Location privacy lends greater physical security for a significant portion of the population. Information privacy keeps our databases of ruin out of the hands of those who would exploit us. And a stronger consumer privacy regime would make it more difficult for firms and others to discover and hence exploit our cognitive biases.[21]

At a basic level, then, one function of privacy is to minimize the exploitation and rendering of vulnerability by hiding the vulnerability itself (e.g., location or peanut allergy) or by protecting the information that, if known, would render us vulnerable in the moment.

As noted above, vulnerability is not distributed evenly across society. On the one hand, certain consumers – those with more resources, for instance, or with cultural influence – might find themselves more often targeted by certain advertisers. On the other hand, factors such as race or socioeconomic status can render individuals or groups vulnerable in more contexts. There is substantial evidence that the more vulnerable a person is in society, the greater the societal expectation that they shed privacy. Work by Khiara Bridges, for examples, illustrates the extent to which "the poor barter their privacy rights in exchange for government assistance."[22] Whereas an

---

[17] Paul Ohm, *Broken Promises of Privacy: Responding to the Surprising Failure of Anonymization*, 57 UCLA L. REV. 1701, 1748 (2010).

[18] MAX BERRY, LEXICON: A NOVEL (2013). Evan Selinger observed, and I agree, that Barry's reference to "Poets" is likely an allusion to Plato's warning in the *Republic* that poets are dangerous to the ideal city because of their capacity to stir the emotions of citizens. PLATO, G. M. A. GRUBE & C. D. C. REEDE, REPUBLIC, Book X (1992).

[19] Mostly. There is a relatively new branch of study that examines how better to persuade consumers and others by determining their psychological make up. It is called persuasion profiling. See, e.g., Maurits Kaptein & Dean Eckles, *Heterogeneity in the Effects of Online Persuasion*, 26 J. INTERACTIVE MARKETING 176 (2012).

[20] Ryan Calo, *Digital Market Manipulation*, 82 GEO. WASH. L. REV. 995 (2014), citing Jon D. Hanson & Douglas A. Kysar, *Taking Behavioralism Seriously: The Problem of Market Manipulation*, 74 N.Y.U. L. REV. 630 (1999).

[21] Or we may wind up turning this information over voluntarily. See Scott R. Peppet, *Unraveling Privacy: The Personal Prospectus and the Threat of Full Disclosure*, 105 Nw. U. L. REV. 1153 (2015).

[22] Khiara M. Bridges, *Privacy Rights and Public Families*, 34 HARV. J.L. & GENDER 113 (2011). Michele Goodwin's contribution to this very symposium also highlights the degree to which debt collection in the health context falls disproportionately on the

insured mother expects privacy around her prenatal care, a mother requiring public assistance must answer a barrage of highly personal questions.[23]

Bridges's observation arises in the context [of] public health services; other examples include welfare, employment, and criminal justice.[24] Common across these contexts and others is a similar compounding effect. The more information you have about a person or group, the greater the potential to take advantage of them. But the less advantages a person or group already enjoys, the lesser their ability to resist the expectations and requirements of turning over information in exchange for support. The result is a vicious cycle – which bears great exploration and may militate in favor of stronger privacy protections for the chronically vulnerable.

PRIVACY AS A SWORD

Thus far the discussion has suggested that greater vulnerability results from an absence of privacy or that privacy's protections are denied to the vulnerable. But privacy bears an even darker relation to vulnerability. Privacy can hide the creation and exploitation of vulnerability itself, both literally and figuratively.

As mentioned, firms might use what they know about consumers to take advantage of them. But firms invoke privacy even as they compromise it. Many companies cling to trade secret protection and other laws to avoid having to describe the processes by which they study and sort consumers at a granular level.[25] The digital environments a company engineers – its websites and apps – are not transparent to the user and attempts to reverse engineer this code can be met with a lawsuit.[26]

Terms of service appear to be written purposefully to maximize allowances while minimizing technical description. Thus a company might say that it uses consumer information to provide services, including advertising, without conveying any real information on how this occurs.[27] When companies talk about how a service works, regulators without technical expertise must largely take the firm's word. Recent developments have seen improvements, however, both in the degree of corporate transparency and in the technical capacity of regulatory bodies to scrutinize information systems.[28]

The idea that privacy can be invoked as a shield against accountability for vulnerability rendering and exploitation is neither limited to the technology context nor particularly novel. Feminist legal scholars such as Catherine MacKinnon and Reva Siegel have long argued that privacy exists in large measure to protect the spaces and practices by which women are subjugated.[29] MacKinnon argues that privacy is foremost a right of the powerful to be left alone

---

already disadvantaged. Michele Goodwin, Hospital Snitches: Privacy, Data Collection and Corporate Responsibility (Jan. 20, 2016). Thank you to conference participant Danielle Keats Citron for pointing me toward Bridges' research.

[23] See also Ryan Calo, *Privacy and Markets: A Love Story*, 91 NOTRE DAME L. REV. 649, 679–81 (2015) (arguing that the market mechanism is at least theoretically more privacy friendly than social distribution).

[24] See Michele Estrin Gilman, *The Class Differential in Privacy Law*, 77 BROOK. L. REV. 1389 (2012).

[25] Nor is this practice limited to the private sector. See David S. Levine, *Secrecy and Unaccountability: Trade Secrets in our Public Infrastructure*, 59 FLA. L. REV. 135 (2007).

[26] The most common arguments involve the anti-circumvention provision of the Digital Millenium Copyright Act and, as in the recent Facebook v. Vachani decision in the Ninth Circuit, the Computer Fraud and Abuse Act prohibition on unauthorized access to a protected computer. Facebook v. Vachani, No. 12–17102 (9th Cir. Jul. 12, 2016).

[27] Ryan Calo, *Against Notice Skepticism in Privacy (and Elsewhere)*, 87 NOTRE DAME L. REV. 1027, 1062 (2012).

[28] The Federal Trade Commission in particular has actively recruited technologists to help the commission identify and redress digital harms.

[29] CATHERINE A. MACKINNON, PRIVACY V. EQUALITY: BEYOND ROE V. WADE, IN APPLICATIONS OF FEMINIST LEGAL THEORY TO WOMEN'S LIVES: SEX, VIOLENCE, WORK, AND REPRODUCTION (D. Kelley Weisberg, ed., 1996); Reva B. Seigel, *"The Rule of Love": Wife Beating as Prerogative and Privacy*, 105 YALE. L.J. 2117 (1996).

by the state – a freedom the powerful use largely to oppress the vulnerable.[30] This idea, while contested, is clearly true to a degree: great harm happens behind closed doors.[31]

Privacy is also deployed against the vulnerable at the level of rhetoric. Recently we have seen the notion of privacy invoked rather explicitly to keep a vulnerable population vulnerable. Specifically, several states passed laws that prohibit local municipalities from establishing mixed gender bathrooms or permitting people to use the bathroom consistent with their gender identity. One such law – called the Public Facilities Privacy and Security Act – requires people to use the bathroom corresponding to the gender on their birth certificate.[32]

These laws reflect back the moral outrage experienced by members of these communities against transgender people. They are about withdrawing protection. But privacy is the way these laws have been formally and publicly justified. The idea is that it violates a person's privacy to be in the same bathroom as someone they conceive of the opposite gender, even if that person's own experience of their gender differs, and even in places – such as women's bathrooms – that consist entirely of stalls with doors.

Note the dual sense in which this privacy rationale enforces vulnerability. First, the target population is already vulnerable (in the classic legal sense grounded in status or relationship) insofar as individuals' gender identities differ from mainstream expectation.[33] And second, the context of the bathroom is one in which everyone – of any gender identity – experiences vulnerability. That is why the privacy rationale gets so much traction and, at the same time, exactly why the violence to the vulnerable target population is particularly intense.[34]

Finally, privacy can obscure the very concept of vulnerability. I have argued that there is a cost to attaching the label "privacy" to contexts where the real harm at issue may involve vulnerability.[35] Thus, for example, *Griswold v. Connecticut* famously invokes privacy (between a doctor and his patient) to place limits on the state's ability to control contraceptive use.[36] *Stanley v. Georgia* invokes privacy to push back against government censorship of obscenity.[37] And *Lawrence v. Texas* invokes privacy to explain why the state cannot prohibit sodomy.[38]

Arguably the values at issue in these and other cases deal less in privacy than in the freedoms citizens should hold to deviate from societal or community expectation. Further, we might wonder whether characterizing the issue as privacy confines the import of these decisions to private spaces. The statement "women should be able to make decisions about their own bodies" or "men should be able to have sex with other men" differs qualitatively from the claim that bedrooms or doctors' offices are private spaces in which the state should not operate.[39]

---

[30] MacKinnon, *supra*.

[31] This is sometimes portrayed as a "radical" argument and, to the extent MacKinnon would conceive of all of privacy as a mask for subjugation, it likely is. But clearly there is truth to the idea that vulnerability rendering and exploitation occurs behind privacy's doors. For an argument that privacy and the subjugation of women are not inexorably linked, see Annabelle Lever, *Must Privacy and Sexual Equalty Conflict? A Philosophical Examination and Some Legal Evidence*, 67(4) Soc. Res. 1137–71 (2000).

[32] Public Facilities Privacy & Security Act, House Bill 2 (2016).

[33] Alternatively, the individual may be in the presumably vulnerable position of exploring the exact contours of gender identity.

[34] Note the parallel to vulnerability theory and its critiques by identity theorists. See *supra*.

[35] Ryan Calo, *The Boundaries of Privacy Harm*, 86 Ind. L. J. 1131 (2011).

[36] 381 U.S. 479 (1965).

[37] 394 U.S. 557 (1969).

[38] 539 U.S. 558 (2003).

[39] A possible counterargument says that privacy acts a bridge to greater tolerance of the underlying conduct. Thus, start by saying that men can have sex in their own bedrooms without state intervention only to later invoke this precedent to strike down a ban on gay marriage. This process may be more comfortable; the question is whether it is necessary. Real people suffered in the years between Lawrence and Obergefell v. Hodges.

PRIVACY AS AFFORDANCE

To summarize the argument so far: the law tends to think of vulnerability as a status held by a person or group or else as a relationship between people or institutions. As the legal literature increasingly recognizes, vulnerability is best understood as layer of personhood – a state that exists more often and to greater degrees in certain people and contexts, perhaps, but exists in everyone sometimes. Moreover, vulnerability is not a naturally occurring phenomenon; it is constructed. Personal information, and therefore privacy, play a crucial role in both rendering and exploiting vulnerability.

Privacy intersects with vulnerability in a variety of complex ways. For example, people or groups without privacy are vulnerable and people who are vulnerable may have fewer opportunities to keep information close. Privacy can help interrupt information asymmetries that permit companies to discover and exploit the ways consumers appear to be vulnerable. At the same time, privacy facilitates vulnerability rendering and exploitation by literally hiding abusive practice, rhetorically as a weapon to justify oppression of the vulnerable, and by figuratively obscuring the real value at issue in a vulnerable context.

A final question might be: given this complex, sometimes contradictory relationship between privacy and vulnerability, how should privacy scholarship approach it? This is not a question I can answer for everyone. The dawning realization that privacy is ultimately about power in myriad forms and ways has led me, personally, to seek a new framework of analysis.[40] Such a framework should recognize the role privacy plays in compromising and protecting privacy for individuals, groups, and institutions. It should be capable of bridging the various senses of privacy as well as the many contexts – private and public, digital and physical – in which privacy arises. And, crucially, it should account for how the very experience and perception of privacy as a sword or a shield varies across the population.

The framework I find most helpful is that of affordance theory. Affordance theory originates in perceptual psychology with the work of James Gibson.[41] Gibson notes that living creatures, including humans, share the same environment. However, they perceive it differently in accordance to their own "affordances," i.e., their capabilities and limitations. Thus, a bird perceives a cliff as irrelevant whereas a person perceives it as dangerous. A tree affords hiding to a squirrel but not to a bear. Gibson invokes the concept of affordances to bridge the divide between the physical properties of the world (e.g., stairs and air currents) and the relational properties they afford to particular organisms (e.g., climbing and flight).

Of particular interest to law and the social sciences is the notion, mentioned by Gibson in passing, that people represent affordances to one another. "The richest and most elaborate affordances of the environment," writes Gibson, "are provide by other animals and, for us, other people."[42] Many factors – social, physical, technical, and cultural – mediate these affordances. I want to focus here on two. The first is the role of *information*. A person is only an affordance if you are able to perceive them as such. Thus, for instance, you may require the assistance of law enforcement and not realize that the plainclothes person a few feet away is a police officer.

[40] The realization has also led others to adopt new methods or justify existing methods in new ways. E.g., Julie E. Cohen, Configuring the Networked Self: Law, Code, and the Play of Everyday Practice (2012); Neil M. Richards, Intellectual Privacy: Rethinking Civil Liberties in the Digital Age (2014).

[41] See, e.g., James J. Gibson, *The Theory of Affordances*, in Robert Shaw and John Bransford, eds, Perceiving, Acting, and Knowing: Toward an Ecological Psychology (1977).

[42] Id.

(Gibson calls these unidentified features of the environment "hidden" affordances.[43]) The second is the role of *law*. A trespasser might think your house affords her shelter, a cannibal that your body affords him nutrition. But property and criminal law say otherwise.[44]

Privacy, too, can be conceptualized as an affordance. Privacy furnishes the capacity to withdraw from the world or to hide information about oneself. As with other features of an environment, what privacy affordances exist varies by personal capacity. A cupboard may afford physical concealment to a child but not an adult. A famous person cannot rely on the anonymity of the crowd. The poor, being reliant upon government and other services, realistically cannot "afford" withdrawal or obscurity – which is why some talk of privacy as a luxury good.[45] People of color may draw greater scrutiny by the surveillance state and hence have both a greater need and lesser chance for privacy's affordances.[46]

Privacy as affordance accommodates the complex role of privacy as both a shield and a sword for vulnerability. Privacy can withdraw information from others about our susceptibilities and help protect against externally imposed conditions that trigger vulnerability. Privacy thus empowers the weak by placing limits on the strong.[47] At the same time, privacy withdraws from public scrutiny – or, in some cases, purports to justify – the manufacture and abuse of vulnerability. Privacy thus empowers the strong by withdrawing abuses from scrutiny.

Gibson's theory of affordances could be usefully applied to the study and development of privacy and privacy law. Elsewhere I argue that reference to affordance theory helps interrogate whether American surveillance law and policy have reached the proper equilibrium between privacy and national security.[48] If the law affords citizens the means by which to resist and reform surveillance, but citizens choose not to do so, a better case can be made that the state is adhering to a social contract that permits a degree of surveillance in the interest of national security. But in practice Americans do not have such affordances, which in turn calls the legitimacy of the surveillance state into doubt.

The most pressing set of problems in consumer privacy – the subject of this anthology – are at their core similar: in the current environment, only firms possess meaningful affordances. Companies can collect data without asking, condition interactions on the provision of other data, and in general underrepresent the utility of data to the firm and the corresponding danger to the consumer. Moreover, companies – having access to consumer behavior and the ability to "code" the technical and legal environment in which transactions take place – are able to shape the affordances of the consumer to a far greater degree than consumers, individually or collectively, can shape those of the firm.

Consumers appear to have choices that would permit them to protect themselves and police the market; however, as a range of scholars have argued over the past decade, those choices are often illusory. Consumers are vulnerable to firms but not the reverse. This asymmetry of information and power is ultimately unhealthy and unsustainable.

The role of the policymaker, broadly understood, may be to help restore balance in the set of respective affordances of consumers and firms. But the argument I wish to advance here has to

---

[43] *Id.*

[44] Law creates, as a minimum, a counter-affordance.

[45] E.g., Julia Angwin, *Has Privacy Become a Luxury Good?*, N.Y. TIMES, Mar. 3, 2014.

[46] For a recent and excellent discussion of the relationship between surveillance and race, see the proceedings of The Color of Surveillance: Government Monitoring of the African American Community, available online at color ofsurveillance.org.

[47] Cf. Samuel Bray, *Power Rules*, 110 COLUM. L. REV. 1172 (2010).

[48] Ryan Calo, *Can Americans Resist Surveillance?*, 83 U. CHI. L. REV. 23 (2016).

do with the approach of privacy scholarship itself. I believe the notion of technical, economic, and legal affordances can help structure and unify the study of consumer privacy. We can ask, within this framework, questions around whether a consumer perceives a set of privacy affordances – including design choices (e.g., encryption), market choices, and legal resources. We can ask whether those perceptions are true, i.e., whether the affordance is actual or "false" or what effect the perception has on consumer behavior. And we can examine whether affordances vary according to demographics or other factors in ways we consider problematic. A complete account of privacy as affordance is beyond the scope of this chapter, but I see it as a promising means by which to explore not only the intersection of vulnerability and privacy but privacy in general.

CONCLUSION

Privacy is a concept that seems to lend itself to an instrumentalist understanding.[49] Privacy exists toward some usually positive end in society. When it comes to the intersection between privacy and vulnerability, however, the picture is rather complex. Privacy can be both a shield against vulnerability and a sword in its service. What is needed to capture this complex interaction is a theoretical lens rooted in the physical and social environment as it exists, but also sensitive to the differing ways people perceive and experience that environment. Although full-throated defense of privacy as affordance is beyond the scope of this chapter, James Gibson's theory is an interesting candidate to capture this complexity.

ACKNOWLEDGMENTS

The author would like to thank law professors Stephan Landsman, Paul Ohm, Julie Cohen, and other participants in the Clifford Symposium, editors at the *DePaul Law Review*, Scott Skinner-Thompson, and Evan Selinger for very helpful comments.

[49] See Ruth Gavison, *Privacy and the Limits of the Law*, 89 YALE L.J. 421 (1980).

12

Ethical Considerations When Companies Study – and Fail to Study – Their Customers

Michelle N. Meyer

Experimentation has been a hallmark of science for 400 years, but only recently – since the advents of the computer and the Internet – have relatively quick, inexpensive experiments at scale become feasible for businesses. Today, the practice of companies studying their customers is ubiquitous. In 2011, Google ran 100–200 experiments per day on its products, services, algorithms, and designs.[1] By 2016, it was running over 10,000 experiments per year.[2] If you are a Bing user, on any given day, you are participating in some fifteen experiments out of the company's 200 or so concurrent daily experiments, each of which exposes several million users to experimental conditions.[3] And if you are a Facebook user, you are a subject in some ten experiments at any given time.[4] Yet frameworks for thinking about the ethical conduct of research – long a mainstay of research throughout the academy and in industries whose research is subject to regulation by the Food and Drug Administration (FDA) – have lagged behind in most business contexts. This chapter considers the ethical implications of company attempts to learn from their customers or users. It also considers the overlooked ethical implications of companies that *fail* to do so.

A FEW WORDS ABOUT TERMINOLOGY

First, this chapter concerns, and refers to, companies' "learning activities." "Research" might be an adequate term, except that in US federal law – and perhaps colloquially – it has a particular meaning, namely, "a systematic investigation ... designed to develop or contribute to generalizable knowledge."[5] As discussed below, many companies study their customers for reasons in addition to, or in lieu of, a desire to contribute to generalizable knowledge. For instance, companies may wish to assure or improve the quality of their products or services. Such quality assurance (QA) and quality improvement (QI) activities fall outside this definition of "research"

---

[1] Erik Brynjolfsson & Andrew McAfee, *The Big Data Boom Is the Innovation Story of Our Time*, THE ATLANTIC (Nov. 21, 2011), https://www.theatlantic.com/business/archive/2011/11/the-big-data-boom-is-the-innovation-story-of-our-time/248215/ (citing Google Chief Economist Hal Varian).

[2] Hal Varian, *Intelligent Technology*, 53 FIN. & DEV. 6, 7 (Sept. 2016).

[3] Ron Kohavi, Alex Deng, Brian Frasca, Toby Walker, Ya Xu & Nils Pohlmann, *Online Controlled Experiments at Large Scale*, PROC. OF THE 19TH ACM SIGKDD INT'L CONF. ON KNOWLEDGE DISCOVERY & DATA MINING 1168, 1168 (2013).

[4] *Radiolab Podcast*, "The Trust Engineers," Feb. 9, 2015, http://www.radiolab.org/story/trust-engineers.

[5] Department of Health and Human Services, Policy for Protection of Human Research Subjects, 45 C.F.R. § 46.102 (d) (1991).

(and, hence, outside of federal regulations governing human subjects research), but comprise an important reason why companies study their customers. The term "learning activities" refers broadly to the range of methods and motivations for studying people, some but not all of which meet the traditional definition of "human subjects research."

Second, although this chapter generally refers to "customers" as the focus of companies' learning activities, when companies such as Google, Bing, and Facebook conduct experiments, they are generally studying their end users rather than their consumers (which tend to be advertisers). Even when this chapter refers solely to "customers," what is said will generally be applicable to users, as well. In addition, some companies study the general public – usually, but not always, because they are potential customers or users, former customers or users, employees or independent contractors, and even suppliers, distributors, and competitors. Because companies have different relationships with these stakeholders than they do with their customers or users, somewhat different ethical issues may be raised. Those nuances, however, are outside the scope of this chapter.

Third, although the traditional term for a person being studied is "subject," a term that federal regulations continue to use even as they undergo the first substantive changes in decades,[6] the trend in the research ethics literature and in research ethics practice (e.g., Institutional Review Board [IRB] deliberations) is towards referring to these individuals instead as "participants." The latter term is widely thought to be more respectful of the goal – if not quite yet the reality – of including individuals who are the focus of study as participants or even partners in the research enterprise. Nevertheless, this chapter generally uses the term "subjects." Because there are many kinds of "participants" in learning activities involving human beings, it often makes for ambiguous prose to refer to those who are the focus of study as participants. More important, the focus of this chapter is learning activities conducted by companies, and most of these proceed without anything like the study-specific, voluntary, informed consent of individuals that is typically (but, importantly, not always) involved in academic research. I defend the ethics of some such activities below, but it strains the normal meaning of the word to refer to unwitting individuals as "participants."

HOW COMPANIES STUDY THEIR CONSUMERS

In order to see when and how studying consumers implicates their privacy and other interests, it will be helpful to briefly review some of the most common types of study design that companies use, and the kinds of ethical issues these study designs raise. The broadest methodological distinction is between *observational* and *experimental* studies.

Observational Studies and the Ethics of Data Collection

A purely observational study involves passively observing customer or user behavior and other phenomena of interest as they occur in a "natural" environment, unchanged by the study. In such a study, where investigators refrain from altering or otherwise intervening in the company's normal business practices, ethical concerns will generally center on potential loss of informational privacy as a result of data collection.

---

[6] Department of Health and Human Services et al., Final Rule: Federal Policy for the Protection of Human Subjects, 82 Fed. Reg. 7,149 (Jan. 19, 2017) (to be codified at 45 C.F.R. 46).

One factor that may help determine the level of ethical concern involved in data collected is the *kind of data* that are collected. Some data are more sensitive than others. Moreover, some data used in a study may already be collected by the company. For instance, customer billing, sales, or inventory information may be analyzed for research purposes. In other cases, however, a company may newly collect additional kinds of data for the purpose of learning. Without appropriate transparency, the collection of additional data may violate a company's terms of service (ToS) or be unexpected by users, whose trust in the company may thereby be undermined. Even when study data have already been collected for routine business purposes, the repurposing of that data for other purposes may be perceived by users to be (or may actually be) problematic.

Different *methods of data collection* also raise different privacy and other ethical concerns. Perhaps the most benign data collection methods are surveys, interviews, and focus groups. Unless the purpose of this data collection is actively hidden from participants, the fact of data collection is necessarily revealed to participants, and consumers may usually choose to participate or not, or to stop at any point. Ethical issues can, of course, be raised by the way this data is stored, how the company uses it (both during and after the study), and with whom the company shares the data (both within and beyond the company).

On the other end of the spectrum, data collection tends to raise the most acute privacy concerns when it is conducted directly by human investigators who watch consumers in real time or who record the relevant phenomena for later viewing. Data collection through audio and visual recordings can involve two particularly troublesome features. First, they are somewhat indiscriminate, and may capture data beyond that which is sought, including data from third party "bystanders." Second, recordings create potentially permanent archives to which investigators (or others) can return repeatedly; this is a substantive difference from mere one-time observations of behavior that are imperfectly preserved in the researcher's memory.

One notable example of proposed human-driven data collection for research purposes occurred in late 2016, when Evernote – the popular platform for creating and sharing notes, photos, and other documents – announced a new policy under which designated employees could read user notes in order to "spot check" the company's efforts to use machine learning to help users automate functions ("like creating to-do lists or putting together travel itineraries").[7] According to the announcement, Evernote users would have been able to opt out of the policy (if they became aware of it – hardly a sure thing). And Evernote did seek to limit the privacy implications of its planned policy: only a few, carefully selected employees would have access to user notes; the company would randomly select notes for inspection (rather than targeting certain users); and the notes would be stripped of names and "any personal information."[8] Still, there was considerable pushback from users, and Evernote quickly reversed course, announcing that users will have to expressly opt *in* before Evernote employees may examine their notes to further the company's efforts to improve the user experience.[9]

---

[7] Chris O'Neill, *A Note From Chris O'Neill about Evernote's Privacy Policy*, EVERNOTE BLOG, Dec. 15, 2016, https://blog.evernote.com/blog/2016/12/15/note-chris-oneill-evernotes-privacy-policy/. Designated employees had always been (and remain) able to access user notes in other, limited circumstances, including "responding to a warrant, investigating violations of [Endnote's] Terms of Service such as reports of harmful or illegal content, and troubleshooting at the request of users." *Id.*

[8] *Id.*

[9] Greg Chiemingo, *Evernote Revisits Privacy Policy Change in Response to Feedback*, EVERNOTE BLOG, Dec. 15, 2016, https://blog.evernote.com/blog/2016/12/15/evernote-revisits-privacy-policy/.

Evernote's announced policy was notable, in large part, for how unusual it was. Much more typically in contemporary business, data are collected by computers and analyzed by humans only in aggregate or anonymized form. Companies typically do not, for instance, directly observe individual customers at their computers as they click an online ad (or not) or in stores as they select one brand of cereal from the grocery aisle over another. Instead, most companies analyze data that *represent* these behaviors. For instance, a company may conduct an A/B test, in which different users are randomly assigned to see one of two versions of an ad, and user click rates for each ad are tracked. Or, during a given time span, a company may compare cereal sales in stores randomized to display boxes relatively higher on store shelves to cereal sales in stores randomized to display boxes relatively lower (say, where they might attract the attention of children).

Experiments and the Ethics of Interventions

Unlike observational studies, in an *experiment*, the investigator actively manipulates for investigational purposes the exposure received by different groups of subjects. Company experiments, for instance, frequently involve altering the existing product or service environment in order to test the effect of that change on customer behavior. In a true experiment, individuals are randomly assigned by the investigator to two or more different exposure conditions. At least one condition is a "treatment" designed to have an effect, and at least one serves as a control. Randomized, controlled trials (RCTs) are generally considered the "gold standard" for establishing a causal relationship between a treatment and a measured outcome. When subjects are sorted into different study conditions by their own preferences or other nonrandom factors, as is the case with observational studies and quasi-experiments, it is likely that the groups themselves will differ, and it may be those group differences, rather than the treatment, that cause any observed differences in outcome.

Between purely observational studies and true experiments lie a variety of other study designs. For instance, a company may impose a treatment on an entire population (or a sample thereof) and collect data both before and after administering the treatment. Or a company may study the outcomes of a "natural experiment" in which a factor external to the investigators (e.g., varying state laws) "assigns" customers to different conditions, approximating true random assignment.

Because all studies depend on some form of data collection, the informational privacy concerns that arise in observational studies (discussed earlier) are also present in experimental and quasi-experimental studies. Experiments pose additional ethical concerns, however, arising from the interventions they impose on some subjects. For instance, treating some consumers differently from others – as is necessarily done in randomized studies – may be said to raise equality concerns. Similarly, assigning customers to one condition or another necessarily deprives them of the ability to sort themselves into conditions. When an experiment proceeds without customers' consent (as is often the case), it may be thought that the experimenter's assignment deprives customers of an important autonomy interest (sometimes characterized as "decisional privacy").

Normally, however, randomizing people to different "treatments" will be ethically problematic on equality grounds only when there is good reason (i.e., evidence) *prior to conducting the experiment* to believe that the risk-benefit profile of one arm is significantly different from that of the other(s) or from what subjects would experience outside of the trial. In clinical research, it is traditionally (if controversially[10]) regarded as an ethical prerequisite of a randomized, controlled

---

[10] See *infra* note 65.

trial for the relevant expert community to be in collective "equipoise" about which condition, on net, most advances patients' interests. Similarly, depriving subjects of a choice between experimental conditions normally will be ethically problematic on autonomy grounds only when individuals have an ethical right to make that choice outside of the experiment.

WHY COMPANIES STUDY THEIR CONSUMERS

So far, we have discussed some of the major methods by which companies learn about their customers and the typical ethically relevant effects – or consequences – for customers of each method. We have yet to consider companies' *reasons* for studying their customers. Few, if any, ethicists believe that intentions are the only thing that counts when considering whether an act (or omission) is morally justified. But count they often do: accidents are generally not as blameworthy as intentional acts, for instance. So, too, with company research: the different purposes behind such research raise different ethical considerations. Of course, companies study their customers for many reasons – and any particular study is often conducted for multiple reasons. With that caveat aside, we now turn to the range of considerations that motivate company research and the ethical relevance of different motivations.

Some company research is conducted, at least in part, in order to contribute to *generalizable knowledge*. Although developing or contributing to generalizable knowledge is typically thought of as the province of academic research, companies such as Facebook and Microsoft compete for the best data scientists, many of whom have academic pasts (and perhaps academic futures or part-time presents) and want to pursue at least some research that is publishable in academic journals. Competitive hiring aside, it is also not implausible to argue that such companies as these have an obligation to conduct some basic research. Some effects are small enough that they require very large study samples to detect. Outside of governments, only companies such as Facebook have large enough user bases for some studies. Some company research may be conducted with this sense of obligation in mind.[11]

Nevertheless, although contributing to generalizable knowledge is an important social good, it may be orthogonal to the consumer's relationship to the company. In the quintessential basic research study, any benefits that result are likely to accrue to others (such as society at large) in the future, while a study's risks are concentrated on subjects. That mismatch in the distribution of research-related risks and expected benefits does not render basic research unethical, but it makes a moral difference. In the ethical and legal frameworks that govern most academic research, this mismatch is addressed in two ways: by a requirement that a study's risks are "reasonable" in relation to its expected benefits,[12] and by a strong default rule (subject to important exceptions) that subjects provide voluntary, informed consent to participating in research,[13] usually as a form of altruism. Study-specific informed consent of this kind is not usually feasible in the kind of continuous, robotically conducted research in which most large companies engage. Yet if a company fails to make it clear to its customers or users that basic research will be conducted, their expectations for what data the company collects, how it uses that data, and how and why it may manipulate the user environment may be upended.

---

[11] Data scientists at large companies are also making advances in statistics and research methodologies, itself a public good.

[12] 45 C.F.R. § 46.111(a)(2).

[13] *Id.* § 46.116.

It is relatively rare, however, that a company's research has no bearing at all on its products and services. Instead, the vast majority of company research aims at either new product development or the quality assurance (QA) or quality improvement (QI) of products and services. While the noble pursuit of generalizable knowledge will generally be orthogonal to the company-customer relationship, research that seeks to develop new products and services may not be, and QA/QI activities are by definition related to the business that brings the company and its users together and are the most likely to directly benefit participants.[14]

Before concluding that the same population that bears any risks of a particular QA/QI activity also stands to enjoy its benefits, however, it is important to distinguish QA/QI activities that aim to assure or improve the quality of a company's products or services *from the customer's or user's point of view* from those that aim to increase business efficiency or maximize profits in ways that are unlikely to benefit customers (and may even set back their interests). For instance, Facebook makes money by selling ad space. Presumably, the longer its users stay on the platform, and perhaps the more they "engage" with the platform (through "likes," shares, and comments), the more likely they are to see and click on these ads – something the company can tout to advertisers when it sets ad prices. But the time that users spend on Facebook and their level of engagement are also reasonably good (if imperfect) proxies for user enjoyment. In this case, then, research designed to determine how best Facebook can maximize user engagement plausibly benefits both Facebook and its users.

In other cases, however, company and user interests diverge, even when it may appear at first blush that they dovetail. Consider, for instance, the differences between people's first order preferences (what we normally mean by preferences) and their second order preferences (the preferences they have *about* their own preferences). Whenever we want to lose weight or remain healthy but also want a second helping of dessert, we have a conflict between our first order preference for the immediate gratification of cake and our second order preference for ranking health above gastronomic delights. To a large extent, it is reasonable to hold individuals responsible for their indulgences, and not the companies who create the products and services in which some customers (over)indulge. If someone were, say, to procrastinate writing a book chapter by indulging in Facebook browsing, we probably ought not to blame Mark Zuckerberg, and still less his employees who conduct A/B tests.

But companies can learn when their customers are most vulnerable to succumbing to such first order preferences, and deliberately use this information to frustrate their second order preferences. For example, a company may try to identify the times of day when users are most susceptible to indulgences (whether sweets or in-app purchases that help boost gamers' play) and offer those indulgences (or ads for them) then.

Some companies take an even more individualized approach. Gary Loveman, who holds a PhD in economics from MIT and is a former Harvard Business School professor, instilled a culture of experimentation[15] at Caesars Entertainment when he took over as COO (he would later become President and CEO before moving on to Aetna). Loveman famously made use of

---

[14] This is more likely to be true the more that a business's customers or users are returning rather than transient. Returning, but not transient, customers may benefit from QA/QI activities that result in improvements to a product or service that they will use in the future.

[15] According to Loveman, "there were three ways to get fired at Harrah's: steal, harass women, or institute a program or policy without first running an experiment." JEFFREY PFEFFER & ROBERT I. SUTTON, HARD FACTS, DANGEROUS HALF-TRUTHS, AND TOTAL NONSENSE: PROFITING FROM EVIDENCE-BASED MANAGEMENT 15 (2006). *See also* Brynjolfsson & McAfee, *supra* note 1 (noting that Loveman is known for saying, "There are two things that will get you fired [at Caesar's]: stealing from the company, or running an experiment without a properly designed control group.").

the large quantities of customer data Caesars collects in its Total Rewards card program to predict which marketing strategies would be effective for different individuals. The results were industry-changing: as of 2014, Caesars boasted 45 million Total Rewards members worldwide.

Soon, however, came charges that Caesars' marketing is predatory and exploits those who are addicted to gambling. Caesars responded to the charge as follows:

> We look for ways to attract customers, and we make efforts to maintain them as loyal customers. When our customers change their established patterns, we try to understand why and encourage them to return. That's no different than a hotel chain, an airline, or a dry cleaner.[16]

The difference harkens back to the distinction between first and second order preferences. Few people have deep second order preferences that conflict with their first order preferences for, say, inexpensive or convenient dry cleaning (unless the cheapest, most convenient dry cleaner engages in practices to which one is ideologically opposed). But too many struggle to reconcile the rush of the quick win with their need to hold down a job, maintain their marriages, or pay for their kids' education.

Similarly, companies may conduct research to determine whether the business can extract more money from its customers without offering anything more of value. Again, Loveman provides a particularly stark example. He wanted to know whether patrons of his casino could tell the difference between a slot machine that pays out only 5 percent of what players put in, as machines in some competitor casinos in Atlantic City did, and one that pays out a slightly more generous 7 percent, as his own casino's slot machines then did. His hypothesis was that they could not, since he calculated that someone would have to play the slots for approximately forty hours before being confident of such a difference, and he suspected that vanishingly few, if any, customers played so long in one sitting. To rigorously test that hypothesis, however, he put two groups of otherwise identical machines on the casino floor: one with the usual 5 percent hold and the other with a 7 percent hold. Sure enough, customers used the 7 percent hold slot machines just as often as the 5 percent machines, but they lost more money when they played those machines, which the house pocketed as a 40 percent increase in gross profit.[17] Caesars used the results of the experiment to set a new policy of 7 percent holds in all slot machines throughout its casinos, leading to over $300 million in profit a decade later.

Of course, most companies extract as much profit from their customers as the market will bear, and the point of this example is not necessarily to suggest that a 7 percent hold rate is unethical (though the addictive nature of gambling for some people makes this business different from many others). Moreover, assuming for the sake of argument that a 7 percent hold rate is ethical (a questions of business ethics well outside the scope of this chapter), discovering through an experiment, as opposed to through luck or trial and error, that the market will bear a 7 percent hold rate does not magically convert that ethical practice to an unethical one. Rather, the point for present purposes is merely that not all company learning activities serve customer interests equally well.

---

[16] Transcript of Episode 466: *Blackjack*, THIS AMERICAN LIFE, June 8, 2012, http://www.thisamericanlife.org/radio-archives/episode/466/transcript.

[17] Ryan Jacobs, *Turning Data Into Profit at Caesars Palace*, INSIDE OPS, Mar. 14, 2014, http://insideops.com/rljacobs/turning_data_into_profit_at_caesars_palace/.

US FEDERAL REGULATION OF HUMAN SUBJECTS RESEARCH:
THE COMMON RULE

With the increase in corporate experimentation and the considerable public attention that some of these experiments have recently received[18] has come increased interest in how company experiments and other forms of learning can be conducted ethically. One obvious source of potential wisdom in this regard is the governance of academic research with human participants. In the United States, much human subjects research is governed directly or indirectly by a set of federal regulations best known as the Common Rule.[19]

The Common Rule reflects the work of the National Commission for the Protection of Human Subjects of Biomedical and Behavioral Research. That ad hoc commission was created by the National Research Act of 1974[20] to distinguish research from practice, identify the ethical principles that should govern the conduct of research with human participants, and recommend specific rules, including the appropriate role of risk-benefit assessment, that local Institutional Review Boards (IRBs) should apply in reviewing and approving research before it may proceed. The Commission's most influential product is known as the Belmont Report, which identified the aforementioned principles as respect for persons, beneficence, and justice.[21]

In prospectively reviewing, and determining whether or not to approve, research, IRBs have three sets of tasks. The first involves *voluntary, informed consent*, which is the main means by which the principle of *respect for persons* is applied to research. The Common Rule provides a list of informational elements (such as a statement that participation is voluntary and a description of the risks and expected benefits of, and individuals' alternatives to, participation) that ordinarily must be disclosed to prospective subjects to help them decide whether or not to participate.[22] Before research may proceed, an IRB must either review and approve the written informed consent that the investigator has drafted to ensure that it accurately and accessibly conveys all appropriate information,[23] or it must determine that Common Rule

---

[18] For instance, Facebook's mood contagion experiment and OkCupid's matching algorithm experiment, discussed later in the chapter, received very strong responses from many privacy and technology critics, regulators, ethicists, and others.

[19] Department of Health and Human Services, Policy for Protection of Human Research Subjects, 45 C.F.R. 46 (1991).

[20] National Research Act, Pub. L. 93–348 (July 12, 1974).

[21] National Commission, Ethical Principles and Guidelines for the Protection of Human Subjects of Research (1978) (hereinafter "Belmont Report," so named because the commission meeting at which its rough outlines were hashed out took place at the Smithsonian Institute's Belmont Conference Center). The commission's staff philosopher, Tom Beauchamp, drafted the Belmont Report. At the time, Beauchamp was simultaneously in intense collaboration with Jim Childress in writing the first edition of what would become perhaps the most influential treatise on method in bioethics, TOM L. BEAUCHAMP & JAMES F. CHILDRESS, PRINCIPLES OF BIOMEDICAL ETHICS (7th ed. 2012) (1979). Although *Principles* and the Belmont Report clearly have much in common, Beauchamp was not able to convince the Commission that the Belmont Report should be written in every aspect exactly as he advised, and as a result there are important differences between the two frameworks. For instance, *Principles* adds to the Belmont principles a fourth principle of non-maleficence, which more completely fills out beneficence by recognizing the importance not only of securing benefits and protecting from harm but also of avoiding harm. In addition, *Principles* refers to respect for autonomy, rather than to the broader principle of respect for persons. Respect for autonomy refers to the prima facie obligation to respect the decision-making capacities of autonomous individuals. The Belmont Report's "respect for persons" awkwardly combines in one principle both that tenet and the idea that *nonautonomous* individuals should be protected. In *Principles*, protection of individuals who are incapable of self-determination is captured by the principles of beneficence, nonmaleficence, and justice, rather than fused with a principle that aims primarily at respect for autonomy.

[22] *Id.* § 46.116(a)–(b).

[23] *Id.* § 46.111(a)(4)–(5).

criteria for waiving some or all of the required elements of informed consent have been met (on which more later).[24]

The second set of tasks that IRBs perform, which is an application of the principle of *beneficence*, is *risk-benefit analysis*. Before it may approve a study, an IRB must find that any research-related physical, psychological, social, legal, or economic risks to subjects are "reasonable in relation to" the study's expected benefits to subjects (if any) and to society (in the form of knowledge production), and it must ensure that these risks are minimized.[25] An IRB must also ensure "adequate protections" to protect subjects' privacy, "when appropriate."[26] And it must – again "when appropriate" – ensure that data collected during the research will be monitored on an ongoing basis to ensure that research risks don't turn out to be higher than expected, possibly necessitating termination of the study.

The third set of tasks broadly concerns *justice* in the *distribution of research risks and expected benefits*. An IRB must ensure that the selection of subjects is "equitable."[27] Investigators should not, for instance, choose vulnerable subjects simply because they are vulnerable or otherwise constitute a convenient sample. IRBs must also ensure that "additional safeguards" are in place if some or all study subjects are likely to be "vulnerable to coercion or undue influence."[28]

By its terms, the Common Rule applies to all activities that (1) meet the regulatory definitions of "research" involving "human subjects," (2) are not exempt from the policy,[29] and (3) are either conducted or funded by one of fifteen federal departments and agencies[30] that have adopted the Common Rule. (Anyone conducting human subjects research involving an item subject to regulation by the Food and Drug Administration – e.g., investigational drugs, medical devices, or biologics – is subject to a similar set of regulations that also includes a requirement of IRB review.[31]) When an institution receives funding to conduct human subjects research, it enters into an agreement with the federal government, called a Federalwide Assurance (FWA), in which it agrees to subject the funded study to IRB review.

However, the current version of the FWA invites institutions to voluntarily subject *all* human subjects research conducted at the institution to IRB review regardless of the source (or even existence) of funding. Institutions that accept this invitation are colloquially referred to as having "checked the box," and historically, somewhere between 74 percent and 90 percent of institutions with an FWA have done so (though with a declining trend).[32] Because the vast majority of colleges, universities, academic medical centers and healthcare systems conduct at least some federally funded human subjects research, and because the majority of those institutions elect to

---

[24] *Id.* § 46.116(c)–(d).
[25] *Id.* § 46.111(a)(1)–(2).
[26] *Id.* § 46.111(a)(7).
[27] *Id.* § 46.111(a)(3).
[28] *Id.* § 46.111(b).
[29] Id. §46.101(b).
[30] The fifteen federal departments and agencies that have codified the Common Rule into their own regulations are the Departments of Agriculture, Commerce, Defense, Education, Energy, Health and Human Services, Housing and Urban Development, Justice, Veterans Affairs, and Transportation and the Agency for International Development, Consumer Product Safety Commission, Environmental Protection Agency, National Aeronautics and Space Administration, and National Science Foundation. In addition, the Central Intelligence Agency complies with the Common Rule pursuant to an Executive Order and the Food and Drug Administration (FDA) has promulgated its own regulations, which are as similar to the Common Rule as possible, commensurate with the limits of the FDA's enabling statute.
[31] *See* Food and Drug Administration, 21 C.F.R. parts 50, 56, 312, and 812.
[32] *See* Carol Weil et al., *OHRP Compliance Oversight Letters: An Update*, 32 IRB 1 (2010) ("informal review of a sample of institutions" showed that in 2000, more than 90% of domestic institutions had agreed to extend the regulations to all human subjects research, while in 2010 only 74% of these institutions did so).

check the box, the vast majority of human subjects research conducted at these institutions is subject to the Common Rule through the FWA.

Federal regulators recently announced their intention to revise the FWA to omit the possibility of checking the box, but it is unclear that this will have a dramatic impact on the scope of IRB review. Even today, virtually every academic and nonprofit research institute requires IRB review of all of its human subjects research as a matter of institutional policy. That is unlikely to change if and when the FWA no longer offers institutions the opportunity to opt into oversight of all its human subjects research by the federal government; the difference is likely to be only that violations would be reportable solely to the relevant authorities at individual institutions, and not also to the federal government.

In sum, the Common Rule is a well-established ethical-regulatory framework for the governance of research involving human subjects. Given the significant overlap between the academy and company data scientists and other researchers – after the US government, Microsoft reportedly employs the largest number of anthropologists in the world – it is also a framework with which many people conducting company research are already familiar.[33]

CHALLENGES IN APPLYING THE COMMON RULE TO COMPANY RESEARCH

There are several problems, however, with simply importing the Common Rule into the company research context.

Limited Substantive Scope of the Common Rule

First, even if the Common Rule applied to research conducted and funded by private companies, much of the research that companies conduct either doesn't meet the Common Rule's definition of "human subjects research" or is human subjects research that is nevertheless exempt from the Common Rule.

The Common Rule defines "research" as "a systematic investigation, including research development, testing and evaluation, designed to develop or contribute to generalizable knowledge."[34] Activities that are instead designed solely to allow companies to measure and either assure or improve the quality of its products or services fall outside the scope of the Common Rule, even if these activities are otherwise identical to research designed to contribute to generalizable knowledge.

Determining when an activity is research, QI/QA, or both is notoriously difficult. Here is a taste of how federal regulatory guidance attempts to thread the needle: an institution engages solely in QI not subject to the Common Rule if it implements a practice that is either untested or "known to be" effective (in some context), with the aim of improving the quality of that institution's work (say, patient care or user experience) and collects (patient or user) data about this implementation for "clinical, practical, or administrative purposes," including in order to determine whether the practice had the expected effects. If, however, these data are *also* collected "for the purpose of establishing scientific evidence to determine how well the

---

[33] Graeme Wood, *Anthropology Inc.*, THE ATLANTIC (Feb. 20, 2013), http://www.theatlantic.com/magazine/archive/2013/03/anthropology-inc/309218.

[34] 45 C.F.R. 46.102(d).

intervention achieves its intended results," then the QI project "may also constitute nonexempt human subjects research."[35]

To see how the research/QI distinction might play out in the (nonmedical) business context, consider the infamous Facebook mood contagion experiment.[36] The purpose of that experiment was to attempt to better understand the effects of exposing users to both positive and negative content in their News Feeds. The mood contagion experiment gave Facebook potentially useful information about the negative effects of its News Feed on users and how to avoid them – a classic QI aim. It also contributed to the academic literature in social psychology pertaining to the general phenomenon of mood contagion. Although mere publication of results, without more, does not render an activity research,[37] the fact that the article reporting the results of the experiment situated them within this broader academic conversation is suggestive of a research, rather than solely a QI, purpose.[38]

Yet the results could have been written up a bit differently – or not published at all – and easily have constituted a pure QI activity not subject to the Common Rule's requirements of IRB review, informed consent, and risk-benefit analysis. The same will be true of virtually all company research.[39] Insistence that company research be subject to the Common Rule will likely only push companies to simply conduct those learning activities as QI, depriving the public of both generalized knowledge and knowledge of the effects of company products and services, and generally reducing transparency about how companies study their users.[40]

Even if an activity involves "research," the Common Rule only applies if that research involves human subjects. Under the Common Rule, a "human subject" is "a living individual about whom an investigator ... conducting research obtains (1) Data through intervention or interaction with the individual, or (2) Identifiable private information."[41] Most company research does not involve interaction with consumers or users but is instead conducted at a distance. Much company research *does* involve intervention, which includes not only physical interventions common in clinical trials such as drawing blood or administering drugs but also "manipulations of the subject or the subject's environment that are performed for research purposes."[42]

---

[35] Off. for Hum. Research Protections, *Quality Improvement Activities FAQs*, U.S. Dep't Health & Hum. Serv., https://www.hhs.gov/ohrp/regulations-and-policy/guidance/faq/quality-improvement-activities (no date; last accessed May 6, 2017).

[36] For background on and a detailed ethical analysis of this experiment, see Michelle N. Meyer, *Two Cheers for Corporate Experimentation: The A/B Illusion and the Virtues of Data-Driven Innovation*, 13 Colo. Tech. L.J. 273 (2015).

[37] *See* Off. for Hum. Research Protections, *Quality Improvement Activities FAQs*, U.S. Dep't Health & Hum. Serv., https://www.hhs.gov/ohrp/regulations-and-policy/guidance/faq/quality-improvement-activities (no date).

[38] *See* Adam D. I. Kramer, Jamie E. Guillory & Jeffrey T. Hancock, *Experimental Evidence of Massive-Scale Emotional Contagion through Social Networks*, 111 Proc. Nat'l Acad. Sci. 8788 (2014).

[39] Perhaps the chief reason why some company research does in fact appear to be designed to contribute to generalizable knowledge (in addition to improving business quality and otherwise guiding business decisions) is that the best data scientists tend to have academic ambitions and therefore are more likely to accept positions in companies that allow them to publish some research in general academic journals such as *PNAS*.

[40] *See* Michelle N. Meyer, John Lantos, Alex John London, Amy L. McGuire, Udo Schuklenk & Lance Stell, *Misjudgements Will Drive Social Trials Underground*, 511 Nature 265 (July 16, 2014).

[41] 45 C.F.R. 46.102(f).

[42] The 2018 Common Rule, however, newly exempts "benign behavioral interventions." Basic HHS Policy for the Protection of Human Research Subjects, 45 C.F.R. § 46.104(d)(3) (2017) (as of this writing, this provision of the revised Common Rule will go into effect on January 19, 2018; it appears in the Code of Federal Regulations following the version of the subpart currently in effect as a convenience to users). The exemption requires, among other things, that the subject "prospectively agrees to the intervention and information collection." *Id.* Until such time as regulators provide guidance interpreting this new exemption, it is unclear whether broad "prospective agreement" to future,

What about research that involves no interaction or intervention, only obtaining data about subjects? For such research to involve "human subjects," the data must be "private," which "includes information about behavior that occurs in a context in which an individual can reasonably expect that no observation or recording is taking place, and information which has been provided for specific purposes by an individual and which the individual can reasonably expect will not be made public (for example, a medical record)."[43] How this rather odd definition of private data applies to the kind of data companies most often use in research is unclear. For example, information knowingly given to a company for business purposes would not seem to qualify as private (since we expect a company to record information given to them), even if its use for company research purposes is contrary to customer expectations.[44]

Even if research data are private, they must also be individually "identifiable" if an activity that only involves obtaining data (without intervention or interaction) is to constitute research with "human subjects." Under the Common Rule, data are "identifiable" only if the subject's identity is either directly associated with the data or is "readily ascertainable" by the researcher.[45] Regulatory guidance further explains that coded data are *not* readily ascertainable if the researcher is denied access to the code key.[46] The vast majority of consumer data used in company research that is not aggregated or anonymous will be "coded" by customer ID, device ID, cookies, and the like. Under federal guidance interpreting the Common Rule, so long as there is an agreement in place under which those conducting research with such data will under no circumstances have access to the key linking these pseudonymous identifiers to actual consumer identities, no "human subjects" are involved and the Common Rule does not apply to the research.

Most data privacy scholars would find this result inadequate for at least two reasons. First, nonidentifiable data can sometimes to be reidentified. Some scholars have argued that HIPAA

unspecified interventions included in something like a ToS would suffice, or whether the exemption requires study-specific agreement. Other exemptions are discussed later in the chapter.

[43] 45 C.F.R. 46.102(f).

[44] *Cf.* Fed. Trade Comm'n, *Privacy Online: A Report to Congress* 7 (June 1998) (describing the Fair Information Practice Principles (FIPPs), including Notice/Awareness, which calls on businesses to disclose their data practices to consumers, usually including "the uses to which the data will be put"); Org. for Econ. Co-operation & Dev. (OECD), *OECD's Privacy Framework* 14 (2013) (orig. 1980) (calling on businesses to respect principles of Purpose Specification ("The purposes for which personal data are collected should be specified no later than at the time of data collection and the subsequent use limited to the fulfillment of those purposes or such others as are not incompatible with those purposes and as are specified on each occasion of change of purpose.") and Use Limitation ("Personal data should not be disclosed, made available or otherwise used for purposes other than those specified in accordance with [the purpose specification principle] except: a) with the consent of the data subject; or b) by the authority of law.")); White House Report, *Consumer Data Privacy in a Networked World: A Framework for Protecting Privacy and Promoting Innovation in the Global Digital Economy*, 4 J. PRIVACY & CONFIDENTIALITY 95, 97, 109–113, 136–7 (2012) (proposing a Consumer Privacy Bill of Rights, including a principle of Respect for Context that calls on companies to "collect, use, and disclose personal data in ways that are consistent with the context in which consumers provide the data"); White House, Administration Discussion Draft: Consumer Privacy Bill of Rights Act of 2015 (Feb. 27, 2015) (requiring that out-of-context data collection, e.g., for research, require either affirmative consumer consent in response to a clear and prominent prompt or approval by an FTC-approved "Privacy Review Board" that finds that such opt-in consent is impractical and that privacy risks have been minimized and are outweighed by "substantial benefits" to those beyond merely the business, e.g., to consumers or society).

[45] 45 C.F.R. 46.102(f).

[46] Off. for Hum. Research Protections, *Coded Private Information or Specimens Use in Research, Guidance*, U.S. DEP'T HEALTH & HUM. SERV., Oct. 16, 2008, https://www.hhs.gov/ohrp/regulations-and-policy/guidance/research-involving-coded-private-information/index.html.

de-identification is inadequate to protect data,[47] and the Common Rule's definition of "non-identifiable" does not set even so high a bar as that. Although federal regulators are aware of the possibility for reidentification, they were unable to achieve consensus among the many federal Common Rule departments and agencies about how to address the problem. As a result, the 2018 Common Rule kicks the ball down the road, merely requiring agencies to regularly reconsider the Common Rule's definition of "identifiable" and whether certain research techniques or technologies (such as genomic sequencing) inherently yield identifiable data.[48]

Finally, several categories of human subjects research are exempt from the Common Rule despite meeting these definitions. For instance, research involving the collection or study of existing data is exempt if the data are publicly available or recorded by the researcher in such a manner that subjects cannot be identified, directly or through identifiers linked to the subjects.[49] Research involving surveys, interviews, and observations of public behavior[50] is exempt if either data are recorded such that subjects cannot be identified directly or through identifiers linked to subjects or, when data are identifiable, if their disclosure would not place subjects at risk of criminal or civil liability or be damaging to the subjects' financial standing, employability, or reputation.[51] Some have worried about "the 'extraordinary' lengths to which food manufacturers go to scientifically engineer craving,"[52] but taste and food quality evaluation and consumer acceptance studies, too, are exempt from the Common Rule.[53] As for the broader social implications of manufacturing ever more addictive food during an obesity epidemic, the Common Rule explicitly instructs, "The IRB should not consider possible long-range effects of applying knowledge gained in the research (for example, the possible effects of the research on public policy) as among those research risks that fall within the purview of its responsibility."[54]

Consent

The Common Rule typically requires researchers to obtain subjects' informed consent to participate in a study. The traditional form such consent takes is often a lengthy written document, signed by the subject, that describes a specific study's purpose, risks, and potential benefits. This kind of formal, study-specific consent is infeasible for the continual A/B testing in which companies such as Facebook, Google, and Bing engage, and for much other business research. A pop-up window that required Facebook users to read and agree to a consent document every time they use the service, for instance, would quickly spell the demise of the platform. Similarly, much company research is behavioral – i.e, designed to investigate which

---

[47] *See, e.g.,* Paul Ohm, *Broken Promises of Privacy: Responding to the Surprising Failure of Anonymization,* 57 UCLA L. REV. 1701 (2010). *But see* Daniel Barth-Jones, *The Debate Over 'Re-Identification' of Health Information: What Do We Risk?,* Health Affairs Blog, Aug. 10, 2012, http://healthaffairs.org/blog/2012/08/10/the-debate-over-re-identification-of-health-information-what-do-we-risk.

[48] *See* Holly Fernandez Lynch & Michelle N. Meyer, *Regulating Research with Biospecimens Under the Revised Common Rule,* 47 HASTINGS CTR. REPORT 3 (May–June 2017).

[49] 45 C.F.R. § 46.101(b)(4).

[50] What constitutes "public behavior" is not well defined.

[51] *Id.* § 46.101(b)(2). *Cf.* Consumer Privacy Bill of Rights Act of 2015 at §4(g) (defining "privacy risk" as the potential of data disclosure to "cause emotional distress, or physical, financial, professional or other harm to an individual").

[52] Calo at 99–100 (citing Michael Moss, *The Extraordinary Science of Addictive Junk Food,* N.Y. TIMES MAG. (Feb. 20, 2013)).

[53] *Id.* § 46.101(b)(6).

[54] *Id.* § 46.111(a)(2).

aspects of the retail environment affect customer behavior – and disclosing the details of these studies in advance would badly (often irreparably) bias their results.[55]

Precisely for these reasons, much company research would meet the Common Rule's criteria for a waiver or alteration of informed consent. That is arguably as it should be (there are sound normative reasons why the criteria for waiver and alteration of informed consent are as they are) – and so this is not an argument for the inapplicability of the Common Rule to company research, per se. But it will not appease those who believe that participating in an experiment or other study should always involve the kind of consent one expects in, say, a clinical trial of an experimental drug.

An increasingly common alternative to study-specific consent is one-time "broad consent," in which participants agree at the time of collection to have their data (or specimens) stored for future, unspecified research. Research institutions have long used broad consent, and the 2018 Common Rule explicitly blesses this alternative in certain circumstances.[56] Broad consent is not a blank check; it requires, among other things, a description of the *kinds* of studies that might be conducted using stored data or tissue.[57] For instance, participants who give broad consent to contribute to a biobank may be told that their tissue and resulting data will be used in health research. Facebook or Google users who will be subject to a variety of A/B testing might be told, in general terms, that they may see one version of a page while others see a different version, and that the length of time they remain on that page, or the extent to which they click through to another page, may be (pseudonymously) recorded and compared with the data of users who see an alternative page in order to help the company decide which page is preferable (either for users or for the business).

Broad consent has been criticized by some: consent that is – by definition – not informed about the specific nature of research, they argue, is insufficiently protective of autonomy.[58] But we knowingly make considered decisions based on incomplete information all the time. As discussed above, however, the prima facie obligation to obtain research subjects' informed consent is primarily rooted in the principle of respect for autonomy. And broad consent need be no less autonomous a decision than study-specific consent: they are simply different kinds of autonomous decisions, one involving an understanding and acceptance of what will happen in a particular study and one involving an understanding and acceptance that the participant's knowledge will be limited to the kinds of studies that may occur.[59]

The closest existing business research analog to broad consent is perhaps the ubiquitous and much-maligned Terms of Service (ToS), or the similarly dense Data Use Policy and Privacy Policy. Whatever the demerits of incompletely informed broad consent, the main difference between it and these company agreements is that virtually everyone "accepts" the ToS without even attempting to read its contents.

There are, however, ways of ensuring that individuals read and even meaningfully comprehend documents such as ToS and consent forms. Research studies increasingly give prospective participants short (online, automatically "graded") comprehension quizzes after they've read the consent (whether broad or study-specific). A company that wants to inform its customers that it learns from customer data in various ways (perhaps including through A/B tests and other experiments) can

[55] *See, e.g.*, Meyer, *supra* note 36, at p. 298 (explaining why study-specific consent would have biased the results of Facebook's mood contagion and OkCupid's matching algorithm experiments).
[56] *See* Fernandez Lynch & Meyer, *supra* note 47.
[57] *See, e.g.*, 45 C.F.R. §46.116(d) (2017). For instance, a biobank might collect tissue under a consent that limits secondary research use of the tissue to health-related research aims.
[58] *See, e.g.*, Björn Hofmann, *Broadening Consent – and Diluting Ethics?*, 35 J. MED. ETHICS 125 (2009).
[59] Mark Sheehan, *Can Broad Consent Be Informed Consent?*, 4 PUB. HEALTH ETHICS 226 (2011).

require one-time passage of such a broad research ToS. Asking customers to agree to a separate Research ToS, labeled as such, is another way of highlighting that particular term of service and prompting those who are concerned to peruse its contents. Assuming that the disclosures and questions are sufficiently clear and accurately reflect the company's learning practices and their implications for customers, a customer who successfully completes the quiz and signs up for the product or service can be said to have given ethically meaningful informed consent.

Users might be required to accept the Research ToS as a condition of opening an account, or they may be given a choice about whether to opt into (or out of) the Research ToS.[60] More customers may be willing to give broad consent to participate in a business's various learning activities than might be expected, especially if some of those learning activities give customers opportunities to be alpha or beta users or the latest innovation. Studying only those customers who opt in to (or fail to opt out of) participation in research, and not the remaining customers, could bias the results, however, because there may be important differences between these two groups of people. Even so, a company might conduct pilot studies on such "empaneled" customers and, if the results are promising, roll out an intervention to successively broader groups of customers.

Whether informed consent-by-ToS is also sufficiently *voluntary* is a separate issue. As with virtually every academic or industry research study, there is no negotiating over the ToS: both research consent forms and commercial ToS are almost always take-it-or-leave-it offers. If a company has a monopoly on a critical product or service, then even if customers understand what they're getting into, thanks to clear ToS and a forced comprehension quiz, they may still lack any meaningful choice over whether to accept those terms or not.[61] The result will be similar if all major companies in a sector require their customers to agree to participate in research and competition has not led to the emergence of an alternative that offers more preferable ToS.

On the other hand, the Common Rule's requirement that subjects are "volunteers"[62] for whom research participation should ordinarily be voluntary – and, indeed, that subjects must ordinarily be told that they may revoke their consent to participate at any time and for any reason, regardless of how that might affect the study[63] – may be less appropriate for an arm's

---

[60] For instance, the direct-to-consumer genetic testing company 23andMe requires all of its consumers to accept both its Privacy Statement and its Terms of Service. These documents disclose (among many other things) that the company and its partners use consumer data not only to provide genetic testing services and to bill consumers for the same, but also to "perform research & development activities, which may include, for example, conducting data analysis and research in order to develop new or improve existing products and services, and performing quality control activities." 23andMe, *Privacy Statement*, https://www.23andme.com/legal/privacy/, §4(a)(viii). The company may also share aggregate or (undefined) "anonymous" consumer data with third parties for various purposes. *Id.* at §4(d)(iii). By contrast, before individual-level consumer data may be used by 23andMe in research designed to contribute to generalizable knowledge, consumers must opt in via a separate "research consent." See 23andMe, *Research Consent*, https://www.23andme.com/about/consent/ (undated; last accessed May 6, 2017); 23andMe, *Privacy Statement*, *supra* at §4(b).

[61] For instance, several people from across the political spectrum have argued that Facebook use is so ubiquitous and central to daily modern life that it should be regulated like a utility. *See, e.g.,* danah boyd, *Facebook Is a Utility: Utilities Get Regulated*, APOPHENIA, May 15, 2010, http://www.zephoria.org/thoughts/archives/2010/05/15/facebook-is-a-utility-utilities-get-regulated.html; Scott Adams, *Should Twitter and Facebook Be Regulated as Utilities?*, SCOTT ADAMS' BLOG, Jan. 25, 2017, http://blog.dilbert.com/post/156377416856/should-twitter-and-facebook-be-regulated-as. *See also* Philip N. Howard, *Let's Nationalize Facebook*, SLATE, Aug. 16, 2012, http://www.slate.com/articles/technology/future_tense/2012/08/facebook_should_be_nationalized_to_protect_user_rights_.html; Timothy B. Lee, *Facebook Has More Influence Over Americans Than Any Media Company in History*, VOX, May 10, 2016, https://www.vox.com/2016/5/10/11640140/facebook-media-influence.

[62] Belmont Report, *supra* note 20, at Part C.1.

[63] 45 C.F.R. § 46.116(a)(8).

length transaction between company and customer. In many cases, it is ethically and legally permissible for a company to offer a product or service premised on certain nonnegotiable conditions that, all else being equal, consumers would not choose. Both law and ethics require that those conditions not be unconscionable, but otherwise a consumer's right to choose may be limited to her initial decision whether to avail herself of a company's product or service or not.

A very great deal of company research easily meets that test. It is hardly unconscionable, for instance, if a company requires its customers or users to agree to have their data used for QI/QA purposes. That is quite routine[64] and the fact that a QI/QA activity may take the form of a randomized, controlled evaluation rather than an observational approach does not, per se, change the moral calculus.[65] Indeed, in some cases – as discussed in the final section of this chapter – it would be unconscionable (or at least ethically inferior) for a company *not* to use nonidentifiable data to ensure that its product or service works the way the company advertises or is safe for users. Nor is it unconscionable if a company decides to exercise its social responsibility (or recruit top data scientists) by conducting research that contributes to the public good of generalizable knowledge.

Many companies conduct pilot studies with their employees. Perhaps ironically, voluntariness is more likely to pose a significant issue in these cases than in cases of customers, who can (barring monopolies) always opt to use a competitor's product or service. Employees, of course, generally have a great deal invested in their employment (financially and professionally, but often also socially and psychologically). This investment can make declining an employer's request to serve as a pilot subject difficult or practically impossible. Employers should therefore generally make such service completely voluntary, especially where studies involve potentially sensitive data or other significant risks.

Similarly, data privacy will generally be more important in this context. Most of us are more concerned about our employers or colleagues learning sensitive things about us than we are about a stranger we are unlikely ever to meet (say, a company data scientist) learning the same thing about us. When employees do opt in to participate in pilot studies, their data should generally be at least coded (if not anonymous), with access to the key linking employee data to their employee identities limited to as few employees as possible (ideally, only one, and strict

---

[64] In the furor over the Facebook mood contagion experiment, much was made of the fact that Facebook had only after the fact included a disclosure in its ToS that it conducted "research." Aside from the important point that the content of a standard ToS is close to morally irrelevant, given the accepted fact that virtually no one reads them, Facebook's Data Use Policy in effect at the time did disclose that the company might use users' data "as part of our efforts to keep Facebook products, services and integrations safe and secure," Kashmir Hill, *Facebook Added "Research" to User Agreement 4 Months After Emotion Manipulation Study*, FORBES (June 30, 2014), http://www.forbes.com/sites/kashmir hill/2014/06/30/facebook-only-got-permission-to-do-research-on-users-after-emotion-manipulation-study/ (referring to users as "guinea pigs made to have a crappy day for science"), a QA/QI purpose that, I have argued, the mood contagion experiment served (even if it also contributed to generalizable knowledge). *See* Meyer, *supra* note 36.

[65] All else being equal, randomized, controlled QA/QI activities are ethically preferable to QA/QI activities using observational methods, because the former permit causal inferences to be made about the effects of a company's goods, services, policies, or practices. The primary ethical issue posed by randomized evaluations is whether different arms have different risk-benefit profiles. The traditional answer of research ethics to this issue is that randomizing subjects to different arms is ethical if the relevant expert community as a whole is in "equipoise" as to which arm, if any, is superior to the other(s). For the seminal statement of this position, see Benjamin Freedman, *Equipoise and the Ethics of Clinical Research*, 317 NEW ENG. J. MED. 141 (1987). Clinical equipoise is, however, the subject of lively and continuing debate in the field of research ethics. *See, e.g.*, Frank G. Miller & Howard Brody, *A Critique of Clinical Equipoise: Therapeutic Misconception in the Ethics of Clinical Trials*, 33 HASTINGS CTR. REPORT 19 (2003).

firewalls should separate these data from company departments such as human resources and benefits), and the key deleted as soon as possible after data collection and analysis.[66]

It is important to note that a different situation is posed by many employer learning activities aimed at assuring or improving workplace policies and conditions. The purpose of such activities – unlike pilot testing a company's new products on its employees – is less orthogonal to the employer–employee relationship. Imagine, for instance, a CEO who worries that some of her employees aren't taking optimal advantage of the company's generous 401(k) matching program.[67] She has a hunch that adding to the usual matching letter information telling each employee what his or her similarly aged peers are saving would nudge the low-savers to save more. The CEO could implement this peer information letter policy in the next enrollment cycle and observe the result, but regardless of whether savings went up or down, she'd never really know what effect, if any, the policy had without running a randomized, controlled experiment in which some employees receive letters with no peer information and others receive letters with peer information. Telling employees in advance that the company would be sending out different letters and why would badly bias the results by altering employees' behavior; no social scientist worth her salt would take the results of such a study seriously.

Although some insist that "human experimentation" always requires informed consent, the CEO would be "experimenting" on her employees no matter what; the only question is whether her experiment will be properly controlled, enabling her to learn from the experience and make sound choices going forward. The CEO will either send the usual matching letter or the alternative letter to all employees, using her intuition to choose between them, without ever knowing which one is better for her employees – and surely without anyone insisting that employees provide informed consent to receive one version of the letter instead of the other. Or she will have the epistemic humility to realize that she does not know which letter will better serve her employees, and will conduct an A/B test to answer that question. To have more qualms about conducting that A/B test than about enacting an untested practice across the board is what I have elsewhere called the "A/B illusion."[68]

Notably, the above challenges in applying the Common Rule's substantive criteria to company research are in addition to the many critiques of it as applied to the academic and biomedical industry context. For instance, many critical terms in the Common Rule are ambiguous or difficult to apply, allowing the processing of IRB review, in which those terms are applied to a study protocol, to be captured by interests other than participant welfare or to reflect various forms of bias. Although the Common Rule requires IRBs to assign each study a single risk-benefit profile, heterogeneity among subjects means that a study will in fact have very different risk-benefit profiles for many subjects.[69] The Common Rule is based on a medical model of research and has crowded out other disciplines' traditions of ethical reflection of research.[70]

---

[66] Selecting employees as pilot subjects may well also bias the data, if employees tend to be more homogeneous than end users.

[67] This scenario, loosely based on actual studies and the challenges that economists tell us they have faced in conducting them, is adapted from Michelle N. Meyer & Christopher F. Chabris, *Please, Corporations, Experiment on Us*, N.Y. TIMES (June 19, 2015), https://www.nytimes.com/2015/06/21/opinion/sunday/please-corporations-experiment-on-us .html.

[68] See Meyer, *supra* note 36. See also the discussion, below, of HiPPOs.

[69] See Michelle N. Meyer, *Regulating the Production of Knowledge: Research Risk-Benefit Analysis and the Heterogeneity Problem*, 65 ADMIN. L. REV. 237 (2013).

[70] See ZACHARY M. SCHRAG, ETHICAL IMPERIALISM: INSTITUTIONAL REVIEW BOARDS AND THE SOCIAL SCIENCES, 1965–2009 (2010).

Different business sectors, if not individual businesses, will benefit from thinking about the right set of ethical principles to guide the particular learning endeavors in which they are engaged. Still, the Common Rule does have some general wisdom to offer: risks and expected benefits are ethically relevant inputs into decisions about the appropriateness of research. Risks to subjects are important to consider, and although the Common Rule directs IRBs not to consider them, businesses that wish to be socially responsible may well wish to consider the risks and costs to third parties of their learning activities. Risks should be minimized to those necessary to achieve the learning aim. The distribution of risks and expected benefits matters: imposing risks on customers is more easily justified if those customers are also among those who stand to benefit from the results of an activity. In the absence of study-specific consent, meaningful notice at the point of service of a company's general research practices and policies can help people make better informed decisions about whether or not to use a product or service. Amending one's products, services, or practices in light of evidence about their effects, or disseminating the results of internal research so that they can guide decision-making by end users, is a good idea.

Indeed, the "basic formula" of Facebook's internal research review process (discussed further below) "is the same as an IRBs [sic]: We consider the benefits of the research against the potential downsides."[71] In particular, the company considers "how the research will improve our society, our community, and Faceboook"; "whether there are potentially adverse consequences that could result from the study," especially due to vulnerable populations or sensitive topics, and "whether every effort has been taken to minimize them"; "whether the research is consistent with people's expectations"; and whether it has "taken appropriate precautions designed to protect people's information."[72]

OVERSIGHT OF COMPANY RESEARCH

Although it is unclear how useful or appropriate it would be to apply the details of the Common Rule's *substantive* criteria to company research, businesses should experiment with adopting something *like* the *process* of IRB review.[73] This somewhat cautious recommendation for a mere approximation of the IRB review process reflects the many legitimate criticisms of that process. For instance, most IRB members are inexpert in both ethical reasoning and the scientific methods of many of the studies they review, and they frequently fail to base their decisions on evidence of risks and expected benefits.[74] Although both researchers and prospective participants

---

[71] Molly Jackman & Lauri Kanerva, *Evolving the IRB: Building Robust Review for Industry Research*, 72 WASH. & LEE L. REV. ONLINE 442, 454 (2016). See also Michelle De Mooy & Shelten Yuen, *Toward Privacy Aware Research and Development in Wearable Health: A Report from the Center for Democracy & Technology and Fitbit, Inc.* (May 2016), available at https://healthblawg.com/images/2016/06/CDT-Fitbit-report.pdf (suggesting that both the Belmont Report and the Common Rule are ethically relevant to wearables companies' research and development processes – but somewhat mischaracterizing both those sources of ethical guidance).

[72] *Id.* at 454–56.

[73] *See, e.g.*, Ryan Calo, *Consumer Subject Review Board: A Thought Experiment*, 66 STAN. L. REV. ONLINE 97 (Sept. 3, 2013), https://www.stanfordlawreview.org/online/privacy-and-big-data-consumer-subject-review-boards/ (proposing that corporations rely on "consumer subject review boards"); De Mooy & Yuen, *supra*, at 20–21 (developing ethical guidance for wearables companies' R&D and proposing that "a company might create a 'Privacy Board' comprised of selected company staff to review the research practices and policies for in-house volunteers and device users, and offer ongoing feedback. Companies may find it useful to bring together privacy experts, advocates, academics, and their R&D teams regularly to discuss existing and emerging privacy issues, market concerns, and technical challenges facing wearable companies.").

[74] *See* ROBERT KLITZMAN, THE ETHICS POLICE? THE STRUGGLE TO MAKE HUMAN RESEARCH SAFE (2015).

are biased in how they approach decisions to participate in research, IRB members are also burdened by their own biases.[75] Finally, compared to other regulators, IRBs are lawless: they are largely unaccountable, have nearly boundless jurisdiction, and typically make ad hoc decisions generally subject to no review or other mechanisms for due process.[76]

Nevertheless, boiled down to its essence, IRB review is simply a mechanism for gathering feedback about a planned learning activity from someone other than the person likely to be most invested in it, who may therefore have a biased view of its risks and potential benefits.[77] In some cases, both the informed consent process and the fact that most prospective participants are free either to leave or take a research offer might plausibly operate as checks on the researcher's self-interest and biased perspective. But because so much of company research neither is nor practically can be conducted with study-specific consent, and because consumers frequently have little choice in choosing to patronize a business that doesn't engage in learning activities, some other check on the researcher's perspective is in order.

Indeed, when the Obama administration was confronted with the dilemma that there will often be important but non-contextual uses of consumer data for which consent is infeasible, it proposed, in its draft Consumer Privacy Protection Act of 2015, that "privacy review boards" be empowered to authorize such non-contextual uses of consumer data if a study met criteria very much like the Common Rule's criteria for waiving consent.[78]

Although the Consumer Privacy Protection Act of 2015 and its privacy review boards did not become law, similar ideas already exist in the business world. Since about 2007, for example, Google has employed an "experiment council" – a group of internal engineers who try to ensure proper experimental design by reviewing proposed experiments using a "lightweight," continually updated checklist of best practices that the experimenter completes. Following the completion of an experiment, results are then presented at a separate "discussion forum" open to anyone at the company but facilitated by experts. The discussion forum aims to ensure that results are valid and properly interpreted, and that there is agreement about the consequences of the interpreted results for the user experience.[79] Although it may appear otherwise, ensuring that experiments are properly designed and that their results are appropriately understood and disseminated are matters not only of scientific and business but also of ethical import. A poorly designed study cannot answer the question it seeks to answer (no matter how important that question may be), rendering any risks or burdens imposed on subjects gratuitous.[80]

---

[75] See Michelle N. Meyer, *Three Challenges for Risk-Based (Research) Regulation: Heterogeneity among Regulated Activities, Regulator Bias, and Stakeholder Heterogeneity*, in HUMAN SUBJECTS RESEARCH REGULATION: PERSPECTIVES ON THE FUTURE 313 (I. GLENN COHEN & HOLLY FERNANDEZ LYNCH EDS., 2014).

[76] See CARL E. SCHNEIDER, THE CENSOR'S HAND: THE MISREGULATION OF HUMAN-SUBJECT Research (2015).

[77] When companies use external IRBs or internal IRB-like boards, the decisions of those boards are almost always advisory only. Ordinarily, as with most business decisions, management will have final say over whether a project goes forward. Often, representatives from various relevant management sectors (e.g., the Chief Privacy Officer, Chief Communications Officer, or in-house counsel) will sit on an internal review board, and if they object to a project for legal or business reasons, that will be the end of the conversation.

[78] White House, *Administration Discussion Draft: Consumer Privacy Bill of Rights Act of 2015* (Feb. 27, 2015), https://www.democraticmedia.org/sites/default/files/field/public/2015/draft_consumer_privacy_bill_of_rights_act.pdf.

[79] Diane Tang, Ashish Agarwal, Deirdre O'Brien & Mike Meyer, *Overlapping Experiment Infrastructure: More, Better, Faster Experimentation*, in PROCEEDINGS OF THE 16TH ACM SIGKDD INTERNATIONAL CONFERENCE ON KNOWLEDGE DISCOVERY AND DATA MINING 17–26 (2010), https://research.google.com/pubs/archive/36500.pdf.

[80] See, e.g., 45 C.F.R. § 46.111 (criteria for IRB approval of research include a determination that "risks to subjects are reasonable in relation to anticipated benefits, if any, to subjects, and the importance of the knowledge that may reasonably be expected to result").

Since about 2009, direct-to-consumer genetics company 23andMe, which also conducts research with genetic data from customers (who provide broad consent to such research), has voluntarily employed an external IRB to review most of its research.[81] That may not be surprising, since the research that 23andMe conducts is similar to research conducted by academic geneticists and is familiar to IRBs. Both Microsoft and Fitbit, Inc. also submit some portion of their research projects to external IRB review and review the remaining projects internally.[82]

Very little is known about such internal review processes, including how common they are among businesses. Following the public fallout over the June 2014 publication of its mood contagion experiment, Facebook announced, in October of the same year, that it was significantly revising (and strengthening) its internal research review process.[83] Employees spearheading that iterative process later published a description of it, which involves training across the company, various research review "checkpoints," and a standing, five-person "research review group" comprised of employees with expertise in policy, ethics, law, and communications (in addition to substantive expertise in Facebook's areas of research) that reviews projects triggered at earlier checkpoints as raising especially complex ethical or other issues.[84] In addition to this internal process, Facebook periodically consults outside subject matter experts.[85]

One important consideration in developing an internal review board is whether and how perspectives external to the company will be brought to bear on decision-making. Two kinds of outside perspective may be especially important: that of professional (usually academic) ethicists and that of laypersons who can represent the end user's experience and expectations. Outsiders may not only be more likely to recognize ethical issues; they may also feel freer than employees to voice concerns about them.[86]

One way to incorporate one or both kinds of perspectives is to include them as external members of a company's otherwise internal review board. The Common Rule, for instance, requires IRBs to include at least one member who is a non-scientist – someone who isn't steeped in the perspective of scientific research and may not see proposed studies the same way — and at least one member who is a non-affiliate of the institution – so that they do not have any inherent financial or other professional investment in the institution being permitted to conduct the research.[87]

Lay perspectives are critical, among other reasons, as a way of correcting insiders' "curse of knowledge." Each of us in an insider in some domain, and in that domain, it is often difficult to

---

[81] *Protecting People in People Powered Research*, 23ANDMEBLOG, July 30, 2014, https://blog.23andme.com/23andme-research/protecting-people-in-people-powered-research. *See also 23andMe Improves Research Consent Process*, 23ANDMEBLOG, June 24, 2010, https://blog.23andme.com/23andme-research/23andme-improves-research-consent-process.

[82] Daniela Hernandez & Deepa Seetharaman, *Facebook Offers Details on How It Handles Research*, WALL ST. J., June 14, 2016, https://www.wsj.com/articles/facebook-offers-details-how-it-handles-research-1465930152.

[83] Reed Albergotti, *Facebook Tightens Oversight of Research*, WALL ST. J., Oct. 2, 2014, https://www.wsj.com/articles/facebook-tightens-oversight-of-research-1412292491.

[84] Molly Jackman & Lauri Kanerva, *Evolving the IRB: Building Robust Review for Industry Research*, 72 WASH. & LEE L. REV. ONLINE 442 (2016).

[85] For example, before conducting "research on trends in the LGBT community on Facebook, [the company] sought feedback from prominent groups representing LGBT people on the value that this research would provide and on what data to collect and report." *Id.* at 453.

[86] The extent to which this relative freedom exists depends, however, on whether and how external members of review boards are compensated. The greater the financial or professional compensation she receives for serving, the more she has to lose by speaking out, and the less she is distinguishable in this regard from an employee.

[87] 45 C.F.R. § 46.107(c)–(d).

know what knowledge we can expect outsiders to share and what knowledge is inside baseball. For instance, lay criticism of the Facebook mood contagion experiment revealed that many users did not realize that their News Feeds have always been curated by an algorithm that prioritizes some posts and deprioritizes others; because they were unaware of this fact, the experimental manipulation was a more dramatic departure from what they believed to be the status quo than it was from Facebook's actual practice, likely increasing the level of outrage. The News Feed algorithm is fundamental to the Facebook platform, and it may never have occurred to some within the company that many users viewed their Facebook News Feed as a simple reverse chronological list of all their friends' posts, unmanipulated by Facebook in any way. Sharing project plans with actual or potential end users can reveal these misunderstandings and suggest ways that research projects should be conducted, telegraphed, or disclosed that will help close the gap between company behavior and end user expectations.

There are advantages and disadvantages to including lay members on internal review boards. Some empirical studies of academic IRBs have found that such members do not always feel empowered to speak up, at least unless there is something like a critical mass of them on the board. Laypersons' lack of expertise in both ethics and the substantive matter under consideration (e.g., data science or wearable technology) can also make it difficult for them to meaningfully participate on the same level as other members.[88] An alternative way of learning about user expectations is through surveys, focus groups, or interviews, which can be tailored to specific planned learning activities.

Ethics experts, too, are critical to ethics review. They have thought long and deeply about certain ethical issues and are therefore well positioned to spot those issues as they arise and bring practical tools to bear in thinking about how to address them. Some companies employ professional ethicists, and more retain professional ethicists as standing consultants. But if a company creates an internal review board, it will be more helpful if ethics experts are included in those discussions as frequently as possible rather than occasionally being consulted.

What roles can internal review boards play? Company Research Review Boards (RRBs) can ensure that research risks are reasonable in light of the expected benefits and in light of the distribution of risks and expected benefits. They can also consider whether the proposed activity would likely match customers' expectations and, if not, whether the project should be abandoned or reconceived to meet expectations, or whether user or consumer expectations should be reset before proceeding. Company RRBs can develop, disseminate, and enforce policies regarding which kinds of data must be anonymous, coded, or de-identified. They can review manuscripts before they are submitted for publication (whether in an academic or trade journal or on a company research blog) to ensure that subject privacy is maintained and that the study results are clearly and accessibly explained and do not needlessly alarm customers. They may also be able to help advise management about the business implications of results.

It must be kept in mind that prospective group review isn't a panacea. IRBs and similar boards don't always prevent unethical activities from occurring, both because their review isn't perfect and because, following approval, they typically exercise minimal oversight over the actual activity. IRBs can also delay, alter, or block valuable and ethical research in ways that can be

---

[88] Institutions sometimes appoint to various boards "lay" members who are actually quite sophisticated about the matter under discussion, whether in order to avoid this problem or because such lay members are more interested in participating. Unfortunately, such lay members begin to look and think more like the "insiders" than like the modal end user, which largely defeats the point of their presence.

harmful to people's welfare. In short, IRBs make Type I and Type II errors (or false positives and false negatives), and both are worth watching out for and trying to mitigate.

HUNGRY, HUNGRY HIPPOS: THE ETHICS OF *NOT* LEARNING

"If we have data, let's look at data. If all we have are opinions, let's go with mine."
— Jim Barksdale, former CEO of Netscape[89]

Most discussions of research ethics limit themselves to the ethical issues raised by *decisions to conduct research* or some other learning activity. This is a mistake (and perhaps the result of a common human bias toward noticing acts more than omissions). An appropriately comprehensive ethical analysis includes not only the risks and expected benefits of studying something, but also the risks and expected benefits of *not studying* that thing. Previous sections of this chapter have alluded to companies' responsibility for learning about the effects on others (and especially on their users or customers) of their products, services, policies and practices and to the critical role that data collection and analysis, experiments, and other learning activities play in meeting that responsibility.

Most business decisions are made on the basis of what Avinash Kaushik and Ron Kohavi call HiPPOs: the Highest Paid Person's Opinions.[90] Some might assume that those who rise to the level of "highest paid person" must have done so by virtue of possessing unique knowledge about what works in business, but the reality is obviously more complex.[91] CEOs and other leaders do often have extensive experience observing the results of various business decisions. But it is rare for such observations to be systemically captured and analyzed, and their lessons extracted and implemented. Moreover, even the best observational study cannot determine whether what is observed is caused by a particular business decision. Instead of evidence, business leaders typically make decisions on the basis of tradition ("how it's always been done," or how their own mentors did things) or instinct. This is problematic because gut instincts – while often romanticized – all too often prove wrong, sometimes leading to harm incurred or to welfare gains foregone.

As an early Amazon engineer, for instance, Greg Linden had the idea of recommending additional purchases to customers based on what they already had in their virtual baskets. A marketing senior vice president was "dead set against it." While Linden's hypothesis was that the feature would tend to result in customers buying more products, the HiPPO's hypothesis was that it would distract customers from checking out, and they would tend not to buy anything at all. The HiPPO forbade Linden from pursuing the project. But Linden decided to test their competing hypotheses on Amazon.com, and his prevailed: "Not only did it win, but the feature won by such a wide margin that not having it live was costing Amazon a noticeable chunk of change." The shopping cart recommendations feature was then rolled out across the platform.[92]

---

[89] This quote has been widely attributed to Barksdale.

[90] Ron Kohavi, Randal M. Henne & Dan Sommerfield, *Practical Guide to Controlled Experiments on the Web: Listen to Your Customers Not to the HiPPO*, in PROC. OF THE 13TH ACM SIGKDD INT'L CONF. ON KNOWLEDGE DISCOVERY & DATA MINING 959, 966 (2007).

[91] *See, e.g.*, then-CEO of OkCupid Christian Rudder, *We Experiment on Human Beings!*, THE OKCUPID BLOG, July 27, 2014, https://theblog.okcupid.com/we-experiment-on-human-beings-5dd9fe28ocd5 ("OkCupid doesn't really know what it's doing. Neither does any other website. It's not like people have been building these things for very long, or you can go look up a blueprint or something. Most ideas are bad. Even good ideas could be better. Experiments are how you sort all this out.").

[92] Greg Linden, *Early Amazon: Shopping Cart Recommendations*, GEEKING WITH GREG blog, Apr. 25, 2006, http://glinden.blogspot.com/2006/04/early-amazon-shopping-cart.html.

Similarly, at JoAnn.com, marketers trying to sell more sewing machines online guessed that the *least* effective promotion of those they were considering would be one that advertised 10 percent off the sale of two machines. The CFO's instinct was that few people wanted two sewing machines, and therefore opting for this promotion would amount to "wast[ing] a week's worth of sales on this promotion." But when the company tested his intuition, they discovered that this promotion increased conversion rates (the rate at which online users who click on a promotion actually purchase the product the promotion advertises) by 70 percent – far more than any of the other promotions they tried. (It turns out that many sewers are members of sewing groups, who simply pursued the promotion in pairs.)[93]

In the Amazon and JoAnn examples, what were primarily at stake were corporate profits. Other business decisions more directly impact customer or user welfare. Consider, again, Facebook's mood contagion experiment. Observational studies by academics of Facebook use had reached contrasting conclusions about what psychological risks, if any, Facebook's News Feed poses to users. Some studies found that friends' positive posts make users feel worse about their own lives (a social comparison effect). Others found that it is friends' negative posts that pose the risk, by depressing users (through a mood contagion effect). Others concluded that both of these hypotheses hold some truth, and that the effect of the News Feed on users depends on an individual user's characteristics (such as personality). Still others believed that the News Feed has no significant psychological effect on users and that studies finding otherwise were mere noise, based on low sample sizes, self-reported outcomes, and other less-than-gold-standard methods.

The News Feed has always been curated by a proprietary algorithm that results in some posts being more likely to be seen than others. Moreover, all users are exposed to undulating levels of both positive and negative content in their feeds, depending on local and national events and other factors. In order to rigorously evaluate the effects on users' mood of exposure to both positive and negative words, Facebook conducted a randomized, controlled experiment in which some user feeds had relatively more positive posts suppressed, others had relatively more negative posts suppressed, and still other feeds served as controls. Experimental exposures to positive and negative words were almost certainly within the range of exposure that users experience over the course of, say, several months of Facebook use. The effects were extremely small, detectable only because the sample size (about 700,000 users across all conditions) was so large. The investigators found that users who were exposed to more positive words themselves used slightly more positive words when writing their own posts, whereas those who were exposed to more negative words used slightly more negative words in their own posts – findings that they interpreted as evidence for the mood contagion hypothesis.

After the results of the experiment were published in an academic journal and reported by the media, widespread public condemnation of Facebook ensued, including contemplated lawsuits and calls for federal and state agency investigations. That condemnation, however, seems mostly misplaced. Facebook's algorithm and other practices almost certainly affect users' exposure to their friends' positive and negative words. The existing evidence about the effects of negative and positive words pointed in different directions: if the social comparison hypothesis was correct, then Facebook's platform poses risks through positive words. If the mood contagion hypothesis was correct, then it is negative words that pose the threat to Facebook's users; positive words actually should be beneficial. If one takes seriously these risks, then the decision that is more

---

[93] Russ Banham, *Power to the Little People*, CFO Magazine, Dec. 14, 2005, http://ww2.cfo.com/technology/2005/12/power-to-the-little-people/.

difficult to ethically defend would have been a decision *not* to try to determine the truth about these risks through a rigorous, yet low-risk, experiment.

A similarly laudable example of a company using research methods to improve the safety of its platform comes from the online gaming company, Riot Games. The company uses social psychology experiments to combat a range of troublesome behaviors, from incivility to harassment, that plague its popular online game, League of Legends.[94] We all wish harassers and those who are uncivil online would just stop or go away. But since that is unlikely to happen, we are better off if companies quickly gather rigorous evidence of what works through low risk, nonconsensual experiments than if they simply guess about how to address the problem.

OkCupid, the online dating company, conducted an experiment that nicely illustrates how research methods can be used to investigate the effectiveness of products and services. OkCupid markets itself as offering customers a science-based approach to dating. And indeed, those pairs of customers who the company's touted "matching algorithm" rates as compatible do tend to engage in longer conversations on the platform. But the company wasn't actually sure whether these pairs engage in more extensive conversation because the matching algorithm accurately predicts compatibility or whether simply telling pairs of people that they are compatible makes them believe and behave as if they were. So it conducted an experiment in which it told some pairs of customers that its algorithm predicted would be compatible that they were not so compatible, it told other pairs that the algorithm predicted would not be compatible that they were, and it compared both of these groups to pairs who were told exactly what the algorithm predicted. As measured by how many messages these pairs of customers exchanged, OkCupid found that although its algorithm did, in fact, predict which pairs would exchange more messages, the act of merely telling pairs that they were compatible (regardless of how compatible the algorithm said they were) was a slightly better predictor.[95] The company reported the results of the experiment on its blog, where customers could use the results to gauge how much reliance to place on the algorithm's suggested pairings.[96]

The Facebook, Riot Games, and OkCupid examples show that nonconsensual "human experimentation" (whether characterized as research or as QI) can be ethically acceptable – indeed, laudable or even ethically obligatory – when the learning activity imposes *no more than minimal risks* on subjects (above and beyond the risks they are already exposed to as customers); when it seeks to *determine the effects of an existing or proposed company practice or product* on those who will be affected by it, so that subjects exposed to (minimal) risks are also those who stand to benefit from the results; and when *the validity of the data* or other practical constraints precludes obtaining fully informed consent.

In the wake of its mood contagion experiment, Facebook was accused of abusing its power, depriving its users of important information, and treating its users as mere means to corporate ends. Yet it is declining to investigate probative, but conflicting and indeterminate, evidence that its platform harms users that would have exhibited these failures, not conducting a QI experiment. Similarly, critics of OkCupid's matching algorithm experiment found it outrageous that the company briefly told some pairs of customers that they were compatible, when the algorithm said that they were not. But the point of the experiment was that, despite its marketing campaign, the company lacked evidence that its algorithm in fact accurately predicted compatibility.

[94] Jeremy Hsu, *Inside the Largest Virtual Psychology Lab in the World*, BACKCHANNEL, Jan. 27, 2015, https://backchannel .com/inside-the-largest-virtual-psychology-lab-in-the-world-7c0d2c43cda5#.3d48yzqzi.

[95] For a more detailed discussion of this experiment and its ethical implications, see Meyer, *supra* note 36, at 312–21.

[96] Rudder, *supra* note 91.

Subjects were not deprived of information known to be accurate or given information known to be false. And in fact, the experiment found that the algorithm is slightly *less* predictive of which pairs will get along well than is simply telling people that they *should* get along well.

It was better, ethically speaking, for Facebook and OkCupid to have conducted these experiments than for them not to have done so, given the probative but inconclusive evidence that emotionally laden Facebook content may post psychological risks to users and that the success of OkCupid's touted matching algorithm may have been partly or wholly due to the power of persuasion rather than to an algorithm that scientifically detects romantic compatibility.[97]

CONCLUSION

There has always been tension between the idea that people need to be protected from research and the idea that people need access to the sometimes considerable benefits of participating in research.[98] Companies increasingly engage in a wide variety of learning activities. These activities may be ethically dubious, praiseworthy, or even obligatory, depending on how much unique privacy and other risks they impose on subjects, whether they are designed to yield important information, whether those who bear the burdens of the learning activity also stand to reap its potential rewards, and whether the learning activity is consistent with subjects' reasonable expectations of how the company will behave. Company learning activities almost always take place outside the jurisdiction of the regulations governing human subjects research. Moreover, even if company learning activities were subject to those regulations, the vast majority would be partly or fully exempt. Nevertheless, companies would benefit from judiciously borrowing elements from both the substance and the process of human subjects regulations, including attention to notice and broad consent, risk-benefit balance and risk minimization, and prospective review of proposed learning activities by a diverse group of individuals who can help anticipate actual and perceived ethical problems.

[97] *See generally* Meyer, *supra* note 36 (discussing both experiments at length and defending this viewpoint).
[98] Anna Mastroianni & Jeffrey Kahn, *Swinging on the Pendulum: Shifting Views of Justice in Human Subjects Research*, 31 HASTINGS CENTER REP. 21 (2001).

13

Algorithmic Discrimination vs. Privacy Law

Alvaro M. Bedoya

In the spring of 2014, the White House published a remarkable report. *Big Data: Seizing Opportunities, Preserving Values* was partly a paean to the economic and social benefits of massive data processing. It also issued an unusually sharp warning: Big data can discriminate.

The "Podesta Report," as it came to be known for its principal author, then-counselor to President Obama, John Podesta, cautioned that automated decision-making systems may work to embed and exacerbate existing inequality, sometimes in ways that are entirely unintentional. If left unchecked, "big data analytics have the potential to eclipse longstanding civil rights protections in how personal information is used in housing, credit, employment, health, education, and the marketplace."[1]

The academy has risen to this challenge with a wave of legal proposals to create transparency and due process protections for automated decision-making systems,[2] and a second wave of proposals for technical safeguards to detect and correct for algorithmic bias.[3] These proposals parallel those of the Podesta Report, which called for greater transparency in algorithmic decision-making systems and recommended that federal agencies expand their technical expertise in order to be able to identify and correct for discriminatory impact.[4]

Curiously, few of these proposals call for a simpler remedy, one that reflects the oldest principle of privacy protection: the right to be let alone.[5] In the face of increasing evidence that automated decision-making systems discriminate, almost no one is arguing that, in order to counter that discrimination, we must empower affected individuals with a greater ability to decide whether or not their data will form a part of those systems.

Why this silence? Why this failure to see collection controls as a critical part of the response to algorithmic bias? The answer, in part, is that ubiquitous data collection is increasingly seen as inevitable and, in fact, desirable. According to the Podesta Report, a "sea of ubiquitous sensors, each of which has legitimate uses, mak[es] the notion of limiting information collection

---

[1] EXECUTIVE OFFICE OF THE PRESIDENT, BIG DATA: SEIZING OPPORTUNITIES, PRESERVING VALUES (2014)(hereinafter "Podesta Report") at iii. *See also ibid* at 51–53.

[2] *See generally, e.g.,* Danielle Keats Citron & Frank Pasquale, *The Scored Society: Due Process for Automated Predictions,* 89 WASH. L. REV. 1 (2014).

[3] *See generally, e.g.,* Joshua Kroll, Joanna Huey, & Solon Barocas et al., *Accountable Algorithms,* 165 UNIV. PENN. L. REV. 633 (2017); Michael Feldman, Sorelle Friedler, & John Moeller et al., *Certifying and Removing Disparate Impact,* arXiv:1412.3756v3 [stat.ML] (July 16, 2015).

[4] *See* Podesta Report at 65.

[5] *See generally* Louis Brandeis & Samuel Warren, *The Right to Privacy,* 4 HARV. L. REV. 193 (1890).

challenging, if not impossible."[6] A companion report, issued by the President's Council of Advisors on Science and Technology (PCAST), argues that "a policy focus on limiting data collection [is] not ... likely to achieve the right balance between beneficial results and unintended negative consequences (such as inhibiting economic growth)."[7] These reports *instead* urge policymakers to rely on use restrictions, limits on how personal information can be used *after* it is collected.[8]

This is a mistake. Post-collection remedies to algorithmic discrimination move the locus of consumer protection out of the hands of consumers and into company boardrooms and government offices. Sometimes, the nature of technology may make this shift necessary. But all big data are not too big for consumer control. Indeed, for some new and highly invasive technologies, collection controls may be the easiest means to protect privacy and prevent discrimination.

This proposed shift from collection controls to use restrictions – and, in turn, from consumer choice to institutional decision-making – also presupposes an alignment of interests between institutions and individuals: between companies and the government, on the one hand, and consumers on the other. These interests are rarely closely aligned. A growing body of evidence suggests that they may be particularly misaligned for people of color and other historically marginalized communities.

This essay makes the case for collection controls as a critical and necessary tool in preventing algorithmic discrimination. To make this argument more accessible, it will focus on one technology – face recognition – which the Podesta Report cited as showing the inevitability of ubiquitous data collection, and which has been documented as producing biased and potentially discriminatory results.[9]

Post-collection remedies to detect and correct bias are urgently needed. But in our rush to address this problem, we must not set aside the most basic right to privacy: the right to decide for ourselves who has access to the private facts of our lives. In many cases, it may be our most effective means to address algorithmic discrimination.

FACE RECOGNITION AND ALGORITHMIC DISCRIMINATION

Face recognition technology involves the automated or semiautomated comparison of two or more facial images in order to determine whether they represent the same person.[10]

---

[6] *See* Podesta Report at 54.

[7] EXECUTIVE OFFICE OF THE PRESIDENT, PRESIDENT'S COUNCIL OF ADVISORS ON SCIENCE AND TECHNOLOGY, BIG DATA AND PRIVACY: A TECHNOLOGICAL PERSPECTIVE (2014)(hereinafter "PCAST Report") at x–xi.

[8] *See* Podesta Report at 56 ("We may need to re-focus our attention on the context of data use"); PCAST Report at xiii ("Recommendation 1: Policy attention should focus more on the actual uses of big data and less on its collection and analysis.").

[9] *See* Podesta Report at 54 ("Facial recognition technologies can identify you in pictures online and as soon as you step outside."); Brendan F. Klare, Mark J. Burge, Joshua C. Klontz et al., *Face Recognition Performance: Role of Demographic Information*, 7 IEEE TRANSACTIONS INFO. FORENSICS SEC. 1789 (2012) (hereinafter "Klare et al.") (showing that face recognition algorithms produce lower accuracy rates for searches of African American, female, and young adult faces); P. Jonathon Phillips et al., *An Other-Race Effect for Face Recognition Algorithms*, 8 ACM TRANSACTIONS ON APPLIED PERCEPTION 14:1, 14:5 (2011) (showing that face recognition algorithms developed in East Asia performed better on East Asians, while algorithms developed in Western countries performed better on whites).

[10] *See* CLARE GARVIE, ALVARO BEDOYA, & JONATHAN FRANKLE, THE PERPETUAL LINE-UP: UNREGULATED POLICE FACE RECOGNITION IN AMERICA (Center on Privacy & Technology at Georgetown Law, 2016)(hereinafter "The Perpetual Line-Up") at 9. The term "face recognition" is also used to describe the process of locating a face in a photo ("face detection") or drawing inferences about the characteristics of that face – regarding gender or age, for example ("face characterization"). This chapter refers to face recognition solely to describe an automated or semiautomated process of

In order for a face to be identified, it must first be detected in an image. Once the "probe" face is detected, it must be standardized so that it can be easily compared to other faces, a process that may involve three-dimensional modeling and rotation of the facial image. Then, a face recognition algorithm extracts a "face template" or "face print" from that probe image, which it compares to all of the face templates or face prints enrolled in its "library" of identified faces.[11] This results in the identification of a "candidate" image and identity (or a series of such candidates) corresponding to the unknown probe face. This is a highly complex process potentially involving millions of variables.[12]

For generations, scientists have known that humans are fairly adept at recognizing individuals of their own race or ethnicity, and are relatively worse at identifying others – a phenomenon known as the "other race" effect.[13] Recent research suggests that face recognition via *computer* vision may suffer from a similar problem.[14]

The most prominent study on the subject, a 2012 investigation co-authored by several of the United States' leading face recognition researchers, found that three commercial algorithms were 5 percent to 10 percent less accurate in identifying African American and female faces.[15] More specifically, the algorithms were more likely to fail to correctly identify – to "miss" – African American and female faces than white and male faces, respectively.

There are various explanations for this bias. Research has not shown which is most influential. One theory cited in the 2012 study has to do with training. If an algorithm is trained on a database that disproportionately represents one race or ethnicity, it may be optimized to identify those individuals, and therefore underperform on other demographics.[16] It is also possible that some demographic groups are, in some respects, more difficult for a computer to recognize. Women's use of cosmetics may render their faces more difficult to distinguish.[17] The facial features of individuals with darker skin tones may be harder to recognize due to lower color contrast.[18] Finally, it is possible that the bias stems from design decisions intended to maximize perform- ance for a particular demographic cohort.[19]

---

identification, as this is the deployment of the technology that raises the most significant privacy concerns. *See* FED. TRADE COMM'N, FACING FACTS: BEST PRACTICES FOR COMMON USES OF FACIAL RECOGNITION TECHNOLOGIES (October 2012)(hereinafter "Facing Facts") at i–ii (differentiating between different uses of face recognition and describing face identification as raising "the most serious privacy concerns because it can identify anonymous individuals in images").

[11] The process can also be used simply to verify a person's claimed identity. In this application, the probe image is compared only to a single library image that corresponds to the individual's claimed identity. This process is known as "face verification" and is not explored in depth here.

[12] The Perpetual Line-Up at 9.

[13] *See, e.g.*, Gustave A. Feingold, *The Influence of Environment on Identification of Persons and Things*, 5 J. AM. INST. CRIM. L. & CRIMINOLOGY 39, (May 1914–Mar. 1915) ("Now it is well known that, other things being equal, individuals of a given race are distinguishable from each other in proportion to our familiarity, to our contact with the race as a whole."); Luca Vizioli, Guillaume A. Rousselet, & Roberto Caldara, *Neural Repetition Suppression to Identity Is Abolished by Other-Race Faces*, 107 PROC. NAT'L ACAD. SCI. U.S., 20081 (2010).

[14] For an overview, see The Perpetual Line-Up at 53–54 and accompanying footnotes.

[15] *See* Klare et al., at 1797.

[16] *See* Klare et al., at 1798.

[17] Klare et al., at 1797.

[18] The Perpetual Line-Up at 54 n. 228.

[19] *Cf.* The Perpetual Line-Up at 54–55 (describing a law enforcement face recognition system using face normalization software customized for only certain demographic categories).

Whatever the origin, if this bias is replicated in a broader population of current commercial algorithms, it could have profound implications for African Americans, women, and any other populations for whom these algorithms underperform.

Initially, the primary commercial deployments of face recognition arose in online social networking. In 2010, for example, Facebook automatically enrolled all of its users in a face recognition system that expedited the process of uploading and labeling user photos.[20]

In recent years, however, face recognition is being used to identify people in real time and real life. Banks are exploring the use of face recognition to verify their customers' identities.[21] Major retail outlets – such as Walmart and Saks Fifth Avenue – have used face recognition systems to spot and identify suspected thieves the moment they set foot in a store.[22] The most recent wave of face recognition companies aims to give private individuals (as opposed to other companies) the ability to identify strangers with the click of a button.[23] One of the first movers in this space, a company called NameTag, promised its users the ability to determine whether a romantic interest was, in fact, a registered sex offender.[24]

The real life application of face recognition heightens the stakes of system accuracy and the hypothetical downsides of systemic bias. It is one thing for a social networking site to suggest the wrong "tag" for a photo. It is entirely another for a bank to mistakenly and systematically reject transactions from female customers at higher rates than those of men, or for a company to mistakenly identify African Americans as shoplifters – or sex offenders – at higher rates than white people.[25]

THE PRACTICAL CASE FOR COLLECTION CONTROLS

The White House is not alone in arguing that ubiquitous data collection is inevitable. This view mirrors industry perspectives. In 2013, the World Economic Forum issued a strong call in favor of the adoption of use restrictions and a retreat from collection controls. "The traditional data-protection approach ... was that the individual is involved in consenting to data use at the time of collection," states the report. Traditional approaches no longer fit, however, because "the torrent of data being generated from and about data subjects imposes an undue cognitive burden

---

[20] Bloomberg News, *Facebook's "Face Recognition" Feature Draws Privacy Scrutiny*, N. Y. TIMES, June 8, 2011, *available at* http://www.nytimes.com/2011/06/09/technology/09facebook.html.

[21] Jonnelle Marte, *Companies Are Betting on a New Way to Protect Your Identity: The Selfie*, WASH. POST, May 6, 2016.

[22] Jeff John Roberts, *Walmart Use of Sci-Fi Tech to Spot Shoplifters Raises Privacy Questions*, FORTUNE, Nov. 9, 2015, *available at* http://fortune.com/2015/11/09/wal-mart-facial-recognition/; Chris Frey, *Revealed: How Face Recognition Has Invaded Shops – And Your Privacy*, THE GUARDIAN, Mar. 3, 2016, *available at* https://www.theguardian.com/cities/2016/mar/03/revealed-facial-recognition-software-infiltrating-cities-saks-toronto

[23] MEDUZA, *The End of Privacy: "Meduza" Takes a Hard Look at FindFace and the Looming Prospect of Total Surveillance*, July 14, 2016, *available at* https://meduza.io/en/feature/2016/07/14/the-end-of-privacy.

[24] Charles Poladian, *NameTag: Facial Recognition App Checks If Your Date Is a Sex Offender but Should You Use It?*, INT'L BUS. TIMES, Jan. 14, 2014, *available at* http://www.ibtimes.com/nametag-facial-recognition-app-checks-if-your-date-sex-offender-should-you-use-it-1539308.

[25] Note that Klare et al., *supra* note 10, suggested 5 percent–10 percent higher false *reject* rates for African Americans and women. The first hypothetical scenario (a bank incorrectly rejecting transactions for female users) involves a straightforward instance of a false reject, an instance where an individual *is present* in a system library but the algorithm fails to verify that person's identity from a probe photo. The second hypothetical, involving individuals being wrongly identified as shoplifters or sex offenders, presupposes a system that is designed to provide, by default, a predetermined number of candidate photos. If a system used an algorithm such as those tested in the 2012 study, a probe photo for an African American would be less likely to correctly return the correct corresponding library image, and thus, would be more likely to return images of similar-looking, "innocent" individuals.

on individual data subjects."[26] The Podesta Report quotes Craig Mundie, senior advisor to the CEO of Microsoft, for a similar proposition: "Simply so much data is being collected, in so many ways, that it is practically impossible to give people a meaningful way . . . to consent to its collection in the first place."[27]

The Podesta Report cites face recognition as one of several new technologies that "make the notion of limiting information collection challenging, if not impossible."[28] This reflects a fundamental misunderstanding about the nature of the technology.

Face recognition is not mere photography; it is a complex process of identification. A walk outside may automatically or inadvertently result in your face being photographed by a range of security cameras or smartphones. However, there is nothing "automatic" about using face recognition to scan, normalize and analyze that face in order to identify it; nor is anyone automatically enrolled in a face recognition database. These are deliberate, and expensive, design decisions.[29] In other words, there is nothing inherent to face recognition that requires automatic enrollment of face templates. Some companies choose to enroll individuals in face recognition systems without their consent. Others do not.

In fact, opt-in consent for the collection and enrollment of face templates is, at least for now, a *de facto* industry best practice for commercial face recognition technology.[30] Despite such prominent outliers as Facebook, most other major companies – such as Google and Microsoft – and prominent industry trade groups have voluntarily decided to ask a person's permission prior to enrolling him or her in an online or real-world face recognition system.[31] Obtaining consent prior to enrollment in a face recognition system may not be trivial, but it is far from impossible.

Indeed, collection controls may afford consumers the simplest and most effective avenue through which to prevent algorithmic discrimination in face recognition systems: to avoid enrollment to begin with. "Information that is not collected in the first place can't be misused," explained Edith Ramirez, then Federal Trade Commission chair.[32] This approach also benefits from the weight of precedent: Two populous states representing an eighth of the American

[26] World Economic Forum Industry Agenda, Unlocking the Value of Personal Data: From Collection to Usage (2013) at 11.

[27] Craig Mundie, *Privacy Pragmatism: Focus on Data Use, Not Data Collection*, Foreign Affairs, Mar./Apr. 2014, *available at* https://www.foreignaffairs.com/articles/2014-02-12/privacy-pragmatism

[28] *See* Podesta Report at 54.

[29] Of course, a store owner's decision to install a security camera is also a deliberate, and costly, design decision. In 2017, however, the care and expense required to operate a functional face recognition system are orders of magnitude greater than those required to set up a simple surveillance video system. Thus, to be clear, the use of "automatic" here is shorthand for the ease with which a particular system may be built and deployed.

[30] *See* Alvaro Bedoya, *Why I Walked Out of Facial Recognition Negotiations*, Slate, June 30, 2015, *available at* http://www.slate.com/articles/technology/future_tense/2015/06/facial_recognition_privacy_talks_why_i_walked_out.html (discussing de facto industry standard).

[31] *See Kinect and Xbox One Privacy FAQ*, Microsoft (last visited Nov. 29, 2016) *available at* https://www.xbox.com/en-US/legal/privacyandonlinesafety ("Kinect ID provides you with the option of signing in to your gamer profile using face recognition technology."); *Making Photo Tagging Easier with Find My Face*, Google+ (last visited Nov. 29, 2016) *available at* https://plus.google.com/+mattsteiner/posts/jKQ35ajJ4EU ("By turning on Find My Face, Google+ can prompt people you know to tag your face when it appears in photos."); Digital Signage Federation, Digital Signage Privacy Standards 7 (Feb. 2011) *available at* http://www.digitalsignagefederation.org/wp-content/uploads/2017/02/DSF-Digital-Signage-Privacy-Standards-02-2011-3.pdf (explaining that the collection of "information that links to individual identity" "requires opt-in consent").

[32] Edith Ramirez, Chair, Fed. Trade Comm'n, Keynote Address at the Technology Policy Institute, Aspen Forum, *The Privacy Challenges of Big Data: A View from the Lifeguard's Chair* (Aug. 19, 2013) at 6.

population, Illinois and Texas, have passed laws requiring consumer consent prior to the collection of biometric information.[33]

In contrast, as Solon Barocas and Andrew Selbst describe in their seminal article, "Big Data's Disparate Impact," post-collection techniques to prevent, detect, and correct for algorithmic discrimination can be painfully difficult.[34] Face recognition is no exception.

Preventing algorithmic discrimination on a large scale will require coordinated action by large groups of academic researchers, face recognition companies, and government standards-setting bodies. As the authors of the 2012 study explain, a leading solution to algorithmic bias involves training algorithms on photosets *primarily composed* of African Americans or other groups on which the software underperforms.[35] But large, publicly available datasets of diverse faces are exceedingly rare.[36] Even then, assuming that such datasets were created and disseminated, companies would have to use them voluntarily to train their algorithms for bias, and companies and the government would need to conduct internal and public testing to ensure that these steps have reduced bias.

At the moment, there is no clear route to eliminate bias in commercial (or government) face recognition systems. But there is a clear means to avoid it: Let people keep their faces out of those systems.

DIVERGENCE OF INTERESTS AND MORAL LAG

For post-collection use limitations to be effective, they require that the interests of companies and consumers align; companies and consumers must, in a sense, agree on which uses of consumers' data are harmful and which are acceptable. The existence of the consumer protection movement speaks to the fact that this is not a foregone conclusion, as does the fact that the push for post-collection use restrictions clearly originates in industry.[37] Interests may be particularly misaligned for technologies, such as face recognition, that allow a company to track an individual without that person's knowledge or consent.

In the case of algorithmic discrimination, companies and consumers need to agree on what constitutes *unacceptable* discrimination. While companies and consumers may disagree on the nuances of data protection, one would think that they would readily agree that discrimination is to be avoided at all costs. Yet a cursory analysis reveals that doing so is not an easy task.

Since a 2012 study by Klare and colleagues, leading face recognition vendors, as well as the government, have known that face recognition algorithms may underperform for certain races,

---

[33] *See* 740 I.L.C.S. 14/1 (2008) (Illinois Biometric Information Privacy Act); Tex. Bus. & Comm. Code 503.001 (2007) (Texas biometric privacy law); *see also* Ben Sobel, *Facial Recognition Technology Is Everywhere: It May Not Be Legal.* WASH. POST (June 11, 2015) *available at* https://www.washingtonpost.com/news/the-switch/wp/2015/06/11/facial-recog nition-technology-is-everywhere-it-may-not-be-legal/?utm_term=.c84153789b09 (quantifying the population covered by these laws and describing their impact).

[34] Solon Barocas & Andrew Selbst, *Big Data's Disparate Impact*, 104 CAL. L. REV. 671, 715–722 (2016) (explaining the difficulties in reforming internal systems to prevent algorithmic discrimination in the employment context).

[35] Klare et al., at 1800. A related recommendation was that algorithms should be "design[ed] … that specifically target different demographic cohorts within the race/ethnicity, gender and age demographics." *Ibid.*

[36] The Perpetual Line-Up at 69 ("Researchers and engineers universally complain about the lack of large, high-quality, diverse datasets of faces.").

[37] *See* Chris Hoofnagle, *The Potemkinism of Privacy Pragmatism*, SLATE (Sept. 2, 2014) *available at* http://www.slate.com/ articles/technology/future_tense/2014/09/data_use_regulation_the_libertarian_push_behind_a_new_take_on_privacy .html ("Use regulations … are part of what appears to be a general strategy to eliminate legal responsibility for data companies.").

genders, and age groups.[38] The authors of that study, which include leading researchers and the FBI's subject matter expert for face recognition, recognized this as a critical finding that should impact deployment: "The experiments conducted in this paper should have a significant impact on the design of face recognition algorithms."[39]

Yet, in 2016 – despite bias issues being public knowledge for some time – two major face recognition companies acknowledged that they did not conduct any testing to identify bias in their algorithms, and the US government body responsible for accuracy testing, the National Institute for Standards and Technology, had conducted only one independent test for algorithmic bias since it began testing for accuracy over fifteen years ago.[40]

Perhaps, with this experience for context, the interests of consumers and companies may be understood in the following way: Consumers have a clear interest in never being discriminated against. Companies may share that interest, but their principal interest lies in not being *perceived* as discriminatory. Tellingly, the 2012 study did not receive significant attention in popular media until 2016.[41]

A more troubling explanation suggests that consumers and companies may simply disagree on what constitutes discrimination. There is a moral lag in data ethics and practices. Powerful entities often take years, even decades, to recognize that a particular use of data was, in fact, discriminatory, when it was more than obvious to the affected individuals at the time. What's more, these realizations frequently come only at significant external prodding.

The most notorious example of this phenomenon involves the US Census's release of Japanese Americans' names and addresses to the US Secret Service during World War II. In the years preceding the war, Japanese Americans volunteered their information to the Census under a strict promise of confidentiality; the Census may release demographic information at the neighbourhood level, but is prohibited from disclosing individual data such as names and addresses. In 1942, however, Congress repealed those confidentiality provisions and allowed individual data to be shared "for use in connection with the conduct of the war." The Census subsequently disclosed such data to government officials to facilitate the detention and internment of Japanese Americans during the war.[42]

It took the US Census close to sixty years to apologize for the sharing of Japanese Americans' data for military purposes, and an additional five years to acknowledge the full extent of such sharing.[43] It is difficult to say when Census officials recognized their grave error; there are indications that, after the war, Census officials genuinely did not understand the extent or nature

---

[38] *See generally* Klare et al., at *supra* n. 9.

[39] Klare et al., at 1800–1801.

[40] The Perpetual Line-Up at 53, 55. *See also See* Patrick J. Grother et. al., *Multiple-Biometric Evaluation (MBE) 2010: Report on the Evaluation of 2D Still-Image Face Recognition Algorithms: NIST Interagency Report 7709*, NATIONAL INSTITUTE OF STANDARDS AND TECHNOLOGY (Aug. 24, 2011), *available at* https://www.nist.gov/publications/report-evaluation-2d-still-image-face-recognition-algorithms, at 55–56.

[41] *See* Clare Garvie & Jonathan Frankle, *Facial-Recognition Software Might Have a Racial Bias Problem*, THE ATLANTIC (Apr. 7, 2016), *available at* https://www.theatlantic.com/technology/archive/2016/04/the-underlying-bias-of-facial-recognition-systems/476991/.

[42] *See* J. R. Minkel, *Confirmed: The U.S. Census Bureau Gave Up Names of Japanese Americans in WWII*, SCIENTIFIC AMERICAN, Mar. 30, 2007 (hereinafter "Minkel, *Confirmed* "), *available at* https://www.scientificamerican.com/article/confirmed-the-us-census-b/; Second War Powers Act, PUB. L. NO. 77-507, § 1402, 56 Stat. 186 (1942) (repealed). The measure passed the House on a near-unanimous voice vote. C. P. Trussell, *Wider War Powers Win Vote of House*, N.Y. TIMES, Mar. 1, 1942, at 1.

[43] *See* Minkel, *Confirmed* (explaining that the Census apologized in 2000 for the sharing of neighborhood-level data but acknowledged the sharing of data on individuals only after independent academic research released in 2007).

of their actions.[44] But the internment of Japanese Americans was itself legally and publicly ratified by the Supreme Court in 1944, and it took the American government more than forty years to apologize and compensate those individuals for that error.[45]

This failure to acknowledge and correct for the mistreatment of vulnerable populations persists today, and it is not limited to the government. In 2013 and 2014, a series of exposés produced a damning picture of the American data broker industry.[46] These investigations revealed that data brokers created and sold marketing lists of vulnerable people, often categorized on the basis of race, age, or health conditions: "Ethnic Second-City Strugglers," "Struggling Elders: Singles," "Aids and Hiv [*sic*] Infection Sufferers."[47]

It is hard to imagine an immigrant, elderly person or HIV-positive individual who is comfortable with having their personal information sold in this way, or being publicly described in this manner. The purpose of these lists is patent: to identify vulnerable people and target them for their vulnerabilities. Yet, two years later, Congress has taken no action to regulate the data broker industry, and marketing lists like these remain freely available. One data broker, NextMark, is currently selling the names and addresses of "Hispanic Multiple Impulse Buyers" and African Americans to target for payday loans.[48]

Why should consumers have faith in post-collection efforts to uncover hidden bias in complex automated systems when *known*, public examples of overt discrimination and mistreatment are left unremedied by the government and private sector alike? Clearly, any meaningful attempt to protect consumers from algorithmic bias must include *both* post-collection mitigation and a renewed commitment to let consumers control the sensitive facts of their lives.

Consumers should not have to wait until the interests of the powerful align with their own. It may be a while.

BLACK BOXES AND COINS

Frank Pasquale describes our modern information ecosystem as a "black box." The term is a double entendre. For the individual, the black box symbolizes extraordinary personal transparency; like the data recording devices in planes and automobiles, the technology and

---

[44] *See Ibid.* In fact, the seminal 1973 report from the US Department of Health, Education & Welfare's Secretary's Advisory Committee on Automated Personal Data Systems – the report that delineated what we now know as the Fair Information Practice Principles – mistakenly indicates that the Census refused to provide name and address data and holds this forth as a model of information protection. *See* U.S. DEP'T HEALTH, EDUC. & WELFARE, RECORDS, COMPUTERS, AND THE RIGHTS OF CITIZENS (1973) at 89–90.

[45] *See* Korematsu v. U.S., 323 U.S. 214 (1944) (upholding the constitutionality of the Japanese American internment); the Civil Liberties Act of 1988 (Pub.L. 100–383, title I, Aug. 10, 1988, 102 Stat. 904, 50a U.S.C. § 1989b et seq.) (providing reparations for internees).

[46] *See, e.g.,* SENATE COMMITTEE ON COM., SCI., AND TRANSP., A REVIEW OF THE DATA BROKER INDUSTRY: COLLECTION, USE, AND SALE OF CONSUMER DATA FOR MARKETING PURPOSES, MAJORITY STAFF REPORT (Dec. 18, 2014) (hereinafter "Senate Commerce Committee Data Broker Report"); FED. TRADE COMM'N, DATA BROKERS: A CALL FOR TRANSPARENCY AND ACCOUNTABILITY (2014); GOV'T ACCOUNTABILITY OFF., INFORMATION RESELLERS: CONSUMER PRIVACY FRAMEWORK NEEDS TO REFLECT CHANGES IN TECHNOLOGY AND THE MARKETPLACE (Sept. 2013).

[47] *See* Senate Commerce Committee Date Broker Report at 24; Pam Dixon, Statement before the Senate Committee on Commerce, Science and Transportation, Hearing on *What Information Do Data Brokers Have on Consumers, and How Do They Use It?* (Dec. 18, 2013) at 12–13.

[48] *See* Mailing list finder, *On the Upsale: Hispanic Multiple Impulse Buyers Mailing list*, NEXTMARK, https://lists .nextmark.com/market?page=order/online/datacard&id=266564); Mailing list, *African-American Payday: Cash Advance*, NEXTMARK, https://lists.nextmark.com/market?page=order/online/datacard&id=332089) (last visited Dec. 2, 2016).

businesses that surround us subject us to a minute and persistent tracking. For businesses, the black box connotes opacity. Once our private data is transferred to the private sector, "we have no clear idea of just how far much of this information can travel, how it is used, or its consequences."[49]

In recent years, however, efforts to protect consumer privacy and prevent algorithmic discrimination have focused on fixing just one of these problems: making institutions more accountable and transparent. We should talk about making humans more opaque.

The industry rebuttal to this argument – that collection controls are difficult, if not impossible – is almost nonsensical. In Silicon Valley, there is a strange, two-sided coin of brilliance and incompetence. When it comes to collecting data, making inferences about that data, and doing so in milliseconds, anything is possible. When it comes to providing consumers meaningful ways to control that collection, defeat is constant. I submit that this failure not only has consequences for privacy, but for equal protection, also.

[49] FRANK PASQUALE, THE BLACK BOX SOCIETY (2015) at 3.

14

Children, Privacy, and the New Online Realities

Stephen Balkam

Getting privacy right for ordinary citizens in an age of connected devices and pervasive tracking is an extraordinary challenge.

How do you provide adequate notice and give the ability to opt out in a world of cloud-based objects and screenless personal assistants? What means does an average person have to determine who or what is collecting her personal details, his precise location or their shopping habits? And how do we square the convenience and sheer magic of our digital devices with the suspicion that large, multinational corporations are peering into the intimate details of our lives in order to seamlessly persuade us to buy their products?

Well, if the challenge of getting the balance right is tough for a typical consumer, it gets far harder and more complex when considering privacy protections for our children. And this balancing act – for parents, for kids and for the companies developing tools, toys and apps – is both helped as well as complicated by current laws and regulations. Adding further complexity to this picture are our ever-evolving ideas about optimal child development and the notion of children's rights in the digital age.

The extraordinary (some would say, unprecedented) rates of change and new developments in the space simply add to the challenge while also forcing us all quickly to address it and find solutions that both protect minors while not squashing innovation or inhibiting the development of compelling content and experiences for kids. And we have to adapt existing privacy laws to this fast-changing landscape while creating new, multi-stakeholder approaches, effective self-regulatory efforts and innovative educational campaigns that address the new online realities of children and their connected devices.

THE BENEFITS AND UNINTENDED CONSEQUENCES OF COPPA

It would be good to begin with look at the most consequential law that governs this space: the Child Online Privacy Protection Act (COPPA) of 1998.

The purpose of COPPA, as it is more commonly known, was to ensure that sites directed at children under the age of thirteen secured verifiable parental permission before collecting personal information. It also specified what responsibilities operators had to ensure the online privacy and safety of those under thirteen and placed restrictions on the marketing to kids.

The Federal Trade Commission (FTC) was given authority to issue regulations and to enforce COPPA. The FTC also encouraged a self-regulatory element in the sanctioning of a number of "safe harbor" programs (e.g., TRUSTe and the ESRB) that would support COPPA compliance by sites and online services for kids. Companies that signed up with these programs could be subject to disciplinary procedures in lieu of FTC sanctions, including hefty financial fines.

In 2011, the FTC put forward revisions to COPPA rule-making and proposed a change to broaden what it means to collect data from kids. The new rules created a data retention and deletion requirement and ordered that children's data be kept only for the necessary length of time needed to achieve the purpose it was collected for in the first place. Also, it required that any third party that might have access to the data, have reasonable measures in place to protect the information.

A year later, the FTC announced[1] further revisions to COPPA, which became effective in the summer of 2013. These included:

- modify the list of "personal information" that cannot be collected without parental notice and consent, clarifying that this category includes geolocation information, photographs and videos;
- offer companies a streamlined, voluntary and transparent approval process for new ways of getting parental consent;
- close a loophole that allowed kid-directed apps and websites to permit third parties to collect personal information from children through plug-ins without parental notice and consent;
- extend coverage in some of those cases so that the third parties doing the additional collection also have to comply with COPPA;
- extend the COPPA Rule to cover persistent identifiers that can recognize users over time and across different websites or online services, such as IP addresses and mobile device IDs;
- strengthen data security protections by requiring that covered website operators and online service providers take reasonable steps to release children's personal information only to companies that are capable of keeping it secure and confidential;
- require that covered website operators adopt reasonable procedures for data retention and deletion; and
- strengthen the FTC's oversight of self-regulatory safe harbor programs.

On the plus side, COPPA has elevated the issue of children's privacy and the potential harm of unscrupulous companies, websites and apps collecting personal information from and marketing to young children. It has brought parents into the center of things and forced a regime of consent and approvals where there was none in the pre-2000 web.

To its credit, the commissioners and staff at the FTC have done a fairly good job of keeping pace with the rapid changes in technology and brought COPPA into a world of social media, apps and mobile devices that simply didn't exist at the time of the act's passage. It has created a level playing field, of sorts, that companies must adhere to and has had an impact internationally, with similar laws and rules applying across much of Europe and beyond. Also, it must be said, the FTC resisted calls to increase COPPA to age sixteen, which many saw as being virtually unenforceable and impinging on the rights of teenagers.

Not surprisingly, COPPA has had its critics and these mostly speak to the unintended consequences of the act and subsequent rulings that have emerged over the years. Chief among

---

[1] "FTC Strengthens Kids' Privacy, Gives Parents Greater Control Over Their Information by Amending Children's Online Privacy Protection Rule," Federal Trade Commission, December 19, 2012.

these is the reality that children, at times encouraged by their parents, lie about their age to access sites that have a thirteen-year-old age minimum.

A widely cited[2] *Consumer Reports* survey suggested that 7.5 million under-thirteens were on Facebook in the United States alone. While Facebook and other social media sites take steps to switch off accounts of underage children, the sheer scale of the "fraud" is daunting for operators.

It is interesting to understand what might be going on with age-related circumvention of COPPA. Naturally, many children under the age of thirteen want to be on the sites and download the apps that many of their older siblings or friends use. After all, Facebook was, originally, a platform for college students. Eventually, once the site opened up, it became hugely popular with high schoolers, and middle school kids weren't far behind in their enthusiasm for the social network. The same has proven true for Snapchat, Instagram and Tumblr.

So, underage kids quickly flocked to these sites and apps and simply lied to gain access. Interestingly, their parents often helped them to get on and even helped their younger kids to lie to do so. When asked about COPPA and the thirteen-year age minimum for most sites, many parents were either unaware of this requirement, or saw the age limit as something similar to the movie rating system. They viewed COPPA's "thirteen" as similar to the MPAA's PG13. In other words, the age limit was seen more as "parental guidance" and not an actual legal requirement.

There are many reasons why a parent might want their ten-, eleven- or twelve-year-old on Facebook or other social media sites. It could be that it is the most efficient way to share family news, photos and upcoming gatherings. Grandparents might actively encourage their grandchildren to join so that they can directly communicate over great distances and have a way to stay connected to their loved ones. Parents might also feel that their child would miss out socially if they were left out of the major online meeting places and, undoubtedly, parents give in to persistent and persuasive nagging by their tweenagers. This holds true for mobile phones, with the average age[3] of a child getting their first phone dropping to just ten years of age.

While lying about your age allows children access to social networks, they can often miss out on the very safety and privacy measures that sites such as Facebook have created for their teen users. For example, if a twelve-year-old chooses to say that she is twenty-one or older when she signs up, her profile will default to public and not friends-of-friends, which is the case for teenage accounts. She will also miss out on safety messages and other targeted posts that would remind her to check who can see her uploads, photos and updates. Suddenly, a middle-school user is widely viewable by the adult world, instead of having the more limited exposure created for teen Facebook users.

Of course, Facebook is not the only social network site with under-thirteens populating their platform. Musical.ly – a very popular app that allows users to video themselves while lip syncing to a song and then post it for their friends to see and like, is skewed particularly young. According to a *New York Times* article,[4] the Shanghai-based company has over 100 million users with many of the most popular profiles amongst kids in the first, second and third grades. The piece quotes a 2011 study that found,

---

[2] Ki Mae Heussner, "Underage Facebook Members: 7.5 Million Users Under Age 13," *ABC News*, May 10, 2011.

[3] Jay Donovan, "The Average Age for a Child Getting Their First Smartphone Is Now 10.3 Years," *Tech Crunch*, May 19, 2016.

[4] John Herrman, "Who's Too Young for an App? Musical.ly Tests the Limits," *The New York Times*, September 16, 2016.

In a study of the law published in 2011 by the academic journal *First Monday*,[5] researchers suggested that COPPA created intractable issues. To remain compliant, tech companies either cut off young users or claimed ignorance of their presence, while parents, for whom the law is meant to provide guidance and comfort, often ended up helping their children circumvent sign-up rules.

In their Privacy Policy, Musical.ly states, "We do not knowingly collect information from children under 13 and we do not want it. We will take steps to delete it if we learn we have collected it." It remains to be seen if this is sufficient notice to parents or if they will fall foul of the law.

Other concerns about COPPA center on the cost of compliance that companies must accept if they are to offer an online product or service to children. In addition, there are real fears about getting things wrong and being hit by a substantial fine. These can be as much as $16,000 for every violation. Given the scale of many online services and apps that figure can multiply quickly.

A recent example[6] of this came from the New York Attorney General's action against Viacom, Mattel, JumpStart and Hasbro totaling $835,000 in fines for violating COPPA and allowing illegal third-party tracking technology at websites for Barbie, Nick Jr., My Little Pony and American Girl, amongst others.

In June 2016, the FTC fined[7] Singapore-based inMobi nearly $1 million for illegally tracking consumers, including kids, without their permission in order to serve up geotargeted ads. Yelp was hit[8] with a $450,000 penalty by the FTC for improperly collecting children's information in violation of COPPA. And Disney-owned Playdom was fined $3 million for illegally collecting and disclosing personally identifiable information of kids under thirteen without their parents' consent.[9]

Given that we as a society want to protect the most vulnerable, perhaps the cost to the tech industry to get their permission and marketing right to our children is the price they have to pay. However, the downside of this financial burden and the potential for punitive fines means that many companies and entrepreneurs are scared off this potential market. This has lead to a dearth of good, compelling content and experiences for younger users. And it has been left to the large, multinational corporations and their lawyers to navigate the under-thirteen space, while individuals and small start-ups simply do not have the means, or the nerve, to compete.

Another avenue of attack against COPPA comes from the children's advocates who argue that the law suppresses children's right to free speech, assembly and self-expression. They reference the UN Convention on the Rights of the Child[10] (which has been ratified by nearly every country in the world, except the United States and Somalia) when arguing that children,

---

[5] danah boyd, Eszter Hargittai, Jason Schultz and John Palfrey, "Why Parents Help Their Children Lie to Facebook about Age: Unintended Consequences of the 'Children's Online Privacy Protection Act,'" *First Monday* 16 (October 21, 2011).

[6] "A. G. Schneiderman Announces Results of "Operation Child Tracker," Ending Illegal Online Tracking of Children at Some of Nation's Most Popular Kids' Websites," press release, *Attorney General Eric T. Schneiderman*, September 13, 2016.

[7] "InMobi Fined $950K By FTC For COPPA Violation; AmEx Unveils Facebook Messenger Bot," *AdExchanger*, June 24, 2016, https://adexchanger.com/ad-exchange-news/ftc-fined-inmobi-950k-amex-builds-facebook-messenger-bot/.

[8] Kimberlee Morrison, "Yelp Pays $450,000 FTC Fine for COPPA Violation." *Social Times*, September 22, 2014.

[9] Chloe Albanesius, "Disney's Playdom Fined $3 Million for Violating Kids' Privacy," *PC Magazine*, May 16, 2011.

[10] "Convention on the Rights of the Child." In *Adopted and Opened for Signature, Ratification and Accession by General Assembly Resolution*, Vol. 44/25. Article 49. United Nations: Human Rights, 1990.

including those under the age of thirteen, have certain rights, including access to the Internet – with or without their parents' permission.

While this is, in itself, a controversial stance, it does raise the question about what rights, if any, an eleven-year-old actually has on- or offline. Under new EU data protection directives, European countries will be able to raise the "digital age of consent" to sixteen. Britain announced that it would opt out of the new ruling, even before the Brexit vote. But the General Data Protection Regulation or GDPR has only fueled the debate about when a child or minor or teenager has a right to go online.

The reality is that kids are already on the Internet. There are tablets[11] for two year olds. There are potty training apps and iPad holders[12] for baby strollers. Increasing numbers of children in elementary and middle school are either provided with or assumed to have a tablet or laptop for work in class or at home. Even the American Academy of Pediatricians is revisiting their guidance to parents, for the first time acknowledging that there is a difference between screen time and screen use.[13]

FCC Commissioner Jessica Rosenworcel has decried what she calls the "homework gap" and is calling on industry, community groups and even McDonalds to help fill the lack of connectivity for many children and teens in poor, remote or tribal areas.[14] Thus not just access to the Internet; broadband connection is seen as a must for children and teens to complete assignments and research and to study topics given to them in schools. This is not the world that existed when COPPA was first introduced towards the end of the 1990s. The new reality is that screens and broadband access and connected devices are fast becoming ubiquitous and being online is considered a fundamental part (some would say right) of childhood.

KIDS AND THE CONNECTED HOME

Keeping the pros and cons of COPPA in mind, it would be good to explore the new and expanding world of the Internet of Things, including web-enabled toys and cloud-based products and services that children, teens and young people increasingly use. Additionally, the exponential growth of artificial intelligence or AI-powered devices, apps and services mean that a child's interaction with everyday objects is undergoing a radical transformation.

Let's begin with Mattel's "Hello Barbie." It is hard to imagine a more universally recognizable doll than Barbie. She has been loved by girls and collected by adults for decades. Barbie has also been at the center of a controversy over attitudes about girls' and women's body shapes.

What's different now is that she's been connected to the web and "cognitized," to use Kevin Kelly's term. She not only speaks (dolls have been doing this since Edison's time) but she also listens and responds to what you say in a conversational reply. She remembers details such as your name, what you want to be when you grow up and whether or not your grandmother is still alive.

And, at the end of the week, parents can opt in to receive a transcript of everything that Barbie and your child has said over the preceding seven days. It is an astonishing achievement by a company called PullString, led by former Pixar CTO, Oren Jacobs. The new Barbie

---

[11] "Fire Kids Edition Tablet, 7" Display, Wi-Fi, 16 GB, Blue Kid-Proof Case," online shopping, *Amazon*, n.d.

[12] "Strollers Stroller Ipad Tablet Stand Holder Baby Can Listen to Songs," online shopping, *AliExpress*, n.d.

[13] Ari Brown, Donald L. Shifrin and David L. Hill, "Beyond 'Turn It Off': How to Advise Families on Media Use," *AAP News & Journals*, 10, 36 (September 28, 2015).

[14] Clare McLaughlin, "The Homework Gap: The 'Cruelest Part of the Digital Divide,'" *neaToday*, April 20, 2016.

incorporates voice recognition, AI smarts, wifi connectivity via cloud-based services and thousands of prerecorded answers as well as prompting questions.

MIT Professor Sherry Turkle worries about the impact of dolls such as Hello Barbie on a young girl's emotional development, saying that she finds such toy's "toxic" and detrimental to a child's emerging ability to converse and make sense of the world. She sees a worrying trend of parents outsourcing their responsibility for interacting with their children to increasingly clever devices and toys.

What might be of more concern are the privacy implications of such a toy. Does the child have any privacy rights implicit in a whispered conversation late at night to her doll in bed? What happens in a stepfamily situation? Do both parents get access to the conversation logs? Do the stepparents? What if Barbie overhears something bad that Dad has said or done to Mom? Will Barbie be subpoenaed to appear in a domestic violence court case? What if hackers gain access to Barbie and fool a young girl into disclosing her and her family's private details or worse, entice her outside to meet up?

Not surprisingly, both Mattel and PullString have spent many development months working on these and other scenarios. They openly work with hackers and provide incentives for those who can find any security loopholes in their systems.

But privacy concerns remain. What's different about Barbie and toys such as Dino,[15] the talking (and listening) dinosaur from CogniToys, is that they come without a screen and keyboard. It is not at all obvious when first interacting with them that they are any different from a child's collection of toys and dolls until you find the on button and, as in *Toy Story*, they come alive.

Dino, like Barbie, can crack jokes and tell stories. But what is remarkable about "him" is that he is connected via the cloud to IBM's Watson, linking a child and his toy to one of the world's most powerful supercomputers. Ask Dino how far away the moon is, and he will tell you in an authentic dinosaur voice that it is 238,900 miles from earth. If you ask Dino what 2 plus 2 are he will calmly tell you 4, but will also tell you that you can ask him more difficult questions. It's not hard to see how children could anthropomorphize such interactive toys, becoming their "friends" and divulging even more personal information to them.

In a somewhat different category is Amazon's Echo and the talking and listening assistant, Alexa. Echo is a simple, black cylindrical tower that sits inconspicuously on a kitchen surface, for example. It was designed with adults in mind, serving up the news, weather, music and much more through a growing galaxy of apps. What was unexpected is the degree to which kids naturally gravitate to Alexa and her calm, reassuring voice. As with Siri, Apple's personal assistant in later versions of the iPhone, Alexa is often used by a busy or harried parent to divert a demanding child. "Ask Alexa," mom may cry. "See what Siri has to say," dad demands as he navigates traffic and passes back his phone.

Kids take to these personal assistants, talking dolls and AI-infused devices as normally as earlier generations mastered the Hula Hoop or Frisbee. Having "cognitized" agents in the house or the car or in their pocket is the new normal. What is different is the amount and degree to which these digitized "helpers" collect, analyze, suggest and serve up ads or purchasing possibilities. And it's hard to see how COPPA applies to something like Echo. Even if a parent gives permission to Amazon for her son to "play" with Alexa, what happens when Johnnie's friend comes over to play? Does his parent also have to give explicit permission? How does a law written and interpreted in a world of websites, screens and keyboards apply to inanimate objects

---

[15] "Meet the CogniToys Dino," *Cogni Toys*, n.d., https://cognitoys.com.

that happen to be connected to the cloud? Will we need a new privacy regime when the Internet of Things becomes artificially intelligent?

VIRTUAL, AUGMENTED AND MIXED REALITY

While dealing with AI and personal assistants such as Alexa is going to test the boundaries of COPPA and our acceptance of personally identifiable information being collected by everyone from Amazon to Zynga, the newly emerging world of artificial reality will provide even more interesting debates.

Artificial reality covers a continuum of experiences from virtual (VR) to augmented (AR) and even mixed reality (MR). And the shape and complexity of the hardware and software that is needed to achieve the desired effect will be determined by where on the artificial reality continuum the developer is trying to land.

Take virtual reality. This is usually a completely immersive, artificial world that uses sensory cues to fabricate a "real" experience. It requires a headset that takes over the user's visual field and can be enhanced by headphones to provide a soundtrack to whatever world they are inhabiting. Examples of VR include Google Cardboard, Samsung's Gear VR, HTC's Vive and, of course, Oculus Rift.

These and others coming onto the market differ between being completely mobile (Cardboard) to totally tethered (Rift), with an equally wide range of pricing.

There is a remarkable realness of the experience. Your brain (and the rest of your body) is tricked into thinking and feeling as if it's on a roller coaster or flying with a flock of seagulls or falling from the top of a skyscraper.

The experience is so real, VR headset manufacturers caution only to use them while sitting down less you crash or hurl yourself out of the way of a bullet or oncoming train or whatever else the software throws at you. Rift is so realistic that it takes a while to readjust to real life. While entertainment and gaming are obvious uses of VR, it could also be used for education, social networking and collaboration. It could just be the killer app of the 2020s.

Then there is augmented reality, which uses the real world and overlays data and digital images, sound and video onto it. Classic examples include the ill-fated Google Glass or the heads-up displays on car windshields. Facebook's plans[16] for AR glasses could not only integrate the data of, say, a football stadium you are about to enter, but also all your friends' photos and videos ever taken there, a list of who else is in the crowd and ways to message them in real time. Rather than entering a completely virtual world, augmented reality promises a data rich interaction with the real world and all the real people – friends included – who inhabit our world.

There are numerous AR glasses either on the market or to be soon. Probably the best known of these is Meta. The TED talk[17] given by Meron Gibetz gives a most tantalizing demo of where this technology is heading. And the reviews[18] from top tech watchers and developers are instructive in their emotional reaction to working and sculpting with virtual 3D objects in a real world environment.

---

[16] Adi Robertson, "Mark Zuckerberg Says Augmented Reality Glasses Are 'What We're Trying to Get To,'" *The Verge*, April 12, 2016.

[17] Meron Gribetz, "A Glimpse of the Future through an Augmented Reality Headset," TED Talk, February 2016.

[18] Meta. *Meta 2 Augmented Reality: Demo Reactions from Robert Scoble, Alexis Ohanian, Will.i.am, and More*, accessed November 15, 2016.

The real breakthrough in augmented reality came with the release of the highly interactive game, Pokémon Go. Rather than using a specially adapted pair of glasses, this AR game uses a smartphone camera interface to overlay virtual characters onto the "real" world that players are in. The phone's GPS capabilities are utilized to track, capture, train and battle characters and the game allows for in app purchases for additional items.

The game has been credited with a surge in children, young people and adults venturing out of doors and into towns, neighborhoods, parks and stores in pursuit of all of the Pokémon characters. It has also been criticized for encouraging large groups to gather in certain city streets, parks and even cemeteries and for being partly to blame for accidents and even deaths. It was claimed that an early version of Pokémon Go allowed the makers of the game to access a user's Google accounts, including their Gmail. This was quickly fixed and no longer appears to be an issue.

Which brings us to the category known as mixed reality. As the name suggests, it borrows aspects of both virtual and augmented reality technologies and overlays the mixed experience on the real world. The best known or, at least, most hyped example of mixed reality is the Florida-based, Magic Leap. In MR, killer whales can suddenly emerge from beneath the wooden floor of a gymnasium and splash below the surface again. Spreadsheets can be projected on to a real desktop, while the planets circle the sun above your head. Virtual objects can appear or disappear depending on your relation to physical pieces of furniture or walls.

Magic Leap and Microsoft's HoloLens are in a multibillion-dollar race to create the next computing platform.[19] But whereas the first iteration of cyberspace, roughly the past twenty-five years, has brought data and images and video to our many and varied screens, MR promises to combine data with presence and even experience into a single pair of glasses or a visor.

It's as if the Internet of the head will be linked to the web of the heart to create a new universe of emotional intelligence. It will have a profound impact on how we see and co-create the world with each other and with an infinite variety of virtual and real objects and encounters. And it will be compelling for our children who, as with earlier technologies, will be early and avid adopters.

MR will require vast new databases, server farms, bandwidth and power to fuel its huge processing demands. Products such as Magic Leap will suck up huge amounts of data about where and how we live, what children's interests are and the kinds of games and films and stories they like to interact with. It will transform how we think and remember and invent and learn and ultimately, how we bring up our kids.

As artificial reality headsets of all kinds enter our homes, there will be a huge temptation on the part of developers and service providers alike to mine the data that is found there. And wherever digital devices go, so do hackers. The real possibility of VR goggles or MR visors being hijacked by a rogue individual or state-sponsored hackers is chilling to consider. Issues of privacy, safety and security will increasingly merge and become part of broader universe of concerns that will take a multi-stakeholder, cross-industry and multinational approach to address.

PARENTS, PRIVACY AND CHILDREN

Government has a crucial role to play in protecting the privacy of children online through laws such as COPPA. The tech industry, on the other hand, has both a business interest and a *moral imperative* to ensure the safety, privacy and security of kids' data and not to exploit them through

---

[19] Microsoft. *Microsoft HoloLens: Transform Your World with Holograms,*" accessed November 15, 2016.

unauthorized marketing. However, it falls to parents to be the first line of defense and the arbiters of what and how their kids share data online.

In a recent Family Online Safety Institute study, 67 percent of parents worry about maintaining the privacy of their child's personal information.[20] The dramatic rise in the numbers of children using smart phones and apps has only exacerbated these concerns. Parents are being challenged to make decisions about their kids' technology use at a younger age than ever before and about devices and services they often don't fully understand.

It is essential that tech companies across the value chain – from ISPs to phone manufacturers to gaming companies and app developers – have easy-to-find and easy-to-understand privacy policies that parents can act on. More educational efforts are needed, such as FOSI's Good Digital Parenting[21] project, which works to empower parents to navigate the web confidently with their kids. This includes tips, tools, resources and even a seven-step guide on how to be a good digital parent.

All of us as consumers, and particularly those of us with kids, will have to take the time to read privacy policies and educate ourselves on how to protect our children's data. There will have to be steady and consistent public education campaigns to keep the issue of digital privacy uppermost in people's minds and to encourage changes in behavior.

A good example of this, in the cyber-security field, is the White House-backed "Lock Down Your Login" campaign. This government/industry/NGO initiative encourages consumers to use multifactor authentication when logging on to a website or app. It is a large-scale, nationwide effort to move the needle on security and to get a majority of users to take an extra step to protect themselves online.

A similar model could be imagined for kids' privacy with an federal administration-led, multi-stakeholder project to raise parental awareness about privacy policies and settings on the most popular sites and apps for kids. It would need the enthusiastic cooperation of industry and the creativity of ad agencies and social media marketers to develop compelling and memorable messages that lead to changes in the rules parents set and the privacy settings their children use.

THE FUTURE OF CHILDREN'S PRIVACY

The current state of children's online privacy is a complex web of COPPA rulemakings, social media privacy policies and NGO efforts to educate parents, and the kids themselves, on how to manage what they post, how they are tracked and who gets to use the data they generate every day. It is a challenge, to say the least, to remain up to date and to take informed decisions based on one's level of concern about a kid's digital footprint and the cyber trail they leave behind through their phones, tablets, laptops and other devices.

What lies ahead with the arrival of the Internet of Things, connected toys, AI personal assistants and artificial reality headsets is an unprecedented public policy challenge that will require thoughtful approaches and multidisciplinary solutions that adequately address the risks and mitigate the harms, while reaping the rewards of this brave new world.

It is not a job for government alone. Nor does the tech industry have all the answers. And the NGO sector, while willing, simply doesn't have the resources to deal adequately with what lies ahead. It will take these three sectors working together along with researchers, academics, psychologists and neuroscientists, to name a few, to tackle the complex legal, business, parental

---

[20] "Parents, Privacy & Technology Use," policy report, *Family Online Safety Institute*, 2015.
[21] "Good Digital Parenting," *Family Online Safety Institute*, n.d.

and ethical concerns that will arise in an always-on, connected, AI-infused, virtually augmented, digital world that our children will inherit.

We owe it to our kids (and their kids) to get this as right as we can, as soon as possible, and to keep iterating our temporary solutions to make sense of the next technological wave. The new online realities will force us to confront this whether or not we believe that "privacy is dead" or that having some control over what the rest of the world can see, access and store about our digital lives is something worth preserving.

15

Stakeholders and High Stakes

Divergent Standards for Do Not Track

Aleecia M. McDonald

INTRODUCTION

In the United States, online privacy is in disarray. As US firms dominate the Internet, those US firms have exported shoddy privacy controls internationally. Many other authors have documented the gaps between user expectations and commercial privacy practices, as well as how little control users have over their own data. This chapter assumes readers are familiar with the general sweep of the past two decades of privacy literature and does not repeat it. In short, users are unable to effectively realize their personal privacy preferences in practice.

The US Federal Trade Commission (FTC) is often the center of policy making around US online privacy. FTC policy powers are limited in scope, both by a design focused on enforcement [1] and from fiscal dependence. The FTC depends upon funding from a Congress that is itself funded by the very companies the FTC might seek to constrain.[1] While quite aware of consumer privacy problems, the FTC tends to merely to request that companies self-regulate or innovate for privacy. Prior attempts at FTC-encouraged privacy controls include the Platform for Privacy Preferences (P3P) [2], a variety of types of opt-out cookies [3] [4], and tiny icons on ads themselves [5] [6].

In contrast, European policy makers take a more direct path of passing privacy laws. Most relevant, the European Parliament adopted the General Data Protection Regulation (GDPR) in April 2016 [7]. Enforcement of the GDPR begins in May 2018 [8].

Do Not Track is yet another voluntary privacy control encouraged by the FTC. In the United States, there are no laws requiring Do Not Track. In the EU, while laws do not explicitly require it, Do Not Track could be the technical means to fulfill the legal requirements of the GDPR.

Section 1 of this chapter presents the evolution of the Do Not Track approach. Section 2 includes reflections upon multi-stakeholder processes generally, using Do Not Track as a case study. Section 3 highlights a subset of the challenges to overcome in order to bring Do Not Track to fruition. Section 4 concludes.

---

[1] The FTC became active in protecting children's health from sugary cereals, which cereal makers fought by persuading Congress to cut FTC funding [8]. Recent FTC enforcement actions resulted in fines against technology companies with large lobbying budgets, including Google (a top-20 contributor to 24 Members of Congress in 2016 via parent company Alphabet), Facebook (a top-20 contributor to 51 Members of Congress in 2016), and Microsoft (a top-20 contributor to 112 Members of Congress in 2016) [9]. More recently, sibling Federal Communications Commission's (FCC's) privacy decisions for opt-in IP data use were reversed by Congress. Media coverage of the congressional vote lists campaign contributions by Internet Service Providers (ISPs) [22].

Of note: while a cochair of the Do Not Track standards work, my role was to create a space for participants to come to agreements if they could. I worked to be fair and keep my personal opinions out of the room, and I believe I largely succeeded. (At the very least, all sides grumbled that I was not doing enough for them, and protested when I explained *that was the point*.) This chapter is nearly the inverse task. Here I present history as I saw it, opinions and all. I hope that a personal account is more interesting and more useful to readers than an attempt at objectivity. You may rely upon other participants to have different perspectives.

1. THE EARLY DAYS OF DO NOT TRACK

Pam Dixon is the Executive Director of the public interest World Privacy Forum organization. In 2007, she introduced the idea of a Do Not Track list [9] for online privacy. Originally, privacy advocates envisioned Do Not Track (also known as DNT) as a direct analog to the Do Not Call list for phone calls. Eight privacy groups joined with the World Privacy Forum in submitting a Do Not Track proposal to the FTC, specifically calling on it to maintain a list of the domain names used to set persistent identifiers for tracking [10]. The domain list could then be used to block trackers, perhaps via browser plug-ins or by networking hardware (e.g., routers). From the very start, Do Not Track was described as a way for people still to see online ads, but stop online tracking [10] [11].

Companies rarely architect their systems to have tracking and content on distinct servers. Blocking servers that track users would also block content from those same servers unless companies invested engineering effort to tease functionality apart and keep it on distinct servers. Advertisers lobbied against Do Not Track as an idea that would "break the Internet." The Do Not Track idea of empowering users to stop tracking caught on, even though the technical mechanism as originally proposed did not. Then-FTC Chairman Jon Leibowitz told Congress he favored a Do Not Track approach, which was followed by an FTC report calling on industry to come up with a better way for users to opt out of tracking [12]. The FTC's support was crucial to moving Do Not Track forward. Three different technical approaches to Do Not Track emerged, each backed by a different web browser maker.

Option 1: *Google's Opt Out Cookie Approach*

Google supported a Do Not Track approach based on industry opt-out cookies. The Digital Advertising Alliance (DAA) offers self-regulatory principles [13] as the basis for a program where web users may opt out of seeing targeted ads, either by visiting each third-party company directly, or opting out for multiple companies at once on the DAA's Ad Choices web interface [4]. The DAA program is a "do not target" approach rather than a "do not track" option. That is, data collection and tracking continue, but ads based on tracking data do not display [14]. Many privacy advocates – and users themselves – found do not target an unacceptably weak substitute for do not track [15].

The DAA's approach had the nontrivial advantage of already existing in the marketplace. However, DAA opt-out cookies suffer from a technical flaw, one not of DAA's making. The DAA opt-out is HTTP cookie-based. That means every time a user deletes her cookies for enhanced privacy, she also deletes her opt-out cookies as well. This is a common use case that undermines what little privacy gains opt-out cookies provide.

Google's solution to DNT was to "harden" DAA opt-out cookies by keeping them even if users delete other cookies [16]. While similar solutions were already possible through browser plug-ins [17], Google offered to build exemptions for DAA opt-out cookies straight into the Chrome browser in a program they called Keep My Opt Outs.

Google added Chrome support for Do Not Track headers (described later in the chapter) in late 2012 [18]. As of 2015, Google announced they had ended their Keep My Opt Outs program in favor of letting the DAA incorporate the technology as a DAA-maintained browser extension. In early 2016, Google Chrome for iOS removed Do Not Track support, which Google described as being due to a technical limitation in changes Apple made to the iOS API rather than a policy change on Google's part [19].

Option 2: *Microsoft's Tracking Protection Lists*

Microsoft took a different approach to answering the FTC's request for user control of tracking. Starting with Internet Explorer 9, Microsoft allowed other parties to create and publish blocking lists. Tracking Protection Lists could simply block content from specific third-party domains, thereby ensuring no tracking cookies (or any other tracking technologies, which is a key advantage) could load in the browser. As a side effect, blocking tracking also blocked ads [20]. Which third-party domains to block were up to the authors of the Tracking Protection Lists, neatly avoiding antitrust issues for Microsoft, and it was entirely up to users to enable any given Tracking Protection List. Tracking Protection Lists follow in the footsteps of the Platform for Privacy Preferences (P3P) [21] and the Platform for Internet Content Selection (PICS) [22]. Microsoft was heavily involved in the W3C standards process for both P3P and PICS, active both on the technology and public policy aspects of each.

The user experience for Tracking Protection Lists was rather dreadful to start, with boxes with Xs across them to indicate blocked content that did not load. Pages often loaded more quickly but were unattractive. Moreover, in the case of conflicting allow and block lists, Microsoft elected to have the domains on allow lists trump the domains on block lists. By very design, privacy protection appeared not to be the top priority for a privacy feature. This was not merely a theoretical problem. One of the initial Tracking Protection Lists came from TRUSTe, and was an allow list of nearly 4,000 domains (including Microsoft's) with no domains blocked [23]. While users could elect not to load Tracking Protection Lists from TRUSTe, having trust issues with TRUSTe right away did not improve Microsoft's own credibility, as Microsoft had crafted a privacy tool that was instantly, and predictably, subverted. Microsoft's commitment to privacy was also tarnished by an expose in the *Wall Street Journal* that established advertising "self-regulation" groups had joined with Microsoft's own advertising team to derail privacy features in Internet Explorer 8 [24].

Along with Tracking Protection Lists, Internet Explorer 9 allowed users to send a Do Not Track header request, albeit through an arcane user interface. Microsoft argued that Tracking Protection Lists were a better privacy approach than Do Not Track headers, since Do Not Track headers were a mere request for privacy while Tracking Protection Lists were a technical mechanism that enforced users' privacy preferences. Advertising trade groups, on the other hand, protested that Tracking Protection Lists would break the advertising model of the Internet, and they favored Google's opt-out cookies over Tracking Protection Lists [25]. The Electronic Frontier Foundation concluded that both Tracking Protection Lists and Do Not Track header signals were best used together, as they have complementary strengths and weaknesses [26].

Option 3: *Mozilla's Header Signals*

Over time, the initial Do Not Track's proposed technical mechanism changed from a list of tracking domains for a web browser to block, into a request for user privacy sent as an HTTP header. Readers may reasonably wonder what an HTTP header is. Imagine visiting a website. In addition to requesting content, a web browser also sends metadata about the device, e.g., which fonts are available, screen size, the browser version, and more. This metadata helps ensure the webserver sends back something suitable to display on a particular device. For a browser with Do Not Track enabled (see Figure 15.1), the web browser translates the user's request into an HTTP header of "DNT:1" to send to web servers along with other metadata (see Figure 15.2). The HTTP header approach is a fairly elegant technical technique to send a signal from a user to all domains the user visits.

Over just a few days in January 2011, Mozilla engineer Sid Stamm added a few dozen lines of code to the Firefox browser to support sending a Do Not Track header [27] [28] with a user interface following a few days later [29]. At that time the technical mechanism to send a Do Not

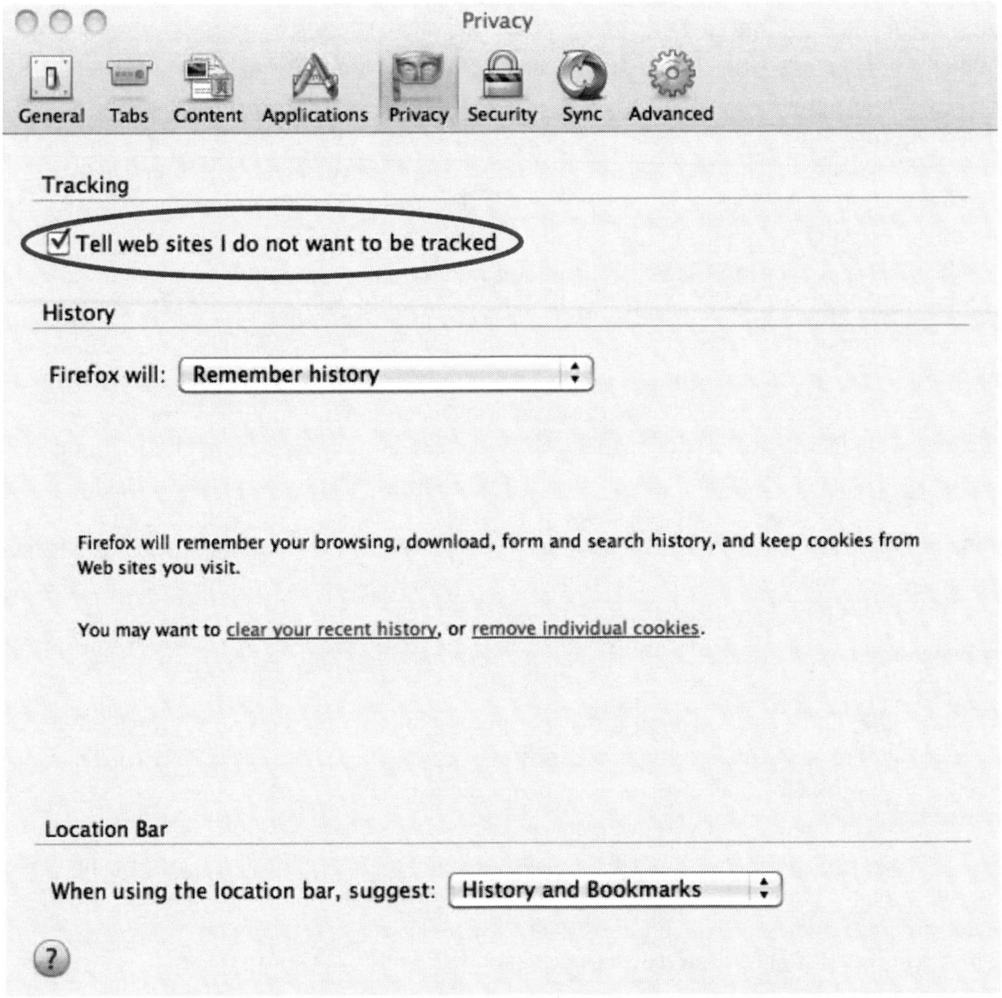

FIGURE 15.1 Mozilla's user interface for Do Not Track in June 2011

```
GET / HTTP/1.1
Host: www.wikipedia.org
User -Agent:  Mozilla/5.0 (Macintosh; Intel
Mac OS X 10.6; rv:2.0.1) Gecko/20100101
Firefox/4.0.1
Accept:
text/html,application/xhtml+xml,application/
xml;q=0.9,*/*;q=0.8
Accept-Language: en-us,en;q=0.5
Accept-Encoding: gzip, deflate
Accept-Charset: ISO-8859-1,utf-
8;q=0.7,*;q=0.7
Keep -Alive: 115
DNT: 1
Connection: keep-alive
[...]
```

FIGURE 15.2 An HTTP header sending a request for no tracking

Track request was fairly well tested, but there remained an open question of what companies should or must do in the face of a user's request not to be tracked.

In March 2011, three coauthors submitted a standards proposal to the Internet Engineering Task Force (IETF) for a Do Not Track header [30] and continued important work crafting code examples and a proof of concept [31]. The IETF declined to work on standardizing Do Not Track. Also in March 2011, the World Wide Web Consortium (W3C) held a call for papers to discuss Do Not Track, resulting in over sixty submissions [32] and leading to a marathon presentation in April [33]. As noted in the workshop report, participants generally supported the idea of a Do Not Track working group within W3C [34]. By then Microsoft had submitted their Tracking Protection Lists for W3C standardization plus a short mention of Do Not Track [35]; that submission eventually turned into the W3C Tracking Protection Working Group which began meeting in September 2011 [36].

One technical benefit to an HTTP header is that it is universal: all parties on a given website get the signal. This contrasts to the opt-out cookie approach where different cookies are set for each company, and indeed must be, because companies (generally) cannot read other companies' cookies. This requires users to set cookies on a per-company basis, even though they may never have heard of the companies and cannot know in advance which ones they will encounter on a given first-party website. Yet because HTTP headers are sent to every party that could read cookies from a device, if a user visits a website that has multiple third parties embedded (say, two ads, a Facebook "Like" button, and a weather widget,) all of those third parties automatically receive the Do Not Track request. There is also no need for the first-party website to coordinate with or even know which third parties are present on their own first-party website. With ad auctions resulting in an ever-changing and unknown landscape of third parties, this technical detail enables Do Not Track to work in practice.

The universal nature of a Do Not Track header not only means there is no need for users to opt out from multiple domains in different ways, it can also mean there is no need to click on countless pop-ups informing users that cookies are in use. Do Not Track settings persist across all interactions from a given web browser. For that matter, Do Not Track could be set for *all* browsers on a device; indeed, an antivirus maker caused quite a controversy when their product turned on Do Not Track in the registry for Windows users, thereby changing the Do Not Track setting that multiple browsers read [37].

Perhaps most important, browsers send HTTP headers *before* setting or sending cookies. That means user consent to tracking can be established before tracking cookies set, not after, as now happens with other cookie-based opt-outs (including Google's hardened opt-out cookies, as described earlier.) Timing is particularly important for compliance with the European Union's General Data Protection Regulation consent rules. To date, there are no purely cookie-based opt-out programs that are able to generally fulfill the requirement of getting prior consent. Such a system is not impossible, but would likely be annoying to implement.

Legislative Proposals for Do Not Track

In addition to the responses of three web browser companies to the FTC, as described earlier, the United States had legislative proposals to limit online tracking. These technical and policy efforts were not completely independent. In particular, fear of legislation motivated some of the industry participation in W3C as an alternative to privacy laws.

In 2010, Senators John Kerry and John McCain proposed the Commercial Privacy Bill of Rights Act of 2011. The bill explicitly gave the FTC the power to design an opt-out for online tracking, which could include Do Not Track [38]. Senator Rockefeller proposed the Do-Not-Track Online Act of 2011, which would have empowered the FTC to design and enforce Do Not Track [39]. Senators Ed Markey and Joe Barton proposed the Do Not Track Kids Act of 2011 by amending the Children's Online Privacy Protection Act of 1998 (COPPA) and barring all ads that are behaviorally targeted to children [40]. In the House, Representative Jackie Speier introduced the Do Not Track Me Online Act, which would have empowered the FTC to design Do Not Track [41]. At the state level, California Senator Alan Lowenthal proposed amending California's existing spyware legislation (SB 761) to have the California Attorney General's Office and the California Office of Privacy Protection draft regulations for a California-wide Do Not Track [42]. Not one of these bills became law.

In 2013, however, California did pass state law AB-370, which requires a company collecting data about Californians to note if and how they respond to an incoming Do Not Track request [43]. The law is strictly a transparency law. AB-370 does not address what Do Not Track should do and does not require companies to do anything at all with an incoming Do Not Track request. In practice, most companies ignore AB-370 [44]. Even when they do not simply ignore the law, companies often note in their privacy policy that they ignore Do Not Track requests. If AB-370 had been intended to shame companies into honoring Do Not Track, it has not succeeded. To date, there are no public enforcement actions against companies for failing to disclose their DNT practices in accordance with AB-370.

In summary, Do Not Track started with a variety of technical approaches before converging upon the Do Not Track header. The work needed to then agree upon the details of technical and policy issues around the Do Not Track header landed in the W3C standards body. The next section discusses how the standards work progressed.

2. SAUSAGE-MAKING: MULTI-STAKEHOLDER STANDARDS

The task of a standards working group is to produce a specification – a technical document – that can be implemented in practice by multiple parties. As a basic example, in the United States there is a standard of PRNDL: cars with automatic transmissions have the same order of Park / Reverse / Neutral / Drive / Low. This enhances safety because, for example, drivers do not accidently put a rental car into reverse out of habit formed from a car at home with a different layout.

In the context of Do Not Track, all user agent software makers (e.g., web browser makers) needed to understand which signals to send or receive. This is largely technical work. Figure 15.3

6.3 Tk Header Field for HTTP Responses

6.3.1 Definition

The **Tk** response header field is a means for indicating the tracking status that applied to the corresponding request. An origin server is REQUIRED to send a Tk header field if its site-wide tracking status value is ? (dynamic) or G (gateway), or when an interactive change is made to the tracking status and indicated by U (updated).

```
Tk-field-name   =  "Tk"
Tk-field-value  =  TSV [ ";" status-id ]
```

The Tk field-value begins with a tracking status value (section 6.2 Tracking Status Value), optionally followed by a semicolon and a status-id that refers to a request-specific tracking status resource (section 6.3.2 Referring to a Request-specific Tracking Status Resource).

FIGURE 15.3 An excerpt from the Tracking Protection Expression candidate release describing a valid response to a Do Not Track signal

presents an excerpt of the Do Not Track standards work. In addition, users should also be able to count on some basic agreement of what privacy is and is not afforded to them from any given company that supports Do Not Track. The details of communication with users are not as well specified. The W3C process explicitly does not address user interface standards, considering them "out of scope," and left to the marketplace. Usually it is browser makers that define user interface issues, but for Do Not Track every first and third party could be communicating differently, particularly if a website asks users for permission to track them despite users previously requesting not to be tracked with Do Not Track settings.

Most W3C standards are by geeks, for geeks, and rather proudly so. Do Not Track, however, attracted a wide variety of participant backgrounds. From the start, the W3C Do Not Track group had over 100 members from companies, privacy non-governmental organizations (NGOs), governments, and academia. Members ranged from geeks, to policy wonks, to lawyers. An advantage to this diversity is the breadth and depth of viewpoints that informed the work. One disadvantage was the absence of a common yet precise working language. Geeks and wonks had to work harder to understand one another than they would to understand other members of their own tribe. The W3C effort became an interdisciplinary multi-stakeholder team by necessity.

If Do Not Track were a movie, the years of work in W3C are a prime candidate for a montage set to peppy music in order to skip the numbing details. Because standards work happens in public, dedicated readers can find source materials online [45]. This chapter presents some broader reflections on multi-stakeholder processes and then a few highlights specific to Do Not Track.

Rough Consensus

The basic work process for most W3C standards is similar to software development: members of the working group identify "issues," akin to software bugs, and submit these issues in writing for group review. In an easy case, everyone can agree upon the problem and a solution, leaving just the task of finding someone to volunteer to draft text as agreed and an editor to update the draft document with the new text. To make decisions stick, W3C process is much like the legal concept of *stare decisis*: unless a working group member presents new information, old decisions stand, thus avoiding endless circular discussions. Resolved issues are procedurally difficult to reopen.

But what of harder cases, where participants do not agree upon the problem let alone a solution? W3C process calls for "rough consensus." This is explicitly different from majority rule. The goal is often to find the least objectionable proposal, rather than the one that gets the most votes by raw count. For example, imagine a political election with five similar candidates, A through E, and one extreme candidate F. If only 20 percent support candidate F, she will win if the support of the other 80 percent splits uniformly across the similar candidates A through E (13 percent each.) This is true even if the 80 percent majority would rather take *any* candidate A through E rather than F. Such suboptimal outcomes are a known flaw of winner-take-all democracy. One of the goals of a consensus process is to avoid this problem. Another consideration in consensus decisions is the intensity of objections. This is not measured by who screams loudest, but rather by a notion of what participants can live with, even if it is not their most favored outcome.

In a collaborative environment these approaches work well. As an example from Do Not Track, advertisers get high economic value from "frequency capping," where a specific ad is shown only a few times to the same person. Privacy advocates had no principled objection to this feature, but found the data collection methods used to track how many times a person saw a given ad as incompatible with their idea of a Do Not Track standard, so they could not support the current implementations of frequency capping for Do Not Track users. Advertisers were adamant that frequency capping is an important and profitable approach, without which they might not be able to support Do Not Track on financial grounds. A majority rule approach would have had each camp hunker down and try to recruit supporters in order to outvote the opposition. Instead, working together, they were able to devise a technical approach [46] that satisfied both the advertisers' priority of frequency capping and the privacy advocates' priority of not tracking users' viewing habits all across the web. The advertising industry would need to write new code, at their expense. Privacy advocates would have a harder time being able to tell if a company fulfilled their promises for user privacy. In both cases, each group would far rather have had a clear "win" for what they wanted in the first place. But both groups also all allowed that they could live with a compromise solution. One of the tools of consensus decisions is taken from the field of integrative bargaining: focus on the outcomes people want, not on their current positions. Often there are ways to get to good enough outcomes for enough people if you can get them to explore the solution space, rather than entrench. At times, this worked.

Less than Good Faith

Consensus tools are not as well suited to participants who actively work to prevent the group from coming to any decision, or have the goal of derailing the process. Most assuredly Do Not Track had participants who were hostile to the idea of any limits on tracking. In some cases I personally encouraged them to join us in order to have a diversity of opinions in the room. As an additional personal observation, the tools used for consensus also worked best in smaller groups, perhaps under fifty participants or so. The Working Group could, and did, break into smaller subgroups with mixed results when reconvened as a full group.

Academic writing does not readily lend itself to a full discussion of how contentious the working group became, nor would it be appropriate, so I will give selected highlights. Most of the working group discussions happened over e-mail, which was all too easy to derail into flame wars. Participants also sniped at each other in the press, including personal attacks and name-calling. There was much more, some of it rather nasty work, including the derailment of a few careers. Tactics such as stalling discussion can be addressed through a normal consensus process (e.g., "Do you have new information to contribute? No? Next speaker in the queue, please.")

However, Do Not Track was not a normal W3C standards process and clearly needed a different approach to continue on to publish a specification.

As an organization, W3C had prior experience with a large, contentious group working on HTML. At one point the HTML working group splintered, with work occurring both within and outside W3C [47]. Do Not Track leveraged the rather messy HTML experience and adopted their decision-making process. This included resolving issues by public text submissions. Once the cochairs wrangled a small set of reasonably final proposed texts, members would submit their objections or support to each proposal, again in writing. The cochairs would go through each response to see which text drew the best consensus, focused on content rather than on raw numbers of responses. The chairs would formally write down their reasoning. Needless to say, this was a great deal of work for chairs and participants, but discussions slowly inched forward.

It was also clear I was drawing a great deal of personal ire. After the transition to text-based issue resolution I recruited a more experienced successor, and I stepped down as cochair. A year later, with no agreement in hand, the group changed leadership again.

As of the summer 2017, Do Not Track survived a recharter vote and the work continues. There are two documents that have moved through several drafts and are at "Candidate Recommendation," or are all but complete. One of those documents is primarily focused on the technical aspects of Do Not Track. The second is primarily focused on what companies must do to comply with Do Not Track, in other words, what it means not to track a user. While the technical document is likely to see final publication in 2017, it seems highly likely that the compliance document will never advance to final stage, despite years of work and a consensus document in hand.

In short, the consensus compliance document had agreement on each individual issue, yet no one liked the final outcome. When reaching decisions in a multi-stakeholder process, there is the risk that one camp likes red, another likes blue, and you end with a purple neither side can stand. With Do Not Track, it was more a patchwork of reds and blues that turned out to be unlovely when taken all together. This outcome is not unique to Do Not Track. A concurrent multi-stakeholder process from the Commerce Department produced a consensus document without corporate plans to implement it [48].

Current Do Not Track efforts address possible ways to move forward with Do Not Track with a technical specification but no compliance document. In the end, there will likely be a set of multiple variants of what Do Not Track means published by different stakeholders, along with individual companies designing their own custom implementations. Not only is this outcome challenging for users, it was foreseeable. Nearly six years ago, prior to my direct involvement with Do Not Track, I coauthored a paper [49] in which we noted that meeting user expectations for Do Not Track conflicted with the easiest path to implementation. We summarized our conclusions in a slide shown here as Figure 15.4.

Do Not Track will not match user expectations to halt all data collection, nor will it have one definition that applies to all companies that implement Do Not Track, and the details of how Do Not Track works per company may or may not be communicated in an automated way. To my surprise, there may not even be details in help files and privacy policies describing what companies do with an incoming Do Not Track signal, despite California's legal requirement to disclose this very information. In short, even my originally most pessimistic scenario now looks like more than companies are willing to do voluntarily.

European enforcement of the General Data Protection Regulation (GDPR) could come as a bit of a shock to some US companies. Indeed, some participants in the Do Not Track standards discussions seem to believe European regulators will somehow change their minds and not enforce parts of the GDPR draft [50]. This seems unlikely as the Eprivacy Regulation

Options to address the expectations gap

- Build DNT to match expectations

- Create one definition of DNT and
  communicate it clearly

- Create one definition plus exceptions
  and communicate them very clearly

- Allow multiple definitions and
  communicate them in novel ways
  Example: HTTP header response

- Put details into privacy policies and
  help files

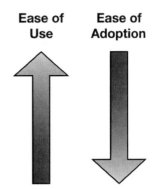

FIGURE 15.4 Ease of use for consumers is inverse to ease of adoption for companies. Predictable results are predictable.

Rapporteurs Draft Report contemplates making Do Not Track both mandatory and stronger on privacy protections [51]. This follows similar recommendations by leading Dutch scholars as well as calls for a mandatory and revised Do Not Track system from the Article 29 Working Party and the European Data Protection Supervisor [52].

3. CHALLENGES

In many ways Do Not Track is just another multi-stakeholder process that has struggled to cross the finish line, similar to many other Internet policy standards that set out with high hopes (PICS, P3P, etc.) Yet there are also aspects of the Do Not Track saga that are unique. A few challenges to a meaningful Do Not Track standard are outlined here. This is not an exhaustive list, but serves to document some of the Do Not Track experience.

Business Model Threats

The most obvious challenge to standardizing Do Not Track was to persuade companies to change their entrenched business models. When Do Not Track work first began, ad blockers were more esoteric. Many companies believed ad blocking would never become so mainstream as to affect their profits in a meaningful way. Privacy advocates claimed otherwise, but their prognostications were often ignored by industry as hyperbole. Today, there is wide agreement that ad blocking is a serious change to the ad ecosystem.

The original value proposition for corporate adoption of Do Not Track was to allow advertisers to segment their audience (this is the flip side of an argument for user choice.) Research finds that some people do not mind being tracked for ads, some people do not mind ads but mind the tracking that powers target ads, and some people do not like ads at all regardless of any privacy implications [53] [54]. Do Not Track was financially interesting because it could let advertisers show untargeted ads to users who only mind the *tracking* for targeted ads rather than mind ads themselves. Do Not Track could be an attractive alternative to losing all revenue when a user turns on ad blocking, particularly for economically valuable contextual ads based on a website's content or the user's current search terms.

Early participants in the Do Not Track work held different expectations about ad blocking. At that time, there was limited use of ad blocking and very limited Do Not Track adoption. In general, advertisers and publishers believed things would continue much as they were. They expected ad blocking to remain limited to a niche market. In part, this view stemmed from the technical acumen required to install ad blockers, which advertisers believed to be an insurmountable barrier for the majority of users. A competing view was that the future web was on a path for ad blockers to catch on in a big way. Privacy advocates saw ad blockers as a threat to existing business models, and also as nearly inevitable if businesses did not stop tracking users. Proponents saw Do Not Track as a way to preserve user privacy choices *and* preserve the ads for free content business model. This was also my personal view, influenced by working for Mozilla at the time.

When businesses do not believe there is change coming, debating the direction of that change is largely pointless. Even if there is belief in change, it is very difficult to convince many businesses to invest in transitioning to uncertain long-term growth when, in the short term, they are still making good money. As such, it was difficult to convince publishers and advertisers to take Do Not Track as seriously as they might have after the rise of ad blockers.

Since the early Do Not Track days, the adoption of ad blocking has increased to the point of threatening revenues and profitability for some publishers [55]. Perhaps the biggest eye opener was when Apple decided to support ad blockers on iOS, which changed the mobile ad landscape substantially in a single decision [56]. But in fairness to some of the companies predicting ad blocking would not affect them much, the "acceptable ads" programs from some ad blockers means some of the biggest advertisers are not blocked. Their ads display, and they continue to gather data, while the ad blockers collect payment for showing ads [57]. This is an interesting outcome, if perhaps not a very stable one.

As of this writing, Google has added selective ad blocking for the next version of Chrome, but will not block tracking [58]. Apple announced Safari will show ads but block tracking, in what is almost an inverse of Google's approach [59]. It will be interesting to see how the market reacts to these different approaches, especially since most users are unlikely to understand the nuances of these quite different approaches that are largely happening invisibly in the background.

What surprised me was the intensity with which companies and self-regulation groups responded. Having worked in software for a decade before taking up privacy, I knew Do Not Track would be unpopular with certain companies. By then Comcast and telecoms generally were well known for questionable tactics and lobbying. Software companies were not. After my experience with Do Not Track I would put software advertisers in the company of telecoms, tobacco companies, and oil and gas companies, willing and able to field sophisticated lobbying efforts.

Forum and Participation

There are many different technical standards bodies. Do Not Track could have proceeded in the IETF instead of the W3C. Had Do Not Track debuted a year later, it might have found a home as part of the Commerce Department's multi-stakeholder efforts [60]. Had any of five different bills passed into law, Do Not Track would have been defined by the Federal Trade Commission [38] [39] [40] [41] or by the California Attorney General's office [42].

W3C offered a few advantages. First, W3C already had worked out legal issues around cooperation and collusion. For example, if a group of companies banded together to impose data restrictions on third parties but largely exempt first parties in most other contexts, that could be anti-competitive and risk legal action. Second, W3C has processes in place for intellectual property issues. Not only does this diminish the chances of someone stealing an idea and profiting from it, but also W3C was able to respond effectively when a patent holder stepped forward to claim Do Not Track infringed on his holding [61].

Not all was rosy. Some industry self-regulation members felt that W3C was essentially encroaching on their turf. They claimed that their own opt-out program was sufficient; the FTC disagreed [62]. Even if self-regulation leaders had otherwise liked a Do Not Track approach from the W3C, that it came from the W3C and not their own groups could pose a problem.

Participation is a problem endemic to multi-stakeholder processes. For Do Not Track, W3C sought to involve participants with a wide range of backgrounds, perspectives, and economic incentives. Microsoft sent five working group members. Some of the privacy groups involved did not have five employees, total. Small companies were unlikely to learn they had the opportunity to join the working group. Large well-funded companies were better able to pay dues to join W3C, to pay to fly participants to far-flung locations, and to staff participation with skilled people over multiple years. W3C waived membership dues for the first year (or longer) in some cases to encourage participation, even by well-funded industry groups, but W3C was not able to address all of the barriers to participation by smaller groups. That necessarily tilts outcomes to be more favorable for large companies just based on who has the resources to be involved. The great part about multi-stakeholder processes is that in theory, everyone can have an equal seat at the table, but in practice, some are more equal than others.

Incorrect Starting Assumptions

Both the FTC and advertising industry groups made two very different miscalculations that made it harder to reach agreement on Do Not Track.

In the FTC's case, they called for Do Not Track to both limit collection and yet also have exceptions for data collection that supports specific uses such as security and billing. Assuming no major new engineering work, when the exceptions were all taken together in aggregate, there would be no limitations on data collection whatsoever. The FTC had reassured industry from the start that important business purposes would continue even for Do Not Track users, and reassured privacy advocates that data collection would reduce for Do Not Track users. This led to Do Not Track participants who believed they were already promised key, yet conflicting, attributes for what Do Not Track would be as a W3C standard, even before W3C became involved. One way to cut through the Gordian knot was to insist upon major software reengineering efforts to change how billing practices work, but of course industry participants were not at all interested in doing so and further believed they had FTC commitments that they would not have to do any such thing.

Meanwhile, advertisers incorrectly believed the rate of Do Not Track adoption would never exceed 5 percent. They based this estimate upon the rate at which users customize browser settings at all. Prior to joining Do Not Track standardization efforts, major businesses calculated that they could afford to lose a small percentage of users who might opt out, which made a voluntary technical standards body preferable to risking privacy legislation. When Mozilla announced a 17 percent adoption rate for Do Not Track, and companies could verify Do Not Track rates on their own web properties, in my opinion that was the end to any meaningful user privacy for a voluntary Do Not Track standard.

Microsoft's Chaos Monkey Moment

The early agreement within the W3C working group in 2011 was to have three options for Do Not Track:

- **dnt:1**, meaning "do not track me"
- **dnt:0**, meaning "tracking is fine"
- no setting at all

No setting at all was a practical necessity because some users would have older browsers without Do Not Track settings. The standard had to account for that common case. The working group compromise agreement was that when DNT is unset, in the United States it means users have not made an active choice for privacy and thus will still be tracked. Any other decision, industry members explained, would be too costly financially and make it impossible for them to adopt Do Not Track voluntarily. This was simply put and understood as a practical reality. However, due to European regulations around data privacy, in Europe no setting at all means that users had not consented to being tracked and therefore companies must not track these users. Simplified, US users would be tracked by default while EU users would not be tracked by default.

Furthermore, the working group also agreed that general purpose web browsers must send signals that are the user's choice. In other words, major web browsers could not set a default of dnt:1 or dnt:0 for all of their users. Specialized user agents with a privacy purpose (e.g., a browser plug-in) might reasonably send dnt:1 for all of their users, with the justification that users installed the plug-in specifically for privacy.

In 2012, Microsoft changed Internet Explorer to send dnt:1 for all users by default, which caused a spot of bother [63] [64]. Worse, this announcement came directly after AVG announced they would set Do Not Track in the registry for all new AVG Windows users. Unquestionably, these decisions wasted a great deal of time and left many people feeling stung. One of the editors for a Do Not Track document created a change to the Apache web server code to ignore Do Not Track signals from all Internet Explorer users, touching off new controversy [65]. It was a right fine mess.

However, despite all of the drama, it is my personal belief that Microsoft did not fundamentally change the Do Not Track landscape. As one advertiser put it, paraphrased from memory, "What is your profit margin? If your profit margin is smaller than the DNT adoption rate, then you must ignore all DNT signals or you will go out of business." For most advertisers, even prior to Microsoft's temporary change to Internet Explorer defaults, the Do Not Track adoption rate was already too high to accept. That left the options of either killing Do Not Track, which proved too difficult to accomplish [66], or attempting to create a standard weak enough on privacy as to be able to accept it at mass scale while still profiting. As privacy advocates saw Do Not Track became weaker on privacy, they were left with the options of either killing Do Not Track, which proved too difficult to accomplish [67], or attempting to strengthen the standard from the outside. Nothing Microsoft did with Internet Explorer defaults changed the underlying tension that Do Not Track adoption rates were too high for industry to voluntarily stop tracking users due to profitability concerns. The topic of browser defaults did get quite a bit of attention, though, and made for less collegial discussions.

Government Mass Surveillance

Recall that Edward Snowden was widely unknown when Do Not Track started. At Do Not Track's inception, it was not clear that the sort of corporate tracking Do Not Track might limit could also impinge upon mass government surveillance. For example, it was not yet public knowledge that Google's PREF advertising tracking cookies were also used by (at least) the US National Security Agency (NSA) and British Government Communications Headquarters (GCHQ) intelligence agencies [68]. Similarly, it was not understood that the NSA used Google's DoubleClick ad network cookies to unmask the IP addresses of Tor users [69] as well as used Google ads to make tracking sites more attractive [70]. If Do Not Track caught on widely, it could have curtailed then-secret state surveillance efforts that piggybacked on corporate tracking.

Law enforcement interests were not formally part of the W3C Do Not Track discussions. In public, Do Not Track was opposed strictly on commercial grounds, by corporations and their industry "self-regulation" groups. Legislative staff asked me if Do Not Track would hinder Google's flu trends project, which surprised me as a question. Flu trends was a big data project that contrasted the set of Google users' searches for flu-related terms in a given city to a set of government health records for actual flu rates [71]. Data mining Google users' search terms raised privacy concerns [72]. Further, as privacy experts and journalists noted, data mining of users' search terms is easily expanded to domains beyond the flu. "You can imagine any number of different scenarios," pointed out EPIC's Marc Rotenberg [73]. At the time that legislative assistants mentioned Google flu trends to me as a reason to back away from reintroducing legislation for Do Not Track, it seemed a baffling non sequitur. Surely flu trends would work as well with the large sample of users who would not take action to enable Do Not Track. For that matter, the flu trends project sounded as if the project could be designed to work for Do Not Track users, too. Years later with more information than I offer here, the flu trends objection may (or may not) have been tied to a national security wish to keep corporate data available for state surveillance programs. Post-Snowden, it now takes little imagination to envision describing Do Not Track as an approach that could hinder antiterrorism efforts. As with many related national security topics, the full history may never be made public.

4. CONCLUSION

Do Not Track is the Energizer Bunny of web standards: first imagined in 2007, a decade later it is still going, and going, and going. Advertisers have ignored millions of users' Do Not Track signals over the past five years. My early concern was that Do Not Track would inherently be a deceptive practice, since despite a catchy name it seemed unlikely to actually stop tracking. Further, user trust has been so abused over the years that another privacy tool that failed to live up to the hype might result in a level of cynicism that precludes the sort of cooperative attempt Do Not Track was hoped to be, leaving users nothing but the arms race of blocking all ads as best they can. That may well be the end point not through the result of Do Not Track being too far away from user expectations, but rather from the delays to have a Do Not Track result at all.

Do Not Track will very likely emerge as a solid technical standard from W3C, paired with a multiplicity of implementations for users to attempt to navigate. There is a Do Not Track version from EFF, plus multiple custom one-off implementations, plus every now and then DAA promises to release their own version. Most significantly, it currently appears likely that Do Not Track will be legally required in Europe. The meaning of Do Not Track for European Internet users would therefore be based upon EU privacy and consent laws.

When I started authoring this chapter there was a serious chance Do Not Track would die in W3C committee after four years of work, which is safe to call a failure. Now it appears not only will Do Not Track emerge as a W3C standard, but it may well become part of a legal requirement to protect the privacy of 400 million European Internet users. It is premature to call anything over, let alone a success: many more twists are likely to occur before the Do Not Track story reaches a stable ending.

Most remarkable is that ten years on, there are still no better options available for privacy choices online. When Do Not Track was first envisioned in 2007, people had flip phones and bluetooth Jawbone headsets with iPhones and Android phones first released that year [74]; MySpace was the most popular website [75]; the most popular web browser was Microsoft Internet Explorer 6.0 and browsers did not auto-update to new versions [76]. And yet, quite a few familiar things were already well established: the *New York Times* online was over a decade old [77] as were HTTP cookies [78]. The European General Data Protection Directive hails from 1995 [79]. It was updated by the General Data Protection Regulation in 2016, and will not be enforced until 2018 [80]. The United States still has no comprehensive privacy legislation. These are a few highlights of how technological and policy protections lag behind innovations in privacy erosion, which is not a new observation.

Do Not Track has not been a sprint, not a marathon, but a relay race. It started in the hands of seasoned privacy advocates, was refined by more technical advocates, picked up and championed by the Federal Trade Commission, bounced through the halls of the US House and Senate as well as the California legislature, dropped into at least three different phases of work in five years within the W3C standards body, and now appears poised to exit W3C, into the waiting hands of the Article 29 Working Party and European policy makers.

While the idea of moving from a voluntary technical standard to a legal mandate is not entirely comfortable, I have hope for incremental improvements in European online privacy. As for the United States, as my former cochair once memorably put it, "tough luck."

5. ACKNOWLEDGMENTS

If it takes a village, I remain a simple villager [81]. Do not track introduced me to some of the most amazing people I have had the privilege to meet. Thank you to everyone inside the W3C working group, as well as many more people not part of the group. It was quite an adventure, wasn't it?

This chapter benefited greatly from the extended patience of, and suggestions from, the book editors, particularly Wendy Nardi. Thanks to R. W. and A. C. for comments with eyes fresh to the entire situation. A particular thank you to editor Evan Selinger for extraordinary kindness as well as good council. All opinions are my own.

6. BIBLIOGRAPHY

[1] *Federal Trade Commission Act*, 1914.
[2] T. Muris, "Protecting Consumers' Privacy: Goals and Accomplishments," *Federal Trade Commission*, 11 June 2002. [Online]. Available: https://www.ftc.gov/public-statements/2002/06/protecting-consumers-privacy-goals-and-accomplishments.

[3] P. Gralla, "Targeted Advertising Cookie Opt-Out (TACO)," *PC World*, 31 March 2009. Available: https://www.pcworld.com/article/232732/targeted_advertising_cookie_optout_taco.html.

[4] "Webchoices: Digital Advertising Alliance's Consumer Choice Tool for Web (Beta)," *Digital Advertising Alliance*. [Online]. Available: http://optout.aboutads.info.

[5] "Advertising Option Icon Application," *Digital Advertising Alliance*. [Online]. Available: https://www.aboutads.info/participants/icon/.

[6] S. Clifford, "A Little 'i' to Teach about Online Privacy," *The New York Times*, 26 January 2010.

[7] "Data Protection Reform: Parliament Approves New Rules Fit for the Digital Era," *European Parliament*, 14 April 2016. [Online]. Available: http://www.europarl.europa.eu/news/en/news-room/20160407IPR21776/Data-protection-reform-Parliament-approves-new-rules-fit-for-the-digital-era.

[8] Official Journal of the European Union, "Regulation (EU) 2016/679 of the European Parliament and of the Council," *European Parliament*, 4 May 2016. [Online]. Available: http://eur-lex.europa.eu/legal-content/EN/TXT/HTML/?uri=OJ:L:2016:119:FULL&from=EN.

[9] "The Origins of Do Not Track, and Its Future," *World Privacy Forum*, 17 June 2013. [Online]. Available: https://www.worldprivacyforum.org/2013/06/the-origins-of-do-not-track-and-its-future/.

[10] A. Schwartz, L. Sherry, C. Cooper, L. Tien, D. Pierce, D. Brandt, R. E. Smith, B. Givens, and P. Dixon, "Consumer Rights and Protections in the Behavioral Advertising Sector," *World Privacy Forum*, October 2007. [Online]. Available: http://www.worldprivacyforum.org/wp-content/uploads/2008/04/ConsumerProtections_FTC_ConsensusDoc_Final_s.pdf.

[11] C. Rampell, "'Do Not Track' Registry Proposed for Web Use," *Washington Post*, 1 November 2007.

[12] Preliminary staff report, "Protecting Consumer Privacy in an Era of Rapid Change: A Proposed Framework for Businesses and Policymakers," *Federal Trade Commision*, December 2010. [Online]. Available: https://www.ftc.gov/sites/default/files/documents/reports/federal-trade-commission-bureau-consumer-protection-preliminary-ftc-staff-report-protecting-consumer/101201privacyreport.pdf.

[13] "The DAA Self-Regulatory Principles," *Digital Advertising Alliance* [Online]. Available: http://www.aboutads.info/principles.

[14] C. Hoofnagle, "A Do-Not-Track Dilemma: DNT ~= Do Not Advertise," *Technology, Academics, Policy*, 10 February 2011. [Online]. Available: http://www.techpolicy.com/Hoofnagle-ADoNotTrackDilemma.aspx.

[15] J. Jones, "'Do Not Track' Means 'Do Not Collect,' FTC Advises," *Response Magazine*, 7 March 2012. Available: http://www.responsemagazine.com/direct-response-marketing/news/do-not-track-means-do-not-collect-ftc-advises-4255.

[16] S. Harvey and R. Moonka, "Keep Your Opt-Outs," *Google Public Policy Blog*, 24 January 2011. [Online]. Available: https://publicpolicy.googleblog.com/2011/01/keep-your-opt-outs.html.

[17] J. Kirk, "Browser Add-On Locks Out Targeted Advertising," *PC World*, 17 March 2009. Available: https://www.pcworld.com/article/161380/article.html.

[18] S. Gilbertson, "Google Chrome Adds 'Do Not Track' Privacy Tools," *Wired*, 7 November 2012. Available: https://www.wired.com/2012/11/chrome-23-skidoos-out-of-beta/.

[19] J. Chokkattu, "Google Chrome for IOS Loses 'Do Not Track' Feature," *Digital Trends*, 29 January 2016. Available: https://www.digitaltrends.com/mobile/chrome-do-not-track-ios/.

[20] E. Bott, "IE9 and Tracking Protection: Microsoft Disrupts the Online Ad Business," *ZDNet*, 13 February 2011. Available: http://www.zdnet.com/article/ie9-and-tracking-protection-microsoft-disrupts-the-online-ad-business/.

[21] World Wide Web Consortium, "Platform for Privacy Preferences (P3P) Project," 20 November 2007. [Online]. Available: https://www.w3.org/P3P/.

[22] World Wide Web Consortium, "Platform for Internet Content Selection (PICS)," 20 November 2009. [Online]. Available: https://www.w3.org/PICS/.

[23] E. Bott, "Privacy Protection and IE9: Who Can You Trust?," *ZDNet*, 11 February 2011. Available: http://www.zdnet.com/article/privacy-protection-and-ie9-who-can-you-trust/.

[24] N. Wingfield, "Microsoft Quashed Effort to Boost Online Privacy," *The Wall Street Journal*, 2 August 2010. Available: https://www.wsj.com/articles/SB10001424052748703467304575383530439838568.

[25] M. Hachman, "The Hidden Feature That Means Microsoft Has Already Won the 'Do Not Track' War," *ReadWrite*, 5 October 2012. Available: https://readwrite.com/2012/10/05/why-microsoft-has-already-won-the-do-not-track-war/.

[26] P. Eckersley, "Tracking Protection Lists: A Privacy Enhancing Technology That Complements Do Not Track," 16 March 2011. [Online]. Available: https://www.eff.org/deeplinks/2011/03/tracking-protection-lists.

[27] "History for Bug 628197," *Mozilla*, 23 January 2011. [Online]. Available: https://bugzilla.mozilla.org/show_activity.cgi?id=628197.

[28] S. Stamm, "Opting Out of Behavioral Ads," 23 January 2011. [Online]. Available: http://blog.sidstamm.com/2011/01/opting-out-of-behavioral-ads.html.

[29] "History for Bug 628198," *Mozilla*, 23 January 2011. [Online]. Available: https://bugzilla.mozilla.org/show_activity.cgi?id=628198.

[30] Mayer, Narayanan and S. Stamm, "Do Not Track: A Universal Third-Party Web Tracking Opt Out," Network Working Group Internet: Draft, 7 March 2011. [Online]. Available: https://www.ietf.org/archive/id/draft-mayer-do-not-track-00.txt.

[31] "Do Not Track Universal Web Tracking Opt Out," *DoNotTrack.Us* [Online]. Available: http://donottrack.us.

[32] World Wide Web Consortium, "Index of /2011/track-privacy/papers," March 2011. [Online]. Available: https://www.w3.org/2011/track-privacy/papers/.

[33] World Wide Web Consortium, "W3C Workshop on Web Tracking and User Privacy: Call for Participation," March 2011. [Online]. Available: https://www.w3.org/2011/track-privacy/.

[34] World Wide Web Consortium, "W3C Workshop on Web Tracking and User Privacy: Workshop Report," March 2011. [Online]. Available: https://www.w3.org/2011/track-privacy/report.html.

[35] A. Zeigler, A. Bateman, and E. Graff, "Web Tracking Protection," 24 February 2011. [Online]. Available: https://www.w3.org/Submission/web-tracking-protection/.

[36] World Wide Web Consortium, "Tracking Protection Working Group Charter," 2011. [Online]. Available: https://www.w3.org/2011/tracking-protection/charter.html.

[37] "AVG 2012," *Should I Remove It*. [Online]. Available: http://www.shouldiremoveit.com/AVG-2012-5825-program.aspx.

[38] J. F. Sen. Kerry, *S.799: Commercial Privacy Bill of Rights Act of 2011*, 2011.

[39] J. D. I. Sen. Rockefeller, *S.913: Do-Not-Track Online Act of 2011*, 2011.

[40] E. J. Rep. Markey, *H.R.1895: Do Not Track Kids Act of 2011*, 2011.

[41] J. Rep. Speier, *H.R.654: Do Not Track Me Online Act*, 2011.

[42] A. Sen. Lowenthal, *S.B. 761: An Act to Add Section 22947.45 to the Business and Professions Code, Relating to Business*, 2011.

[43] Office of the Attorney General, Xavier Becerra, "Attorney General Kamala D. Harris Issues Guide on Privacy Policies and Do Not Track Disclosures," *State of California Department of Justice*, 21 May 2014. [Online]. Available: https://oag.ca.gov/news/press-releases/attorney-general-kamala-d-harris-issues-guide-privacy-policies-and-do-not-track.

[44] F. J. Zuiderveen Borgesius and A. M. McDonald, "Do Not Track for Europe," in *43rd Research Conference on Communication, Information and Internet Policy (Telecommunications Policy Research Conference)*, 2015.

[45] World Wide Web Consortium, "Tracking Protection Working Group," 2011. [Online]. Available: https://www.w3.org/2011/tracking-protection/.

[46] E. Felten, "Privacy by Design: Frequency Capping," *Federal Trade Commission*, 3 July 2012. [Online]. Available: https://www.ftc.gov/news-events/blogs/techftc/2012/07/privacy-design-frequency-capping.

[47] "Welcome to the WHATWG Community," *WhatWG*. Available: https://whatwg.org.

[48] G. Gross, "Some Privacy Advocates Question Mobile Apps Agreement," *Network World*, 26 July 2013. Available: https://www.networkworld.com/article/2168530/mobile-apps/some-privacy-advocates-question-mobile-apps-agreement.html.

[49] A. M. McDonald and J. M. Peha, "Track Gap: Policy Implications of User Expectations for the 'Do Not Track' Internet Privacy Feature," in *39th Research Conference on Communication, Information and Internet Policy (Telecommunications Policy Research Conference)*, 2011.

[50] S. M. Wiley, "Re: What Additional Optional Information Is ESSENTIAL in Europe to Document a Informed That Has Been Given?," 28 March 2017. [Online]. Available: https://lists.w3.org/Archives/Public/public-tracking/2017Mar/0035.html.

[51] M. Lauristin, "Draft Report on the Proposal for a Regulation of the European Parliament and of the Council Concerning the Respect for Private Life and the Protection of Personal Data in Electronic

Communications and repealing Directive 2002/5 8/EC (Regulation on Privacy and Electronic Communications)," *European Parliament*, 9 June 2017. [Online]. Available: http://www.europarl.europa.eu/sides/getDoc.do?type=COMPARL&reference=PE-606.011&format=PDF&language=EN&secondRef=01.

[52] F. Zuiderveen Borgesius, J. Van Hoboken, R. Fahy, K. Irion, and M. Rozendaal, "An Assessment of the Commission's Proposal on Privacy and Electronic Communications: Study for the LIBE Committee," *European Parliament*, May 2017. [Online]. Available: http://www.europarl.europa.eu/RegData/etudes/STUD/2017/583152/IPOL_STU(2017)583152_EN.pdf.

[53] A. M. McDonald and L. F. Cranor, "Beliefs and Behaviors: Internet Users' Understanding of Behavioral Advertising," in *38th Research Conference on Communication, Information and Internet Policy (Telecommunications Policy Research Conference)*, 2010.

[54] J. Turow, J. King, C. J. Hoofnagle, A. Bleakley, and M. Hennessy, "Americans Reject Tailored Advertising and Three Activities That Enable It," 2009. Available: https://papers.ssrn.com/sol3/papers.cfm?abstract_id=1478214.

[55] M. Scott, "Rise of Ad-Blocking Software Threatens Online Revenue," *The New York Times*, 30 May 2016. Available: https://www.nytimes.com/2016/05/31/business/international/smartphone-ad-blocking-software-mobile.html.

[56] P. Elmer-DeWitt, "Let the iOS 9 Ad Block Wars Begin!," *Fortune*, 19 September 2015. Available: http://fortune.com/2015/09/20/apple-ad-block-ios9/.

[57] M. Geuss, "Over 300 Businesses Now Whitelisted on AdBlock Plus, 10% Pay to Play," *Ars Technica*, 3 February 2015. Available: https://arstechnica.com/information-technology/2015/02/over-300-businesses-now-whitelisted-on-adblock-plus-10-pay-to-play/.

[58] D. Dayen, "Be Careful Celebrating Google's New Ad Blocker: Here's What's Really Going On," *The Intercept*, 5 June 2017. Available: https://theintercept.com/2017/06/05/be-careful-celebrating-googles-new-ad-blocker-heres-whats-really-going-on/.

[59] J. Wilander, "Intelligent Tracking Prevention," *Apple, Inc.*, 5 June 2017. [Online]. Available: https://webkit.org/blog/7675/intelligent-tracking-prevention/.

[60] National Telecommunications & Information Agency, "Multistakeholder Process to Develop Consumer Data Privacy Codes of Conduct," 29 February 2012. Available: https://www.ntia.doc.gov/federal-register-notice/2012/multistakeholder-meetings-develop-consumer-data-privacy-code-conduct-co.

[61] N. Doty, "Tracking Preference Expression Patent Advisory Group Charter (DNT PAG)," 3 April 2015. [Online]. Available: https://www.w3.org/2012/06/dnt-pag-charter.html.

[62] K. Bachman, "FTC Chair Stuns Advertisers," *AdWeek*, 17 April 2013. Available: http://www.adweek.com/digital/ftc-chair-stuns-advertisers-148644/.

[63] E. Bott, "Microsoft Sticks to Default Do Not Track Settings in IE 10," *ZDNet*, 7 August 2012. Available: http://www.zdnet.com/article/microsoft-sticks-to-default-do-not-track-settings-in-ie-10/.

[64] G. Keizer, "Yahoo to Ignore Microsoft's 'Do Not Track' Signal from IE10," *Computer World*, 29 October 2012. Available: https://www.computerworld.com/article/2493048/data-privacy/yahoo-to-ignore-microsoft-s–do-not-track–signal-from-ie10.html.

[65] K. Noyes, "Apache Web Servers Will Ignore IE10's 'Do Not Track' Settings," *PC World*, 11 September 2012. Available: http://www.pcworld.com/article/262150/apache_web_servers_will_ignore_ie10s_do_not_track_settings.html.

[66] E. Bott, "Major Advertising Group Quits Do Not Track Standards Body," *ZDNet*, 17 September 2013. Available: http://www.zdnet.com/article/major-advertising-group-quits-do-not-track-standards-body/.

[67] J. Aquino, "Jonathan Mayer to 'Do Not Track' Working Group: I Quit," 31 July 2013. Available: http://www.businessinsider.com/jonathan-mayer-quits-do-not-track-standardization-group-2013-7?op=1

[68] A. Soltani, A. Peterson, and B. Gellman, "NSA Uses Google Cookies to Pinpoint Targets for Hacking," *The Washington Post*, 10 December 2013. Available: https://www.washingtonpost.com/news/the-switch/wp/2013/12/10/nsa-uses-google-cookies-to-pinpoint-targets-for-hacking/.

[69] "'Tor Stinks' Presentation: Read the Full Document," *The Guardian*, 4 October 2013. [Online]. Available: https://www.theguardian.com/world/interactive/2013/oct/04/tor-stinks-nsa-presentation-document.

[70] P. Paganini, "How NSA Tries to Compromise Tor Anonymity: Tor Stinks Document," *Security Affairs*, 6 October 2013.

[71] J. Ginsberg, M. Mohebbi, R. S. Patel, and L. Brilliant, "Detecting Influenza Epidemics Using Search Engine Query Data," *Nature*, pp. 1012–4, December 2008.

[72] C. Matyszczyk, "Sick? Google Shares Health Searches with Govt.," *C|net*, 12 November 2008. Available: https://www.cnet.com/news/sick-google-shares-health-searches-with-govt/.

[73] C. Metz, "When You Sneeze, Does Google Tell the Feds?," *The Register*, 15 November 2008. Available: http://www.theregister.co.uk/2008/11/15/google_flu_trends_privacy/.

[74] "17 Weird Things You Did on the Internet in 2007 That You Forgot All About," *BuzzFeed*, 20 January 2017. Available: https://www.buzzfeed.com/geico/2007-internet.

[75] D. Kirkpatrick, "As Facebook Takes Off, MySpace Strikes Back," *Fortune*, 19 September 2007. Available: http://archive.fortune.com/2007/09/18/technology/myspace_strikes.fortune/index.htm.

[76] R. MacManus, "Browser Market Share: Maxthon May Stop Firefox's Slow Climb," *ReadWrite*, 17 January 2007. Available: https://readwrite.com/2007/01/17/browser_market_share_maxthon_vs_firefox/.

[77] "Our History," *The New York Times*, 2017. [Online]. Available: http://www.nytco.com/who-we-are/culture/our-history/.

[78] D. Kristol, "HTTP State Management Mechanism," memo, Network Working Group, February 1997. [Online]. Available: https://tools.ietf.org/html/rfc2109.

[79] European Parliament and the Council, "Directive 95/46/EC of the European Parliament and of the Council of 24 October 1995 on the Protection of Individuals with regard to the Processing of Personal Data and on the Free Movement of Such Data," 24 October 1995. [Online]. Available: http://data.europa.eu/eli/dir/1995/46/oj.

[80] European Parliament and the Council, "Regulation (EU) 2016/679 of the European Parliament and of the Council of 27 April 2016: On the Protection of Natural Persons with Regard to the Processing of Personal Data and on the Free Movement of Such Data, and Repealing Directive 95/46/EC (General Data Protection Regulation)," 7 April 2016. [Online]. Available: http://data.europa.eu/eli/reg/2016/679/oj.

[81] A. ". Plotkin, "Werewolf," online game, 14 February 2010. [Online]. Available: http://www.eblong.com/zarf/werewolf.html.

[82] B. Fung, "The FTC Was Built 100 Years Ago to Fight Monopolists: Now, It's Washington's Most Powerful Technology Cop," *The Washington Post*, 25 September 2014. Available: https://www.washingtonpost.com/news/the-switch/wp/2014/09/25/the-ftc-was-built-100-years-ago-to-fight-monopolists-now-its-washingtons-most-powerful-technology-cop/.

[83] "Open Secrets," *Center for Responsive Politics*, 2016, [Online]. Available: http://www.opensecrets.org.

[84] "DAA's Self-Regulatory Program for Online Behavioral Advertising Frequently Asked Questions," *Digital Advertising Alliance*, August 2011. [Online]. Available: http://www.aboutads.info/resource/download/DAA-Website-FAQ.pdf.

[85] T. Sottek, "The 265 Members of Congress Who Sold You Out to ISPs, and How Much It Cost to Buy Them," *The Verge*, 29 March 2017. Available: https://www.theverge.com/2017/3/29/15100620/congress-fcc-isp-web-browsing-privacy-fire-sale.

16

Applying Ethics When Using Data beyond Individuals' Understanding

Martin E. Abrams and Lynn A. Goldstein

THE BIG BANG

The big bang in digitally based decision making requires data users to determine whether what one is doing with data is right or wrong. That is ethics.

Most organizations make use of data to forecast the future in an ever-accelerating manner. Much of that data pertains directly to individuals, and many of those forecasts will have a direct impact on individuals. Furthermore, those actions based on data will have an impact on society as a whole.

Using data to forecast the future is not new. Actuarial tables have been used by insurance companies for centuries. Actuaries used data from the past, and data about a particular person was used to predict when he or she would likely die. The data used to build the tables was limited but was better at planning risk than no predictions at all. Those early predictions were limited because all the inputs – data, methodology, and computing power – were limited.

The first use of broad data sets to predict individual behavior over large populations was the adoption of credit scoring in the 1980s. This use followed the computerization of credit files in the 1960s and 1970s. The first credit scores made use of historic data to predict the likelihood of an individual with a particular credit history going bankrupt over a five-year period. Credit scores revolutionized consumer lending to the point that the World Bank encouraged credit reporting as a necessary infrastructure for economic development.[1]

However, scoring requires mountains of objective data that is observed rather than self-reported. The introduction of the first Internet browser in 1993 sparked the growth of this objective data. Individuals' interactions with websites, as well as the websites they visited, created mountains of observed data. This data could then be processed to predict the advertisement that would most likely spark the interest of the individual. At the same time as observed data was accelerating, computer and communications technologies were getting faster and less expensive. This convergence sparked the digitalization of almost everything, from the items purchased at the grocery store to every heartbeat in a hospital. This development continues today, when technology has resulted in our sensor-based society, where everything from the tires on our cars to the toothbrushes in our mouths has the ability to record and share observed data.[2]

---

[1] Martin Abrams, "The Origins of Personal Data and Its Implications for Governance," OECD *Expert Roundtable Discussion*, 21 March 2014 [hereinafter Origins of Personal Data].

[2] *Id*. Examples of observed data are facial images from CCTV, WIFI readers in buildings that establish location, time paused in a pixel on the screen of a tablet, and data from sensor technology.

The last piece of the puzzle is methodology. A decade ago, computer scientists figured out how to use unstructured data in analytic processes. In the past, data had to be in indexed fields, meaning only like data could be processed together in order to be analyzed. With the new methodologies, diverse data sets could be processed together, creating the infrastructure for big data analysis. This evolution moved analytics beyond statistical orthodoxy, based on limited data sets and the testing of a predetermined hypothesis, to letting data correlations drive the questions the data would address.[3]

This growth means data and analytics may be used to improve education, prolong lives, build economies, and enhance opportunities. It also means data may be used to move stale inventories and predict what credit card you will want, when you will want it, and when you are vulnerable to a seller's siren song. Lastly, data may predict who is a sucker and how to defraud the elderly.

LIMITS OF CONSENT AND THE NEED FOR ASSESSMENTS

Legacy privacy systems established consent as the best means for assuring individuals have primacy over their data. This made sense when privacy law was theorized in the 1960s and first established in the 1970s in Germany and Sweden. Data came primarily from the individual, and a purpose specification notice could easily be provided to the individual. However, the US Fair Credit Reporting Act (FCRA)[4] was enacted in 1970 as a fair processing statute. It was the FCRA that established the basis for credit scoring, along with consumer protection laws that protected against age, gender, and race discrimination.

The 1980 OECD Guidelines on the Protection of Privacy and Transborder Flows of Personal Data (OECD Privacy Guidelines) established that consent alone was not enough, that data needed to be processed in a fair manner, and that the organization is accountable for doing so. The OECD Privacy Guidelines established consent and accountability as clear pillars for the law, with accountability assuring fair processing. The 1995 European Union (EU) Data Protection Directive[5] established six legal bases for processing data, reinforcing the concept of fair processing. While consent might be the primary means of establishing a legal basis for processing, there were five others that have been carried forth to the General Data Protection Regulation[6] enacted in 2016.

The Article 29 Data Protection Working Party, established by the EU Directive, published an opinion on the use of legitimate interests as a legal basis to process.[7] The Legitimate Interests Opinion first establishes the difference, in European law, between privacy, which equates to autonomy assured by consent, and data protection, which assures the full range of fundamental rights including privacy, when processing data. The use of legitimate interests requires an assessment of the balance between the value created for the organization and the risks to fundamental rights and freedoms of the individual.

The Canadian private sector privacy law, the Personal Information Protection and Electronic Documents Act (PIPEDA),[8] modeled after the OECD Privacy Guidelines, also has consent and

---

[3] *Id.*

[4] 15 U.S.C. § 1681 [hereinafter FCRA].

[5] Directive 95/46/EC of the European Parliament and of the Council of 24 October 1995 on the protection of individuals with regard to the processing of personal data and on the free movement of such data [hereinafter EU Directive].

[6] Regulation (EU) 2016/679 [hereinafter GDPR].

[7] Opinion 06/2014 on the notion of legitimate interests of the data controller under Article 7 of Directive 95/46/EC, 844/14/EN, WP 217, adopted on 9 April 2014 [hereinafter Legitimate Interests Opinion].

[8] S.C. 2000, c. 5.

accountability as the foundations for privacy protection. While consent is the primary ground, part of accountability is the assurance that processing is reasonable and responsible, suggesting that an assessment process is necessary when processing is complex.

US privacy norms, beyond sector-specific laws such as the FCRA, are built on concepts of deception and unfairness. As data use gets more complex, as sensor-rich technologies generate more and more observed data, it gets much more difficult to drive internal data use purely based on a consumer decision driven by a lengthy privacy notice. The Obama Administration's proposed Consumer Privacy Bill of Rights Act[9] and the Federal Trade Commission's report on protecting consumer privacy[10] recommend businesses have privacy by design processes that assure data is used in context. This means that privacy by design should include assessment processes.

LEGAL, FAIR, AND JUST

Accountability as a principle was first established by the OECD Privacy Guidelines. It has since explicitly been adopted in the legal regimes of Canada, Mexico, Colombia, and the new GDPR. The essential elements of accountability were defined by a multi-stakeholder process in 2009 that published the essential elements of accountability.[11] The second essential element covers the mechanisms to put privacy policies in place, including risk assessments.[12] The new GDPR requires data protection impact assessments when privacy by design processes indicate that a processing will create a high degree of risk for individuals.[13] The GDPR's provision on legitimate interests requires an assessment when used to permit a processing.[14]

An assessment must establish that the use of data is in context, creates value for stakeholders that out balances risks to individuals, and does not create inappropriate discriminatory effects. This might be characterized as requiring an assessment process to determine that a processing of data is legal, fair, and just and then stand ready to demonstrate how that determination was reached.

The assessment of what is legal, fair, and just increasingly becomes an interpretation against societal norms, and that is ethics.

THINKING WITH DATA, ACTING WITH DATA

The first computerized business systems were designed to conduct data-intensive processes such as billing and payroll. Data was used to facilitate legacy processes.[15] That is acting with data.

Most consumer credit took place at stores. A consumer would apply for credit, a credit report would be requested, and a credit clerk would input the data into a scorecard, which would yield a credit decision. The scoring algorithm was based on the best judgment of the credit manager.[16] The application of the credit score is still acting with data. The predictive credit score was developed in the 1980s when statisticians began to test the hypothesis developed by the credit

---

[9] Administration's Discussion Draft: Consumer Privacy Bill of Rights Act of 2015 (Feb. 27, 2015).

[10] Federal Trade Commission, "Protecting Consumer Privacy in an Era of Rapid Change: Recommendations for Businesses and Policymakers (Mar. 26, 2012).

[11] Information Accountability Foundation, The Essential Elements of Accountability.

[12] *Id.*

[13] GDPR Article 35.

[14] GDPR Article 6.

[15] Origins of Personal Data.

[16] *Id.*

managers. Using historic files, statisticians used five-year-old credit data (historic data) to predict bankruptcies over the next five years (current data).[17] We believe the development of the predictive credit score was the first instance of thinking with consumer data.

Thinking with data uses old outcomes to predict a future state. Thinking with data has a risk profile, that is significant, but is very different than acting with data. Those risks are less to the individuals to whom the data pertains, and more to the future individuals to whom it is implied. It is with this thinking with data, and the transition to acting with data, that we see the real ethical issues.

What Do We Mean by Ethics?

Today there is a renewed discussion of what is meant by ethics. Ethics was used to drive the first adoption of privacy laws in the 1970s. One could argue the 1890 *Harvard Law Review* article "The Right to Privacy," by Louis Brandeis and Samuel Warren, established that privacy was necessary to assure dignity.[18] When Alan Westin published "Privacy and Freedom" in 1967,[19] it was this concept of dignity that needed to be protected as electronic computers began to process data that pertained to people. Westin was picking up on 18th-century German philosopher Immanuel Kant's argument that autonomy is the highest level of dignity. Consent is therefore the sole means for assuring autonomy and therefore dignity. By extension, numerous data protection authorities believe that the ethic dignity through autonomy is the sole ethic governing data protection.

However, ethics is also a basis for fair processing. This foundation can be seen in the fundamental rights treaties that were developed, in part, because of the horrors of World War II. The fundamental rights treaties include much more than privacy, reaching into fields such as education, healthcare, employment, and technology, namely sharing in the benefits. In other words, the fair processing of data should enhance dignity through data-driven innovations that improve the lives of individuals. This articulation would suggest that the "golden rule" ethic, do unto others as you would have them do unto you, has standing as well. This ethic would suggest processors would look both at the context of their agreement with individuals as well as at the value they are creating for individuals when determining if a processing is appropriate.

The EU Directive and the new GDPR establish data protection as a means for assuring the full range of fundamental rights when processing data. This establishment argues for ethics that go beyond autonomy. Giovanni Buttarelli, European Data Protection Supervisor (EDPS), issued an opinion September 11, 2015 entitled "Towards a New Digital Ethics: Data, Dignity and Technology."[20] In the EDPS Opinion, Buttarelli stated "that data should serve people, people should not serve data," in setting out the prerequisite for dignity in a data-driven era.[21] Buttarelli's views would suggest that ethics proportionally balance autonomy and the "golden rule" is the basis for ethical analysis.[22]

---

[17] *Id.*

[18] 4 HARVARD L. REV. 193 (Dec. 15, 1890).

[19] ALAN F. WESTIN, PRIVACY AND FREEDOM (The Bodley Head Ltd. 1970).

[20] European Data Protection Supervisor, "Towards a New Digital Ethics: Data, Dignity and Technology," Opinion 4/ 2015, September 11, 2015 [hereinafter EDPS Opinion].

[21] *Id.*

[22] The EDPS established an Ethics Advisory Board in January 2016. That Board will issue guidance in 2017.

IAF History with Ethical Assessments

At the end of 2013, the Information Accountability Foundation (IAF) was challenged to develop a process for assessing whether big data projects were appropriate. The companies that made the challenge were companies that had very successful privacy impact assessments but felt those assessments were missing the emerging issues related to big data. In order to respond to the challenge, a brainstorming team was created. The key issue that emerged from the brainstorming was that big data touches many stakeholders and that these stakeholders had conflicting ethical frames. The intersection of these ethical frames was the spot where data serves people, rather than people serving data. The result of that brainstorming is the Unified Ethical Frame (UEF).[23]

Development of the UEF began with European concepts that data protection assures the full range of fundamental rights and freedom. It is fundamental to the UEF that ethical processing should facilitate those rights, not abridge them.

However, criteria are needed in order to measure. Since data protection is broader than privacy, criteria are needed that go beyond privacy. The brainstorming team adopted five values for assessment. Those values, which are described more completely in a later section, are:

- Beneficial
- Progressive
- Sustainable
- Respectful
- Fair

The product of the assessment is a set of questions that guides decision makers and documentation to facilitate oversight.

To be effective, the UEF needed to be translated into tools organizations could use to conduct actual assessments. The first experimental tool was developed in 2015 with questions based on the five values listed here. That initial "strawman" tool was then customized for digital marketing through a multi-stakeholder process. As part of that process, IAF learned the assessment tool works best if it follows normal business process, with the values integrated throughout the questionnaire. This shortened the questionnaire, because some questions reference more than one value.

The IAF has since customized the assessment process yet again for big data processing that would comply with Canada's private sector privacy law, the Personal Information Privacy and Electronic Documents Act. Working with approximately twenty Canadian organizations or Canadian offices of multinational companies and Access Privacy, the Osler Hoskins Harcourt LLP privacy and data management consulting service, the IAF customized the assessment document created by IAF for Canadian law. This draft document was then finalized in a multi-stakeholder session, which was funded by a grant from the Office of the Privacy Commissioner of Canada. That multi-stakeholder session was held in December 2016.

The section that follows is taken from the preamble for that assessment. The final report for the Canadian project was posted to the IAF website in March 2017, where the assessment questionnaire as well as the preamble is accessible. The draft that follows was current as of September 20, 2016.

---

[23] The UEF was reviewed in a plenary session at the International Conference of Data Protection and Privacy Commissioners in Mauritius in October 2016.

A CUSTOMIZED ETHICAL ASSESSMENT

Introduction

Organizations need to engage in advanced analytics to be successful today, and to do so, they need to be able to determine that their big data analytics are legal, fair, and just. The purpose of this document is to introduce an assessment process that helps an organization determine whether its big data[24] activities are legal, fair, and just and demonstrate how that determination was reached.

Big data is critical to innovation, and innovation is critical to a healthy, sustainable economy. The Commissioner of Competition, Innovation and Infrastructure recently remarked that "strong competition drives innovation, which in turn drives productivity, efficiency and economic growth" and that "the collection, analysis and use of data is increasingly becoming an important source of competitive advantage, driving innovation and product improvement."[25] For "consumers, innovation brings more choices and higher quality products and services in a dynamic marketplace."[26]

The PIPEDA sets out a helpful framework for a healthy, sustainable economy derived from big data analytics.[27] PIPEDA is technology and sector neutral. By recognizing both the right of privacy of individuals with respect to their personal information and the need of organizations to collect, use or disclose personal information for purposes that a reasonable person would consider appropriate in the circumstances, PIPEDA balances the interests of individuals and organizations.[28] PIPEDA requires accountability, specifying that organizations must be responsible for the personal information under their control.[29] However, big data analytics can create accountability challenges, and an assessment to determine whether big data activities are legal, fair, and just may be part of an organization's privacy management program.[30]

Generally, under PIPEDA, organizations must obtain an individual's consent, whether express or implied, in order to collect, use or disclose an individual's personal information.[31] PIPEDA's consent requirements establish a helpful framework for advanced data analytics by contemplating circumstances where organizations must process personal information in

[24] "Big data can be described as data sets so large, lacking in structure, and changeable from one moment to another that traditional methods of data analysis no longer apply." Office of the Privacy Commissioner of Canada (OPC), *Consent and Privacy: A Discussion Paper Exploring Potential Enhancements to Consent under the Personal Information Protection and Electronic Documents Act* ("Consent Discussion Paper"), 2016, at 6.

[25] Remarks by John Pecman, Commissioner of Competition, Innovation and Infrastructure, in Toronto, Ontario, on May 25, 2016.

[26] *Id.*

[27] PIPEDA in its current form is equally applicable to private sector and health sector privacy law.

[28] PIPEDA's purpose is to establish rules to govern the collection, use, and disclosure of information in an era in which technology increasingly facilitates the circulation and exchange of information. Section 3 of PIPEDA. PIPEDA's purpose provision, which attempts to reconcile two competing interests, privacy and organizational needs, should be interpreted with flexibility, common sense, and pragmatism. *Englander v. Telus Communications Inc.*, 2004 FCA 387 at ¶ 46.

[29] Principle 4.1 in Schedule 1 to PIPEDA.

[30] Office of the Information and Privacy Commissioner of Alberta, Office of the Privacy Commissioner of Canada, and Office of the Information and Privacy Commissioner for British Columbia, *Getting Accountability Right with a Privacy Management Program* ("Joint Accountability Guidance") 2012, at p. 1 (Privacy management programs help "promote trust and confidence on the part of consumers, and thereby enhance competitive and reputational advantages for organizations.").

[31] Principles 4.3.1 and 4.3.6 in Schedule 1 to PIPEDA.

connection with the provision of a product or service.[32] Specifically, under PIPEDA, organizations can require an individual to consent – within the terms and conditions of the product or service – to data analytics provided that (i) the organization complies with the specified transparency and data minimization requirements (both of which are consistent with other PIPEDA requirements)[33] and (ii) the collection, use, and disclosure in question are required to fulfill "legitimate purposes." Although the phrase "legitimate purposes" is not defined, it is informed by Section 5(3) of PIPEDA, which describes appropriate purposes as those that are "appropriate in the circumstances" as considered by a reasonable person,[34] and by the balancing of interests within the Purpose Section of PIPEDA.[35]

As a general proposition, a reasonable person would consider it to be entirely appropriate and legitimate for an organization to engage in data analytics. In order to bolster their ability to maintain that their particular types of data analytics are reasonable, legitimate, and appropriate in a given set of circumstances, organizations may conduct an assessment process that considers the ethical impact of big data analytics. The Information Accountability Foundation (IAF) has developed such an assessment process. The IAF's assessment process supplements the fair information practice principles and relies on five values: Beneficial, Progressive, Sustainable, Respectful, and Fair.[36] The consideration of these five values enhances an organization's privacy management program and its compliance with its accountability obligations under PIPEDA. Ultimately, by providing a framework for establishing that the purpose and nature of a big data analytics activity are reasonable, legitimate, and appropriate in a given set of circumstances, the assessment process helps an organization, as part of its privacy management program, determine whether big data activities are legal, fair, and just and demonstrate how that determination was reached.

The Five Key Values

To understand these five values, it is important to appreciate that not all big data analytics are equally impactful on the individuals to whom the data pertains. Big data analytics can be separated into two phases: "thinking with data" and "acting with data." Generally, "thinking with data" is where new insights, which go beyond experience and intuition and come instead from correlations among data sets, are discovered. "Acting with data" is where these insights are put into effect and where individuals may be affected as these insights are employed in an individually unique manner. The "acting with data" phase often is individually impactful; the "thinking with data" phase often is not (the risks related to false insights usually are the primary concern in that phase). Often it is necessary to distinguish between "thinking with data" and "acting with data" when considering the five key values: Beneficial, Progressive, Sustainable, Respectful and Fair.

BENEFICIAL The purpose of assessment is achieving the benefits that come with data-driven activities while mitigating the possible risks. Both the "thinking with data" and "acting with data" phases require an organization to define the benefits that will be created by the analytics and

---

[32] Principle 4.3.3 in Schedule 1 to PIPEDA provides: "An organization shall not, as a condition of the supply of a product or service, require an individual to consent to the collection, use or disclosure of information beyond that required to fulfill the explicitly specified, and legitimate purposes."

[33] The phrase "explicitly specified" is informed by PIPEDA Principle 4.2 Identifying Purposes and Principle 4.8 Openness, and the data minimization wording ("beyond that required") is informed by and consistent with Principle 4 Limiting Collection and Section 5(3) Appropriate Purposes.

[34] Section 5(3) of PIPEDA.

[35] Section 3 of PIPEDA.

[36] Unified Ethical Frame for Big Data Analysis, Information Accountability Foundation, October 7, 2014.

should identify the parties that gain tangible value from the effort. The act of big data analytics may create risks for some individuals. Those risks must be counterbalanced by the benefits created for all individuals, organizations, or society as a whole. This balancing concept is consistent with PIPEDA's stated purpose

> to establish, in an era in which technology increasingly facilitates the circulation and exchange of information, rules to govern the collection, use and disclosure of personal information in a manner that recognizes the right of privacy of individuals with respect to their personal information and the need of organizations to collect, use or disclose personal information for purposes that a reasonable person would consider appropriate in the circumstances.[37]

To define benefits, one must have an understanding of why the data is being collected, used or disclosed. While big data does not always begin with a hypothesis, it usually begins with a sense of purpose about the type of problem to be solved.[38] Data scientists, along with others in an organization, should be able to define the usefulness or merit that comes from solving the problem, so it might be evaluated appropriately. The risks should also be clearly defined so that they may be evaluated as well. If the benefits that will be created are limited, uncertain, or if the parties that benefit are not the ones at risk from the processing, those circumstances should be taken into consideration, and appropriate mitigation for the risk should be developed before the analysis begins.[39]

PROGRESSIVE Since bringing large and diverse data sets together and looking for hidden insights or correlations may create some risks for some individuals, the value from big data analytics should be materially better than not using big data analytics. If the anticipated improvements can be achieved in a less data-intensive manner, then less intensive processing should be pursued.[40] Precision is not required. One might not know the level of improvement in the "thinking with data" phase. Yet, by the time one is proposing "acting with data," the organization should be better equipped to measure the level of improvement. This application of new learning to create materially better results is what drives innovation.

Progressive must be assessed in the context in which the processing takes place. There are examples of big data being used to reduce congestion, manage disaster relief, and improve medical outcomes where the level of improvement would not have been possible without big data analytics. However, there are other examples where an organization may analyze data and achieve only marginal improvements, only using big data analytics because they are new and interesting. If there are other methods that will accomplish the same objectives, organizations should consider pursuing those methods rather than using big data analytics to produce the same or lesser results with greater risks.[41]

---

[37] Section 3 of PIPEDA.

[38] *See* OPC, *Expectations: A Guide for Submitting Privacy Impact Assessments to the Office of the Privacy Commissioner of Canada* (OPC Expectations), March 2011 (federal entities undertaking particularly intrusive or privacy-invasive initiatives or technologies are expected to first demonstrate that the activity or program is necessary to achieve a specific or legitimate purpose.).

[39] *Id.* (The assessment should help determine whether the initiative raises privacy risks; measures, describes and quantifies these risks; and proposes solutions to eliminate privacy risks or mitigate them to an acceptable level.)

[40] *Id.* (The OPC also expects federal entities to demonstrate that the intrusion on privacy is proportional to the benefit to be derived.) The concept of proportionality comes into play when conducting assessments on all of the values, but it particularly comes into play on the progressive value.

[41] *Id.* (The OPC also expects federal entities to demonstrate that no other less privacy intrusive alternative would achieve the same purpose.)

SUSTAINABLE Sustainable covers two issues. The first is understanding how long an insight might be effective, while the second relates to whether the data used for the insight might be available when acting with data.

All algorithms have an effective half-life: a period in which they effectively predict future behavior. Some half-lives are very long; others are relatively short. Big data analysts should understand this concept and articulate their best understanding of how long an insight might endure once it is reflected in application. Big data insights, when placed into production, should provide value that is sustainable over a reasonable time frame. Considerations that affect the longevity of big data analytics include whether the source data will be available for a period of time in the future, whether the data can be kept current, and whether the discovery may need to be changed or refined to keep up with evolving trends and individual expectations. These considerations are consistent with PIPEDA's Accuracy and Collection Limitation Principles.[42]

There are situations where data, particularly de-identified data, might be available for the "thinking with data" phase but would not be available in the "acting with data" phase because of legal or contractual restrictions.[43] These restrictions affect sustainability.

RESPECTFUL Respectful relates directly to the context in which the data originated and to the contractual or notice-related restrictions on how the data might be applied. As the OPC stated in its recent discussion paper on consent and privacy, "the principle of "respect for context" bears some conceptual resemblance to the idea of "consistent use" employed in the federal Privacy Act in which a use or disclosure that is consistent with the purpose for which the information was originally collected may not require the individual's consent. The key to employing either concept is the way in which the original "context" or original "use" is defined, since this will determine how broad a range of other uses can be considered "respectful" or "consistent."[44]

Big data analytics may affect many parties in many different ways. Those parties include individuals to whom the data relates, organizations from whom the data originates, organizations that aggregate the data, and those that might regulate the data. All of these parties have interests in the data that must be taken into consideration and respected.

An example is data scraped online for commercial purposes in violation of the sites' terms and conditions that prohibit such site scraping. Users of big data analytics must respect those terms and conditions.

Organizations using big data analytics should understand and respect the interests of all the stakeholders involved in, or affected by, the analytics. Anything less would be disrespectful.

FAIRNESS While "respectful" speaks to the conditions related to, and the processing of, the data, "fair" relates to the insights and applications that are a product of big data. The impacts of that processing must be fair.

---

[42] Principle 4.4 in Schedule 1 to PIPEDA ("Information shall be collected by fair and lawful means."); Principle 4.6.1 ("The extent to which personal information shall be accurate, complete, and up-to-date will depend upon the use of the personal information, taking into account the interests of the individual. Information shall be sufficiently accurate, complete and up-to-date to minimize the possibility that inappropriate information may be used to make a decision about the individual.").

[43] *Id.* at Principle 4.4 ("information shall be collected by fair and lawful means.").

[44] Consent Discussion Paper at 17.

Canadian law prohibits discriminatory practices based on race, national or ethnic origin, color, religion, age, and sex.[45] Yet, big data analytics may predict those characteristics without actually looking for fields labeled race, national or ethnic origin, color, religion, age, or sex. The same can be said about genotypes, particularly those related to physical characteristics. Inferring characteristics and using them to make decisions based on prohibited grounds is not fair. Big data analytics, while meeting the needs of the organization that is conducting or sponsoring the processing, must be fair to both the individuals to whom the data pertains and to whom it will be applied.[46]

The analysis of fairness needs to protect against unseemly or risky actions but also to enhance beneficial opportunities. There are risks related to being too reticent with data. Human rights speak to shared benefits of technology and broader opportunities related to employment, health, and safety. Preempting such opportunities is also a fairness issue.[47]

In considering the value of being fair, organizations should take steps to balance individual interests in a manner that gives real weight to the interests of other stakeholders, particularly those individuals who will be impacted by the analysis.[48] Results should not be gamed to favor the data users.

How This Assessment Document May Be Used

The purpose of this assessment document is to assist organizations to leverage the potential of big data that pertains to individuals in a manner that is consistent with Canadian law while protecting individuals from the risks of both using and not using data. This assessment document raises additional considerations that may not be covered in a typical privacy impact assessment (PIA). This assessment document does not replace PIAs; it should be used in conjunction with PIAs. It assists organizations in looking at the rights and interests impacted by data collection, use, and disclosure in data-driven activities.

Organizations may incorporate this assessment document in whole or in part into their own unique processes and programs and may use a triage process to determine the questions that are appropriate to ask considering their own circumstances and the level of assessment necessary. For example, if the activity in question is only minimally changed from the past, no assessment might be necessary. If data is being used in a manner that is crystal clear from privacy notices and context, then a PIA might be all that is necessary.

This assessment document may be used as big data activities reach key milestones or decision points. Some level of assessment may be appropriate at each phase of a big data activity. Big data analytics may include phases when the activity is first conceived, then approved for

---

[45] Canadian Human Rights Act, R.S.C. 1985, c. H-6.

[46] PIPEDA's stated purpose "is to establish, in an era in which technology increasingly facilitates the circulation and exchange of information, rules to govern the collection, use and disclosure of personal information in a manner that recognizes the right of privacy of individuals with respect to their personal information and the need of organizations to collect, use or disclose personal information for purposes that a reasonable person would consider appropriate in the circumstances." Section 3 of PIPEDA.

[47] Principle 4.4 in Schedule 1 to PIPEDA ("Information shall be collected by fair and lawful means.").

[48] *See* OPC Expectations (The OPC asks government departments to answer the following four questions, which are based on the test used in *R. v. Oakes* to weigh reasonable limitations on rights and freedoms in a free and democratic society:

- Is the measure demonstrably necessary to meet a specific need?
- Is it likely to be effective in meeting that need?
- Is the loss of privacy proportional to the need?
- Is there a less privacy-invasive way of achieving the same end?).

programming, put into operation, and eventually reviewed. Questions need not be repeated in later phases if underlying conditions have not changed. If there have been changes to the activity that impact answers, the questions may need to be repeated. If questions between the two assessments are duplicated, they may need not to be repeated, and organizations may need to determine where in their processes it makes sense for the questions to be asked.

Benefits and risks, and their likelihood, may be determined based on an organization's approach to risk. As new data analysis and new applications of insights can change over time, the process of assessing benefits and risks may need to be repeated. Regardless of when the assessment is conducted, the results of each assessment may be presented to decision makers for a determination on whether to proceed with an activity.

The assessment document identifies key issues that decision makers in organizations may consider. No score is generated that makes decisions for users. Rather, if decision makers take into account what they learn from the assessment process, decisions may be made in a manner that gives real weight to the interests of other stakeholders, particularly those individuals who will be impacted by the data analysis.

The sample questions help evaluate whether, based on the assessment, the activity is reasonable, appropriate, and legitimate. Use of the assessment document helps determine whether the decisions reached on the appropriateness of an activity were well reasoned and demonstrate how that determination was reached. Organizations may disclose that they use this assessment document or one based on it.

While developed for big data activities, this assessment document and the "thinking and acting with data" distinction may be used to assess any activities within an organization where data is collected, used, and disclosed in a manner that may not have been anticipated by the individuals to whom the data pertains but is otherwise reasonable, appropriate, and legitimate.

CONCLUSION

Thinking with data is compelling to data driven organizations. Using the insights that come from thinking with data has the potential to improve almost all processes from medical procedures to personalized products and services. However, the risks to all stakeholders are different when an organization thinks with data and uses those insights in a manner that has impact on individuals. What is similar is that the law and regulation will lag both the benefits and the risks and harms that come from using analytics more robustly. This lag leads to the need for ethical assessments.

For organizations to be "ethical," they need to make an assessment of whether an activity applying analytics is appropriate. Assessments must be conducted against criteria. The criteria that the IAF has applied are the concepts of legal, fair, and just. "Legal" is fairly simple. Are there laws, regulations, or contracts that explicitly prohibit or permit an application. "Fair" is more complex. Fair requires considering whether a reasonable set of individuals would consider such an activity to be within bounds, based on a balancing of risks and benefits. Beyond fair is "just." Are there societal norms that would preclude such an activity? For example, the use of an individual's gender might not explicitly be prohibited, and might be fair, but a societal norm might suggest the use to be unjust. Being both fair and just can only be understood within the context of the activity.

To establish whether an activity is legal, fair, and just, IAF suggests an organization should evaluate an activity against five very broad values: beneficial, progressive, sustainable, respectful, and fair. The questionnaire IAF developed is based on those five values, but it is applied from a business process orientation. The introduction to the questionnaire and the actual questions create a framework that is customizable by industry and organizations.

The questionnaire does not drive a score. Rather it derives the key facts that would lead to a decision that is legal, fair, and just.

The essential elements of accountability, the foundation for this assessment process, requires an organization to be responsible and answerable. The questionnaire facilitates accountability by driving responsible processes that are demonstrable both to internal reviewers and to external oversight agencies. All systems need to have an enforcement mechanism, and the ability to demonstrate on request facilitates enforcement by oversight agencies. The presence of enforcement agencies then creates the incentives for organizations to use the assessment process with competency and integrity.[49]

[49] Information Accountability Foundation, "Enforcing Big Data Assessment Processes."

PART IV

International Perspectives

17

Profiling and the Essence of the Right to Data Protection

Bilyana Petkova and Franziska Boehm

In 2012, when the European Commission launched its data protection reform package, "a Eurobarometer survey showed that in the case of behavioral advertising, 54% of Europeans feel uncomfortable with practices which involve online profiling and a large majority of them (74%) would like to be given the opportunity to give (or refuse) their specific consent before the collection and processing of their personal data."[1] Whereas the specific case of targeted advertising under EU law has been extensively studied, and the pitfalls of "informed consent" for privacy protection convincingly exposed,[2] this chapter focuses on a wider conceptualization of profiling in the context of consumer privacy. Although the respondents to the Eurobarometer study were not asked for their opinions in other areas of the law where automated decision-making may play a role, the risks of profiling stretch well beyond behavioral advertising. If life opportunities are based on predictive scoring, people can be sorted into the "wheat" and the "chaff" for, inter alia, their health, housing, employment, and travel opportunities.[3] Crucially, the economic possibilities of individuals can be significantly reduced due to the vast information asymmetries that extensive data collection creates in favor of organizations having access to the collected data.

First, we review the legislative history of Article 15 of the 1995 EU Data Protection Directive[4] (the 1995 Directive), as it was amended through Article 22 in the process of adopting a new EU General Data Protection Regulation[5] (GDPR) that would enter into force in 2018. Next, we discuss profiling in the context of the case law of the Court of Justice of the European Union

---

[1] TNS Opinion & Social Report, *Special Eurobarometer (EB) 359: Attitudes on Data Protection and Electronic Identity in the EU,* European Commission (2011), available at: http://ec.europa.eu/public_opinion/archives/ebs/ebs_359_en.pdf.

[2] Frederik J. Zuiderveen Borgesius, *Improving Privacy Protection in the Area of Behavioural Targeting* (Wolters Kluwer, 2015). *See* also Frederik J. Zuiderveen Borgesius, "Singling Out People Without Knowing Their Name: Behavioural Targeting, Pseudonymous Data, and the New Data Protection Regulation," 32 *Computer Law & Security Review* 256 (2016).

[3] Frank Pasquale, *The Black Box Society: The Secret Algorithms That Control Money Information,* Harvard University Press, 3, 11 (2015), Chapter 2; Danielle Keats Citron & Frank Pasquale, "Then Scored Society: Due Process for Automated Predictions," 89 *Washington Law Review* 1, 13–16 (2014).

[4] Directive 95/46/EC of the European Parliament and of the Council of 24 October 1995 on the Protection of Individuals with regard to the Processing of Personal Data and on the Free Movement of Such Data, [1996] OJ L 281/31.

[5] Regulation 2016/679 of the European Parliament and of the Council of 27 April 2016 on the Protection of Natural Persons with regard to the Processing of Personal Data and on the Free Movement of Such Data (General Data Protection Regulation) [2016] OJ L 119/59.

(CJEU). We argue that a combined reading of the *Google Spain*,[6] *Digital Rights Ireland*,[7] and *Schrems*[8] cases in conjunction with the GDPR and especially in light of the EU Charter of Fundamental Rights (the Charter)[9] renders certain types of profiling to affect the very essence of the right to data protection enshrined in Article 8 of the Charter. In conclusion, we bring a few hypotheticals of algorithmic decision-making from the employment context, which illustrate how the relevant legislative framework might be applied.

REFORM OF THE EU DATA PROTECTION PROVISION ON AUTOMATED DECISION-MAKING

The Implications of "Decisions Based 'Solely' on Automated Processing"

Article 15 of the 1995 EU Directive can be traced back to the French Data Protection Act of 1978, which aimed to prohibit automated court decisions.[10] The 1995 Directive's provision grants individuals the right not to be subject to a decision that is based solely on automated processing of data intended to evaluate personal aspects of the data subject. The prohibition is valid when an automated decision produces legal effects concerning the individual or similarly significantly affects her. Since the 1995 Directive's provision has never been evoked before the CJEU, the consequences of the provision can so far only be theorized in the abstract. In what concerns profiling, the impact assessment of the Commission in 2012 highlighted that the 1995 Directive only applies to decisions based *solely* on automated processing. Therefore, there is a risk that including a merely formal human intervention in the decision-making process, with no influence on the outcome of that process, easily circumvents the provision. The Commission gave examples for such procedures including the conditions of a telephone service or insurance contract, where offers and tariffs are adjusted on the basis of a scoring of the potential customers through the use of general and individual data related to them. "While the decision to make a specific offer is formally with the sales staff, this person's decision is defined by the outcome of an automated system so that he or she effectively has no margin [of discretion] to deviate from that suggestion."[11] The same problem can arise in a range of other contexts, for example if a company decides to use credit scoring to assess the financial credibility of a potential leaser: although the decision on whether to grant a housing contract is formally made by a real estate agent and hence, is not solely based on the automated processing of the data, in effect the outcome of that decision ends up being almost entirely influenced by automated processing. Another ready example is the use of legal software that facilitates sentencing – the ban on the use of automated decisions in the judiciary that was likely at the core of enacting Article 15 in the first place thus becomes controversial. Arguably, this loophole can be closed through judicial interpretation that requires human reevaluation in the form of an appeal's procedure. In any event, even if the amendments introduced in Article 22 of the GDPR did not expressly address this issue, certain

---

[6] Case C-131/12, *Google Spain and Google*, EU:C:2014:317.

[7] Joined Cases C-293/12 and C-594/12, *Digital Rights Ireland Ltd. v. Minister for Communications, Marine and Natural Resources and Kärntner Landesregierung and Others*, EU:C:2014:238.

[8] Case C-362/14, *Maximillian Schrems v. Data Protection Commissioner*, EU:C:2015:650.

[9] Charter of Fundamental Rights of the European Union, OJ 2012 C326/39.

[10] Loi Informatique Et Libertés [Act on Information Technology, Data Files and Civil Liberties] (Act N°78–17 of 6 January 1978), last amended 17 March 2014: "No court decision involving the assessment of an individual's behaviour may be based on an automatic processing of personal data intended to assess some aspects of his personality."

[11] Commission Staff Working Paper Impact Assessment, SEC/2012/0072 final (2012), available at: http://eur-lex.europa .eu/legal-content/EN/TXT/?uri=CELEX:52012SC0072.

parts of the preamble (Recital) of the GDPR provide a hook for judicial interpretation that aims to avoid merely formal human intervention.[12] Under European law, the preambles of legislative acts do not formally carry binding legal force. However, they present important indicators of legislative intent and as such should provide guidance for the judiciary.

New Requirements in the GDPR

Instead, some of the innovations initially discussed in the context of the GDPR included an absolute prohibition of automated decision-making for children[13] and the introduction of an obligation for Data Protection Officers (DPOs) for larger economic operators.[14] One of the rationales behind the insertion of an obligation for DPOs for large private companies and the insistence in the initial drafts of the GDPR on concrete parameters that would delineate such obligation was that significant data protection risks such as profiling activities done by head-hunting companies can be mitigated by DPOs. The expectation was that on a cost-benefit analysis, the burden on companies would be justified by the risky nature of the processing and the added value for individuals. However, in the course of interinstitutional negotiations on the new Regulation, the requirements on DPOs were somewhat watered down.[15] What remained from the early stages of the legislative process are the absolute prohibition of automated decision-making for children,[16] as well as the intention of the Commission to insert in the reformed legal framework an obligation on data controllers to carry out a data protection impact assessment in certain cases. For instance, such impact assessments are mandated when sensitive data are being

---

[12] It is worth quoting at length, for example, the relevant part of Recital 71 of the GDPR: "The data subject should have the right not to be subject to a decision, which may include a measure, evaluating personal aspects relating to him or her which is based solely on automated processing and which produces legal effects concerning him or her or similarly significantly affects him or her, such as *automatic refusal of an online credit application or e-recruiting practices* without any human intervention. Such processing includes 'profiling' that consists of any form of automated processing of personal data evaluating the personal aspects relating to a natural person, in particular to analyse or predict aspects concerning the data subject's performance at work, economic situation, health, personal preferences or interests, reliability or behaviour, location or movements, where it produces legal effects concerning him or her or similarly significantly affects him or her," emphasis added, *supra* n. 5.

[13] The Commission thought that there is a need for specific rules on consent for children below 13 years in the online environment – specifying that parental consent would always be required – to help protecting a very vulnerable category of data subjects because of their young age, *supra* n. 11.

[14] Compare the Proposal for a Regulation of the European Parliament and of the Council on the Protection of Individuals with regard to their Personal Data and on the Free Movement of Such Data, COM (2012) 11 final with the European Parliament Legislative Resolution of Mar. 12, 2014 on the Proposal for a Regulation of the European Parliament and of the Council on the Protection of Individuals with regard to their Personal Data and on the Free Movement of Such Data.

[15] Both the Commission's and European Parliament's (EP) versions were more concrete in that respect since the requirements on DPOs in the private sector were more detailed: in the Commission's version, a DPO needed to be employed by any enterprise that has 250 or more employees; and in the EP's version when data processing is carried out "by a legal person and relates to more than 5000 data subjects in any consecutive 12-month period; or the core activities of the controller or the processor consist of processing special categories of data ... location data or data on children or employees in large scale filing systems.", *id.* The final version of the GDPR provides that DPOs should be rather used if "core activities of the controller or the processor consist of processing operations which, by virtue of their nature, their scope and/or their purposes, require regular and systematic monitoring of data subjects on a large scale," Art. 37.1b, *supra* n. 5.

[16] Art. 8.1 GDPR provides that "Where the child is below the age of 16 years ... processing [of personal data] shall be lawful only if and to the extent that consent is given or authorised by the holder of parental responsibility over the child. Member States may provide by law for a lower age for those purposes provided that such lower age is not below 13 years." *See* also the relevant part of Recital 71 of the GDPR that in relation to measures based on automated processing explicitly holds that: "Such measure should not concern a child," *supra* n. 5.

processed, but also when the type of processing involves such specific risks as profiling. Thus, the final text of the GDPR requires impact assessments in cases of:

> A systematic and extensive evaluation of personal aspects relating to natural persons which is based on automated processing, including profiling, and on which decisions are based that produce legal effects concerning the natural person or similarly significantly affect the natural person.[17]

Derogations from the Ban on Automated Decision-Making

Like its predecessor Article 15 of the 1995 Directive, the new Article 22 of the GDPR provides for a number of derogations to the right of individuals not to be subject to a decision based solely on automated processing of data. The exceptions provided for in the GDPR are almost identical to those provided by the Directive: on the one hand, they are based on contractual relationships between the data subject and data controller,[18] and on the other can be authorized by Union or Member State law provided that there are appropriate safeguards for the data subject.[19] However, Article 22 inserts a new derogation based on consent.[20] As pointed out by Frederik Borgesius and others, a literal interpretation of the exceptions to Article 15 of the 1995 Directive, and by extension of Article 22 of the GDPR, substantially limit the remit of the provision.[21] For example, in the case of an application for a housing contract, a real estate agency can apply automated processing arguing that such processing (in the form of credit scoring) is justified by the person's request to enter into a contract. Despite the insistence of the European Parliament on detailing minimum standards in the field of national employment law,[22] regarding the second derogation, Article 22 of the final text of the Regulation provides little guidelines on when the standard "of suitable measures to safeguard the data subject's rights and freedoms and legitimate interests" is met. However, more so than the 1995 Directive, the language of the GDPR's Preamble offers additional safeguards for the individual. When interpreted in conjunction with Recital 71, all derogations to Article 22, whether based on contract, EU or Member State law, or on consent should be read narrowly. According to the Recital, minimum suitable safeguards for the data subject include the provision of information, the possibility to express his or her point of view and obtain an explanation of the decision, as well as the possibility to challenge that decision.[23] Likely on a case-by-case basis, courts would have to make the difficult assessment of what appeal procedures involving human intervention satisfy the requirement for "suitable safeguards." It should be noted that on first reading, the European Parliament (EP) suggested an amendment that finally did not make it to the final text of the Regulation; that amendment would have inserted a prohibition on profiling which leads to measures

---

[17] Article 35.3a of the GDPR. *See also* Recitals 75 and 90–91, *id.*

[18] Art. 22.2.a of the GDPR, *supra* n. 5.

[19] Art.22.2.b, *id.*

[20] Art. 22.2.c., *id.*

[21] *Supra* n. 2, *Improving Privacy Protection* Chapter 9, and the literature cited there.

[22] European Parliament Legislative Resolution of Mar. 12, 2014 on the Proposal for a Regulation of the European Parliament and of the Council on the Protection of Individuals with regard to their Personal Data and on the Free Movement of Such Data, amendment 192.

[23] Recital 71 of the GDPR in relevant parts reads: "In any case, such processing should be subject to suitable safeguards, which should include specific information to the data subject and the right to obtain human intervention, to express his or her point of view, to obtain an explanation of the decision reached after such assessment and to challenge the decision," *supra* n. 5.

producing legal effects concerning the data subject or similarly significantly affecting the interests, rights or freedoms of the concerned data subject not based solely but also *predominantly* on automated processing.[24] Parliament also wanted to include directly in the wording of Article 22, rather than in the preamble, the requirement for an explanation of the decision reached after an automated assessment.[25]

Special Protection of Sensitive Data

In addition, in what concerns measures based on sensitive data, the final version of the GDPR introduced a new provision that provides special protection for such categories of data in the context of automated decision-making,[26] thereby circumscribing the derogations enshrined in Article 22.2. Special categories of sensitive data are those based on personal data revealing race or ethnic origin, political opinions, religious or political beliefs, or trade-union membership, and the processing of genetic data, as well as biometric data, for the purpose of uniquely identifying a natural person, as well as data concerning health or concerning a natural person's sex life or sexual orientation.[27]

In the part of the stakeholders' debate[28] about definitions that surrounded the original European Commission's proposal for the GDPR, some expressed the view that a broad definition of personal data per se would be desirable, suggesting that identification should not be the only element in defining personal data in view of the possible evolution of new technologies and behavioral profiling. A counterproposal suggested excluding from the definition of personal data any information whose processing does not interfere with the values of privacy, fairness, and nondiscrimination. Yet others (primarily some Data Protection Authorities – DPAs) wanted to revisit the categories of sensitive data by moving towards a definition that would examine the content and use of data as sensitive rather than prescribing an exhaustive list of sensitive data at the outset. A more radical proposal consisted of eliminating the general prohibition to process sensitive data and foreseeing instead a special obligation to ensure appropriate safeguards for the processing.

The debate about defining personal data and sensitive data is important for present purposes as it also impacts the legal treatment of profiling measures. It is widely acknowledged that algorithmic predictions about sensitive data can be made even if such data is not fed into an algorithmic model. The example given most often is that if a certain geographic region has a high number of low-income or minority residents, an algorithm that employs simply geographic data is likely to indirectly determine loan eligibility based on race or ethnic origin.[29] However, the definition of sensitive data in the Regulation may be interpreted to offer a broader view of what "sensitive data" is, one that is not limited to the variables explicitly mentioned but also

---

[24] *Supra* n. 27, amendment 115.

[25] *Id.*

[26] Art. 22.4 of the GDPR, *id.* The derogation is in turn subject to exceptions based on consent and in the public interest, provided that there are safeguards for the individual. The notion of consent is problematic as the individual might feel pressured to give their consent in order to enter into contractual obligations.

[27] Art. 9 of the GDPR, *id.*

[28] *Supra* n. 11.

[29] "For example, a bank could use software to deny credit to people who live in a particular neighbourhood, because many people in that neighbourhood don't repay their debts. If primarily immigrants live in that neighbourhood, such profiling measures might discriminate against immigrants, by accident or on purpose. But such practices wouldn't be covered by the prohibition of profiling measures based solely on special categories of data. Similarly, the software could deny credit to somebody who lives in a poor neighbourhood, even though that person always repays his or her debts." *Supra* n. 2, *Improving Privacy Protection* at p. 289.

extends to variables with which they correlate. Such interpretation is in fact in tune with Recital 51, which clarifies that sensitive data are to be understood as personal data that are particularly sensitive in relation to fundamental rights and freedoms to which their processing might pose significant risks. Since offering a special legal regime to sensitive data was designed primarily to address issues of discrimination, a broader interpretation of the category of sensitive data seems warranted.[30]

Right to Explanation?

Related to the possibility to obtain an explanation about an automated decision, the 1995 Directive, as well as the GDPR, grant the data subject a right to learn about the logic involved in automated personal data processing. Whereas Article 12a of the Directive gives this right to individuals for automated decisions with significant effects, the respective Article 13.2(f) of the GDPR offers a somewhat broader wording: it grants the data subject the right to receive *meaningful* information about the logic involved, as well as the significance and the envisaged consequences of such processing. Read in particular in the light of Recital 63 of the GDPR, which explicitly requires that the logic involved in *any* automated personal data processing be revealed, regardless of an assessment of significant effects on the data subject, the new provision arguably further enhances transparency. Moreover, Recital 60 specifies that individuals need not proactively seek information the existence of which they might not always be aware of, i.e., they need to be informed upfront if they are being profiled.[31] However, as with the 1995 Directive, the GDPR's Recitals preserve the requirement that the information given to individuals should not adversely affect the rights and freedoms of others, pointing out in particular trade secrets or intellectual property rights, as well as copyrights protecting software.[32]

Apart from proprietary concerns however, the right to obtain information on the logic behind automated decision-making remains uncertain for technical reasons. Jenna Burrell explains this problem as the "opacity that stems from the mismatch between mathematical optimization in high-dimensionality characteristic of machine learning and the demands of human-scale reasoning and styles of semantic interpretation."[33] Her study shows that probing into the "why" of a particular classification decision requires human interpretation that in some cases may "provide an understanding that is at best incomplete and at worst false reassurance."[34] In any event, it is noteworthy that Article 13.2(f) of the GDPR does not tie the requirement for

---

[30] As pointed out by Bryce Goodman and Seth Flaxman however, whereas with small datasets it might be possible to account for correlations between sensitive and nonsensitive data, as datasets become increasingly large, correlations can become complex and difficult to detect a priori. Bryce Goodman & Seth Flaxman, European Union Regulations on Algorithmic Decision-Making and a "Right to Explanation," paper presented at the Workshop on Human Interpretability in Machine Learning (2016), New York, NY.

[31] Recital 60 reads in relevant parts: "Furthermore, the data subject *should be informed of the existence of profiling and the consequences of such profiling.* Where the personal data are collected from the data subject, the data subject should also be informed whether he or she is obliged to provide the personal data and of the consequences, where he or she does not provide such data. That information may be provided in combination with standardised icons in order to give in an easily visible, intelligible and clearly legible manner, a meaningful overview of the intended processing. Where the icons are presented electronically, they should be machine-readable," emphasis added, *supra* n. 5.

[32] Recital 63 of the GDPR, *id.*

[33] Jenna Burrell, "How the Machine 'Thinks': Understanding Opacity in Machine Learning Algorithms," *Big Data & Society* 10 (2016). "Machine optimizations based on training data do not naturally accord with human semantic explanations. The workings of machine learning algorithms can escape full understanding and interpretation by humans, even for those with specialized training, even for computer scientists."

[34] *Id.*

revealing the logic behind automated personal data processing to the logic behind an algorithm. Therefore, the provision might also be interpreted as giving the individual a right to receive an explanation about the logic behind a measure that affects him as a result of the processing.

DEFINITION AND CASE-LAW ON PROFILING

Definition of Profiling in the GDPR

The European Parliament (EP) insisted on a definition of profiling in the GDPR. Further, on first reading the main text of the GDPR, the EP suggested a definition of profiling to be inserted that with some minor changes made it into the final text of the Regulation, which now states that:

> "profiling" means any form of automated processing of personal data consisting of the use of personal data to evaluate certain personal aspects relating to a natural person, in particular to analyse or predict aspects concerning that natural person's performance at work, economic situation, health, personal preferences, interests, reliability, behaviour, location or movements.[35]

On first reading of the Regulation, the EP suggested an insertion into the Preamble that specified: "Profiling based solely on the processing of pseudonymous data should be presumed not to significantly affect the interests, rights or freedoms of the data subject."[36] However, at the same time the EP also acknowledged the limits of pseudonymization: "Where profiling, whether based on a single source of pseudonymous data or on the aggregation of pseudonymous data from different sources, permits the controller to attribute pseudonymous data to a specific data subject, the processed data should no longer be considered to be pseudonymous."[37] The final text of the GDPR includes a Recital that addresses the difficulties associated with de-identification.[38]

The Google Spain *Case*

The development of the legislative process on the GDPR coincided with some important decisions delivered by the Court of Justice of the European Union. In the first one, *Google Spain*,[39] on the substance, the question focused on the data protection rights of an individual to prevent Google from displaying links to information that was too outdated to be relevant to that individual's current circumstances. The CJEU interpreted Article 12(b) of the 1995 Directive, which provides a right to appeal to the national DPA to compel the correction, removal or blocking of false and inaccurate information, and Article 14(a), which provides the right to object to the inclusion of false information in a database (and when the objection is justified, requires the controller of the database to remove the objectionable data). Unlike the Advocate General, who did not find a search engine to be the data controller,[40] the CJEU emphasized the need to

---

[35] Art. 4.4 of the GDPR, *supra* note 5.
[36] *Supra* n. 27, amendment 34.
[37] *Id.*
[38] Recital 30 of the GDPR reads: "Natural persons may be associated with online identifiers provided by their devices, applications, tools and protocols, such as internet protocol addresses, cookie identifiers or other identifiers such as radio frequency identification tags. This may leave traces which, in particular when combined with unique identifiers and other information received by the servers, may be used to create profiles of the natural persons and identify them," *supra* n. 30.
[39] *Supra* n. 6.
[40] C-131/12, *Google Spain*, Opinion of Advocate General Jääskinen, EU:C:2013:424, para. 72.

secure the effectiveness of the EU data protection regime and decided that Google was indeed the controller of the data. When a person is searched for by name in Google's search engine, even if the links lead to lawfully displayed material, Google needs to remove them if they contravene the provisions of EU data protection law.

In relation to profiling, the CJEU reasoned that "the organization and aggregation of information published on the internet by search engines" may, "when users carry out their search on the basis of an individual's name, result in them obtaining through the list of results *a structured overview* of the information relating to that individual that can be found on the internet enabling them to establish a more or less detailed profile of the data subject."[41] Further, the Court emphasized that the search engine is "liable to affect *significantly* the fundamental rights to privacy and to the protection of personal data," stressing that the

> processing enables any internet user to obtain through the list of results *a structured overview* of the information relating to that individual that can be found on the internet – information which potentially concerns a vast number of aspects of his private life and which, without the search engine, could not have been interconnected or could have been only with great difficulty – and thereby to establish a more or less detailed profile of [the data subject]. Furthermore, the effect of the interference with those rights of the data subject is *heightened* on account of the important role played by the internet and search engines in modern society, which render the information in such a list of results ubiquitous.[42]

The CJEU therefore read the provisions of the 1995 Directive in the light of the Charter in emphasizing the need to ensure the effectiveness of the data protection regime, as well as the significant interference with the rights of privacy and data protection that profiling, understood as a structured overview of personal information, might entail. In a way, the CJEU also anticipated Article 21 of the GDPR, which lays down an individual right to object to data processing, including profiling. In particular, Article 21.1 postulates that the data subject shall have the right to object at any time to the processing of personal data, which produces legal effects concerning him or her or similarly significantly affects him or her.[43] The burden of proof then falls on the controller, who cannot process any longer the personal data unless they can demonstrate compelling legitimate grounds for the processing. The decision on whether the processing can be allowed would therefore depend on a balancing test. In *Google Spain*, the CJEU merely sketched the contours of such a balancing exercise in the context of profiling by search engines, leaving it to the national courts to put flesh on the bones of that test. Whereas the Court reasoned that in the particular circumstances of the case at stake, the commercial interest of the search engine in the processing cannot trump the individual rights to privacy and data protection of the individual,[44] it recognized that the balance may depend, on a case-by-case analysis, on:

---

[41] *Supra* n. 6, para. 37, emphasis added.

[42] *Id.*, para. 80, emphasis added.

[43] Article 22.1 of the GDPR reads: "The data subject shall have the right to object, on grounds relating to his or her particular situation, at any time to processing of personal data concerning him or her which is based on point (e) or (f) of Article 6(1), including profiling based on those provisions. The controller shall no longer process the personal data unless the controller demonstrates compelling legitimate grounds for the processing which override the interests, rights and freedoms of the data subject or for the establishment, exercise or defence of legal claims," *supra* n. 5. In the final version of the GDPR, Article 22 is more detailed compared with the original Commission's proposal and includes provisions on the right to individuals to object to the processing of their data for direct marketing purposes.

[44] "In the light of the potential seriousness of that interference [with the rights to privacy and data protection under the EU Charter], it is clear that it cannot be justified by merely the economic interest which the operator of such an engine has in that processing," supra n. 6, para. 81.

the nature of the information in question and its sensitivity for the data subject's private life and on the interest of the public in having that information, an interest which may vary, according to the role played by the data subject in public life.[45]

The CJEU gave particular emphasis to the nature of the information in *Google Spain*: it concerned the display of links to pages of a daily newspaper that mentioned the applicant's name in relation to the recovery of social security debts incurred sixteen years earlier.[46] Such information could hardly be in the interest of the public. Further, the CJEU did not assess the sensitivity of the data based on the categories outlined in the 1995 Directive (and later in the GDPR). Given the limited reasoning characterizing the CJEU's decisions, one can only assume that the sensitivity of the data in *Google Spain* was judged based on the fact that it could potentially have significant effects on the individual. For instance, the applicant's financial credibility for a number of contractual applications could be severely hampered based on the outdated information about his debts. However, the CJEU also acknowledged that public interest considerations could trump individual rights (and the objection to profiling), for example depending on whether the individual is a public figure or not. Ultimately, although with *Google Spain* the CJEU pointed to the significant dangers that profiling might pose to individual rights, the judgment did not disentangle the different aspects of the rights to privacy and data protection in relation to profiling, an opportunity that the Court missed also in its *Digital Rights Ireland* and *Schrems* decisions.

The Digital Rights Ireland *and* Schrems *Cases*

The European Court of Human Right's (ECtHR) case law on profiling in cases condemning state surveillance served as a springboard for the CJEU in its rulings in *Digital Rights Ireland* and *Schrems*. In particular, in *Digital Rights Ireland*[47] where the CJEU invalidated the European Data Retention Directive in its entirety and with retroactive effect, the Court extensively cited the case law of the ECtHR on profiling.[48] The Data Retention Directive aimed to harmonize the obligations of the providers of publicly available electronic communications services or of public communications networks with respect to the retention of data generated or processed by them, in order to ensure that the data are available for the purpose of the investigation, detection and prosecution of serious crime, as defined by each Member State in its national law. Retention concerned so-called traffic or meta data, necessary to identify subscribers but excluded the content of their communications.

One of the primary grounds on which the CJEU based its conclusion that the Data Retention Directive is invalid was the Court's concern about the significant effects that profiling may produce on the life of individuals. The CJEU held that that the "data, taken as a whole, may allow very precise conclusions to be drawn concerning the private lives of the persons whose data has been retained, such as the habits of everyday life, permanent or temporary places of

---

[45] *Id.*, para. 81. A discussion on balancing freedom of expression with privacy and data protection rights goes beyond the scope of this chapter. *See* Bilyana Petkova, "Towards an Internal Hierarchy of Values in the EU Legal Order: Balancing the Freedom of Speech and Data Privacy," 23 *Maastricht Journal of European and Comparative Law*, 3 (2016).

[46] *Id.*, para. 97.

[47] *Supra* n. 7.

[48] In particular, the CJEU drew inspiration from the ECtHR's *S. and Marper v. the United Kingdom*, Judgment of 4 December 2008, Application No. 30562/04 and 30566/04. In this case, the Strasbourg Court referred to the "risk of stigmatization" stemming from the entry of the applicants' personal data into a big database.

residence, daily or other movements, the activities carried out, the social relationships of those persons and the social environments frequented by them."[49] It stated that in view of the important role played by Articles 7 and 8 of the Charter on data protection and privacy, and given the serious interference that data retention for national security purposes entails, "the EU legislature's discretion is reduced, with the result that review of that discretion should be *strict*."[50]

The *Digital Rights* decision concerned measures of profiling in the context of state surveillance, but due to the specificities of the EU data protection regime which extends protections to personal data held both by the private and the public sector, its relevance is broader. Importantly, the Court, quoting the opinion of the Advocate General, put a special emphasis on the fact that the "data … [are] subsequently used *without the subscriber or registered user being informed*, [something that can] generate in the minds of the persons concerned the feeling that their private lives are the subject of constant surveillance."[51] Finally, based on a distinction between content and traffic data, the CJEU declared that neither the essence of the right to privacy nor the essence of the right to data protection are affected since the challenged Directive did not require the acquisition of content. Instead, the Court proceeded in invalidating the Data Retention Directive based on a proportionality assessment, finding the measures enshrined in it to disproportionately affect both Articles 7 and 8 of the Charter, read in conjunction. The Court's reasoning can be criticized in that it did not explicitly acknowledge the blurring line between content and meta data. In fact, a very detailed profile of the individual can be constructed based on meta data only.

In any event, in the *Schrems*[52] case which invalidated the Safe Harbor agreement on data transfers between the United States and the European Union, the Court found that the essence of the right to private life is affected in the case of mass surveillance that gives the government access to the content of intercepted communications.[53] Similarly, the Court found that the essence of the right to effective judicial protection is affected by the lack of any possibility for the individual to pursue legal remedies (in order to have access to personal data relating to him or her, or to obtain the rectification or erasure of such data). When the essence of a fundamental right is affected under EU law, this excludes any further balancing tests with countervailing interests.[54] It is noteworthy that with *Schrems*, the Court established for the first time that the very essence of a fundamental right is affected. However, as with *Digital Rights Ireland* and *Google Spain* before, the CJEU did not discuss further the differences, if any, between Article 7 and 8 of the Charter.

---

[49] *Supra* n. 7, para. 27.
[50] *Id.*, para. 48, emphasis added.
[51] *Id.*, para. 37, emphasis added.
[52] *Supra* n. 8.
[53] *Id.*, para. 94. Although the referring Irish Court and the Advocate General did not reach the same conclusions about the essence of fundamental rights being affected, both largely shared the CJEU's assessment on the incompatibility of the Safe Harbor decision with the Charter in what refers to the necessity of massive surveillance and the insufficiency of US oversight mechanisms such as the Foreign Intelligence Surveillance Court (FISC). See Opinion of Advocate General Bot in Case C-362/14, *Maximillian Schrems v. Data Protection Commissioner* (Oct. 6, 2015).
[54] "The identification of an intrusion as compromising the essence of privacy meant that there was no need for a proportionality assessment under Article 52 (1.2) of the Charter," Martin Scheinin, "The Essence of Privacy and Varying Degrees of Intrusion," *Verfassunsblog*, available at: http://verfassungsblog.de/the-essence-of-privacy-and-varying-degrees-of-intrusion-2/ (2015).

THE RIGHTS TO PRIVACY AND DATA PROTECTION

Separate or Derivative?

A closer look at the cases described earlier against the background of the GDPR's provision on automated decision-making leads to several questions. First, could the rights to private life and data protection under the Charter be disentangled and to what effect? Second, if so, under what circumstances would the essence of the right to data protection be affected?

As in other areas of EU law where the law is yet to be settled[55] and despite the fact that the CJEU has not explicitly elaborated yet on such a distinction, the debate on distinguishing the right to privacy[56] from the right to data protection[57] under the Charter has been triggered by interpretations given by Advocates General. On the one hand, Advocate General Eleanor Sharpston[58] and more recently, Advocate General Pedro Cruz Villalòn[59] supported the view that the two rights are separate. On the other, Advocate General Dámaso Ruiz-Jarabo Colomer thought the right to data protection to be merely copying some of the provisions of the 1995 Directive and essentially subsumed by the right to privacy.[60] The emerging consensus in the academic community, despite differences in opinion about which of the two rights should be ascribed broader scope, converges around the view that the two rights need to be afforded different legal treatments.[61] Some anchor this view in the understanding that data protection is a positive right, which requires intervention by the state in order to ensure the observance of that right, whereas privacy is viewed as a negative right that guards against state or corporate surveillance (or the reverse). In his opinion in *Digital Rights Ireland*, Advocate General Cruz Villalòn continued the discussion fueled by academics under this header by stating that: "Article 8 of the Charter enshrines the right to the protection of personal data as a right which is distinct from the right to privacy. Although data protection seeks to ensure respect for privacy, it is, in particular, subject to an autonomous regime."[62] The Advocate General sought to hypothesize

---

[55] For a recent example, *see* Opinion of Advocate General Kokott in Case C-157/15, *Samira Achbita and Centrum voor gelijkheid van kansen en voor racismebestrijding v. G4S Secure Solutions NV* (2016) and Opinion of Advocate General Sharpson in Case C-188/15, *Bougnaoui and ADDH v. Micropole SA*. Both cases concerned forms of prohibition on wearing a headscarf at work but the Advocates General suggested a somewhat different conclusion.

[56] Article 7 of the Charter reads: "Everyone has the right to respect for his or her private and family life, home and communications," *supra* n. 9.

[57] Article 8 of the Charter reads: "1. Everyone has the right to the protection of personal data concerning him or her. 2. Such data must be processed fairly for specified purposes and on the basis of the consent of the person concerned or some other legitimate basis laid down by law. Everyone has the right of access to data which has been collected concerning him or her, and the right to have it rectified. 3. Compliance with these rules shall be subject to control by an independent authority."

[58] Opinion of Advocate General Sharpston for Case C-92/09 and C-93/09, *Volker und Markus Schecke and Hartmut Eifert* [2010] ECR I-11063, para. 71.

[59] Opinion of Advocate General Cruz Villalòn in Joined Cases C-293/12 and C-594/12, *Digital Rights Ireland Ltd. v. Minister for Communications, Marine and Natural Resources and Kärntner Landesregierung and Others* (Dec. 12, 2013).

[60] Opinion of Advocate-General Ruiz Jarabo Colomer, delivered on 22 December 2008 for Case C-553/07, *College van burgemeester en wethouders van Rotterdam v. M.E.E. Rijkeboer*, para. 25.

[61] Gloria González Fuster and Raphaël Gellert, "The Fundamental Right to Data Protection in the European Union: In Search of an Unchartered Right," 26 *International Review of Law, Computers & Technology* 73 (2012); Juliane Kokott and Christoph Sobotta, "The Distinction between Privacy and Data Protection in *the* Jurisprudence of the CJEU and the ECtHR," 3 *International Data Privacy Law* (2013). See also Orla Linskey, "Deconstructing Data Protection: The 'Added-Value' of a Right to Data Protection in the EU Legal Order," 63 *International and Comparative Law Quarterly* 3 (2014).

[62] *Supra* n. 59, para. 55.

about situations where one of the two rights might be considered to legitimately pass a proportionality assessment (i.e., the right to data protection), whereas the other (the right to privacy) can be disproportionately affected. For the Advocate General, provided that there are sufficient guarantees, the mere processing of personal data, even if such data identify an individual,[63] cannot be seen as disproportionately affecting Article 8 of the Charter. However, the Advocate General distinguished the nature of the data: without going into the explicitly enumerated categories of sensitive data, he isolated a category of "data which are in a sense more than personal. These are data which, qualitatively, relate essentially to private life, to the confidentiality of private life, including intimacy."[64] Further, the Advocate General describes the data as "not personal data in the traditional sense of the term, relating to specific information concerning the identity of individuals, but 'special' personal data, the use of which may make it possible to create a both faithful and exhaustive map of a large portion of a person's conduct strictly forming part of his private life, or even a complete and accurate picture of his private identity."[65] It would seem that what the Advocate General was truly concerned with was the effects of profiling. In his reasoning, even the mere upstream collection of such "more personal data" might need to be curtailed in order to safeguard private life under Article 7 of the Charter.

What to make of all these loose ends? First of all, it would appear that the CJEU places special importance on the Charter rights to privacy and data protection that, read together with the 1995 Directive or the GDPR, establish a regime of high protection. Second, there is a particular emphasis in the GDPR, as well as in the CJEU's case law, on providing safeguards for the individual to prevent undesirable profiling. One could imagine that in a world of big data, both the right to data protection and privacy's remit stretch beyond issues of identification[66] and go into issues of profiling. Profiling precedes automated decision-making and as such, might constitute serious interference with the rights to privacy and data protection if it significantly affects the individual. Significant effects on the individual in turn cannot be confined to the processing of sensitive data as defined in the 1995 Directive or the GDPR and instead need to be assessed on a case-by-case basis. The standard of judicial review that applies is, to use the vernacular of the US Supreme Court, that of strict scrutiny or strict proportionality. Interferences therefore with the right to both data protection and privacy might be justified but the threshold that poses requirements for sufficient safeguards is elevated. When should limitations to these rights be deemed so incongruent with the overall European data protection regime as to preclude any assessment of proportionality?

The Essence of the Rights to Privacy and Data Protection: Hypotheticals from the Employment Context

As discussed in the previous section, in *Schrems* the CJEU was concerned with indiscriminate surveillance that reaches the content of intercepted telecommunications. Potentially, the accumulation of such data can lead to very detailed profiling of the individual; the Court thought that this affects the very essence of the right to private life. Following Advocate General

---

[63] *Id.*, paras. 64 and 59–60.

[64] *Id.*, para. 65.

[65] *Id.*, para. 74.

[66] The mere identification of an individual by their name may be thought to go outside of the scope of protection afforded to private life, or alternatively, dismissed on a balancing. For these two alternative approaches, *see* T-194/04 *Bavarian Lager v. Commission* [2007] ECR II-3201 and Opinion of Advocate General Sharpston in Case C-28/08 P, *European Commission v. Bavarian Lager*, EU:C:2009:624, paras. 153 and 217.

Cruz Villalòn's reasoning from his opinion in the *Digital Rights Ireland* case, a dignitary understanding of the core values that privacy underpins must be linked to the individual's intimate, inner sphere of which the content of communications forms a part. The CJEU did not spell out what might constitute an infringement of the essence of the right to data protection but some have speculated that data security is at the core of Article 8 of the Charter. Such an interpretation stems from the *Digital Rights Ireland* case:

> Nor is that retention of data such as to adversely affect the essence of the fundamental right to the protection of personal data enshrined in Article 8 of the Charter, because Article 7 of Directive 2006/24 provides, in relation to data protection and data security, that, without prejudice to the provisions adopted pursuant to Directives 95/46 and 2002/58, certain principles of data protection and data security must be respected by providers of publicly available electronic communications services or of public communications networks. According to those principles, Member States are to ensure that appropriate technical and organisational measures are adopted against accidental or unlawful destruction, accidental loss or alteration of the data.[67]

However, a broader understanding of the right to data protection as ensuring the fair processing of data would lead to a different interpretation. In certain cases, even though the intimate sphere of the individual would not be touched upon and therefore the essence of the right to privacy not adversely affected, we could imagine situations in which algorithmic profiling is performed without any suitable safeguards, i.e., without the individual being informed about the profiling and its consequences or being given the possibility to recur to any appeal's procedure. Unfair processing under Article 8 of the Charter could thus infringe the very essence of the right to data protection.

One example might come from the employment context. Increasingly, private companies sell predictive algorithms to inform employment decisions based on data analytics – the science of mining raw data to make predictions. "People analytics" positions itself to analyze big data for human resource applications. In the United States, one company alone, Kenexa – bought by IBM for $1.3 billion in 2012 – reportedly does 20 million assessments each year.[68] For millions of available jobs in the United States, particularly entry-level hourly jobs, an online personality test determines whether the applicant even gets a chance to have their resume looked at by an actual human being. Estimates show that in 2014, 60–70 percent of prospective workers faced these tests, up from 30 percent to 40 percent just five years earlier, with a growth rate of 20 percent annually.[69] Algorithms can uncover correlations between seemingly unrelated personal characteristics; an anecdotal example includes the tendency of job applicants to like Manga animations, which correlates with their good job performance in coding. Proponents argue that data analytics enhance business and efficiency but also diversity by helping employers make better decisions and facilitating the hiring of individuals otherwise difficult to place. Critics claim that reliance on big data promotes labor discrimination and adversely affects human rights. Beyond

---

[67] *Supra* n. 7, paras. 39–40. Recently, also Advocate General Mengozzi espoused a similar interpretation of the essence of data protection as data security in his opinion in the PNR-Canada case: "As regards the essence of the protection of personal data, it should be observed that, under Article 9 of the agreement envisaged, Canada is required, in particular, to 'ensure compliance verification and the protection, security, confidentiality and integrity of the data', and also to implement 'regulatory, procedural or technical measures to protect PNR data against accidental, unlawful or unauthorised access, processing or loss'. In addition, any breach of data security must be amenable to effective and dissuasive corrective measures which might include sanctions," *see* Opinion 1/15, September 8, 2016, ECLI:EU: C:2016:656 at paras. 185–187.

[68] Andrew Leonard, "Your Boss Wants to Be Nate Silver," *Salon* (Dec. 13, 2013), available at: http://bit.ly/1jWKQ8N.

[69] "Exacerbating Long-Term Unemployment: Big Data and Employment Assessments, Employment Testing: Failing to Make the Grade," *Employee Assessment Blog* (June 13, 2014), available at: http://bit.ly/2a9ARAX.

the question of workplace discrimination, the research of Nathan Newman shows that prehire personality testing taken to the next level by algorithms helps employers screen out employees who will insist on higher wages and organize or support unionization.[70] For instance, an analysis of employment practices has shown that Walmart managers use personality tests to screen out those likely to be sympathetic to unions, emphasizing that finding the most skilled employee is a subordinate goal to finding the most compliant one. In another example a screening test designed for nurses was advertised as weeding out "undesirable behavior" described as "focus on pay, benefits or status".[71]

Equally troubling, as Newman shows, for employees who are already hired, companies have massively expanded data-driven workplace surveillance that allows employers to algorithmically assess which employees are most likely to leave and thereby limit pay increases largely to them, lowering wages over time for workers either less able to find new employment because of their age or less inclined in general to risk doing so. At least in the United States, monitoring workers' actions through office computers and e-mail, and tracking web searching or access to social media to electronically analyse the data seems to be on the way of becoming the rule rather than the exception for employers. Similarly, every work cellphone can perform a monitoring function, delivering location data on every step a worker makes. Data analytics empowers companies to assess who is looking for a new job and who is not, who might leave, and who will stay no matter what. Annual pay raises and bonuses could then be calibrated accordingly. A report by McKinsey based on a case study of a European industrial company found out that when the company applied data analytics to that effect, they were able to slash their annual budget for compensation increases by 75 percent compared to their previous across-the-board compensation approach.[72] As one can summarize the matter, it really comes down to segmentation and differentiation by the employer. This trend in the employment context is not unlike strategies that companies implement in the financial sector and consumer marketing to profile people in order to give them very different offers for products and services. However, arguably the long-lasting, significant effects that screening employment practices have on the individual are even greater.

In the near future, perhaps algorithmic personality tests will be designed also for employees so that their data would not need to be scraped from e-mail or social media, something that might on its face be contravening the purpose limitation principle under EU data protection law.[73] In 2015 the police department in the city council in Charlotte, North Carolina, piloted an algorithm that used officers' past history of citizens' complaints against them along with less obvious factors such as incidents that the officers deemed stressful in order to predict the probability of their committing future police misconduct.[74] Thus, policemen classified as more prone to violence were recommended for counselling programs.

---

[70] Nathan Newman, "UnMarginalizing Workers: How Big Data Drives Lower Wages and How Reframing Labor Law Can Restore Information Equality in the Workplace," *Cincinnati Law Review* (forthcoming).

[71] *Id.*

[72] Sabine Cosack, Matthew Guthridge, and Emily Lawson, "Retaining Key Employees in Times of Change, *McKinsey Quarterly* (Aug. 2010), available at: http://www.mckinsey.com/businessfunctions/organization/our-insights/retaining-keyemployees-in-times-of-change.

[73] For an interpretation possibly divergent from EU law on workplace privacy rights by the ECtHR, see *Bărbulescu v. Romania,* Judgment of 12 January 2016, Application No. 61496/08. However, the decision in *Bărbulescu* is not final as it is pending review by the Grand Chamber of the Strasbourg Court. See also Steve Peers, "Is Workplace Privacy Dead? Comments on the Barbulescu Judgment," *EU Law Analysis Blog* (2016), available at: http://eulawanalysis .blogspot.com/2016/01/is-workplace-privacy-dead-comments-on.html.

[74] Rob Arthur, "We Now Have Algorithms to Predict Police Misconduct: Will Police Departments Use Them?" *Five Thirty Eight* (2016), available at: http://fivethirtyeight.com/features/we-now-have-algorithms-to-predict-police-miscon duct/.

Would "people analytics" be legal under EU law? Algorithmic personality tests would fall under the statutory definition of personal data. With the processing of personal data of workers next to the 1995 Directive (and soon the GDPR),[75] the application of the Charter can be triggered. In the hypotheticals described earlier, algorithmic employment screening practices can be reasonably understood as covering the definition of profiling, outlined both in statute and in the CJEU's case law. Under the GDPR, the deployment of such practices by employers would require impact assessments and might be considered to cover the definition of sensitive data, even if questions on trade union membership are not explicitly asked. Read in the light of the GDPR's preamble and the CJEU's case law, the derogations to the prohibition on automated decision-making under Article 22 of the GDPR that are based on contract, consent, and Member State or EU law would need to be read narrowly. People analytics realized through algorithms would therefore only be possible with minimum suitable safeguards for the data subject such as the upfront provision of information about employment profiling (the emphasis on information is also enshrined in the *Digital Rights Ireland* case); the possibility to express his or her point of view and obtain an explanation of the decision (e.g., why a pay raise is not granted to one employee but is to another or why a policeman is not allowed to participate in a particular police operation),[76] as well as the possibility to challenge that decision (e.g., in an appeals procedure). Furthermore, under Article 21.1 of the GDPR individuals would be empowered to object to such processing of their data, perhaps arguing in light of *Google Spain* that the mere commercial interest of the employer in using a prehiring algorithm or algorithmic personality test cannot justify interference with their rights to privacy and data protection. On a proportionality assessment, courts might then need to assess the relevance of public or general interest arguments[77] that can be evoked in defense by the employer, for instance in the case of algorithmic profiling for crime prevention, or in the case mentioned earlier, for predicting police misbehavior. Under the Charter, profiling in the context of people analytics may not necessarily reach the level of impinging on the very essence of the right to privacy understood as intimacy (although it could still fail the proportionality test). It can however, depending on the circumstances of the case, be viewed as infringing upon the essence of the right to data protection, and in particular on the fairness of the data processing prong.

---

[75] Under EU law, unlike directives, which need to be transposed into domestic law and therefore often give discretion to the national lawmaker as to the measures to be adopted in order to achieve the results set by the directive, regulations have directly binding effect on the Member States. However, the GDPR has still left a considerable margin of discretion to the national lawmaker in various areas, including the employment context. Art. 88.1 of the GDPR and para. 155 of the Recital lay down that Member States may, by law or by collective agreements, provide for more specific rules to ensure the protection of the rights and freedoms in respect of the processing of employees' personal data in the employment context. However, Art. 88.2 require that such rules include suitable and specific measures to safeguard the data subject's human dignity, legitimate interests and fundamental rights, *supra* n. 5.

[76] Combined reading of Art. 21.1 and Art. 13.2(f) of the GDPR, *supra* n. 5.

[77] The GDPR still leaves public interest considerations to be defined by national law, *see* primarily Art. 6.3b and para. 10 of the Recital of the GDPR. Subject to sufficient safeguards for the individual, such considerations may in certain cases trump the purpose limitation principle, including in the employment context, *see* mainly Art. 5.1.b, Art. 6e and paras. 50–52 of the Recital of the GDPR. Importantly, Article 52.1 of the Charter provides that: "Any limitation on the exercise of the rights and freedoms recognised by this Charter must be provided for by law and respect the essence of those rights and freedoms. Subject to the principle of proportionality, limitations may be made only if they are necessary and genuinely meet *objectives of general interest recognised by the Union* or the need to protect the rights and freedoms of others," *supra* n. 9.

TENTATIVE CONCLUDING REMARKS

The comprehensive overhaul of the European data protection regime, which started as far back as in 2012 and is still ongoing beyond the adoption of the GDPR, holds a lot of promise for the protection of the personal data of Europeans in a digital world. In particular, the guarantees enshrined in the revised provisions on automated decision-making of the GDPR, when read in conjunction with the recital, provide wider protections to the individual than the 1995 Directive. Certainly, the European Charter of Fundamental Rights and the case law of the CJEU interpreting the statutory provisions in light of the Charter secure a robust constitutional layer of protection against undesirable profiling. In spite of fluctuations in the definitions of personal and sensitive data during the legislative process that led to the adoption of the GDPR, it seems that the CJEU might be making a subtle move in its interpretation of the Charter toward protecting against undesirable profiling measures instead of merely protecting against the identification of an individual. We have argued that in this sense, the essence of the right to data protection can be harmed when there is unfair profiling in the context of automated decision-making.

However, many open questions still remain. One of them relates to the explainability of algorithmic decision-making. At a technical and/or methodological level, what does explainability entail? Finally, what appeal procedures with human intervention can be deemed to satisfy the standard of suitable safeguards?

18

Privacy, Freedom of Expression, and the Right to Be Forgotten in Europe

Stefan Kulk and Frederik Zuiderveen Borgesius

INTRODUCTION

In this chapter, we discuss the relationship between privacy and freedom of expression in Europe.[*] For readers who are not familiar with the complex legal order in Europe, we introduce the Council of Europe and its European Court of Human Rights (Section 1), and the European Union and its Court of Justice (Section 2). We discuss how those two courts deal with privacy and freedom of expression. We illustrate the tension between these two fundamental rights by looking at the judgment of the Court of Justice of the European Union in the *Google Spain* case, sometimes called the 'right to be forgotten' case (Section 3). The court decided in *Google Spain* that people have, under certain conditions, the right to have search results for their name delisted.

We then describe the development of the right to be forgotten, and discuss some open questions (Section 4). Delisting requests illustrate that a case-by-case analysis is required when balancing the rights to privacy and freedom of expression (Section 5). We can expect much more case law, that hopefully provides more guidance on how to strike the balance between these fundamental rights.

We consider how the two most important European courts deal with balancing privacy and freedom of expression.[1] We focus on the right to be forgotten, especially in its sense as the right to have search results removed. The General Data Protection Regulation (GDPR),[2] applicable from 2018, also introduces a broader 'right to erasure'.[3] That GDPR provision is outside the scope of this chapter.[4]

---

[*] As in their earlier publications, both authors equally contributed to this chapter. We would like to thank David Erdos, Bojana Kostic, Marijn Sax, Nico van Eijk, Joris van Hoboken, and Kyu Ho Youm for their helpful comments. Any errors are our own.

[1] There are different traditions in European countries regarding the right balance between privacy and freedom of expression. See M. Verpaux, *Freedom of Expression* (Europeans and Their Rights, Council of Europe 2010), pp. 17–27; pp. 197–199.

[2] European Parliament and Council Regulation (EU) 2016/679 of 27 April 2016 on the Protection of Natural Persons with regard to the Processing of Personal Data and on the Free Movement of Such Data, and Repealing Directive 95/46/EC (General Data Protection Regulation) [2016] OJ L 119/1.

[3] See on the right to erasure ('to be forgotten') in the GDPR: J. V. J. Van Hoboken, 'The Proposed Right to Be Forgotten Seen from the Perspective of Our Right to Remember: Freedom of Expression Safeguards in a Converging Information Environment (Prepared for the European Commission)' (May 2013); C. Bartolini and L. Siry, 'The Right to Be Forgotten in the Light of the Consent of the Data Subject' (2016) 32(2) *Computer Law & Security Review* 218.

[4] The chapter builds on and borrows some sentences from our earlier work: S. Kulk and F. J. Zuiderveen Borgesius, '*Google Spain v. Gonzalez*: Did the Court Forget about Freedom of Expression' (2014) 5(3) *European Journal of Risk Regulation* 389 ; S. Kulk and F. J. Zuiderveen Borgesius, 'Freedom of Expression and "Right to Be Forgotten" Cases in

1 THE COUNCIL OF EUROPE AND ITS EUROPEAN COURT OF HUMAN RIGHTS

The Council of Europe was founded in 1949, just after the Second World War, and is the most important human rights organisation in Europe. It is based in Strasbourg and now has forty-seven Member States.[5] In 1950, the Council of Europe adopted the European Convention on Human Rights.[6] This Convention lists human rights that Member States must guarantee. The Council of Europe also set up a court: the European Court of Human Rights, based in Strasbourg. That court decides on alleged violations of the rights in the European Convention on Human Rights.[7]

1.1 *Privacy*

The European Convention on Human Rights contains a right to privacy (Article 8)[8] and a right to freedom of expression (Article 10). Article 8 of the Convention protects the right to private life. (In this chapter, we use 'privacy' and 'private life' interchangeably.[9]) Article 8 in principle prohibits interference with the right to privacy. Yet, paragraph 2 shows that this prohibition is not absolute. In many cases the right to privacy can be limited by other interests, such as public safety, or for the rights of others, such as freedom of expression. Article 8 reads as follows:

> 1. Everyone has the right to respect for his private and family life, his home and his correspondence.
> 2. There shall be no interference by a public authority with the exercise of this right except such as is in accordance with the law and is necessary in a democratic society in the interests of national security, public safety or the economic well-being of the country, for the prevention of disorder or crime, for the protection of health or morals, or for the protection of the rights and freedoms of others.

The European Court of Human Rights interprets the right to privacy generously, and refuses to define the ambit of the right.[10] The court 'does not consider it possible or necessary to attempt an exhaustive definition of the notion of private life'.[11] The court says it takes

---

the Netherlands after *Google Spain*' (2015) 1(2) *European Data Protection Law Review* 113; F. J. Zuiderveen Borgesius and A. Arnbak, 'New Data Security Requirements and the Proceduralization of Mass Surveillance Law after the European Data Retention Case,' Amsterdam Law School research paper No. 2015–41 (23 October 2015) http://ssrn .com/abstract=2678860; F. J. Zuiderveen Borgesius, *Improving Privacy Protection in the Area of Behavioural Targeting* (Kluwer Law International 2015).

[5] 'Who We Are,' *Council of Europe* www.coe.int/en/web/about-us/who-we-are, accessed 6 September 2017.

[6] European Convention on Human Rights [1950].

[7] Articles 19 and 34 of the European Convention on Human Rights. In exceptional situations, the Grand Chamber of the Court decides on cases (Articles 30 and 43 of the European Convention on Human Rights). Judgments by the Grand Chamber have more weight than judgments of other chambers of the Court.

[8] Article 8 of the European Convention on Human Rights: 'Right to respect for private and family life'.

[9] See on the difference between 'privacy' and 'private life': G. González Fuster, *The Emergence of Personal Data Protection as a Fundamental Right of the EU* (Springer 2014) 82–84; 255.

[10] See generally on the Article 8 case law of the European Court of Human Rights: D. Harris et al., *Law of the European Convention on Human Rights* (Oxford University Press 2014) 522–591; R. Ivana, *Protecting the Right to Respect for Private and Family Life under the European Convention on Human Rights* (Council of Europe 2012); A. W. Heringa and L. Zwaak, 'Right to Respect for Privacy' in P. Van Dijk et al. (eds), *Theory and Practice of the European Convention on Human Rights* (Intersentia 2006) 663–750.

[11] See e.g. *Niemietz v. Germany* App no 13710/88 (ECtHR 16 December 1992), para. 29. The court consistently confirms this approach. See e.g. *Pretty v. United Kingdom*, App no 2346/02 (ECtHR 29 April 2002), para. 61; *Marper v. United Kingdom* App no 30562/04 and 30566/04 (ECtHR 4 December 2008) para. 66.

'a pragmatic, common-sense approach rather than a formalistic or purely legal one'.[12] The court uses a 'dynamic and evolutive' interpretation of the Convention, and says 'the term "private life" must not be interpreted restrictively'.[13] In several cases, the court acknowledged that people also have a right to privacy when they are in public, such as in restaurants[14] or on the street.[15] The court's dynamic approach towards the interpretation of the Convention has been called the 'living instrument doctrine'.[16] The living instrument doctrine could be seen as the opposite of the US doctrine of originalism. The latter doctrine entails that the US Constitution is to be interpreted according to the original meaning that it had at the time of ratification.[17] In sum, the European Court of Human Rights gives extensive protection to the right to privacy interests, but the right is not absolute.

1.2 *Freedom of Expression*

The right to freedom of expression is protected in Article 10 of the European Convention on Human Rights. Paragraph 2 of Article 10 permits limitations on the right to freedom of expression, similar to paragraph 2 of Article 8. Hence, the right to freedom of expression may be limited 'for the protection of the reputation or rights of others',[18] including the right to privacy. Article 10 reads as follows:

> 1. Everyone has the right to freedom of expression. This right shall include freedom to hold opinions and to receive and impart information and ideas without interference by public authority and regardless of frontiers. This Article shall not prevent States from requiring the licensing of broadcasting, television or cinema enterprises.
> 2. The exercise of these freedoms, since it carries with it duties and responsibilities, may be subject to such formalities, conditions, restrictions or penalties as are prescribed by law and are necessary in a democratic society, in the interests of national security, territorial integrity or public safety, for the prevention of disorder or crime, for the protection of health or morals, for the protection of the reputation or rights of others, for preventing the disclosure of information received in confidence, or for maintaining the authority and impartiality of the judiciary.

Article 10 does not only protect the 'speaker' but also the 'listener', who has the right to *receive* information. As the European Court of Human Rights puts it, 'The public has a right to receive information of general interest.'[19] The court also notes that 'Article 10 applies not only to the content of information but also to the means of transmission or reception since any restriction imposed on the means necessarily interferes with the right to receive and impart information.'[20] Moreover, 'the internet plays an important role in enhancing the public's

---

[12] *Botta v. Italy* App no 21439/93 (ECtHR 24 February 1998) para. 27.

[13] *Christine Goodwin v. United Kingdom*, App no 28957/95 (ECtHR 11 July 2002), para. 74; *Amann v. Switzerland*, App no 27798/95 (ECtHR 16 February 2000), para. 65.

[14] *Von Hannover v. Germany (I)*, App no 59320/00 (ECtHR 24 September 2004).

[15] *Peck v. the United Kingdom*, App no 44647/98 (ECtHR 28 January 2003). See also N. Moreham, 'Privacy in Public Places' (2006) 65(3) *The Cambridge Law Journal* 606.

[16] A. Mowbray, 'The Creativity of the European Court of Human Rights' (2005) 5(1) *Human Rights Law Review* 57. The court puts it as follows: 'That the Convention is a living instrument which must be interpreted in the light of present-day conditions is firmly rooted in the Court's case-law' (*Matthews v. United Kingdom* App no 24833/94 (ECtHR 18 February 1999), para. 39). The court started the 'living instrument' approach in: *Tyrer v. United Kingdom*, App no 5856/72 (ECtHR 25 April 1978) para. 31.

[17] B. Boyce, 'Originalism and the Fourteenth Amendment' (1998) 33 *Wake Forest Law Review* 909.

[18] Paragraph 2 of Article 10 of the European Convention on Human Rights.

[19] *Társaság a Szabadságjogokért v. Hungary*, App no 37374/05 (ECtHR 14 April 2009), para. 26.

[20] *Autronic v. Switzerland* App no 12726/87 (ECtHR 22 May 1990), para. 47.

access to news and facilitating the sharing and dissemination of information generally.'[21] Or as the European Court of Human Rights highlighted in another case, 'User-generated expressive activity on the Internet provides an unprecedented platform for the exercise of freedom of expression.'[22]

Privacy and freedom of expression have equal weight in the case law of the European Court of Human Rights: 'As a matter of principle these rights deserve equal respect.'[23] Which right should prevail depends on the circumstances in a particular case. The court has developed a large body of case law on balancing privacy and freedom of expression. The court takes a nuanced approach, taking all circumstances of a case into account.[24]

To balance privacy and freedom of expression, the European Court of Human Rights has developed a set of criteria. For instance, expression that advances public debate receives extra protection in the court's case law: an 'essential criterion is the contribution made by photos or articles in the press to a debate of general interest'.[25] And if a publication concerns a politician or a similar public figure, rather than an ordinary citizen, the European Court of Human Rights is more likely to rule that freedom of expression outweighs privacy.[26] The court summarises the main criteria as follows:

> Where the right to freedom of expression is being balanced against the right to respect for private life, the relevant criteria in the balancing exercise include the following elements: contribution to a debate of general interest, how well known the person concerned is, the subject of the report, the prior conduct of the person concerned, the method of obtaining the information and its veracity, the content, form and consequences of the publication, and the severity of the sanction imposed [on the party invoking freedom of expression].[27]

The Convention's provisions primarily protect people against their states. States should not interfere too much in people's lives – states thus have a negative obligation towards their citizens. States may only interfere with a person's right to freedom of expression if such interference is proportionate and necessary in a democratic society. However, in the late 1960s, the European Court of Human Rights started to recognize that the Convention could also imply positive obligations.[28] Hence, on some occasions, states must also take action to protect people against breaches of their human rights.[29] For instance, a state may have an obligation to protect

---

[21] *Fredrik Neij and Peter Sunde Kolmisoppi v. Sweden* App no 40397/12 (ECtHR 19 February 2013), p. 9.

[22] *Delfi v. Estonia* App no 64569/09 (ECtHR 16 June 2015), para. 110.

[23] *Axel Springer AG v. Germany* App no 39954/08 (ECtHR 7 February 2012), para. 87. See similarly: *Von Hannover v. Germany* App nrs 40660/08 and 60641/08 (ECtHR 7 February 2012), para. 100; *Węgrzynowski and Smolczewski v. Poland* App no 33846/07 (ECtHR 16 July 2013), para. 56. See on this balancing approach: E. Barendt, 'Balancing Freedom of Expression and Privacy: The Jurisprudence of the Strasbourg Court' (2009) 1(1) *Journal of Media Law* 49.

[24] M. Oetheimer, *Freedom of Expression in Europe: Case-Law Concerning Article 10 of the European Convention on Human Rights* (Council of Europe Publishing 2007).

[25] *Axel Springer AG v. Germany* App no 39954/08 (ECtHR 7 February 2012), para. 90.

[26] *Axel Springer AG v. Germany* App no 39954/08 (ECtHR 7 February 2012), para. 91.

[27] *Satakunnan Markkinapörssi Oy And Satamedia Oy v. Finland* App no 931/13 (ECtHR 21 July 2015), para. 83.

[28] J. Akandji-Kombe, *Positive Obligations under the European Convention on Human Rights: A Guide to the Implementation of the European Convention on Human Rights* (Council of Europe Publishing 2007).

[29] See e.g. *Z v. Finland* App no 22009/93 (ECtHR 25 February 1997), para. 36; *Mosley v. United Kingdom*, App no 48009/08 (ECtHR 10 May 2011), para. 106. See generally: J. Akandji-Kombe, 'Positive Obligations under the European Convention on Human Rights: A Guide to the Implementation of the European Convention on Human Rights', 7 (Human Rights Handbooks 2007); P. De Hert, 'From the Principle of Accountability to System Responsibility? Key Concepts in Data Protection Law and Human Rights Law Discussions', International Data Protection Conference 2011 www.vub.ac.be/LSTS/pub/Dehert/410.pdf accessed 6 September 2017.

journalists from violent attacks. If the state fails to meet that obligation, the state infringes the right to freedom of expression.[30]

People cannot bring a claim against other people before the European Court of Human Rights.[31] But people can complain to the court if their state does not adequately protect their rights against infringements by other people. The rights in the European Convention on Human Rights can also indirectly protect people against human rights violations by other non-state actors.

To illustrate how the European Convention on Human Rights balances privacy and freedom of expression, we briefly discuss the 2012 *Axel Springer* case. Springer publishes the mass-circulation German daily newspaper, *Bild*. In 2004, *Bild* wrote about the arrest of a well-known German actor during the Munich beer festival (*Oktoberfest*) for possession of 0.23 gram of cocaine. The actor plays a police superintendent in a popular TV series. *Bild* put a picture of the actor on its front page with the text: 'Cocaine! Superintendent [name] caught at the Munich beer festival' (publication 1). In a later publication (2), *Bild* reported that the actor was convicted for cocaine possession and fined 18000 euro.

The actor went to court, claiming *Bild* had invaded his privacy. German courts decided, in several instances, that Springer violated the actor's privacy, because there was no public interest in knowing about his offence. The German courts prohibited further publication of the *Bild* article and ordered Springer to pay a 1000-euro penalty. German courts gave similar judgments regarding publication 2.

Springer went to the European Court of Human Rights, and claimed that Germany violated its right to freedom of expression. Germany and Springer agreed that Springer's freedom of expression was interfered with, that the interference was prescribed by law, and that the aim of the interference was legitimate: protecting the reputation and privacy of the actor. But the parties disagreed on whether the interference with freedom of expression was 'necessary in a democratic society' (see Article 10(2) of the European Convention on Human Rights).

The European Court of Human Rights confirms that freedom of expression, as a general principle, is essential for democracy:

> Freedom of expression constitutes one of the essential foundations of a democratic society and one of the basic conditions for its progress and for each individual's self-fulfilment. Subject to paragraph 2 of Article 10, it is applicable not only to 'information' or 'ideas' that are favourably received or regarded as inoffensive or as a matter of indifference, but also to those that offend, shock or disturb. Such are the demands of pluralism, tolerance and broadmindedness without which there is no 'democratic society'. As set forth in Article 10, freedom of expression is subject to exceptions, which must, however, be construed strictly, and the need for any restrictions must be established convincingly.[32]

The European Court of Human Rights reaffirms that freedom of expression can be limited in view of the rights of others, such as privacy. The court agrees with the German courts' assessment that Springer's sole interest in writing about the actor was that he was a well-known actor who was arrested. However, the court emphasises that he was arrested in public, during the *Oktoberfest*. Moreover, the actor had revealed details about his private life in a number of interviews. Therefore, his legitimate expectation of privacy was reduced.[33] Furthermore, the publications had a sufficient factual basis.

---

[30] See e.g. *Gundem v. Turkey* App no 23144/93 (ECtHR 16 March 2000).
[31] Article 34 of the European Convention on Human Rights.
[32] *Axel Springer AG v. Germany* App no 39954/08 (ECtHR 7 February 2012), para. 78. Internal citations omitted.
[33] Ibid., para. 101. Internal citations omitted.

According to the European Court of Human Rights, a balancing exercise was needed between the publisher's right to freedom of expression, and the actor's right to privacy. The court says 'there is nothing to suggest that such a balancing exercise was not undertaken' by Springer. As Springer had received the information about the actor from the police, it did not have strong grounds for believing that it should preserve his anonymity. Therefore, says the court, Springer did not act in bad faith. Additionally, Springer's publications did not 'reveal details about [the actor's] private life, but mainly concerned the circumstances of and events following his arrest'.[34] Nor did the publications contain disparaging expressions or unsubstantiated allegations.[35]

Regarding the severity of the sanctions imposed on Springer, the court notes, 'Although these were lenient, they were capable of having a chilling effect on the applicant company.'[36] The European Court of Human Rights concludes that Germany violated the right to freedom of expression of the publisher Springer.[37] In short, Springer's freedom of expression right prevails, in this case, over the actor's privacy right.

In sum, the European Convention on Human Rights protects both privacy and freedom of expression. The Convention's privacy and freedom of expression rights can have a horizontal effect, which means that these rights are also relevant in disputes among citizens. The European Court of Human Rights says privacy and freedom of expression are equally important.

2 THE EUROPEAN UNION AND ITS COURT OF JUSTICE

The European Union has its origin in the European Coal and Steel Community, which was formed in 1951, and the European Economic Community and European Atomic Energy Community, which were formed in 1957. These communities and other forms of cooperation developed into the European Union (EU), which was formally established in 1992 by the Maastricht Treaty. The EU has grown into an economic and political partnership between twenty-eight (soon twenty-seven)[38] European countries. The 2007 Lisbon Treaty was the latest treaty to structurally reform the European Union.

The EU itself is not a party to the European Convention of Human Rights.[39] However, each of the EU member states is also a member of the Council of Europe, and must thus also adhere to the Convention on Human Rights.[40]

The Court of Justice of the European Union, based in Luxembourg, is one of the core EU institutions.[41] National judges in the EU can, and in some cases must, ask the Court of Justice of the European Union for a preliminary judgment concerning the interpretation of EU law.[42] As noted, the European Union has its roots in economic cooperation. Until 1969 the Court of

---

[34] Ibid., para. 108.
[35] Ibid., para. 108.
[36] Ibid., para. 109.
[37] Ibid., paras. 110–111.
[38] The United Kingdom is likely to leave the EU: the so-called Brexit.
[39] See also Opinion 2/13, ECLI:EU:C:2014:2454, in which the European Court of Justice advised against accession of the EU to the European Convention on Human Rights.
[40] 'Our Member States', *Council of Europe* www.coe.int/en/web/about-us/our-member-states, accessed 6 September 2017.
[41] Article 13(1) of the Treaty on European Union (consolidated version) ([2016] OJ C 202).
[42] Article 19(3)(b) of the Treaty on European Union (consolidated version).

Justice of the European Union did not consider itself competent to rule on fundamental rights.[43] Nowadays, the Treaty on the European Union codifies the importance of fundamental rights.[44] Article 6(3) of the Treaty reads: 'Fundamental rights, as guaranteed by the European Convention for the Protection of Human Rights and Fundamental Freedoms and as they result from the constitutional traditions common to the Member States, shall constitute general principles of the Union's law.' Moreover, in 2000 the Charter of Fundamental Rights of the European Union was adopted. It lists the fundamental rights and freedoms recognized by the EU.[45] Since the Charter became a legally binding instrument in 2009,[46] the number of cases in which the Court of Justice of the European Union cited the Charter has increased substantially.[47] Recently, the court has also given influential privacy and data protection-related judgments,[48] such as the *Google Spain* judgment (see Section 4.3).

2.1 *Privacy and Freedom of Expression*

The Charter of Fundamental Rights of the European Union contains a right to privacy and a right to freedom of expression that resemble the corresponding rights in the European Convention on Human Rights.[49] In addition to the right to privacy, the Charter contains a separate right to the protection of personal data.[50]

2.2 *Data Protection Law*

Article 8 of the Charter of Fundamental Rights of the European Union grants people the right to protection of personal data:

> 1. Everyone has the right to the protection of personal data concerning him or her.
> 2. Such data must be processed fairly for specified purposes and on the basis of the consent of the person concerned or some other legitimate basis laid down by law. Everyone has the right of access to data which has been collected concerning him or her, and the right to have it rectified.
> 3. Compliance with these rules shall be subject to control by an independent authority.

---

[43] In 1969, the Court of Justice of the European Union said that 'fundamental human rights [are] enshrined in the general principles of Community law and protected by the Court' (Case C-29/69 *Stauder v. Stadt Ulm* [1969] ECR 419, para. 7). Also see: G. González Fuster, *The Emergence of Personal Data Protection as a Fundamental Right of the EU* (Springer 2014) 164.

[44] Article 6(3) of the Treaty on the European Union (consolidated version).

[45] The phrases 'fundamental rights' and 'human rights' are roughly interchangeably. See on the slight difference: G. González Fuster, *The Emergence of Personal Data Protection as a Fundamental Right of the EU* (Springer 2014) 164–166.

[46] Article 6(1) of the Treaty on European Union (consolidated version).

[47] G. de Búrca, 'After the EU Charter of Fundamental Rights: The Court of Justice as a Human Rights Adjudicator?', (2013) 20(2) *Maastricht Journal of European and Comparative Law* 168.

[48] See e.g. joined Cases C-293/12 and C-594/12 *Digital Rights Ireland and Seitlinger and others v. Minister for Communications and Others*, ECLI:EU:C:2014:238, invalidating the Data Retention Directive; and Case C-362/14 *Maximillian Schrems v. Data Protection Commissioner*, ECLI:EU:C:2015:650, invalidating the Safe Harbor agreement. See generally: L Laudati *Summaries of EU court decisions relating to data protection 2000–2015* (OLAF European Anti-Fraud Office 2016) https://ec.europa.eu/anti-fraud/sites/antifraud/files/caselaw_2001_2015_en.pdf accessed 6 September 2017.

[49] See Article 7 (privacy) and Article 11 (freedom of expression) in the Charter of Fundamental Rights of the European Union. See Article 52 in the Charter on the possible limitations on the exercise of the Charter's rights.

[50] The European Convention on Human Rights does not explicitly protect personal data. However, many cases that concern personal data are also covered by the Convention's right to privacy. See: P. de Hert and S. Gutwirth, 'Data Protection in the Case Law of Strasbourg and Luxemburg: Constitutionalisation in Action' in S. Gutwirth et al. (eds), *Reinventing Data Protection?* (Springer 2009) 3–44.

Since the 1990s, the EU has played an important role in the field of data protection law. Data protection law developed in response to the increasing amounts of personal information that were gathered by the state and large companies, typically using computers.[51] In the 1970s, several European countries adopted data protection laws. Some of those national data protection laws contained restrictions on the export of personal data. National lawmakers wanted to prevent that their citizen's data would be exported to countries without sufficient legal protection of personal data.[52]

In 1981, the Council of Europe (not the European Union) adopted the first legally binding international instrument on data protection, the Data Protection Convention.[53] The Data Protection Convention requires signatories to enact data protection provisions in their national law.[54] The European Commission, which is a European Union institution, had called on Member States to ratify the Data Protection Convention in 1981. However, in 1990 only seven Member States had done so.[55] Moreover, the Data Protection Convention left possibilities for countries to raise barriers for personal data flows at the borders.[56] Many stakeholders feared that national authorities would stop the export of personal data to other European countries.

In 1990, the EU stepped in to harmonise data protection law in the European Union, and presented a proposal for a Data Protection Directive.[57] After five years of debate, the EU adopted 'Directive 95/46/EC of the European Parliament and of the Council of 24 October 1995 on the Protection of Individuals with regard to the Processing of Personal Data and on the Free Movement of Such Data.'[58] This Data Protection Directive is probably the most influential data privacy text in the world.[59]

The Data Protection Directive has two aims. First: to 'protect the fundamental rights and freedoms of natural persons, and in particular their right to privacy with respect to the processing of personal data'.[60] Second: to safeguard the free flow of personal data between EU member states. Under the Data Protection Directive, EU 'Member States shall neither restrict nor

---

[51] C. J. Bennett, *Regulating Privacy: Data Protection and Public Policy in Europe and the United States* (Cornell University Press 1992).

[52] Ibid. See also F. W. Hondius, *Emerging Data Protection in Europe* (North-Holland Publishing Company 1975); V. Mayer-Schönberger, 'Generational Development of Data Protection in Europe' in P. E. Agre and M. Rotenberg (eds), *Technology and Privacy: The New Landscape* (MIT Press 1997).

[53] Convention for the Protection of Individuals with regard to Automatic Processing of Personal Data CETS No.: 108, 28 January 1981. The Convention is under revision: see http://www.coe.int/en/web/data-protection/modernisation-convention108.

[54] Article 4(1) of the Data Protection Convention.

[55] European Commission, Recommendation 81/679/EEC of 29 July 1981 relating to the Council of Europe Convention for the Protection of Individuals with regard to the Automatic Processing of Personal Data [1981] OJ L246/31; N. Platten, 'Background to and History of the Directive' in D. Bainbridge (ed), *EC Data Protection Directive* (Butterworth 1996) 17–18, 23.

[56] Article 12.3 of the Data Protection Convention allows states to derogate from the prohibition of interfering with cross border data flows, in brief because of the special nature of personal data, or to avoid circumvention of data protection law.

[57] P. M. Schwartz, *Managing Global Data Privacy: Cross-Border Information Flows in a Networked Environment* (Privacy Projects 2009) 11; A. C. M. Nugter, Transborder Flow of Personal Data within the EC: A Comparative Analysis of *Princiepstat* (Kluwer Law International 1990).

[58] European Parliament and Council (EC) 95/46 on the Protection of Individuals with Regard to the Processing of Personal Data and on the Free Movement of Such Data [1995] OJ L281/31.

[59] See M. Birnhack, 'The EU Data Protection Directive: An Engine of a Global Regime' (2008) 24(6) *Computer Law & Security Review* 508; M. Birnhack, 'Reverse Engineering Informational Privacy Law' (2012) 15(1) *Yale Journal of Law and Technology* 24; A. Bradford, 'The Brussels Effect' (2012) 107 *Northwestern University Law Review* 1.

[60] Article 1(1) of the Data Protection Directive. See also Article 1(2) of the General Data Protection Regulation.

prohibit the free flow of personal data between Member States for reasons connected with the protection [of personal data].'[61]

EU data protection law grants rights to people whose data are being processed (data subjects),[62] and imposes obligations on parties that process personal data (data controllers).[63] The Data Protection Directive contains principles for fair data processing, comparable to the Fair Information Practice Principles.[64]

For instance, personal data must be processed lawfully, fairly and transparently (lawfulness, fairness and transparency).[65] Personal data that are collected for one purpose may not be used for incompatible purposes (purpose limitation).[66] Data must be adequate, relevant and limited to what is necessary in relation to the processing purposes (data minimisation).[67] Data must be 'accurate and, where necessary, kept up to date; every reasonable step must be taken to ensure that personal data that are inaccurate, having regard to the purposes for which they are processed, are erased or rectified without delay' (accuracy).[68] Data must be 'kept in a form which permits identification of data subjects for no longer than is necessary for the purposes for which the personal data are processed' (storage limitation).[69] Appropriate security of personal data must be ensured (integrity and confidentiality).[70]

In 2018, the GDPR will replace the Data Protection Directive. While based on the same principles as the Directive, the Regulation brings significant changes. For instance, unlike a directive, a regulation has direct effect in the Member States. A regulation does not require implementation in the national laws of the Member States to be effective.[71] Hence, the Regulation should lead to a more harmonised regime in the European Union.[72] Moreover, the Regulation aims to improve compliance and enforcement. Under the Regulation, Data Protection Authorities can, in some situations, impose fines of up to 4 per cent of a company's worldwide turnover.[73]

The Charter's right to protection of personal data and the right to privacy partly overlap. But in some respects, the right to protection of personal data has a broader scope than the right to privacy. The right to protection of personal data, and data protection law, apply as soon as personal data – any data relating to an identifiable person – are processed. Data protection law aims to ensure fairness when personal data are processed: such data must be processed 'lawfully, fairly and in a transparent manner in relation to the data subject'.[74] Data protection law deals

---

[61] Article 1(2) of the Data Protection Directive. See also Article 1(3) of the General Data Protection Regulation.

[62] Article 2(a) of the Data Protection Directive. See also Article 4(1) of the General Data Protection Regulation.

[63] Article 2(d) of the Data Protection Directive. See also Article 4(7) of the General Data Protection Regulation.

[64] See on the Fair Information Practices: R. Gellman, 'Fair Information Practices: A Basic History' (Version 2.16, 17 June 2016, continuously updated) http://bobgellman.com/rg-docs/rg-FIPShistory.pdf accessed 6 September 2017.

[65] Article 5(a) of the General Data Protection Regulation. Article 5 of the General Data Protection Regulation corresponds with Article 6 of the Data Protection Directive.

[66] Article 6(b) of the Data Protection Directive; Article 5(b) of the General Data Protection Regulation.

[67] Article 6(c) of the Data Protection Directive; Article 5(c) of the General Data Protection Regulation.

[68] Article 6(d) of the Data Protection Directive; Article 5(d) of the General Data Protection Regulation.

[69] Article 6(e) of the Data Protection Directive; Article 5(e) of the General Data Protection Regulation.

[70] Article 6(f) of the Data Protection Directive; Article 5(f) of the General Data Protection Regulation.

[71] Article 288 of the Treaty on the Functioning of the EU (consolidated version 2012).

[72] The extent to which the Regulation will actually harmonize data protection rules is a matter of discussion, see e.g. P. Blume, 'The Myths Pertaining to the Proposed General Data Protection Regulation' (2014) 4(4) *International Data Privacy Law* 269.

[73] Article 79 of the General Data Protection Regulation.

[74] Article 5(1)(a) of the General Data Protection Regulation, which replaces Article 6(1)(a) of the Data Protection Directive.

with 'information privacy'[75] and 'data privacy',[76] but it also aims, for instance, to protect people against discriminatory effects of data processing.[77]

In some respects, privacy has a broader scope than data protection law. For example, a stalker often violates the victim's privacy. However, if the stalker does not collect or process the victim's personal data, data protection law does not apply.[78]

In conclusion, both the European Convention on Human Rights of the Council of Europe and the Charter of Fundamental Rights of the European Union protect privacy and freedom of expression.[79] The more recent Charter also explicitly protects the right to the protection of personal data.

3 THE *GOOGLE SPAIN* JUDGMENT OF THE COURT OF JUSTICE OF THE EUROPEAN UNION

We now turn to the *Google Spain* judgment of the Court of Justice of the European Union to see how this court has applied the rights to privacy, data protection and freedom of expression in a concrete case. The *Google Spain* judgment was triggered by a Spanish dispute between, on the one hand, Google, and on the other hand, Mario Costeja González and the Spanish Data Protection Authority. Costeja González took issue with a link in Google's search results to a 1998 newspaper announcement concerning a real estate auction to recover his social security debts.[80] Without Google's search engine, the newspaper announcement would probably have faded from memory, hidden by practical obscurity.[81]

Costeja González wanted Google to delist the search result for searches on his name, because the information suggesting he had financial problems was outdated. Costeja González complained to the Spanish Data Protection Authority, which upheld the complaint against the search engine. Court proceedings commenced, and eventually a Spanish judge asked the Court of Justice of the European Union on guidance on how to interpret the Data Protection Directive.[82]

In *Google Spain*, the Court of Justice of the European Union states that a search engine enables searchers to establish 'a more or less detailed profile' of a data subject, thereby

---

[75] D. J. Solove and P. M. Schwartz, *Information Privacy Law* (Aspen 2014).

[76] L. A. Bygrave, *Data Privacy Law: An International Perspective* (Oxford University Press 2014).

[77] See E. Brouwer, *Digital Borders and Real Rights: Effective Remedies for Third-Country Nationals in the Schengen Information System* (Martinus Nijhoff Publishers 2008) 200. See also Recital 71 and Article 21 of the General Data Protection Regulation, on profiling and automated decisions. See about that provision the chapter by Boehm and Petkova in this book.

[78] See on the scope of privacy and data protection: G. González Fuster, *The Emergence of Personal Data Protection as a Fundamental Right of the EU* (Springer 2014); F. J. Zuiderveen Borgesius, *Improving Privacy Protection in the Area of Behavioural Targeting* (Kluwer Law International 2015), chapter 5, section 2; O. Lynskey, *The Foundations of EU Data Protection Law* (Oxford University Press 2015).

[79] See: K. Lenaerts and J. A. Gutiérrez Fons, 'The Place of the Charter in the EU Constitutional Edifice' in S. Peers et al. (eds), *The EU Charter of Fundamental Rights: A Commentary* (Hart Publishing 2014) 1559–1594.

[80] See for the original publication: http://hemeroteca.lavanguardia.com/preview/1998/01/19/pagina-23/33842001/pdf .html accessed 6 September 2017.

[81] We borrow the 'practical obscurity' phrase from the US Supreme Court: *Dep't of Justice v. Reporters Comm. for Freedom of the Press*, 489 U.S. 749, 762 (1989). For an analysis see: K. H. Youm and A. Park, 'The "Right to Be Forgotten" in European Union Law Data Protection Balanced with Free Speech.' (2016) 93(2) *Journalism and Mass Communication Quarterly* 273.

[82] See on delisting requests in Spain: M. Peguera, 'In the Aftermath of *Google Spain*: How the "Right to Be Forgotten" Is Being Shaped in Spain by Courts and the Data Protection Authority' (2015) 23(4) *International Journal of Law and Information Technology* 325.

'significantly' affecting privacy and data protection rights.[83] According to the court, search results for a person's name provide 'a structured overview of the information relating to that individual that can be found on the internet – information which potentially concerns a vast number of aspects of his private life and which, without the search engine, could not have been interconnected or could have been only with great difficulty'.[84]

The Court of Justice of the European Union says that search engine operators process personal data if they index, store and refer to personal data available on the web.[85] Moreover, the court sees search engine operators as 'data controllers' in respect of this processing.[86] Data controllers must comply with data protection law. The court also reaffirms that data protection law applies to personal data that are already public.

The Data Protection Directive contains provisions that aim to balance data protection interests and freedom of expression. For example, the directive provides for an exception for data that are processed for journalistic purposes or artistic and literary expression, if 'necessary to reconcile the right to privacy with the rules governing freedom of expression'.[87] But the court states that a search engine operator cannot rely on the exception in data protection law for data processing for journalistic purposes.[88]

The court holds that people have, under certain circumstances, the right to have search results for their name delisted. This right to have search results delisted also applies to lawfully published information. The court bases its judgment on the Data Protection Directive and the privacy and data protection rights of the Charter of Fundamental Rights of the European Union.[89] More specifically, the court bases its decision on the Data Protection Directive's provisions that grant data subjects, under certain conditions, the right to request erasure of personal data, and the right to object to processing personal data.[90]

The Data Protection Directive grants every data subject the right to correct or erase personal data that are not processed in conformity with the directive.[91] In *Google Spain*, the court clarifies that not only inaccurate data can lead to such unconformity, but also data that are 'inadequate, irrelevant or no longer relevant, or excessive' in relation to the processing purposes, for instance because the data have been stored longer than necessary.[92] In such cases, a search engine operator must delist the result at the request of the data subject.

The *Google Spain* judgment focuses on searches based on people's names. For instance, a search engine may have to delist an article announcing a public auction of a house at 10 Eye Street for a search for 'John Doe' who is mentioned in the article. But after a successful delisting

---

[83] Case C-131/12 *Google Spain v. Agencia Española de Protección de Datos (AEPD) and Mario Costeja González*, ECLI: EU:C:2014:317, paras. 37 and 80.

[84] Ibid., para. 80.

[85] Ibid., para. 28.

[86] Ibid., para. 28.

[87] Article 9 Data Protection Directive. See also Article 85 of the General Data Protection Regulation.

[88] Case C-131/12 *Google Spain v. Agencia Española de Protección de Datos (AEPD) and Mario Costeja González*, ECLI: EU:C:2014:317, para. 85. The English version of the judgment says Google 'does not appear' to be able to benefit from the media exception. However, in the authentic language of the judgment, Spanish, the CJEU says Google cannot benefit from the media exception. See on the media exception: D. Erdos, 'From the Scylla of Restriction to the Charybdis of Licence? Exploring the Scope of the "Special Purposes" Freedom of Expression Shield in European Data Protection' (2015) 51(1) *Common Market Law Review* 119.

[89] Case C-131/12 *Google Spain v. Agencia Española de Protección de Datos (AEPD) and Mario Costeja González*, ECLI: EU:C:2014:317, para. 99.

[90] Articles 12(b) and 14(a) of the Data Protection. See Articles 15, 17 and 21 of the General Data Protection Regulation.

[91] Articles 12(b) and 14(a) of the Data Protection Directive. See also Articles 16–19 of the General Data Protection Regulation.

[92] Case C-131/12 *Google Spain v. Agencia Española de Protección de Datos (AEPD) and Mario Costeja González*, ECLI: EU:C:2014:317, para. 93.

request of John Doe, the search engine can still legally refer to the same article when somebody searches for '10 Eye Street'. Making a publication harder to find, but only for searches based on a name, reintroduces some practical obscurity: the information is still available, but not as easily accessible in relation to the person's name.[93]

The Court of Justice of the European Union says in *Google Spain* that a 'fair balance' must be struck between the searchers' legitimate interests, and the data subject's privacy and data protection rights.[94] However, the court says that the data subject's privacy and data protection rights override, 'as a rule', the search engine operator's economic interests, and the public's interest in finding information.[95] With that 'rule', it seems that the Court of Justice of the European Union takes a different approach than the European Court of Human Rights, which says that freedom of expression and privacy have equal weight. However, the Court of Justice of the European Union makes this remark specifically in the context of delisting requests. Hence, the Court did not say that privacy and data protection rights generally override other rights.

The Court of Justice of the European Union also stresses that data subjects' rights should not prevail if the interference with their rights can be justified by the public's interest in accessing information, for example, because of the role played by the data subject in public life. This approach resembles the approach of the European Court of Human Rights when balancing privacy and the freedom of expression. As mentioned, the European Court of Human Rights considers how well-known the person is about whom a publication speaks. Public figures such as politicians must accept more interference with their privacy than do ordinary citizens.

When a search engine operator delists a search result, freedom of expression may be interfered with in at least three ways.[96] First, those offering information, such as publishers and journalists, have a right to freedom of expression. As noted, the right to freedom of expression protects not only the expression (such as a publication), but also the means of communicating that expression.[97] Therefore, if delisting makes it more difficult to find the publication, the freedom to impart information is interfered with.[98] Second, search engine users have a right to receive information. Third, a search engine operator exercises its freedom of expression when it presents its search results; an organised list of search results could be considered a form of expression.[99]

The *Google Spain* judgment was controversial. Many feared that freedom of expression would receive insufficient protection after the judgment. The NGO Index on Censorship said: 'The Court's decision . . . should send chills down the spine of everyone in the European Union who

---

[93] See P. Korenhof and L. Gorzeman, 'Who Is Censoring Whom? An Enquiry into the Right to Be Forgotten and Censorship,' working paper, July 15, 2015, https://ssrn.com/abstract=2685105.

[94] Ibid., para. 81.

[95] Ibid., para. 99.

[96] J. V. J. van Hoboken, *Search Engine Freedom: On the Implications of the Right to Freedom of Expression for the Legal Governance of Web Search Engines* (Kluwer Law International 2012) 350.

[97] *Autronic v. Switzerland* App no 12726/87 (ECtHR 22 May 1990), para. 47.

[98] J. V. J. van Hoboken, *Search Engine Freedom: On the Implications of the Right to Freedom of Expression for the Legal Governance of Web Search Engines* (Kluwer Law International 2012) 350.

[99] Case C-131/12 *Google Spain v. Agencia Española de Protección de Datos (AEPD) and Mario Costeja González*, Opinion of AG Jääskinen, para. 132. J. V. J. van Hoboken, *Search Engine Freedom: On the Implications of the Right to Freedom of Expression for the Legal Governance of Web Search Engines* (Kluwer Law International 2012) 351. In the United States, some judges have granted search engines such freedom of expression claims (on the basis of the First Amendment of the US Constitution). E.g. *Search King, Inc. v. Google Technology, Inc.*, 2003 WL 21464568 (W.D. Okla. 2003). For a discussion see: E. Volokh and D. M. Falk, 'Google First Amendment Protection for Search Engine Search Results' (2011–2012) 82 *Journal of Law, Economics and Policy* 883. For criticism on granting such claims, see: O. Bracha, 'The Folklore of Informationalism: The Case of Search Engine Speech' (2014) 82 *Fordham Law Review* 1629.

believes in the crucial importance of free expression and freedom of information.'[100] Others welcomed the judgment.[101]

In sum, the Court of Justice of the European Union recognised a right to be delisted. The right to be delisted requires from search engine operators that they delist, at the request of a data subject, outdated search results for name searches. But national courts and data protection authorities must decide on actual delisting requests. In the next section, we discuss how Google, Data Protection Authorities and courts deal with delisting requests after the *Google Spain* judgment.

4 AFTER THE *GOOGLE SPAIN* JUDGMENT

4.1 *Google*

After the *Google Spain* judgment, Google created an online form that enables people to request the delisting of particular results for searches on their name.[102] If such a request is made, Google will 'balance the privacy rights of the individual with the public's interest to know and the right to distribute information.'[103] Google will look at 'whether the results include outdated information about you, as well as whether there's a public interest in the information – for example, we may decline to remove certain information about financial scams, professional malpractice, criminal convictions, or public conduct of government officials'.[104] Between fifty and one hundred people are working full time at Google to deal with delisting requests.[105]

As of August 2017, Google had received over 588,000 requests and has evaluated more than 2.1 million URLs. Google has delisted roughly 43 per cent of those URLs.[106] The top ten sites impacted by delisting requests include Facebook, YouTube, Twitter and Profile Engine (a site that crawls Facebook).

Google gives twenty-three examples of how it dealt with delisting requests. Examples of granted requests, quoted from Google, include:

- 'An individual who was convicted of a serious crime in the last five years but whose conviction was quashed on appeal asked us to remove an article about the incident.'
- 'A woman requested that we remove pages from search results showing her address.'
- 'A victim of rape asked us to remove a link to a newspaper article about the crime.'
- 'A man asked that we remove a link to a news summary of a local magistrate's decisions that included the man's guilty verdict. Under the UK Rehabilitation of Offenders Act, this conviction has been spent.'[107]

---

[100] 'Index blasts EU Court Ruling on 'Right to Be Forgotten', *Index on Censorship* https://www.indexoncensorship.org/2014/05/index-blasts-eu-court-ruling-right-forgotten accessed 6 September 2017.

[101] See e.g. J. Powles, 'The Case That Won't Be Forgotten' 2015-47 *Loyola University Chicago Law Journal* 583; H. Hijmans, *The European Union as Guardian of Internet Privacy: The Story of Art 16 TFEU* (Springer, 2016).

[102] 'Removing Content from Google', *Google*, https://support.google.com/legal/troubleshooter/1114905?hl=en#ts=1115655%2C6034194 accessed 6 September 2017.

[103] 'Search Removal Request under Data Protection Law in Europe', *Google* https://support.google.com/legal/contact/lr_eudpa?product=websearch accessed 6 September 2017.

[104] Ibid.

[105] As reported by Peter Fleischer, Google's Global Privacy Counsel, at the Privacy & Innovation Conference at Hong Kong University, 8 June 2015, www.lawtech.hk/pni/?page_id=11 accessed 6 September 2017.

[106] 'European Privacy Requests for Search Removals', *Google* www.google.com/transparencyreport/removals/europeprivacy/?hl=en accessed 30 August 2017.

[107] Ibid.

In all these cases Google delisted the search result for the individual's name.

Examples of denied requests include:

- 'We received a request from a former clergyman to remove 2 links to articles covering an investigation of sexual abuse accusations while in his professional capacity.'
- 'An individual asked us to remove a link to a copy of an official state document published by a state authority reporting on the acts of fraud committed by the individual.'
- 'An individual asked us to remove links to articles on the internet that reference his dismissal for sexual crimes committed on the job.'[108]

In all these cases, Google denied the request.

The examples suggest that Google does a reasonable job when dealing with delisting requests. However, Google could be more transparent about how it deals with delisting requests. More transparency could enable regulators, academics and members of the public to keep an eye on removal practices. As noted, Google delisted over 785,000 URLs. It is unclear whether those URLs concerned news articles, blog posts, revenge porn, or other materials. Moreover, we do not know whether requests mainly come from ordinary citizens, politicians, criminals or other people.

4.2 *Data Protection Authorities*

The EU's national Data Protection Authorities cooperate in the Article 29 Working Party, an advisory body.[109] The Working Party published guidelines on the implementation of the *Google Spain* judgment. The Working Party says that 'in practice, the impact of the de-listing on individuals' rights to freedom of expression and access to information will prove to be very limited.'[110] Nevertheless, Data Protection Authorities 'will systematically take into account the interest of the public in having access to the information'.[111] The Working Party also called on search engine operators to be transparent about their decisions: 'The Working Party strongly encourages the search engines to publish their own de-listing criteria, and make more detailed statistics available.'[112]

The Working Party developed a set of criteria to help Data Protection Authorities to assess, on a case-by-case basis, whether a search engine operator should delist a search result. The Working Party states, 'It is not possible to establish with certainty the type of role in public life an individual must have to justify public access to information about them via a search result.'[113] Nevertheless, the Working Party says that 'politicians, senior public officials, business-people and members of the (regulated) professions' can usually be considered to play a role in public life. Regarding minors, the Working Party notes that Data Protection Authorities are more inclined to delist results.[114] Data Protection Authorities are also more likely to intervene if search results

---

[108] Ibid.
[109] See S. Gutwirth and Y. Poullet, 'The Contribution of the Article 29 Working Party to the Construction of a Harmonised European Data Protection System: An Illustration of "Reflexive Governance"?' in V. P. Asinari and P. Palazzi (eds), *Défis du Droit à la Protection de la Vie Privée: Challenges of Privacy and Data Protection Law* (Bruylant 2008) 570–610.
[110] Article 29 Working party, 14/EN WP 225 (2014) 2 and 6.
[111] Ibid., 2.
[112] Ibid., 3 and 10.
[113] Ibid., 13.
[114] Ibid., 15.

reveal 'sensitive data'.[115] The criteria developed by the Working Party offer guidance to both search engines and Data Protection Authorities when they decide on de-listing requests.[116]

4.3 *Open Questions*

Below we discuss some open questions regarding delisting requests after *Google Spain*. More specifically, we consider how the right to be forgotten relates to public registers and open data policies. We also highlight the uncertainties surrounding sensitive personal data the processing of such data by search engines. And we consider whether search engines should delist search results only on EU-domains, or also on other domains.

4.3.1 *Public Registers and Open Data*

Nowadays, many personal data are made accessible online. For instance, through open data initiatives and public registers, personal data are generally available on the web. If a public register is published online, its data can be collected and republished by data brokers, journalists, search engines and others. Such data reuse can serve important goals, such as fostering transparency, innovation and public sector efficiency. However, data reuse can also threaten privacy.[117] Questions also arise about how the publication of such data relates to the right to be forgotten. Information may have to be removed, depending on factors such as the type of information, the information's relevance and the time that has elapsed.

The Court of Justice of the European Union has given the beginning of an answer in the *Manni* case.[118] This case dealt with the removal of information in the official chamber of commerce of Lecce, Italy. Salvatore Manni asked the chamber of commerce to erase, anonymise, or block the information linking him to the liquidation of a company in 1992. According to Manni, he cannot sell properties of a tourist complex, because potential purchases have access to that information in the company register.

In this case, the Italian Court of Cassation asked the Court of Justice of the European Union how the principle of data minimisation related to the duty for Member States to disclose information in a company register under the Company Law Directive.[119] The Italian court also asked whether Member States may limit access to information about dissolved companies. To determine whether people have a right to erasure, the Court of Justice of the European Union considers the purpose of the company register. The disclosure of information as prescribed by the Company Law Directive essentially aims to protect the interests of third parties in relation to companies with limited liability.[120] The directive is silent on whether

---

[115] See on sensitive data: Section 5.3.2.

[116] See for an analysis of factors to take into account when deciding on delisting requests: J. Ausloos and A. Kuczerawy, 'From Notice-and-Takedown to Notice-and-Delist: Implementing the Google Spain Ruling' (2016) 14(2) *Colorado Technology Law Journal* 219.

[117] F. J. Zuiderveen Borgesius, J. Gray and M. van Eechoud, 'Open Data, Privacy, and Fair Information Principles: Towards a Balancing Framework' (2015) 30 *Berkeley Technology Law Journal* 2073.

[118] Case C-131/12 *Camera di Commercio, Industria, Artigianato e Agricoltura di Lecce v. Salvatore Manni*, ECLI:EU: C:2017:197.

[119] First Council Directive 68/151/EEC of 9 March 1968 on coordination of safeguards which, for the protection of the interests of members and others, are required by Member States of companies within the meaning of the second paragraph of Article 58 of the Treaty, with a view to making such safeguards equivalent throughout the Community (OJ 1968 L 65, p. 8), as amended by Directive 2003/58/EC of the European Parliament and of the Council of 15 July 2003 (OJ 2003 L 221, p. 13).

[120] Case C-131/12 *Camera di Commercio, Industria, Artigianato e Agricoltura di Lecce v. Salvatore Manni*, ECLI:EU: C:2017:197, paras. 49 and 51.

information should also be available after a company has dissolved. Yet, according to the court, information must remain available because rights and legal relations may continue to exist.[121] Moreover, given the diversity of national laws regarding time limits, the court finds that it is impossible to identify a certain period of time that must elapse before someone has the right to erase information.[122]

The Court of Justice of the European Union also considers the right to privacy and the right to protection of personal data, as protected by the Charter of Fundamental Rights of the European Union.[123] The court finds that these rights are not disproportionately interfered with for two reasons. First, because the types of information are limited to information about a particular person in relation to the company.[124] Second, because those who trade with joint-stock companies and limited liability companies have as safeguards only the assets of the latter companies. The court notes, 'It appears justified that natural persons who choose to participate in trade through such a company are required to disclose the data relating to their identity and functions within that company, especially since they are aware of that requirement when they decide to engage in such activity.'[125]

Yet, the Court of Justice of the European Union also notes that 'it cannot be excluded' that in exceptional cases, access to information is limited to parties who have a specific interest in the information, but only after a 'sufficiently long period' after the dissolution of a company.[126] In such cases, people may have a right to object against the processing of their data.[127] But the court also stresses that Member State law may restrict this right to object.[128] According to the Court of Justice of the European Union, the Italian court must determine the extent to which Italian law enables or limits the right to object, and whether the facts and circumstances of the case justify the limitation of access to the data concerning Manni.[129] The Court of Justice of the European Union also highlights that 'the mere fact that ... the properties of a tourist complex built by Italiana Costruzioni, of which Mr Manni is currently the sole director, do not sell because of the fact that potential purchasers of those properties have access to that data in the company register' does not constitute a reason to limit to the information in the company register.[130]

In sum, the Court of Justice of the European Union requires, in principle, that the personal data must be available in the company register, even after a company has dissolved. Yet, the court also leaves room for Member States to enable individuals to apply, in exceptional cases, for a limitation of the availability of information about them in company registers.

4.3.2 *Sensitive Data*

The *Google Spain* judgment has caused a problem regarding search engine operators and 'special categories of data'. Such special categories of data are 'personal data revealing racial or ethnic origin, political opinions, religious or philosophical beliefs, trade-union membership,

---

[121] Ibid., para. 53.
[122] Ibid., paras. 54–56.
[123] Arts. 7 and 8 of the Charter of Fundamental Rights of the European Union.
[124] Case C-131/12 *Camera di Commercio, Industria, Artigianato e Agricoltura di Lecce v. Salvatore Manni*, ECLI:EU: C:2017:197, para. 58.
[125] Ibid., para. 59.
[126] Ibid., para. 60.
[127] Article 14(a) of the Data Protection Directive.
[128] Case C-131/12 *Camera di Commercio, Industria, Artigianato e Agricoltura di Lecce v. Salvatore Manni*, ECLI:EU: C:2017:197, paras. 61 and 62.
[129] Ibid., paras. 62–63.
[130] Ibid., para. 63.

and the processing of data concerning health or sex life'.[131] Regarding data relating to offences and criminal convictions, the Data Protection Directive states that processing 'may be carried out only under the control of official authority, or if suitable specific safeguards are provided under national law, subject to derogations which may be granted by the Member State under national provisions providing suitable specific safeguards'.[132] All these categories of data receive extra protection in the Data Protection Directive, because such data 'are capable by their nature of infringing fundamental freedoms or privacy'.[133] For brevity, we refer to 'sensitive data', rather than to special categories of data.

As noted, the Court of Justice of the European Union chose to see search engines operator as data controllers when they index, store, and refer to personal data on websites. That choice has caused a problem with sensitive data. The Data Protection Directive only allows personal data processing if the controller can rely on a legal basis for processing.[134] In *Google Spain*, the Court of Justice of the European Union ruled that, for the processing at issue, a search engine could rely on the legitimate interests provision.[135] This provision, also called the balancing provision, permits processing if the controller's legitimate interests, or those of a third party, outweigh the data subject's fundamental rights.

However, the processing of sensitive data is only allowed after the data subject gave his or her explicit consent, or if an exception applies that can legalise the processing of sensitive data.[136]

In practice, many websites that are indexed by a search engine may include sensitive data. For example, a website might include a picture of an identifiable person in a wheelchair: personal data concerning that person's health. And the website of a Catholic choir may include a member list: personal data indicating religion.

Because processing sensitive data requires explicit consent, a search engine operator would need the data subject's explicit consent for processing web pages that include such data. Asking hundreds of millions of people for their consent would be impossible. The Data Protection Directive contains exceptions to the in-principle prohibition of processing sensitive data, such as exceptions for churches and for the medical sector. But in many cases, search engine operators cannot rely on any of the exceptions.[137]

Therefore, it seems that a search engine operator's practices are, formally, partly illegal – when the operator processes sensitive data included on web pages, and no exceptions apply. That formal illegality is a side effect of the choice of the Court of Justice of the European Union to see a search engine operator as a controller regarding the processing of personal data on third-party web pages.

To avoid that search engine activities would be rendered partly illegal, the advocate general in *Google Spain* did not want to regard a search engine operator as a controller regarding the

---

[131] Article 8(1) of the Data Protection Directive. See also Article 9(1) of the General Data Protection Regulation.

[132] Article 8(5) of the Data Protection Directive. See also Article 10 of the General Data Protection Regulation.

[133] Recital 33 of the Data Protection Directive.

[134] Article 8(2) of the Charter of Fundamental Rights of the European Union; Article 7 of the Data Protection Directive; Article 6 of the General Data Protection Regulation.

[135] Article 7(f) of the Data Protection Directive. Case C-131/12 *Google Spain v. Agencia Española de Protección de Datos (AEPD) and Mario Costeja González*, ECLI:EU:C:2014:317, para. 73.

[136] Article 8 of the Data Protection Directive. See also Article 9 of the General Data Protection Regulation. In some member states, data subjects cannot override the in-principle prohibition of processing sensitive data by giving their explicit consent. See European Commission, Commission Staff Working Paper, *Impact Assessment Accompanying the proposal for the General Data Protection Regulation*, SEC(2012) 72 final, Annex 2, http://ec.europa.eu/justice/data-protection/document/review2012/sec_2012_72_en.pdf accessed 6 September 2017, p. 29.

[137] See in more detail: S. Kulk and F. J. Zuiderveen Borgesius, '*Google Spain v. Gonzalez*: Did the Court Forget about Freedom of Expression' (2014) 5(3) *European Journal of Risk Regulation* 389.

processing of personal data made available on third party web pages.[138] In contrast, the Court of Justice of the European Union did not explicitly consider consequences of seeing search engine operators as data controllers. After the *Google Spain* judgment, Google, Data Protection Authorities, and courts have solved the sensitive data problem by ignoring it.

But a 2016 judgment by a Dutch lower court (which was later overruled) illustrates how this sensitive data problem may play out. An attorney submitted a delisting request to Google, regarding a blog post about a criminal conviction of the attorney in another country. Under Dutch law, personal data regarding criminal convictions are sensitive data.[139] The court held that Google could not link to the blog post, because the post contained sensitive data. Google had not asked the attorney for his consent for referring to the blog post, and therefore Google could not legally link to it.[140] Google appealed the decision.

The Dutch Court of Appeals mitigated the sensitive data problem. In short, the Court of Appeals decided that Google can rely on an exception for journalistic purposes. (The Court of Appeals seems to come to a decision that is contrary to the Court of Justice of the European Union.)[141] Hence, the Court of Appeals says that, under certain conditions, Google is allowed to process sensitive data for its search engine.[142]

Still, a coherent Europe Union-wide solution must be found for the sensitive data problem. Perhaps the Court of Justice of the European Union can find such a solution. A French judge asked preliminary questions to the Court of Justice of the European Union, regarding this sensitive data problem in the context of delisting requests. Perhaps the Court of Justice of the European Union can think of a creative solution to solve the problem.[143]

Otherwise, the EU legislator must take action. One possibility would be to introduce a new exception to the in-principle prohibition of processing sensitive data, specifically for search engines. However, it does not seem plausible that the EU lawmaker will revise the GDPR anytime soon.

4.3.3 *Delisting Requests Only for EU Domains?*

The domain-related scope of the right to be delisted is contentious.[144] Google chose to delist search results only on its European domains (e.g. google.de or google.fr). Hence, Google did not delist search results on its google.com domain.[145] The Article 29 Working Party, however, says that 'limiting de-listing to EU domains on the grounds that users tend to access search engines via their national domains cannot be considered a sufficient mean to satisfactorily guarantee the rights of data subjects according to the [*Google Spain*] ruling.'[146]

---

[138] Case C-131/12 *Google Spain v. Agencia Española de Protección de Datos (AEPD) and Mario Costeja González*, Opinion of AG Jääskinen, para. 90.

[139] Article 16 of the Dutch Data Protection Act.

[140] Rechtbank Rotterdam, 29 March 2016, ECLI:NL:RBROT:2016:2395 http://deeplink.rechtspraak.nl/uitspraak?id= ECLI:NL:RBROT:2016:2395. See F. J. Zuiderveen Borgesius, 'Het "right to be forgotten"' en bijzondere persoons-gegevens: geen ruimte meer voor een belangenafweging?' ['The "right to be forgotten" and sensitive personal data: no room for balancing?'] (2016) 4 *Computerrecht* 220.

[141] See Section 4 of this chapter.

[142] Hof Den Haag, 23 May 2017, www.rechtspraak.nl, ECLI:NL:GHDHA:2017:1360.

[143] See http://english.conseil-etat.fr/Activities/Press-releases/Right-to-be-delisted accessed 6 September 2017.

[144] B. Van Alsenoy and M. Koekkoek, 'Internet and Jurisdiction after *Google Spain*: The Extraterritorial Reach of the "Right to be Delisted"' 5(2) *International Data Privacy Law* 105; C. Kuner, 'The Court of Justice of the EU judgment on Data Protection and Internet Search Engines: Current Issues and Future Challenges' in: H. Hijmans and H. Kranenborg (eds.), *Data Protection Anno 2014: How to Restore Trust?* (Intersentia 2014) 19–44.

[145] See: J. Powles, 'The Case That Won't Be Forgotten' 2015–47 *Loyola University Chicago Law Journal* 583, 596.

[146] Article 29 Working party, 14/EN WP 225 (2014) 3.

It is difficult to defend that the domain name of a search engine website should be the main factor when deciding which national law applies. If that were the main factor, a search engine operator could easily escape the application of national laws by opting for a particular domain name.[147] However, Google – a company from the United States, where freedom of expression is strongly protected – does not want to delist search results on its .com domain. Google argues that it usually sends users from Europe to their local domain, for instance Google.fr for France and Google.de for Germany.[148]

The Court of Justice of the European Union will have to decide about the domain-related scope of delisting requests. In 2015 the French Data Protection Authority, *Commission Nationale de l'Informatique et des Libertés* (CNIL) demanded that Google delisted results not only for searches on their European domains such as Google.fr, but on all its domains, including google. com. According to CNIL, 'To be effective, delisting must be carried out on all extensions of the search engine.'[149]

Google did not comply. CNIL responded by starting formal proceedings against Google. In the meantime, Google implemented geolocation technology to ensure search results are delisted on Google domains if these domains are accessed from the country of the data subject.[150] To illustrate: an internet user with a French IP address would not see delisted search results on Google.com. An internet user with an IP address from the United States would see all search results on Google.com, including results that were delisted in France.

CNIL, however, was not satisfied, as the delisted results would still be available to search engine users outside France. Moreover, people could circumvent the geo-block by using a virtual private network, which enables people to access a website using a foreign IP-address.[151] CNIL fined Google 100,000 Euros. Google appealed the decision with the French *Conseil d'État* – the highest administrative court in France.[152] The *Conseil d'État* has asked the Court of Justice of the European Union preliminary questions. In short, the Court of Justice of the European Union is asked for the correct interpretation of data protection law regarding the domain-related scope of delisting requests.[153]

5 CONCLUDING THOUGHTS

The *Google Spain* judgment of the Court of Justice of the European Union illustrates how, under European law, freedom of expression can be limited by privacy and data protection rights. Privacy and data protection rights require that, under certain conditions, search engine operators

---

[147] Y. Fouad, 'Reikwijdte van het Europese dataprotectierecht na Google Spanje: wat is de territoriale werkingssfeer en wordt eenieder beschermd?' ['Scope of the European data protection law after *Google Spain*: what is the territorial scope and is everyone protected?'], Master's thesis 2015, Institute for Information Law (University of Amsterdam), on file with authors.

[148] P. Fleischer, 'Reflecting on the Right to Be Forgotten', *Google In Europe Blog* www.blog.google/topics/google-europe/reflecting-right-be-forgotten accessed 6 September 2017.

[149] 'CNIL Orders Google to Apply Delisting on All Domain Names of the Search Engine', *CNIL* www.cnil.fr/en/cnil-orders-google-apply-delisting-all-domain-names-search-engine accessed 6 September 2017.

[150] 'Adapting Our Approach to the European Right to Be Forgotten', *Google* https://europe.googleblog.com/2016/03/adapting-our-approach-to-european-right.html accessed 6 September 2017.

[151] CNIL, decision no. 2016–054, unofficial translation by CNIL www.cnil.fr/sites/default/files/atoms/files/d2016-054_penalty_google.pdf accessed 6 September 2017.

[152] M. Scott, *Google Appeals French Privacy Ruling,'* New York Times (New York, 19 May 2016) www.nytimes.com/2016/05/20/technology/google-appeals-french-privacy-ruling.html accessed 6 September 2017.

[153] 'Portée territoriale du droit au déréférencement', *Le Conseil d'État* http://www.conseil-etat.fr/Actualites/Communiques/Portee-territoriale-du-droit-au-dereferencement accessed 6 September 2017.

must delist outdated search results for name searches, if the relevant individual requests delisting. Yet, when assessing whether a search result must be delisted, search engine operators, Data Protection Authorities and national courts must also consider the extent to which delisting affects freedom of expression. Searchers have the right to receive information, and publishers, bloggers, journalists etc. have the right to impart information. National courts and Data Protection Authorities must therefore consider all relevant facts and circumstances and decide on a case-by-case basis whether a particular search result should be delisted for name searches.

In principle, privacy and freedom of expression have equal weight in Europe: which right prevails depends on the circumstances of a case. Balancing privacy-related and freedom of expression-related interests will always remain contentious and difficult. A case-by-case analysis is required, and all circumstances of a case should be taken into account. The Court of Justice of the European Union gave limited guidance as to when a search result should be delisted. But, the European Court of Human Rights has developed rich and nuanced case law on balancing privacy and freedom of expression, in which it provides a list of criteria to determine the right balance. We can expect much more case law on delisting requests; hopefully that will give more guidance for deciding about delisting requests.

The discussion on the right to be forgotten is part of a broader discussion on how to balance different rights and interests when personal information is accessible online. Similar questions arise with regard to, for instance, open data initiatives, and online archives of newspapers or case law. The discussion on the right to be forgotten is only the beginning of how the rights to privacy and freedom of expression should be weighed in the online world.

* * *

19

Understanding the Balancing Act behind the Legitimate Interest of the Controller Ground

A Pragmatic Approach

Irene Kamara and Paul De Hert

1 INTRODUCTION

The new legislation of the European Union regulating the protection of personal data has finally been adopted, after a legislative process that lasted nearly four years. The General Data Protection Regulation (GDPR) is a legal instrument of 99 articles and 173 recitals, directly applicable to all EU Member States of the European Union.[1]

The GDPR, which replaced the Data Protection Directive, aims to modernise and render more effective data protection law, aiming among others to respond to technological challenges and the risks emerging technologies pose to the protection of personal data. Fundamental rights concerns partly explain the reform. The protection of personal data received the status of a fundamental right in the European Union with the adoption of the Lisbon Treaty.[2] Another important concern is the need for enabling free movement of personal data, or, as Recital (10) of the Regulation provides, to 'remove the obstacles to flows of personal data'. One of the corner-stones of the protection of personal data in that respect is the lawfulness of processing. Lawfulness of processing is one of the fundamental principles relating to processing of personal data, established in art. 5(1) (a) GDPR, according to which: 'Personal data should be processed lawfully, fairly and in a transparent manner in relation to the data subject.' Article 6 provides six grounds for lawfulness of processing: the consent of the data subject (6(1) (a)), the legal obligation of the controller (6(1) (c)), the performance of a contract (6(1) (b)), the vital interests of the data subject (6(1) (d)), the performance of a task carried out in the public interest or the exercise of official authority (6(1) (e)) and the legitimate interest of the controller (6(1) (f)). The GDPR requires that at least one of these six grounds applies in each data processing operation for the processing to be deemed lawful. The grounds are to a large extent same as the Data Protection Directive 95/46/EC. Despite the numerous opinions and essays on other grounds, mainly relating to the conditions for a valid consent, the legitimate interest of the controller has not been at

---

the spotlight. Some comments on the topic deal critically with this ground as a basis for lawful processing, sometimes going as far as to characterise the ground as a 'loophole' for the protection of personal data, for the reason of being flexible enough in comparison with some stricter or at least more straightforward requirements for the other grounds for lawful processing of art. 6 GDPR (and relevant art. 7 of the Data Protection Directive). While authorities and academics are in general hesitant to discuss in depth the legitimate interest of the controller ground (except for the Article 29 Data Protection Working Party opinion in 2014), this does not seem to be the case for actual practice and data controllers, which quite often rely on that ground.[3]

Taking these points into account , this chapter proposes a formalisation of the balancing act of art. 6(1) (f) GDPR. We propose three steps, establishing: the legitimacy of the interest of the controller, the necessity of the pursued aim and the balancing of the opposing interests of the controller and the data subject. We also discuss essential components of each step that help determine the outcome of the test. We argue that the legitimate interest of the controller ground is largely based on context and might significantly differ on a case-by-case level. The legitimate interest ground is not a loophole in the new EU data protection law. Rather, it is an equally important ground for legitimate processing. If misinterpreted or applied in bad faith, the ground can be seen as too lenient or a loophole. The newly introduced accountability principle, the other principles of art. 5 GDPR and of course art. 8 and 52(2) Charter, however, set the proper framework for the grounds of lawful processing, including the legitimate interest of the controller or a third-party ground of art. 6(1) (f) GDPR.

The contribution is structured as follows: First, we briefly refer to the fundamental right to protection of personal data, enshrined in the Charter of Fundamental Rights and the conditions for interference to the right, set in art. 52(2) Charter. Section three presents the grounds for lawful processing in the Data Protection Directive and the criticism exercised on the legitimate interest ground. This section provides the background of the transition from the Directive to the Regulation regime, which is thoroughly discussed in section four. Section four includes the main discussions in the preparation of the GDPR and the proposed conceptualisation of the legitimate interest of the controller ground of art. 6(1) (f). Following that, the fifth and the sixth sections provide further clarifications on the concept of legitimate controller by examining placing the legitimate interest ground in the wider context of the GDPR. The seventh section provides an overview and analysis of the most relevant case law of the Court of Justice of the European Union in relation to the legitimate interest ground, with the aim to shed light to the analysis. Last, section eight provides examples of legitimate interest grounds and examines the suitability of the ground in these cases. The chapter ends with conclusions which provide a summary of the discussion and reflections for the application of the provision.

2 THE FUNDAMENTAL RIGHT TO PROTECTION OF PERSONAL DATA

2.1 *Charter of Fundamental Rights: Not an Absolute Right and the Limitations to the Rights Provided for in Art. 52 (1) Charter*

The right to the protection of personal data is established as an autonomous self-standing right in the Charter of the Fundamental Rights of the European Union. The Charter was declared

---

[3] For instance a paper published by the think tank CIPL, which, based on insights shared by the industry participants of CIPL, identifies a list of current practices, where legitimate interest is used as a ground for processing. The paper highlights that 'organisations in all sectors currently use legitimate interest processing for a very large variety of processing personal data and this trend is likely to continue under the GDPR'. Centre for Information Policy Leadership (CIPL) Recommendations for Implementing Transparency, Consent and Legitimate Interest under the GDPR" May 2017, https://www.informationpolicycentre.com/uploads/5/7/1/0/57104281/cipl_recommendations_on_transparency_consent_and_legitimate_interest_under_the_gdpr_-19_may_2017-c.pdf (accessed 30 May 2017).

legally binding with the Lisbon Treaty in 2009. Art. 8 of the Charter 'constitutionalised' the right by protecting it separately than the right to the respect of private life protected in art. 7 of the Charter. Paragraph 2 of art. 8 Charter already provides the legal basis for processing. Processing may be based on the consent of the individual concerned or another legitimate basis laid down by law. The right to the protection of personal data is not an absolute right. Limitations to the right are provided in art. 52 of the Charter, which should be read in combination with art. 8(2). Limitations need to be provided for by law, respect the essence of the right and be necessary and proportionate. The primary law of the European Union, therefore, already provides the frame-work in which a limitation to the right of art. 8 can take place. Due to the hierarchy of EU legislation (primary and secondary laws) and the fact that the EU data protection legislation has its legal basis in the EU primary law, including art. 16 Treaty on the Functioning of the European Union (TFEU) and the Charter, any limitation cannot deviate, or go further than the conditions of arts. 8 and 52 Charter.

2.2 *European Convention of Human Rights and the Proportionality Test*

Beyond the Charter and the European Union, the European Convention of Human Rights has long protected the right for the protection of personal data, as an aspect of the right to respect for private life (art. 8 ECHR). Art. 8(2) ECHR provides that by means of exception, interference with the right to respect for private life is allowed under conditions. The article establishes a proportionality test to assess whether an interference is allowed. The interference has to be in accordance with the law ('legality'), have a legitimate basis ('legitim-acy') and be necessary in a democratic society ('proportionality stricto sensu').[4] The article provides exhaustively a list of broadly framed interests, which qualify to provide a legitimate basis for the interference to the right to respect for private life. These are national security, public safety, the economic wellbeing of a country, the prevention of disorder or crime, the protection of health, the protection of morals and the protection of the rights and freedoms of others. Even though EU data protection legislation is not legally based on the ECHR, to which the European Union is only one of the member parties, we take notice of the significant influences of the Convention to the EU data protection law. The new GDPR explicitly acknowledges that restrictions to data protection principles and the rights of the individuals should be 'in accordance with the requirements set out in the Charter and in the European Convention for the Protection of Human Rights and Fundamental Freedoms'.[5]

Balancing conflicting interests and rights has been a doctrinal tool with which the Courts, both the European Court of Human Rights and the Court of Justice of the European Union, are following the doctrine in cases that involve conflicts of rights.[6] Several scholars have developed

---

[4] Read further Douwe Korff, 'The Standard Approach under Articles 8–11 ECHR and Article 2 ECHR', European Commission, 2008, http://ec.europa.eu/justice/news/events/conference_dp_2009/presentations_speeches/KORFF_Douwe_a.pdf, (accessed 15 October 2016).

[5] Recital 73 GDPR.

[6] The balancing doctrine has been criticised by Habermas for depriving constitutional rights of their normative power, in the sense that rights are downgraded to the level of policies, goals and values. Habermas also criticises the balancing approach for an underlying 'irrationality'. He argues that 'because there are no rational standards here, weighing takes place either arbitrarily or unreflectively, according to customary standards and hierarchies' (see comments in Robert Alexy, 'Constitutional Rights, Balancing, and Rationality', *Ratio Juris*, vol. 16 no. 2, 2003, p. 134). Jurgen Habermas, *Between Facts and Norms*, Cambridge: Polity, 1992.

theories and frameworks on the principle of proportionality,[7] how to balance conflicting interests and ultimately whether 'balancing' is an appropriate doctrine when conflicts between interests occur.[8] According to Robert Alexy's theory, the Law of Balancing, balancing can be broken down into three stages:

> The first stage is a matter of establishing the degree of non-satisfaction, of, or detriment to, the first principle. This is followed by a second stage, in which the importance of satisfying the competing principle is established. Finally, the third stage answers the question of whether or not the importance of satisfying the competing principle justifies the detriment to, or non-satisfaction of, the first.[9]

Alexy in his theory refers to *competing* instead of *conflicting* principles. In balancing, this would have consequences as to what the expected outcome of the assessment is. In conflicting principles, the conflict must be resolved in an all-or-nothing fashion, whereas in the case of two competing principles, one of the principles must be outweighed, without this meaning that the outweighed principle is invalid.[10] From that perspective, the concept of competing principles is an interesting theoretical tool to read the legitimate interest of the controller ground in the GDPR. An interesting discussion relates to whether rights should be perceived as principles or rules.[11] Harbo, when interpreting Alexy's conceptualisation, asserts that perceiving rights as principles rather than rules, implies that rights are not absolute, and can be thus weighted against other principles, i.e. against other individual rights but also policies laid down in legislative measures'.[12] On the other hand, Dworkin's theory supports the view, 'Rights are only law, i.e. trumps vis-à-vis arguments of policy, or collective rights expressed through legislative acts.'[13] In terms of the right to the protection of personal data as enshrined in art. 8 of the Charter, as extended to whether rights are absolute or relative, this discussion has been solved with art. 52 Charter, as mentioned earlier, which provides that the right of art. 8 can be subject to limitations. Despite this, the influence of such theories can be traced in the provisions of EU data protection law, and the balancing test of the legitimate interest ground, even though an one-to-one application of the one or the other theory is not visible.[14]

3 EU DATA PROTECTION LEGISLATION: THE 1995 EU DATA PROTECTION DIRECTIVE

Taking the analysis to the secondary law of the European Union, the 1995 Data Protection Directive introduces the grounds for lawful processing ('criteria for legitimate data processing') in art. 7. The criteria are listed exhaustively and severally ('*or … or*'). If at least one of the grounds is fulfilled, the data processing operation is allowed.[15]

---

[7] Sybe A. De Vries, 'Balancing Fundamental Rights with Economic Freedoms according to the European Court of Justice', *Utrecht Law Review*, vol. 9 no. 1, 2013, pp. 169–192.

[8] See Tor-Inge Harbo, 'The Function of the Proportionality Principle in the EU law', *European Law Journal*, vol. 16 no. 2, 2010, pp. 158–185; Kai Möller, 'Proportionality: Challenging the Critics', *International Journal of Constitutional Law*, vol. 10 no. 3, 2002, pp. 709–731.

[9] Robert Alexy, *A Theory of Constitutional Rights*, Oxford: Oxford University Press, 2002.

[10] Harbo (2010) p. 166.

[11] The distinction between rights and principles is clarified in art. 51(1) of the Charter: '*Subjective rights shall be respected, whereas principles shall be observed.*'

[12] Harbo (2010) p. 166.

[13] Ibid.

[14] Further analysis however evades the scope of this contribution.

[15] See for extensive analysis read subsection 4.3 of this chapter.

3.1 *Consent in Art. 7(a) of the Directive*

Art. 7(a) requires the unambiguous consent of the data subject. Much discussion has revolved around the question of when consent is unambiguous, whether it has to be active or whether passive action is also sufficient and how relevant consent is in the context of technological emergence and automated processing (e.g. big data).[16] By definition, consent includes several requirements. It has to be a freely given, specific and informed indication of the data subject's wishes by which the data subject *signifies his or her agreement* for the processing of personal data relating to him or her. The Article 29 Data Protection Working Party (WP29) has provided practical guidance on the conditions of valid consent.[17] Data controllers often rely on this ground, especially in the context of the Internet or mobile applications. An (even not legitimately acquired) agreement of the data subject itself often offers a *false assurance* to the controller of legality of the data processing. However, it is very important that all the conditions for valid consent – including the possibility of its withdrawal – are fulfilled. An agreement to data processing without proper information being provided to the data subject in advance is not valid, and a processing operation based solely on such agreement ('consent') is not legitimate. This is an issue that the GDPR aims to tackle, as is discussed later in this chapter.

3.2 *Contract, Compliance with Legal Obligation, Protection of Vital Interests of the Data Subject and Public Interest in Art. 7(b) to 7(e) of the Directive*

Grounds 7(b) to 7(e) of the Data Protection Directive all require a necessity test, performed by the data controller. The Directive allows for the processing of personal data only if processing is necessary either for the performance of a contract, the compliance of the controller with a legal obligation, the protection of the vital interests of the data subject, or public interest. The necessity test is inevitably performed initially from the data controller himself, prior to the processing of the personal data.[18] Nevertheless, the decision of the controller to process personal data on the basis of the outcome of the necessity test is subject to administrative control from the supervisory (data protection) authority and judicial control from the competent courts. If the outcome of the necessity test is negative – this is that processing is not necessary – then there is no legal interest of the authorities to check the decision. However, if the outcome of the necessity test is positive, and the controller will start processing personal data, the lawfulness of processing is subject to control, as well as the ground(s) of lawfulness, and the decision (including the rationale) of the controller that justify that the conditions of the ground are fulfilled. The Directive left it to the national legislation of each Member State to determine the meaning of the concepts of 'public interest' and 'essential interest for data subject's life'. For instance, with regard to the concept of 'important public interest' some countries required approval by an ethics committee (e.g. Sweden), while others did not

---

[16] Read further danah boyd and Kate Crawford, 'Critical Questions for Big Data: Provocations for a Cultural, Technological, and Scholarly Phenomenon', *Information, Communication & Society*, vol. 15 no. 5, 2012, pp. 662–679. Fred H. Cate and Viktor Mayer-Schönberger, 'Notice and Consent in a World of Big Data', *International Data Privacy Law*, vol. 3 no. 2, 2013, pp. 67–73. Daniel J. Solove, 'Privacy Self-Management and the Consent Dilemma', *Harvard Law Review*, vol. 126 no. 1880, 2013.

[17] Article 29 Data Protection Working Party, Opinion 15/2011 on the definition of consent, WP187, 13 July 2011.

[18] Lee A. Bygrave and Dag Wiese Schartum, 'Consent, Proportionality and Collective Power', in Gutwirth Serge, Yves Poullet, Paul De Hert, Cécile de Terwangne and Sjaak Nouwt (eds.), *Reinventing Data Protection?*, Springer Netherlands, Dordrecht, 2009, pp. 157–173.

(e.g. Germany and Finland).[19] Such flexibility which apparently aimed to embrace the diversity of legal standards in the legislature of the EU Member States led to non-harmonised results. The non-harmonised approaches in turn led to compliance difficulties for data controllers operating in more than one EU Member State. This is a difficulty that is expected to be overcome with the directly applicable GDPR.[20]

3.3 *Legitimate Interest of the Controller in Art. 7(f) of the Directive*

The last ground of art. 7 is the legitimate interest of the controller or third parties. Art. 7(f) provides:[21]

> "Processing is necessary for the purposes of the legitimate interests pursued by the controller or by the third party or parties to whom the data are disclosed, except where such interests are overridden by the interests for fundamental rights and freedoms of the data subject which require protection under Article 1 (1)."

The provision was amended several times during the legislative process, but the amendments did not substantially differ from one another. The first proposal,[22] the amended proposal[23] and the final text of art. 7(f) all included the condition that the legitimate interest of the controller is a ground for lawful processing if the interests of the data subject did not prevail. Thus, all versions included what is often called as a 'balancing' test between the legitimate interests of the data controller and the interests of the data subjects.[24] The final text of art. 7(f) Directive specified further the two sides of the balancing test: on the one hand, there was the legitimate interest(s) pursued by either the controller or a third parties and on the other hand the interests for fundamental rights and freedoms of the data subject under art. 1(1) of the Data Protection Directive. However, the provision does not provide pointers or criteria on how to perform the balancing act.

3.4 *Criticism*

The Directive entrusted EU Member States with the task of specifying conditions for the balancing test. As was shown in the Report concerning the implementation of the Directive, published in 2003 in line with art. 33 of the Directive, the implementation of art. 7 into national legislation was unsatisfactory and showed divergences.[25] Federico Ferretti highlights that a loose

---

[19] Douwe Korff, 'EC Study on Implementation of Data Protection Directive 95/46/EC', 2002, https://ssrn.com/abstract= 1287667 (accessed 10 September 2016).

[20] Article 288 of the Treaty on the Functioning of the EU European Union, OJ C 326, 26.10.2012.

[21] Art. 7(f) Directive 95/46/EC. The elements of the provision are further elaborated in the section on the General Data Protection Regulation.

[22] Proposal for a Council Directive Concerning the Protection of Individuals in Relation to the Processing of Personal Data, COM (1990) 314–2, 1990/0287/COD.

[23] Mark Powell, 'Amended Proposal for a Council Directive on the Protection of Individuals with regard to the Processing of Personal Data and on the Free Movement of such Data (92/C 311/04) COM (92) 422 final — syn 287', *Computer Law & Security Review*, vol. 10, 1994, pp. 43–46, ISSN 0267–3649, http://dx.doi.org/10.1016/ j.clsr.2006.03.004.

[24] The *balancing* even though included as a term in the provision of art. 7(f) stems from the Recital 30 of Directive 95/46/EC provides ('in order to maintain a balance between the interests involved while guaranteeing effective competition').

[25] Commission of the European Communities, Report from the Commission. First Report on the Implementation of the Data Protection Directive (95/46/EC), COM (2003) 265 final. See further on the implementation of the Directive: Yves Poullet, 'EU Data Protection Policy: The Directive 95/46/EC: Ten Years after', *Computer Law & Security*

application of the legitimate interest ground provision could lead to uncertainty and potentially be a 'tool for circumvention' of the legal protection offered to individuals.[26]

Apart from the diversity in the implementation of the provision in the national legislatures of the Member States, the legitimate interest ground has often been characterised as a loophole in the protection of personal data.[27] Paolo Balboni et al. pinpoint the subjectivity of the data controller's judgement as a key issue in that respect.[28] Moreover, another issue is that one cannot verify that the balancing test actually took place, unless this is challenged in court.[29]

Criticism also targets the lack of useful guidance in the Directive for the interpretation of the legitimate interest of the controller.[30] This point is regularly made for provisions of principles-based legislation that are not descriptive enough. In the case of the legitimate interest, indeed some pointers or criteria as to when data subjects' rights override the legitimate interests are missing in the Directive. As we see further in this contribution, the GDPR introduces new concepts such as the reasonable expectations of the data subject and provides examples of legitimate interests in the Recitals with the aim to address the criticism.

4 LEGITIMATE CONTROLLER'S INTEREST IN THE 2016 GENERAL DATA PROTECTION REGULATION

4.1 *Preparatory Works: Commission, EP, Council Versions of Art.6(1) (f)*

The Commission proposal (2012)[31] introduced the legitimate interest of the controller ground with a substantial differentiation from the Directive and the final version of the provision. The EC proposal simply excluded the legitimate interests of third parties from the scope of art. 6(1) (f). In addition, as with many provisions in the 2012 proposal, the Commission would be empowered to adopt delegated acts for the purpose of further specifying the conditions of the legitimate interest ground for various sectors and data processing situations, including the processing of personal data related to a child.[32] Even though such guidance would be useful, the choice of the Commission as a competent body, and the means of delegated acts, were criticised for several reasons.[33] One argument was that the vital decisions for the interpretation of the ground should not be left to an executive body, with limited competence for such task.

Review, vol. 22 no. 3, 2006, pp. 206–217, ISSN 0267–3649, http://dx.doi.org/10.1016/j.clsr.2006.03.004 (accessed 15 September 2016).

[26] Federico Ferretti, 'Data Protection and the Legitimate Interest of Data Controllers: Much Ado about Nothing or the Winter of Rights?' *Common Law Market Review*, vol. 51 no.3, 2014, pp. 843–868.

[27] 'A Loophole in Data Processing: Why the "Legitimate Interests" Test Fails to Protect the Interests of Users and the Regulation Needs to Be Amended', *Bits of Freedom*, 11 December 2012, https://www.bof.nl/live/wp-content/uploads/20121211_onderzoek_legitimate-interests-def.pdf, (accessed 10 August 2016).

[28] Paolo Balboni, Daniel Cooper, Rosario Imperiali and Milda Macenaite, 'Legitimate Interest of the Data Controller. New Data Protection Paradigm: Legitimacy Grounded on Appropriate Protection', *International Data Privacy Law*, 2013: ipt019, p.247f.

[29] Bits of Freedom (2012), section 4.

[30] Balboni, et al. (2013), p. 247.

[31] European Commission, Proposal for a Regulation of the European Parliament and of the Council on the Protection of Individuals with regard to the Processing of Personal Data and on the Free Movement of Such Data (General Data Protection Regulation) COM (2012) 11 final – 2012/0011 (COD), 25.01.2012.

[32] Art. 6(5) Proposal for a GPDR (2012).

[33] Christopher Kuner doubted the feasibility of such prior guidance from the Commission due to the complexity of the issue and the dependence on the particular facts of each case. Christopher Kuner, 'The European Commission's Proposed Data Protection Regulation: A Copernican Revolution in European Data Protection Law', *Privacy & Security Law Report*, vol. 11 PVLR 06, 2012

Instead the role of the WP29 in interpreting and providing guidance on the Directive could be continued by the European Data Protection Board in the GDPR.[34]

The European Parliament (EP) First Reading[35] reinstated the legitimate interest of the third party in the provision of art. 6(1) (f). The EP added a condition to the legitimate interest of the controller ground. This is the *reasonable expectation of the data subject* based on the relationship with the controller.[36] The EP also proposed the deletion of the provision on delegated acts of the Commission. An interesting proposed amendment of the EP was made regarding the processing of *pseudonymous data*. The Parliament suggested that the processing of such data should be presumed to meet the reasonable expectations of the data subject.[37] However, the WP29 strongly recommended omitting this phrase from the GDPR, as it could 'give rise to misinterpretation and could be understood as an exemption to the obligation of the controller to carry out the balancing test'.[38]

A discussion that emerged during the preparatory works of the GDPR revolved around the inclusion (or not) of an exhaustive list of acceptable legitimate interests. The Report of the Committee on Civil Liberties, Justice and Home Affairs to the European Parliament in 2012 ('Albrecht report') included such a list in art. 6(1) (b).[39] The article provided a list of cases when the legitimate interest of a controller overrides the interests, fundamental rights and freedoms of the data subject *as a rule*. Proposed cases included in the list were the processing of personal data taking place as part of the exercise of the right to freedom of expression, and the processing of personal data in relation to the media and the arts.[40] However, such a solution was not embraced by either the regulators or the industry as it would involve the risk of being 'misleading' and 'unnecessarily prescriptive'.[41] The industry advised against such a restrictive list, which, it argued, would not anticipate the trajectory of new technologies and business models.[42] The Council First Reading is very close to the final version, which we discuss in the following section.[43]

---

[34] Judith Rauhofer, 'One Step Forward, Two Steps Back? Critical Observations on the Proposed Reform of the EU Data Protection Framework'. *Journal of Law and Economic Regulation*, vol. 6 no. 1, 2013, pp. 57–84.

[35] European Parliament (2014) Legislative Resolution of 12 March 2014 on the Proposal for a Regulation of the European Parliament and of the Council on the Protection of Individuals with regard to the Processing of Personal Data and on the Free Movement of such Data (General Data Protection Regulation) (COM(2012)0011 – C70025/2012 – 2012/0011(COD)).

[36] The concept of 'reasonable expectations' is further discussed in Section 5.3 of this chapter.

[37] Recital 38 European Parliament First Reading (2014).

[38] Article 29 Data Protection Working Party, Working Party Comments to the vote of 21 October 2013 by the European Parliament's LIBE Committee, Annex to letter to Greek Presidency, 11 December 2013, http://ec .europa.eu/justice/data-protection/article-29/documentation/other-document/files/2013/20131211_annex_letter_to_ greek_presidency_wp29_comments_outcome_vote_libe_final_en_.pdf, (accessed 10 June 2016).

[39] Committee on Civil Liberties, Justice and Home Affairs, Draft Report on the Proposal for a Regulation of the European Parliament and of the Council on the Protection of Individual with regard to the Processing of Personal Data and on the Free Movement of such Data (General Data Protection Regulation) (COM(2012)0011 – C7–0025/2012 – 2012/0011(COD)), http:// www.europarl.europa.eu/meetdocs/2009_2014/documents/libe/pr/922/922387/922387en.pdf (accessed 10 June 2016).

[40] Other cases provided in the article were the processing of personal data necessary for the enforcement of the legal claims of the data controller (art. 6(1) (b)(b)), when personal data would be provided by the data subject and the personal data would be used for direct marketing for its own and similar products and services (art. 6(1) (b)(c)), the processing of personal data in the context of professional business-to-business relationships (art. 6(1) (b)(d)) and when processing would be necessary for registered non-profit associations, foundations, and charities for the purpose of collecting donations (art. 6(1) (b)(e)).

[41] Article 29 Data Protection Working Party, WP217, p. 12.

[42] 'ICC Position on Legitimate Interests', ETD/STM, *International Chambers of Commerce*, 28 October 2015, http:// www.iccgermany.de/fileadmin/user_upload/Content/Digitale_Wirtschaft/373-537legitimateint1-2015.pdf (accessed 25 September 2016).

[43] European Council (2015) Preparation of a General Approach. 9565/15, 11 June 2015, adopted at JHA Council Meeting on 15 June 2015.

4.2 *Lawful Processing Grounds under Art. 6 GDPR*

While a detailed analysis of the grounds of legitimate processing is beyond the scope of this chapter, it suffices to mention that the GDPR kept almost intact the list of criteria for lawful processing as we know it from the Directive. The new listing of grounds is contained in art. 6 of the Regulation: consent (art. 6(1) (a)), performance of a contract (art. 6(1) (b)), legal obligation of the controller (art. 6(1) (c), vital interests (art.6(1) (d)), performance of a task carried out in the public interest (art. 6(1) (e)) and the legitimate interest of the controller (6(1) (f)) synthesise the exhaustive list of grounds for lawful processing of personal data. A new addition is article 7 GDPR, the conditions for consent. As a general comment, despite the broad criticism of over-reliance on consent as a legal ground, the EU regulator chose to emphasise the consent ground with a separate provision. This choice of the further specification of the consent ground is on the one hand partly justified by the wide discussions on the conditions for a valid consent. On the other hand, it instigates the risk of being misinterpreted as a prioritisation of consent over the other grounds of art. 6 GDPR.

4.3 *Framing the Balancing Act of Art. 6(1) (f) GDPR*

The final version of the legitimate interest of the controller ground in Regulation 679/2016 is mostly based on the Directive provision (art.7(f)). Two novelties are introduced regarding children's personal data, which merit attention from the side of the controller, and the public authorities, which cannot ground their data processing operation on art. 6(1) (f). The provision art. 6(f) GDPR reads:

> "Processing is necessary for the purposes of the legitimate interests pursued by the controller or by a third party, except where such interests are overridden by the interests or fundamental rights and freedoms of the data subject which require protection of personal data, in particular where the data subject is a child."[44]

In comparison to the provision of art. 7(f) of the Directive 95/46/EC, art. 6(1) (f) does not have many new elements to offer. The wording was improved in several instances.[45] One significant differentiation is the de-linking of the scope of the data subjects' interests, rights and freedoms that should not be overridden, from the material scope of the legal instrument. The legitimate interest of the controller provision (art. 7(f)) of the 95/46/EC Directive referred explicitly to art. 1 (1) of the Directive,[46] and thus linked the scope of the data subject's interests, rights and freedoms to scope of the Directive. The GDPR provision of art. 6(1) (f) drops the reference to the subject matter and refers to 'interests or fundamental rights and freedoms of the data subject which require protection of personal data'. The change in the wording can be considered as broadening of the scope. *Any* interests, rights and freedoms that merit the protection of personal data should be assessed by the controller when considering the legitimate interest ground for its processing activities.

[44] Art. (1) (f) GDPR.
[45] 'Legitimate interest' is now 'legitimate interests' in art. 6(1) (f) GDPR, 'overridden by the interests for fundamental rights and freedoms' of the Directive is now 'overridden by the interests or the fundamental rights and freedoms'. The last amendment was also highlighted by the WP29 in its Legitimate Interest opinion. The WP29 indicated that the wording of the Directive was a misspelling ('or' instead of 'for').
[46] Article 1(1) Directive 95/46/EC read: 'In accordance with this Directive, Member States shall protect the fundamental rights and freedoms of natural persons, and in particular their right to privacy with respect to the processing of personal data.'

4.3.1 *Step One: Legitimacy*

One of the first questions arising from the legitimate interest ground, also relevant to the different theoretical approaches to the balancing doctrine,[47] is the choice of the legislator of balancing between disparate interests: the interests of the controller or a third party on the one hand and the rights and freedoms of the data subject on the other. In principle, the disparity leads to the general rule that data subject rights override in principle the legitimate interests of the controller.[48] However, the ground of art. 7(f) implies that a legitimate interest pursued by a controller or a third party can prevail over the rights and freedoms of the data subject.

Regarding the interests of the data subject, the WP29 opines that the omission of the word 'legitimate' intentionally broadens the scope of the data subjects' interests that need to be balanced, so as to include even *illegitimate* interests of the data subject. The WP29 provides the example of an individual who has committed theft in a supermarket, and his interest not to have his picture disclosed on the Internet by the owner of the shop. However, this example does not directly respond to the argument made by the WP29, as the interest of the data subject in this case is still legitimate. The right to the protection of personal data is not automatically abolished once the individual has committed an illegal act, in this case, theft. Nevertheless, the argument on the illegitimate interests of the data subject is still valid.

The very choice of 'legitimate'[49] instead of *legal interest* of the controller is also interesting. A legal interest would be an interest stemming from a legal instrument, reflecting the 'aggregate of the legal relations of a person with respect to some specific physical object or the physical relations of specific objects'.[50] A legitimate interest on the other hand, might not be specifically foreseen in a legal instrument, but in any case has to be in accordance with the law, in the sense that it does not violate the law.[51] As such, the legitimate interest of the controller can be a fundamental right established in the Charter of Fundamental Rights, a legal right provided in a Union or national law, or it can be any other interest (including commercial) pursued by the controller, as long as it is in line with the law. The nature of the source of the interest of the controller is not important to determine its legitimacy. It does however play a role in the balancing test against the interests, rights or freedoms of the data subject, as we discuss later. The Article 29 Data Protection Working Party (WP29) proposes two conditions for the legitimacy of the interest of the controller. It must represent a *real* and *present* interest, and it has to be sufficiently *clearly articulated*.[52] As often in civil law, legal claims have to be real and present, especially when interest overrides the rights of another party. According to this interpretation of the WP29, a future interest, an interest depending on the fulfilment of a condition or an expectation for an interest are not sufficient under art. 6(1) (f). The broad scope of the concept of the legitimate interest of the controller invites a spectrum of different interests under the legitimate interest ground, as are further discussed in this chapter.[53]

[47] See discussion in Section 2 of this chapter.
[48] Case C-131/12 *Google Spain and Google*, EU:C:2014:317, paragraph 81.
[49] The choice of the word 'legitimate' *interest* instead of conflicting *rights* has been discussed by Ferretti, who interprets the 'legitimate interest' as meaning a legally protected interest. Federico Ferretti (2014).
[50] Arthur Corbin, 'Legal Analysis and Terminology', 29 *Yale Law Journal* 163, 1919–1920, p.173.
[51] By 'law' here is meant 'any law', not only the data protection law.
[52] Article 29 Data Protection Working Party 'Opinion 06/2014 on the notion of legitimate interests of the data controller under Article 7 of Directive 95/46/EC' WP217, April 2014.
[53] See Section 8 of this chapter.

4.3.2 *Third Parties*

The provision of 6(1) (f) GDPR retains the same terminology as regards the legitimate interest pursued by the controller or by a third party. The Directive included the phrase '*by the third party or parties to whom the data are disclosed*', but this phrase, especially *in fine* ('to whom the data are disclosed') is redundant due to the definition for 'third parties' in art. 4(10). A third party in the GDPR is a natural or legal person, public authority, agency or body, other than 'the data subject, controller, processor, and persons who under the direct authority of the controller or processor' are authorised to process personal data. The term is not far from the way it is used in civil law, that is a person which is not party to an agreement.[54] The GDPR explicitly provides that the third party has to be other than the data controller, processor, data subject, or the persons under the direct authority of the controller or processor. In the data protection context, the third party is not part of the relationship data controller–data subject, nor of the relationship data processor–data subject. In practice, it will be challenging to determine *who* is a third party. The third party would need to be processing data not on behalf of the controller (as it would then be a processor), nor have its own personal data be processed (as it would then be a data subject), but would however need to pursue a legitimate interest to process the personal data of the data subject. The legitimate interest of the third party is distinct from the legitimate interest of the controller (although they can both constitute a ground for lawful processing). Thus, the third party needs to have its own separate legitimate interest to process the personal data. This is problematic, as once the 'third party' pursues its own interests to process the data, and is granted access to the data, it will then most probably qualify as a data controller in its own right (provided that the other conditions for the controllership are met). With the definition of the third party included in art. 4 GDPR, the list of potential third parties is shortened due to the broad list of actors that are exempted from the definition of 'third party'. Taking the example of a cloud computing environment, searching for possible actors to qualify as third parties could be troublesome. Broader categories, such as Internet users, would perhaps qualify as third parties in that case, but crystallising a legitimate interest pursued by such a broadly defined third party could be problematic.[55] Another actor that could qualify as a third party could be a person that has legal claims against the data subject, and needs therefore to process the personal data of the data subject in order to proceed with its legal claims.[56] It is recommended therefore to interpret the provision regarding the third party strictly, as in principle, any third party receiving personal data would be considered a data controller or processor.[57]

4.3.3 *Step Two: Necessity*

Necessity is part of all the grounds of art. 6(1) GDPR, apart from consent.[58] As in the Directive,[59] the legitimacy of the interest pursued by the controller does not suffice for the ground of art. 6(1) (f) GDPR to be fulfilled. The processing also needs to be *necessary* for the purposes of the legitimate interests pursued by the controller or by a third party. Necessary in this case means that the processing of personal data is the measure least restrictive to the rights of the data

---

[54] Article 29 Data Protection Working Party 'Opinion 1/2010 on the Concepts of "Controller" and "Processor"' WP169, 2010, p. 33f.

[55] The WP29 assesses the interests of a wider community in the balancing test by including it under the legitimate interest of the *controller* together with any business or other interest of the controller itself. WP217, p. 35.

[56] See Section 7.5 RIGAS SATIKSME case: *Suing the Data Subject for Property Damages Is a Legitimate Interest.*

[57] Article 29 Data Protection Working Party, Opinion 1/2010 on the concepts of 'controller' and 'processor', WP169, 2010, p.33f.

[58] Art. 6(1) (a) GDPR.

[59] See p. 324 of the Handbook (section 3 of this chapter).

subjects. If there is another way of meeting the legitimate interest pursued by the controller or the third party, that interferes less with the right to the protection of personal data of the individuals, then processing is not necessary.[60] The European Data Protection Supervisor, in a recent background policy paper providing a 'toolkit' for assessing the necessity of a (legislative) measure, characterised the concept of necessity in data protection law as a 'facts-based' concept.[61] Indeed, whether a processing operation is necessary highly depends on the facts of the specific case under examination. But external boundaries to *what is necessary* in each case are to be set by the principles relating to processing of personal data, provided in art. 5 GDPR, such as lawfulness, fairness, data minimization and integrity.

4.3.4 *Step Three: Balancing Test*

Art. 6(1) (f) involves the *obligation* to weigh the legitimate interests of the controller on the one hand and the interests, rights and freedoms of the data subject on the other in order to determine in each specific case whether the data subject's rights override the legitimate interest of the controller or the third party ('balancing test'). Many elements should be considered in this balancing test. That is, elements that can affect the outcome to the one or the other side. The nature of the data is one such element (sensitive, open, public, etc.). Another element relates to the power and status of the two parties (controller or third party and data subject).[62] An employer intending to process the personal data of an employee is in a relatively stronger position than the employee. The source of the legitimate interest of the controller or the third party is also significant. An interest stemming from a fundamental right established in the Charter of Fundamental Rights such as the freedom of expression has different weight than a commercial interest to attract customers through targeted advertising.[63] Other issues include the purpose and impact of processing.

5 FURTHER CLARIFICATIONS ON THE BALANCING TEST

5.1 *Impact Assessment*

A crucial element of *balancing* is the assessment of the *impact* of the processing operation at stake to the interests, rights and freedoms of the data subject. The impact should be understood as including *both benefits and risks* to the individual stemming from the processing operation. Risk assessment is not unusual to data and information security. Several methodologies exist for the identification and classification of risk, the determination of their severity and the recommendation of mitigation measures. The Open Web Application Security Project (OWASP),[64] a non-profit organisation working on open source software, has proposed a methodology of five main steps, starting from risk identification, the estimation of likelihood, estimation of impact,[65] the determination of the severity of risk and prioritisation of risks for mitigation. Standardisation

---

[60] 'Big Data and Data Protection', ICO, version 1.0, 2014, paragraph 64 p. 20, https://ico.org.uk/media/for-organisations/documents/1541/big-data-and-data-protection.pdf (accessed 10 September 2016).

[61] European Data Protection Supervisor 'Developing a "Toolkit" for Assessing the Necessity of Measures that Interfere with Fundamental Rights, Background Paper', June 2016, p. 8.

[62] Article 29 Data Protection Working Party (2014).

[63] See for instance the Opinion of the Advocate General in CJEU *Google Spain and Google* case, Section 7.2 of this chapter.

[64] Website of OWASP, https://www.owasp.org/index.php/About_OWASP (accessed 18 September 2016).

[65] According to OWASP methodology, this stage includes both technical impact factors such as loss of confidentiality, availability, integrity, availability and accountability, and business impact factors, such as financial damage, loss of reputation and others.

bodies have also developed standards and guidelines on risk management. For instance, NIST, the US Institute for Standards and Technology, has proposed a privacy risk management framework, which includes a Privacy Risk Assessment Methodology.[66] The ISO has published the ISO 31000 on risk management, but also the ISO/IEC 27005 which is specific to information security risk management.[67] While existing risk assessment methodologies could be useful for the balancing of the legitimate interest ground, assessing 'benefits' and positive impact is challenging, due first to the subjectivity involved in such a benefit analysis and second to the nature of the impact on rights and freedoms of individuals.

Colin J. Bennett and Robin M. Bayley argue that the legitimate interest ground is structured by a context in which there is 'pro-active assessment of risk' and demonstration of accountability.[68] Although, as we said, the assessment goes further than just a risk assessment, the argument on the demonstration of accountability is important. Indeed, in the framework of the accountability principle of art. 5(2) GDPR, the concept of legitimate interest is seen as a continuous exercise for the controller to demonstrate that his interest prevails over the interests, rights and freedoms of the data subject. This is different from the Data Protection Directive, where the accountability of the controller was implied. With the introduction of the accountability principle and the element of demonstration, the controller needs to document the decision (and its justification) to rely on the legitimate interest ground not only at the moment of the decision, but as long as he grounds processing on the legitimate interest.

5.2 *What Should Be the Weight of Mitigation Mseasures in the Balancing Test?*

There can be two approaches to the balancing test under art. 6(1) (f). A sensu stricto balancing test responds to the literal interpretation of the provision. Such a test would omit including in the balancing test as self-standing criteria any mitigation measures and *safeguards*, such as organisational or technical measures, taken by the controller for the protection of the data subject's rights. The rationale for this approach is simple. The ground of art. 6(1) (f) asks for a balancing test between two *values*, the legitimate interests of the controller (or a third party) and the interests, rights and freedoms of the data subject, and the mitigation measures are not inherent to any of those values. As discussed earlier, an interest lies with a controller when he has a present and real need to process personal data. By definition, a legitimate interest does not include mitigation measures and safeguards to reduce adverse impacts. An argument in favour of adopting this approach is that making 'safeguards' part of the test would unfairly influence the assessment in favour of the legitimate interest of the controller. Any *scheduled* safeguards and mitigation measures would most likely weigh in favour of the controller and 'at the expense' of data subject's interests, rights and freedoms, by softening the impact and consequences of interference. In case the legitimate interest of the controller prevails, the controller still needs to take safeguards to protect data subjects' rights, on the basis mainly of art. 5, 13 and 21 GDPR. Prevailing should in no case be interpreted as *abolishing*.

---

[66] National Institute for Standards and Technology (NIST), 'Privacy Risk Management for Federal Information Systems', NISTIR 8062 draft, http://csrc.nist.gov/publications/drafts/nistir-8062/nistir_8062_draft.pdf, (accessed 18 September 2016).

[67] International Standardisation Organisation (ISO), ISO 31000:2009 Risk Management-Principles and guidelines, ISO/IEC 27005:2011, Information technology – Security techniques – Information security risk management.

[68] Colin J. Bennett and Robin M. Bayley, 'Privacy Protection in the Era of "Big Data": Regulatory Challenges and Social Assessments', in Bart van der Sloot, Dennis Broeders and Erik Schrijvers (eds.), *Exploring the Boundaries of Big Data*, Amsterdam University Press, Amsterdam, 2016.

Another approach is the one proposed by the WP29. To prevent undue impact, balancing would include mitigation measures, such as the use of anonymization techniques and privacy enhancing technologies (PETs).[69]

From a teleological perspective, the WP29 approach fits better with the aim of the protection of the right, not to look at concepts bare from their context, but to adopt a more pragmatic approach and investigate the protection and impact on data subjects' rights. Thus, including mitigation measures in the assessment would lead to a representation of the actual expected impact of the processing on data subjects' rights, and would still allow the legitimate interests to prevail. This approach does not 'punish' the controller that takes mitigation measures and safeguards, by not including them in the balancing test. On the contrary it encourages the controller to do so. On the other hand, one should keep in mind that the weight of future safeguards and mitigation measures is always relevant to their realisation and effectiveness. Such measures therefore should be considered, but not play a significant role in determining to which side the scale leans.

5.3 *Reasonable Expectations of the Data Subject*

A new concept in the GDPR is the *reasonable expectations* of data subjects based on the relationship with the controller.[70] The concept of reasonable expectations is known in other fields of law,[71] and in the case law of the European Court of Human Rights (ECtHR) on the art. 8 of the European Convention of Human Rights (ECHR).[72] The introduction of the concept was in general received positively from data protection advocates,[73] even though not without exceptions.[74]

Even though included only in a recital of the final text of the GDPR, the reasonable expectations criterion will be a significant element of the balancing test. According to this criterion, the controller would need to assess whether the data subject reasonably expects the collection of personal data *at the time* and in *the context* of the collection for the specific purpose.[75] The example of a client–provider relationship stands out in that respect. When an individual orders a product online, he would expect that the service provider would process his personal data. The controller pursues the interest to conduct business[76] and carry out the

---

[69] Article 29 Data Protection Working Party (2014)

[70] Recital 47 GDPR.

[71] The 'reasonable expectations' criterion in GDPR could be compared to the 'reasonable expectations' doctrine in other fields of law such as consumer protection law, contract law, insurance law and administration law. See Clarisse Girot, *User Protection in IT Contracts: A Comparative Study of the Protection of the User against Defective Performance in Information Technology.* Vol. 11. Kluwer Law International, The Hague, 2001. Also, CJEU, Judgment of the Court of First Instance 8 May 2007, *Citymo v Commission*, Case T-271/04, EU:T:2007:128.

[72] See for instance European Court of Human Rights, Judgement of 24 June 2004, *von Hannover v. Germany.*

[73] Simon Davies, "The Data Protection Regulation: A Triumph of Pragmatism over Principle?" *European Data Protection Law Review*, vol. 2:3, 2016, pp. 290–296.

[74] See Colette Cuijpers et al. who relate the 'reasonable expectations' criterion in the GDPR to the criticism attached to the reasonable expectations test in the US Informational Privacy literature and argue that 'the legal protection is conditioned by people's expectations of privacy, but these expectations are significantly formed by the legal protection.' C. M. K. C. Cuijpers, N. N. Nadeszda Purtova and Eleni Kosta, "Data Protection Reform and the Internet: The Draft Data Protection Regulation" in A. Savin and J. Trzaskowski (eds.), *Research Handbook on EU Internet Law*, Edward Elgar, Cheltenham, 2014, pp. 543–568.

[75] Recital 47 GDPR.

[76] According to article 16 of the Charter of Fundamental Rights EU, '*The freedom to conduct a business in accordance with Union law and national laws and practices is recognised.*'

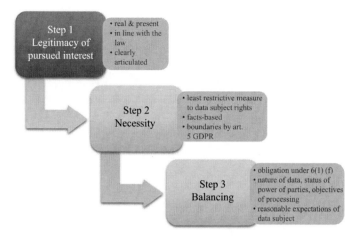

FIGURE 19.1 Conceptualisation of the balancing act framework of art. 6(1) (f) GDPR

product order.[77] A reasonable expectation relates strongly to the circumstances *before* processing takes place, including the provision of clear and timely information to the data subject. A reasonable expectation of processing therefore relates to the *foreseeability* and *acceptance* from the side of the data subject of the processing operation. While the foreseeability needs to be articulated objectively (a clear, timely and transparent information notice, justified for the purposes it serves, etc.) by the data controller, the acceptance of the data subject can also be implied (otherwise, we would refer to 'consent'). Scholars raise a flag of over-reliance on *reasonable* expectations; what is reasonable might be influenced by previous (not necessarily fair) practices of dominant players in a field.[78]

6 UNDERSTANDING THE LEGITIMATE INTEREST GROUND IN THE WIDER CONTEXT OF THE GDPR

6.1 *The Right to Access and the Right to Object*

If processing takes place based on the legitimate interest of the controller or a third party, the GDPR provides the data subject with safeguards, aiming to counteract interference with the data subject's interests, rights, and freedoms. Article 13 GDPR, which concerns the information to be provided where personal data are collected from the data subject, and art. 14, concerning the information to be provided where personal data have not been obtained from

---

[77] In the *Google Spain and Google* case, the Advocate General recognised the fundamental right to conduct business, established in art. 16 of the Charter of Fundamental Rights, as within the meaning of legitimate interests of art. 7(f) of the Directive. The AG opined, 'An internet search engine service provider lawfully exercises both his freedom to conduct business and freedom of expression when he makes available internet information location tools relying on a search engine.'

[78] Nicolo Zingales argues, 'Consumers tend to recognize the rules and policies adopted by the dominant players as part of the general cultural and societal expectation.' Arguably, this could lead, according to Zingales, to contractual practices being used as a shield against certain contractual obligations used in the market. Nicolo Zingales, 'Unreasonable v. Unfair Data Processing: Contrasting Two Rising Modes of Protection Against Over-reaching Terms of Service', unpublished paper presented at the Amsterdam Privacy Conference 2015. However, in a recent case brought to the Supreme Court of Canada, the Court ruled that there are limitations to such contractual clauses. Such limitations are imposed by public policy concerns. The judge in the case *Douez v. Facebook Inc.*, concluded: '*In general, then, when online consumer contracts of adhesion contain terms that unduly impede the ability of consumers to vindicate their rights in domestic courts, particularly their quasi-constitutional or constitutional rights, in my view, public policy concerns outweigh those favouring enforceability of a forum selection clause.*' Supreme Court of Canada, Douez v. Facebook, Inc. 2017 SCC 33, https://scc-csc.lexum.com/scc-csc/scc-csc/en/item/16700/index.do (accessed 29 June 2017).

the data subject, establish the obligation of the controller to inform the data subject that processing is based on the ground of art. 6(1) (f), the legitimate interests pursued by the controller or a by a third party.[79] This is an additional obligation to the disclosure of the legal basis of processing.[80] The controller needs to inform the data subject on *which* are the legitimate interests that the controller or the third party pursues and prevail over the rights of the data subject. Paul De Hert and Vagelis Papakonstantinou draw attention to the exception to the information obligation of the controller in cases where 'the data subject already has the information',[81] as such broad exemptions could in practice render the right to information irrelevant.[82] The provision of this information is a prerequisite for the exercise of the right to object.

The right to object to processing based on the legitimate interest of the controller (or a third party) is established in art. 21 GDPR. This is not a new provision in the EU data protection law.[83] What is new is the reversal of the burden of proof. In art. 14 of the Data Protection Directive, the data subject could object on *compelling legitimate grounds* and the controller would stop processing those personal data if the objection would be *justified*. Art. 21(1) GDPR provides:

> The controller shall no longer process the personal data unless the controller demonstrates compelling legitimate grounds for the processing which override the interests, rights and freedoms of the data subject or for the establishment, exercise or defence of legal claims.[84]

Once the data subject objects, the controller is obliged to stop processing personal data, unless the controller demonstrates compelling grounds for processing. The data subject's right to have his personal data not processed based on the legitimate interest of the controller is granted *ab initio*.[85] The compelling grounds provided by the controller need to override the interests, rights and freedoms of the data subject or be important for legal claims. A new element in the legislation is the use of personal data for legal claims.[86] If interpreted broadly, the 'legal claims' term could include a broad range of cases, and could leave room for misuse, or even abuse by data controllers in bad faith. It should be accepted that such legal claims should stem from the relationship of the controller with the data subject. There should also be a strong *causal link* of the claim with the personal data at stake. This means that the legal claim cannot be otherwise established, exercised or defended unless the processing of personal data objected to takes place ('*compelling*'). The right to information and the right to object are granted along the other data subject rights (access, restriction of processing, erasure, etc.). The data protection principles of art. 5 GDPR and the accountability principle constitute a framework of safeguards for the data subject.

6.2 *Processing of Sensitive Data and Further Processing on the Ground of Legitimate Interest*

The provision on the processing of special categories of data is enriched in the GDPR with the introduction of genetic and biometric data, as distinct categories from the data concerning health.

---

[79] Art. 13(1) (d) and art. 14(2) (b) GDPR.

[80] Art. 13(1) (c) and art. 14(1) (c).

[81] Art. 13(4) and art. 14(5) GDPR.

[82] Paul De Hert and Vagelis Papakonstantinou, 'The New General Data Protection Regulation: Still a Sound System for the Protection of Individuals?', *Computer Law & Security Review*, vol. 32:2, 2016, pp. 179–194.

[83] Art. 21 GDPR corresponds to art. 14 Directive 95/46/EC.

[84] Art. 21(1) GDPR.

[85] Rauhofer (2013).

[86] It is not new in the case law however. See *I. v. Finland*, despite the fact that the parties had reverse roles: the data subject wanted access to her personal data to support her legal claims against the controller. European Court of Human Rights, Case of I v. Finland (Application no. 20511/03), Strasbourg, 17 July 2008, Final 17–10–2008.

Although the legitimate interest of the controller is not as such a ground constituting an exception to the general prohibition of processing of sensitive personal data in art. 9(1), elements of the legitimate interest ground can be identified in two of the grounds of art. 9(2) GDPR. First, there is the ground of 'legitimate activities' by a non-profit body.[87] The legitimate activities ground is closely linked to the legitimate interest ground of art. 6(1) (f), but has a more limited scope ('activities' instead of 'interests') and is conditioned on appropriate safeguards, the type of the controller (non-profit body), the aim of activity of the controller ('political, philosophical, religious or trade union') and the relationship of the data subjects with the controller (members, former members or persons with regular contact with the controller). The other ground of art. 9 is the ground of the establishment, exercise or defence of legal claims.[88] Legal claims usually fall within the legitimate interest of a controller (as is also obvious in the right to object provision), although the provision also includes not only claims of the controller, but also of the data subject.[89] The careful and limited introduction of elements of the legitimate interest of the controller ground in the processing of sensitive data confirms the aim of the GDPR to impose a stricter regime on the processing of such data and offers a good example for comparison with the broader and more flexible conditions of art. 6(1) (f)[90]

Regarding further processing, the GDPR makes use of the criterion of reasonable expectations of the data subject also in the case of further processing.[91] If the data subject does not reasonably expect further processing given the circumstances of each case, then further processing is not allowed with the original legal ground for processing. A critical issue is what can be considered as 'compatible' with the original purposes. Apart from the criterion of 'reasonable expectations' other criteria can also help the controller determine the compatibility of original with further processing purposes: any links between the purposes, the context in which the personal data have been collected, the nature of the personal data, the consequences to the data subjects and the existence of safeguards in both original and further (intended) processing.[92] The controller needs therefore to conduct comprehensive compatibility and impact assessment before engaging in any further processing. The GDPR regards the indication and transmission of criminal acts or threats to public security in individual cases or in several cases relating to the same criminal act or threats to public security as being in the legitimate interest pursued by the controller. It recognises however that often such disclosure of personal data could be incompatible with 'legal, professional or other binding obligation of secrecy' and thus includes an exception to the compatibility rule, when such obligations are involved and conflict with the processing.

6.3 *Children and Public Authorities*

Children are vulnerable to risks such as the unwanted dissemination of their personal data on online social networks, and targeted advertising,[93] but also to online and offline abuse,

---

[87] Art. 9(2) (d) GDPR.

[88] Art. 9(2) (f) GDPR.

[89] See discussion later in this chapter.

[90] Even though the extension of the 'exceptions' list in comparison to art. 8 of the Directive 95/46/EC can be considered as achieving the opposite result.

[91] Recitals 47 and 50 GDPR.

[92] Article 6(4) GDPR and recital 50 GDPR.

[93] European Data Protection Supervisor, 'Opinion of the European Data Protection Supervisor on the Communication from the Commission to the European Parliament, the Council, the European Economic and Social Committee and the Committee of the Regions, "European Strategy for a Better Internet for Children"', July 2012, https://secure.edps .europa.eu/EDPSWEB/webdav/shared/Documents/Consultation/Opinions/2012/12–07–17_Better_Iternet_Children_ EN.pdf, (accessed 25 September 2016).

cyberbullying and others. In line with the increased attention the GDPR draws to the protection of children,[94] the provision of art. 6(1) (f) emphasises the balancing needed when the data subject is a child (*'in particular when the data subject is a child'*). When the data subject is a child, this element should weigh in the balancing test in favour of the interests, rights and freedoms of the data subject. The GDPR includes the condition on children only in the legitimate interest ground of art. 6 and consent (art. 8). This heightened protection for children comes to outweigh the vulnerability of children as data subjects – in the forms of information asymmetry, the exercise of data subjects' rights to access or object, etc. – as opposed to data controllers, which may be organisations and corporations such as online social networks and search engines. A practical difficulty for the controller in applying the special attention to the rights of the children is that the age of the data subject, which is personal data, requires that the controller already engage in a processing operation, i.e. collection of the information, for which the controller already needs a legal ground.

Another novelty is the inapplicability of the legitimate interest of the controller ground to public authorities. The final text of the GDPR does not allow public authorities to use the legitimate interest ground for data processing activities in the performance of their tasks[95] Public authorities may however use one of the other grounds for lawful processing of art. 6 GDPR.

7 COURT OF JUSTICE OF THE EU: LANDMARK CASES, BUT FEW 'CONCRETE' ANSWERS FOR LEGITIMATE INTEREST GROUND

The role of the Court of Justice in interpreting EU data protection law has been of fundamental significance. Landmark cases such as the *Digital Rights Ireland* case,[96] the *Google Spain* case[97] and the *Schrems* case[98] have elevated the role of the CJEU as gatekeeper of EU data protection law. Vassilios Skouris, former president of the Court, stated:[99]

> European justice is a fundamental guarantee for the application of the rule of law and democracy. But it is also a major factor of adjusting the legislative choices to ongoing societal changes. The institutional setup is such that calls for the European judge to make sure that legislative solutions adopted under given circumstances maintain their value even in view of novel phenomena.

Despite the significance of the judgements in the data protection field, the CJEU did not have many occasions to interpret the ground of art. 7(f) of the Data Protection Directive, and in the few occasions there was such an opportunity, it was not fully exploited. As will be seen, the CJEU missed for instance the opportunity to interpret the necessity condition of the ground in the *ASNEF* case. It provided some answers however in the recent *Breyer* case, as analysed in this chapter. The following

---

[94] Recital 38 and art. 8 GDPR. Results from Cookie Sweep of EU Data Protection Authorities and report on children online (in French): 'Vie privée des enfants: une protection insuffisante sur les sites Internet', *CNIL*, 2 September 2015, https://www.cnil.fr/fr/vie-privee-des-enfants-une-protection-insuffisante-sur-les-sites-internet-0, last accessed 25 September 2016. Read further about this issue and on the age for consent of children in Lina Jasmontaite and Paul De Hert, 'The EU, Children under 13 Years, and Parental Consent: A Human Rights Analysis of a New, Age-Based Bright-Line for the Protection of Children on the Internet', *International Data Privacy Law*, vol. 5 no. 1, 2015, pp. 20–33.

[95] Art. 6(1) and recital 47 GDPR. The Data Protection Directive 95/46/EC did not preclude public authorities from using the ground of legitimate interest of art. 7(f). In the *Manni* case, the Court of Justice EU found that the processing of personal data by an authority legally responsible to keep a register satisfies *inter alia* the ground of legitimate interest of the controller of art. 7(f) Directive 95/46/EC, Case C-398/15, EU:C:2017:197.

[96] Joined Cases C-293/12 and C-594/12 *Digital Rights Ireland and Others*, EU:C:2014:238.

[97] Case C-131/12 *Google Spain and Google*, EU:C:2014:317.

[98] Case C-362/14 *Schrems*, EU:C:2015:650.

[99] Vassilios Skouris, 'After 12 Years', *Maastricht Journal of European and Comparative Law*, vol. 23 no. 2, 2016.

cases are the most relevant jurisprudence with focus on the ground of legitimate interest. They are presented here in order to explore the stance of the CJEU on the matter under discussion.

7.1 *ASNEF Case: Legitimate Interest Ground Is* Not Strictly for Personal Data Appearing in Public Sources[100]

The CJEU was asked to issue a preliminary ruling referred by the Supreme Tribunal Court of Spain. The parties in the two joined cases were the Asociación Nacional de Establecimientos Financieros de Crédito (ASNEF) and the Federación de Comercio Electrónico y Marketing Directo (FECEMD) against the Spanish state Administration. References for the preliminary ruling concerned the interpretation of art. 7(f) of Data Protection Directive.

7.1.1 *Facts and Preliminary Questions*

ASNEF and FECEMD brought administrative proceedings before the national courts of Spain complaining that the national legislation transposing the Data Protection Directive to the national law violated art. 7(f) of the Directive. The argument of the plaintiffs was that the Spanish Royal Decree added conditions to the ground of art. 7(f), in breach of the Data Protection Directive. According to the plaintiff, the breach lay on the condition that for the interest of the controller to be legitimate, the controller should process personal data which *appear in public sources* (files of the Spanish Organic law 15/1999).

The Supreme Court of Spain took the view that such restriction in the Spanish Decree is a *barrier* to the free movement of personal data, which is incompatible with the Data Protection Directive. Since the outcome of the cases depended on the interpretation of the Directive, the Supreme Court referred two questions to the CJEU. The first question related to the interpretation of art. 7(f) as allowing the processing of personal data necessary to pursue a legitimate interest of the controller or of third parties when fundamental rights and freedoms are not being prejudiced, *and* the data to be processed appear in *public sources*. The second question referred to whether art. 7(f) of Data Protection Directive had *direct effect*.[101]

7.1.2 *Ruling*

The Court of Justice EU confirmed that the list of grounds for lawful processing of art. 7 Data Protection Directive is exhaustive and restrictive.[102] Member States therefore cannot include additional grounds or provide for additional requirements amending the scope of a principle of art. 7. Guidance and national measures which provide a clarification of the ground are in line with the Directive. Regarding the content of the legitimate interest ground, the Court found two conditions that must cumulatively be fulfilled. The first is the *necessity* condition. Processing needs to be necessary for the legitimate interests of the controller or third parties or parties to whom the data are disclosed. The second condition is that such legitimate interests *must not be overridden* by the fundamental rights and freedoms of the data subject.[103] The Court did not provide further interpretation of the 'necessity' condition. However, it provided further explanation of the second condition.

---

[100] Joined Cases C-468/10 and C-469/10, *ASNEF*.
[101] The direct effect of EU law is a fundamental principle of EU law, which enables individuals to immediately invoke European law before courts, independent of whether national law exists http://eur-lex.europa.eu/legal-content/EN/TXT/HTML/?uri=URISERV:l14547&from=EN (accessed 10 September 2016).
[102] Joined Cases C-468/10 and C-469/10, para. 30.
[103] Joined Cases C-468/10 and C-469/10, para. 38.

The Court noted the need for *balancing* between opposing rights and freedoms included in the second condition of art. 7(f). The ruling went further on to specify that balancing depends in principle on the *individual circumstances* of each case. In the context of those individual circumstances, the person or the institution carrying out the balancing test should take into account the data subject's rights of arts. 7 and 8 of the Charter of Fundamental Rights of the European Union.[104] Here the Court included within the scope of balancing both the right for respect for private and family life and the right to the protection of personal data. The reason for the inclusion of both fundamental rights, as provided in the ruling, is the close connection of the right to respect for private life with the right of art. 8(1).[105] The fundamental rights of arts. 7 and 8 of the Charter are not absolute rights. Therefore, interference with non-absolute rights can be allowed when the conditions of art. 52 of the Charter are fulfilled. In the case under discussion, when referring to the limitations to the fundamental right to protection of personal data, the Court recalled art. 8(2) and art. 52(1). The Court therefore interpreted the balancing condition of art. 7(f) as depending on a case by case basis. The Court kept a reservation ('*in principle*') for this rule, without however further specifying exceptions. In relation to the elements of the balancing test, the Court said that it is possible to take into consideration the fact that the *seriousness of the infringement* can vary depending on whether the data in question already appear in public sources.

The Court replied to the first question that art. 7(f) of Directive 95/46 must be interpreted as *precluding* national rules to require not only that the fundamental rights and freedoms of the data subject be respected, but also that those data should appear in public sources, thereby excluding, in a categorical and generalised way, any processing of data not appearing in such sources.[106] In addition, the reply to the second preliminary question regarding the direct effect of the art. 7(f) of the Directive, the Court found that art. 7(f) has direct effect.

7.2 *AEPD v. Google* Case: The Balancing Test Depends in Principle on Individual Circumstances[107]

The Audiencia Nacional (Spanish national high court) requested a preliminary ruling concerning the application of the Directive 95/46/EC to Internet search engines and the right to be de-listed from search results. The case was about a decision of AEPD, the Spanish Data Protection Authority, upholding a complaint by a Spanish citizen against Google Spain and Google Inc. and ordering Google Inc. to 'adopt the measures necessary to withdraw personal data relating to Mr Costeja González from its index and to prevent access to the data in the future'. In short, preliminary questions related to the interpretation of the territorial application of the Data

---

[104] Article 7 Charter protects the right to respect for private and family life. Art. 8 establishes the right to protection of personal data.

[105] In fact, the Court referred to '*the right to respect for private life with regard to the processing of personal data, recognised by Articles 7 and 8 of the Charter*', citing the two distinct rights of art. 7 and art. 8 Charter as one. This is not new in the case law of the CJEU. Gloria Gonzalez Fuster discusses inconsistencies in the case law of the CJEU in separation and disentanglement of the rights of art. 7 and art. 8 of the Charter. Gloria Gonzàlez Fuster, 'Fighting for Your Right to What Exactly: The Convoluted Case Law of the EU Court of Justice on Privacy and/Or Personal Data Protection', *Birkbeck Law Review* 2:2, 2014, p. 263.

[106] Joined Cases C-468/10 and C-469/10, para. 49.

[107] An extensive analysis of the judgement is not in the scope of this contribution. Read further Christopher Kuner, 'The Court of Justice of the EU Judgment on Data Protection and Internet Search Engines: Current Issues and Future Challenges', in Burkhard Hess and Cristina M. Mariottini (eds.), *Protecting Privacy in Private International and Procedural Law and by Data Protection*, Farnham, Surrey: Ashgate, 2015, pp. 19–55. Paul De Hert and Vagelis Papakonstantinou, '*Google Spain*: Addressing Critiques and Misunderstandings One Year Later', *Maastricht Journal of European and Comparative Law*, vol. 22 no. 4, 2015, pp. 624–638.

Protection Directive, the activity of search engines as providers of content in relation to the Directive and the scope of the right to erasure.[108] The Advocate General (AG) in his Opinion recognised that the provision of Internet search engine services falls within the legitimate interests of the controller ground for lawful processing (art. 7(f) Directive). Further on the AG provided that this activity breaks down to three purposes:

> (i) making information more easily accessible for internet users; (ii) rendering dissemination of the information uploaded on the internet more effective; and (iii) enabling various information society services supplied by the internet search engine service provider that are ancillary to the search engine, such as the provision of keyword advertising'.[109]

The AG related those purposes to freedom of Internet users to receive information (art. 11 Charter), freedom of expression (art. 11 Charter) and freedom of search engine service providers to conduct business (art. 16 Charter).

The judgement did not explicitly uphold the AG's arguments on the legitimate interest of Internet search engine providers. It limited the references to the legitimate interest ground of art. 7 (f) to what was strictly necessary for the judgement. The Court referred to the two cumulative conditions of the legitimate interest ground and confirmed the requirement for a balancing test in the second condition (*except where such interests are overridden by the interests for fundamental rights and freedoms of the data subject*). As in the ASNEF case, the Court provided that the balancing test depends, in principle, *on the individual circumstances* of each case, stressing at the same time the need to consider the data subject's rights of arts. 7 and 8 Charter.[110]

7.3 *RYNES* Case: Protection of Property, Health, and Life of Family and the Individual as Legitimate Interests[111]

The case concerned the interpretation of art. 3(2) of the Directive 95/46/EC, which is the so-called household exemption.[112] Rynes had installed a surveillance system at his home which recorded the entrance, the public footpath and the entrance to the house opposite. In examining on whether the activity of Rynes fell under the exemption of art. 3(2), the Court of Justice EU also referred to the legitimate interest of the controller ground. The Court provided that the protection of the property, health and life of family and the individual (claimant himself) may constitute legitimate interests pursued by the controller.[113] The Court ruled that art. 3(2) of Directive 95/46/EC must be interpreted as meaning that the activity of Rynes did not fall under the household exemption.[114] This case is interesting because even though it does not elaborate

---

[108] C-131/12, EU:C:2014:317.
[109] AG Opinion C-131/12, EU:C: 2013:424 para. 95.
[110] C-131/12 paragraph 40.
[111] C-212/13, EU:C:2014:2428.
[112] Art. 3(2) Directive 95/46/EC provides:

> 'This Directive shall not apply to the processing of personal data: by a natural person in the course of a purely personal or household activity'.

[113] Para. 34 C-212/13.
[114] The Court provided, 'The second indent of Article 3(2) of Directive 95/46/EC of the European Parliament and of the Council of 24 October 1995 on the protection of individuals with regard to the processing of personal data and on the free movement of such data must be interpreted as meaning that the operation of a camera system, as a result of which a video recording of people is stored on a continuous recording device such as a hard disk drive, installed by an individual on his family home for the purposes of protecting the property, health and life of the home owners, but which also monitors a public space, does not amount to the processing of data in the course of a purely personal or household activity, for the purposes of that provision.'

on the balancing test, it uses the legitimate interest ground to show that even when Directive 95/46/EC applies (thus not under the household exemption), the interests of the controller are co-considered in the provisions of the law. The Court gave a broader role to the legitimate interest ground, one of bringing balance among conflicting interests and rights, and reminded us of the relativity of the right to protection of personal data.

7.4 *BREYER* Case: Ensuring Operability of Online Media Services May Constitute a Legitimate Interest

The German Federal Court of Justice requested a preliminary ruling on a case concerning a German citizen (Breyer) seeking a prohibitory injunction against the Federal Republic of Germany for storing IP addresses.[115] Breyer required the Federal Republic to refrain from storing, or arranging for third parties to store, the IP address of the host system from which he sought access, except when necessary to restore the availability of the telemedium in a case of a fault. In his Opinion delivered in May 2016, the Advocate General proposed:

> Article 7(f) of Directive 95/46 must be interpreted as meaning that the objective of ensuring the functioning of a telemedium can, in principle, be regarded as a legitimate interest, the purposes of which justify the processing of personal data, subject to an assessment that that interest prevails over the interests or fundamental rights of the person concerned. A national provision which did not allow that legitimate interest to be taken into account would be incompatible with that article.

The Advocate General classified the *functioning* of a telemedium among the legitimate interests of art. 7(f) Data Protection Directive. Breyer rejected the argument that the storage of dynamic IP addresses is necessary to protect the proper functioning of Internet services against possible attacks. The AG responded that he did not think that 'a categorical answer can be given in relation to that problem, whose solution, on the contrary, must be preceded, in each particular case, by a balancing of the interests of the website owner and the rights and interests of users'.[116] The AG asserted that art. 7(f) Directive asks for a *case-by-case* balancing test.

On 19 October 2016, the Court of Justice published its judgement on the case. The Court decided that a dynamic IP address registered by an online media services provider constitutes personal data, where the provider 'has the legal means which enable it to identify the data subject with additional data which the internet service provider has about that person'.[117] The Court then went on to reply to the second question posed by the German Court on whether the storage of those IP addresses at the end of the (website) consultation period is authorised by art. 7(f) of the Data Protection Directive. The Court first said that German national law[118] had a more restrictive scope than the Directive. In explaining art.7(f), the Court interpreted the legitimate interest ground provision as precluding 'Member States from excluding, categorically and in general, the possibility of processing certain categories of personal data without allowing the opposing rights and interests at issue to be balanced against each other in a particular case'. The Court provided (65§2):

> Article 7(f) of Directive 95/46 must be interpreted as precluding the legislation of a Member State, pursuant to which an online media services provider may collect and use personal data

---

[115] Case C-582/14, *Breyer*.
[116] Case C-582/14, Opinion of Advocate General Campos Sánchez-Bordona delivered on 12 May 2016, footnote 40.
[117] Case C-582/14, *Judgment of the Court 19 October 2016*, ECLI:EU:C:2016:779.
[118] Telemediengesetz (Law on telemedia) of 26 February 2007.

relating to a user of those services, without his consent, only in so far as that the collection and use of that data are necessary to facilitate and charge for the specific use of those services by that user, even though the objective aiming to ensure the general operability of those services may justify the use of those data after a consultation period of those websites.

The Court therefore confirmed with its ruling, first, the opinion of the AG as to the case-by-case element of the legitimate interest ground ("in a particular case"). Second it confirmed the ASNEF case approach about the (lack) of powers of Member States to restrict the scope of the legitimate interest ground. Third, it confirmed the approach of the Court in the Rynes case, namely that the legitimate interest ground guarantees that the (legitimate) interests of the data controller are not disregarded, but considered and balanced against the interests, rights and freedoms of the data subject. In addition, the case offers a new example of a legitimate interest of art. 7(f), not examined by the CJEU in this context before: that is, the interest of an online media service provider to collect and use data relating to the use of online media services that are necessary to facilitate and charge for the specific use of the services by the user, with the aim to ensure operability of those services.[119]

7.5 *RIGAS SATIKSME* Case: Suing the Data Subject for Property Damages Is a Legitimate Interest

The Rīgas satiksme case[120] concerned a request by a Latvian Court for a preliminary ruling on whether the phrase of art. 7(f) Directive 95/46/EC 'is necessary for the purposes of the legitimate interests pursued by the third party or parties to whom the data are disclosed' should be interpreted as to allow National Police to disclose personal data to the public transportation company of Riga (Rīgas satiksme) in the civil proceedings.

7.5.1 *Facts*

A car accident occured in Latvia, after the passenger of a taxi opened the door of the vehicle while a trolleybus of the company Rīgas satiksme was passing next to the taxi. Initially the company sought damages against the taxi driver. The latter, however, claimed that the passenger was liable for the damages caused to the trolleybus. When Rīgas satiksme requested the personal data of the passenger from the national police, the latter provided the first and last names of the taxi passenger, but declined to provide the identity document number and the address of the passenger. The trolleybus company brought an administrative law action against the competent Administrative Court of Latvia, which at first instance, upheld the action of the trolley company and ordered the national police to provide the requested information. The national police appealed against the ruling, and requested the opinion of the national Data Protection Agency. The latter opined that the national Data Protection Act cannot be used as a legal basis to provide personal data, as the law does not oblige the controller to process the data, but 'simply permits it'[121]. The referring court however takes the view that in order to bring a civil action the applicant would need to know the residence of the taxi passenger. Following that, the referring court had doubts over the interpretation of the 'necessity' concept of art. 7(f) of the Data Protection Directive 95/46/EC.

---

[119] For detailed commentary on the significance of the Breyer case, read Paul De Hert (2017).
[120] Case C-13/16, Request for a preliminary ruling from the Augstākā tiesa (Latvia) lodged on 8 January 2016 – Valsts policijas Rīgas reģiona pārvaldes Kārtības policijas pārvalde v Rīgas pašvaldības SIA (Rīgas satiksme).
[121] EU:C:2017:336, para. 18.

7.5.2 *Ruling*

The CJEU ruled that art. 7(f) of the Directive 95/46/EC expresses the *possibility* of processing data such as 'the communication to a third party of data necessary for the purposes of the legitimate interests pursued by that third party'.[122] Thus, there is *no obligation* to process the personal data on the basis of art. 7(f). This does not mean however that art. 7(f) precludes such processing if the conditions set in the article are met.

The Court went on to examine the three cumulative conditions of the legitimate interest ground. The first condition is the pursuit of a legitimate interest by the data controller by the third party or parties to whom the data are disclosed. The Court confirmed the AG's opinion by ruling, 'There is no doubt that the interest of a third party in obtaining the personal information of a person who damaged their property in order to sue that person for damages can be qualified as a legitimate interest.'[123] Regarding the *necessity* condition, the Court reinstated that limitations to the protection of personal data must take place only in so far as is strictly necessary. In the case of the provision of the first and last names of the taxi passenger however, the Court found that merely those data do not make it possible to identify the passenger with 'sufficient precision' in order to bring action against him. In that sense, the Court identified a 'functional element' in the necessity condition of art. 7(f). As for the third condition of the legitimate interest ground, the Court followed the Breyer case argumentation, and ruled that the balancing of the opposing rights and interests depends 'in principle on the specific circumstances of the particular case'.[124] The Court, however, provided an additional criterion for consideration in the balancing act, and in particular, the seriousness of the infringement to right to protection of personal data; namely, the possibility of accessing the data public sources. The Court referred to the ASNEF case, which also provided that the 'seriousness of the infringement of the data subject's fundamental rights resulting from that processing can vary depending on whether or not the data in question already appear in public sources'.[125]

7.6 *Remarks*

The preceding cases do not provide elaborate interpretation of the legitimate interest ground, but a fragmented compilation of elements that are part of the legitimate interest ground and its components, namely the legitimacy of the interest of the controller or the third party, necessity and the balancing act. The recent Breyer case seems to show a new stance from the CJEU not to miss opportunities to provide interpretation of the legitimate interest ground, as in the ASNEF case. In replying to the second question for preliminary ruling, the Court could just have assessed whether national German law restricts the scope of the legitimate interest ground of the Directive. However, the Court went further to clarify that under conditions, the data used by online media service providers to ensure the operability of such services could serve a legitimate aim. The Rigas Satiksme case is a prominent example where the CJEU interpreted the three conditions of the balancing test of art. 7(f) of the Directive. Such interpretations are more than valuable. Despite that all the foregoing case law refers to the Directive, the small changes of the provision in the GDPR text render the case-law findings a good first basis for interpretation also of the GDPR legitimate interest ground.

---

[122] EU:C:2017:336, para. 26.
[123] EU:C:2017:336, para. 29.
[124] EU:C:2017:336, para. 31.
[125] EU:C:2011:777, para. 44.

8 SELECTED CASE STUDIES FOR THE NEW LEGITIMATE INTEREST GROUND

As seen in the previous section, a broad variety of interests can be brought under the legitimate interest ground. The ultimate reality check of the legitimate interest ground in the GDPR is done by the judicial authorities. The national courts and the Court of Justice of the EU will be the gatekeepers of the correct implementation of the GDPR, but also of what Skouris calls the need 'to adjust the legislative choices to societal challenges'. Prior to that, supervisory authorities, controllers and data subjects are have called each from a different perspective, to check whether the provision is applied in a harmonised way, whether the data subject's rights are protected and whether processing based on the legitimate interest ground can allow business models to develop, while respecting the right to the protection of personal data of the individuals.

The aim of this subsection is to illustrate some of the questions, prepositions and practical issues regarding the application of the legitimate interest ground in several cases. As a starting point we take the examples provided in the Recitals of the GDPR and further elaborate on them. In the recitals of the GDPR,[126] we see a first distinction of legitimate interests of the controller, that is those that constitute prima facie 'legitimate interest' overriding the data subject's interests, rights and freedoms, and the ones that *may* override the interests of the data subject. It should be noted that the first category is in principle considered as a legitimate interest, even though the GDPR relates it to a series of conditions (strictly necessary and proportionate) and it should be contextualised. In the first category,[127] the GDPR includes the processing of personal data for preventing fraud (Rec. 47) and network and information security (Rec.49). In the second category, direct marketing purposes (Rec. 47) is brought as an example.[128]

8.1 *Network, Information Security and Anti-Fraud Measures*

As discussed in this chapter, an operator of a website may have a legitimate interest in storing certain personal data relating to visitors to that website in order to protect itself against cyber-attacks. Network and information security purposes are in principle seen as legitimate interests pursued by a controller.[129] The GDPR highlights that this is the case, when strictly necessary and proportionate. The foregoing approach in the GDPR recital, treating (under conditions) network and information security as legitimate interests pursued by the controller, is also compatible with the Directive on Information Systems (Cybercrime Directive).[130] The Cybercrime Directive provides that the identification and reporting of threats and risks posed by cyberattacks is a pertinent element of effective prevention (Rec. 12).

Such a purpose would in principle be legitimate, if real and present, in line with the law and clearly articulated. Regarding the necessity element, it can be assumed that in specific cases (not as a general rule), processing for the purpose of ensuring network and information security could

---

[126] Recitals 47, 48 and 49 GDPR.

[127] This categorisation is not formalised in the GDPR, but we follow it in this contribution in order to group the types of legitimate interests and facilitate the discussion.

[128] Recital 48 GDPR also provides the example of processing, including transmission, for internal administrative purposes within a group of undertakings or institutions that may constitute a legitimate interest of the controller.

[129] Recital 49 GDPR.

[130] Directive 2013/40/EU of the European Parliament and of the Council of 12 August 2013 on attacks against information systems and replacing Council Framework Decision 2005/222/JHA, L 218/8, 12 August 2013.

be regarded as necessary, when for instance there is an ongoing attack or an identified threat. The critical issue with network and information security purposes will be the balancing stage, which will determine whether and to what extent such purposes pursued by the controller or a third party can prevail over the interests of the data subject. Processing for information security purposes should not be abused as a generic clause that fits all cases.

In practice, it is rare that only the controller runs the information security activities. The processor should also provide sufficient guarantees to implement appropriate technical and organisational measures (art. 28 GDPR). In fact, often it is a processor, for instance in cloud computing, that provides day-to-day information security measures. In addition, the obligation of art. 32 GDPR on secure processing applies to both controller and processor. It follows that the processor may also have a legitimate interest to process data in such cases, but this interest does not qualify as prevailing over the interest, rights and freedoms of the individual based on art. 6(1) (f) GDPR. It should however be accepted that such processing activity aligns with the legitimate interest of the controller for information security, and subsequently, is covered by this concept.

Another case is the prevention of fraud (Recital 47 GDPR). A processing operation which supports such purposes is unlikely to be based on one of the other grounds of art. 6 GDPR. The consent of the data subject – who in the case of fraud investigation is the suspect criminal – will most probably not be provided by the data subject, due to the exercise of its right to avoid self-incrimination. Contract, vital interest, and public interest grounds are not relevant, with the exception of public interest when fraud is committed or attempted against the public sector. The only alternative to the legitimate interest of the controller ground in the case of the prevention of fraud or crime in general is compliance with a legal obligation to which the controller is subject. Nevertheless, such obligation is often difficult to establish in the preliminary stages of a criminal investigation. The legitimate interest of the controller would qualify for the prevention of fraud, on the condition that the requirements are met and the principles of art. 5 GDPR are respected. A generic 'prevention of fraud' purpose is not a legitimate interest prevailing over the data subject's interests. Specific circumstances that justify the processing for the prevention of fraud as the proportionate measure.

8.2 *Big Data and Profiling*

In a recent study, Lokke Moerel and Corien Prins pinpoint deficiencies of legal norms of the data protection regulatory framework in Europe. One of the examples the authors put forward is the new age of systems based on algorithms, which are able to combine and analyse vast amounts of data gathered from numerous sources. According to the authors, this activity brings the legitimate interest of the controller to the forefront. The authors propose a test based on the legitimate interest ground for data collection and processing purposes. Other scholars suggest that 'personal data processing for behavioural targeting that involves tracking people over various Internet services cannot be based on Article 7(f) of the Data Protection Directive, necessity for the legitimate interests of the controller'.[131]

This discussion reflects two things: first that the processing personal data in the case of profiling, for instance for direct marketing purposes, may be a legitimate interest pursued by the controller. Recital 47 of the GDPR provides, 'The processing of personal data for direct marketing purposes may be regarded as carried out for a legitimate interest.' Second, opinions

---

[131] Frederik Borgesius, 'Personal Data Processing for Behavioural Targeting: Which Legal Basis?', *International Data Privacy Law*, vol. 5 no. 3, 2015, pp. 163–176, ipv011.

on whether the legitimate interest ground is an appropriate legal basis for processing are diverse. It is not far-fetched to assume a similar multi-vocal approach on the part of supervisory authorities. For instance, the UK Information Commissioner (ICO) suggests that 'an organisation may have a number of legitimate interests that could be relevant, including, for example: profiling customers in order to target its marketing; preventing fraud or the misuse of its services; physical or IT security'. At the same time, other DPAs might be more reluctant to point towards the direction of legitimate interest ground in the case of big data, profiling and even marketing. In general, despite that in the case of big data, legal bases such as 'consent' might be difficult, we are not convinced that the legitimate interest ground is appropriate for each case of big data profiling. Instead, due to the problematic application of some of personal data principles (such as purpose limitation and specification)[132] in the big data context, the risk of the (un)lawfulness of processing is increased.

9 CONCLUSIONS

The methodological tool of balancing is fundamental in EU law to achieve a proportionate result between conflicting (or 'competing') rights. The EU data protection law, both the Data Protection Directive and the new GDPR, introduce the proportionality principle in the grounds for lawful processing, in art. 6(1) (f), the legitimate interest of the controller ground. The rationale of the legitimate interest ground is that under certain conditions such interests might be strong and justified enough to prevail over the interests, rights and freedoms of the data subject. *When* and *how* the prevailing of the legitimate interests of the controller or third party over the data subject's rights can take place under the GDPR provisions is not a one-dimensional assessment.

The legitimate interest ground as provided in the previous regime of the Data Protection Directive has been criticised as a loophole in the EU data protection law, as being vague and flexible to allow for broad interpretations of what may constitute a legitimate interest of the controller or a third party. The Regulation does not substantially alter the wording of the relevant provision in relation to the Directive. In fact, the examples of legitimate interest provided in the Recitals of the GDPR partially confirm the foregoing critique referring to a broad range of interests that can 'slip through' under the provision of art. 6(1) (f) GDPR. Network and Information Security, anti-fraud measures, internal administrative purposes within a group of undertakings or direct marketing (Recitals 47–49) demonstrate this argument. However, we do not agree that the legitimate interest ground is a loophole in the EU data protection law. First, the ground is not a self-standing provision, but one of the 'safeguards' established in the EU data protection secondary law, aiming to protect the fundamental right of art. 8 Charter. As such, the ground should be read through the lens of the data protection principles of art. 5 GDPR (i.e. the lawfulness and fairness of processing). In that respect, the GDPR introduced a significant improvement in relation to the Directive; that is the principle of accountability: the positive obligation of the controller to respect, comply, document and demonstrate compliance with the Regulation. Along with data protection principles, the legitimate interest ground's 'boundaries' are framed by art. 8 of the Charter. Thus, even if the interests of the controller prevail over the data subject's interests on one specific occasion, this only means that the controller has a base for lawful processing of the data subject's personal data. The ground and

---

[132] Omer Tene and Jules Polonetsky characterise the relationship of data minimization with big data business models as antithetical. Tene and Polonetsky (2013).

the weighing included in the provision should not be seen as having a broader effect than they have. The interests, rights and freedoms of the data subject are not abolished. On the contrary, once the controller is subject to the GDPR, he or she needs to comply with his or her legal obligations derived from the Regulation, including the data subject's rights, the organisational and technical measures and the whole set of obligations established in the GDPR.

This brings us to the second point. The legitimate interest ground is first necessarily determined by the controller himself or herself. It is of utmost importance that the supervisory authorities (DPAs), and subsequently the national courts, thoroughly check the continuous justification of the ground for as long as processing takes place on the basis of this ground.

Ultimately, the CJEU will play a significant role in interpreting the provision in line with the Charter, but also in light of the societal needs and technological developments. To date, the Court has delivered landmark decisions in the EU data protection law field, but has not fully taken the opportunity to interpret the legitimate interest ground. The recent *Breyer* and *Rigas satiksme* cases showed the intention of the Court to provide answers.

In this chapter, we suggested a formalisation of the legitimate interest ground steps towards the decision of the controller on whether to base his or her processing on the legitimate interest ground. The proposed three steps and their components are informed primarily by the GDPR provision of art. 6(1) (f) and GDPR recitals, but also other sources, such as guidance provided by the WP29 and the European Data Protection Supervisor. Such a framework, with its essential components ('reasonable expectations of the data subject', impact assessment, and others), provides tools to protect against controllers in bad faith, who are over-broadening the concept of legitimate interest, and help controllers in good faith make a proper decision on whether the ground of art. 6(1) (f) is an appropriate legal basis for their intended personal data processing activity.

10 LITERATURE

- Alexy, Robert, 'Constitutional Rights, Balancing, and Rationality', *Ratio Juris*, vol. 16 no. 2, 2003
- Article 29 Data Protection Working Party, Opinion 06/2014 on the notion of legitimate interests of the data controller under Article 7 of Directive 95/46/EC, WP217, April 2014
- Article 29 Data Protection Working Party, Opinion 1/2010 on the concepts of 'controller' and 'processor', WP169, 2010
- Article 29 Data Protection Working Party, Opinion 15/2011 on the definition of consent, WP187, 13 July 2011
- Article 29 Data Protection Working Party, Working Party Comments to the vote of 21 October 2013 by the European Parliament's LIBE Committee, Annex to letter to Greek Presidency, 11 December 2013,
- Bagger Tranberg, Charlotte, 'Proportionality and Data Protection in the Case Law of the European Court of Justice', *International Data Privacy Law*, 2011, vol. 1 no. 4, pp.239–248
- Balboni, Paolo, Daniel Cooper, Rosario Imperiali and Milda Macenaite, 'Legitimate Interest of the Data Controller: New Data Protection Paradigm: Legitimacy Grounded on Appropriate Protection', *International Data Privacy Law*, vol. 3:4, 1 November 2013, Pages 244–261
- Bennett, Colin J. and Robin M. Bayley, 'Privacy Protection in the Era of "Big Data": Regulatory Challenges and Social Assessments', in Bart van der Sloot, Dennis Broeders and

Erik Schrijvers (eds.), *Exploring the Boundaries of Big Data*, Amsterdam University Press, Amsterdam, 2016

- Bits of Freedom, 'A Loophole in Data Processing: Why the "Legitimate Interests" Test Fails to Protect the Interests', 2012
- Borgesius, Frederik J. Zuiderveen, 'Personal Data Processing for Behavioural Targeting: Which Legal Basis?" *International Data Privacy Law*, vol. 5, no 3, 1 August 2015, Pages 163–176
- boyd, danah, and Kate Crawford, 'Critical Questions for Big Data: Provocations for a Cultural, Technological, and Scholarly Phenomenon', *Information, Communication & Society*, vol. 15, no. 5, 2012, pp. 662–679
- Bygrave, Lee A. and Dag Wiese Schartum, 'Consent, Proportionality and Collective Power', in Serge Gutwirth, Yves Poullet, Paul de Hert, Cécile de Terwangne and Sjaak Nouwt (eds.), *Reinventing Data Protection?* Springer Netherlands, Dordrecht, 2009, pp. 157–173
- Cate, Fred H. and Viktor Mayer-Schönberger, 'Notice and Consent in a World of Big Data', *International Data Privacy Law*, vol. 3, no. 2, 2013, pp. 67–73
- Centre for Information Policy Leadership (CIPL) 'Recommendations for Implementing Transparency, Consent and Legitimate Interest under the GDPR', 2017
- Commission of the European Communities, Report from the Commission. First Report on the Implementation of the Data Protection Directive (95/46/EC), COM(2003) 265 final
- Corbin, Arthur, 'Legal Analysis and Terminology', *Yale Law Journal*, vol. 29, no. 163, 1919–1920, p. 173
- Cuijpers, C. M. K. C., Purtova, N.N. and Kosta, E., 'Data Protection Reform and the Internet: The Draft Data Protection Regulation', in A. Savin and J. Trzaskowski (eds.), *Research Handbook on EU Internet Law*, Edward Elgar, 2014, pp. 543–568
- Davies, S., 'The Data Protection Regulation: A Triumph of Pragmatism over Principle?' *European Data Protection Law Review*, vol. 2, no. 3, 2016, pp. 290–296
- De Hert, Paul, 'Data Protection's Future without Democratic Bright Line Rules: Co-existing with Technologies in Europe after *Breyer*', *European Data Protection Law Journal*, vol. 1, 2017, p. 20–35
- De Hert, Paul and Vagelis Papakonstantinou, 'The New General Data Protection Regulation: Still a Sound System for the Protection of Individuals?', *Computer Law & Security Review*, vol. 32, 2016, pp. 179–194
- De Hert, Paul and Serge Gutwirth, 'Privacy, Data Protection and Law Enforcement: Opacity of the Individual and Transparency of Power', Erik Claes, Antony Duff and Serge Gutwirth (eds.), *Privacy and the Criminal Law*, Antwerp and Oxford: Intersentia, 2006, pp. 61–104
- De Hert, Paul and Vagelis Papakonstantinou, '*Google Spain*: Addressing Critiques and Misunderstandings One Year Later', *Maastricht Journal of European and Comparative Law*, vol. 22, no. 4, 2015, 624–638
- European Data Protection Supervisor, 'Developing a "Toolkit" for Assessing the Necessity of Measures that Interfere with Fundamental Rights,' Background paper, June 2016
- European Data Protection Supervisor, Opinion of the European Data Protection Supervisor on the Communication from the Commission to the European Parliament, the Council, the European Economic and Social Committee and the Committee of the Regions: 'European Strategy for a Better Internet for Children', July 2012

- Ferretti, Federico, 'Data Protection and the Legitimate Interest of Data Controllers: Much Ado about Nothing or the Winter of Rights?' *Common Law Market Review*, vol. 51, 2014, pp. 843–868,
- Fuster, Gloria Gonzàlez, 'Fighting for Your Right to What Exactly: The Convoluted Case Law of the EU Court of Justice on Privacy and/Or Personal Data Protection', *Birkbeck Law Review*, vol. 2, 2014, p. 263.
- Girot, Clarisse, *User Protection in IT contracts: A Comparative Study of the Protection of the User against Defective Performance in Information Technology*. Vol. 11. Kluwer Law International, 2001.
- Habermas, Jurgen, *Between Facts and Norms*, Cambridge: Polity, 1992
- ICO, 'Big Data and Data Protection', version 1.0, 2014
- Harbo, Tor-Inge, 'The Function of the Proportionality Principle in the EU law', *European Law Journal*, vol. 16, no. 2, 2010, pp. 158–185
- International Chambers of Commerce, 'ICC Position on Legitimate Interests', ETD/ STM – 28 October 2015
- ISO 31000:2009, Risk management: Principles and Guidelines, ISO/IEC 27005:2011, Information technology: Security Techniques: Information Security Risk Management
- Jasmontaite, Lina, and Paul De Hert, 'The EU, Children under 13 Years, and Parental Consent: A Human Rights Analysis of a New, Age-Based Bright-Line for the Protection of Children on the Internet', *International Data Privacy Law*, vol. 5, no. 1, 2015, pp. 20–33
- Korff, Douwe, 'The Standard Approach Under Articles 8–11 ECHR and Article 2 ECHR', 2008
- Kuner, Christopher, 'The Court of Justice of the EU Judgment on Data Protection and Internet Search Engines: Current Issues and Future Challenges', in Burkhard Hess and Cristina M. Mariottini (eds.), *Protecting Privacy in Private International and Procedural Law and by Data Protection*, Farnham, Surrey: Ashgate, 2015, pp. 19–55
- Kuner, Christopher, 'The European Commission's Proposed Data Protection Regulation: A Copernican Revolution in European Data Protection Law', *Privacy & Security Law Report*, vol. 11 PVLR 06, 2012
- Moerel, Lokke and Corien Prins, 'Privacy for the Homo Digitalis: Proposal for a New Regulatory Framework for Data Protection in the Light of Big Data and the Internet of Things', 2016
- Mark Powell, 'Amended Proposal for a Council Directive on the Protection of Individuals with regard to the Processing of Personal Data and on the Free Movement of Such Data (92/C 311/04) COM (92) 422 final — syn 287', *Computer Law & Security Review*, vol. 10, 1994, pp. 43–46, ISSN 0267-3649
- National Institute of Standards and Technology, 'Privacy Risk Management for Federal Information Systems', NISTIR 8062 draft, http://csrc.nist.gov/publications/drafts/nistir-8062/ nistir_8062_draft.pdf (accessed 18 September 2016)
- Poullet, Yves, 'EU Data Protection Policy: The Directive 95/46/EC: Ten Years after', *Computer Law & Security Review*, vol. 22, no. 3, 2006, pp. 206–217, ISSN 0267-3649
- Rauhofer, Judith, 'One Step Forward, Two Steps Back? Critical Observations on the Proposed Reform of the EU Data Protection Framework', *Journal of Law and Economic Regulation*, vol. 6, no. 1, 2013, pp. 57–84.
- Skouris, Vassilios, 'After 12 Years', *Maastricht Journal of European and Comparative Law*, vol. 23 MJ 2, 2016

- Solove, Daniel J., 'Privacy Self-Management and the Consent Dilemma', *Harvard Law Review*, vol. 126 1880 2013
- Tene, Omer and Jules Polonetsky, 'Big Data for All: Privacy and User Control in the Age of Analytics', Northwestern Journal of Technology and Intellectual Property , vol. 11, 2013, p. 239
- Zingales, N., 'Unreasonable v. Unfair Data Processing: Contrasting Two Rising Modes of Protection Against Over-reaching Terms of Service', unpublished paper presented at Amsterdam Privacy Conference, 2015

—

- Directive 2013/40/EU of the European Parliament and of the Council of 12 August 2013 on attacks against information systems and replacing Council Framework Decision 2005/222/ JHA, L 218/8, 14.8.2013
- Directive 95/46/EC of the European Parliament and of the Council of 24 October 1995 on the protection of individuals with regard to the processing of personal data and on the free movement of such data, L 281, 23.11.1995
- European Parliament, Legislative resolution of 12 March 2014 on the proposal for a regulation of the European Parliament and of the Council on the protection of individuals with regard to the processing of personal data and on the free movement of such data (General Data Protection Regulation). (COM(2012)0011 – C70025/2012 – 2012/0011(COD))
- European Commission, Proposal for a Regulation of the European Parliament and of the Council on the protection of individuals with regard to the processing of personal data and on the free movement of such data (General Data Protection Regulation) COM (2012) 11 final – 2012/0011 (COD), 25.01.2012
- European Council, Preparation of a general approach. 9565/15, 11.6.2015, adopted at JHA Council Meeting on 15.6.2015
- Proposal for a Council Directive concerning the protection of individuals in relation to the processing of personal data, COM (1990) 314–2, 1990/0287/COD
- Regulation (EU) 2016/679 of the European Parliament and of the Council of 27 April 2016 on the protection of natural persons with regard to the processing of personal data and on the free movement of such data, and repealing Directive 95/46/EC (General Data Protection Regulation)
- Treaty on the Functioning of the EU European Union, OJ C 326, 26.10.2012

—

- Court of Justice of the European Union, Judgment of the Court of First Instance 8 May 2007, *Citymo v. Commission*, Case T-271/04, EU:T:2007:128
- Court of Justice of the European Union, Judgement of 24 November 2011, *ASNEF, FECEMD*, Joined Cases C-468/10 and C-469/10, EU:C:2011:777
- Court of Justice of the European Union, Judgement of 8 April 2014, *Digital Rights Ireland, Seitlinger*, Joined Cases C-293/12 and C-594/12, EU:C:2014:238
- Court of Justice of the European Union, Judgement of 11 December 2014, *Ryneš*, C-212/13, EU:C:2014:2428
- Court of Justice of the European Union, Judgement of 13 May 2014, Case C-131/12, *Google Spain and Google*, EU:C:2014:317
- Court of Justice of the European Union, Judgement of 6 October 2015, *Schrems*, Case C-362/14, EU:C:2015:650
- Court of Justice of the European Union, Opinion of Advocate General Campos Sánchez-Bordona of 12 May 2016, *Breyer*, C-582/14, EU:C:2016:339

- Court of Justice of the European Union, Judgement of 19 October 2016, *Breyer*, Case C-582/14, EU:C:2016:779
- Court of Justice of the European Union, Judgement of 9 March 2017, *Manni*, Case C-398/15 EU:C:2017:197
- Court of Justice of the European Union, Judgement of 4 May 2017, *Rīgas satiksme*, Case C-13/16, EU:C:2017:336
- Supreme Court of Canada, *Douez v. Facebook, Inc.*, 2017 SCC 33
- European Court of Human Rights, Judgement of 24 June 2004, *von Hannover v. Germany*, (Application no. 59320/00)
- European Court of Human Rights, Judgement of 17 July 2008, *I v. Finland* (Application no. 20511/03)

ACKNOWLEDGMENT

The authors would like to thank Omer Tene for his comments on a previous version of this chapter.

PART V

New Approaches to Improve the Status Quo

20

The Intersection of Privacy and Consumer Protection

Julie Brill

American belief in the value of privacy is deeply rooted. Supreme Court Justice Louis Brandeis wrote that our founding fathers "sought to protect Americans in their beliefs, their thoughts, their emotions and their sensations," and did so by conferring on us "the right to be let alone – the most comprehensive of rights and the right most valued by civilized men."[1] Brandeis was writing in the context of government wiretapping of phone calls, and today there is a well-established doctrine of constitutional rights protecting against unwarranted government intrusion,[2] as well as statutory requirements involving law enforcement access[3] and intelligence surveillance.[4] Elsewhere, the right to privacy has also given rise to protections related to contraception use,[5] abortion,[6] familial relationships,[7] and more.

But privacy encompasses more than just rights-based protections: some aspects of privacy focus not on individual rights but on principles of consumer harm. In this way, the US privacy framework differs from the European approach, which rests on fundamental rights in the Charter,[8] the EU-wide protections in the General Data Protection Regulation,[9] and Member State legislation. Privacy protection in the United States is more of a hybrid between rights-based protections and protections designed to prevent consumer harm.

The network of privacy protections intersecting with consumer protections begins with narrowly focused privacy laws designed to protect sensitive information, where inappropriate disclosure, inaccuracies, and misuse of the data could harm consumers. These sector-specific laws cover financial information,[10] medical data,[11] information about children,

---

[1] *Olmstead v. United States*, 277 U.S. 438, 478 (1928) (Brandeis, J., dissenting).

[2] *See* U.S. Const. amend. IV, *available at* https://www.law.cornell.edu/constitution/fourth_amendment.

[3] *See, e.g.*, 18 U.S.C. §§ 2510–22, 2701–12.

[4] *See, e.g.*, 50 U.S.C. § 1801 *et seq.*

[5] *Griswold v. Connecticut*, 381 U.S. 479 (1965).

[6] *Roe v. Wade*, 410 U.S. 113 (1973) *holding modified by Planned Parenthood of Se. Pennsylvania v. Casey*, 505 U.S. 833 (1992).

[7] *Moore v. City of E. Cleveland, Ohio*, 431 U.S. 494 (1977).

[8] Charter of Fundamental Rights of the European Union, 2012/C 326/02 (Oct. 26, 2012), *available at* http://eurlex .europa.eu/legal-content/EN/TXT/?uri=CELEX:12012P/TXT.

[9] European Union General Data Protection Regulation, 2016/679 (Apr. 27, 2016), *available at* http://eur-lex.europa.eu/ legal-content/EN/TXT/?uri=uriserv:OJ.L_.2016.119.01.0001.01.ENG&toc=OJ:L:2016:119:TOC.

[10] 15 U.S.C. §§ 6801–09.

[11] Health Insurance Portability and Accountability Act, Pub. L. No.104–191, 110 Stat. 1936 (1996) (codified in scattered sections of 18, 26, 29, and 42 U.S.C.).

and information used to make decisions about consumers' credit, insurance, employment,[12] and housing.[13]

For example, the Fair Credit Reporting Act[14] (FCRA) governs the use of credit reports, which were developed as a way to help lenders decide whether specific consumers are worthy of credit. Many of the FCRA's provisions are intended to help ensure that credit reports – and the credit, employment, housing, and other major decisions that are based on them – are accurate. The information in credit reports is also deeply personal, so the FCRA limits how companies can use credit reports and provides other protections that follow Fair Information Practice Principles.[15] Among other things, these comprehensive protections allow consumers to know when information is being used to make important decisions about them and to have the opportunity to correct the information at these critical junctures.

The Fair Debt Collection Practices Act[16] also falls at the intersection of privacy and consumer protection concerns. It limits how and when a debt collector may contact consumers, as well as restricting debt collectors from revealing the existence of a debt to third parties. The main purpose of the Fair Debt Collection Practices Act is to prevent debt collectors from using abusive or fraudulent tactics to make consumers pay debts. But it also protects consumers' privacy by limiting the circumstances under which the existence of a debt, which may be deeply embarrassing to a consumer or threaten her employment, may be revealed.

Yet another example is the Telemarketing Sales Rule,[17] which targets deceptive or abusive telemarketing practices. It requires specific disclosures and prohibits misrepresentations in telemarketing calls. But in addition to addressing these consumer protection concerns, the Rule also protects consumer privacy by setting limits on the times telemarketers may call consumers at home and prohibiting calls to a consumer who has asked not to be called again.

Still other laws protect particularly sensitive information or information about particularly vulnerable consumers. For example, the Children's Online Privacy Protection Act[18] restricts the online collection of information from children. The Gramm-Leach-Bliley Act[19] and its implementing regulations restrict the sharing of personal information by financial institutions and require them to keep consumers' information secure. And the Health Insurance Portability and Accountability Act[20] (HIPAA) protects health information in the hands of health care providers, insurers, and their business associates.

The states have many additional privacy laws that limit employers' ability to view their employees' social network accounts,[21] prohibit employers and insurers from using information about

---

[12] *See* Children's Online Privacy Protection Act, 15 U.S.C. §§ 6501–06.

[13] 15 U.S.C. § 1681 *et seq.*

[14] *Id.*

[15] For a general overview of the Fair Information Practice Principles, see FED. TRADE COMM'N, INTERNET OF THINGS: PRIVACY AND SECURITY IN A CONNECTED WORLD 19–20 (2015), *available at* http://www.ftc.gov/system/files/documents/reports/federal-trade-commission-staff-report-november-2013-workshop-entitled-internet-things-privacy/150127iotrpt.pdf.

[16] *See* Fair Debt Collection Practices Act, 15 U.S.C. § 1692 *et seq.*

[17] Telemarketing Sales Rule, 16 C.F.R. § 310.

[18] 15 U.S.C. § 6501 *et seq.* and Children's Online Privacy Protection Rule, 16 C.F.R. § 312.

[19] 15 U.S.C. § 6801 *et seq.* and Safeguards Rule, 16 C.F.R. § 314.

[20] Pub. L. No. 104–191, 110 Stat. 1936 (1996) (codified in scattered sections of 18, 26, 29, and 42 U.S.C.).

[21] *See State Social Media Privacy Laws*, NAT'L CONFERENCE OF STATE LEGISLATURES, *available at* http://www.ncsl.org/research/telecommunications-and-information-technology/state-laws-prohibiting-access-to-social-media-usernames-and-passwords.aspx (last updated July 6, 2016) (noting that twenty-five states have enacted social media laws that apply to employers).

certain medical conditions,[22] require online services to allow minors to delete information they have posted,[23] require companies to protect the security of information,[24] and require companies to notify consumers when they suffer a security breach involving personal information.[25]

In addition to these laws, which are focused on specific industries, specific types of data, and particularly vulnerable consumers, another network of protections lying at the intersection of privacy and consumer protection arises under section 5 of the Federal Trade Commission Act.[26] With its prohibition against unfair or deceptive acts or practices in commerce, section 5 is a broad, flexible, and remedial consumer protection statute that has allowed the FTC to address some key privacy concerns. The FTC has used its deception authority against companies that have misled consumers in a material way about their data practices. The FTC has used its unfairness authority when a company's data practices have harmed consumers in a way consumers cannot avoid, with no offsetting benefit to consumers or competition. Consumer harm in these contexts has included financial harm, of course; but it has also included inappropriate collection of information on consumers' mobile devices,[27] unwarranted intrusions into private spaces,[28] the exposure of health and other sensitive information,[29] the exposure of previously confidential information about individuals' networks of friends and acquaintances,[30] and the disclosure of sensitive information to third parties who in turn victimize consumers.[31] Thus, although the FTC generally targets privacy and data security practices that cause harm to consumers, the notion of harm is broadly defined.

Through its law enforcement and policy work, the FTC grapples with how technological advances affect our nation's concept of privacy and data security, and how to best give consumers knowledge, control, and choice about how their personal information is collected and used. The

---

[22] *See, e.g., Employment and Your Medical Privacy (California Medical Privacy Series)*, Privacy Rights Clearinghouse, *available at* https://www.privacyrights.org/consumer-guides/employment-and-your-medical-privacy-california-medical-privacy-series (last updated July 1, 2012).

[23] *See* Cal. Bus. & Prof. Code § 22580 *et seq., available at* http://leginfo.legislature.ca.gov/faces/codes_displaySection.xhtml?lawCode=BPC&sectionNum=22580.

[24] *See, e.g.,* 201 Mass. Code Regs. 17.04, *available at* http://www.mass.gov/courts/docs/lawlib/201-209cmr/201cmr17.pdf.

[25] *See Security Breach Notification Laws*, Nat'l Conference of State Legislatures, http://www.ncsl.org/research/telecommunications-and-information-technology/security-breach-notification-laws.aspx (last updated Jan. 4, 2016) (noting that forty-seven states have enacted legislation requiring security breach notifications).

[26] *See generally* 15 U.S.C. § 45.

[27] *See, e.g.,* Goldenshores Techs. LLC C-4446 (F.T.C. Mar. 31, 2014) (decision and order), *available at* https://www.ftc.gov/system/files/documents/cases/140409goldenshoresdo.pdf.

[28] *See* Press Release, Federal Trade Commission, *Aaron's Rent-to-Own Chain Settles FTC Charges That It Enabled Computer Spying by Franchisees* (Oct. 22, 2013), *available at* https://www.ftc.gov/news-events/press-releases/2013/10/aarons-rent-own-chain-settles-ftc-charges-it-enabled-computer.

[29] *See* Press Release, Federal Trade Commission, *FTC Files Complaint against LabMD for Failing to Protect Consumers' Privacy* (Aug. 29, 2013), *available at* https://www.ftc.gov/news-events/press-releases/2013/08/ftc-files-complaint-against-labmd-failing-protect-consumers (describing FTC complaint alleging that LabMD failed to reasonably protect the security of consumers' personal data, including medical information). *But see* Timothy Tobin, *FTC ALJ: Embarrassment/Emotional Harm and Risk of Harm Does Not Satisfy "Substantial Consumer Injury" Prong of Unfairness*, Hogan Lovells Chronicle of Data Protection (Nov. 17, 2015), *available at* http://www.hldataprotection.com/2015/11/articles/consumer-privacy/ftc-alj-embarrassmentemotional-harm-and-risk-of-harm-does-not-satisfy-substantial-consumer-injury-prong-of-unfairness/ (describing the Administrative Law Judge's dismissal of the FTC complaint because emotional harm is not sufficient to make an injury unfair).

[30] *See* Facebook, Inc., C-4365 (F.T.C. July 27, 2012) (decision and order), *available at* https://www.ftc.gov/sites/default/files/documents/cases/2012/08/120810facebookdo.pdf.

[31] FTC v. Sitesearch Corp., d/b/a LeapLab (D. Az. Dec. 22, 2014) (complaint), *available at* https://www.ftc.gov/system/files/documents/cases/141223leaplabcmpt.pdf.

FTC has taken action against some of the biggest names on the Internet, including Google[32] and Facebook,[33] as well as many smaller players, for deceiving consumers about their data practices or using consumers' data in an unfair manner. And the FTC keeps a close eye on emerging new technologies – such as user-generated health information,[34] facial recognition technology,[35] cross-device tracking,[36] retail mobile location tracking,[37] and mobile payments[38] – to help ensure they are developed in a manner that will not harm consumers. The Commission's modus operandi includes penalties – it has obtained hundreds of millions of dollars in penalties and restitution in its privacy and data security cases over the past several decades. And to settle the FTC's investigations where the agency has found data use and security practices to be amiss, the agency will place the company under a twenty-year order with robust injunctive provisions requiring corrective action and monitoring of the company's privacy and data security practices.

In this way, the FTC has used its consumer protection authority under section 5 to become one of the leading privacy enforcement agencies in the United States. Unlike Europe's data protection authorities, which typically focus exclusively on data protection, the FTC has a much broader mandate: to protect the nation's consumers, making sure they are not cheated or misled in the marketplace; and to protect competition, making sure that the marketplace is offering up a wide range of goods and services at the fairest price.[39] It is this broad mandate that has allowed the Commission to leverage its authority to become a key player in privacy enforcement and policy development in the United States.

The FTC's role in privacy enforcement is likely to continue growing. Privacy violations are often linked to a variety of consumer harms, such as deceptive financial practices and fraud. This connection grows stronger as technological advances create new opportunities and uses – resulting in both benefits and risks to consumers – for players in the complex marketplace for personal data. These players include data brokers, data analytics companies, lead generators, payday lenders, debt collectors, and credit reporting agencies.

In order to understand the depth of the connection between privacy and consumer harm, one has to look behind the statements that companies make in their privacy policies and beyond the data practices that eventually become evident to consumers and enforcers. Behind the scenes, invisible to consumers and ordinary observers, vast amounts of data about consumers are flowing from their laptops, smartphones, connected devices – and from offline sources such as driving records, mortgage liens, and tax assessments – to create detailed, individual profiles. These

[32] Google, Inc., C-4336 (F.T.C. Oct. 13, 2011) (decision and order), *available at* https://www.ftc.gov/sites/default/files/documents/cases/2011/10/111024googlebuzzdo.pdf.

[33] Facebook, Inc., C-4365 (F.T.C. July 27, 2012) (decision and order), *available at* https://www.ftc.gov/sites/default/files/documents/cases/2012/08/120810facebookdo.pdf.

[34] Press Release, Federal Trade Commission, *Spring Privacy Series: Consumer Generated and Controlled Health Data* (May 7, 2014), *available at* https://www.ftc.gov/news-events/events-calendar/2014/05/spring-privacy-series-consumer-generated-controlled-health-data.

[35] *See generally* FED. TRADE COMM'N, FACING FACTS: BEST PRACTICES FOR COMMON USES OF FACIAL RECOGNITION TECHNOLOGIES (2012), *available at* https://www.ftc.gov/sites/default/files/documents/reports/facing-facts-best-practices-common-uses-facial-recognition-technologies/121022facialtechrpt.pdf.

[36] Press Release, Federal Trade Commission, *FTC to Host Workshop on Cross-Device Tracking Nov. 16* (Mar. 17, 2015), *available at* https://www.ftc.gov/news-events/press-releases/2015/03/ftc-host-workshop-cross-device-tracking-nov-16.

[37] Press Release, Federal Trade Commission, *Spring Privacy Series: Mobile Device Tracking* (Feb. 19, 2014), *available at* https://www.ftc.gov/news-events/events-calendar/2014/02/spring-privacy-series-mobile-device-tracking.

[38] *See* FED. TRADE COMM'N, WHAT'S THE DEAL? AN FTC STUDY ON MOBILE SHOPPING APPS (2014), *available at* https://www.ftc.gov/system/files/documents/reports/whats-deal-federal-trade-commission-study-mobile-shopping-apps-august-2014/140801mobileshoppingapps.pdf; FED. TRADE COMM'N, PAPER, PLASTIC ... OR MOBILE? AN FTC WORKSHOP ON MOBILE PAYMENTS (2013), *available at* https://www.ftc.gov/sites/default/files/documents/reports/paper-plastic-or-mobile-ftc-workshop-mobile-payments/p0124908_mobile_payments_workshop_report_02-28-13.pdf.

[39] *See* 15 U.S.C. § 45(a)(2) (granting the FTC the authority to prevent "unfair methods of competition in or affecting commerce and unfair or deceptive acts or practices in or affecting commerce").

profiles contain a seemingly endless array of information about consumers: what they buy, where they live, and how much money they spend on a specific occasion.

Some of this information is mundane when viewed in isolation. And granted, much of this data is collected to fuel targeted advertising, a practice that solves the problem posed over a century ago by the great merchant and philanthropist John Wanamaker, who said, "Half the money I spend on advertising is wasted; the trouble is I don't know which half." Targeted advertising benefits consumers as well as companies: many consumers prefer to see ads they are interested in, rather than random ads for products and services they would never purchase. Also, since companies are willing to pay significantly more for targeted advertisements, the advertisements fund much of the online free content we all enjoy.

However, the information that can be gleaned extends well beyond a customer's preference for action movies or pink boots. Often, it can be far more disconcerting, and far more sensitive, including information about a consumer's financial status, race, sexual orientation, and health conditions.

Data brokers and data analytics firms combine a multitude of data points into comprehensive profiles that create highly revealing pictures about each of us. And because such entities do not directly engage with consumers, they are essentially invisible to us. One of the largest data brokers reportedly has information on about 700 million active consumers worldwide,[40] with some 1,500 data points per person.[41] Such data brokers learn about consumers from the cookies that hitch rides as users travel online and from the social media sites where users post everything from home addresses to pictures to magazine subscriptions and store purchases, as well as deeds on file in towns and counties. They load all this data into sophisticated algorithms that spew out alarmingly personal predictions about health, financial status, interests, sexual orientation, religious beliefs, politics, and habits. The data in our profiles may determine what offers we receive, what rates we pay, even what jobs we get. It may be used to make determinations about whether we are too risky to do business with or aren't right for certain clubs, dating services, schools, or other programs.

The FTC has focused on how this data can be used in a manner that harms consumers. A report that the FTC issued in 2014[42] found that data brokers collect a wide range of financial information about consumers. Some segment consumers into groups of the "Rural and Barely Making It," "Ethnic Second-City Strugglers," "Tough Start: Young Single Parents," and "Credit Crunched: City Families."[43] This information could help banks find low-income consumers and offer them safe, low-cost financial products. But such products likely also appeal to purveyors of payday loans and other financially risky products and help them identify vulnerable consumers most likely to need quick cash. For these reasons, it is important for data brokers to give consumers more control over the information that goes into their profiles, and to be more accountable for how these profiles are used – and misused – by their customers.

Further, the sheer volume and vulnerability of personal data collected, traded, and stored has created significant problems. Data breaches are rampant. In the span of only a few months, we

[40] *See* Adam Tanner, *Finally You'll Get to See the Secret Consumer Dossier They Have on You*, FORBES (June 25, 2013), *available at* http://www.forbes.com/sites/adamtanner/2013/06/25/finally-youll-get-to-see-the-secret-consumer-dossier-they-have-on-you/#52b8b81b27ce.

[41] Natasha Singer, *Mapping, and Sharing, the Consumer Genome*, N.Y. TIMES (June 16, 2012), *available at* http://www.nytimes.com/2012/06/17/technology/acxiom-the-quiet-giant-of-consumer-database-marketing.html?ref=natashasinger.

[42] *See generally* FED. TRADE COMM'N, DATA BROKERS: A CALL FOR TRANSPARENCY AND ACCOUNTABILITY (2014), *available at* https://www.ftc.gov/system/files/documents/reports/data-brokers-call-transparency-accountability-report-federal-trade-commission-may-2014/140527databrokerreport.pdf.

[43] See COMM. ON COMMERCE, SCIENCE, AND TRANSP., A REVIEW OF THE DATA BROKER INDUSTRY: COLLECTION, USE, AND SALE OF CONSUMER DATA FOR MARKETING PURPOSES 12, 24 (2013), *available at* https://www.commerce.senate.gov/public/_cache/files/0d2b3642-6221-4888-a631-08f2f255b577/AE5D72CBE7F44F5BFC846BECE22C875B.12.18.13-senate-commerce-committee-report-on-data-broker-industry.pdf.

saw the online marketing company Epsilon expose the e-mail addresses of millions of customers of the nation's largest firms, including JP Morgan, Citigroup, Barclaycard US, and Capital One.[44] And many consumers panicked when Sony's PlayStation online network was hacked, resulting in the exposure of the personal information of about 77 million gamers worldwide.[45]

The risks for consumers are particularly serious when data brokers fail to keep financial information secure. For example, the FTC sued two debt brokers in 2014 for posting files containing information about tens of thousands of consumers on publicly accessible websites, free for anyone to download.[46] These files not only listed debtors by name – and thus revealed who has unpaid debts, a fact that can be sensitive on its own[47] – but also contained full bank account numbers and other sensitive financial information.

Lead generators are another set of important players in the market for personal, sensitive information, and their activities can cause concrete and immediate harm to consumers. For example, the FTC took action against a "lead generator" that collected information about consumers who were interested in payday loans.[48] The Commission alleged that the company sold information about consumers who applied for payday loans to anyone who wanted to buy it. The FTC believes the vast majority of information went to non-lenders, including some who used the information to commit fraud.[49]

In addition, the abundance of information that is available about consumers and their finances can help make a variety of financial scams more convincing and ultimately more damaging to consumers. One of the most common complaints that the FTC receives from consumers is about debt collectors, including so-called "phantom debt collectors," who demand that consumers pay debt that they do not actually owe. By adding personal details in their fraudulent telemarketing schemes, including portions of a Social Security number, the name of a store where a consumer owed money, or the amount of an old, paid-off debt, phantom debt collectors make their demands much more convincing. Or the scammers might simply find out about a consumer's debt and demand payment, even though the scammer has no right to the payment. The FTC has taken several actions against phantom debt collectors.[50]

Other imposters are using the same techniques – obtaining sensitive and personal financial information about consumers – to convince consumers that a fraudulent call is real. The FTC has seen a dramatic rise in complaints about imposters who claim to be from the Internal Revenue Service or other government agencies. Their conversations with consumers are laced with the consumer's Social Security number and other personal information, thereby convincing the consumer that the call is legitimate, and she needs to comply with the caller's demand to pay immediately or else face wage garnishment or arrest. These

---

[44] Josh Halliday, *Epsilon Email Hack: Millions of Customers' Details Stolen*, THE GUARDIAN (Apr. 4, 2011), *available at* https://www.theguardian.com/technology/2011/apr/04/epsilon-email-hack.

[45] Ben Quinn & Charles Arthur, *PlayStation Network Hackers Access Data of 77 Million Users*, THE GUARDIAN (Apr. 26, 2011), *available at* https://www.theguardian.com/technology/2011/apr/26/playstation-network-hackers-data.

[46] *See* FTC v. Bayview Solutions, LLC, Case 1:14-cv-01830-RC (D.D.C. Oct. 31, 2014), *available at* http://www.ftc.gov/system/files/documents/cases/111014bayviewcmp.pdf and FTC v. Cornerstone and Co., LLC, Case 1:14-cv-01479-RC (D.D.C. Aug. 27, 2014), *available at* http://www.ftc.gov/system/files/documents/cases/141001cornerstonecmpt.pdf.

[47] *See* Fair Debt Collection Practices Act, 15 U.S.C. § 1692(a) (associating abusive debt collection practices with "personal bankruptcies, to marital instability, to the loss of jobs, and to invasions of individual privacy").

[48] FTC v. Sitesearch Corp., d/b/a LeapLab (D. Az. Dec. 22, 2014) (complaint), *available at* https://www.ftc.gov/system/files/documents/cases/141223leaplabcmpt.pdf.

[49] *Id.* ¶¶ 19–23.

[50] *See, e.g.*, Press Release, Federal Trade Commission, *FTC, Illinois Attorney General Halt Chicago Area Operation Charged with Illegally Pressuring Consumers to Pay "Phantom" Debts* (Apr. 10, 2015), *available at* https://www.ftc.gov/news-events/press-releases/2015/04/ftc-illinois-attorney-general-halt-chicago-area-operation-charged.

misuses of financial information give particularly vivid illustrations of the harms consumers face from data breaches and inadequate accountability regarding data brokers and lead generators.

Finally, some uses of these vast amounts of data may have discriminatory impacts or may perpetuate and exacerbate existing discrimination. A risk assessment tool used in the sentencing of criminal defendants may inappropriately weigh race in predicting an individual's risk of recidivism.[51] The FTC also discussed these concerns in its recent report, called *Big Data: A Tool for Inclusion or Exclusion?*[52] For instance, the FTC raised concerns that machine learning techniques used to make hiring decisions may produce a workforce that reflects the current workforce with its existing gender and race disparities.[53]

The confluence of privacy and consumer protection concerns also arises in the context of alternative scoring models, such as those employed by ZestFinance, Affirm, and Earnest. In this realm, past is prologue: the origins of the FCRA have something to teach us about the potential of future concerns with respect to alternate scoring. The FCRA was our nation's first "big data" law. The seeds for it were planted in the growing economy after World War II. Businesses formed cooperatives to enable quicker and more accurate decisions about creditworthiness by sharing information about consumers who were in default or delinquent on loans. Over time, these agencies combined, paving the way for consumers to gain access to credit, insurance, and jobs. As credit bureaus increased their ability to draw inferences and make correlations through ever-larger databases, unease about the amount of information that credit bureaus held – as well as its accuracy and its use – also increased. Congress passed the FCRA in 1970 to address these concerns.[54]

The FCRA governs the use of information to make decisions about consumer credit, insurance, employment, housing and other transactions initiated by consumers. It covers not only credit bureaus but also their sources and clients. The FCRA gives consumers important rights. For instance, consumers are entitled to access their data, challenge its accuracy, and be notified when they are denied credit or get a loan at less than favorable rates because of negative information in their files.

The use of credit scores has thrived under the FCRA's rights of notice, access, correction, relevancy, and accuracy, and the FCRA has enabled the credit reporting enterprise to serve a purpose useful not only to the credit reporting agencies and their clients, but also to consumers. The credit scores that first emerged from analysis of consumers' credit files broadened access to credit,[55] and they made determinations of a particular consumer's creditworthiness more

---

[51] *See* Julia Angwin, Jeff Larson, Surya Mattu & Lauren Kirchner, *Machine Bias*, ProPublica (May 23, 2016), https://www.propublica.org/article/machine-bias-risk-assessments-in-criminal-sentencing (providing an overview of studies in this area).

[52] *See generally* Fed. Trade Comm'n, Big Data: A Tool for Inclusion or Exclusion? (2016), *available at* https://www.ftc.gov/system/files/documents/reports/big-data-tool-inclusion-or-exclusion-understanding-issues/160106big-data-rpt.pdf.

[53] *See id.* at 28.

[54] *See generally* Mark Furletti, *An Overview and History of Credit Reporting*, Fed. Reserve Bank of Philadelphia Payment Cards Ctr., 3–4 (2002), *available at* https://www.philadelphiafed.org/consumer-credit-and-payments/payment-cards-center/publications/discussion-papers/2002/CreditReportingHistory_062002.pdf.

[55] *See* Bd. of Governors of the Fed. Reserve Sys., Report to the Congress on Credit Scoring and Its Effects on the Availability and Affordability of Credit S-1 (2007), *available at* http://www.federalreserve.gov/boarddocs/rptcongress/creditscore/creditscore.pdf ("The large savings in cost and time that have accompanied the use of credit scoring are generally believed to have increased access to credit, promoted competition, and improved market efficiency.").

efficient and more objective than was the case with prior, more subjective determinations.[56] As scoring models began to proliferate and enter into new types of decisions – including employment, insurance, and mortgage lending – consumers and regulators grew concerned about what exactly was going on within these models.[57] Some of the most important questions were whether credit-related scores were using variables that act as proxies for race, ethnicity, age, and other protected categories.

In 2003, Congress directed the FTC and the Federal Reserve to study these questions in the context of credit-based insurance scores and traditional credit scores.[58] After extensive and rigorous studies, both agencies found that the scores they examined largely did not serve as proxies for race or ethnicity.[59] The FTC and Federal Reserve reports shed a lot of light on traditional credit scores and assuaged some important concerns, which was good for everyone involved: consumers, credit bureaus, and credit score users.

Fast forward to today. We're now seeing a proliferation of other types of scores being used to make FCRA-covered eligibility determinations.[60] While these scores are subject to the same obligations of access, accuracy, security, and other requirements imposed by the FCRA, they have not yet been subject to the same kind of scrutiny that Congress and the federal agencies brought to bear on traditional credit scores. The use of new sources of information, including information that goes beyond traditional credit files, to score consumers raises fresh questions about whether these alternate scores may have disparate impacts along racial, ethnic, or other lines that the law protects, or that should be addressed.

Those questions are likely to linger and grow more urgent unless and until the companies that develop these alternate scores go further to demonstrate that their models do not contain racial, ethnic, or other prohibited biases. These companies may learn that their models have unforeseen inappropriate impacts on certain populations. Or they might simply find their algorithms should eliminate or demote the importance of certain types of data because their

---

[56] *See, e.g.,* Fed. Trade Comm'n, Prepared Statement of the FTC on Credit Scoring Before the House Banking and Financial Services Committee 1 (2000), *available at* https://www.ftc.gov/sites/default/files/documents/public_statements/prepared-statement-federal-trade-commission-credit-scoring/creditscoring.pdf ("With credit scoring, lending decisions are likely to be more objective, faster and less costly than traditional 'judgmental' decisions.").

[57] *See* H. Rep. 108–263, at 26, *available at* https://www.congress.gov/108/crpt/hrpt263/CRPT-108hrpt263.pdf (reporting on a hearing of the House Subcommittee on Financial Institutions and Consumer Credit that explored how credit scores and other credit reporting information "are used by the lending, mortgage, consumer finance, insurance, and non-financial industries").

[58] Fair and Accurate Credit Transactions Act of 2003 § 215, Pub. L. 108–159 (Dec. 4, 2003), *available at* https://www.congress.gov/bill/108th-congress/house-bill/2622/text.

[59] *See* Bd. of Governors of the Fed. Reserve Sys., Report to the Congress on Credit Scoring and Its Effects on the Availability and Affordability of Credit S-1 – S-2 (2007), *available at* http://www.federalreserve.gov/boarddocs/rptcongress/creditscore/creditscore.pdf (concluding that "the credit characteristics included in credit history scoring models do not serve as substitutes, or proxies, for race, ethnicity, or sex"); Fed. Trade Comm'n, Credit-Based Insurance Scores: Impacts on Consumers of Automobile Insurance 62–73 (2007), *available at* https://www.ftc.gov/sites/default/files/documents/reports/credit-based-insurance-scores-impacts-consumers-automobile-insurance-report-congress-federal-trade/p044804facta_report_credit_based_insurance_scores.pdf (finding that credit-based insurance scores "do not act solely as a proxy" for membership in the racial, ethnic, and income groups studied in the report but finding a small proxy effect with respect to African Americans and Hispanics).

[60] *See generally* Fed. Trade Comm'n, Transcript of Spring privacy Series: Alternative Scoring Products (2014), *available at* https://www.ftc.gov/system/files/documents/public_events/182261/alternative-scoring-products_final-transcript.pdf; Pam Dixon & Robert Gellman, *The Scoring of America: How Secret Consumer Scores Threaten Your Privacy and Your Future,* World Privacy Forum (Apr. 2, 2014), http://www.worldprivacyforum.org/wp-content/uploads/2014/04/WPF_Scoring_of_America_April2014_fs.pdf.

predictive value is questionable, as FICO discovered with respect to paid-off collection agency accounts and medical collections.[61]

Unfortunately, it's not realistic to rely on the approach that the FTC took to gain an understanding of the full spectrum of scoring models used today. It took the FTC nearly four years to conduct its study. The FTC – and all other federal agencies for that matter – simply would not have the capacity to study every score out there. That approach will not scale.

Moreover, scoring algorithms and other forms of big data analytics rely on statistical models and data system designs that few on the outside understand in detail. Even if we on the outside could peer into the hundreds of scoring algorithms that could potentially affect consumers, what would we learn? We might learn which features of a data set are used in a given algorithm, and what weight a company attaches to them. These details might be so abstract, and so rapidly changing, that they do not tell government, consumers, or other concerned stakeholders much at all about what really matters – which is how the algorithms are actually used and whether they have discriminatory or other inappropriate effects.

This suggests that testing the effects of big data analytics may be a promising way to go. Companies using scoring models should themselves do more to determine whether their own data analytics result in unfair, unethical, or discriminatory effects on consumers. In addition to scrutinizing their own practices, companies should do much more to inform consumers of what is happening with their data. Companies can get creative with user interfaces to provide consumers with more meaningful, usable access to their data. This will serve two purposes: meaningful usable access for consumers will help address questions about the role that big data analytics plays in the marketplace and whether consumers are being treated fairly, and it will provide a helpful check on potentially troublesome data practices. As Louis Brandeis famously said, "sunlight is said to be the best of disinfectants."

These examples of problematic data broker behaviors, data breach risks, and potentially discriminative data uses demonstrate the interconnected nature of privacy concerns and consumer protection issues. While big data and new information infrastructures, such as mobile broadband systems, offer many benefits to consumers – and promise even more – these benefits will be realized only if consumer protection regulators enforce safeguards for privacy and data security as well as safeguards against financial fraud and other consumer harms.

Given these challenges, how could the United States strengthen its privacy framework? On the legislative front, we need Congress to enact consumer privacy laws to address the highly connected, data-intensive world we now live in. For example, baseline privacy legislation would help companies understand how to protect the sensitive information that now flows outside the decades-old silos of our laws protecting financial, health, and credit reporting data.[62] Data broker

---

[61] *See* Annamaria Andriotis, *FICO Recalibrates Its Credit Scores*, WALL ST. J. (Aug. 7, 2014), http://online.wsj.com/ articles/fico-recalibrates-its-credit-scores-1407443549; *FICO Score 9 Introduces Refined Analysis of Medical Collections*, FICO (Aug. 7, 2014), http://www.fico.com/en/newsroom/fico-score-9-introduces-refined-analysis-of-medical-collec tions. FICO's changes followed a report by the Consumer Financial Protection Bureau, which found that (1) "consumers with more medical than non-medical collections had observed delinquency rates that were comparable to those of consumers with credit scores about 10 points higher"; and (2) "consumers with paid medical collections were less likely to be delinquent than other consumers with the same credit score." CONSUMER FINANCIAL PROTEC-TION BUREAU, DATA POINT: MEDICAL DEBT AND CREDIT SCORES 5–6 (2014), *available at* http://files.consumerfinance .gov/f/201405_cfpb_report_data-point_medical-debt-credit-scores.pdf.

[62] As FTC Commissioner, I called on Congress to enact such legislation. *See, e.g.*, Julie Brill, *A Call to Arms: The Role of Technologists in Protecting Privacy in the Age of Big Data*, FED. TRADE COMM'N (Oct. 23, 2013), https://www.ftc.gov/ sites/default/files/documents/public_statements/call-arms-role-technologists-protecting-privacy-age-big-data/131023nyu polysloanlecture.pdf.

legislation would provide much needed transparency, rights of access, and rights of correction to the consumer profiles that are created and sold by data brokers.

Much can also be done by companies themselves. Companies need to build privacy protections into their everyday business practices. They need to write simplified privacy policies that consumers can understand without having to retain counsel. And generally, there needs to be greater transparency around data collection, use, and retention.

And the FTC will continue to address these challenges by engaging in discussions with a wide variety of stakeholders to inform its policy initiatives. This includes academics, companies, and advocates, as well as data protection and consumer protection enforcement colleagues around the world. In addition, the FTC will continue building its own capacity to analyze and understand new technologies. Together, all of these perspectives not only help keep the FTC informed but also provide a forum for different stakeholders to debate and discuss consumer protection challenges.

ACKNOWLEDGMENT

Thank you to Laurie M. Lai for her assistance in preparing this manuscript.

21

A Design Space for Effective Privacy Notices[*]

Florian Schaub, Rebecca Balebako, Adam L. Durity, and Lorrie Faith Cranor

INTRODUCTION

Personal information is everywhere. Individuals share personal details on social media. Websites and mobile apps collect usage and purchasing habits. Advertisers and data brokers analyze behavioral data to deliver targeted advertising. Fitness wearables, smartwatches, and mobile apps – and their manufacturers – trace every step of their users and know about potential health issues before they do. Voice assistants, smart thermostats, and smart TVs provide companies with unprecedented access to people's homes.

The widespread adoption of such potentially privacy-invasive technologies could indicate that many individuals do not care about privacy and are happy to surrender it for added comfort and convenience. However, privacy research suggests a more complex explanation. Surveys and experiments frequently show that many individuals are concerned about their privacy, but feel helpless and resigned when trying to balance privacy needs with other considerations [2, 122]. While benefits of a new technology or service are often evident, privacy implications are rarely as clear. Opaque information flows involving multiple entities in the collection, processing, and sharing of personal data make it difficult to judge how data shared for one reason today may affect privacy in other contexts in the future. The progression towards the Internet of Things (IoT) exacerbates this issue as more devices gain extensive sensing capabilities and are highly connected with each other and the cloud.

To be able to understand the privacy implications of using a system or device and make informed privacy decisions, users need to be aware of the system's data practices, i.e., what personal information is collected, used, retained and shared. Indeed, lab experiments with a search engine that displayed a compact "privacy meter" summarizing privacy practices associated with each search result demonstrated that users take privacy information into account when it is simplified and made salient in search results, and that many users will pay a small premium to shop at more privacy protective websites [39].

This need for transparency – and the associated need for freedom to decide whether to entrust personal information to a certain entity – is recognized in data protection and privacy laws and regulations around the world [56]. Despite privacy notice and choice being considered essential

---

[*] This is an updated and slightly extended version of a paper first published at the Symposium on Usable Privacy and Security (SOUPS) 2015, July 22–24, 2015, Ottawa, Canada.

aspects of privacy and data protection for decades, today's privacy notices are surprisingly ineffective at informing users.

Smartphones and mobile apps introduce additional privacy issues as they support the recording of sensor and behavioral information that enables the inference of behavior patterns and profiling of users. Yet, comparatively smaller screens and other device restrictions constrain how users can be given notice about and control over data practices. The increasing adoption of wearable devices, such as smart watches or fitness trackers, as well as smart home devices, such as smart thermostats, connected lightbulbs, or smart meters, represents a trend towards smaller devices that are even more constrained in terms of interaction capabilities, but are also highly connected with each other and the cloud. While providing notice and choice is still considered essential in the IoT [47, 73], finding appropriate and usable notice and choice mechanisms can be challenging.

The challenges of providing usable privacy notice have been recognized by regulators and researchers. For instance, former FTC chairwoman Edith Ramirez [106] stated in the IoT context: "In my mind, the question is not whether consumers should be given a say over unexpected uses of their data; rather, the question is how to provide simplified notice and choice." An extensive body of research has studied usability issues of privacy notices (e.g., [14, 33, 63, 50]) and proposed improved notice interfaces (e.g., [34, 65, 66]), as well as technical means to support them (e.g., [74, 127, 131]). Multi-stakeholder processes have been initiated in the wake of the Obama White House's proposed Consumer Bill of Rights [121] to tackle the transparency and control issues of mobile privacy [91] and facial recognition [92]. While such efforts have resulted in guidance for notices in the context of particular systems, they have given little consideration to usability [14].

Existing frameworks and processes for building privacy-friendly systems, such as Privacy by Design [36] or privacy impact assessments (PIAs) [138], focus on the analysis of a system's data practices and less so on the design of notices. Even the OECD report on "making privacy notices simple" [93] basically states that one should design a simplified notice, conduct usability tests, and deploy it – the crucial point of *how* to design a simplified notice is not addressed. Common proposals to improve the usability of privacy notices are the use of multilayered notices [9, 26] or just-in-time notices [46].

Despite the previous work on privacy notices, transparency tools, and privacy mechanisms, a system designer or developer has very little guidance on how to arrive at a privacy notice design suitable and appropriate for their specific system and its respective characteristics. Existing best practices are spread throughout the literature and have not previously been organized into a comprehensive design framework. As a result, privacy notices are often hastily bolted on rather than integrated well into a system's interaction design. Designers may not be aware of the many alternatives for designing usable privacy notices and therefore do not systematically consider the options. Furthermore, designers and researchers do not yet have a standard vocabulary for describing privacy notice options.

In this paper, we make multiple contributions to ease the design of privacy notices and their integration into a system. The goal is to help developers embed privacy notices and choice options into their system design where relevant, with minimal disruption to the system's interaction flow. First, we identify challenges, requirements, and best practices for the design of privacy notices. Based on a survey of existing literature and privacy notice examples, we develop a design space of privacy notices. This design space and its dimensions provide a systemization of knowledge and a taxonomy to foster understanding of and reasoning about opportunities for privacy notices and controls. We demonstrate the utility of our design space by discussing existing privacy notice approaches in different domains.

PRIVACY NOTICES

The concept of privacy notices is founded on the idea that users of services and systems that collect or process personal information should be informed about what information is collected about them and for which purposes, with whom it is shared, how long it is stored, and what their options may be for controlling or preventing certain data practices [44, 94]. Given such transparency, users should be able to make informed privacy and consent decisions. Thus, the purpose of a privacy notice is to make a system's users or a company's customers aware of data practices involving personal information. The privacy notice acts as a public announcement of internal practices with regard to the collection, processing, retention, and sharing of personal information.

Privacy notices can take different shapes and leverage different channels, ranging from a privacy policy document posted on a website, or accessible by links from mobile app stores or mobile apps, to signs posted in public places indicating CCTV cameras are in operation. Even an LED indicating that a camera or microphone is active and recording constitutes a privacy notice, albeit one with limited information about the data practices associated with the recording. Providing notice about data practices is an essential aspect of data protection frameworks and regulation around the world [56]. While transparency has been emphasized as an important practice for decades, existing privacy notices often fail to help users make informed choices. They can be lengthy or overly complex, discouraging users from reading them.

Multiple Roles of Privacy Notices

Privacy notices serve different roles depending on a stakeholder's perspective. Consumers, companies, and regulators see privacy notices in different ways.

For *companies*, privacy notices serve multiple purposes, including demonstrating legal compliance and building customer trust. Privacy notices are often primarily a necessity to ensure compliance with legal and regulatory requirements, rather than a tool to create transparency for users. For instance, the European Data Protection directives have strict notice requirements [40, 42]. In the United States, not providing notice could be interpreted as a deceptive trade practice by the FTC [44] or violate federal, state, or sector-specific privacy legislation, such as CalOPPA [95] or HIPAA [27].

Yet, there are also intrinsic reasons why businesses and system designers should aim to provide privacy notices that are meaningful to users. Being up front about data practices – especially about those that may be unexpected or could be misinterpreted – provides the opportunity to explain their purpose and intentions in order to gain user acceptance and avoid backlash. Furthermore, companies that provide privacy-friendly and secure systems can leverage privacy notices to make users aware of privacy-friendly data practices. Implementing and highlighting good security and privacy practices can further create a competitive advantage as users may perceive the system as more trustworthy.

Regulators, such as data protection authorities or the FTC, rely on companies' privacy notices – primarily their privacy policies – as an important tool to investigate and enforce regulatory compliance [31]. If a company violates its privacy policy, it provides regulators with a basis to take action; for example, the FTC may treat a violation as an unfair or deceptive trade practice [44, 115]. Further, data protection authorities in Europe and other countries may assess whether the described practices meet more stringent criteria, such as use limitation, the proportionality of data practices, and user access options [40, 42].

Hurdles to Effective Privacy Notices

While privacy notices fulfill many roles for different stakeholders, in practice most privacy notices are ineffective at informing consumers [33, 82]. This ineffectiveness stems from hurdles that can be attributed not only to general shortcomings of the notice and choice concept [25, 33, 115], but also to the challenges in designing effective privacy notices.

Notice complexity. The different roles of privacy notices result in a conflation of requirements. Besides informing users about data practices and their choices, privacy notices serve to demonstrate compliance with (self-) regulation and limit the system provider's liability [23]. As a result, privacy notices often take the shape of long privacy policies or terms of service that are necessarily complex because the respective laws, regulations, and business practices are complex [25]. For instance, website privacy policies are typically long, complex documents laden with legal jargon. Indeed it has been estimated that to read the privacy policies for all the websites an American Internet user visits annually would take about 244 hours per year [82]. Privacy policies also read like contracts because regulators aim to enforce them like contracts [25]. Notices may further be purposefully vague to avoid limiting potential future uses of collected data [115]. The effect is that these notices are difficult for most people to understand [82, 110].

Lack of choices. Many privacy notices inform people about data practices but do not offer real choices. Using a website, an app, a wearable device, or a smart home appliance is interpreted as consent to the data practices – regardless of the user having seen or read them. Even if notices are seen by users, they largely describe a system's data practices, with few choices to opt out of certain practices, such as sharing data for marketing purposes. Thus, users are effectively left with a take-it-or-leave-it choice: give up your privacy or go elsewhere [115]. Users almost always grant consent if required to receive the service they want [25]. In the extreme case, privacy notices are turned into mere warnings that do not empower individuals to make informed choices [25] (e.g., "Warning: CCTV in use" signs). Yet, privacy notices can only be effective if they are actionable and offer meaningful choices [33]. Awareness of data practices can enable users to make informed privacy decisions, but privacy controls are needed in order to realize them [112].

Notice fatigue. Notice complexity and the lack of choices mean that most privacy notices are largely meaningless to consumers [25]. Users may feel it is pointless to read them, and most users don't. A recent White House report [105] stated, "Only in some fantasy world do users actually read these notices and understand their implications before clicking to indicate their consent." Furthermore, businesses may change their data practices and notices at any time, which means any effort spent on understanding the notice may have been in vain [115]. Privacy notices and security warnings are often shown at inopportune times when they conflict with the user's primary task [62], and are therefore dismissed or accepted without scrutiny. Frequent exposure to seemingly irrelevant privacy notices results in habituation, i.e., notices are dismissed without users even registering their content [6, 55]. Further, a notice's framing, user distractions, or the passage of time between when a user reads a notice and is asked to provide information can reduce the notice's effectiveness [3].

Decoupled notices. Some systems decouple a privacy notice from the actual system or device, for example by providing it on a website or in a manual. Privacy notices are not only relevant for websites, mobile apps, or surveillance cameras, but for the whole gamut of systems and devices that process user information. Designing and providing appropriate notices for novel systems, such as smart home appliances or wearable devices, is challenging [47]. The straightforward approach is to decouple the privacy notice from the system. For example, many manufacturers of fitness tracking devices provide a privacy policy on their websites, while the actual device does not provide any privacy notices [102]. As a result, users are less likely to read the notice and may therefore be surprised when they realize that their mental models do not match the system's actual data practices [47].

These issues paint a somewhat dire picture of the state of privacy notices. However, just abandoning the concept of notice is not a viable option, as the transparency that notices should provide is essential for users, businesses, and regulators alike [106]. We argue that many of these issues can be addressed by placing the emphasis on how privacy notices are designed. Instead of providing notice merely to fulfill legal and regulatory requirements, notices should effectively inform users about data practices and provide appropriate choices. Some proposed solutions point in that direction, such as multilayered privacy notices [9], just-in-time notices [100], and notices focused on unexpected data practices [47, 106]. However, so far, there is little guidance on the actual design and integration of such notices into real-world systems. Next, we identify requirements and best practices for effective and usable privacy notice design.

REQUIREMENTS AND BEST PRACTICES FOR PRIVACY NOTICE DESIGN

In order to make privacy notices effective and usable, they should not be tacked on after the system has been completed but instead be integrated into a system's design. Privacy notices and choice options can then be designed for specific audiences and their notice requirements, and take into account a system's opportunities and constraints.

In this section, we identify common requirements, necessary considerations, and best practices for privacy notices. These aspects are based on a survey of the usable privacy literature and an analysis of existing privacy design and assessment frameworks, such as Privacy by Design [36], PIAs [138], and proposals for layered notice design [9, 26, 93].

Together with the design space presented in the next section, the requirements and best practices discussed in this section provide guidelines and a toolbox for system designers and researchers that can aid them in the development of usable and more effective privacy notices for their systems.

Understand Privacy in the System

The first step in designing effective privacy notices is to understand a system's information flows and data practices in order to determine whether privacy notices are needed, who should be notified, and about what. Such an assessment can be conducted as part of a PIA [138], which further serves the purpose of identifying privacy risks associated with the system and making recommendations for privacy-friendly systems design. PIAs are becoming an essential – in some countries mandatory – aspect of systems design [136]. They serve the broader goal of ensuring a system's legal and regulatory compliance, as well as informing Privacy by Design and risk mitigation. A common approach in existing PIA frameworks [137, 138] is to first assess if the system collects or processes privacy-sensitive information to determine if a full PIA is required. The next step is to describe the system in detail, including its information flows and stakeholders. This description is the basis for analyzing the system's privacy implications and risks [36, 37]. A PIA produces a report detailing identified issues and recommendations on how to address them.

The resulting recommendations for privacy improvements may include changing collection practices, or identifying opportunities for data minimization. Data minimization reduces the risk of using data in ways that deviate from users' expectations as well as liability risks associated with data theft and unintended disclosure [47]. As an additional benefit, it also reduces the complexity of data practices that need to be communicated to users in privacy notices. If done early in a system's design process, this may also be an opportunity to consider and improve system constraints related to privacy. For example, recognizing that a video camera is collecting information, the device designers may decide to include a light or other signal indicating when the camera is on. The PIA report and data practices should be updated to reflect any privacy-friendly improvements. This process may involve multiple iterations.

Conducting a PIA informs notice design by helping to determine if notices are necessary in the first place, providing an overview of data practices for which notice should be given, potentially reducing the complexity of data practices, and determining the audiences that need to be considered in notice design. The outcome of a PIA is a deep understanding of a system's privacy characteristics, which can be codified in a comprehensive privacy policy.

A privacy policy describes a system's data practices including all relevant parameters, namely what data is being collected about users (and why), how this information is being used (and why), whether it is shared with third parties and for what purposes, how long information is retained, as well as available choice and access mechanisms [44]. This full privacy policy serves as the definitive (and legally binding) privacy notice. As such, it may be a long and complex document, which primarily serves the company to demonstrate transparency and regulatory compliance. It is therefore mainly relevant for businesses and regulators and less interesting or useful to users. However, a well-defined privacy policy can serve as the basis for designing concise, user-friendly privacy notices as it maps out the different data practices about which users may need to be informed.

Different Notices for Different Audiences

PIAs and the creation of privacy policies are well-known and established concepts, but notice design often stops with the privacy policy. Whereas the full privacy policy may be sufficient for businesses and regulators, the key challenge is to design effective privacy notices for users. Therefore, one needs to understand which audiences have to be addressed by notices [23]. While determining a website's audience may be straightforward (typically the visitors of the website), mobile applications, wearables, smart cars, or smart home appliances expand the audiences and user groups that need to be considered. Such systems may have a primary user, but potentially also multiple users with different privacy preferences. For example, a home lock automation system may collect information about all family or household members, including guests [123]. Wearables, such as Google Glass, may incidentally collect information about bystanders. Social media and mobile applications enable users to share information with and about others, e.g., by tagging someone in a geo-referenced photo.

To determine the different audiences for privacy notices, the set of all data practices specified in the privacy policy needs to be analyzed to determine which data practices affect which audience. Typical audience groups are the *primary user* of a system; *secondary users*, such as household members, having potentially less control over the system; and *incidental users*, such as bystanders, who may not even be aware that information about them is collected by a system. Depending on the system, other or additional audience groups may need to be considered. There may also be regulatory requirements applying to specific audience groups, such as children [84], that have to be considered.

While some audience groups may be affected by the same data practices (e.g., data collection about the primary user and other household members by a smart home system), other groups may only be affected by very specific data practices (e.g., while all of a wearable's data practices affect the primary user, bystanders are only affected if they're incidentally recorded by the device, for instance, when the primary user takes a photo or video with a wearable device).

Relevant and Actionable Information

To be effective and draw the user's attention, privacy notices must contain relevant information. For each audience, one should identify those data practices that are likely unexpected for this audience in the prevalent transaction or context. Those practices are relevant because they cross contextual boundaries [81] and thus violate contextual integrity [15, 90]. Providing notice and choice for such practices should be prioritized. The FTC notes with respect to the IoT that not every data collection requires choice, but that users should have control over unexpected data practices, such as data sharing with third parties [47]. FTC chairwoman Ramirez explains this rationale as follows [106]: "Consumers know, for instance, that a smart thermostat is gathering information about their heating habits, and that a fitness band is collecting data about their physical activity. But would they expect this information to be shared with data brokers or marketing firms? Probably not." In these cases, users need clear privacy notices.

If possible, one should not only rely on estimations of what may be expected or unexpected. User surveys and experiments can reveal actual privacy expectations. Creating personas [89] that represent different members of a specific audience group can help ensure that less obvious concerns are appropriately considered.

For each data practice, all parameters relevant for creating a notice should be gathered. For instance, for a data collection practice this may include by whom information is collected, why, how it is used, for how long it is retained, and if and how it is eventually deleted. For third-party sharing practices, it is relevant with whom information is shared, why, and whether and how usage is restricted or limited in time. Data protection regulation may also provide specific notice requirements (e.g., [40, 41, 42]).

Regardless of regulatory requirements, additional information should be compiled about data practices – especially unexpected ones – to ensure the effectiveness of notices provided to users. The notice should help the recipient make informed privacy decisions. This can be achieved by identifying reasons or benefits for the practice with regard to a specific audience, determining implications and risks for the respective audience, and identifying remedies or choices available to the respective audience. Providing reasons offers the opportunity to explain the purpose of a potentially unexpected, yet benign data practice [84]. Communicating risks [16], for instance with examples [58], supports an individual's assessment of privacy implications, especially when data practices are complex or abstract. Offering specific choices makes the information actionable.

System Constraints and Opportunities

A specific system may impose constraints on privacy notices that need to be considered in their design. In general, aspects to consider are the different interfaces provided by a system, including their input and output modalities, as well as their relation to specific audience groups. Specific interfaces may have further constraints, such as limited screen real estate. For instance, the FTC [47] notes that providing notice and choice in the context of the IoT can be challenging due to the ubiquity of devices, the persistence of collection, and practical obstacles for providing information if devices lack displays or explicit user interfaces. Similar issues have already been recognized in the context of ubiquitous computing [73]. Designing notices for specific audiences may further be limited by how the respective audience can be reached or how they can communicate their privacy choices [102].

Systems may also provide opportunities that can be leveraged to provide a layered and contextualized notice concept for each audience, and potentially even integrate privacy notices and controls into a user's primary activity [112]. By recognizing the constraints, designers may be able to find creative and perhaps novel ways for giving notice. For instance, the lack of explicit user interfaces on a device can be compensated with privacy dashboards, video tutorials, privacy icons or barcodes on the device, and offering choices at the point of sale or in setup wizards [47]. Identified constraints may also be addressed by considering notice mechanisms as part of the system design, i.e., adjusting system features to accommodate notices and controls.

Layered and Contextualized Notices

While it may be essential to be transparent about many aspects of a system's data practices, showing everything at once in a single notice is rarely effective. Instead, all but the simplest notices should consist of multiple layers. Multilayered notices constitute a set of complementary privacy notices that are tailored to the respective audience and the prevalent contexts in which they are presented. The granularity of information provided in a specific notice layer must be appropriate for the respective context. For example, a full privacy policy can be complemented by short and condensed notices summarizing the key data practices [9, 84]. Just-in-time or transactional notices provide notice about a specific data practice when it becomes relevant for the user [46], for example, informing people about how contact information is used or whether it is shared with third parties when a user registers on a website.

A multilayered notice concept combines notices shown at different times, using different modalities and interfaces, and varying in terms of content and granularity in a structured approach. For example, some data practices may not require an immediate notice, particularly those that are consistent with users' expectations [45]. It can be expected that a fitness tracker collects information about the user's physical activities – this is the main purpose of the device – thus this collection does not necessarily require prior notice. Automatically uploading a user's activity data to a server or sharing it with other apps may be less expected, thus appropriate notice and choice should be given [84].

Any specific notice should include only the information and control options most relevant and meaningful to a specific audience at that time. Following the details-on-demand pattern [117], initial notices can either point towards additional information and controls or be complemented with alternative user interfaces to review data practices or privacy settings. Deciding what information to include in an initial short notice is a crucial aspect at this stage, because users are more likely to provide consent to the short notice than click through to a more detailed privacy notice. Thus, if such a short notice does not capture all relevant information it may hide information and impair transparency [83]. This is especially an issue for unexpected data practices. Therefore, the notice concept should structure notice layers hierarchically in such a way that the smallest notice either already captures the main aspects of the data practice or draws attention to more expressive notices. Subsequent layers may add additional characteristics.

Designers further need to be aware of not overwhelming users with privacy notices. While many data practices may warrant a notice, providing too many or repetitive privacy notices can result in habituation – users click notices away without considering their content. After a few repetitions, the content of a warning literally does not register anymore in the user's brain [5, 6].

Finding the appropriate number of notices may require user testing. Polymorphic messages [5] or forcing interaction with the notice [21, 22] can reduce habituation effects. A good practice is to prioritize what and when notices are shown based on privacy risks associated with the respective data practice [48].

An example for multilayered design is the Microsoft Kinect sensor. This device uses video, depth-cameras, and audio to enable users to interact with games through motion and speech. The Kinect has two LEDs that indicate whether motion detection is active or whether video and audio are being recorded and potentially sent to a server. Users can further access a full privacy notice through the screen to which the Xbox is connected, as well as on the Xbox website [139]. Unfortunately, LED indicators alone cannot make users aware of what information is being collected or shared for what purposes, whereas most users will likely ignore the policy. Thus, additional notice layers could enhance awareness and obtain informed consent from users.

In Section 4 we introduce a design space for privacy notices that supports the development of a layered and contextualized notice concept by exposing the relevant dimensions that can be leveraged in the design of individual notices, namely the *timing*, *channel*, and *modality* of notices, as well as the *control* options a notice may provide.

User-Centered Design and Evaluation

Once a notice concept has been developed for each audience, individual notices can be designed and evaluated in a user-centered design process, or by engaging users in participatory design [130]. When conceptual notices for different audiences overlap in terms of timing, channel, modality and content, they can potentially be combined into a single notice serving multiple audiences, as long as the resulting notice meets the requirements of each audience group.

User testing and the usability evaluation of notices can be integrated into a system's overall evaluation and quality assurance processes. One should evaluate individual notices, as well as their combination and the overall notice concept. Notices should be evaluated in the context of the actual system or system prototypes to ensure that they integrate well into the system's interaction design. The effectiveness of notices and warnings can be evaluated along multiple dimensions, such as user attention, comprehension, and recall [8, 13]. It is also important to evaluate whether notices help users make informed choices, both about using a particular service and about exercising choice options [39, 65, 66].

Typically, notices should be evaluated in rigorous user studies. However, budget and time constraints may not always allow for extensive evaluation. In such cases, expert evaluation with usability heuristics [88] can provide at least some indication of the notices' effectiveness. Crowdsourcing platforms also offer an opportunity for conducting quick and inexpensive evaluations of privacy notice design [14].

The outlined best practices support the development of a comprehensive set of privacy notices tailored to a system's different audiences. In the next section, we describe the design space of privacy notices in detail to effectively support the design of individual notices as well as audience-specific notice concepts.

DESIGN SPACE OF PRIVACY NOTICES

The design practices outlined in the previous section help to integrate notice design into a system's development process. The purpose of the design space described in this section is to aid the design of specific notices by supporting system designers and privacy engineers in considering the design dimensions of privacy notices. The design space also provides a taxonomy and vocabulary to compare, categorize, and communicate about different notice designs – within a product team as well as with other involved stakeholders, such as the legal department, responsible for drafting the privacy policy, and management. The design space approach has also been used in other privacy and security research, for example, for the creation of a taxonomy of social network data [111], the investigation of web browser Privacy Enhancing Technologies (PETs) [140], and the examination of interfaces for anti-phishing systems [28].

We constructed our design space according to design science principles [101, 126]. Following Ken Peffers et al.'s research methodology [101], we developed and refined the design space in an iterative process, starting with an extensive literature review and the collection and assessment of multiple existing information systems and their privacy notices. This resulted in an initial privacy notice taxonomy, for which we collected feedback in informal discussions with about twenty privacy experts and professionals in summer 2014 at the Symposium on Usable Privacy and Security [119] and at the Workshop on the Future of Privacy Notice and Choice [30]. In further iterations, we refined the design space by taking the expert feedback into consideration and assessing the applicability and expressiveness of the design space in the context of several scenarios grounded in existing privacy notices.

Figure 21.1 provides an overview of the design space. Its main dimensions are a notice's *timing* (when it is provided), *channel* (how it is delivered), *modality* (what interaction modes are used), and *control* (how choices are provided). In the following, we describe each dimension in detail. Note that it often makes sense to consider these dimensions in parallel rather than in sequence, as different dimensions can impact each other. Furthermore, the options for each dimension presented here are not meant to be exclusive. The design space can be extended to accommodate novel systems and interaction methods.

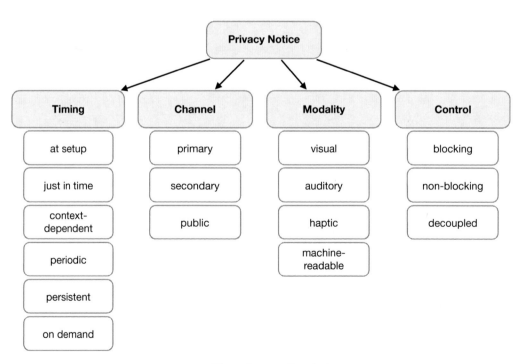

FIGURE 21.1 The privacy notice design space.

Timing

Timing has been shown to have a significant impact on the effectiveness of notices [13, 39, 55, 99]. Showing a notice at an inopportune time may result in users ignoring the notice rather than shifting their attention to it [134]. Delays between seeing a notice and making a privacy decision (e.g., caused by distractions) can change the user's perception of the notice [97] and even cancel out a notice's effect [3]. Thus, users may make different decisions at different points in time, depending on what primary task they are engaged in, the information provided in a notice, and other contextual factors [2]. A comprehensive notice concept should provide notices at different times tailored to a user's needs in that context. We describe six possible timing opportunities here.

At Setup

Notice can be provided when a system is used for the first time [84]. For instance, as part of a software installation process users are shown and have to accept the system's terms of use. Receiving and acknowledging a HIPAA privacy notice [125] when checking into a doctor's office in the United States can also be considered a setup notice – even if provided on paper. Typically, privacy notices shown at setup time are complemented by a persistently available privacy policy that can be accessed retrospectively by users on demand.

An advantage of providing notices at setup time is that users can inspect a system's data practices before using or purchasing it. The system developer may also prefer to provide information about data practices before use for liability and transparency reasons. Setup notices can be used to make affirmative privacy statements to gain user trust. For example, a form to sign up for an e-mail newsletter may contain a concise statement that e-mail addresses are not shared with third parties [24]. Setup notices also provide the opportunity to explain unexpected data practices that may have a benign purpose in the context of the system [84]. Such explanations can be integrated into the system's setup wizard or video tutorials. Showing privacy information before a website is visited can even impact purchase decisions. Serge Egelman et al. found that participants were more likely to pay a premium at a privacy-protective website when they saw privacy information in search results, as opposed to on the website after selecting a search result [39].

However, privacy notices at setup also have shortcomings. Users have become largely habituated to install-time notices, such as end-user license agreements, and ignore them [19]. At setup time, users may have difficulty making informed decisions because they have not used the system yet and cannot fully assess its utility or weigh privacy trade-offs. Furthermore, users may be focused on the primary task, namely completing the setup process to be able to use the system, and fail to pay attention to notices [55]. Therefore, privacy notices provided at setup time should be concise and focus on data practices immediately relevant to the primary user rather than presenting extensive terms of service [84]. Integrating privacy information into other materials that explain the functionality of the system may further increase the chance that users do not ignore it.

Just in Time

A privacy notice can be shown when a data practice is active, for example when information is being collected, used, or shared. Such notices are referred to as "contextualized" or "just-in-time" notices [12, 67, 84]. Andrew Patrick and Steve Kenny [100] first proposed just-in-time click-through agreements in order to provide notice and obtain consent with a concise dialog specific to a certain data practice or transactional context. Examples of notices triggered by data collection are the cookie consent notices shown on websites in Europe [42]. Just-in-time notices can complement or replace setup notices.

Just-in-time notices and obtaining express consent are particularly relevant for data practices considered sensitive or unexpected [47, 84]. For instance, in the case of mobile apps, access to sensitive information such as the user's location, contacts, photos, or calendars, or the ability to record audio and video, should be accompanied by just-in-time notices [46]. Another example is automatic car headlamps that continually sense ambient light conditions; providing notice about this type of data collection might not be necessary. However, privacy expectations may be violated when this information is shared with an insurance company to determine how often the car is driven at night. In such cases, privacy notice as well as choices should be provided. While just-in-time notices enhance transparency and enable users to make privacy decisions in context, users have also been shown to more freely share information if they are given relevant explanations at the time of data collection [67].

Typically, just-in-time notices are shown before data are collected, used, or shared if express user consent is required. On websites, information about how collected data will be used can be presented near input fields in online forms [67]. Just-in-time summary dialogs [7] can show summarized transaction data before it is sent to a service provider. This approach is often used before applications send error or crash reports. Small delays to avoid interrupting the user's primary task may be acceptable [99, 97].

Context-Dependent

The user's and system's context can also be considered to show additional notices or controls if deemed necessary [112]. Relevant context may be determined by a change of location, additional users included in or receiving the data, and other situational parameters. Some locations may be particularly sensitive, and therefore users may appreciate being reminded that they are sharing their location when they are in a new place, or when they are sharing other information that may be sensitive in a specific context. For example, Yang Wang et al. [129] proposed a notice that provides cues to Facebook users about the audience of their future post to help avoid over-sharing. Facebook introduced a privacy checkup message in 2014 that is displayed under certain conditions before posting publicly. It acts as a "nudge" [1, 29] to make users aware that the post will be public and to help them manage who can see their posts (see Figure 21.2). In sensor-equipped environments, such as smart homes, new users or visitors should also be made aware of

Privacy Checkup   Skip

Hi Charlie — Sorry to interrupt. You haven't changed who can see your posts lately, so we just wanted to make sure you're sharing this post with the right audience. (Your current setting is Public, though you can change this whenever you post.) Learn more.

Who do you want to share this post with?

| 👥 Friends | 🌐 Public | ⚙ More Options |

FIGURE 21.2 Facebook's privacy checkup notice warns the user before posting publicly.

what information is being collected and how it is used [73]. Privacy-preserving proximity testing could help determine when the user is near a sensor [10, 74].

Detecting relevant situations and context changes are challenges in providing context-dependent notices. Furthermore, determining whether a context is relevant to an individual's privacy concerns could in itself require access to that person's sensitive data and privacy preferences [112]. However, providing context-specific support may help users make privacy decisions more aligned with their desired level of privacy in the respective situation and thus foster trust in the system.

Periodic

Notices can be shown once, the first couple of times a data practice occurs, or every time. The sensitivity of the data practice may determine the appropriate frequency. Additionally, if the notice includes a consent or control option, it may be appropriate to obtain consent on different occasions, depending on the context, user action, or data being collected. However, showing a notice more than once can be overbearing and can lead to notice fatigue [18] and habituation [6, 22]. Thus, repeating notices need to be designed carefully [5] and their frequency needs to be balanced with user needs. Data practices that are reasonably expected as part of the system may require only a single notice, whereas practices falling outside the expected context of use may warrant repeated notices. In general, it is also advisable to show a notice anew if a data practice has changed.

Periodic reminders of data practices can further help users maintain awareness of privacy-sensitive information flows. Reminders are especially appropriate if data practices are largely invisible [10]. For example, in the health domain, patient monitoring devices in the home may remind users on a weekly basis that data is being collected. Those messages make the user aware of the on-going practice and can provide control options. Hazim Almuhimedi et al. [4] find that periodic reminders of how often a user's location and other information have been accessed by mobile apps caused participants to adjust and refine their privacy settings. Another example of periodic reminders are the annual privacy notices US financial institutions must provide to customers [35].

A challenge with periodic notices is that they must be relevant to users in order not to be perceived as annoying. Reminders should not be shown too frequently and should focus on data practices about which users may not be aware. If a system has too many data practices requiring reminders, data practices can be prioritized based on their potential privacy impact or a combined notice can remind users about multiple data practices. Individual reminders can also be integrated into an overall notification schedule to ensure that users are not overwhelmed. Rotating warnings or changing their look can further reduce habituation effects [5, 134].

Persistent

Persistent notices can provide awareness of ongoing data practices in a less obtrusive manner. A persistent indicator is typically non-blocking and may be shown whenever a data practices is active, for instance when information is being collected continuously or when information is being transmitted [34, 46]. When inactive or not shown, persistent notices also indicate that the respective data practice is currently not active. For instance, Android and iOS display a small icon in the status bar whenever an application accesses the user's location. (In theory, if the icon is not shown users should assume their location is not being accessed. However, researchers have shown that applications sometimes access location when the icon is not being displayed [132].) Privacy browser plugins, such as Privacy Bird [34] or Ghostery [53], place an icon in the browser's toolbar to inform users about the data practices or third party trackers of the website visited. Recording lights are examples of persistent notices that indicate when a sensor is active. Camcorders, webcams, the Kinect sensor, Google Glass, and other devices feature such indicators.

An issue with such ambient indicators is that they often go unnoticed [104] and that most systems can only accommodate such indicators for a small number of data practices. A system should only provide a small set of persistent indicators to indicate the activity of especially critical data practices. Furthermore, persistent indicators should be designed to be noticeable when they are active.

On Demand

All previous timing options pertain to the system actively providing notices to users. Users may also actively seek privacy information and request a privacy notice. Therefore, systems should expose opportunities to access privacy notices on demand [84]. A typical example is posting a privacy policy at a persistent location [73] and providing links to it from a website, app, or other privacy notices in the system. Better options are privacy settings interfaces or privacy dashboards within the system that provide information about data practices; controls to manage consent; summary reports of what information has been collected, used, and shared by the system; as well as options to manage or delete collected information. Contact information for a privacy office should be provided to enable users to make written requests.

Channel

Privacy notices can be delivered through different channels. We distinguish *primary*, *secondary*, and *public* channels. A system may leverage multiple channels to provide different types of notices.

Primary

When a privacy notice is provided on the same platform or device a user interacts with, a primary channel is used for delivering the notice. One example is a privacy notice shown on the user's smartphone that is either provided by the app in use or the operating system. Another example is a privacy notice shown on a website. The defining characteristic of a primary channel is that the notice is provided within the user's interaction with the system, i.e., the user is not required to change contexts. Thus, a browser plugin that provides privacy information about a website (e.g., Privacy Bird [34]) would also be considered a primary channel as the notice is provided within the browsing context.

Using a primary channel is typically preferable, because the notice is presented within the context of the system, which supports users in evaluating privacy implications and their privacy preferences [96, 112]. The primary channel is particularly suitable to provide notice to primary users, but can also be used to provide notices to secondary users. For instance, other household members can also be addressed by a smart home appliance's privacy indicators.

Secondary

Some systems may have no or only limited primary channels that can be leveraged for privacy notices and obtaining consent [10]. Wearables, smart home appliances, and IoT devices are examples of systems with constrained interaction capabilities. Such devices may have very small or no displays, which makes it difficult to display notices in an informative way [102].

For instance, privacy policies are more difficult to read on mobile devices [118]. LEDs and other output features could serve as persistent privacy indicators but are often insufficient to communicate relevant aspects of data practices, such as for what purposes data is being collected or with whom it is being shared. Moreover, IoT devices may be installed in remote or less accessible locations. The user may not be near the sensor device when a notice is generated. The user's context may further constrain the use of primary channels for privacy notices. For instance, car owners cannot read detailed privacy notices while driving; users of Internet-connected gym equipment may only want basic information about data sharing while they exercise, but may be interested in learning more about privacy implications when at home.

In such cases, privacy notices can be provided via secondary channels, i.e., outside the respective system or context. A secondary channel leverages out-of-band communication to notify primary and secondary users. For instance, secondary channels can be used to provide setup notices. Rather than showing privacy information on the respective device, choices could be provided at the point of sale (e.g., opt-outs or opt-ins for specific data practices) or as part of video tutorials [47]. Just-in-time, context-dependent, and periodic notices can be delivered as text messages or e-mails, or any other available communication channel. This requires that the user agrees to receive such notices and provides respective contact information during setup [47]. For instance, the iOS update process gives the option to e-mail oneself the terms of service instead of reading them on the phone.

On-demand notices can be made persistently available at a well-defined location [73], such as posting a (multilayered) privacy policy on the system's website. Pointers to the privacy policy from the system or device (e.g., using visual markers [10, 47]) can ease access to that privacy notice layer.

An increasingly common approach is to make privacy notices and controls available on a companion device, e.g., on a paired smartphone rather than directly on the wearable or IoT device. Such companion devices provide larger displays and more input and output options to make notices more accessible. Companion devices can also act as privacy proxies [74] for a larger number of constrained devices and systems. Examples are centralized control centers for smart home and IoT devices [47], or privacy and permission managers on mobile devices [4, 46].

Public

Primary and secondary channels are targeted at specific users. However, some systems are not aware of the identity of their users, especially secondary and incidental users. In such cases, public channels can be leveraged to provide notice and potentially choices. Examples of public channel privacy notices are signs posted in public places to inform people about video surveillance or a camera's recording indicator.

Public notices can also be supported by technology. IoT devices and other systems may broadcast data practice specifications wirelessly to other devices nearby [10] in so-called privacy beacons [74]. For instance, a camera could inform people about the purpose of its recordings, how long recordings are retained, and who may access them. Such beacons can also inform people about available privacy controls [68].

Public channels can also be leveraged by users to communicate their privacy preferences. Markers can be placed on physical objects to control object or face recognition [108]. A privacy beaconing approach can be used to broadcast preferences to others nearby, for instance transmitting the wish to not be photographed to camera phones nearby [69].

Modality

Different modalities can be used to communicate privacy notices to users. Which modality should be selected depends on what the specific notice strives to achieve, the user's likely attention level, and the system's opportunities and constraints. According to the C-HIP model [32, 134], users process warning messages by switching their attention to them, extracting relevant information from the warning, and comprehending the information; a user's attitudes and beliefs determine if the user acts on the warning. Privacy notices can target each aspect of this process and the choice of modality can increase the effectiveness. For example, if users are engaged in a task that requires visual attention (e.g., driving), using audio to convey privacy information may be more appropriate. Note that not all modalities may be consistently available or effective. Accessibility issues due to physical or visual impairments need to be considered in notice design [128]. Users also may not hear or see a notice due to distractions, a blocked line of sight, or headphone use. Thus, it is important to evaluate the saliency of different modalities used in notice design [134].

We first discuss visual notices, including text and icons, as they are most common. Auditory and haptic signals can also be used to communicate privacy information. However, they have a lower capacity for conveying information compared to visual notices, which may result in a user preference for visual or textual notices [28]. Quite often, modalities are combined; for example, an audio signal may be used to draw attention to a visual notice displayed on a screen. Finally, machine-readable privacy notices enable the use of different modalities and representations depending on context.

Visual

Visual notices can be provided as text, images, icons, or a combination thereof. Presentation and layout are important aspects in the design of visual notices [134], including colors, fonts, and white space, all of which can impact users' attention to and comprehension of the notice [28, 29].

Textual notices can convey complex ideas to users. However, linguistic properties have been shown to influence the perception of warning messages [57]; a notice's framing affects sharing decisions [3]. Specialized terms and jargon may lead to low understanding or the inability to make appropriate privacy decisions [14, 76]. Thus, designers should pay attention to a notice's wording [134], including user testing [14].

While today's website privacy policies are often lengthy [63, 82], privacy notices do not have to be. Relevant information can often be expressed more concisely than in prose. For instance, short notices for smartphone apps have been proposed that convey useful privacy information in the form of risk or expectation scores [52, 78, 79, 87]. Privacy tables and privacy nutrition labels have also been proposed to summarize websites' data practices [65, 83, 86]. Some privacy notice formats have also been standardized by industry or regulators, e.g., financial privacy notices in the United States [51]. Standardized notices offer a familiar interface for users and ease the comparison of products [65].

The effectiveness of notices can be increased by personalizing them to the specific user; for instance by including the user's name in the notice [135] or leveraging other characteristics of the user, such as their demographics or familiarity with a system [134]. An aspect related to personalization is the translation of textual privacy notices into the user's language. Failing to translate may leave international users uninformed about the privacy policy or unable to exercise control over their privacy settings [124].

Images, icons, and LEDs are further options for conveying privacy information visually. Icons can quickly convey privacy settings or currently active data practices. They can be combined with a control switch to activate or deactivate the data practice [47]. However, due to privacy's often abstract nature, images or icons depicting privacy concepts can be difficult to develop. A number of icon sets have been proposed to represent various privacy concepts, both in industry [38, 77, 103, 107] and in research projects [29, 34, 54, 60], with varying levels of success. For example, the AdChoices icon used by the online advertising industry and placed on web ads has been shown to have low user comprehension [77]. Physical indicators, such as LEDs, may use light to visually indicate data practices. LEDs do not have to be binary (on or off) but could leverage colors and blinking patterns to convey different information [59]. Google Glass' display is a transparent glass block that is visibly illuminated if the device is in use, which gives bystanders an indication of whether the device is active.

The meaning of abstract indicators, such as icons or LEDs, often needs to be learned, thus requiring user education. Users also may not notice them [104]. However, when done well, pictorial symbols increase the salience and likelihood of a warning being noticed [134], thus, combining icons with textual explanations in privacy notices may improve the effectiveness of the notice, yet, does not require that users learn the exact meaning of the icon.

Visceral notices take an experiential rather than descriptive approach [23]. For example, eyes appearing and growing on a smartphone's home screen relative to how often the user's location has been accessed [113] can leverage strong reactions to anthropomorphic design [23] to provide an ambient sense of exposure.

Auditory

Auditory notices can take at least two forms: spoken word and sounds. Spoken word may be the form of an announcement, prerecorded or otherwise. One familiar example is the announcement when calling a customer service line that the call might be recorded.

Sounds can be specialized for the device, or based on well-known sounds in that culture. Ryan Calo discusses several examples of visceral notices in which audio signals can "leverage a consumer's familiarity with an old technology" [23]. One example is digital cameras; although some digital cameras and smartphones do not have a physical shutter, they are often configured to emit a shutter sound to make secondary users (i.e., the subjects of the picture) and passersby (incidental users) aware that the device is collecting data by taking a picture. A bill was proposed in the US Congress in 2009 to make such camera shutter sounds mandatory [23]. The bill was not passed; however, some Asian countries have had such requirements for many years.

Auditory warnings can also draw attention to data practices or other notices [134]. For example, the P3P browser plugin Privacy Bird emitted different bird-chirping sounds depending on whether the website's privacy policy matched the user's specified privacy preferences [34]. Rebecca Balebako et al. [12] used sounds to draw attention to occasions when game apps accessed the user's location and other data during game play. Auditory notices face similar challenges as icons – unless familiar [23], their meanings need to be learned. However, they can draw attention to ongoing data practices or privacy notices requiring user attention, especially for systems and devices with constrained interaction capabilities.

Haptic and Other

While not widely used for privacy notices yet, haptic feedback provides a potential modality to communicate privacy information. For instance, Balebako et al. [12] combined sound and vibration to notify users about data sharing on smartphones. Similar approaches could be used in wearable devices without displays.

Other modalities taking advantage of human senses, such as smell, wind, ambient lighting, or even taste [70], could be potentially leveraged for privacy notices as well. For instance, olfactory displays [71] could use chemical compounds to generate a pleasant or disgusting smell depending on whether a system or app is privacy-friendly or invasive. Such approaches may warrant further exploration.

Machine-Readable

The previous modalities directly engage the user's senses. An additional modality offered by computer systems is to encode data practices in a machine-readable format and communicate them to a user's device where the information is rendered into a privacy notice. This way, the data collection system only needs to specify the data practices and can leave it to the device how the information is presented to the user, leveraging it's input and output capabilities. This also provides the opportunity to present notices in different formats on different devices, or differently for specific audiences. However, there is also a risk that machine-readable data practices are misinterpreted or misrepresented by a device. Transparent documentation, certification, or established guidelines on how the machine-readable format should be interpreted may alleviate this issue [109].

Gabriel Maganis et al. equipped devices with small displays that show active QR codes, which encode recent data collection history and the device's privacy policy [80]. Privacy beacons [74] have already been mentioned as an approach to transmit machine-readable data practices to other devices.

The Platform for Privacy Preferences (P3P) is a standard machine-readable format for expressing data practices. Websites provide a P3P policy that P3P user agents, such as Privacy Bird [34] or Internet Explorer, can obtain and render. While P3P failed to reach widespread adoption [33], communicating data practices in a machine-readable format may gain acceptance in the IoT context [10, 112]. Smartphone apps or centralized command centers could aggregate privacy information from multiple constrained devices and offer a unified notice format and privacy controls.

Control

Whenever possible, privacy notices should not only provide information about data practices but also include privacy choices or control options. Choices make the information in privacy notices actionable and enable users to express their consent and their privacy preferences.

The typical choice models are *opt-in*, i.e., the user must explicitly agree to a data practice, and *opt-out*, i.e., the user may advise the system provider to stop a specific practice. However, choices need not be binary. Instead users can be provided with controls to refine purposes for which collected information can be used, specify recipients of information sharing, or vary the granularity of information collected or shared. The goal should be to provide means for users to express preferences globally and selectively [73] instead of a take-it-or-leave-it approach. Controls need to be designed well in order to not overwhelm the user with choices [114].

Furthermore, offering elaborate privacy controls can lead to oversharing over time, either because users feel in control and thus share more [20], or just because of the usability cost of managing the settings [64]. Therefore, default settings need to be carefully considered [84], as they may be kept unchanged out of convenience or because they are interpreted as implicit recommendations [2]. Notice can also give explicit recommendations, for example, as nudges that highlight beneficial choices [1, 4], or with social navigation cues that inform about others' privacy choices [17, 98].

Controls can be directly integrated into the notice, in which case they may be blocking or non-blocking, or they can be decoupled to be used on demand by users. Decoupling may be desirable if the control panel is complex or if the notice provides only limited opportunities for integrating control. To reduce user burden a system may learn a user's preferences and adjust privacy controls automatically [133].

Blocking

Setup, just-in-time, context-dependent, and periodic notices may include blocking controls. A blocking notice requires the user to make a choice or provide consent based on the information provided in the notice. Until the user provides a choice he or she cannot continue and the respective data practice is blocked. Blocking notices typically constitute opt-in consent, e.g., when terms of service must be accepted in order to use the service, but ideally should provide more meaningful choices. For example, if a smartphone privacy notice states that the camera app can access the device's location, users should be able to selectively allow or deny this access while still being able to use the app.

An issue with such click-through agreements [100] is that users may click without reading the provided information. Moving away from just presenting yes and no buttons can increase engagement with the dialog. For instance, Simone Fischer-Hübner et al. propose using a map metaphor on which the user has to drag and drop data onto areas corresponding to their sharing preference [49]. Cristian Bravo-Lillo et al. found that forcing users to interact with relevant information in the notice, e.g., by having to move the mouse cursor over a specific text, can effectively address habituation [21, 22].

Non-Blocking

Blocking controls require engagement, which can be obtrusive. Non-blocking controls can provide control options without forcing user interaction. For instance, Facebook and Google+ provide integrated sharing controls when users create a post. Users who do not interact with these controls have their posts shared according to the same settings as their previous posts. The control mechanisms can also inform about a post's audience [129]. Privacy notices can also link to a system's privacy settings to ease access to privacy controls without blocking the interaction flow.

Decoupled

Some notices may not provide any integrated privacy controls due to system or device constraints. They can be complemented by privacy controls that are decoupled from the specific privacy notice. For instance privacy dashboards and privacy managers enable users to review and change privacy settings when needed [46, 47]. Online companies, such as Google, offer such privacy dashboards to control privacy settings across more than one of their services; advertising associations provide websites to allow web users to opt out of targeted advertising for all partners. Apple's iOS provides a settings menu to control privacy settings for installed apps.

Decoupled privacy controls may also take a more holistic approach by attempting to learn users' privacy preferences from their control choices. Those learned preferences could then be applied to other systems, for example, when a new device is connected to the user's smart home system [47].

USE CASES

The description of the privacy notice design space highlights the variety of potential privacy notice designs. In this section, we discuss privacy notice approaches in three different domains and how they map onto our design space, and identify potential design alternatives.

Website and Social Media Privacy Policies

The prevalent approach for providing notice on websites is to post the website's privacy policy on a dedicated page. Audiences of a website's privacy policy are primary and secondary users, as well as regulators. Websites typically provide notices on demand (*timing*), i.e., users need to seek and access the privacy policy if they want to learn about a website's data practices. Website notices typically use the *primary channel*, because websites are not tied to a specific hardware or screen size, and are largely visual (*modality*). Privacy controls are often decoupled from a privacy notice (*control*), i.e., the privacy policy may point to a settings page that allows users to manage privacy, typically by opting out of certain practices, such as data sharing with advertisers.

The status quo of website privacy notices is a major reason why the notice and choice approach is considered ineffective [25, 33, 115]. However, some websites have developed more effective notice concepts. For instance, Microsoft [85], Facebook [43], and others have implemented multilayered privacy policies that are also interactive. Explanations are integrated into the privacy page and details are provided on demand rather than showing a long privacy policy. But improving the presentation of the privacy policy is not sufficient if users do not access it. Users require notices integrated into the website in addition to a privacy policy.

One approach is to leverage different timing options, such as just-in-time and contextual notices. Notices can be shown when a data practice occurs for the first time or when the user uses a specific feature for the first time. Notices can be integrated into online forms to make users aware of how their provided data is used and with whom it may be shared. Browsers also provide just-in-time notices for resource access, e.g., when a website wants to use the user's location. Contextual notices can be used to warn about potentially unintended settings. For instance, Facebook introduced a privacy checkup warning when posting publicly, see Figure 2. This blocking notice explains the potential issue and offers integrated privacy controls. The same notice could be realized with non-blocking controls, e.g., as a banner below the post entry field; by blocking the publishing of the post, users are forced to validate their settings. Also note that the dialog does not contain an "OK" button; the user needs to make a specific choice.

Varying a notice's channel is not meaningful for most websites, because the primary channel is well accessible. However, secondary channels – such as e-mail, SMS, and mobile app notifications – are being used by social media sites to provide privacy-relevant notifications, for instance, when one has been tagged in a photo or receives a friend request.

Most privacy controls on websites are decoupled from specific notices. But account registration forms may require users to provide opt-in consent for certain data practices before the account can be created. Cookie consent notices as required by European data protection regulation have been implemented as blocking notices, as well as non-blocking notices, e.g., a banner shown at the top of a page that does not impair use of the website.

Smartphone App Permissions

In contrast to websites' privacy policies, privacy and permission management on smartphones employs a more interactive approach. Mobile platforms regulate apps' access to sensors and user resources (e.g., contacts and text messages). The two major platforms, Android and iOS, take different approaches in terms of how they provide privacy notices and controls to users concerning apps' access to resources, although this varies somewhat by version. In the following, we

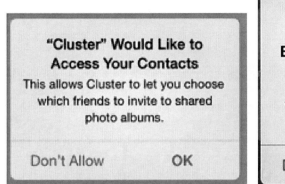

FIGURE 21.3 iOS's just-in-time notice with purpose explanation (left) and periodic reminder (right).

discuss how their approaches utilize different parts of the design space. We focus on iOS 8.x and Android 5.x, the latest versions available in 2015, which illustrate two different approaches.

For both iOS and Android the smartphone itself is the *primary channel*. Both systems show privacy notices mainly on the device. Apps can also be installed via a *secondary channel*, namely a Web store for Android and the iTunes application for iOS. While this secondary channel is available via a computer, the notice design is almost identical to app installation directly on the device. In terms of *modality*, both systems primarily use *visual notices*. Android further requires apps to declare requested permissions in a manifest (*machine-readable*), while iOS apps may specify usage descriptions for access of restricted resources (e.g., location or contacts).

In their app stores, both platforms provide links to an app's privacy policy, which users may access *on demand*. Android further integrates privacy notices into an app's installation process (*at setup*). The user sees a screen that lists the requested app permissions, and the user must either accept all permissions (*blocking*) or not install the app. When an app update changes the requested permissions, a similar notice is shown (*periodic*).

The app installation process on iOS does not include any privacy notices. Instead, iOS shows notices when an app wants to access a resource for the first time, as shown on the left in Figure 3. These notices are *blocking* and ask the user to allow or deny the access request. The notice may contain a developer-specified explanation [120]. In addition, many iOS apps integrate explanations into the application flow before the access request is shown. As of iOS 8, the app developer can also choose to show the authorization notice in advance, but iOS enforces that a resource cannot be accessed without user authorization. In iOS 8, permission requests are not periodic and are only requested once [75]. However, iOS shows periodic reminders for apps that have permission to access the user's location in the background, as shown on the right in Figure 21.3. Both iOS and Android also use a *persistent* location icon in the toolbar indicating that location information is being accessed.

On iOS, users can access a privacy settings menu that facilitates the inspection and adjustment of privacy settings for specific resources, globally as well as for specific apps (*on demand* and *decoupled*). Android provided a similar option (AppOps) in a previous version, but version 5 does not allow users to change an app's permissions. Users can inspect an app's permissions in the app store, but the only option for privacy control is to uninstall the app.

Thus, a major difference between the platforms in 2015 was the level of control afforded to the user. iOS users could choose to deny an app access to any specific resource requested, yet continue to use the app. In contrast, Android users had to accept all of an app's permissions in order to use it. Google introduced the ability to allow users to grant or revoke permissions selectively in Android 6.

Photo and Video Lifelogging

Lifelogging [116] aims to support the memorization and retrieval of everyday events. A common aspect of lifelogging approaches is the recording of photos and videos at frequent intervals, e.g., with GoPro cameras or neck-worn cameras that automatically take a picture every few minutes. A major issue with those technologies is that they not only record the primary user but also bystanders (*incidental users*) [61]. Yet, privacy notices for lifelogging devices, such as the Autographer camera [11] or Google Glass, are mainly targeted at the primary user. They typically provide a privacy policy on the manufacturer's website, privacy settings in a mobile companion app, or a web portal to control sharing and access to the data stream (*secondary channel, on demand,* and *decoupled*). Incidental users neither receive privacy notices nor have options to control being recorded, except for a recording indicator light or a shutter sound on some devices.

   Based on the design space, we can consider alternatives to notify and give control to incidental users. Ideally, incidental users should be informed at the moment they are being recorded or soon afterwards (*just-in-time*) and should be given the opportunity to withdraw consent (*control*). Notices on the device (*primary channel*) are likely not effective, as they may not be salient. In order to leverage a secondary channel, e.g., send a notification to the bystander's smartphone, the bystander would need to be identified in order to determine whom to contact, which introduces additional privacy implications. Another option is to use a *public channel*, for instance by wirelessly broadcasting a *machine-readable* notice that a photo has been taken. The incidental user's device could render the notice visually and use sound or vibration to draw attention to the visual notice (*modalities*). A blocking control option does not make much sense in the context of taking photos and videos, as the primary user would have to wait until consent is collected from all bystanders, even though bystanders and the user may be in motion. Thus, incidental users could be given the *non-blocking* option to retroactively opt out of being photographed. This choice would need to be relayed back to the primary user's device, which could then either delete the photo or detect and remove or blur the incidental user (which poses additional technical challenges that would need to be addressed). While this could provide a viable solution, it also requires bystanders to express their consent any time someone takes a photo nearby, which may become cumbersome in crowded places or at popular tourist spots. An incidental user's preferences could either be stored on their device, which then could automatically respond to such photo notifications, or the incidental user's photo preferences could be broadcast to photographers nearby [69].

CONCLUSIONS

We have presented a design space that provides a structured approach and vocabulary to discuss and compare different privacy notice designs. This can support the design of privacy notices and controls. The design space should be leveraged as part of a comprehensive design process that focuses on audience-specific privacy notice requirements and considers a system's opportunities and constraints, in order to develop a notice and choice concept that is well integrated with the respective system, rather than bolted on. Notices should be evaluated in user studies.

A key aspect of effective notice design is the realization that a privacy policy, which may be necessary for regulatory compliance, is insufficient and often unsuitable for informing users. Privacy policies need to be accompanied by a notice concept that leverages the options provided in the notice design space to provide information relevant to the targeted audience and to make that information actionable by providing real choices. Actionability is important, because privacy notices without control may leave users feeling helpless [99]. Empowering users with privacy controls increases their trust and may result in increased use and disclosure [20].

Novel technologies and integrated devices, such as wearables or the IoT, pose new challenges for the design of privacy notices and controls. Information collection is continuous and sharing paramount [72]. Public policy, legislation, and technological approaches need to work together to enable users to manage their privacy in such systems. The identified best practices and the proposed design space provide the means to reason about meaningful design options for notice and control in such systems. For instance, by leveraging alternative channels or modalities, and providing notices and control options at different times in the information life cycle. A future challenge is to develop and provide tools to support the identification of notice requirements, system opportunities, and applicable options in the design space, and explore the automated and semiautomated generation of notice and control interfaces.

ACKNOWLEDGMENTS

This research was partially funded by NSF grants CNS-1012763, CNS-1330596, and DGE-0903659, as well as by Facebook. The authors would like to thank Aditya Marella and Maritza Johnson for initial contributions to this project; the privacy and usability experts who provided feedback on iterations of the design space; as well as Alessandro Acquisti, Sameer Patil, Yang Wang, our SOUPS shepherd Andrew Patrick, and our reviewers for feedback on earlier drafts.

REFERENCES

[1] A. Acquisti. Nudging privacy: The behavioral economics of personal information. *IEEE Security Privacy*, 7(6):82–85, 2009.

[2] A. Acquisti, L. Brandimarte, and G. Loewenstein. Privacy and human behavior in the age of information. *Science*, 347(6221):509–514, 2015.

[3] I. Adjerid, A. Acquisti, L. Brandimarte, and G. Loewenstein. Sleights of privacy: Framing, disclosures, and the limits of transparency. In *Proc. SOUPS '13*, article 9, 11 pages. New York: ACM, 2013.

[4] H. Almuhimedi, F. Schaub, N. Sadeh, I. Adjerid, A. Acquisti, J. Gluck, L. F. Cranor, and Y. Agarwal. Your location has been shared 5,398 times! A field study on mobile app privacy nudging. In *Proc. CHI '15*, pages 787–796. New York: ACM, 2015.

[5] B. Anderson, B. Kirwan, D. Eargle, S. Howard, and A. Vance. How polymorphic warnings reduce habituation in the brain: Insights from an fMRI study. In *Proc. CHI '15*, pages 2883–2892. New York: ACM, 2015.

[6] B. Anderson, A. Vance, B. Kirwan, D. Eargle, and S. Howard. Users aren't (necessarily) lazy: Using NeuroIS to explain habituation to security warnings. In *Proc. ICIS '14*, 2014.

[7] J. Angulo, S. Fischer-Hübner, T. Pulls, and U. König. HCI for Policy Display and Administration. In *Privacy and Identity Management for Life*, pages 261–277. Berlin: Springer, 2011.

[8] J. J. Argo and K. J. Main. Meta-analyses of the effectiveness of warning labels. *Journal of Public Policy & Marketing*, 23(2):193–208, Oct. 2004.

[9] Article 29 Data Protection Working Party. Opinion 10/2004 on More Harmonised Information Provisions. WP 100, Nov. 2004.

[10] Article 29 Data Protection Working Party. Opinion 8/2014 on the Recent Developments on the Internet of Things. WP 223, Sept. 2014.

[11] Autographer. http://www.autographer.com, 2012. Accessed: June 1, 2015.

[12] R. Balebako, J. Jung, W. Lu, L. F. Cranor, and C. Nguyen. "Little brothers watching you": Raising awareness of data leaks on smartphones. In *Proc. SOUPS '13*, Article 12, 11 pages. New York: ACM, 2013.

[13] R. Balebako, F. Schaub, I. Adjerid, A. Acquisti, and L. Cranor. The impact of timing on the salience of smartphone app privacy notices. In *Proceedings of the 5th Annual ACM CCS Workshop on Security and Privacy in Smartphones and Mobile Devices*, SPSM '15, pages 63–74, New York: ACM. 2015.

[14] R. Balebako, R. Shay, and L. F. Cranor. Is your inseam a biometric? A case study on the role of usability studies in developing public policy. In *Proc. USEC '14*, 2014.

[15] L. Barkhuus. The mismeasurement of privacy: Using contextual integrity to reconsider privacy in HCI. In *Proc. CHI '12*, pages 367–376, New York: ACM, 2012.

[16] L. Bauer, C. Bravo-Lillo, L. F. Cranor, and E. Fragkaki. Warning design guidelines. Tech. report CMU-CyLab-13-002, CyLab, Carnegie Mellon University, 2013.

[17] A. Besmer, J. Watson, and H. R. Lipford. The impact of social navigation on privacy policy configuration. In *Proc. SOUPS '10*, article 7, 10 pages, New York: ACM, 2010.

[18] R. Böhme and J. Gros99klags. The security cost of cheap user interaction. In *Proc. Workshop on New Security Paradigms*, pages 67–82, New York: ACM, 2011.

[19] R. Böhme and S. Köpsell. Trained to accept? A field experiment on consent dialogs. In *Proc. CHI '10*, pages 2403–2406, New York: ACM, 2010.

[20] L. Brandimarte, A. Acquisti, and G. Loewenstein. Misplaced confidences: Privacy and the control paradox. *Social Psychological and Personality Science*, 4(3):340–347, 2013.

[21] C. Bravo-Lillo, L. F. Cranor, S. Komanduri, S. Schechter, and M. Sleeper. Harder to ignore? Revisiting pop-up fatigue and approaches to prevent it. In *Proc. SOUPS '14*, pages 105–111, Berkeley: USENIX Association, 2014.

[22] C. Bravo-Lillo, S. Komanduri, L. F. Cranor, R. W. Reeder, M. Sleeper, J. Downs, and S. Schechter. Your attention please: Designing security-decision UIs to make genuine risks harder to ignore. In *Proc. SOUPS '13*, article 6, 12 pages, New York: ACM, 2013.

[23] R. Calo. Against notice skepticism in privacy (and elsewhere). *Notre Dame Law Review*, 87(3):1027–1072, 2012.

[24] J. Cannon. *Privacy in Technology*. IAPP, 2014.

[25] F. Cate. The limits of notice and choice. *IEEE Security Privacy*, 8(2):59–62, Mar. 2010.

[26] Center for Information Policy Leadership. Ten steps to develop a multilayered privacy notice. White paper, Mar. 2007.

[27] Centers for Medicare & Medicaid Services. *The Health Insurance Portability and Accountability Act of 1996 (HIPAA)*. http://www.cms.hhs.gov/hipaa/, 1996.

[28] Y. Chen, F. M. Zahedi, and A. Abbasi. Interface design elements for anti-phishing systems. In *Service-Oriented Perspectives in Design Science Research*, pages 253–265. Berlin: Springer, 2011.

[29] E. Choe, J. Jung, B. Lee, and K. Fisher. Nudging people away from privacy-invasive mobile apps through visual framing. In *Proc. INTERACT '13*, pages 74–91, Berlin: Springer, 2013.

[30] CMU CyLab. Workshop on the future of privacy notice and choice. https://www.cylab.cmu.edu/news events/events/fopnac/, June 27, 2015.

[31] L. Cranor. Giving notice: Why privacy policies and security breach notifications aren't enough. *IEEE Communications Magazine*, 43(8):18–19, Aug. 2005.

[32] L. F. Cranor. A framework for reasoning about the human in the loop. In *Proc. UPSEC '08*, article 1, 15 pages, Berkeley: USENIX Assoc., 2008.

[33] L. F. Cranor. Necessary but not sufficient: Standardized mechanisms for privacy notice and choice. *Journal on Telecommunications and High Technology Law*, 10(2):273–308, 2012.

[34] L. F. Cranor, P. Guduru, and M. Arjula. User interfaces for privacy agents. *ACM TOCHI*, 13(2):135–178, 2006.

[35] L. F. Cranor, K. Idouchi, P. G. Leon, M. Sleeper, and B. Ur. A large-scale evaluation of U.S. financial institutions' standardized privacy notices. *ACM Trans. Web* 10, 3, Article 17 (August 2016), 33 pages.

[36] G. Danezis, J. Domingo-Ferrer, M. Hansen, J.-H. Hoepman, D. Le M'etayer, R. Tirtea, and S. Schiffner. Privacy and data protection by design: From policy to engineering. Report, ENISA, Dec. 2014.

[37] M. Deng, K. Wuyts, R. Scandariato, B. Preneel, and W. Joosen. A privacy threat analysis framework: Supporting the elicitation and fulfillment of privacy requirements. *Requirements Engineering*, 16(1):3–32, Nov. 2010.

[38] Disconnect.me. Privacy policies are too complicated: We've simplified them. https://disconnect.me/ icons, Dec. 2014. Accessed: June 1, 2015.

[39] S. Egelman, J. Tsai, L. F. Cranor, and A. Acquisti. Timing is everything?: The effects of timing and placement of online privacy indicators. In *Proc. CHI '09*, pages 319–328, New York: ACM, 2009.

[40] European Parliament and Council. Directive 95/46/EC on the protection of individuals with regard to the processing of personal data and on the free movement of such data. *Official Journal of the European Communities* (L 281):31–50, 1995.

[41] European Parliament and Council. Directive 2002/58/EC concerning the processing of personal data and the protection of privacy in the electronic communications sector (Directive on privacy and electronic communications). *Official Journal of the European Communities* (L 201), pages 37–47, 2002.

[42] European Parliament and Council. Directive 2009/136/EC. *Official Journal of the European Communities*, (L 337), pages 11–36, 2009.

[43] Facebook. Data policy. https://www.facebook.com/privacy/explanation, 2015. Accessed: June 1, 2015.

[44] Federal Trade Commission. Privacy online: A report to Congress. FTC report, 1998.

[45] Federal Trade Commission. Protecting consumer privacy in an era of rapid change. FTC report, 2012.

[46] Federal Trade Commission. Mobile privacy disclosures: Building trust through transparency. FTC staff report, Feb. 2013.

[47] Federal Trade Commission. Internet of Things: Privacy & security in a connected world. FTC staff report, Jan. 2015.

[48] A. Felt, S. Egelman, M. Finifter, D. Akhawe, and D. Wagner. How to ask for permission. In *Proc. HOTSEC '12*, Berkeley: USENIX, 2012.

[49] S. Fischer-Hübner, J. S. Pettersson, M. Bergmann, M. Hansen, S. Pearson, and M. C. Mont. HCI designs for privacy-enhancing identity management. In *Digital Privacy: Theory, Technologies, and Practices*, pages 229–252. Boca Raton: Auerbach Pub., 2007.

[50] H. Fu, Y. Yang, N. Shingte, J. Lindqvist, and M. Gruteser. A field study of run-time location access disclosures on android smartphones. In *Proc. USEC '14*, Reston: Internet Society, 2014.

[51] L. Garrison, M. Hastak, J. M. Hogarth, S. Kleimann, and A. S. Levy. Designing evidence-based disclosures: A case study of financial privacy notices. *Journal of Consumer Affairs*, 46(2):204–234, June 2012.

[52] C. Gates, N. Li, H. Peng, B. Sarma, Y. Qi, R. Potharaju, C. Nita-Rotaru, and I. Molloy. Generating summary risk scores for mobile applications. *IEEE Transactions on Dependable and Secure Computing*, 11(3):238–251, May 2014.

[53] Ghostery. https://www.ghostery.com. accessed: June 1, 2015.

[54] J. Gomez, T. Pinnick, and A. Soltani. Know privacy. Final report, University of California, Berkeley, School of Information, 2009.

[55] N. S. Good, J. Grossklags, D. K. Mulligan, and J. A. Konstan. Noticing notice: A large-scale experiment on the timing of software license agreements. In *Proc. CHI '07*, pages 607–616, New York: ACM, 2007.

[56] G. Greenleaf. Sheherezade and the 101 data privacy laws: Origins, significance and global trajectories. *Journal of Law, Information and Science*, 23(1):4–49, 2014.

[57] M. Harbach, S. Fahl, P. Yakovleva, and M. Smith. Sorry, I don't get it: An analysis of warning message texts. In *Proc. USEC '13*, pages 94–111. Berlin: Springer, 2013.

[58] M. Harbach, M. Hettig, S. Weber, and M. Smith. Using personal examples to improve risk communication for security & privacy decisions. In *Proc. CHI '14*, pages 2647-2656, New York: ACM, 2014.

[59] C. Harrison, J. Horstman, G. Hsieh, and S. Hudson. Unlocking the expressivity of point lights. In *Proc. CHI '12*, pages 1683–1692, New York: ACM, 2012.

[60] L. E. Holtz, H. Zwingelberg, and M. Hansen. Privacy policy icons. In *Privacy and Identity Management for Life*, 279–285. Berlin: Springer, 2011.

[61] G. Iachello, K. N. Truong, G. D. Abowd, G. R. Hayes, and M. Stevens. Prototyping and sampling experience to evaluate ubiquitous computing privacy in the real world. In *Proc. CHI '06*, pages 1009–1018, New York: ACM, 2006.

[62] P. G. Inglesant and M. A. Sasse. The true cost of unusable password policies: Password use in the wild. In *Proc. CHI '10*, pages 383–392, New York: ACM, 2010.

[63] C. Jensen and C. Potts. Privacy policies as decision-making tools: An evaluation of online privacy notices. In *Proc. CHI '04*, pages 471–478, New York: ACM, 2004.

[64] M. J. Keith, C. Maynes, P. B. Lowry, and J. Babb. Privacy fatigue: The effect of privacy control complexity on consumer electronic information disclosure. In *Proc. ICIS '14*. 2014.

[65] P. G. Kelley, L. Cesca, J. Bresee, and L. F. Cranor. Standardizing privacy notices: An online study of the nutrition label approach. In *Proc. CHI '10*. New York: ACM, 2010.

[66] P. G. Kelley, L. F. Cranor, and N. Sadeh. Privacy as part of the app decision-making process. In *Proc. CHI '13*, pages 3393–3402, New York: ACM, 2013.

[67] A. Kobsa and M. Teltzrow. Contextualized communication of privacy practices and personalization benefits: Impacts on users' data sharing and purchase behavior. In *Proc. PETS '05*, pages 329–343, Berlin: Springer, 2005.

[68] B. Könings, F. Schaub, and M. Weber. PriFi beacons: Piggybacking privacy implications on wifi beacons. In *Ubicomp '13 Adjunct Proceedings*, pages 83–86, New York: ACM, 2013.

[69] B. Könings, S. Thoma, F. Schaub, and M. Weber. Pripref broadcaster: Enabling users to broadcast privacy preferences in their physical proximity. In *Proc. MUM '14*, pages 133–142, New York: ACM, 2014.

[70] P. Kortum. *HCI beyond the GUI: Design for haptic, speech, olfactory, and other nontraditional interfaces*. Burlington: Morgan Kaufmann, 2008.

[71] S. Landau. Control use of data to protect privacy. *Science*, 347(6221):504–506, Jan. 2015.

[72] M. Langheinrich. Privacy by Design – principles of privacy-aware ubiquitous systems. In *Proc. UbiComp '01*. Berlin: Springer, 2001.

[73] M. Langheinrich. A privacy awareness system for ubiquitous computing environments. In *Proc. UbiComp '02*. Berlin: Springer, 2002.

[74] M. Lazer-Walker. Core location in iOS 8. http://nshipster.com/core-location-in-ios-8/, 2014. accessed: June 1, 2015.

[75] P. Leon, B. Ur, R. Shay, Y. Wang, R. Balebako, and L. Cranor. Why Johnny can't opt out: A usability evaluation of tools to limit online behavioral advertising. In *Proc. CHI '12*, pages 589–598, New York: ACM, 2012.

[76] P. G. Leon, J. Cranshaw, L. F. Cranor, J. Graves, M. Hastak, B. Ur, and G. Xu. What do online behavioral advertising privacy disclosures communicate to users? In *Proc. WPES '12*, pages 19–30, New York: ACM, 2012.

[77] I. Liccardi, J. Pato, D. J. Weitzner, H. Abelson, and D. De Roure. No technical understanding required: Helping users make informed choices about access to their personal data. In *Proc. MOBIQUITOUS '14*, pages 140–150, ICST, 2014.

[78] J. Lin, S. Amini, J. I. Hong, N. Sadeh, J. Lindqvist, and J. Zhang. Expectation and purpose: Understanding users' mental models of mobile app privacy through crowdsourcing. In *Proc. UbiComp '12*, pages 501–510, New York: ACM, 2012.

[79] G. Maganis, J. Jung, T. Kohno, A. Sheth, and D. Wetherall. Sensor tricorder: What does that sensor know about me? In *Proc. HotMobile '11*, pages 98–103, New York: ACM, 2011.

[80] G. Marx. Murky conceptual waters: The public and the private. *Ethics and Information technology*, 3(3):57–169, 2001.

[81] A. M. McDonald and L. F. Cranor. The cost of reading privacy policies. *I/S: A Journal of Law and Policy for the Information Society*, 4(3):540–565, 2008.

[82] A. M. Mcdonald, R. W. Reeder, P. G. Kelley, and L. F. Cranor. A comparative study of online privacy policies and formats. In *Proc. PETS '09*, pages 37–55. Berlin: Springer, 2009.

[83] Microsoft. Privacy Guidelines for Developing Software Products and Services. Technical Report version 3.1, 2008.

[84] Microsoft. Microsoft.com privacy statement. https://www.microsoft.com/privacystatement/en-us/core/default.aspx, 2014. Accessed: June 1, 2015.

[85] G. R. Milne, M. J. Culnan, and H. Greene. A longitudinal assessment of online privacy notice readability. *Journal of Public Policy & Marketing*, 25(2):238–249, 2006.

[86] A. Mylonas, M. Theoharidou, and D. Gritzalis. Assessing privacy risks in android: A user-centric approach. In *Workshop on Risk Assessment and Risk-Driven Testing*, pages 31–37, Berlin: Springer, 2014.

[87] J. Nielsen and R. Molich. Heuristic evaluation of user interfaces. In *Proc. CHI '90*, pages 249–256, New York: ACM, 1990.

[88] L. Nielsen. Personas. In *The Encyclopedia of Human-Computer Interaction*. The Interaction Design Foundation, 2nd ed., 2014. https://www.interaction-design.org/encyclopedia/personas.html.

[89] H. Nissenbaum. A contextual approach to privacy online. *Daedalus*, 140(4):32–48, 2011.

[90] NTIA. Short form notice code of conduct to promote transparency in mobile app practices. Redline draft, July 2013. http://www.ntia.doc.gov/files/ntia/publications/july25codedraft.pdf.

[91] NTIA. Privacy multistakeholder process: Facial recognition technology, 2014. http://www.ntia.doc.gov/other-publication/2014/privacy-multistakeholder-process-facial-recognition-technology. Accessed: June 1, 2015.

[92] OECD. Making privacy notices simple: digital economy papers 120, July 2006. http://www.oecd-ilibrary.org/science-and-technology/making-privacy-notices-simple231428216052.

[93] OECD. The OECD privacy framework. Report, 2013. http://www.oecd.org/sti/ieconomy/oecdprivacyframework.pdf.

[94] Official California legislative information. *The Online Privacy Protection Act of 2003*, 2003.

[95] L. Palen and P. Dourish. Unpacking "privacy" for a networked world. In *Proc. CHI '03*. New York: ACM, 2003.

[96] S. Patil, R. Hoyle, R. Schlegel, A. Kapadia, and A. J. Lee. Interrupt now or inform later? Comparing immediate and delayed privacy feedback. In *Proc. CHI '15*, pages 1415–1418, New York: ACM, 2015.

[97] S. Patil, X. Page, and A. Kobsa. With a little help from my friends: Can social navigation inform interpersonal privacy preferences? In *Proc. CSCW '11*, pages 391–394, New York: ACM, 2011.

[98] S. Patil, R. Schlegel, A. Kapadia, and A. J. Lee. Reflection or action? How feedback and control affect location sharing decisions. In *Proc. CHI '14*, pages 101–110, New York: ACM, 2014.

[99] A. Patrick and S. Kenny. From privacy legislation to interface design: Implementing information privacy in human-computer interactions. In *Proc. PET '03*, pages 107–124, Berlin: Springer, 2003.

[100] K. Peffers, T. Tuunanen, M. A. Rothenberger, and S. Chatterjee. A design science research methodology for information systems research. *Journal of Management Information Systems*, 24(3):45–77, 2007.

[101] S. R. Peppet. Regulating the Internet of Things: First steps toward managing discrimination, privacy, security, and consent. *Texas Law Review*, 93(85):85–176, 2014.

[102] T. Pinnick. Privacy short notice design. TRUSTe blog, Feb. 2011. http://www.truste.com/blog/2011/02/17/privacy-short-notice-design/. Accessed: June 1, 2015.

[103] R. S. Portnoff, L. N. Lee, S. Egelman, P. Mishra, D. Leung, and D. Wagner. Somebody's watching me? Assessing the effectiveness of webcam indicator lights. In *Proc. CHI '15*, pages 1649–1658, New York: ACM, 2015.

[104] President's Concil of Advisors on Science and Technology. Big data and privacy: A technological perspective. Report to the President, Executive Office of the President, May 2014.

[105] E. Ramirez. Privacy and the IoT: Navigating policy issues. CES Opening Remarks, 2015. FTC public statement.

[106] A. Raskin. Privacy icons: Alpha release. http://www.azarask.in/blog/post/privacy-icons/. Accessed: June 1, 2015.

[107] N. Raval, A. Srivastava, K. Lebeck, L. Cox, and A. Machanavajjhala. Markit: Privacy markers for protecting visual secrets. In *UbiComp '14 Adjunct Proceedings*, pages 1289–1295, New York: ACM, 2014.

[108] J. Reidenberg and L. F. Cranor. Can user agents accurately represent privacy policies? Available at SSRN: http://papers.ssrn.com/abstract=328860, 2002.

[109] J. R. Reidenberg, T. Breaux, L. F. Cranor, B. French, A. Grannis, J. T. Graves, F. Liu, A. M. McDonald, T. B. Norton, R. Ramanath, N. C. Russell, N. Sadeh, and F. Schaub. Disagreeable privacy policies: Mismatches between meaning and users' understanding. *Berkeley Technology Law Journal*, 30(1):39–88, 2015.

[110] C. Richthammer, M. Netter, M. Riesner, J. Sänger, and G. Pernul. Taxonomy of social network data types. *EURASIP Journal on Information Security*, 11, 2014.

[111] F. Schaub, B. Könings, and M. Weber. Context-adaptive privacy: Leveraging context awareness to support privacy decision making. *IEEE Pervasive Computing*, 14(1):34–43, 2015.

[112] R. Schlegel, A. Kapadia, and A. J. Lee. Eyeing your exposure: Quantifying and controlling information sharing for improved privacy. In *Proc. SOUPS '11*, article 14, New York: ACM, 2011.

[113] B. Schwartz. *The Paradox of Choice: Why More Is Less*. HarperCollins Publishers, 2004.

[114] P. M. Schwartz and D. Solove. Notice and choice. In *The Second NPLAN/BMSG Meeting on Digital Media and Marketing to Children*, 2009.

[115] A. J. Sellen and S. Whittaker. Beyond total capture: A constructive critique of lifelogging. *Commun. ACM*, 53(5):70–77, May 2010.

[116] B. Shneiderman. The eyes have it: A task by data type taxonomy for information visualizations. In *Proc. Symp. on Visual Languages*, pages 336–343, New York: IEEE, 1996.

[117] R. I. Singh, M. Sumeeth, and J. Miller. Evaluating the readability of privacy policies in mobile environments. *International Journal of Mobile Human Computer Interaction*, 3(1):55–78, 2011.

[118] SOUPS 2014 organizing committee. Tenth symposium on usable privacy and security. http://cups.cs .cmu.edu/soups/2014/, July 9–11, 2014.

[119] J. Tan, K. Nguyen, M. Theodorides, H. Negr´on-Arroyo, C. Thompson, S. Egelman, and D. Wagner. The effect of developer-specified explanations for permission requests on smartphone user behavior. In *Proc. CHI '14*, pages 91–100, New York: ACM, 2014.

[120] The White House. Consumer data privacy in a networked world. Technical report, Feb. 2012. http:// www.whitehouse.gov/sites/default/files/privacy-final.pdf.

[121] J. Turow, M. Hennessy, and N. Draper. The tradeoff fallacy: How marketers are misrepresenting American consumers and opening them up to exploitation. Technical report, Annenberg School for Communication, University of Pennsylvania, Philadelphia, PA, June 2015.

[122] B. Ur, J. Jung, and S. Schechter. Intruders versus intrusiveness: Teens' and parents' perspectives on home-entryway surveillance. In *Proc. UbiComp '14*, pages 129–139, New York: ACM, 2014.

[123] B. Ur, M. Sleeper, and L. F. Cranor. {Privacy, Privacidad, Приватност} Policies in Social Media: Providing Translated Privacy Notice. *I/S: A Journal of Law and Policy for the Information Society*, 9(2), pages 201–243, 2013.

[124] U.S. Department of Health & Human Services. Notice of privacy practices for protected health information, April 2003, https://www.hhs.gov/hipaa/for-professionals/privacy/guidance/privacy-prac tices-for-protected-health-information/index.html.

[125] R. H. von Alan, S. T. March, J. Park, and S. Ram. Design science in information systems research. *MIS quarterly*, 28(1):75–105, 2004.

[126] W3C. Tracking protection working group. http://www.w3.org/2011/tracking-protection/. Accessed: June 1, 2015.

[127] W3C. Web accessibility and usability working together. http://www.w3.org/WAI/intro/usable. Accessed: June 1, 2015.

[128] Y. Wang, P. G. Leon, A. Acquisti, L. F. Cranor, A. Forget, and N. Sadeh. A field trial of privacy nudges on facebook. In *Proc. CHI '14*, pages 2367–2376, New York: ACM, 2014.

[129] S. Weber, M. Harbach, and M. Smith. Participatory design for security-related user interfaces. In *Proc. USEC '15*, 2015.

[130] R. Wenning, M. Schunter, L. Cranor, B. Dobbs, S. Egelman, G. Hogben, J. Humphrey, M. Langheinrich, M. Marchiori, M. Presler-Marshall, J. Reagle, and D. A. Stampley. The platform for privacy preferences 1.1 (P3P 1.1) specification. http://www.w3.org/TR/P3P11/, 2006.

[131] P. Wijesekera, A. Baokar, A. Hosseini, S. Egelman, D. Wagner, and K. Beznosov. Android permissions remystified: A field study on contextual integrity. In *Proc. USENIX Security*, 2015.

[132] P. Wijesekera, A. Baokar, L. Tsai, J. Reardon, S. Egelman, D. Wagner, and K. Beznosov. The feasibility of dynamically granted permissions: Aligning mobile privacy with user preferences. In *Proc. of the 2017 IEEE Symposium on Security and Privacy (Oakland '17)*, 2017.

[133] M. S. Wogalter, V. C. Conzola, and T. L. Smith-Jackson. Research-based guidelines for warning design and evaluation. *Applied Ergonomics*, 33(3):219–230, 2002.

[134] M. S. Wogalter, B. M. Racicot, M. J. Kalsher, and S. Noel Simpson. Personalization of warning signs: The role of perceived relevance on behavioral compliance. *International Journal of Industrial Ergonomics*, 14(3):233–242, Oct. 1994.

[135] D. Wright. Should privacy impact assessments be mandatory? *Communications of the ACM*, 54(8):121–131, Aug. 2011.

[136] D. Wright. Making privacy impact assessment more effective. *The Information Society*, 29(5):307–315, Oct. 2013.

[137] D. Wright, K. Wadhwa, P. D. Hert, D. Kloza, and D. G. Justice. A Privacy Impact Assessment Framework for data protection and privacy rights. Deliverable September, PIAF project, 2011.

[138] Xbox.com. Kinect and Xbox One privacy FAQ. http://www.xbox.com/en-US/kinect/privacyandonlinesafety.

[139] H. Xu, R. E. Crossler, and F. B´elanger. A value sensitive design investigation of privacy enhancing tools in web browsers. *Decision Support Systems*, 54(1):424–433, 2012.

Enter the Professionals

Organizational Privacy in a Digital Age

J. Trevor Hughes and Cobun Keegan

THE PRIVACY PRACTICE

The privacy profession has arrived. Today, more than 35,000 individuals self-identify as privacy professionals. They are lawyers, technologists, and administrators who work in privacy programs in governments and businesses all over the world. According to a survey by the International Association of Privacy Professionals (IAPP), the typical privacy professional works in the compliance department of a private company at the director level or higher.[1] On an average day, privacy professionals "work on privacy policies, procedures and governance structures; provide privacy related awareness and training throughout the organization; respond to privacy and security incidents; manage privacy communications; design and implement privacy controls; manage privacy issues arising with new and existing products; conduct privacy-related employee monitoring and investigations; help with privacy staff development; and participate in privacy-related data committees."[2]

In the general scheme of modern vocations, privacy has developed into a fully fledged profession in relatively short stretch of time – in tandem with the surge of the data economy. Just twenty years ago, a privacy profession in the United States barely existed. It is a uniquely modern profession, brought to prominence at a time when companies are more likely to worry about losing private data than intellectual property or other proprietary information,[3] and consumers are expected to generate more than a million gigabytes of sensitive health data during their lifetime.[4] Privacy professionals approach problems with a unique set of tools, undergo specialized training, receive certification, comply with particularized regulations, and belong to their own professional associations. To understand the exponential growth of privacy practice and test whether privacy is here to stay, this chapter compares privacy with other more established professions, such as medicine and the practice of law.

THE RISE OF PROFESSIONS

Before the industrial revolution, the expertise-based occupations that we now call "professions" did not exist. At the time, there were only three "recognized gentlemanly professions" in

---

[1] INTERNATIONAL ASSOCIATION OF PRIVACY PROFESSIONALS & EY, IAPP-EY ANNUAL PRIVACY GOVERNANCE REPORT 2016 xiii (Sept. 2016), https://iapp.org/media/pdf/resource_center/IAPP-2016-GOVERNANCE-SURVEY-FINAL2.pdf.

[2] *Id.* at xx.

[3] Sarah Tonigan Hatch, *New Wells Fargo Insurance Cyber Security Study Shows Companies More Concerned with Private Data Loss Than with Hackers*, BUS. WIRE (Sept. 7, 2016, 10:00 AM), http://www.businesswire.com/news/home/20160907005311/en/Wells-Fargo-Insurance-Cyber-Security-Study-Shows.

[4] Ariana Eunjung Cha, *Watson's Next Feat? Taking on Cancer*, WASH. POST (June 27, 2015), http://wapo.st/watson.

Western European society: divinity, law, and medicine.[5] Unlike the educated classes of earlier European society, restricted to rigidly defined priesthoods, these professions required only a formal education for entrée.[6] However, one's success in this system depended more on an ability to secure patronage and connections with prominent professionals than on proven merit or educational achievement.[7] The high social status of the gentlemanly professions was reinforced by "scholarly prestige, restrictive practices through the enforcement of licensing, [and] relatively high personal income," making them unique among the occupations of the time.[8]

Much more common were occupations and trades that were learned outside of formal educational institutions, passed down from mentor to apprentice through on-the-job training.[9] This was a firsthand way of conveying expertise, suitable to the community-oriented society of the time where reputation depended more on word of mouth than any paper certificate. Small communities in a barter economy had less need for their would-be professionals to adhere to formalized ethical codes or rigid standards. If someone wondered about the pedigree and reputation of the craftsman they were hiring, they need only have asked their neighbors.

The nineteenth century brought with it a surge in the specialization of labor, leading to cash-based markets, increasingly hierarchical workplaces, and the urbanization of populations.[10] In such a rapidly modernizing society, "community and aristocratic tradition were no longer sufficient to guarantee credit and credibility."[11] Instead, there was an increasing need for highly trained individuals who could be relied upon for consistent quality without the personal knowledge or direct supervision of those who hired them.

The growing need to organize expertise in a way that could guarantee trustworthiness among strangers was solved by guilds. In their book *The Future of the Professions*, Richard and Daniel Susskind point to medieval guilds, such as the master masons, as the progenitors of modern professions – and professional associations.[12] As guilds of merchants and craftsmen developed, from the twelfth century onwards, these formerly isolated tradesmen "came together to set standards, [to] control competition, to look after the interests of their members and families, and to enjoy the prestige of being part of a group of recognized experts."[13] With association came prestige, recognition, and the ability to self-regulate. As rules and standards were established, entrée into these professional groups began to depend less on social class and more on demonstrated merit.

PROFESSIONS DEFINED

Today, professions are so widespread and varied that it is difficult to define precisely what a modern "profession" is. As the Susskinds observe, many trades and vocations, from baking to management consulting, lay claim to the title of profession.[14] But in popular consciousness, as well as the academic literature, a more limited definition emerges. The Susskinds point to four overlapping similarities of

---

[5] Magali Sarfatti Larson, The Rise of Professionalism: A Sociological Analysis 4–5 (1977).

[6] *Id.* at xiv, *citing* Karl Mannheim, Ideology and Utopia 155–56 (1936).

[7] *Id.* at 5–9.

[8] Carlo M. Cipolla, Before the Industrial Revolution: European Society and Economy, 1000–1700 70 (1976).

[9] *See id.*

[10] Larson, *supra* note 5, at 5.

[11] *Id.* at 10–11.

[12] Richard Susskind & Daniel Susskind, The Future of the Professions: How Technology Will Transform the Work of Human Experts 19–20 (2015).

[13] *Id.* at 20.

[14] *Id.* at 15.

modern professions: "(1) they have specialist knowledge; (2) their admission depends on credentials; (3) their activities are regulated; and (4) they are bound by a common set of values."[15]

Thus, not all trades, occupations, and specialties can count themselves among the professions. Some lack the requisite standardization of values – political pundits come to mind. Some, such as door-to-door salesmen, are not adequately organized. Some, data scientists for instance, are too new or amorphous to have gained recognition. Some, such as wedding officiants, are too specialized to reach a critical mass. And some, dog whisperers, for example, do not require the level of training to justify the prestige that the title of "profession" brings. In the following sections, we show how information privacy has matured as a profession – one vital to the modern economy – while drawing comparisons to older, more established, trades.

Specialist Knowledge

The use of specialist knowledge is the first and predominant characteristic of a profession.[16] Professionals are trained specialists who are paid to apply their expertise to the real-world needs of their employers, customers, patients, or clients. Those who seek professional services do so with a pronounced information asymmetry, so professionals "help people overcome their limited understanding, and they act as gatekeepers who maintain, interpret and apply the practical expertise from which we wish to benefit."[17] In turn, it is the application of the "special knowledge of the profession that justifies its autonomy."[18]

The expertise that professionals apply in practice is derived from their own practical experience as well as the body of knowledge of their profession – usually built up by generations of academics and practitioners. For example, in Western medicine, the body of knowledge has existed for far longer than the profession itself, extending at least back to the Hippocratic physicians, who first developed an understanding of disease based on natural rather than supernatural causes.[19] The professional knowledge of lawyers, too, is built on a foundation of academic scholarship. In addition, the legal profession's body of knowledge benefits from the constant accretion of rules and principles through legislative edict and judicial interpretation.

Often, professions also have officially prescribed bodies of knowledge, endorsed by professional associations. For example, the International Information Security System Certification Consortium (ISC)² – a professional association of data security professionals – maintains textbooks for each of its professional certifications.[20] Each of these textbooks, appropriately called a Body of Knowledge (BOK), "defines global industry standards, serving as a common framework of terms and principles that our credentials are based upon and allows professionals worldwide to discuss, debate, and resolve matters pertaining to the field."[21]

The body of knowledge of the privacy profession is a mixture of all these sources, from scholarly writing and legal precedent to practical training manuals. At its foundation is a long history of philosophical thought about the relation between individuals and society and the importance of privacy in human life. In his book, *Nothing to Hide*, Daniel Solove summarizes ancient privacy texts: "The Code of Hammurabi protected the home against intrusion, as did ancient Roman law. The early Hebrews had laws safeguarding against surveillance. And in

---

[15] *Id.*

[16] *Id.* at 16.

[17] *Id.* at 42.

[18] Eliot Freidson, Profession of Medicine: A Study of the Sociology of Applied Knowledge 343 (1988).

[19] *Id.* at 13–15.

[20] *About (ISC)²*, Int'l Info. Sec. Sys. Certification Consortium, https://www.isc2.org/aboutus/default.aspx (last visited Jan. 3, 2018).

[21] *Id.*

England, the oft-declared principle that the home is one's 'castle' dates to the late fifteenth century."[22] Some scholars have even characterized the need for privacy from social interaction as a universal human drive – also apparent in nonhuman animals[23] – the desire to regulate interactions and determine whether or not to engage with others.[24]

Built on this foundation is the work of legal scholars such as Louis Brandeis and Samuel Warren, whose 1890 law review article is often cited as the first to closely examine the legal right to privacy.[25] Seventy years later, William Prosser categorized this general right to privacy "into a taxonomy of four torts and introduced it as a major topic in both academic and practical understandings of tort law."[26] These four torts – intrusion on seclusion, public disclosure, false light, and appropriation – represented the core of privacy law in the United States for decades.[27] Yet as technology increased the availability and distribution of personal information, the understanding of the types of privacy entitled to legal protection continued to shift.

By the 1960s, the emergence of what were then known as "computerized data processing systems" and "databanks" began to signal significant changes in organizations' impact on privacy. Alan Westin, then a law professor at Columbia University, realized that such technologies had profound implications for the capacity of governments to engage in surveillance of their citizens and corporations of their customers and employees: "The issue of privacy raised by computerization is whether the increased collection and processing of information for diverse public and private purposes, if not carefully controlled, could lead to a sweeping power of surveillance by government over individual lives and organizational activity."[28] Westin, then, foresaw an age of big data, which would accentuate an imbalance of power between individual data subjects, on the one hand, and data-rich organizations in business and government on the other hand. With these concerns in mind, Westin reinterpreted the right to privacy as rooted in a human need to control how personal information about ourselves is obtained and used by others, helping to found the field of information privacy.[29]

In his book, Westin called for "definite criteria that public and private authorities can apply in comparing the claims for disclosure or surveillance through new devices with the claims to privacy."[30] By the 1970s, government recognition of the need to address information privacy began to further expand the privacy body of knowledge. In the wake of the Watergate scandal, the executive branch recognized the need for more rigorous record-keeping policies within the federal government, starting with President Richard Nixon's creation of the Domestic Council Committee on the Right to Privacy in the White House.[31] The sudden emphasis on the impact of computers on the privacy of government records led the Department of Health, Education,

---

[22] DANIEL J. SOLOVE, NOTHING TO HIDE: THE FALSE TRADEOFF BETWEEN PRIVACY AND SECURITY 4 (2011).

[23] Alan Westin, *The Origins of Modern Claims to Privacy*, in PHILOSOPHICAL DIMENSIONS OF PRIVACY: AN ANTHOLOGY 56, 56–59 (Ferdinand David Schoeman ed., 1984).

[24] Irwin Altman, *Privacy Regulation: Culturally Universal or Culturally Specific?*, 33 J. SOC. ISSUES 66, 82–86 (1977).

[25] Samuel D. Warren & Louis D. Brandeis, *The Right to Privacy*, 4 HARV. L. REV. 193 (1890).

[26] Neil M. Richards & Daniel J. Solove, *Prosser's Privacy Law: A Mixed Legacy*, 98 CAL. L. REV. 1887, 1888 (2010).

[27] *Id.* at 1889. *See* William L. Prosser, *Privacy*, 48 CAL. L. REV. 383, 388–89 (1960).

[28] ALAN WESTIN, PRIVACY AND FREEDOM 154 (1967).

[29] Andrew Clearwater & J. Trevor Hughes, *In the Beginning ... An Early History of the Privacy Profession*, 74 OHIO STATE L.J. 899 (2013). *See* WESTIN, *supra* note 28, at 7.

[30] WESTIN, *supra* note 28, at 364. The *Privacy and Freedom* list focused on balancing privacy and security when developing surveillance, factoring in (1) the seriousness of the need for surveillance, (2) alternative methods, (3) the reliability of the surveillance instrument, (4) whether consent to surveillance has been given, and (5) the capacity for limitation and control. *Id.* at 364–71.

[31] *See* Clearwater & Hughes, *supra* note 29, at 899 (2013).

and Welfare to publish a report entitled *Records, Computers, and the Rights of Citizens,*[32] which answered Westin's call for policymaking criteria by enumerating the first set of fair information practices for government use of automated personal data systems.[33] Notably, these principles describe such fundamental privacy concepts as notice of data collection, purpose-based limitations on data use, consent to new uses of collected data, and access to and correction of inaccurate records.[34] The report also drew heavily on the conclusions of the National Research Council-funded study *Databanks in a Free Society,* led by Alan Westin, which had developed a similar list of recommended "areas of priority for public policy" related to government record systems.[35]

Congress expanded upon these fair information practices in the Privacy Act of 1974, codifying rules for the collection and use of data concerning individuals by the federal government.[36] The Privacy Act also authorized the creation of the U.S. Privacy Protection Study Commission, which released a report a few years later with its recommendations for improving the fair information practices.[37] The report provided specific findings about the guiding principles of the Privacy Act, which it summarized as openness, individual access, individual participation, collection limitation, use limitation, disclosure limitation, information management, and accountability.[38]

Though the U.S. government never incorporated the fair information practices into a generalized privacy law, the Organization for Economic Cooperation and Development (OECD) endorsed its own version of these principles in 1980, issuing a set of guidelines to help harmonize OECD member country privacy protections.[39] The OECD principles included collection and use limitations, purpose-specification, data quality, openness, and individual participation.[40] Though the OECD guidelines are nonbinding, they proved instrumental in the progression of the privacy law of OECD member countries, most notably in Europe. This set the stage for the enactment in Europe of the 1995 EU Data Privacy Directive, which embraced and expanded on the same principles.[41]

As rapidly evolving technology continued to impact individual privacy in new ways, the law also adapted. In 1976, a decision of the U.S. Supreme Court that there was no right to privacy in information once it was placed into the stream of commerce, sparked swift legislative action to provide privacy protection for financial information.[42] This set the stage for the introduction of

---

[32] U.S. Dep't of Health, Educ., & Welfare, *Records, Computers and the Rights of Citizens: Report of the Secretary's Advisory Committee on Automated Personal Data Systems* (July 1, 1973), https://aspe.hhs.gov/report/records-computers-and-rights-citizens.

[33] *Id.*; U.S. Dep't of Homeland Sec., *Privacy Policy Guidance Memorandum* (Dec. 29, 2008), https://www.dhs.gov/sites/default/files/publications/privacy_policyguide_2008-01_0.pdf.

[34] U.S. Dep't of Health, Educ., & Welfare, *supra* note 32.

[35] Alan F. Westin & Michael A. Baker, Databanks in a Free Society: Computers, Record-Keeping, and Privacy 355 (1972). These "areas of priority" included the citizen's right to see his record, rules for confidentiality and data-sharing, and limiting unnecessary data collection. *Id.* at 355–92.

[36] Privacy Act of 1974, 5 U.S.C. § 552a (2012).

[37] U.S. Privacy Prot. Study Comm'n, Personal Privacy in an Information Society (July 1977), https://epic.org/privacy/ppsc1977report/.

[38] *Id.* at App. 4.

[39] Michael Kirby et al., *The History, Achievement and Future of the 1980 OECD Guidelines on Privacy* 1, 3 (Mar. 10, 2010), http://www.oecd.org/sti/ieconomy/44945835.doc. *See* Clearwater & Hughes, *supra* note 29, at 902–03.

[40] Org. for Econ. Cooperation & Dev., OECD Guidelines on the Protection of Privacy and Transborder Flows of Personal Data (Sept. 23, 1980).

[41] Julia M. Fromholz, *The European Data Privacy Directive,* 15 Berkeley Tech. L.J. 461, 466 (2000). *See* Directive 95/46/EC of the European Parliament and of the Council of 24 October 1995 on the Protection of Individuals with Regard to the Processing of Personal Data and on the Free Movement of Such Data, 1995 O.J. (L 281).

[42] Clearwater & Hughes, *supra* note 29, at 901. *See* United States v. Miller, 425 U.S. 435 (1976).

the dozens of industry-specific information privacy laws and regulations in the United States today.[43] At the federal level, these cover a broad range of industries including consumer finance (FCRA),[44] healthcare (HIPAA),[45] education (FERPA),[46] financial services (GLBA),[47] websites directed to children (COPPA),[48] and even video rental companies (VPPA).[49] State governments have stepped in to provide additional protections. In fact, nearly every U.S. state now has laws requiring data breach notifications and student privacy protections.[50] Additionally, due to the "California effect," where companies set policies based on the most stringent rules of the states in which they do business, some states have passed privacy protective laws with a national impact.[51] For example, the California Online Privacy Protection Act of 2003 (CalOPPA) is the first U.S. law to require web-based companies to post privacy policies.[52] Meanwhile, both Massachusetts[53] and Nevada[54] have shaped industry practices by mandating minimum data security measures.[55]

Yet the privacy body of knowledge goes beyond compliance with laws and regulations. Privacy professionals also apply a body of knowledge based on best practices, often developed through information sharing within industries, at conferences, or as part of a certification process.[56] Professional associations and trade groups have been instrumental in furthering privacy best practices, helping to implement guidelines, stabilize operations, and develop mechanisms for assessing risk.[57] For example, two groups of online advertisers, the Digital Advertising Alliance and the Network Advertising Initiative, created self-regulatory codes of conduct influenced by fair information practices including notice, choice, transparency, and control.[58] Similarly, the World Wide Web Consortium (W3C), a group of hundreds of organizations from industry, academia, and civil society, works to unify "Do Not Track" standards to allow for user choice in online tracking.[59] Other voluntary technical standards, such as those developed by the International Organization for Standardization (ISO), have also proven instrumental in shaping

---

[43] For a comprehensive survey of U.S. federal privacy laws covering record-keeping, education, health, financial, Internet, and communications, see ANITA L. ALLEN, PRIVACY LAW AND SOCIETY (2007).

[44] Fair Credit Reporting Act, 15 U.S.C. § 1681 (2012).

[45] Health Insurance Portability and Accountability Act of 1996, 42 U.S.C. §§ 1320d(1)–(9) (2012); 45 C.F.R. §§ 160, 164 (2015).

[46] Family Educational Rights and Privacy Act, 20 U.S.C. § 1232g (2012); 34 C.F.R. Part 99 (2016).

[47] Gramm–Leach–Bliley Act, 15 U.S.C. §§ 6801–6809 (2012).

[48] Children's Online Privacy Protection Act of 1998, 15 U.S.C. 6501–6505 (2012); 16 C.F.R. Part 312 (2016).

[49] Video Privacy Protection Act, 18 U.S.C. § 2710 (2012).

[50] For surveys of these state laws, see, respectively: DAVIS WRIGHT TREMAINE LLP, SUMMARY OF U.S. STATE DATA BREACH NOTIFICATION STATUTES (July 2016), http://www.dwt.com/statedatabreachstatutes/; CTR. FOR DEMOCRACY & TECH., STATE STUDENT PRIVACY LAW COMPENDIUM (Oct. 2016), https://cdt.org/files/2016/10/CDT-Stu-Priv-Compendium-FNL.pdf.

[51] Ganka Hadjipetrova & Hannah G. Poteat, *States Are Coming to the Fore of Privacy in the Digital Era*, 6 ABA LANDSLIDE 12, 14 (2014).

[52] *Id. See* California Online Privacy Protection Act of 2003, CAL. BUS. & PROF. §§ 22575–79 (2016).

[53] MASS. GEN. LAWS ch. 93H (2016); 201 MASS. CODE REGS. 17 (2016).

[54] NEV. REV. STAT. § 603A (2015).

[55] *See* ORACLE, MASSACHUSETTS DATA SECURITY LAW SIGNALS NEW CHALLENGES IN PERSONAL INFORMATION PROTECTION (2010), http://www.oracle.com/us/products/database/data-security-ma-201-wp-168633.pdf.

[56] See the Certification section of this chapter for a longer discussion of these factors.

[57] *See* Clearwater & Hughes, *supra* note 29, at 921–22.

[58] Digital Advertising Alliance, *DAA Self-Regulatory Principles*, http://digitaladvertisingalliance.org/principles (last visited Jan. 3, 2018); NETWORK ADVERTISING INITIATIVE, 2015 UPDATE TO THE NAI CODE OF CONDUCT (2015), http://www.networkadvertising.org/sites/default/files/NAI_Code15encr.pdf.

[59] W3C, *Tracking Protection Working Group*, https://www.w3.org/2011/tracking-protection/ (last visited Jan. 3, 2018).

privacy practices.[60] At times government agencies, such as the National Telecommunications and Information Administration (NTIA), have facilitated the development of industry best practices. Through its multistakeholder format, the NTIA has worked with industry and advocacy groups to create privacy best practices for facial recognition and unmanned aerial vehicles.[61] Other regulators have shaped industry norms by issuing practice guides or advisory regulatory interpretations, including the Federal Trade Commission (FTC) in the United States,[62] the Information Commissioner's Office (ICO) in the United Kingdom,[63] and the Article 29 Working Party in the European Union.[64]

Importantly, the privacy body of knowledge transcends the field of law and regulation and increasingly extends into organizational management, technology, and design. In fact, a recent survey of privacy professionals found that fewer than half of respondents had legal degrees, with the rest coming from a background in IT, information security, engineering, or business management.[65] The privacy governance skill-set of these privacy professionals is reflected in the IAPP's Certified Information Privacy Manager (CIPM) certification.[66] Professionals with this credential fulfill privacy program management roles within their organizations, operationalizing privacy into business processes using applied tools such as data inventories and risk assessments and integrating privacy considerations into product life cycles from the design through the manufacturing stages.[67]

The final set of unique competencies within the privacy body of knowledge are those held by privacy professionals with technical backgrounds. Whether they work on the design, acquisition, or administration of IT systems, technologists are increasingly required to understand privacy rules and operations.[68] Privacy professionals who are technologists develop and implement privacy-protective systems and techniques. Their body of knowledge therefore includes a technical understanding of methods of putting privacy policies into practice including encryption, de-identification, authentication, and obfuscation.[69] This set of skills is reflected in the IAPP's Certified Information Privacy Technologist (CIPT) certification.[70]

Professionals are trained masters of interpretation, applying their conceptual knowledge to solve problems they encounter in the real world.[71] As we have shown, privacy professionals draw from a vast body of legal, technological, and management knowledge in solving the problems they encounter. On top of its philosophical and sociological foundations, privacy professionals

---

[60] *See, e.g.,* ISO, ISO/IEC 27018:2014: *Code of Practice for Protection of Personally Identifiable Information (PII) in Public Clouds Acting as PII Processors* (2014), http://www.iso.org/iso/catalogue_detail.htm?csnumber=61498.

[61] For each of these reports, see Nat'l Telecomm. & Info. Admin., *Internet Policy Task Force: Privacy*, https://www.ntia.doc.gov/category/privacy (last updated June 21, 2016).

[62] *See, e.g.,* Fed. Trade Comm'n, Final Model Privacy Form under the Gramm-Leach-Bliley Act (2010); Fed. Trade Comm'n, Complying with Coppa: Frequently Asked Questions (2015); Fed. Trade Comm'n, Start with Security: A Guide for Business (2015).

[63] Information Commissioner's Office, Privacy Notices, Transparency and Control: A Code of Practice on Communicating Privacy Information to Individuals (2016).

[64] *See* Article 29 Working Party, *Opinions and Recommendations*, European Commission, http://ec.europa.eu/justice/data-protection/article-29/documentation/opinion-recommendation/index_en.htm (last visited Jan. 3, 2018).

[65] International Association of Privacy Professionals, 2015 Privacy Professionals Salary Survey 69 (2015), https://iapp.org/media/pdf/resource_center/2015_Salary-Survey_Full-Report_Final.pdf.

[66] International Association of Privacy Professionals, Privacy Manager Certification (2013), https://iapp.org/media/pdf/certification/CIPM_BoK.pdf.

[67] *Id.* Privacy Impact Assessment (PIA) is a primary example of the way in which privacy processes are operationalized. *See* David Wright & Paul de Hert, Privacy Impact Assessment 149–60 (2012).

[68] Travis Breaux, Introduction to IT Privacy: A Handbook for Technologists 2–3 (2014).

[69] *See id.*

[70] International Association of Privacy Professionals, IT Privacy Certification (2015), https://iapp.org/media/pdf/certification/CIPT_BoK.pdf.

[71] Susskind & Susskind, *supra* note 12, at 131.

have enhanced this body of knowledge with academic scholarship, legal precedent, regulatory principles, and industry best practices. This diverse set of legal, managerial, and technical competencies allows privacy professionals to specialize within their field, creating a wide range of sets of expertise. As technology and regulations develop, so too does the expertise of individual professionals, eventually shaping the body of knowledge of the profession.

Regulation

The second major characteristic of professions is regulatory recognition. Government regulation of professions is often noninterventionist, effectively transforming recognized professions into regulated monopolies. In exchange for exclusive purview over the professional activity, regulations require professions to standardize and institute credentialing programs. The Susskinds quote Donald Schön, a social scientist and scholar of professions at MIT, who writes, "In return for access to their extraordinary knowledge in matters of great human importance, society has granted [professionals] a mandate for social control in their fields of specialization, a high degree of autonomy in their practice, and a license to determine who shall assume the mantle of professional authority."[72] The recognition that government regulation provides is important to developing professions because it affords them official acknowledgment of their value, generates upward mobility for practitioners, and raises the public profile of their work.[73]

Recognition can occur directly, with laws establishing monopoly power for a profession, or indirectly with regulations that simply acknowledge the importance of a profession. In either case, the regulatory recognition of a profession leads to increased autonomy and legitimacy for professionals. Direct recognition often comes in the form of licensing requirements, which ensure quality while at the same time restricting competition, thereby rewarding professionals for their investment in their expertise.[74] Enhanced autonomy also allows professions to regulate themselves through professional associations. For example, in 1858 the United Kingdom established the General Medical Council with the goal of regulating medical practitioners by instituting a registration system and enforcing minimum training requirements.[75] This official government recognition established medical professionals apart from unqualified practitioners such as traditional healers or "traveling quacks," who had all been competing for the same clients.[76]

Indirect government recognition can lead to similar results, though without the additional benefit to a profession of establishing a legal monopoly over its professional activity. One example of this can be seen in the early profession of psychology. After World War I, the U.S. government began to recognize clinical psychologists due to their substantial contributions in classifying personnel for the war effort.[77] Unlike in the medical field, this did not come in the form of a government-established professional association. Instead, the U.S. government merely began to mandate the use of psychological assessments when hiring personnel, first in the military and then throughout the government.[78] This helped to transform psychology from a

---

[72] SUSSKIND & SUSSKIND, *supra* note 12, at 21, *quoting* DONALD A. SCHÖN, EDUCATING THE REFLECTIVE PRACTITIONER: TOWARD A NEW DESIGN FOR TEACHING AND LEARNING IN THE PROFESSIONS 7 (1987).

[73] *Id.* at 17.

[74] *See* LARSON, *supra* note 5, at 104–35 (1977).

[75] Ivan Weddington, *The Movement toward the Professionalization of Medicine*, 301 BMJ 688(1990).

[76] *Id.*

[77] DONALD S. NAPOLI, THE ARCHITECTS OF ADJUSTMENT: THE HISTORY OF THE PSYCHOLOGICAL PROFESSION IN THE UNITED STATES 11 (1981).

[78] *Id.* at 12–15.

purely academic discipline to an applied profession by establishing permanent positions for professional psychologists and providing them with a platform to prove their utility.[79]

The field of privacy has recently seen an increase in this latter type of indirect government recognition. As one example, much as in early clinical psychology, regulators have recognized the importance of the privacy profession by requiring organizations to hire or train privacy professionals. The U.S. federal government has recently proposed or issued multiple regulations that require the use of privacy professionals for adequate compliance.

Most notably, the Office of Management and Budget (OMB) recently released an update to Circular A-130, a document governing the management of information resources within the federal government.[80] The new rules require each federal agency to designate a Senior Agency Official for Privacy (SAOP) to oversee management of all personal information controlled by that agency. This embeds a position for at least one privacy professional in every federal agency, codifying the role of privacy professionals within the U.S. government. The SAOP in each federal agency is responsible for managing its "privacy continuous monitoring program," including "maintaining ongoing awareness of privacy risks and assessing privacy controls at a frequency sufficient to ensure compliance with applicable privacy requirements and to manage privacy risks."[81] This requirement is expected to result in the appointment of up to 500 new privacy leaders in the U.S. federal government alone.[82] A recent memorandum to agency heads reiterated that "agencies should recognize that privacy and security are independent and separate disciplines" that "raise distinct concerns and require different expertise and different approaches."[83] This reinforces the fact that privacy and security are distinct disciplines, requiring a different skillset and consequently separate staff. Also notable in the revised circular is the requirement that "all employees and contractors" of federal agencies receive information security and privacy awareness training.[84]

Government recognition of the privacy profession has also occurred on the international level. As discussed in the previous section, the OECD's 1980 guidelines on privacy and data transfers attempted to harmonize national laws between its member states by creating internationally recognized basic principles.[85] The OECD updated these guidelines in 2013, adding a recommendation that all data controllers implement "privacy management programs" to give effect to the guidelines and provide for "appropriate safeguards based on privacy risk assessment."[86] The OECD recommended that member countries implement the guidelines through "the adoption of complementary measures, including education and awareness raising, skills development, and the promotion of technical measures which help to protect privacy."[87] As the OECD explained, this was meant as a direct endorsement of the need for privacy

---

[79] *Id.*

[80] Office of Mgmt. & Budget, Exec. Office of the President, Circular No. A-130 (July 27, 2016), https://www.whitehouse.gov/sites/default/files/omb/assets/OMB/circulars/a130/a130revised.pdf. *See* Revision of OMB Circular No. A–130, "Managing Information as a Strategic Resource," 81 Fed. Reg. 49,689 (July 28, 2016), https://www.gpo.gov/fdsys/pkg/FR-2016-07-28/pdf/2016-17872.pdf.

[81] Circular No. A-130 at 33 (Definitions #59).

[82] Tony Scott et al., *Managing Federal Information as a Strategic Resource*, WHITE HOUSE BLOG (Jul. 27, 2016), https://www.whitehouse.gov/blog/2016/07/26/managing-federal-information-strategic-resource.

[83] Office of Management and Budget, Executive Office of the President, Memorandum No. M-16–24: Role and Designation of Senior Agency Officials for Privacy 2 (Sept. 15, 2016), https://www.whitehouse.gov/sites/default/files/omb/memoranda/2016/m_16_24_0.pdf.

[84] Circular No. A-130 at Appendix I.4.h.

[85] ORG. FOR ECON. COOPERATION & DEV., *supra* note 40.

[86] ORG. FOR ECON. COOPERATION & DEV., THE OECD PRIVACY FRAMEWORK, para. 15(a) (2013), http://www.oecd.org/sti/ieconomy/oecd_privacy_framework.pdf.

[87] *Id.* at para. 19(g).

professionals: "Privacy professionals play an increasingly important role in the implementation and administration of privacy management programs. ... Credential programs in data protection and privacy, as well as specialized education and professional development services may contribute to the development of the necessary skills."[88]

In its recently enacted Global Data Protection Regulation (GDPR), the European Union has gone a step further, requiring companies that control or process personal information to designate Data Protection Officers (DPOs) in charge of managing compliance with the regulation.[89] Under the GDPR, any entity that engages, as part of its "core activities," in "processing operations which ... require regular and systematic monitoring of data subjects on a large scale" must designate a DPO.[90] A DPO must be provided with the resources necessary to ensure compliance with the GDPR, as well as resources to "maintain his or her expert knowledge."[91] Estimates for the number of privacy professionals necessary to comply with this requirement range as high as 75,000.[92] The EU Data Protection Supervisor previously provided guidance on the DPO role when it was required only in government organizations, explaining that DPOs should have at least three years of "relevant experience," defined as "experience in implementing data protection requirements and experience within the appointing institution/organization resulting in knowledge of how it functions."[93] The guidance goes on to recommend that each DPO be "given the opportunity to develop his/her skills" through certification as a privacy professional.[94]

In addition to setting forth new regulations, governments can recognize privacy professionals through the enforcement of existing laws. The broad regulatory mandate of the FTC to bring enforcement actions against companies engaging in "unfair or deceptive acts or practices"[95] has led it to pursue more than 175 cases for privacy or security breaches, effectively becoming the primary regulator of privacy practices in the United States.[96] Due to these enforcement actions, companies often enter into consent decrees with the FTC, agreeing to abide by additional rules to settle allegations brought against them by the agency. In dozens of consent decrees imposed on companies, the FTC has explicitly endorsed the professional practice of privacy, requiring those companies to implement comprehensive privacy management programs.[97] For example, in its consent orders entered against Google in 2011[98] and Facebook in 2012,[99] the FTC explained:

> The privacy programs that the orders mandate must, at a minimum, contain certain controls and procedures, including: (1) the designation of personnel responsible for the privacy program; (2) a

---

[88] *Id.* at 32.

[89] 2016 O.J. (L 119) 55–56, Arts. 37–39.

[90] 2016 O.J. (L 119) 55, Art. 37(1)(b). In addition, a private entity must designate a DPO if its core activities consist of processing special categories of data (defined under Article 9) on a "large scale." Art. 37(1)(c). All public entities, except for courts, must also designate a DPO. Art. 37(1)(a).

[91] 2016 O.J. (L 119) 56, Art. 38(2).

[92] Rita Heimes & Sam Pfeifle, *Study: GDPR's Global Reach to Require at Least 75,000 DPOs Worldwide*, INTERNATIONAL ASSOCIATION OF PRIVACY PROFESSIONALS (Nov. 9, 2016), https://iapp.org/news/a/study-gdprs-global-reach-to-require-at-least-75000-dpos-worldwide/.

[93] European Data Protection Supervisor, Professional Standards for Data Protection Officers of the EU institutions and bodies working under Regulation (EC) 45/2001 4, fn. 2 (Oct. 14, 2010), http://ec.europa.eu/dataprotectionofficer/docs/dpo_standards_en.pdf.

[94] *Id.* at 5, describing IAPP certification as "the most relevant certification at this stage."

[95] 15 U.S.C. § 45(a)(1).

[96] KENNETH A. BAMBERGER & DEIRDRE K. MULLIGAN, PRIVACY ON THE GROUND: DRIVING CORPORATE BEHAVIOR IN THE UNITED STATES AND EUROPE 187–89 (2015); Daniel J. Solove & Woodrow Hartzog, *The FTC and the New Common Law of Privacy*, 114 COLUM. L. REV. 583, 605 (2014).

[97] FED. TRADE COMM'N, PROTECTING CONSUMER PRIVACY IN AN ERA OF RAPID CHANGE 31 (2012).

[98] Fed. Trade Comm'n, Decision and Order, In the Matter of Google Inc., FTC Docket No. C-4336 (Oct. 24, 2011).

[99] Fed. Trade Comm'n, Decision and Order, In the Matter of Facebook, Inc., FTC Docket No. C-4365 (July 27, 2012).

risk assessment that, at a minimum, addresses employee training and management and product design and development; (3) the implementation of controls designed to address the risks identified; (4) appropriate oversight of service providers; and (5) evaluation and adjustment of the privacy program in light of regular testing and monitoring.[100]

Furthermore, both orders require the companies to engage a "qualified, objective, independent, third-party professional, who uses procedures and standards generally accepted in the profession" to conduct biennial assessments of the ordered comprehensive privacy programs over a period of two decades.[101] The FTC must approve each person hired to conduct these assessments and the assessor must have "a minimum of three years of experience in the field of privacy and data protection."[102] Through Freedom of Information Act (FOIA) requests, the privacy advocacy group EPIC gained access to portions of these assessments, which show that the public accounting firm PwC acted as the initial assessor of Google's comprehensive privacy program.[103] In its assessment, PwC explains that its "privacy compliance, information security, and risk management professionals hold leadership positions in many organizations that define privacy leading practices and standards."[104]

The Federal Communications Commission (FCC) has recognized, through both regulatory and enforcement actions, the importance of hiring – and properly training – privacy professionals. Though later rescinded through Congressional action, the FCC's 2016 Broadband Privacy Order encouraged privacy training for employees of U.S. broadband providers.[105] The regulation would have required broadband Internet service providers to "take reasonable measures to secure" customer proprietary information (PI) and provided guidance for the types of measures that count as "reasonable."[106] As part of this guidance, the FCC recommended that each broadband provider designate "an official responsible for its privacy practices," focus on "training employees and contractors on the proper handling of customer PI," and, to that end, "seek out expert guidance and best practices on the design and implementation of efficacious training programs."[107] The FCC has also issued consent orders under its enforcement authority requiring companies to improve their privacy and security practices as a result of a data breach. For example, in an order from 2015, the FCC required AT&T to

> develop and implement a compliance plan to ensure appropriate processes and procedures are incorporated into AT&T's business practices to protect consumers against similar data breaches in the future. In particular, AT&T will be required to improve its privacy and data security practices by appointing a senior compliance manager who is privacy certified, conducting a privacy risk assessment, implementing an information security program, preparing an appropriate compliance manual, and regularly training employees on the company's privacy policies and the applicable privacy legal authorities.[108]

---

[100] Fed. Trade Comm'n, *supra* note 97, at 31.

[101] In the Matter of Google, *supra* note 98, at Part IV; In the Matter of Facebook, *supra* note 99, at Part V.

[102] *Id.*

[103] Dione J. Stearns, Assistant General Counsel, *Federal Trade Commission, FOIA-2012–01156 Re: Google's Initial Privacy Assessment,* Elec. Privacy Info. Ctr. (Sept. 25, 2012), https://epic.org/privacy/ftc/googlebuzz/FTC-Initial-Assessment-09–26-12.pdf.

[104] *Id.*

[105] Fed. Communications Comm'n, Report and Order, *Protecting the Privacy of Customers of Broadband and Other Telecommunications Services,* WC Docket No. 16–106 (Oct. 27, 2016), *rescinded by* Act of Apr. 3, 2017, Pub. L. No. 115-22.

[106] *Id.* at paras. 238–55.

[107] *Id.* at para. 252.

[108] Fed. Communications Comm'n, *News Release: AT&T to Pay $25 Million to Settle Consumer Privacy Investigation* (April 8, 2015), https://www.fcc.gov/document/att-pay-25m-settle-investigation-three-data-breaches-0.

Over the past two decades, governments have increasingly provided an official seal of recognition to the role of the privacy professional, at times even regulating this role directly. Certain trends are apparent in government practice, including requirements for the designation of a single officer with final reporting authority as to privacy practices – whether in European companies or U.S. government agencies. Regulations have also required other privacy-specific obligations, such as the completion of risk assessments or implementation of comprehensive privacy programs. As it has with other professions before, government recognition is leading to increased autonomy for privacy professionals, legitimizing their roles and enabling them to better advocate for needed resources.[109]

However, as Berkeley professors Kenneth Bamberger and Deirdre Mulligan found in their extensive qualitative research into the practice of privacy in the United States and Europe, specific regulations often "played only a limited role in animating corporate processes and practices" among privacy professionals.[110] Instead, best practices and industry norms, shared through professional associations and informal information sharing, have driven much of the growth of the privacy profession. These factors are discussed further in the following sections.

Credentials and Self-Regulation

The third characteristic the Susskinds identify in professions is the use of credentials.[111] It is not enough for an individual to have relevant knowledge and expertise in a professional field. To gain government and professional recognition of their competence to practice, their knowledge and abilities must also be certified, usually after extensive training followed by some form of standardized testing. In addition, professions often require evidence of good character in order to admit new members to their ranks, whether by means of background checks, recommendations, or academic records. Control over credentialing also implies the ability of professions to decertify members whose practices fall outside the accepted standards of the profession.

A professional typically earns his or her first required credential by completing a formal course of education through an accredited institution. In the United States, many professions require a four-year bachelor's degree plus a graduate degree: lawyers go to law school, doctors to medical school. This has not always been the case. The medical field, once lacking in standardized education requirements, took a large leap toward professionalization with the publication of the Flexner Report in 1910, which concluded that "a vast army of men is admitted to the profession and practice of medicine who are untrained in science fundamental to the profession."[112] Following the recommendations of the report, dozens of medical schools that fell short of its recommendations had to be closed.[113] Many other professions still require only a four-year degree with a certain amount of relevant coursework. For example,

[109] OMB Circular A-130 provides a good example of this legitimizing effect. *See* Angelique Carson, *U.S. Gov't Is Changing How It Does Privacy*, IAPP: THE PRIVACY ADVISOR (Sept. 27, 2016), https://iapp.org/news/a/u-s-govt-is-changing-how-it-does-privacy-x/.

[110] BAMBERGER & MULLIGAN, *supra* note 96, at 60.

[111] SUSSKIND & SUSSKIND, *supra* note 14, at 16.

[112] ABRAHAM FLEXNER, MEDICAL EDUCATION IN THE UNITED STATES AND CANADA, x (1910), http://archive.carnegiefoundation.org/pdfs/elibrary/Carnegie_Flexner_Report.pdf.

[113] JENNY SUTCLIFFE & NANCY DUIN, A HISTORY OF MEDICINE 89 (1992).

the field of accounting usually requires 150 hours of coursework – often completed in five years of study – but only an undergraduate degree.[114]

Separate from academic degrees, most professions also require an additional credential: certification through a professional body, often through the completion of a standardized exam. Certification ensures that those entering the profession in fact have the requisite qualifications, competencies, and knowledge to practice and are endorsed by a group of their peers.[115] This helps to unify professional practice, which in turn increases public trust in the profession.[116] Two prime examples of high-stakes certification tests are the legal and medical professions. In the United States, where the practice of law is regulated by individual state courts, lawyers take arduous bar exams after graduating from law school in order to determine their admission to practice.[117] Similarly, once doctors have completed their residency requirements, they are sponsored by a board in their chosen specialty to take a board examination, which they must pass in order to practice medicine.[118] Most other professions have certification programs "created, sponsored, or affiliated with professional associations and trade organizations interested in raising standards," though many professions, including privacy, do not require a particular certification as a prerequisite to practice.[119]

The privacy profession includes practitioners from a variety of educational backgrounds. Roughly 40 percent of privacy professionals have legal degrees, while others come from backgrounds in technology or business.[120] As the profession has grown, privacy experts have developed certifications to help regulate entry into the profession. Professional associations such as the IAPP manage such certifications, providing the structure on which to grow norms and professional practices. In their interviews with leading privacy managers, Bamberger and Mulligan find a great appreciation for the role that associations have played in encouraging the professionalization of privacy.[121] Those interviewed cited the importance of associations in their practice for developing best practices, sharing information across firms, and responding quickly and uniformly to changing regulation.[122]

In 2016, a survey of privacy professionals showed that 54 percent of respondents hold certifications from the IAPP.[123] Most other respondents hold other professional certifications, with only 20 percent reporting that they lack a certification beyond their educational degree.[124] Nearly 12,000 IAPP members have been certified under the association's various bodies of knowledge. These include the Certified Information Privacy Professional (CIPP) program, which covers privacy laws and regulations and has branched out to feature specializations in the United States (CIPP/US), European Union (CIPP/E), Canada (CIPP/C), Asia (CIPP/A), and U.S. government (CIPP/G); the Certified Information Privacy Manager (CIPM) program, which presents professionals with the business management practices that allow organizations to operationalize privacy standards in privacy programs on the ground; and the Certified

---

[114] Nat'l Ass'n of State Boards of Accountancy, Draft: Education and Licensure Requirements for Certified Public Accountants 4 (July 2008), https://media.nasba.org/files/2011/03/120_150_Hour_Education_Paper-Jul08.pdf.

[115] Phillip M. Harris, The Guide to National Professional Certification Programs xvii–xviii (2001).

[116] Id.

[117] California Bar Examination: Information and History, The State Bar of California, http://admissions.calbar.ca.gov/Portals/4/documents/Bar-Exam-Info-History.pdf (last visited Oct. 26, 2016).

[118] Harvard Medical School, Harvard Medical School Family Health Guide 18 (2005).

[119] Phillip M. Harris, supra note 115, at xviii.

[120] International Association of Privacy Professionals, supra note 65, at 69.

[121] Bamberger & Mulligan, supra note 96, at 74–75.

[122] Id.

[123] International Association of Privacy Professionals & EY, supra note 1, at 5–6.

[124] Id.

Information Privacy Technologist (CIPT) program, which trains technologists who are charged with securing data privacy at all stages of IT product and service lifecycles.

The CIPM, CIPP/E, CIPP/US, and CIPT credentials have been accredited by the American National Standards Institute (ANSI) under the International Organization for Standardization's (ISO) standard 17024: 2012, which assesses and accredits certification programs that meet rigorous criteria of impartiality, timeliness, and job relevance.[125] In an article published in *International Data Protection Law*, an Oxford University Press journal, in 2014, University of Tilburg scholar Eric Lachaud explored a variety of qualifications, training, and certification requirements for the DPO role under the GDPR. Lachaud concluded that the IAPP's certification scheme is best suited to address the multilayered job requirements of privacy and data protection professionals. Referring to article numbers in the European Commission proposal in place at the time, he stated, "Brought together, the schemes proposed by the IAPP are those that best fit the requirements of the GDPR concerning DPOs. The CIPM fulfills the requirements of Article 37 by attesting to the theoretical capacities of candidates to lead a data protection policy, while the CIPP/E attests to the comprehensive knowledge that a candidate must have of the European legal framework according to Article 35(5)."[126]

In addition to obtaining professional certifications, professionals are also expected to keep their knowledge up to date with continued training on new developments in their field. As the Susskinds put it, "It is the role of the professionals to curate the knowledge over which they have mastery, on behalf of their professions and the recipients of their services."[127] To encourage such continual advancement of knowledge, professions usually have strong academic branches and professional associations, both of which work to train new professionals and extend the collective knowledge of the profession through academic journals and conferences. In addition, professional governing bodies often require professionals certified within their ranks to complete continuing education in order to maintain their professional status.[128] For example, lawyers and doctors are required to earn a certain number of continuing education credits to retain good standing in their profession. Similarly, the IAPP requires all privacy professionals it certifies to maintain their certification with at least twenty hours of continuing education credits every two years. Privacy professionals can earn such credits by attending conferences and Web-conferences, participating in online training, or other demonstrated involvement with the field.[129]

Credentialing provides professions such as privacy a vital method of regulating the behavior of their members. While privacy professionals have a diverse set of formal educational backgrounds, their involvement in professional associations helps to standardize practices across the profession. Though certification is not a professional requirement in privacy, more than half of all privacy professionals currently hold at least one certification. As the ranks of the privacy profession continue to grow, the trend toward certification and other means of standardizing practice is likely to continue.

---

[125] Jennifer Saunders, *IAPP Certifications Granted ANSI Accreditation under International ISO Standard*, IAPP: THE PRIVACY ADVISOR (Aug. 11, 2015), https://iapp.org/news/a/iapp-certifications-granted-ansi-accreditation-under-international-iso-standard/; Elizabeth Gasiorowski-Denis, *New and Improved ISO/IEC 17024 Standard for Personnel Certification Programmes*, ISO (July 24, 2012), http://www.iso.org/iso/home/news_index/news_archive/news.htm?refid=Ref1625.

[126] Eric Lachaud, *Should the DPO Be Certified?*, 4(3) INT'L DATA PRIVACY L. 189, 198 (2014).

[127] SUSSKIND & SUSSKIND, *supra* note 14, at 15.

[128] Rosemary M. Lysaght & James W. Altschuld, *Beyond Initial Certification: The Assessment and Maintenance of Competency in Professions*, 23 EVALUATION & PROGRAM PLANNING 95, 101 (2000).

[129] International Association of Privacy Professionals, *Maintaining Your Certification*, https://iapp.org/certify/cpe/ (last visited Jan. 3, 2018).

Norms and Ethics

Ethical codes are the basis of the fourth and final feature of professions the Susskinds identified. They suggest that professionals are "bound by a common set of values over and above any formal regulations that apply to them."[130] These values often include behavioral traits such as "honesty, trustworthiness, and commitment to serving and reassuring others."[131] Many professionals are drawn to their occupation by a commitment to uphold these values, while "serving the public good, fulfilling certain social responsibilities, ensuring access to their services, and even some degree of altruism."[132]

Famously, the medical profession can trace its guiding ethical principles to the Hippocratic Oath – in part, "primum non nocere," or "first do no harm"– initially written more than two millennia ago.[133] Though it cannot claim such a long history, the privacy profession is similarly guided by the foundational ethical principles implied by a "right to privacy." However, unlike medicine, the practice of privacy is yet to uniformly embrace a single client-centered moral principle. Privacy professionals encounter ethical questions frequently, by the very nature of their work, but distilling these choices into a uniform privacy ethics has proven difficult.[134] In the European Union, privacy has been recognized as a fundamental human right since its inclusion as Article 8 of the European Convention for the Protection of Human Rights and Fundamental Freedoms.[135] Thus the practice of privacy in Europe is often framed in terms of the goal of protecting these individual rights.[136] In contrast, though privacy is protected from government intrusion by the Fourth Amendment to the U.S. Constitution, privacy professionals in the United States are more likely to frame their work in terms of building "consumer trust" than pursuing a constitutional ideal of morality.[137]

Beyond these generalized ethical values that inspire professionals to behave ethically, professions also embrace explicit ethical codes of conduct. Professional ethical codes serve several important functions: they make clear that professionals are responsible not only for the product of their labor but also for the consequences of their actions; they serve as a backup to legal rules; they inform the public about risks and consequences; and they remind professionals that they belong to a single group with a uniform baseline of beliefs.[138] More directly, codes of conduct guide professional practice, drawing clear lines between acceptable and unacceptable behaviors.

Professional associations can play an important role in bringing about these standardized codes of ethical mores. As with the other steps in its professionalization, the medical field can trace the development of standardized ethical codes of conduct to medical associations. In 1948, the World Medical Association, which took responsibility for establishing ethical guidelines for the medical profession, first adopted a revised version of the Hippocratic Oath, recommending

---

[130] SUSSKIND & SUSSKIND, *supra* note 14, at 17.

[131] *Id.* at 18.

[132] *Id.*

[133] Emil Disckstein, Jonathon Erlen, & Judith A. Erlen, *Ethical Principles Contained in Currently Professed Medical Oaths*, 66 ACADEMIC MED. 622 (1991).

[134] *See* LUCIANO FLORIDI, THE ETHICS OF INFORMATION (2015) (arguing that establishing processes to weigh the ethics of data usage on a case by case basis is important because individual privacy must sometimes give way to other social goods).

[135] Convention for the Protection of Human Rights and Fundamental Freedoms, Nov. 4. 1950, art. 8, 213 U.N.T.S. 221, 230 (entered into force Sept. 3, 1953).

[136] For an exploration of the importance of the fundamental right to privacy to the practice of privacy in Germany and France, see BAMBERGER & MULLIGAN, *supra* note 96, at 89, 129.

[137] BAMBERGER & MULLIGAN, *supra* note 96, at 184–86.

[138] KARL DE LEEUW & JAN BERGSTRA, THE HISTORY OF INFORMATION SECURITY: A COMPREHENSIVE HANDBOOK 755 (2007), *citing* JACQUES J. BERLEUR, ETHICS OF COMPUTING: CODES, SPACES FOR DISCUSSION AND LAW (1996).

that its member medical schools and faculties adopt the oath as part of their training, a practice that continues to this day.[139] Associations may also require members to abide by certain codes of conduct in order to maintain their continued membership, ensuring that the work of member professionals complies "with clearly stated standards of conduct and ethical codes."[140] In the United Kingdom, the same law that established the General Medical Council gave the doctors who ran the Council the power to remove any of their fellow medical practitioners from the official register if they judged them guilty of "infamous conduct in any professional respect."[141]

Though a professional association is by no means synonymous with its profession, it "indicates the maturity of the professional project" and often has a vested interest in policing the conduct of its members.[142] The accounting profession provides a good example of a professional association that has created safeguards to ensure ethical conduct on the part of its members. The International Federation of Accountants – a consortium of accounting organizations around the world representing more than three million members – funds an independent standards-setting board that publishes detailed ethical guidelines for the profession, updated every few years.[143] These guidelines include a set of fundamental principles, which act as a minimum set of standards that member institutions are required to enforce through monitoring and disciplinary procedures as well as third-party auditing.[144]

Lawyers, too, are bound by a code of professional ethics enforced by professional associations. In the United States, the American Bar Association (ABA) first adopted the Canons of Professional Ethics in 1908, attempting to establish a unified set of standards of professional responsibility.[145] Over the years, the ABA updated these rules many times, but most significantly in 1983, after a six-year study by a specially established commission.[146] The new Model Rules of Professional Conduct have been adopted by all fifty states and the District of Columbia. Along with the published opinions of the ABA's Standing Committee on Ethics and Professional Responsibility, the model rules are used as guidance for determining attorney misconduct.[147] These rules include provisions on conflicts of interest, confidentiality, and proper communications; regulate attorney duties and behavior in various contexts; and prohibit practices such as self-dealing and dishonesty.[148]

Professionals in fields such as medicine, accounting, and law, rely on professional codes of conduct to determine their behavior vis-à-vis their clients. But in the privacy profession, ethical questions are often framed in relation to consumers, who are typically not the direct clients of a privacy professional. Thus, ethics remains a nascent aspect of the privacy profession, though some progress has been made in establishing codes of conduct that guide ethical decision making in privacy. For example, the Cybersecurity Credentials Collaborative (C3), a consortium of professional cybersecurity associations, adopted the Unified Framework of Professional

---

[139] World Medical Association, *History*, https://www.wma.net/who-we-are/history/ (last visited Jan. 3, 2018).

[140] SUSSKIND & SUSSKIND, *supra* note 12, at 17.

[141] Weddington, *supra* note 75, at 689.

[142] LARSON, *supra* note 5, at 5.

[143] INTERNATIONAL ETHICS STANDARDS BOARD FOR ACCOUNTANTS, HANDBOOK OF THE CODE OF ETHICS FOR PROFESSIONAL ACCOUNTANTS 2 (2016).

[144] *Id.* at § 100.5. The fundamental principles of the accounting profession are integrity, professional competence and due care, confidentiality, and professional behavior. *Id.*

[145] American Bar Association, *Model Rules of Professional Conduct: Preface*, http://www.americanbar.org/groups/profes sional_responsibility/publications/model_rules_of_professional_conduct/model_rules_of_professional_conduct_pref ace.html (last visited Jan. 3, 2018).

[146] *Id.*

[147] *Id.*

[148] *Id.*

Ethics for Security Professionals.[149] Through the framework, C3 member associations agree to require individuals certified through their professional certifications to agree to specific standards of integrity, objectivity, confidentiality, and professional competence.[150] As a member of this group, the IAPP has adapted this code of conduct beyond the cybersecurity context, creating a professional code that every privacy professional must sign before completing a certification.[151]

Creating enforceable ethical standards is the primary remaining challenge for privacy as it continues to professionalize. Though privacy professionals often share common values, and are increasingly subject to professional codes of conduct of associations or other professions, they still lack an enforceable unifying ethical code of conduct specific to the privacy profession as such, as distinct from, for example, legal ethics for privacy lawyers.[152] The development of such a code of ethics depends in part on other changes to the profession, including stronger regulations that would create the sort of professional monopoly that enjoys authority to regulate the behavior of its members. Until that time, the privacy profession will continue to rely on strengthening norms and best practices.

A PROFESSION FOR THE DIGITAL AGE:
INTERDISCIPLINARY AND INTERNATIONAL

Despite its currently vigorous growth, the profession of privacy did not exist until the final decade of the twentieth century. Companies, governments, and nonprofits only began to bake privacy practices into organizational culture as they became aware of the legal, operational, and reputational risks of ignoring the privacy of citizens, consumers, and employees. Organizations increasingly found that they needed a single officer – a privacy professional – to ensure that their privacy practices fell within the norms and best practices of the field and to guarantee that other employees were aware of privacy risks.[153] To fill this need, the privacy profession developed its own body of knowledge, based on the ever-growing body of privacy laws, regulations, and best practices, as well as organizational governance mechanisms and technological innovations. With governments around the world recognizing, and sometimes regulating, the role of the privacy officer, the position has been cemented into standard organizational structures. Thus, privacy has professionalized, developing certification regimes, codes of conduct, and professional associations to further organize its practice.

As in other professions, privacy professionals have entered into a social contract with those they serve. Richard and Daniel Susskind describe this contract between professions and society in terms of a "grand bargain":[154]

> In acknowledgment of and in return for their expertise, experience, and judgment, which they are expected to apply in delivering affordable, accessible, up-to-date, reassuring, and reliable services, and on the understanding that they will curate and update their knowledge and methods, train their members, set and enforce standards for the quality of their work, and that

---

[149] Cybersecurity Credentials Collaborative (C3), *Ethics*, http://www.cybersecuritycc.org/ (last visited Jan. 3, 2018).

[150] *Id.*

[151] International Association of Privacy Professionals, IAPP Privacy Certification Candidate Handbook 33 (2015), https://iapp.org/media/pdf/certification/IAPP_Privacy_Certification_Candidate_Handbook.pdf.

[152] Notably, privacy lawyers are subject to the Model Rules of Professional Conduct. The IAPP is currently working with the ABA to establish an authorized Privacy Law accreditation, which would require the passage of a privacy ethics exam. *See* Debra Cassens Weiss, *ABA House Is Asked to Accredit Program that Certifies Lawyers as Privacy Law Specialists*, ABA J. (Nov. 15, 2016), http://www.abajournal.com/news/article/groups_asks_aba_house_to_accredit_program_that_certifies_lawyers_as_privacy/.

[153] *See* Bamberger & Mulligan, *supra* note 96, at 76.

[154] Susskind & Susskind, *supra* note 14, at 22.

they will only admit appropriately qualified individuals into their ranks, and that they will always act honestly, in good faith, putting the interests of clients ahead of their own, we (society) place our trust in the professions in granting them exclusivity over a wide range of socially significant services and activities, by paying them a fair wage, by conferring upon them independence, autonomy, rights of self-determination, and by according them respect and status.

The Susskinds explore this "grand bargain" and the effects it has on our current society – asking whether it is the optimal way to organize the expertise of professions in a digital economy marked by labor market disruptions and rapid change.[155] Though for now the professions are our "current solution to the challenge in society of supporting people who need access to practical expertise," the Susskinds predict that this will soon change as knowledge becomes increasingly distributed and distributable.[156]

In contrast to older vocations, however, the privacy profession is itself a product of the information age. It is markedly different from other professions that the Susskinds explore in embodying two traits: it is inherently *interdisciplinary* and *international*. Combining knowledge and skills that are interdisciplinary, spanning laws and ethics, management and technology, the privacy profession is well situated to respond to these predicted shifts in the distribution of knowledge. Though privacy professionals craft solutions based on their expert knowledge, their focus more often is on distributing knowledge – implementing privacy decisional tools such as privacy impact assessments, guideline documents, and privacy audits throughout their organizations.[157] Importantly, privacy professionals impart guidance and advice to policymakers, decision makers and individual consumers as they tackle the challenges of protecting personal information in an age of data abundance. The privacy profession is thus already focused on distribution of expertise, with privacy professionals integrating privacy into corporate decision-making, product design, business processes, and information technology systems.[158] This does not make the privacy profession less professional, but simply more in tune with the shifting needs of a connected society.

The international scope of the privacy profession has also prepared it for the future. While cultural perceptions of privacy continue to differ, regulations and management practices around the world are converging, shaping privacy into an increasingly unified global practice. The rise of the global data economy, with commerce and communication less impeded by national borders, has contributed to this trend.[159] But, early in the development of the profession, privacy professionals also intentionally embraced an international focus. For example, the International Conference of Data Protection and Privacy Commissioners (ICDPPC) first met in 1979 and now coordinates the efforts of 110 privacy regulators around the world through its annual conference.[160] Additional conferences with an international reach, hosted by the IAPP and

---

[155] *See* Martin Kenney & John Zysman, *The Rise of the Platform Economy*, Issues Sci. & Tech. 61 (Spring 2016) (describing implications of the new "platform economy" for labor, business, and society); Erik Brynjolfsson & Andrew McAfee, The Second Machine Age: Work, Progress, and Prosperity in a Time of Brilliant Technologies (2014) (exploring solutions to prepare society for the new normal).

[156] Susskind & Susskind, *supra* note 14, at 250.

[157] Bamberger & Mulligan, *supra* note 96, at 101.

[158] *Id.* at 32.

[159] *See* Organization for Economic Cooperation and Development, *Dismantling the Barriers to Global Electronic Commerce* (Oct. 16, 1997), http://www.oecd.org/sti/ieconomy/dismantlingthebarrierstoglobalelectroniccommerce.htm; Asia-Pacific Economic Cooperation, APEC Privacy Framework (2005).

[160] International Conference of Data Protection and Privacy Commissioners, *History of the Conference*, https://icdppc .org/the-conference-and-executive-committee/history-of-the-conference/ (last visited Nov. 26, 2016). For a thorough analysis of the history of ICDPPC resolutions, see Calli Schroeder, *When the World's DPAs Get Together: Resolutions of the ICDPPC*, International Association of Privacy Professionals (Nov. 28, 2017), https://iapp.org/news/a/ when-the-worlds-dpas-get-together-resolutions-of-the-icdppc/.

other organizations, help to encourage knowledge sharing and a cross-border sense of community on all levels of the privacy profession.[161]

The emergence and growth of the privacy profession reflects the need of public and private sector organizations in all sectors of the economy all over the world to develop and implement effective information governance, including data classification, de-identification, data minimization, and policies around data collection, processing, retention, and use. Meaningful privacy protection depends on integrating varied understandings of privacy impacts into each organization's value structure and decision-making. Hiring privacy professionals at all levels of an organization is necessary to fulfill this goal, but the profession must also be ready to enhance the level of trust that organizations – and society – will place in innovative technologies and new business models. To that end, the privacy profession must focus on professionalism, by strengthening codes of conduct and standardizing practices while continuing to celebrate diverse cultural perspectives and organizational norms.

---

[161] BAMBERGER & MULLIGAN, *supra* note 96, at 80.

23

Privacy Statements

Purposes, Requirements, and Best Practices

Mike Hintze

It's popular (and easy) to criticize privacy statements. They are full of legalese and technical jargon. They are unclear. They don't have enough detail. They are too long. Nobody reads them. While some critiques are valid, others reflect a misunderstanding of what a privacy statement can and must accomplish.

Some shortcomings of privacy statements can be addressed through careful and informed drafting. But while drafting a privacy statement may be considered by some to be one of the most basic tasks of a privacy professional, doing it well is no simple matter. One must understand and reconcile a host of statutory and self-regulatory obligations. One must consider different audiences who may read the statement from different perspectives. One must balance pressures to make the statement simple and readable against pressures to make it comprehensive and detailed. A mistake can form the basis for an FTC deception claim. And individual pieces can be taken out of context and spun into public relations debacles.

This chapter explores the art of crafting a privacy statement. It explains the multiple purposes of a privacy statement. It lists and discusses the many elements included in a privacy statement – some required by law, and others based on an organization's objectives. Finally, it describes different approaches to drafting privacy statements and suggests best practices based on a more complete understanding of a privacy statement's purposes and audiences.

PART I: WHAT IS A PRIVACY STATEMENT?

A privacy statement is primarily a legal document. It fulfils numerous, specific legal requirements imposed by a growing number of privacy laws and regulations worldwide. Conversely, it creates legal obligations, since inaccuracies in a privacy statement can lead to legal liability.

Privacy statement obligations are designed to advance both individual and broader objectives. At the individual level, privacy statements can inform individual users about an organization's practices with regard to data and privacy. Privacy statements can play a role in the need to obtain user consent for data collection and use activities. Under most privacy laws that require consent for certain types of data collection or use, that consent must be informed. A privacy statement that contains sufficient detail to help individuals make informed consent decisions can play a critical role in meeting those legal obligations.

Privacy statements also play broader roles in creating transparency and accountability regarding an organization's practices. Forcing organizations to publicly articulate their practices creates incentives for those organizations to adopt practices they are not embarrassed to describe.

It also amplifies the need to develop internal organizational processes to track and document what data the organization collects and how it uses that data. And it gives regulators a hook to hold organizations accountable for the representations they make.

Because a privacy statement is typically the primary document explaining an organization's privacy-related practices, it is also the place where the organization conveys whatever additional messaging it wants to (beyond what it is legally required to say). It's the place where the organization can tell its privacy story.

Determining how best to fulfil each of these purposes requires an understanding of the audiences of a privacy statement. Individual consumers are just one audience, and the one least likely to read privacy statements. On the other hand, journalists, advocates, regulators, and others are more likely to read them, and to take action based on them. Thus, a well-crafted privacy statement must take into account these different audiences and the information and story it wishes to convey to each of them.

PART II: WHAT GOES INTO A PRIVACY STATEMENT?

A. *Overview*

There are three key tasks you must achieve to produce a complete privacy statement:

1. Get the facts.
2. Meet your legal obligations.
3. Tell your story.

Large parts of a privacy statement consist of factual descriptions of what the organization does: what data it collects and how, how that data is used, whether and with whom the data is shared, how long the data is retained, etc. Getting a complete and accurate understanding of the relevant facts may be the most important and challenging aspect of creating a privacy statement. A privacy statement that contains factual inaccuracies provides an easy target for regulators and others.

A privacy statement must also meet all applicable legal requirements. These requirements largely come from privacy statutes, but they can also come from self-regulatory programs,[1] contractual obligations, and other sources. An organization subject to European privacy law must meet the notice requirements of the 1995 Privacy Directive and will soon need to meet the requirements of the General Data Protection Directive. An organization that owns or operates a commercial website or online service that collects personal information from a California resident must meet the requirements of the California Online Privacy Protection Act. Depending on the nature of the company and its business, sectoral privacy laws can impose additional privacy statement requirements.[2] Collecting information from children can trigger additional requirements.[3] A company that operates globally, or that offers products and services

---

[1] For example, the TRUSTe privacy seal program requirements include eighteen items that must be included in a privacy statement. See TRUSTe Enterprise Privacy Certification Standards (revised on: March 12, 2015), available at https://www.truste.com/privacy-certification-standards/program-requirements/. Companies involved in online targeted advertising may choose, or find themselves contractually bound, to comply with the requirements of the Network Advertising Initiative (NAI) and/or Digital Advertising Alliance (DAA).

[2] See, e.g., the Gramm-Leach-Bliley (GLBA) Act, 15 U.S.C. § 6801 (applies to a broadly-defined set of financial institutions), and the Health Insurance Portability and Accountability Act of 1996 (HIPAA), 42 U.S.C. § 1306 (applies to health plans, health care clearinghouses, health care providers, and business associates of covered entities).

[3] In the United States, the Children's Online Privacy Protection Act (COPPA), 15 U.S.C. § 6501.

that are available globally, can be subject to requirements stemming from dozens of privacy statutes and other sources from around the world.

Many organizations choose to go beyond baseline legal compliance in terms of privacy protections. For those organizations, the privacy statement is one place it can tout those practices to seek a competitive advantage, increase brand loyalty, or simply make its customers feel good about its products. Often, a privacy statement will be used to tell readers not just *what* data is collected and *how* it is used, but also *why* the organization collects and uses that data and how the data collection and use provide value to the individual and/or society. Privacy statements provide an opportunity for an organization to tell its story and to communicate its values.

There is one additional point to keep in mind when determining the content to include in a privacy statement. The facts will be different for every organization and for every product or service. Every organization should tell its own story. The specific legal obligations often will be different from organization to organization (as will the risk tolerance at play in interpreting those obligations). There may be small bits of boilerplate language that could be used across different privacy statements. And looking to other statements for examples and inspiration can be helpful. But for the bulk of a privacy statement, the text cannot simply be copied from other privacy statements. Crafting a good privacy statement involves drafting and building a unique document from the ground up.

B. *Common Legal Requirements*

The following surveys the elements commonly required to be included in a privacy statement.

1. *The Identity of the Data Controller*

The privacy statement must identify the entity or entities that ultimately own the data and/or determine how the data will be used.[4] For example, if a vendor hosts a website on behalf of the data controller, the privacy statement for that website must identify the controller rather than (or in addition to) the vendor. This also means that if a product or service is offered under the brand of a wholly owned and controlled subsidiary, the privacy statement typically should identify the controlling corporate parent. Thus, in the context of an acquisition, the acquired company's privacy statement(s) should be updated to disclose the identity of the new corporate parent.

2. *What Data Is Collected or Otherwise Obtained*

The privacy statement must describe the categories of personal data collected or obtained.[5] Obviously, for an organization that collects many different types of data, such a disclosure could be quite lengthy. Often, a long list of data collected, by itself and without context, can appear overly invasive. Thus, it may be better to combine the disclosures of *what* data is collected with descriptions of *why* it is collected and *how* it will be used.

3. *How Data Is Collected or Obtained*

A privacy statement should also describe how data is collected.[6] Where data is requested from an individual and is explicitly provided, such as in a web form, how the data is collected is self-

---

[4] 1995 EU Data Protection Directive, Article 10(a) ("the identity of the controller and of his representative, if any").

[5] California Business and Professions Code § 22575(b), EU General Data Protection Regulation (GDPR) Articles 14(1)(d) and 15(1)(b).

[6] See, e.g., Australian Privacy Act 1988, APP 1.

evident. But increasingly, the bulk of the data collected about individuals is collected through a variety of passive means, and/or is acquired from third parties.

4. *Whether Providing Data Is Required and the Consequences of Not Providing Data*

European privacy rules require privacy statements to state whether providing data is mandatory, as well as stating the consequences of not providing data.[7] In practice, these disclosures tend to be quite general. For example, a privacy statement might declare that some services require a certain amount of data to function correctly, and that refusal to provide that data means that the person will not be able to use the service.

5. *Third-Party Sources of Data*

Where personal data is obtained from a source other than the data subject, the privacy statement must describe the source(s) from which the personal data originate, and if applicable, state whether data comes from publicly accessible sources.[8] While it remains unclear whether European regulators will interpret this provision to require the disclosure of every individual third-party source of data, organizations will at least need to list categories of third-party data sources (data brokers, social networks, other partners, public sources, etc.), perhaps illustrated with key examples for each category.[9]

6. *How Data Is Used*

Another basic element of a privacy statement is a description of how the data is used.[10] As with the descriptions of the data collected, organizations should decide what level of specificity to use for these descriptions. Often, categories or types of uses will be described. Common uses include:

- Operating and providing the product(s) and/or service(s),
- Improving the product(s) and service(s),
- General business operations,
- Security (including fraud detection, keeping the product(s) safe and secure, and securing the organization's systems and infrastructure),
- Personalization (either within the particular product or service, or across products and services),
- Direct marketing, and
- Advertising.

If the privacy statement lists categories of uses, it is best to illustrate each category with some key examples. In structuring these descriptions, it may be useful to distinguish "primary purposes" over which the organization does not offer choice (such as providing services, business

---

[7] 1995 EU Data Protection Directive, Article 10(c) ("whether replies to the questions are obligatory or voluntary, as well as the possible consequences of failure to reply"). GDPR Article 13(2)(e) ("Where the personal data is collected from the data subject, whether providing the data is required, including: whether it is a requirement necessary to enter into a contract, whether it is otherwise required by statute or contract, and the possible consequences of the failure to provide such data").

[8] GDPR Articles 14(2)(f) and 15(1)(g).

[9] See GDPR Recital 61 ("Where the origin of the personal data cannot be provided to the data subject because various sources have been used, general information should be provided").

[10] See, e.g., 1995 EU Data Protection Directive, Article 10(b) ("the purposes of the processing for which the data are intended"). GDPR Articles 13(1)(c), 14(1)(c), and 15(1)(a).

operations, and security) from secondary uses over which users have some choice (such as direct marketing and ad targeting).

7. *Use of Data for Automated Decision-Making or Profiling*

When the GDPR comes into effect in 2018, the use of personal data "for automated decision-making, including profiling" must be disclosed.[11] The notice must describe the existence of such processing, meaningful information about the logic involved, and the significance and anticipated consequences for the data subject.[12]

8. *Disclosures of Data to Third Parties*

A privacy statement must disclose the categories of third parties to which personal data may be shared.[13] Some privacy statements make the implausible claim that "we never share your data with anyone." But every organization either discloses data to at least some third parties, or is likely to at some point – and those disclosures and potential disclosures should be described in the privacy statement. Any organization could be compelled to turn over data to law enforcement.[14] Virtually every organization is likely at some point to use a vendor or service provider that will need some access to personal data (accountants, auditors, law firms, payment processors, IT support providers, customer service vendors, etc.). Nearly any company could be involved in a merger, acquisition, divestiture, or similar transaction that would require sharing some personal data with the other company or companies involved. Many organizations have ongoing commercial relationships with other parties that involve some sharing of data between them: ad service providers, social networks, etc.

Many privacy statements also state that data is shared with affiliates and subsidiaries. But care should be taken to avoid characterizing controlled affiliates and subsidiaries as "third parties." In other words, it may be beneficial to differentiate (a) transfers of, or access to, data within a corporate family of controlled affiliates and subsidiaries, from (b) disclosures of data to third parties.

9. *Transfers of Data in an HTTP Referral Header*

In *Gaos v. Google*,[15] Google faced a class-action lawsuit due to the practice of its Internet search service including a user's search query terms in the "referral header." As a result of this practice, when that user arrived on a third-party website as the result of clicking on a link or ad on Google search results page, that website would know the search terms the user entered that resulted in the display of that link or ad. The essence of the claims was that Google shared this information with a third party without the knowledge or consent of the user. As part of the settlement, Google agreed to disclose this practice to its users. In order to avoid litigation, organizations that engage

---

[11] See GDPR Articles 13(2)(f), 14(2)(g), and 15(1)(h). See also Article 22 for what constitutes automated decision-making, including profiling.

[12] *Id.*

[13] California Business and Professions Code § 22575(b) ("the categories of third-party persons or entities with whom the operator may share that personally identifiable information"), 1995 EU Data Protection Directive, Article 10(c) ("the recipients or categories of recipients of the data"). See also GDPR Articles 13(1)(e), 14(1)(e), and 15(1)(c).

[14] Some legal standards require the potential disclosure of data to law enforcement to be specifically called out. For instance, the EU-U.S. Privacy Shield Framework requires a privacy statement to include "a description of the requirement to disclose personal information in response to lawful requests by public authorities, including to meet national security or law enforcement requirements." See EU-U.S. Privacy Shield Framework Principles Issued by the U.S. Department of Commerce, at § II.1.a.xii. Available at http://ec.europa.eu/justice/data-protection/files/privacy-shield-adequacy-decision-annex-2_en.pdf.

[15] 5:10-CV 4809 (N.D. Cal.; Mar. 29, 2012).

in equivalent or analogous practices that reveal data about a user to a third party may feel compelled to add equivalent disclosures.[16]

10. *Use of Cookies*

The EU ePrivacy Directive requires consent for cookies and similar technologies, and consent requires clear notice regarding the use of cookies.[17] Some organizations have chosen to maintain a separate "cookie policy" that their cookie banners or cookie consent experiences can point to. However, because a privacy statement would typically need to contain some discussion of cookies, and several references to them throughout, it will frequently be more efficient for the organization and easier for the customer to have all privacy-related cookie disclosures in the privacy statement. Plus, having cookie disclosures in multiple documents creates the risk of real or perceived inconsistencies.

Note that cookies are easy to detect, and privacy watchdogs have been known to test websites to see how many cookies are being set, what domains they come from, and what their expiration dates are. So if the cookie disclosures are inaccurate or incomplete, such errors may be readily detectable.

11. *Third-Party Tracking*

CalOPPA requires operators of websites and online services to "disclose whether other parties may collect personally identifiable information about an individual consumer's online activities over time and across different Web sites when a consumer uses the operator's Web site or service."[18] This requirement will likely apply to any website or service that uses a third-party ad network, analytics service, content provider, or social plug-in.

12. *Use of Third-Party Analytics Services*

In particular, organizations should disclose is the use of third party analytics services. Some analytics services assert that (a) the data they collect is not "personally identifiable" and/or (b) the data they collect is not combined across different websites in a way that would trigger the CalOPPA requirements related to third-party tracking. However, these services are nevertheless collecting data about users' interactions with the site, and under some privacy laws, such as those in Europe, such activity would constitute the collection of personal data and/or a disclosure of personal data to a third party, and should therefore be disclosed.

Additionally, many analytics providers contractually require their customers to include certain disclosures in their privacy statements. For example, the Flurry Analytics Terms of Use requires that the privacy policy of an organization using the analytics service "must (i) provide notice of your use of a tracking pixel, agent or any other visitor identification technology that collects, uses, shares and stores data about end users of your applications (whether by you, Flurry or your Ad Partners) and (ii) contain a link to Flurry's Privacy Policy and/or describe Flurry's opt-out for the Analytics Service to your end users in such a manner that they can easily find it and opt-out of the Analytics Service tracking."

---

[16] Google added this disclosure to its privacy FAQs. But placing such disclosures in the privacy statement has the advantage of not requiring readers to look across multiple documents to find relevant privacy information.

[17] Directive on privacy and electronic communications 2002/58/EC, as amended by Directive 2009/136/EC, Article 5(3) ("the storing of information, or the gaining of access to information already stored, in the terminal equipment of a subscriber or user is only allowed on condition that the subscriber or user concerned has given his or her consent, having been provided with clear and comprehensive information ...").

[18] Calif. Business and Professions Code § 22575(b)(6).

13. *Use of Data for Online Behavioral Advertising*

The use of data for online advertising has been a particular focus of regulatory scrutiny. As a result, privacy regulators expect that the use of data for online behavioral advertising should be called out with some specificity.[19]

As a practical matter, this means that website publishers and app providers that enable the display of targeted ads should describe:

- That data will be used to create a profile for ad targeting purposes,
- The types of data collected and used for that purpose,
- How that data is collected (e.g., via cookies or other means),
- Whether, how, and for what purposes the data will be transferred to third parties.

If the website or app provider works with one or more third-party ad network(s) or other advertising service providers that collect and combine data across unrelated apps, sites, or services, the notice should also include:

- The name(s) of the third-party ad network(s) or similar advertising service provider(s),
- A general description of how third-party ad targeting and delivery work, and that data collected from the current website or app may be combined with data collected from the individual's interactions with other websites or apps.

Additional disclosures regarding online behavioral advertising, including how to opt out from such use, may be necessary.

Further, these and other specific notice obligations related to online behavioral advertising are also required by the self-regulatory programs described in section 14. These self-regulatory requirements may apply to an organization as a result of direct participation in these programs. But it is worth noting that they can also apply if an organization is working with a program participant, and that participant contractually passes through those requirements to website publishers and its other customers or partners.[20]

14. *Participation in Online Behavioral Advertising Self-Regulatory Programs*

Most companies that provide online behavioral advertising services participate in one or more of the self-regulatory programs offered by the Network Advertising Initiative (NAI),[21] Digital Advertising Alliance (DAA),[22] European Interactive Digital Advertising Alliance (EDAA),[23] and Digital Advertising Alliance of Canada (DAAC).[24] Each of these programs requires that

---

[19] For example, the Article 29 Working Party has stated that ad networks and publishers "should ensure that individuals are told, at a minimum, who (i.e. which entity) is responsible for serving the cookie and collecting the related information. In addition, they should be informed in simple ways that (a) the cookie will be used to create profiles; (b) what type of information will be collected to build such profiles; (c) the fact that the profiles will be used to deliver targeted advertising and (d) the fact that the cookie will enable the user's identification across multiple web sites." Art. 29 Working Party Opinion 2/2010.

[20] The Network Advertising Initiative (NAI) obligates members to "require the websites where they collect data for Interest-Based Advertising to clearly and conspicuously post notice that contains: (a) A statement of the fact that data may be collected for Interest-Based Advertising; (b) A description of types of data that are collected for Interest-Based Advertising purposes; (c) An explanation of how, and for what purpose, the data collected will be used or transferred to third parties; and (d) A conspicuous link to an Opt-Out Mechanism." NAI Self-Regulatory Code of Conduct (2013) Section II.B.3.

[21] See http://www.networkadvertising.org/.

[22] See http://www.aboutads.info/.

[23] See http://www.youronlinechoices.com/.

[24] See http://youradchoices.ca/.

participants disclose in their privacy statements that they participate in and adhere to the principles of the program.[25] In that disclosure, more organizations also provide links to the program's website.

15. *Online Behavioral Advertising Opt-Out*

All the online behavioral advertising self-regulatory programs require participating companies to provide notice of how to opt out from receiving this type of advertising.[26] And as noted earlier, participating companies may pass through this requirement to web publishers, app developers, and other customers and partners. The opt-out disclosure will typically include a link to an opt-out mechanism offered by the company itself, opt-out mechanisms offered by the third-party ad network(s) with which the company works, and/or industry-wide opt-out tools operated by the self-regulatory programs.

16. *Use of Sensitive Data, Including Health Data, for Online Behavioral Advertising*

The EDAA requires members not only to describe the types of data collected and used for behavioral advertising purposes, but also "whether any data is ... 'sensitive personal data' as defined by the national implementation of Directive 95/46/EC."[27] Generally, this would include any personal data that reveals a person's racial or ethnic origin, political opinions, religious or philosophical beliefs, trade-union membership, health, or sex life.[28]

Additionally, the NAI requires that "members that use standard interest segments for Interest-Based Advertising that are based on health-related information or interests shall disclose such segments on their websites."[29] While this disclosure does not necessarily need to be in the privacy statement to meet the NAI obligation, to the extent that there are other privacy disclosures about the use of data for online behavioral advertising purposes in the privacy statement, regulators are likely to expect this related information to be included in the same place.

Depending on the nature of the health segments used, the organization may wish to characterize them as "non-sensitive" (for example, to differentiate interest in topics such as hay fever or fitness from more serious medical condition such as HIV or cancer). However, if the privacy statement is global, such characterization may be challenged in Europe and other countries where *any* health-related data would likely be considered "sensitive personal data" under local data protection laws.

17. *Response to Do Not Track Signals*

CalOPPA requires any website or online service that collects information about a consumer's online activities over time and across third-party websites or online services to disclose how it responds to Web browser "do not track" (DNT) signals or similar mechanisms.[30] Because the DNT standard has not been widely adopted, many organizations include language in their privacy statements stating that they do not respond to browser DNT signals. For organizations that have implemented a response to the DNT signals from the major browsers (such as Google

---

[25] See, e.g., NAI Self-Regulatory Code of Conduct (2013) Section II(B)(1)(e); DAA Self Regulatory Principles for Online Behavioral Advertising (2009) Section II(A)(1)(d).

[26] Network Advertising Initiative (NAI) Self-Regulatory Code of Conduct (2013) Section II(B)(1)(g). Digital Advertising Alliance (DAA) Self Regulatory Principles for Online Behavioral Advertising (2009) Section II(A)(1)(c).

[27] IAB Europe EU Framework for Online Behavioural Advertising (2011), Principle I.A.1.b.

[28] See Directive 95/46/EC, Art 8.

[29] NAI Self-Regulatory Code of Conduct (2013) Section II(B)(2).

[30] Calif. Business and Professions Code § 22575(b)(5) & (7).

Chrome, Mozilla Firefox, or Microsoft Edge), the privacy statement should specify that the implementation is limited to the major browsers since there are numerous web browsers beyond the mainstream browsers that could adopt different DNT-like mechanisms, and it could be difficult or impossible to ensure adherence to all of them.

18. *Data Retention*

Today, several factors may compel organizations to disclose their data retention practices, and such disclosures will become a clear legal requirement in the near future. Participants in the TRUSTe privacy seal program must include "a general description of the Participant's information retention policies."[31] The NAI Code of Conduct requires each member to disclose the "approximate length of time [it retains] data used for Interest-Based Advertising or Ad Delivery and Reporting."[32] While the current EU Data Protection Directive does not explicitly require the disclosure of retention time frames, European regulators have been pushing companies to be more transparent about retention. And by 2018, the GDPR will require the privacy notice to describe "the period for which the personal data will be stored, or if that is not possible, the criteria used to determine that period."[33]

19. *Data Security*

Most privacy laws do not explicitly require data security as part of a privacy statement. But it is required by some laws,[34] it is implicit in others,[35] and it has become a common element of privacy statements. To the extent data security is included, the description need not go into great detail. As with most factual disclosures in the privacy statement, getting into too much detail increases the risk of making a mistake and/or rendering the privacy statement quickly out-of-date. Further, making absolute security promises (e.g., "your data is secure with us") can increase the risk of liability in the event of a data breach. Thus, most organizations choose to limit data security disclosures to high-level statements about taking reasonable steps to help protect the security of the personal data they collect and maintain.

20. *The Individual's Right to Access Personal Data*

A number of privacy laws give individuals the right to access personal data about them that the organization holds, and further require that the privacy statement inform them of that right.[36]

---

[31] TRUSTe Enterprise Privacy Certification Standards (revised on: March 12, 2015), available at https://www.truste.com/privacy-certification-standards/program-requirements/.

[32] Network Advertising Initiative (NAI) Self-Regulatory Code of Conduct (2013) Section II(B)(1)(f).

[33] GDPR Articles 13(2)(a), 14(2)(a), and 15(1)(d).

[34] For example, the Gramm-Leach-Bliley Act (GLBA), which applies to financial institutions, requires that a privacy notice include "the financial institution's policies and practices with respect to protecting the confidentiality and security of nonpublic personal information." 16 CFR § 313.6.

[35] For example, the Health Information Portability and Accountability Act (HIPAA) Privacy Rule, does not explicitly state that security must be addressed. Rather it says a privacy notice must include: "A statement that the covered entity is required by law to maintain the privacy of protected health information, to provide individuals with notice of its legal duties and privacy practices with respect to protected health information, and to notify affected individuals following a breach of unsecured protected health information" 45 CFR 164.520(b)(1)(v)(A). However, security measures are among the legal duties a HIPAA-covered entity has to maintain the privacy of protected health information, and the Model Notices of Privacy Practices published by the US Department of Health and Human Services (HHS) contains language about data security: See, e.g., http://www.hhs.gov/sites/default/files/ocr/privacy/hipaa/npp_fullpage_hc_provider.pdf.

[36] 1995 EU Data Protection Directive, Article 10(c) ("the existence of the right to access to and the right to rectify the data concerning him"). GDPR Articles 13(2)(b), 14(2)(c), and 15(1)(e) (the existence of the right of a data subject to request from the controller access to and rectification or erasure of personal data); see also Article 15 (right of access).

21. *The Individual's Right to Correct or Amend Personal Data*

Most privacy laws that provide a right to access also provide a right to collect or amend that data – particularly if the data is inaccurate – and likewise require that the privacy statement inform individuals of that right.[37]

22. *The Individual's Right to Delete Personal Data*

The trend in privacy law is to extend the rights of access and correction to include a right to delete data. The GDPR, for example, adds a right of erasure that the 1995 EU Data Protection Directive lacked. And this right, too, must be described in the privacy statement.[38]

Note that the GDPR notice requirements related to the access, correction, and deletion of personal data all state that the privacy statement must disclose the individual's right to *request* from the controller access, correction, or deletion. Stating these rights as a "right to request" rather than an absolute right to access, correct, or delete will avoid overstating these rights and will preserve the organization's ability to deny such a request where there is a legal basis for doing so.

23. *The Right of Data Portability*

Another new right introduced in the GDPR is the right of data portability. Specifically, the regulation states that the privacy statement must disclose "the existence of the right of a data subject to receive data he or she has provided to the controller in a structured, commonly used and machine-readable format, and transmit that data to another controller."[39]

24. *The Right to Withdraw Consent*

Where an organization processes personal data based on the consent of the data subject under GDPR Articles 6(1)(a) or 9(2)(a), the regulations require the privacy statement to disclose the existence of the right to withdraw consent at any time (without affecting the lawfulness of processing based on consent before its withdrawal).[40]

25. *The Right to Object to, or Restrict, the Processing of Personal Data*

Additional GDPR rights that must be disclosed in the privacy statement are the right of a data subject to object to the processing of personal data and the right to obtain a restriction of such processing under certain circumstances.[41] The right to object applies to processing based on Article 6(1)(e) ("necessary for the performance of a task carried out in the public interest or in the exercise of official authority vested in the controller") or Article 6(1)(f) ("necessary for the purposes of the legitimate interests pursued by the controller or by a third party"), or for the purposes of marketing.[42] The right to obtain a restriction on processing applies under four narrow circumstances described in Article 18(1). Organizations may choose to include detail on the limitations of these rights so as to discourage individuals from asserting them in circumstances when they do not apply.

---

[37] 1995 EU Data Protection Directive, Article 10(c) ("the existence of the right to access to and the right to rectify the data concerning him"). GDPR Articles 13(2)(b), 14(2)(c), and 15(1)(e) ("the existence of the right to request from the controller access to and rectification or erasure of personal data"), see also Article 16 (right to rectification).
[38] GDPR Articles 13(2)(b), 14(2)(c), and 15(1)(e), see also Article 17 (right to erasure).
[39] GDPR Articles 13(2)(b) and 14(2)(c). See also Article 20 for the scope of the data portability obligations.
[40] GDPR Articles 13(2)(c) and 14(2)(d).
[41] GDPR Articles 13(2)(b), 14(2)(c), and 15(1)(e).
[42] See GDPR Article 21(1) and (2).

26. *European Legal Basis for Processing*

The GDPR will also require organizations to describe in their privacy statements the legal basis or bases for processing personal data as set out in the regulation (e.g., consent, performance of a contract, "legitimate interests," etc.).[43]

In addition, where processing is based on the legitimate interests pursued by the controller or a third party under Article 6(1)(f), the privacy statement must include a description of those interests.[44] This information may be partially provided as part of privacy statement language about how data is used and shared with third parties. But most organizations will likely need to add additional new language to their privacy statements to specifically identify the legal bases relied on, and in particular the legitimate interests. Something such as:

> We collect and process personal data about you with your consent and/or as necessary to provide the products you use, operate our business, meet our contractual and legal obligations, protect the security of our systems and our customers, or fulfil other legitimate interests.

Note that this disclosure, along with the several preceding rights that the GDPR requires to be disclosed in a privacy statement, are based on very specific elements of European privacy law. As a result, organizations may wish to put some or all of this language in a dedicated "European Privacy Rights" section – particularly if they are concerned about extending these rights to individuals in jurisdictions where they do not otherwise apply.

27. *Collection of Data from Children*

In the United States, the Children's Online Privacy Protection Act (COPPA)[45] requires any organization that collects data online from children under the age of thirteen to meet certain obligations, including notice obligations. These requirements can apply to any site or service that is directed to children, but also to any organization that could find itself with actual knowledge that it has collected data from children under thirteen.

Some organizations, in order to stake out a position that they are not subject to COPPA obligations, state in their privacy statement that they do not knowingly collect data from children under thirteen, and if they learn of any such collection, the data will be deleted. However, great care should be taken to ensure that such a statement is accurate, in light of FTC cases that have found similar statements to be deceptive.[46] If it is convinced it is not subject to COPPA, a company may do better to stay silent on this topic.

Acknowledging that they are or could be subject to COPPA, other organizations should include sections in their privacy statements that discuss the collection of information from children and include the more specific disclosures described in sections 28-30.

28. *Whether a Service Enables a Child to Publicly Disclose Personal Data*

The COPPA Rule requires disclosure of a "description of what information the operator collects from children, including whether the Web site or online service enables a child to make personal

---

[43] GDPR Articles 13(1)(c) and 14(1)(c). See also Article 6 for a list of the legal bases for processing personal data.

[44] GDPR Articles 13(1)(d) and 14(2)(b).

[45] 15 U.S.C. §§ 6501–6506 (Pub. L. 105–277, 112 Stat. 2681–728, enacted October 21, 1998), implementing regulations at 16 CFR Part 312.

[46] See, e.g., United States of America v. Sony BMG Music Entertainment, Case No. 08 CV 10730 (2008) (claiming statements in the Sony Music privacy policy that users indicating they are under 13 will be restricted from Sony Music's web page activities to be false and misleading given Sony accepted registrations from users providing date of birth indicating that they were under 13).

information publicly available."[47] This requirement has been interpreted to mean that any service with a feature that allows users to communicate with other users, and that therefore could be used by a child to reveal personal information, would trigger this notice obligation.

29. *A Parent's Right to Revoke Consent*

The COPPA Rule requires that the notice state that "the parent can review or have deleted the child's personal information, and refuse to permit further collection or use of the child's information [and] the procedures for doing so."[48]

30. *A parent's Right to Access or Delete a Child's Data*

Likewise, the COPPA-mandated notice must disclose that "the parent can review or have deleted the child's personal information" and "state the procedures for doing so."[49]

31. *Global Data Transfers*

Various privacy laws around the world restrict cross-border data flows, the best-known being those in Europe. To support an argument that users are on notice, organizations should disclose that data it collects may be transferred to and processed or stored in other jurisdictions. Some organizations do this at a very high level, noting that data may be transferred to any country where the organization or its service providers operate. However, beginning in 2018 when the EU General Data Protection Regulation (GDPR) comes into effect, these disclosures will need to be more detailed. Specifically, where a data controller intends to transfer personal data to a country outside the European Economic Area (EEA) or to an international organization, the privacy notice must describe the fact of such transfer and either:

- the existence or absence of an adequacy decision by the European Commission, or
- in the case of transfers based on "suitable safeguards" under Articles 46, 47, or 49(1)(b) (such as contractual provisions or binding corporate rules), such safeguards and how to obtain a copy of them.[50]

32. *EU-U.S. Privacy Shield Framework*

If an organization participates in the Privacy Shield, an extensive and explicit set of notice requirements apply. Some requirements are unique to the Privacy Shield and would likely be grouped together in a paragraph or two. These include:

- a statement of the organization's participation in the Privacy Shield,[51] and its adherence to Privacy Shield Principles with respect to all personal data received from the European Union in reliance on the Privacy Shield;[52]
- a link to, or the web address for, the Privacy Shield List maintained by the Department of Commerce (https://www.privacyshield.gov);[53]

---

[47] 16 CFR 312.4(d)(2).
[48] 16 CFR 312.4(d)(3).
[49] *Id.*
[50] GDPR Articles 13(1)(f), 14(1)(f), and Article 15(2).
[51] See EU-US Privacy Shield Framework Principles Issued by the US Department of Commerce, § II.1.a.i. Available at http://ec.europa.eu/justice/data-protection/files/privacy-shield-adequacy-decision-annex-2_en.pdf.
[52] *Id.*, at §§ II.1.a.iii and II.6.d.
[53] *Id.*, at § II.1.a.i.

- the entities or subsidiaries of the organization also adhering to the Principles, where applicable;[54]
- a description of when exceptions to the organization's adherence to the Principles based on statute, government regulation, or case law that creates conflicting obligations or explicit authorizations "will apply on a regular basis";[55]
- the independent dispute resolution body designated to address complaints and provide appropriate recourse free of charge to the individual, and whether it is: (1) the panel established by DPAs, (2) an alternative dispute resolution provider based in the EU, or (3) an alternative dispute resolution provider based in the United States,[56] and a link to the website or complaint submission form of the independent recourse mechanism that is available to investigate unresolved complaints;[57] and
- a statement of the possibility, under certain conditions, for the individual to invoke binding arbitration for claimed violations of the Principles.[58]

The right of the individual to invoke binding arbitration applies to only to those "residual" claims that remain unresolved after pursuing the other available means of recourse under the Privacy Shield.[59] Organizations wishing to avoid creating a broader right to arbitration than exits under the Privacy Shield will likely choose to describe this limitation and/or otherwise qualify the privacy statement language regarding the right to arbitration.

Other notice requirements under the Privacy Shield Framework are common elements that are likely already in an organization's privacy statement in some form, and do not necessarily need to be repeated in the statement's specific section or paragraphs regarding the Privacy Shield.

- The types of personal data collected.[60]
- The purposes for which it collects and uses personal information about individuals.[61]
- The type or identity of third parties to which it discloses personal information, and the purposes for which it does so.[62]
- A description of the requirement to disclose personal information in response to lawful requests by public authorities, including to meet national security or law enforcement requirements.[63]
- The right of individuals to access their personal data.[64]
- The choices and means the organization offers individuals for limiting the use and disclosure of their personal data.[65]
- Information about how to contact the organization with any inquiries or complaints, including any relevant establishment in the EU that can respond to such inquiries or complaints.[66]

---

[54] *Id.*, at § II.1.a.ii.
[55] *Id.*, at § I.5.
[56] *Id.*, at § II.1.a.ix.
[57] *Id.*, at § II.6.d.
[58] *Id.*, at § II.1.a.xi.
[59] See *id.*, Annex I.
[60] *Id.*, at § II.1.a.ii.
[61] *Id.*, at § II.1.a.iv.
[62] *Id.*, at § II.1.a.vi.
[63] *Id.*, at § II.1.a.xii.
[64] *Id.*, at § II.1.a.vii. Note that the right to access personal data is subject to certain limitations set out in Principle II.8. An organization will likely wish to carefully state those limitations in its privacy statement so as to avoid overstating the scope of the right.
[65] *Id.*, at § II.1.a.viii.
[66] *Id.*, at § II.1.a.v.

Additionally, there are two notice requirements under the Privacy Shield that may have broader applicability, but that may be prudent to include with the specific Privacy Shield language. The first is:

- The organization's liability for damage in cases of onward transfers to third parties.[67]

Under the Privacy Shield, the organization's liability in the case of onward transfers does not apply when "the organization proves that it is not responsible for the event giving rise to the damage."[68] An organization will likely wish to include a description of this limitation in its privacy statement to avoid creating strict liability for damage resulting from onward transfers.

The Privacy Shield also requires the organization's privacy statement to include:

- A statement regarding the organization being subject to the investigatory and enforcement powers of the FTC, the Department of Transportation, or any other US-authorized statutory body.[69]

While this is generally true irrespective of the Privacy Shield Framework, it's not something most organizations would typically include in their privacy statements. Thus, organizations may choose to group it with the rest of the specific Privacy Shield disclosures.

Finally, the Commerce Department has asked companies applying for the Privacy Shield to include language regarding it "above the fold" (i.e., in the top layer of a layered notice or near the top of a long statement). This does not mean that all the language required under the Privacy Shield Framework should be at the top of the statement, but it does mean that some brief statement regarding the Privacy Shield should be near the top, which can then link to more information deeper in the statement.

33. *Contact Information*

Privacy laws commonly require that privacy statements include the entity's contact information.[70] In Europe, starting in 2018, the privacy statement will also need to provide the contact information for the organization's data protection officer.[71]

While seemingly a straightforward and simple requirement, providing contact information can be surprisingly fraught with challenges. Whatever contact information is provided will likely be used by customers or other individuals with privacy questions, concerns, or complaints. So it is important to be sure that those inquiries are received by those with the capability and expertise to respond to them quickly and appropriately. It is also a best practice to have processes in place to track those inquires in order to maintain appropriate records, flag and fix instances of noncompliance, and identify trends that can indicate reputational or other risks. Thus, especially in large organizations, just providing the organization's street address or the phone number of the main switchboard may not be the best approach.

In some countries, regulators have encouraged publishing local contact information. One way to address this while still maintaining a consistent global privacy statement is to point to a separate page that lists an organization's local affiliates along with local contact information. However, this approach also runs the risk of privacy inquiries being misrouted or misplaced.

---

[67] *Id.*, at § II.1.a.xiii.
[68] See *id.*, § II.7.d.
[69] *Id.*, at § II.1.a.x.
[70] GDPR Articles 13(1)(a) and 14(1)(a).
[71] GDPR Articles 13(1)(b) and 14(1)(b). See also Article 37 for the requirements for designating a data protection officer.

In some cases, publishing a postal address may be sufficient. But other types of contact information are often required. For example, for organizations subject to COPPA, the privacy statement must contain "the name, address, telephone number, and email address of the operator."[72] Unfortunately, publishing an e-mail address in a privacy statement often results in that address receiving large amounts of spam and other non-privacy-related messages, which can overwhelm the organization's ability to respond expeditiously to legitimate privacy concerns and inquiries.

Many organizations have chosen to implement a web form that can help prevent spam and route the electronic message to the appropriate recipient. Presenting such a web form as the most prominent and preferred contact method, even if other contact methods are also provided, can help address these challenges. However, whether providing such a form meets the COPPA requirement of including an "email address" in the privacy statement remains unclear.

Finally, any approach that doesn't point to a single address or contact method should consider the aforementioned needs to ensure that inquiries are routed to the right people and answered in a consistent way, and that there is a comprehensive way to globally track and manage such inquires.

34. *How to Lodge a Complaint*

A privacy statement should inform individuals how they can lodge a complaint about the organization's privacy practices.[73] Most organizations will want to encourage users first to contact the organization itself, rather than lodge a complaint with a regulator, so this information is best placed in conjunction with the organization's contact information. If the organization works with a third-party dispute resolution service, such as that offered by TRUSTe, this information should also contain details about how to invoke that process, should the individual not succeed in resolving the matter directly with the organization.[74]

35. *The Right to Lodge a Complaint with a Supervisory Authority*

The European GDPR will require organizations to state specifically in their privacy statements that individuals have a right to lodge a complaint with a supervisory authority.[75] This language could be placed adjacent to the organization's contact information, along with language encouraging the individual to contact the organization directly to resolve any complaints before contacting a supervisory authority. Alternatively, it could be included in a Europe-specific section that lists all the rights required to be disclosed under the GDPR.

36. *Last Updated or Effective Date*

The privacy statement should include the date it is updated or comes into effect.[76] Many organizations choose to list just the month and year, rather than a precise date.

---

[72] COPPA Rule, 16 CFR 312.4(d)(1)

[73] See EU-US Privacy Shield Framework Principles Issued by the US Department of Commerce, § II.1.a.v. Available at http://ec.europa.eu/justice/data-protection/files/privacy-shield-adequacy-decision-annex-2_en.pdf. See also Australian Privacy Act 1988, APP 1.4(e).

[74] TRUSTe, Enterprise Privacy Certification Standards (last updated Apr. 3, 2017), § II(A)(1)(o). Available at https://www.truste.com/privacy-certification-standards/program-requirements/.

[75] GDPR Articles 13(2)(d), 14(2)(e), and 15(1)(f).

[76] The California Online Piracy Protection Act (CalOPPA) requires that a privacy policy state its effective date. Calif. Business and Professions Code § 22575(b)(4).

37. *Notification of Material Changes*

The privacy statement must describe how individuals will be notified of a material change.[77] Many privacy statements describe how *any* change will be communicated (for example, by updating the effective date on the statement), and then state or suggest that some more robust method of notice will be provided if the change is material. The FTC has provided guidance that a material change requires affirmative express consent,[78] so privacy statements should avoid suggesting that material changes can be made without meeting that standard. However, there is no clear standard for what changes must be considered "material." A reasonable interpretation could limit this to retroactive changes that in some significant way "change the deal" under which the data was collected.

PART III: OTHER KEY CONSIDERATIONS

Once the content of the privacy statement has been assembled, the final drafting, editing, design, translation, and publication, and ongoing maintenance, can raise additional issues and considerations.

A. *Style, Tone, and Terminology*

The use of technical or legal jargon reduces the clarity of a privacy statement for the average reader. Instead, those drafting privacy statements should use plain language to describe data practices in the clearest possible way.[79] There are excellent resources and guidance available on plain language writing, many aimed at increasing the clarity of government documents, but which can be utilized for privacy statement drafting as well.[80]

The tone of a privacy statement can vary significantly. Good privacy statements tend to find a middle ground that is friendly and conversational, and aligns with the image the organization wishes to convey. Privacy statements that sound overly formalistic and legalistic are likely to be criticized as undermining transparency. And privacy statements that try to be cute or humorous are likely to be criticized as not taking privacy seriously enough (especially to audiences outside the United States).

Language designed to obscure or "sugarcoat" a fact that some readers might view negatively can backfire and lead to more negative attention. For example, over-reliance on generalities and the word "may" or other similar term is another common pitfall. If a service collects location data in only some specific circumstances, the privacy statement should not say "we may collect location data." Instead, it should say "when you do X, we will collect location data." In some cases, such choice of language will cross the line onto deception. For example, saying the

---

[77] Calif. Business and Professions Code § 22575(b)(3).

[78] Federal Trade Commission, Protecting Consumer Privacy in an Era of Rapid Change: Recommendations for Businesses and Policymakers (March 2012), at viii. See also the FTC settlements with Google and Facebook.

[79] For a comparison of several companies' privacy statements using criteria for plain language writing, see Katy Steinmetz, "These Companies Have the Best (And Worst) Privacy Policies," Time.com, 6 August 2015, available at http://time.com/3986016/google-facebook-twitter-privacy-policies/. Full report available at http://centerforplainlanguage.org/wp-content/uploads/2015/09/TIME-privacy-policy-analysis-report.pdf.

[80] See, for example, http://www.plainlanguage.gov/ is a US federal government site focused on fostering plain language writing in US government documents and publications. Texts of plain language laws that have been adopted in various US states is available at http://www.languageandlaw.org/TEXTS/STATS/PLAINENG.HTM. The Center for Plain Language (http://centerforplainlanguage.org/) provides resources for the use of plain language and serves as a watchdog for unclear writing by the government and private sector.

organization "may" do something when it, in fact, will do that thing is misleading. In a small number of cases, generalities are unavoidable, but drafters of privacy statements should make a determined effort to eliminate as many as possible.

Privacy statements should avoid characterizing data as "anonymous" when it likely is not. There is a broad spectrum of de-identification, and a growing consensus that anonymous data is at the far end of that spectrum.[81] Data that is characterized as anonymous must be devoid of any unique identifiers, be aggregated with the data of many different individuals, and have no known possibility of being reversed so as to identify or single out an individual. Characterizing data as anonymous when a lesser level of de-identification has been applied could be viewed as deceptive. Instead, characterizing the data as de-identified or pseudonymous – or simply describing the de-identification methodology – may be more accurate and less risky.

Likewise, some privacy statements attempt to define a term such as "personal information" narrowly, and then go on to claim that a service does not collect any personal information. However, the clear trend in privacy regulation is toward a broad view of what data is covered, including any data that is linkable to a person or a device, and any data that can be used to single out or individually impact a person. Thus, IP addresses, cookie IDs, and other unique identifiers (as well as all data linked to such IDs) should be considered in scope (even if the organization does not actually know the identity of the person from whom the data is collected), and should be covered by the privacy statement. Privacy statements for services that collect such data, yet claim that they do not collect "personal information" are likely to be viewed by regulators as inaccurate or misleading.

And it is best to avoid the term "personally identifiable information" or "PII" – especially if the privacy statement is intended for a global audience. While that term is widely used in the United States, it is less common elsewhere. Especially for a European audience, the use of that term makes the company appear to be an American company that is unaware of European privacy rules and sensitivities. Instead, use the term "personal data" (the term used in European privacy laws), or a slightly more acceptable compromise "personal information." "Personal data" has the advantage of being slightly shorter (which, given the number of times it will be used in a statement, can have a material impact on the length of the statement). It also has the advantage of being distinguishable from other uses of the term "information" – "data" refers to what is collected from or about users and is subject to privacy law, whereas "information" refers to the details that are provided to inform readers about the organization's privacy practices (e.g. the company's privacy statement provides *information* about the *data* it collects).

B. *Design and Accessibility*

A well-structured privacy statement helps the reader find the relevant information quickly and easily. It makes it unnecessary to read the entire statement in order to locate the information that is relevant to a particular reader or to find the answer to a particular question. A well-organized and structured privacy statement will reduce redundancies. Using clear headings will help the reader find the relevant information quickly. If the privacy statement is long, the use of a table of contents or similar navigation aid will also increase usability.

---

[81] See Jules Polonetsky, Omer Tene, and Kelsey Finch, "Shades of Gray: Seeing the Full Spectrum of Practical Data De-Identification" (2016) Santa Clara Law Review, Forthcoming. Available at http://ssrn.com/abstract=2757709. See also, Ira S. Rubinstein and Woodrow Hartzog, "Anonymization and Risk," 91 Wash. L. Rev. 703 (2016). Available at https://www.law.uw.edu/wlr/print-edition/print-edition/vol-91/2/anonymization-and-risk/.

Likewise, adopting a layered format can provide quick summaries and a roadmap for finding more detail in the full statement. A typical layered privacy statement will have a short "top layer" that provides a short summary (often designed to fit on one page or one screen) of a privacy statement's key points and provides a roadmap for navigating the full statement. Layered privacy statements have been used successfully for over a decade and are regularly encouraged by privacy regulators and others.[82]

The design should also take into account the different form factors on which the privacy statement may be read so that it will render correctly on both large screens and small. A related consideration is accessibility; care should be taken to ensure that the privacy statement is compatible with screen readers and other assistive technologies.

C. *Publishing and Linking to the Statement*

The privacy statement should be easy to find and links to it should be provided in prominent locations and in consistent ways across an organization's experiences. For example, every web page should have the link to the statement in the same conspicuous location and using the same words (and that link should contain the word "privacy").[83] The link should be even more prominent where users are asked to provide personal data, are asked to make a choice with regard to personal data, or where more sensitive personal data is collected.

An important question related to how a privacy statement is presented and linked to involves whether or how it should be accepted as a condition of using a product or service. Should it be agreed to when the user agrees to the terms or service? Should it be incorporated by reference – in whole or in part – into the terms of service, End User License Agreement (EULA), or other terms that the user agrees to? Or should it be "acknowledged" in some way that falls short of explicit agreement? There is little consensus on these questions, and different organizations have taken different approaches.

A theoretical advantage of having the privacy statement formally accepted or acknowledged is that it might bolster a consent argument – that the individual consented to the data collection and use described in the privacy statement. However, reliance on that type of consent argument is somewhat dubious, and even more so if agreement to the privacy statement is accomplished by being incorporated by reference in a longer legal agreement (like a terms of service). It is highly unlikely that a European regulator would view such an approach as constituting valid consent. In fact, language that requires broad consent to data use practices as a condition of use has been criticized as violating consumer protection rules – especially in Germany where consumer groups have successfully brought actions against companies that have done this.[84]

---

[82] For example, the Article 29 Working Party's recommendations to Google on its 2012 privacy statement included a recommendation that Google adopt a layered privacy statement. See letter to Larry Page from the Article 29 Working Party, 16 October 2012, available at http://ec.europa.eu/justice/data-protection/article-29/documentation/other-docu ment/files/2012/20121016_letter_to_google_en.pdf.

[83] CalOPPA requires that the privacy statement be posted "conspicuously," and it defines "conspicuously post" to include providing a test link that "does one of the following: (A) Includes the word 'privacy.' (B) Is written in capital letters equal to or greater in size than the surrounding text. (C) Is written in larger type than the surrounding text, or in contrasting type, font, or color to the surrounding text of the same size, or set off from the surrounding text of the same size by symbols or other marks that call attention to the language." See California Business and Professions Code § 22577(b).

[84] See, for example, http://www.pcworld.com/article/2065320/berlin-court-rules-google-privacy-policy-violates-data-pro tection-law.html.

However, in the United States, one advantage is that incorporating the privacy statement, in whole or in part, into an agreement that also has an arbitration clause can give the organization an argument that the arbitration clause applies to any individual complaints about the organization not adhering to its privacy statement.[85] And that, in effect, could create a significant barrier to class action litigation. Bottom line: don't do it in Europe. However, in the United States, the pros likely outweigh the cons.

D. *Translation and Localization*

Privacy statements should be translated into every language in which the products and services it covers are available. As a general matter, it is best to keep a privacy statement as consistent as possible worldwide. Ideally, the localization of privacy statements can largely be a direct translation.[86]

Having different privacy statements in different jurisdictions can raise questions from customers, advocates, and regulators – especially if it appears to some readers as if they are being provided with less information or fewer privacy protections than customers in other jurisdictions. Further, making different privacy commitments in different markets creates compliance challenges for global services. If the organization has to track different processes, different data usage disclosures, etc. for different markets, the resulting complexity would be difficult and costly to manage, could lead to incompatibilities, and would increase the likelihood of error, thereby creating additional legal risk. By contrast, maintaining one global version of a privacy statement not only simplifies compliance, it dramatically increases the simplicity and ease of maintenance of the statement itself.

This approach means that the statement would meet a single high bar internationally that reasonably accommodates varying national requirements. In most cases, a global approach is achievable because there is significant overlap and consistency in notice obligations found in privacy laws worldwide. As reflected in Part B.2, some laws require disclosures that other laws do not, but it is rare that a law would prohibit exceeding its requirements or prohibit additional disclosures beyond the minimum required.

Nevertheless, it is prudent to seek local review and feedback on a privacy statement translation. Doing so can help spot translation errors, flag local sensitivities, and identify local custom and legal requirements. But because of the benefits of maintaining global consistency to the extent possible, suggested changes from local counsel or other experts should be carefully and critically reviewed. In many cases, it may make sense to push back or reject a suggested change. Thus, when seeking local review, it is best to set the expectation from the outset that a suggested change will be accepted only if it is based on a legal requirement that is unambiguous and there is a consensus that there is a significant legal risk. Where there is agreement that a change is warranted, consider incorporating the change into the privacy statement for all markets worldwide. This approach may raise the bar internationally, but will maintain consistency.

---

[85] See Susan Lyon-Hintze, "'I Agree' Privacy Policy as Contract," IP Issues in Business Transactions Course Handbook, PLI (2016).

[86] Often, localized privacy statements will remove references to specific services or product features that are not available in the local market. But another approach would be to simply state near the beginning of the privacy statement that not all products or features mentioned in the privacy statement are available in all markets.

E. *Updating*

Privacy statements must be kept up-to-date. Organizations should have processes in place to regularly review the privacy statement and/or identify changes in practices and policies that would necessitate a privacy statement update.

When it comes time to publish and update, the organization will need to decide how to notify its users. Different organizations employ a range of choices. Sometimes, the organization will merely update the effective date on the privacy statement itself. Others will add the word "updated" next to their privacy statement links on their websites. And some go further and provide popup notices on their sites, and/or send email notifications to registered users. As noted in Part B.2, some privacy laws require that when there is a "material" change, users must not only be notified, but must provide explicit consent to the change. Related considerations include whether to maintain archived versions of past privacy statements, publish redlined versions of the update showing each change, or publish a change log describing each change.

Each organization will need to decide which approach is most appropriate given the circumstances – including the nature of the changes and the relationship it has with its customers. But it's important to recognize that privacy statement changes are frequently highlighted by journalists and bloggers, and are rarely portrayed in a light favorable to the organization. Thus, in considering the steps to take in notifying users of the changes, organizations should consider the advantages of describing the changes in their own words, rather than abdicating that role to bloggers who may misread, misunderstand, or mischaracterize the changes.

CONCLUSION

Crafting a privacy statement is both an art and a science. Creating a good privacy statement requires an understanding of regulatory requirements and other legal obligations across jurisdictions, a thorough command of the relevant facts, and a sensitivity to how the statement will be viewed by different audiences with different motivations for reading it. Every privacy statement is unique. It cannot be copied from other statements and it must be actively maintained to ensure it stays accurate and complete.

Most organizations have found their privacy statements to be a source of criticism more often than praise. And errors and ambiguities in privacy statements have led to legal challenges. But done well, a privacy statement can demonstrate transparency and explain practices in ways that enhance customer trust and bolster the organization's reputation. Taking the task seriously, devoting the time and resources necessary, and following some key best practices can significantly reduce the risks and increase the potential benefits inherent in drafting and publishing a privacy statement.

24

Privacy versus Research in Big Data

Jane R. Bambauer

INTRODUCTION

Humans are hard to study.

First, humans are uncooperative research material because they are each so different from one another. Unlike minerals, where an experiment on one pile of sodium produces the same results as it would on another pile of sodium, the same treatment can have very different effects on different people. What's worse, when it comes to behavioral research, even the same human can make different decisions at different points in time or in different contexts. These problems can be overcome to some extent through good research design, but the methods for doing so often involve some trivial or significant deceit – secret observations and interventions.

These mechanisms to achieve research validity provoke a different set of problems. Humans are also less cooperative as research subjects because they have autonomy, dignity, and safety interests that are simply not relevant in geology and astrophysics. A thick layer of legal and ethical restrictions apply to researchers in the health and social science fields, and some research that stays within the bounds of research norms can nevertheless spark national controversy and contempt if it transgresses popular expectations.

A wary young scientist would be wise to avoid studying humans altogether. Rocks are safer. But research that enlightens us about the human condition is too valuable to abandon. Moreover, the big data era marks a critical change in opportunity. Sensors, the Internet of Things, and other means of passive data collection give researchers unprecedented access to information that would have been forgotten (if it was ever observed in the first place) in a small data world. Algorithms allow our devices and apps to run hundreds of little experiments a day. We finally have the means to study humans almost as thoroughly and rigorously as we study rocks.

This new frontier invites renewed thought about the wisdom of Western research policy. This chapter explores three major concerns about corporate and academic social science.

Repurposing Data: Generally speaking, people do not appreciate when data collected for one purposes is used to study something else entirely. For example, in 2014, a group of Danish researchers scraped, cleaned, and released information about 70,000 people using the dating website OK Cupid.[1] Even though the information was accessible to all other OK Cupid

---

[1] Emil O. W. Kirkegaard & Julius D. Bjerrekaer, *The OkCupid Dataset: A Very Large Public Dataset of Dating Site Users*, OPEN DIFFERENTIAL PSYCHOLOGY, available at https://openpsych.net/forum/showthread.php?tid=279.

members (and to any member of the public willing to sign up with an account), the researchers were roundly criticized for sharing and using the data for research purposes without permission from the website or its users.[2]

Reidentification Risk: Apart from concerns about repurposing data, research subjects also have legitimate concerns that sensitive information in a research database may be attributed to them, causing embarrassment and other harms. For example, in 2006, Netflix released an anonymized dataset for members of the public to use to design their own recommendation algorithms. When two computer science researchers showed that the anonymized data could potentially be linked to information on IMdB or elsewhere on the Internet to reveal identities, a consumer class action was filed and Netflix canceled the release of future research databases.[3]

Intervention: The autonomy interests of human subjects are greater still when the research team not only observes the person's data but actively manipulates the person's environment or experience in order to study the response. In 2014, Facebook came under scrutiny for changing the news feeds that some of its users saw in order to see whether the changes had an effect on the content of their posts.[4] Since this was done surreptitiously, without any specific or generic notice that Facebook was conducting research, the controversy spurred a debate about whether the law requiring Institutional Review Board (IRB) review prior to the implementation of research plans should be extended to cover research at private companies.[5]

Each of these problems has something to teach about our instincts when it comes to research. Each controversy has sparked debate over the need for effective notice and consent. Without effective notice, big data research violates Fair Information Practice Principles (FIPPs) and shared notions of autonomy and respect. Left unexamined, these instincts can drive policy-makers to privacy and ethics rules that replicate the Common Rule for private industry research. But a close examination exposes some flaws in the traditional approach. The expansion of IRB rules to private American companies would exacerbate some existing dysfunction in American research law and would further impede health and social science research without serving the intended public interests.

This chapter first describes in broad strokes the legal scheme that applies to research in the United States. Next, it addresses the risks from repurposing data, reidentifiability, and surreptitious interventions and shows that these risks are not as severe as they are often presumed to be. It concludes with an examination of the incentives that are created by current and proposed laws restricting research.

BASIC REGULATORY SCHEME FOR RESEARCH

The American Common Rule provides mandates for some researchers to comply with a basic set of research ethics. Even in areas where the Common Rule does not apply, it provides a backbone for the norms and expectations in the field, and becomes a basis for comparison when firms deviate from those norms.

---

[2] Robert Hackett, *Researchers Caused an Uproar by Publishing Data from 70,000 OkCupid Users*, FORTUNE.COM (May 18, 2016).

[3] Steve Lohr, *Netflix Cancels Contest Plans and Settles Suit*, N.Y. TIMES (March 12, 2010).

[4] Adam D. I. Kramer et al., *Experimental Evidence of Massive-Scale Emotional Contagion through Social Networks*, 111 PROC. NAT'L ACAD. SCI. 8788 (2013).

[5] *See generally* the essays published in a special symposium issue of the *Colorado Technology Law Journal*, WHEN COMPANIES STUDY THEIR CUSTOMERS: THE CHANGING FACE OF SCIENCE, RESEARCH, AND ETHICS, 13 COLO. TECH. L. J. 193–368 (2015).

Under the Common Rule, research is treated very differently depending on whether it involves an intervention or merely the analysis of existing data. For research on observational data – that is, data that was observed for some other purpose – data can be shared and used for research purposes if it has been deidentified.[6] It can also be used in identified (or identifiable) form with the consent of the research subjects. An Insitutional Review Board can approve research on observational data without consent and de-identification if there is sufficient research-related justification and if the privacy risks are minimized in some other way, but deidentification and consent are the standard options.[7]

De-identification is the most commonly adopted means to balance research interests with privacy. Generally speaking, companies can hand off data collected incident to their business to a team of researchers without consent. In most fields, unless the researchers receive federal funding or are employed by a federally funded research institution, companies would not be under any formal legal mandate to anonymize the data. But in the health field, HIPAA regulations require health providers to prepare a de-identified database for sharing with researchers except in limited circumstances.[8] Educational institutions have similar requirements under the Family Education Rights and Privacy Act.[9] Even outside the health and education fields, the Federal Trade Commission (FTC) advises firms to take this precaution and there is significant public pressure to do so as well.[10]

Generally, observational data can be analyzed with consent OR with proper de-identification.

When researchers are actually performing an intervention – that is, if they are interacting with the subjects or affecting their environment in real time – then the legal requirements are more robust. The Common Rule generally requires researchers to get clearance from an IRB charged with assessing and protecting the interests of the putative research subjects, and researchers usually have to get consent from research subjects (although as with deidentification, there are exceptions to the consent requirement if risk is minimized and if there is a research-related reason to keep subjects in the dark about the intervention.) However, the Common Rule requiring IRB review and consent only applies to federally funded research organizations, so institutional review of research performed by private firms is entirely voluntary.

Research interventions require consent and IRB review IF conducted by a federally-funded research organization.

[6] 45 CFR 46.102 (defining "human subject" research based on an intervention or the collection of identifiable private information).

[7] 45 CFR 46.101 (b) (defining categories of research that are exempt from IRB review).

[8] OFFICE OF CIVIL RIGHTS, GUIDANCE REGARDING METHODS FOR DE-IDENTIFICATION OF PROTECTED HEALTH INFORMATION IN ACCORDANCE WITH THE HEALTH INSURANCE PORTABILITY AND ACCOUNTABILITY ACT (HIPAA) PRIVACY RULE (2012).

[9] FREQUENTLY ASKED QUESTIONS: DISCLOSURE AVOIDANCE, PRIVACY TECHNICAL ASSISTANCE CENTER, DEPARTMENT OF EDUCATION (2012).

[10] FEDERAL TRADE COMMISSION, PROTECTING CONSUMER PRIVACY IN AN ERA OF RAPID CHANGE: RECOMMENDATIONS FOR BUSINESSES AND POLICYMAKERS (2012).

This has led some to worry that research at private firms is a free-for-all without any enforceable checks.[11] However, all conduct at private firms operates against a backdrop of generally applicable tort law and regulation. Generally applicable laws protect research subjects from unreasonable risks regardless of whether those risks are created for a research purpose or some other purpose. Moreover, compliance with IRB rules and even consent should not shield a researcher from civil and criminal penalties if he should have foreseen the risks.

Nevertheless, this basic scheme has come under significant attack over the last few years for understandable reasons: the distinction between federally funded research and private corporate research is senseless at best, backwards at worst.

Today, there are two strong calls for legal reform. First, many influential legal scholars and computer scientists argue that de-identified data is so easy to reidentify that it cannot be relied on as a useful tool to manage the conflict between privacy and research, and regulators are taking these arguments seriously (although to date, none have abandoned de-identification as a key determinant of legal status for data).

At the same time, there has also been a push to expand the Common Rule to apply to all research, not just research performed by academic and other federally funded research organizations.

Together, these proposals would significantly raise the costs and administrative burdens of research. In the next three parts, we will get a sense of where these calls for reform are coming from.

DATA REPURPOSING

OK Cupid routinely uses data from its dating website to reveal all sorts of interesting things about how humans behave when attracting mates. The company's research has confirmed that racial preferences or implicit bias affects the dating market. On the bright side, they have also found that people still care about grammar. Initial messages are much less likely to receive a response when they use the letter "U" instead of "you."[12]

Their practices are, strictly speaking, violations of FIPPs.[13] FIPPs require firms to provide notice and choice before repurposing data that was collected for a legitimate business purpose. This privacy interest would have a severe effect on research if lawmakers were to imbed it in enforceable legal rights.

Although FIPPs provide the underpinnings for modern privacy law and policy around the world, the principle against data repurposing is rarely applied to research. Indeed, one of the defining features of big data is the practice of combining and analyzing data to reveal patterns unrelated to the original transactions. Data analytics frequently uses data that was collected for one purpose and uses it for some other unexpected processing. Strict adherence to FIPPs would require OK Cupid to give effective notice and consent before studying the data it

---

[11] Daniel Solove, Facebook's Psych Experiment: Consent, Privacy, and Manipulation, HUFFINGTON POST (Aug. 30, 2014); Ryan Calo, *Consumer Subject Review Boards: A Thought Experiment*, 66 STAN. L. REV.ONLINE 97 (2013).

[12] OKTRENDS BLOG, https://blog.okcupid.com/.

[13] HEW REPORT, *supra* note 16, at xx; see also ROBERT GELLMAN, FAIR INFORMATION PRACTICES: A BASIC HISTORY (Feb. 11, 2015), http://bobgellman.com/rg-docs/rg-FIPShistory.pdf (providing a history of FIPPs).

collects about its users, and would also require outside researchers to get consent before observing, scraping, and reusing data even if they have lawful access to the information. With respect to repurposing, the "insider" and "outsider" distinction would not matter – both the company and the user would be equally guilty of exploiting their access to information in order to do something other dating or facilitating dating. Thus, as a purely descriptive matter, the FIPP honoring the right to prevent data repurposing would either halt data analytics as we know it or would force courts to water down the concept of "consent" so that it serves little value to data subjects.

This raises the question: Is data repurposing actually an affront to human dignity? The demand for notice and consent is closely related to another factor that has drifted through the commentary without a lot of reflection: As a species, we simply do not like to be studied. We have a natural aversion to the accumulation of power by others who have observed us. This aversion has ancient origins and has an evolutionary explanation. Recall, in the Old Testament, God punishes King David with a plague on his people not because David killed many people in his conquests, but because David had the hubris to take a census. *That* kind of social information belonged to God, not to man.

This longstanding discomfort ought to be acknowledged and confronted explicitly because the instincts may not serve us well, now that we live in a collaborative and more civilized society.

The limitation on repurposing data raises two significant problems. First, the original context or purpose of the data collection is usually ambiguous. For example, perhaps we *should* assume that OK Cupid will study many facets of dating in case some of the findings affect the medium- and long-term designs of the platform.

Second, good research often has to be disrespectful of context. US Census data, which serves the primary purpose of allocating resources and voting interests across the country, is used for a wide array of public policy research. Google has received a lot of praise for using search terms to identify previously unknown side effects of prescription drugs. Outside researchers have used search data that Google makes available to study the chilling effects caused by Edward Snowden's revelations that the federal government secretly collected private Internet communications. Thomas Piketty's critique of wealth distribution policies used repurposed tax records. The study conclusively finding that the drug Vioxx caused a significant increase in the risk of cardiac arrest used repurposed insurance data from Kaiser Permanente. More generally, all of the most important health social science relies to some extent on repurposed data, and the consequences of forbidding that research would be hard for anybody to stomach.

Thus, it is not surprising that just about every law that has used FIPPs as its guide has also recognized a research exception. That exception typically permits researchers to access data collected for some other purpose as long as the data is first de-identified so that the sensitive information cannot be linked back an associated with any specific research subject.

REIDENTIFICATION RISK

Next, we consider heightened concerns about the validity of data anonymization techniques in light of recent demonstration reidentification attacks. IRBs and lawmakers are increasingly worried that common de-identification techniques may not actually offer much protection. However, the demonstration attacks tend to exaggerate the risks of reidentification.

Let's use the famous Latanya Sweeney reidentification of then-Governor William Weld to illustrate how reidentification attacks usually work.[14] At the time, Sweeney was a graduate student at MIT who saw a problem with the way many public health databases were prepared– by removing names and doing little else. She used voter registration records to reidentify Governor Weld in a public-use research database containing hospital admissions information in Massachusetts. The William Weld attack was a matching attack, and all matching attacks work, more or less, as so:

An intruder takes a deidentified database and tries to find a set of records that describes the general population, includes identities, and shares at least some of the variables with the deidentified data. These circles represent the information in the variables that the two databases have in common.

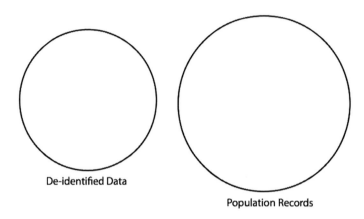

Next, the intruder looks for research subjects who have some unique combination of values across a number of variables in the de-identified data. And she then looks for unique combinations of those same variables in the de-identified data.

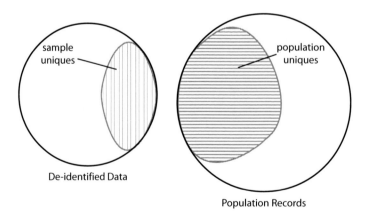

---

[14] Latanya Sweeney, *k-Anonymity: A Model for Protecting Privacy*, 10 INT'L J. UNCERTAINTY, FUZZINESS & KNOWLEDGE-BASED SYS. 557 (2002).

Next the intruder links up all the uniques that he can. Some of the population uniques will not be in the sample of de-identified data, and some of the sample uniques won't be linkable because there will actually be two or more people in the population who share those characteristics. But those who are unique in both can be reidentified.

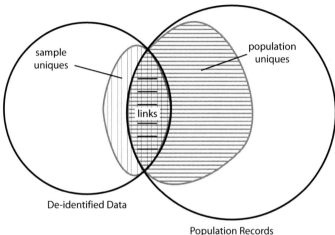

Latanya Sweeney performed just this sort of attack. She found Governor Weld's birthdate and zip code using voter registration records, which are public. Moreover, Governor Weld was the *only* person in the voter registration records with his combination of sex, birth date, and zip code. She then used the Massachusetts de-identified hospital records which at the time (this is before the passage of HIPAA) included the birth date, full zip code, and gender of each patient. One of the hospital patients had the same unique combination of demographics as Governor Weld, so a unique was matched to a unique, and voilà – the demonstration attack was born.

Moreover, Sweeney went on to show that Governor Weld was not special. Using census data, Sweeney estimated that about 87 percent of Americans have a unique combination of birthdate, home zip code, and gender, thus putting most of us at risk of such an attack. (During replication the figure has since been corrected to 63 percent, but the point remains that most of us are unique along those three variables.)

However, even this reidentification attack, which was exceedingly influential in the design of HIPAA and in subsequent policy discussions, actually exaggerates the opportunities for reidentification because it does not account for the very high chance of false matches.

First, remember that in theory the intruder has population records so that he knows that he is linking a record in the deidentified data to some unique person in the general population. In fact, neither Latanya Sweeney nor any real intruder will ever have a complete set of population records. Even voter registration records are incomplete (we know a sizable portion of our population isn't registered to vote), and information collected from the Internet in an ad hoc way is even more porous.

Daniel Barth-Jones, an epidemiologist at Columbia's School of Public Health, has replicated the William Weld attack.[15] By comparing voter registration records to the census records from

[15] Daniel C. Barth-Jones, The "Re-identification" of Governor William Weld's Medical Information: A Critical Re-Examination of Health Data Identification Risks and Privacy Protections, Then and

the same time, he found that 35 percent of adults in Massachusetts were NOT registered to vote. Moreover, it would have been quite likely for an *unregistered* person to share a birth date, gender, and zip code with someone who looks unique in the voter registration data. He used pigeonhole calculations to predict the chance that another man shared Governor Weld's sex, birth date, and zip code. There was a 35 percent chance that somebody may have shared Governor Weld's demographics. Even after ruling out everybody in the voter registration rolls (who obviously did not share Weld's demographics), there *still* would have been a good chance – about 18 percent – that somebody who wasn't registered to vote shared the same combination.

So a match of the sort that Latanya Sweeney did could come with an 82 percent confidence rate, which is quite good, but might not be good enough for an intruder to bother carrying out a mass matching attack.

Today, norms and laws push data holders to do a better job deidentifying their research data. The HIPAA privacy rule provides two routes to making health data de-identified. Under the most common, safe harbor method, data providers remove all or part of eighteen different types of variables. The list of course includes zip code and birth date, though year of birth and coarsened geographic information can be included (45 C.F.R. §164.514(b)(2)). Under the expert approach, data is handed over to somebody versed in statistical disclosure control techniques who deidentifies it in a way that preserves a lot more utility than the safe harbor method can afford without significantly increasing the opportunities for reidentification. The expert must certify that the de-identified data poses "a very low probability of identifying individuals" (45 C.F.R. §164.514(b)(1)).

This does add some cost and drag on research, of course, but from the privacy perspective HIPAA-deidentified data has had a good showing. For example, a study performed by the Office of the National Coordinator for Health Information Technology (ONC) put HIPAA deidentification to the test by taking a sample of 15,000 HIPAA-compliant deidentified records and asking a team of experts to try to reidentify them using public records and commercially available databases.[16] They found that two out of the 15,000 files were successfully matched to patient identities. That's a risk of .013 percent. This is an exceedingly small risk. To give you a sense – the data subjects are more likely to die in an auto accident this year than they are to be reidentified if an attack is attempted. (For comparison's sake, the chance of dying from an auto accident this year is approximately .017 percent.)

More importantly, the research team *thought* they had correctly identified twenty-eight of the records. This further proves that reidentification attacks take time and effort and, even after all that, can be overwhelmed with false matches.

Another more recent study published in *Science* illustrates how commonly the technical literature ignores the problem of false positives. The study, called "Unique in the Shopping Mall," made headlines in the *New York Times* and many other major news outlets for purportedly showing that de-identified credit card data could easily lead to reidentification of the credit card holders.[17] The authors used a database consisting of three months of purchasing

Now (2012), available at https://fpf.org/wp-content/uploads/The-Re-identification-of-Governor-Welds-Medical-Informa tion-Daniel-Barth-Jones.pdf.

[16] Deborah Lafky, *The Safe Harbor Method of De-Identification: An Empirical Test*, DEPT. OF HEALTH & HUMAN SERVICES OFFICE OF THE NATIONAL COORDINATOR FOR HEALTH INFORMATION TECHNOLOGY (2009), available at http://www.ehcca.com/presentations/HIPAAWest4/lafky_2.pdf.

[17] Yves-Alexander de Montjoye, *Unique in the Shopping Mall: On the Reidentifiability of Credit Card Metadata*, 347 SCIENCE 536 (2015).

records for 1.1 million credit card clients in an undisclosed OECD country. The credit card company removed names and other direct identifiers, and the authors used the database to evaluate uniqueness. More specifically, the authors calculated the chance that any given person in the database is unique (compared to the other cardholders whose data is included in the database) based on X number of purchase transactions. So, for example, if Jim was the only person in the database who made a purchase at a particular bakery on September 23 and at a particular restaurant on September 24, he would be unique with only two transactions.

The authors used these "tuples" – place-date combinations – to estimate the chance that a person in the database looks unique in the database, and found that 90 percent of the data subjects were unique based on just four place-date tuples. They thus concluded that 90 percent of credit card users are reidentifable based on just 4 four transactions. In other words, the authors treated sample uniqueness as equivalent to reidentification risk. The authors completed this step of finding sample uniques and then stopped.

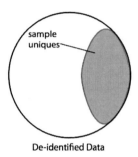

De-identified Data

The problem is that there's still a lot of work to do after finding that somebody is unique in a database in order to link them to a specific, identified person in the world. Indeed, knowing that somebody is unique in the research data doesn't even tell us whether they really are unique in the general population. This credit card data only describes a sample of the general population, so it's missing a lot of information about the rest of the population. If the data came from a country with tens of millions of credit card holders, uniqueness within the anonymized database would be a poor measure of uniqueness within the general population.

All the *Science* article did was show that data subjects tend to be unique within their database. Those accustomed to working with research data would not be surprised by this finding; the whole point of working with individual-level data is to make use of the unique combinations of factors that people in the database have. Otherwise, aggregated tables would do.

None of this critique is meant to suggest that deidentified research data is risk-free. But there are flaws in the reporting that tend to distort the public perception of risk. A malicious attack on expertly deidentified data would be costly and difficult, and even attacks on inexpertly deidentified data would be more error-prone than commentators tend to acknowledge.

Today, policymakers are very nervous about the risk of reidentification. They are persuaded that something fundamental has changed in the balance between research and privacy, and that data subjects are now exposed to too much risk. This perception is inspired in part by the work of Paul Ohm, a legal scholar and former advisor to the FTC. Based on demonstration attacks on public research data from AOL and Netflix, Ohm concluded that anonymization is dead, that people can be reidentified with "astonishing ease," and that consequently, every privacy law that relies on the concept of anonymization must be rewritten to restrict access to data.[18]

In other words, Ohm persuasively argued that de-identification does not strike a safe balance between privacy and research benefits. Yet the value proposition for anonymization is still very good.

One way to understand how well deidentification has performed as a form of good-enough privacy is by comparing it to the risks of privacy breaches that we are very familiar with managing: the risk of data breaches from hacking and data spills. The Privacy Rights Clearing-house currently reports over 900 million breached records based on 5,113 reported data breaches since 2005. 47 million of these records contained health data. These breaches involved data in identified form. By contrast, there is no reliable evidence that bad actors are reidentifying anonymized research data.

The comparison to data breaches is also valuable for shedding light on the precautions that should and should not be taken. Although the current rate of data breach may be too high, nobody seriously argues that the appropriate level of data breach risk is zero. That standard would be too costly for firms and for society more broadly. The same is true for data anonymization.

Deidentification cannot eliminate the risk of an intrusive attack, but the risk is outweighed by the value society gets in return for the ability to share research data more widely. De-identified data facilitates replication efforts and allows researchers to study data pooled from multiple sources. De-identified data also allows the public to access government records that would otherwise be exempted from public records laws because of privacy interests. A rejection of de-identification as a tool for data-sharing will have little consequence for the businesses and agencies that collect the data and great consequence to outside, independent researchers.

Data de-identification and repurposing have not been seriously challenged by existing and proposed laws regulating research. Research interventions on the other hand have traditionally been viewed with skepticism. The next part asks whether current policies that subject research interventions to significant restrictions and review are serving important interests for research subjects.

SURREPTITIOUS INTERVENTIONS

In 2012, Facebook teamed up with researchers at Cornell University to investigate whether mood is affected by the moods of our friends as expressed through Facebook status updates. The researchers took a sample of about 300,000 randomly selected Facebook users and divided them into two related experiments. The control groups saw the usual newsfeed on their home pages – the same newsfeed they would have seen if they weren't in the experiment. The experimental groups saw newsfeeds for which either positive or negative emotional expressions by their friends were reduced by 10 percent.

The researchers found that sure enough, people who saw fewer negative postings were very slightly less likely to post a negative status update themselves. And conversely, people who saw fewer positive postings were less likely to post a positive update, and more likely to post a negative one. It is not clear that this study documented any actual changes in mood as opposed to changes in what was expressed, and the effect was small in absolute terms. Nevertheless, it was an interesting finding, in part because it conflicted with other studies finding that people feel

---

[18] Paul Ohm, *Broken Promises of Privacy: Responding to the Surprising Failure of Anonymization*, 57 UCLA L. REV. 1701 (2010).

better about themselves when their friends share bad news, and feel worse about their status when friends share good news. (This could be known as the Gore Vidal theory of emotion contagion based on his quotable "every time a friend succeeds, I die a little.")

The Facebook emotion contagion experiment received a lot of press not because of its findings, but because the study was conducted surreptitiously, without any specific consent from Facebook users. It is not clear why this particular study captured the imagination and fears of the general public. It was not the first secret study that Facebook had conducted, nor was it the most significant in terms of its implications about Facebook's potential power. For example, an earlier study had compared a control group of Facebook users who saw a generic "Get out the Vote" message to an experimental group who saw a social stimulus – the same get-out-the-vote message paired with pictures of six friends who had reported that they have already voted.[19] The experimental group was slightly more likely to vote than the control group. In terms of substance, the "poke to vote" study seems to have far greater implications for the potential influence that Facebook could have over behavior. (Even for this study, though, it is worth keeping in mind that the size of the effect, while statistically significant, was very small – increasing voting by 0.39 percent. The effect may be marginal as compared to other media effects such as news coverage or media company endorsements.)

For whatever reason, the emotion contagion study was the one that set off a public debate about the law and ethics of research in the Internet era.

How important is it that Facebook did more than study the data it incidentally collected for operations and actually intervened, changing the newsfeed algorithm for some users? Experimental intervention is not at all unusual among information technology companies – indeed it is an entirely standard part of metrics-driven business practices. Google regularly engages in so-called "A/B testing," experimenting with the placement, phrasing, and design of its web pages to see how experimental groups compare to control groups. We know that the company constantly tweaks the algorithms used to generate search results based on the responsive behavior of its users. One longtime Google graphic designer even resigned in protest when he got tired of the testing he was asked to do to figure out which of forty-one different shades of blue produced the greatest click-through rate.[20]

These data-driven business practices are not actually all that new. Well before the Internet, retail spaces meticulously observed foot traffic and purchasing information to figure out how to optimize the layout of their stores and shelves. Nevertheless, the fact that a practice is popular is not a good justification on its own if the practice strikes many people as disrespectful or harmful.

The significance that research ethicists attach to experimental intervention does not hold up to careful scrutiny. The legal significance of a research intervention has two major flaws. First, it organizes law and policy around a research intent rather than around risky conduct. Second, it protects consumers only from systematic and methodologically sound research, and not from the myriad ad hoc experiments that happen as a matter of course.

Let's focus first on research intent. The very concept of an experimental "intervention" or "manipulation" suggests that there is some platonic neutral state of the world, but of course this is not so. People and firms constantly interact and "intervene" in others' lives. When Facebook changes its newsfeed algorithm for nonresearch purposes, Facebook users will be affected in all

[19] Robert M. Bond et al., *A 61-Million-Person Experiment in Social Influence and Political Mobilization*, 489 NATURE 295 (2012).

[20] Douglas Bowman, *Goodbye, Google*, STOPDESIGN (Mar. 20, 2009), http://stopdesign.com/archive/2009/03/20/goodbye-google.html.

the same ways as they would if they were in an experiment. The only thing that distinguishes a research intervention from the rest of life is an intention to learn from it. So we are left with an important question: Why is it legally and socially acceptable to manipulate people for business purposes, or for personal purposes, or even just for sport, but not for the sake of science? The explanation must reside in abstract notions of autonomy.

To be clear, if a research intervention exposes people to unreasonable risk of physical or emotional harm, it should be regulated. But this would be just as true for the same conduct performed without a research intent. Tort law and safety regulations will limit the researcher in these circumstances just as it limits other actors.

Second, research regulation does not really prevent experimental interventions. Rather, it protects us only from *good* research interventions – that is, from systematic studies that use random assignment. If a doctor picks a treatment for patient from among two equally standard and accepted treatments and is then curious to know how his patient fares, he is conducting a sort of experiment. It is not a particularly reliable one, to be sure, but the doctor made a choice that changed the status quo and then observed the results with interest. The same would be true if the doctor had ten patients, and recommended the same treatment for all ten. But if the doctor were to take the ten patients and randomly assign them to the two accepted treatments, his conduct would cross into the domain of formal research, and the doctor could not proceed without informed consent.

Together, these problems should raise serious doubts about traditional research policy. Existing laws and proposals for their expansion are fueled by moral objections to the intent to create generalized knowledge. Put as plainly as that, the laws are not even constitutional, let alone sensible.[21]

To be clear, nothing should inhibit regulators from restricting conduct that causes known or plausible harm to consumers. If Facebook *uses* its research findings to depress its users into shopping more often, or to stifle the vote in an election, then of course something sinister may be occurring, and the law may need to step in. But the initial research should not be objectionable unless the intervention is itself harmful conduct (regardless of intent). My critique here extends only to research interventions that could be implemented for nonresearch purposes without violating any law or shared social norms.

Indeed, the research may reveal ways that Facebook can *enhance* public welfare, particularly when it is willing to share its findings with the world rather than treating them as proprietary. Unfortunately, Facebook was punished for doing that.

In fact, the individuals who received the greatest disapprobation were the academic researchers at Cornell. The publication of their study led to an unprecedented focus on their compliance with IRB regulations, and under current law at least at the national level, only researchers at institutions that receive federal research funding are required to comply with the rules. The Cornell researchers were criticized for exploiting a sort of IRB loophole. The researchers structured the study such that they gave input to Facebook about designing the intervention, then let Facebook actually implement it, and later collected the data. This arguably kept the Cornell researchers' involvement within the definition of "exempt research" under the Common Rule so that IRB review was not required. This was controversial.[22] Even the journal that published the article published a statement of concern about the Cornell researchers'

[21] Philip Hamburger, *The New Censorship: Institutional Review Boards*, 6 Sup. Ct. Rev. 271 (2006).
[22] Meeting Notes, Council for Big Data, Ethics & Society, http://bdes.datasociety.net/wpcontent/uploads/2015/02/minutes-2014-11-14.pdf (calling the Facebook Emotion Contagion study a "research scandal"); James Grimmelmann, *The Law and Ethics of Experiments on Social Media Users*, 13 Colo. Tech. L. J. 219 (2015) (calling it "IRB laundering").

decision to proceed without full IRB review or consent. Yet IRB review may not have made a difference; the low stakes of this particular intervention would have permitted the researchers to use expedited review, and very likely would have permitted them to proceed without consent. The excessive focus on IRB rules that may have been mere technicalities is a symptom that public reaction is based on unsettled instincts without a clear theory of harm.

CONCLUSIONS

In the end, popular research policy has produced four unfortunate lessons for big data companies.

First, a company or institution should not share data with outside researchers since they may become the next target of a demonstration reidentification attack.

Second, a company is at a disadvantage when working with researchers at academic or federally funded research institutions since they run legal and public perceptions risks related to IRB regulations.

Third, companies are at a disadvantage when they formalize and carefully test their predictions about consumer behavior rather than operating on the basis of assumptions, conventional wisdom, or untested theories.

And fourth, certainly from a public relations perspective, a company is much better off hoarding its findings rather than sharing them with the public.

Proposals to expand the Common Rule reduces the second of these four problems but exacerbates the others. Instead of increasing the regulations of research at private firms to match the regulation of publicly funded researchers, lawmakers should consider reorienting the law to reduce concrete risks while removing some of the unnecessary costs of research.

25

A Marketplace for Privacy

Incentives for Privacy Engineering and Innovation

Courtney Bowman and John Grant

INTRODUCTION

To what extent should the government further regulate consumer privacy protection or will the free market drive businesses to augment and/or provide these protections themselves? There has been much discussion of the market effects of consumer demand (or lack thereof) for privacy, but we contend that this consumer-oriented focus loses sight of a second – and potentially just as significant – market: the talent-oriented market for the programmers and engineers at the heart of the information technology industry. In this chapter, we aim to explore privacy not as *a value*, but as *value itself*, exploring the dual markets of privacy-enhancing products, services, and corporate practices on the one hand and privacy-motivated engineering talent on the other.

Commentators tend to situate their defense of informational privacy interests in the field of rights, ethics, and moral inquiry, i.e., treating privacy as a value to be defended as such. We do not wish to suggest that such defenses are not worth pursuing; on the contrary, we believe that the recognition and defense of privacy as a value is essential and we therefore assume some normative grounding of privacy interests as a critical point of departure for the chapter to follow. We do, however, wish to argue that privacy interests can and should also be evaluated in market terms, as a competitive force driving *both* corporate responses to consumer demands *and* the placement of prized and limited engineering talent. This is a suggestion that is often overlooked in technology and informational privacy discussions, but we aim to demonstrate its time has come.

DO CONSUMERS CARE ABOUT PRIVACY?

In determining whether concerns about privacy influence consumer choices, we begin by looking at the consumers themselves: Do they believe that privacy is important? At first glance, research suggests that they do highly value privacy, as both consumers themselves and the companies that court them expressly state. However, actual consumer actions may not always be consistent with their stated preferences, making it unclear just how much of an effect these stated preferences actually have when a consumer is standing at the cash register or about to click the "Purchase" button online. Given the inherent complexity of surveying individuals about a complex concept such as privacy and the challenge of isolating a single factor from the myriad factors influencing a purchasing decision, we then examine whether corporate behavior appears to be influenced by a belief that consumer choice – and therefore profitability – depends upon a market driven by consumer demand for privacy.

Expressed Consumer Preferences

There is no shortage of public opinion polling on privacy questions. Whether in the form of a directly expressed opinion or manifested as a preference for a privacy-enhancing policy or practice, consumers overwhelmingly favor privacy.

When posed as a direct question, preference for privacy has scored high marks for nearly two decades. In April 2001, the American Society of Newspaper Editors found that 81 percent of those polled were either "very concerned" or "somewhat concerned" that a commercial entity might violate their privacy.[1] A UPI-Zogby poll from April 2007 found that 85 percent of respondents said that privacy is important to them as consumers.[2] A 2015 survey by Gigya – a "customer identity management platform" provider – found that a whopping 96 percent of US respondents "admit to being somewhat or very concerned about data privacy and how companies are using customer data."[3]

Privacy concerns often present themselves as suspicion of new technologies. In March 2000, 89 percent of respondents said they were uncomfortable with tracking user behavior on the Internet, while a Pew Internet & American Life survey in 2008 on cloud computing found that 90 percent of respondents were concerned that their personal data might be sold by cloud providers, and 68 percent objected to the scanning and analysis of the data to inform targeted advertising.[4] A 2014 PwC survey found that 82 percent of Americans are worried that so-called wearable technology will invade their privacy and suggested that this worry "thwart[s] greater adoption of wearable devices."[5]

Concerns about general privacy protection were significant enough to translate into support for enhanced government regulation in the space. In August 2000, a Pew Internet and American Life report found that an overwhelming 94 percent of respondents thought that privacy violators should face some sort of government discipline for their actions.[6] A Markle Foundation study a year later found 64 percent support for more rules designed to protect privacy on the Internet.[7] In February 2002, a Harris poll found a similar number (63 percent) thought that the current law was inadequate to protect online privacy.[8]

Consumer preferences for privacy are also manifest in support for privacy-enhancing policies and technologies. Polls have found overwhelming support for opt-in consent before websites share data (86 percent of respondents in two 2000 polls[9]) as well as the posting of privacy notices clearly explaining how data will be used (75 percent of respondents in 2000[10]). Support for the "Right to Be Forgotten" provision of the forthcoming European Union General Data Protection

---

[1] *Public Opinion on Privacy*, Electronic Privacy Information Center, *available at* https://epic.org/privacy/survey/ (last visited Feb. 23. 2017).

[2] *Id.*

[3] Gigya, *The 2014 State of Consumer Privacy and Personalization, available at* http://www.gigya.com/blog/survey-the-state-of-consumer-privacy-personalization/ (last visited Feb. 23, 2017).

[4] *Public Opinion on Privacy*, Electronic Privacy Information Center, *available at* https://epic.org/privacy/survey/ (last visited Feb. 23. 2017).

[5] William Welsh, "Wearable Devices: Privacy, Security Worries Loom Large," *InformationWeek* (Oct. 22, 2014), *available at* http://www.informationweek.com/healthcare/mobile-and-wireless/wearable-devices-privacy-security-worries-loom-large/d/d-id/1316833.

[6] *Public Opinion on Privacy*, Electronic Privacy Information Center, *available at* https://epic.org/privacy/survey/ (last visited Feb. 23. 2017).

[7] *Id.*

[8] *Id.*

[9] *Id.*

[10] *Id.*

Regulation (GDPR) – under which individuals can request that data controllers delete identifiable information about themselves – hovers around numbers that any world leader would covet – 61 percent in 2015, according to Software Advice.[11]

Of course, as Homer Simpson reminds us, "People can come up with statistics to prove anything. Forfty [sic] percent of all people know that."[12] It would be quite easy to cherry-pick surveys that prove our general point, and other polling data suggests that consumers may quickly abandon a preference for privacy for the sake of convenience, financial benefit, or just because the "product" has more appeal than any loss of personal privacy. For example, in the afore-mentioned Gigya survey that found 96 percent of customers concerned about data privacy, 56 percent of respondents reported using a "social login" (e.g., a Facebook account) to access multiple websites because they preferred not to "spend time filling in registration forms in order to register on a site." The inconvenience of filling out a registration for each website visited (which can be quite minimal given the Autofill capabilities on most Web browsers) clearly outweighs any concerns about allowing a single entity to collect more information about users' Web browsing and purchasing habits.

Polling on privacy can be particularly fraught due to any number of factors. First and foremost, the ambiguous nature of the very concept of privacy means that any single respondent will likely have a different conception of the term.[13] Consequently, unlike other consumer polling where the options are going to be clearly defined – a sample of Coca Cola is the same for every participant – in the case of privacy it will be almost impossible to determine the nuanced definition of that term that sits inside each respondent's head. This ambiguity further muddies the water when respondents are given a choice between privacy and something more tangible such as a product or access to information or entertainment. The immediate gratification of a desire to see exclusive media content may trump the ambiguous longer-term individual and societal harms that might arise from a lack of individual privacy. The context of the polling can also be significant. Societal attitudes toward privacy can be significantly affected by current events. Consequently, sensitivity about privacy may differ significantly depending on whether the survey was taken after a frightening security event such as the terrorist attacks of September 11, 2001, versus a paranoia-inducing revelation such as those about mass government surveillance by former US National Security Agency contractor Edward Snowden.

A full assessment of consumer attitudes regarding privacy and the strengths and weaknesses of public opinion polling on the topic is beyond the scope of this chapter. Although attitudes toward privacy can differ greatly between individuals and may be affected by any number of factors, we suggest that the surveys cited above provide – if nothing else – an indication that many consumers are at least conscious of some concept of privacy when interacting with commercial entities. We do not attempt to pinpoint exactly how this privacy consciousness plays into the complex mélange of factors that go into any single purchasing decision – and indeed it may be different for every consumer – but the fact that it registers at all should be of interest to marketers, particularly in an age of precisely calibrated personalized consumer interactions.

---

[11] Cheryl Kemp, "61 Percent of Americans Support the Right to Be Forgotten as California Enacts New Law," *WHIR*, Sep. 29. 2014, *available at* http://www.thewhir.com/web-hosting-news/61-percent-americans-support-right-forgotten-california-enacts-new-law (last visited Dec. 26, 2017).

[12] *The Simpsons: Homer the Vigilante* (Fox television broadcast, Jan. 6, 1994).

[13] Daniel J. Solove, *Understanding Privacy* (Cambridge, MA: Harvard University Press, 2008), 1.

Corporate Perspective

MA TYLER: Most round here do [believe in a superstition]. And when most believe, that do make it true.

JACK TYLER: Most people used to believe that the Earth was flat, but it was still round.

MA TYLER: Ah ha, but they behaved as if 'twere flat.[14]

Whether or not consumers *actually* consider privacy to be a deciding factor in their decisions to buy a product or visit a website, corporations seem to believe that they do and indeed have stated so directly. Furthermore, the actual behavior of consumers notwithstanding, commercial entities have taken actions – particularly in response to recent government and intelligence law enforcement behaviors – that suggest that they expect the market to reward privacy protection.

Commercial entities directly extoll the importance of privacy to their customers both on and off the record. Kenneth Bamberger and Deirdre Mulligan, in their book *Privacy on the Ground*, interviewed a number of corporate executives from around the world about their approach to privacy and their relationships to privacy regulators. The interviews were conducted with "corporate professionals identified as leading the field of privacy protection" from "large firms," but the quotes are unattributed to encourage candor.[15] These executives were quick to cite consumer concerns about privacy as a factor in the increase in the number of privacy offices and their powers within these entities. According to Bamberger and Mulligan, "Every one of our respondents identified consumer expectations as a touchstone for developing corporate privacy practices."[16]

Corporate privacy officers interviewed suggested that customers saw concern about privacy as responsive to their demands: "Your customers will hold you to a higher standard than laws will, and the question is: Do you pay attention to your customers?"[17] This in turn builds consumer confidence in the company and strengthens the relationship with the customer as corporations consider "always what's the right thing to do to maintain the company's trusted relationship with our employees, with our clients, with any constituency in society that has a relationship to us."[18] Interestingly, while privacy is not a new concept, the perception of its value to consumers seems to be relatively recent, with one interviewee suggesting while "a number of years ago" consumers did not place privacy "high on the radar," now "we're seeing it pop up in RFPs [requests for proposals] in almost every selling instance."[19] According to Bamberger and Mulligan, executives attribute this heightened consciousness of privacy to "high-profile activities of the FTC [Federal Trade Commission] and the disclosures mandated by security breach notification laws" in combination with "already occurring social and technological changes."[20]

These off-the-record comments are echoed on-the-record as well – often quite prominently by high-level executives. Tim Cook, current CEO at Apple Inc. ("Apple"), has taken direct aim at consumers with a number of high profile statements on the importance of privacy. At a February 2015 White House-organized cybersecurity conference at Stanford University, Cook warned of the "dire consequences" of sacrificing privacy and called for a corporate commitment to its protection: "If those of us in positions of responsibility fail to do everything in our power

[14] *Doctor Who: Image of the Fendahl* (BBC television broadcast, Nov. 12, 1977). Forgive the indulgence as one of the authors has a (probably unhealthy) obsession with this show.

[15] Kenneth A. Bamberger and Deirdre K. Mulligan, *Privacy on the Ground* 11 (Cambridge, MA: MIT Press, 2015).

[16] *Id.* at 65.

[17] *Id.*

[18] *Id.* at 67.

[19] *Id.* at 66.

[20] *Id.* at 73.

to protect the right of privacy, we risk something far more valuable than money. We risk our way of life."[21] This was followed in September 2015 by an open letter to Apple's customers promising, amongst other things, that Apple does not build profiles of its customers and monetize the information that consumers entrust to them nor will it provide governments with "backdoor access" to its products or direct access to its servers.[22] Cook too equates privacy protection with maintaining the trust of its customers: "At Apple, your trust means everything to us. That's why we respect your privacy and protect it with strong encryption, plus strict policies that govern how all data is handled."

Other major companies have similarly recognized that consumers at some level crave privacy protections. Mark Zuckerberg, CEO of Facebook, famously suggested in 2010 that privacy was no longer a "social norm."[23] A few years later, Zuckerberg announced that Facebook was "looking for new opportunities to ... open up new, different private spaces for people where they can then feel comfortable sharing and having the freedom to express something to people that they otherwise wouldn't be able to. Because at some level there are only so many photos you're going to want to share with all your friends."[24] In 2007, Bill Gates – then CEO of Microsoft Corporation – advocated for a consumer privacy bill that would give consumers greater control over their personal data.[25]

Consumer privacy interests are recognized not just by these major players in the market but also by a number of new entrants who promote rigorous privacy protection as a key selling point. Messaging service SnapChat touts its ability to enable users to "express whatever is on your mind ... without automatically creating a permanent record of everything you've ever said."[26] Another messaging service – WhatsApp (now owned by Facebook) – declared itself:

> built ... around the goal of knowing as little about you as possible: You don't have to give us your name and we don't ask for your email address. We don't know your birthday. We don't know your home address. We don't know where you work. We don't know your likes, what you search for on the internet or collect your GPS location. None of that data has ever been collected and stored by WhatsApp, and we really have no plans to change that.[27]

Corporate Action

Of course, a statement that one recognizes a concern for privacy does not necessarily indicate true belief, leaving us to look for behavior consistent with the expressed mindset. Silicon Valley's behavior in this regard is decidedly mixed.

[21] Ashley Armstrong, "Tim Cook: Cyber Privacy Is a Life or Death Issue," *The Telegraph*, Feb. 13, 2015, *available at* http://www.telegraph.co.uk/finance/11412625/Tim-Cook-Cyber-privacy-is-a-life-and-death-issue.html (last visited Dec. 26, 2017).

[22] Apple's Commitment to Your Privacy, *available at* https://www.apple.com/privacy/ (last visited Feb. 23, 2017).

[23] Bobbie Johnson, "Privacy No Longer a Social Norm, Says Facebook Founder," *The Guardian*, Jan. 10, 2010, *available at* https://www.theguardian.com/technology/2010/jan/11/facebook-privacy (last visited Dec. 26, 2017).

[24] Will Oremus, "Facebook's Privacy Pivot," *Slate*, July 25, 2014, *available at* http://www.slate.com/articles/technology/future_tense/2014/07/facebook_s_privacy_pivot_mark_zuckerberg_s_plan_to_win_back_trust.html (last visited Dec. 26, 2017).

[25] "Microsoft's Bill Gates Wants New Privacy Law," *CIO*, Mar. 8, 2007, *available at* http://www.cio.com/article/2441839/security-privacy/microsoft-s-bill-gates-wants-new-privacy-law.html (last visited Dec. 26, 2017).

[26] "Snaps and Chats," *available at* https://www.snap.com/en-US/privacy/our-approach/ (last visited Feb. 23, 2017).

[27] Philip Bates, "Everything You Need to Know About Your WhatsApp Privacy Settings," *Make Use Of*, Nov. 21, 2014, *available at* http://www.makeuseof.com/tag/everything-need-know-whatsapp-privacy-settings/ (last visited Dec. 26, 2017).

Google and Facebook lead a veritable pack of Silicon Valley companies that seek to build their fortunes in large part on the ever-expanding mountain of data that they collect, store, and ultimately monetize in various formats. In order to return relevant search results, Google's automated web crawlers constantly scour the Internet for new content and then update their 95-pedabyte-and-growing index, which is used to return customized search results.[28] Google's popular "free" email service, Gmail, further adds to the mountain of data stored in their servers in the form of the email content and metadata of more than 1 billion users.[29] This in turn can be further combined with profile information and user activities from any of Google's many other offerings – including YouTube subscribers, Android mobile phone users, Google+ social media platform members, and other services.[30] The end result is an often startlingly accurate user profile.[31] Facebook similarly has amassed a substantial amount of personal information provided by its 1.79 billion active monthly users (as of the third quarter of 2016).[32] This data is again analyzed and used to generate targeted advertising for Facebook users as they navigate the social media platform and beyond.[33]

Meanwhile, armies of developers build a dizzying variety of mobile device applications ("apps") that do everything from simulate a *Star Wars* lightsaber to providing insight into the best seat selection on airlines while often simultaneously – both overtly and covertly – mining contact lists and other mobile device information to be sold to data brokers, retailers, and advertisers all trying to most efficiently match consumers to the products they are most likely to buy.[34] As of June 2016, the Android app store offered 2.2 million apps to users, while Apple device users could choose from approximately 2 million.[35]

Unsurprisingly given the intrinsic link between this data and their overall success, these companies zealously and often at great cost defend this gold mine of data and their freedom to use it as they please, drawing the ire of privacy advocates and even regulators. In 2010, Google asserted that all Gmail users expressly consent to automated scanning of emails in support of targeted advertising and even individuals who do *not* have a Gmail account "impliedly" consent to such scanning when they email a Gmail user as it fought a class action lawsuit by a number of its users alleging violations of the Federal Wiretap Act and the California Invasion of Privacy Act.[36] Ultimately the case fell apart when the judge refused to certify the class, and Google later quietly settled with the plaintiffs with undisclosed terms and without admitting any fault – or

---

[28] Scott Matteson, "How Does Google Search Really Work?" *Tech Republic*, Dec. 11, 2013, *available at* http://www .techrepublic.com/blog/google-in-the-enterprise/how-does-google-search-really-work/ (last visited Dec. 26, 2017).

[29] Craig Smith, "By the Numbers: 15 Amazing Gmail Statistics," *DMR*, Aug. 4, 2016, *available at* http://expandedram blings.com/index.php/gmail-statistics/ (last visited Dec. 26, 2017).

[30] "Google to Track Users … Like Never Before," *RT*, Jan. 25, 2012, *available at* https://www.rt.com/news/google-privacy-policy-tracking-671/ (last visited Dec. 26, 2017).

[31] Brian R. Fitzgerald, "Google to Sell User Profiles, Photos in Ads," *Wall Street Journal*, Oct. 11, 2013, *available at* http:// blogs.wsj.com/digits/2013/10/11/google-to-sell-user-profiles-and-photos-in-ads/ (last visited Dec. 26, 2017).

[32] "Number of Monthly Active Facebook Users Worldwide as of 4th Quarter 2016," *The Statistics Portal*, *available at* https://www.statista.com/statistics/264810/number-of-monthly-active-facebook-users-worldwide/ (last visited Feb. 23, 2017).

[33] "How to Target Facebook Ads," *available at* https://www.facebook.com/business/a/online-sales/ad-targeting-details/ (last visited Feb. 23, 2017).

[34] Sam Biddle, "How iPhone Apps Steal Your Contact Data and Why You Can't Stop It," *Gizmodo*, Feb. 15, 2012, *available at* http://gizmodo.com/5885321/how-iphone-apps-steal-your-contact-data-and-why-you-cant-stop-it (last visited Dec. 26, 2017).

[35] "Number of Apps Available in Leading App Stores," *The Statistics Portal*, *available at* https://www.statista.com/ statistics/276623/number-of-apps-available-in-leading-app-stores/ (last visited Feb. 23, 2017).

[36] Defendant's Motion to Dismiss at 2, In Re: Google Inc. Gmail Litigation, Northern District of California (2013).

committing to any change in its practices.[37] Google took center stage again in 2014, wading into battle with European courts and regulators as they championed a so-called "right to be forgotten" that data subjects can assert in requesting that information about them be deleted from an entity's servers. The case was widely reported, and the world watched while Google argued that freedom of speech protections gave them substantial discretion to continue to display search results over a data subject's objection.[38] When the European Court of Justice (EJC) disagreed and ruled that Google must entertain and under certain conditions grant requests to remove personal data from their search results, Google responded (arguably somewhat petulantly) by broadly granting deletion requests even when not necessarily meeting the conditions set out in the ECJ's opinion.[39]

Company privacy values are not just reflected in the corporation–consumer relationship but also in the willingness of the company to cooperate with government requests for data. Rather than conduct direct surveillance on individuals, governments have found that they can access troves of personal information with minimal legal process. In 2007, Yahoo!, an Internet search engine, content producer, and email provider came under fire when it provided emails of supposed "dissidents" to the Chinese government upon request.[40] Ultimately, Yahoo! changed its policy for responding to such requests, but further revelations have indicated ongoing willingness to collaborate with government surveillance demands in other instances where legal authority is murky at best. Most recently, Yahoo! was reported to have collaborated with US intelligence agencies to modify "its email security program to flag the appearance of a digital 'signature' the U.S. had linked to a foreign terrorist group backed by another government" – a program deemed by the American Civil Liberties Union to be "unprecedented and unconstitutional."[41] Apple too has in the past collaborated closely with US government law enforcement agencies in assisting them in accessing customer data stored on physical devices as well as in cloud storage accounts.[42] This in spite of its carefully cultivated rebellious counterculture image.[43] Facebook frequently provides law enforcement and intelligence agencies with mountains of data from its social media platform, including the content of communications between multiple individuals via its messaging application.[44] Given their willingness to spend significant resources defending their own rights to data, the fact that they have – until recently (as we will see) – done so little to defend the privacy interests of their customers vis-à-vis the government suggests a disconnect between their professed devotion to privacy and their actions.

---

[37] Cara Salvatore, "Google Unveils Settlement in Email Scanning Suit," *Law360*, Dec. 14, 2016, *available at* https://www.law360.com/articles/872757/google-unveils-settlement-in-email-scanning-suit (last visited Dec. 26, 2017).

[38] Alan Travis and Charles Arthur, "EU Court Backs 'Right to Be Forgotten': Google Must Amend Results on Request," *The Guardian*, May 13, 2014, *available at* https://www.theguardian.com/technology/2014/may/13/right-to-be-forgotten-eu-court-google-search-results (last visited Dec. 26, 2017).

[39] Case C-131/12, Google Spain SL and Google Inc. v. Agencia Española de Protección de Datos (AEPD) and Mario Costeja González, ECLI:EU:C:2014:317 (2014).

[40] Ewen MacAskill, "Yahoo Forced to Apologise to Chinese Dissidents Over Crackdown on Journalists," *The Guardian*, Nov. 14, 2007, *available at* https://www.theguardian.com/technology/2007/nov/14/news.yahoo (last visited Dec. 26, 2017).

[41] Bree Fowler and Michael Liedtke, "Reported Yahoo Email Scanning Revives Surveillance Concern," *US News and World Report*, Oct. 5, 2013.

[42] Dave Gershgorn, "Apple Cares about Your Privacy Unless You Use iCloud," *Popular Science*, Feb. 19, 2016, *available at* https://www.popsci.com/apple-cares-about-your-privacy-unless-you-use-icloud (last visited Dec. 26, 2017).

[43] Luke Dormehl, *The Apple Revolution: Steve Jobs, the Counter Culture, and How the Crazy Ones Took Over the World* (London: Virgin Books, 2012).

[44] *Facebook Government Requests Report*, https://govtrequests.facebook.com/country/United%20States/2016-H2/ (accessed on May 7, 2017).

The so-called "gag orders" that can sometimes accompany these requests can limit the options of a company that does want to challenge a government order. And, given the sensitive or classified nature of many government investigations, it may be that these companies calculate a very low probability that government collaboration would be exposed, thus presenting a low risk of negative market effects. This calculation may have changed, however, with the 2013 revelations of former National Security Agency contractor Edward Snowden. The trove of documents provided by Snowden revealed extensive collaboration between Silicon Valley and the US government in the collection of information on individual users of assorted platforms and products.[45] In addition, the Snowden documents also suggested that US intelligence agencies had covertly accessed information systems of some of these same companies, at once absolving them of the sin of collaboration while exposing their security protocols as inadequate to protect their customers' data.[46]

Following the Snowden revelations, Silicon Valley displayed an apparently newfound interest in publicly questioning government authority to acquire information. The Microsoft Corporation fought to prevent government access to the content of a user's Hotmail email account, arguing that even though the user was in the United States and accessed the account from within the United States, the data was physically stored on a server located in Ireland and therefore outside US jurisdiction.[47] To the surprise of many observers, Microsoft's argument has prevailed – at least temporarily.[48] Microsoft has also challenged a gag order accompanying a court order for information, arguing that its First Amendment rights are violated by the imposed silence in the name of security.[49]

Social media platform Twitter has also taken a more aggressive stance toward government requests for information. Although the Twitter platform is generally widely accessible, the sheer volume of data can make collection and analysis of its content difficult. To facilitate this, Twitter can provide paying customers with "firehose" access – a means by which expansive streams of the platform's public content can be consumed by paying customers.[50] Twitter's Developer Agreement now explicitly cites international privacy law as a condition of using its data, expressly prohibiting developers "to display, distribute or otherwise make available Content to any person or entity that you reasonably believe will use such data to violate the Universal Declaration of Human Rights."[51] Twitter has even moved to cut off access to the firehose for US and other intelligence agencies.[52]

Apple made headlines in 2016 when it challenged a court order to assist the Federal Bureau of Investigation (FBI) in overriding security protocols in one of its iPhone devices. The phone was known to belong to one of the gunmen involved in the February 2015 mass shooting in San Bernardino, California, and the FBI sought access to the device in its pursuit of potentially

---

[45] Glenn Greenwald, *No Place to Hide* (New York: Picador, 2015).

[46] Barton Gellman, "NSA Infiltrates Links to Yahoo, Google Data Centers Worldwide, Snowden Documents Say," *Washington Post*, Oct. 30, 2013, *available at* https://www.washingtonpost.com/world/national-security/nsa-infiltrates-links-to-yahoo-google-data-centers-worldwide-snowden-documents-say/2013/10/30/e51d661e-4166-11e3-8b74-d89d714ca4dd_story.html?utm_term=.7941fd9bbff4 (last visited Dec. 26, 2017).

[47] Brief for Appellant, *Microsoft v. United States of America*, U.S. Second Circuit Court of Appeals, 2014 *available at* http://digitalconstitution.com/wp-content/uploads/2014/12/Microsoft-Opening-Brief-120820141.pdf.

[48] Orin Kerr, "2nd Circuit Denies Rehearing in Microsoft Ireland Case by an Evenly Divided Vote," *Washington Post*, Jan. 24, 2017.

[49] Shira Ovide, "Microsoft Also Challenges Government Surveillance Gag Order," *Wall Street Journal*, Jun. 26, 2013.

[50] Firehose access does not include messages exchanged between users through a Direct Messaging feature nor does it include content to which access has been restricted by the user.

[51] "Twitter Developer Agreement," *available at* https://dev.twitter.com/overview/terms/agreement.html.

[52] Brian Barrett, "Twitter May Have Cut Spy Agencies Off From Its Flood of Data," *Wired*, May 9, 2016, *available at* https://www.wired.com/2016/05/twitter-dataminr-intelligence-community/ (last visited Dec. 26, 2017).

useful intelligence information.[53] Failing to gain access to the locked device via its own means, the FBI first requested assistance from Apple and, having been rebuffed, sought and received a court order directing Apple to provide "reasonable technical assistance to assist law enforcement" in bypassing security features of the iPhone.[54] Apple immediately appealed the order – announcing its decision both in the judicial court but also in the court of public opinion. On February 16, 2016, Apple posted "A Message to Our Customers" on its website from CEO Tim Cook:

> The government could extend this breach of privacy and demand that Apple build surveillance software to intercept your messages, access your health records or financial data, track your location, or even access your phone's microphone or camera without your knowledge. While we believe the FBI's intentions are good, it would be wrong for the government to force us to build a backdoor into our products. And ultimately, we fear that this demand would undermine the very freedoms and liberty our government is meant to protect.[55]

The FBI and the Department of Justice might be forgiven for their expressed surprise and dismay in the face of Apple's vociferous opposition to the government order, as it was reported that Apple had unlocked iPhones for authorities in similar cases at least seventy times since 2008.[56] Some observers argued that this apparently inconsistent position was made more on "reputational grounds" than out of any concerns about legal precedent or technical capacity.[57]

Ultimately, a courtroom showdown between the most valuable company in the world and the most powerful government in the world never came to pass as the Department of Justice dropped its case against Apple, claiming that it had unlocked the phone without the help of Apple's engineers.[58] Nonetheless, others in the Valley quickly moved to avoid Apple's dilemma by introducing end-to-end encryption in their communications offerings – including Facebook Messenger, WhatsApp, Viber, Signal, and Telegram, amongst others.[59] Such encryption would make it nearly impossible for even app developers themselves to read the contents of communications carried across their platforms. Consequently, law enforcement and intelligence agencies renewed their concerns about the risk of "going dark" (i.e., losing the ability to collect vital intelligence information and/or evidence of criminal activity, even under the condition of a probable cause warrant), but there seemed to be little sympathy within the Silicon Valley community.[60] Battle lines appear to have been drawn.

---

[53] Sam Thielman, "*Apple v. the FBI*: What's the Beef, How Did We Get Here and What's at Stake?" *The Guardian*, Feb. 20, 2016, *available at* https://www.theguardian.com/technology/2016/feb/20/apple-fbi-iphone-explainer-san-bernardino (last visited Dec. 26, 2017).

[54] Dustin Volz and Joseph Menn, "Apple Opposes Order to Help Unlock California Shooter's Phone," *Reuters*, Feb. 17, 2016, *available at* https://www.reuters.com/article/california-shooting-timcook/apple-opposes-order-to-help-unlock-california-shooters-phone-idUSKCN0VQ0YG (last visited Dec. 26, 2017).

[55] "A Message to Our Customers," *available at* http://www.apple.com/customer-letter/ (last visited Feb. 23, 2017).

[56] Shane Harris, "Apple Unlocked iPhones for the Feds 70 Times Before," *The Daily Beast*, Feb. 17, 2016, *available at* https://www.thedailybeast.com/apple-unlocked-iphones-for-the-feds-70-times-before (last visited Dec. 26, 2017).

[57] *Id.*

[58] Laurie Segall, Jose Pagliery, and Jackie Wattles, "FBI Says It Has Cracked Terrorist's iPhone without Apple's Help," *CNN Money*, Mar. 28, 2016, *available at* http://money.cnn.com/2016/03/28/news/companies/fbi-apple-iphone-case-cracked/index.html (last visited Dec. 26, 2017).

[59] Rachel Ranosa, "9 Messaging Apps with End-to-End Encryption: Facebook Messenger, WhatsApp, iMessage and More," *Tech Times*, Jul. 9, 2016, *available at* http://www.techtimes.com/articles/169154/20160709/9-messaging-apps-with-end-to-end-encryption-facebook-messenger-whatsapp-imessage-and-more.htm (last visited Dec. 26, 2017).

[60] Majority Staff of House Homeland Security Committee, *Going Dark, Going Forward: A Primer on the Encryption Debate*, June 2016, *available at* https://homeland.house.gov/wp-content/uploads/2016/07/Staff-Report-Going-Dark-Going-Forward.pdf.

Was the Snowden leak the Silicon Valley equivalent of Paul's conversion on the road to Damascus, knocking tech CEOs out of their Teslas on the road to the Consumer Electronics Show with the Good Word of privacy? The relationships between these companies, the government, and consumers are complex and likely defy any simple explanation. While taking a stand against powerful government agencies with the occasional history of aggressive tactics against the private sector may seem bold and principled, there may in fact be little risk to companies of this size, which field global operations and control such a significant source of information and communication that the US government ultimately cannot afford to alienate them. In addition, if the desire to protect communications was indeed so strong within these companies, then why did the rush to implement end-to-end encryption only occur following a very public dispute? The technology behind this capability is not new, and the risk that the government's (or anyone else's) prying eye might stray to online communication has been anticipated since Whitfield Diffie and Martin Hellman first shook hands in 1974.[61]

The Whole Story?

Why then spend time and resources waging legal battles against government surveillance in the name of individual privacy while at the same time also aggressively opposing the pro-privacy initiatives of regulators, advocates, and even customers themselves? Clearly there is some advantage to having the company name associated with privacy in a public way. However, if consumers were truly making purchasing decisions based on privacy, they would surely be more attentive to the actual privacy protective features of a product or service and at least the more discerning ones might even be turned off by aggressive regulatory battles to weaken privacy controls.

We suggest that the corporate privacy strategy cannot be solely attributed to a concern for the consumer market, but that it makes more sense when considered in light of a second market in which technology companies must compete: the market for talent.

DO ENGINEERS CARE ABOUT PRIVACY?

While the first half of this chapter suggests that there is strong and growing (albeit imperfect) demand for a consumer interest driven privacy market, as we have seen there are also compelling reasons to doubt that privacy markets will take flight without added lift. Beyond consumer demand, we propose that privacy, as a market force, must also be buoyed by the need to recruit and retain talented engineering workers who are themselves highly motivated to care about the ethical and political implications of their professional undertakings. Moreover, we suggest that such a motive force cannot be relegated to a perfunctory or check-the-box compliance-oriented approach (e.g., mandatory review of a privacy memo or thirty-minute training session). Rather, satisfying the engineering market's demand for a workplace that substantively addresses privacy concerns requires (re)shaping the corporate ethos such that privacy considerations are made as central to an employee's sense of workplace identity and corporate loyalty as other employee offerings including compensation (i.e., salary, equity), benefits and workplace perks, titles and responsibilities, personal growth and development opportunities, reporting structures, work

---

[61] Diffie and Hellman created one of the encryption key exchange methods that became an essential component of secure information movement across the Internet. The authors commend Steven Levy's excellent book *Crypto* to any reader – technical and nontechnical alike – who has an interest in the battle over encryption started by these men and their contemporaries and continuing to this day.

environment, and organizational divisions. As we hope to demonstrate in the remainder of this chapter, programmers are uniquely situated as highly skilled, valued, and empowered workers to effectuate this kind of principled shift.

Further, the increasing competition on employee regard for privacy has a self-reinforcing effect, such that as more privacy-motivated talent comes on board because of the espoused corporate orientation, those employees will in turn bolster expectations – through both subtle and more assertive means, as we shall later discuss – for additional privacy-respectful business developments. Corporations, consequently, will increasingly experience internal pressures to put themselves out on the line as a demonstration of their commitment to meeting employee expectations. As public displays of these shifting corporate convictions and word-of-mouth employee testimonials multiply, workers are likely to experience an ever-stronger draw to firms that provide them with an opportunity to direct their talents towards more virtuous engineering endeavors.

Hacker Roots

Computer science engineers (or programmers) comprise the raw talent that drives information technology innovation and enables the success of the technology sector. "Hacking" or the assignation of "hacker" in some admixture of the historical, cultural, and operational senses,[62] is core to the identity of most computer programmers, whether or not they explicitly acknowledge it. The term has its roots in 1950s MIT with train enthusiasts who "hacked" their train sets to optimize, customize, or simplify modify how they functioned to perform in a manner that had not been enabled by the sets in their given form.[63] The efforts of these earlier hackers were largely benign in the sense that their interests, which later expanded into emerging computer systems, was directed at tinkering with machines and learning how they worked, and to "push [ing] computer systems beyond the defined limits."[64]

Hacking took on a more explicit ethical dimension in the 1970s with a divergent subculture focused on telephone systems. These phone hackers (or "phreakers") plied their craft to the exploitation of vulnerabilities in telephonic switch systems to make free long-distance phone calls.[65] With the advent and spread of the personal computer in the 1980s, hacking acquired its more nefarious or countercultural overtones. Fueled in part by dystopian science fiction narrative visions such as William Gibson's *Neuromancer*, individual hackers and hacker groups including the 414s, Legion of Doom, and Chaos Computer Club exploited developments in modem technology that enabled computers to communicate over telephone lines to go beyond "benign exploration of systems,"[66] and began to engage in acts to disrupt or shutdown remote systems, as well as acts of outright fraud that would soon become criminalized. Most prominent

---

[62] We might distinguish at least three senses of the term "hacking." The historical sense relates to the etymological roots of the phrase briefly rendered in the next paragraphs. The cultural sense tends to evoke characterizations popularized in science fiction (see n. 79). The operational sense is a functional definition that draws on notions of rapid design and implementation and is often distinguished from more robust, commercially viable "development" efforts. In this last sense, a "hacked" programming effort may eventually be supplanted by a production worthy undertaking or it may be employed in rough-and-ready fashion for proximate purposes. None of these senses are mutually exclusive and the term is often used in loose fashion implying any one or a mix of the connotations.

[63] Ben Yagoda, "A Short History of 'Hack,'" *The New Yorker*, Mar. 6, 2014, *available at* http://www.newyorker.com/tech/elements/a-short-history-of-hack (last visited Dec. 26, 2017).

[64] Spyd3r, "The History of Hacking," *HelpNet Security*, Apr. 8, 2002, *available at* https://www.helpnetsecurity.com/2002/04/08/the-history-of-hacking/ (last visited Dec. 26, 2017).

[65] Id.

[66] Id.

among 1980s legislative efforts to address the emerging threats of computer-based malefactors were the Comprehensive Crime Control Act of 1984,[67] which established a statutory prohibition on unauthorized access and/or use of computers and established the Secret Service as enforcement authority over credit and computer fraud, and the Computer Fraud and Abuse Act (CFAA) of 1986, which further extended the scope of computer-related criminal acts to include the trafficking of passwords, distribution of malicious code, and denial of service attacks, inter alia.[68]

As the culture evolved, hackers competed for renown by carrying out increasingly audacious acts of fraud, intrusion, and theft through the late 1980s and 1990s. The divergence of the term "cracker" from "hacker" was effectuated by traditionally benign hackers responding to "the vilification of their good name" and wishing to distinguish themselves from the mold of "vandals and thieves whose sole purpose is unauthorized 'cracking' into secure systems for personal gain."[69] Reclamation of hacker identity was facilitated in part by the writings of journalist Steven Levy, who provided a more structured account of hacker culture and helped to codify more socially oriented principles in the form of a Hacker Ethic.[70,71] While a regard for privacy as such is not explicit within this early formulation, the Hacker Ethic provides an early reference point for programmers seeking to evaluate the ethical content of their craft. In describing a "new way of life, with a philosophy, an ethic and a dream,"[72] the ethic emphasizes principles and tenets inflected with broad societal implications, such as openness, transparency, decentralization, access (to computers), freedom of information, and improvement of the quality of life, which collectively bear more than a passing resemblance to privacy concepts enshrined in staple privacy frameworks such as the Fair Information Practices (FIPs).[73]

From Hacking to Hacktivism

Over time, the hacker identity has acquired an increasingly more overt political and ethical focus. "Hacktivism," a portmanteau term mashing the digital profile of computer hackers with the socially conscious motives and movements of traditional political activism, represents a further step in the restoration of hacker identity and mainstreaming of an ethical orientation of the programming discipline. Hacktivism reflects a desire to apply the programming trade as an

---

[67] *Comprehensive Crime Control Act of 1984*, HR 648, 98th Cong., 2nd sess., Congressional Record 130, 1-224, *available at* http://www.legisworks.org/GPO/STATUTE-98-Pg1837.pdf.

[68] Robert Trigaux, "A History of Hacking," *St. Petersburg Times Online*, June 14, 1998, *available at* http://www.sptimes.com/Hackers/history.hacking.html (last visited Dec. 26, 2017). For a fully amended current version of the CFAA, see also *Computer Fraud and Abuse Act*, U.S. Code 18 (1986), §§ 1030 et seq *available at* https://www.law.cornell.edu/uscode/text/18/1030 (last visited Dec. 26, 2017).

[69] Zuley Clarke, James Clawson, and Maria Cordell, "A Brief History of Hacking," (Nov. 2003), *available at* http://steel.lcc.gatech.edu/~mcordell/lcc6316/Hacker%20Group%20Project%20FINAL.pdf (last visited Jun. 1, 2017).

[70] Steven Levy, *Hackers: Heroes of the Computer Revolution* (Garden City: Anchor Press/Doubleday, 1984).

[71] Ethical hacking may have even deeper roots in earlier analogue computer systems, including the Hollerith punch card tabulators initially used by various international census bureaus: "It's worth remembering that back in the early 1940s, when everything looked hopeless, the Resistance leader René Carmille sabotaged the Hollerith infrastructure in occupied France by leaving the eleventh column of the punch cards, which indicated Jewish identity, blank. Carmille has been described as one of the first ethical hackers." Kate Crawford, "Letter to Silicon Valley," *Harper's Magazine*, Feb. 2017, 38.

[72] Steven Levy, *Hackers: Heroes of the Computer Revolution*, (Garden City: Anchor Press/Doubleday, 1984), 26.

[73] Various formulations of the FIPs exist along with a variety of naming conventions, including Fair Information Practice Principles (FIPPs) and Fair Information Principles (FIPs). See Robert Gellman, *Fair Information Practices: A Basic History*, for a definitive account of the origin, evolution, and implementation of the FIPs, *available at* https://bobgellman.com/rg-docs/rg-FIPshistory.pdf (last visited Dec. 26, 2017).

instrument in the service of ends that have real (though sometimes misguided) social and political implications.[74] Prominent hacktivist figures such as Aaron Swartz, whose suicide in 2013 was allegedly motivated by pressure from a federal indictment for charges of wire fraud and violating the Computer Fraud and Abuse Act, have become role models for a generation of socially conscious hackers. Swartz, who was affiliated with various progressive causes in life,[75] became a posthumous inspiration for hackathons devoted to the development of software tools for enhancing privacy, transparency, and information access, among other aims.[76] Indeed, hackathon events organized around social impact objectives, as well the prominence of organizations such as Code for America,[77] provide more mainstream outlets for the once-subversive culture of hacking to further integrate with more normalized political and social movements and civic objectives. Civil society and even government agencies draw upon well-intentioned programmers who crave opportunities to volunteer their craft for the good of society.[78]

Though hacktivism can be pursued as a hobby, the underlying impulse towards ethical practices in programming as well as coding for the benefit of social impact has nontrivial carryover to professional pursuits. While the popularized notion of the hacker living a dual life – by day, droll corporate hack toiling in a cubicle flooded in the unflattering flicker of florescent office lighting; by night, antihero ensconced in dimly lit, lair-like basement computer lab wired up to multiple terminals panning a cascade of indecipherable computer code and myriad other cyber-chic trappings[79] – may carry some cachet in the hacker community, there is a dissonance to this Janus-faced character that may only be sustainable in fiction.[80] In the real world, programmers who are overtly or more subtly influenced by this lineage would likely, if given the choice, elect for a job or career that is fulfilling and dignified (or at least morally neutral) in the manner demanded by their values and choose to embrace in their daily breadwinning a sense of virtuous labor that might otherwise have to be sought independently (or clandestinely) as a kind of moral offset or supplement.

While expansive surveys of the field are – as yet – lacking, there is mounting evidence that the younger generation of programmers powering the technology industry both respect and identify with this hacker lineage. As a 2013 *Time* magazine poll indicated, Americans aged eighteen to thirty-four diverged significantly from their elders in espousing a belief that Edward Snowden's actions exposing the scope of NSA surveillance programs constituted a "good thing."[81]

---

[74] Katherine Noyes, "The Rise of the Ethical Hacktivist," *Linux Insider* (Feb. 24, 2014), *available at* http://www .linuxinsider.com/story/80042.html (last visited Dec. 26, 2017).

[75] John Naughton, "Aaron Swartz Stood Up for Freedom and Fairness: And Was Hounded to His Death," *The Guardian* (Feb. 7, 2015), *available at* https://www.theguardian.com/commentisfree/2015/feb/07/aaron-swartz-suicide-internets-own-boy (last visited Dec. 26, 2017).

[76] "Worldwide Aaron Swartz Memorial Hackathon Series," *Noisebridge* (last modified Feb. 1, 2017), *available at* https:// noisebridge.net/wiki/Worldwide_Aaron_Swartz_Memorial_Hackathon_Series (last visited Dec. 26, 2017).

[77] "About Us," *Code for America*, *available at* https://www.codeforamerica.org/about-us (last visited Dec. 26, 2017).

[78] The White House Office of Science and Technology Policy under President Obama has promoted, encouraged, and co-hosted a number of civic oriented hackathon events. (https://www.whitehouse.gov/sites/whitehouse.gov/files/ images/Try%20This%20At%20Home-01-2017.pdf). Hackathon efforts sponsored by state and local governments have similarly taken root, e.g., the California Department of Justice's Hack for Justice (https://storify.com/richards1000/ hack-for-justice).

[79] As popularized in such films as *Terminator 2* (1991), *The Lawnmower Man* (1992), *The Net* (1995), *Hackers* (1995), *Johnny Mnemonic* (1995), and *The Matrix* (1999).

[80] "You can't buy ethics offsets for the terrible things you do at your day job." Mike Monteiro, "Ethics Can't Be a Side Hustle," *Dear Design Student* (Mar. 20, 2017), *available at* https://deardesignstudent.com/ethics-cant-be-a-side-hustle-b9e78c090aee#.j66s1z83c (last visited Dec. 26, 2017).

[81] Zeke Miller, "TIME Poll: Support for Snowden – and His Persecution," *Time*, Jun. 13, 2013, *available at* http://swampland .time.com/2013/06/13/new-time-poll-support-for-the-leaker-and-his-prosecution/ (last visited Dec. 26, 2017).

Philosophy professor and New York Times contributor Peter Ludlow went even further in asserting that the deeds of whistle-blowers and hacktivists such as Snowden, Jeremy Hammond, Chelsea Manning, and Aaron Swartz signal a broader generational determination to assert moral convictions in the face of and as a correction to systemic evils.[82] That Edward Snowden continues to command sizeable audiences (and speaking fees) as a virtual keynote speaker at major technology conferences and universities[83] may not signal a unified ethos amongst engineers, but it does suggest a strong demand to engage on challenging and topical ethical questions affecting the industry at large.

These precedents for ethical proclivities in the engineering profession will not, by themselves, fully demonstrate the thesis of a privacy-driven marketplace for talent. They do, however, provide a hint as to the cultural affinities that factor into a programmer's employment preferences, all else being equal. Computer programmers who have come of age in a culture influenced by the hacker ethos are given to a worldview that is at least partially inflected with a sense of social responsibility that may carry them beyond the idea of coding for coding's sake (as hobbyists) or purely for pecuniary reasons (as professionals). Given the choice, many programmers will be inclined to opt for work that is socially aware (if not more outwardly virtuous), or at least infused with a high regard for admirable conduct and upright trade practices, including the respect for privacy. While it may still be too early to point to industry-wide surveys as indicators of a general trend of favoring engineering jobs at firms devoted to privacy-protective practices and business models, the anecdotal evidence abounds and employers may be taking notice.

Are Employers Aware That Their Engineers Demand a Sense of Purpose?

On the margin at least, we can begin to construct an argument about how corporations may be increasingly aware of the fatigue of engineers focusing their lives' work on trivial problems. Jeffrey Hammerbacher's lament on Charlie Rose that, "The best minds of my generation are thinking about how to make people click ads,"[84] was both a personal entreaty to leave the cozy ranks of advertisement-funded Facebook to found Cloudera and a more general industry admonishment.

This perceived dearth of substance amongst many talented engineers in the computer programming world may be at least a partial motive for the growing prominence of the "mission-focused" technology firm. A cursory review of the "About" or "Mission" pages of any number of prominent startups and Silicon Valley establishments will display a bewildering array of formulaic techno-cant describing some treacly and amorphously feel-good aspiration.[85] Whether these platitudes match in any meaningful way with the operational reality of these

---

[82] Peter Ludlow, "The Banality of Systemic Evil," *New York Times*, Sep. 15, 2013, *available at* https://opinionator.blogs .nytimes.com/2013/09/15/the-banality-of-systemic-evil/?smid=fb-share&_r=2 (last visited Dec. 26, 2017).

[83] Michael Isikoff and Michael B. Kelley, "In Exile, Edward Snowden Rakes in Speaking Fees while Hoping for a Pardon," *Yahoo!*, Aug. 11, 2016, *available at* https://www.yahoo.com/news/edward-snowden-making-most-digital-000000490.html (last visited Dec. 26, 2017).

[84] Drake Baer, "Why Data God Jeffrey Hammerbacher Left Facebook to Found Cloudera," *Fast Company*, Apr. 18, 2013, *available at* https://www.fastcompany.com/3008436/takeaway/why-data-god-jeffrey-hammerbacher-left-facebook-found-cloudera (last visited Dec. 26, 2017).

[85] E.g., Twitter: "to give everyone the power to create and share ideas and information instantly without barriers"; Google: "to organize the world's information and make it universally accessible and useful"; Facebook: "to give people the power to share and make the world more open and connected"; Asana: "To help humanity thrive by enabling all teams to work together effortlessly." Etc.

businesses is a separate question,[86] but it is sufficient to note that these mission statements are at least *intended* to signify more than corporate slogans and to factor into the perception that candidates and employees have of their (prospective) employers.

Corporate Motivations for Favoring Privacy Interests in Talent Markets

For technology companies vying for a narrow pool of exceptional engineering talent, there is a limited set of levers available to entice new candidates and retain seasoned employees. When compensation, benefits, and perks are relatively undifferentiated, technology firms are given to exploring more extreme measures to win over workers.[87] Cultural factors, including privacy-protective mission commitments, can serve as the critical dial to turn a candidate in favor of one offer over another. And, indeed, when it comes to employee satisfaction, a substantive connection that goes beyond fiscal incentives does seem to matter. As a recent Gallup survey indicates, millennials (the target candidate demographic for most technology firms) tend to be significantly more engaged and less likely to become retention risks when they connect with the mission or purpose of their employer.[88]

One of the ways that technology firms seek to entice the best engineering talent is through managerial models that subvert traditional hierarchies and instead promote organizational "flatness."[89] Companies that empower employees through less rigid, more distributed management structures in order to encourage creativity, engender trust, or improve efficiency, must also grapple with the spreading of risk through more diffuse decision-making. Engineers who, in a more traditional hierarchical environment, take orders and are expected to merely act on those orders, gain authority and greater agency in directing the course of their own work within flat(ter) organizations. If those diffuse decision-makers lack the tools (including ethical aptitudes) for sound decision-making, they become a liability to the organization. In this way, nonhierarchical or flat technology firms have an incentive to hire, cultivate, and/or reward ethically-minded coders who are capable of acting semiautonomously without exposing the firm to unnecessary risk.

Companies may also choose to adopt open source standards as a way of promoting a certain type of engineering culture that may appeal to engineers' ethical sensibilities, including a strong regard for privacy-enhancing engineering. As a prominent standard in software development, "the open source way" offers a model framework for exposing code to be evaluated by and shared

---

[86] As examples in the preceding footnote suggest, there is often a comically sprawling disconnect between the prosaic gravity of the company's purported aim and the actual nature of the gadgetry or ever-so-slightly-differentiated advertising platform offerings.

[87] For a discussion of the extreme compensatory measures that technology startups are willing to explore and the countervailing concerns, see Daniel Terdiman "Silicon Valley Talent Wars: Engineers, Come Get Your $250K Salary," *CNET*, Sept. 22, 2014, *available at* https://www.cnet.com/news/silicon-valley-talent-wars-engineers-come-get-your-250k-salary/ (last visited Dec. 26, 2017). For an additional portrait of the rich array of perks and benefits offered as enticements to tech candidates in the Seattle area, see Rachel Lerman, "Tech Startups Working Hard to Sell Culture That Job Hunters Will Buy Into," *Seattle Times*, Jan. 30, 2016, *available at* http://www.seattletimes.com/business/technology/tech-startups-working-to-sell-a-culture-job-hunters-will-buy/ (last visited Dec. 26, 2017).

[88] Brandon Rigoni and Bailey Nelson, "Millennials Not Connecting with Their Company's Mission," *Gallup* , Nov. 15, 2016, *available at* http://www.gallup.com/businessjournal/197486/millennials-not-connecting-company-mission.aspx (last visited Dec. 26, 2017). "Rallying millennials around a mission and purpose dramatically increases their employee engagement: 67% of millennials are engaged at work when they strongly agree that the mission or purpose of their company makes them feel their job is important."

[89] For an explanation of "flat" and "bossless" organizational structure as an approach to building unique corporate cultures, see Walter Chen, "Bosslessness: What It Is and Why It's All the Rage in Silicon Valley," *Entrepreneur*, Nov. 22, 2013, *available at*: https://www.entrepreneur.com/article/229977 (last visited Dec. 26, 2017).

amongst one's peers. From the employer's perspective, this model is believed to promote meritocracy and to enable more creative, rapid, and community-oriented development.[90] By emphasizing transparency in the development process, the open source way can also promote accountability and oversight, key principles of privacy-protective technology. In the open source environment, poor quality code or projects that enable overtly nefarious activities are more likely to incur opprobrium, thereby incentivizing open source coders to exercise greater care in developing software that may raise the hackles of their peers.

Openness and Transparency Promote Self-Examination and Market Fluidity

In elevating the principles of sharing, transparency, and community development, the open source model and the companies that draw upon its engineering advantages may have unwittingly influenced other, more social aspects of engineering culture. Channels intended for sharing programming information may also become de facto public spaces for examining peripheral ethics considerations. In November 2016, for example, blogger, teacher, and computer engineer Bill Sourour incited a wave of self-examination within a computer programming forum on the popular discussion website Reddit when he wrote of a coding project early in his career working for an interactive marketing firm whose primary clientele were large pharmaceutical companies. When required to build an online quiz which directed respondents to a specific client's drug regardless of how they answered the questions, Sourour carried out his charge without a second thought until he later learned that a young girl treated with the drug had taken her own life possibly as a result of severe depression and suicidal ideation, which were known side effects of the drug.[91] The resulting Reddit channel "went viral" as other confessions and self-recriminations of programmers emerged, culminating in calls by Sourour and others to, "start talking about the ethical responsibilities that come along with writing code," and to create organizations to more formally govern and regulate the programming profession.[92]

Transparency is on display directly in the forums that facilitate talent entry and job seeking. Sites such as Glass Door allow engineers to comment on and rate their current and former employers. Job seekers thereby gather insights into potential employers' cultures, compensation regimes, managerial practices, job listings, interview processes, and benefits. Free-form fields provide reviewers with occasion to comment on any number of other considerations, including the companies' ethical and privacy postures. In a market in which top talent is extremely coveted, these forums further tilt the playing field in favor of applicants, whose opinions may be skewed even by small numbers of outlying but damning reviews from former employees.

The technology industry is already commonly identified as one of the most fluid employment markets with the highest turnover rate amongst Fortune 500 companies.[93] Because of the strong demand for highly skilled computer programmers, engineers who care about the ethical

---

[90] "What Is Open Source?" *Opensource.com, available at* https://opensource.com/resources/what-open-source (last visited Dec. 26, 2017).

[91] Bill Sourour, "The Code I'm Still Ashamed Of," *Medium*, Nov. 13, 2016, *available at* https://medium.freecodecamp .com/the-code-im-still-ashamed-of-e4c021dff55e#.xqfqe2y1p (last visited Dec. 26, 2017). See also the Reddit forum tracking the full discussion, available at https://www.reddit.com/r/programming/comments/5d56fo/the_code_im_ still_ashamed_of/?sort=qa (last visited Dec. 26, 2017).

[92] Julie Bort, "Programmers Are Having a Huge Discussion about the Unethical and Illegal Things They've Been Asked to Do," *Business Insider*, Nov. 20, 2016, *available at* http://www.businessinsider.com/programmers-confess-unethical-illegal-tasks-asked-of-them-2016-11 (last visited Dec. 26, 2017).

[93] "Tech Companies Have Highest Turnover Rate," *TechRepublic, available at* http://www.techrepublic.com/blog/ career-management/tech-companies-have-highest-turnover-rate/ (last visited Dec. 26, 2017).

positions of their employers may feel freer (i.e., less motivated by job security and economic concerns) to express their moral indignation and, if necessary, vote with their feet and seek employment elsewhere.[94] With an abundance of information at their disposal with which to make decisions about the cultural affinity of employers, programmers are in a powerful position to express their ethical leanings at the companies and in the positions they choose. And as personal responsibility and ethical decision-making are cultivated in one workplace, those expectations and normative practices will diffuse, spread, and influence expectations elsewhere as engineers shift positions across a highly mobile industry.

Engineers Are Consumers and Citizens Too

Programmers are themselves consumers and often unusually discerning ones, as they've seen firsthand how the proverbial sausage is made. Living as both programming agent of the technology milieu and inextricable consumer of that self-constructed world is bound to trigger some level of reflexive regard for the implications of their direct handiwork. Much like nontech consumers and citizens, engineers are also affected by broader cultural trends, including developments in media coverage around privacy issues, law, enforcement actions, and policy debates.

If not the most informed (out of interest for an issue set so close to their daily lives), programmers, at the very least, tend to be amongst the first informed (by virtue of proximity) when technology issues implicate privacy and other ethical concerns. As avid participants on social media, when omissions, failures, or egregious errors in technology systems surface, computer programmers have demonstrated a willingness to respond quickly and with proportionate censure. When, for example, Google came under fire because its photo app tagged an image of an African American couple as "gorillas," (at the time) Google Engineer and Chief Social Architect Yonatan Zunger was quick to tweet an apology, identifying the failing as, "100% Not OK."[95]

When engineers such as Zunger react publicly in this manner, they both serve as positive and empowering examples to other engineers and build awareness and support for similar deeds, which further drives the general demand for privacy-sensitive engineering talent.

More directly, in specialized fields criticized as the locus for past imprudence or reckless practice, there is a growing recognition of formal calls to rein in tradecraft and inculcate a baseline adherence to common principles and practices. Following the 2008 market crash, for example, financial engineers Emanual Derman and Paul Wilmette drafted a "Modeler's Oath" akin to the physician's Hippocratic Oath.[96] This oath includes the commitment to "understand that my work may have enormous effects on society and the economy, many of them beyond my comprehension."[97] In the network security industry, an accreditation model for "Certified

---

[94] It's possible that such freedom presents a double-edged sword. A force that eases the transition out of a firm that neglects privacy and other ethical engineering practices may in turn leave that organization bereft of moral agents who are willing to stand on principle. If such a phenomenon leads to ethically minded talent "pooling" at some companies while ethical "desertification" transpires at others, it would be a somewhat perverse outcome if the companies unencumbered by more conscientious engineers secured a competitive advantage by being able to innovate more rapidly even with somewhat less talented resources than their privacy-conscious competitors. Consumer demand for privacy may, however, provide a counterbalance to nullify the advantage.

[95] Loren Grush, "Google Engineer Apologizes after Photos App Tags Two Black People as Gorillas," *The Verge*, Jul. 1 2015, *available at* http://www.theverge.com/2015/7/1/8880363/google-apologizes-photos-app-tags-two-black-people-gorillas (last visited Dec. 26, 2017).

[96] Emanuel Derman and Paul Wilmott, "The Financial Modelers' Manifesto" (Jan. 8, 2009), *available at* SSRN: https://ssrn.com/abstract=1324878.

[97] *Id.*

Ethical Hackers" through the International Council of E-Commerce Consultants has been established to provide a framework for legitimizing and professionalizing authorized penetration testing techniques and distinguishing the trade from its evil twin, "Black Hat hacking," which often entails applying similar techniques for unauthorized, illegal, and often nefarious ends.[98]

Building on the tradition of Levy's aforementioned Hacker Ethic, a number of domain-specific society Codes of Ethic have been adopted to explicitly address privacy concerns, amongst other ethical and social considerations. The Australian Computer Society Code of Ethics calls on its practitioners to "consider and respect people's privacy which might be affected by my work."[99] Similarly, the Association for Computing Machinery Code of Ethics asserts recognition that "there is increased potential for violating the privacy of individuals and groups," and thus "it is the responsibility of professionals to maintain the privacy and integrity of data describing individuals."[100] As a final example, the League of Professional System Administrators Code of Ethics commits its members to submit, "I will access private information on computer systems only when it is necessary in the course of my technical duties. I will maintain and protect the confidentiality of any information to which I may have access regardless of the method by which I came into knowledge of it."[101]

Grassroots efforts among Silicon Valley engineers have, in recent months, only served to further demonstrate the strength of the talent market in influencing the ethical trajectory of their employers and the technologies they develop. As speculation around immigration reforms and eventual Executive Orders from the new Trump administration surfaced, Silicon Valley engineers embarked on pledge campaigns,[102] demonstrations, and other protests demanding prominent companies to commit to disavowing support of potential privacy-, civil rights-, and civil liberties-intrusive policies such as implementing a Muslim registry.[103] As one Silicon Valley community organizer and technologist Dave McClure remarked, "You don't have a voice with the president if you didn't vote for him. . . . But employees and customers have a voice with the tech companies. Silicon Valley should be demonstrating at the front doors of Google, Facebook and Twitter to make sure they share our values."[104] In this and numerous other ways, engineers program the world in which they too must live.

---

[98] *Certified Ethical Hacking Certification*, EC-Council, *available at* https://www.eccouncil.org/programs/certified-ethical-hacker-ceh/ (last visited Dec. 26, 2017).

[99] "Australian Computer Society Code of Ethics," *available at* http://courses.cs.vt.edu/professionalism/WorldCodes/Australia.Code.html (last visited Feb. 23, 2017).

[100] "Association for Computing Machinery Code of Ethics and Professional Conduct," *available at* https://www.acm.org/about-acm/acm-code-of-ethics-and-professional-conduct (last visited Dec. 26, 2017).

[101] "The League of Professional System Administrators Code of Ethics," *available at* https://lopsa.org/CodeOfEthics (last visited Dec. 26, 2017).

[102] Jon Sharman, "Hundreds of Silicon Valley Tech Workers Pledge Not to Build Donald Trump's Muslim Registry," *Independent*, Dec. 14, 2016, *available at* http://www.independent.co.uk/news/world/americas/silicon-valley-tech-workers-pledge-not-build-donald-trump-muslim-registry-a7474561.html (last visited Dec. 26, 2017). "Employees of Google, Microsoft, Amazon, Apple and more have signed the neveragain.tech promise to 'refuse to build a database of people based on their constitutionally-protected religious beliefs' and have said they 'are choosing to stand in solidarity with Muslim Americans, immigrants, and all people whose lives and livelihoods are threatened by the incoming administration's proposed data collection policies.'"

[103] Levi Sumagaysay, "Palantir, Oracle, Amazon Urged to Reject Creation of Muslim Registry," *SiliconBeat*, Jan. 18, 2017, *available at* http://www.siliconbeat.com/2017/01/18/palantir-oracle-amazon-urged-reject-creation-muslim-registry/ (last visited Feb. 23, 2017).

[104] David Streitfeld, "Tech Opposition to Trump Propelled by Employees, Not Executives," *The New York Times*, Feb. 6, 2017, *available at* https://www.nytimes.com/2017/02/06/business/trump-travel-ban-apple-google-facebook.html?_r=1 (last visited Dec. 26, 2017).

CONCLUSION

A consumer's choose of a product or service is potentially influenced by myriad factors such that it might be almost impossible to determine the but-for cause of any given purchasing decision. Similarly, the decision as to where to seek employment is equally – if not more so – complex. However, we suggest that our supposition herein is at least plausible and can be quite readily tested through surveys directed at employees taking jobs with employers with varying reputations for the protection of privacy.

Should our hypothesis prove true, then we have potentially uncovered a far more reliable mechanism for evaluating the privacy commitment of an organization. Whereas consumers can only ever have a limited view of a company's operations, an employee is likely to have a far more comprehensive view of the privacy practices followed. Should those practices fail to accord with the employer's public image, then those employees whose job selection depended in part on their privacy values would be less likely to stay. Consequently, the number of graduates from colleges and universities where surveys indicated that privacy was highly valued, who accept positions at a company, may represent a further indicator of said company's commitment to privacy. Ultimately, a strong indicator of whether privacy has taken root as a market force may be a firm's willingness to risk or forego near- and medium-term fiscal gains for the end of fostering a long-term competitive advantage both in building privacy-respectful technology, products, services, and in fomenting a culture that satisfies employee demands that their handiwork is held to higher standards for societal impact of privacy protections. Future work will be needed to examine whether such telling signs have come to pass.

Finally, this should suggest to the advocacy community the value of educating and appealing to young computer scientists and engineers. Given the importance of high-quality talent to the success of a technology-focused company, there may be enormous value in instilling engineering and computer science students with a sense of the importance of privacy and thus motivating them to select (and therefore strengthen and perpetuate) privacy-conscious businesses and technologies.

26

The Missing Role of Economics in FTC Privacy Policy

James C. Cooper and Joshua Wright

I INTRODUCTION

The Federal Trade Commission (FTC) is the leading US privacy regulator.

In addition to specific statutory authority to promulgate rules under the Gramm-Leach-Bliley Act (GLBA)[1] and the Children's Online Privacy Protection Act (COPPA),[2] the FTC enjoys broad authority under Section 5 of the FTC Act to combat "unfair and deceptive acts and practices."[3] Since the dawn of the modern Internet, the FTC has used this enforcement power against companies that have failed to honor privacy-related promises,[4] and against companies engaged in conduct that the FTC has found sufficiently harmful to consumers' privacy as to be an unfair act or practice.[5] Another key weapon in the FTC's privacy arsenal has been a series of influential policy reports that are often treated as *de facto* guidelines by the private bar. The FTC's 2012 Privacy Report, for example, laid out mainstays of its privacy framework, such as "privacy by design" and "notice and choice." Subsequent reports applied these concepts to areas such as the Internet of things (IOT), data brokers, and big data.

At its root, privacy regulation is about restricting information flows, which – to borrow a tired cliché – are the lifeblood of today's digital economy. As such, the FTC's authority to limit firms' abilities to collect and use personal information stands to have a considerable impact on economic activity. It's not an exaggeration to say that privacy regulation is increasingly becoming as significant economically as antitrust policy. Indeed, antitrust policy's focus on monopoly power and its acquisition naturally restricts the domain of competition law. Privacy regulation knows no such bounds. The intellectual and analytical underpinnings of privacy regulation are considerably weaker than antitrust, which relies nearly exclusively upon the tools of microeconomics to illuminate its priorities and substantive parameters.

Given the potential economic significance of privacy regulation on the modern economy, it would be desirable to have a privacy policy that is as economically coherent as antitrust, but sadly

---

[1] 15 U.S.C. § 6801.

[2] 15 U.S.C. § 91.

[3] 15 U.S.C. § 45(n).

[4] *See, e.g., Nomi Tech., Inc.* (Sept. 3, 2015), *available at* https://www.ftc.gov/enforcement/cases-proceedings/132-3251/ nomi-technologies-inc-matter. *See, e.g., GeoCites, Corp.* (Feb. 5, 1999), at https://www.ftc.gov/sites/default/files/docu ments/cases/1999/02/9823015cmp.htm.

[5] *See, e.g., Facebook, Inc.,* (Aug. 10, 2012), *available at* https://www.ftc.gov/enforcement/cases-proceedings/092-3184/ facebook-inc; *DesignerWare, LLC,* (Apr. 15, 2012), *available at* https://www.ftc.gov/enforcement/cases-proceedings/ 112-3151/designerware-llc-matter.

this isn't the case.[6] Each of the FTC's privacy enforcement actions has resulted in consent orders, which are private agreements between the FTC and the defendant to settle allegations that the defendant's conduct violated the FTC Act. As such, the extent to which the challenged conduct harms, or is likely to harm, consumers – a necessary condition to invoke the FTC Act – remains unclear. The complaints and analyses to aid public comment do little more than recite the elements of an unfairness claim – the practice caused unavoidable harms that were not outweighed by benefits to consumers or competition. Further, the FTC reports are devoid of any economic analysis or empirical evidence, and instead are based almost solely on anecdotes and hypotheticals presented at workshops.[7]

It's not much of an exaggeration to say that privacy regulation today stands where antitrust regulation stood in the 1970s – it is rudderless and incoherent.[8] Mergers and practices were condemned not for their impact on consumers, but merely because they either led to an accretion of market share or impacted smaller companies. Consumers suffered, as antitrust proscribed efficient practices. A series of Supreme Court cases beginning in the late 1970s, however, charted a new course, announcing that consumer welfare would be antitrust's guiding principle.[9] From then on, the reach of antitrust law would be confined to practices that were likely to raise prices, reduce output, or otherwise threaten to diminish the fruits of competition. The economic revolution allowed antitrust to escape its incoherent state in the 1960s and 1970s and is widely looked upon as a remarkable shift in the law to the benefit of consumers and economic growth.[10]

Privacy is ripe for a similar intellectual revolution. In this chapter, we argue that consumers would benefit immensely if economics were to play as central a role in privacy regulation as it does in antitrust. In recent years, the FTC has drifted from an *ex post* harms-based approach to privacy – one triggered by conduct that injures consumers directly or through material deception – to an approach increasingly centered on notice and choice, as well as *ex ante* prophylactic measures, such as "data minimization" and "privacy by design."[11] Returning to a harm-based approach – guided by economic theory and empirical evidence – is crucial, because only then can one be assured that FTC action is actually providing a benefit to consumers. Four areas in particular stand out.

First, as a threshold matter, the FTC needs to be more precise in articulating the privacy harms its policy recommendations are intended to remedy. For example, merely asserting that sharing certain information with third parties for marketing purposes may go beyond consumer

[6] *See, e.g.,* Joshua D. Wright, *FTC & Privacy, The Missing Role of Economics,* at 7 (Nov. 12, 2012) (noting how slogans like "privacy by design" are devoid of analytic content).
[7] FTC, Big Data: A Tool for Inclusion or Exclusion: Understanding the Issues (Jan. 2016) ("Big Data Rep."), *available at* https://www.ftc.gov/system/files/documents/reports/big-data-tool-inclusion-or-exclusion-understanding-issues/160106big-data-rpt.pdf; FTC, Internet of Things: Privacy & Security in a Connected World (Jan. 2015) ("IOT Rep."), *available at* https://www.ftc.gov/system/files/documents/reports/federal-trade-commission-staff-report-november-2013-workshop-entitled-internet-things-privacy/150127iotrpt.pdf; FTC, Data Brokers: A Call for Transparency and Accountability (May 2014) ("Data Brokers Rep."), *available at* https://www.ftc.gov/system/files/documents/reports/data-brokers-call-transparency-accountability-report-federal-trade-commission-may-2014/140527databrokerreport.pdf; FTC, Protecting Consumer Privacy in an Era of Rapid Change: Recommendations for Businesses and Policymakers (March 2012) ("2012 Privacy Rep."), *available at* https://www.ftc.gov/reports/protecting-consumer-privacy-era-rapid-change-recommendations-businesses-policymakers.
[8] *See* Douglas H. Ginsburg, *Originalism and Economic Analysis: Two Case Studies of Consistency and Coherence in Supreme Court Decision Making,* 33 HARV. J.L. & PUB. POL. 217 (2010).
[9] *See Reiter v. Sonotone Corp.,* 442 U.S. 330, 343 (1979); *Continental T.V., Inc. v. GTE Sylvania,* 433 U.S. 36 (1977).
[10] *See* Sandeep Vaheesan, *The Evolving Populisms of Antitrust,* 93 NEB. L. REV. 370, 395.
[11] *See* J. Howard Beales, III & Timothy J. Muris, *Choice or Consequences: Protecting Privacy in Commercial Information,* 75 U. CHI. L. REV. 109 (2008).

expectations does not *ipso facto* convert this conduct into substantial consumer injury. Absent a material lie or some obvious affront to privacy, such as a loss of dignity, autonomy, or seclusion, a mere failure to meet expectations should not trigger the FTC Act.

Second, and relatedly, the FTC should, to the extent feasible, quantify the alleged consumer harm from the data flows in question. The "consumer expectations" that undergird current FTC privacy policy are derived from a combination of survey responses and workshop testimony. Hypotheticals and stated preferences, however, are no substitute for revealed preference: the former trivially tell us only that privacy has value; we need the latter to tell us how much. A focus on revealed preference tells a very different story.[12] For example, there are 1.3 billion daily Facebook users,[13] 150 million people use Snapchat daily,[14] health-tracking apps and wearables continue to grow apace,[15] and nearly half of US households have an Amazon Prime account.[16] Economic studies, moreover, find nearly universally that consumers are willing to provide personal information for small amounts of compensation, or, alternatively, are only willing to pay very little to avoid personal data collection.[17] The FTC needs to incorporate this extant research – which broadly suggests that consumers are comfortable with the trade-offs they are making in their digital lives – into its privacy policy-making. In addition, the FTC should train its formidable research capabilities on the task. The FTC has a long and distinguished history of conducting first-rate empirical research with important policy impact;[18] given the significance of privacy to the Commission's current mission, it should invest the resources to conduct empirical research into consumers' valuation of privacy.

A third area that requires more serious attention from economics relates to the FTC's use of its deception authority. As noted earlier, much of the FTC's privacy enforcement has been centered on promises made in firms' privacy policies. For a practice to be deceptive under Section 5, it must not only be untrue, but also be material, in that the falsehood impacts consumers' decision-making. The FTC enjoys a presumption of materiality for express claims. This policy seems sensible for the print and television advertising that weaned the FTC's modern deception authority – why would an advertiser make a claim in an advertisement if not to draw consumers to its product? But applying this presumption to statements in privacy policies seems a stretch; these policies are drafted by lawyers and intended to comply with state laws and self-regulatory organizations. What's more, the empirical evidence shows that few

---

[12] The gap between stated and revealed preference has come to be known as the "privacy paradox," and much of the policy-making in privacy can be seen as aimed to close this gap by getting consumer behavior to match their survey responses.

[13] *Company Info*, FACEBOOK, http://newsroom.fb.com/company-info/ (last visited Oct. 10, 2016).

[14] Sarah Frier, *Snapchat Passes Twitter in Daily Usage*, BLOOMBERG NEWS, June 2, 2016, *available at* https://www .bloomberg.com/news/articles/2016-06-02/snapchat-passes-twitter-in-daily-usage.

[15] By 2015, an estimated 500 million people worldwide will use a mobile health app. Stephen McInerney, *Can You Diagnose Me Now? A Proposal to Modify the Fda's Regulation of Smartphone Mobile Health Applications with a Pre-Market Notification and Application Database Program*, 48 U. MICH. J.L. REFORM 1073 (2015) (*citing* Kevin Pho, *Health App Users Beware*, USA TODAY (Apr. 2, 2014), *available at* http://www.usatoday.com/story/opinion/2014/04/02/ medical-app-fitness-health-fda-technology-column/7224837/). Andrew Meola, *Wearables and Mobile Health App Usage Has Surged by 50% Since 2014*, BUSINESS INSIDER (Mar. 7, 2016) (health tracker use increased from 16% in 2014 to 33% in 2015), *at* http://www.businessinsider.com/fitbit-mobile-health-app-adoption-doubles-in-two-years-2016-3. *See also* Susannah Fox, *The Self-Tracking Data Explosion*, PEW RESEARCH CENTER (June 4, 2013), *available at* http:// www.pewinternet.org/2013/06/04/the-self-tracking-data-explosion/.

[16] *See* Krystina Gustafson, *Half of America Could Have an Amazon Prime Account by the End of the Year*, CNBC, *available at* http://www.cnbc.com/2016/09/26/amazon-prime-signing-up-members-at-a-faster-clip.html.

[17] *See* Section IV.A.2, *infra*.

[18] For a survey of FTC policy research *see* William E. Kovacic, *The Federal Trade Commission as Convenor: Developing Regulatory Policy Norms without Litigation or Rulemaking*, 13 COLO. TECH. L.J. 17 (2015).

people ever read, much less comprehend, these policies.[19] And when they do, it appears to have no impact on their behavior.[20] Here again is an area that would benefit greatly from economic analysis. In the 1980s, the FTC produced a large body of pathbreaking research on advertising, laying the foundation for its advertising enforcement authority, especially as related to health claims and advertising substantiation generally.[21] A similar employment of economic resources to develop a more comprehensive understanding of the extent to which representations made in privacy policies impact consumer behavior is warranted. Unless consumers can be shown to read and respond to privacy policies, the FTC should rethink its preoccupation with "notice and choice" regimes designed to promote competition around privacy, and focus instead on cognizable consumer privacy harms.[22]

Finally, the FTC should employ economic rigor in considering the negative impacts on competition and consumers when developing its privacy policy. The digital economy, which accounts for an estimated six percent of GDP annually, lives on consumer data.[23] Policies such as "privacy by design" and "data minimization" necessarily limit collection and use of data, and are thus likely to exacerbate problems associated with a lack of marketplace information, such as adverse selection and moral hazard.[24] The vast amount of empirical literature examining the problems that arise when markets lack information must be incorporated into the FTC's policy-making. What's more, when the FTC enters into consent agreements that limit the ability of firms to collect and use data for twenty years, or restricts their ability to merge complementary data sets without opt-in consent, it necessarily will diminish the ability of firms to innovate and

---

[19] *See* Aleecia M. McDonald & Lorrie Faith Cranor, *The Cost of Reading Privacy Policies*, 4 I/S: A J. L. & Pol'y Info. Soc'y 543 (2008) (estimating the cost of reading privacy policies to be $3,534/year). Some contend that the lack of consumer interest in privacy policies stems from poor design, and can be ameliorated though improved disclosures. *See* Patrick Gage Kelley et al., *A "Nutrition Label" for Privacy* (2009), *at* https://cups.cs.cmu.edu/soups/2009/proceed ings/a4-kelley.pdf; Patrick Gage Kelley et al., *Standardizing Privacy Notices: An Online Study of the Nutritional Labeling Approach*, CyLab (2010), *at* http://repository.cmu.edu/cgi/viewcontent.cgi?article=1002&context=cylab. Others, however, see consumer indifference to privacy policies as evidence of rational ignorance– consumers purposely avoid privacy policies because the benefits from comprehension are too small. *See* J. Howard Beales, III & Timothy J. Muris, *Choice or Consequences: Protecting Privacy in Commercial Information*, 75 U. Chi. L. Rev. 109, 113–15 (2008).

[20] *See, e.g.,* Omri Ben-Shahar & Adam S. Chilton, *Simplification of Privacy Disclosures: An Experimental Test*, 45 J. Leg. Stud. 41 (2016); Lior Strahilevitz & Matthew B. Kugler, *Is Privacy Policy Language Irrelevant to Consumers ?*, 45 J. Leg. Stud. 69 (2016) (among a panel of Gmail users who find privacy concerns with Gmail scanning, 85% of consumers would not pay anything to avoid scanning). *But see* Lori Cranor et al., *The Effect of Online Privacy Information on Purchasing Behavior: An Experimental Study*, 22 Info. Sys. Res. 254 (2010) (finding that privacy sensitive consumers are willing to pay a premium to purchase from online merchants with higher privacy scores).

[21] *See, e.g.,* Pauline Ippolito & Janis Pappalardo, Advertising Nutrition & Health: Evidence from Food Advertising 1977–1997 (2002); Pauline Ippolito & Alan Mathios, Information and Advertising Policy: A Study of Fat and Cholesterol Consumption in the United States, 1977–1990 (1996); Pauline Ippolito & Alan Mathios, Health Claims in Advertising and Labeling: A Study of the Cereal Market (1989); John Calfee and Janis Pappalardo, How Should Health Claims for Foods Be Regulated? An Economic Perspective (1989). *See also* J. Howard Beales, III & Timothy J. Muris, *In Defense of the* Pfizer *Factors*, in James Campbell Cooper ed., The Regulatory Revolution at the FTC: A Thirty-Year Perspective on Competition and Consumer Protection at 91 (2013).

[22] *See, e.g.,* Florencia Marotta-Wurgler, *Does Contract Disclosure Work?*, 168 J. Inst. Theo. Econ. 94, 95 (2012) (explaining that for competition over standard form contract terms to be effective, a threshold number of consumers need to read and respond to their terms).

[23] Stephen Siwek, *Measuring the U.S. Internet Sector*, Internet Association (Dec. 10, 2015), *available at* http://inter netassociation.org/wp-content/uploads/2015/12/Internet-Association-Measuring-the-US-Internet-Sector-12–10–15.pdf.

[24] "Adverse selection" occurs when one party has hidden information about their true quality, resulting in lower quality types being selected into a market. "Moral hazard" refers to the situation that arises when one does not bear the full costs of their actions.

compete.[25] Without taking these considerations into account, the FTC almost surely underestimates the costs of its actions surrounding privacy. Indeed, one feature of the FTC's application of its enforcement authority in the privacy context – as is the case with its competition authority – is the lack of adjudication. In other words, the most frequent resolution of the FTC's privacy enforcement efforts is the consent agreement, not adjudication. As we will discuss, the heavy emphasis upon settlement rather than adjudication introduces challenges to closely integrating economics into the FTC's regulatory approach.

The remainder of this chapter is organized as follows. Part II examines the history of FTC privacy enforcement and policy-making, with special attention paid to the lack of economic analysis. In Part III, we focus on the unique ability of economic analysis – both theoretical and empirical – to ferret out conduct that is likely to threaten consumer welfare, and how this toolkit has proven so valuable to antitrust analysis. Part IV suggests lessons from antitrust's history that the FTC could apply as it forms privacy policy going forward. The final section offers some concluding thoughts.

II FTC'S PRIVACY TOOL KIT

The FTC has used its enforcement authority under Section 5 as well as softer methods, such as reports and speeches, to enforce norms in the collection and use of personal data. We will discuss these tools and how, at least as currently applied, they are insufficiently guided by economics and in some instances, altogether untethered from economic analysis.

A Enforcement

The FTC's consumer protection authority derives from the FTC Act's declaration that "unfair and deceptive acts and practices" are unlawful.[26] Although at one time there was a conflation of unfairness and deception, the modern evolution of the FTC's consumer protection jurisdiction has given distinct analytic content to these powers. The touchstone of both the unfairness and deception authority is consumer harm. As will be seen, both of the FTC's enforcement tools are triggered by consumer harm, rendering economics an almost requisite component of any coherent analysis.

1 Deception

The mainstay of the FTC's privacy program is deception. For a practice to be deceptive under the FTC Act, there must be a "representation, omission or practice that is likely to mislead consumers" who are "acting reasonable in the circumstances."[27] The representation, omission or practice also must be "material," in that it "is likely to affect the consumer's conduct or decision with regard to a product or service."[28] Although deception under the FTC Act does not require a specific showing of harm, the materiality requirement serves as a proxy.[29] Any express claims are presumed to be material.[30] The rationale for this is simple and makes sense. Rather than requiring the FTC to prove that an advertiser made a claim with the intention of attracting

---

[25] *See* James C. Cooper, *The WhatsApp Privacy Policy Change: No Cause for Alarm*, FORBES (Sept. 7, 2016), *available at* http://www.forbes.com/sites/jamesccooper1/2016/09/07/the-whatsapp-privacy-policy-change-no-cause-for-alarm/#5b85 cc5204db.

[26] 15 U.S.C. § 45(a).

[27] Deception Statement at 1.

[28] *Id.*

[29] *See id.* (if a practice is material "consumer injury is likely, because consumers are likely to have chosen differently but for the deception."); *Id.* at 6 ("injury and materiality are different names for the same concept.").

[30] *Id.* at 5.

consumers to its product, the burden falls to the defendant to show that consumers were not impacted by the claims – a steep burden.[31] The Commission also considers claims or omissions that "significantly involve health, safety, or other areas with which the reasonable consumer would be concerned."[32]

In privacy enforcement, the FTC uses its deception authority to hold companies to their promises regarding data collection and use, which most often are found in privacy policies. The earliest case was against Geocities, a website that hosted a virtual community of personal homepages.[33] The Commission alleged that while Geocities' privacy policy represented that collected personal information would be used only for e-mail offers they requested, in fact Geocities sold this information to third parties, which constituted a deceptive act.[34] More recently, the Commission brought deception charges against a company, Nomi Technologies, that provided a way for retailers to track consumer movements in their stores. Nomi had said in its privacy policy that consumers could opt out of tracking online and in retail locations using Nomi's product, yet retail opt-out was largely unavailable.

The FTC has also used its deception authority to challenge disclosure that while present, was deemed to be inadequate. For example, *Sears Holdings Mgm't Corp* (SHC) involved software that consumers could load on their computers to provide feedback on purchases made from Sears retailers.[35] The Privacy Statement and End User License Agreement (PSULA) disclosed, beginning on line 75, that the application would monitor almost all of the user's Internet activity.[36] Nonetheless, the FTC alleged that this disclosure was inadequate, and that the only representation consumers reasonably would take away is that the application would track "online browsing."[37] Accordingly, the Commission alleged that SHC's practices were deceptive.

The FTC has also looked beyond the four corners of privacy policies to find implied promises in user interfaces.[38] For example, the FTC focused on an FAQ section explaining how to disable tracking on a Safari browser,[39] and similarly focused on Snapchat's FAQs and marketing for allegedly deceptive claims regarding the disappearance of messages,[40] to identify allegedly deceptive claims.

2 *Unfairness*

The FTC's modern unfairness authority mandates a benefit-cost test. Formally, for an act or practice to be unfair it must "cause[] or [be] likely to cause substantial injury to consumers which is not reasonably avoidable by consumers themselves and not outweighed by

---

[31] *See Kraft Inc. v. FTC*, 970 F.2d 311 (7th Cir. 1992).

[32] Deception statement at 5. The Commission notes that materiality has been found when the information pertains to the "central characteristics of the product or service," such as "the purpose, safety, efficacy, or cost." *Id.*

[33] *GeoCites, Corp.* (Feb. 5, 1999), *available at* https://www.ftc.gov/sites/default/files/documents/cases/1999/02/9823015cmp .htm. *See also* Toysmart, Eli Lilly.

[34] GeoCities Compl, at ¶¶12–16, 18–20.

[35] *In the Matter of Sears Holdings Mgm't Corp.* (Aug. 31, 2009), *at* https://www.ftc.gov/enforcement/cases-proceedings/ 082-3099/sears-holdings-management-corporation-corporation-matter.

[36] *Id.* at ¶ 8.

[37] *Id.* at ¶13.

[38] *See* Woodrow Hartzog & Daniel Solove, *The FTC's Common Law of Privacy*, 114 Columbia L. Rev. 583 (2014).

[39] *See United States v. Google, Inc.*, Cv 12–04177 SI (N.D. Ca. Nov. 16, 2012), *available at* https://www.ftc.gov/sites/ default/files/documents/cases/2012/11/121120googleorder.pdf.

[40] *Snapchat, Inc.*, (Dec. 1, 2014), *available at* https://www.ftc.gov/system/files/documents/cases/141231snapchatcmpt.pdf. *See also HTC America Inc.*, FTC (June 25, 2013), *available at* https://www.ftc.gov/sites/default/files/documents/cases/ 2013/07/130702htccmpt.pdf (instruction manual); *Google Inc.*, FTC (Oct. 13, 2011), *available at* https://www.ftc.gov/ sites/default/files/documents/cases/2011/10/111024googlebuzzcmpt.pdf (interface).

countervailing benefits to consumers or to competition."[41] Unlike deception, which requires no direct proof of harm and does not contemplate defenses, unfairness incorporates an explicit benefit cost analysis. In this manner, there is a clear analogy between the FTC's enforcement tools and antitrust's standards: deception is akin to a *per se* prohibition, whereas unfairness bears more than a passing semblance to antitrust's rule of reason.

The FTC's early forays into data security relied on unfairness. Applying unfairness in most data security contexts is relatively straightforward – harm is apparent in the form of documented fraudulent charges and the practices challenged by the FTC are obviously sub par.[42] Take, for example, large data breach cases like DSW[43] or Choicepoint.[44] Lax security standards caused substantial consumer injury to the tune of several million dollars. There were no discernable benefits from, e.g., allowing bad actors posing as customers access to a database of millions of credit card numbers. Also, because consumers had no say over them, data security standards were not reasonably avoidable. In this manner, the application of unfairness is similar to a negligence standard: given the stakes, the level of care of care chosen by these curators of consumer data was too low.

Whereas unfairness has been a mainstay of data security enforcement, the FTC largely has avoided use of its unfairness authority for pure privacy issues. This fact is likely due to the "substantial injury" requirement, which is less straightforward for issues involving the collection and use of personal data without any financial harm. Although unfairness does not necessarily cover only tangible harm,[45] the Unfairness Statement explains that "emotional impact and other more subjective types of harm ... will not ordinarily make a practice unfair."[46] Thus, the extent to which practices such as online tracking or sharing data with third-party advertisers would constitute "substantial consumer injury" for the purposes of unfairness remains unclear.

The uncertain role of subjective harm in unfairness may explain why the FTC has relied almost exclusively on its deception authority to enforce specific promises made with respect to data collection and use rather than alleging that certain data practices are injurious in and of themselves. Indeed, two of the three cases alleging unfairness for unwanted surveillance involved allegations that the observation of the personal data could lead to physical harm, which is specifically allowed in the Unfairness Statement.[47] For example, in *TrendNet*, a case involving allegedly unsecure feeds for personal webcams, the Commission alleged that "the exposure of sensitive information through the respondent's IP cameras increases the likelihood that consumers or their property will be targeted for theft or other criminal activity."[48] Similarly, *DesignerWare* involved software licensed to rent-to-own establishments, which was used to monitor the location of rented computers and was capable of surreptitiously taking screenshots,

---

[41] 15 U.S.C. § 45(n).

[42] An issue can arise, however, with respect to showing "likely" harm from data breaches that have occurred in the past with no evidence of actual harm. *See LabMD, Inc.*, Final Order, (July 28, 2016), *available at* https://www.ftc.gov/system/files/documents/cases/160729labmdorder.pdf.

[43] *See DWS, Inc.* (Mar. 14, 2005), *available at* https://www.ftc.gov/sites/default/files/documents/cases/2006/03/0523096c4157dswcomplaint.pdf.

[44] *See United States v. Choice Point, Inc.*, Civ. No. 1–06-CV-0198 (N.D. Ga. Jan. 301, 2006), *available at* https://www.ftc.gov/sites/default/files/documents/cases/2006/01/0523069complaint.pdf.

[45] Indeed, *International Harvester*, the case announcing the Unfairness Statement, involved physical harm from exploding gas tanks. *See International Harvester Co.*, 104 F.T.C. 949 (1984).

[46] Unfairness Statement at 3.

[47] *Id.*

[48] TrendNet Compl. at ¶13.

logging keystrokes, and photographing people from the computer's webcam.[49] As in *TrendNet*, the unwanted surveillance by third parties was alleged to cause "financial and physical injury."[50]

Another theme in both *TrendNet* and *DesignerWare* was the unwanted surveillance of intimate activities that interfered with consumers' "peaceful enjoyment of their homes."[51] For example, the Commission alleged that "consumers are harmed by DesignerWare's unwarranted invasion into their homes and lives and its capture of the private details of individual and family life, including for example, images of visitors, children, family interactions, partially undressed individuals, and couples engaged in intimate activities."[52] These allegations again move the injury further away from purely subjective harm toward tangible harm – the Unfairness Statement specifically notes "harassing late-night telephone calls" as the type of conduct where "emotional effects might possibly be considered as the basis for a finding of unfairness" because "tangible injury could be clearly demonstrated."[53]

The FTC's complaint against Facebook is the only other unfairness action based solely on privacy concerns. The FTC's charges stem from privacy policy changes Facebook made in 2009 that left more personal information public and accessible by friends' applications.[54] As in *TrendNet* and *DesignerWare*, the FTC's allegations intimated the potential of physical harm from "unwanted contacts" by those who would be "able to infer [a Facebook user's] locale" based on the newly available information, but the complaint also alleged that the potential disclosure to third parties of information that a user may not want to share also constituted injury sufficient to make a practice unfair.[55] Specifically, the complaint identifies "exposing potentially controversial political views or other sensitive information," "potentially sensitive affiliations, that could, in turn reveal a user's political views, sexual orientation, or business relationships" to "prospective employers, government organizations or business competitors."[56] Perhaps left unstated was a looming reputational harm that had the potential to impair employment prospects, which again nudges the injury into the more familiar terrain of losses that are capable of being monetized.

B *Reports*

The FTC has a long and distinguished history as a leader in what some have dubbed "policy R&D."[57] For example, in the 1980s, FTC economists and attorneys were responsible for pathbreaking work in industrial organization theory,[58] the economics of

---

[49] *See DesignerWare, LLC*, FTC (Apr. 15, 2012), *available at* https://www.ftc.gov/enforcement/cases-proceedings/112-3151/designerware-llc-matter.

[50] *Id.* ¶19.

[51] *Id. See also TrendNet* at ¶13 ("This risk impairs consumers' peaceful enjoyment of their homes, increases consumers' susceptibility to physical tracking or stalking").

[52] *Id. See also TrendNet* at ¶13 ("The exposure of sensitive information through respondent's IP cameras . . . increases the likelihood that consumers' personal activities and conversations or those of their family members, including young children will be observed and recorded by strangers over the Internet.").

[53] UFS at n. 16. What's more, invasion of the home represents the quintessential "intrusion on seclusion" tort, *see* Restatement (Second) of Torts § 652B (1977). Further, it is the privacy interest underlying the "Do Not Call" list. *See* J. Howard Beales, III & Timothy J. Muris, *Choice or Consequence: Protecting Privacy in Commercial Information*, 75 U. CHI. L. REV. 109, 119 (2008).

[54] *See Facebook* Compl. at ¶¶ 19–24.

[55] *Id.* at ¶26.

[56] *Id.* at ¶26 b–d.

[57] *See* Kovacic, *supra* note 18.

[58] *See* Thomas G. Krattenmaker & Steven C. Salop, *Anticompetitive Exclusion: Raising Rivals' Costs to Achieve Power over Price*, 96 YALE L.J. 209 (1986).

advertising,[59] and the impact of government restraints on the professions.[60] More recently, the FTC's empirical work on competition in the pharmaceutical industry, restrictions on e-commerce, and intellectual property have had a large policy impact.[61]

FTC privacy reports have had at least as much policy impact as enforcement actions. The FTC typically assembles a workshop consisting of several panels of experts – typically a mixture of industry representatives, privacy advocates, and academics – over a day or series of days to discuss issues of interest. Following the workshop, the FTC will solicit comments. FTC staff will then release a report based on workshop testimony and transcripts.

There have been four major recent privacy reports: the 2012 Report, which laid out the FTC's core privacy framework; the Internet of Things (IOT) Report; the Data Brokers Report; and the Big Data Report. Although these reports do not put forth binding rules, they act as *de facto* guidelines for privacy professionals advising companies.[62] The 2012 Privacy Report, for example, sets out a framework, which includes the now-familiar concepts of "Privacy By Design," "Simplified Consumer Choice," and "Transparency" as its core pillars. The FTC also dispelled any notions that this report was an academic exercise by urging companies to "accelerate the pace of its self-regulatory measures" to implement the FTC's privacy framework.[63] This frame-work, laid out in the 2012 Privacy Report, has become the lodestar for FTC privacy policy and enforcement. Further, the other reports contain sections such as, "Best Practices" or "Consider-ations for Companies." For example, the IOT Report suggests that companies engage in practices such as "security by design," "data minimization" and "notice and choice."[64] Similarly, the Data Brokers Report recommends that data brokers implement "privacy by design,"

---

[59] Pauline M. Ippolito & Alan D. Mathios, *Information, Advertising and Health Choices: A Study of the Cereal Market*, 21 RAND J. ECON. 459 (1990); Howard Beales et al., *The Efficient Regulation of Consumer Information*, 24 J.L. & ECON. 491, 513 (1981); John Kwoka, *Advertising the Price and Quality of Optometric Services*, 74 AM. ECON. REV. 211 (1984).

[60] R. S. BOND, J. J. KWOKA, J. J. PHELAN, & I. T. WHITTEN, EFFECTS OF RESTRICTIONS ON ADVERTISING AND COMMERCIAL PRACTICE IN THE PROFESSIONS: THE CASE OF OPTOMETRY (FTC Bureau of Economics Staff Report 1980).

[61] FTC, POSSIBLE ANTICOMPETITIVE BARRIERS TO E-COMMERCE: WINE (July 2003), *at* https://www.ftc.gov/sites/default/files/documents/advocacy_documents/ftc-staff-report-concerning-possible-anticompetitive-barriers-e-commerce-wine/winereport2.pdf; FTC, POSSIBLE ANTICOMPETITIVE BARRIERS TO E-COMMERCE: CONTACT LENSES (2004), *available at* www.ftc.gov/sites/default/files/documents/reports/possible-anticompetitive-barriers-e-commerce-contact-lenses-report-staff-federal-trade-commission/040329clreportfinal.pdf.

[62] *See, e.g.,* Dana Rosenfeld & Alysa Hutnik, *FTC Releases Best Practices for Protecting Consumer Privacy*, KELLEY DRYE & WARREN (Apr. 2, 2012), *available at* http://www.kelleydrye.com/publications/client_advisories/0735:

> The FTC's final privacy framework, which combines best practices with principles that are already interpreted as requirements under the FTC Act, represents the Commission's current stance on the protection of consumer privacy rights. Entities should be prepared for this framework to guide the FTC's actions regarding its policy-making initiatives, legislative support, and enforcement actions to the extent that it has authority under existing statutes, including the FTC Act. *Entities that implement the FTC's recommendations will be in a better position to defend privacy and data security practices in the event of an enforcement action, as well as quickly adapt to privacy legislation if and when it is enacted.*

> The Privacy and Data Security Group, *Internet of Things: Federal Agencies Offer Privacy and Data Security Best Practices*, BALLARD SPAHR LLP (Jan. 29, 2015), *available at* http://www.ballardspahr.com/alertspublications/legalalerts/2015-01-29-internet-of-things-federal-agencies-offer-privacy-data-security.aspx:

> Although the FTC best practices do not have the force of law, they provide businesses with insight into regulators' expectations for how consumer data is collected and used, and highlight the issues the FTC will focus on in future actions. Companies (including utilities) should regularly assess how their information and security practices compare with regulators' expectations, especially when launching IoT-enabled devices and services.

[63] 2012 Privacy Rep. at v.

[64] *See* IOT Rep.

implement better methods to refrain collecting information from teens and children, and "take reasonable precautions to ensure that downstream users of their data" do not use it for illegal purposes.[65] Some of the reports also recommend legislation. The 2012 Privacy Report called for baseline privacy legislation,[66] a call the IOT Report echoed.[67] The Data Brokers Report suggested comprehensive FCRA-like legislation for data brokers.[68] Importantly, none of the reports contain any original empirical evidence or economic analysis, and almost never mention, let alone incorporate, the relevant academic literature.[69] Instead they rely primarily on supposition or hypothetical scenarios posited by panelists or commenters to support their conclusions.[70]

III THE BENEFICIAL ROLE OF ECONOMICS IN REGULATION: LEARNING FROM THE ANTITRUST EXPERIENCE

The argument that economic analysis should be incorporated into the FTC's privacy enforcement actions under its Section 5 authority has been around as long as the FTC has been present in the privacy space.[71] The rationale for this incorporation is clear: economic analysis is in Section 5's DNA – unfairness explicitly calls for a benefit-cost analysis, and deception rests on evidence that a practice altered consumer decision-making. Yet in the privacy domain, the FTC appears to eschew economic analysis.[72] As seen earlier, the FTC's privacy policy has evolved despite little use of this powerful tool.[73] Because all of the unfairness cases involve consent agreements, these cases do little more than recite the elements of the claim in the complaint, never grappling with the complex trade-offs between privacy harms and benefits to information flows. Many of the FTC's deception cases, moreover, rest on the notion that consumers make decisions based on promises related to routine data collection and use,[74] but the FTC has never done the hard work to discover whether this is really true. Finally, none of the FTC's privacy reports – which are at least as important as its enforcement actions in setting policy – employ anything resembling economic analysis.

The roots of the FTC's institutional reluctance to engage with economic thinking are well known and understandable. The Bureau of Consumer Protection (BCP) simply does not

---

[65] Data Broker Rep. at ix.

[66] 2012 Privacy Rep. at viii.

[67] IOT Rep. at 48–49.

[68] Data Brokers Rep. at viii.

[69] *See* Section IV.A.2, *infra.*

[70] *See, e.g.,* Big Data Rep. at 10–11 (positing how big data hypothetically could be used to "create or reinforce existing disparities" or charge higher prices to people in lower income communities); IOT Rep. at 16 (positing how wellness trackers could be used to price health or life insurance, or infer suitability for employment).

[71] *See, e.g.,* Privacy Online: Fair Information Practices in the Electronic Marketplace: A Federal Trade Commission Report to Congress, Dissenting Statement of Commissioner Orson Swindle 16 (May 25, 2000), *available at* https://www.ftc.gov/sites/default/files/documents/reports/privacy-online-fair-information-practices-elec tronic-marketplace-federal-trade-commmission-report/swindledissent.pdf. *See also* J. Howard Beales, III & Timothy J. Muris, *FTC Consumer Protection at 100: 1970s Redux or Protecting Markets to Protect Consumers?,* 83 Geo. Wash. L. Rev. 2157, 2204 (2015); Richard Craswell, *Regulating Deceptive Advertising: The Role of Cost-Benefit Analysis,* 64 S. Cal. L. Rev. 549, 552 (1991).

[72] Joshua D. Wright, *The FTC and Privacy Regulation: The Missing Role of Economics,* Briefing on Nomi, Spokeo, and Privacy Harms, George Mason University Law and Economics Center (Nov. 12, 2015), *available at* http://masonlec.org/site/rte_uploads/files/Wright_PRIVACYSPEECH_FINALv2_PRINT.pdf.

[73] There are some bright spots. For example, the FTC's new conference, PrivacyCon, brings together academics, including economists, to present and discuss research on privacy and data security. The recent workshop on Informational Injuries similarly explored some of the economic dimensions of privacy.

[74] *See, e.g., Nomi Tech., supra* note 4; *Google Safari, supra* note 39; *HTC America, supra* note 40.

frequently engage with economic analysis.[75] The FTC consumer protection mission largely involved business practices tending to create significant consumer harm with little or no generation of offsetting consumer benefits in the context of fraud.[76] There is little need for an economist to weigh the costs and benefits of business practices that are obviously harmful. As such, incorporating a team – or even one – of the FTC's PhD economists has historically been unnecessary and shied away from by the BCP.[77]

That is not to say that the FTC has entirely rejected economic analysis as irrelevant or inapplicable to consumer protection actions. To the contrary, the FTC began formally embracing the role of economic analysis in consumer protection as early as the 1980s when it adopted its statements on unfairness, deception, and advertising substantiation.[78] Even if there is currently a conflict between the BCP's historical approach to evaluating consumer protection cases at the FTC and the realities of privacy enforcement actions,[79] the historical incorporation and acceptance of economic analysis in consumer protection – especially as it relates to advertising – bodes well for the eventual integration of economic analysis into privacy regulation. Later, we explore antitrust's experience with economics as a guide to adopting a deeper integration of economics and cost-benefit analysis into the privacy framework.[80]

It is well founded that economics is a uniquely situated set of tools that can assess the tradeoffs facing consumers: the consumer welfare benefits of new and enhanced products and services against the potential harm to consumers.[81] Antitrust law was slow to embrace and integrate the insights of economics. Congress passed the Sherman Act in 1890, effectively outlawing "every contract, combination or conspiracy in restraint of trade" and "monopolization." In the early years, economics played little to no role in antitrust analysis.[82] However as early as the 1930s, economics began seeping into the margins of antitrust law and policy debates.[83] In the 1960s and

---

[75] Wright, *The Missing Role of Economics, supra* note 72.

[76] *Id.*

[77] *Id.*

[78] 1980 Policy Statement on Unfairness; 1983 Policy Statement on Deception. In 1994, Congress codified the unfairness standard into Section 5 of the FTC Act. 15 U.S.C. § 45(n). Under the Section 5 unfairness prong, the Commission must not declare an act or practice unfair unless it "causes or is likely to cause substantial injury to consumers which is not reasonably avoidable by consumers themselves *and not outweighed by countervailing benefits to consumers or to competition.*" 15 U.S.C. § 45(n)." Effectively, this incorporates an economic cost-benefit test in those cases that fall under the unfairness prong of Section 5, with the last step requiring the Commission to evaluate countervailing benefits. In the case of the deceptive prong, the Commission will only declare an act to be deceptive if there has been a material representation, omission, or practice likely to mislead reasonably acting consumers under the circumstances that ultimately harms consumers. FTC Policy Statement on Deception, appended to Cliffdale Associates, Inc., 103 F.T.C. 110, 174 (1984), *available at* https://www.ftc.gov/public-statements/1983/10/ftc-policy-statement-decep tion. The only relevant element is materiality and whether the act or practice likely to affect the consumers' decision with respect to a particular product or service. FTC Policy Statement on Deception, appended to Cliffdale Associates, Inc., 103 F.T.C. 110, 174 (1984), *available at* https://www.ftc.gov/public-statements/1983/10/ftc-policy-statement-decep tion. *See also* Geoffrey A. Manne et al., In the Matter of Nomi Technologies, Inc.: The Dark Side of the FTC's Latest Feel-Good Case 5 (2015).

[79] Joshua D. Wright, *The FTC and Privacy Regulation: The Missing Role of Economics*, Briefing on Nomi, Spokeo, and Privacy Harms, GEORGE MASON UNIVERSITY LAW AND ECONOMICS CENTER (Nov. 12, 2015), *available at* http:// masonlec.org/site/rte_uploads/files/Wright_PRIVACYSPEECH_FINALv2_PRINT.pdf.

[80] *Id.*

[81] *Id.*

[82] William E. Kovacic & Carl Shapiro, *Antitrust Policy: A Century of Economic and Legal Thinking*, 14 J. ECON. PERS. 43 (2000).

[83] Hovenkamp 1985.

1970s, antitrust lawyers and the agencies were just as – if not more – reluctant to allow economic analysis to permeate into antitrust law.[84]

In the 1960s, a "new learning" in antitrust economics began to evolve as a number of now well-known scholars at Harvard University, Yale University, and the University of Chicago inserted into antitrust law the view that their purpose should be to promote economic efficiency and consumer welfare instead of protecting small traders and individuals from competitive market forces.[85] In essence, these scholars began questioning many of the per se illegality rules of the Supreme Court. In fact, they went so far as to argue that at least some conduct under antitrust laws, e.g., vertical restraints, were so frequently pro-competitive – or at least neutral – in their effects that the Supreme Court should actually hold them to a rule of per se *legality*.[86]

By the mid-1970s, the Supreme Court had begun rewriting its antitrust doctrine, overturning long-standing precedent in order to bring it into alignment with this new development and understanding in antitrust economics.[87] By *Continental T.V., Inc. v. GTE Sylvania*,[88] the Supreme Court had clearly shifted its analysis to take into consideration the impact of firms' behaviors and actions on the market and, ultimately, the consumer.[89] In *GTE Sylvania*, the Supreme Court determined that it was the overall market impact of an alleged restraint of trade that was of utmost concern, recognizing that vertical nonprice restrictions had the potential actually to promote interbrand competition, and ultimately stating this to be the "primary concern of antitrust law."[90] It was *GTE Sylvania* that really solidified antitrust's shift to embrace the economic approach, and in fact it was not too long before the Supreme Court determined that Congress had actually "designed the Sherman Act as a 'consumer welfare prescription.'"[91]

The evolution of antitrust to include economic welfare as the leading driver in its analysis transformed this body of law. In fact, the shift to a welfare-based antitrust standard and its inherent reliance upon economic thinking has created benefits for consumers, competition, and the economy as a whole by leading "to greater predictability in judicial and agency decision making."[92] Incorporating economics into antitrust benefits consumers in a number of related ways. First, it focuses the antitrust enforcement and regulatory enterprise on the goal of consumer welfare and solves a longstanding dilemma for a body of law that has long been plagued by serving too many masters. For example, the integration of economics into antitrust facilitated the Supreme Court's move away from rules of *per se* illegality to a rule of reason approach, relying upon on cost-benefit analysis tethered to scientific method to analyze competitive behavior on a case-by-case basis rather than through the idiosyncratic intuition and

[84] Up until the 1960s and 1970s, the Supreme Court had only interpreted the antitrust statutes to be providing a set of "vague and, ironically, anti-competitive social and political goals." Douglas A. Ginsburg, *Originalism and Economic Analysis: Two Case Studies of Consistency and Coherence in Supreme Court Decision Making*, 33 Harv. J. L. & Pub. Pol. 217, 218 (2010). *See also* United States v. Aluminum Co. of Am., 158 F.2d 416, 428–29 (2d Cir. 1945) (Judge Learned Hand described antitrust as having the goal of reducing the "helplessness of the individual" and to ensure that industries were organized into small units for "its own sake and spirit in spite of possible cost.").

[85] Ginsburg, *supra* note 84, at 218. These scholars include Phillip Areeda at Harvard Law School, Robert Bork and Ward Bowman at Yale Law School, and Frank Easterbrook and Richard Posner at the University of Chicago Law School. *Id.*

[86] Kovacic & Shapiro, *supra* note 82, at 53.

[87] Ginsburg, *supra* note 84, at 218.

[88] 433 U.S. 36 (1977).

[89] Joshua D. Wright & Douglas A. Ginsburg, *The Goals of Antitrust: Welfare Trumps Choice*, 81 Fordham L. Rev. 2405, 2406 (2013).

[90] *Id.*

[91] *Reiter v. Sonotone Corp.*, 442 U.S. 330, 343 (1979).

[92] Wright & Ginsburg, *supra* note 89, at 2407.

presumptions of the individual judge or agency at a particular point in time. Second, antitrust's economic toolkit allows courts and agencies to identify and eliminate theories of liability and defenses that, if allowed, would provide incentives for behavior that would harm competition consumers.[93] Third, the integration of economics into antitrust provides an analytical approach for testing novel theories of consumer harm – that is, novel theories of harm will be tolerated, but tested rigorously with the available data in individual cases.

Economics has transformed antitrust law and the methods antitrust enforcement agencies use to analyze cases. The combination of deep integration of economics with antitrust law and a singular focus on economic welfare has been cause for an important and intellectually coherent shift in the focus of antitrust laws and enforcement agencies over the past fifty years. Economics provides a number of useful analytical tools to inform antitrust analysis in terms of how various forms of conduct will influence consumer welfare. These tools have influenced several areas of antitrust law and competition enforcement agency behavior, including, merger analysis, the relationship between concentration and price in antitrust policy, price discrimination enforcement, and tying law.

IV AREAS FOR IMPROVEMENT

As explained earlier, antitrust was rescued from incoherence by mooring it to consumer welfare and economic analysis. As privacy regulation has grown in importance, it's time that the analysis develop accordingly. One could not imagine the FTC attempting to block a merger based exclusively upon consumer surveys or the staff's impressions of a workshop. Yet, that is exactly the state of play in privacy.

Facebook's 2014 acquisition of WhatsApp brings this dichotomy in analytic rigor into sharp relief. On the antitrust side of the FTC's regulatory enterprise, the FTC's Bureau of Competition applied the cost-benefit framework laid out in the Horizontal Merger Guidelines (HMG) to determine that the combination didn't pose a threat to competition.[94] Accompanying the FTC's closing of its antitrust investigation into the merger, however, was a letter from the BCP, cautioning that if WhatsApp fails to "obtain consumers' affirmative consent" before using their data "in a manner that is materially inconsistent" with the promises it made at the time of collection, it may be in violation of the FTC Act.[95] Although the concept of notice for a change in data sharing is not novel and (assuming the changes in data use were material) would be consistent with a deception theory, the opt-in requirement was new. It was accompanied by no analysis of the costs or benefits, and the only authority that the FTC relied on were complaints from settled cases that had *nothing* to do with opt-in versus opt-out consent for privacy policy changes, but rather with alleged failures adequately to *notify* consumers about privacy policy changes.[96]

---

[93] *Id.*

[94] *See* Chelsey Dulaney, *Facebook Completes Acquisition of WhatsApp*, WALL ST. J. (Oct. 4, 2014), *available at* http://www.wsj.com/articles/facebook-completes-acquisition-of-whatsapp-1412603898.

[95] Letter from Jessica L. Rich to Erin Egan & Anne Hoge (Apr. 10, 2014), *available at* https://www.ftc.gov/public-statements/2014/04/letter-jessica-l-rich-director-federal-trade-commission-bureau-consumer. The letter called for "affirmative express consent" for changes, and a blog posting from a BCP staffer later clarified that merging parties needed to obtain "express opt-in consent" for material changes to data practices. *See Mergers and Privacy Policies* (Mar. 25, 2015), *available at* https://www.ftc.gov/news-events/blogs/business-blog/2015/03/mergers-privacy-promises.

[96] *In re Facebook, Inc.* Decision and Order, No. C-4365 (2012), *available at* http://www.ftc.gov/enforcementcases-proceedings/092-3184/facebook-inc.; *In re Gateway Learning Corp.*, Decision and Order, No. C-4120 (2004), *available at* http://www.ftc.gov/enforcementcases-proceedings/042-3047/gateway-learning-corp-matter.

Because opting in will result in less data than opting out,[97] this new requirement will surely deter some companies from engaging in beneficial changes to their current data collection, or from having access to less data when they do. That the FTC developed a requirement with huge potential impact on the way data are used in such an ad hoc manner, without any analysis of likely impact on consumers, is troubling.

As the WhatsApp-Facebook experience demonstrates, the chasm between antitrust analysis and privacy analysis couldn't be wider. Perhaps this gap would be fine if the stakes weren't so high, but that's not the case. To use a tired cliché, data is today's currency, and by regulating these data flows, privacy regulation has enormous impacts on one of the most vibrant sectors of the US economy. Just as privacy regulation has grown in importance, so should the analysis on which it relies grow in coherence and sophistication. To be fair, the difference in sophistication cannot be entirely laid at the feet of the FTC. There is an important difference between privacy law and antitrust law: the lack of development outside of the FTC. The FTC shares antitrust jurisdiction with the Department of Justice (DOJ), and there is a private right of action under the Sherman Act. Accordingly, modern antitrust jurisprudence is well developed, providing both guidance and restraint on the FTC's competition mission. The development of privacy policy, on the other hand, has been completely without external constraint; absent a well-developed body of case law, it has been left entirely to the FTC's discretion. This is likely to be the state of play for the foreseeable future, so the FTC has a special responsibility to get it right.

We believe that privacy enforcement and policy-making are ripe for a revolution similar to the one that transformed antitrust forty years ago. As follows, we sketch out an analytic structure – one that borrows from antitrust in examining in detail the benefits and costs related to FTC privacy interventions – that could help move privacy closer to the type of rigorous analysis that is needed when the stakes are so high.

A *Identifying Cognizable Harm*

The foundation of all the FTC's privacy work rests on the notion of consumer harm from the collection of personal data – directly in unfairness, and indirectly in deception through materiality. It's easy to see actual or potential harm in the context of stolen credit card, bank account, and insurance information. But increasingly, FTC focus is on collection and use involving nonmonetizeable data, as is evident in the recent reports on the IOT, data brokers, and big data. In antitrust, a plaintiff must articulate a theory of *why* the conduct in question is likely harmful to competition and consumers. For example, the agencies may challenge a merger on a unilateral or coordinated effects theory.[98] Or, a plaintiff may challenge a dominant firm's conduct because it is foreclosing its rivals' access to a necessary input. In addition to articulating

---

[97] *See, e.g.,* Jin-Hyuk Kim & Liad Wagman, *Screening Incentives and Privacy Protection in Financial Markets: A Theoretical and Empirical Analysis*, 46 RAND J. ECON. 1 (2015) (finding evidence that screening was less accurate when an opt-in requirement for sharing was in place, because it limited revenue from selling to third parties); Avi Goldfarb & Catherine E. Tucker, *Privacy Regulation and Online Advertising*, 57 MGM'T SCI. 57 (2011) (finding that EU privacy regulations governing web tracking, some of which require opt-in consent, reduce advertising effectiveness); *id.* at 60 (executives from large European companies report that it costs 15 Euros for each opt-in consent); HOWARD BEALES, THE VALUE OF BEHAVIORAL TARGETING (2010), *available at* http://www.networkadvertising.org/pdfs/Beales_NAI_Study.pdf.

[98] As explained in the Horizontal Merger Guidelines:

> A merger can enhance market power simply by eliminating competition between the merging parties. This effect can arise even if the merger causes no changes in the way other firms behave. Adverse competitive effects arising in this manner are referred to as "unilateral effects." A merger also can enhance market

a theory of harm, antitrust plaintiffs must present evidence that the practice has had, or is likely to have, an effect on competition, either directly with evidence of reduced output or higher prices, or with proxies such as market share and foreclosure percentages.[99] This demonstration exists to guard against the erroneous condemnation of benign or beneficial conduct.

Although the analog with antitrust law is not perfect, requiring the FTC to articulate the privacy value being harmed and attempting to provide some measurement of its magnitude would be an improvement over the status quo. This exercise would impose a discipline and structure on the FTC's privacy analysis, thereby increasing the likelihood that its actions actually improve consumer welfare.

1 *What Is the Privacy Value at Stake?*

Privacy is a complex, multifaceted concept, capable of meaning a variety of things and promoting different values. For example, in one of its earliest and most famous articulations, privacy was called the "right to be let alone."[100] Privacy also has been referred to as isolation, anonymity in a crowd, or the ability to control the information others have about us.[101] Privacy is seen as instrumental to the human condition, or "personhood."[102] For example, some see privacy as a fundamental human right, the deprivation of which is a direct affront to one's dignity.[103] More instrumentally, privacy also gives rise to autonomy – breathing space to make your own choices and experiment without surveillance and the concomitant fear of societal (or governmental) reprobation.[104] In this manner, autonomy is seen as a necessary component to development. Indeed, the Supreme Court has embraced this conception of privacy in some of its more controversial substantive due process jurisprudence, finding that the Constitution provides a zone in which intimate decisions can be made free from interference by the state.[105] Not only is autonomy a requirement for internal development, moreover, some argue that it is a necessary condition for a democratic and pluralistic society.[106]

Surprisingly, however, the FTC's reports that map out its regulatory posture do little to identify exactly which of these privacy values are implicated by the commercial data flows that are the subject of FTC scrutiny. Indeed, most of its reports do little more than suggest that the regulatory framework – notice and consent requirements, coupled with "privacy by design" and "data minimization" – are needed to bring commercial data practices into line with consumer expectations. It is true that expectations often may correspond closely with harm. Expected data

---

power by increasing the risk of coordinated, accommodating, or interdependent behavior among rivals. Adverse competitive effects arising in this manner are referred to as "coordinated effects."

See U.S. DEPARTMENT OF JUSTICE & FEDERAL TRADE COMMISSION, HORIZONTAL MERGER GUIDELINES *at* 2 (2010).

[99] *See National Collegiate Athletic Ass'n v. Board of Regents*, 468 U.S. 85 n. 49 (1984)

[100] Samuel Warren & Louis Brandeis, *The Right to Privacy*, 4 HARV. L. REV. 193 (1890).

[101] *See* Daniel J. Solove, *Conceptualizing Privacy*, 90 CAL. L. REV. 1087, 1110 (2002).

[102] *Id.* at 1116.

[103] Universal Declaration of Human Rights, G.A. Res. 217A (III), U.N. Doc. A/810 at Art. 12 (1948), *available at* http://www.un.org/en/universal-declaration-human-rights/.

[104] *See* Julie E. Cohen, *Examined Lives: Informational Privacy and the Subject as Object*, 52 STAN. L. REV. 1373, 1424–25 (2000). *See also* Julie E. Cohen, *What Privacy Is For*, 126 HARV. L. REV. 1904, 1911 (2013) ("Lack of privacy means reduced scope for self-making ... privacy is one of the resources that situated subjects require to flourish.").

[105] *See Griswold v. Connecticut*, 381 U.S. 479 (1965); *Roe v. Wade*, 381 U.S. 479 (1973); *Planned Parenthood of Se. Pennsylvania v. Casey*, 505 U.S. 833 (1992).

[106] *See* Anita L. Allen, *Coercing Privacy*, 40 WM. & MARY L. REV. 723, 746 (1999) ("It is not simply that people need opportunities for privacy; the point is that their well-being, and the well-being of the liberal way of life, requires that they in fact experience privacy."); Paul M. Schwartz, *Privacy & Democracy in Cyberspace*, 52 VAND. L. REV. 1609 (1999). *See also* Paul M. Schwartz, *Property, Privacy, and Personal Data*, 117 HARV. L. REV. 2055 (2004) (arguing that privacy is like a public good or a "commons" that requires management to prevent a reduction in beneficial social interactions).

practices in a voluntary transaction can never be harmful. For example, exposure of sensitive medical information to third parties is likely to intrude on privacy. But if there has been consent for such third-party sharing, it is expected, and hence we can assume that the consumer has been adequately compensated for any privacy intrusion.

Importantly, the converse is not true: unexpected data practices do not always equate to privacy harm. Consider two cases. First, one would not expect a computer provider surreptitiously to record intimate household activities, and such recording would clearly give rise to privacy harms – being observed in intimate settings is an intrusion into the home, which has long be held to be a sanctum in privacy law, and such observation would offend basic human dignity, and likely negatively impact autonomy.[107] Here, the practice consumers didn't expect clearly intruded on privacy. Now consider a "smart oven" app that records oven-usage information. According to the FTC, providing these data to third parties, such as data brokers or ad networks, would be inconsistent "with the context of the consumer's relationship with the manufacturer," and thus would require opt-in consent.[108] But if there is privacy harm, it flows from the collection and use of the data, not a failure to meet expectations. They are separate considerations. Whether the data sharing met expectations is an issue of the contract between the consumer and the app maker, which may be mediated through the market or the legal system. But focusing on consumer expectations is a distraction from determining whether a necessary condition for FTC action has been met: is the transfer of these data to third parties likely to create substantial consumer injury? For example, does having these data in the hands of a third party constitute an affront to dignity or reduce autonomy? Or perhaps the targeted ads that may result from such data sharing will intrude into one's seclusion?[109] Accordingly, a focus on expectations, rather than harm, necessarily will be overly inclusive.

2 *The Need for Empirical Evidence to Fuel Evidenced-Based Consumer Protection Policy*

Harm is the focal point of FTC enforcement. As explained in Part II, in the domain of privacy, the FTC has put a great deal of reliance on workshop testimony, distilled by staff and without input from the Bureau of Economics, to identify harmful practices. It can, and should, do better. There is a growing literature that attempts to measure consumers' valuation of privacy through revealed (as opposed to stated) preference, yet none of this work appears in the FTC's reports. The FTC, however, needs to reconcile its policy positions with the fact that most research in the area suggests that consumers are comfortable with the type of data sharing involved in the day-to-day functioning of an ad-supported online world.

In general, research finds that consumers are willing to accept small discounts and purchase recommendations in exchange for personal data,[110] and that they exhibit low

---

[107] See *DesignerWare, LLC*, FTC (Apr. 15, 2012), *available at* https://www.ftc.gov/enforcement/cases-proceedings/112-3151/designerware-llc-matter

[108] See IOT Rep. at 40 (contending that such sharing would be inconsistent with the context of the consumer's relationship with the manufacturer).

[109] This type of privacy harm was used as the justification for perhaps the most famous of all FTC regulatory programs, the "do not call" list. *See* Beales & Muris, *supra* note 11, at 119–20. *See also Mainstream Marketing Servs., Inc. v. FTC*, 358 F.3d 1228 (10th Cir. 2004) (protecting individuals from unwanted intrusions in their homes is a substantial government interest); *Rowan v. U.S. Post Office Dep't*, 397 U.S. 728 (1970) (same).

[110] See Dan Cvrecek, Marek Kumpost, Vashek Matyas & George Danezis, *A Study on the Value of Location Privacy*, PROCEEDINGS OF THE 5TH ACM WORKSHOP ON PRIVACY IN THE ELECTRONIC SOCIETY (2006). For a full review of this literature *see* Alessandro Acquisti et al., *The Economics of Privacy*, 54 J. ECON. LIT. 442, 478 (2016).

willingness to pay for protection from telemarketers.[111] For example, one study finds that consumers are willing to pay an additional $1 to $4 for a hypothetical smartphone app that conceals location, contacts, text content, or browser history from third-party collectors.[112] Recent research also reports that while a representative sample of Google users find Gmail's practice of scanning e-mails to be privacy-intrusive, two-thirds would not be willing to pay anything for a Gmail service that didn't scan e-mails, and the median payment for the remaining one-third of consumers was only $15 per year.[113]

These results, moreover, are consistent with real world behavior in which consumers increasingly participate in online activities that reveal personal data to both known and unknown parties. For example, there are 1.3 billion daily Facebook users,[114] 150 million people use Snapchat daily,[115] the percentage of consumers using health tracking apps and wearables has doubled since 2014,[116] and nearly half of US households have an Amazon Prime account.[117] Further, very few people bother to opt-out of online tracking or to adopt privacy-protecting technology, such as the TOR browser or searching via Duck, Duck, Go![118] Indeed, Acquisti, Taylor, and Wagman conclude in a recent survey of the literature that the adoption of privacy-enhancing technologies has lagged substantially behind the use of information-sharing technologies.[119] Thus, although consumers tell survey-takers that they are concerned about being observed, their revealed preference suggests that privacy concerns are not sufficient to slow the adoption of services that rely on the collection and use of their data.

Who's doing the watching also seems to matter. Benjamin Wittes and Jodie Liu find that people are more concerned about privacy with proximate observation by individuals than distant observation by computers.[120] For example, the authors find evidence from Google Autocomplete that people often search for information on topics such as HIV and sexual identification, suggesting that the ability to search anonymously online for information about these topics

---

[111] *See* Hal R. Varian, Glenn Woroch & Fredrik Wallenburg, *Who Signed Up for the Do Not Call List?* (2004), *available at* http://eml.berkeley.edu/~woroch/do-not-call.pdf; Ivan P. L. Png, *On the Value of Privacy from Telemarketing: Evidence from the "Do Not Call" Registry* (2007), *available at* http://papers.ssrn.com/sol3/papers.cfm?abstract_id=1000533.

[112] Scott Savage & Donald M. Waldman, *The Value of Online Privacy* (2013), *available at* http://papers.ssrn.com/sol3/papers.cfm?abstract_id=2341311.

[113] Lior Strahilevitz & Matthew B. Kugler, *Is Privacy Policy Language Irrelevant to Consumers?*, 45 J. Leg. Stud. 69 (2016).

[114] *Company Info*, Facebook, http://newsroom.fb.com/company-info/ (last visited Oct. 10, 2016).

[115] Sarah Frier, *Snapchat Passes Twitter in Daily Usage*, Bloomberg News, June 2, 2016, *available at* https://www.bloomberg.com/news/articles/2016-06-02/snapchat-passes-twitter-in-daily-usage.

[116] By 2015, an estimated 500 million people worldwide will use a mobile health app. Stephen McInerney, *Can You Diagnose Me Now? A Proposal to Modify the FDA's Regulation of Smartphone Mobile Health Applications with A Pre-Market Notification and Application Database Program*, 48 U. Mich. J. L. Reform 1073 (2015) (*citing* Kevin Pho, *Health App Users Beware*, USA Today (Apr. 2, 2014), *available at* http://www.usatoday.com/story/opinion/2014/04/02/medical-app-fitness-health-fda-technology-column/7224837/). Andrew Meola, *Wearables and Mobile Health App Usage has Surged by 50% Since 2014*, Business Insider (Mar. 7, 2016) (health tracker use increased from 16% in 2014 to 33% in 2015), *available at* http://www.businessinsider.com/fitbit-mobile-health-app-adoption-doubles-in-two-years-2016-3. *See also* Susannah Fox, *The Self-Tracking Data Explosion*, Pew Research Center (June 4, 2013), *available at* http://www.pewinternet.org/2013/06/04/the-self-tracking-data-explosion/.

[117] See Krystina Gustafson, *Half of America Could Have an Amazon Prime Account by the End of the Year*, CNBC, *available at* http://www.cnbc.com/2016/09/26/amazon-prime-signing-up-members-at-a-faster-clip.html.

[118] See Maurice E. Stucke & Allen P. Grunes, *No Mistake About It: The Important Role of Antitrust in the Era of Big Data*, Antitrust Source at 8–9 (April 2015).

[119] *See* Alessandro Acquisti et al., *The Economics of Privacy*, 54 J. Econ. Lit. 442, 476 (2016).

[120] Benjamin Wittes & Jodie Liu, *The Privacy Paradox: The Privacy Benefits of Privacy Threats*, Center for Technology Innovation at Brookings (May 2015), *available at* http://www.brookings.edu/~/media/research/files/papers/2015/05/21-privacy-paradox-wittes-liu/wittes-and-liu_privacy-paradox_v10.pdf.

provides an important privacy benefit and probably spurs increased information generation. Research in a similar vein finds that self-checkout in libraries has increased the number of LGBT books checked out by students, again suggesting that privacy concerns are reduced when human interaction is removed from the situation.[121] This research suggests that privacy harms may be overstated to the extent that these predictions are made, and known, only by algorithms rather than people.

In addition to incorporating the extant research into their privacy policy, the FTC should train its formidable research capabilities on the task. The FTC has a long and distinguished history of conducting first-rate empirical research with policy impact.[122] Given the importance of privacy to the Commission's current mission, it should invest the resources to conduct empirical research into consumers' valuation of privacy and the impact of privacy regulation on market outcomes. If need be, moreover, the FTC could use its unique "6(b)" power to subpoena data from companies to examine these questions.[123]

As seen, the available literature tells a different story than found in the FTC reports. The take-away is not that privacy is valueless, or that data practices do not give rise to privacy concerns, but rather that the privacy intrusions associated with most of the online ecosystem are small and that most consumers are comfortable with the typical bargain of sharing information with faceless servers in return for free content and services, such as e-mail and social networking platforms. Accordingly, the FTC's enforcement posture is likely to be too aggressive by failing to consider this empirical evidence and by placing too much weight on opinions from the most privacy-sensitive constituents. Similarly, the same considerations also raise serious questions for mainstays in the FTC's privacy program, such as "data minimization" and "privacy by design." It would appear that these concepts are based on the preferred mix of privacy and functionality for the most privacy sensitive, which implies that the FTC is using its bully pulpit to cajole companies into supplying too much privacy. This posture would be welfare-enhancing only if consumers are incapable of making informed choices because they systematically underestimate privacy harms. If this is the case, the FTC should state their position clearly and engage in research to demonstrate what seems to us to be a necessary predicate for its current posture.

3 *Distinguishing Strategic Privacy from Beneficial Privacy*

The IOT, Big Data, and Data Broker reports identify as a potential harm the possibility of being treated differently based on accurate data.[124] But the FTC needs to distinguish between privacy harms and harms to individuals when they suffer worse terms because a counterparty has a more accurate view of their characteristics. True, such a person is harmed by virtue of a concealed trait becoming public, but the harm stems from terms of trade that more accurately reflect one's type, rather than directly from the invasion of privacy. Using privacy strategically to get a larger share of surplus is wholly dissipative, and it exacerbates the problems associated with adverse selection and moral hazard, which are always present with asymmetric information.[125]

---

[121] *See also* Stephanie Mathson & Jeffry Hancks, *Privacy Please? A Comparison between Self-Checkout and Book Checkout Desk for LGBT and Other Books,* 4 J. ACCESS SERVS. 27, 28 (2007).

[122] *See* notes 57–61, and accompanying text, *supra.*

[123] 15 U.S.C. § 46(b). Since 2000, it has used this power to examine data brokers, pharmacy benefit managers, and patent assertion entities.

[124] See, *e.g.,* Data Brokers Rep. at v–vi; IOT Rep. at 15–16; Big Data Rep. at 10–11.

[125] *See, e.g.,* Richard A. Posner, *The Economics of Privacy,* 71 AM. ECON. REV. 405 (1981); Richard A. Posner, *The Right of Privacy,* 12 GA. L. REV. 393 (1978).

Any regulation to prevent classification based on traits that big data analytics can ferret out should be rooted in antidiscrimination law[126] – which embodies the choices that society has made about which traits are fair game for classification – rather than the FTC Act. That is, when privacy is solely strategic, unless there are other socially beneficial reasons for preventing discrimination based on the trait in question, it makes no sense to bar such classification on privacy grounds.[127] For example, although it is clearly correct to prevent lenders from basing terms on race, gender, or religion, it would be odd – and socially wasteful – to prevent them from discriminating based on credit history. Using antidiscrimination law rather than privacy law to prevent certain classifications also has the advantage of discouraging wasteful investments in signaling. Even if privacy law prevents a firm from attempting to find the value of some hidden trait, nothing prevents a consumer from attempting to signal her value of that trait.[128] But if a firm is forbidden from making decisions (e.g., hiring, pricing, and insurance) based on the trait in question, signaling no longer has value. Further, an antidiscrimination regime would save resources that risky types would devote to concealing the negative values of the trait in question, which would increase the amount of information available to society.

It is true that it may be difficult to disentangle the inherent and strategic dimensions of privacy. For example, health privacy has a strategic dimension: keeping the presence of diabetes or bipolar disorder secret likely will lead to advantages in the labor and insurance markets. But most people also would suffer privacy harm from having health conditions made public. In these cases, where there is a legitimate privacy interest at stake, it is appropriate for policy makers to consider privacy regulation.

B Reevaluating the Materiality Presumption

As discussed previously, many of the FTC's privacy cases rest on broken promises found primarily in privacy policies. Enforcing promises makes sense, and has a strong economic pedigree.[129] Disclosure of product attributes – for example, nutritional content or health benefits – allows heterogeneous consumers to select their preferred bundle of price and nonprice attributes, and it spurs competition over dimensions that consumers value.[130] To the extent that consumers view data practices as an important determinant of which web sites or platforms to use, one would expect firms voluntarily to disclose how they collect and use personal information – unravelling means that consumers will infer the worst from silence.[131] Although this theory is sound, competition over privacy can break out only if consumers respond to privacy disclosures, or stated another way, if privacy promises are material. In its deception cases, the FTC has presumed that these privacy-related statements are material in the same way

---

[126] *See, e.g.,* Equal Credit Opportunity Act, 15 U.S.C. § 1691 *et seq.*; Fair Housing Act, 42 U.S.C. § 12101 *et seq.*; Genetic Information Nondiscrimination Act, 42 U.S.C. § 2000ff *et seq.*

[127] For a formal exposition of this point, *see* James C. Cooper, *Separation Anxiety,* 20 VA. J. L. & TECH. 1 (2017).

[128] Scott Peppet, *Unraveling Privacy: The Personal Prospectus & the Threat of a Full Disclosure Future,* 105 NW. U. L. REV. 1153 (2011).

[129] *See* Howard Beales et al., *The Efficient Regulation of Consumer Information,* 24 J.L. & ECON. 491, 513 (1981) ("information remedies allow consumers to protect themselves according to personal preferences rather than place on regulators the difficult task of compromising diverse preferences with a common standard.").

[130] *See* Pauline M. Ippolito & Alan D. Mathios, *Information, Advertising, and Health Choices: A Study of the Cereal Market,* 21 RAND J. ECON. 459 (1990).

[131] Beales et al., *supra* note 129, at 523; Paul Milgrom, *What the Seller Won't Tell You: Persuasion and Disclosure in Markets,* 22 J. ECON. PERSP. 115, 119–21 (2008).

that any express marketing claim is presumed material. But there are serious reasons to doubt the validity of this presumption in the context of privacy policy.

First, unlike advertisements or other marketing materials, firms do not develop privacy policies to attract consumers but rather to comply with state regulation or self-regulatory regimes.[132] Second, the evidence is overwhelming that almost nobody reads privacy policies.[133] Third, experimental evidence finds that even when consumers read these policies, they are still willing to trade personal data for free services. For example, consider two recent papers. Omri Ben-Shahar and Adam S. Chilton present to a random sample of representative consumers six different privacy policies – including "best practices" and a warning label – for a dating app that was purposely designed to be a poster-child for the kind of data practices that should frighten consumers.[134] Each privacy policy explained that the app collects highly sensitive information (e.g., sexual history and preferences) that is identifiable, used for advertising and future communications, shared with third parties, including advertisers and insurers, and retained forever. Yet, the authors find that regardless of the privacy policy shown, consumer comprehension and willingness to share personal information remained the same. Although most participants clearly didn't read the policies closely (spending only a few seconds on the disclosure page regardless of treatment), even for those who did, there were no differences in the amount of personal data shared. In similar work, Strahilevitz and Kugler focus on real-world services and privacy policies.[135] They present various versions of Gmail privacy policies to a random sample of representative Gmail users. Although the subjects generally comprehended the policy and believed that Gmail's automated content analysis was intrusive, two-thirds were unwilling to pay anything to avoid the practice – they perceived some privacy cost, but it was not as large as the value of free e-mail. For the rest of the subjects, the median annual payment they were willing to make to avoid e-mail scanning was only $15. Finding such a small willingness to pay for privacy is consistent with most of the empirical work in this area,[136] and is consistent with consumers remaining rationally ignorant of privacy policy terms.[137]

It is true that materiality is judged based on the intended audience, but the FTC should not be able to claim materiality by assuming that privacy policies are aimed only at the most privacy

---

[132] *See, e.g.,* Cal. Bus. & Prof. Code Sec. 22575–78; Del. Code Tit. 6 Sec. 205C.

[133] *See* Aleecia M. McDonald & Lorrie Faith Cranor, *The Cost of Reading Privacy Policies*, 4 I/S: J.L. & POL'Y INFO. SOC'Y 543 (2008). *See also* Florencia Morotta-Wurgler, *supra* note 22, at 99 (noting that empirical evidence on disclosure regimes is "piecemeal and mixed"); OMRI BEN-SHAHAR & CARL E. SCHNEIDER, MORE THAN YOU WANTED TO KNOW: THE FAILURE OF MANDATED DISCLOSURE 33–57 (2014) (surveying empirical evidence on the failure of mandated disclosure).

[134] *See* Omri Ben-Shahar & Adam S. Chilton, *Simplification of Privacy Disclosures: An Experimental Test*, 45 J. LEG. STUD. 41 (2016). *See also* Jane R. Bambauer et al., *A Bad Education*, 2017 IL. L. REV. 109 (2017) (finding evidence that privacy disclosures are usually wasteful and may cause consumers to overreact).

[135] Lior Strahilevitz & Matthew B. Kugler, *Is Privacy Policy Language Irrelevant to Consumers?*, 45 J. LEG. STUD. 69 (2016).

[136] *See* Alessandro Acquisti et al., *The Economics of Privacy*, 54 J. ECON. LIT. 442 (2016). *But see* Janice Y. Tsai et al., *The Effect of Online Privacy Information on Purchasing Behavior: An Experimental Study*, 22 INFO. SYS. RES. 254 (2011) (finding that privacy-sensitive consumers are willing to pay more to purchase small items (batteries and sex toys) from websites with higher privacy ratings).

[137] *See* Beales & Muris, *supra* note 11, at 113–15. Others have focused on the complexity of privacy policies as the driving force behind lack of consumer uptake. For example, Kelley et al. find that simplifying information in a standardized table format helps increase comprehension. *See* Patrick Gage Kelley et al., *A "Nutrition Label" for Privacy* (2009), *at* https://cups.cs.cmu.edu/soups/2009/proceedings/a4-kelley.pdf; Patrick Gage Kelley et al., *Standardizing Privacy Notices: An Online Study of the Nutritional Labeling Approach*, CYLAB (2010), *at* http://repository.cmu.edu/cgi/viewcontent.cgi?article=1002&context=cylab. The lack of attention to privacy policies may also be the result of a free-rider problem: consumers may assume that consumer watchdog organizations (or a sufficient number of their peers) are aware of privacy policy terms, which would obviate their need to read these policies.

sensitive, and then defining this group as those who responded to the privacy policy.[138] Such reasoning reduces materiality to a tautology, stripped of all content. Under this standard, every statement is material as long as at least one person responds to it, because, by definition, that person was the intended audience. Instead, materiality for privacy policies must be judged by some threshold impact on all consumers. Otherwise, we allow the preferences of a small minority of the most privacy sensitive consumers to strike the balance between privacy and the benefits from data sharing – a balance that clearly would be harmful to most consumers.

Importantly, our call to reevaluate the materiality presumption will not mean that firms can make and break privacy promises with impunity. It merely eliminates the Commission's ability to rely on a presumption of materiality, and forces it to carry its burden of production. For example, the Materiality Statement says that when the Commission cannot presume materiality, evidence, based on a reliable survey or expert testimony, can demonstrate that the product costs more than one with the feature.[139] Further, materiality need not be demonstrated in every case. The FTC could perform a large-scale empirical study of how consumers respond to privacy policies, perhaps using its 6(b) authority. If such a study were to show that some threshold number of consumers responded to changes in privacy promises, it would lay a predicate for materiality in any subsequent individual case, leaving the defendant to provide evidence that the study should not apply to its situation.

Untethered from the materiality requirement, the FTC's consumer protection efforts in privacy regulation are no longer about consumer harm – or promoting consumer welfare – but rather, they are about micromanaging privacy policies and placing broad sectors of the digital economy under the thumb of a single agency. Faced with potential liability for trivial misstatements, firms have increased incentives to take down voluntary privacy policies or not generate them at all. This will leave consumers and privacy watchdogs with even less information than they are already receiving about website activity – exacerbating the very problem the FTC was attempting to solve. This unintended consequence is one that is easily foreseeable; and one that is obvious to most economists. But the Commission's analysis simply ignores these trade-offs.

C *Identifying Benefits from Information Flows (or the Costs of Intervention)*

The lack of information can severely impact the abilities of markets to generate welfare for consumers. Because privacy regulation almost by definition restricts information flows, it can exacerbate the problems associated with informational asymmetries. Further, restricting firms' ability to collect and use consumer data can impact their ability to compete. These problems can be especially difficult for new entrants or firms subject to lengthy consent orders.

1 *Adverse Selection, Moral Hazard, and Better Matching*

Increased information improves market performance by reducing the costs of determining hidden quality or the distribution of prices. But privacy regulation by definition interferes with the free flow of information, and hence imposes costs on markets. For example, markets with asymmetric information often suffer from adverse selection, which occurs when a firm's offerings attract a disproportionate amount of "bad" types – e.g., risky borrowers, unproductive

---

[138] *See, e.g., Nomi Tech., Inc.* Statement of Chairwoman Ramirez and Commissioners Brill and McSweeny (Sept. 3, 2015) ("Consumers who read the Nomi privacy statement would likely have been privacy-sensitive, and claims about how and when they could opt out would likely have especially mattered to them."), *available at* https://www.ftc.gov/enforcement/cases-proceedings/132-3251/nomi-technologies-inc-matter.

[139] Deception Statement at 5.

workers, bad drivers, those with unhealthy lifestyles, and the like. In addition to adverse
selection, markets characterized by asymmetric information are often subject to moral hazard.
Whereas adverse selection concerns hidden information about parties before they enter into a
relationship, moral hazard concerns hidden actions – actions that impact the value of the
relationship – that occur *after* the parties enter into a contract. For example, drivers can reduce
the probability that they will get into an accident by choosing to drive more slowly, less often,
and on less congested roads. Adverse selection and moral hazard can be found in a variety of
markets in which one party is likely to have private information.[140] Both adverse selection and
moral hazard impose costs on society. To deal with adverse selection, "good" types typically
enjoy worse terms than they would in markets with full information, and may incur costs
associated with signaling. Firms often address moral hazard by rationing (e.g., deductibles,
and down payments). At the margin, good types exit markets or enjoy too little insurance or
credit. Thus, privacy regulations – especially those concerning the use of data to make predictions – that limit the ability to discover private information in employment, healthcare, and
insurance markets are likely to impose welfare cost on society.[141]

There are also direct consequences from privacy regulation that have to do with matching.
For example, Jin-Hyuk Kim and Liad Wagman present empirical evidence that an opt-in
requirement for selling consumers' financial information reduces the marketability of these
data, and hence firms' incentives to assure its accuracy[142] They find that counties with opt-in
requirements had lower loan-denial rates and concomitantly higher foreclosure rates. Similarly,
Amalia R. Miller and Catherine E. Tucker find that increased consent requirements for sharing
health care data reduces incentives to adopt health information technology (HIT). Their results
show that lower HIT adoption rates are associated with worse health outcomes, especially for
minority babies.[143] Avi Goldfarb and Catherine E. Tucker examine the impact of EU privacy
regulation that makes collection of consumer data more expensive and difficult on advertising
effectiveness.[144] Their results suggest that the EU Privacy Directive decreased advertising
effectiveness in the EU by 65 percent on average compared to the rest of the world.

---

[140] *See* Lawrence M. Ausbel, *Adverse Selection in the Credit Card Market*, (1999) (credit card markets); Wendy
Edelburg, *Risk-Based Pricing of Interest Rates for Consumer Loans*, 53 J. MONETARY ECON. 2283 (2006) (consumer
loan market); Liran Einav, Mark Jenkins & Jonathan Levin, *The Impact of Credit Scoring on Consumer Lending*, 44
RAND J. ECON. 249 (2013) (subprime auto loan market); William Adams, Liran Einav, & Jonathan Levin, *Liquidity
Contraints and Imperfect Information in Subprime Lending*, 99 AM. ECON. REV. 49 (2009) (subprime auto loan
market); Bev Dahlby, *Testing for Asymmetric Information in Canadian Automobile Insurance in* CONTRIBUTIONS TO
INSURANCE ECONOMICS 423 (1992) (auto insurance); Daniel Altman, David M. Cutler & Richard Zeckhauser,
Adverse Selection and Adverse Retention, 88 AM. ECON. REV. 122 (1998) (health insurance); Amy Finkelstein & James
Poterba, *Testing for Asymmetric Information Using "Unused Observables" in Insurance Markets: Evidence from the
U.K. Annuity Market*, 81 J. RISK & INS. 709 (2014); Dean Karlan & Jonathan Zinman, *Expanding Credit Access: Using
Randomized Supply Decisions to Estimate the Impacts*, 23 REV. FIN. STUD. 433 (2010) (South African subprime
lender); Robery Puelz & Arthur Snow, *Evidence on Adverse Selection: Equilibrium Signaling and Cross-Subsidization
in the Insurance Market*, 102 J. POL. ECON. 236 (1994). *But see* Pierre-Andre Chiappori & Bernard Salanie, *Testing for
Asymmetric Information in Insurance Markets*, 108 J. POL. ECON. 56 (2000) (no evidence in French auto insurance
market for first time drivers); James H. Cardon & Igal Hendel, *Asymmetric Information in Health Insurance: Evidence
from the National Medical Expenditure Survey*, 32 RAND J. ECON. 408 (2001) (health insurance).
[141] *See* James C. Cooper, *Separation Anxiety*, 20 VA. J. L. TECH. 1 (2017).
[142] Jin-Hyuk Kim & Liad Wagman, *Screening Incentives and Privacy Protection in Financial Markets: A Theoretical and
Empirical Analysis*, 46 RAND J. ECON. 1 (2015).
[143] Amalia R. Miller & Catherine E. Tucker, *Can Health Care Information Technology Save Babies?*, 119 J. POL. ECON.
289 (2011); Amalia R. Miller & Catherine E. Tucker, *Privacy Protection and Technology Diffusion: The Case of
Electronic Medical Records*, 55 MGM'T SCI. 1077 (2009).
[144] Avi Goldfarb & Catherine E. Tucker, *Privacy Regulation and Online Advertising*, 57 MGM'T SCI. 57 (2011).

It's important to note that merely identifying costs associated with restrictions on data collection and use doesn't mean that the FTC's actions are necessarily welfare-reducing. To the contrary; these costs may be justified if the privacy harms are sufficient. But these harms need to be identified, not assumed. In FTC enforcement actions, benefits from data sharing are never mentioned in the complaints or analyses to aid public comment. This practice is perhaps understandable, as these are documents from settled cases written by the plaintiff. Less understandable, however, is the sparse treatment given to benefits in the FTC's reports, and the complete lack of acknowledgement on the vast economic literature on the problems that arise when markets are deprived of information. The FTC needs to incorporate this highly germane body of knowledge when shaping policy positions – otherwise, its actions are likely to be welfare-reducing.

2 The Impact of Restricting Data Flows on Innovation and Competition

To the extent that it's unguided by economic analysis, the FTC's privacy policy is likely to have an adverse effect on innovation. For example, in the wearables industry, companies are working together to create devices that can detect pneumonia, optimize health care, and in some cases, share information with health care providers with the goal of lowering the costs on insurance premiums. The increases to consumer welfare from these innovations are obvious. However, if a generalized fear of data sharing restricts this flow between patients and health care provides – or generally, consumers and producers – then the benefits from such innovation may not be realized. Further, placing businesses under twenty-year orders that carry intrusive monitoring and reporting requirements seems especially likely to squelch innovation in the digital economy when a firm's half-life is closer to two years than to ten.[145]

Producer responses to consumer concerns also can be negatively affected by restricting data flows. Software companies such as Apple and Microsoft often release patches after a new – or updated – product release to ensure that the consumer has the best product available. Determining what aspects of these products need to be patched can only occur if consumers share their data with the software companies. Restrictions on such flows of data may result in firms inefficiently substituting a higher level of *ex ante* research into potential software issues for *ex post* discovery through beta testing and otherwise responding to issues that are only observable after a product's release. What's more, excessive *ex ante* development will delay the benefits the consumer reaps from receiving the product at an earlier date.

Overly restrictive privacy regulation deters firms from innovating practices that promote consumer choice and transparency – the very principles that lie at the heart of the Commission's consumer protection mission. Indeed, innovation in new privacy-enhancing tools and technologies might be at risk. If a company might face legal action for incorrectly yet harmlessly describing an opt-out feature they did not need to provide in the first place, then why bother? So long as economic analysis is a marginal player in privacy regulation at the FTC, this unfortunate equilibrium will remain.

---

[145] The FTC can obtain substantial monetary penalties for violations of orders and certain statutes: Google paid $22.5 million for violating its consent decree with outdated FAQs, and *Spokeo* paid $800,000 for violations of the Federal Credit Reporting Act. FTC, GOOGLE WILL PAY $22.5 MILLION TO SETTLE FTC CHARGES IT MISREPRESENTED PRIVACY ASSURANCES TO USERS OF APPLE'S SAFARI INTERNET BROWSER (Aug. 9, 2010), *available at* https://www.ftc .gov/news-events/press-releases/2012/08/google-will-pay-225-million-settle-ftc-charges-it-misrepresented; FTC, SPOKEO TO PAY $800,000 TO SETTLE FTC CHARGES COMPANY ALLEGEDLY MARKETED INFORMATION TO EMPLOYERS AND RECRUITERS IN VIOLATION OF FCRA (June 12, 2012), *available at* https://www.ftc.gov/news-events/press-releases/2012/ 06/spokeo-pay-800000-settle-ftc-charges-company-allegedly-marketed.

Finally, it's important to acknowledge the impact that privacy regulation can have on competition. First, when the Commission places certain firms under twenty-year orders that limit their abilities to use data, it can hinder them as competitors. For example, the order against Facebook, which appears to require it to obtain opt-in consent for material changes to its privacy policy, has impacted its ability to use WhatsApp's data, making it a less effective rival against other social media companies without such strictures.[146] Further, these types of restrictions are likely to create incentives for firms to inefficiently substitute internal for external expansion. This also may discourage innovation by start-ups in data-driven sectors, to the extent that acquisition by a larger company is a less viable outcome.

Second, limiting the ability of firms to collect and use data to identify and target potential customers can soften competition.[147] For example, if a firm is able to discern that a particular consumer enjoys its style of clothing, but tends to purchase from a rival, it can target this consumer with advertising and discounts. This type of targeting intensifies competition in two ways: it reduces search costs by allowing consumers more easily to identify competing firms; and it allows firms to compete directly for consumers, potentially to lower prices for everyone.

V CONCLUSION

The FTC has been in the privacy game for almost twenty years. In that time span, the digital economy has exploded. We live much of our lives in an interconnected web of information – we're constantly sending and receiving all matter of media through smart phones, tablets, and health trackers. As a consequence, the importance of privacy regulation to the economy has grown as well. Unfortunately, its sophistication has yet to keep pace with its stature. The FTC's privacy policy has been built on a foundation devoid of any economic content, instead based almost solely on anecdotes and hypotheticals presented at workshops, as filtered through staff. The FTC can, and should, do better. Privacy stands today where antitrust stood in the 1970s. Antitrust's embrace then of economics helped transform it into a coherent body of law that – despite some quibbles at the margin – almost all agree has been a boon for consumers. Privacy is ripe for a similar revolution. The sooner that the FTC begins to incorporate serious economic analysis and rigorous empirical evidence into its privacy policy, the sooner consumers will begin to reap the rewards.

ACKNOWLEDGMENT

We thank Elise Nelson for comments on an earlier draft.

[146] *See* James C. Cooper, *The WhatsApp Privacy Policy Change: No Cause for Alarm*, FORBES (Sept. 7, 2016), *available at* http://www.forbes.com/sites/jamesccooper1/2016/09/07/the-whatsapp-privacy-policy-change-no-cause-for-alarm/#5b85 cc5204db.

[147] *See* James C. Cooper et al., *Does Price Discrimination Intensify Competition? Implications for Antitrust*, 72 ANTITRUST L.J. 327 (2005). Total welfare can increase when markets exhibit "best response asymmetry" – i.e., one firm's weak market is another's strong market – and they place relatively more weight on their strong market. *See* Kenneth S. Corts, *Third Degree Price Discrimination in Oligopoly: All-Out Competition and Strategic Commitment*, 29 RAND J. ECON. 306 (1998); Lars A. Stole, *Price Discrimination & Competition* in HANDBOOK OF INDUSTRIAL ORGANIZATION 3 (2007); Thisse & Vives, *On the Strategic Choice of Spatial Price Policy*, 78 AM. ECON. REV. 122 (1998). *See also* James Campbell et al., *Privacy Regulation and Market Structure*, 24 J. ECON. & MGM'T STRATEGY 47 (2015) (showing in a theoretical framework how privacy regulation can distort competition by disproportionately impacting small new firms).

27

Big Data by Design

Establishing Privacy Governance for Analytics

Dale Skivington, Lisa Zolidis, and Brian P. O'Connor

COMPLIANCE BY DESIGN

In 2011 Dell decided to rebrand its compliance program to send a message to the business that we are not the department that stops you from innovation, but rather we are the one that will help you meet your business objectives in a compliant manner. We launched Compliance By Design to strategically align more than fifteen Dell compliance programs in order to assist the business and engage it in a consistent and meaningful way.

Our first step in implementing this program was to develop a common framework and taxonomy. We developed a maturity assessment tool based upon the AICPA/CICA Privacy Maturity Model tool,[1] which we modified to meet the needs of the various compliance programs. Each year, we track our development in each component of our program and identify where we have moved the needle toward higher levels of maturity. We also use these benchmarks to plan priorities for the next upcoming year.

Privacy Maturity Model

Our Global Compliance and Global Audit groups worked with each Compliance program owner to fairly assess the maturity of each component of their program and, after considering gaps in light of the risks to the company, developed specific Key Performance Indicators to address them. We also developed action plans, working across the programs to leverage common control needs.

A key focus of control development was ensuring that the compliance programs were engaged in risk assessment during the envisioning stages of product or application development life cycles. For privacy, this engagement was critical to ensure that Privacy Impact Assessments (PIAs) occurred at a juncture where we could influence the outcome. We brought together more than 100 stakeholders in a two-day session, where we reviewed our various product, services, and software development life cycles to consider how to enhance and develop systemic controls.

We also took the opportunity to review our standard Privacy Impact Assessment (PIA) tool and content to determine if new and emerging risks required new or different content. One area of focus was analytics, or Big Data.

---

[1] American Institute of Certified Public Accountants and Canadian Institute of Chartered Accountants, respectively. *See* https://www.isaca.org/chapters1/phoenix/events/Documents/aicpa_cica_privacy_maturity_model.pdf.

	1 Ad hoc	2 Initial	3 Formal	4 Validated	5 Monitored
Policy	None written	Limited distribution & understanding	Formal but may be inconsistent	Globally consistent & enforceable	Regularly reviewed & updated
Governance	None established	Discrete, informal, & limited	Corporate oversight & exec level	Management involvement at all levels	Scorecard reporting
Risk management	Incomplete & inconsistent	Risk assessment, not management	Risk assessment & management	Cross-functional, executive validation	Component of ERM
Procedures & controls	None written	Limited coverage	Consistent & global	Subject to self-assessment & audit	Exception reporting & resolution
3rd party management	No standards	Some standards May be inconsistent	Consistent, cross-functional coordination	Proactive monitoring & self-assessment	Independent external audits
Compliance & monitoring	None established	Informal & limited	Audit-driven, remedial actions endorsed	Analytics technology; cross-functional	Accountability-driven, extends beyond enterprise
Incident management	Ad hoc & inconsistent	Some consistency Little analysis	Root cause analysis, global standards	Issue tracking Technology in place	Effectiveness & efficiency metrics
Training & awareness	None	General, infrequent, single media	Custom-tailored, recurring, multi-media	Role-specific awareness; 3rd parties	Ongoing awareness

Big Data analytics projects present unique risks given the volume of data frequently considered, the changing nature of the field, and the sometimes imprecise goals of finding beneficial uses of seemingly unconnected data elements. Conscientious use of data enables beneficial uses of data, while keeping privacy considerations in mind.

With Big Data projects, we enhance privacy by expanding what responsible companies such as Dell already do – use good governance both before we launch a product or service and after the launch to make sure we consider privacy and security. Dell's governance processes therefore include both Privacy Impact Assessments and specific internal reviews for Big Data product proposals. Thinking about potential pitfalls in the development stage – knowing what could go wrong when deciding to use Big Data techniques for a particular purpose – helps reduce the risk of causing some potential negative consequences.

THE ROLE OF PRIVACY IMPACT ASSESSMENTS

Big Data tools can serve a number of different purposes to meet a wide variety of goals. Large volumes of seemingly unrelated data can be analyzed to draw conclusions that can improve product performance and enhance researchers' capabilities. Projects based on Big Data analytics can range from crime-mapping software for predictive policing to crowd-sourced medical diagnoses produced by "medical detectives" to targeted product recommendations on websites to thermostats tailored to your personal habits and temperature preferences at home. Some researchers may use Big Data to search for relationships between two unrelated behaviors and others may use it to analyze what messages elicit the strongest behavior from individuals. Few Big Data projects are exactly alike.

Yet, a PIA process must be repeatable and trackable in order to provide the most value for a company. The PIA must analyze a proposed new product or service, or a significant proposed change to an existing product or service, to identify risks, offer proposed changes to mitigate risk, and support the relevant business goals within the bounds of privacy law. Given the variability of Big Data projects, building the structure for an effective PIA process can be a challenge.

Dell approached this task by building on its existing PIA process. The Dell PIA process recommends a PIA for all projects or programs involving personal data, and requires a privacy review for initiatives, projects or programs that will handle personal data in a novel way or that could raise significant risk. The Dell team uses project owner input, a set of triggers and risk ratings that determine whether a PIA requires additional review by and consultation with one of Dell's global privacy managers. Dell's internal counsel can also request that additional PIA review be conducted.

Fostering good working relationships with business team leaders and the legal counsel supporting those leaders has been an essential element to making Dell's PIA program work. For a number of years, Dell's privacy, knowledge assurance, and compliance teams have worked closely with leaders from each key business unit selected to serve as data management stewards in addition to their day jobs.

Each data management steward attends quarterly meetings with Dell's chief privacy officer and compliance leaders to review issues most important to the company and discuss needs of each area of the business. Dell privacy managers also frequently meet with data management stewards or participate in periodic business unit team meetings, to better understand the business and learn about new projects or initiatives in the formative stages. Teaming with the business helps identify projects in need of a PIA early so that privacy can be more easily and effectively built into the project design. Understanding the business and its goals also helps the privacy team identify and understand the privacy risk associated with any given project so that risk can be effectively mitigated. Knowing that privacy managers strive to support the business and reduce risk for new projects adds to the business teams' incentives to take responsibility for providing full information for the determination of whether a PIA is required. Together, the business and the privacy team add value to new initiatives and changes to existing programs.

Another way the Dell privacy team has moved to enhance its relationship with business teams is in saving time for its business leaders by streamlining and automating Dell's PIA questionnaires. Once a bulky, one-size-fits-all, manually processed questionnaire, Dell's newly updated question-naire is designed to try to present only those questions most relevant to a particular project or area of the business. Some baseline questions are presented to every user. Responses to those questions may trigger the presentation of additional questions tailored to the type of project. For example, there may be questions presented to someone completing the questionnaire for a human resources project that would not be presented to someone with a marketing project. The baseline questions gather data on the type of project under development, the type of personal data to be collected or processed, and the business area initiating the PIA. Answers to these questions then trigger subsequent questions built upon and extending from the opening set of responses.

One of Dell's privacy managers reviews the questionnaire responses. Questions and answers are risk rated. PIAs scored as "low risk" are documented in the tool but may not require further action from the project owner or the privacy manager. Projects involving Big Data analytics are identified early and receive tailored examination based on a set of review questions developed by Dell's privacy counsel.

Privacy managers explore with the appropriate business team the specific business goals of the project, what data will be collected, and how it will be used. They discuss how the data will be collected, the purposes for which it will be processed, who will be able to see and use the data, and whether any potential discriminatory impact might be imputed. Data storage and retention, including whether personal data should be stored in aggregated or anonymized form, also comprise important considerations that privacy managers will discuss and assist the business in planning.

In some instances, a checklist of standard requirements may be issued to the project owner. At times, a checklist of tasks may require completion before a project submitted to the PIA process is approved. If the business team's responses indicate significant potential risk associated with the project, the privacy manager will work with the business to identify mitigating controls and reduce the risk before the project can go forward.

The ultimate goal of the PIA process for big data projects is to ensure that projects going forward both further business goals and exercise conscientious uses of data. Perhaps the most challenging step is to determine how to help the company balance risk against benefit.

INTERNAL REVIEW BOARDS AND BENEFIT-RISK ANALYSIS TOOLS FOR BIG DATA PROJECTS

As it becomes easier for government agencies and private companies to store ever-greater amounts of data, and as new software is developed to help analyze large stores of data created in different formats and applications, we have also seen increasing concerns on the part of individuals, privacy regulators, and privacy advocates. One area of concern is the possibility that Big Data analysis could result in decisions about credit or product pricing, based on various personal and societal attributes, which could have an adverse impact on members of certain disadvantaged groups.[2]

A second major area of concern relates to the collection of large databases of personal information from a variety of sources that will be used for data analysis projects that were never anticipated when the personal data was initially collected. These new uses are at odds with the Fair Information Principles of Notice and Choice, which are essential elements of data privacy laws around the globe. As Jules Polonetsky, Omer Tene, and Joseph Jerome discuss in a recent law review article,[3] it is often impractical to obtain consent from large numbers of individuals to new uses of data. For one thing, it may not even be possible to locate certain individuals due to the passage of time. Providing notice at the time of data collection is also impractical, because the controller cannot predict all possible and yet-to-be determined data analysis projects that may be valuable at a later date.[4]

While some may view this seemingly intractable conflict as an appropriate limit on the use of personal data, others view the potential benefits of Big Data projects as so great that we must find an alternative to traditional concepts of notice and choice. Ryan Calo was perhaps the first to suggest that an alternative might be derived from the concept of Internal Review Boards (IRBs) that have been created to examine the ethical issues surrounding human-subject medical research.[5] He suggests the creation of Consumer Subject Review Boards (CSRBs), comprised of employees with diverse skill sets, and operating according to predetermined rules. The Federal Trade Commission (FTC) has also recognized the potential for the strict application

[2] *See generally* Exec. Office of the President, *Big Data: Seizing Opportunities, Preserving Values* (2014) [hereinafter White House Big Data Report], *available at* http://www.whitehouse.gov/sites/default/files/docs/big_data_privacy_report_may_1_2014.pdf.

[3] Jules Polonetsky, Omer Tene & Joseph Jerome, *Beyond the Common Rule: Ethical Structures for Data Research in Non-Academic Settings*, 13 J. TEELECOMM. & HIGH TECH. L. 333 (2015), *available at* http://ctlj.colorado.edu/?page_id=238#tabs-238-0-6.

[4] Kate Crawford & Jason Schultz, *Big Data and Due Process: Toward a Framework to Redress Predictive Privacy Harms*, 55 B. C. L. REV. 93, 108 (2014); *see also* Danielle Keats Citron, *Technological Due Process*, 85 WASH. U. L. REV. 1249 (2008).

[5] Ryan Calo, *Consumer Subject Review Boards: A Thought Experiment*, 66 STAN. L. REV. ONLINE 97 (2013), http://www.stanfordlawreview.org/online/privacy-and-big-data/consumer-subject-review-boards.

of notice and choice principles to restrict unexpected new uses of personal data that could have societal benefits.[6]

Polonetsky, Tene, and Jerome have elaborated on Calo's "thought experiment" and have proposed that CSRBs use the substantive principles developed to address the ethics of research on human subjects when evaluating Big Data projects. These principles are: respect for the individual, beneficence, justice, and respect for law. In the Big Data context, beneficence is the desire to determine whether the benefits of data use outweigh the potential harms. Although it is rare that a CSRB could employ quantitative techniques to assess proposals, the authors argue that "beneficence calls for organizations to perform a rational, non-arbitrary, systematic assessment."[7]

What would go into such an assessment? Fortunately, in a separate article, Polonetsky, Tene, and Jerome have outlined an evaluation tool that could be used to weight the benefits, risks, and possible risk mitigations related to a given Big Data project.[8] The two components of this tool are (1) a Privacy Impact Assessment (PIA) that takes into account the more varied set of risks presented by Big Data and (2) a Data Benefit Analysis (DBA) that takes into account the broad array of benefits and beneficiaries of Big Data projects.

The authors state that Big Data presents risks that go beyond the tangible harms that we see with a more restricted set of personal data, e.g., identity theft, financial loss, and the exposure of sensitive data. They posit that Big Data creates other risks, which they categorize as "Intangible" (e.g., "creepy inferences" about data subjects, and reputational damage) and "Abstract" (e.g., panoptic surveillance, and chilling effects on activities).[9] The PIA must take these risks into account, and then assess the likelihood of occurrence.

The DBA looks at the unique variety of potential benefits inherent in Big Data projects, and the fact that potential beneficiaries can extend beyond the data subject and the organization that initially collected the data, and possibly to a particular community or society as a whole. For example, one reported project identified harmful drug interactions by comparing de-identified internet search queries against indicators of adverse side-effects.[10] This result, once confirmed, benefitted all current and potential users of the relevant drugs.

The DBA produces a "raw score" based on the magnitude of the benefit, which is then discounted by the probability that the benefit will result. However, the authors provide no description of how this score would be calculated, what the scale would be (e.g., 1–10), or how the probability discount would be applied to the score. In any event, the final step of the process is a comparison of the weighted risks (from the PIA) with the weighted benefits (from the DBA).

The authors suggest that the results would fall into one of the quadrants shown in Figure 27.1.

In 2015, members of the Conference Board's Council of Chief Privacy Officers (hereinafter "CPO Council")[11] attempted to develop a more granular Benefit-Risk Tool, based on the concepts outlined by Polonetsky, Tene, and Jerome. They discussed possible ways to assign

---

[6] FTC Staff Report, *Internet of Things: Privacy & Security in a Connected World* (2015), *available at* http://www.ftc.gov/system/files/documents/reports/federal-trade-commission-staff-report-november-2013-workshop-entitled-internet-things-privacy/150127iotrpt.pdf.

[7] Polonetsky, Tene & Jerome, *supra* note 5, at 358–59.

[8] Jules Polonetsky, Omer Tene & Joseph Jerome, *Benefit-Risk Analysis for Big Data Projects*, FUTURE OF PRIVACY FORUM (Sept. 2014), *available at* https://fpf.org/wp-content/uploads/FPF_DataBenefitAnalysis_FINAL.pdf.

[9] *Id.* at 3.

[10] Nicholas Tatonetti et al., *Detecting Drug Interactions from Adverse-Event Reports: Interaction between Paroxetine and Pravastatin Increases Blood Glucose Levels*, 90 CLIN. PHARM. & THER. 133 (2011); Nicholas Tatonetti et al., *A Novel Signal Detection Algorithm for Identifying Hidden Drug-Drug Interactions in Adverse Event Reports*, 12 J. AM. MED. INFORMATICS ASS'N 79 (2011).

[11] Margaret P. (Peggy) Eisenhauer, Program Director for the Conference Board's Council of Chief Privacy Officers, Brian O'Connor, Dell, Inc., Jonathan Fox, Cisco Systems, Inc., and John Gevertz, ADP, Inc.

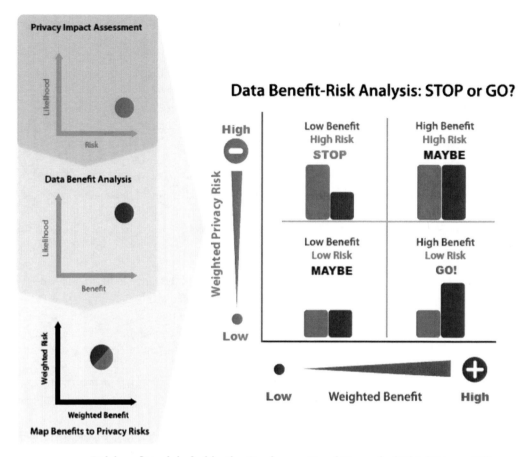

FIGURE 27.1 Risk-benefit tool drafted by the Conference Board Council of Chief Privacy Officers

numerical values to the risks and benefits of Big Data projects, but quickly concluded that it was not possible to quantify these factors objectively. This led to discussions of possible alternatives to numerical scores. At the suggestion of Jules Polonetsky, the CPO Council looked at another tool, described in a 2011 paper entitled "Incident Response and Data Protection," by Andrew Cormack, Chief Regulatory Advisor at JANET (UK Joint Academic Network).[12] It examines justifications for various types of Computer Security Incident Response Team (CSIRT) activities under European law, applying the balancing test set out by European regulators. Under this test, entities may process personal data provided that the processing is necessary, that it furthers the legitimate interest of the entity (or a third party), and that these legitimate interests are not overridden by the fundamental rights and freedoms of the data subjects.

Cormack presents a visual model for comparing and balancing the legitimate interests of CSIRTs with the rights of data subjects, to determine if (and when) those data subject rights might override the legitimate interests of CSIRTs in processing personal data (or data that may be personal data) for various computer security activities.

This is the model that Cormack proposes:[13]

---

[12] Andrew Cormack, *Incident Response and Data Protection*, Draft 2.0, JANET(UK) (Sept. 2011), *available at* http://www
.terena.org/activities/tf-csirt/publications/data-protection-v2.pdf.
[13] *Id.* at 9.

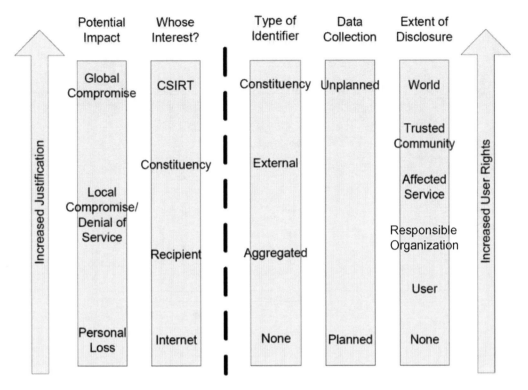

FIGURE 27.2

Cormack's paper contains several examples of this model in use, with scenarios ranging from CSIRTs' use of malware honeypots to forensic analysis of compromised computers, network intrusion analysis, DoS attack analysis, and creation of IP address threat lists. The CPO Council considered how Cormack evaluated these use cases with his balancing test. This model presented some distinct advantages in its presentation of "legitimate use" (justification) on one side of the visual diagram and "rights and freedoms" (user rights) on the other side.

Modifying the Cormack model to more broadly evaluate Big Data and analytics initiatives, the group agreed upon the following specific changes:

- Adjusting the words used to describe the potential impact, interests and extent of disclosure to be less CSIRT-centric and more general to reflect the broader application of the tool;
- Replacing Cormack's "Type of Identifier" column with two new columns: one listing levels of data sensitivity, and a second describing likelihood of personal identification; and
- Overlaying the FPF concepts of risk types and risk mitigation.

The CPO Council created an initial model and modified it after a number of group discussions in which additional factors were added. The most current version is shown here as Figure 27.3:[14]

The first three columns in Figure 3 describe potential Program Benefit Factors relating to a Big Data project. The fourth and fifth columns describe Decision Support Factors, which relate to the controller's confidence that the benefits will be realized, and the availability of risk

---

[14] The tool is provided as "open source" – it may be freely used, modified, and shared, provided that it remains open source. *See* http://opensource.org/licenses/GPL-3.0. The original version is in color, using red, yellow, and green rather than black, gray, and white.

Proposed Risk-Benefits Analysis Tool for Analytics and Big Data Initiatives

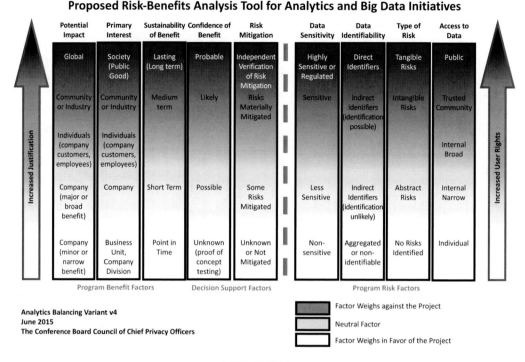

FIGURE 27.3

mitigation methods. The remaining columns describe four aspects of privacy risk associated with a particular project.

In the first five columns, the factors weighing against the project are at the bottom, neutral factors are found in the middle, and those in favor of the project are at the top. The risk factor columns are reversed, with the risks weighing against the project at the top, neutral factors in the middle, and low risks weighing in favor of the project found at the bottom of each column. As each column is "scored," users place a slider with the appropriate shade (black, gray, or white) on that column. Once all the columns are scored, users end up with a graphic representation of risks and benefits. Ideally, the overall pattern will be weighted heavily toward white or black, and clearly indicate whether a given project should proceed or should be abandoned.

Further Guidance on Certain Columns

The CPO Council has provided some additional guidance on the how an internal review board might interpret the factors in several of the columns. This guidance will help facilitate review board discussions, and suggest the types of information that should be requested from those proposing a given Big Data project.

Program Benefits Factors

Potential Impact (Column 1): Identify the potential beneficial impact of the program on different stakeholder groups.
- **Global or Societal:** The program can provide a material benefit to global communities or societies. *Examples*: improved malware detection, improved health outcomes, reduction of discriminatory bias in decision-making, smart grid initiatives. This analytics initiative has the potential to make the world a better or safer place.

- **Community or Industry:** The program can provide a material benefit to local communities or industry members. *Examples*: improved authentication for financial transactions, improved educational outcomes for particular schools, smart cities initiatives. Reduction of security, compliance or other risk could also present a material benefit, such as use of analytics to identify cross-industry fraud.
- **Individuals:** The program can provide a material benefit to particular individuals associated with the program. *Examples*: analytics to identify low-risk individuals who can be excluded from certain scrutiny measures (i.e. "TSA Pre-check"), analytics to identify high-risk individuals (such as people at risk of depression) for enhanced outreach by health care professionals.
- **Company Major Benefit:** This program has a major impact on the company overall, including significant cost reduction, risk reduction or improved efficiency. *Examples*: analysis of customer or employee flight risk, analytics for loss prevention or improved authentication. If the analytics program supports legal compliance (such as demonstrating nondiscrimination or meeting security requirements), that is also a major company benefit.
- **Company Minor Benefit:** This program benefits the company in a particular way. *Examples*: improved targeting of marketing messages for particular products and services, business intelligence for a particular business unit or brand, analytics for a company website.

Whose Interest (Column 2): Indicate the stakeholder most likely to benefit from the program.
Sustainability of Benefit (Column 3): Indicate the expected duration of the anticipated benefits.

Decision Support Factors

The Decision Support Factors are designed to assist in the evaluation of the process by considering (1) how likely the expected benefit actually is and (2) how well the identified risks are mitigated.

Confidence of Benefit (Column 4): An analytics or Big Data initiative will be more justified if the likelihood of success is high. While the likelihood of success may be difficult to gauge, the company should use reasonable efforts to assess its confidence that the expected benefit will be fully achieved. The scale can also be used to reflect the possibility that the initiative will produce positive outcomes, even if the full benefit is not achieved.

Risk Mitigation (Column 5): An analytics of Big Data initiative will be more justified if the risks identified in the Program Risk Factors section are mitigated. Risks may be mitigated using technological controls as well as by policies and contracts. Risks may also be mitigated by program design changes, such as reducing identifiers, using a smaller pool of data for tests/proof of concept programs, and/or establishing controls to evaluate inferences for intangible risks (such as creepiness). Use of an independent entity (such as an IRB) could allow the company to demonstrate that risks are fully mitigated.

Program Risk Factors

Sensitivity of Data Elements (Column 6): Identify the sensitivity of the data elements used in or generated by the program. If the program is going to generate propensities, consider the sensitivity of the inferences that will be drawn in addition to the underlying data elements. *Example*: if nonsensitive consumer grocery purchasing data is used to predict consumers who may have heart disease, then the program should be classified as "highly sensitive." *Example*: if general demographic data is used to infer sexual orientation or income, the program should be classified as "sensitive."

- **Highly sensitive elements** include information about medical conditions (diseases, prescription medicines, mental health conditions/addictions, etc., including propensity for a disease), biometrics, genetic information, financial account information (including account numbers and balances), credit information or credit scores, and government-issued identification numbers, along with any other data elements regarded as highly sensitive by the company.
- **Sensitive elements** include other types of health information and propensities (including pregnancy, disability status, seasonal allergies, weight loss), income and financial/credit propensities, race, ethnicity, gender, sexual orientation, criminal records or propensity for criminal activity, children's data, and precise location data along with any other data elements regarded as sensitive by the company.
- **Less sensitive data elements** include general consumer and demographic data and propensities, such as interests (including fitness and wellness interests), presence of children/pets in home, marketing preferences, languages spoken, household-level demographics, consumer product purchasing data, and census data. Data elements that allow individuals to be contacted may also be less sensitive, such as email addresses and physical addresses. Data elements that consumers have permissioned for publication (such as likes and tweets) are also less sensitive.
- **Nonsensitive data elements** include those data elements whose attributes do not pertain to specific individuals (such as nonassociated telemetry or machine data, aggregated transactional or product usage data, aggregated consumer data for modeling, and company-focused information on devices/apps/websites).

Identifiability of Data Elements (Column 7)

- **Direct Identifiers** are those data elements that generally allow you to identify, contact, locate or target a person, including: (i) names, (ii) usernames, (iii) all physical address information other than state or the first three digits of a zip code, (iv) dates of birth except year, (v) telephone and fax numbers, (vi) e-mail addresses, (vii) government-issued identification numbers, (viii) company-issued identification numbers, including account numbers, employee identification numbers, reward program numbers, etc., (ix) device identifiers and serial numbers (e.g., MAC addresses), (x) Web Universal Resource Locators (URLs), Internet Protocol (IP) addresses, (xi) identifiers associated with cookies or other online tracking methodologies (browser fingerprints), (xii) individual biometrics and/or photographs, and (xiii) any other unique identifying number, characteristic or code.
- **Indirect Identifiers** are those data elements which, when taken together, can be used to identify, contact, locate or target individuals (or narrow the population for identification). These elements include: (i) race, (ii) age, (iii) zip code or other geographic information, (iv) specific conditions (such as pregnancy status, disability status, specific health condition, blood type, etc.), (v) transaction records, or (vi) other characteristics (number of children, length of employment, etc.). Indirect identifiers also include those data elements that allow targeting of communications to individuals via devices, browsers or other channels.

For programs where identifiability is not needed, the company should use statistical methods to reduce the likelihood that individuals could be identified, located, contacted or targeted from the dataset. This analysis will determine the possibility of unintended identification.

- **Nonidentifiable Data (no PI):** The program does not include any direct or indirect data elements. For example, the program may only use aggregated data or data captured from telemetry. There is no risk that individuals will be identified or that data elements may be associated with an individual or used for targeted communications.

Type **of Risk (Column 7):** This assessment leverages the Future of Privacy Forum risk spectrum.[15] In this column, we consider the types of potential risks likely to result from the program.

- **Tangible Risks** include threats of damage to physical well-being, financial loss or exposure to fraud, damage to livelihood, administrative inconvenience, security breaches, or confidentiality breaches. Tangible risks also include risks that the program may result in discrimination or may have a discriminatory impact.
- **Intangible Risks** include damage to reputation, "creepy" inferences, anxiety, embarrassment, loss of control or autonomy, exclusion or isolation.
- **Abstract Risks** include panoptic surveillance, social stratification, filter bubbles, paranoia or loss of trust, limits of free expression, or threats to democracy.

Access to Data (Column 8): This assessment identifies the recipients of program results: the individual to whom the result pertains, a small group of recipients within the company, a large group of individuals within the company, a trusted community (such as fraud data collaboration or industry working group) or the public (such as to an industry group generally or other unrestricted audience).

Applying the Tool to a Hypothetical Project Proposal

As a hypothetical example of how to use this tool, Acme Defense Corp. (ADC) is a government contractor whose employees need to maintain security clearances in order to access classified data. The government imposes numerous requirements relating to physical and systems security, as well as the evaluation of ADC personnel assigned to government projects. Regulations require ADC to maintain an "insider threat" identification program, the purpose of which is to identify individuals who are more likely than others to steal classified data and engage in espionage.

ADC has purchased software applications that allow it to collate personal information from many of its own systems, as well as data from public sources, and then look for unusual activity or patterns that suggest an employee presents a heightened risk of data theft or espionage.

Data about employees will be gathered from the following internal and external sources:

- HR data regarding performance reviews, performance counseling; disciplinary actions; citizenship, country of birth; passed over for promotion
- Business expense system data: unusual expense patterns
- Badge access data: unusual entry patterns
- Ethics Investigations Database: any references to an employee with a clearance
- All activity on company network with focus on failed login attempts, unusual copying, downloading, printing, e-mailing of data and documents
- Database of all social media activity by relevant employees using certain key words indicating negative attitude toward US government, employer, secrecy, defense industry, etc.
- Database of all web surfing activity (using company equipment) to sites associated with groups or countries hostile to US interests, employer, secrecy, defense industry, etc.
- Government data containing all travel records relating to relevant employees, indicating unusual travel patterns or travel to countries of concern
- Credit Reports on relevant employees: data on debt and repayment issues

Applying the criteria in the tool generates the following assessments, from white to black, in each of the columns:

---

[15] Polonetsky, Tene and Jerome, *supra* note 10.

Hypothetical Use: Evaluation of Company Insider Threat Detection Initiative – Documentation

	Program Goal	Apply analytics to data sets relating to employees working on classified projects in order to identify unusual activity or patterns that suggest an employee presents a heightened risk of data theft or espionage.
	Description of Data	HR data (pay, performance, expense), network data (monitoring based on keywords), compliance hotline reports, facilities data (badge access records), travel records, social media (Twitter, other public), credit reports.
Benefits	Potential Impact	Global – company processes highly sensitive data, the compromise of which would put individuals at real risk. Company also must protect (trade secrets). Company is required by law to have an insider threat program.
	Primary Interest	Society – the program helps company reduce risks to all individuals whose data it processes.
	Sustainability of Benefit	Lasting – the program would be ongoing to detect current and future threats.
Support	Confidence of Benefit	Possible. Program may also detect employee behavior that presents risk for the company (such as inadvertent exposure of sensitive information), even if the employee does not intend harm.
	Risk Mitigation	Material mitigation – defined controls for handling program flags (including employee "due process"), access and security controls, and documented or audited policies to restrict any secondary use of the datasets.
Risks	Data Sensitivity	Highly sensitive, including HR and financial records.
	Data Identifiability	Direct identifiers – required because we have to identify precisely those employees who present risk.
	Type of Risk	Tangible – including possible misidentification of a non-risky employee as a risk, inappropriate job loss or restrictions, financial and reputational harm to the individual. If not properly designed, program could also have a discriminatory impact, flagging employees based on race, religion, national origin or languages spoken. Risk to company includes loss of trust by employees due to the intrusive nature of the program.
	Access to Data	Internal narrow – a small team will review program results. If a flagged employee is determined to actually pose a risk, the matter will follow the existing confidential HR process for investigation and resolution.
	Other Relevant Factors	Company will provide notice regarding the program to all employees and respond to questions/concerns.

FIGURE 27.4

Proposed Risk-Benefits Analysis Tool for Analytics and Big Data Initiatives
Hypothetical Use: Evaluation of Company Insider Threat Detection Initiative

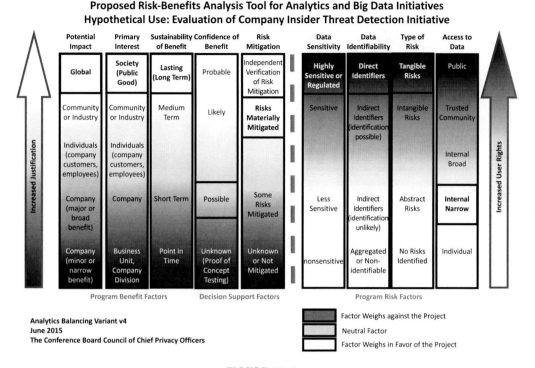

	Potential Impact	Primary Interest	Sustainability of Benefit	Confidence of Benefit	Risk Mitigation		Data Sensitivity	Data Identifiability	Type of Risk	Access to Data	
Increased Justification	Global	Society (Public Good)	Lasting (Long Term)	Probable	Independent Verification of Risk Mitigation		Highly Sensitive or Regulated	Direct Identifiers	Tangible Risks	Public	Increased User Rights
	Community or Industry	Community or Industry	Medium Term	Likely	Risks Materially Mitigated		Sensitive	Indirect Identifiers (identification possible)	Intangible Risks	Trusted Community	
	Individuals (company customers, employees)	Individuals (company customers, employees)								Internal Broad	
	Company (major or broad benefit)	Company	Short Term	Possible	Some Risks Mitigated		Less Sensitive	Indirect Identifiers (identification unlikely)	Abstract Risks	Internal Narrow	
	Company (minor or narrow benefit)	Business Unit, Company Division	Point in Time	Unknown (Proof of Concept Testing)	Unknown or Not Mitigated		nonsensitive	Aggregated or Non-identifiable	No Risks Identified	Individual	

Program Benefit Factors   Decision Support Factors   Program Risk Factors

Analytics Balancing Variant v4
June 2015
The Conference Board Council of Chief Privacy Officers

Factor Weighs against the Project
Neutral Factor
Factor Weighs in Favor of the Project

FIGURE 27.5

Next, the colored "sliders" placed on the nine columns in the tool generate a holistic view of overall risks and benefits, as seen in Figure 27.5.

If the results were heavily weighted toward white or black values, the IRB's decision on whether to move forward would be an easy one. However, in this hypothetical the results are more evenly balanced, if one assumes that each column carries equal weight (which can be debated and adjusted by each IRB). The result is three white and three black sliders. Two of the columns show light gray results, and a third shows a dark gray result. Consequently, the overall balance of the nine columns falls on the white side of the spectrum, but just barely.

With this close result, the decision on whether to move forward should not hinge on a numerical tally of blacks and whites, i.e., five white versus four black sliders in this hypothetical. Rather, these results should lead to a full discussion of the benefits, risks, supporting factors, and mitigations. The IRB will likely need to agree that the benefits are such that the balance is truly tipped in favor of moving forward. Perhaps the IRB can identify additional controls that will further reduce the privacy risks.

CONCLUSION

Dell has taken a two-pronged approach to addressing the challenging area of big data. We began with robust risk analysis, strengthened and added automation to our PIA process, and are working to leverage the Conference Board's Proposed Risk-Benefit Analysis Tool. Dell's business leaders have reacted very positively to the tool and its graphical presentations of risk. We plan to incorporate it formally in both our PIA processes.

Risk assessment and a robust PIA process are key cornerstones in evaluating any business's Big Data projects. The findings from those processes and a strong partnership with business teams lead to improved privacy considerations built into the projects. An IRB process brings these pieces together for the most complex project proposals.

Dell believes the Conference Board's Proposed Risk-Benefit Analysis Tool, combined if possible with an IRB process, can also form a useful component for a wide variety of organizations as they evaluate Big Data projects that leverage personally identifiable information. Every organization should consider whether the tool can be improved, clarified, or tailored to its specific business interests or public mission.

28

The Future of Self-Regulation Is Co-Regulation

Ira S. Rubinstein[*]

INTRODUCTION

Privacy policy in the United States has long relied on a combination of sectoral law, market forces, and self-regulation. Over the years, the Department of Commerce (DOC) and the Federal Trade Commission (FTC) have favored a self-regulatory approach. Their preference follows from familiar arguments suggesting that self-regulation can protect privacy in a more flexible and cost-effective manner than direct regulation without impeding the rapid pace of innovation in Internet-related businesses.

Privacy self-regulation generally involves individual firms, a trade association, or an ad hoc group of firms establishing substantive rules concerning the collection, use, and transfer of personal information, as well as procedures for applying these rules to participating firms. Self-regulation most often takes the form of industry groups promulgating *voluntary* codes of conduct that members agree to adhere to. Many critics view privacy self-regulation as a failure due to an overall lack of accountability and transparency, incomplete realization of robust privacy principles, free rider issues, and weak oversight and enforcement.[1] For these observers the real purpose of voluntary self-regulation is to avoid government regulation. Not surprisingly, they see comprehensive privacy legislation as the only viable alternative.[2]

Under this government regulation model, Congress would define substantive privacy requirements for commercial firms based on the Fair Information Practice Principles (FIPPs), which undergird modern privacy law, authorize agency regulation, and spell out which agencies have enforcement authority, what remedies are available, and whether individuals have a private right of action to recover damages for any injuries they might suffer when a firm violates the law.

These opposing sides in the privacy debate view voluntary self-regulation and government regulation as mutually exclusive options between which policy makers have to choose. But this is short sighted and stultifying. Modern regulatory theory has long treated self-regulation as a

[*] This chapter draws on the author's prior work on this topic, *see infra* note 1.
[1] *See* Ira S. Rubinstein, *Privacy and Regulatory Innovation: Moving Beyond Voluntary Codes*, 6 I/S J. L. Pol. 355 (2011); *see also* Bert-Jaap Koops, et al., *Should Self-Regulation Be the Starting Point? in* STARTING POINTS FOR ICT REGULATION: DECONSTRUCTING PREVALENT POLICY ONE-LINERS 125 (Bert-Japp Koops, Mariam Lips, Corien Prins & Maurice Schellekens, eds., 2006).
[2] *See* CHRIS JAY HOOFNAGLE, ELEC. PRIVACY INFO. CTR., PRIVACY SELF-REGULATION: A DECADE OF DISAPPOINTMENT (2005), http://epic.org/reports/decadedisappoint.pdf; Robert Gellman and Pamela Dixon, *Failures of Privacy Self-Regulation in the United States, in* ENFORCING PRIVACY: REGULATORY, LEGAL AND TECHNOLOGICAL APPROACHES (D. Wright & P. De Hert, eds. 2016).

"highly malleable term which may encompass a wide variety of instruments."[3] On this view, voluntary codes and direct government regulation are opposing ends of a regulatory continuum, with most self-regulatory schemes falling somewhere in the middle. This chapter explores the middle ground. It examines *co-regulatory* approaches, in which industry enjoys considerable flexibility in shaping self-regulatory guidelines, consumer advocacy groups have a seat at the table, and government sets default requirements and retains general oversight authority to approve and enforce these guidelines.[4] Privacy co-regulation is generally understood as a collaborative, flexible, and performance-based approach to privacy regulation that draws on the theoretical insights of collaborative governance theory.[5] This chapter argues that self-regulation in the form of voluntary codes has had a sufficiently long run to prove its worth but has failed. Now is the time to make the transition to co-regulation, especially in the United States.

The chapter is organized into three sections. The first considers in detail the differences between self-regulation and co-regulation. The second looks at the failure and stubborn persistence of voluntary codes of conduct. The third shifts the discussion to three case studies of privacy codes and practices that have benefited from a co-regulatory approach. In the past few years, there have been some notable developments in co-regulatory schemes as well some important empirical studies. These new materials provide an opportunity to understand the conditions for the success (and failure) of co-regulatory solutions in the privacy field and what this implies for the future of regulatory innovation. The chapter concludes by offering a few recommendations on how the U.S. Congress can implement co-regulatory approaches in any future legislation to optimally protect online consumer privacy while preserving innovation and economic growth.

SELF-REGULATION VS. CO-REGULATION

Self-regulation defies easy definition, but at a minimum involves a firm or private organization assuming responsibility for its own rules or practices and overseeing any sanctions for noncompliance, as opposed to a government agency regulating the firm under public law. As Colin Bennett and Charles Raab note, self-regulation encompasses a variety of policy instruments such as privacy commitments, privacy codes, privacy standards, and privacy seals.[6] This chapter focuses mainly on privacy codes of conduct as well as corporate privacy management practices, which may or may not be subject to a legal mandate or reflected in a code of conduct.[7] In analyzing these codes and practices, we distinguish two main forms of regulatory efforts relied on by private firms, self-regulation and co-regulation, which differ in terms of the role that government plays in industry rulemaking and enforcement.[8] When private firms carry out both tasks independent of direct government involvement, we will refer to this as voluntary codes of conduct. As described by Margot Priest, such codes arise when a group of like-minded firms or the members of a trade association agree to operate according to rules and procedures as defined

---

[3] Darren Sinclair, *Self-Regulation Versus Command and Control? Beyond False Dichotomies*, 19 LAW & POL'Y 529, 532 (1997).

[4] *Id.* at 544.

[5] *See* Dennis D. Hirsch, *Going Dutch? Collaborative Dutch Privacy Regulation and the Lessons It Holds for U.S. Privacy Law*, 2013 MICH. ST. L. REV. 83 (2013).

[6] COLIN BENNETT & CHARLES RAAB, THE GOVERNANCE OF PRIVACY 153 (2006).

[7] Bennett and Raab identify five types of privacy codes (organizational, sectoral, functional, technological, and professional), *id.* at 155; here we examine only the first three types.

[8] *See* JOSEPH V. REES, REFORMING THE WORKPLACE: A STUDY OF SELF-REGULATION IN OCCUPATIONAL SAFETY (1988).

by the code, which typically reflects industry best practices.[9] The firms (or their trade associations) handle virtually all of the regulatory functions ordinarily reserved for government. Thus, participating firms are *accountable* to each other or the trade association but not directly to the government; they engage in *rulemaking* consensually by members who adopt the code; there is neither *adjudication* (except perhaps by a peer review committee) nor a dispute resolution mechanism, and only limited *sanctions* apart from ejection of noncompliant firms from the trade association; and *coverage* of relevant industry principles suffers from free rider problems due to the voluntary nature of the regulatory regime. Finally, there is little *public involvement*, although firms developing a code may engage in public consultation at their discretion.[10]

Voluntary codes of conduct are the most prevalent form of privacy self-regulation in the United States, where trade associations or firms engage in self-regulatory efforts in the hopes of staving off increased enforcement by regulatory agencies or the enactment of privacy laws that would be tougher than industry-devised privacy codes. A number of U.S. industry sectors illustrate this pattern quite nicely.[11]

In contrast, co-regulation exhibits a much higher degree of government involvement.[12] As with self-regulation, there are several forms of co-regulation but here we focus on their common characteristics. First, they tend to be cooperative rather than adversarial, taking full advantage of corporate social responsibility as a motivating factor in firm behavior.[13] Second, co-regulatory models rely on firms or trade associations to perform a variety of government functions.[14] Third, co-regulatory guidelines are both less prescriptive than state regulations (which tend to define required actions) and more open-ended (stating broad intentions or a desired outcome), thereby allowing regulated firms more discretion in developing specific implementation plans.[15] Fourth, firms tend to be more committed to rules that they had a hand in shaping, resulting in increased compliance rates.[16] Finally, co-regulation shifts the role of government from one of rulemaking and imposing sanctions when industry violates these rules, to that of providing incentives for implementing regulatory programs while maintaining "a credible residual program" of oversight and enforcement.[17] In short, co-regulatory strategies are distinguishable from voluntary codes not only in the degree of government involvement but across all relevant dimensions, i.e., accountability, rulemaking, adjudication, sanctions, and public involvement.

In a pathbreaking article published in 2006, Dennis Hirsch first discussed the possibilities of developing a new, co-regulatory model for privacy based on a number of innovative environmental policy tools that have emerged over the past thirty years. Hirsch contrasted the older, command-and-control model of environmental regulation with "second generation" regulations

---

[9] *See* Margot Priest, *The Privatization of Regulation: Five Models of Self-Regulation*, 29 OTTAWA L. REV. 233, 240–41 (1997–98).

[10] *Id.* at 242.

[11] *E.g.*, the marketing industry, HOOFNAGLE, *supra* note 2, at 2 (analyzing the Telephone Preference Service of the Direct Marketing Association); the data broker industry, Gellman and Dixon, *supra* note 2, at 55–56 (analyzing the Individual Reference Service Group Principles); the online advertising industry, HOOFNAGLE, *id.* at 9–10, Gellman and Dixon, *id.* at 59–61, Rubinstein, *supra* note 1, at 384–90, and Dennis D. Hirsch, *The Law and Policy of Online Privacy: Regulation, Self-Regulation, or Co-Regulation?* 34 SEATTLE UNIV. L. REV. 438, 460–64 (2011) (analyzing the Network Advertising Initiative (NAI) Principles).

[12] The following discussion is based on Rubinstein, *supra* note 1, at 370–74.

[13] *See* Douglas C. Michael, *Cooperative Implementation of Federal Regulations*, 13 YALE J. REG. 535, 541–42 (1996).

[14] Priest, *supra* note 9, at 238.

[15] Michael, *supra* note 13, at 544.

[16] IAN AYRES & JOHN BRAITHWAITE, RESPONSIVE REGULATION: TRANSCENDING THE DEREGULATION DEBATE 113 (1992).

[17] Michael, *supra* note 13, at 541.

that encouraged "the regulated parties themselves to choose the means by which they will achieve environmental performance goals" resulting in "more cost-effective and adaptable" strategies.[18] The defining characteristic of second generation strategies is that they "allow these self-directed actions to count towards regulatory compliance."[19] This radical departure from a command-and-control regime spurs regulatory innovation by harnessing a firm's own ingenuity in devising environmental solutions that meet or exceed legal requirements yet fit a firm's business model and the needs of its customers.

Hirsch contends that privacy regulation has much to learn from these second-generation environmental strategies and proposes several ideas for adapting them to protect information privacy without deterring innovation. In particular, he emphasizes environmental covenants, which are contractual agreements negotiated between regulators and regulated firms. In this form of co-regulation, "government and an industry trade association might negotiate the proper regulatory goals, collaborate on the drafting of standards, and work cooperatively to enforce the standards against specific firms that violate them."[20] In these negotiations, other stakeholders, such as environmental advocacy groups or members of the public, frequently have a seat at the bargaining table and the rules of engagement are established to support the overall goal of achieving greater flexibility and responsiveness to specific conditions and more rapid improvements than would otherwise occur under prescriptive government regulation. Industry finds these negotiated covenants attractive because they have more input into the final agreement than with conventional rulemaking efforts; the covenants take the form of performance goals rather than technology mandates; and their longer time frame better fits the normal business planning and investment cycle, while the government and society benefit from this approach by achieving better results (such as steeper pollution reductions) than might otherwise be politically achievable.[21]

Legal scholars have sought to explain why this approach sometimes achieves better solutions to environmental problems than do traditional command-and-control regulations. Richard Stewart offers an explanation based on the logic of Coasian bargaining principles:

> The premise is that legal rules will advance society's welfare if they are voluntarily agreed to by all relevant interests. If those with a stake in the regulatory requirements – the regulated, the regulator, and perhaps third party environmental or citizen interests – agree on an alternative to the standard requirements, the agreement may be presumed to be superior to the standard.[22]

Similarly, other scholars explain the success of the covenanting approach in terms of the very nature of the underlying process, which emphasizes "stakeholder representation, face-to-face negotiation, [and] consensus-based decision making."[23] What both explanations have in common is a focus on information sharing, direct negotiations, self-interested mutual compromises, and voluntary agreement.[24] All of the case studies to be discussed represent illuminating examples of the co-regulatory approach at work in the field of privacy.

[18] Dennis D. Hirsch, *Protecting the Inner Environment: What Privacy Regulation Can Learn from Environmental Law*, 41 GA. L. REV. 1, 8 (2006).
[19] *Id.* at 37–40
[20] Hirsch, *The Law and Policy of Online Privacy, supra* note 11, at 465.
[21] *See* Richard B. Stewart, *A New Generation of Environmental Regulation?*, 29 CAP. U. L. REV. 21, 60–94 (2001).
[22] *Id.* at 61.
[23] Jody Freeman & Laura I. Langbein, *Regulatory Negotiation and the Legitimacy Benefit*, 9 N.Y.U. ENVTL. L. J. 60, 71 & 132–35 (2000).
[24] *See* Hirsch, *Going Dutch?, supra* note 5, at 100–2.

THE FAILURE (AND PERSISTENCE) OF VOLUNTARY CODES OF CONDUCT

When the Clinton administration began to develop a regulatory framework for electronic commerce and the Internet in the late 1990s, it promoted self-regulation as the preferred approach to protecting consumer privacy online. Clinton officials believed that private sector leadership would cause electronic commerce to flourish, and specifically supported efforts "to implement meaningful, consumer-friendly, self-regulatory privacy regimes" in combination with technology solutions.[25] While arguing that unnecessary regulation might distort market developments by "decreasing the supply and raising the cost of products and services" or by failing to keep pace with "the break-neck speed of change in technology,"[26] they also asserted that if industry failed to address privacy concerns through self-regulation and technology, the pressure for a regulatory solution would increase.

Not surprisingly, industry embraced this view. For example, at a 1995 public privacy workshop, industry representatives cited three reasons that regulating privacy would be counterproductive. First, it would stifle innovation in a developing market. Second, it might drive marketing activity off the Internet entirely by adding unnecessary costs to online advertising. And third, it would interfere with the market definition of consumer privacy preferences and the appropriate industry response.[27] Privacy advocates in attendance expressed a contrary view, warning that self-regulation would remain ineffective without enforceable privacy rights, which were necessary to deter bad actors and outliers and ensure the widest possible participation in any self-regulatory schemes, also noting that technology alone was no substitute for enshrining FIPPs in law.[28]

In the past twenty-two years, these two positions have hardly changed at all, although Congress has tried and failed to enact online privacy legislation, and the FTC has fluctuated between supporting legislation and giving industry self-regulation yet another try. What is most striking about the ensuing policy debate is neither the opposing views of advocates and industry nor the FTC's ambivalence. Rather, it is the assumption at the heart of the debate that policy makers must choose exclusively between these two options. This is a false dichotomy and one that neglects the wide variety of co-regulatory alternatives that could be playing a larger role in the privacy arena.

That said, the main problems with industry self-regulation based on voluntary codes of conduct are well-known. This author previously identified six normative factors for evaluating self-regulatory initiatives: efficiency (the self-regulatory principles should harness industry expertise to achieve tailored solutions at the lowest attainable costs for government, industry, and the public); openness (the self-regulatory system should enable the public to participate in developing substantive rules and enforcement mechanisms) and transparency (the system should require disclosure of both substantive standards and how participating firms perform against these standards); completeness (the principles should address all aspects of the applicable standards – in this case, the full set of FIPPs); free rider problems (strategies should minimize firms refusing to abide by or falsely claiming adherence to self-regulatory principles); oversight and enforcement (the system should provide complaint resolution mechanisms, audit or other forms of verification, and impose consequences for firms that fail to comply with substantive

---

[25] WILLIAM J. CLINTON & ALBERT GORE, JR., A FRAMEWORK FOR GLOBAL ELECTRONIC COMMERCE 18 (1997).

[26] *Id.* at 4.

[27] *See* FED. TRADE COMM'N, STAFF REPORT: PUBLIC WORKSHOP ON CONSUMER PRIVACY ON THE GLOBAL INFORMATION INFRASTRUCTURE 27–29 (1996), http://www.ftc.gov/reports/privacy/privacy.pdf.

[28] *Id.*

requirements); and use of second-generation design features (which mainly consist in the benefits associated with formulating principles through direct negotiations among the parties, based on information sharing, Coasian bargaining, and mutual buy-in to outcomes).[29] Voluntary privacy codes often are deficient in one or more of these normative factors.

A case in point is the Network Advertising Initiative (NAI) Principles, a voluntary code of conduct established in 2001 by an ad hoc industry advertising group, and revised several times since then. The author's 2011 case study of this code showed that the NAI Principles fared poorly on all six normative factors.[30] Assessments by Hirsch, Gellman and Dixon, and Hoofnagle all reach similar conclusions, even factoring in positive steps taken by NAI in the ensuing years.[31] And yet, as the more recent Do Not Track saga nicely illustrates, the FTC has not given up on self-regulation as a preferred solution,[32] which it also turns to when faced with emerging technologies such as the Internet of Things.[33]

What, then, accounts for the persistence of voluntary codes of conduct in the regulatory toolbox despite the record of failure of privacy self-regulation? It is beyond the scope of this chapter to analyze this question fully, but it is possible to voice a few tentative hypotheses. One is industry's success in ensuring that regulators support flexible, market-based solutions and, hence, self-regulation. Indeed, certain FTC Commissioners are quite explicit about this preference.[34] Chris Hoofnagle offers a second hypothesis, namely, that "From the FTC's perspective, even weak self-regulatory regimes assist the Agency."[35] Finally, it is worth noting that the FTC has very limited authority to prescribe rules defining "unfair or deceptive acts or practices," and therefore is in no position to issue privacy rules except indirectly through its case-by-case enforcement activity.[36] This would change if Congress enacted a new, omnibus privacy law and explicitly granted the FTC rulemaking authority, which it currently enjoys only under sectoral laws such as the Children's Online Privacy Protection Act (COPPA) and the Gramm-Leach-Bliley Act. But Congressional inactivity on omnibus privacy bills over the past 15 years makes the FTC's prospects for broader rulemaking authority very grim. In short, one way to understand the FTC's tolerance of deeply flawed self-regulatory codes is as a pragmatic response to an imperfect set of regulatory options.

---

[29] Rubinstein, *supra* note 1, at 380–83. Koops et al. use a very similar set of factors to assess self-regulatory solutions; *see* Koops, *supra* note 1, at 136–40.

[30] Rubinstein, *id.* at 384–90.

[31] *See supra* note 11.

[32] Brendan Sasso, *FTC Shows Little Interest in "Do Not Track" Mandate*, THE HILL (Aug. 20, 2013), http://thehill.com/policy/technology/317925-ftc-shows-little-interest-in-mandating-do-not-track.

[33] Chase Gunter, *FTC in No Rush to Regulate Internet of Things*, FCW (Feb. 9, 2016), https://fcw.com/articles/2016/02/09/gunter-ftc-iot-regs.aspx (noting that FTC Commissioner Terrell McSweeny, speaking at an Internet of Things event, "emphasized the importance of relevant industries having strong, voluntary self-regulation and best practices, rather than having the FTC impose rigid, sweeping standards").

[34] *See, e.g.,* Fed. Trade Comm'n, *Remarks of Commissioner Maureen K. Ohlhausen at the Digital Advertising Alliance Summit* (June 5, 2013), https://www.ftc.gov/sites/default/files/documents/public_statements/remarks-commissioner-maureen-k.ohlhausen/130605daasummit.pdf; Fed. Trade Comm'n, *Remarks of Chairman Deborah Platt Majoras at the Council of Better Business Bureaus* (Apr. 11, 2005), https://www.ftc.gov/sites/default/files/documents/public_state ments/self-regulatory-organizations-and-ftc/050411selfregorgs.pdf.

[35] CHRIS JAY HOOFNAGLE, FEDERAL TRADE COMMISSION PRIVACY LAW AND POLICY 181 (2016). Hoofnagle, *id.*, gives three reasons: voluntary codes take work off the Agency's plate and bind companies to promises that, even if weak, are likely to be broken; it is easier to police broken promises under the FTC's deception authority than to employ unfairness; and voluntary codes may evolve into industry standards, "giving the FTC traction in proceedings to argue that a consensus exists about a certain practice being unreasonable."

[36] For an explanation, *see* Rubinstein, *supra* note 1, at 411, n. 206.

CO-REGULATORY ALTERNATIVES

The main advantages of co-regulation as an alternative to self-regulation or government regulation are fourfold: it draws on industry knowledge and expertise; yields rules that are more cost-effective, workable, and innovative; creates a stronger sense of industry ownership over rules and thus better compliance; and results in rules that are more politically practicable and efficient.[37] Are these advantages borne out in practice? To answer this question, we look at three very different scenarios. In the first, individual firms identified as leaders in the privacy field devise their own privacy management practices in response to a complex mix of social, business, and regulatory factors. There are strict privacy laws in some settings but not in others and very little discussion of codes of conduct as a means of demonstrating accountability. This first case study offers some critical reflections on an important study by Ken Bamberger and Deirdre Mulligan analyzing the regulatory dynamic shaping privacy management best practices at leading multi-nationals.[38] In the second, firms agree to participate in a multistakeholder process to devise voluntary but enforceable privacy codes on narrow topics. A U.S. government agency – the National Telecommunication and Information Administration (NTIA) – runs the process in an open and transparent manner but neither the underlying procedures nor the substantive outcome have any explicit basis in law.[39] Here the author undertakes his own investigation of three codes recently developed through the NTIA's multistakeholder process. In the third, Dutch privacy law encourages the creation of codes of conduct that are best characterized as "legally stipulated" in the sense that national laws spell out the code making process, the substantive requirements any code must satisfy, and the legal consequences of approved codes.[40] This case study relies on a detailed examination of Dutch privacy codes by Dennis Hirsch.[41]

Accountability and Privacy Management Programs or "Privacy on the Ground"

Over the past few decades, the concept of "accountability" has emerged as an important trend in global data privacy law, policy, and organizational practices.[42] The concept has its origins in the 1980 Organization for Economic Cooperation and Development (OECD) guidelines for privacy protection (OECD Privacy Guidelines), which articulate eight key principles for the protection of personal information and represent an early and influential version of the FIPPs.[43] Principle 8 (the "Accountability Principle") imposes on data controllers (i.e., organizations that make decisions about the content and use of personal data) an obligation "for complying with measures which give effect" to the remaining OECD principles.[44] It is not an oversimplification to say that accountability in the privacy field boils down to data controllers implementing

---

[37] *See* Hirsch, *Law and Policy of Online Privacy*, *supra* note 11, at 464–68.

[38] KENNETH A. BAMBERGER AND DEIRDRE K. MULLIGAN, PRIVACY ON THE GROUND: DRIVING CORPORATE BEHAVIOR IN THE UNITED STATES AND EUROPE (2016).

[39] *See* Multistakeholder Process to Develop Consumer Data Privacy Codes of Conduct, 77 Fed. Reg. 13098 (March 5, 2012).

[40] Koops, *supra* note 1, at 121–22.

[41] Hirsch, *Going Dutch?*, *supra* note 5.

[42] *See generally*, Center for Information Policy Leadership (CIPL), *Evolving Accountability*, https://www.informationpo licycentre.com/evolving-accountability.html (describing CIPL's multiyear Accountability-Based Privacy Governance Project).

[43] Org. for Econ. Co-operation & Dev. [OECD], *Guidelines Governing the Protection of Privacy and Transborder Flows of Personal Data*, OECD Doc. C(80)58/FINAL (Sept. 23, 1980), http://www.oecd.org/intemet/ieconomy/oecdguide linesontheprotectionofprivacyandtransborderflowsofpersonaldata.htm.

[44] OECD Guidelines, *id.*, § 14.

comprehensive privacy management programs. In 2013, the updated OECD privacy guidelines added a new Article 15, requiring that a data controller must have in place a privacy management program that

> is tailored to the structure, scale, volume and sensitivity of [a data controller's] operations; provides for appropriate safeguards based on privacy risk assessment; is integrated into its governance structure and establishes internal oversight mechanisms; includes plans for responding to inquiries and incidents; and is updated in light of ongoing monitoring and periodic assessment.[45]

Furthermore, accountability so understood has been enshrined in both E.U. data protection law[46] and U.S. privacy law.[47]

Bamberger and Mulligan's book, however, suggests that complying with strict legal mandates matters far less in developing sound accountability practices than what they aptly call "privacy on the ground" by which they mean "the combination of social, market, and regulatory forces that drive privacy decisions and how these forces interact with formal privacy laws in successful and unsuccessful ways."[48] The coauthors reached this conclusion based on a series of semistructured qualitative interviews with chief privacy officers (CPOs) at large firms (which privacy experts had identified as engaging in best practices), regulators and scholars in five countries (the United States, Germany, Spain, France, and the United Kingdom).

Despite differences in national privacy laws and the activity levels of regulators across the five countries, the authors found that companies exhibited remarkably similar approaches to protecting consumer privacy. The successful firms operated privacy management programs that exhibited three common characteristics.[49] First, they employed powerful and relatively autonomous privacy professionals with access to high-level firm management. Second, these privacy professionals had the ability to mediate between external privacy demands and internal corporate privacy practices. They engaged in "beyond compliance" behavior driven less by law and more by the wish to maintain consumer trust and avoid reputational sanctions. Third, they ran programs that integrated privacy measures into existing risk management processes through (a) distributing privacy expertise within business units and empowering these experts to surface privacy issues and offer advice on how to reduce privacy risks and (b) assigning specialized staff to data-intensive processes and systems.

Surprisingly, the authors found the strongest evidence of these characteristics among U.S. and German firms, despite the radically different legal climates in which these firms operated. U.S. firms respond to the FTC's "common law" approach to understanding consumer expectations, which it develops in the course of sanctioning unfair and deceptive practices, and to the agency's use of "soft law" tools designed to increase transparency, motivate self-regulatory systems, and empower privacy advocates.[50] In addition, state security breach notification laws and extensive

---

[45] OECD, Recommendation of the Council Concerning Guidelines Governing the Protection of Privacy and Transborder Flows of Personal Data [C(80)58/FINAL], as amended on July 11, 2013 [C(2013)791], § 15(a).

[46] For example, both art. 7(f) of the E.U. Data Protection Directive (DPD) and art. 24 of the recently approved General Data Protection Regulation (GDPR) are based on the accountability principle. The E.U. also permits the use of Binding Corporate Rules (BCRs) to satisfy the adequacy test for data transfers under both art. 25 of the DPD and art. 46 of the GDPR and BCRs also reflect the accountability principle.

[47] For example, many FTC consent decrees require that companies remedy findings of unfair or deceptive acts or practices by developing and maintaining "comprehensive information privacy programs," which require very similar elements to Article 15 of the updated OECD Guidelines.

[48] BAMBERGER & MULLIGAN, *supra* note 38, at 10.

[49] *Id.* at 173–80.

[50] *Id.* at 189–90.

press coverage of privacy incidents helped tie corporate privacy performance to market reputation.[51] Although German firms operate under one of the strictest data protection laws in the world, their data protection officers (DPOs) exercise strategic and operational leadership within forward-looking companies due to several unique aspects of German law and policy. First, the DPOs enjoy independence and clout because they operate under a legal mandate requiring their independence. Second, German Data Protection Agencies (DPAs) seem more interested in providing oversight and guidance than in prescriptive regulation, which allows an ongoing dialogue with the DPOs over the meaning of privacy. Finally, work councils play an unusual role in Germany, negotiating practices involving the use of employee data and creating a nexus between privacy and workers' rights that "stimulates internal conversations regarding ... the appropriate balance between individual rights against company and societal interests."[52]

Based on their study of U.S. and German privacy best practices, the authors identify three common properties for catalyzing an approach to accountability that they refer to as "bringing the outside in." The three properties are: (1) "Ambiguity with accountability," which refers to the flexibility and discretion of privacy professionals in the face of ambiguous privacy mandates, on the one hand, and the demand for accountability, on the other, which results from the combination of activist regulators and third-party stakeholders (privacy advocates in the United States and independent work councils in Germany), whose scrutiny helps shape the contours of corporate behavior; (2) a "boundary-spanning community," which refers not only to other CPOs but to a large and diverse privacy community that regularly exposes CPOs to skeptics and critics, thereby avoiding insularity while facilitating new ideas and approaches to problem solving[53]; and (3) "disciplinary transparency" brought about in response to high-profile enforcement actions and security breach incidents that not only enhance the relative power of CPOs but help push firms "away from compliance and toward risk management."[54]

Does "privacy on the ground" amount to co-regulation? In most ways it does, but not in all ways. As noted earlier, collaborative governance requires a shift from self-regulation to co-regulation in the form of negotiated codes of conduct. The co-authors recognize that regulatory styles matter and fully embrace "new governance" approaches over command-and-control regulatory models.[55] And their analysis of "bringing the outside in" suggests that firms displaying the relevant properties will achieve all four of the main advantages of co-regulation.[56] But their book hardly mentions direct negotiations among diverse parties (government, industry, *and* advocates) or Coasian bargaining resulting in mutual buy-in to codes of conduct.[57] One likely reason for this omission is that the CPOs interviewed by Bamberger and Mulligan did not discuss codes of conduct (perhaps because they considered them ineffective tools for achieving accountability). Here we pursue a different line of thought in which the omission of this topic signals shortcomings in how the authors analyze corporate behavior aimed at achieving accountability.

To begin with, Bamberger and Mulligan's study raises methodological concerns. The authors acknowledge that their sample is limited to a subset of large firms identified as privacy leaders using a snowball sampling technique and that this limits their ability to generalize from their

---

[51] *Id.* at 192–94.
[52] *Id.* at 197–216.
[53] *Id.* at 228–29.
[54] *Id.* at 231.
[55] *Id.* at 34–35.
[56] *See supra* text accompanying notes 20–24 and 37.
[57] Nor does the CIPL accountability project provide a role for direct negotiations.

findings.[58] However, they offer policy guidance to regulators without such qualifications, even though small and medium enterprises (SMEs) and start-ups are largely absent from their study. Another problem, as Chris Hoofnagle points out, is that while the interviewed CPOs freely report on their own successes, they do not seem to discuss programmatic failures or firm behaviors that outsiders might view as highly problematic.[59] The authors acknowledge that reporting on "'well-practiced narratives'" runs some risks of distortion and describe their efforts to contextualize CPO interviews with other materials.[60] And yet, while they provide a deeply nuanced account of successful CPOs "bringing the outside in," they omit any discussion of the dynamics at play _inside_ of for-profit corporations or what determines whether competing corporate priorities prevail over worthwhile privacy initiatives. As an in-house privacy counsel for many years at a large multinational identified as a leader in the privacy field, this author observed first-hand how privacy goals do not always align with primary business goals – sometimes they did but at other times they had to be balanced against pressing corporate needs such as responding to competitive challenges, increasing revenues, or meeting budgetary targets.[61] Furthermore, a review of FTC actions against brand-name corporations confirms that when shifts occur in a firm's business priorities, privacy is often the loser.[62] As a theoretical matter, the authors acknowledge that "public values and regulatory mandates predictably encounter systematic resistance when they create tension" with a firm's primary goals.[63] But they offer no account of how these tensions play out in practice.

Third, the authors emphasize the importance of reputational concerns in creating what they call "a social license to operate." They found that when a firm decides to establish or maintain a positive reputation for privacy, this enhances a CPO's ability to obtain resources and achieve her strategic goals. Less clear is the meaning or measure of "positive reputation" (is it increased market capitalization, revenue, profit, good will, or all of these combined?) or whether the avoidance of reputational sanctions is a truly sustainable source of a CPO's status and power within a corporate hierarchy. Moreover, as Hoofnagle rightly points out, some industries simply lack reputational pressure points. For instance, consumer reporting agencies and behavioral advertising companies "lack direct consumer relationships, and often have incentives to act in a maximally privacy-invasive way."[64]

---

[58] BAMBERGER & MULLIGAN, _supra_ note 38, at 11.

[59] _See_ HOOFNAGLE, FEDERAL TRADE COMMISSION, _supra_ note 35, at 314.

[60] BAMBERGER & MULLIGAN, _supra_ note 38, at 43.

[61] The author was an in-house counsel at Microsoft Corporation from 1990 to 2007, and served as chief privacy counsel for the last seven years of his tenure; his clients during this period included the company CPOs.

[62] _See, e.g., In the Matter of Google, Inc._, FTC File No. C-4336 (Oct. 13, 2011) (Google decided to use available customer data in a new way to jump start its social networking service (Buzz) in competition with Facebook); _In the Matter of Facebook_, FTC File No. 092 3184 (July 27, 2012) (Facebook retroactively revised its privacy statements and privacy settings in order to enhance its advertising revenue). Nor are these isolated cases; _see_ Ira S. Rubinstein & Nathan Good, _Privacy by Design: A Counterfactual Analysis of Google and Facebook Privacy Incidents_, 28 BERKELEY TECH. L.J. 1333 (2013) (analyzing multiple privacy incidents in both firms).

[63] BAMBERGER & MULLIGAN, _supra_ note 38, at 28.

[64] HOOFNAGLE, FEDERAL TRADE COMMISSION, _supra_ note 35, at 315. The authors emphasize the importance of breach notification laws in drawing attention to privacy issues, BAMBERGER & MULLIGAN, _id._ at 72. However, the reputational impact of data breaches may be fading now that data breaches have become so ubiquitous, _see_ Lewis Morgan, _List of Data Breaches and Cyber Attacks in 2016 — 1.6 Billion Records Leaked_, IT GOVERNANCE BLOG (Dec. 12, 2016), http://www.itgovernance.co.uk/blog/list-of-data-breaches-and-cyber-attacks-in-2016-1-6-billion-records-leaked/. Additionally, breach incidents impose relatively low costs on affected firms, _see_ Sasha Romanosky, _Examining the Costs and Causes of Cyber Incidents_, 2 J. CYBERSECURITY 121 (2016) (analyzing a sample of 12,000 cyber incidents and concluding that the cost of a typical cyber incident is less than $200,000 or only 0.4% of a sample firm's estimated annual revenue). There are exceptions. For example, after Yahoo disclosed two massive data breaches affecting 500 million and a billion users respectively, its suitor Verizon sought to lower the price it had offered to acquire the company; _see_

Notwithstanding these criticisms, Bamberger and Mulligan's analysis of corporate privacy practices is deeply insightful. The authors rightly conclude that firms achieve greater success in protecting privacy not when regulatory agencies grow "the number, specificity and uniformity of regulations" and their own regulatory power,"[65] but rather when they push "more of the responsibility for meaningfully defining, interpreting, and enforcing privacy back toward corporations."[66] This author concurs in their conclusions, which seem wholly consistent with the co-regulatory approach previously outlined. But a problem remains unresolved insofar as "bringing the outside in" occurs at the individual firm level, which seems like a highly unstable foundation for privacy regulation. Moreover, in valorizing CPOs and corporate best practices, the authors seem to assume that corporate objectives remain constant, which is highly unlikely. As already noted, CPOs are subject to powerful internal pressures that may undercut their ability to deliver on privacy-protective objectives, especially when the bloom is off the rose. Nor does this approach overcome the incomplete realization of the FIPPs as dictated by more urgent business needs or free rider problems. The market for privacy reputation simply isn't strong enough to carry that weight. Rather, what seems to be needed is a co-regulatory approach that builds on the coauthors' penetrating analysis by transforming "bringing the outside in" from a maxim into a code of conduct, one that reflects direct negotiations and Coasian buy-in by the affected parties. Such codes also have the advantage of allowing implementation not only by large firms but also by SMEs and start-ups in diverse sectors.

The NTIA Multistakeholder Process

In February 2012, the White House released a privacy report with two central elements: (1) a Consumer Privacy Bill of Rights (CPBR), which is a comprehensive set of FIPPs for governing personal data processing in commercial settings and (2) a multistakeholder process, which NTIA would convene, to develop legally enforceable codes of conduct specifying how the CPBR applies in specific business contexts.[67] Although the Administration encouraged Congress to enact legislation based on the CPBR and later floated a Discussion Draft[68] that went nowhere, the White House forged ahead anyway by encouraging firms to work with privacy advocates, consumer protection enforcement agencies, and others to implement the CPBR in what it called "voluntary enforceable codes of conduct." The White House Framework described the process as follows:

> The Administration will convene open, transparent forums in which stakeholders who share an interest in specific markets or business contexts will work toward consensus on appropriate, legally enforceable codes of conduct. Private sector participation will be voluntary and companies ultimately will choose whether to adopt a given code of conduct. The participation of a broad group of stakeholders, including consumer groups and privacy advocates, will help to

---

Melissa Etehad, *Yahoo's Latest Data Breach Could Mean an Even Bigger Price Cut for Verizon*, L.A. TIMES (Dec. 17, 2016), http://www.latimes.com/business/technology/la-fi-tn-yahoo-shares-verizon-20161216-story.html. But even if the deal moves ahead despite these developments, it remains to be seen whether Verizon will adopt stronger security practices that avoid future data breaches.

[65] BAMBERGER & MULLIGAN, *id.* at 245.

[66] *Id.* at 246.

[67] The White House, *Consumer Data Privacy in a Networked World: A Framework for Protecting Privacy and Promoting Innovation in the Global Digital Economy*, Feb. 2012, http://www.whitehouse.gov/sites/default/fi les/privacy-final.pdf (the "Privacy Blueprint").

[68] Administration Discussion Draft: Consumer Privacy Bill of Rights Act of 2015, https://www.whitehouse.gov/sites/default/files/omb/legislative/letters/cpbr-act-of-2015-discussion-draft.pdf.

ensure that codes of conduct lead to privacy solutions that consumers can easily use and understand. A single code of conduct for a given market or business context will provide consumers with more consistent privacy protections than is common today, when privacy practices and the information that consumers receive about them varies significantly from company to company.[69]

According to the administration, this multistakeholder processes would offer three advantages over traditional rulemaking, "flexibility, speed, and decentralization necessary to address Internet policy challenges."[70] This "open, transparent multistakeholder processes" would differ radically from traditional agency rulemaking because the stakeholders, rather than the government, would control the process and its results, including both what issues should be addressed, how to structure the process to encourage broad participation, how best to share timely and relevant information to ensure transparency, and how to reach an orderly conclusion, preferably in the form of consensus on a proposed code.[71] The Administration cited as a precedent the work of Internet standards groups, noting that these organizations "frequently function on the basis of consensus and are amenable to the participation of individuals and groups with limited resources" and that these characteristics "lend legitimacy to the groups and their solutions" as does the use of open and transparent processes.[72]

As for the role of the NTIA in the multistakeholder process, it would be limited to providing a forum for discussion and consensus-building among stakeholders and, even when stakeholders disagreed over how best to interpret the CPBR, NTIA's only role would be to "help the parties reach clarity on what their positions are and whether there are options for compromise toward consensus, rather than substituting its own judgment."[73] Finally, the Administration identified two incentives for participation by industry stakeholders: first, building consumer trust by engaging directly with consumers and other stakeholders during the process and by adopting a code of conduct and, second, assisting participating firms via a (weak) safe harbor such that "in any enforcement action based on conduct covered by a code, the FTC will consider a company's adherence to a code favorably."[74] Based on the three completed projects to date, however, it is not clear that the current design of the multistakeholder process fully achieved any of the three advantages previously identified or benefited as much from a co-regulatory approach to privacy codes as the Administration had hoped it would.[75]

Mobile Apps. In March 2012, the Administration sought public comment both on which consumer data privacy issues lent themselves to legally enforceable codes of conduct established through a multistakeholder process, as well as what procedures would best foster the development of these codes.[76] In response to more than eighty comments expressing an interest in mobile application (app) transparency, and given the support of a broad range of additional stakeholders, the NTIA then selected this issue as the focus of the first privacy multistakeholder process. The mobile app stakeholder group held its initial meeting in July 2012 and over the next year met for a total of sixteen times. In terms of process, the early meetings were shepherded by

[69] Privacy Blueprint, *supra* note 67, at 2.

[70] *Id.* at 23.

[71] *Id.* at 24–27.

[72] *Id.* at 23.

[73] *Id.* at 27.

[74] *Id.* at 24.

[75] For similar assessments, *see* Gellman and Dixon, *supra* note 2, at 69–72; Margot E. Kaminski, *When the Default Is No Penalty: Negotiating Privacy at the NTIA*, 94 Denv. L. Rev. 923, 944–47 (2016).

[76] Multistakeholder Process, *supra* note 39.

an independent facilitator and debates over process carried over from the earlier comment period.[77] At the second meeting, consumer advocates threatened to walk out if the meeting did not develop a concretely defined process,[78] and concerns over the lack of clear procedural rules recurred throughout subsequent meetings. The first draft of a mobile app code of conduct was promulgated almost a year later but to a mixed reception – two participants endorsed it, twenty supported it, seventeen sought further consideration, and one abstained.[79]

The code of conduct required mobile application developers to show users an easy-to-understand description of the kinds of data the app collects and the kinds of entities with which the app shares this data.[80] According to one participant who supported the code, "app developers, industry groups and advocates were initially substantially far apart in their approaches to mobile app transparency," but the code as adopted reflected "a flexible approach to communicating data collection and sharing practices to consumers, while also providing substantial grounds for enforcement by the Federal Trade Commission."[81] Alternatively, detractors objected to both the process and the substance of the code. A dissenting consumer advocacy group stated that the app code effort "exposed the futility of the multistakeholder process" and that because companies were allowed to state their support for the draft without assuming any compliance obligations, this would encourage free-riding.[82] Despite these criticisms, several industry stakeholders decided to implement solutions that adhered to the draft code.[83] This first multistakeholder charter was very narrow, however, and only addressed one aspect of a single element of the CPBR (transparency), while neglecting the other six principles, making it a modest success at best.

Facial Recognition. In February 2014, the NTIA initiated a second multistakeholder process devoted to "how best to ensure that consumers' rights to control, transparency, security, access and accuracy, focused collection, and accountability are respected within the context of current and emerging commercial uses of facial recognition technology."[84] This second effort was both more ambitious and more structured than the mobile app process, setting defined dates for future meetings and relying on predetermined agendas, discussion panels, and question-and-answer sessions to ensure that stakeholders had an adequate factual background before

[77] *See Privacy Multistakeholder Process: Mobile Application Transparency*, NAT'L TELECOMM. & INFO. ADMIN., (Nov. 12, 2013), https://www.ntia.doc.gov/other-publication/2013/privacy-multistakeholder-process-mobileapplication-transparency.
[78] NTIA Holds Second Meeting on Mobile Apps, IAPP DAILY DASHBOARD (Aug. 23, 2012), https://iapp.org/news/a/2012-08-23-ntia-holds-second-meeting-on-mobile-apps/.
[79] Press Release, *Consumer Watchdog, Effort to Craft Apps "Transparency Code" Shows Futility of Multi-Stakeholder Process*, CONSUMER WATCHDOG (July 25, 2013), http://www.consumerwatchdog.org/newsrelease/effort-craft-apps-%E2%80%9Ctransparency-code%E2%80%9D-shows-futility-multi-stakeholder-process.
[80] NTIA, *Short Form Notice Code of Conduct to Promote Transparency in Mobile Applications* (June 17, 2013), http://www.ntia.doc.gov/files/ntia/publications/july_17_code_draft.pdf.
[81] NTIA, *Multistakeholder Process Delivers Increased App Transparency*, CENTER FOR DEMOCRACY & TECHNOLOGY BLOG, July 25, 2013, https://cdt.org/blog/ntia-multistakeholder-process-delivers-increased-app-transparency/.
[82] Press Release, *supra* note 79.
[83] As of early 2016, privacy guidelines based on the code were present in apps used by more than 200 million customers; see *Keynote Address of Assistant Secretary Strickling at Silicon Flatirons Conference on the Digital Broadband Migration*, NAT'L TELECOMM. & INFO. ADMIN. (Jan. 31, 2016), https://www.ntia.doc.gov/speechtestimony/2016/keynote-address-assistant-secretary-strickling-silicon-flatirons-conference-dig.
[84] *Privacy Multistakeholder Meetings Regarding Facial Recognition Technology: February–June 2014*, NAT'L TELECOMM. & INFO. ADMIN., (Dec. 3, 2013), https://www.ntia.doc.gov/otherpublication/2013/privacy-multistakeholder-meetings-regarding-facial-recognition-technology-feb.

addressing issues of substance. However, it was also more contentious and adversarial, and the differences between industry representatives and some advocates proved irreconcilable.

Over the next sixteen months, the working group met only sporadically due in part to consumer advocacy groups strongly opposing a draft code created by an industry group. At the June 2015 meeting, the American Civil Liberties Union sought to counter the industry draft by introducing "An Ethical Framework for Facial Recognition," which required that facial recognition users receive informed, written consent for each distinct use of the technology.[85] The two sides were unable to find common ground and a short time later, nine civil liberties groups staged a walkout. In a joint statement announcing their withdrawal, they expressed frustration over the process's failure to reach consensus on fundamentals, emphasizing that in recent NTIA meetings, "industry stakeholders were unable to agree on any concrete scenario where companies should employ facial recognition only with a consumer's permission."[86] The process then limped along for three more meetings until June 2016, when the remaining stakeholders finally reached consensus on a weak set of best practice recommendations, which several consumer groups dismissed out of hand.[87]

Drones. The third multistakeholder process started later but finished earlier and more successfully than the facial recognition effort. At the first meeting in August 2015, the NTIA provided background material in an effort to ensure all stakeholders had an adequate knowledge base to proceed from. The meeting featured a stakeholder question-and-answer session and a presentation on the current state of drone operation. Additionally, the NTIA facilitated stakeholder discussions regarding how to identify the privacy, transparency, and accountability issues that could be addressed by the best practices, as well as how best to structure the stakeholder work.[88]

The drone process quickly took the form of a dialectic between two of the best practice discussion drafts: one from the Center for Democracy & Technology (CDT) and one from the Hogan Lovells law firm, representing a coalition of drone operators.[89] Although originating from an advocacy organization, the CDT draft enjoyed broad support from industry and advocacy groups. After CDT presented a comparison of the two drafts, the major industry and advocacy stakeholders reached consensus on a combined draft, which was adopted over the objections of the ACLU and a few other advocacy groups. The dissenters criticized this combined draft for being at odds with widely accepted privacy principles and conditioned their support on a number of changes that, in the end, were not adopted.[90]

In sum, the mobile app code group met sixteen times over a period of twelve months and produced a code of conduct devoted to a single principle (transparency) that enjoyed some uptake; the facial recognition group met eight times over a period of twenty nine months and produced a weak code of conduct covering six out of seven principles, and most advocates rejected this code; and the drone group met six times over a period of nine months and

---

[85] Zack Martin, *ACLU: Facial Recognition Needs Ethical Framework,* Secure ID News (May 27, 2014), http://www.secureidnews.com/news-item/aclu-facial-recognition-needs-ethical-framework/.

[86] *Privacy Advocates Quit Commerce Department Facial Recognition Talks,* Consumer Watchdog Blog, June 15, 2015, http://www.consumerwatchdog.org/blog/privacy-advocates-quit-commerce-department-facial-recognition-talks.

[87] Press Release, *Statement on NTIA Privacy Best Practice Recommendations for Commercial Facial Recognition Use,* Consumer Federation of America (June 15, 2016), http://consumerfed.org/press_release/statement-ntia-privacy-best-practice-recommendations-commercial-facial-recognition-use/.

[88] *See Multistakeholder Process: Unmanned Aircraft Systems,* Nat'l Telecomm. & Info. Admin (June 21, 2016), http://www.ntia.doc.gov/other-publication/2016/multistakeholder-process-unmanned-aircraft-systems.

[89] *Id.*

[90] *Id.*

produced a fairly robust code covering five principles. This averages out to ten meetings per project with an average duration of thirteen plus months per project.

In terms of the purported advantage of the NTIA process, the three projects were somewhat flexible, allowing each group to devise its own methods and structure, learn from, and somewhat improve the process as they went along.[91] They were not exactly speedy, but that judgment depends on selecting an alternative rulemaking process for the sake of comparison, although there is no obvious standard.[92] The issue of "decentralization necessary to address Internet policy challenges" is addressed later in this chapter.

*　*　*　*　*

It is too soon to assess the three codes of conduct in terms of the six normative factors identified earlier, but a few tentative conclusions may be stated (excluding the first factor (efficiency) and the fifth (oversight and enforcement)). Certainly, the NTIA process was open and transparent, although it remains to be seen if the firms that have agreed to abide by the codes also will disclose how well they perform against the applicable standards. As already noted, the codes are incomplete in the sense that they do not all address all the CPBR principles. The least successful aspects of the codes by far, however, are the fourth factor (handling free rider problems) and the sixth (using second-generation design features).[93]

In thinking about free rider problems and the industry incentives to participate in the NTIA process, it is helpful to divide firms into two categories: (1) those already voluntarily adhering to an industry code of conduct (e.g., NAI) and (2) those not already doing so. In the absence of legislation, both groups have an incentive to refrain from participating in the NTIA process. Those in the first group have already drafted industry codes of conduct with no or limited consumer input. If they choose to participate in a NTIA process relevant to their sector, one can safely predict that consumer groups will seek to strengthen the existing industry codes. Thus, most firms would have a strong incentive to sit out the process (or not adopt any codes that emerge) rather than subject themselves to more restrictive rules. Those in the second group have even stronger reasons not to participate. If they have not yet promised to comply with a voluntary code, then they are not subject to FTC enforcement for "deceptively" failing to live up to such commitments. If they sign on to a NTIA code, however, they would thereby expose themselves to such enforcement actions. Thus, firms in both the first and second groups will likely have limited incentives to participate.[94]

---

[91] Some of those improvements were the result of informal norms the groups developed in collaboration with the NTIA, while others came about from more formal discussions, such as the August 29, 2013 "lessons learned" meeting the NTIA held to take written and verbal comments from the community. *See Notice of Meeting* (Aug. 9, 2013), https://www.ntia.doc.gov/federal-register-notice/2013/multistakeholder-meeting-develop-consumer-data-privacy-code-conduct-con.

[92] For example, the original COPPA rule took just over six months from the (combined) Notice of Proposed Rulemaking (NPRM) and Request for Comment (RFC) to the Final Rule (and by law the final rule had to be completed within one year of the date of enactment of COPPA), while the revised COPPA rule took almost seventeen months from the RFC to the initial NPRM, an additional ten months for the supplemental NPRM, and a total of thirty-four months from the RFC to the Final Rule. On the other hand, the FTC averaged about seven months per decision in reviewing applications for the COPPA safe harbor programs. *See generally*, Fed. Trade Comm'n, *Children's Privacy*, https://www.ftc.gov/tips-advice/business-center/privacy-and-security/children%27s-privacy.

[93] Letter from Ira Rubinstein & Dennis Hirsch, to the Nat'l Telecomm. & Info. Admin., NAT'L TELECOMM. & INFO. ADMIN (Mar. 26, 2012), https://www.ntia.doc.gov/files/ntia/ntia_comments_rubinstein_hirsch_final.pdf.

[94] *See* Kaminski, *supra* note 75, at 939 (noting that "in the absence of a worse regulatory alternative…industry has little incentive to meaningfully participate in the NTIA process").

Nor are the incentives to participate as identified by the Administration (building consumer trust and favorable treatment by the FTC if there is an enforcement action) sufficient to overcome this reasoning. At least some companies (especially those that are mainly domestic and thus not subject to European or other stricter privacy regimes) may view the gain in consumer trust as speculative or marginal and prefer to wait until Congress enacts privacy legislation before committing to a code of conduct that imposes new legal obligations. As for favorable FTC treatment, companies that sit out the NTIA process and free ride on other firms that do participate are indifferent to being treated favorably by the FTC because they have not agreed to adhere to a code and so cannot be charged with acting "deceptively" if they ignore it (unless the code becomes a standard that determines what constitutes reasonableness, which is discussed below). Moreover, during the mobile apps process, the FTC declined to move beyond its commitment to "favorable treatment" and treat compliance with an NTIA code as a safe harbor.[95]

Of course, if Congress enacted new privacy legislation in keeping with the Administration's proposal, this would alter the regulatory calculus by subjecting all covered entities to the seven principles of the CPBR, regardless of whether they participated in the NTIA process. This would bring free riding to an end because companies would have to follow an approved code of conduct or be subject to the general obligations of the legislation. Moreover, as the Administration recommended in the Discussion Draft, the legislation could establish a binding safe harbor mechanism that might provide firms with significant incentives to participate in the NTIA process. Additional benefits would include greater clarity and certainty about how the CPBR applies to a specific industry and the opportunity to negotiate the specific terms of an eventual code that the industry would agree to abide by.

The question, then, is how to change the incentives in the absence of legislation and get companies to participate in the NTIA process now. The most obvious lever is for the FTC to change its current enforcement policy. First, the FTC could devote new resources to enforce voluntary codes of conduct more vigorously under the deception prong of section 5, treating any failure by a company to abide by a code they have agreed to follow as a presumptive violation.[96] To increase the incentive to participate in the NTIA process, the FTC should also develop a policy under which firms that decline to abide by a completed NTIA code and instead follow self-regulatory codes devised by trade associations are not entitled to any favorable treatment in the event of enforcement. Thus, to receive favorable treatment these companies, too, would

---

[95] According to Gellman and Dixon, "In the first multi-stakeholder process, the FTC was very clear that they would not be offering a "safe harbor" for companies that chose to voluntarily comply with the code. This position from the FTC denied the NTIA an important negotiating tool. It is unclear what long-term impact this might have. The initial impact, however, appears to have been deleterious to the process, making it less attractive to app developers and publishers." *Supra* note 2, at 71. Perhaps the FTC never supported anything stronger than "favorable treatment" because it worried that the NTIA codes would be too weak or limited to justify full-fledged safe harbor treatment. *See, e.g.,* Fed. Trade Comm'n, Staff Report: Mobile Privacy Disclosures: Building Trust through Transparency iii (Feb. 2013), https://www.ftc.gov/sites/default/files/documents/reports/mobile-privacy-disclosures-building-trust-through-transparency-federal-trade-commission-staff-report/130201mobileprivacyreport.pdf (noting that firms would be treated favorably only if they adhered to "strong privacy codes").

[96] Although this is current policy, Gellman and Dixon argue that the FTC has not been very diligent about using its section 5 powers to enforce the promises made by firms regarding their adherence to voluntary codes; *see* Gellman and Dixon, *supra* note 2, at 56–69, 73–74. Indeed, apart from cases charging firms with falsely claiming certification under the E.U.–U.S. Safe Harbor Agreement (SHA) or having violated the terms of the SHA, a survey of more than 200 privacy or data security actions suggests that the FTC has brought only *one* case in which it directly charges a firm with violating a self-regulatory code. *See* Complaint at 4, U.S. v. Google Inc., No. CV 12–04177 SI (N.D. Cal. Nov. 16, 2012) (charging Google with misrepresenting its compliance with the NAI Principles by failing to disclose properly its data collection and use practices).

have to submit themselves to a NTIA process, even if this results in changes to their existing code.

Second, the FTC can give all firms – including those who have not adopted a NTIA code – a strong incentive to participate in the multistakeholder process by embarking on a new strategy that treats approved codes of conduct as establishing industry standards, thereby making them relevant to determining "reasonableness" under the unfairness prong of section 5. This enforcement strategy would be a departure from existing FTC policy but is not beyond the pale. As Margot Kaminski points out, initially the FTC might be reluctant to look to NTIA codes alone to determine reasonableness. "However, if the NTIA process works the way the White House envisions, it will result in standards widely adopted by industry leaders, which would consequently nudge or dictate the industry standards on which FTC enforcement relies."[97] In other words, if the NTIA process succeeds in creating industry codes of conduct that are then actually adopted by the majority of players in an industry, "it is hard to imagine the FTC will not eventually look to the codes for guidance as to the industry standard in a sector in determining which enforcement actions to pursue."[98]

While it is always difficult to predict how companies will respond to such regulatory initiatives as this one, suffice to say that the history of privacy self-regulation in the United States teaches that firms are far more willing to develop and commit to a voluntary code of conduct when faced with a credible threat of stricter government regulation if they fail to act than when no such threat exists.[99] In the present case, this threat is absent, at least in the short term if not in the long term (given Congress' poor track record on privacy legislation). Thus, the FTC should consider using both the "deceptive" and "unfair" prongs of its existing section 5 authority, as outlined earlier, to pursue a new enforcement strategy that gives firms more incentive to participate in the NTIA process.

Finally, this assessment considers whether the Administration has been successful in using second-generation regulatory strategies to achieve the desirable goal of fostering voluntary codes of conduct that meet the requirements of the CPBR. As noted earlier, the Privacy Blueprint claims that the NTIA process has several advantages that sound in co-regulation including flexibility, speed, decentralization, and creativity and cites as a precedent the work of Internet standards groups. However, the analogy to Internet standards processes seems rather strained. Such standard-setting processes differ from the NTIA process in at least two important ways. To begin with, the main goal of Internet standards is interoperability, which is achieved by defining protocols, messaging formats, schemas, and languages. Interoperability motivates company participation for the simple reason that unless a company's products or services interoperate with the network infrastructure, hardware, and software that make up the Internet, it is out of business. Moreover, companies with specific views on how to achieve interoperability recognize that they are far more likely to influence a standard if they are at the table than if they stay away. Thus, the goal of interoperability naturally draws participants to the table and makes them amenable to a joint solution.

In addition, Internet standards bodies such as the Internet Engineering Task Force (IETF) emphasize "rough consensus and running code," which is a shorthand way of saying that while everyone who participates has an opportunity to be heard, consensus requires not just verbal

---

[97] Kaminski, *supra* note 75, at 928.
[98] *Id.*
[99] Rubinstein, *supra* note 1, at 401; Kaminski, *id.* at 941–43 (making a similar point by reference to contract law and the idea of penalty defaults).

persuasion but the evidence of two or more independently developed interoperating implementations. The IETF standards process relies on working implementations both as an objective (or at least a pragmatic) measure of expertise (i.e., which participants are worth listening to) and of progress (how to know when the process is complete). But the NTIA process lacks both characteristics. As was discussed earlier, companies may boycott the process with relative impunity – doing so would certainly not prevent them from selling a product that both works and turns a profit. Nor is there an objective measure of success analogous to running code. Although the Administration emphasizes consensus, diversity of participation, openness, and transparency as the characteristics that will ensure the legitimacy of the NTIA process, the dissimilarities with the Internet standards process are striking.

Arguably, environmental covenants are more analogous to, and offer a better model for, the Administration's proposed multistakeholder process than do Internet standards processes.[100] In particular, several points stand out as lessons learned from earlier experiments by the Environmental Protection Agency (EPA) in using a consensus-based multistakeholder process to develop "cheaper, cleaner and smarter" approaches to environmental regulation.[101] First, it is vital to develop ground rules at the beginning of the process, which should address the nature of consensus, the development of agendas, the expected level of participation, approaches to resolving conflicts, and the removal of participants who are unduly obstructing the process, rather than counting on each multistakeholder group to develop its own ground rules.[102] Second, working groups that utilized trained, neutral facilitators performed better than those that did not.[103] Third, the lack of specific deadlines contributed to the slow pace of negotiations. Once the EPA imposed deadlines, this "helped to galvanize action."[104] Thus, future multistakeholder processes should consider establishing comprehensive ground rules at the outset, using trained neutral facilitators for all negotiations, and setting specific deadlines for the termination of the process.[105]

Dutch Privacy Codes of Conduct

In an important 2013 paper, Dennis Hirsch seeks to test the proposition that co-regulation does a better job of developing commercial privacy rules than do either government regulation or self-regulation.[106] As already noted, proponents of co-regulation (or "collaborative governance") believe that it combines the flexibility and industry expertise of voluntary self-regulation with the heightened accountability and administrative norms of government regulation.[107] Does this imply that collaborative governance is the best way to protect personal information? Hirsch tries to answer this question through a detailed study of Dutch codes of conduct. As Hirsch describes it, the Dutch Personal Data Protection Act (PDPA) – which is a comprehensive statute implementing the very broad principles of the E.U. Data Protection Directive – allows industry sectors

---

[100] Letter from Rubinstein & Hirsch, *supra* note 93.
[101] *See* Kerr, Greiner, Anderson & April, Inc., *Analysis and Evaluation of the EPA Common Sense Initiative* (July 29, 1999), nepis.epa.gov/Exe/ZyPURL.cgi?Dockey=9101PDAX.TXT (study funded by EPA); Cary Coglianese & Laurie K. Allen, *Building Sector-Based Consensus: A Review of EPA's Common Sense Initiative* (2003), Scholarship at Penn Law, Paper 107, http://scholarship.law.upenn.edu/cgi/viewcontent.cgi?article=1102&context=faculty_scholarship.
[102] Coglianese & Allen, *id.* at 42.
[103] *Id.* at 43.
[104] *Id.* at 44.
[105] *See* Letter of Rubinstein & Hirsch, *supra* note 93.
[106] Hirsch, *Going Dutch?*, *supra* note 5.
[107] *Id.* at 88.

to draw up codes specifying how the statutory requirements apply to their specific sector. These codes are then submitted to the Dutch Data Protection Authority (DPA) for review and approval.[108] Specifically, organizations that are considered "sufficiently representative" of a sector and that are planning to draw up a code of conduct may ask the DPA for a declaration that "given the particular features of the sector or sectors of society in which these organizations are operating, the rules contained in the said code properly implement" Dutch law.[109] Article 25 (4) of the PDPA further provides that such declarations shall be "deemed to be the equivalent to" a binding administrative decision, making it similar in effect to "safe harbor" treatment under U.S. law.[110] Over the past twenty years, Dutch privacy regulators have approved codes for twenty sectors including banks, insurance firms, and direct marketers.[111] As Hirsch points out, these codes thus provide a highly suitable body of practical experience for testing the claims of privacy co-regulation in a setting where there is a statutory basis for both their process and their substance.[112]

Hirsch interviewed regulators, industry representatives, and privacy advocates who had drafted and negotiated the codes and found that (1) the need to clarify the broad terms of the PDPA as they applied to specific sectors and in some cases to forestall direct government regulation created sufficient incentives for companies to participate; also, the negotiation process (2) built sufficient trust between regulators and industry to promote both information sharing and joint-problem solving between them, thereby taking advantage of industry expertise, and (3) led to more tailored, workable, and cost-effective rules. However, Hirsch also identified a number of significant weaknesses in the Dutch co-regulatory approach and offered several thoughtful recommendations for improving them, which he classified as either minimizing weaknesses or maximizing strengths.[113]

The most important weakness Hirsch identifies is the lack of public involvement in the Dutch code of conduct program. Dutch privacy law requires the DPA to reach a preliminary decision on a proposed code of conduct within thirteen weeks of submission and to then publish notice of its draft decision in an official government publication, which makes it available for public inspection. Interested parties then have six weeks to submit comments, and the DPA has six months from the date of the initial application to decide whether the code properly embodies the statute.[114] But Hirsch discovered that none of this works in practice because the parties need far more than thirteen weeks to complete the negotiation process (ten to twenty meetings over several years was not uncommon). Most importantly, this unrealistically short deadline "has the unintended effect of encouraging the industry and the DPA to negotiate the code informally

---

[108] *See Dutch Personal Data Protection Act* (PDPA, art. 25(1)), available and translated at http://www.dutchdpa.nl/downloads_wetten/wbp.pdf.

[109] *Id.*

[110] Hirsch, *Going Dutch?*, *supra* note 5, at 119–20.

[111] *Id.* at 89.

[112] Outside of Europe, Australia and New Zealand have adopted a similar approach to privacy covenants; *see* Rubinstein, *supra* note 1, at 401. In the United States, there is only one example of an industry negotiating privacy covenants with regulators – the safe harbor program under COPPA, which has a variety of shortcomings and relatively few participants; Rubinstein, *id.* at 394–99 (assessing the COPPA safe harbor against the six normative factors and identifying as the main flaw a lack of regulatory flexibility due to structural defects).

[113] Throughout his article, Hirsch also calls attention to the flurry of recent U.S. privacy bills that contain safe harbor provisions, *see* Hirsch, *Going Dutch?*, *supra* note 5, at 96–99 (describing three recent bills). In particular, the Obama Administration's Draft Discussion bill contains a provision, section 301, entitled "Safe Harbors for Enforceable Codes of Conduct." Thus, Hirsch's recommendations are also meant to shed some light on how the United States should approach privacy safe harbors; *id.* at 152.

[114] *Id.* at 117.

before the sector formally applies for approval . . . This, in turn, reduces interested parties' ability to influence the DPA with their comments since, by the time the comment period occurs," the DPA and the sector have usually worked through all their differences and reached agreement on the key provisions. As a result, the DPA is already strongly committed to the code prior to receiving any public comments."[115]

The obvious fix to this problem is opening up the code negotiation process to include other stakeholders such as consumer or privacy advocacy groups. This is par for the course in the United States but does not work as well in the Dutch setting because such groups are comparatively rare and not very powerful. Hirsch reports on an interesting proposal that would enhance public involvement while preserving the fragile trust between regulators and sectors that fosters candid discussion. Under this proposal, the drafting and negotiation process would be divided into two phases. "In the first, industry and government would collaborate on an initial, tentative draft. In the second, public interest stakeholders such as consumer or privacy groups would join the discussion and provide their reactions and ideas."[116] Thereafter, the DPA would follow existing procedures and publish the code for public comment, giving stakeholders another chance to weigh in. According to Hirsch, "Stakeholders participating in the second stage would not be able to exercise veto power over the document. However, they would be able to review it and 'cry foul' to the policymaking community, or even the media, if they believed it to be one-sided."[117] This proposal might be a very hard sell in the United States, where advocacy groups would likely insist on equal participation rights to those of industry from the outset, yet this staged approach seems like an interesting way to manage the NTIA multistakeholder process and preserve information sharing and public involvement alike.

Hirsch identifies several other weaknesses and responds to them accordingly. The Dutch program demonstrates a weakness with respect to monitoring, enforcement, and compliance, hence Hirsch proposes a third-party certification program.[118] He does not, however, address issues of cost or scalability. As noted previously, the Dutch codes – which remain in effect for five years – are also "slow-moving, largely static instruments" and it is considered a hardship to renegotiate new codes every five years. Thus, the process might benefit from a more streamlined form of reapproval and a commitment from the parties to approved codes to continue meeting on an ongoing basis to discuss code implementation problems and possible improvements. This would also make the code negotiation process more adaptive by institutionalizing "continuous monitoring, feedback, and adjustment" while preventing the negotiation process from becoming "ossified and, at the same time, increase monitoring and accountability."[119] Finally, Hirsch also offers five self-explanatory recommendations for maximizing the strengths of the Dutch code program, all of which apply equally well to U.S. safe harbor programs:[120] (1) make safe harbor programs sector-based to preserve the benefits of information sharing;[121] (2) allow industry sectors to address all aspects of a statute in their codes of conduct (which is not the case for two of the proposed U.S. privacy codes discussed in his article); (3) enact baseline privacy legislation to address free-rider problems; (4) provide public recognition to safe harbor participants to boost

---

[115] *Id.* at 118.
[116] *Id.* at 155 (citations omitted).
[117] *Id.*
[118] *Id.* at 152–53.
[119] *Id.* at 156–57.
[120] *Id.* at 157–61.
[121] This is easier said than done given the inherent difficulties in setting sectoral boundaries. For example, what sector controls debit card purchases of health-related services using a mobile health app?

reputational capital; and (5) use codes to create a global standard (this is essentially a proposal to harmonize code approval standards by regional entities such as the FTC, the Article 29 Working Group, and APEC), resulting in a single, globally interoperable, approved set of privacy rules. Taken together, Hirsch's two sets of recommended improvements address all six of the normative factors previously discussed.

CONCLUSION

We are at a crossroads in privacy regulation. With the GDPR, the European Union has cast its lot with a belt-and-suspenders approach that retains broad principles (such as processing data only for legitimate interest and subject to purpose limitations), and inter alia, toughens consent requirements, limits profiling absent appropriate safeguards, imposes new obligations (such as the right to be forgotten and data portability), adds new accountability measures (such as data protection by design and default and certain required risk assessments), permits codes of conduct along with certifications, privacy seals, and trust marks, and imposes huge new fines for violations (up to 4 percent of the global annual turnover for severe infringements).[122] These many different provisions may be defensible singly or in the aggregate; they are mentioned here mostly to suggest that the GDPR embraces prescriptive regulation with a vengeance, while simultaneously enhancing the power of regulatory agencies. Meanwhile, the United States has failed to enact new privacy legislation during the past fifteen years, and the FTC remains a moderately effective but cautious enforcement agency. And yet, if Congress were to enact new privacy legislation, it would have almost a clean slate to write on in devising a co-regulatory approach that follows the recommendations spelled out earlier. That is to say, a baseline privacy statute with broad privacy principles and a safe harbor program that strongly incentivizes firms to adopt codes of conduct. These codes should be sectoral, comprehensive, and highly flexible, and rely on direct negotiations in which industry representatives and advocates have seats at the table and bargain for mutual advantage, while the government retains an oversight role as to both approval and enforcement. Co-regulation is far from a perfect solution to regulating privacy (there are none) but we have had enough experience with various forms of co-regulation to learn some valuable lessons, avoid foolish errors, and forge ahead with something new – and hopefully better – than either self-regulation or prescriptive statutes. Now is the time to seize the middle ground.

ACKNOWLEDGMENTS

The author would like to thank Kiel Brennan-Marquez, Robert Gellman, Christopher Hoofnagle, Ronald Lee, and John Verdi for their comments on an earlier draft of this chapter, Jacob Bollinger for his excellent research assistance, and the Future of Privacy Forum for its support.

---

[122] *See generally* Cedric Burton et al., *The Final European Union General Data Protection Regulation*, BLOOMBERG BNA PRIVACY & SEC. L. REP. (Jan. 25, 2016), https://www.wsgr.com/publications/pdfsearch/bloombergbna-0116.pdf.

29

Privacy Notices

Limitations, Challenges, and Opportunities[*]

Mary J. Culnan and Paula J. Bruening

INTRODUCTION

The first principle of fair information practices (FIPPS) states that "there shall be no personal-data record-keeping system whose very existence is secret and there shall be a policy of openness or transparency about an organization's personal-data record-keeping policies, practices, and systems" (US HEW, 1973). This principle requires that organizations make their information practices visible to the public. Because consumers suffer from deficits of information and control about how their personal information will be used after it is disclosed, transparency is essential to the fair use of personal information (Culnan & Williams, 2009). Lack of openness potentially enables organizations to collect and use information without protections and outside the scrutiny of consumers, regulators, or others due to information assymetries. Since the late 1970s, what has commonly been referred to as "notice" has been used to create openness.

Notice arguably fosters openness by requiring companies to make public the business models, vendor relationships, and data practices that drive the digital economy. However, since the mid-1990s, regulators, privacy advocates, and businesses have criticized both online and offline notices as being too complex, legalistic, lengthy, and opaque. Questions about how notices could be improved figure prominently in nearly every discussion about privacy. Businesses complain of the challenge of writing notices that meet regulators' requirements for completeness, while consumer advocates call for clarity and concise, consumer-friendly language. Notices that support individual choice about the subsequent use of personal information often are written in language that allows companies such latitude that consent authorizes nearly any data use. As a result, notices are often perceived as doing little to promote the individual's informed decisions about their personal information.

Rapid changes in technology further strain companies' ability to provide useful notice. The Internet of Things (IoT), the ubiquitous deployment of sensors, advances in big data analytics, and the complex vendor relationships and data sharing partnerships that characterize today's data ecosystem challenge organizations' ability to explain their data practices. The need to use data robustly and in innovative ways clashes with requirements that notices specify a particular purpose or use for the data collected. The degree to which data collection is integrated through the use of sensors into environments such as cities, retail locations and other public spaces can

---

[*] The views expressed in the paper are those of the authors. Earlier versions of this paper were presented at the 8th Annual Privacy Law Scholars Conference, Berkeley, California, June 2015, and published in the *University of North Carolina Journal of Law and Technology*, vol. 17, no. 4, May 2016.

make posting notice difficult, and new technologies such as mobile devices with small screens create new challenges for providing meaningful notice. For these and other reasons, the White House identified transparency as a key challenge for privacy in its *National Privacy Research Strategy* (2016).

We argue that to achieve the openness required by FIPPS, data protection and privacy should move from a "notice" model to one based on an environment of "transparency." We also assert that the terms "notice" and "transparency" are not synonymous and that different definitions apply to each. We define notice as the posted articulation of a company's privacy practices and policies. In contrast, transparency is a condition of disclosure and openness jointly created by companies and policy makers through the use of a variety of approaches, including notice.

We further argue that notice is an essential tool but that establishing openness requires far more than notice. Rather it requires an *environment of transparency*. Whether transparency is achieved depends not only on posting a notice but also on the *perceived quality* of the disclosure (Schnackenberg & Tomlinson, 2016). We argue that our experience with notice over the last twenty years demonstrates that a single notice cannot fully inform consumers, regulators, and the public about data practices. Rather, to achieve the openness required by the first principle of fair information practices – particularly given the complexity of the emerging data ecosystem – organizations must employ a variety of tools that support the various functions notice alone was once intended to serve. This environment of transparency – and the openness that it fosters – is necessary to support the fair use of personal information.

We begin by reviewing the history of notice in the United States and its traditional role in privacy and data protection. We consider the challenges and limitations of notice; the attempts of a range of stakeholders to address them; and the lessons learned from these efforts. We also examine the implications of emerging technologies and data uses for notice. Finally, we propose ways in which effective transparency can be achieved, including the role of notice. It is important to note that this chapter is limited to the issues related to notice and to fostering transparency. We recognize the importance of the full complement of FIPPS and that transparency alone is not sufficient to assure the fair use of data. We also recognize the importance of meaningful choice or consent and that notice as it is currently implemented is the mechanism by which individuals now learn about their opportunity, if available, to consent or choose. However, issues related to the current implementation of the other FIPPS are beyond the scope of this chapter. Finally, articulations of fair information practices take different forms in different jurisdictions (Gellman, 2016). While the history of notice reflected in this chapter is admittedly limited to the United States, many of the strengths and limitations of notice revealed by this experience are relevant across jurisdictions.

BACKGROUND: A HISTORY OF NOTICE

In his seminal work, *Privacy and Freedom*, Westin (1967) discussed individuals' awareness about the collection, processing, and storage of data as one means to protect against the unfair treatment that can result when inaccurate information is used or shared to make decisions about them. His work emphasized that when individuals do not know that information systems exist, they cannot challenge either a particular use or disclosure, or the decisions that result.

Notice first emerged as a mechanism to achieve awareness and a basis for promoting the legitimate use of personal information when large-scale computerized systems emerged in the

1970s. In the 1990s, the Internet and e-commerce renewed discussion about the need to provide notice to individuals about the collection and use of personal data. Our chapter briefly reviews the evolution of notice in the United States beginning in the 1970s through the release in 2012 of major privacy reports by both the White House and the Federal Trade Commission (FTC).

The Origins of Notice

In the early 1970s, then-Secretary of Health, Education, and Welfare Elliot Richardson established the Secretary's Advisory Committee on Automated Data Systems in response to growing public concerns about the harmful consequences of the widespread use of computer and telecommunications technology. The committee's report, *Records, Computers, and the Rights of Citizens* (1973) articulated the original Code of Fair Information Practices with openness as the first principle. The report called for any organization maintaining an administrative personal data system to provide public notice once a year and detailed what information the notice should include.

In 1974, Congress passed the Privacy Act (5 USC § 552), designed to regulate the federal government's collection and protection of information about citizens. The act requires federal agencies collecting information to inform each individual whom it asks to supply information (1) the authority which authorizes the solicitation of the information and whether disclosure of such information is mandatory or voluntary; (2) the principal purpose(s) for which the information is intended to be used; (3) the routine uses which may be made of the information, and (4) the effects on individuals, if any, of not providing all or any part of the requested information The act's key requirements are based on the FIPPS.

The Privacy Act also called for the creation of the Privacy Protection Study Commission (PPSC), charging it with examining a wide range of record-keeping practices and privacy issues arising in the public sector and in a variety of commercial environments. In its report, the PPSC articulated objectives for data protection systems and reiterated the importance of openness to fairness (US PPSC, 1977). The report included recommendations related to a variety of data uses, among them direct marketing mailing lists. The PPSC was asked to investigate whether a party that engages in interstate commerce and maintains a mailing list should be required to remove an individual's name and address from that list, absent an exception in law. However, the report instead recommended that private sector organizations that share their mailing lists with third parties provide notice of this practice to the individuals on the list and provide an opportunity for individuals to opt out of sharing. This recommendation effectively articulated what is now referred to as "notice and choice" for the first time.

Online Privacy and Notice

In the 1990s, the promise of a new National Information Infrastructure (NII) brought with it the recognition that new privacy risks threatened the benefits the Internet promised. In 1993, Vice President Al Gore created the Information Infrastructure Task Force (IITF), and charged it with developing comprehensive policies and programs that would promote the development of the NII. A Privacy Working Group was created within the IITF, and in June 1995 it released its report, which proposed a framework for the collection and use of telecommunications-related personal information. The framework included a notice principle requiring that individuals be given sufficient information to make informed decisions about the collection, use, and protection of their personal information (IITF, 1995). The IITF framework built on the OECD Guidelines (1980), which established notice as a global principle and have served as the basis for law, regulation, and international agreements around the world. The role of notice was subsequently reinforced in the White House *Framework for Global Electronic Commerce* which stated that the IITF privacy principles require data gatherers to inform consumers about what information they collect and how they plan to use it (White House, 1997).

During the 1990s, the FTC began a separate consumer privacy initiative to examine and understand online privacy issues. In 1996, it reported that participants in a workshop on online privacy generally agreed that notice of information practices is essential to advancing privacy online; they disagreed, however, about the substance of privacy notices (FTC, 1996). In 1998, the FTC analyzed the content of a sample of commercial websites to determine how many of them posted privacy notices, and among those that did, whether those notices contained the core elements of FIPPS. In its report to Congress, the FTC asserted "the most fundamental principle is notice" (FTC, 1998). Georgetown University and the FTC conducted follow-up sweeps in 1999 and 2000, respectively (FTC, 1999; FTC, 2000). In the 2000 sweep, the FTC found that 62 percent of the sites in its random sample and 97 percent of the websites the report characterized as "busiest" posted a privacy notice. While Congress did not enact comprehensive federal online privacy legislation as a result of these findings, online privacy notices nonetheless emerged as a best practice. However, in 2003 California enacted the California Online Privacy Protection Act (CAL. BUS. & PROF. CODE § 22575–22579), which required operators of commercial websites collecting personal information from California residents to post a privacy notice that meets certain requirements. Because online businesses typically serve a national audience, the California law effectively imposed a requirement for all U.S. online businesses to post a privacy notice.

Both the White House and the FTC revisited notice when they issued major reports on privacy in 2012, each of which discuss notice in the context of *transparency*. In each report, notice remains the fundamental mechanism for providing transparency to consumers. The White House report extensively references notice in its discussion of transparency, highlighting the role of notice, the challenges faced by organizations providing it in light of emerging technologies, and the significance of the consumer-company relationship in determining how notice is provided (White House, 2012). In its report, the FTC emphasized greater transparency as one means to advance its consumer privacy goals. It argued for measures that could make companies' data practices more transparent, including improved privacy notices that promote information practices and enable consumers to compare privacy practices among organizations and choose among them on that basis (FTC, 2012).

In summary, over more than four decades the privacy discussions in the United States have centered on a common theme: technology holds the potential to provide enormous benefit to the economy, firms and individuals, if the privacy concerns raised by successive generations of technology are addressed. Notice, despite its limitations, remains the primary method for promoting awareness and addressing these privacy concerns.

THE ROLES OF TRADITIONAL NOTICE

Since the principles of fair information practices were articulated in the 1970s, traditional notice has evolved to serve different functions for individuals, businesses, regulators, advocates, and the media.

Supporting Consumer Privacy Decisions

Perhaps the essential role for notice is to inform individuals' decisions about the use of their personal information. In theory, notice supports autonomy by raising awareness and placing decisions in the hands of the individual (Calo, 2012). As previously described, there is widespread agreement that awareness promotes fairness and is the first principle of fair information use. Notice provides the basis for two types of decisions. First, if choice or consent is available, the information in notices about an organization's data practices helps individuals decide whether to engage with the organization or to allow subsequent uses of their personal information. Second, notices enable individuals who value privacy to compare the data practices of different organizations and to choose which companies they wish to do business with based on those practices. In this way, privacy notices could serve as the basis for a market solution for privacy.

Supporting a Market Solution for Privacy

The Clinton administration's strategy for increasing consumer and business confidence in the use of electronic commerce proposed a market approach to privacy (White House 1997). After consulting with industry, consumer groups, and the Internet community, the administration issued principles to guide government support for the development of electronic commerce.

To help realize this vision, the Department of Commerce engaged in a parallel effort to urge companies to post privacy notices (Department of Commerce, 1995). Based on the privacy practices articulated in notices posted across the commercial sector, individuals could inform themselves, compare notices, and determine whether or not to do business with a particular company, or whether to choose to look elsewhere for a good or service. Privacy could serve as a brand differentiator, arguably attracting individuals who valued companies that collected, shared, and used data responsibly.

The Clinton administration's 1997 *Framework* also reinforced the role of private sector leadership, and the role of market forces in guiding the development of the Internet. It further urged that the Internet should not be subject to unnecessary regulation. It highlighted the need to support the efforts of private sector organizations to develop mechanisms to facilitate the successful operation of the Internet. The National Telecommunication and Information Administration (NTIA) of the Department of Commerce highlighted this support for self-regulation as a mechanism to protect privacy and published a compendium of papers authored by experts in law, economics, and business, which examined the strengths and limitations of self-regulation as an approach to protecting personal information (Department of Commerce, 1997).

Serving as a Basis for Regulation: The Federal Trade Commission

In theory, notice is an attractive regulatory vehicle for several reasons. It is based on an assumption that information provides the basis for better individual decisions when individual preferences vary. Notices also allow for flexibility in an environment characterized by a wide variety of business models. A notice regime is also relatively easy to enforce, as regulators only have to verify that the description of the practices is accurate. Notices differ from warnings, as the purpose of warnings is to prevent a high-risk activity related to health or safety, while the goal of a notice is to inform decisions (Ben-Shahar & Schneider, 2011; Calo, 2012; Fung, Graham, & Weil, 2007).

The FTC's original authority was limited to "unfair methods of competition." However, in 1938, Congress expanded the FTC's formal authority to include consumer protection. Section 5 of the FTC Act (15 USC § 45) empowers the FTC to investigate and halt any "unfair" or "deceptive" conduct in almost all industries affecting interstate commerce. This authority includes the right to investigate a company's compliance with its own asserted data privacy protection policies (Hoofnagle, 2016; Solove & Hartzog, 2014). The FTC acts under this power to investigate organizations whose practices do not conform to the policy articulated in the privacy notice. Three early examples of these "broken promise" actions include *In the Matter of Geocities* (1998) where the FTC challenged the accuracy of a website's representations about marketing uses of information collected from visitors to its website; *FTC v. Toysmart.com* (2000) where customer information was sold as part of a bankruptcy settlement in violation of a promise made in the online privacy notice; and *In the Matter of Microsoft Corp.* (2002) where the accuracy of statements made about privacy and security for the Passport service was challenged. For more detailed information about these and other FTC enforcement actions, see Solove and Hartzog (2014) and Hoofnagle (2016).

The FTC Act also has been used to provide oversight and enforcement for the U.S. self-regulatory regime. In the 1990s, industry-wide codes of conduct (as opposed to company-specific practices) served as important tools in FTC enforcement of the terms of notices (Hoofnagle 2016). FTC oversight of compliance with these codes in conjunction with the oversight of state and local authorities complements such self-regulatory enforcement by providing an independent legal incentive for each member company, and the group as a whole, to live up to its promised standard of behavior.

Informing the Public Dialogue about Data Use and Protection

An organization's posted notice make its data and privacy practices public. Notices enable nongovernmental organizations, advocates, and the press to monitor an individual company's activity with respect to data. Taken together, the notices posted by companies provide a window into the evolution of data-gathering technology and data practices. In doing so, privacy notices and the information they make available foster a public conversation about data collection and use, and make possible a role for the public in the debate about how data is used and protected. In some instances, privacy watchdogs, advocacy organizations, and interested individuals have discovered discrepancies in privacy notices or have tested a company's practices against the assertions in their notice and then brought their findings to the press and regulators.

Providing an Opportunity for Internal Review of Data Practices

The development and articulation of an accurate, current privacy notice requires considerable effort on the part of companies. To write a clear, comprehensive notice, a company must fully understand its data practices including the types of data they collect, how data is used and with whom it is shared; where and how it is stored and how long it is kept; and how it is secured and protected from loss, wrongful access, or inappropriate use. It also requires that companies understand the data protection and privacy rules and laws that apply.

While not originally envisioned to function in this way, the drafting of a privacy notice provides a company with an opportunity to inventory and assess its internal practices. This review can also serve as a platform for decision-making about whether to continue with a data practice or deployment of technology in light of considerations related to brand, and developments in law, policy, or market practices. As a result, it provides the added benefit of helping companies keep abreast of data collection and use across the organization, stay aware of the privacy impact and potential risks of data use, and make reasoned decisions about appropriate data use and protection (Calo, 2012).

CHALLENGES AND LIMITATIONS OF CURRENT NOTICES

Critics often argue that notices are of limited utility. They assert that notices are not drafted in a way that makes them useful to individuals, and that because meaningful consent is rarely available to individuals, notice is no longer needed to inform individual choice. This section addresses these arguments.

Notices Are Often Found to Be Complex, Unclear, and Too Lengthy to Be Useful to Consumers

As discussed previously, the FTC can hold companies to the assertions in their posted policies. Thus, even if the law does not require a company to post a notice, once a company does post one, it is subject to the enforcement of its terms. Because a company opens itself to liability by posting a notice, corporate counsel offices are understandably motivated to limit legal exposure and draft notices that are overly general, or lengthy and legalistic. Reidenberg et al. (2014) argue that such broad or vague statements about collection practices are the functional equivalent of no notice. In another recent study, Martin (2015) argues that the "designed obscurity" of privacy notices achieved through the use of ambiguous language sends a false signal to individuals and may undercut the ability of notices to support market decisions based on differences in information practices. As a result, notices lack the attributes needed to provide consumers with the basis for making informed decisions about privacy.

Moreover, notices were originally intended to facilitate a one-on-one relationship between individuals and websites. Today, the complex technologies, business models and data practices, and networks of vendor relationships that support digital services (e.g., Internet of Things, cloud computing, big data, behavioral advertising) are difficult to explain and challenge attempts to draft simple, readable notices. Nissenbaum (2011) suggests that even if at a given moment a notice could reasonably describe an organization's information flows and data protection measures, the rapid change in technology, analytics, and business relationships can quickly render it inaccurate.

To make traditional privacy notices useful to individuals, drafters face the challenge of communicating large amounts of complex, often technical information in a succinct, reader-friendly way. The notices that result often are hard to read (and even more difficult to understand), are read infrequently, and do not support rational decision making about privacy (Milne & Culnan, 2004). Because the ability of individuals to process information is limited, traditional notices produce information overload and do not promote informed decisions (Calo, 2012). Researchers estimate that the time invested in reading the privacy notices for the websites an individual visits on average in a given year is approximately 201 hours per year per person (McDonald & Cranor, 2008). Further, privacy notices are only one type of disclosure that individuals encounter in a typical day, resulting in what Ben-Shahar and Schneider (2011) describe as the "accumulation problem" where people encounter too many disclosures overall to digest the majority of them.

Whether a notice is clear or not depends upon whether the target audience reasonably can be expected to be able to read and comprehend it. Research has revealed significant readability issues with current privacy notices. For example, Jensen and Potts (2004) and Milne, Culnan, and Greene (2006) criticize existing notices as written at an educational level exceeding that of a large proportion of the population. Further, recent studies also found that a majority of the public incorrectly assumes that the existence of a privacy policy necessarily means that the firm will protect the confidentiality of all of their personal information (Smith, 2014; Turow, Hennessey, & Draper, 2015).

A notice's usefulness also depends in part on whether or not an individual can easily locate it. When privacy notices are difficult to access – obscured by their location or posted in lettering that blends with other text – they provide little help to individuals attempting to understand data practices or choose whether or not to engage with a company or use a device or service, as the 2009 FTC consent decree with Sears Holding Management Corporation illustrates (Hoofnagle, 2016).

Consent Is Increasingly Less Meaningful, Appropriate and/or Available to the Consumer, Raising the Question of Why Notice Is Relevant or Necessary At All

In the OECD Guidelines (1980), consent was articulated to allow individuals to limit secondary use when personal information was collected for one purpose and used for other purposes. In practice, consent is offered for a limited set of practices such as the receipt of subsequent marketing communications. As data sharing and processing drive more and more of society's most essential functions, individual consent to the collection, processing, and secondary uses of data has become more circumscribed. Use of data for socially valuable purposes, e.g., law enforcement, locating lost children, tracking deadbeat parents, medical research, fraud detection, and network security argue against restricting collection and the subsequent use of certain kinds of data on the basis of consent.

In the emerging data ecosystem, characterized by sensor-rich environments, complex vendor relationships, and the analytic processing of big data, the ability of individuals to consent to any particular instance of data collection or use may be vastly more limited than it was in the era when data was collected almost exclusively through websites, and where the individual interacted with a single entity, typically the web publisher. Given this diminished role of consent, some commenters question whether notice remains relevant at all. For example, Fred H. Cate (2006) argues that a system of data protection based on consumer choice no longer works and that notices provide individuals only with an "illusion of enhanced privacy." Cate proposes an approach that would require notice only where the collection of data is not reasonably obvious to the individual. In contrast to the critics of notice, we believe that even when not used or acted upon by consumers, traditional notices remain essential to transparency, serving the additional functions of notice we described previously.

ADDRESSING THE CHALLENGES OF NOTICE

Attempts to address the challenges encountered when informing the individual and the limitations of traditional privacy notices have taken two forms: (1) efforts to improve written privacy notices – both offline notices distributed on paper and online privacy notices and (2) efforts to create alternatives to written notices.

Efforts to Improve Written Privacy Notices

One early attempt to improve notices was an effort to design short or layered notices that would aid compliance with the provisions of the Gramm-Leach-Bliley Act of 1999 (Pub. L. 106–102, 113 Stat. 1338). GLBA requires that financial institutions issue privacy notices to their customers, and specifies the content – but not the format – of the notice. Subsequently, the Regulatory Relief Act of 2006 (Pub. L. 109–351) directed the eight GLB agencies jointly to develop a model form that companies could use to issue their GLBA privacy notices. The agencies released a model form in March 2007. The final rule issued on December 1, 2009 specified the content and format for institutions choosing to adopt the standardized GLBA notice (FTC, 2009a).

In 2001, the Centre for Information Policy Leadership (CIPL) at the law firm of Hunton and Williams LLP undertook a project to develop a layered online privacy notice that would complement an organization's existing "long" privacy notice. The goal of the project was to design a standard, simplified format that would promote better consumer decisions about whether or not to share personal information with a particular organization. The simplified format was expected to communicate effectively with individuals about how an organization collects, uses, shares, and protects personal information; individuals wishing more detail about the organization's practices could also consult the long notice (CIPL, 2006).

A third effort to improve written notices began in summer 2012 when the NTIA launched a multi-stakeholder process to address how to provide notices for mobile apps. The White House *Consumer Privacy Bill of Rights* called for the use of a multi-stakeholder process to develop voluntary, enforceable codes of conduct to address privacy questions raised by new technologies and specific data practices (White House, 2012); this was the first such process. On July 25, 2013, the Department of Commerce released a draft of the code, which required adopters to describe the types of data collected, how user-specific data is shared, where an individual can access a long form privacy notice if one exists, and the identity of the entity providing the app. The draft code includes design guidelines for the notice (Department of Commerce, 2013).

Alternatives to Traditional Notice

Efforts to develop alternatives to traditional notice have included technology solutions. The Platform for Privacy Preferences (P3P) and the AdChoices icon represent two attempts to use technology to improve online disclosures. In addition, some organizations independently have begun to develop their own tools to help inform their users.

The Platform for Privacy Preferences

P3P is a standard developed by the World Wide Web Consortium (W3C) through a multiyear process that began in 1997 and concluded in September 2001 when the W3C issued a final specification. P3P provides a syntax with which websites can code the privacy practices described in their traditional privacy notices. Web browsers and other types of software can automatically retrieve the P3P notice if one exists. The software then interprets the P3P notice and communicates the results to the user. The user learns about the site's information practices without having to read the written privacy notice (Cranor, 2002).

The adoption of P3P was voluntary. However, many perceived P3P as too difficult and complicated to use, and it never was widely implemented. Microsoft was the only major browser to support P3P; Internet Explorer 6 used P3P to implement cookie filtering. Two standalone applications also implemented P3P: Privacy Bird (http://privacybird.org) and Privacy Finder (http://www.privacyfinder.org). Both tools search for P3P privacy policies at the websites a user visits and if a policy is found, the tools then match the policy with the user's privacy preferences.

AdChoices Icon

The research projects previously described were early attempts to better inform the individual in an environment where website content was provided by a single source, typically the site owner. Today, a web page is likely to be supported by many vendors and comprise content from many different sources, each of which may follow different information practices. In February 2009, the FTC issued a staff report articulating self-regulatory principles that applied to online advertising where ad networks target online ads based on tracking individuals over time (FTC, 2009b). The principles excluded contextual advertising where an ad was based on a single visit to a web page or a single search request, and "first party" advertising where data was not shared with third parties.

In response to the FTC report, the online advertising industry formed the Digital Advertising Alliance (DAA) to promote implementation of FTC principles and to create a clickable icon, which would appear on online ads. The AdChoices icon represents an attempt to provide greater awareness in an environment where networks of online advertisers track browsing behavior across websites. Stakeholders hoped that over time, the icon would become as recognizable to consumers as the recycling symbol (http://www.aboutads.info). The DAA program appears to have been widely adopted; however researchers found instances of non-compliance (Komanduri et al., 2011). Further, the effectiveness of the program has not been extensively assessed (Kaye, 2014).

Company-Generated Tools

Organizations have taken independent steps to create tools by which consumers can view and control their own personal information. For example, the Google privacy policy includes a section on "Transparency and Choice," which describes tools generated by Google that allow users to access their account history, view and edit their preferences about the Google ads they receive, and control the sharing of their information with others through their Google Account. Facebook offers similar help to its users. Acxiom, a large data broker, offers "About the Data," a tool to help consumers learn about the data Acxiom has collected about them.

Lessons Learned and Unresolved Challenges

While it is widely acknowledged that most traditional privacy notices are too long, lack uniformity, and are difficult to comprehend, notice is still viewed as the primary means whereby organizations make the public aware of their data practices (FTC, 2012; White House, 2012). The efforts to improve notices described above yielded mixed results. For example, only two of these efforts, the AdChoices icon and the GLB model form, were widely adopted (4A's, 2012; Cranor et al., 2013). Further, questions have been raised about the effectiveness of all three, due in part to a lack of rigorous testing. Only the GLB model form was subjected to quantitative consumer testing, which assessed the performance of the final notice (Levy & Hastak, 2008). While focus groups were used in the design of the CIPL layered notice, neither the CIPL notice nor the NTIA notice for mobile applications were subject to quantitative performance testing by the designers.

Carnegie Mellon University researchers subsequently tested traditional privacy notices and layered notices (McDonald et al., 2009). They found that consumers processed information provided in layered notices faster than that found in long notices, but that readers of the layered notices such as the one developed by CIPL came away with a less accurate sense of an organization's data and privacy practices. They also found that people chose not to continue to read the long notice when they did not find the information they sought in the short notice. In another study, they tested the mobile applications notice generated by the NTIA process. They found that many users had limited understanding of the terms used in the NTIA notice (Balebako, Shay, & Cranor, 2014). This argues that testing should be an integral part of the design of alternative notices if the alternatives are to be useful and deserving of wide adoption. Nonetheless, these efforts, particularly the GLB model form, provide useful insights about what enhances or inhibits the ability to provide more effective notices.

Lessons of the GLB Model Form

GLBA requires that covered organizations disseminate privacy notices that meet the criteria established in the law's disclosure requirements and the privacy rule implementing the law. The legislation and implementing rules offer organizations incentives to adopt the GLB model form that may not exist when a notice is not required by regulation. While the use of the model privacy form is voluntary, organizations that do so benefit from the certainty that they comply with the regulations. Moreover, the standardized format and content of the model form creates efficiencies for consumers by better enabling choice about information use (to the extent available under the law) and allowing consumers to compare choices across financial institutions. Finally, the notice as articulated in the model form continues to provide a basis for FTC regulation.

Moreover, because the GLBA implementing rule does not provide the assurances of a safe harbor, some companies perceive that posting a notice in a way other than that prescribed by the model form increases their risk of exposure to an FTC enforcement action. The model's clear rules for content and format arguably lessen that exposure. Finally, rigorous consumer testing increased the probability that the form would be effective (Levy & Hastak, 2008). However, it should also be noted that the model form was developed for a single industry and for a limited set of business practices. Even so, the design and testing of the form took several years before it became final, raising questions about its ability to scale.

In 2013, researchers at Carnegie Mellon University assessed over 3,000 GLBA policies based on data collected using an automated web crawler (Cranor et al., 2013). The study highlighted the challenges faced by that organizations using the form when disclosing what types of information they collect. Restrictions on what language may be used to describe how information is collected also posed problems. While standardized language facilitated transparency and comparisons across institutions, the researchers found some of the terms used were redundant or ambiguous. However, when researchers compared privacy practices across similar institutions, they found differences in their privacy practices, suggesting that making a company's data practices more conspicuous could highlight these differences and thereby empower consumers' decision-making. Despite the issues raised by this research, the standardized table format used in the GLB model form nonetheless appears to hold promise for a better way to provide individuals necessary information about data and privacy practices.

Promise and Challenges of a "Nutrition Label" Format for Privacy Notices

Carnegie Mellon University researchers tested alternative forms of privacy notices, comparing them to natural language, full-text policies (Kelley et al., 2010). They found that of the options they tested, the standardized table often compared to a "nutrition label" format yielded the best results. They concluded that the success of this approach resulted both from the table format and the standardized language, which improved accuracy, the ability to locate information, the speed with which an individual could locate information, and the individual's experience in reading notices. These findings argued for developing a format for short privacy notices similar to that of nutritional labels.

Despite its promise, developing a privacy notice modelled after food nutrition labels poses significant challenges. The nutrition content of food can be analyzed and quantified, and the numerical values posted on the labels can be objectively tested and verified by a third party. The result is a set of reliable numbers the consumer can compare easily. In the United States, consumers can also use the label to compare products against numerical government nutrition recommendations. These values are unlikely to change quickly, and if they do, their accuracy can be readily tested in a lab. Creating an accurate nutritional label involves simply filling in the boxes on the form. As a result, the nutrition label has been at least moderately effective at promoting consumer choice, creating a basis for regulation, and providing a source of information for consumer advocates and the media (Fung, Graham, & Weil, 2007; Hadden, 1986).

However, privacy notices pose challenges not faced by entities adopting the nutrition label for food. The content and format of the nutrition label are fixed by regulation and apply across products; by contrast, data practices and protections do not lend themselves to quantified expression. For example, while nutrition labels are based on "percent of Recommended Daily Allowance," there is no comparable standard for information practices given the variety of business models and industries (Bambauer et al., 2017). Moreover, for food, the product is fixed at purchase and the individual controls its use after purchase. For information, the individual currently has little comparable control as the company controls future uses of the data. All future uses are unlikely to be known at the time of disclosure and may be subject to change. While the effectiveness of both nutrition labels and privacy notices depends on consumers' ability to understand the information disclosed in the notice and make appropriate comparisons, these issues challenge attempts to accurately describe the organization's data practices in a standard format across industries and business models.

Looking Ahead

In its 2012 report, the FTC proposed that to promote better comprehension and comparison of privacy practices, notices should be "clearer, shorter, and more standardized" (FTC, 2012, p. 61). It recognized that a rigid format for use across all sectors is not appropriate, and that it would be necessary to accommodate differences in business models across industry sectors. It stated that to allow individuals to compare privacy practices across companies and encourage companies to compete on privacy, privacy notices should contain some standardized elements such as terminology and format. How this would work in practice remains an open question. Further, the time required by efforts aimed at improving notices described previously suggest that creating new forms of effective notice is a long-term project and that these efforts are unlikely to be successful unless consumer testing is part of the design process. New technologies such as mobile applications and the Internet of Things (IoT) pose further challenges to providing notice.

EMERGING TECHNOLOGICAL CHALLENGES

The prior sections focused primarily on issues related to providing notice in traditional computing on desktops and laptops. Here we review the challenges raised by new technologies and data ecosystems, which may provide little opportunity to interface with the consumer. This limited opportunity for interaction with the consumer makes providing notice difficult and sometimes impossible.

The broad implementation of notices starting in the 1990s began in a data environment that centered primarily on the collection of data via websites. Privacy protections were based on a theory of control – individuals who were made aware of data practices and protection measures and provided the opportunity to choose based on assertions in a posted privacy policy could make decisions about the collection, use, and sharing of data pertaining to them.

The advent of big data and new technologies such as mobile applications, the IoT, and sensor-rich environments where personal information may be collected, shared, and processed silently and ubiquitously, and for a wide range of purposes, poses new privacy concerns and challenges for addressing these concerns. Privacy concerns arise when information practices conflict with an individual's reasonable expectations about how their information should be used. The physical characteristics of these new technologies may make it difficult to make such new uses visible to the individual, issues exacerbated in a global environment with varying literacy levels.

Big Data Analytics

Using analytics to process what is commonly referred to as "big data" raises its own challenges. Analytics are often applied to data originally collected for another purpose and combined with data from other sources. The individual may be aware of the initial collection and uses of data, but not of the subsequent analytic processing. Further, the information may also be shared with and used by third parties of whom the individual is not aware. Some of these third parties may collect data on behalf of consumer-facing companies such as data brokers, advertising networks or mobile analytics providers. Because these third parties do not have relationships or direct contact with consumers, providing notice about these activities is problematic. There are also calls for increased transparency around algorithms when they are used to make automated decisions (Citron & Pasquale, 2014).

Perhaps the aspect of big data analytics that poses the greatest challenge is the nature of the processing itself. Researchers do not approach large data sets in search of the answer to a question; rather, they explore the data for what it may reveal. Thus, data may be used in ways that could not have been anticipated and therefore would not have been included in a privacy notice (Cate & Mayer-Schoenberger, 2012).

Providing effective notice later, when these new uses actually occur, is not practical. Data may have been collected long before its use and amassed from many different sources, and it may no longer be possible to locate and contact what could be thousands of individuals whose data was used. Further, using big data analytics to create personal information from nonpersonal information after collection, poses additional challenges (Crawford & Schultz, 2014). For example, Target used analytics to infer that a customer was pregnant based on a record of her purchases, thereby creating new personal information (Duhigg, 2012). Absent new restrictions on data collection and use, proposals for addressing some of the privacy and other fairness challenges of the secondary use of big data include companies' implementation of privacy impact assessments, privacy-by-design processes, accountability programs, and ethical reviews to avoid undertaking legal but questionable data uses (Calo, 2013).

Mobile Applications

Mobile applications also pose challenges to notice that do not exist with applications that run on a traditional PC. First, the small screens on mobile devices provide limited space to display a privacy notice. Second, applications can access information on the user's phone such as contacts, photos, or actual location, even when that information is not necessary for the application to function. Users may be unaware of these information practices if they are not disclosed. Without awareness, it may be impossible for individuals to make informed choices about using a particular application (Balebako et al., 2013). Finally, the constraints of the application environment raise questions about how and when notice should be provided, where the notice should be stored, and when it should be displayed.

Internet of Things and Sensors

The IoT refers to the ability of everyday objects to connect to the Internet and to send and receive data. The "smart devices" that make up the IoT can include automobiles, home appliances, or wearable fitness devices, to name only a few. Mobile devices with WI-FI or Bluetooth turned on enable sensors in physical places to receive signals from nearby devices. For example, sensors in retail stores can use a unique identifier broadcast by the mobile device to track how customers move through the store; often a third-party analytics firm may do this tracking without the customer's knowledge (Soltani, 2015). As is the case with mobile applications, individuals are unlikely to be aware of the information capabilities of these devices or the fact their device is being tracked, highlighting the need for awareness at the time the individual makes a purchase decision about a device or chooses to enable a particular feature.

RECOMMENDATIONS: MOVING FROM NOTICE TO TRANSPARENCY

Until recently, the term "organizational transparency" primarily was used as a rhetorical device or as an *ad hoc* construct, the meaning of which varied by field of study (Schnackenberg & Tomlinson, 2016). For example, the meaning of transparency differed depending on whether one referred to, for example, financial markets, organizational governance or trust in online commerce. While Schnackenberg and Tomlinson did not specifically address privacy notices, their conclusions appear to be relevant to privacy as well. In this review of the literature on transparency, the authors define transparency as a *perception of the quality of information received from a sender* which includes three dimensions of information quality: the *degree* of information disclosure (including the perception that relevant information is complete and received in a timely fashion), the *clarity* of the disclosure, and the *accuracy* of the disclosure.

In the context of privacy, some have argued that transparency is a mechanism that promotes trust in organizations because quality disclosures can enhance perceptions that an organization is trustworthy (Richards & Hartzog, 2016; Schnackenberg & Tomlinson, 2016). Trust affects consumers' willingness to assume the risks of disclosing personal information and is important to building a long-term customer relationship where consumers are vulnerable and must rely on "strangers" to protect their interests due to information asymmetries (Culnan & Williams, 2009; Richards & Hartzog, 2016). Organizations foster trust if they provide assurances that they will not behave opportunistically. Therefore, good quality disclosures can signal to individuals that a company can be trusted with their personal information, provided that the company abides by the practices disclosed in the notice (Culnan & Bies, 2003).

As a practical matter, notice will continue to serve as the starting point for transparency. However, given the growing complexity of the emerging data ecosystem, the ubiquity of data collection, and the incidence of real-time processing, a single notice can no longer reasonably be expected to serve the many purposes of supporting individual choice, regulation, and public awareness and education. Currently, some argue that the broader goal of transparency has been reduced to notice based on a set of procedural rules against which compliance could be measured (Cate, 2006). We propose instead that to achieve an *environment of transparency*, organizations should deploy, and policy makers should support a variety of methods for reaching all stakeholders. We now turn to our specific recommendations for improving transparency including the need for business buy-in and regulatory guidance.

Organizations Should Continue to Provide Comprehensive, Technical Notices to Facilitate the Roles of Regulators and Advocates

Long notices often read like legal documents and may include comprehensive technical descriptions of data collection and use. Such notices often are of little use to individuals, who are unwilling and uninterested in investing the time to read them, and are often ill equipped to understand them. In spite of these familiar shortcomings, these notices are still important and necessary to transparency, as they provide a basis for oversight by regulators and others. However, these notices lack the clarity and accuracy needed by individuals and therefore fail to provide transparency to an important group of stakeholders.

Organizations Should Also Develop Alternative Forms of Disclosure for Individuals, Providing Them with Relevant Information in Clear, Understandable Language, in a Format That Promotes Comprehension and That Is Delivered at the Appropriate Time

Traditional comprehensive notices do not support transparency for individuals because they are perceived as being unclear, and they may not be available at the appropriate time. Alternative disclosures for consumers are needed that are brief, succinct, and accurate yet include the relevant information that promotes individual understanding about data collection and use. In some situations, disclosure should be designed and delivered just in time to facilitate choice when choice is available, such as whether or not to allow a mobile application to make use of the individual's exact location. To create these disclosures, organizations will need to understand how to communicate effectively with their target audiences. Firms will need to understand what information individuals need, and develop methods for communicating this information quickly and clearly. Existing research on labels and warnings may prove instructive here.

The IoT in particular will require creative approaches to notice, particularly where devices may not have a screen and where collection of information is unexpected or not obvious or visible. The FTC has called for such innovation in notices for the IoT (FTC, 2015).

Notices Should Be Developed as Part of the System Development Process

Because privacy notices have served an integral role in regulation, legal counsel is often tasked with drafting notices independent of the development of the applications described in the notice. Typically these notices are designed to be comprehensive and to avoid liability. Importantly, because notices are often viewed as a vehicle for compliance, they customarily are drafted at the end of the system development process, after decisions about data practices have been implemented. When privacy notices are viewed as a compliance responsibility and overseen by the legal department, the rapid pace of system development makes it difficult to coordinate the privacy notice with new features of the application. Given this disconnect, the rapid development cycles in many firms increases the likelihood that their privacy notice will not accurately reflect the details of their current data practices.

Privacy by design (PbD) is an approach to protecting privacy by embedding it into the design specifications of technologies (Cavoukian, 2011). While PbD is increasingly considered fundamental to responsible governance within organizations, it has focused almost exclusively on data practices, often as they are implemented in technology. Yet privacy by design also offers an opportunity to build and improve transparency. Rather than add the privacy notice on at the end, notices can be integrated into the design of the system.

Early research on risk communication for products may also provide helpful insights. Researchers have argued for a *system* of warnings consisting of multiple disclosures designed for a variety of audiences. The design of the warnings would be considered an integral part of the overall product design process (Laughery & Hammond, 1999). This approach can advance privacy notices that are more relevant, communicate better to individual users, and integrated into the user's interaction with a device or system. Designers, supported by legal and other appropriate personnel, can work together to address the constraints of the system when designing notice. By integrating the creation of notice into the design process, designers ideally can take advantage of opportunities to deliver visual or auditory notices at times they are most useful. It can also allow developers to take advantage of a variety of channels by which notices can be delivered, depending on the audience, and the constraints or opportunities of the system (Schaub et al., 2015).

Contextual Expectations Should Serve as a Key Consideration for Improving Consumer Notices

Individual privacy expectations recently have been defined in terms of social norms (Nissenbaum, 2010). These norms define what information practices are acceptable and do not raise privacy concerns in a given context. For example, a recent national public opinion survey found that 87 percent of individuals were concerned about the sharing of their information with others without their knowledge and consent, suggesting this practice violates social norms (NCSA, 2015). Reusing information in a way that is related to the original purpose of the collection generally does not raise privacy concerns because such use conforms to established social norms (Martin, 2015; Nissenbaum, 2010). These can include sharing an address with a carrier who will deliver a purchase, providing a credit card number to a bank for payment processing, internal operations, fraud prevention or first-party marketing (FTC, 2012). Because these uses are obvious and/or widely accepted and often do not involve consent, it may be necessary to mention them only briefly in the consumer notice, if at all. On the other hand, heightened transparency is needed when information is processed in ways that violate consumer expectations and are unexpected in light of the context. Potential contextual issues should be assessed separately, as part of a privacy impact assessment or ethical review (White House, 2015)

Technology Should Promote Transparency by Supporting the Availability and Utility of Notice

While initial efforts at technological solutions have enjoyed limited success, technology may still play a significant role in fostering more effective transparency that empowers individuals. One example of such work is the Usable Privacy Policy Project at Carnegie Mellon University (http://www.usableprivacy.org/learn_more). The project responds to the limitations of natural language, privacy notices, and other obstacles by using machine natural language processing. For users, the project holds out the possibility of access to notices that would inform privacy decision-making. For website operators, it promises a way to overcome the limitations of existing natural language notices without imposing new requirements.

In addition to machine-readable notices, technology can also provide alternatives to traditional text notices. These can include images, icons, LEDs, or auditory notices in the form of sounds or spoken word. The mode by which a notice is delivered is best selected to attract the individual's attention.

Public Education Should Work at the Core of Efforts to Promote Transparency

Transparency also requires that the public be broadly informed about data collection and use – not only on an application-by-application basis, but also as a foundation for navigating the data ecosystem at large. This public awareness fosters greater understanding about data uses, their benefits to the individual and to society, and the risks that they may pose. Because it is difficult to explain complexity to people who are unfamiliar with a particular practice or technology (Ben-Shahar & Schneider, 2011), privacy notices cannot both educate individuals and be timely and succinct. Therefore, public education must be a separate and ongoing initiative. Brief, one-time attempts at public education prompted by some event or the release of some product or application will not be sufficient. For example, the success of the nutrition label is due in part because the label was accompanied by an extensive, distinct consumer education effort that continues today (Fung, Graham, & Weil, 2007). As the experience with the nutrition label also demonstrated, public education is not a one-time event. It is also a responsibility that should be shared by the public and private sectors. Ideally it should begin when children are young, in the same way that we begin to educate them at an early age about health, financial literacy, and various safety issues.

But while public education is critical, it does not obviate the need we described earlier for the comprehensive notice and the consumer-focused notice. Nor does it relieve companies of the responsibility to engage in responsible, ethical data practices. Rather, education is an essential complement to notice as it enables the public to make rational choices about data use based on a full understanding of the risks and benefits of a particular data ecosystem (Bambauer et al., 2017). Moreover, if individuals are educated, abbreviated notices or notification icons are more likely to effectively provide them with needed information.

Better Transparency Will Depend on Regulatory Guidance and Business Buy-In

Proposals for providing consumers with notices that are not comprehensive but that highlight key information that supports decision-making have met with some resistance. In particular, companies have voiced concerns that posting such abbreviated notices may open them to liability. Requiring companies to post both an abbreviated and a comprehensive notice would address such concerns. Regulators must provide business with clarity and assurances about their legal responsibilities with respect to notice to reduce industry concerns about the risk of exposure to regulatory action.

If regulators are unable or unwilling to motivate companies to act, the business community will likely resist a call for better consumer notices. For example, Smith (1993) found that given an ambiguous external environment, executives rarely take active steps to develop new privacy practices absent some external event that forces them to act. Recent events support his findings. The FTC content analysis of websites and its report on online behavioral advertising respectively resulted in the adoption of online privacy notices and the development of the AdChoices icon without new legislation (FTC, 2000; FTC, 2009b). Regulators could advance transparency for consumers, for example, by conducting web surveys to assess whether firms are complying with existing regulations related to notice visibility and usability, issuing guidance and policy statements, and nudging business through other nonregulatory methods.

Further, where appropriate, the FTC should decline to endorse any solution that has not been subjected to rigorous consumer testing to determine its effectiveness. This would include new disclosure mandates as well as self-regulatory requirements articulated either through industry-led processes or those established through a government-led multi-stakeholder process. Typically, two types of research should inform the design of new disclosures. Qualitative research (e.g., focus groups) is used to design initial prototypes. Quantitative research is used to test prototypes to see which performs best in meeting the objectives of the new disclosure. Quantitative testing is important because *ad hoc* theories about what works best are not always reliable and must be validated against objective criteria. For example, the FTC conducted both qualitative and quantitative research to design the GLB model form and to assess its usefulness to consumers before releasing the final rule.

Absent pressure from government, business community leadership, and collaboration with consumer and privacy advocates, notices will fail to provide individuals with the usable information they need about data practices. Richards and Hartzog (2016) argue that viewing transparency through a lens of trust could move privacy from procedural compliance to a basis for building trusted and sustainable relationships. For companies adopting this perspective, transparency should not pose a threat. In fact, for responsible companies, transparency should both enhance their relationship with consumers and promote the innovative, responsible use of data. One study found that when privacy information is made more salient, some consumers are willing to pay a small premium to purchase from privacy-protective websites. What is particularly interesting about this study is that it is based on actual purchase behavior, rather than on the participants' stated intentions, which may or may not reflect how they will actually behave. Here, the participants in the experiment used their own credit cards to make actual purchases. The authors hypothesize that where there are transparency and privacy protections, privacy may serve as a selling point (Tsai et al., 2011). Where companies provide value in exchange for the use of their data, transparency enables consumers to evaluate the risk-benefit trade-off for disclosure (Awad & Krishan, 2006). Given that transparency is unlikely to be achieved solely through new regulation, it is ultimately up to companies to take steps to ensure their data practices are fair, rather than merely complying with a set of procedural guidelines.

CONCLUSION

Privacy notices currently serve many purposes: they provide a basis for individual choice, they serve as the basis for regulation, they promote public awareness of data practices, and they enable oversight by privacy experts and advocates of issues related to the collection, processing, and protection of information about individuals. The process of creating notices also provides an opportunity for organizations to review and understand their data collection practices and make responsible decisions about internal data flows and external data uses. We have discussed the shortcomings of traditional notices as a tool for promoting individual choice. We also have described the results of efforts to improve them through the use of layered or short notices, reviewed attempts to develop technological alternatives to traditional notice, and identified the challenges that new technologies pose to notice. We further argued that the way data is collected, used, processed, and stored in the emerging data ecosystem requires not simply improved notices, but a multipronged approach to informing the individual about data and privacy practices based on an overall *environment of transparency*.

Moving from notice to transparency challenges both regulators and business in ways that could not have been envisioned in 1973 when the original FIPPS were created. While there is agreement across a range of stakeholders that current privacy notices are simply not working, new approaches grounded in procedural compliance, whether mandatory or voluntary, are unlikely to deliver transparency. We believe that our calls for the integration of the design of notices into the system development process as part of privacy by design, public education, and new technological solutions hold promise for delivering the transparency that is central to fairness. For this to happen, organizations need to recognize the business value that transparency can yield. Finally, while transparency is a necessary condition for the fair use of personal information envisioned by the FIPPS, transparency alone is not sufficient, since all of the fair information principles contribute to fairness.

REFERENCES

Awad, Naveen F. and Krishan, M. S. Krishan. 2006. The Personalization Privacy Paradox: An Empirical Evaluation of Information Transparency and the Willingness to Be Profiled Online for Personalization. *MIS Quarterly*, 30(1): 13–28.

Balebako, Rebecca, Jung, Jaeyeon, Lu, Wei, Cranor, Lorrie Faith, and Nguyen, Carolyn. 2013. "Little Brother's Watching You": Raising Awareness of Data Leaks on Smartphones. In *Symposium on Usable Privacy and Security* (SOUPS). Newcastle. https://cups.cs.cmu.edu/soups/2013/proceedings/a12_Balebako.pdf.

Balebako, Rebecca, Shay, Richard, and Cranor, Lorrie Faith. 2014. *Is Your Inseam a Biometric? A Case Study on the Role of Usability Studies in Developing Public Policy*. Workshop on Usable Security (USEC 2014), San Diego. http://lorrie.cranor.org/pubs/usec14-inseam.pdf

Bambauer, Jane R., Loe, Jonathan, and Winkelman, D. Alex. 2017. A Bad Education. *University of Illinois Law Review*, 2017(1): 109–166.

Ben-Shahar, Omri and Schneider, Carl. 2011. The Failure of Mandated Discourse. *University of Pennsylvania Law Review*, 159(3): 647–749.

Calo, Ryan. 2012. Against Notice Skepticism in Privacy (and Elsewhere). *Notre Dame Law Review*, 87(3): 1027–1072.

Calo, Ryan. 2013. Consumer Subject Review Boards: A Thought Experiment. In *Big Data & Privacy: Making Ends Meet Digest*. Washington: Future of Privacy Forum. http://www.futureofprivacy.org/big-data-privacy-workshop-paper.

Cate, Fred H. 2006. The Failure of Fair Information Practice Principles. In Jane K. Winn (ed.), *Consumer Protection in the Age of the Information Economy*: 360–363. Burlington: Ashgate.

Cate, Fred H. and Mayer-Schoenberger, Viktor. 2012. Notice and Consent in a World of Big Data, *Microsoft Global Privacy Summary Report and Outcomes*. http://www.techpolicy.com/NoticeConsent-inWorldBigData.aspx.

Cavoukian, Ann. 2011. *Privacy by Design: The Seven Foundational Principles.* Information and Privacy Commissioner of Ontario, Canada. https://www.ipc.on.ca/images/Resources/7foundationalprinciples.pdf.

Centre for Information Policy Leadership. 2006. *Ten Steps to Develop a Multilayered Privacy Notice.* https://www.huntonprivacyblog.com/wp-content/files/2012/07/Centre-10-Steps-to-Multilayered-Privacy-Notice.pdf.

Citron, Danielle Keats and Pasquale, Frank A. 2014. The Scored Society: Due Process for Automated Protections. *Washington Law Review,* 89(1): 2–33.

Cranor, Lorrie Faith. 2002. *Web Privacy with P3P.* Sebastapol: O'Reilly & Associates.

Cranor, Lorrie Faith, Idouchi, Kelly, Leon, Pedro Giovanni, Sleeper, Manya, and Ur, Blase. 2013. Are They Actually Any Different? Comparing Thousands of Financial Institutions' Privacy Policies. In *Twelfth Workshop on the Economics of Information Security* (WEIS), Washington, DC. http://weis2013.econinfosec.org/papers/CranorWEIS2013.pdf.

Crawford, Kate and Schultz, Jason. 2014. Big Data and Due Process: Toward a Framework to Redress Predictive Privacy Harms. *Boston College Law Review,* 55(1): 93–127. http://bclawreview.org/files/2014/01/03_crawford_schultz.pdf.

Culnan, Mary J. and Bies, Robert J. 2003. Consumer Privacy: Balancing Economic and Justice Considerations. *Journal of Social Issues,* 59(2): 323–342.

Culnan, Mary J. and Williams, Cynthia Clark. 2009. How Ethics Can Enhance Organizational Privacy: Lessons from the ChoicePoint and TJX Data Breaches. *MIS Quarterly,* 33(4): 673–687.

Duhigg, Charles. 2012. How Companies Learn Your Secrets. *New York Times Magazine,* February 16. http://www.nytimes.com/2012/02/19/magazine/shopping-habits.html?_r=0

4A's. 2012. *DAA Announces "Your AdChoices" Consumer Education Campaign.* Press Release, Jan. 20. http://www.aaaa.org/news/press/Pages/012012_daa_adchoices.aspx.

Fung, Archon, Graham, Mary, and Weil, David. 2007. *Full Disclosure: The Perils and Promise of Transparency.* New York: Cambridge University Press.

Gellman, Robert. 2016. *Fair Information Practices: A Basic History.* Version 2.16. http://bobgellman.com/rg-docs/rg-FIPShistory.pdf.

Hadden, Susan G. 1986. *Read the Label: Reducing Risk by Providing Information.* Boulder: Westview Press.

Hoofnagle, Chris Jay. 2016. *Federal Trade Commission: Privacy Law and Policy.* New York: Cambridge University Press.

Jensen, Carlos and Potts, Colin. 2004. Privacy Policies as Decision-Making Tools: An Evaluation of Online Privacy Notices. In *CHI 04 Proceedings:* 471–478, Vienna.

Kaye, Kate. 2014. Study: Consumers Don't Know What AdChoices Privacy Icon Is. *Advertising Age:* January 29. http://adage.com/article/privacy-and-regulation/study-consumers-adchoices-privacy-icon/291374/.

Kelley, Patrick Gage, Cesca, Lucian, Bresee, Joanna, and Cranor, Lorrie Faith. 2010. *Standardizing Privacy Notices: An Online Study of the Nutrition Label Approach,* Carnegie Mellon CyLab Report CMU-CyLab-09-014. https://www.cylab.cmu.edu/files/pdfs/tech_reports/CMUCyLab09014.pdf.

Komanduri, Saranga, Shay, Richard, Norcie, Greg, Ur, Blase, and Cranor, Lorrie Faith. 2011. *AdChoices? Compliance with Online Behavioral Advertising Notice and Choice Requirements.* Carnegie Mellon CyLab Report 11-005. https://www.cylab.cmu.edu/files/pdfs/tech_reports/CMUCyLab11005.pdf.

Laughery, Kenneth R. and Hammond, Amy. 1999. Overview. In Michael S. Wogalter, David M. DeJoy, and Kenneth R. Laughery (eds.). *Warnings and Risk Communication:* 1–11. Philadelphia: Taylor & Frances Inc.

Levy, Alan S. and Hastak, Manoj. 2008. *Consumer Comprehension of Financial Privacy Notices.* http://www.ftc.gov/privacy/privacyinitiatives/Levy-Hastak-Report.pdf.

Martin, Kirsten. 2015. Privacy Notices as Tabula Rasa: An Empirical Investigation into How Complying with a Privacy Notice Is Related to Meeting Privacy Expectations Online. *Journal of Public Policy and Marketing,* 34(2): 210–227.

McDonald, Alecia M. and Cranor, Lorrie Faith. 2008. The Cost of Reading Privacy Policies. *I/S, A Journal of Law and Policy for the Information Society,* 4(3):540–565.

McDonald, Alecia M., Reeder, Robert W., Kelley, Patrick Gage, and Cranor, Lorrie Faith. 2009. A Comparative Study of Online Privacy Policies and Formats. In Ian Goldberg and Mikhail J. Atallah (eds.). *Privacy Enhancing Technologies: 9th International Symposium PETS 2009:* 37–55, Seattle.

Milne, George R. and Culnan, Mary J. 2004. Strategies of Reducing Online Privacy Risks: Why Consumers Read (or Don't Read) Online Privacy Notices. *Journal of Interactive Marketing*, 18(3): 15–29.

Milne, George R., Culnan, Mary J., and Greene, Henry. 2006. A Longitudinal Assessment of Online Privacy Notice Readability. *Journal of Public Policy and Marketing*, 25(2): 238–249.

National Cyber Security Alliance. 2015. *Results of Consumer Data Privacy Survey Reveal Critical Need for All Digital Citizens to Participate in Data Privacy Day.* https://staysafeonline.org/about-us/news/results-of-consumer-data-privacy-survey-reveal-critical-need-for-all-digital-citizens-to-participate-in-data-privacy-day.

Nissenbaum, Helen. 2010. *Privacy in Context.* Palo Alto: Stanford Law Books.

Nissenbaum, Helen. 2011. A Contextual Approach to Privacy Online. *Daedalus*, 140(4): 32–48.

Organization for Economic Co-operation and Development (OECD). 1980. *Guidelines Governing the Protection of Privacy and Transborder Data Flow of Personal Data.* http://www.oecd.org/sti/ieconomy/oecdguidelinesontheprotectionofprivacyandtransborderflowsofpersonaldata.htm.

Reidenberg, Joel R., Russell, N. Cameron, Callen, Alexander J., Qasir, Sophia, and Norton, Thomas B. 2014. Privacy Harms and the Effectiveness of the Notice and Choice Framework. *TPRC, 42nd Research Conference on Communication, Information, and Internet Policy.* http://papers.ssrn.com/sol3/Papers.cfm?abstract_id=2418247.

Richards, Neil M. and Hartzog, Woodrow. 2016. Taking Trust Seriously in Privacy Law. *Stanford Technology Law Review.* 19(3): 431–472.

Schaub, Florian, Balebako, Rebecca, Durity, Adam L., and Cranor, Lorrie Faith. 2015. A Design Space for Effective Privacy Notices. In *Symposium on Usable Privacy and Security (SOUPS)*. Ottawa, Canada. http://ra.adm.cs.cmu.edu/anon/isr2015/CMU-ISR-15-105.pdf.

Schnackenberg, A. K. and Tomlinson, E. C. 2016. Organizational Transparency: A New Perspective on Managing Trust in Organization–Stakeholder Relationships. *Journal of Management.* 42(7): 1784–1810.

Smith, Aron. 2014. Half of Online Americans Don't Know What a Privacy Policy Is. *Fact Tank. Pew Research Center.* December 4. http://www.pewresearch.org/fact-tank/2014/12/04/half-of-americans-dont-know-what-a-privacy-policy-is/.

Smith, H. Jeff. 1993. Privacy Policies and Practices: Inside the Organizational Maze. *Communications of the ACM*, 36(12): 105–22.

Solove, Daniel J. and Hartzog, Woodrow. 2014. The FTC and the New Common Law of Privacy. *Columbia Law Review*, 114(3): 583–676.

Soltani, Ashkan. 2015. *Privacy Trade-offs in Retail Tracking.* Federal Trade Commission, Apr. 30. https://www.ftc.gov/news-events/blogs/techftc/2015/04/privacy-trade-offs-retail-tracking.

Tsai, Janice Y, Egelman, Serge, Cranor, Lorrie Faith, and Acquisti, Alessandro. 2011. The Effect of Online Privacy Information on Purchasing Behavior: An Experimental Study. *Information Systems Research*, 22(2): 254–68.

Turow, Joseph, Hennessy, Michael, and Draper, Nora. 2015. *The Tradeoff Fallacy.* Philadelphia: Annenberg School of Communication, University of Pennsylvania. https://www.asc.upenn.edu/sites/default/files/TradeoffFallacy_1.pdf.

U.S. Department of Commerce. 1995. *Privacy and the NII: Safeguarding Telecommunications-Related Personal Information.* https://www.ntia.doc.gov/legacy/ntiahome/privwhitepaper.html.

U.S. Department of Commerce. 1997. *Privacy and Self Regulation in the Information Age.* http://www.ntia.doc.gov/report/1997/privacy-and-self-regulation-information-age.

U.S. Department of Commerce, National Telecommunications & Information Administration. 2013. *Short Form Notice Code of Conduct to Promote Transparency in Mobile App Practices.* https://www.ntia.doc.gov/files/ntia/publications/july_25_code_draft.pdf.

U.S. Department of Health Education and Welfare. 1973. *Records, Computers and the Rights of Citizens: Report of the Secretary's Advisory Committee on Automated Personal Data Systems.* http://epic.org/privacy/hew1973report/default.html.

U.S. Federal Trade Commission. 1996. *Staff Report: Public Workshop on Consumer Privacy on the Global Information Infrastructure.* http://www.ftc.gov/reports/staff-report-public-workshop-consumer-privacy-global-information-infrastructure.

U.S. Federal Trade Commission. 1998. *Privacy Online: Report to Congress.* https://www.ftc.gov/sites/default/files/documents/reports/privacy-online-report-congress/priv-23a.pdf.

U.S. Federal Trade Commission. 1999. *Self-Regulation and Privacy Online: FTC Report to Congress.* https://www.ftc.gov/news-events/press-releases/1999/07/self-regulation-and-privacy-online-ftc-report-congress.

U.S. Federal Trade Commission. 2000. *Privacy Online: Fair Information Practices in the Electronic Marketplace: A Report to Congress.* https://www.ftc.gov/sites/default/files/documents/reports/privacy-online-fair-information-practices-electronic-marketplace-federal-trade-commission-report/privacy2000 text.pdf.

U.S. Federal Trade Commission. 2009a. *Final Model Privacy Form Under the Gramm-Leach-Bliley-Act, Final Rule.* 16 CFR Part 313. https://www.ftc.gov/sites/default/files/documents/federal_register_notices/final-model-privacy-form-under-gramm-leach-bliley-act-16-cfr-part-313/091201gramm-leach.pdf.

U.S. Federal Trade Commission. 2009b. *Self-Regulatory Principles for Online Behavioral Advertising.* https://www.ftc.gov/sites/default/files/documents/reports/federal-trade-commission-staff-report-self-regu latory-principles-online-behavioral-advertising/p085400behavadreport.pdf.

U.S. Federal Trade Commission. 2012. *Protecting Consumer Privacy in an Era of Rapid Change: Recommendations for Businesses and Policymakers.* https://www.ftc.gov/sites/default/files/documents/reports/federal-trade-commission-report-protecting-consumer-privacy-era-rapid-change-recommendations/120326privacyreport.pdf.

U.S. Federal Trade Commission. 2015. *Internet of Things: Privacy & Security in a Connected World.* https://www.ftc.gov/system/files/documents/reports/federal-trade-commission-staff-report-november-2013-work shop-entitled-internet-things-privacy/150127iotrpt.pdf.

U.S. National Information Infrastructure Task Force. 1995. *Privacy and the National Information Infrastructure: Options for Providing and Using Personal Information.* https://aspe.hhs.gov/report/options-promoting-privacy-national-information-infrastructure).

U.S. Privacy Protection Study Commission. 1977. *Personal Privacy in an Information Society: The Report of the Privacy Protection Study Commission.* Washington. https://www.epic.org/privacy/ppsc1977report/

Westin, Alan F. 1967. *Privacy and Freedom.* New York: Atheneum.

The White House. 1997. *A Framework for Global Electronic Commerce.* Washington, DC. http://clinton4 .nara.gov/WH/New/Commerce.

The White House. 2012. *Consumer Data Privacy in a Networked World: A Framework for Protecting Privacy and Promoting Innovation in the Global Digital Economy.* https://www.whitehouse.gov/sites/default/files/privacy-final.pdf.

The White House. 2015. *Discussion Draft: Consumer Privacy Bill of Rights Act.* https://www.whitehouse .gov/sites/default/files/omb/legislative/letters/cpbr-act-of-2015-discussion-draft.pdf.

The While House. 2016. *National Privacy Research Strategy.* https://www.whitehouse.gov/sites/default/files/nprs_nstc_review_final.pdf.

30

It Takes Data to Protect Data

David A. Hoffman and Patricia A. Rimo

In October 2011, at the Halted Hacker conference in Miami, McAfee employees demonstrated the ability to remotely access insulin pumps.[1] While most of the press attention focused on the ability to remotely inject a fatal dose of insulin, the privacy team at Intel Corporation (the company that would soon acquire McAfee and rename it Intel Security) started analyzing the impact similar breaches could have if sensitive personal data, such as the medical information available in an insulin pump, were stolen. Cybersecurity attacks on companies' networks were occurring all the time, but this particular hack signaled a change in focus. The insulin pump hack demonstrated the need for robust cybersecurity to protect lives and revealed an entirely new universe of connected devices – now known as the Internet of Things (IoT) – that collect, store, and process personal data.

Researchers at Intel Security quickly turned their attention to the problem of how to provide better predictive protections against cyber attackers. They seized upon the idea of using data from machines that were being hacked to predict and protect against attacks on other machines. The researchers learned that this approach could be highly effective, but also understood the need to demonstrate the responsible use of the data to ensure both security and privacy.

While some would pit security and privacy against each other, arguing that individuals must choose one over the other, the two actually can and should reinforce each other. It's this model that forms the basis of this chapter: Privacy and security should be pursued hand in hand as we move toward an increasingly connected, digital world. To fully realize the benefits of information technology, big data, and the IoT, individuals must be confident that their devices are designed in a way that protects their data and that any data being collected and processed from those devices is used responsibly.

"We must make security and privacy ubiquitous, simple, and understood by all," said entrepreneur and tech investor David Gorodyansky. "[We must make] sure privacy and access are part of the equation at product inception and that policy and legislation account for privacy and access in the new Internet-driven world."[2] That's the desired state: security and privacy reinforcing each other. And to get there – to make security and privacy ubiquitous and to ensure both privacy and access – it's often necessary to process personal data.

---

[1] Goodin, Dan, "Insulin Pump Hack Delivers Fatal Dosage over the Air," *The Register*, October 27, 2011, http://www.theregister.co.uk/2011/10/27/fatal_insulin_pump_attack/.

[2] Gorodyansky, David, "Privacy and Security in the Internet Age," *Wired.com*, January 1, 2015, https://www.wired.com/insights/2015/01/privacy-and-security-in-the-internet-age/.

While it might seem odd that data would be needed to secure data, if you want to be protected against cyber attacks, you need a trusted entity to scan Internet traffic to prevent malicious code from running on your machine. If you want to be confident the links you're going to click on aren't harmful, you need software to know both where you are on the web and what's waiting for you there – and the same holds true for preventing terrorism or providing effective law enforcement.

The point is this: It takes data, to protect data. The environment we live in is changing. How we collect, store, and process data has never presented so many opportunities – and risks – and to adapt to this change we must accept that the more data we have access to, the better protected it must be. The rest of this chapter makes the case that more data can lead to increased safety and privacy, if we implement the right programs and controls. To make that case, however, we must first understand the changing threat landscape that exists today.

THE GROWING CYBER THREAT

Cybersecurity professionals say it's not a question of whether an organization or individual will be subject to a cyber intrusion; it's a question of when. This is largely because of what Chris Young, CEO of McAfee, calls the "cyber debt" – which must be paid down. As IT innovation has accelerated and technology has assumed a dominant place in our lives and economy, we have invested very little in cybersecurity.[3] Many companies thought they were investing, as they hired consultants, licensed tools, and started information security organizations. In retrospect, however, the investment was not nearly enough to mitigate the growing risks.[4] With each passing week, enterprises and individuals are exposed to more cyber breaches for which they're often unprepared. That's because of the cyber debt – the gap between the investment needed and the one actually made to secure many of those systems, devices, and networks. It now seems that with so many high-profile cyber attacks, organizations are beginning to understand the need to close that gap.

The U.S. government, for instance, created a Cybersecurity National Action Plan that calls for the creation of a $3.1 billion Information Technology Modernization Fund to enable the retirement, replacement, and modernization of legacy information technology that is difficult to secure and expensive to maintain.[5] Steve Morgan, the founder and editor-in-chief of Cybersecurity Ventures, predicts spending on cybersecurity products and services will eclipse $1 trillion over the next five years.[6] Organizations now see the increased risks and would like to pay off the cyber debt. They are struggling, however, to understand where to invest the money to gain the most impact.

Meanwhile, cyber adversaries have had plenty of incentives: money, fame, a political or social cause, or just demonstrating technical prowess. To counter these adversaries, enterprises, governments, and individuals have access to strong cybersecurity tools – and more importantly, sophisticated cybersecurity platforms and architectures. Fortunately, the cybersecurity market is

---

[3] Young, Christopher. "Cybersecurity Recommendations for the Next Administration: Keep Cybersecurity Front and Center," *Lawfare*, November 3, 2016, https://www.lawfareblog.com/cybersecurity-recommendations-next-administration-keep-cybersecurity-front-and-center.

[4] Hoffman, David A. "Paying Down the Cybersecurity Debt: A Shared Responsibility," *Policy@Intel*, July 27, 2015, http://blogs.intel.com/policy/2015/07/27/paying-down-the-cybersecurity-debt-a-shared-responsibility/.

[5] "Fact Sheet: Cybersecurity National Action Plan," The White House, February 9, 2016, https://www.whitehouse.gov/the-press-office/2016/02/09/fact-sheet-cybersecurity-national-action-plan.

[6] Morgan, Steven C., "CyberSecurity Market Report," Cybersecurity Ventures, June 9, 2016, http://cybersecurityventures.com/cy6bersecurity-market-report/.

innovating constantly, trying to keep up with the seemingly universal appetite for faster, bigger data sets and streams. For instance, McAfee Labs estimates that over the next three years, network traffic will increase 132 percent, and the number of IP-connected devices will increase from 16.3 billion to 24.4 billion. Over the next four years, the number of IoT devices is expected to grow from 15 billion to 200 billion, and the global market size of the public cloud will rise 64 percent, to $159 billion.[7]

As societies become more mobile and integrated through the IoT and data, nearly all aspects of personal and business life have been enhanced. But the attack surface has also expanded and will continue to do so. There are 316 new threats experienced every minute, according to McAfee Labs' Threats Report of September 2016.[8] Total instances of reported use of ransomware has grown 128 percent in 2016, and the reported use of mobile malware grew 151 percent. In the future, as data continues to travel outside the organizational perimeter – in clouds and personal devices – that data becomes much more vulnerable to both unintentional leaks and targeted attacks. Specialists say they are trying to figure out how to extend the sphere of trust while maintaining better control.[9]

As long as individuals and organizations value their digital assets, there will be adversaries who want to steal or alter those assets. Instead of just stealing a person's name, address, phone number, email address or purchasing history, criminals will begin to steal frequently visited locations, what people eat, watch, and listen to, their weight, blood pressure, prescriptions, sleeping habits, daily schedule, exercise routine, and yes, even their blood sugar levels. The threat to privacy has never been greater.

CYBER THREATS PUT PERSONAL DATA AT RISK

When we talk about personal data, we're talking about data that reasonably relates to an individual person. This definition continues to need interpretation and application to innovative ways of collecting and processing data. Nevertheless, cyber criminals are targeting personal data – either to offer it for sale, embarrass prominent individuals, hold it hostage in a ransomware attack, achieve a political objective or for any other purpose one can imagine such as blackmail or recruiting an insider to hand over log-in credentials. The growing value of personal data makes it even more important to protect.

Over the last few years, numerous high-profile data breaches have exposed personal data in just about every sector of the economy:

- Retail – Target, Home Depot
- Entertainment & Communications – Sony, Yahoo
- Healthcare – Anthem, France's Mutuelle Générale de la Police
- Finance – JPMorgan Chase, Vietnam's Tien Phong Bank
- Government – Office of Personnel Management (OPM), the Philippines' Commission on Elections
- Online Platforms – eBay, Myspace
- Transportation – Uber, British Airways

---

[7] Brad Antoniewicz et al., "McAfee Labs Report: 2016 Threats Predictions," McAfee Labs, November 2, 2015, http://www.mcafee.com/us/resources/reports/rp-threats-predictions-2016.pdf.

[8] "McAfee Labs Threats Report: September 2016," McAfee Labs, September 13, 2016, http://www.mcafee.com/us/resources/reports/rp-quarterly-threats-sep-2016.pdf.

[9] "McAfee Labs 2017 Threats Predictions," McAfee Labs, November 29, 2016, http://www.mcafee.com/us/resources/reports/rp-threats-predictions-2017.pdf.

And as we've seen during the presidential elections in the United States, the personal e-mail correspondence of candidates, campaign managers, party officials, and others in the political system was even fair game for WikiLeaks, which announced in advance it would leak hacked information.

One of the most far-reaching personal data breaches in the United States – the effects of which are yet to be fully calculated – was the breach of the OPM in June 2015. The stolen personal information included detailed files and personal background reports on more than 21.5 million individuals, and the fingerprint data of 5.6 million.[10] Much of this information was highly sensitive, including data on individuals who were consulting professionals for mental health, controlled substance abuse or financial difficulties. In this case, the information stolen has value far beyond damage to the individual; it could potentially damage national security.

Not surprisingly, healthcare has become a new favorite of cyber criminals, with some asserting that cybersecurity in that sector is not as advanced as in others. Not only is personal information stolen in healthcare breaches, but it is offered for sale on the dark web. This kind of data is particularly valuable to cyber criminals because, unlike financial information, it's nonperishable. Whereas credit card or password information can quickly be changed, information about a person's chronic conditions, prescription medicines, mother's maiden name, insurance data, and Social Security number has a longer shelf life. One owner of such nonperishable information even offered to sell a database containing the personal medical data of 397,000 patients, according to a recent report from Intel Security.[11]

Another recent study revealed that one-third of respondents in the United Kingdom do not trust the National Health Service (NHS) with their personal information.[12] Ironically, the study was conducted by an EU-funded advocacy group, European Translational Information and Knowledge Management Services, advocating for a new culture of openness in sharing personal health information and seeking to encourage people to share their medical information for research purposes.

The further personal data travels outside an organization's network perimeters, the more at risk it could be. Recent distributed denial of services (DDoS) attacks using compromised IoT devices – primarily security cameras with Internet connected digital recording devices – illustrate this point.[13] The distributed ability to access security camera feeds inside peoples' homes shows just how personal the theft of information is, and will become.

THE DISTRIBUTED NATURE OF THE THREAT

We live in a dangerous world that many would argue is getting more dangerous. Ben Wittes and Gabriella Blum detail these increased risks in their book, *The Future of Violence*.[14] In it, they describe a future where malware, 3D printing of weapons, biological labs in basements and undetectable bug-sized drones will challenge our existing concepts of how to protect populations, nation states, and personal data. What does it mean for protecting personal data when an

[10] Krebs, Brian, "Congressional Report Slams OPM on Data Breach," *Krebs on Security* (blog), September 7, 2016, https://krebsonsecurity.com/2016/09/congressional-report-slams-opm-on-data-breach/.

[11] Beek, Christiaan, Charles McFarland, and Raj Samani, "Health Warning Cyberattacks Are Targeting the Health Care Industry," McAfee Labs, October 2016, http://www.mcafee.com/mx/resources/reports/rp-health-warning.pdf.

[12] Martin, Alexander J., "NHS Patients Must Be Taught to Share Their Data, Says EU Lobby Group," *The Register*, October 18, 2016, http://www.theregister.co.uk/2016/10/18/nhs_patients_need_to_learn_to_give_their_data_to_us_says_lobby_group/.

[13] Leetaru, Kalev, "The Dyn DDOS Attack and the Changing Balance of Online Cyber Power," *Forbes*, October 31, 2016, http://www.forbes.com/sites/kalevleetaru/2016/10/31/the-dyn-ddos-attack-and-the-changing-balance-of-online-cyber-power/.

[14] Wittes, Benjamin, and Gabriella Blum, *The Future of Violence: Robots and Germs, Hacker and Drones: Confronting a New Age of Threat* (New York: Basic Books, 2015).

individual can weaponize an IoT botnet attack from their basement? The malicious actors who present these risks could come from anywhere. Wittes and Blum lay out four main changes in the world that create difficulty in addressing these risks:

- Modern technology enables individuals to wield the destructive power of nation states.
- Individuals, including you personally, can potentially be attacked with impunity from anywhere in the world.
- Technology makes less relevant many of the traditional concepts around which our laws and political organization for security have evolved. National borders, jurisdictional boundaries, citizenship, and the distinctions between national and international, an act of war and crime, state and private action, all offer divides less sharp than they used to.
- Our nation – and every nation – can face attack through channels controlled and operated not by governments, but by the private sector and by means against which governments lack the ability to defend, making private actors pivotal to defense.[15]

Because of the need to protect against these risks, the mission of government security agencies is growing in criticality. Never before in history has a single individual been able to cause so much harm to so many people. To provide privacy and security, governments now must focus not just on providing protection from other nation states, but increasingly from small groups or single actors. It is not likely that government agencies will be able to address these risks alone, as this function is not provided by traditional law enforcement and intelligence tools.

DIFFICULTY OF GOVERNMENTS ALONE TO PROTECT AGAINST THE THREAT

Security is now more about target identification than about learning information from known targets. While technology does contribute to this risk, it also provides tools to mitigate it. We live in a big data environment where we have the opportunity to use complex analytical algorithms to better predict where threats will come from and who may be causing them. Many of these innovative tools are created by the private sector, and the companies that develop them operate globally and have the ability to work across jurisdictional boundaries in ways that are more difficult for governments.

While worldwide governments have a legitimate interest in making sure cyber threats are addressed powerfully and comprehensively, governments alone cannot protect against them – nor should they try. As Wittes and Blum point out, governments have required private sector contractors to provide security, going back to the hiring of sentries to protect travel on Roman roads.[16] The road metaphor is especially apt for our distributed global Internet infrastructure. Unlike the Persians, the Romans created their road network not just as a trade route, but as a fundamental way of free travel for all citizens of the empire. Similarly, the internet was created as a democratized open platform to ease the distribution of information. This global infrastructure is largely comprised of hardware and software solutions developed for use and sale with little country-specific customization. Those solutions are based on technical standards created to preserve international interoperability and efficiency. Technology companies that create the infrastructure and the applications that operate on it, however, are in many ways better positioned to protect the "travelers on this information highway."

---

[15] Ibid., 5.
[16] Ibid., 177–179.

This need for private sector participation and leadership is why governments are increasingly calling for voluntary public-private partnerships (PPPs) and collaboration. The Obama administration recognized this in the various cybersecurity policies they issued. For example, a Presidential Policy Directive (PPD) from July 2016 states:

> The private sector and government agencies have a shared vital interest in protecting the Nation from malicious cyber activity and managing cyber incidents and their consequences. The nature of cyberspace requires individuals, organizations, and the government to all play roles in incident response. Furthermore, effective incident response efforts will help support an open, interoperable, secure, and reliable information and communications infrastructure that promotes trade and commerce, strengthens international security, fosters free expression, and reinforces the privacy and security of our citizens.[17]

The creation of the Framework for Improving Critical Infrastructure Cybersecurity in 2014 (known as the Cybersecurity Framework), developed by the National Institute of Standards and Technology (NIST), is a prime example of this shared responsibility in action. NIST actively engaged with public and private stakeholders, including Intel, in all phases of the framework development process. The resulting Cybersecurity Framework is widely acknowledged as a clear road map for organizations to follow in order to evaluate and enhance their cybersecurity readiness. The PPD of 2013 that initiated the Framework process intended for it to be collaborative and nonregulatory. The executive summary of the Framework itself states it well:

> In enacting this policy, the Executive Order calls for the development of a voluntary risk-based Cybersecurity Framework – a set of industry standards and best practices to help organizations manage cybersecurity risks. The resulting Framework, created through collaboration between government and the private sector, uses a common language to address and manage cybersecurity risk in a cost-effective way based on business needs without placing additional regulatory requirements on businesses.[18]

Several international governments have expressed interest in the Framework, which they see as a rational way to evaluate risk, and Intel has written a use case white paper on how to implement it.[19] Other PPPs in the United States include the President's National Security Telecommunications Advisory Committee, the DHS information sharing standards working groups, and NIST's National Cybersecurity Center of Excellence.

The United States is not alone in valuing PPPs to advance cybersecurity. One of the foundations of the UK's soon-to-be-finalized national cybersecurity strategy is a deeper reliance on private-public partnership, defining more efficient mechanisms for collaboration between industry, government, and academia:

> The Government will fund a "grand challenge" to identify and provide innovative solutions to some of the most pressing problems in cyber security. CyberInvest, a new industry and Govern-

---

[17] Obama, Barack, "Presidential Policy Directive: United States Cyber Incident Coordination," The White House, July 26, 2016, https://www.whitehouse.gov/the-press-office/2016/07/26/presidential-policy-directive-united-states-cyber-incident.

[18] "Framework for Improving Critical Infrastructure Cybersecurity," National Institute of Standards and Technology (NIST), February 12, 2014, https://www.nist.gov/sites/default/files/documents/cyberframework/cybersecurity-framework-021214.pdf.

[19] Tim Casey et al., "An Intel Use Case for the Cybersecurity Framework in Action," *Intel Security*, February 12, 2014, http://www.intel.com/content/www/us/en/government/cybersecurity-framework-in-action-use-case-brief.html.

ment partnership to support cutting-edge cyber security research and protect the UK in cyber-space, will be part of our approach to building the academic-government-industry partnership.[20]

Nations such as Canada, Australia, South Africa, Finland, France, Japan, India, the Netherlands, and others have included private-public partnerships as a key tenet of their cybersecurity strategies as well.

Approaches to such partnerships vary, according to Intel's Dr. Claire Vishik[21]:

- The national cybersecurity strategy released in **France** in 2011 calls for the establishment of a PPP to assist in threat detection and other areas without specifying the characteristics of such a partnership.
- In **Germany**, the approach to the partnership mechanism is more concrete, putting forward a recommendation for the National Cybersecurity Council with a clear charter. Other PPPs in cybersecurity are already active in Germany, including UP KRITIS and Alliance for Cybersecurity.
- **Japan,** which like Germany has a mature private-public partnership space in cybersecurity, used the national cybersecurity strategy to describe the sector-based approach to PPPs, with the objective of ensuring new threats are not overlooked and the strategic cybersecurity solutions are developed by experts.
- The National Cyber Security Policy developed in 2013 in **India** considers private-public partnership as a key strategy and outlines various areas of emphasis, including the creation of a think tank to address complex issues. In addition, the national CERT has an active role in areas that require collaboration between government and the private sector.
- The National Cybersecurity Policy Framework in **South Africa** stresses the importance of PPPs in cybersecurity and directs them to address both national and international problems in this area.

According to Vishik , the critical role private-public partnerships play in so many national cybersecurity strategies may be a precursor of the greater international collaboration achieved through this mechanism.

THE ROLE OF GLOBAL TECHNOLOGY COMPANIES

When the Roman government hired private sentries to guard Roman roads, it wasn't because they didn't understand the problem at hand or how to solve it. The government realized it was not equipped to solve the problem on its own and required private partnerships with sentries to secure the road network. The analogy to our modern cyber networks could not be clearer. From a cyber perspective, the government does two things very well. First, they understand what is happening on their own networks, which are very attractive targets. And second, they can aggregate security intelligence about bad actors from several information sources not available to the private sector.

Over the past fifty years, governments have taken advantage of centralized telecommunications networks, gaining the ability to intercept signals and analyze them for intelligence. Now

---

[20] Cabinet Office, National Security and Intelligence, The Rt. Hon. Philip Hammond MP, and HM Treasury, *National Cyber Security Strategy 2016–2021*, HM Government, November 1, 2016, https://www.gov.uk/government/uploads/system/uploads/attachment_data/file/567242/national_cyber_security_strategy_2016.pdf.

[21] Vishik, Claire. "Private-Public Partnerships in Cybersecurity: Cornerstone of Cybersecurity Strategies Worldwide." *Policy@Intel* (blog), December 27, 2016, http://blogs.intel.com/policy/2016/12/27/private-public-partnerships-in-cybersecurity-cornerstone-of-cybersecurity-strategies-worldwide/.

that the threats are so widespread and reach well beyond telecommunications networks, however, governments realize they need private partners and shared expertise. Add to this the fact that in many countries – certainly in the United States – the government does not own the critical infrastructure that needs protecting from cyber threats, and the need for PPPs increases. Power, water, and transportation systems are generally in private sector hands, and these systems have varying degrees of regulation already. Rather than imposing more regulation, governments should take advantage of the wealth of threat information that private companies already have and add to it, rather than replace it.

Private partners such as global technology companies are in the best position to get advance warning of threats and protect personal data from them. These companies operate hardware and software on a global scale, meaning they collect and manage data from thousands of information sources in multiple countries. They're also adept at creating trusted relationships with various governments around the world. The most advanced information security companies are constantly collecting, analysing, and disseminating threat intelligence from their own security tools, which are deployed around the globe. What's more, they can fold in and correlate threat information from other sources such as government and individuals. These companies' operations span several continents, putting them at the perfect intersection between the flow of data in the global digital infrastructure and making them the best stakeholders to improve the state of data management and protection.

THE NEED TO SCAN AND PROCESS DATA

While much of the data that global security companies process is reputation information about threat actors, individuals' personal information is certainly included in those data flows. As stated earlier, when we talk about personal data, we're talking about data that reasonably relates to an identifiable individual. Regulators are struggling to determine the degree to which information needs to relate to a person to be considered personal data – or personally identifiable information (PII), as it is sometimes called. To fall under the law or regulation, for example, they ask, how easy does it have to be to trace the data back to a specific individual? Due to their frequent use by internet companies to serve targeted online advertising, one of the most prominent and controversial debates in this area has been whether IP addresses should be considered personal data.[22]

The fundamental analysis in both the European Union and the United States rests on the likelihood that the information will be used in a way to relate to an identifiable individual. As innovations in data analytics improve the ability to draw inferences from more diverse data sets, it is likely that more information will have the potential to be related to identifiable individuals. Yet the use of these innovations is also one of the best prospects for improving cybersecurity.

The fact is, in order for data to be helpful in mitigating cyber threats, it will likely need to include IP addresses. If security experts don't scan a significant amount of the data, they can't catch what is malicious. This access to information is different from the debate about accessing encrypted communications. The data subject to cybersecurity scanning will most often be unencrypted, so it's worth noting that we are not talking about the encryption issue here. When we talk about using data to protect data, we're discussing the need to capture key indicators in

---

[22] *FCC Adopts Privacy to Give Broadband Consumers Increased Choice, Transparency and Security for Their Personal Data*, October 27, 2016, http://transition.fcc.gov/Daily_Releases/Daily_Business/2016/db1027/DOC-341937A1.pdf.

the information transiting the internet and individual devices, process the information, and use that feedback to protect against cyber attacks.

By processing the data, malware and ransomware can be identified and prevented from harming an individual's or organization's technology. The argument is not whether the government or private partners should have the right to break encryption, but rather how those organizations may use data they already have the right and ability to access. Once the information is deemed legitimate to process by a governing body, responsible actors ought to be able to use the data for cybersecurity purposes as long as privacy is maintained.

THE POWER THAT DATA ANALYTICS WILL BRING TO IDENTIFY THREATS

In a well-publicized TED Talk in 2014, *Economist* editor Kenneth Cukier stated, "Big data is going to transform how we live, how we work and how we think."[23] Big data's value extends to cybersecurity as well. Yet the term "big data" has been used – and overused – in so many different contexts that its value is sometimes hard to discern. "The fundamental idea isn't about the bigness of the data; it's about wide varieties and different types of data that can be brought together," said Bryan Ware, CEO of Haystax Technology, a Virginia-based security analytics firm.[24] "There have been big databases for many years, but the ability to pull them together, store them in the cloud and use analytics gives us a way to harness all those different pieces of data." Adversaries are already using big data against us for crimes such as identity theft and can even pull little bits of data from various sources and compile an identity, says Ware. Likewise, cybersecurity professionals can use the same tools and techniques to protect people. For example, by combining many sources of data and analytical techniques, they can infer what types of attacks are most likely to occur and how to protect against them.[25]

Having access to multiple data sources is useful only if you have a way to make sense of that data and apply it toward a specific problem – that's why analytics are so important and why the field is booming. Ginni Rometty, CEO of IBM, told *Forbes* that big data analytics will radically change the way businesses operate and make decisions: "Many more decisions will be based on predictive elements versus gut instincts."[26] The same article notes that the big data and analytics industry will grow from its current $103 billion to $203 billion by 2020, as predicted by research company IDC. As analytics tools grow more sophisticated, they will become better and better at being predictive.

Big data analytics can also be a boon to homeland and national security efforts, as well as to public safety efforts on the local level. But individuals have to be assured that their personal information is well protected. The global IT governance association ISACA makes this point about big data analytics and privacy:

> Enterprises eager to reap the benefits of big data and its vast potential are recognizing their responsibility to protect the privacy of the personal data gathered and analyzed with big data.

---

[23] Cukier, Kenneth, "Big Data Is Better Data," Lecture, *TEDSalon Berlin* 2014, Berlin, Germany, June 2014, https://www.ted.com/talks/kenneth_cukier_big_data_is_better_data.

[24] Bryan Ware, CEO of Haystax Technology, interviewed by Patricia Rimo and Hakeem S. Allen, Washington, D.C., October 6, 2016.

[25] Ibid.

[26] Markman, Jon, "Big Data Unleashes Business Opportunity," *Forbes*, November 1, 2016, http://www.forbes.com/sites/jonmarkman/2016/11/01/big-data-unleashes-business-opportunity/#5f1c613a416e.

The success of enterprises will depend on how they meet and deal with the various big data challenges and impacts.[27]

COMPANIES AS DATA FIDUCIARIES

Allowing companies to collect and process the type of information needed to protect personal data means those companies need to demonstrate they will use that information responsibly. Jack Balkin and Jonathan Zittrain commented on this requirement in their recent article, "A Grand Bargain to Make Tech Companies Trustworthy."[28] Balkin and Zittrain recommend we treat technology service providers as "fiduciaries" over people's data and expect certain assurances of how they will handle it. Fiduciaries in other areas of the law owe duties to individuals and have expectations of responsible behavior placed on them (such as doctors, lawyers, and accountants). Balkin and Zittrain propose a trade-off that in exchange for federal preemption of state privacy legislation and immunity from some class action liability, companies would agree to abide by a set of information best practices that include limitations on how the data is used and sold.

This idea of treating tech companies as fiduciaries is similar to proposals Intel Corporation and other companies have made to pass comprehensive U.S. privacy legislation based on the Organization for Economic Cooperation and Development's (OECD) implementation of the Fair Information Practice Principles (the FIPPs).[29] The underlying commonality of the proposals is that society needs to allow organizations to use data in innovative ways to reap the substantial benefits of advances in technology, but part of the bargain must be that those organizations demonstrate they will behave responsibly. A flexible, but rigorous, regulatory structure is a necessary part of the solution.

THE GLOBAL COMMON LANGUAGE OF PRIVACY

Paula Bruening at Intel succinctly captured the importance of the FIPPs when she described them as a global "common language of privacy."[30] The eight OECD FIPPs have been the foundation of privacy law for more than forty years, and they lay out a model to think about privacy that is much greater than just minimizing the collection and use of data. The FIPPs have proven to be flexible enough to apply to decades of technology innovation and are still adaptable to our current environment.

Bruening and the Intel privacy team have embarked on an effort to explain how these FIPPs provide an opportunity to optimize both the innovative AND ethical uses of data. *Rethinking Privacy* encourages policymakers and industry leaders to use the full set of FIPPs to protect the privacy of individuals.[31] The effort also developed guidance on how to apply each of the FIPPs to

---

[27] "Privacy & Big Data," Information Systems Audit and Control Association, 2013, http://www.isaca.org/Knowledge-Center/Research/ResearchDeliverables/Pages/Privacy-and-Big-Data.aspx.

[28] Balkin, Jack M., and Jonathan Zittrain, "A Grand Bargain to Make Tech Companies Trustworthy," *The Atlantic*, October 3, 2016, http://www.theatlantic.com/technology/archive/2016/10/information-fiduciary/502346/.

[29] *The OECD Privacy Framework*, Organisation for Economic Co-operation and Development, July 11, 2013, http://www.oecd.org/sti/ieconomy/oecd_privacy_framework.pdf.

[30] Bruening, Paula, "Fair Information Practice Principles: A Common Language for Privacy in a Diverse Data Environment," *Intel Security* (blog), January 28, 2016, https://blogs.intel.com/policy/2016/01/28/blah-2/.

[31] Hoffman, David A., and Paula J. Bruening, "Rethinking Privacy: Fair Information Practice Principles Reinterpreted," *Intel Security* (blog), November 5, 2015, http://blogs.intel.com/policy/files/2015/11/Rethink2015finalforprint.pdf.

a new data environment shaped by advances in the IoT, cloud computing, and advanced data analytics. This work is directly relevant to showing how companies that will use data to protect data can also demonstrate they are doing so responsibly. Let's now take each of the FIPPs and apply it to the task of using data to provide better cybersecurity.

Collection Limitation Principle

There should be limits to the collection of personal data and any such data should be obtained by lawful and fair means and, where appropriate, with the knowledge or consent of the data subject.

(OECD Guidelines on the Protection of Privacy and Transborder Flows of Personal Data[32])

Evolving methods for delivering internet services are changing what it means to "collect" data. Often the data is just passing through machines comprised of different hardware and software. That hardware and software have the ability to analyze the data and isolate information that causes concern. For example, security software can automatically scan information coming onto a server, determine what packets are associated with malicious code, and transmit back to the security software vendor the information relating to those packets (likely including an IP address that could be used, if combined with other information, to identify an individual person). It is unclear whether we should think that the developer of that software has "collected" all of the data that the software scanned, or just the data that has been transmitted back. We contend that there are fewer privacy implications from scanning the data at the source and only transmitting back the relevant information relating to cybersecurity risks. That approach seems consistent with the intent of the Collection Limitation Principle.

Data Quality Principle

Personal data should be relevant to the purposes for which they are to be used, and to the extent necessary for those purposes, should be accurate, complete and kept up-to-date.

(OECD Guidelines on the Protection of Privacy and Transborder Flows of Personal Data[33])

The greater the consequences to the individual from the processing of personal data, the more important it is that the data be relevant and accurate. Data quality can be aided by having more – specifically more diverse – data on which to apply analytics, thereby creating a greater likelihood of evaluating data that is accurate, up-to-date, and necessary. It will be critical that cybersecurity companies have a robust data quality program, coupled with the ability for individuals to understand what data relating to them has been processed and how an algorithm has decided that they, their data or their machine has created a cybersecurity risk (see Individual Participation Principle later in this chapter).

Purpose Specification Principle

The purposes for which personal data are collected should be specified not later than at the time of data collection and the subsequent use limited to the fulfillment of those purposes or such others as are not incompatible with those purposes and as are specified on each occasion of change of purpose.

(OECD Guidelines on the Protection of Privacy and Transborder Flows of Personal Data[34])

---

[32] http://www.oecd.org/sti/ieconomy/oecdguidelinesontheprotectionofprivacyandtransborderflowsofpersonaldata.htm
[33] *See supra* n. 32.
[34] Ibid.

The Purpose Specification Principle allows for the processing of data when that use is "not incompatible" with the purposes that are obvious to the individual, either implicitly from the context or explicitly in some sort of notice. The Article 29 Working Party's opinion on Purpose Specification notes that the 95/46 Directive allows the processing of data for purposes that are "specified, explicit and legitimate," and "not incompatible" with the original purpose.[35] It articulates key factors to be considered when assessing whether a purpose is "not incompatible," including:

- The relationship between the purposes for which the data has been collected and the purposes of further processing
- The context in which the data has been collected and the reasonable expectations of the data subjects as to the data's further use
- The nature of the data and the impact of the further processing on data subjects
- The safeguards applied by the controller to ensure fair processing and to prevent any undue impact on the data subjects

Applying these criteria, one can make a strong case that providing robust cybersecurity over the networks and machines that process data should almost always be viewed as "not incompatible."

Use Limitation Principle

Personal data should not be disclosed, made available or otherwise used for purposes other than those specified in accordance with [purpose specification principle] except: a) with the consent of the data subject; b) by the authority of law.

(OECD Guidelines on the Protection of Privacy and Transborder Flows of Personal Data[36])

To use data to protect data, companies need either to restrict the use of data to just providing robust cybersecurity, or provide prominent notice that the information will be used for other purposes. The increased sharing of cybersecurity information between companies in the private sector and with various governments has been a top priority across the cybersecurity community. To enable this sharing in a responsible manner, it will be critical to establish legal restrictions on the use of shared information for other purposes.

Security Safeguards Principle

Personal data should be protected by reasonable security safeguards against such risks as loss or unauthorized access, destruction, use, modification or disclosure of data.

(OECD Guidelines on the Protection of Privacy and Transborder Flows of Personal Data[37])

It should go without saying that cybersecurity companies should deploy robust measures to protect their networks, facilities, and data. It will also be important for any recipients of shared information in the private sector or the government to prioritize security.

---

[35] "Opinion 03/2013 on Purpose Limitation," Article 29 Data Protection Working Party, April 2, 2013, http://ec.europa .eu/justice/data-protection/article-29/documentation/opinion-recommendation/files/2013/wp203_en.pdf.
[36] Ibid.
[37] Ibid.

Openness Principle

There should be a general policy of openness about developments, practices and policies with respect to personal data. Means should be readily available of establishing the existence and nature of personal data and the main purposes of their use, as well as the identity and usual residence of the data controller.

(OECD Guidelines on the Protection of Privacy and Transborder Flows of Personal Data[38])

Openness is about much more than just posting privacy policies or providing direct notice to the providers of personal data. Intel has recommended that openness may best be achieved through the implementation of two kinds of communications:

- Comprehensive disclosures, which provide an in-depth explanation of how an organization collects, processes, and protects data. Civil society, advocates, and experts may review these notices to develop a detailed view of a company's practices or gain an understanding of developments across the digital marketplace. Regulators may compare these statements with the company's activities to determine whether their representations are valid and whether their practices fall within the bounds of law and commonly accepted guidance.
- Context-specific notices, which provide concise, targeted information about data collection, use, storage, and protection so individuals can determine whether to make a purchase, engage in an activity or interact with an online vendor. Focused, tailored, context-specific notices that are made available to the consumer at the appropriate times support individuals' real-time decision making about collection and use of their data.[39]

For cybersecurity companies, the personal data they collect will often relate to individuals who may not have had any connection with the company. For example, an individual sending an e-mail message to a friend may not know that it will be scanned by cybersecurity software loaded on a server at a data hosting intermediary in the internet backbone. For that reason, it is important that cybersecurity companies invest in the type of comprehensive disclosure that will instill confidence in regulators and privacy advocates. Also, to best serve the public, those companies should supplement the disclosures with consumer education to best educate the public on the critical importance of using data to protect data. An example of this type of consumer education is the work that industry supports through the National Cybersecurity Alliance, the organization that coordinates both Cybersecurity Awareness Month and International Data Privacy Day.

Individual Participation Principle

An individual should have the right to: a) obtain from a data controller, or otherwise, confirmation of whether or not the data controller has data relating to him; b) have communicated to him, data relating to him within a reasonable time, at a charge, if any, that is not excessive in a reasonable manner; and in a form that is readily intelligible to him; c) be given reasons if a request made under (a) or (b) is denied, and to be able to challenge such denial; and d) challenge data relating to him and, if the challenge is successful to have the data erased, rectified, completed or amended.

(OECD Guidelines on the Protection of Privacy and Transborder Flows of Personal Data[40])

---

[38] Ibid.
[39] Hoffman, David A., and Paula J. Bruening, "Rethinking Privacy," 14.
[40] *See supra* n. 32.

The ability for individuals to understand the data collected about them, and challenge the processing of that data, has been an important aspect of privacy for decades. The collection of cybersecurity information presents unique difficulties for individual participation, as often the individual to whom the data relates may not know their data has been collected, processed or used. Additionally, the individual may not know an algorithm has identified that the collected data relates to a cybersecurity threat.

However, there are still mechanisms cybersecurity companies can provide to foster individual participation. People who observe that their computing devices are being blocked from signing onto networks should have an opportunity to inquire with cybersecurity companies to understand whether their devices have been flagged as at risk of being infected with a virus, or that they may be part of a botnet. Some cybersecurity situations may require only providing limited information back to the individual about the processing, to reduce the risk malicious actors will game the system, but all companies should be able to at least tell individuals their inquiry has been appropriately reviewed.

Accountability Principle

A data controller should be accountable for complying with measures which give effect to the principles stated above.

(OECD Guidelines on the Protection of Privacy and Transborder Flows of Personal Data[41])

The Accountability Principle was not robustly defined or applied for decades. However, in the past ten years tremendous work has been done to describe what organizations need to put in place to demonstrate they are behaving responsibly.[42] Accountability requires not just policies that company employees will follow, but also resources, staffing, organizational structures, and business processes to ensure the company implements those policies. In their book *Privacy on the Ground: Driving Corporate Behavior in the United States and Europe*, University of California, Berkeley professors Kenneth Bamberger and Deirdre Mulligan compare over fifty privacy programs and convincingly show the benefits to privacy from putting in place accountability structures.[43]

Companies should not implement the FIPPs as disconnected, individual rules. Instead, depending on the context of the data's use, organizations should rely on some of the FIPPs more than others. The principles interrelate with each other, and regulators and other policy stakeholders should evaluate privacy protections based on a company's implementation of all eight FIPPs. For example, to accomplish robust cybersecurity, Collection Limitation and Openness may be less useful, while Use Limitations and Accountability can provide better protections. To mitigate privacy concerns and ensure data is used solely to enhance cybersecurity, companies should implement FIPPs and establish strong privacy programs with robust oversight.

As described in *Rethinking Privacy*:

In this way, the FIPPs can be viewed as a system of levers to be pulled and adjusted, or requirements to be given the weight necessary to provide the best protection possible in the

---

[41] Ibid.

[42] Alhadeff, Joseph et al., "Demonstrating and Measuring Accountability," The Centre for Information Policy Leadership, October 2010, http://www.huntonfiles.com/files/webupload/CIPL_Accountability_Phase_II_Paris_Project.PDF.

[43] Bamberger, Kenneth A., and Deirdre K. Mulligan, *Privacy on the Ground: Driving Corporate Behavior in the United States and Europe* (Cambridge, MA: MIT Press, 2015).

context of a particular technology or data application. The heightened focus on accountability places greater burden on companies to make thoughtful, judicious decisions about how best to apply FIPPs in a way that practically yields effective protections.[44]

We need to make certain we implement the FIPPs in these cybersecurity mechanisms so we can reap these benefits without creating privacy risks. We will need these protections for future challenges we will inevitably face for the use of data, such as using security analytics to enhance national security and securing the IoT.

USING DATA TO PROTECT MORE THAN JUST DATA

To use data to protect data, cybersecurity companies will potentially need to process large amounts of information that could relate to identifiable individuals. Robust and accountable privacy programs that include a chief privacy officer who reports to senior management, adequate staffing and resources, robust risk management processes, and privacy by design mechanisms integrated into product development can provide protections for individuals while also allowing for the use of data to protect data.

As we improve real-time, automated, cybersecurity information sharing, we will have the potential to quickly mitigate attacks and minimize their potential for harm. Using cybersecurity data in this way will have a substantial net benefit for privacy – if organizations build the right protections in place. These cybersecurity protections, however, will safeguard much more than just data. They'll also protect the power grid, water treatment plants, Internet-connected vehicles, and hospitals and medical devices, such as insulin pumps. Improved cybersecurity will not only protect data – it will save lives. And that's the benefit of using data to protect data.

ACKNOWLEDGMENTS

We would like to acknowledge the writing and research support provided by Hakeem S. Allen, RH Strategic Communications, and Cameron Rohde, RH Strategic Communications at Intel Corporation.

---

[44] Hoffman, David A., and Paula J. Bruening, "Rethinking Privacy," 19.

31

Are Benefit-Cost Analysis and Privacy Protection Efforts Incompatible?

Adam Thierer

I. INTRODUCTION: WHY TRY TO QUANTIFY THE UNQUANTIFIABLE?

Any attempt to quantify values that some believe are inherently unquantifiable is bound to generate controversy. But there are good reasons to try to do so anyway.

For example, how much is "a little peace and quiet" or a "pristine view" worth? It is tempting to say that such things are "priceless."[1] Despite the challenges of placing a monetary value on such things, indirect measures do exist. People put a price on a little peace and quiet or a pristine view each time they rent a cabin in the woods, vacation at a secluded beach, or move from the city to a less congested area.[2]

These individual valuations can be aggregated and studied by economists and market analysts to estimate how much those settings or experiences are worth and those valuations can then be used for a wide variety of other purposes. Such estimates can be used by firms to plan where to build new residences or vacation units, for example. Or the valuations might be used by governments to make land use decisions, or to help determine how best to allocate taxes.

Consider other examples. What is the value of a park or nature preserve? What is the value of an animal that might be threatened by extinction? Even more controversially, what is the value of a human life?

In each case, a seemingly insurmountable challenge exists in terms of placing a monetary valuation on highly subjective – and sometimes seemingly sacrosanct – values.[3] For such reasons, some skeptics will insist that it is impossible – perhaps even distasteful or unethical – to place monetary values on such important values based on what is an exercise in crude utilitarianism.[4]

But the reason we should seek to "put a value on values" or "quantify the unquantifiable" is because we live in a world of limited resources and inescapable trade-offs. When certain

---

[1] Frank Ackerman and Lisa Heinzerling, *Priceless: On Knowing the Price of Everything and the Value of Nothing* (New York: The New Press, 2004).

[2] John Morrall and James Broughel, *The Role of Regulatory Impact Analysis in Federal Rulemaking* (Arlington: Mercatus Center at George Mason University, 2014): 22. ("Actually, people demonstrate with their own actions every day that they do not place an infinite value on their own life. There is a cost to safety, and people are willing to trade off a little bit of safety in exchange for paying a lower price.")

[3] Justin Zhan and Vaidyanathan Rajamani, "The Economics of Privacy," *International Journal of Security and Its Applications*, vol. 2, no. 3 (July, 2008): 104. ("The problem is that it is difficult to quantify the cost, benefits, and risks involved in information disclosure as most of the evaluation boils down to a subjective nature.")

[4] Steven Kelman, "Cost-Benefit Analysis: An Ethical Critique," *Regulation*, (January/February 1981): 33–40, http://object.cato.org/sites/cato.org/files/serials/files/regulation/1981/1/v5n1–7.pdf.

subjective values become a matter of public policy concern, society is forced to consider the costs and benefits of various potential solutions to perceived problems.

There is no escaping this task even when it seems complicated, illogical, or distasteful. Instead of viewing such an exercise as outlandish or offensive, it should be welcomed as an enlightening endeavor and a useful tool that can help us "improve the quality of difficult social choices under conditions of uncertainty,"[5] thus reaching superior results within a deliberative democracy.[6]

All this is equally true when we ponder how to value "privacy," perhaps one of the most amorphous concepts and subjective personal conditions that we might ever try to quantify. This chapter considers some of the complexities of subjecting privacy-related public policy proposals to formal benefit-cost analysis and makes the case for attempting to do so despite the formidable challenges at hand.

II. BENEFIT-COST ANALYSIS: THE BASICS

First, some general background on benefit-cost analysis (BCA). BCA attempts to formally identify the opportunity costs associated with regulatory proposals and, to the maximum extent feasible, quantify the benefits and costs of those rules.[7]

In the United States, BCA has become a fixed part of the federal rule-making process and it generally enjoys bipartisan support.[8] Many other countries now employ some variety of BCA during the rule-making process,[9] but few have developed as rigorous a BCA process as has the United States. For that reason, this article will focus on how BCA works in the United States.

In the United States, the BCA process is guided by various presidential executive orders and guidance documents promulgated by the Office of Information and Regulatory Affairs (OIRA).[10] OIRA was created as part of the Paperwork Reduction Act of 1980 and made part of the Office of

---

[5] James V. DeLong, "Defending Cost-Benefit Analysis: Replies to Steven Kelman," *Regulation*, (March/April 1981): 39.

[6] Morrall and Broughel, at 5. ("It is important to stress that benefit-cost analysis is an aid to decision-making, not a strict decision rule in itself. It informs decisions; it does not replace decisions. Benefit-cost analysis is just one factor among many that decision makers should consider before setting policy. There are, of course, other factors that regulators should also take into account that may not be captured in figures about benefits and costs.")

[7] *See* Susan E. Dudley and Jerry Brito, *Regulation: A Primer* (2d ed., 2012): 97–98. ("The cost of a regulation is the opportunity cost – whatever desirable things society gives up in order to get the good things the regulation produces. The opportunity cost of alternative approaches is the appropriate measure of costs. This measure should reflect the benefits foregone when a particular action is selected and should include the change in consumer and producer surplus."); Jerry Ellig & Patrick A. McLaughlin, "The Quality and Use of Regulatory Analysis in 2008," *Risk Analysis*, vol. 32 (2012): 855.

[8] Cass R. Sunstein, "The Stunning Triumph of Cost-Benefit Analysis," *Bloomberg View*, September 12, 2012, http://www.bloomberg.com/news/2012-09-12/the-stunning-triumph-of-cost-benefit-analysis.html. ("It is not exactly news that we live in an era of polarized politics. But Republicans and Democrats have come to agree on one issue: the essential need for cost-benefit analysis in the regulatory process. In fact, cost-benefit analysis has become part of the informal constitution of the U.S. regulatory state. This is an extraordinary development.")

[9] *See, e.g., Canadian Cost-Benefit Analysis Guide* (Treasury Board of Canada Secretariat, 2007), https://www.tbs-sct.gc.ca/rtrap-parfa/analys/analys-eng.pdf; *Cost-Benefit Analysis Guidance Note* (Australian Government Office of Best Practice Regulation, February 2016), https://www.dpmc.gov.au/resource-centre/regulation/cost-benefit-analysis-guidance-note; *Guide to Social Cost Benefit Analysis* (The Treasury of the New Zealand Government, July 2015), http://www.treasury.govt.nz/publications/guidance/planning/costbenefitanalysis/guide; *Impact Assessment Guidelines* (European Commission, January 15, 2009), http://ec.europa.eu/smart-regulation/impact/commission_guidelines/docs/iag_2009_en.pdf.

[10] *See* Richard B. Belzer, "Risk Assessment, Safety Assessment, and the Estimation of Regulatory Benefits," (Arlington: Mercatus Center at George Mason University, 2012): 5, http://mercatus.org/publication/risk-assessment-safety-assessment-and-estimation-regulatory-benefits.

Management and Budget (OMB).[11] "OIRA reviews … significant proposed and final rules from federal agencies ([except for] independent regulatory agencies) before they are [finalized and] published in the *Federal Register*."[12]

Since 1981, various presidential executive orders have required executive branch agencies to utilize BCA in the regulatory policymaking process.[13] The most important regulatory policy-making guidance is found in Executive Order 12866, issued by President Bill Clinton in September 1993,[14] and OMB's Circular A-4, issued in September 2003.[15] Circular A-4 and subsequent agency guidance issued by OIRA list the steps agencies must follow when conducting a regulatory impact analysis (RIA).[16]

Several elements of the RIA process are relevant when considering how to conduct BCA for complicated issues such as privacy protection. For example, according to OIRA, RIAs must include a "statement of the need for the regulatory action" that also explains "whether the action is intended to address a market failure or to promote some other goal."[17] RIAs are also supposed to include a "clear identification of a range of regulatory approaches," which includes "the option of not regulating."[18]

OIRA also requires that alternatives to federal regulation be considered such as "state or local regulation, voluntary action on the part of the private sector, antitrust enforcement, consumer-initiated litigation in the product liability system, and administrative compensation systems."[19] Agencies are supposed to assess the benefits and costs of all these alternatives.[20] If federal regulation is still deemed necessary, OIRA also encourages agencies to consider flexible policy approaches.[21] After evaluating those considerations, OIRA requires a formal "estimate of the benefits and costs – both quantitative and qualitative."[22] The quantification of benefits and costs is strongly encouraged but, when impossible, agencies are required to describe them qualitatively and make a clear case for regulatory action.[23]

---

[11] Curtis W. Copeland, "The Role of the Office of Information and Regulatory Affairs in Federal Rulemaking," *Fordham Urban Law Journal*, vol. 33 (2005): 102.

[12] US General Accounting Office, "OMB's Role in Reviews of Agencies' Draft Rules and the Transparency of Those Reviews," GAO-03-929, (2003): 3, http://www.gao.gov/products/GAO-03-929.

[13] *See* Executive Order 12291, 46 Federal Register 13193, February 19, 1981.

[14] *See* Executive Order 12866, 58 Federal Register 51735, September 30, 1993.

[15] See Office of Management & Budget, Circular A-4 (2003), http://www.whitehouse.gov/sites/default/files/omb/assets/omb/circulars/a004/a-4.pdf [hereinafter OMB, Circular A-4].

[16] *See* Office of Information & Regulatory Affairs, *Regulatory Impact Analysis: A Primer* (2011), http://www.whitehouse.gov/sites/default/files/omb/inforeg/regpol/circular-a-4_regulatory-impact-analysis-a-primer.pdf, [hereinafter OIRA, RIA Primer]; Richard Williams and Jerry Ellig, "Regulatory Oversight: The Basics of Regulatory Impact Analysis" (Arlington: Mercatus Center at George Mason University, 2011): 17, http://mercatus.org/publication/regulatory-oversight.

[17] OIRA, *RIA Primer, supra* note 16, at 2.

[18] Ibid.

[19] Ibid.

[20] Ibid. at 7.

[21] Ibid. at 2, 5.

[22] OIRA, *RIA Primer*, at 3.

[23] Ibid. at 3–4.

President Barack Obama issued several executive orders attempting to clarify and improve the federal regulatory rulemaking process.[24] Importantly, Executive Order 13563, issued in January 2012, noted that:[25]

> In applying these principles, each agency is directed to use the best available techniques to quantify anticipated present and future benefits and costs as accurately as possible. Where appropriate and permitted by law, each agency may consider (and discuss qualitatively) *values that are difficult or impossible to quantify*, including equity, human dignity, fairness, and distributive impacts.[26]

Finally, ongoing cultural and technological change must be factored into the BCA process in accordance with Executive Order 13610, which President Obama issued in May 2012. It specified that "it is particularly important for agencies to conduct retrospective analyses of existing rules to examine whether they remain justified and whether they should be modified or streamlined in light of changed circumstances, including the rise of new technologies."[27]

These various caveats found in presidential executive orders illustrate the nuances of modern BCA, which lets agencies consider a broad array of issues and values, including those that defy easy quantification.

III. ANALYZING PRIVACY TRADE-OFFS

When we turn to the potential application of BCA to privacy-related policy proposals, a variety of complications become evident.

To keep things conceptually simple, we can group these issues into two general categories related to (1) the value that individuals place on their personal privacy, and (2) the value they place on various goods or services that might require them to sacrifice a certain degree of their privacy.

Unsurprisingly, the first bucket of issues is riddled with definitional difficulties and computational complexities. By contrast, the latter category lends itself more easily to explanation and quantification. Regardless, an examination of each set of issues through the prism of BCA can help inform the policymaking process and lead to better decisions.

A. *The Value of Privacy*

Legal scholars have observed that attempts to define privacy are "notoriously contentious"[28] and can quickly become a "conceptual jungle,"[29] "because privacy means so many different things to so many different people."[30] Economists who have studied privacy issues agree,

---

[24] *Regulatory Matters*, White House, http://www.whitehouse.gov/omb/inforeg_regmatters (last visited Dec. 23, 2012). *See, e.g.*, Identifying and Reducing Regulatory Burdens, Exec. Order No. 13610, 77 Fed. Reg. 28,469 (May 12, 2012), *available at* http://www.whitehouse.gov/sites/default/files/docs/microsites/omb/eo_13610_identifying_and_reducing_regulatory_burdens.pdf; Improving Regulation and Regulatory Review, Exec. Order No. 13,563, 76 Fed. Reg. 3,821, Jan. 18, 2011, *available at* http://www.whitehouse.gov/sites/default/files/omb/inforeg/eo12866/eo13563_01182011.pdf.

[25] Improving Regulation and Regulatory Review, 76 Fed. Reg. at 3,822.

[26] Improving Regulation and Regulatory Review (emphasis added).

[27] Identifying and Reducing Regulatory Burdens, 77 Fed. Reg. at 28,469.

[28] Maureen K. Ohlhausen and Alexander P. Okuliar, "Competition, Consumer Protection, and the Right [Approach] to Privacy," *Antitrust Law Journal*, vol. 80 (2015): 150. ("Attempting to craft a universal definition of privacy is notoriously contentious and, likely, impossible.")

[29] Daniel J. Solove, *Understanding Privacy* (2008): 196.

[30] Cord Jefferson, "Spies Like Us: We're All Big Brother Now," *Gizmodo*, September 27, 2012, http://gizmodo.com/5944980/spies-like-us-were-all-big-brother-now.

noting that "privacy is a subtle good, whose economic character varies widely"[31] and that a "leading complaint about BCA is the utilitarian one that a dollar of benefit or cost to one person may carry considerably more ethical weight than a dollar of benefit or cost to another person."[32]

Creating a taxonomy of privacy "harms" is, therefore, quite complicated[33] and often hinges on a contextual analysis of each particular case and controversy.[34] The analysis of privacy harms is further complicated by which actors are being accused of violating privacy: governments, corporations or private organizations, or other individuals.[35]

The irony of policy debates about privacy is that public officials sometimes simultaneously speak of privacy as being what economists would call a "merit good," while others think of it as a "demerit good." Merit goods are goods or services that have widespread benefits, even if citizens may not fully appreciate (or properly value) those benefits. Educational services and museums are two commonly cited examples of merit goods that produce positive externalities for the general public, but which may not be produced to a sufficient degree without government action. Demerit goods, by contrast, are goods or services which are considered socially undesirable or harmful to the public, usually because they are overconsumed by individuals and have negative externalities for others. Pollution and smoking are two commonly cited examples of demerit goods.

The definitions of both merit and demerit goods hinge on somewhat paternalistic opinions about what is good (or bad) for consumers or the general public. Governments often tax or regulate to encourage the production of merit goods or, conversely, to discourage the production of demerit goods.

Some policymakers speak of privacy as a type of merit good when they suggest new laws or regulations are needed to protect privacy even if the public is not clamoring for such protections, or when it is simply unwilling to pay for such protections. Conversely, other policymakers seemingly view privacy as a demerit good when they suggest that it is undesirable for citizens (or perhaps specific groups) to have too much of it relative to other values, namely "safety" and "security," which also represent quite amorphous values or objectives.

Consider how this tension played out in recent debates over smartphone encryption. Leading smartphone software makers such as Apple, Google, and Microsoft have offered increasingly sophisticated cryptography protections on their devices to help consumers better protect their personal data and communications. In early 2016, following a mass shooting in San Bernardino, California, the US Federal Bureau of Investigation (FBI) requested Apple's assistance in unlocking an encrypted cell phone that belonged to one of the shooters.[36] Apple pushed back against the request, leading some policymakers to suggest, as Senator Tom

[31] Joseph Farrell, "Can Privacy Be Just Another Good?" *Journal on Telecommunications and High Tech Law*, vol. 10 (2012): 261.

[32] Timothy J. Brennan, "Behavioral Economics and Policy Evaluation," *Journal of Benefit Cost Analysis*, vol. 5, no. 1 (2014): 93.

[33] M. Ryan Calo, "The Boundaries of Privacy Harm," *Indiana Law Journal*, vol. 86, no. 3 (2011): 1131–62.

[34] Helen Nissenbaum, *Privacy in Context: Technology, Policy, and the Integrity of Social Life* (Stanford: Stanford University Press, 2010).

[35] Ryan Hagemann, "What Does Privacy Mean?" *Medium*, July 25, 2016, https://medium.com/niskanen-center/what-does-privacy-mean-32d5497e7b3#.fldomn1dz, (suggesting the need for "a tripartite contextual distinction for conceptualizing privacy based on possible harms that may result from violations: harms that result from invasions of privacy by (1) government, (2) corporations, and (3) individuals. Each of these actors have substantially different harms associated with their violation of individual privacy, and each will accordingly warrant varying degrees of control.").

[36] Eric Lichtblau and Katie Benner, "Apple Fights Order to Unlock San Bernardino Gunman's iPhone," *New York Times*, February 17, 2016, http://www.nytimes.com/2016/02/18/technology/apple-timothy-cook-fbi-san-bernardino.html.

Cotton of Arkansas did, that "Apple chose to protect a dead Isis terrorist's privacy over the security of the American people."[37] This represented a view of privacy as sort of demerit good that the public has too much of (i.e., that strong smartphone cryptography could undermine the ability of law enforcement agencies to protect public safety). Other policymakers pushed back, however, and suggested that Apple was wise to default to strong cryptography "by design" because it would help safeguard the privacy and security of individuals, even if they didn't know they needed such protection.[38]

This sort of intellectual schizophrenia over the value of privacy is also often on display in public policy debates about the privacy implications of commercial data collection and use. It is often the case that the exact same commercial good or service that is proclaimed to be privacy-invasive is, at once, also privacy-enhancing. Benjamin Wittes and Jodie C. Liu of the Brookings Institution observe that:

> Many new technologies whose privacy impacts we fear as a society actually bring great privacy boons to users, as well as significant costs. Society tends to pocket these benefits without much thought, while carefully tallying and wringing its hands about the costs. The result is a ledger in which we worry obsessively about the possibility that users' internet searches can be tracked, without considering the privacy benefits that accrue to users because of the underlying ability in the first instance to acquire sensitive material without facing another human, without asking permission, and without being judged by the people around us.[39]

Three good examples, they argue, are online searches, online shopping, and e-book readers. Each technology has raised its share of privacy concerns. Generally speaking, the most common privacy-related complaint about all three is that they can be used to more closely track and share a user's browsing, shopping, and reading habits.

To be sure, these three technologies introduce such privacy risks. On the other hand, all three enhance privacy in other ways. They let users engage in information retrieval efforts or purchases in the seclusion of their own homes, which in the past might have required embarrassing interactions with others at libraries or bookstores. Thus, it has never been easier, Wittes and Liu say, for people to view or purchase potentially controversial content or goods which, in a past era, would have brought the uncomfortable gaze of others in physical environments.

For these reasons, they conclude that "the American and international debates over privacy keep score very badly and in a fashion gravely biased towards overstating the negative privacy impacts of new technologies relative to their privacy benefits."[40] By extension, if public policies were introduced aimed at limiting the capabilities of these services, it could not be regarded as an unambiguous benefit for end-user privacy because if users began substituting

---

[37] Quoted in Danny Yadron, Spencer Ackerman and Sam Thielman, "Inside the FBI's Encryption Battle with Apple," *The Guardian*, February 18, 2016, https://www.theguardian.com/technology/2016/feb/17/inside-the-fbis-encryption-battle-with-apple.

[38] Eric Geller, "Pro-Encryption Lawmakers See 'Apple vs. FBI' fight as a Chance to Educate Congress," *The Daily Dot*, February 23, 2016, http://www.dailydot.com/layer8/apple-fbi-iphone-encryption-backdoors-congress-ron-wyden-zoe-lofgren (quoting US Senator Ron Wyden: "If criminals and hackers can get [Americans'] information, because strong encryption has been gutted by their government, those criminals and hackers can use [the vulnerability] to hurt Americans. And I don't think the American people are going to react very well to that kind of policy when people really break this down in the way I've described.").

[39] Benjamin Wittes and Jodie C. Liu, "The Privacy Paradox: The Privacy Benefits of Privacy Threats," Center for Technology Innovation at Brookings, (May 2015): 2, https://www.brookings.edu/research/the-privacy-paradox-the-privacy-benefits-of-privacy-threats.

[40] Ibid., 2.

other (or older) services or technologies for them, they might actually be losing privacy in other ways.

Because "consumers have wildly divergent preferences based on their individual needs and tempered by the costs they are willing to bear,"[41] economists employ "willingness to pay" and "willingness-to-accept" analysis in an attempt to sort through these valuation issues such as these. The OMB's Circular A-4 explains the difference as follows:

> The principle of "willingness-to-pay" (WTP) captures the notion of opportunity cost by measuring what individuals are willing to forgo to enjoy a particular benefit. In general, economists tend to view WTP as the most appropriate measure of opportunity cost, but an individual's "willingness-to-accept" (WTA) compensation for not receiving the improvement can also provide a valid measure of opportunity cost.[42]

As applied to proposals to protect privacy, willingness-to-accept represents "the lowest price a person would be willing to accept to part with a good (protection of personal data) she initially owned," whereas willingness-to-pay is "the maximum price a person would be willing to pay to acquire a good (protection of personal data) she did not own."[43] Experimental evidence suggests that "WTA tends to be larger than WTP," because of loss aversion, or "the disproportionate weight that people tend to place on losses relative to gains."[44]

Regardless of which measure is used, WTP and WTA analysis can help inform regulatory decision-making through the BCA process. Robert M. Solow, a Nobel Prize–winning economist, once noted that it makes more sense to describe "willingness to pay" as "willingness to sacrifice," precisely because "the underlying rationale of cost-benefit analysis is that the cost of the good thing to be obtained is precisely the good thing that must or will be given up to obtain it."[45] Stated more simply, as the old saying goes: There is no such thing as a free lunch. Trade-offs are inevitable, and that is particularly true when public policy is being made for all consumers who have wildly divergent views on privacy. Using WTP/WTA analysis at least gives policymakers some rough proxies for how much *some* or *most* consumers are willing to sacrifice to gain a bit more privacy.

Exactly how much are most consumers willing to sacrifice to protect privacy? We will return to that question and WTP analysis more generally in Section V. But first we introduce the other side of the BCA equation: the value of services and products created through data collection practices.

B. *The Value of Services and Products*

Privacy-related regulatory proposals can be subjected to BCA analysis, because both "the protection and disclosure of personal data are likely to generate trade-offs with tangible

---

[41] Meredith Kapushion, "Hungry, Hungry HIPPA: When Privacy Regulations Go Too Far," *Fordham Urban Law Journal*, vol. 31 (2003): 1491.

[42] OMB, Circular A-4, at 18.

[43] Alessandro Acquisti, Leslie K. John, and George Loewenstein, "What Is Privacy Worth?" *The Journal of Legal Studies*, vol. 42, no. 2 (June 2013): 255, https://www.cmu.edu/dietrich/sds/docs/loewenstein/WhatPrivacyWorth.pdf.

[44] Ibid. ("Applied to privacy, this explanation of the WTA-WTP gap would predict that someone who enjoyed a particular level of privacy but was asked to pay to increase it would be deterred from doing so by the prospect of the loss of money, whereas someone who was asked to sacrifice privacy for a gain in money would also be reluctant to make the change, deterred in this case by the loss of privacy.")

[45] Robert M. Solow, "Defending Cost-Benefit Analysis: Replies to Steven Kelman," *Regulation* (March/April 1981): 40.

economic dimensions."[46] This is certainly the case as it relates to the potential value of services and products that are generated through online data collection and use.

"Using Facebook is a trade," observes Tom Simonite of *MIT Technology Review*. "You get a way to socialize over the Internet, and the company gets to rent out your eyeballs to advertisers."[47] The quid pro quo Simonite describes here is at work not just for Facebook but also with countless other online platforms and services that the public enjoys today. Instead of charging a fee for the content or services they provide, most online platforms or application providers instead allow free access to the platform or service in exchange for a certain amount of data collection to better target ads or to offer additional services.[48]

This value exchange is not usually well articulated by producers or particularly well understood by consumers.[49] Nonetheless, that value exchange is real and creates substantial benefits for both producers and consumers of these online goods and services. Moreover, "customers have come to expect personalized services and simple access to information systems" thanks to this process.[50]

New York Times technology columnist Farhad Manjoo has documented "the substantial benefits that free, ad-supported services have brought to consumers worldwide. Many hundreds of millions of people now have access to more information and communication technologies because of such services," he argues.[51]

Many studies have documented the benefits associated with commercial data collection and data-driven marketing.[52] A 2016 report from the Direct Marketing Association revealed that, in 2014, data-driven marketing added $202 billion in revenue to the US economy and created more than 1 million jobs.[53] Consultants at Gartner[54] and McKinsey Global Institute[55] have also

---

[46] Alessandro Acquisti, Curtis R. Taylor, and Liad Wagman, "The Economics of Privacy," *Journal of Economic Literature*, vol. 52, no. 2 (2016): 444.

[47] Tom Simonite, "Facebook Has Nuked Ad Blockers, For Now," *MIT Technology Review*, August 9, 2016, https://www.technologyreview.com/s/602138/facebook-has-nuked-ad-blockers-for-now.

[48] Adam Thierer, "A Framework for Benefit-Cost Analysis in Digital Privacy Debates," *George Mason University Law Review*, vol. 20, no. 4 (Summer 2013): 1080.

[49] Jeff Green, "Protecting Behavioral Marketing," *ClickZ*, February 2, 2011, https://www.clickz.com/protecting-behavioral-marketing/53047. ("What makes this conversation so difficult is that marketers need to discuss data rights and leave that discussion with a simple articulation of the quid pro quo. What do you give and what do you get? Until we have that discussion, it's hard to talk about protecting data. In its simplest form, here is how the data protection conversation needs to start: Advertiser says to consumer: 'When you come to my site and give me data, here is how I use it, and here is what I give you in return.' Technology company using data says to publishers: 'When you place this pixel on your website, I will gain these insights and use them in this way, and here is what I give you in return.' It sounds simple. But the reality is that to date, most players in the industry have avoided this discussion. Others have tried burying the details in their terms and conditions and calling that a discussion. It's not.")

[50] Zhan and Rajamani, "The Economics of Privacy," at 101.

[51] Farhad Manjoo, "What Apple's Tim Cook Overlooked in His Defense of Privacy," *New York Times*, June 10, 2015, http://www.nytimes.com/2015/06/11/technology/what-apples-tim-cook-overlooked-in-his-defense-of-privacy.html?_r=0.

[52] Software & Information Industry Association, *Data-Driven Innovation, A Guide for Policymakers: Understanding and Enabling the Economic and Social Value of Data* (May 2013), http://www.siia.net/Divisions/Public-Policy-Advocacy-Services/Priorities/Data-Driven-Innovation.

[53] John Deighton and Peter Johnson, *The Value of Data 2015: Consequences for Insight, Innovation & Efficiency in the U.S. Economy* (2016): 5, http://ddminstitute.thedma.org/#valueofdata.

[54] Gartner, "Gartner Says Big Data Will Drive $28 Billion of IT Spending in 2012," October 17, 2012, http://www.gartner.com/newsroom/id/2200815

[55] James Manyika, Michael Chui, Brad Brown, Jacques Bughin, Richard Dobbs, Charles Roxburgh, and Angela Hung Byers, "Big Data: The Next Frontier for Innovation, Competition, and Productivity," McKinsey Global Institute Report (May 2011): 97–106, http://www.mckinsey.com/insights/business_technology/big_data_the_next_frontier_for_innovation.

produced major reports documenting the significant consumer benefits from "big data" across multiple sectors of the economy.

Commercial data collection efforts enable better targeting of advertising and marketing by producers, which in turn generates a variety of consumer benefits that they may not otherwise have at their disposal.[56] Manjoo notes that "the economic logic of [digital] services" is that "many of them would never work without a business model like advertising. Services like social networks and search engines get substantially better as more people use them – which means that the more they cost to users, the worse they are. They work best when they're free, and the best way to make them free is to pay for them with another business that depends on scale – and advertising is among the best such businesses."[57]

How much more effective are these services thanks to data collection and ad-targeting efforts? Howard Beales, who is a Professor of Strategic Management and Public Policy at George Washington University School of Business and former Director of the Bureau of Consumer Protection at the FTC, has found that "the price of [behaviorally targeted] advertising in 2009 was 2.68 times the price of run of network advertising," and this increased return on investment is important because it creates "greater utility for consumers [from more relevant advertisements] and clear appeal for advertisers" because of the increased conversion of ads into sales.[58]

Generally speaking, the more data that is collected, the better this sort of ad tailoring gets. This enables the creation of even more free (or at least very inexpensive) content and services for consumers.[59] Regulatory enactments aimed at limiting data collection in the name of protecting privacy would, therefore, likely make the production of such services more expensive or even lead them to disappear entirely.

Data aggregation also has broad benefits for low-income populations. James C. Cooper of George Mason University notes that, in recent decades, "the largest increases in credit card ownership are in the bottom half of income earners," and "there was a 77 percent increase in access to consumer credit by the lowest quintile compared to a 14 percent increase for the highest quintile. The poor also appeared to gain from automated underwriting for mortgages."[60] Increased data collection helped make this result possible.

---

[56] Adam Thierer, "Relax and Learn to Love Big Data," *US News & World Report* (blog), September 16, 2013, http://www.usnews.com/opinion/blogs/economic-intelligence/2013/09/16/big-data-collection-has-many-benefits-for-internet-users.

[57] Farhad Manjoo, "What Apple's Tim Cook Overlooked in His Defense of Privacy," *New York Times*, June 10, 2015, http://www.nytimes.com/2015/06/11/technology/what-apples-tim-cook-overlooked-in-his-defense-of-privacy.html?_r=0.

[58] Howard Beales, *The Value of Behavioral Advertising*, (Washington, DC: Network Advertising Initiative, March 2010): 3. http://www.networkadvertising.org/pdfs/Beales_NAI_Study.pdf. A more recent study from Beales and economist Jeffrey Eisenach, which was sponsored by the Digital Advertising Alliance, revealed that advertisers place significantly greater value on users for whom more information is available, and … the availability of cookies to capture user-specific information is found to increase the observed exchange transaction price by at least 60 percent relative to the average price (for users with "new" cookies), and by as much as 200 percent (for users with longer-lived cookies). J. Howard Beales and Jeffrey A. Eisenach, "An Empirical Analysis of the Value of Information Sharing in the Market for Online Content," (January 2014): 1, http://papers.ssrn.com/sol3/papers.cfm?abstract_id=2421405.

[59] Beales and Jeffrey A. Eisenach, ibid., at 16 ("At a time when 'traditional media' face considerable challenges to their underlying business models, online advertising constitutes a dynamic and rapidly expanding component of the digital economy. The advent of information sharing in the market for online content has created unprecedented opportunities for the exchange of information to more efficiently connect consumers with the ultimate suppliers of the products they value the most." The authors continue on to note that "the largest publishers rely on third-party technology models for approximately half of their advertising needs, while 'long-tail' publishers rely even more heavily on these models.").

[60] James C. Cooper, "Separation, Pooling, and Big Data," George Mason University Legal Studies *Research Paper Series* LS 15–15, *Virginia Journal of Law & Technology* (2016): at 20.

Consider another example of how data collection enables the creation of new services that might be particularly valuable for low-income consumers. When Google launched its free e-mail service Gmail in 2004, some privacy advocates reacted angrily about how Google was going to target ads based on the content of e-mails. Critics even encouraged lawmakers to ban such algorithmic contextual targeting[61] and legislation was subsequently introduced in California that would have done so.[62] The legislation did not pass, however, and consumers quickly adapted their privacy expectations to accommodate this new service, somewhat to the dismay of some privacy advocates.[63]

Today, Gmail has over 1 billion monthly actives users and the free service is taken for granted by many consumers.[64] But it is worth remembering that before the service existed, major e-mail providers offered users less than 10 megabytes of e-mail storage, far more limited functionality, and charged them a price for those services (typically $10–20 per month). This makes the value exchange clear and even quantifiable for purposes of a hypothetical BCA: If privacy-related regulation had made a service such as Gmail illegal, consumers would have been paying more for a lesser service. That would have disadvantaged many low-income consumers, who might struggle to pay monthly fees for such services.

This is not to say there are no privacy concerns related to the contextual targeting of digital ads based on the content of e-mail messages. Rather, it is simply meant to illustrate the trade-offs at work when public policy acts to limit data collection and use. Once policymakers have a feel for the potential downsides of limiting data collection in contexts like this, they will be in a better position to determine whether the benefits of proposed regulation will outweigh these costs.

Privacy regulation could have other costs that could be estimated as part of the BCA process. Today's "app economy" has given small innovators the chance to compete on an even footing with larger players.[65] Data limitations could deleteriously impact new business formation or the expansion of existing firms and services. By raising the cost of doing business, regulation can act as a barrier to new entry and innovation, especially for smaller operators and new start-ups that may find it difficult to comply with such rules or absorb the costs of doing so.

"In a setting where first-party advertising is allowable but third-party marketing is not, substantial advantages may be created for large incumbent firms," argue economists Avi Goldfarb and Catherine Tucker.[66] "For example, if a large website or online service were able to use its data to market and target advertising, it will be able to continue to improve and hone its advertising, while new entrants will find it difficult to challenge the incumbent's predominance by compiling other data or collecting their own data."[67] This could, in turn, affect market

---

[61] *See* Letter from Chris Jay Hoofnagle, Electronic Privacy Information Center, Beth Givens, Privacy Rights Clearinghouse, and Pam Dixon, World Privacy Forum, to California Attorney General Lockyer, May 3, 2004, http://epic.org/privacy/gmail/agltr5.3.04.html.

[62] S.B. 1822, 2003–04 Reg. Sess. (Cal. 2004).

[63] Paul Ohm, "Branding Privacy," *Minnesota Law Review*, vol. 97 (2013): 907 (noting that the Gmail case study "serves as a reminder of the limits of privacy law, because sometimes the consuming public, faced with truthful full disclosure about a service's privacy choices, will nevertheless choose the bad option for privacy, at which point there is often little left for privacy advocates and regulators to do").

[64] Frederic Lardinois, "Gmail Now Has More Than 1B Monthly Active Users" (February 1, 2016), https://techcrunch.com/2016/02/01/gmail-now-has-more-than-1b-monthly-active-users.

[65] Michael Mandel, "Where the Jobs Are: The App Economy," *TechNet* (February 7, 2012), http://www.technet.org/wp-content/uploads/2012/02/TechNet-App-Economy-Jobs-Study.pdf. ("The App Economy now is responsible for roughly 466,000 jobs in the United States, up from zero in 2007 when the iPhone was introduced.")

[66] Avi Goldfarb and Catherine Tucker, "Comments on 'Information Privacy and Innovation in the Internet Economy,'" Comments to the US Department of Commerce (Jan. 24, 2011), at 4, http://www.ntia.doc.gov/comments/101214614-0614-01/attachments/NTIA_comments_2011_01_24.pdf.

[67] Ibid.

structure and the overall competitiveness of certain sectors of the economy, which could also act to limit consumer choices or raise their costs. Again, these are the sort of costs that can be considered and estimated as part of the BCA process.

IV. SYNTHESIS AND SOLUTIONS

If it is the case that aggregating millions of individual privacy preferences is riddled with thorny philosophical challenges, yet estimating the cost of regulatory enactments is far more feasible, some skeptics might insist that the deck is stacked against privacy when it comes to BCA efforts.[68] But just because estimating the benefits of proposed regulations is more difficult than quantifying their potential costs, it does not automatically foreclose the possibility of policy action.

To reiterate, at least in the United States, the BCA process has repeatedly acknowledged that values "including equity, human dignity, fairness, and distributive impacts" (Executive Order 13563) should be considered alongside other issues.[69] It may be the case that after a thorough review of all the costs associated with proposed regulatory enactments that policymakers still find the case for regulation compelling because of the various perceived benefits associated with new rules. Making that determination will never be an exact science, but the democratic process is better off for weighing these costs and benefits as best it can.

This section considers a few additional factors that may come into play as regulators undertake such a review.

A. *The Importance of WTP Analysis*

As noted earlier, WTP/WTA analysis is likely to be an extremely important part of any privacy-related BCA. Using public polling results to gauge consumer privacy valuations will not be sufficient.[70] Public opinion polls about privacy-related matters often ask binary, simplistic questions that do not force respondents to consider the costs or other trade-offs associated with their answers.[71] How questions are framed in polls also has a strong influence on how much people say they value privacy.[72]

---

[68] Julie Cohen, "The Regulatory State in the Information Age," *Theoretical Inquiries in Law*, vol. 17, no. 2 (2016): 35. ("Because cost-benefit analysis contemplates that even serious harms may be outweighed by higher levels of overall economic benefit, and because it tends to weigh the concrete costs of regulatory implementation more heavily than the more diffuse benefits to be realized from compliance, it offers a particularly congenial technique for achieving that result. At the same time, the increasingly tight conflation of cost-benefit review with regulatory rationality has meant that critics have found themselves placed in the unenviable role of Luddites, advancing complex conceptions of dignity and fairness to counter a simpler, more accessible narrative.")

[69] Improving Regulation and Regulatory Review, 76 Fed. Reg. at 3,822.

[70] Kai-Lung Hui and I. P. L. Png, "The Economics of Privacy," in Terrence Hendershott, ed., *Handbooks in Information Systems*, vol. 1 (2006): 17, http://www.comp.nus.edu.sg/~ipng/research/privacy_HISE.pdf. ("Clearly, it would be misleading to judge the importance of privacy from opinion polls alone. Rigorous experiments are necessary to gauge the actual value that people attach to their personal information under various circumstances.").

[71] Jim Harper and Solveig Singleton, "With a Grain of Salt: What Consumer Privacy Surveys Don't Tell Us," Competitive Enterprise Institute (June 2001): 1, http://papers.ssrn.com/sol3/papers.cfm?abstract_id=299930. ("Privacy surveys in particular ... suffer from the 'talk is cheap' problem. It costs a consumer nothing to express a desire for federal law to protect privacy. But if such law became a reality, it will cost the economy as a whole, and consumers in particular, significant amounts that surveys do not and cannot reveal."); Berin Szoka, "Privacy Polls v. Real-World Trade-Offs," Progress & Freedom Foundation, *Progress Snapshot* (November 2009), http://www.pff.org/issues-pubs/ps/2009/pdf/ps5.10-privacy-polls-tradeoffs.pdf.

[72] Daniel Castro, "New Survey Shows Some Privacy Scholars Lack Objectivity," *Innovation Files* (October 14, 2012), http://www.innovationfiles.org/new-survey-shows-some-privacy-scholars-lack-objectivity.

The end result is that polls inevitably show strong demand for "more privacy" without providing much context about what that means relative to the other factors in play. "To understand and model privacy," argue Harvard researchers Luc Wathieu and Allan Friedman, "more information is needed about consumer preferences, beyond 'people want privacy.'"[73] Simply because people say they are concerned about privacy or want more of it does not mean they will pay a premium for it.[74] "Most studies ask for personal opinion, rather than measure the digital choices people make," notes *New York Times* reporter Somini Sengupta.[75] Willingness-to-pay analysis can help *partially* remedy this problem by more rigorously evaluating consumer decisions in both real-world environments and laboratory experiments.

Exactly how much are consumers willing to sacrifice to gain a bit more privacy? Evidence suggests that the answer is: not as much as they say they do. The most comprehensive surveys of the literature on the economics of privacy have been conducted by Alessandro Acquisti of Carnegie Mellon University along with various coauthors. His research has found that "surveys of US respondents have repeatedly highlighted privacy as one of the most significant concerns of Internet users" but "at the same time as they profess their need for privacy, most consumers remain avid users of information technologies that track and share their personal information with unknown third parties."[76] This is the so-called "privacy paradox" or the fact that, generally speaking, even though many people say they want their privacy protected, "they are willing to trade off personal information for small rewards, or are unwilling to change their behavior when privacy threats arise."[77]

In the economics literature, this sort of phenomenon is commonly referred to as "hypothetical bias," or "the difference between hypothetical and actual statements of value, where actual statements of value are obtained from experiments with real economic commitments."[78] Economists also speak of "revealed preference," which refers to how "people may reveal their valuations of nonmarket goods through their actions."[79] Economists use "contingent valuation" surveys to determine how much consumers would actually pay for certain goods and services as compared to their stated preferences. A 2001 meta-analysis of twenty-nine experimental studies found that "on average subjects overstate their preferences by a factor of about 3 in hypothetical settings."[80]

---

[73] Luc Wathieu and Allan Friedman, "An Empirical Approach to Understanding Privacy Valuation," Harvard Business School Division of Research, Working Paper No. 07–075 (2007): 8, http://www.hbs.edu/faculty/Publication%20Files/07-075.pdf.

[74] Jessica Guynn, "Gmail Is Target of New Microsoft Privacy Campaign against Google," *Los Angeles Times*, February 6, 2013, http://www.latimes.com/business/technology/la-fi-tn-microsoft-privacy-campaign-against-google-gmail-20130206,0,6815888.story (quoting SearchEngineLand.com founding editor Danny Sullivan as saying, "While people in polls say they are concerned, in reality they are really not that concerned").

[75] Somini Sengupta, "What Would You Pay for Privacy?" *New York Times Bits Blog*, March 19, 2012, http://bits.blogs.nytimes.com/2012/03/19/what-would-you-pay-for-privacy.

[76] Alessandro Acquisti, Curtis R. Taylor, and Liad Wagman, "The Economics of Privacy," *Journal of Economic Literature*, vol. 52, no. 2 (2016): 476.

[77] Jens Grossklags and Alessandro Acquisti, "When 25 Cents Is Too Much: An Experiment on Willingness-To-Sell and Willingness-To-Protect Personal Information," unpublished manuscript (June 7, 2007): 3, http://people.ischool.berkeley.edu/~jensg/research/paper/Grossklags_Acquisti-WEIS07.pdf.

[78] John A. List and Craig A. Gallet, "What Experimental Protocol Influence Disparities between Actual and Hypothetical Stated Values?" *Environmental and Resource Economics*, vol. 20 (2001): 243. ("Understanding why people misstate their actual preferences for a good when asked a hypothetical question remains an important issue in nonmarket valuation. While biases have been observed in both directions, much work in this literature suggests that people tend to overstate their actual willingness to pay in hypothetical situations." Ibid., at 241.)

[79] Morrall and Broughel, at 22.

[80] John A. List and Craig A. Gallet, "What Experimental Protocol Influence Disparities between Actual and Hypothetical Stated Values?" *Environmental and Resource Economics*, vol. 20 (2001): 241.

Several privacy-related studies have documented this hypothetical bias or revealed preference in action. For example:

- A 2005 experiment involving 206 online shoppers conducted by German analysts from Humboldt University in Berlin noted that consumers "do not always act in line with their stated privacy preferences, giving away information about themselves without any compelling reason to do so."[81] In this case, "[personal information] disclosure was alarmingly high across all clusters, belying the previously expressed reluctance to disclose information online."[82]
- A 2007 study coauthored by Acquisti and Jens Grossklags found that, when confronted with the option to protect or sell their information, "individuals almost always chose to sell their information and almost never elect[ed] to protect their information even for values as little as $0.25."[83]
- A 2012 study by the European Network and Information Security Agency that combined laboratory and field experiments revealed a strong interest in privacy-friendly services among consumers when price was not a consideration.[84] However, where price differs among similar services, the survey found that "the market share of the privacy-friendly service provider drops, below or close to one third" relative to the "privacy-invasive" offering.[85]
- A 2013 study of smartphone apps and privacy by Scott J. Savage and Donald M. Waldman of the University of Colorado at Boulder found that "the representative consumer is willing to make a one-time payment for each app of $2.28 to conceal their browser history, $4.05 to conceal their list of contacts, $1.19 to conceal their location, $1.75 to conceal their phone's identification number, and $3.58 to conceal the contents of their text messages. The consumer is also willing to pay $2.12 to eliminate advertising," the authors noted.[86] These are not significant WTP sums when compared to higher estimated benefits of $5.06 per app for consumers. However, the authors did find that "more experienced" consumers were willing to spend more to protect their information when compared to "less experienced" consumers.[87]
- A 2016 experimental analysis by law professors Lior Strahilevitz of the University of Chicago Law School and Matthew B. Kugler of Northwestern University School of Law reveals that only one-third of participants "expressed a willingness to pay any amount of money to receive a version of their e-mail service that did not use automated e-mail content analysis to deliver personalized ads" and that "the median willingness to pay was $15 per year. Just 3% of the sample expressed a willingness to pay more than $120 per year for such an e-mail service," they found.[88]

---

[81] Bettina Berendt et al., "Privacy in E-Commerce: Stated Preferences vs. Actual Behavior," *Communications of the ACM*, vol. 48, no. 4 (April 2005): 104, http://cacm.acm.org/magazines/2005/4/6247-privacy-in-e-commerce/abstract.

[82] Ibid., at 104.

[83] Jens Grossklags and Alessandro Acquisti, "When 25 Cents Is Too Much: An Experiment on Willingness-to-Sell and Willingness-to-Protect Personal Information," unpublished manuscript (June 7, 2007): 6, http://people.ischool.berkeley.edu/~jensg/research/paper/Grossklags_Acquisti-WEIS07.pdf.

[84] Nicola Jentzsch et al., European Union Agency for Network & Information Security, *Study on Monetizing Privacy: An Economic Model for Pricing Personal Information* (2012): 37–9, https://www.enisa.europa.eu/publications/monetising-privacy.

[85] Ibid., at 1, 5.

[86] Scott J. Savage and Donald M. Waldman, "The Value of Online Privacy," University of Colorado at Boulder, Discussion Papers in Economics, Working Paper No. 13–02 (October 2013): 1, http://www.colorado.edu/Economics/papers/Wps-13/wp13-02/wp13-02.pdf.

[87] Ibid., at 29, 1.

[88] Lior Strahilevitz and Matthew B. Kugler, "Is Privacy Policy Language Irrelevant to Consumers?" *Journal of Legal Studies*, vol. 45, http://papers.ssrn.com/sol3/papers.cfm?abstract_id=2838449.

Tellingly, consumer behavior also does not change much in the aftermath of major data breaches, even though the public has a more visceral feel for the potential losses. As a 2013 *ZDNet* headline by Steve Ranger put it: "Everyone worries about data leaks, but shares everything anyway."[89] Ranger continued on the note that:

> Consumer concern about privacy had led some to warn that – if privacy concerns are not addressed – a privacy black hole could emerge and undermine the internet economy, which is based on the permanent and easy availability of personal data that can be harvested, repackaged and resold. However, according to the Economist Intelligence Unit report only 38 percent of respondents said they had stopped dealing with a company after it suffered a data breach, suggestion that tolerance of such events is greater than some may have thought.[90]

Scholars interpret such WTP results differently with one camp suggesting that "actions really do speak louder than words, and that consumers are comfortable with the way things are."[91] It is undoubtedly doubt true that "if privacy were free, we would all want more,"[92] but that assertion does not incorporate real-world trade-offs. When faced with the potential for higher prices, lesser service, lower quality products, or even just greater inconvenience, many consumers reveal that they are unwilling to pay much to better protect their privacy. These insights might better inform BCA analysis for privacy-related matters.

However, another view of the WTP literature and results is that "consumers are rarely (if ever) completely aware about privacy threats and the consequences of sharing and protecting their personal information."[93] It may be the case that more and better disclosures about data collection policies could help remedy this problem. Unfortunately, new research from Omri Ben-Shahar and Adam Chilton, both of the University of Chicago Law School, finds that simplified privacy disclosures that warned users of more sensitive data collection about sexual issues were no more likely to alter consumer behavior than other disclosures.[94] This again reflects a general unwillingness by consumers to pay for better privacy protections.

Then again, there aren't many services on the market today that offer consumers an alternative experience for what we might think of as a "privacy premium," or a surcharge for a more privacy-enhancing experience. Even though current WTP literature suggests that consumers would not be willing to pay much (or anything) for such services, we may not know their true value to the public unless more of those services are offered.

For that reason, some privacy advocates and analysts have clamored for more pay-for-privacy options, with some of those advocates going so far as to beg online service and application

---

[89] Steve Ranger, "The End of Privacy? Everyone Worries about Data Leaks, but Shares Everything Anyway," *ZDNet*, April 19, 2013, http://www.zdnet.com/article/the-end-of-privacy-everyone-worries-about-data-leaks-but-shares-everything-anyway.

[90] Ibid.

[91] James Cooper, "Rational Ignorance and the Privacy Paradox," *Forbes*, July 18, 2016, http://www.forbes.com/sites/jamesccooper1/2016/07/18/rational-ignorance-and-the-privacy-paradox/#2eff27641f70.

[92] Kapushion, at 1487.

[93] Alessandro Acquisti, Curtis R. Taylor, and Liad Wagman, "The Economics of Privacy," *Journal of Economic Literature*, vol. 52, no. 2 (2016): 444.

[94] Omri Ben-Shahar and Adam S. Chilton, "Simplification of Privacy Disclosures: An Experimental Test," University of Chicago Coase-Sandor Institute for Law & Economics Research Paper No. 737, April 13, 2016, http://papers.ssrn.com/sol3/Papers.cfm?abstract_id=2711474; (altering the formal properties of the privacy disclosures had essentially no effect on respondents' comprehension of our disclosure, willingness to disclose information, or expectations about their privacy rights.").

providers to make them pay for their sites and services.[95] "Truly, the only way to get around the privacy problems inherent in advertising-supported social networks is to pay for services that we value," argues Alexis Madrigal of *The Atlantic*.[96] "It's amazing what power we gain in becoming paying customers instead of the product being sold," he says.[97]

Again, it is not clear that consumers would really choose any differently even if they were offered more priced service models which focused on privacy protection. Alternatively, consumers might choose an upsell model that optimized other values: better functionality, additional content, greater security, etc. Finally, it is worth nothing that when privacy advocates suggest higher prices can better help protect privacy, those same price increases would constitute a diminution of consumer welfare in the eyes of most regulatory economists, who have traditionally advocated regulation to lower consumer prices, not raise them.

B. *The Role of PETs*

There are other variables that could affect the decision about whether or not new regulations are warranted. As was noted in Section III, the BCA process requires that alternatives to regulation be considered when evaluating the need for new rules. One potential factor in this regard is the market for privacy enhancing technologies (PET), which are digital "self-help" tools that let users block or limit various types of advertising and data collection or enjoy a more anonymous online experience.

Many different types of PETs are available today.[98] For example, "ad preference managers" that let users manage their advertising preferences are available from major online search and advertising providers. Apple, Google, Microsoft, Yahoo! and others also offer advertising opt-out tools as well as variations on "private browsing" mode, which allows users to turn on a stealth browsing mode to avoid data collection and other forms of tracking. Similarly, some variant of a "Do Not Track" mechanism or an opt-out registry is now included in all major browsers to complement the cookie controls they had already offered.

Independent ad-blocking tools and cookie-blocking technologies are quite popular and easy to download and configure. Meanwhile, new privacy-oriented search engines such as Duck-DuckGO[99] and Oscobo[100] offer a search experience that blocks data collection altogether.[101] Many leading instant messaging apps also offer end-to-end encryption, including Facebook Inc.'s WhatsApp, Apple's iMessage, and Signal by Open Whisper Systems.[102] There also exists

---

[95] Zeynep Tufekci, "Mark Zuckerberg, Let Me Pay for Facebook," *New York Times*, June 4, 2015, http://www.nytimes .com/2015/06/04/opinion/zeynep-tufekci-mark-zuckerberg-let-me-pay-for-facebook.html.

[96] Alexis C. Madrigal, "Why You Should Want to Pay for Software, Instagram Edition," *The Atlantic*, December 17, 2012, http://www.theatlantic.com/technology/archive/2012/12/why-you-should-want-to-pay-for-software-instagram-edi tion/266367.

[97] Ibid.

[98] "66 Ways to Protect Your Privacy Right Now," *Consumer Reports*, September 20, 2016, http://www.consumerreports .org/privacy/66-ways-to-protect-your-privacy-right-now.

[99] "We Don't Collect or Share Personal Information," DuckDuckGo, http://duckduckgo.com/privacy.html. (last visited September 16, 2016);

[100] Ryan Chiavetta, "Oscobo Lets Users Search without Fear of Tracking," *Privacy Tech*, August 8, 2016, https://iapp.org/ news/a/oscobo-lets-users-search-without-fear-of-tracking.

[101] Jennifer Valentino-DeVries, "Can Search Engines Compete on Privacy?" *Wall Street Journal Digits* (blog), January 25, 2011, http://blogs.wsj.com/digits/2011/01/25/can-search-engines-compete-on-privacy.

[102] Nathan Olivarez-Giles, "Messaging Apps Vary Widely When It Comes to Privacy," *Wall Street Journal*, September 26, 2016, http://www.wsj.com/articles/messaging-apps-vary-widely-when-it-comes-to-privacy-1474920203.

a large and growing market of independent digital security tools, including antivirus and anti-malware technologies and services.[103]

On the one hand, the existence of such a broad class of PETs suggests that consumers have ways of addressing privacy concerns even in the absence of new regulation. This could be factored into the BCA process when determining the need for new rules and might weigh against imposing new restrictions on data collection. On the other hand, public adoption of these technologies tends to be quite low. This may be because not every individual or household has the same privacy needs. Or it could be the case due to a lack of adequate information or public education about these options.

Does the low adoption of PETs tell us anything about WTP analysis for privacy more generally? In some cases the relationship between the price and adoption of PETs seems perfectly logical. For example, the Blackphone, a smartphone "that prioritizes privacy over everything else," was announced in October 2014 for a retail price of $629.[104] It offered fully encrypted messaging and voice calls. A successor (the Blackphone 2) was launched the following summer for $800 and billed as a way to "test whether security is a priority for smartphone buyers."[105] "Now that there's an alternative that boasts strong security," Chris O'Brien of *VentureBeat* noted at the time, "it's going to be intriguing to see whether buyers have indeed changed their attitudes about security. Or whether we're just as lazy and indifferent as ever."[106] Less than a year later, however, Blackphone was losing money, laying off employees, and "flirting with failure."[107]

Blackphone's difficulties may indicate that expecting consumers to pay a privacy premium of $800 is simply too steep a price. Then again, even less expensive PETs or ones that are entirely free of charge to consumers are not being widely adopted. Regardless, real-word data about these choices can help inform the BCA process when policymakers are considering new regulations. At a minimum, policymakers can probably safely conclude that any new regulation that significantly raises costs to consumers – or which requires them to purchase expensive services to better protect their privacy – are unlikely to achieve widespread public adoption.

C. *Alternative Legal Remedies*

Alternative legal or regulatory remedies are also regularly considered as part of the BCA process in an attempt to determine whether existing policies might provide solutions to perceived problems. For privacy-related matters, many such alternatives to new regulation exist.

In the United States, targeted federal statutes exist that address sensitive issues related to health,[108] financial,[109] and children's privacy,[110] among other concerns. This probably reflects

---

[103] Online security and digital privacy are related, but also distinct in some ways. For example, technically speaking, antivirus and other anti-malware technologies are considered security tools, but they can also help protect a user's privacy by guarding information she wishes to keep private.

[104] Jamie Rigg, "Blackphone Review: Putting a Price on Privacy," *Engadget*, October 3, 2014, https://www.engadget.com/2014/10/03/blackphone-review.

[105] Chris O'Brien, "Blackphone 2 from Silent Circle Will Test Whether Security Is a Priority for Smartphone Buyers," *VentureBeat*, August 21, 2015, http://venturebeat.com/2015/08/21/blackphone-2-from-silent-circle-will-test-whether-security-is-a-priority-for-smartphone-buyers.

[106] Ibid.

[107] Thomas Fox-Brewster, "Sorry Privacy Lovers, the Blackphone Is Flirting with Failure," *Forbes*, July 6, 2016, http://www.forbes.com/sites/thomasbrewster/2016/07/06/silent-circle-blackphone-losses-layoffs-geekphone-lawsuit/#55eadf3060df.

[108] *See* Health Breach Notification Rule (2009), 16 C.F.R. § 318.1 (2012).

[109] *See* Truth in Lending Act, 15 U.S.C. §§ 1601–1667(f) (2006); Fair Credit Billing Act, 15 U.S.C. §§ 1666–1666(j) (2006); Fair Credit Reporting Act of 1970, 15 U.S.C. §§ 1681–1681(u) (2006).

[110] *See* Children's Online Privacy Protection Act (COPPA) of 1998, 15 U.S.C. § 6501 (2006).

the fact that "the most stable and widely accepted privacy rights in the United States have long been those that are tethered to unambiguous tangible or physical rights, such as rights in body and property, especially the sanctity of the home."[111]

Other legal remedies are available through lower state courts including torts,[112] contract law,[113] and targeted state statutes.[114] "Privacy class actions have become a major financial liability for technology companies"[115] and class action lawsuit activity is particularly intense following data breaches.[116] For example, in September 2016, just days after news broke that it had suffered a massive data breach, Yahoo! was hit with lawsuits accusing the company of gross negligence.[117]

The US Federal Trade Commission (FTC) also possesses broad enforcement authority to monitor unfair and deceptive information practices and the agency has been using that authority more aggressively in recent years.[118] The FTC's approach to policing such practices originated with its statutorily granted authority under Section 5 of the Federal Trade Commission Act,[119] which prohibits "unfair or deceptive acts or practices in or affecting commerce."[120]

The FTC's interpretation of this authority was clarified in its 1980 *Policy Statement on Unfairness*, in which the agency noted that, "[t]o justify a finding of unfairness the injury must

---

[111] Adam Thierer, "The Pursuit of Privacy in a World Where Information Control Is Failing," *Harvard Journal of Law & Public Policy*, vol. 36 (2013): 416.

[112] See Jim Harper, *The Privacy Torts: How U.S. State Law Quietly Leads the Way in Privacy Protection* (2002), http:// www.privacilla.org/releases/Torts_Report.html.

[113] See Jim Harper, "Understanding Privacy – and the Real Threats to It," Cato Institute, *Policy Analysis* (August 4, 2004): 3, www.cato.org/pub_display.php?pub_id=1652: "Contract law, for example, allows consumers to enter into enforceable agreements that restrict the sharing of information involved in or derived from transactions. Thanks to contract, one person may buy foot powder from another and elicit as part of the deal an enforceable promise never to tell another soul about the purchase."

[114] State governments and state attorneys general also continue to advance their own privacy policies, and those enforcement efforts are often more stringent than federal law. Christopher Wolf, "Targeted Enforcement and Shared Lawmaking Authority as Catalysts for Data Protection," (2010): 3, http://www.justice.gov.il/NR/rdonlyres/8D438C53-82C8-4F25-99F8-E3039D40E4E4/26451/Consumer_WOLFDataProtectionandPrivacyCommissioners.pdf. (At the state level, legislatures have become the proving grounds for new statutory approaches to privacy regulation. Some of these developments include the enactment of data security breach notification laws . . . as well as highly detailed data security laws, enacted largely in response to data breaches. This partnership has resulted in a set of robust standards for the protection of personal data.")

[115] Lior Strahilevitz and Matthew B. Kugler, "Is Privacy Policy Language Irrelevant to Consumers?" *Journal of Legal Studies*, vol. 45 (2016): 10, http://papers.ssrn.com/sol3/papers.cfm?abstract_id=2838449.

[116] Peter Fleischer, "Privacy-Litigation: Get Ready for an Avalanche in Europe," *Peter Fleischer: Privacy?* (blog) (October 26, 2012), http://peterfleischer.blogspot.com/2012/10/privacy-litigation-get-ready-for.html?m=1: "Within hours of any newspaper headline (accurate or not) alleging any sort of privacy mistake, a race begins among privacy class action lawyers to find a plaintiff and file a class action. Most of these class actions are soon dismissed, or settled as nuisance suits, because most of them fail to be able to demonstrate any 'harm' from the alleged privacy breach. But a small percentage of privacy class actions do result in large transfers of money, first and foremost to the class action lawyers themselves, which is enough to keep the wheels of the litigation-machine turning."

[117] Horia Ungureanu, "Yahoo Sued for Gross Negligence over Massive Data Breach," *Tech Times*, September 24, 2016, http://www.techtimes.com/articles/179224/20160924/yahoo-sued-for-gross-negligence-over-massive-data-breach.htm#s thash.jhtF6aWq.dpuf.

[118] In its March 2012 report, *Protecting Consumer Privacy in an Era of Rapid Change*, the FTC noted that, using its Section 5 authority and other powers, the agency has carried out many privacy and data security-related actions just since December 2010. Federal Trade Commission, *Protecting Consumer Privacy in an Era of Rapid Change: Recommendations for Businesses and Policymakers* (2012) at ii, http://ftc.gov/os/2012/03/120326privacyreport.pdf. The FTC has brought many other privacy and data security-related cases using its Section 5 powers since that 2012 report was released.

[119] See J. Howard Beales, "The FTC's Use of Unfairness Authority: Its Rise, Fall, and Resurrection," Federal Trade Commission (May 30, 2003), http://www.ftc.gov/public-statements/2003/05/ftcs-use-unfairness-authority-its-rise-fall-and-resurrection; J. Thomas Rosch, Federal Trade Commission, "Deceptive and Unfair Acts and Practices Principles: Evolution and Convergence," Speech at the California State Bar, (May 18, 2007), https://www.ftc.gov/public-statements/2007/05/deceptive-and-unfair-acts-and-practices-principles-evolution-and.

[120] 15 U.S.C. § 45(a) (2012).

satisfy three tests"[121]: "It must be substantial; it must not be outweighed by any countervailing benefits to consumers or competition that the practice produces; and it must be an injury that consumers themselves could not reasonably have avoided."[122] Two former FTC officials have noted that this "is essentially a cost-benefit test."[123] The FTC's *Policy Statement* also specified that "the Commission is not concerned with trivial or merely speculative harms ... Emotional impact and other more subjective types of harm ... will not ordinarily make a practice unfair."[124]

In practice, this means that the agency demands that firms live up to the privacy and security promises they make to the public and that they avoid "overt misrepresentations about privacy practices that are presumptively material," as current FTC Commissioner Maureen K. Ohlhausen has noted. "The deception approach helps to protect consumers who choose a particular product based upon the company's representations about that product's privacy impact."[125]

Finally, in additional to these legal remedies, ongoing cultural and technological change is often factored into the BCA process. Again, President Obama's Executive Order 13610 noted that agencies "conduct retrospective analyses of existing rules to examine whether they remain justified and whether they should be modified or streamlined in light of changed circumstances, including the rise of new technologies."[126] This could be particularly important as relates to privacy-related proposals because public attitudes about privacy tend to evolve over time – sometimes quite rapidly.[127]

V. CONCLUSION

Benefit-cost analysis and privacy protection efforts are not incompatible. Merely because the calculation of the benefits and costs associated with privacy proposals is challenging does not mean the analysis should be avoided.[128] In the end, we return to the fact that *context matters*. As Acquisti and his coauthors note, "It is not possible to conclude unambiguously whether privacy protection entails a net 'positive' or 'negative' change in purely economic terms: its impact is context specific."[129]

While imperfect, benefit-cost analysis can help policymakers and the public make better decisions about how to spend scarce societal resources, no matter what the context. Deliberative democracy works better when policymakers have more information at their disposal to make challenging decisions such as these.

[121] Letter from the Federal Trade Commission to Wendell H. Ford, Chairman, Consumer Subcommittee, US Senate Committee on Commerce, Science, & Transportation, & John C. Danforth, Ranking Minority Member, Consumer Subcommittee, US Senate Committee on Commerce, Science & Transportation (December 17, 1980), http://www.ftc.gov/bcp/policystmt/ad-unfair.htm [hereinafter FTC Policy Statement on Unfairness].
[122] FTC, *Policy Statement on Unfairness*.
[123] J. Howard Beales, III and Timothy J. Muris, "Choice or Consequences: Protecting Privacy in Commercial Information," *University of Chicago Law Review*, vol. 75 (2008): 109.
[124] FTC, *Policy Statement on Unfairness* (footnotes omitted).
[125] Maureen K. Ohlhausen and Alexander P. Okuliar, "Competition, Consumer Protection, and the Right [Approach] to Privacy," *Antitrust Law Journal*, vol. 80 (2015).
[126] "Identifying and Reducing Regulatory Burdens," *Federal Register*, Vol. 77, at 28,469.
[127] Adam Thierer, "Technopanics, Threat Inflation, and the Danger of an Information Technology Precautionary Principle," *Minnesota Journal of Law, Science & Technology*, vol. 14, no. 1 (2013): 312–50.
[128] Morrall and Broughel, at 28. ("Organized, objective, and transparent information is generally necessary for good decisions, especially if they are complicated. 'It's complicated' is not an excuse for not doing benefit-cost analysis. In fact it is a reason to do it. Imperfect information is better than no information as long as it is not intentionally biased.")
[129] Alessandro Acquisti, Curtis R. Taylor, and Liad Wagman, "The Economics of Privacy," *Journal of Economic Literature*, vol. 52, no. 2 (2016): 443–44.

32

Privacy after the Agile Turn

Seda Gürses and Joris van Hoboken[*]

1 INTRODUCTION

The objective of this chapter is to explore how recent paradigmatic transformations in the production of digital functionality have changed the conditions for privacy governance. We are motivated by the lack of scholarship that focuses on these transformations and how they matter to privacy in the future.[1] The introduction of information systems in different spheres of societal activity continues to spark privacy issues. But for those who are trying to understand the issues and come up with solutions, what is our mental model of how information systems and digital functionality are produced? Are privacy research and policy sufficiently informed by the predominant modes of production? This chapter originates from the realization that this may not sufficiently be the case.

Generally, the aim of this chapter is twofold. First, we wish to stimulate privacy researchers and policy makers to pay more attention to the production of digital functionality, instead of merely looking at the results of such production for privacy. Second, our goal is to help construct a starting point for doing so. To get there, this chapter looks at a combination of three transformations in the production of digital functionality, which we jointly denote "the agile turn." In short, these are the shifts from waterfall to agile development, from shrink-wrap software to services, and from the PC to the cloud. After clarifying and situating the agile turn, we study its implications for privacy governance through the lens of three high-level perspectives: modularity, temporality and capture. These perspectives allow us to foreground the directions in which the agile turn requires privacy research and policy to focus more of their attention. In the process, we also underline when and how privacy scholarship and policy implicitly rely on modes of software production that are long outdated.

Academic work on privacy has focused on several framings to grasp, reflect on and criticize the developments in technology and society. One theme has emerged under the overarching frame of *data*, paralleling the focus in data privacy regulation on personal data. Privacy concerns in this frame are expressed in terms of the effects of data flows. Accumulations of personal data and the exchange of data in markets are seen to have the potential to lead to information and power asymmetries between individuals and data-hoarding organizations. Such asymmetries can have negative consequences for the freedom to have a private life, informational

[*] The research for this paper was conducted as a Postdoctoral Research Fellow at the Information Law Institute (ILI), New York University and Visiting Scholar at the NYU Stern Center for Business & Human Rights, New York University.
[1] One notable exception is the work on privacy decisions of IOS developers by Shilton and Greene 2016.

self-determination, autonomy and contextual social norms. In this approach, data in itself has great agency in determining the conditions of surveillance, knowledge, and violations of privacy.

A second frame has taken to analyzing algorithms (that crunch data) as its main direction of inquiry. Algorithms are seen as (opaque) gatekeepers of access, life chances, decision making and social formation. Their implementations trouble some of the core concepts of liberal democracies such as accountability, fairness, autonomy and due process (Ziewitz, 2016). The algorithmic lens brings into focus the relational and messy agency of artifacts in socio-technical systems, exploring ways to demonstrate and make accountable the potential of mathematical constructs to influence everyday activities in complex ways.

Finally, much scholarship has focused on the social turn, user agency and privacy. With the rise of Web 2.0, a more dynamic and participatory environment was created, which gave rise to social networks and related technologies. In a deliberate attempt to resist techno-centric narratives, critical work in this area focuses on how users interpret and make meaning in social platforms (Jamieson, 2016). Researchers in this context identify the many ways in which users, far from being victims of surveillance or passive receivers of consumer design, actively shape everyday technologies.

All this scholarship is very valuable, but falls short of asking why these particular constellations of data and algorithms and user experiences that we confront have come into being in the first place. In examining how data and algorithms are deployed in digital infrastructures, and how these come to matter for users specifically and society generally, existing scholarship on data and algorithms makes great strides in understanding how current day technologies are *consumed*. However, the ideological markers, pools of desirable knowledge and practices of technology *production* that bring these sets of conditions forth and not others tend to go unquestioned. With the exception of some scholars who have focused on different framings, such as platforms and infrastructures (Helmond, 2015; Jamieson, 2016), most privacy scholarship assumes that data flows and algorithms are inevitable building blocks of our current socio-technical systems.

But if data flows and the algorithms we experience today are not just the product of a natural progression of technological innovation, why are they so prominent, and how have they come to be as such? To do justice to such questions and their policy implications, we argue that exploring their roots in the context of *software production* should also be the subject of critical inquiry and technology policy. As we discuss later, our claim is not that the production and consumption of software can be neatly separated – especially not after the agile turn. This is also because technologies continue to evolve after reaching the consumer market. Yet, our claim is that the ongoing focus on their consumption only is insufficient. Rather, we believe that inquiries into their production can help us better engage with new configurations of power (Zuboff, 2015) that have implications for fundamental rights and freedoms, including privacy.

We are aware that because of the broad aims and subject matter of this chapter the reader will be confronted with a variety of omissions. We cannot cover software production in all its historical and political economic glory, but only highlight major shifts in the industry relevant to our inquiry. In addition, and to give force to our argument, we sometimes rely on idealized depictions of industry practices as indicated in online materials and in the articulations of interviewees – software developers and product managers – we reached out to in the research leading to this chapter. We do hope that questions such as the discrepancy between ideals and actual practice, with an eye on the discursive work that some of these depictions do, will also be the subject of future research.

While we are interested in studying the wider societal implications of the agile turn, this chapter is concerned with its implications for privacy governance. We understand privacy governance as the combination of technical, organizational and regulatory approaches for the governance of privacy. Privacy engineering is an emerging field of research that focuses on designing, implementing, adapting and evaluating theories, methods, techniques and tools to systematically capture and address privacy issues in the development of sociotechnical systems (Gürses and del Alamo, 2016). Regulatory approaches to privacy include data privacy frameworks such as the FIPPS, self-regulatory guidance and sectoral laws or general data privacy laws such as those that exist in the EU and many other countries. On the interface of regulatory and organizational approaches to privacy governance one finds what Bamberger and Mulligan have denoted as "privacy on the ground" (Bamberger and Mulligan, 2015). We further refer to and rely in particular on two normative theories of privacy in our analysis; Helen Nissenbaum's theory of contextual integrity (Nissenbaum, 2009) and Philip E. Agre's theory of capture (Agre, 1994).

For the sake of our analysis, we make a distinction between three parties involved in the configuration of software and services, and their privacy implications in the world. These are: (1) *developers and operators*, i.e., the parties that develop software, architect services and operate the cloud infrastructure. Typically, service operators themselves use other services for development and may integrate services into their offering to their customers; (2) *curators*, i.e., the end-user-facing entities that integrate software structured as services into their own operations (this includes so-called enterprise customers). Curators pick and choose which services to use with implications for their end-users. These curators can be IT departments, local web development teams or individual developers; (3) *end-users*, i.e., the individual users, consumers, employees, workers, students, patients and audiences, whose privacy is affected by the structuring of software as services after the agile turn. We are aware that calling these parties "users" may hide that they are the product or provide essential labor for the service to operate (see, e.g., Fuchs, 2013; Scholz, 2012). We use the term end-users to emphasize that they tend to have little agency in the design of the services discussed in the chapter. We are also aware that from a privacy perspective the different underlying "roles" will have normative implications for the appropriate flow of personal information, considering contextual integrity (Nissenbaum, 2009).

Because of the broad aims of this chapter, we have relied on a combination of methodologies. This includes over twenty in-person and telephone interviews with relevant industry experts, including software developers, devops, product managers and developers, data engineers, a/b testers, AI experts and privacy officers. During these conversations, we inquired how the production of software and services is organized, as well as how relevant transformations have come to affect the conditions for privacy governance. In addition to the interviews, we have relied on industry white papers, legal, policy and technical documents, as well as relevant scientific literature, in particular from the fields of computer science and engineering, industrial management, software studies, regulation and law. We build on Christopher S. Yoo and Jean-François Blanchette's volume on the regulation of the cloud and the infrastructural moment of computing (Yoo and Blanchette, 2015) as well as Kaldrack and Leeker's edited volume on the dissolution of software into services (Kaldrack and Leeker, 2015).

In the coming sections, we first describe the three shifts that constitute what we call the agile turn. For each of the shifts, we touch on the historical roots and sketch some of its current motions. Next, we introduce the three perspectives through which we explore the implications of the agile turn to privacy governance, namely modularity, temporality and capture. These perspectives also allow us to question some of the underlying assumptions of privacy research and policy when it comes to the production of software and digital functionality more generally.

2 THE AGILE TURN

Over the last decade and a half, the production of (noncritical) software has been fundamentally transformed as the result of three parallel developments. First, increasingly software producers have moved from the use of heavyweight and planned development models for information systems such as the so-called waterfall model, to lightweight and lean methods.[2] These latter models are categorized under the umbrella term "agile" software development and involve an emphasis on user-centricity, short development cycles, continuous testing and greater simplicity of design (Douglass, 2015).

Second, pervasive connectivity and advances in flexible client-server models have made possible a shift from "shrink-wrapped software" products to software as services as the model for architecting and offering digital functionality. In this so-called service-oriented architecture (SOA) model, software no longer runs only on the client side, but is redesigned to run on a *thin client* that connects to a *server* which carries out most of the necessary computation. In addition, the core functional components of a service (e.g., authentication and payment) can now be modularized into self-contained units and integrated on demand through automated programming interfaces (APIs), optimizing business agility.

Third, the service model came along with scaling and performance challenges that have boosted the development of large data centers offering flexible computing resources, also known as cloud computing (Blanchette, 2015; Weinman, 2015). As computing resources in the hands of consumers have become mobile, smaller and, hence, constrained in capacity, cloud services have gotten further cemented as the dominant way to produce and provide digital functionality and host the related processing and data storage capabilities.

As a result, "hardware, once objectivized as a physical computer, is becoming distributed across different data centers and dissolving completely into infrastructures. And software ... is dissolving in a cascade of services that organize access to data and its processing" (Kaldrack and Leeker, 2015). Driven by an interest in programmer and code productivity, cost-efficiency and an increased volatility in responding to customer requirements, the agile turn has offered the possibility of programming, business and computing on demand (Neubert, 2015).

2.1 *From Waterfall to Agile Development*

Around 1968 software engineering came to be recognized as an engineering discipline of its own (Mahoney, 2004; Neubert, 2015). This recognition came shortly before IBM decided to unbundle its hardware and software, paving the way to the commodification of software products (Neubert, 2015). While a variety of management and engineering literature proposed wildly different models on how to produce software, structured processes, such as the waterfall or spiral model, dominated the industry until the 1990s. These models rely on rigorously regimented practices, extensive documentation and detailed planning and management (Estler et al., 2014). In waterfall models, software projects have a clear beginning during which the requirements and design are settled, and a final stage during which a version of a software is tested and released to its users.

---

[2] A 2015 survey conducted by Hewlett Packard as part of their report titled "State of Performance Engineering" with 601 IT developers in 400 US companies indicated that two thirds of these companies are either using "purely agile methods" or "leaning towards agile." "Is agile the new norm?," http://techbeacon.com/survey-agile-new-norm

Starting with the 1980s, and continuing in the 1990s, programmers started proposing more lightweight models that promoted greater autonomy to developer teams. One of these proposals culminated in what was titled the "Manifesto for Agile Software Development" in 2001. The supporters of this manifesto value:

> Individuals and interactions over processes and tools
> Working software over comprehensive documentation
> Customer collaboration over contract negotiation
> Responding to change over following a plan (Beck et al., 2001).

Like many of its contemporaries, the manifesto underlines a "no design up front" attitude and brings together a series of lightweight software engineering methodologies. Some of these methodologies focus on techniques (e.g., pair-programming), while others focus on managerial processes (e.g., stakeholder involvement and stand-up meetings), with an overall emphasis on continuous testing (starting with test codes and extending to integration testing), communication and the visibility of progress (Parson, 2011). Most importantly, the introduction of agile methods helps produce software in much shorter iterations (weeks vs years, or multiple times a day), in greater simplicity (always do the simplest thing that could possibly work and don't design more than what you need right now), and continuous code reviews (Fox and Patterson, 2013).

2.2 From Shrink-Wrap Software to Service-Oriented Architectures

Legend has it that in 2001, Jeff Bezos sent Amazon developers a memo demanding that "henceforth, all teams will expose their data and functionality through service interfaces and will communicate with each other through these interfaces" (Yegge, 2011). Bezos had a vision for the architecture of Amazon's offering as composed of services, internally and externally, a vision that has contributed to the company's leadership in services and the cloud.[3]

The primary technical benefits of the shift to service-oriented architectures are the extensibility, integrability and interoperability of software components in a distributed environment (Exposito and Diop, 2014). In concert with web service standards, service-oriented architectures make it easier for modularized service components to connect and cooperate within an enterprise or across the industry. The goal is to allow service operators to rapidly extend existing services, integrate additional service components (or create service-composites) and allow service components to be accessed through different channels, e.g., fixed and mobile devices (Newcomer and Lomow, 2005). This way of architecting the offering as a set of microservices[4] allows companies to adhere to the mantra of "doing one thing really really well" and relying on others for everything else (Carlson, 2014; Google, 2016). It contributes to the ability of businesses to rapidly respond to market and environmental changes – in other words, it offers business agility.

The move to services has varying impacts on different software products and their users. Companies and organizations offering (information) goods and services through digital channels (shortly, curators) can now integrate themselves into the service environment, often through the mere addition of a few basic lines of code,[5] outsourcing basic functionality such as

---

[3] The memo ended with a clear indication of the gravity of noncompliance: "Anyone who doesn't do this will be fired."

[4] More recently, the industry has started to use the term microservices for the components in SOA, signaling a trend to further decompose services into modular parts. For a discussion see e.g., Fowler and Lewis (2014).

[5] Add SDK integration possibility. See e.g., Button for an example of a *service* to facilitate such integration: https://www.usebutton.com/developers.

authentication, advertisement placement, or security to a third-party provider. Consequently, what to the end-user looks like a seamless website offered by a single provider is often in reality a mix of a Frankenstein and a Matryoshka doll concealing dozens of services.

For software that used to be offered through a shrink-wrap model, the implications for users are just as significant. First, pay-as-you-go access to service models replaces software ownership and licensing, creating a more attractive business model for producers. In shrink-wrap software, the binary of the application used to run under the control of the user, typically on the user's device. New versions would be released intermittently. Software vendors would have to make sure that their software matched the requirements of all permutations of user hardware. Updates and maintenance would be cumbersome. Users would typically have to manage them on their own.

In contrast, with services end-user data is to be secured by the service provider and the code that provides the functionality resides mainly on the server side. This allows for iterative feature development, and more control over the costs of maintenance, monitoring, support and third-party service licensing.[6] Instead of waiting for the release of new versions, users can benefit from continuous updates. This is a big advantage in an industry where as much as 60 percent of software costs are for maintenance, and of those costs 60 percent are for adding new functionality to legacy software (Fox and Patterson, 2013). Services that support collaborative work (such as document sharing or processing) can now also better attend to the needs of end-users, even across organizational borders. The collaborative and social implications of the agile turn, under the heading Web 2.0 (O'Reilly, 2005), have been the subject of significant privacy research and policy debates, while other structural characteristics have received significantly less attention.[7]

What used to be structured and marketed as shrink-wrap software, such as Microsoft Word, has transformed into a service such as Office 365 or Google Docs. A music player such as RealPlayer now finds its counterpart in music streaming services such as Spotify that not only play your favorite music, but offer recommendations, social network features and intelligent playlists. Thus, different types of software users are pulled into service offerings replacing the software that used to run on their own hardware. Surely, this was not a painless transition for those in the software industry that had "a dearly held belief that installable applications can and should be treated as packaged products, to be sold to consumers at retail like a bottle of shampoo or a box of dried pasta" (Stutz, 2003). And, providing some reassurance to its adherents, shrink-wrap software will continue to exist, for instance in operating systems or in the "clients" of the client-server model such as browsers or apps, as well as in safety and security critical settings. Yet, while these may still look and feel like software products, they are increasingly likely to operate under the control of producers and bundled with update, security, or performance services.

2.3 *From PCs to the Cloud*

Finally, the agile turn is made possible by, and continues to shape, what is called cloud computing. At the basic level, Infrastructure as a Service (IaaS) cloud computing involves the economic and physical restructuring of computing resources (processing, databases and storage)

---

[6] See e.g., John Vincent's argument against running a private version of a SaaS on customer premises: http://blog.lusis.org/blog/2016/05/15/so-you-wanna-go-onprem-do-ya/.

[7] O'Reilly's Web 2.0 explanation discussed many of the software production transformations, including lightweight development and the shift to services. With respect to privacy, he anticipates a "Free Data movement within the next decade" because of the centrality of user data collection and power struggles over its control in the industry (O'Reilly, 2005).

into flexible, scalable utilities, available on demand (Blanchette, 2015; Weinman, 2015). Cloud computing also stands for a similar restructuring at the level of software production and software usage, encompassing the rise of Platform as a Service (PaaS) and Software as a Service (SaaS) offerings. Cloud computing offerings continue to develop and diversify rapidly in the various layers of development, storage and processing. Recent developments include Data as a Service (DaaS), including the possibility for services to integrate specialized data products (Pringle et al., 2014), machine learning and AI services (Hook, 2016), and the rise of container models for service deployment (Cloud Native, 2016).

Historically, the emergence of cloud computing reflects a return to the mainframe, after the rise and decline of the PC, which became dominant in the 1980s and '90s. In earlier days, computing hardware was very costly and the mainframe model in combination with time-sharing provided the most cost-efficient access to computing for predominantly large, organizational users. The invention of the PC in the 1970s and its subsequent mass adoption in the following decades turned the tide. People had access to and control over their own, personal computing resources to run software (or develop it) themselves. This, in combination with the rise of internet connectivity provided the basis of what Zittrain has called "the generative internet" (Zittrain, 2008). Mobility and the rise of the service model have significantly changed the user device landscape. Today, users have less and less actual control over their devices as their data and software increasingly moves to servers in the cloud.

Cloud computing entails significantly more than the mere relative shift of hardware capacity from users to server farms. It involves the development of a variety of layers to manage these computing resources to the benefit of different users. Considering our focus on the *production* of digital functionality, it's worth noting that many significant developments related to these technical management layers first became common practice inside dominant Web-native service companies, such as Amazon or Google. Around 2004 and shortly after its adoption of the service-oriented architecture paradigm, Amazon realized that its internal solutions for the production and management of virtual machines could be the basis of an external offering as well (Black, 2009). To phrase it differently, Amazon's cloud offerings emerged from internally oriented engineering innovations related to the efficient production of their services in a new production paradigm. Amazon's cloud services are leading the industry (Knorr, 2016).

More recently, a similar move can be observed in the proliferation of the container model for the production and management of service components in a cloud environment (Metz, 2014). This container model involves a further advancement in the use of the cloud for the production of digital functionality. It involves an abstraction away from the virtual machine and a focus on making the service component the dominant building block, both for development as well as for operations. In the words of the Cloud Native Computing Foundation (CNCF), which is spearheading the container model, "Cloud native applications are container-packaged, dynamically scheduled and microservices-oriented" (Fay, 2015). The foundation includes the likes of Cisco, Google, Huawei, IBM, Red Hat, Intel, Docker and the Linux Foundation. Google's contribution involves the donation of open sourced container manager 'Kubernetes',[8] an open sourced solution derived from its internal solution called Borg (Metz, 2014).

The agile turn has accelerated software production while transforming business operations. Clearly, this has great implications for different aspects of privacy governance. Many of the elements of the agile turn have been addressed by privacy researchers and policymakers in some way, but an integrated perspective on the implications of the agile turn for privacy governance

---

[8] Kubernetes is derived from κυβερνήτης and is Greek for "helmsman" or "pilot."

has so far been missing. In the next sections, we develop three perspectives that allow us to look at the privacy implications of the agile turn and to start reflecting upon the ability of existing privacy governance frameworks to address some of the related challenges.

3 MODULARITY

The agile turn comes with an increase in modularity in software as a service environment. The term modularity is used to describe the degree to which a given (complex) system can be broken apart into subunits (modules), which can be coupled in various ways (Baldwin, 2015). As a design or architectural principle modularity refers to the "building of a complex product or process from smaller subsystems that can be designed independently yet function together as a whole" (Baldwin and Clark, 1997). The concept of modularity and its application have been the subject of research in different engineering disciplines and industrial management (Dörbecker and Böhmann, 2013). It is generally used to manage complexity of systems and to allow for independent implementation and reuse of system components (Clark et al., 2002) and is an important design and policy principle for the internet (Van Schewick, 2012; Yoo, 2016). Modular design involves the mantra that the independence of system components is optimized after which they are 'loosely coupled' (Van Schewick, 2012). Its origins lay in the study of complex systems more generally (Simon, 1962).

The implications of modularity in software and service offerings for privacy are varied and have not been systematically studied until now.[9] We observe an incentive for the pooling of data in the industry along the lines of specialized services offering basic functionality, creating what could be called a variety of functional data brokers. Second, the unbundling of service components leads to a situation in which users, when using one service, are pulled into a whole set of service relationships. Each of those relationships has its own (dynamic) privacy implications for end-users. This dynamic also lends urgency to the question of how privacy is addressed in the various business to business (B2B) arrangements between service components, internally and externally, and as a matter of engineering as well as policy. Finally, the resulting network of relationships between different services and users raises the question of who is the proper addressee for privacy norms in such an environment. Which industry players can and should take what responsibility for addressing privacy after the agile turn?

3.1 *Service Use and Production in a Modular World*

Before discussing some of the main implications of modularity for privacy, it is useful to further clarify the implications of modularity from the perspectives of the service curators, as well as the developers of software as service (while focusing on the privacy implications for end-users). Organizations of various kinds are pulled into using "software as a service" delivered by third parties when structuring their offerings to their own end-users, thereby taking on the role of "service curators." Second, the developers of software as a service may develop specific new functionality, while integrating existing software and services of third parties.

---

[9] Siani Pearson discusses the relevance of certain characteristics of modularity for privacy governance in her discussion of privacy and cloud computing but doesn't explicitly refer to the concept (Pearson, 2009). Pauline Anthonysamy and Awais Rashid state the emergence of novel challenges for privacy governance because of the massive collection, processing and dissemination of information in hyperconnected settings (Anthonysamy and Rashid, 2015).

The integration of services by curators is well illustrated by the concept of the mashup, which was pioneered by services such as HousingMaps. HousingMaps was an early Google Maps mashup, created even before there was a Google Maps API.[10] It combined Craigslist apartment and housing listings on a Google Map, giving end-users a new interface for searching apartments that addressed a clear user need. The range of basic service components available for integration into the offering of companies and organizations[11] has matured significantly over the last decade. Many of these services have direct privacy implications for end-users. Typical service components for publishers, retailers and other organizations include:[12] user analytics,[13] UX-capture,[14] advertisement,[15] authentication,[16] captcha,[17] performance and (cyber)security,[18] maps and location,[19] search,[20] sales and customer relation management,[21] data as a service,[22] payment,[23] event organizing and ticketing,[24] stockage,[25] shipping,[26] reviews,[27] sharing and social functionality,[28] commenting,[29] and embedded media.[30]

The strength and attraction of these third-party services derive from the fact that these services are structured so they can be offered across curators and domains, at so-called internet scale. For instance, authentication services can use intelligence gathered across websites to the benefit of smaller players unable to gather such information effectively (iOvation, 2016). Even a curator with a small end-user count, can benefit from the knowledge gathered by a service operator that serves many many others. The emergence of third-party advertising and tracking over the last two decades is just one example of modularization and its implications for publishers.[31] For small

---

[10] See http://www.housingmaps.com/.

[11] Here, we consider all companies and organizations that are offering (information) goods and services, connecting to end-users through digital channels.

[12] This list, while not exhaustive, is meant to illustrate the argument. The question of what the current array of service components in different online service sectors looks like is the kind of future research that we think needs to happen and is likely to provide further insights into how privacy governance may be organized.

[13] Statcounter (https://statcounter.com/) or market leader Google Analytics (https://analytics.google.com/analytics/web/provision).

[14] Fullstory (https://www.fullstory.com) for user session replays and UX recorder (http://www.uxrecorder.com) for recording the users' face and audio during interaction.

[15] Revenue Hits (http://www.revenuehits.com/) or market leader Google AdSense (http://www.revenuehits.com/).

[16] See e.g., SwiftID by CapitalOne (2-factor authentication) https://developer.capitalone.com/products/swiftid/homepage/, OpenID (http://openid.net/) or Facebook Login (https://developers.facebook.com/docs/facebook-login).

[17] See e.g., sweetCaptcha (http://sweetcaptcha.com/) and market leader Google reCaptcha (https://www.google.com/recaptcha/intro/index.html).

[18] See e.g., CloudFlare (https://www.cloudflare.com/), Symantec's Web security, including Web filtering (https://www.symantec.com/en/uk/web-security-cloud/) or the free and open https as a service, Let's Encrypt (https://letsencrypt.org/).

[19] OpenStreetMap (https://www.openstreetmap.org/) or market leader Google (https://developers.google.com/maps/).

[20] See e.g., Google Custom Search (https://cse.google.com/cse/).

[21] See one of the earliest movers to the cloud, Salesforce (http://www.salesforce.com/).

[22] See e.g., Oracle Data Cloud (https://www.oracle.com/applications/customer-experience/data-cloud/index.html) or Acxiom's LiveRamp connect (http://www.acxiom.com/liveramp-connect/).

[23] See e.g., PayPal's Braintree v.zero SDK (https://developer.paypal.com/).

[24] See Eventbrite (https://developer.eventbrite.com/) or Ticketmaster (http://developer.ticketmaster.com/).

[25] See e.g., Fulfillment by Amazon (https://services.amazon.com/fulfillment-by-amazon/benefits.htm).

[26] See e.g., Deliver with Amazon (for delivery suppliers) (https://logistics.amazon.com/ and UPS Shipping AP (for delivery demand) (https://www.ups.com/content/us/en/bussol/browse/online_tools_shipping.html).

[27] See e.g., Feefo (https://www.feefo.com/web/en/us/).

[28] See e.g., AddThis (http://www.addthis.com/) and Facebook Sharing (https://developers.facebook.com/docs/plugins).

[29] See e.g., Facebook Comments (https://developers.facebook.com/docs/plugins/comments/) or Disqus (https://disqus.com/).

[30] See e.g., Google's YouTube (https://www.youtube.com/yt/dev/api-resources.html) and Soundcloud (https://developers.soundcloud.com/docs/api/sdks).

[31] On the displacement of publishers, see e.g., Turow (2012).

and medium-sized organizations, it is unlikely to be economical to consider the in-house development of any of the functionality previously mentioned. When in-house development is pursued successfully, it will often make sense to split off the result as a separate service offering. As a result, curators regularly default end-users into other services and the choices these third parties make with respect to privacy governance. In some cases, third-party services may integrate services of their own, further challenging control and oversight over the experience of privacy of end-users. With such complexity built into its logic, the service environment responds by doing what it knows best: it introduces a service. Ghostery, for example, helps curators (and end-users) regain some oversight. Its Marketing Cloud Management service helps curators manage third-party trackers on their websites.[32]

For the developers and operators of software structured as a service, something similar is going on in terms of service integration as in the case of the mere curators. Many of the basic service functionality components mentioned earlier may well be desirable to integrate into a developed software as a service offering. For instance, a music streaming software service such as Spotify may integrate sharing features and authentication solutions from third parties such as Facebook, Google or Twitter. It will likely build its own recommendation engine, but may use a third-party service for the actual streaming of music to mobile users or the analysis of potential fraudulent use. Moreover, those producing software as a service will use a range of developer tools with direct implications for user privacy, e.g., because of their access to usage data. More often than not, those tools themselves will be offered as a service[33] or be integrated into a Platform as a Service (PaaS) offering.[34] These services may sometimes be doubled[35] and replaced on demand depending on developers' needs. As we will discuss in Sections 4 and 5 of this chapter, developer tools often continue to be in use after the service has been deployed to end-users.

3.2 *Pooling of Data*

A central ramification of modularity for privacy is the incentive towards the pooling of end-user data across services and domains by specialized service providers. Such pooling of data, in various modalities, can allow for the most cost-efficient provisioning of core functionality, but results in significant concentration of data in the hands of specialized service providers affecting large numbers of end-users.[36] For instance, a recent empirical study found that Google is tracking end-users on 92 out of the 100 most popular websites, as well as on 923 of the top 1,000 websites (Altaweel et al., 2015). More specifically, the researchers found that Google Analytics were tracking visitors on 52; DoubleClick on 73; and YouTube on 19 of the top 100 sites (Altaweel et al., 2015).

The business-to-business arrangements between curators and service operators with respect to the use, storage, ownership and analysis of data and the treatment of end-users' privacy interests more generally are crucial to understand privacy governance after the agile turn. Research and

---

[32] The Ghostery brand, which was owned by Evidon, was sold to Cliqz GmbH in early 2017.
[33] Trello, https://trello.com.
[34] Platform as a Service may maintain Software Development Kits (SDKs) or mediate the complete service cloud production cycle, as in the case of Cloud Foundry https://www.cloudfoundry.org.
[35] A software company may integrate multiple analytics services such as Google Mobile Analytics https://www.google.com/analytics/mobile/ and Mixpanel https://mixpanel.com.
[36] As we discuss in Section 5, the usage of this data increasingly constitutes a core ingredient for developing these services and further strengthens this dynamic.

data on such relationships, however, is currently minimal.[37] Clearly, increasing market concentration and seemingly winner-take-all dynamics are at play in some of these service markets.[38] Such market power further decreases the leverage that curators have to demand privacy-friendly standards for the treatment of end-users, assuming that they may have some incentives to do so.

What choices do curators have that want to cater to the privacy of end-users? Services such as Google data analytics, Facebook authentication and advertising networks are likely to present curators with take-it-or-leave-it options. Clearly, such take-it-or-leave-it options across different types of curators and end-users are unlikely to take account of the contextual nature of privacy norms. In certain domains, it is still unlikely that data is being pooled at the individualized level, partly, as such pooling of data may amount to a data privacy violation. Generally, however, what starts to emerge is a landscape of what could be called functional data brokers.

3.3 *Bundled Relationships*

As a direct result of modularity, end-users are increasingly confronted with bundles of service relationships when using digital functionality. The explosive rise in tracking website visitors is best documented. Recent research established that by merely visiting the top 100 most popular sites, end-users collect a staggering 6,000 HTTP cookies in the process (Altaweel et al., 2015). The researchers conclude that a user who browses the most popular websites "must vet dozens, even hundreds of policies to understand the state of data collection online" (Altaweel et al., 2015). Notably, such web privacy measurement studies tend to be limited to the study of tracking that is visible to the researchers (Englehardt and Narayanan, 2016). The exchange and collection of data through first- and third-party services that are not visible to end-users is typically unaccounted for. Advertising networks are known to exchange data amongst each other through ad exchanges, parallel to bidding on advertisement placement options. First parties may also end up having to track and share data about multiple devices belonging to an individual end-user, and precisely monitor their consumption of services on these devices (e.g., number of installations, deletions and amount of use), due to the licensing of third-party services.

Some of the services into which curators default their users are by now well known to end-users, as they are operated by major internet companies that have a large and growing offering of services, such as Google or Facebook. While these internet companies may produce and organize their offering based on the modularity principle, this does not have to be the case for the way in which they negotiate privacy with end-users. For instance, Google consolidated its privacy policy across all its different services into one privacy policy that generally allows user data to be shared amongst the different service components operated by the company (Google, 2012), resulting in regulatory action in Europe (Schechner and Ifrati, 2012). The company does provide end-users a host of specific privacy controls with respect to the different service components, but in many cases only the use of data for particular features can be controlled. Thus, the benefits that modularity could offer in allowing for the negotiations around privacy with end-users on a more granular level generally do not seem to materialize. What such benefits are, and which privacy engineering

---

[37] Examples that come to mind are the Facebook-Datalogix deal that allows advertisers to evaluate the impact of their advertising on in-store sales on an individualized level (see https://www.facebook-studio.com/news/item/making-digital-brand-campaigns-better) or the Foursquare American Express deal that closes the loop between location check-ins and purchases (see http://www.nytimes.com/2011/06/23/technology/23locate.html).

[38] Many of the resulting services, such as Facebook authentication, amount to what economists would call two-sided market platforms, serving both end-users and organizational users.

solutions could be deployed to accrue these benefits, are questions that a more systematic study of the implications of modularity for privacy could help to answer.

We have used the term end-users to refer to a multiplicity of roles that individuals can have. These roles include the roles of the consumer, shopper, employee, student, patient, voter, traveller and fan. The fact that the same services are integrated by curators along a wide variety of domains without differentiation in privacy governance is one of the reasons why privacy may be eroded, or perhaps better, flattened to notice and choice/consent negotiations. The case of curators in the spheres of government and education has received some discussion in the privacy literature. Christopher Soghoian, for instance, called attention to the exposure of White House website visitors to YouTube tracking in 2009, in ways that were problematic considering the rules relating to the use of cookies on federal agency websites (Soghoian, 2009). The White House later reconfigured the YouTube integration to prevent tracking users that were not watching YouTube videos on the site. In the education context, service providers have also been challenged to adopt more context-appropriate privacy practices. Google Apps for Education switched off its Gmail-related advertising for students after a legal complaint about the scanning of the e-mails of students and alumni from the University of California at Berkeley (Brown, 2016). In Germany, the integration of Facebook like-buttons on shopping sites has been the subject of successful litigation (Bolton, 2016). While these cases indicate that certain actors may use legal or other means to demand service providers respect contextual privacy norms, this result may not be attainable for actors with insufficient economic, social or legal leverage.

3.4 *Responsibility for Privacy in a Hyperconnected Service Environment*

The modularization of services raises the question of who exactly is and should be responsible to ensure privacy as a matter of policy, law and principle. In the hyperconnected service environments that have emerged over the last decades, this question is nontrivial to answer, and policy makers continue to struggle to find the right answers. What responsibility does and should a curator have with respect to the privacy governance of integrated services affecting its end-users? How realistic is it to allocate responsibility to curators, if they have no bargaining power over increasingly dominant service operators? Conversely, what role could the operators of services have in ensuring that the use of their offerings respects privacy? And who could and should develop and implement which engineering solutions to address privacy issues in business-to-business relations?

In Europe, where a comprehensive data privacy framework exists to ensure the lawful, fair and transparent processing of personal data, regulators have struggled to allocate legal responsibility as a result of modularization. European data protection imposes its interlinked obligations on the so-called data controller, i.e., the entity that determines the purposes and means of a particular personal data processing operation. In addition, the EU legal framework entails the concept of processors, which are entities that process personal data under the instruction and authority of data controllers, but do not process personal data for their own purposes.

The Article 29 Working Party, i.e., the EU-level body of independent data privacy regulators, has signaled the willingness of European regulators to attribute significant responsibility to curators.[39] For instance, in the case of behavioral advertising, it has asserted that "publishers

---

[39] Cloud computing services, including IaaS subcontracting, has led to a similar (ongoing) discussion of controller and processor responsibilities under EU data protection law. Notably, the GDPR contains additional obligations for processors.

should be aware that by entering into contracts with ad networks with the consequence that personal data of their visitors are available to ad network providers, they take some responsibility towards their visitors" (Article 29 Working Party, 2010b). While remaining somewhat vague about their precise responsibility, including the extent to which publishers become (joint) data controllers for the processing of personal data by third-party advertising networks operating on their website, it has concluded that such responsibility exists at least for the initial processing of visitor data in the case of redirects (Article 29 Working Party, 2010b). More broadly, one of the criteria the Article 29 Working Party has developed for establishing who is the controller, is whether there is control over the processing of personal data as a result of "implicit competence" (Article 29 Working Party, 2010a). An educational institution's implicit competence over the processing of (its) student data or the employer's implicit competence over the processing of its employee's data (by third-party services) could be seen as examples of this. In practice, this principle would imply that end-user-facing curators have significant responsibility over the data privacy governance by service operators they have integrated. While EU regulators have taken a similar stance over the obligations of curators in service integration decisions, we still see little evidence that they have made much progress in enforcing this principle.

4 TEMPORALITY

In addition to modularization, the agile turn comes with a number of changes in the temporal relationships between end-users and service developers and operators. First, in shrink-wrap software, the transaction between developers and end-users is limited to a short moment at the point of sale (or download). With services, the transaction gets prolonged throughout the use and, as regards privacy, sometimes beyond that. Second, service users are subject to a continuously evolving relationship with a cascade of curated services – an end-user facing service may integrate or remove third-party services, which similarly may integrate or remove third parties. Finally, any such service is optimized over time to capture relevant user activities and interactions through the management of a dynamic feature space.[40] Consequently, the distinction between the production and use phases of digital functionality that was inherent to shrink-wrap software is blurred significantly.

The blurring of the distinction between the production phase and use in combination with the acceleration in the dynamic production of services has serious implications for privacy governance. Privacy governance still implicitly and predominantly relies on this distinction, from the era of the waterfall model and its temporal underpinnings. To explore these implications for privacy governance, we juxtapose some of the temporal assumptions that seem to underlie the agile turn. This helps to expose certain gaps in current privacy theory and data protection regimes that need to be addressed in research as well as practice.

4.1 *Temporality and Privacy*

Privacy theories and models tend to consider spatial aspects of privacy more explicitly than temporal ones. Specifically, visibility, location, intimacy and information flow (from A to B in an abstract space) are prioritized, while temporal aspects are often only addressed incidentally or implicitly. It is not that these aspects are separable. Every spatial description has a temporal aspect: when we discuss being in public or private space, time is always implied. At the level of

---

[40] For our discussion of capture, see Section 5.

privacy theory, even if contextual integrity "is not conditioned on dimensions of time, location, and so forth" (Nissenbaum, 2009), it could still be seen as a theory that requires looking back in time with the intent of identifying the relevant social norms for the appropriate flow of information, that can inform the design of future socio-technical systems. This complex time construction that is inherent to contextual integrity nicely illustrates that time is not linear but a complex concept that may provide a rich lens through which to consider what is happening in the increasingly dynamic privacy relationship between end-users and services.

Data privacy regimes, such as the FIPPS or EU data protection, can at times be more explicit with respect to temporal aspects of the different principles. Data retention and the so-called right to be forgotten are clearly expected to regulate how long into the future captured data can be projected. Yet, data protection principles often assume the use of the planned and up-front design development and the associated long production phases of shrink-wrap software. For example, it is common to hear that privacy by design is to be applied from the very beginning of software design and not as an afterthought when the system is ready for deployment. However, "the beginning" of digital functionality that is offered as a bundle of services is hard to establish and, even if it could be established, not the only moment at which privacy by design is required. In addition, it seems likely that "the end" of a service, a service component, or the removal of a feature may be just as relevant for privacy.

Notice and choice/consent and purpose limitation all assume (for their effectiveness) that the functionality on offer can be stabilized enough to present to the users and that relevant changes to the functionality are rare enough to make a renegotiation of consent feasible. The introduction of frequent updates and dynamic permissions that prompt users during the use of a service show that for the current software ecosystem, the consent of a user may be under continuous re-evaluation. Absent a substantial stability in the service, these principles can easily lose meaning in establishing privacy protection and lead to symbolic industry practices (Van Hoboken, 2016). As a result of "big data," many have already given up on the possibility of continuing to give meaning to these principles (Cate and Mayer-Schönberger, 2013). The widely heard calls for focus on the regulation of the use of personal data instead of the regulation of collection could be seen as a response to the temporal dimension of privacy, although these proposals may concede too much to be taken as serious proposals to address privacy (Nissenbaum, 2016), as opposed to throwing in the towel.

Some privacy scholars have explicitly discussed temporal aspects of privacy and design. Leysia Palen and Paul Dourish build on Irwin Altman's theory of privacy management to argue that people inform their privacy practices in the present based on past experiences as well as in anticipation of future actions (Palen and Dourish, 2003). In contrast, Agre's theory of capture tries to understand privacy in relation to the practice of producing socio-technical systems. More specifically, the "grammar of action" model claims that the reorganization of existing activity is inherent to the development and operation of socio-technical systems (Agre, 1994, 11). This means that the design of functionality builds on past activities, but also implies that the observation of end-users allows for the regulation of future activities in ways that may infringe upon end-users' autonomy. The introduction of the Facebook like button, its dissemination across the web and its recent diversification into "Facebook reactions" can be seen in this light as one instance of the evolution of regulation of "self-expression" over time (Kant, 2015).

4.2 *A Dynamic Environment of Services and Features*

The temporal dimension plays out in relation to privacy in digital functionality at multiple levels thanks to the three shifts in software production. An agile service operator can shape the temporal relationship with its users by successfully leveraging the increased control developers have in curating and designing the server-side functionality. Thanks to the high degree of modularity, which allows for the loose coupling of service components, service curators can integrate, switch or remove services throughout deployment. Further flexibility and scalability is achieved by relying on the shift to cloud computing and the available services for development and programming, in addition to dynamic functionality and associated business development.

Specifically, agile programming practices allow developers across services to continuously tweak, remove, or add new features using "build-measure-learn feedback loops."[41] Weekly sprints, scrums and daily standup meetings are the rituals of this accelerated production of features that is unleashed into the world.[42] This includes experimental features, minimum viable products and alpha releases, and may be best captured by the term "perpetual beta," which stands for a never-ending development phase (O'Reilly, 2005). Minor changes to existing features happen daily, while major changes can be introduced every two weeks to two months.[43] For example, Microsoft Bing boasts that they are "deploying thousands of services 20 times per week, with 600 engineers contributing to the codebase," "pushing over 4000 individual changes per week, where each code change submission goes through a test pass containing over 20,000 tests."[44] For smaller companies the numbers are of course smaller, but the time intervals of daily tweaking, weekly releases and quarterly feature overhauls are common.

Yet, the constant evolution of the feature space is not just a compulsive programming activity but also a way to situate the business in the marketplace. Companies big and small will opt for new features to gain advantage over or to catch up with competitors. Features provide the distinctive flavors that distinguish one service from another. Venture capitalists may evaluate investments based on feature portfolios.[45] Given these influence factors, dominant companies and investors in a given market can play an important role in feature design trends across the industry.

In practice, the management of the introduction, change or removal of features is mainly the responsibility of product managers who keep an eye out on competitors or talk with clients to drive decisions on new features. Depending on their standing in the company, user experience (UX) engineers or sales teams may also ask for new features. The demand for features may also originate from the developers themselves. For example, due to accelerated production, engineering teams may incur what is coined *technical debt*: the quality of engineering suffers due to speedy production and code hacks to release features, which may lead to increasing costs, system brittleness and reduced rates of innovation.[46] Features may be redesigned to pay off the

---

[41] "Build-measure-learn feedback loops" is a term coined by lean methodology proponents who claim that "the fundamental activity of a startup is to turn ideas into products, measure how customers respond, and then learn whether to pivot or persevere." See http://theleanstartup.com/principles/.

[42] Research as well as the interviews we conducted in preparation for this chapter show that there are great differences between start-ups and large companies in how agile methods are applied. Often there is a divergence between the ideals of the manifestos for agile programming and actual practice, which we do not discuss further. We are also brushing over the challenges of applying agile methods in distributed teams, where knowledge, economic and racial hierarchies exist between those developers located in Silicon Valley or its competitor sites in the Global North and those predominantly located in the Global South.

[43] While we make it sound as if rapid feature release is an easy feat, in reality it is a complex management challenge and may result in problems such as overproduction (see e.g., https://www.oreilly.com/ideas/overproduction-in-theory-and-practice) and feature drifts.

[44] See http://stories.visualstudio.com/bing-continuous-delivery/.

[45] And their effectiveness and scalability in terms of capturing unique user data.

[46] Technical debt may include the intensification of interdependencies that break modularity, in which case teams may start talking about concepts such as "changing anything, changes everything" (Sculley et al., 2014).

technical debt accrued from rapid feature release. In total, features provide refined and flexible units for defining and evaluating business ambitions in sync with development activities.

4.3 *Changes of the Feature Space and Autonomy*

For end-users, the result of this feature inflation means that they may interact with features that look the same but do different things, interact with multiple features that do the same thing, and in some cases, may see their favorite features simply disappear. On the surface, using a service implies agreeing to changes in functionality across time. Under the hood, it implies that the relationship between a user and services is constantly reconfigured by a line-up of service providers and their curatorial choices in services, as well as agile programming practices.

This continuous reconfiguration is barely communicated in privacy policies and terms of use and is generally not open to negotiation. In this constellation, informed consent runs into its temporal limits. Even if the service bundle remains stable, changes to features means that the information captured by the services is easily likely to be repurposed. This raises the question whether and under what conditions changes to features require re-establishing informed consent.

So, what happens to the relationship between end-users and services once the service is no longer in use? In general, data privacy regimes are very concerned with the governance of information collection and processing activities, but they are silent as to what happens when a functionality is removed or a service relationship ends. Depending on the functionality, the removal of features may impact end-users' ability to complete tasks, organize their work with and in relation to others, or access related data. In contrast, with every removal of a service from a curator's bundle, the relationship between the user and the removed service becomes ambiguous.

Finally, the conflation of production and use may have its advantages, too. If a feature is seen as a privacy disaster, it can be easily redesigned, or simply removed. At the same time, the ability to silently change features also means that service providers are more susceptible, for example, to requests from government agencies to design features or break privacy functionality for surveillance purposes, as was the case for Lavabit (Van Hoboken and Rubinstein, 2013). We also heard many examples of service providers being subject to the interests of intellectual property holders. Such developments are not independent of these temporal shifts inherent to the production of services. The increased ability of service providers to fiddle with functionality at the request of powerful third parties, together with their ability to use features to optimize user activities for business goals illustrates that services are likely to amplify potential infringements upon the autonomy of users.

5 CAPTURE

The agile turn takes the capture model to its logical extreme. Capture is an alternative privacy concept developed by Agre in the 1990s to highlight the conditions of privacy in relation to the construction of socio-technical information systems (Agre, 1994). Capture involves the reorganization of everyday human activities through improvements of their legibility and evaluation for economic purposes. Specifically, it implies the development and imposition of "grammars of action" – specifications of possible activities that are enabled by systems and can be mixed and matched by users – that, when put into use, can come to reconfigure everyday activities while subjecting them to commodification and economic incentives. In contrast to surveillance models of privacy that focus on how technological advances intrude upon private space and that derive from histories of government surveillance, the capture model has its roots in automation, industrial management (including Taylorism) and systems engineering.

In this section, we question the reasonableness of treating information flows as the central concern to privacy, and as something that can be discussed independent of the design and production of functionality. Leveraging capture, service providers may accumulate power through their ability to reorganize and optimize user activities, leading to a host of other problems. We argue that discussions of privacy need to consider capture through service and feature production in a way that recognizes their impact on user activities, autonomy, labor and markets.

5.1 *The Ingredients of Capture*

Agre described how capture is produced based on software engineering practices in the beginning of the 1990s, well before the agile turn. He defines capture in five (potentially iterative) phases. In phase one, someone *analyzes* human activities of interest and their fundamental units. For example, a requirements engineer may study a bank to identify relevant activities which may include opening an account, and making and auditing transactions. Next the developer team *articulates* this ontology in a technical system with which end-users will be able to put those units of activity together into possible *grammars of action*. When eventually the bank deploys this system, these designed units of action are *imposed* onto the users and employees of the bank who inevitably have to reorganize their activities (or resist doing so) in a way compatible with the grammars of action inherent to the system. The bank system can now maintain a running parse of all activities that can be *instrumented* through their system. Once trackable, records of the reorganized activity of the bank customers and employees can be stored, inspected, audited, merged and employed as the basis of optimization, performance measurement and quality assurance (*elaboration*).

In comparison to the 1990s, the way capture functions has transformed in technical and economic terms, due to the modularization and the new temporalities of software and service production. It is realized through an assemblage of features, services and multilayered testing in which the end-users are being tracked and enlisted to test capture's efficiency. Specifically, every feature is a real-time probe into the continuous reorganization of users' activities. End-user activity becomes a key ingredient in managing the system. Or, as Tim O'Reilly asserts: "Users must be treated as co-developers" (O'Reilly, 2005). The mantra "release early and release often" translates to an imperative to closely monitor how features are used to decide whether and how they will remain part of a service. As O'Reilly further highlights, "If users don't adopt [features], we take them down. If they like them, we roll them out to the entire site" (O'Reilly, 2005).

This refashioning of the user into a codeveloper and evaluator is worthy of greater attention. When features are offered to millions of users, data analysts state that user anecdotes are not a reliable source of intelligence for the developers. Instead, captured data are assumed to reflect users' desires, interests, constraints and opinions. Thus, user (inter)actions as captured by the system can easily be conflated with user intentions. As a result, people are made complicit in the capturing and reorganization of their own behavior and in the "rapid development of features that are able to identify, sequence, reorder and transform human activities" (Agre, 1993). Again, this also illustrates that captured data is not a mere "byproduct of the digital mediation of otherwise naturally occurring activities. The data are, at least in part, evidence of the purposeful design of the system that 'happens' to generate them" (Barocas, 2012).

5.2 *The Merging of Digital Functionality and Data*

The tight feedback loops between features and captured data means that they may eventually melt into each other. In order to capture the success of a feature, developers may need to develop new metrics. For example, sometimes developers may want to know if the user has "considered" the contents of a new feature, say a new information box, before taking an action. Researchers have shown that eye-mouse coordination patterns are reliable enough to provide just such an indicator (Rodden et al., 2008). So, now the developer may integrate an analytics service that captures mouse movements to evaluate the use of the information box. Once the service is integrated, mouse movements may be used in the evaluation of other features, too.

Beyond evaluation, captured data becomes a key ingredient in producing services and their features. For example, traditionally authentication would be a binary decision problem, i.e., matching user credentials to an authorization database. After the agile turn, it can be turned into a classification problem based on user keystrokes, browser information, and time of log-in. Mouse movement data, for example, can be used for continuous authentication. This example illustrates that user and behavior analytics and A/B testing, which were essential for the evaluation of data products such as recommender systems, search ranking and voice recognition, are increasingly incorporated into core functionality. Finally, all the captured data can support business agility. Data analysts in small start-ups may use captured data and behavioral data to analyze user churn or compute pricing, as well as for evaluating future programming efforts.

5.3 *Grammars of Action, Flexible Ontologies and Testing*

Agility demands that capture operates recursively and in a multilayered fashion. Specifically, service operators need to keep track of users and their activities. They need to keep track of their service components. But they also need to keep track of how well they are keeping track of their users and service components. Each service that a feature resides in is a specialized unit loosely coupled into a dynamic ontology of market and organizational activities. Rapid feature release and loose coupling of services (and components) simplify programming and management but create complex interdependencies that need to be orchestrated to produce a seamless and adaptive environment for user tracking in support of the grammars of action that are imposed on the users.

Mastering capture involves an elaborate system of automation and testing. New software may be released dozens of times a day, where each release may be subject to thousands of automated tests[47]. This shifts the problem of managing interdependencies and user tracking to the management of tests. Specifically, while service and feature optimization is realized through A/B testing, and user and behavioral analytics, continuous software delivery is guaranteed through a host of internal tests that track interfaces, dependencies and users' response to changes.[48] Capturing user behavior and tracking the different service components bleeds into capturing the behavior

---

[47] In a popular blog post from 2009, IMVU developer Timothy Fitz writes: "We have around 15k test cases, and they're run around 70 times a day." (Fitz, 2009). How well such testing is integrated across the industry, e.g., in companies of different sizes and maturity, are a topic of future research.

[48] Developers are often encouraged to write their unit tests before writing their code. Further tests include integration testing, system testing, acceptance testing and regression testing. The last one refers to making sure that a new release is compatible with past versions (Humble and Farley, 2010). The automation of testing and the management of testing results has become a science in itself (Wiedemann, 2013).

of the operator's capture models. In conclusion, with the agile turn, the mastery of keeping track of tracking becomes central to the production of digital functionality.

5.4 *Limitations of Privacy as Information Flow or Accumulation*

If every form of digital functionality has the potential to be transformed into a data intensive machine learning product, the application of principles such as data minimization, purpose specification and policies that enforce some sort of control over data on the side of end-users is going to be challenging. At the same time, much of service capture creates prime opportunities to apply privacy technologies such as differential or pan privacy. The application of these techniques could protect users from individual harms due to reidentification of data. Furthermore, the interviews taught us that metrics for user behavior in services are still in the developing phase, meaning this field is open for greater study, theorizing and regulatory intervention. Policy makers could pay attention to services that provide detailed user analytics, including intrusive techniques that facilitate the replay of individual users' gestures and video of their environment.[49] Computer scientists can leverage their techniques to provide automated privacy support that allows users to evaluate which information flows they want to engage in and how they can control these when they use services. However, all of these measures fall short of addressing the privacy implications of the capture model.

The conflation of user intentions with observations of their actions raises a fundamental question of what it means to consider users as stakeholders in the governance of services. Just because users are tracked very intensely, doesn't mean they can express themselves. Studies that purport the "privacy paradox," that users say they want their privacy but then act otherwise, are symptomatic of the same ideology that suggests that actions are intentions. It is a challenge for privacy research to express the fundamental damage of such positions and the practice of user capture to people's autonomy and human dignity (Cohen, 2012; Rouvroy and Poullet, 2009).

Finally, we are doubtful that constraints on information flows, derived from contextual values or regulatory frameworks, will be able to fully address the implications of services for the reorganization and optimization of everyday activities. First, this would require the development of a framework for evaluating agile production practices using appropriate information flows, which will be a considerable challenge. Data privacy regimes rarely attend to the conditions of production, nor do they easily address the implication of users being enlisted as labor in the production of services through the process of capture. The experimentation with user populations in the process of feature production requires a debate on the conditions under which these practices remain legitimate under the disguise of digital innovation. All in all, given how fundamental services have become to people's everyday lives, their work activities, their education and their enjoyment of (health)care, the agile turn raises the question whether other, or complementary regulatory approaches are called for. Rather than turning them into questions of information flows and data privacy, consumer protection, software regulation or the treatment of certain services as new types of utility providers may be better suited to address these deeper challenges associated with the agile turn.

---

[49] FullStory captures every detail of your customer's experience on your site or web app, http://www.fullstory.com; Jaco, "We Collect Everything. Jaco records and plays exactly what your users are seeing. No matter how complex your application is," http://getjaco.com; Mixpanel, "Mixpanel gives you the ability to easily measure what people are doing in your app on iOS, Android, and web," http://mixpanel.com.

6 CONCLUSION

In exploring questions of privacy governance in light of the agile turn, much of this chapter's attention has been directed to framing its consequences and the best ways to start exploring these in more depth. We conclude that modularity, temporality and capture are central to understanding the way in which digital functionality comes into the world and affects privacy and the conditions for its governance. This is the case from a regulatory as well as technical and organizational perspectives.

The modularity in production presents us with a fine paradox of sorts. There is significant independence of basic service components but at the higher level and the way in which the world presents itself to end-users, interdependency is king. Service curators are key in production and default end-users into bundles of service relationships. Production has become increasingly dynamic and puts stress on the temporal dimensions of privacy. It also drives the capture of user activities and data to a new level. End-users are often depicted as mere consumers, while the capture of their activity and the data derived from it has become an essential ingredient in service production.

Much of privacy scholarship has decoupled the consideration of information flows from the dynamic construction of functionality for users, not engaging in depth in the latter. Not only should privacy scholarship pay more attention to how current-day software is produced, it should also more centrally focus on what functionality ends up being offered and how it reorganizes user activities. The study of algorithms as a lens is likely to fall short of addressing the complexities of the production of different types of digital functionality for similar reasons. We believe that our argument for studying the conditions of production is more broadly applicable, especially considering the collapse of the distinction between consumption and production we discuss in this chapter.

Finally, this chapter forcefully raises the question, what kinds of privacy solutions are most likely to work after the agile turn. Which aspects of production should be embraced as they allow for effective privacy governance and which aspects should be constrained since they are incompatible? Or should the focus simply be placed on creating alternatives to centralized data-driven service production? From the industry itself, we expect the further emergence of "privacy as a service" offerings in which specialized services, internally and externally, help curators and operators comply with data privacy regulations and the strategic challenges inherent in intrusive and data-intensive offerings. Perhaps the production of privacy-friendly alternatives should be stimulated for essential types of functionality. However, the economics of service modularity pose a significant challenge for independent privacy applications. Privacy is not the "doing one thing really well" kind of problem.

REFERENCES

Agre, Philip E. "Surveillance and capture: Two models of privacy." *The Information Society*, vol. 10, no. 2 (1994): 101–127.

Altaweel, Ibrahim, Nathan Good, and Chris Jay Hoofnagle. "Web privacy census." *Technology Science* (2015). Available at http://techscience.org/a/2015121502/.

Anthonysamy, Pauline, and Awais Rashid. "Software engineering for privacy in-the-large." In *Software Engineering (ICSE), 2015 IEEE/ACM 37th IEEE International Conference on Software Engineering*, vol. 2, pp. 947–948. Florence: IEEE, 2015.

Article 29 Working Party. (2010a). "Opinion 1/2010 on the concepts of 'controller' and 'processor,'" Brussels, 2010. Available at http://ec.europa.eu/justice/policies/privacy/docs/wpdocs/2010/wp169_en.pdf.

Article 29 Working Party. (2010b). "Opinion 2/2010 on online behavioural advertising," Brussels, 2010. Available at http://ec.europa.eu/justice/policies/privacy/docs/wpdocs/2010/wp171_en.pdf.

Article 29 Working Party. "Opinion 05/2012 on cloud computing," Brussels, (2012). Available at http://ec .europa.eu/justice/data-protection/article-29/documentation/opinion-recommendation/files/2012/ wp196_en.pdf.

Baldwin, Carliss Y. "Modularity and organizations." In *International Encyclopedia of the Social & Behavioral Sciences*. Orlando, FL: Elsevier, 2nd ed. (2015): 718–723.

Baldwin, Carliss Y., and K. B. Clark. "Managing in an age of modularity." *Harvard Business Review* vol. 75, no. 5 (1997): 84–93.

Bamberger, Kenneth A., and Deirdre K. Mulligan. *Privacy on the Ground Driving Corporate Behavior in the United States and Europe*. Cambridge, MA: MIT Press, 2015.

Barocas, Solon. "Big data are made by (and not just a resource for) social science and policy-making" (Abstract), *Internet, Politics, Policy 2012 Conference*, Oxford University (2012). Available at http://ipp .oii.ox.ac.uk/2012/programme-2012/track-c-data-methods/panel-1c-what-is-big-data/solon-barocas-big-data-are-made-by-and.

Beck, K., Beedle, M., Van Bennekum, A., Cockburn, A., Cunningham, W., Fowler, M., . . . & Kern, J. *Manifesto for Agile Software Development* (2001).

Black, Benjamin. "EC2 origins." Jan. 25, 2009. Available at http://blog.b3k.us/2009/01/25/ec2-origins.html.

Blanchette, Jean-François. "Introduction: Computing's infrastructural moment." In Christopher S. Yoo and Jean-François Blanchette (eds.), *Regulating the Cloud: Policy for Computing Infrastructure*. Cambridge, MA: MIT Press (2015): 1–21.

Bolton, Doug. "Facebook 'Like' button may be against the law, German court rules." *The Independent*, Mar. 10, 2016. Available at http://www.independent.co.uk/life-style/gadgets-and-tech/news/facebook-like-button-illegal-data-protection-germany-court-a6923026.html.

Bonneau, Joseph, Edward W. Felten, Prateek Mittal, and Arvind Narayanan. "Privacy concerns of implicit secondary factors for web authentication." In *SOUPS Workshop on "Who are you?! Adventures in Authentication (WAY)."* Menlo Park, CA, July 9, 2014.

Brown, Emma. "UC-Berkeley students sue Google, alleging their emails were illegally scanned." *The Washington Post*, Feb. 1, 2016. Available at https://www.washingtonpost.com/news/grade-point/wp/2016/02/01/uc-berkeley-students-sue-google-alleging-their-emails-were-illegally-scanned/.

Carlson, Lucas. "4 ways Docker fundamentally changes application development." *InfoWorld*, Sept. 18, 2014. Available at http://www.infoworld.com/article/2607128/application-development/4-ways-docker-fundamentally-changes-application-development.html.

Cohen, Julie E. "What privacy is for." *Harvard Law Review*, vol. 126, no. 7 (2012): 1904.

Cate, Fred H., and Viktor Mayer-Schönberger. "Notice and consent in a world of Big Data." *International Data Privacy Law*, vol. 3, no. 2 (2013): 67–73.

Clark, David D., John Wroclawski, Karen R. Sollins, and Robert Braden. "Tussle in cyberspace: Defining tomorrow's internet." In *ACM SIGCOMM Computer Communication Review*, vol. 32, no. 4 (2002): 347–356.

Cloud Native Computing Foundation (2016). Available at https://cncf.io/.

Dörbecker, Regine, and Tilo Böhmann. "The concept and effects of service modularity: A literature review." In *System Sciences (HICSS), 2013 46th Hawaii International Conference on System Sciences*, pp. 1357–1366. Wailea, Maui, HI: IEEE, 2013.

Douglass, Bruce P. *Agile Systems Engineering*. Waldman, MA: Morgan Kaufmann, 2015.

Englehardt, Steven, and Arvind Narayanan (2016). "Online tracking: A 1-million-site measurement and analysis." In *Proceedings of the 2016 ACM SIGSAC Conference on Computer and Communications Security (CCS'16)*, pp. 1388–1401.

Erickson, Seth, and Christopher M. Kelty. "The durability of software." In Irina Kaldrack and Martina Leeker (eds.), *There Is No Software, There Are Just Services*. Lüneburg, Germany: Meson Press (2015): 39–56.

Estler, Hans-Christian, Martin Nordio, Carlo A. Furia, Bertrand Meyer and Johannes Schneider. "Agile vs. structured distributed software development: A case study." *Empirical Software Engineering*, vol. 19, no. 5 (2014): 1197–1224.

Exposito, Ernesto, and Code Diop. *Smart SOA Platforms in Cloud Computing Architectures*. Hoboken, NJ: John Wiley & Sons, 2014.

Fay, Joe. "Assembly of tech giants convene to define future of computing." *The Register*, Dec. 18, 2015. Available at http://www.theregister.co.uk/2015/12/18/cloud_native_computer_cloud_native/.

Fitz, Timothy. "Continuous deployment at IMVU: Doing the impossible fifty times a day." *Blog Post*, February 10, 2009. Available at https://www.timothyfitz.com.

Fox, Armando, and David Patterson. *Engineering Software as a Service: An Agile Approach Using Cloud Computing*, Strawberry Canyon LLC, 2nd ed., 2013.

Fuchs, Christian. "Class and exploitation on the internet." In Scholz Trebor (ed.), *Digital Labor: The Internet as Playground and Factory*. New York and London: Routledge (2013): 211–224.

Google. "Updating our privacy policies and terms of service." *Official Blog*. Jan. 24, 2012. Available at https://googleblog.blogspot.com/2012/01/updating-our-privacy-policies-and-terms.html.

Google. "Ten things we know to be true." (2016). Available at https://www.google.com/about/company/philosophy/.

Gürses, Seda, and Jose M. del Alamo. "Privacy engineering: Shaping an emerging field of research and practice." *IEEE Security & Privacy*, vol. 14, no. 2 (2016): 40–46.

Helmond, Anne. "The platformization of the web: Making web data platform ready." *Social Media+ Society*, vol. 1, no. 2, 2015: 1–11.

Hook, Leslie. "Cloud computing titans battle for AI supremacy," *Financial Times*, Dec. 5, 2016. Available at https://www.ft.com/content/bca4876c-b7c9-11e6-961e-a1acd97f622d.

Humble, Jez, and David Farley. *Continuous Delivery: Reliable Software Releases through Build, Test, and Deployment Automation (Adobe Reader)*. London: Pearson Education, 2010.

iOvation. "iOvation launches passwordless security for consumer-facing websites." Feb. 29, 2016. Available at https://www.iovation.com/news/press-releases/iovation-launches-passwordless-security-for-consumer-facing-websites.

Jamieson, Jack. "Many (to platform) to many: Web 2.0 application infrastructures." *First Monday*, vol. 21, no. 6 (2016). doi:10.5210/fm.v21i6.6792.

Kaldrack, Irina, and Martina Leeker. "Introduction." In Irina Kaldrack and Martina Leeker (eds.), *There Is No Software, There Are Just Services*. Lüneburg, Germany: Meson Press (2015): 9–20.

Kant, Tanya. "FCJ-180 'Spotify has added an event to your past':(Re) writing the self through Facebook's autoposting apps." *The Fibreculture Journal*, vol. 2015, no. 25, 2015: Apps and Affect (2015).

Knorr, Eric. "2016: The year we see the real cloud leaders emerge," *InfoWorld*, Jan. 4, 2016. Available at http://www.infoworld.com/article/3018046/cloud-computing/2016-the-year-we-see-the-real-cloud-leaders-emerge.html.

Fowler, Martin, and James Lewis. "Microservices a definition of this new architectural term" (2014). Available at http://martinfowler.com/articles/microservices.html.

Mahoney, Michael S. "Finding a history for software engineering." *IEEE Annals of the History of Computing*, vol. 26, no. 1 (2004): 8–19.

Metz, Cade. Google open sources its secret weapon in cloud computing. *WIRED*, Oct. 10, 2014. Available at https://www.wired.com/2014/06/google-kubernetes/

Neubert, Christoph. "'The tail on the hardware dog': Historical articulations of computing machinery, software, and services." In Irina Kaldrack and Martina Leeker (eds.), *There Is No Software, There Are Just Services*. Lüneburg, Germany: Meson Press (2015).

Newcomer, Eric, and Greg Lomow. *Understanding SOA with Web services*. Upper Saddle River, NJ: Addison-Wesley, 2005.

Nissenbaum, Helen. *Privacy in Context: Technology, Policy, and the Integrity of Social Life*. Stanford University Press, 2009.

Nissenbaum, Helen. "Must privacy give way to use regulation?" *Lecture at the Watson Institute, Brown University, March* 15, 2016. Available at http://watson.brown.edu/events/2016/helen-nissenbaum-must-privacy-give-way-use-regulation.

O'Reilly, Tim. "What is web 2.0: Design patterns and business models for the next generation of software" (2005). Retrieved March 2006. Available at http://www.oreilly.com/pub/a/web2/archive/what-is-web-20.html.

Palen, Leysia, and Paul Dourish. "Unpacking privacy for a networked world." In *Proceedings of the SIGCHI conference on Human factors in computing systems*, pp. 129–136. Ft. Lauderdale, FL: ACM, 2003.

Parson, D. "Agile software development methodology, an ontological analysis." Massey University, Aukland (2011). Available at http://www.davidparsons.ac.nz/papers/agile%20ontology.pdf.

Pearson, Siani. "Taking account of privacy when designing cloud computing services." In *Proceedings of the 2009 ICSE Workshop on Software Engineering Challenges of Cloud Computing*, pp. 44–52. Washington, DC: IEEE Computer Society, 2009.

Pringle, Tom, T. Baer and G. Brown. "Data-as-a-service: The next step in the as-a-service journey." In *Oracle Open World Conference*, San Francisco, 2014.

Rodden, Kerry, Xin Fu, Anne Aula, and Ian Spiro. "Eye-mouse coordination patterns on web search results pages." In: Mary Czerwinski, Arnie Lund and Desney Tan. *CHI'08 Extended Abstracts on Human Factors in Computing Systems*. Florence, Italy: ACM (2008): 2997–3002.

Roy, Jacques. *The Power of Now: Real-Time Analytics and IBM Infosphere Streams*. New York: McGraw Hill Education, 2015.

Rouvroy, Antoinette, and Yves Poullet. "The right to informational self-determination and the value of self-development: Reassessing the importance of privacy for democracy." In: Gutwirth S., Poullet Y., De Hert P., de Terwangne C., Nouwt S. (eds.), *Reinventing Data Protection?* Dordrecht: Springer (2009): 45–76.

Schechner, Sam, and Amir Efrati. "EU privacy watchdogs blast Google's data protection." *The Wall Street Journal*, Updated Oct. 16, 2012. https://www.wsj.com/articles/SB10000872396390443675404578060501067902658

Scholz, Trebor, ed. *Digital Labor: The Internet as Playground and Factory*. New York and London: Routledge, 2012.

Sculley, D., Todd Phillips, Dietmar Ebner, Vinay Chaudhary and Michael Young. "Machine learning: The high-interest credit card of technical debt." NIPS 2014 Workshop on Software Engineering for Machine Learning. Saturday December 13, 2014. Montreal, QC, Canada. (2014).

Shilton, Katie, and Daniel Greene. "Because privacy: Defining and legitimating privacy in ios development." *IConference 2016 Proceedings, Philadelphia, PA* (2016).

Simon, Herbert A. "The architecture of complexity." *Proceedings of the American Philosophical Society*, vol. 106, no. 6 (1962): 467–482.

Stutz, David. "The failure of shrinkwrap software" (2003). Available at http://www.synthesist.net/writing/failureofshrinkwrap.html.

Turow, Joseph. *The Daily You: How the New Advertising Industry Is Defining Your Identity and Your Worth*. New Haven: Yale University Press, 2012.

Van Hoboken, Joris. "From collection to use in privacy regulation? A forward looking comparison of European and U.S. frameworks for personal data processing." In Van der Sloot, Bart, Dennis Broeders and Erik Schrijvers (eds.), *Exploring the Boundaries of Big Data*. Amsterdam: Amsterdam University Press (2016): 231–259.

Van Hoboken, Joris, and Ira Rubinstein. "Privacy and security in the cloud: Some realism about technical solutions to transnational surveillance in the post-Snowden era." *Maine Law Review*, vol. 66, no. 2 (2013): 488.

Van Schewick, Barbara. *Internet Architecture and Innovation*. Cambridge, MA: MIT Press (2012).

Weinman, Joe. "Cloud strategy and economics." In Christopher S. Yoo and Jean-François Blanchette (eds.), *Regulating the Cloud: Policy for Computing Infrastructure*. Cambridge, MA: MIT Press (2015): 21–60.

Wiedemann, Christin. The Science of Testing, Christin's Blog on Testing. Available at: https://christintesting.wordpress.com/2013/04/07/the-science-of-testing/

Xu, Lai, and Sjaak Brinkkemper. "Concepts of product software: Paving the road for urgently needed research." In *the First International Workshop on Philosophical Foundations of Information Systems Engineering (PHISE'05)*. Porto, Portugal: FEUP Press (2005): 523–528.

Yegge, Steve. "Stevey's Google platforms rant." (2011). Available at https://gist.github.com/chitchcock/1281611.

Yoo, Christopher S. "Modularity theory and internet regulation." *University of Illinois Law Review*, vol. 2016 (2016): 1–62.

Yoo, Christopher S., and Jean-François Blanchette (eds.) *Regulating the Cloud: Policy for Computing Infrastructure*. Cambridge, MA: MIT Press, 2015.

Ziewitz, Malte. "Governing algorithms myth, mess, and methods." *Science, Technology & Human Values*, vol. 41, no. 1 (2016): 3–16.

Zittrain, Jonathan. *The Future of the Internet And How to Stop It*. New Haven and London: Yale University Press, 2008.

Zuboff, S. Big other: Surveillance capitalism and the prospects of an information civilization. *Journal of Information Technology*, vol. 30, no. 1 (2015): 75–89.